에듀윌
편입영어

**편입 교육
브랜드만족도
1위**

**3년 연속
100%
합격**

2022 대한민국 브랜드만족도
편입 교육 1위 (한경비즈니스)
산출근거 후면표기

기출심화 완성
독해

에듀윌 편입 컨텐츠연구소, 홍준기 공저

eduwill

3년 연속 100% 합격자 배출
교수진이 만든 교재

에듀윌과 함께 시작하면,
당신도 합격할 수 있습니다!

편입 합격 후 대학에 진학했으나 학과 전공이 맞지 않아
휴학 후 다시 편입을 결심하여 서강대에 합격한 3학년 대학생

직장생활을 하며 2년간 편입공부를 해
인서울 대학에 당당히 합격한 30대 직장인

대학진학을 포기하고 20살 때 학점은행제 독학사를 통해 전문학사를 취득하고
편입을 준비하여 합격한 21살 전문학사 수험생

군복무 중 취업에 대해 고민하다 공대계열 학과로 편입을 결심하여
1년 만에 한양대에 합격한 복학생

누구나 합격할 수 있습니다.
시작하겠다는 '다짐' 하나면 충분합니다.

마지막 페이지를 덮으면,

에듀윌과 함께
편입 합격이 시작됩니다.

6년간 아무도 깨지 못한 기록

합격자 수 1위
에듀윌

KRI 한국기록원 2016, 2017, 2019년 공인중개사 최다 합격자 배출 공식 인증 (2022년 현재까지 업계 최고 기록)

에듀윌을 선택한 이유는 분명합니다

편입 교육 브랜드만족도

1위

3년 연속 서성한반 서울소재 대학 합격

100%

합격 시 업계 최대 환급

500%

업계 최초 불합격 시 환급

100%

에듀윌 편입을 선택하면 합격은 현실이 됩니다.

---

* 2022 대한민국 브랜드만족도 편입 교육 1위 (한경비즈니스)
* 서성한반(P사) 교수진 전격입성 | 2019~2021년 서성한반(P사) 수강생 합격자 서울소재 20개 대학 기준 3년 연속 100% 합격자 배출 (서울소재 20개 대학: 연세, 고려, 서강, 성균관, 한양, 중앙, 이화, 한국외, 경희, 서울시립, 건국, 국민, 동국, 숭실, 홍익, 숙명, 세종, 명지, 광운, 서울여)
* 서강, 성균관, 한양, 중앙, 경희, 서울시립, 한국외, 건국, 숭실, 동국 중 5곳 최종 합격 시 500% 환급 (서울캠퍼스 기준-성균관, 경희 제외)
* 상품 구매일부터 종료일까지 기준, 수강 익일부터 출석률, 진도율 각 90% 이상, 최종 배치고사 3회 모두 응시 & 1회 이상 80점 이상 달성하고 서울소재 20개 대학 중 3개 대학 불합격 인증 시 수강료 100% 환급 (제세공과금 22% 제외)

편입 교육 1위

업계 최고! 완벽한 교수 라인업
스타 교수진 대규모 입성

3년 연속 서성한반 100% 합격자 배출* 에듀윌 교수진에
위드스타 1타 교수진* 대규모 입성

기본이론부터 문제풀이까지 6개월 핵심압축 커리큘럼

기본이론 완성	핵심유형 완성	기출심화 완성	적중실전 완성	파이널
기본이론 압축 정리	핵심포인트 집중 이해	기출문제 실전훈련	출제유력 예상문제 풀이	대학별 예상 모의고사

* 서성한반(P사) 교수진 전격입성 | 2019~2021년 서성한반(P사) 수강생 합격자 서울소재 20개 대학 기준 3년 연속 100% 합격자 배출
 (서울소재 20개 대학: 연세, 고려, 서강, 성균관, 한양, 중앙, 이화, 한국외, 경희, 서울시립, 건국, 국민, 동국, 숭실, 홍익, 숙명, 세종, 명지, 광운, 서울여)
* 1타 교수진 : W사 2022년 프리패스 수강 데이터 산출 (저스틴, 권윤아, 고하늬, 홍석기 2022.01~2022.12)

에듀윌 편입

에듀윌 편입 시리즈
전격 출간

3년 연속 100% 합격자 배출* 교수진이 만든 교재로
합격의 차이를 직접 경험해 보세요.

* 본 교재 이미지는 변동될 수 있습니다.
* 여러분의 합격을 도와줄 편입 시리즈 정보는 에듀윌 홈페이지(www.eduwill.net)에서 확인하세요.

* 서성한반(P사) 교수진 전격입성 | 2019~2021년 서성한반(P사) 수강생 합격자 서울소재 20개 대학 기준 3년 연속 100% 합격자 배출
 (서울소재 20개 대학: 연세, 고려, 서강, 성균관, 한양, 중앙, 이화, 한국외, 경희, 서울시립, 건국, 국민, 동국, 숭실, 홍익, 숙명, 세종, 명지, 광운, 서울여)

편입 교육 1위

노베이스 수험생을 위한
쌩기초 풀-패키지 무료배포

클라쓰가 남다른 1타 교수진*으로 새롭게 탄생!
한 달이면 기초 탈출! 신규회원이면 누구나 신청 가능!

1타 교수진의 쉽고 알찬 쌩기초 입문 강의
- 1타 교수진 노하우 총 집합
- 기초 지식부터 입문 이론까지
- 초단기 쌩 노베이스 완벽 탈출

토익 베이직 RC/LC 강의
- 첫 토익부터 700+ 한 달이면 끝
- 편입 공인영어성적 준비를 위한 토익 기초 지원

합격비법 가이드
- 대학별 최신 편입 전형 제공
- 최신 편입 관련 정보 모음
- 합격전략 및 합격자 수기 제공

기출어휘 체크북
- 편입생이 꼭 알아야 할 편입 어휘의 모든 것
- 최신 기출 어휘를 빈도순으로 구성

편입 합격!
에듀윌과 함께하면 현실이 됩니다.

쌩기초 풀패키지
무료 이벤트

* 1타 교수진 : W사 2022년 프리패스 수강 데이터 산출 (저스틴, 권윤아, 고하늬, 홍석기 2022.01~2022.12)
* 본 혜택과 경로는 예고 없이 변경되거나 대체될 수 있습니다.

에듀윌 편입

에듀윌 편입의
독한 관리 시스템

전문 학습매니저의 독한 관리로
빠르게 합격할 수 있도록 관리해 드립니다.

독한 담임관리

· 진단고사를 통한 수준별 학습설계
· 일일 진도율부터 성적, 멘탈까지 관리
· 밴드, SNS를 통한 1:1 맞춤 상담 진행
· 담임 학습매니저가 합격할 때까지
  독한 관리

독한 학습관리

· 학습진도 체크 & 학습자료 제공
· 데일리 어휘 테스트
· 모의고사 성적관리 & 약점 보완 제시
· 대학별 배치상담 진행

독한 생활관리

· 출석 관리
· 나의 학습량, 일일 진도율 관리
· 월별 총 학습시간 관리
· 슬럼프 물리치는 컨디션 관리
· 학원과 동일한 의무 자습 관리

eduwill

편입 교육 1위

친구 추천하고
한 달 만에 920만원 받았어요

2021년 2월 1달간 실제로 리워드 금액을 받아가신
*a*o*h**** 고객님의 실제사례입니다.

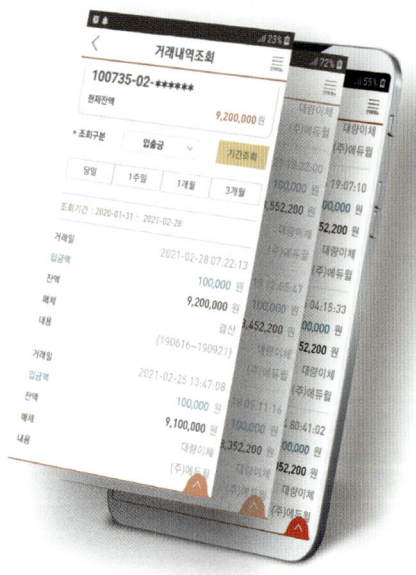

에듀윌 친구 추천 이벤트

친구 1명 추천할 때마다
현금 10만원

추천 참여 횟수
무제한 반복

에듀윌 친구 추천 검색

친구 추천 이벤트

※ 추천 참여 횟수 무제한   ※ 해당 이벤트는 예고 없이 변경되거나 종료될 수 있습니다.

자세한 내용이 궁금하다면 1600-6700

에듀윌
편입영어

기출심화 완성

독해

머리말
PREFACE

영문을 제대로 이해하기 위해서는 영어의 이해, 사회와 문화의 이해, 그리고 진정한 글의 이해로 나눠서 생각해 볼 수 있다. 영어의 이해는 어휘와 문법과 구문 실력이 필요한 단계이며, 학습 초기에는 어휘와 문법만 알면 글을 이해할 수 있을 것 같지만, 어느 정도 난도가 높아지면 이 단계로는 해결이 안 된다. 그 다음이 바로 사회적·문화적 이해인데, 여기에는 영미권의 사회와 문화를 이해해야만 알 수 있는 부분이 상당수 있으며, 많은 글을 읽으면서 어느 정도 해소되어 간다. 마지막으로 이 단계를 넘어서면 진정한 글의 이해로 개인 각자의 지적인 이해 능력이 필요한 단계로 간다. 읽어도 알 수 없고, 추상적인 글을 구체화시키지 못했던 기억들이 있다면 바로 이 단계의 문제인 셈이다. 이러한 생각 이상의 어려운 독해 영역을 정복 한다는 것은 어불성설이며, 원어민들조차도 모든 글을 이해할 수는 없다. 마치 우리가 한국어 원어민이지만, 자신의 전공과 무관한 어려운 논문을 이해할 수 없는 것과 마찬가지 이치이다.

그렇다면 시험에 나오는 정도의 글을 이해하고 해결해 나갈 수 있는 독해력을 갖춘다는 것은 가능한 일일까? 시험에 관한 한 가능하다는 게 저자의 생각이다. 물론 올바른 학습법과 수많은 노력을 한다는 전제하에서 그러하다. 가능한 일이라면 올바른 학습법은 무엇인가? 체계적으로 독해력을 향상시킬 수 있는 프로그램과 이에 적합한 교재들, 이러한 방법을 체계적으로 전달할 수 있는 교수법이 동반되어야 한다는 것이다. 저자의 4단계 시리즈를 따라가다 보면 독해에 대해서는 실력 향상뿐 아니라 자신감을 가지게 될 것이라 자부한다. 물론 저자가 쓴 교재가 최고라고 단정할 수는 없지만, 서점에서 여러 책을 보면서 각각의 책들이 지향하는 바, 그 책을 통해서 달성하고자 하는 목표를 제대로 살펴본다면, 어떤 책이 좋은 책인지 남에게 휘둘리지 않고 수험생 스스로 올바르게 판단할 수 있을 것이다.

편입 시험에서 독해 분야는 여타 시험과 비교해 볼 때 상상을 넘어설 정도로 어렵다. 주어진 시간에 문제를 푸는 것도 어려운데, 읽어야 하는 내용도 까다로운 글들이 많다. 여기에 덧붙여 지문으로 출제되는 내용의 면면을 보면 만만치가 않다. 더불어 편입 시험의 독해 분야는 너무나도 방대한 주제를 다루고 있어서 대단한 주의를 요한다. TIME이나 THE ECONOMIST와 같은 유수의 잡지뿐 아니라 NEW YORK TIMES와 USA TODAY 같은 일간지에서 인용되기도 한다. 최근에는 NEW YORKER와 THE ATLANTIC과 같은 수준 높은 잡지에서도 지문이 발췌되기도 한다. 이렇게 시사적인 것만 출제되는 것이 아니라 세월이 흘러도 변하지 않는 헨리 데이빗

소로우(Henry D. Thoreau)의 월든(Walden)과 같은 고전에서도 지문을 발췌하며, 스탠포드 대학교의 철학대사전과 같은 고급 지문들을 선보이기도 한다. 여기에 각 전공 분야의 원서에서 인용하는 지문들이 날로 많아지고 있다. 이런 상황에서 우리가 할 수 있는 최적의 대비는 출제된 문제들에 대해서 철저히 살펴보고 나올 수 있는 부분에 대한 독서를 통해 출제 가능한 영역의 배경지식을 쌓아 두는 것이다.

그러나 제한된 시간에 여러 영역을 공부하는 수험생들이 이러한 모든 배경지식을 쌓기 위해 독서를 하는 것은 불가능한 일이다. 그렇다면 최적의 대안은 무엇일까? 바로 풍부한 내용을 주제별로 일목요연하게 정리한 교재를 가지고 학습하여 비슷한 부류의 지문이 나오면 당황하지 않고 대처할 수 있는 학습을 하는 것이 최선의 방책일 것이다. 그러기에 이 〈기출심화 완성 독해〉 교재는 2006년부터 2020년까지의 기출문제를 완벽히 분석하여 총 800문제를 선정한 후 이를 체계적으로 분류하였다. 이렇게 선정된 중요 지문들을 사회과학, 자연과학, 인문학, 그리고 문화·예술 분야로 나누어 구성하였다. 이렇게 크게 4개로 나눈 후에 다시 각 분야를 세부적으로 분류해 총 20개의 Chapter를 구성하여 어떠한 테마의 독해에도 만전을 기할 수 있도록 하였다.

다시 처음으로 돌아가서 진정으로 독해를 잘 하는 비결은 많이 읽고 많이 생각하는 것이다. 하지만 우리에게 남은 시간은 그리 많지 않기에, 인위적으로 글을 읽는 방식을 습득하고 다양한 문제의 글을 이해하려고 해야 한다. 글을 읽으면서 내가 지금 무엇을 읽고 있고, 글의 어떤 부분을 읽고 있는지 끊임없이 스스로 피드백을 하면서, 핵심 키워드를 중심으로 요약하는 훈련을 열심히 하길 바란다. 이런 훈련이 자연스럽게 되어 가면서 읽는 양이 늘어나고 읽는 글의 난도가 올라가면 실력 역시 이에 비례하여 늘어 가는 것이다. 지금보다는 두 달 뒤에 더 성장하고, 그 두 달 뒤에는 더욱더 성장하여, 12월이 되면 적어도 편입 시험의 독해 부분은 완성된 상태로 시험장에 들어가는 것을 목표로 하루하루 열심히 한다면 소망하는 학교에 들어가서 새로운 봄을 맞이할 것이다. 언제나 초심을 잃지 말고 성실하고 겸손하게 학업에 정진하여 편입이라는 어려운 관문을 멋지게 통과하는 학생들이 되길 소망한다.

에듀윌과 함께 합격을 기원하며

저자 홍준기

독해 4단계 커리큘럼
GUIDE

1 기본이론 완성 독해

글의 서술 방식과 구성 방식을 살펴보고, 문제 유형들을 간단하게 점검한다. 끊어 읽기를 비롯한 문장의 해석 연습을 위한 단계이다. 200여 개에 이르는 독해 지문의 연습을 통해 문장을 이해하고, 단락을 이해하는 연습을 통해 독해의 확실한 기본을 정립할 수 있다. 발췌가 아닌 전체 독해 지문 모두에 속독 속해를 연습할 수 있도록 배려하였다. 독해에 대한 기본적인 훈련을 통하여 어려운 지문으로 나아갈 수 있는 발판을 만드는 과정이며, 이 과정에서 편입 독해에 대한 방향을 정립할 수 있도록 구성하였다.

2 핵심유형 완성 독해

지난 20년간의 학교별 편입 독해를 철저히 분석하여, 출제되는 문제 유형을 분석한 교재이다. 편입 독해 교재의 표준이 되어 다년간 편입 독해 문제 유형 분야에서 정상을 지켜 왔던 저자의 IRUM 유형 독해를 개정하였고, 유형을 좀 더 세분화하고 새로운 유형을 추가하여 향후 편입 독해의 유형을 예측할 수 있다. 추론 등의 복잡한 문제를 해결하는 요령 등을 상세히 서술하였고, paraphrase 유형 해결 방안도 살펴본다. 최근의 새로운 문제 유형에 대해서도 소개하였다. 유형 독해 800제에서는 최신 경향을 반영하여 다양한 문제에 대한 접근법을 소개하였으므로, 추론과 같은 문제들뿐 아니라 순서 연결과 같은 논리적 전개 등 특정한 유형에 약한 수험생들에게 역시 도움이 될 것이다.

3 기출심화 완성 독해

2006년부터 2020년까지의 12년간의 기출문제를 철저히 분석하고, 분야별로 나눠 400여 지문을 수록하였다. 2021과 2022년 기출문제는 학교별 연습을 위하여 수록하지 않았으며, 별도의 기출문제집에 수록될 예정이다. 철저한 해설과 분석을 바탕으로 한 난도가 높은 대략 400여 개의 지문을 학습하고 나면 편입 기출문제에 대한 두려움은 사라질 것이다. 더불어 다양한 소재의 수많은 지문으로 구성되어 있으므로 배경지식에 대한 두려움도 많이 해소될 것이다.

4 적중실전 완성 독해

총 20회로 구성되는 난도 높은 예상 문제집으로 회당 10개 지문에 20~30문제씩 구성되어 있다. 매년 마무리 특강으로 자료를 만들고 마무리 수험생들을 대상으로 그 결과를 비교 분석하여 실전에 가장 근접한 문제들로 구성하였다. 실제보다 다소 어려운 문제들도 있지만, 이렇게 훈련한 학생들이 시험에서 좋은 성과를 거두었고, 이제는 입소문으로 실전 독해를 찾는 독자들이 많아졌다. 단순한 문제와 해설뿐 아니라, 애매하고 어려운 문장은 구조를 분석해 두었고, 문제의 보기 하나하나까지 출제 원리에 근거해 가장 최적화된 예상 문제로 준비하였다.

독해 학습 노하우
GUIDE

1 편입 시험의 독해는 어떠한가?

편입 시험에서 독해가 차지하는 비중은 절대적이다. 독해만으로 편입 시험을 출제하는 학교뿐만 아니라 문법이나 어휘를 출제하는 경우에도 독해 지문 내에서 물어보는 등 독해를 활용한 문제들이 주류를 이루고 있다. 일반적으로 전체 문제 가운데 70% 이상을 독해가 차지하고 있는 셈이다. 특히 상위권 대학들을 중심으로 '원서 해독 능력'에 초점을 맞추면서 정확하게 읽고 이해하지 못하면 풀 수 없는 문제가 다수 출제되고 있다. 한마디로 말해서 영어로 된 글을 읽어 낼 수 있는 능력을 시험하는 것이라 하겠다.

2 독해의 전반적인 경향은 어떠한가?

(1) 일반적인 특징

① 단문과 중문에서 중문과 장문으로 전환되었다.

독해가 예전의 경향과 달라진 것은 지문이 길어지고 있다는 것이다. 짧은 지문으로 문제를 구성하는 것이 아니라 긴 지문으로 문제를 구성하는 것이 최근의 경향이다. 또 주제도 과거와 다르게 시사적인 지식을 요구하는 문제에서 영미의 소설이나 에세이 등 문학 작품에 이르기까지 다양하게 출제되고 있다. 그러므로 제대로 된 독해 능력을 갖춰야 한다. 더불어 좋은 기사나 글의 일부를 발췌해서 출제하기 때문에 앞뒤 관계가 생략된 채로 출제되는 지문을 읽고 추론할 수 있는 능력이 요구된다.

② 지문 개수가 절대적으로 증가하였다.

대표적으로 외대의 경우를 보면 60분에 50문제가 출제되는데 12개의 독해 지문에 30문제가 출제된다. 그렇다면 어휘, 문법, 논리를 제외하면 12개 지문을 40~45분 내에 풀어야 하는데, 시간이 턱없이 부족할 수밖에 없다. 성균관대의 경우 역시 50문제 중 독해에서 30문제를 출제하는데 평균적으로 11~12개의 지문이 출제된다. 중앙대의 경우도 10개의 지문에서 18문제가 독해 영역에서 나온다. 한양대는 20문제를 13개의 지문 속에서 묻고 있다. 이렇듯 지문 개수가 학교마다 증가하고 있으므로 상당한 독해력이 요구되고 있으며, 극단적으로 독해력의 보강 없이는 상위권 대학의 편입 시험을 통과할 수 없다는 이야기가 된다.

③ 지문 자체보다도 어려운 문제가 나온다.

최근 편입 시험의 대표적인 경향은 지문 자체보다도 문제가 어렵다는 것이다. 과거의 경우는 지문이 난해해도 문제가 간단하기 때문에 정답을 쉽게 고를 수 있었지만, 이제는 지문을 해석해 놓고도 문제를 풀 때 딱 떨어지는 정확한 정답을 고르기가 애매한 문제가 많다는 뜻이다. 그러므로 비슷하지만 왜 답이 안 되는지에 대한 정확한 훈련이 없이는 함정에 빠질 수밖에 없게 된다. 예전처럼 대강 읽고 글이 요구하는 바를 찾는 문제보다는 글 속의 단서를 바탕으로 추론하는 문제가 많이 나오므로 글을 완전히 장악하는 제대로 된 독해 실력이 요구된다고 하겠다.

(2) 문제 유형의 변화

① 문제 유형이 다각화되어 간다.

과거에는 제목, 주제, 요지, 내용 일치 등 일반적인 문제 유형들이 다수였지만, 요즘의 경향은 추론, 독해 지문 내에서의 문장 완성, 재진술 등을 많이 묻고 있다. 단순히 내용을 알고 있는지만 묻는 것이 아니라 제대로 알고 있는지를 묻는 문제 유형이 늘어나고 있다.

② 사라지는 문제 유형이 있다.

과거에는 독해 지문 속에서 문법 사항을 확인하는 문제들이 상당수 출제되었지만, 이제는 상위권 대학을 중심으로 문법보다는 글의 이해에 초점을 맞춘 문제들로 대체되고 있다. 더불어 지문에서 한 단어를 밑줄 긋고 동의어를 묻는 문제들 역시 사라져 가고 있다. 문법과 어휘 영역에서 묻고 있는 것을 독해에서 되물을 필요가 없다는 이유에서이다.

③ 부각되는 문제 유형이 있다.

단순한 의미 파악을 넘어서 그 의미의 변형을 골라낼 수 있는지를 묻는 재진술(paraphrase) 영역 등은 문제의 수준이 높아진 단적인 사례라고 할 수 있다. 더불어 글을 제대로 이해하고 글 속에 내포된 의미를 파악해야 하는 추론 문제 역시 여러 대학에서 많이 나오는 유형이고, 독해 지문 내에서의 문장 완성 문제는 전체 독해 문제의 1/3 이상을 차지할 만큼 비중이 높은 유형이다.

3 최근 상위권 대학들의 출제 경향

(1) 난이도의 상승

① 인문학 지문이 강화되었다.

지문의 난도를 높이기 위하여 인문학 분야의 추상적인 글을 많이 사용한다. 서강대에서는 조지 오웰의 글이 단골로 출제되고, 한양대에서는 학술 서적의 글이 매년 인용되고 있다. 외대의 경우 버트란트 러셀의 The Conquest of Happiness에서 최근 10년간 4개의 지문이 인용되기도 하였다. 이렇게 고전을 출제하는 주된 이유는 학문을 목적으로 하는 대학에서 원서 해독 능력을 갖춘 인재를 뽑기 위해서 영어뿐 아니라 추상적인 글을 이해하는 능력을 봄과 동시에 변별력을 높이기 위해서 더욱더 난해한 글을 인용하는 경향이 있다.

② 전문적인 내용도 출제된다.

전문적인 지식을 요하는 지문들이 다수 출제되고 있다. 2012년 서강대의 경우에도 미술사에 있어 모더니즘의 대표적인 저서인 Five Faces of Modernity에서 인용한 지문이 출제되었다. 벤야민과 아도르노와 같은 미학과 철학 분야의 대가들의 글 역시 서강대 등에서 출제되고 있다.

독해 학습 노하우
GUIDE

(2) 시사적인 지문의 변화

① 최신 시사뿐 아니라 지속적인 시사 현상에 주목한다.
한때는 시험 보기 직전의 시사적인 글이 주류를 이뤘던 적도 있었지만, 이제는 시간이 흘러도 여전히 사회 문제가 되는 내용들이 소재로 빈번히 출제된다. 언론의 책임이나 제한, 인종 차별과 소수 보호 등은 시대를 초월한 대표적인 주제가 되었다. 지구 온난화나 기후 변화 협약 등 환경 관련 주제들 역시 많이 출제되고 있다. 그렇다고 최신의 주제가 빠진 것은 아니다. 스마트폰, 자율주행차, 유전자 가위 등 첨단 기술에 관한 내용 역시 자주 등장한다.

② 미국만의 주제가 아닌 세계적인 현상에 주목한다.
과거에는 시사적인 지문들이 미국적 소재에 한정되고, 미국의 정치·경제와 관련된 지문이 많았다면, 이제는 세계 각지의 소식들이 문제화되고 있다. 가령 이슬람의 문화나 중국, 일본 등과의 관계 역시 소재가 되고 있다. 더불어 유럽의 문화적 이해를 요하는 지문도 다수 출제되고 있다. 더불어 부르카와 같은 여성의 인권과 관련한 문제들 역시 자주 선보이고 있다.

③ 전반적으로 압축해서 전체를 보여준다.
과거와 다르게 지문을 시사적인 글에서 인용할 때에도 일부를 막연히 인용하는 것이 아니라, 글의 흐름을 고려하여 앞뒤의 부연 설명에 해당하는 부분을 제외하고 핵심을 인용하고 있다. 글이 어려워지게 되는 배경이 된다. 가령 2쪽 이상의 글을 1/2쪽으로 인용하면서 핵심을 추리다 보면, 전후 관계가 연결이 안 되는 난해한 글이 될 수 있다.

④ 소재가 다양화되고 있다.
과거에는 Time, Newsweek, Economist에 한정되었던 출제가 이제는 영미의 수많은 신문과 잡지들에서 인용되고 있다. New Yorker나 The Atlantic과 같은 수준 높은 잡지들 역시 상위권 대학을 중심으로 인용된다. 그렇지만 Time이나 Newsweek는 여전히 전통적으로 강하며, 전 학교에 걸쳐 The New York Times와 The Guardian의 기사가 많이 인용되고 있다.

(3) 글의 진술 방식을 고려

① 설명의 형태가 아닌 '논증' 형태의 글이 늘어났다.
지문의 길이가 길어지면서 이에 동반하여 나타나는 현상이다. 서강대의 경우 New York Times의 opinion 란의 room for debate 코너를 이용하여 독해 지문을 구성하였고, 여러 상위권 대학들도 저자의 주장을 바탕으로 독자를 설득하는 논증 구조의 글이 다수 지문으로 선보이고 있다. 중앙대에서는 ACRO MASTER THE GMAT에서 인용한 논증 문제를 출제하기도 하였다.

② 에세이를 활용한 지문도 눈에 띄게 늘었다.
서사의 이야기 구조를 활용하거나, 에세이를 활용하는 문제가 늘어나고 있다. 한양대의 경우 에세이를 Free College Essays.com에서 인용하기도 하였다. 더불어 소설에서의 출제도 눈에 띄는데, 성균관대 오후 지문 중 하나는 The Best American Science and Nature Writing 2011에서 출제하기도 하였다.

4 어떻게 독해를 준비해야 하는가?

① 지금 당장 독해를 시작하라.

문법이나 어휘를 끝내 놓고 독해를 하려는 학생들이 많다. 문법이나 어휘가 되어야 독해가 된다고 생각하는 것 같다. 그렇다면 문법이나 어휘가 안 된 어린아이들은 동화책 역시 글인데 어떻게 글을 읽을까? 이에 대한 해답은 수준에 알맞은 글을 읽어야 한다는 것이다. 아직 초급이라면 그에 맞는 글을, 중급이라면 그에 맞는 글을 읽어 나가야 글을 이해하는 힘이 생긴다. 지금 당장 읽어 나가야 한다. 독해는 시간이 오래 걸리고 성과가 더디게 나는 영역이므로 빠른 대비가 필요하다.

② 문법이나 구문을 넘어 글의 이해로 가야 한다.

영문 해석 자체가 안 되는 경우라면 문법과 구문을 활용한 구문 독해가 초급에 도움이 되는 것은 사실이다. 하지만 상위권을 준비하는 경우라면 글을 이해하고 의미를 파악하는 단계로 넘어가야지 문장의 분석에만 매달리면 결국 빠르고 정확한 독해를 해낼 수 없다. 마치 언어 영역의 글을 읽는 것처럼 글의 핵심을 파악하고 진정한 글의 의미를 이해하여야 한다. 이제는 70%가 아니라 95% 이상 이해하여야 난해한 문제를 풀 수 있다. 문법과 구문과 어휘로 풀 수 있는 문제를 넘어서면, 이해력이나 영미의 사회와 문화를 바탕으로 해야 해결할 수 있는 문제에 직면하게 됨을 명심하라.

③ 가능하면 영어로 된 글을 많이 읽어라.

전반기에는 전공과 관련된 글이든, 인터넷상에 올려 놓은 글이든, 소설책이든 닥치는 대로 영어로 된 글을 많이 읽어야 한다. 읽어 가면서 서서히 글을 읽는 요령이 생기고, 글의 전후 관계를 바탕으로 이해하고 추론하는 능력이 생긴다. 하지만 후반기에는 막연한 글을 읽기보다는 시험에 알맞게 구성된 자료를 풀고 읽어 가는 것이 더 효율적이다.

④ 기출문제의 철저한 분석을 해라.

최근 10년간의 기출 독해 지문을 철저히 풀어 보고 검토하여야 한다. 다양한 소재의 다양한 글을 읽으면서 최근의 경향에 익숙해져야 한다. 오래되고 경향과 동떨어진 오래된 기출문제가 아니라 최근의 내용을 빠짐없이 다룬 기출 독해를 봐야 한다.

⑤ 경향과 일치하는 예상 문제로 시험을 대비하라.

막연히 아무런 독해 문제집을 풀면 되는 게 아니다. 최신 경향을 제대로 대비한 독해 교재를 풀어야 한다. 각 학원에서 제시하는 예상 문제 역시 좋은 대비가 되지만, 검증이 되지 않았다는 약점이 있다. 이렇게 독해 교재를 풀 때에 유념할 것은 기존에 본 적이 없는 지문이어야 시험에 대한 대비가 되는 것이며, 독해의 경우 어디선가 풀었던 것은 잠재의식에 남아 있어 연습이 별로 도움이 되지 않는다. 기출문제를 푼 이후라면 문제집을 제대로 선택할 수 있으리라 본다.

구성과 특징
FOREWORD

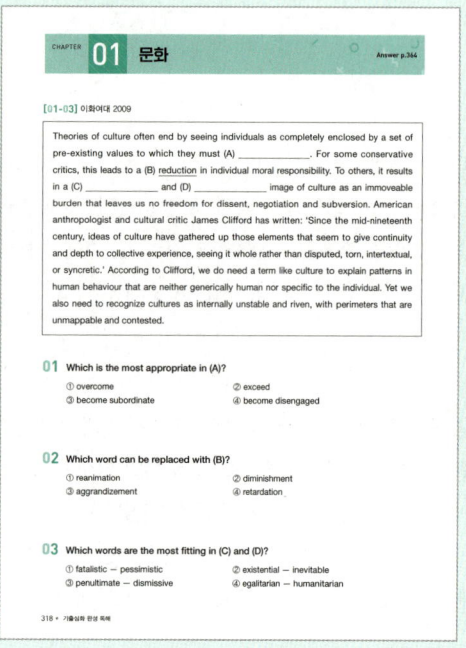
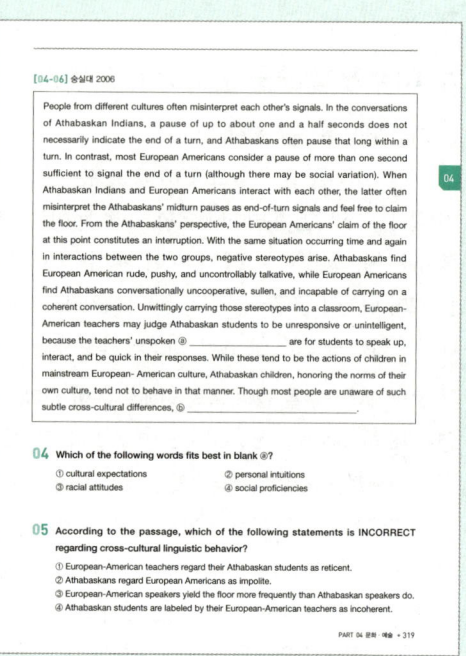

1 기출문제 완벽 분석

제한된 시간에 여러 영역을 공부하는 수험생들에게 최적의 대안은 풍부한 내용을 주제별로 일목요연하게 정리한 교재로 학습하는 것이기에 2006년부터 2018년까지의 기출문제를 완벽히 분석하여 총 800문제를 선정하였다.

2 테마별 체계적 구성

이렇게 선정된 중요 지문들을 사회과학, 자연과학, 인문학, 문화·예술 분야의 지문으로 나누어 800문제로 구성하였다. 이렇게 크게 4개로 나눈 후에 다시 각 분야를 세부적으로 분류해 총 20개의 Chapter로 구성하여 어떠한 테마의 독해에도 만전을 기할 수 있도록 하였다.

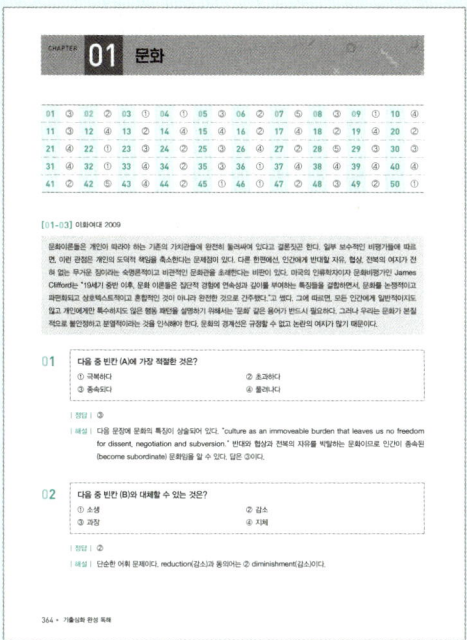
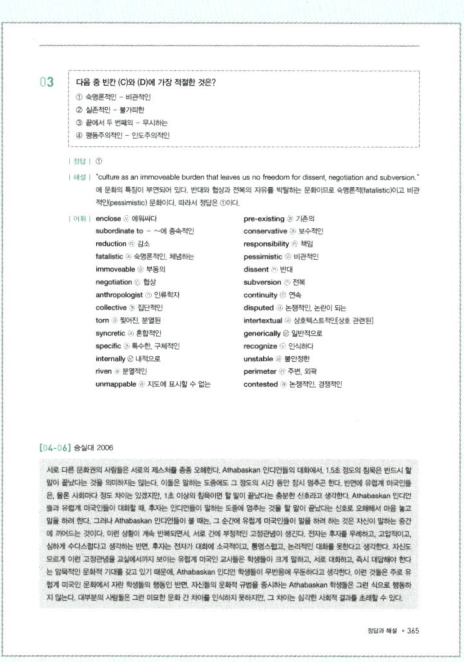

3 문제와 해설의 분리

독해는 그 속성상 해석이나 해설이 옆에 달려 있으면 효과가 반감되기에, 문제편과 해설편을 분리하여 학습의 편의를 도모하였다. 하지만 해설은 전체를 대조하듯이 보는 것이 아니라 부족한 부분만 살펴보는 것이 바른 학습법이다.

4 지문과 보기의 철저한 해설

지문 전체에 대한 해석과 해설, 어휘 정리뿐 아니라 문제 하나하나의 보기마저도 꼼꼼하게 해석을 하였다. 교재를 쓰는 입장에서는 대단히 지루한 작업이지만, 수험생들에게 도움이 되는 작업이기에 성실히 임하였다.

5 4단계 학습 커리큘럼

단계별 시리즈 구성으로 단발성 학습이 아닌, 체계적인 학습이 가능하도록 구성하였다. 〈기본 ⇨ 유형 ⇨ 심화 ⇨ 실전〉으로 이어진다. 에듀윌 편입 영어시리즈를 마치고 나면 독해력이 원하는 만큼 향상되어 있으리라 확신한다.

차례
CONTENTS

PART 01 사회과학

CHAPTER 01 법학·정치 16

CHAPTER 02 사회 29

CHAPTER 03 언론·광고 44

CHAPTER 04 교육 58

CHAPTER 05 경제·경영 74

PART 02 자연과학

CHAPTER 01 기초 과학 102

CHAPTER 02 지구·환경 116

CHAPTER 03 생물 138

CHAPTER 04 인간 161

CHAPTER 05 의학·건강 178

PART 03 인문학

CHAPTER 01 역사 · 고고학 — 204

CHAPTER 02 철학 · 종교 — 223

CHAPTER 03 문학 — 243

CHAPTER 04 언어 — 267

CHAPTER 05 심리 — 287

PART 04 문화 · 예술

CHAPTER 01 문화 — 318

CHAPTER 02 정보 · 기술 — 341

CHAPTER 03 지역 · 지리 — 356

CHAPTER 04 음악 · 미술 — 366

CHAPTER 05 영화 · 스포츠 — 388

정답과 해설

PART 01

사회과학

CHAPTER 01 법학 · 정치
CHAPTER 02 사회
CHAPTER 03 언론 · 광고
CHAPTER 04 교육
CHAPTER 05 경제 · 경영

CHAPTER 01 법학·정치

[01-02] 한양대 2016

> Voter opinion polls are often disparaged because they are seen as inaccurate or misused by network news shows eager to boost ratings. However, those who want to discredit voter opinion polling for elections overlook a few facts. First, the last week or two before an election is notoriously _____. Voters finally decide whether or not to vote, and undecided voters make up their minds about the candidates for whom they will vote. This means that polls taken too far in advance of an election cannot possibly forecast with precision the outcome of that election. Second, exit polls differ from most other types of scientific polling, mainly because dispersed polling places preclude exit pollsters from using normal sampling methods. However, debating whether voter polls are accurate or not misses the point. Voter polls are not intended to forecast winners and losers. They are designed to describe the broad spectrum of public opinion and to elucidate what voters are really thinking and what policies are most important to them. In fact, most of what we know about voter behavior and policy preferences come from past opinion polls about elections.

01 빈칸에 들어갈 가장 알맞은 것은?

① fussy
② volatile
③ elevated
④ tranquil

02 윗글의 내용과 가장 거리가 먼 것은?

① Media outlets are often believed to misuse voter opinion polls in order to increase their viewership.
② Voter opinion polls taken too early cannot predict the outcome of an election accurately.
③ The value of voter opinion polls resides in predicting winners and losers.
④ The discrepancy between exit polls and other types of polls is largely due to the fact that exit polls do not utilize normal sampling methods.

[03-05] 동국대 2006

Among those sympathetic to the general idea of equality a debate is taking place about how best to achieve what might be called a society of equals; a society which achieves an egalitarian idea of social justice. One view—which we can call the "distributive" idea—is well put by G. A. Cohen. "I take for granted that there is something which justice requires people to have equal amounts of…." On this view a society of equals is one in which people have something in equal measure; perhaps wealth, happiness or standard of living. The alternative—"social"—view is that an equal society consists not in equal shares of something but in a particular type of social relations between individuals. On this view the enemy of equality is not so much unequal division but, for example, snobbery and servility. An earlier defence of social equality is to be found in the English socialist R. H. Tawney's book *Equality*, and more recent versions can be found in the work of David Miller and Richard Norman. It is hard not to be sympathetic to the general approach of both distributive and social equality, yet, at the same time, to find that extreme versions seem to be missing something.

03 What is the main purpose of the passage?

① to introduce the two kinds of ideas of equality
② to show that the social view of equality is better than the distributive view
③ to inform that social equality has been advocated by more scholars
④ to explain why it is hard not to be sympathetic to the idea of equality

04 Which of the following does NOT related to the distributive idea?

① hierarchy
② possessions
③ welfare
④ joy in life

05 Which is true according to the passage?

① It is not hard to object to the general approach of both types of equality.
② Tawney, Miller and Norman are the scholars who do not support the distributive idea.
③ The extreme form of social equality has more drawbacks than that of distributive equality.
④ The social view believes that unequal distribution is more serious than servitude.

[06-07] 한양대 2008

When you are plagued with inner fears and you are forever fighting a degenerating sense of "nobodiness," then you will understand why we find it difficult to wait. There comes a time ⓐ when the cup of endurance runs over, and men are no longer willing to be plunged into an abyss of injustice where they experience frustration. I hope that you can understand our unavoidable impatience. You express a great deal of anxiety over our willingness to break laws. This is certainly a legitimate concern. Since we so diligently urge people to obey the Supreme Court's decision of 1954 outlawing segregation in the public schools, it is rather strange and paradoxical to find us consciously breaking laws. One may well ask, "How can you advocate breaking some laws and obeying others?" The answer is found in the fact that there are two types of laws. There are just laws and there are unjust laws. I would be the first to advocate obeying just laws. One has not only a legal but moral responsibility to obey just laws. I would agree with Saint Augustine that ⓑ _____.

06 Which of the following is closest in meaning to ⓐ?

① when men are satisfied with justice
② when men spill endurance into the cup
③ when the cup is brimming with patience
④ when men cannot stand delay any longer

07 Which of the following is most appropriate for ⓑ?

① every law is unjust in essence
② an unjust law is no law at all
③ an unjust law is a law all the same
④ it is meaningless to tell just laws from unjust laws

[08-11] 성균관대 2007

Opponents of capital punishment argued that inflicting death was not necessary to control crime and properly punish wrongdoers. Instead, alternative punishment such as imprisonment could effectively deter other potential offenders from committing offenses. ⓐ According to this logic, the (가) of punishment, rather than its (나), can be a better deterrent. ⓑ Death penalty supporters contended that capital punishment self-evidently prevents more crime because death is so much more feared than mere restrictions on one's liberty. Supporters and opponents of capital punishment still debate its (다). ⓒ Social scientists have collected statistical data on trends in homicide before and after jurisdictions have abolished capital punishment. ⓓ They have also compared homicide rates in places with and without the death penalty. The great majority of these statistical comparisons indicate that the presence or absence of capital punishment of executions does not visibly influence the rate of homicide. Opponents of capital punishment maintain that these studies refute the argument that (라). ⓔ Many capital punishment opponents consider the deterrence argument fully negated and no longer part of the debate. However, capital punishment advocates note that because the death penalty is reserved for the most aggravated murders, the deterrent effect of capital punishment on such crimes may not be apparent in data on homicide rates in general.

08 When the above passage can be divided into two paragraphs, which would be the best boundary?

① ⓐ
② ⓑ
③ ⓒ
④ ⓓ
⑤ ⓔ

09 Which of the following is the best for the pair of blanks (가) and (나)?

① certainty – severity
② severity – certainty
③ presence – absence
④ absence – improvement
⑤ proof – data

10 Which of the following is the best for the blank (다)?

① origin
② morality
③ objectivity
④ effectiveness
⑤ cost

11 In the context of the passage, which of the following is most appropriate for the blank (라)?

① the death penalty increases crime
② the death penalty cannot prevent crime
③ the death penalty deters crime
④ the death penalty is irrelevant to crime
⑤ alternative punishments can deter crime

[12-13] 단국대 2011

The widespread sale and use of illegal drugs poses a major challenge to governments throughout the world. In the war on drugs, several countries, including Singapore, have adopted a "zero tolerance" law regarding drug trafficking and possession. For anyone caught trafficking in illegal drug, the penalty in Singapore since 1975 has been death. In order to incur the death penalty, the accused must be found in possession of more than a certain quantity of illegal drugs. In addition to the harsh penalty for drug trafficking, Singaporean law also <u>imposes</u> a "presumption of intent" to be a drug trafficker in all cases where the amount of drugs in the possession of a person exceeds a certain limit. To understand how the presumption works, first consider the presumption that a person is "innocent until proven guilty beyond reasonable doubt." Normally the presumption of innocence means that two things must be shown: that the accused physically committed the crime, and intended to do it.

12 Choose the word which is closest in meaning to imposes.

① inflicts
② reproaches
③ dilates
④ secedes

13 Which of the following is NOT true according to the passage?

① Singapore does not tolerate illegal drugs.
② Drug trafficking provokes the death penalty in Singapore.
③ Singapore is a country with some of the toughest measures regarding trafficking drugs.
④ A "presumption of intent" is no longer valid in drug trafficking cases.

[14-17] 숙명여대 2008

> The term "Federal Government" refers to a system of government in which the powers are divided between the national and the local government by a constitution in such fashion as to assure the local governments a considerable measure of autonomy. The hallmark of federal systems is that the powers of the local and of the national governments are constitutionally distinguished. There are local governments in all systems, however centralized, and since they are not museum pieces they always possess some measure of authority. In a federal system the powers of the principal local governments are constitutionally guaranteed to them. Most governmental systems of the world are unitary and not federal in their basic patterns of organization. In the unitary systems, the powers of the principal local governments are subject to definition by the central government, and may be expanded or contracted by the latter without the permission or concurrence of the former. On the other hand, in federal systems, the local governments, whatever they may be called ("states" in the United States; "provinces" in Canada), possess an area of authority blocked out for them by a constitution which is the fundamental law of the land.

14 In a federal system the powers of the principal local governments are _____.

① automatically denied
② autonomous
③ guaranteed equal to those of the national government
④ constitutionally guaranteed
⑤ expanded or contracted by the government without permission

15 Most governmental systems of the world are _____.

① democratic
② fundamental
③ blocked out
④ federal
⑤ unitary

16 What does the underlined phrase "museum pieces" mean?

① invaluable
② lacking authority
③ archaic properties
④ not without merit
⑤ small but powerful

17 Which of the following statements about local governments in a federal system is NOT true?

① They are autonomous to a significant degree.
② They have powers which are guaranteed by constitution.
③ They have rights to oppose to the decisions of the central government.
④ Constitution separates the powers of the local government from those of the central government.
⑤ They possess some degree of authority.

[18-20] 이화여대 2010

> The authority of government, even such as I am willing to submit to, is still an impure one; to be strictly just, it must have the ㉠_____ of the governed. It can have no pure right over my person and property but what I concede to it. The progress from an absolute to a limited monarchy, from a limited monarchy to a democracy, is a progress toward a true respect for the individual. Even the Chinese philosopher was wise enough to regard the individual as the basis of the empire. There will never be a really free and enlightened State until the State comes to recognize the individual as a higher and independent power, from which all its own power and authority are derived, and treats him accordingly. I please myself with imagining a State which ㉡_____; which even would not think it inconsistent with its own repose if a few were to live aloof from it, not meddling with it, who fulfilled all the duties of fellow men.

18 Which of the following may fit ㉠ best?

① debate and suspicion
② support and reservation
③ sophistication and credibility
④ sanction and consent

19 Which of the following best completes ㉡?

① can be just to all men and treat the individual with respect
② should protect the individual from the external threat
③ should force the individual to obey the rules of society
④ can present the individual with the high ideas of the nation

20 Which of the following represents the author's main point?

① Individuals' challenge to their government is always legitimate
② The best government is one which esteems the individual's right
③ The power of government can be justified by democratic leaders
④ Individuals can hardly be alienated from society

[21-23] 가천대 2017

Everyone has heard of "the banality of evil" and you might even know which political theorist coined the phrase. In 1961, Hannah Arendt was engaged by *The New Yorker* to go to Jerusalem to report on the trial of Adolf Eichmann, whom Isreli security forces had captured a year prior. In 1963 the articles Arendt wrote were further developed and published as *Eichmann in Jerusalem*: *A Report on the Banality of Evil*. In her writing, Arendt suggested that Eichmann, who was known as the "father" of Hitler's "final solution" was actually not so much a monster as just a regular guy who was following orders and trying to move his bureaucratic career ahead. She further argued that the evil of the holocaust stemmed from (A) _____, and she blamed ordinary people for not taking responsibility for their actions. This condition is what she termed "the banality of evil." Furthermore, she implied that in the corrupt environment resulting from Nazi rule, the Nazi-appointed local Jewish councils were in part responsible for the six million deaths because of their (B) _____, albeit fractured, with the Nazis. Her assertions caused an outcry of scathing commentary and censure around her book, which is still considered her most provocative work.

21 Which of the following is appropriate for the blank (A)?

① Hitler's violent policies
② commonplace inattentiveness
③ noticeable cooperation
④ evil nature of humanity

22 Which of the following is most appropriate for the blank (B)?

① competition
② conflict
③ disillusionment
④ alliance

23. Which of the following is not true of the passage?

① Eichmann was arrested in 1960.
② According to Arendt, Eichmann was not an evil figure but merely an ordinary person who wanted to get promoted in his bureaucratic career.
③ The Holocaust was mainly caused by local Jewish councils who fully recognized Nazi's brutality.
④ Arendt suggests that evil occurs when ordinary people relinquish responsibility for their own actions.

[24-25] 국민대 2014

> Questions about the nature of law have long been dominated by the classic dispute between legal positivists and theorists of natural law. [A] Positivists hold that whether a legal system exists in a given society, and if so what the answer is in that society to any particular legal question, are matters of fact about how power is exercised in that society. [B] Natural lawyers believe that law is in the first instance a set of moral norms embodied in the way things are. [C] So, according to natural law theory, we cannot say whether an edict enforced in a particular society has the status of law without considering whether it passes a certain threshold of objective right, whereas according to legal positivism, the judgment that something is the law is a judgment of social fact which commits us to no such evaluation. [D]

24. Which is the best place for the following sentence?

> They associate law with objective principles of justice and right, which can be used as standards to judge the exercise of human power.

① [A]   ② [B]
③ [C]   ④ [D]

25 Which is true according to the passage?

① Neither legal positivism nor natural law theory concerns the ethical aspects of the law.
② From the positivists' point of view, the concept of legal justice would be a social product.
③ Both legal positivism and natural law theory maintain that the law is based on objective standards.
④ According to natural law theory, the law of a particular society is inherently deviant from the natural law.

[26-28] 단국대 2018

> If the democratic alternative to the totalitarian one-way broadcasts is a row of separate soapboxes, then I submit that the alternative is unworkable, is unreasonable, and is humanly unattractive. It is above all a false alternative. It is not true that liberty has developed among civilized men when anyone is free (A) to set up a soapbox, is free to hire a hall where he may expound his opinions to those who are willing to listen. On the contrary, freedom of speech is established to achieve its essential purpose only when different opinions are expounded in the same hall to the same audience. For, while the right to talk may be the beginning of freedom, the necessity of listening is what makes the right important. What matters is not the utterance of opinions. What matters is the confrontation of opinions in debate. (B) No man can care profoundly that every fool should say what he likes.

26 Which is the closest meaning to the underlined part (A)?

① to say his (her) individual opinions
② to build his (her) small rooms
③ to establish his (her) own worlds
④ to make his (her) theaters

27 What is implied by the underlined part (B)?

① Every fool should be respected.
② Discussing different opinions is more important than listening to all opinions.
③ Every man has the right to say what he (she) likes.
④ Nobody likes any fool's opinions.

28 According to the passage, which is true?

① There is no actual alternative to the totalitarian broadcasts.
② To get the freedom of speech, different opinions should be exposed in the same condition.
③ Separate soapboxes are the alternatives to totalitarianism.
④ To allow the freedom to speak one's own opinions is the most important thing.

[29-30] 국민대 2016

Attitudes to climate change seems to have been sharply polarized along political lines at least in America. A large-scale survey in 2013 shows that 70% of Democratic voters saw evidence of man-made climate change in recent weather patterns, whereas only 19% of Republican voters did. It is not that conservatives are ignorant. Knowledge of science makes little difference to people's beliefs about climate change, except that it makes them more certain about what they believe. Republicans with a good knowledge of science are more skeptical about global warming than less knowledgeable Republicans.

The best explanation for the gap is that people's beliefs about climate change have become determined by feelings of identification with political groups. When people are asked for their views on climate change, they seem to translate this into a broader question: whose side are you on? The issue has become associated with Democrats, causing conservatives to dig in against it. The divide may not be resolved within a few years.

29 Which best describes the main idea of the passage?

① Political conservatives are generally more optimistic.
② The progress of global warming is still under debate.
③ Scientific knowledge has nothing to do with people's beliefs.
④ People's views on climate change depend more on political orientation than on facts.

30 According to the passage, which is the most likely reason for conservatives to be more skeptical about global warming?

① Scientific knowledge is always limited and can be falsified.
② Conservatives are generally more certain in what they believe.
③ There are not many man-made changes in recent weather patterns.
④ Democrats are more concerned about climate change than are conservatives.

CHAPTER 02 사회

[01-03] 숭실대 2012

> Korea's rigid social model aggravates the nation's extreme demographic problems. Korean women have stopped having anywhere near enough babies to provide the country with the workforce it will need in the future.
>
> Since Korean women started entering the labour force in large numbers, the opportunity costs of having children have risen sharply. The workplace makes few allowances for women who want to take a career break. If a woman drops off the career track for a couple of years, Korean firms are far less likely than Western ones to welcome her back. And if a firm does take back a working mother, she will face a stark choice: drop off the fast track or work long and inflexible hours.
>
> Flexible and working from home are frowned on. This makes it staggeringly hard to combine work and child care, especially since Korean mothers are expected to bear most of the responsibility for pushing their children to excel academically.
>
> The direct costs of raising children who can pass that all-important exam are also hefty. Sending one child to a $1,000-a-month *hagwon* is hard enough. Paying for three is murder. Parents engage in an educational arms race. Those with only one child can afford higher fees, (1) so they bid up the price of the best *hagwon*. This gives other parents yet another incentive to have fewer children.
>
> Since 1960 the fertility rate in Korea has fallen faster than nearly anywhere on earth, from six children per woman to 1.15 in 2009. That is a recipe for demographic collapse. If each Korean woman has only one baby, each generation will be (2) _____ as large as the one that came before. Korea will age and shrink into global irrelevance.

01 Which of the following best rephrases the underlined part (1)?

① so they are willing to pay more for the best education
② so they will go to the auction for the best price
③ so they want to take a career break for their children
④ so they will pay as little as possible

02 Which one of the following fits best in the blank (2)?

① twice
② half
③ less
④ one fifth

03 According to the passage, which of the following is NOT true?

① Korea is facing a serious problem of aging along with very low rate of child birth.
② The average number of children per family in 2009 was 1.15, but it used to be five times larger in the 1960s.
③ It is generally difficult for Korean women to go back to the workplace after giving birth.
④ Korean women are bearing enough babies to provide the workforce now, but soon they won't be able to do so.

[04-06] 단국대 2011

The most recent data hint that life span is no longer growing. And, according to a new study, we may spend more years sick than we did even a decade ago. A recent study suggests that the goal of a long life marked by mostly healthy years may not be possible for most of humanity.

According to the analysis, the average age of _____ —which is defined as the period of life spent with serious illness and lack of functional mobility—has increased in the last two decades. For example, a 20-year-old man in 1998 could be expected to live an additional 45 years without at least one of these diseases; heart disease, cancer or diabetes. But that number fell to 43.8 in 2006. "There is substantial evidence that we have done little to date to eliminate or delay disease or the physiological changes that are linked to age." the authors wrote.

"We have always assumed that each generation will be healthier and live longer than the prior one." they said, "The growing problem of lifelong obesity and increases in hypertension and high cholesterol among cohorts reaching old age are a sign that health may not be improving with each generation. We do not appear to be moving to a world where we die without experiencing disease, functioning loss, and disability."

04 What would be the best title for the passage?

① Significance of Living Longer
② Secret of Longevity
③ Health Tips for Senior Citizens
④ Long and Unhealthy Life

05 What is the most appropriate word for the blank?

① morbidity
② fatality
③ humility
④ senility

06 Which of the following is LEAST likely to be inferred from the passage?

① People live longer with serious illness, but even growth of life expectancy may be nearing an end.
② The goal of a long life marked by mostly healthy years may not be possible for most of humanity.
③ The number of people who report a lack of mobility, such as not being able to walk up steps or walk a quarter mile, has increased.
④ Life expectancy plummeted as treatments for major diseases improved and infectious diseases were quelled by vaccines and better treatment.

[07-09] 동국대 2011

East Asia's booming economies have for years been the envy of the world, but ㉮ <u>a shortfall in one crucial areas—babies—threatens to render yesterday's tigers toothless</u>. Some of the world's lowest birth rates look set to slash labor forces in Singapore, South Korea and Taiwan, where fewer workers will support more retirees and their ballooning health care and pension costs. Shuffling along in the vanguard of ageing Asia is Japan, whose population started slowly shrinking three years ago, and where almost a quarter of people are over 65 while children make up just 13 percent. On current trends, Japan's population of 127 million will by 2055 decline to 90 million, its level when it kicked off its post-war boom in 1955. Asian population giant China may still be near its prime, with armies of young rural workers flocking to its factories. But, ㉯ _____ the 30-year-old one-child policy, its demographic time bomb is also ticking.

07 The underlined sentence ㉮ most nearly means that the falling birth rates _____.

① are threatening tigers living in Asia
② will likely weaken Asian economies
③ may drive up Asia's emerging markets
④ will put Asian economies at overheating risk

08 Which of the following best fills in the blank ㉯?

① despite
② prior to
③ as opposed to
④ thanks to

09 According to the passage, which of the following is true?

① In Taiwan there is a growing need for an unskilled labor force.
② Singapore may see its young workers assume heavy pension burdens.
③ Japan's post-war boom will come to an end in 2055.
④ China's population growth will defy gravity for decades to come.

[10-12] 성균관대 2011

In 1798 Thomas Malthus, an English priest and economist, enunciated his general law of population: that it necessarily grows faster than the food supply, until war, disease, and famine arrive to reduce the number of people. As is turned out, the last plagues great enough to put a dent in global population had already happened when Malthus wrote. World population hasn't fallen, historians think, since the Black Death of the 14th century.

In the two centuries after Malthus declared that population couldn't continue to soar, that's exactly what it did. The process started in what we now call the developed countries, which were then still developing. The spread of New World crops like corn and the potato, along with the discovery of chemical fertilizers, helped banish starvation in Europe. Growing cities remained cesspools of disease at first, but from the mid-19th century on, sewers began to channel human waste away from drinking water, which was then filtered and chlorinated; that dramatically reduced the spread of cholera and typhus.

Moreover in 1798; the same year that Malthus published his dyspeptic tract, his compatriot Edward Jenner described a vaccine for small-pox—the first and most important in a series of vaccines and antibiotics that, along with better nutrition and sanitation, would double life expectancy in the industrializing countries, from 35 years to 77 today.

10 What does the underlined that's exactly what it did mean?

① the number of people decreased a lot
② too many people were killed in the World War
③ people began to live longer than before
④ the world population continued to grow fast
⑤ everything went as he predicted

11 Malthus' general law of population turned out to be false because he _____.

① couldn't think of the modern development
② didn't know the exact population
③ published his tract too late
④ got the idea from the Bible
⑤ didn't count the world wars

12 Which one did NOT contribute to the growth of population?

① vaccines
② chemical fertilizers
③ growing cities
④ the sewers
⑤ crops in the USA

[13-15] 한국외대 2006

> Many people believe that the Civil Rights Movement in America began on December 1, 1955, when an African-American woman named Rosa Parks refused to give up her seat on a Montgomery, Alabama, bus so that a white person could sit there. At that time local laws unjustly allowed African-Americans to be treated as second-class citizens. Many hotels, restaurants, and even drinking fountains throughout the South were for whites only. And in Montgomery, the state capital of Alabama, as elsewhere throughout the South, city buses were segregated; the front ten seats were set aside for whites, and African-American passengers had to ride in the back.
>
> Because she found it degrading to have to sit in the "Colored" section of the bus, Rosa Parks usually walked home from her job. But on that winter evening, Parks was feeling tired and decided to take the bus home. Soon all ten seats in the front of the bus were occupied by white people, and when another white man got on, the driver told Parks and three others to give up their seats so that he could extend the "Whites Only" section. The three others gave up their seats, but Parks refused to move. The driver called the police, who took her into custody.

13 Rosa Parks usually didn't take the bus home from work, because _____.

① she thought it was illegal to distinguish bus seats according to ethnic groups
② she thought it was humiliating to sit in seats designated for colored people
③ she wanted to walk home from her job to save money
④ she believed it was not appropriate for only white people to sit in comfortable seats
⑤ she believed that it was not efficient to separate bus seats by different colors

14. How many African-Americans sat in the front ten seats of the bus in question?

① 0
② 1
③ 2
④ 3
⑤ 4

15. Which of the following is stated or implied in the passage?

① The Civil Rights Movement in America was sparked by a car accident.
② In the 1950s, it was illegal in Alabama to discriminate against people based on their skin color.
③ Most hotels and restaurants in America were for white people only.
④ Rosa Parks was detained at a police station for a certain period of time.
⑤ African-Americans in Montgomery boycotted the city buses for the high bus fare.

[16-18] 홍익대 2016

However, most Jews in the North remained too insecure in their status to act altruistically toward blacks in a consistent way. Instead, they usually fell into a much more ambivalent pattern, continuously asserting their social superiority as whites but expressing concern and sympathy for blacks when it did not bring their own status into question. The issue of residential segregation provides an instructive example. Jews supported neighborhood "protective" associations in New York and Chicago, but the Jewish press often found it appropriate to criticize such movements. The editors of the *American Hebrew*, however, ultimately understood the dilemma faced by status-conscious Jews, who they thought would surely encourage black social advancement, education, and self-sufficiency as long as "the negro advanced anywhere (A) but in their own neighborhood." Many Jews who lived in transitional neighborhoods avoided the uncomfortable question of residential restriction altogether, preferring to sell their homes to African Americans and move. In this manner, they were able to fulfill their contradictory desires to put distance between themselves and the changing neighborhood and to avoid participating directly in the segregation efforts. These dual impulses were at work in 1919, when members of Chicago's Temple Isaiah voted to relocate away from the encroaching "Black Belt" but ignored the pleas of the Hyde Park-Kenwood Association not to sell to an African American congregation.

16 According to the above passage, which of the following is not true?

① The social status of Jews in the North was not secure enough.
② The issue of residential restriction indicated that Jewish Americans were altruistic.
③ Jews were supportive of the education and social uplift of African Americans.
④ The Jewish American attitude towards race-relations were ambivalent.

17 Which of the following is closest in meaning to (A) but?

① yet
② only
③ still
④ except

18 Which of the following can be inferred from the above passage?

① Jews emphasized their whiteness by keeping their neighborhoods white.
② Jews were consistent in their actions for African Americans.
③ The residential issue often brought Jews' status into question.
④ Jews often felt torn between their impulses for inclusion and distinctiveness.

[19-21] 가톨릭대 2016

One of the central claims of feminist thought is that biological 'sex' is a separate thing from 'gender', which is a matter of cultural convention. Notions as to which traits 'masculinity' and 'femininity' involve vary from one society to another. What is thought of as 'feminine' behaviour in one context might be seen as more 'masculine' behaviour in another. Ⓐ People conform to the cultural norms as to 'male behaviour' and 'female behaviour' set by the social context in which they live. From being born onwards, they are socialized into accepting unconsciously, and acting upon the basis of, such norms. A central element of growing up involves learning how to be 'male' or how to be 'female.' Ⓑ And the person comes to think that the culturally derived gender norms that have shaped them are actually natural and unchangeable. In this way, ways of thinking and acting that we tend to think are naturally either 'feminine' or 'masculine' are in fact the products of the inculcation of specific cultural expectations. Ⓒ

As a result, we might think that cultural norms of gender would influence a person as they grow up not just in terms of their ways of thinking, but also in terms of their corporeality, that is, the ways in which they move and experience their bodies. In most societies, men tend to occupy more positions of power than women. In patriarchal form of social organization, men as a group both have more power than women and also have power over women. Ⓓ In a society like that, cultural forces tend simultaneously to reflect and to justify this situation. Men are seen as being somehow naturally superior to women. This superiority is taken as if it were an unchanging fact of life. Gender norms characteristic of a patriarchal society create an essence of 'femininity' that is not a natural essence, but a _____. 'Femininity' generally is defined in negative ways, stressing the inferiority of the female psychologically and physically.

19 Choose the best expression for the blank.

① linguistic expression
② historical accident
③ social change
④ cultural fabrication

20. Choose the best place where the following sentence should be put.

> Generally these learning processes happen at an unconscious and semi-conscious psychological level.

① Ⓐ 　　　　　　　　　② Ⓑ
③ Ⓒ 　　　　　　　　　④ Ⓓ

21. Which of the following is NOT true, according to the passage?

① In most societies, cultural norms reflect the way things actually are, and are accepted as natural.
② Culture exerts influence not only on the way we think but also on the way we use our bodies.
③ In a patriarchal society, men's superiority to women is regarded as an unchanging fact of life.
④ The ideas of what constitutes femininity or masculinity are not identical in all social organizations.

[22-23] 한양대 2018

Among the central preoccupations of Durkheim is the question of what holds societies together. His answer points to the crucial role of law in promoting and maintaining this social _____. He shows how, as society advances from religion to secularism, and from collectivism to individualism, law becomes concerned less with punishment than compensation. But punishment performs a significant role in expressing the collective moral attitudes by which social solidarity is preserved. He distinguishes between what he calls mechanical solidarity and organic solidarity. The former exists in simple, homogeneous societies which have a uniformity of values and lack any significant division of labour. These uncomplicated communities tend to be collective in nature. In advanced societies, however, where there is division of labour, a high degree of _____ exists. There is substantial differentiation, and collectivism is replaced by individualism. These forms of social solidarity are, he argues, reflected in the law: classify the different types of law and you will find the different types of social solidarity to which it corresponds. According to Durkheim, while mechanical solidarity operates in traditional and small-scale societies, organic solidarity comes from individuals' reliance on each other to perform their specified tasks.

22 윗글의 제목으로 가장 적절한 것은?

① Types of Social Solidarity, Types of Society
② Coming Full Circle?: Law and Punishment
③ Division of Labor: How Societies Have Progressed
④ Making Room for Compromise: Solidarity & Individuality

23 빈칸에 들어갈 가장 적절한 것은?

① bond – diversity
② cohesion – interdependence
③ solidarity – collectivism
④ homogeneity – distinctiveness

[24-25] 성균관대 2013

> Researchers have a hard time measuring how common bullying is because (A) _____. Is bullying only verbal, or does there have to be a physical act? If you hear a schoolyard taunt that you know how to brush off, were you bullied or just annoyed? Does it have to be repeated behavior to count as bullying, or can it happen just once? Does it have to disrupt a whole class, or can it affect only one or two kids? None of this is clear to those who study and make laws to prevent bullying. Most state laws differ on the precise motivations and consequences required for a harassing event to count as bullying. If one 12-year-old boy taunts another, most state laws wouldn't call it bullying unless there is both demonstrable harm—the victim is injured(at least psychologically)—and demonstrable intent. (B) _____, for a bully to be a bully, he can't have just been any insensitive kid. He had to want to hurt his classmate.

24 Which is most appropriate for the blank (A)?

① there are so many kinds of bullying pattern
② it is not possible to check all the schools in the US
③ there's no single definition
④ it is not common among college kids
⑤ there's no way to understand the human mind

25 Which is most appropriate for the blank (B)?

① In other words
② On the contrary
③ On the other hand
④ By contrast
⑤ By all means

[26-28] 한국외대 2013

The massacre of children at an elementary school in Newtown, Conn., has caused (A) <u>a profound change in Americans' views on guns</u>, galvanizing the broadest support for stricter gun laws in about a decade, according to a *New York Times/CBS* News poll. The poll found that a majority of Americans—54 percent—think gun control laws should be tightened, up markedly from a *CBS* News poll last April that found that only 39 percent backed stricter laws. The rise in support for stricter gun laws stretched across political lines, including an 18-point increase among Republicans. A majority of independents now back stricter gun laws. Whether the Newtown shooting—in which 20 first graders and 6 adults were killed—will have a long-term effect on public opinion of gun laws is hard to assess just a month after the rampage. But (B) _____ the smaller increases in support for gun control immediately after other mass shootings, including after the 2011 shooting in Tucson that severely wounded Representative Gabrielle Giffords, the latest polling results suggest a deeper, and possibly more resonating shift.

26 Which of the following is true of the passage?

① An increasing number of Republicans support stricter gun laws.
② Two recent polls on gun laws reveal contradictory results.
③ The recent mass shooting permanently changed American views on guns.
④ Americans are unaffected by mass-shooting incidents.

27 Which of the following is being referred to by the underlined (A)?

① An urgent call for tighter gun laws among Republicans
② A record-breaking increase in gun purchases for self-protection
③ Majority support for gun control among conservatives
④ Sharply increased nationwide support for stricter gun laws

28 According to the context, which of the following best fits into the blank (B)?

① owing to
② unlike
③ just as
④ in addition to

[29-30] 항공대 2018

Economists often assume that markets are inert, that they do not touch or taint the goods they exchange. Market exchange, they assume, doesn't change the meaning or value of the goods being exchanged. This may be true enough if we're talking about material goods. If you sell me a flat screen television or give me one as a gift, it will be the same good. It will work the same either way. But the same may not be true if we're talking about non-material goods and social practices such as teaching and learning or engaging together in civic life. In those domains, bringing market mechanisms and cash incentives may undermine or crowd out non-market values and attitudes worth caring about. Once we see that markets and commerce, when extended beyond the material domain, can change the character of the goods themselves, can change the meaning of the social practices, as in the example of teaching and learning, we have to ask where markets belong and where they don't, and where they may actually undermine values and attitudes worth caring about. But to have this debate, we have to do something we're not very good at, and that is to reason together in public about the value and the meaning of the social practices we prize, from our bodies to family life, to personal relations, to health, to teaching and learning, and to civic life. Now these are controversial questions, and so we tend to shrink from them. In fact, during the past three decades, when market reasoning and market thinking have gathered force and gained prestige, our public discourse during this time has become hollowed out, empty of larger moral meaning. For fear of disagreement, we shrink from these questions. But once we see that markets change the character of goods, we have to debate among ourselves these bigger questions about how to value goods. One of the most corrosive effects of putting a price on everything is on commonality, the sense that we are all in it together. Against the background of rising inequality, marketizing every aspect of life leads to a condition where those who are affluent and those who are of modest means increasingly live separate lives. We live and work and shop and play in different places. Our children go to different schools. This isn't good for democracy, nor is it a satisfying way to live, even for those of us who can afford to buy our way to the head of the line. Here's why. Democracy does not require perfect equality, but what it does require is that citizens share in a common life. What matters is that people of different social backgrounds and different walks of life encounter one another, and bump up against one another in the ordinary course of life, because this is what teaches us to negotiate and to abide our differences. And this is how we come to care for the common good.

29 Which of the following statement is NOT true?

① We have to debate among ourselves bigger questions about how to value goods.
② Serious debate about the role and reach of markets remains largely absent from our life.
③ We worry that we are moving toward a society which everything is up for sale.
④ Recently market reasoning has been replaced by market exchange.

30 It can be inferred from the passage that _____.

① maximizing utility should be a principle to build a fair society
② a society should involve reasoning together about the good life
③ the highest morality is to maximize happiness
④ one needs to follow an unconditional or a categorical imperative rather than market norms

[01-02] 단국대 2016

In the Philippines, television has become all things to all people: friend, teacher, lover, mother. With the decline in local movie production, viewers now have the biggest stars of Philippine cinema in their homes every single day. The two largest TV networks now advertise themselves as *kapuso* (of the same heart) and *kapamilya* (member of the family), underscoring their intimate personal relationships with the viewers. News anchors don't just read the day's news, they also blast erring government officials, often without benefit of any investigation. They host public-service programs that provide everything from medical assistance to scholarships to karaoke machines (apparently a basic necessity).

In a country where about half of the population lives in poverty, TV is the easiest avenue of escape. Not only does it offer variety shows, soap operas and superhero fantasies, but it also gives away millions of cash in game shows and contests. Of course, <u>the ultimate escape</u> is via the new "American Idol"-type shows, in which viewers pick the winner by text-message voting. This is democracy in action: unfiltered and instantaneous.

01 According to the passage, which is true?

① Viewers should send instant text-messages to win a lot of cash prize.
② Buying TV sets is the easiest way to overcome the poverty in the Philippines.
③ News anchors often criticise corrupted government officials with insufficient proofs.
④ In the Philippines, TV networks air movies frequently to promote local movie industry.

02 Which is implied by the underlined part?

① reliable excuse
② final destination
③ safe fire exit
④ becoming rich

[03-05] 한국외대 2010

Media tycoon Rupert Murdoch recently stated the newspaper business model of providing content online for free was "malfunctioning." Murdoch, who owns the *Wall Street Journal*, a rare newspaper with a profitable, subscription-based website, has vowed to boost the earning power of his digital properties by increasing the number of his sites that charge for content. Other publishers are suggesting that, while subscriptions to online newspapers and magazines might be a tough sell to consumers ㉮_____, readers might be willing to pay small fees, from a few pennies to a few dollars, for each story that grabs their attention.

Of course, publishers are not the first to view so-called micropayments as a potential source of revenue for digital content. Apple's iTunes store showed it was possible to build a billion-dollar business by selling songs for 99 cents each. And, although many analysts doubt publishers can make the switch from free to fee, there is another industry that is currently making a similar transition: online gaming.

Two of the online-gaming world's fastest-growing segments—multiplayer role-playing games and social games—are increasingly generating impressive revenues from tiny transactions. They originally relied primarily on subscriptions for income. But the trend is the free-to-play, or 'freemium' model. Under this system, gamers can play for no cost, but they usually find the games are more entertaining when pay small fees.

03 Which of the following best fits into ㉮?

① who are likely to buy news online
② accustomed to getting their news for free
③ who are eager to read news
④ who are very generous otherwise
⑤ inclined to read papers offline

04 Which of the following is NOT stated or implied in the passage?

① Most online newspapers do not have profitable, subscription-based websites.
② Some digital content providers have already made a huge sum of money.
③ Media corporations have found a way out in online service.
④ Many experts are skeptical about charging fees for news articles.
⑤ Online gamers either play for free or pay for more fun.

05 What are online publishers most likely to do after benchmarking the game industry?

① They are likely to increase the subscription fee for online newspaper.
② They are likely to charge small fees for the stories that may attract reader's attention.
③ They are likely to sell some offline news companies in order to expand the online journals.
④ They are likely to enter into game industry because of its profitable business model.
⑤ They are likely to lower subscription fees for online newspapers.

[06-08] 성균관대 2008

The cream of the contemporary crop of slogans is still found in the creations of the advertizing trade, which of course was the first to exploit psychology and behaviorism to turn the art of persuasion into a quasi-science. The success of its catchwords is confirmed by retail sales figures that make even the national deficit seem a trifle. More to the point, anyone can confirm the sticking power of business's best slogans simply by scavenging around in the mind: "Fly now, pay later." "You're in safe hands." "Say it with flowers." "A diamond is forever." Such a list could go on almost forever. This fact indeed suggests one possible explanation for 'sloganosis', that diminishes the spark of the current slogan output. Could it be that we are witnessing a weird new form of inflation? Is it conceivable that just as an oversupply of money drives down the value of currency, an excess of sloganizing diminishes the catchiness of catchwords and the public's vulnerability to their magic?

There are those, of course, who would like to see sloganeering die off entirely. Precisely because the art appeals to emotion, some idealists and intellectual purists disdain it in favor of cool, rational discourse. This crowd is clearly trying to swim against a very strong human current. Moreover, they are out of touch with the problems of both leadership and the human dilemma. The problem has never been to get people to think about doing something. The difficulty has always been to get them to act. From time immemorial, leaders have found that one of the best ways, for good or ill, is to say, "Rally round the slogan, folks."

06 Which would be the best title of the passage?

① History of Slogan
② Overuse of Slogan in Modern Society
③ Economic Gains of Slogan
④ Slogan and Public Education
⑤ Complete Decline of Slogan in Modern Society

07 According to the author, what causes 'sloganosis'?

① the pubic's distrust
② economic inflation
③ oversupply of slogans
④ weak leadership
⑤ excessive use of psychology in advertizing

08 According to the passage, the author suggests _____.

① the main purpose of slogans is to let the public act
② sloganeering will be disappearing in the future
③ the language of slogans should be more intellectual
④ national economy is deeply related with the future of slogans
⑤ slogans have been used to exploit human weakness

[09-10] 한양대 2016

A company has a great product and naturally wants consumers to think of it as the best they can buy. So the marketing team rolls out an advertising campaign showing why the product is superior to the competition in terms of features and price, and is rewarded with robust sales. Instead of being able to bask in that success, however, the company starts to hear a lot of complaints and get a lot of returns. Clearly, the strategy (A) _____. But why? It turns out that comparative ads and "Ours is the best!" product positioning activate something known as the maximizing mind-set, which leads people to regard anything that's less than perfect as a waste of money. Our research has found that although some people are "maximizers" by nature, and others tend to be content with "good enough," those attitude aren't fixed. The maximizing mind-set can be induced by situations that encourage people to make comparisons and to look for the very best. When marketing messages inadvertently induce it, the results may be post-purchase regret and brand switching at the slightest hint of (B) _____.

09 빈칸에 들어갈 표현으로 가장 적절한 것은?

	(A)	(B)
①	failed	adversity
②	recoiled	improvement
③	backfired	disappointment
④	floundered	gratification

10 윗글의 내용과 거리가 먼 것은?

① Comparative ads do not always pay off.
② Maximizers tend to entice other people to make comparisons.
③ The maximizing mind-set is contingent upon situations.
④ Consumers with a maximizing mind-set are inclined to seek after the very best.

[11-13] 성균관대 2010

The marketing world is full of folklore about consumer reactions to color. Color preference can often sound like a mix of fad and cultural custom, especially when the French will eat gray tinned peas and beans, while the British will not, and we prefer green apples to the Americans' glossy red. [Ⅰ] However, there is more to color than meets the eye. The idea that color can affect the nervous system in some way seems strengthened by the fact that experiments have recorded raised blood pressure in red surroundings and lowered blood pressure in blue surrounding. [Ⅱ] Red evokes subjective reactions of increased energy and hunger; blue evokes tranquility and relaxation. Whether knowingly or otherwise, the effects of seeing red have been cleverly exploited by fast food chains. [Ⅲ] As well as making people hungry, red and its close relation, orange, cause people to feel ㉮_____. By using these colors, places like Mcdonald's create an atmosphere which increases the appetite but subtly dissuades the customer from hanging around for very long. [Ⅳ] Color has also been used to strike effect in the marketing of consumer products. A group of housewives was once asked to test samples of identical soap powder in three different boxes, one yellow, one blue and one a mix of blue and yellow. [Ⅴ] Extraordinary results ensued: the powder in the yellow packet was judged to be so powerful that some said it had damaged their clothes, while the blue was said to be so weak that it left stains behind; the powder in the mix of blue and yellow was assessed as just right. Yet the only difference was in ㉯_____.

11 When the above passage can be divided into three paragraphs, which would be the best boundary?

① [Ⅰ] and [Ⅲ]
② [Ⅰ] and [Ⅳ]
③ [Ⅱ] and [Ⅲ]
④ [Ⅲ] and [Ⅳ]
⑤ [Ⅲ] and [Ⅴ]

12 Which of the following is most appropriate for the blank ㉮?

① peaceful
② generous
③ nervous
④ hurried
⑤ comfortable

13 Which of the following would be best for the blank ㉯?

① the color of the powder
② the color of the packet
③ the color of the clothes
④ the quality of the powder
⑤ the quality of the packet

[14-15] 한양대 2008

> While journalists profess their faith in this objective world, they have little confidence in their ability to recognize it. The norms of "objective" reporting thus involves presenting "both sides" of an issue regardless of their veracity. We thus have the poignant irony that a journalist who systematically attempts to verify facts-to say which set of facts is more accurate-runs the risk of being accused of abandoning his or her objectivity by favoring one side over another. Interestingly, this objective reporting tends to promote a specific ideology. Lurking within it is a specific philosophical assumption about where truth lies. Since the objective reporting tends to assume that both sides will always be speaking partial truth, it is easy to infer that (A).

14 Which of the following is the best title for the passage?

① Ideology and Journalism
② The Verification of Truth
③ The Pitfall of Objective Reporting
④ The Norms of Objective Reporting

15 Which of the following best fits into (A)?

① the whole truth must be within us
② the whole truth must be within our reach
③ the whole truth must lie somewhere out there
④ the whole truth must lie somewhere in the middle

[16-17] 한양대 2014

A mainstay of American newspapers since the early nineteenth century, political cartoons use graphic art to comment on current events in a way that will inform, amuse, provoke, poke, and persuade readers. Cartoons take on the principal issues and leaders of the day, skewering hypocritical or corrupt politicians and depicting the ridiculous, the ironic, or the serious nature of a major event in a single, deftly drawn image. Cartoons use few words, if any, to convey their message. Some use caricature, a technique in which a cartoonist exaggerates the features of well-known people to (A) _____ them. Because they have the ability to evoke an emotional response in readers, political cartoons can serve as a vehicle for swaying public opinion and can contribute to reform. Thomas Nast (1840–1902), the preeminent political cartoonist of the second half of the nineteenth century, demonstrated the power of his medium when he used his art to end the corrupt Boss Tweed Ring in New York City. His images are still in currency today: Nast created the tiger as the symbol of Tammany Hall, the elephant for the Republican Party, and the donkey for the Democratic Party. Created under tight deadlines for (B) _____ formats like newspapers, cartoons still manage to have influence. Although they tackle the principal issues and leaders of their day, they often provide a vivid historical picture for generations to come.

16 빈칸에 들어갈 가장 알맞은 것을 고르시오.

	(A)	(B)
①	make fun of	ephemeral
②	look down on	fleeting
③	find fault with	collateral
④	get the upper hand of	improvising

17 윗글의 내용과 가장 어울리는 견해를 고르시오.

① The more mean-spirited a political cartoon is, the more effective.
② Political cartoons are a powerful means of influencing the public.
③ Political cartoonists must maintain their objectivity on controversial subjects.
④ Because of their relevance to current affairs, political cartoons rarely serve as historical documents.

[18-20] 이화여대 2017

Most industry discourse about convergence begins and ends with what I call the black box fallacy: sooner or later all media is going to be flowing through a single black box in our living rooms and all we have to do is to figure out which black box it will be. Media convergence is not an endpoint; rather, [A] _____ at various intersections between media technologies, industries, content, and audiences. Thanks to the [B] _____ of channels and the increasingly [C] _____ nature of computing and telecommunications, we are entering an era where media will be everywhere and we will use all kinds of media in relation to each other.

Media convergence is more than simply a technological shift; it alters the relationship between existing technologies, industries, markets, genres, and audiences. This initial wave of media changes exerts a destabilizing influence, resulting in a series of lurches between exhilaration and panic. Yet, media convergence is also sparking creative innovation in almost every sector of popular culture; our present media environment is marked by a proliferation of differences.

18 What is the most appropriate title of the passage above?

① Black Box Fallacy: The Beginning and the Ending of Media Convergence
② Black Box Fallacy and the Technological Shift
③ Media Convergence and Its Destabilizing Influence
④ Media Convergence and the Changing Environment
⑤ The Intersections of Media and the Fallacy of Convergence

19 Which expression best fits [A]?

① it overturned the black box fallacy
② it is an ongoing process occurring
③ it is the disintegrating situation happening
④ it confused audiences
⑤ it misled the industry

20 Which pair best fits [B] and [C]?

① multiplication – ambivalent
② privatization – proactive
③ proliferation – ubiquitous
④ diffusion – circumscribed
⑤ dispersion – displaced

[21-24] 동국대 2008

American society has a long-standing tradition of criticizing violence in the media. During the nineteenth century, educators and others warned about the effects of ⓐ lurid dime novels and newspaper crime stories on the young. In the early twentieth century, motion pictures and radio were both viewed as significant social threats. Today, concerns are expressed about violence in computer games, popular songs, and on the Internet. Throughout the evolving changes in media technology, a fundamental question has remained the same: Do depictions of violence in the media somehow contribute to real-life violence? Since the 1950s, television has been at the center of the debate over media violence. There are several reasons for the focus on television. It is pervasive and thus it is heavily watched. More worse, television shows are frequently violent. In one 1982 study, researchers who analyzed 180 hours of programming counted 1,846 acts of violence. The net result of television's popularity and violent content is that the average American child witnesses eight thousand murders and one hundred thousand other acts of violence by the time he or she finishes elementary school. Many argue that exposure to such quantities of violent depictions damages children and contributes to violence in real life. In particular, critics claim that television violence teaches children that violence is an acceptable solution to problems and fosters a fearful attitude by leading viewers to think that the world is more violent than it really is.

21 The word ⓐ lurid closest in meaning to _____.

① dirty
② grisly
③ ludicrous
④ boring

22 Which of the following is the best title of the passage?

① History of Media Violence in American Society
② Internet Violence Drives Back TV Violence
③ The Evolving Changes in Media Technology
④ The Impact of TV Violence on Young Americans

23 Which of the following is true according to the passage?

① American society has long been afflicted with acts of violence.
② Both radio and newspaper still pose a major threat to the fabric of today's society.
③ Since the mid-twentieth century, American people have blamed TV as the main source of media source of media violence.
④ The 1982 study refuted the claim that media violence had been directly responsible for the promotion of aggression.

24 Which of the following is NOT mentioned as the reasons for the focus on TV?

① It is widely distributed.
② It is very popular.
③ It is scandalous.
④ It has violent contents.

[25-26] 성균관대 2012

Perhaps the most significant problem with the media hyperbole concerning cloning is the easy assumption that humans simply are a product of their genes—a view usually called "genetic essentialism." Television hosts and radio personalities have asked whether it would be possible to stock an entire basketball team with clones of Michael Jordan. In response, philosophers, theologians, and other experts have reiterated wearily that, although human behavior undeniably has a genetic component, a host of other factor—including uterine environment, family dynamics, social setting, diet, and other personal history—play important roles in an individual's development. Consequently, a clone produced from the DNA of an outstanding athlete might not be interested in sports. What's more, the cloning issue reveals the way in which the mass media foster attitudes of technological and scientific determinism by implying that scientific 'progress' cannot be halted. Of course, many scientists share the attitudes, and too often, they refuse to accept moral responsibility for their participation in research that may contribute to human suffering.

25 The best title of the passage would be _____.

① Benefits of Scientific Progress
② Media and the Ethics of Cloning
③ Media's Contribution to Anti-cloning Campaigns
④ Sports and Scientific Determinism
⑤ Regulation of Cloning through Laws

26 According to the passage, which of the following is true?

① Scientists are entitled to adopt the objective attitude towards moral controversy.
② The media seem to be obsessed with the idea of DNA as fate.
③ Most scientists admit that cloning research needs to be limited.
④ Most theologians have very little knowledge of science.
⑤ There has been too much negative media attention on human cloning.

[27-30] 숙명여대 2017

The mass media serves as an important part of the cultural context in which women experience eating disorders. The consequences of an eating disorder include harm not only to their physical bodies through severe dieting, strenuous exercise, or purging, but harm to their emotional well-being. Eating disordered women become caught up in feelings of unworthiness and low self-esteem, which then succeeds only in driving them to become even more thin in order to have control over their own bodies. Research shows that there is a correlation between the amount of media exposure one has and body dissatisfaction. Studies often point to the media's portrayal of an unattainable cultural ideal as having a(n) [A] _____ impact on females' self-perception of their own bodies, as well as [B] _____ their self-esteem. Some females inaccurately perceive the shape of their own body due to a dualistic combination of lowered self-esteem and perfectionist values that may have been instilled through familial relations or other primary groups. There are many industries profiting off of this unrealistic body model. The cosmetic surgery industry is profiting at an all-time high. Women are paying over six billion dollars for purely cosmetic surgeries. Many women are spending an extraordinary amount of money to subject themselves to unnecessary surgery, which includes the use of anesthetics and oftentimes invasive procedures that require long recovery times, only to look more like our society's cultural ideal, which is significantly below a healthy weight according to the medical model.

27 Which pair of words best completes [A] and [B]?

① negative – pulling down
② overwhelming – upholding
③ ineligible – heightening
④ enormous – demanding
⑤ bad – condemning

28 What is the side effect of using anesthetics in cosmetic surgery?

① Anesthetics makes plastic surgery unnecessary.
② It summons women to spend enormous money.
③ It causes eating disorders.
④ It requires long recovery time after surgery.
⑤ It makes women to find an alternative way to imitate the role model reflected on TV.

29 Which of the following is NOT TRUE for the eating disordered women?

① They usually do extreme dieting.
② They construct their own body images autonomously and multidimensionally.
③ They are spending lots of money for unrequired plastic surgery.
④ They may perceive their own images through perfectionist values inculcated from outside.
⑤ None of the above

30 Which of the following statements is NOT TRUE for the above passage?

① Women who are dissatisfied with the shape of their own bodies usually do exercise strenuously.
② The cosmetic surgery industry gets high profit nowadays.
③ Mass media advertises the improbable type of female body.
④ Women's eating disorders are quite natural in the present age.
⑤ None of the above

CHAPTER 04 교육

[01-03] 숭실대 2006

If we say that "x is a necessary condition for y," we mean that if we don't have x, then we won't have y. Or put differently, without x, you won't have y. To say that x is a necessary condition for y does not mean that x guarantees y. If we say that "x is a sufficient condition for y," then we mean that if we have x, we know that y must follow. In other words, x guarantees y. To illustrate, some educators argue that there is a causal connection between improved performance by public school students (as measured by the SAT) and the expenditure of dollars on schools by state governments, that more money spent yields better learning. This claim is in some degree undermined by those who point out that during the years 1992-1993 none of the five states with the highest teachers' salaries was among the 15 U.S. states with the top SAT scores; and of the 10 states with the highest per-pupil expenditures, only one (Wisconsin) was among the 10 states with the highest SAT scores; and the state with the highest per-pupil expenditure, New Jersey, ranked 39th in SAT scores—all evidence tending to show that high expenditure is not a ⓐ_____ condition of student achievement. But the 10 states with the lowest per-pupil spending included four (North Dakota, South Dakota, Tennessee, and Utah) among the 10 states with the top SAT scores; and while North Dakota ranked 44th in expenditures it ranked second in SAT scores; and while South Dakota ranked last in teachers' salaries it ranked third in SAT scores—all evidence tending to show that high expenditure is not a ⓑ_____ condition of student achievement.

01 According to the passage, data collected from 1992-1993 demonstrate that _____.

① some scholars argue that states should spend more money on education
② student academic achievements will invariably improve if more money is spent on education
③ necessary conditions are more important regarding school performance than sufficient conditions
④ money spent on education does not always result in higher student academic achievements

02 According to the passage, which of the following states best illustrates that higher expenditures do not inevitably produce higher student achievements?

① Tennessee
② New Jersey
③ Wisconsin
④ South Dakota

03 Choose the most appropriate words for blanks ⓐ and ⓑ.

	ⓐ	ⓑ
①	sufficient	necessary
②	necessary	necessary
③	necessary	sufficient
④	sufficient	sufficient

[04-06] 이화여대 2013

> The major philosophical issue affecting treatment of the gifted is whether education should be aimed at elevating the masses or at nurturing those who evidence the greatest potential. The issue has often been posed as a dichotomy between [A] _____ and democratic equality. Another perspective is that the democratic practice of educating equally individuals of unequal intelligence—that is, having the same expectations and standards for the bright and the dull—is a false conception of equality that leads to [B] _____ and wasted talent. True equality consists rather in providing each individual [C] "_____" (Tsuin-chen, 1961). Throughout history the prevailing philosophy with regard to equality of opportunity has been manifested in the treatment of gifted individuals.
>
> What society values has also helped determine the definition and identification of gifted individuals over time. When visual arts have been prized—for example, in Renaissance Europe—society has sought out and supported the artistically gifted. Acute needs based on emergencies such as war or famine, and chronic needs existing over time, have also influenced society's identification of gifted individuals. The warrior society of ancient Sparta, for instance, required and hence nurtured individuals gifted with military prowess.

04 Choose a statement that may be inferred from the passage above.

① Parents of gifted children are often overly assertive individuals.
② Gifted individuals should be given an education according to their ability.
③ The definition of gifted individuals has stayed the same over time.
④ Parents of gifted children should provide stimulating materials in the home.
⑤ Economic differences may affect child-rearing practices.

05 Which pair best fits [A] and [B]?

① superiority – competence
② clique – achievement
③ dregs – ordinariness
④ elitism – mediocrity
⑤ extract – skillfulness

06 Which best suits the quote in [C]?

① an equal opportunity to profit by education according to his intelligence
② specialized resources and intensive instructional efforts
③ a supportive home environment as well as personal commitment and excellent teaching
④ stimulating materials in the home
⑤ more elaborate speech, explanation, reasoning, praise, and specific feedback

[07-09] 경희대 2012

Home schooling could affect children's relationships with their peers and other adults because of prolonged periods spent with their parents, educationalists have claimed. Most academics concede that education will in the future be increasingly centered around the home, and fear children could become isolated and withdrawn. Professor Michael Barber, of London University's Institute of Education, said pupils could spend half their time at school and half at home as a compromise. He said home tuition would play an increasingly significant role in educating children in the coming years. "I believe very strongly that children need to have the experience of school," he added. "There is the quality control issue of ensuring pupils are taught the basics and assessed. Children also need to spend time with their peers to learn the rules of work in a democratic society and learn to deal with relationships with adults other than their parents." Margaret Rudland, head teacher of Godolphin and Latymer School, said children needed to experience the ⓐ 'rough and tumble' of peer associations.

07 윗글의 주제로 가장 알맞은 것은?

① Children's relationship with peers and adults
② The role of home schooling in education
③ Home is the center for education
④ Danger of home schooling

08 윗글로부터 알 수 없는 것은?

① Some people believe isolating home schoolers from their peers can be dangerous.
② Home schooling may affect children's socialization skills because they spend little time with peers.
③ Some educators believe traditional schools will not exist in the future.
④ Most experts believe the center of educations will be the home in the future.

09 ⓐ **rough and tumble**이 의미하는 것은?

① hard or demanding aspects
② physical exercises
③ feeling of competition
④ conversations with other pupils

[10-11] 성균관대 2012

In the depths of every exam candidate's nightmares lurks the toad-like examiner, dripping red ink all over the painfully written exam script and laughing fiendishly. But examiners are remarkably tolerant people. They all stress that they try to find good work and would far rather pass somebody than fail them. However, there are certain things which are guaranteed to irritate the most friendly of examiners. A chief examiner says, "Any paper that's roughly presented starts off as a loser. How can we be fair to someone if we can't read what they have written?" The one thing that most infuriates them all is _____. Some candidates pick out one or two words in the written question and they think, 'Ah. I remember those words,' and just pour out what they did in class. It should be statutory that no exam candidate is allowed to pick up a pen for the first quarter of an hour. They should spend that time just making sure they understand what's wanted and then planning answers. Some pupils pride themselves on their ability to waffle—but there are no prizes for writing a longer script than anybody else, so don't pad. On the other hand, it's better to resort to waffle rather than leave one question out.

10 Which of the following is most appropriate for the blank?

① forgetting the writing kits
② spending too much time working out one question
③ being late for the exam
④ not answering the questions as set
⑤ not submitting the paper in time

11 According to the passage, which of the following is true?

① Some students have too much pride to admit that they failed the exams.
② Some exam candidates tend to add unnecessary materials to their answers.
③ The worst nightmare for the examiners is the rude attitudes of the exam candidates.
④ Writing at great length is always the best way for doing well on exams.
⑤ The examiners are rarely affected by the poor handwriting of the exam candidates.

[12-13] 중앙대 2015

Whatever their initial motivations, fundamentalist groups were occasionally successful in pursuing anti-evolution goals in the South and Southwest during the first few decades of the last century. By the end of the 1920s, fundamentalists had introduced antievolution bills into a majority of U.S. state legislatures, and had passed some in various southern states. Probably the most famous confrontation between evolution and biblical creationism during that period was the 1925 trial of a schoolteacher, John Scopes, who was convicted of ignoring the ban against teaching evolution in Tennessee schools.

Although many biologists felt that the Scopes trial essentially defeated the intellectual validity of the creationist position, creationists apparently lost little ground in these regions and managed to have an impact on public education far beyond the South and Southwest. As Nelkin pointed out, by influencing textbook adoption procedures in various local and state school boards in the United States, creationists successfully minimized evolutionary explanations in secondary school textbooks for a long time.

The impetus for an increase of evolutionary teaching in U.S. secondary schools was the result of a movement to reform the science curriculum in the late 1950s and early 1960s, when it was realized that science education lagged behind that of other countries, specifically the Soviet Union, which in 1957 had launched the first space satellite, Sputnik. Among these innovations were new high school textbooks in both biological and social sciences that discussed evolution and analyzed changes in human social relationships. By the end of the 1960s anti-evolution laws were either repealed or declared unconstitutional. Within the last decade, a number of societies and institutes established by fundamentalists for the propagation of creation science/intelligent design have entered the fray with the aim of including creationism in the science curriculum. Despite the name, there is little (if any) recognizable science in creation science. Although considerable literature deals with creationist attacks on evolution, the refusal of fundamentalist creationists to accept the scientific evidence shows no promise of ever being resolved.

12 윗글을 통해 추론할 수 있는 것으로 가장 적합한 것을 고르시오.

① The increase of the evolutionary teaching resulted in the public belief that creationists deteriorated the quality of science education.
② The author is skeptical about the arguments in intelligent design proposed by fundamentalists.
③ Fundamentalists were successful in introducing anti-evolution bills to the entire states of the U.S. in the 1920s.
④ Fundamentalists' essential claims are based on the premises of evolutionary biology.

13 윗글의 제목으로 가장 적합한 것을 고르시오.

① Contribution of Science Education to the Development of Space Science
② Science Curriculum Reform in U.S. Secondary Schools
③ Eulogy to the Propagation of Creationism
④ Creationist-Evolutionist Conflict in the U.S. Science Education

[14-17] 경희대 2013

To find the origins of Yale University, don't go to New Haven, Conn., the New England city where this ⓐ hallowed American institution of higher learning sits. Instead, head to the old British redoubt of Fort St. George in Chennai, India. This was where, in the 17th century, a certain Elihu Yale made his fortune as a top official of the East India Co. His riches enabled him to eventually donate a carton of books and cloth in 1718 to an obscure college across the oceans in colonial Connecticut. Those items, summarily sold for the kingly sum of £562, helped shore up the ⓑ fledgling school that would take his name. What later became the training ground for five U.S. Presidents, myriad world leaders, and generations of American cognoscenti would not be what it is today ⓒ _____. Fast-forward almost three centuries and Yale's connections to the East are once again dominating events on campus. A controversial venture into Singapore—another creation of East India Co.—is proceeding apace: the Yale-National University of Singapore (NUS) College is set to open its doors to students in August 2013. Yale's administrators have touted it as one of Asia's first liberal-arts colleges, an institution that emphasizes "critical thinking and classroom interaction." Last year Yale president Richard Levin said, "Just as Yale shaped liberal-arts education in the U.S. in the 19th century, we believe the new Yale-NUS College can play a ⓓ pivotal role in shaping the many liberal-arts colleges likely to be built in Asia in the coming decades."

14 윗글의 제목으로 적절한 것은?

① Yale University's Connections to the East
② How Elihu Yale Made His Fortune
③ The Yale-National University of Singapore College
④ The Importance of Liberal-Arts Education

15 밑줄 친 ⓒ에 들어갈 알맞은 표현은?

① were it not for its ties with Asia
② because it had ties with Asia
③ because it did not have ties with Asia
④ were if not for its ties with Asia

16 밑줄 친 ⓐ **hallowed**, ⓑ **fledgling**, ⓓ **pivotal**의 가장 적절한 의미의 조합은?

① sacred – soaring – central
② sacred – skyrocketing – important
③ consecrated – young – principal
④ consecrated – renowned – main

17 윗글의 내용과 일치하는 것은?

① 예일 대학교는 인도에서 처음으로 개교하였다.
② 예일 대학교는 처음부터 세계적으로 유명했다.
③ 예일–싱가포르 국립대의 교양대학은 논란이 되고 있다.
④ 예일 대학교는 영국의 동인도회사에 의해 설립되었다.

[18-19] 중앙대 2013

During the 1890s, the map of higher learning changed profoundly in the United States. As pressures to organize learning around post-Darwinian conceptions of science mounted with growing acceptance of natural evolution, belief in human agency apart from divine intervention grew apace. This altered preferred modes of scientific investigation and explanation. Increasingly, innovation and progress came to be associated with specialization and experimentation, one result being that new disciplines multiplied. _____. Once almost exclusively the province of men with ministerial training, it now became a secular academic profession. In addition, having been an expansive, even comprehensive, field in scope, philosophy now became, more narrowly focused. Just as natural philosophy had earlier evolved into the various natural sciences, so now moral philosophy evolved into various social sciences. Those aspects of mental philosophy or psychology that might be studied in a laboratory also gained distinct disciplinary definition. Before the opening of the twentieth century, psychologists had developed their own professional association and journals to facilitate communication and mark the autonomy of their new community. (A) The separation of psychology from philosophy had important consequences for education, which was just then beginning to gain acceptance as a subject of university study. (B) Because psychology involved the study of mental functions and structures, its relevance to education was clear. (C) What is more, unlike philosophy, a discipline in which one's search for truth was guided by abstract values or theological beliefs, psychology involved empirical research. (D) Seeming to provide education with a scientific basis, psychology quickly became a popular topic among teachers and reformers interested in education.

18 논지의 흐름상 빈칸에 들어가기에 가장 적합한 것을 고르시오.

① Despite the innovative movements, philosophy remained impeccable inside the Beltway.
② Challenged by these developments, philosophy underwent a thoroughgoing transformation.
③ Motivated by the paradigm shift, philosophy embraced contradictions from a diversity of domains.
④ As things turned out, philosophy shunned the objective inquiry approach from natural science.

19 아래의 문장이 들어갈 위치로 가장 적합한 곳을 고르시오.

This lent an aura of "objective science" to psychology that philosophy lacked.

① (A) ② (B)
③ (C) ④ (D)

[20-21] 중앙대 2013

Dyslexia has traditionally been defined by exclusionary criteria. The term is used to describe a child's significant difficulty, for no clearly apparent reason, in acquiring efficient reading skills. The difficulties cannot be attributed to sensory, intellectual, or neurological impairments, obvious speech and language disorders, emotional or behavioral disorders, or lack of educational opportunity. Terms such as "specific reading disability" and "reading disorder" have been used interchangeably to refer to this condition. This exclusionary definition of dyslexia is fraught with assumptions that have yet to be proven. It assumes that children who have reading difficulties in the presence of average intellectual ability (i.e., reading discrepancy criteria) have different types of difficulties than children whose reading difficulties are commensurate with their lower intelligence.

As researchers argued, there is little consistent evidence to validate this hypothesis. For example, children diagnosed as having dyslexia _____ children whose reading difficulties were consistent with their lower intellectual abilities. A large-scale developmental study demonstrated that the performance of two groups of young children with reading ability, who also demonstrated differing levels of verbal intellectual ability, did not differ on a number of sound awareness tasks. Furthermore, not only has the validity of intelligence tests been questioned, in general, but their relevance to the reading-disabled population is problematic, because they include tasks whose performance may be fostered by reading experience itself. It is established, however, that dyslexia can be present in individuals who have markedly superior intellectual abilities. Thomas Edison, Albert Einstein, and Auguste Rodin are examples of "men of eminence" who all struggled with acquiring efficient reading or spelling skills.

20 빈칸에 들어가기에 가장 적합한 것을 고르시오.

① demonstrated very different behavioral patterns from
② revealed very similar recovery resilience to
③ displayed very different intellectual abilities from
④ exhibited very similar decoding processes to

21 윗글을 통해 추론할 수 있는 것으로 가장 적합한 것을 고르시오.

① In general, children with lower intelligence will be more likely to experience difficulties in acquiring reading skills than those with higher intellectual abilities.
② The findings from developmental studies are of a great use in accounting for the positive correlation between children's intelligence test scores and their reading difficulty.
③ There could be a number of different factors for a child's significant difficulty with reading skills, but speech and language disorders are the crucial ones.
④ Children may differ in the ease of the acquisition of reading skills even though they do not differ in the ability of sound awareness.

[22-24] 성균관대 2017

We use the terms "college" and "university" interchangeably. "She went to Michigan," we say, or "he goes to Oberlin"—not bothering with the noun that follows the name as if a college and a university were the same thing. They are not. They are, to be sure, interconnected and a college may exist as a division of "school" within a university. But a college and a university have a different purposes. [A] The former is about transmitting knowledge of and from the past to undergraduate students so they may draw upon it as a living resource in the future. The latter is mainly an array of research activities conducted by faculty and graduate students with the aim of creating new knowledge in order to supersede the past. [B] Both of these are worthy aims, and sometimes they converge, as when a college student works with a scholar or scientist doing cutting-edge or groundbreaking research. More often, however, these purposes come into competition, if not conflict, especially as one moves up the ladder of prestige. [C] As the man who created one of the world's great universities, the University of California, acknowledged with unusual honesty, "a superior faculty results in an inferior concern for undergraduate teaching." [D] It has been nearly fifty years since Clark Kerr identified this "cruel paradox" as one of our more pressing problems. Today it is more pressing than ever. [E] But what, exactly, is at stake in college, and why should it matter how much or little goes on there? F At its core, a college should be a place where young people find help for navigating the territory between adolescence and adulthood. It should provide guidance, but not coercion, for students trying to cross that treacherous terrain on their way toward self-knowledge. It should help them develop certain qualities of mind and heart requisite for reflective citizenship.

22 The underlined "Both of these" refer to _____.

① college and university
② graduate and undergraduate
③ education and research
④ past and future
⑤ tradition and cutting-edge science

23 The underlined "cruel paradox" means that _____.

① a college might be better than a university
② great scholars are not necessarily great teachers
③ college diploma does not guarantee a decent job
④ a university professor may teach better than a college one
⑤ students don't learn much from their college life

24 If the above passage is divided into three paragraphs, the best boundary would be _____.

① A   C
② A   D
③ B   D
④ B   E
⑤ C   F

[25-27] 홍익대 2018

Lawrence Kohlberg's stages of moral development have been hugely influential and are widely accepted. Kohlberg built on Piaget's work by creating a series of dilemmas in which he used to see the moral reasoning that children, young people, and adults were using in order to provide a solution. He concluded that moral development consists of three stages: pre-conventional (ages 6-13), conventional (ages 13-16), and post-conventional (ages 16+).

In the pre-conventional stage, children are not being guided by their own moral reasoning, but follow their parents and carers. They are doing this either to seek reward or to avoid punishment. Through punishment and obedience, the child finds out about what is right and wrong through seeing consequences of their actions. Individualism and instrumental purposes result in the child learning that some actions and behaviors are rewarded. The child is also learning to avoid behaviors that might mean punishment. By the end of the pre-conventional stage the child is also beginning to enjoy helping people and has learned the 'If I help you, you might be able to help me' approach.

The conventional stage consists of an awareness of group behavior and the ideas of what is and is not acceptable in society. In this stage, children become aware of mutual interpersonal expectations, relationships, and interpersonal conformity. Children come to believe that good behavior pleases other people, e.g., parents, friends, and teachers. They are also becoming aware of the motive factor, e.g., 'He didn't mean to drop it. He meant to help.' Also, they become more aware of society's needs and interests, and what is deemed by society to be right or wrong. They are keen to obey regulations and laws.

25 What is the main purpose of the passage?

① To explain early childhood moral development
② To describe child ages and mental growth
③ To persuade importance of parents in childhood
④ To provide examples for intellectual development

26 According to the passage, which of the following is true?

① A child in the age of 14 shows the moral development in the pre-conventional stage.
② Piaget criticized Kohlberg's research work, and presented three-stage childhood development.
③ Children at 13-16 ages come to understand the motives underlying human behavior.
④ In moral development, the conventional stage is followed by the pre-conventional stage.

27 Which of the following would be most likely to follow the passage?

① Kohlberg's critical review on the Piaget's work
② Effects of friendship on moral development
③ Reasons for moral and cognitive development
④ Children's post-conventional moral development

[28-30] 국민대 2016

All across the U.S. kids troop back to school each year in late August or early September. However, for youngsters at Moton Elementary School, summer ended this year on July 10. On that date, the kids returned for the third year of an experimental program that adds 40 extra days to the usual 180-day school year. They were breaking a long-standing American tradition of summer vacation—dating back to a time when family labor was vital to the late-summer harvest—that gives the U.S. one of the shortest school years in the industrialized world. There is surely a connection between that distinction and the Ⓐ dismal academic performances of American students, compared with their peers elsewhere. A growing number of ordinary Americans support the idea. The Gallup Organization, which has been polling on the subject since 1958, found that last week for the first time a majority of its sample favored a longer year. Most parents of Moton Elementary School also strongly support the longer school session and worry about a return to the old system. It is clear that the time for a hard look at the longer school year has come. It seems a litmus test on how serious we are about education. The summer time harvest that America needs to reap these days is not down on the farm, but up in the mind.

28 Which is the best title of the passage?

① Need for a Longer School Year
② Kids' Expectation for Vacation
③ Return to the Old School System
④ Farm Harvests in America and Elsewhere

29 Which is closest in meaning to the underlined Ⓐ dismal?

① miserable
② consistent
③ improved
③ exceptional

30 Which is true according to the passage?

① Parents at Moton Elementary School are not serious about education.
② We find a longer school year in most industrialized countries than in the U.S.
③ Moton Elementary School started to have a longer school session last year.
④ The second Gallup survey on the school year was conducted long after the first.

CHAPTER 05 경제·경영

[01-02] 중앙대 2008

Several arguments have been brought forward to suggest that a rising population hinders the economic growth of an underdeveloped economy. First, such an economy will have a high burden of dependency, that is to say the number of children will be large relative to the working population that has to support them. A rise in population will increase this burden, since it will lead to a rise in the number of children. ⓐ Furthermore, resources that might have been used for investment purposes will be needed to satisfy current consumption. ⓑ Linked with this, funds which might have been used to raise the amount of capital per worker will instead be needed to duplicate exiting facilities, whether these are productive capital or social overhead capital. ⓒ It has been demonstrated that the faster a population grows, the more investment is needed to keep constant the amount of capital per worker. ⓓ In numerical terms, it is reckoned that if a population is increasing by 1% per annum, an investment of 2.5% to 5% of national income is needed, merely to keep constant the amount of equipment per worker.

01 윗글에서 다음 문장이 들어갈 곳으로 가장 적합한 것을 고르시오.

> This will mean that even more labor will be tied up in caring for them.

① ⓐ ② ⓑ
③ ⓒ ④ ⓓ

02 윗글에 제시된 내용과 가장 일치하는 것을 고르시오.

① A rising population impedes the use of resources for investment purposes in an underdeveloped economy.
② A rising population in an underdeveloped economy leads to a fall in labor cost.
③ A rising population in an underdeveloped economy leads to an immediate increase in the working population.
④ A rising population is compatible with an economic growth in an underdeveloped economy.

[03-05] 한국외대 2016

Ever since the 2008 financial crisis, predictions of the dollar's demise have come repeatedly. As the U.S. economy sank into recession, so too did confidence that the greenback could maintain its long-held position as the world's premier reserve currency. But here we are, several years after the crisis, and the dollar is showing just how (A) _____ it is. The dollar index, which measures its value against other currencies, recently reached a four-year high. And the policymakers who criticized the dollar show little interest in dumping it. The buoyancy of the greenback reflects the fact that the U.S. is a rare bright spot among the world's major economies. American GDP in the third quarter grew an annualized 3.5% — far higher than what most other industrialized economies have been posting. The fact remains too that no other currency can truly (B) _____ the dollar. The uncertain stability of the euro was exposed by its multiyear sovereign-debt crisis and the chaotic response that followed from Europe's leaders. How long the dollar's run lasts depends on everything from the future growth of U.S. GDP to the health of the global economy. There are plenty of factors that could undercut the dollar over the long term. Russia and China are settling more trade between the two nations in rubles and yuan. If other economic powerhouses follow suit, that could begin to chip away at the dollar's utility. (C) But for now, that's a very big if.

03 From the context, which of the following ordered pairs best fits into (A) and (B)?

① priceless – eliminate
② improbable – supplement
③ sensitive – beat
④ almighty – rival

04 Which of the following is implied by (C)?

① The dollar's stability will last for a while.
② Other economic powerhouses will trade more in dollars.
③ The global economy will remain unhealthy.
④ Russia and China may threaten the dollar's utility.

05 Which of the following is NOT true of the passage?

① People have anticipated the fall of the American currency.
② There is potential for other currencies, such as ruble and yuan, to challenge the greenback.
③ The growth rate of the American GDP has outstripped those of its rivals recently.
④ Despite European debt, the euro has maintained its strong utility.

[06-07] 광운대 2007

Years ago, when I was a young assistant professor at the Harvard Business School, I thought that the key to developing managerial leadership lay in raw brain power. I thought the role of business schools was to develop future managers who knew all about the various functions of business—to teach them how to define problems succinctly, analyze these problems and identify alternatives in a clear, logical fashion, and, finally, to teach them to make an intelligent decision. My thinking gradually became tempered by living and working outside the United States and by serving seven years as a college president. During my presidency of Babson College, I added several additional traits or skills that I felt a good manager must possess. The first is the ability to express oneself in a clear, ⓐ _____ fashion. Good oral and written communication skills are absolutely essential if one is to be an effective manager. Second, one must possess that intangible set of qualities called leadership skills. To be a good leader one must understand and be sensitive to people and be able to inspire them toward the achievement of common goals. Third, I concluded that effective managers must be broad human beings who not only understand the world of business but also have a sense of the cultural, social, political, historical and, particularly, the international aspects of life and society. This suggests that exposure to the liberal arts and humanities should be part of every manager's education.

06 글쓴이의 주장이 아닌 것을 고르시오.

① Managers should be able to understand and inspire people.
② Managers should possess good communication skills.
③ The author thinks that managers should be broadly knowledgable.
④ Managers should be a man of integrity.

07 윗글의 ⓐ에 들어갈 수 있는 가장 적절한 표현을 고르시오.

① blunt
② articulate
③ lengthy
④ perplexing

[08-10] 항공대 2017

The real difference between Malthus and Ricardo did not revolve around gluts, rents, or protection but rather method. Both lived in an age of scientific discovery. Both searched for cause and effect links. Both predicted what would occur because of these links. But Ricardo focused more intensely on the intricate sequence of steps along the way. Malthus seemed content to find a general principle and then apply it to the world. Recall Ricardo's careful seven step path to the stationary world. Malthus did not construct such rigorous models. Under the guidance of James Mill, Ricardo attempted long deductive chains of reasoning. He wanted to derive propositions as certain as Euclidean geometry or Newtonian mechanics. Sometimes his assumptions or first premises were simply wrong. But given those premises, his theory was impregnable. Impregnable, yes; useful, perhaps not. Keynes and Joseph Schumpeter both accused Ricardo of choosing assumptions or examples that ensured the result he desired. Schumpeter called this the "_____."

08 Choose the best answer to fill in the blank.

① Malthusian Trap
② Ricardian Virtue
③ Ricardian Vice
④ Schumpeterian Creative Destruction

09 It can be inferred from the passage _____.

① Malthus and Ricardo defined cause, a major concept in classical economics, exactly the same
② James Mill had inconsiderable influence on the methodological thinking of Ricardo
③ Ricardo was never criticized for this disregard of experience and practice
④ Ricardo believed that economy was a strict science like mathematics

10 Which of the following statements is true?

① Malthus did not construct any model to explain his theory.
② Ricardo's theory was useful in all situations.
③ One of the crucial points separating Ricardo from Malthus was the emphasis Ricardo placed on steps to derive economic principles.
④ Ricardo's assumptions and premises were invincible.

[11-13] 경희대 2009

The fact is that recent economic numbers have been terrifying, not just in the U. S., but around the world. Manufacturing, in particular, is plunging everywhere. Banks aren't lending; businesses and consumers aren't spending. Let's not mince words: This looks an awful lot like the beginning of a second Great Depression.

We weren't supposed to find ourselves in this situation. For many years most economists believed that preventing another Great Depression would be easy. In 2003, Robert Lucas of the University of Chicago, in his presidential address to the American Economic Association, declared that the central problems of depression-prevention has been solved, for all practical purposes, and has in fact been solved for many decades."

Milton Friedman, in particular, persuaded many economists that the Federal Reserve could have stopped the Depression in its tracks simply by providing banks with more liquidity, which would have prevented a sharp fall in the money supply. Ben Bernanke, the Federal Reserve chairman, famously apologized to Friedman on his institution's behalf: "You're right. We did it. We're very sorry. But thanks to you, we won't do it again."

It turns out, however, that preventing depressions isn't that easy after all. Under Mr. Bernanke's leadership, the Fed has been supplying liquidity like an engine crew trying to put out a five-alarm fire, and the money supply has been rising rapidly. Yet credit remains scarce, and the economy is still in free fall.

Friedman's claim that monetary policy could have prevented the Great Depression was an attempt to refute the analysis of John Maynard Keynes, who argued that monetary policy is ineffective under depression conditions and that fiscal policy—large-scale deficit spending by the government—is needed to fight mass unemployment. The failure of monetary policy in the current crisis show that Keynes had it right the first time.

11 According to the passage, many economists in favor of Friedman's theory _____.

① developed effective preventive measures for economic depressions
② preferred monetary policy to curtail the economic crisis
③ were successful in predicting causes of the Great Depression
④ provided a large fiscal spending plan to stop economic depressions

12 The underlined part indicates that the Federal Reserve chairman, Bernanke, _____.

① trusts current economic policy and will not change its direction
② agrees that spending should not be encouraged for more employment
③ acknowledges the problems in Friedman's market-oriented economic policy
④ disagrees with Friedman who believed in lending more money to the poor than to the rich

13 Which one is true about Keynesian economists?

① They demand less control of the government for free market.
② They believe that government intervention is more effective during the economic crisis.
③ They want unlimited bank loans and other monetary support to prevent credit default.
④ They argue against a small government which provides fiscal policy for the unemployed.

[14-15]

> The race to the bottom is a socioeconomic concept that occurs between nations. When competition becomes fierce between nations over a particular area of trade and production, the nations are given increased incentive to dismantle currently existing regulatory standards. It may be seen that with the global push towards free trade, labor is now _____ the race to the bottom model. With an extremely large labor pool to draw from worldwide and a virtually unrestricted ability to move capital, multi-national corporations may now freely move their operations from country to country, following the most affordable labor. This in turn affects labor laws, particularly in developing countries, where things such as minimum wage or required overtime pay create a large barrier to lowest-cost labor. The race to the bottom therefore, dictates that more and more nations (again, particularly in the developing world) will eliminate their labor laws.

14 Which of the following can be inferred from the passage?

① The race to the bottom model results in changes in labor laws.
② International trade restricts the capital flow to developing nations.
③ Cheap labor is concentrated more in developed rather than developing nations.
④ Outsourcing is less common for multinational companies.

15 Choose the one that best fills in the blank.

① thoroughly resisting
② entirely immune to
③ very susceptible to
④ debating whether it needs

[16-17] 중앙대 2009

A margin account sounds mysterious to the uninformed. Actually, it is nothing more than a loan the stockbroker makes to you using your securities as collateral to support the loan. Here's how it works: Say you open a margin account by depositing $3,000. (All brokers require a minimum deposit for a margin account, and the Board of Governors of the Federal Reserve System requires an initial margin requirement of 50 percent of the value of securities purchased.) Then, you buy 100 shares of ABC stock at $___ⓐ___ a share. Thus, you bought $5,000 worth of stock, ignoring commissions, with only a $3,000 deposit; obviously the other $2,000 came from your broker. Now, what happens if the stock goes up or down in value? No problem, if it goes up. You can sell whenever you like and repay the $2,000 loan plus interest and pocket the difference. If it goes down, keep one simple fact in mind—the loss is all yours. You don't share it with the broker. So if ABC goes down to $30 a share and you then sell, the broker still gets $2,000, plus interest, and you still pocket the difference—$1,000 in this case. You lose $2,000, which is $20 a share times the ___ⓑ___ shares.

16 How does the author define a margin account?

① what one loses from investment in stocks
② what one gets from investment in stocks
③ what the stockbroker pays to you
④ what the stockbroker lends to you

17 밑줄 친 ⓐ와 ⓑ에 들어가기에 가장 적합한 것을 고르시오.

① 30 – 50
② 30 – 100
③ 50 – 50
④ 50 – 100

[18-20] 숭실대 2010

For years, American educators have been touting the rise of the "knowledge economy" and shifting focus away from the manual trades, encouraging teens onto the four-year college track in preparation for our supposedly postindustrial society. Meanwhile, ㉮ <u>cubicle jobs are increasingly going the route of manufacturing work</u> as corporations outsource any task that can be delivered over a wireless connection. In addition, thanks to the financial crisis, the drain is only likely to accelerate. So perhaps it is time to reconsider where the future of work is headed as the century unfolds. It's a subject that is starting to gain traction, first in the writings of Princeton economist Alan Blinder and most recently in a clever book called *Shop Class as Soul-craft*, by philosopher (and motorcycle repairman) Matthew Crawford.

Crawford makes some compelling arguments about the link between independent thinking, self-reliance, and working with one's hands. The connection is hardly new: ancient Greek notions of 'knowledge' (sophia) and 'craftiness' (techne) also implied manual dexterity (Athena was patron goddess of both wisdom and craftsmen) and Heidegger identified man as a fundamentally tool-using animal. Blinder predicts that work will soon be divided between ㉯ 'personal services' requiring face-to-face contact and ㉰ 'impersonal services' that don't, and can thus be sent abroad. He counts 30 million to 40 million of these impersonal jobs and predicts that the economic upheaval for white-collar workers is just beginning. For manual labor, however, his analysis suggests a future of rising wages and demand.

18 According to the passage, which of the following is true?

① Educators have been critical of the advent of "knowledge economy."
② The popularity of manual labor has continued since ancient Greek times.
③ Technological development has contributed to changes in the labor market.
④ Crawford and Blinder predict that cubicle jobs will be turned into manual labor in the future.

19 What does ㉮ cubicle jobs are increasingly going the route of manufacturing work mean?

① The demands for cubicle jobs are increasing.
② Cubicle jobs are transferred to manufacturing work.
③ The processes of cubicle jobs are similar to those of manufacturing work.
④ Cubicle jobs are disappearing more and more.

20 What are good example of ㉯ 'personal services' and ㉰ 'impersonal services', respectively?

① chef – repairman
② radiologist – interior designer
③ nurse – book publisher
④ typist – customer service clerk

[21-22] 한양대 2015

The relevance of formal economic models to real-world policy has been a topic of some dispute. The economists R. D. Norton and S. Y. Rhee achieved some success in applying such a model (A) _____ to the Korean economy over a fourteen-year period; the model's figures for output, prices, and other variables closely matched real statistics. The model's value in policy terms, however, proved less clear-cut. Norton and Rhee performed simulations in which, keeping long-term factors constant, they tried to pinpoint the effect of short-term policy changes. Their model indicated that rising prices for imported oil would increase inflation; reducing exports by five percent would lower Gross Domestic Product and increase inflation; and slowing the growth of the money supply would result in slightly higher inflation. These findings are somewhat (B) _____. Many economists have argued that reducing exports will lessen, not increase, inflation. And while most view escalating oil costs as inflationary, few would think the same of slower monetary growth. The Norton-Rhee model can perhaps be viewed as indicating the pitfalls of a formalist approach that stresses statistical "goodness of fit" at the expense of genuine policy relevance.

21 윗글의 목적으로 가장 알맞은 것은?

① to propose a new type of economic analysis
② to suggest an explanation for Korean inflation
③ to determine the accuracy of Norton and Rhee's analysis
④ to describe the limitations of a formal economic model

22 빈칸에 들어갈 가장 알맞은 것은?

	(A)	(B)
①	retrospectively	startling
②	reflectively	promising
③	prospectively	anticipating
④	intensively	disappointing

[23-25] 경희대 2013

> The Japanese say they suffer from an economic disease called ⓐ "structural pessimism." Overseas too, there is a tendency to see Japan as a harbinger of all that is doomed in the economies of the euro zone and America—even though figures released on November 14th show its economy grew by an annualised 6% in the third quarter, rebounding quickly from the March tsunami and nuclear disaster. Look dispassionately at Japan's economic performance over the past ten years, though, and "the second lost decade," if not the first, is a misnomer. Much of what tarnishes Japan's image is the result of demography—ⓑ _____. In aggregate, Japan's economy grew at half the pace of America's between 2001 and 2010. In short, Japan's economy works better for those middle-aged and older than it does for the young. But it is not yet in crisis, and economists say there is plenty it could do to raise its potential growth rate. The trouble is that the downbeat narrative is deeply ingrained. The current crop of leading Japanese politicians, bureaucrats, and businessmen are well past middle age. Mr. Weinstein says they suffer from "diminished-giant syndrome," nervously watching the economic rise of China.

23 문맥상 밑줄 친 ⓐ <u>structural pessimism</u>과 관계가 없는 것은?

① Japanese social milieu of doom
② Japanese economic accomplishment
③ Japanese narratives of negative self-image
④ Japanese sense of loss

24 빈칸 ⓑ _____ 에 들어갈 가장 알맞은 어구는?

① its net debt as a share of GDP is one of the highest in the OECD
② Japan's unemployment rate is now higher than in 2000
③ most Japanese have grown richer over the decade
④ more than half its population is over 45

25 윗글의 내용과 맞지 않는 것은?

① Japan falls behind its European counterparts in economic growth.
② Japan recovers from both economic and natural disasters.
③ Figures contradict the international image of Japan in economic crisis.
④ Japan's real crisis is its morale having impact on Japanese people's psyche.

[26-28] 숭실대 2011

The word conflict has both negative and positive ㉠ connotations. People with a negative attitude toward conflict tend to view the opposing party as the enemy. To these people, conflict suggests aggression, violence, and destructive competition. It is true that intense conflict can lead to biased perceptions and gross ㉡ distortions of reality. In the heat of such situations, we often concentrate so hard on making our own point that we neglect the other person's needs and point of view. Winning becomes more important than coming up with a mutually beneficial solution. Thus negative personal emotion can interfere with a fair resolution of the issues that started the conflict.

Conflict within organizations can be destructive when management expects interdependent individuals or groups to compete with one another. In such situations, one person's or group's success is achieved at the expense of the other individual or group. Employees involved in frequent, high levels of conflict may experience stress and respond by withdrawing from the situation. Their discomfort may be expressed psychologically (apathy and indifference) or physically (tardiness, absenteeism, or turnover). In more extreme cases, they may react with aggressive and hostile behavior, such as stealing or damaging company property.

Some managers believe that any conflict within organizations is undesirable. They attempt to reduce or eliminate conflict through careful selection of people, training, detailed job descriptions, elaborate rules, and incentive systems. These methods are useful for preventing some undesirable conflicts but aren't the complete answer.

Managers having a more positive attitude toward conflicts may view conflict situations as exciting, intriguing, and challenging. From a decision-making standpoint, conflict may result in better choices if it does not take place in a setting where people try to score points and beat one another. Instead, conflict can stimulate a search for the reasons behind conflicting viewpoints and for ways to resolve disagreements. The positive approach tends to lead to innovation and change. By providing managers with information about their organization's operations, conflict can show where corrective actions are needed.

26 Which of the following would be the best title for the passage?

① Why Managers Enjoy Conflicts
② Different Attitude toward Conflict
③ Conflicts and Competition
④ Benefits of Conflict

27 According to the passage, which of the following is true?

① Conflicts do not lead to fair resolution of issues.
② To negative people, mutually beneficial solution is more important than winning.
③ Any conflict within organizations is undesirable so that we have to reduce it.
④ The positive attitude toward conflict tends to lead to innovation and change.

28 Choose the one that is closest in meaning to ㉮ connotations and ㉯ distortions.

① resolution – implication
② resolution – twist
③ implication – perversion
④ implication – resolution

[29-31] 경희대 2012

Psychologists and behavioral economists are identifying the personality types and other traits that distinguish savers from spenders, showing that people who aren't good savers are neither stupid nor irrational—but often simply don't accurately foresee the consequence of not saving. Rewire the brain to find pleasure in future rewards, and you're on the path to a future you really want.

In one experiment, neuroeconomist Paul Glimcher of New York University wanted to see what it would take for people to willingly delay gratification. He gave a dozen volunteers a choice; $21 in a month—to essentially wait a month in order to gain just $1. In economics-speak, this kind of person has a "flat discount function," meaning he values tomorrow almost as much as today and is therefore able to delay gratification. At the other end was someone who was willing to wait a month only if he got $68, a premium of $48 from the original offer. This is someone economists call a "step discounter," meaning the value he puts on the future (and having money then) is dramatically less than value he places on today; when he wants something, he wants it ⓐ_____. The $21 person was, tellingly, an M.D.—Ph.D. student. "If you're willing to get to grad school for eight years, you're really willing to delay ⓑ_____." says Glimcher.

29 윗글의 주제로 알맞은 것은?

① How to start your financial technology with $20
② Two types of personality in money-spending
③ How to get prepared for going to graduate school
④ An effective way to suppress an desire to spend

30 글의 흐름상 빈칸 ⓐ에 들어갈 표현으로 알맞은 것은?

① again   ② once
③ later   ④ now

31 윗글에 사용된 표현 중에서 빈칸 ⓑ에 가장 알맞은 것은?

① consequence
② gratification
③ value
④ premium

[32-33] 숭실대 2012

Let's hear it for Volkswagen at the start or 2012. The German automaker has responded to demands from its works council by agreeing to stop the e-mail server to its BlackBerry-using employees a half-hour after their shift ends, only restoring it 30 minutes before work begins the next day.

The agreement for now only affects about 1,150 of Volkswagen's more than 190,000 workers in Germany, but it's a start in encouraging employees to switch off, curb the twitchy reflex to check e-mail every couple of minutes, and take a look out at things—like family and the big wide world—without the distraction of a blinking red light.

Now I know we're all supposed to be grown-ups and (1) switching off should be a simple enough decision, but the fact is addictions to BlackBerries and other hand-held devices are powerful and nobody expects addicts to self-administer the right medicine without some help. The Volkswagen decision reflects growing up evidence of stress-related burnout tied to employees' inability to separate their working and private lives now that developed societies live in a 24/7 paroxysm of connection.

Employee burnout has become an issue on socially conscious Germany—the object of a *Spiegel* cover story following the resignation in September of a prominent Bundesliga soccer coach, Ralf Rangnick of Schalke, who complained of exhaustion. A Volkswagen spokesman in Wolfsburg told Bloomberg News the company had to balance the benefits of round-the-clock access to staff with protecting their private lives.

---

32 Which of the following is the urgent issue in German society?

① the works council
② employee burnout
③ the values on family life
④ Spiegel's cover story

33 Which or the following is NOT the benefit of (1) switching off?

① reducing worktime outside workplaces
② relieving workers' nerve
③ providing time for families
④ strengthening employees' will

[34-36] 이화여대 2012

The strict systematization at fast food restaurants creates mass products. It raises the throughput. And it gives fast food companies an enormous amount of power over their employees. "When management determines exactly how every task is to be done ... and can impose its own rules about pace, output, quality, and technique," the sociologist Robin Leidner has noted, "[it] makes workers increasingly interchangeable." The management no longer depends upon the talents or skills of its workers—those things are built into the operating system and machines. Jobs that have been "de-skilled" can be filled cheaply. The need to retain any individual worker is greatly reduced by the ease with which he or she can be replaced.

Teenagers have long provided the fast food industry with the bulk of its workforce. The industry's rapid-growth coincided with the baby-boom expansion of that age group. Teenagers were in many ways the ideal candidates for these low-paying jobs. Since most teenagers still lived at home, they could afford to work for wages too low to support an adult, and until recently, their limited skills attracted few other employers. The flexible terms of employment in the fast food industry also attracted housewives who needed extra income. As the number of baby-boom teenagers declined, the fast food chains began to hire other marginalized workers: recent immigrants, the elderly, and the handicapped.

The fast food industry now employs some of the most disadvantaged members of society. It often teaches basic job skills—such as getting to work on time—to people who can barely read, whose lives have been chaotic or shut off from mainstream. Many individual franchisees are genuinely concerned about the well-being of their workers. But the stance of the fast food industry on issues involving employee training, the minimum wage, labor unions, and overtime pay strongly suggest that its motives in hiring the young, the poor, and the handicapped are hardly [A] _____.

34 As used in the fast food industry, which of the following can be inferred as the usage of term <u>throughput</u>?

① generating a sociable dining atmosphere to create more comfort and familiarity for customers who frequent the restaurant
② increasing the speed of assembly and doing every step faster to produce more in a given time
③ shortening the amount of time customers eat their meals inside the restaurant, thus ensuring faster customer turnover and higher profits
④ minimizing the number of items on the restaurant's menu so that more reserved employees are needed to assemble the food
⑤ augmenting the number of customers through advertising and the development of promotional deals

35 Of fast food restaurants and their operations, which two chief characteristics does the writer above ultimately emphasize?

① career opportunities and fringe benefits
② friendliness and familiarity
③ regimentation and standardization
④ reasonable price and customer satisfaction
⑤ the ethos of the assembly line and salubrious cooking

36 Based on the tone of the passage above, which best fits [A]?

① altruistic   ② exploitative
③ lucrative   ④ conciliatory
⑤ malignant

[37-38] 중앙대 2012

When Michael Bloomberg announced a 2007 teachers' union agreement to pay cash bonuses to teachers at schools where test scores increase, he said. "In the private sector, cash incentives are proven (A) motivators for producing results. The most successful employees work harder, and everyone else tries to figure out how they can improve as well," Eli Broad, whose foundation promotes incentive pay plans for teachers, added. "Virtually every other industry compensates employees based on how well they perform. We know from experience across other industries and sectors that linking performance and pay is a powerful incentive." These claims misrepresent how private sector firms motivate employees. Although incentive pay systems are commonplace, they are almost never based exclusively or even primarily on (B) qualitative output measurement for professionals. Indeed, while the share of private sector workers who get performance pay has been increasing, the share of workers who get such pay based on numerical output measures has been decreasing. The business management literature nowadays misleads people to accept warnings about incentives that rely heavily on quantitative rather than qualitative measures. Because of the ease with which most employees game purely quantitative incentives, most private sector accountability systems (C) blend quantitative and qualitative measures, with most emphasis on the latter. This method characterizes accountability of relatively low- and high-level employees. McDonald's, for example, does not evaluate its store managers by sales volume or profitability alone. Instead, a manager and his or her supervisor establish targets for easily quantifiable measures such as sales volume and costs, but also for product quality, service, cleanliness, and personnel training, because these factors may affect long-term profitability as well as the reputation (and thus, profitability) of other outlets. Certainly, supervisory evaluation of employees is (D) less reliable than numerical output measurements such as storewide sales (or student test scores). Supervisory evaluation maybe tainted by favoritism, bias, inflation and compression (narrowing the range of evaluations to avoid penalizing or rewarding too many employees), and even kickbacks or other forms of corruption. Yet the widespread management use of subjective evaluations, despite these flaws, suggests that as one personnel management review concludes, "it is better to imperfectly measure relevant dimensions than to perfectly measure irrelevant ones."

37 윗글에서 논지의 흐름상 가장 적합하지 않은 것을 고르시오.

① (A) ② (B)
③ (C) ④ (D)

38 윗글의 제목으로 가장 적합한 것을 고르시오.

① The Way to Promote Employees' Empowerment
② How to Measure the Quality of Teachers for Proper Salary
③ Critical Dilemma: Who Can Evaluate Employees?
④ The Accountable Way of Measuring Employees' Performance

[39-40] 한국외대 2012

> Sales of Tata Motors' low-cost Nano model have been limited by public perceptions of what it was designed to be. Unveiled in 2007 and dubbed "the people's car," the Nano made headlines as the world's lowest-priced car. It was intended to be a safe upgrade for the millions of families who crowd four people or more onto motorcycles and mopeds in India.
>
> But due to the heavy media attention, the wrong kind of buyers started buying the Nano. Rather than being seen as a step up from a motorcycle, it became known as a cut-price car and many Nanos were bought as third cars or novelties. People upgrading from a two-wheeler got safety and comfort in the rainy monsoon months, but gave up the ease of parking of a motorbike in cities. Also, because its top speed is 105 km/hour, the Nano has limited appeal for anyone who drives long distances on the highway.
>
> Finally, the auto market in India is dominated by small cars at entry-level prices, and the Nano is not as low-cost as it used to be. If there is a choice between a low-priced car and a car that is 25% higher but a "proper car," then people would choose the latter. <u>Even for buyers at the bottom of the pyramid, a car is an aspirational thing, so they don't want their car to be called the cheapest car in India.</u>

39 Which of the following best explains why the Nano has not achieved its sales goals?

① The marketing campaign has not clearly identified the target customers.
② Its top speed is only 105 km/hour.
③ It is now considered a top-end model and too expensive compared to other cars in the market.
④ The number of people who will buy it as a novelty is limited.

40 What is the best interpretation of the underlined sentence?

① Rich people do not want to be seen driving a car known as "the cheapest car in India."
② Buyers want the cheapest model available and they want people to know how little they paid.
③ Poor people want to raise their social status when buying a car so they are sensitive to its reputation.
④ Indian customers value quality over price and are willing to pay more for a good car.

[41-43] 경희대 2013

Globalization, argues *New York Times* columnist Tom Friedman, is "making it possible for corporations to reach farther, faster, cheaper, and deeper around the world" and is fostering "a flowering of both wealth and technological innovation the likes of which the world has never before seen." To David Korten, a former Ford Foundation official and now a prominent globalization critic, it is "market tyranny extending its reach across the planet like a cancer, ⓐ _____, and feeding on life in an insatiable quest for money." The careful listener to this by-now-familiar debate can actually discern a striking point of agreement. (ⓑ) Yet there's mounting evidence that multinational firms may be less capable of delivering competitive products than national or local firms. (ⓒ) Any first-year economics student learns that firms can lower average costs by expanding, but only up to a point. Beyond that point (according to the law of diminishing returns to scale), complexities, breakdowns, and inefficiencies begin to drive average costs back up. (ⓓ) The collapse of massive state-owned enterprises in the old Soviet Union and the bankruptcies of Chrysler and New York City are notable reminders of a lesson we should have absorbed from the dinosaur: Bigger is not always better. (ⓔ)

41 윗글의 내용과 맞지 않는 것은?

① Multinational companies producing less competitive products
② Unlimited lowering of costs by large-scaled marketing
③ Historical instances of colossal companies' downfall
④ The two contrary views on global corporations

42 빈칸 ⓐ _____ 에 들어갈 어구 중 적합하지 않은 것은?

① colonizing ever more of the planet's living spaces
② destroying livelihoods
③ displacing people
④ rendering democratic institutions active

43 다음 문장이 삽입될 본문의 가장 적합한 곳을 고르시오.

In short, both sides assume, one with euphoria and the other with fear, that global-scale business is the wave of the future.

① ⓑ　　　　　　　　　　② ⓒ
③ ⓓ　　　　　　　　　　④ ⓔ

[44-46] 숭실대 2016

There are today about 190 million people in the world who live in a country other than the one in which they were born—nearly 60 percent of them are in rich countries (about 36 million in Europe and 38 million in the United States). People migrate primarily for economic reasons, but some do so to escape political and religious oppression. The 38 million foreign-born people who live in the United States represent 12.6 percent of the U.S. population. Of these, 11 million, or nearly 30 percent, entered the nation illegally. Most nations impose restrictions on immigration to reduce the inflow of low-skilled people (while often encouraging the immigration of highly skilled and technical people). Migration is generally more restricted and regulated than the international flow of goods, services and capital.

In general, capital flows more freely across national boundaries than people. Financial or portfolio capital (bank loans and bonds) generally move to nations and markets where interest rates are higher, and foreign direct investments in plants and firms flow to nations where expected profits are higher. This leads to more efficient use of capital and generally benefits both lenders and borrowers. During the 1970s, Middle Eastern nations deposited a great deal of their huge earnings from petroleum exports in New York and London banks, which then lent (recycled) them to Latin American and Asian governments and corporations. During the 1980s, Japan invested a large chunk of its huge export earnings in financial assets and real estate and set up corporate subsidiaries in the United States.

Since the mid-1980s, the United States has become an increasingly large net borrower from the rest of the world to cover its excess of spending over production. Global banks established branches in major international monetary centers around the world, nearly $3 trillion of foreign currencies are exchanged each day by around-the-clock trading in world financial centers, and newly-established sovereign funds (financial institutions owned by Middle Eastern petroleum exporting nations, Singapore, China, Russia, and Brazil) are making huge investments of all kinds all over the world. Financial markets are globalized as never before. The downside is that when a financial crisis starts in one country it quickly spreads to others.

44 Which of the following would be best for the title?

① The Modern Aspects of International Trade
② The Globalization of Immigrants
③ The International Flow of Labor and Capital
④ The Role of U.S. in the Globalized Financial Markets

45 Which of the following is NOT true?

① The chief reason for migration is economic.
② People have fewer chances to move than money.
③ Money moves to where there are big profits.
④ The U.S. became the largest loan-lender from the mid-1980s.

46 Which of the following is true about the globalized markets?

① Money is the primary agency.
② It is dependent mainly on the migrating labors.
③ Foreign investments require lower interest rates for safety reasons.
④ Free flow of money is a defensive mechanism for financial crisis.

[47-48] 성균관대 2018

The rise of a handful of vast corporate powerhouses whose business models have no instructive precedent from the analogue-era forces a reappraisal of the way capitalist economies work. The top seven highest valued companies in the world are all in the technology sector. Titans such as Alphabet (which owns Google) and Facebook specialize in products that do not exist in three-dimensional space. Apple and Amazon sell real-world objects as well as concepts, but their fortunes and market dominance have been built on nebulous concepts—models, brands and algorithms.

Wealth is no longer in factories, pipelines or retail outlets. Their capital is not anchored to specific fields. That makes them hard to regulate and hard to tax. These are patterns of economic globalization that pre-date the digital revolution. While some intangibles like software and data strongly rely on computers, others do not: brands, for example.

What makes the new era different is the extent to which value has become detached from the tangible, and the corresponding social and economic consequences. This is the dynamic described by Jonathan Haskell and Stian Westlake as "capitalism without capital". In their book of that title, the authors illuminate ways in which the scale of intangibility deforms the familiar mechanisms of a market economy.

47 The underlined "capitalism without capital" means _____.

① the collapse of capitalist economy
② capitalism with the intangible capital
③ the importance of global network in business
④ the inequality of wealth in capitalism
⑤ the global expansion of tangible assets in capitalism

48 The best headline of the above editorial is "_____."

① The Necessity of Globalism in Capitalism
② The Globalization of Capitalism
③ The Rise of the Intangible Wealth
④ The Changing Nature of Capitalism
⑤ The Guide to the Success in the New Era

[49-50] 광운대 2018

Is the bitcoin boom about to turn into one of history's biggest busts? The digital currency's massive surge this year—it's up more than 1,400%—has all the hallmarks of a huge ⓐ_____ bubble, according to people such as Warren Buffett. And if it bursts, the results are likely to be ⓑ_____. "In terms of how it ends, bubble history suggests it will be with a bang, rather than a whimper," said Sharon Zoller, an economist at ANZ. (A) "I can't think of any reason why this time would be different." To better understand what may lie ahead, here's the lowdown on one famous financial bubble in history: Tulip mania. In the early 17th century, speculation helped drive the value of tulip bulbs in the Netherlands to previously unheard of prices. (B) Newly imported from Turkey, tulips were a big novelty at the time. Hard data from those days is ⓒ_____, so it's difficult to gauge exactly how much prices soared. (C) But people were putting up their homes as collateral. Like many bubbles, prices were driven by greed or the fear of missing out. Speculators were buying bulbs in the hope that they could sell them on at an even higher price. (D) Again, it didn't last. A flurry of sales caused a domino effect, and prices collapsed. (E) "Prices will become so out of reach of the common man that ultimately demand fades," he said.

49 다음 주어진 표현이 들어갈 가장 적절한 위치는?

> Stephen Innes, head of Asian trading at currency broker Oanda, believes bitcoin bubble could go the same way.

① (A) ② (B)
③ (C) ④ (D)
⑤ (E)

50 빈칸 ⓐ, ⓑ, ⓒ에 들어갈 가장 적절한 모둠은?

① scarce – spectacular – speculative
② speculative – spectacular – scarce
③ scarce – speculative – scarce
④ speculative – scarce – spectacular
⑤ spectacular – scarce – speculative

에듀윌 편입영어 **기출심화 완성 독해**

PART 02

자연과학

CHAPTER 01   기초 과학
CHAPTER 02   지구·환경
CHAPTER 03   생물
CHAPTER 04   인간
CHAPTER 05   의학·건강

CHAPTER 01 기초 과학

[01-05] 경기대 2010

> Thomas Kuhn made some controversial claims about the overall direction of scientific change. According to a widely-held view, science progresses towards the truth in a linear fashion, as older incorrect ideas get replaced by newer, correct ones. ㉮ _____ This 'cumulative' conception of science is popular among laymen and scientists alike, but Kuhn argued that it is both historically inaccurate and philosophically naive. For example, he noted that Einstein's theory of relativity is in some respects more similar to Aristotelian than Newtonian theory—so the history of mechanics is not simply a linear progression from wrong to right. ㉯ _____, Kuhn questioned whether the concept of objective truth actually makes sense at all. The idea that there is a fixed set of facts about the world, independent of any particular paradigms, was of dubious coherence, he believed. Kuhn suggested a radical alternative: the facts about the world are paradigm-relative, and thus change. If this suggestion is right, then it ㉰ _____ to ask whether a given theory corresponds to the facts 'as they really are', nor therefore to ask whether it is objectively true.

01 Which of the following is the most appropriate for the blank ㉮?

① But earlier theories are subjectively better than later ones.
② Later theories are thus objectively better than earlier ones.
③ So both earlier and later theories exist side by side.
④ So later theories are not necessarily better than earlier ones.

02 Choose one that best fits in the blank ㉯?

① On the contrary ② Nonetheless
③ Ironically ④ Moreover

03 Choose one that is closest in meaning to the underlined word "dubious".

① questionable
② trustworthy
③ enduring
④ intermittent

04 Which of the following is the most appropriate for the blank ㉯?

① holds good
② is of vital importance
③ makes no sense
④ makes a great difference

05 According to the above passage, which of the following is NOT true?

① Before Kuhn, people generally believed that the history of science is a straightforward progression towards the truth.
② Kuhn doubted whether the concept of objective truth is valid.
③ Kuhn believed that he could find a fixed set of facts about the world outside any particular paradigm.
④ Kuhn thought that Einstein's theory of relativity had something in common with Aristotelian theory.

[06-08] 숭실대 2009

Kepler's laws describe the way that planets move in their orbits around the sun. Galileo's discoveries, including the law of compound motion and the equations for accelerated motion, describe the way that objects move in a laboratory here on the surface of the earth. Neither of these sets of laws, however, contains any suggestion that there is any way in which a planet might be similar to a cannonball, or that the laws that operate on the earth might also operate in the heavens. In other words, after Kepler and Galileo had completed their work, physics and astronomy were two separate, unconnected areas of science. It was Isaac Newton (1642~1727) who first showed us that what happens on the earth is in no way different from what happens anywhere else in the universe.

Newton, perhaps the most brilliant scientist who ever lived, synthesized the work of Galileo and others into a statement of the basic principles that govern the motion of everything in the universe, from stars and planets to clouds, cannonballs, and the muscles in your body. We call these results Newton's Laws of Motion. They sound so simple and obvious that it's hard to realize that they represent the results of centuries of experiment and observation, and ever harder to appreciate what an extraordinary effect they had on the development of science. Three basic laws formed the centerpiece of Newton's description of motion.

06 According to the passage, which of the following is NOT true?

① Newton's Laws of Motion are based on the results of centuries of research.
② Newton replicated Kepler's research over a long period.
③ Thanks to Newton, astronomy and physics became interrelated.
④ The laws of motion may be applied to any object moving in the universe.

07 Which of the following would be the topic of the next paragraph?

① Newton's biographical episodes
② The importance of Galileo's discoveries
③ Detailed explanations of Newton's three laws of motion
④ A brief introduction to Kepler's laws

08 In which of the following books would you most likely find the passage?

① An introductory book of physics
② A biography of Galileo Galilei
③ A book about the Milky Way
④ A motion picture guide book

[09-11] 한국외대 2006

Mathematical theorems rely on a logical process and, once proven, are true until the end of time. Mathematical proofs are absolute. To appreciate the value of such proofs they should be compared with their poor relation, the scientific proof. In science a hypothesis is put forward to explain a physical phenomenon. If observations of the phenomenon compare well with the hypothesis, this becomes evidence in favor of it. Experiments may be performed to test the predictive power of the hypothesis, and if it continues to be successful then this is even more evidence to back the hypothesis. Eventually the amount of evidence may be overwhelming and the hypothesis becomes accepted as a scientific theory.

However, the scientific theory can never be proven to the same absolute level of a mathematical theorem: it is merely considered highly likely based on the evidence available. So-called scientific proof relies on observation and perception, both of which are fallible and provide only ⓐ _____ of the truth. This weakness in scientific proof leads to scientific revolutions in which a theory that was assumed to be correct is replaced with another theory, which may be merely a refinement of the original theory, or which may be a complete contradiction.

09 Which of the following best fits into ⓐ?

① clarifications
② simulations
③ negation
④ approximations
⑤ counter-examples

10 What is the passage mainly about?

① Experiments as the best way of testing hypotheses
② Scientific theories as compared to mathematical theorems
③ Reliable evidence in scientific proofs
④ Contradictions in scientific revolutions
⑤ The importance of experiments in science and mathematics

11 Which of the following is stated or implied in the passage?

① A scientific theory considered undoubtedly true one day can be proven false the next day.
② Scientific theories as well as mathematical theorems are absolute and devoid of doubt.
③ Mathematics crucially relies either on evidence from experimentation or infallible logic.
④ The scientific proof is no less powerful and rigorous than the mathematical proof.
⑤ Both scientific theories and mathematical theorems need sufficient observations of the relative phenomenon.

[12-14]

The phenomenon of simultaneous discovery—what science historians call "multiples"—turns out to be _____. The law of the conservation of energy, so significant in science and philosophy, was formulated four times independently in 1847, by Joule, Thomson, Colding and Helmholz. They had been anticipated by Robert Mayer in 1842.

The sheer number of multiples could mean only one thing: scientific discoveries must, in some sense, be inevitable. They must be in the air, products of the intellectual climate of a specific time and place. It should not surprise us, then, that calculus was invented by two people at the same moment in history. Leibniz and Newton may never have actually sat down together and shared their work in detail. But they occupied a common intellectual milieu.

Of course, that is not the way Newton saw it. He had done his calculus work in the mid-1660s, but never published it. And after Leibniz came out with his calculus, in the 1680s, people in Newton's circle accused Leibniz of stealing his work, setting off one of the great scientific scandals of the 17th century. That is the inevitable human response. We're reluctant to believe that great discoveries are in the air. We want to believe that great discoveries are in our heads.

12 Choose the one that best fills in the blank.

① relatively timed
② bafflingly mysterious
③ extremely common
④ absolutely novel

13 Which of the following can be inferred about "multiples"?

① They do not transcend time and place.
② They happen without prior knowledge of one another.
③ They enhance the reputation of the discoverer.
④ They add importance to an already made discovery.

14 What is the main idea of the passage?

① Plagiarism of ideas is rampant among rivals.
② Credit must be given to multiple scientists for the same discovery.
③ Multiples are evidence that scientific discoveries are predestinated.
④ Science historians must record multiples objectively.

[15-17] 국민대 2013

You might ask why we cannot teach physics by just giving the basic laws on page one and then showing how they work in all possible circumstances, as we do in Euclidean geometry, where we state the axioms and then make all sorts of deductions. (So, not satisfied to learn physics in four years, you want to learn it in four minutes?) We cannot do it in this way for two reasons. First, we do not yet know all the basic laws: there is an expanding frontier of ignorance. Second, the correct statement of the laws of physics involves some very unfamiliar ideas which require advanced mathematics for their description. Therefore, one needs a considerable amount of preparatory training even to learn what the words mean. No, it is not possible to do ⓐ it that way. We can only do it piece by piece. Each piece, or part, of the whole of nature is always merely an approximation to the complete truth, or the complete truth so far as we know it. In fact, everything we know is only some kind of approximation, because we know that we do not know all the laws as yet. Therefore, things must be learned only to be unlearned again or, more likely, to be corrected.

15 Which best describes the type of the passage?

① lecture script
② academic paper
③ newspaper article
④ physics textbook

16 Which is NOT true according to the passage?

① As knowledge increases, so ignorance decreases.
② What we learn about things can never be the ultimate truth.
③ You cannot teach physics in such a way that you teach Euclidean geometry.
④ The laws of physics can only be properly described with the help of advanced mathematics.

17 What does the underlined ⓐ it refer to?

① teaching physics
② knowing all the basic laws
③ learning what the words mean
④ the correct statement of the laws of physics

[18-20] 홍익대 2013

Another value of science is the fun called intellectual enjoyment which some people get from reading and learning and thinking about it, and which others get from working in it. This is a very real and important point and one which is not considered enough by those who tell us it is our social responsibility to reflect on the impact of science on society.

Is this mere personal enjoyment of value to society as a whole? No! But it is also a responsibility to consider the value of society itself. Is it, in the last analysis, to arrange things so that people can enjoy things? If so, the enjoyment of science is as important as anything else.

But I would like not to underestimate the value of the world view which is the result of scientific effort. We have been led to imagine all sorts of things infinitely more marvelous than the imaginings of poets and dreamers of the past. It shows that the imagination of nature is far, far greater than the imagination of man. For instance, how much more remarkable it is for us all to be stuck—half of us upside down—by a mysterious attraction, (A) _____ a spinning ball that has been swinging in space for billions of years, than to be carried on the back of an elephant supported on a tortoise swimming in a bottomless sea.

18 Which of the following is most suitable for (A)?

① as
② to
③ off
④ up

19 Which of the following can NOT be inferred from the above?

① One of the examples of the imagination of nature is to be carried on the back of an elephant supported on a tortoise swimming in a bottomless sea.
② People have fun from reading and learning science, apart from the enjoyment they get from working in it.
③ The imagination of nature is far greater than the imagination of poets and dreamers in the past.
④ The author believes that the intellectual enjoyment of science is important.

20 What is the main topic of the above passage?

① how to get intellectual enjoyment
② the greatness of poetic imagination
③ the importance of a unique worldview
④ the value of science

[21-22] 중앙대 2014

Some people believe that mathematics is a difficult, dull subject that is to be pursued only in a clear-cut, logical fashion. This belief is perpetuated because of the way mathematics is presented in many textbooks. Often mathematics is reduced to a series of definition, methods to solve various types of problems, and theorems. Theorems are statements whose truth can be established by means of deductive reasoning and proofs. This is not to minimize the importance of proof in mathematics, for it is the very thing that gives mathematics its strength. But the power of the imagination is every bit as important as the power of deductive reasoning.

The long history in the development of a concept or any of the unproductive approaches that were taken by early mathematicians is not always addressed in mathematics courses. The fact is that the mathematician seeks out relationships in simple cases, looks for patterns, and only then tries to generalize. It is often much later that the generalization is proved and finds its way into an actual textbook.

One way we can learn much about mathematics and in the meantime find enjoyment in the process is by studying numerical relationships that exhibit unusual patterns. For example, children may find it easier to learn their multiplication tables by exploring the patterns that the numbers display. _____. Given a difficult problem, a mathematician will often try to solve a simpler, but similar, problem. This type of reasoning—first observing patterns and then predicting answers in complicated problems—is an example of inductive reasoning. It involves reasoning from particular facts or individual cases to a general statement that may be true. The more individual occurrences that are observed, the better able we are to make a correct generalization. For instance, we can predict the exact time of sunrise and sunset each day. Thus there is a very high probability that the prediction will be successful.

21 윗글의 제목으로 가장 적합한 것을 고르시오.

① Unconventionality of Mathematical Reasoning
② Inductive Reasoning in the Study of Math
③ The Developmental Patterns of Generalization
④ The Power of Math Theorems in Complex Problems

22 윗글에서 빈칸에 들어가기에 가장 적합한 것을 고르시오.

① Even complicated arithmetic problems can sometimes be solved by using patterns
② Arithmetic problems are perceived difficult by most school-aged children
③ Children's arithmetic ability will be enhanced by solving a series of difficult problems
④ Mathematical arguments follow unpredictable thinking trajectories

[23-25] 항공대 2017

A large element of chance is inherent in natural processes. The spacing between trees in a natural forest, for example, is random. (A) If you discovered a forest where all the trees were equally spaced, you would conclude that it had been planted. (B) It would be highly unlikely to find the leaves laid out in perfectly straight rows. (C) We can express the results of such observations by saying that a disorderly arrangement is much more probable than an orderly one if the laws of nature are allowed to act without interference. (D) Entropy originally found its place in thermodynamics, but its importance grew tremendously as the field of statistical mechanics developed. This analytical approach employs an alternate interpretation of entropy. In statistical mechanics, the behavior of a substance is described by the statistical behavior of the atoms and molecules contained in it. One of the main conclusions of the statistical mechanical approach is that isolated systems tend toward greater disorder, and entropy is a measure of that disorder. When all systems are taken together to form the Universe, the entropy of the Universe always increases. Ultimately, the entropy of the Universe should reach a maximum. When it does, the Universe will be in a state of uniform temperature and density. All physical, chemical, and biological processes will cease, because a state of perfect disorder implies no available energy for doing work.

23 Choose the most appropriate place for the sentence below.

> Likewise, leaves fall to the ground with random arrangements.

① (A) 　　　　　　　　　　② (B)
③ (C) 　　　　　　　　　　④ (D)

24 Which of the following is true?

① The idea of entropy originally started from statistical mechanics and applied to thermodynamics later.
② An analytical approach to entropy may illustrate the statistical behaviors of the atoms and molecules.
③ The entropy of the Universe decreases in all natural processes.
④ All systems naturally tend to move from a state of disorder to a state of order.

25 What would be the best title of the passage above?

① entropy and disorder
② entropy and metabolism
③ the reversible impact of entropy
④ the difference between natural entropy and artificial entropy

[26-27] 인하대 2018

Heat is everywhere. It's raw energy, and it boils down to matter in motion. Atoms and molecules, the building blocks of everything around us including ourselves, move constantly and randomly; the faster they move, the warmer the substance they make up. Every object in this world—no matter how frigid it may seem—contains some heat. Even a jug of ice water harbors so much molecular motion that if you gently place a drop of ink on the surface, it will diffuse evenly throughout the liquid within hours. In fact, if you could extract and store all the thermal energy contained in a single snowy ski slope in January, you could heat your house with it for days. Scientists have determined that, at least in theory, there's a point called absolute zero where all motion—and hence all heat—ceases to exist. But it remains unattainably cold: -460°F.

Heat always travels in whatever direction tends to equalize temperatures; that is, from region of high thermal energy and relative warmth to colder areas. Bring enough heat together in one place, and you may be able to overcome the forces of attraction between atoms and molecules, causing a change of state from solid to liquid or liquid to gas. Such changes require additional energy, called latent heat, which doesn't raise the substance's temperature but is needed just to change state. Consequently, _____ to raise the temperature of a quart of water from 210°F (liquid) to 220°F (steam) than it does to raise its temperature from 85°F (liquid) to 95°F (liquid).

26 Which of the following is not true according to the passage?

① Heat moves to colder places.
② Even cold water has thermal energy.
③ People have not experienced absolute zero.
④ A ski slope does not contain thermal energy in winter.
⑤ A drop of ink on the surface of ice water will diffuse throughout the water.

27 Which of the following is most appropriate for the blank?

① it takes more energy
② it gets more dangerous
③ it requires less heat
④ it becomes less expensive
⑤ it gets more perceivable

[28-30] 가톨릭대 2017

When we digest a slice of bread, we break the carbohydrates into simple sugars and its proteins into amino acids. At the same time, we also break down and rebuild the proteins of our own skin, muscles and bones. All organisms continually break down macromolecules and reuse the building blocks.

Organisms have to assemble and disassemble macromolecules easily. The bonds that hold macromolecules together must be strong enough so that the macromolecules will not fall apart. But the bonds must not be so strong that organisms can't easily take them apart when they need to. Like children's pop beads and Legos bricks, the building blocks of life easily snap together and easily snap apart.

Amazingly, biological building blocks all snap together in the same way. The building blocks of all the major macromolecules join by the same simple chemical reaction. In every case, enzymes (molecules that help make and break chemical bonds) remove two hydrogen atoms and one oxygen atom from between pairs of building blocks, forming a bond. Removing two hydrogens and an oxygen—the equivalent of one molecules of water—is called a dehydration condensation reaction, because one water molecule is removed.

To snap apart macromolecules, organisms reverse the dehydration condensation reaction, adding one water molecule to each pair of water, a process called hydrolysis [Greek, *hydro* = water + *lysis* = breaking].

Although all the building blocks are joined by similar dehydration condensation reactions, the exact bonds that form are different in each case. For example, sugars form *glycosidic bonds*, while amino acids form *peptide bonds*.

28 What is the topic of the passage?

① the way organisms store and consume energy
② the types of chemical bonds formed by enzymes
③ the intricate structure of bonds holding macromolecules together
④ the role of enzymes in the mechanism of the building blocks of life

29 Based on the passage, choose the best words for the blanks on the following statement.

> • Enzyme link two building blocks by _____ the equivalent of one water molecule.
> • Enzyme add a water molecules to _____ a long chain into two single building blocks.

① taking away – break
② taking away – form
③ adding – break
④ adding – form

30 Which of the following is NOT true according to the passage?

① All living things including humans constantly break down macromolecules.
② Macromolecular bonding is so strong that building blocks do not snap apart.
③ How biological building blocks are linked is identical for all the major molecules.
④ The bonds that form from dehydration are different in each case.

CHAPTER 02 지구·환경

[01-03] 숭실대 2010

One of the many remarkable properties of water is the unwillingness of bodies of water of substantially different temperature to mix together. This property is responsible for the formation in fresh water lakes of a phenomenon known as the thermocline, a phenomenon that can play an important role in a lake's summertime ecology. Consider the annual temperature fluctuations in a typical deep-water impoundment in the southern United States. In late winter, whatever ice may have previously formed at the surface of the lake melts, and the water temperature measures a uniform 38-42 degrees. Wave action stirs oxygen into the water at the lake's surface, and the temperature uniformity allows distribution of this dissolved oxygen to all depths. With oxygen plentiful, many of the reservoir's fish species, both predator and forage, are found throughout the water column.

In sunny days of early spring, the surface temperature increases and water expands. Because 50-degree water is lighter than 40-degree water, a layer of warmer water builds at the surface of the lake, resting like a pillow on the mass of colder water below. The pillow of warm surface water slowly increases in thickness, as heat is transferred into the depths by the limited stirring of wave action. By early summer, a remarkable stratification has occurred, and a sharp boundary separates two independent bodies of water within the lake. The boundary is a temperature gradient called the thermocline, and it acts as a barricade to prevent any further mixing of oxygen into the chilly depths. The temperature barrier prevents oxygen from circulating from the surface to replace the oxygen consumed by fish and dying zooplankton. In order to survive, fish are forced ㉮ _____ into the relatively narrow zone between the thermocline and the surface. ㉯ <u>The cold nights of autumn reverse the trend.</u>

01 According to the passage, which of the following is NOT true?

① The increase of warm surface water leads to the lack of oxygen in the depths.
② Oxygen is sufficiently provided in all parts of the lake in late winter.
③ Thermocline is formed on warm surfaces by hot temperatures.
④ The temperature barrier limits the movement of water and oxygen.

02 Choose the word that would fit best in ㉮.

① backward
② downward
③ upward
④ forward

03 According to ㉯ The cold nights of autumn reverse the trend, what would happen in autumn?

① The temperature barrier would become thinner.
② The cold surface water would plunge into the depth.
③ The depths would contain less oxygen than before.
④ The surface would expand faster and thicker.

[04-05]

Eclipses happen only during the new moon phase, when the moon moves to the side of Earth facing the sun. However, because the moon orbits Earth at a slight angle, the three bodies will only periodically line up on the same plane to create an eclipse. Interestingly, total eclipses are only possible on Earth because of a _____: The moon's diameter and distance from Earth make its relative size just big enough to cover the sun. If the moon were any smaller or farther away, we would only see partial eclipses. In fact, in a billion years or so, the moon will have drifted so far from Earth that solar eclipses will no longer occur. Another type of solar eclipse, the annular eclipse, occurs when the moon's elliptical orbit carries it far enough from Earth that it becomes too small to totally block the sun. In this case, the eclipse appears as a blackened circle rimmed by sunlight. Total eclipse occurs every one or two years, while total and partial eclipses together average about two and a half incidences per year. But because they are visible from such a small area on Earth each time, the chance of observing a total eclipse from any single spot is less than once in a lifetime.

04 Choose the one that best fills in the blank.

① hypothetical pattern
② systematic illusion
③ catastrophic interaction
④ serendipitous coincidence

05 Which of the following can be inferred from the passage?

① The slight angle of the sun allows it to align with Earth and the moon so it becomes hidden.
② The increasing distance between the moon and Earth will ultimately eliminate eclipses.
③ Nowadays, total eclipses are more commonly observed than partial eclipses.
④ The annular eclipse is an atypical and the rarest form of partial eclipse.

[06-07] 성균관대 2009

> Most scientists now accept the theory that the universe had an instant of creation, that it came to be in a vast fireball explosion 15 or 20 billion years ago. This so-called Big Bang theory makes some scientists acutely uncomfortable; science believes that every effect has a cause, but, according to the Big Bang theory, the birth of the universe has an uncaused effect. On the other hand, the theory ignites in many religious minds a small thrill of confirmation; they believe that the divine intellect willed all into being, *ex nihilo*. For the scientist who has lived by his faith in the power of reason, (가) this story ends like a bad dream. He has scaled the mountains of ignorance; he is about to conquer the highest peak; as he pulls himself over the final rock, he is greeted by a band of theologians who have been sitting there for centuries.

06 The underlined (가) "this story" refers to the idea that _____.

① The faith of science in "the power of reason" collapsed
② Theologians had already foreseen what science proved
③ Science did not succeed to prove the birth of the universe
④ The universe was created by the God ex nihilo
⑤ The Big bang Theory is finally accepted by scientists

07 The best theme of the passage is _____.

① Science over theology
② Conflict between science and theology
③ Where science meets theology
④ Science prevails where theology fails
⑤ The Big Bang Theory: A biblical account of the origin of the universe

[08-10] 서강대 2008

Scientists who study meteorites do so in a (　　　) way. Rather than looking at objects from afar, they actually hold the products of stars and remnants of scattered planets in their hands in the form of meteorites. Locked within these rocks from space are tiny pieces of the solar system that predate even the planets. Tens of thousands of meteorites have been recovered from the far corners of our world. Although these space rocks can be classified in dozens of ways, meteoriticists divide them into two main categories: those that preserve a record of the solar nebula—the growth of microscopic grains to planet-size bodies—and those that preserve evidence of subsequent planetary processes—such as volcanism, interior melting, impacts, and fragmentation.

08 Which one of the following words would fill in the parenthesis best?

① simple
② tangible
③ spectacular
④ scientific

09 Which one of the following words from the passage refers to a different thing from the rest?

① meteorites
② tiny pieces of the solar system
③ space rocks
④ microscopic grains

10 Which one of the passages is not true?

① Meteorites are evidence of creation of solar system.
② Meteorites can show the evidence of volcanic activities.
③ Meteoriticists study planetary processes through meteorites.
④ Solar system usually comes well before the creation of planets.

[11-12] 중앙대 2010

Life on Earth uses 20 amino acids to build up the thousands upon thousands of different proteins that perform a myriad of cell functions. ㉮ One of the first experiments aimed at reproducing the primordial Earth and its chemistry was undertaken by Stanley Miller in 1953. He was able to synthesize amino acids using lightning-like discharges in a reducing atmosphere of methane, ammonia and water-similar to what exists on Jupiter. Since that pioneering work, researchers have come to believe that Earth's early atmosphere was in fact more oxidative, containing mostly nitrogen and carbon dioxide. ㉯ However, Dr. Emily Blank states a different view: "Without the reducing atmosphere, the Miller mechanism becomes much less efficient at producing amino acids." One way to get around this is to make the amino acids in space and have them come crashing down on-board meteorites and comets. There is ample evidence that meteorites carry amino acids. And just recently, an amino acid was discovered in comet material brought back by NASA's Stardust spacecraft. ㉯ Blank and her colleagues were curious as to what happens to these biomolecules when the "space capsule" they are riding in smacks into the Earth. The team has focused their work on comets, rather than meteors. Although comets are less prevalent in the inner solar system, they have a few possible advantages over their dry rocky counterparts when it comes to delivering biologically relevant material to a planet's surface. First of all, a comet impact is thought to be less harsh than that of a meteorite because comets are less dense, which means their impact generates lower temperatures and pressures. ㉰ Blank says that the blow would be further softened on a comet arriving at an oblique angle. The second advantage of comets is that they carry water, which is key for the chemical reactions that beget life. When the comet lands, its ice melts, forming a little puddle near the crash site. "Comets give you all the ingredients, like a compact evolution kit," Blank says.

11 아래의 문장이 들어갈 위치로 가장 적합한 곳을 고르시오.

> Astrobiologists often focus on the origins of amino acids in order to understand where life may have come from.

① ㉮ ② ㉯
③ ㉰ ④ ㉱

12 윗글을 통해 추론할 수 있는 것으로 가장 적합한 것을 고르시오.

① Comet crashes helped spark Earth life.
② Amino acids are optional for the living creatures on Earth.
③ A meteor impact produces relatively lower pressures than that of a comet.
④ Electronic discharge is an economic means for the production of amino acids.

[13-15] 덕성여대 2007

> Like all weather, hurricanes are fueled by heat—the heat of sun-drenched tropical seas, which powers the storms by sending warm, moist air rushing toward the frigid upper atmosphere like smoke up a chimney. As surrounding air is sucked in at the base of the storm, Earth rotation gives it a twist, creating a whorl of rain bands. These whip-tails of thunderstorm activity are strongest where they converge in a ring of rising, spinning air, the eyewall, which encloses the cloud-free eye. Hurricanes (called typhoons in the western Pacific and tropical cyclones in the Indian Ocean) can propel themselves to an altitude of 50,000 feet or more, where the rising air finally vents itself in spiraling exhaust jets of cirrus clouds. The largest ever, the 1997 Pacific typhoon Tip, sent gale-force of winds across more than 650 miles. Even an average hurricane packs some 1.5 trillion watts of power in its wind—equivalent to about half the world's entire electrical generating capacity.

13 In order for a hurricane to be made _____.

① moist air must be above the upper atmosphere
② it must be a very sunny day
③ seas must be heated enough
④ clouds must enclose tropical seas

14 The thunderstorms of hurricanes are strongest in the _____.

① eyewall   ② eye
③ spinning air   ④ rain band

15 The wind power of an average hurricane _____.

① is about 15 trillion watts
② makes the rising air vent
③ enables sea water to soar to an altitude of 50,000 feet or more
④ can not exceed the world's entire electrical generating capacity

[16-18] 아주대 2016

[A] The atmosphere is divided into five layers. It is thickest near the surface and thins out with height until it eventually merges with space. Ozone is found in the two different parts of the Earth's atmosphere: the troposphere and the stratosphere. The former is ground level ozone, a human health irritant and component of smog, while the latter accounts for the vast majority of atmospheric ozone that protects human health as it absorbs ultraviolet radiation from the sun, thereby preventing the radiation from hitting Earth's surface and harming living organisms from this biologically dangerous radiation. ❶

[B] The term 'ozone hole' refers to recent depletion of this protective layer of stratospheric ozone over the polar regions. People, plants, and animals living under the ozone hole are harmed by the solar radiation now reaching the Earth's surface—where it causes health problems from eye damage to skin cancer. ❷

[C] Scientists discovered that the ozone layer was thinning in the lower stratosphere, with particularly dramatic ozone loss—known as the ozone hole—in the Antarctic springtime. This is caused by increasing concentrations of ozone-depleting chemicals in the stratosphere, called chlorofluorocarbons or CFCs, which remain in the atmosphere for decades to over a century. When the sun comes out again in the polar spring, the ice particles melt, releasing the ozone-depleting molecules which in turn do their dirty work, breaking apart the molecular bonds in ultraviolet radiation-absorbing ozone. ❸

[D] The ozone hole, however, is not the mechanism of global warming. Ultraviolet radiation represents less than one percent of the energy from the sun—not enough to be the cause of the excess heat from human activities. Global warming is caused primarily from putting too much carbon into the atmosphere when coal and oil are burned to generate electricity or to run our cars. These gases spread around the planet like a blanket, capturing the solar heat that would otherwise be radiated out into space. ❹

[E] Both of these environmental problems do, however, have a common cause—human activities that release gases into and alter the atmosphere. Ozone depletion occurs when CFCs—formerly found in aerosol spray cans and refrigerants—are released into the atmosphere. These gases, through several chemical reactions, cause the ozone molecules to break down, reducing ozone's ultraviolet radiation-absorbing capacity. ❺

16 Which of the following questions is NOT answered in the passage?

① What is the ozone hole?
② What causes the ozone hole?
③ How does the ozone hole influence people?
④ How does the ozone hole contribute to global warming?
⑤ Does climate change have an impact on the stratospheric ozone layer?

17 The following is removed from the passage. In which parts ❶~❺ may it be inserted to support the argument made by the author?

> Because our atmosphere is one connected system, it is not surprising that ozone depletion and global warming are related in some other ways. For example, evidence suggests that climate change may contribute to thinning of the protective ozone layer.

① ❶   ② ❷
③ ❸   ④ ❹
⑤ ❺

18 According to the passage, which of the following is NOT true?

① The "ozone hole" in the troposphere do harm to people and animals.
② Ozone depleting molecules are released from the ice particle due to global warming.
③ CFCs, a human-developed compound, are quite destructive and long-lived in the atmosphere.
④ The thickness of the polar stratospheric ozone layer represents the intact function of its protection by the atmosphere.
⑤ As carbon chemicals and other heat-trapping gases rise into the atmosphere, spread around the globe, and act like a blanket holding in heat around Earth.

[19-21] 단국대 2017

Modern forecasting methods are fairly accurate when it comes to short-range predications, but the longer the forecast, the more chances there are that the forecasts are going to be incorrect. (A) The current method of mathematically calculating weather conditions confines accurate predictions to about five days in advance due to the chaotic nature of the weather. (B) Meteorologists combine the results of the computational data collection methods with the actual atmospheric conditions occurring in the present. (C) Current information concerning the temperature, dew point, and winds at various levels is gathered throughout the day all around the world to provide clues that are compared to computer models based on past conditions to come up with probable weather patterns. (D) As a result, an experienced meteorologist who has seen a great variety of weather conditions and is knowledgeable about the changes and shifts that they are likely to make stands nearly as good of a chance at accurately predicting future weather conditions as a computer-generated model does.

19 Which has the closest meaning to the underlined word?

① changes
② degrees
③ speeds
④ elevations

20 Choose the most suitable position of the following sentence in the above passage.

However, though the science and methodology of meteorological methods have improved, there are still large gaps in the understanding of atmospheric and weather-related activity.

① (A)
② (B)
③ (C)
④ (D)

21 According to the passage, which is NOT true?

① Computer-generated models are quite reliable to predict longer-term weather patterns.
② Experienced meteorologists can make predictions as accurately as computer-generated models do.
③ Accurate weather predictions can only be made for the near future since weather changes rapidly.
④ The modern forecasting takes data into account, particularly temperature, humidity and wind patterns to determine future weather patterns.

[22-25]

> A hot spot is a giant underground caldron of molten rock in one of the world's many volcanically active areas. The steamy geysers, thermal pools, and mud pots of Yellowstone National Park owe their origins to hot spots.
>
> Annually, more than 200 geysers erupt in Yellowstone, making this one of the most interesting places in the world for geologists. Over 100 geysers lie within the Upper Geyser Basin, a one-square-mile area near Old Faithful, the most famous geyser in the world. The Yellowstone hot spot was created around ten million years ago, and the center of the park is still volcanically active, with molten rock only a mile or two beneath the Earth's surface.
>
> When rain and melted snow seep down through tiny cracks in the Earth, the water eventually reaches underground chambers of lava-heated rock. The rock heats the water, and the boiling water and steam often make their way back up to the surface in the form of a geyser, a thermal pool, or a mud pot.
>
> In a geyser, water trapped in an underground chamber heats up beyond the boiling point and forms steam. Since steam takes up 1,500 times more space than water, pressure builds up, eventually forcing the superheated water to burst to the surface as a geyser. A thermal pool is formed when the water from the hot spot reaches the surface before cooling off. If the water does not make it all the way to the surface, steam and gases may dissolve rocks and form a bubbling mud pot instead.

22 Where do hot spots occur?

① In rocky regions near the equator
② Below the ground near active volcanoes
③ About a mile above a volcano's crater
④ In the center of ancient volcanoes

23 According to the passage, why is Yellowstone National Park an interesting place for geologists?

① There are 100 square miles of hot spots.
② Over 200 geysers erupt there each year.
③ There are more than 100 different kinds of geysers.
④ More than 200 types of rock are found there.

24 How do hot spots contribute to the formation of geysers?

① Hot spots melt all of the snow falling into a volcano's crater.
② Water is trapped in an underground chamber and cannot escape.
③ Hot rocks create boiling water, steam, and pressure underground.
④ Water from hot spots rises to the surface before it cools off.

25 When do mud pots form?

① When steam and gases dissolve rocks near the surface
② When underground water exceeds the boiling point
③ When snow melts in Yellowstone's geyser basins
④ When superheated water bursts to the surface

[26-28] 서울여대 2013

The theory Charles Hapgood alluded to in his book entitled *Earth's Shifting Crust: A Key to Some Basic Problems of Earth Science* was one first propounded in 1908 by an amateur American geologist named Frank Bursley Taylor. Taylor came from a wealthy family and had both the means and freedom from academic constraints to pursue unconventional lines of inquiry. He was one of those struck by the similarity in shape between the facing coastlines of Africa and South America, and from this observation he developed the idea that the continents had once slid around. He suggested that the crunching together of continents could have thrust up the world's mountain chains. He failed, however, to produce much in the way of evidence, and the theory was considered too crackpot to merit serious attention.

In Germany, however, Taylor's idea was picked up, and effectively appropriated, by a theorist named Alfred Wegener, a meteorologist at the University of Marburg. Wegener investigated the many plant and fossil anomalies that did not fit comfortably into the standard model of Earth history and realized that very little of it made sense if conventionally interpreted. Animal fossils repeatedly turned up on opposite sides of oceans that were clearly too wide to swim. How, he wondered, did marsupials travel from South America to Australia? How did identical snails turn up in Scandinavia and New England? And how, come to that, did one account for coal seams and other semitropical remnants in frigid spots like Spitsbergen, four hundred miles north of Norway, if they had not somehow migrated there from warmer climates?

26 What is "The theory" in line 1?

① The Big Bang theory
② The Baked Apple theory
③ The Continental Drift theory
④ The Evolution theory

27 Which of the following is NOT true about Frank Bursley Taylor?
① His theory had influence on Charles Hapgood's geological study.
② He was rich enough not to put a limit on his geological inquiry.
③ He insisted that the world's mountains were formed by the moving continents.
④ He proved his own theory that the continents had once slid around.

28 Which of the following did Wegener NOT use to prove his theory?
① His contemporary meteorological studies
② Marsupials' fossils found in South America and Australia
③ Coal layers found underneath the ground
④ Snails found in Scandinavia and New England

[29-30] 인하대 2013

According to Dr. M. Kerry O'Banion and his research team, astronauts of the future, those taking long journeys to Mars, may have even more to worry about. O'Banion says, "In addition to the known risks that are already out in space including potential risks of cancer or cataracts, there is also the potential that you could exacerbate neuro-degenerative disease." The researchers exposed lab mice to high levels of cosmic radiation, the same amount an astronaut would be exposed to over the three years it would take to get to Mars. They found that the mice began showing signs of Alzheimer's disease. O'Banion says current spacecraft technology works well to protect against solar radiation, but it isn't designed to shield against increased levels of cosmic radiation found outside of Earth's orbit. O'Banion says, "The galactic cosmic radiation has a very high velocity, high mass charged particles. These particles are very challenging to shield against with conventional materials. One needs large thicknesses of water, concrete or lead. My understanding is that currently we don't have the technology to shield effectively in spacecraft against these events because we can't carry that much material." O'Banion is confident that over the next few years, researchers will develop methods to protect against these radioactive particles, ensuring that in the future, astronauts can focus on their mission, without having to worry about their exposure to _____.

29 Which of the following is most appropriate for the blank?

① solar radiation
② cosmic radiation
③ conventional materials
④ potential risks of cancer and cataracts

30 Which of the following is true according to the passage?

① It will take over three years for the astronauts to reach Mars.
② There are no risks that the astronauts take during the journeys to Mars.
③ The mice showed no signs of Alzheimer's disease in the experiment.
④ The researchers developed the method to protect against the radioactive particles that arise in space.

[31-32] 중앙대 2013

The Aswan High Dam, built in Egypt with Russian support, was supposed to provide hydroelectric power and to increase Egypt's food supply by controlling the unpredictable Nile River. The project meant that great art treasures were flooded as submerged land was drained for cultivation. (A) _____, only one-tenth of an acre of land was made available for each person added to Egypt's population during the period of construction. One result of the dam was that the Nile no longer flooded the delta farmlands annually. These annual floods served to restore the farmland fertility with deposited silt. This no longer the case, the quality of the farmland decreased. The dam also cut off the nutrients that had been washed to the Mediterranean Sea as a result of the annual floodings. (B) _____ this, or the change in the salinity of the sea that the dam produced, the sardine catch dropped from 18,000 tons per year to 500 tons per year. The stable lake created by the dam allowed aquatic snails to flourish. The snails serve as an intermediate host to a blood fluke that bores into humans causing the dreaded disease, schistosomiasis. The construction of the dam had important political implications at the time.

31 밑줄 친 (A), (B)에 들어가기에 가장 적합한 것을 고르시오.

① Therefore – Due to
② However – Because of
③ Consequently – Despite
④ Nonetheless – According to

32 윗글의 제목으로 가장 적합한 것을 고르시오.

① Environmental Problems Caused by the Aswan High Dam
② The Economic Effects of the Aswan High Dam in Egypt
③ Benefits and Problems of Floodings in the Nile River
④ The Influence of Politics on the Aswan High Dam Construction

[33-35] 한국외대 2014

As a tsunami leaves the deep water of the open-ocean and travels into the shallower water near the coast, it transforms. A tsunami travels at a speed that is related to the water depth—hence, as the water depth decreases, the tsunami slows. The tsunami's energy flux is dependent on both its wave speed and wave height. As it travels into shallower water, its height grows. This is called shoaling. Because of (A) this shoaling effect, a tsunami that is unnoticeable at sea, may grow to be several meters or more in height near the coast. When it finally reaches the coast, a tsunami may appear as a rapidly rising or falling tide, as a series of breaking waves, or even a bore. Just like other water waves, tsunamis begin to lose energy as they rush onshore—part of the wave energy is reflected offshore, while the shoreward-propagating wave energy is dissipated through bottom friction and turbulence. Despite these losses, tsunamis still reach the coast with tremendous amounts of energy. Tsunamis have great erosion potential, stripping beaches of sand that may have taken years to accumulate and undermining trees and other coastal vegetation. Capable of inundating, or flooding, hundreds of meters inland past the typical high-water level, the fast-moving water associated with the incoming tsunami can crush homes and other coastal structures. Additionally, their destructive power can be enormous and they can affect entire ocean basins.

33 Which of the following is the passage mainly about?

① How tsunamis are similar to typhoons
② How tsunamis effect the ocean basin
③ How tsunamis transform in their way onshore
④ How to evacuate when tsunamis come

34 Which of the following is true in accordance with (A)?

① The higher the wave is, the faster the tsunami runs.
② When a tsunami slows down, its height decreases.
③ The height of tsunamis increases as they slow down.
④ The tsunami's energy has no association with wave speed and height.

35 Which of the following is true of the passage?

① Tsunamis are likely to converge far offshore.
② Tsunami's energy decreases when approaching coasts.
③ Tsunamis can easily be detected in the deep ocean.
④ Tsunami's influence is limited to coastal areas.

[36-38] 항공대 2016

Further encouragement for the existence of black holes came in 1967 with the discovery by a research student at Cambridge, Jocelyn Bell-Burnell, of objects in the sky that were emitting regular pulses of radio waves. At first Bell and her supervisor, Antony Hewish, thought they might have contact with an alien civilization in the galaxy. In the end, however, they came to the less romantic conclusion that these objects, which were given the name pulsars, were in fact rotating neutron stars that were emitting pulses of radio waves because of a complicated interaction between their magnetic fields and surrounding matter. This was bad news for writers of space westerns, but very hopeful for the small number of us who believed in black holes at that time: it was the first positive evidence that neutron stars existed. A neutron star has a radius of about ten miles, only a few times the critical radius at which a star becomes a black hole. If a star could collapse to such a small size, it is not unreasonable to expect that other stars could collapse to even smaller size and become black holes. How could we hope to detect a black hole, as by its very definition it does not emit any light? It might seem a bit like looking for a black cat _____. Fortunately, there is a way. As John Michell pointed out in his pioneering paper in 1783, a black hole still exerts a gravitational force on nearby objects.

36 The passage above is mainly about _____.

① the legacy of black hole
② the function of black hole
③ the discovery of black hole
④ the latent power of black hole

37 Choose the one that best fills in the blank.

① in a coal cellar
② in an inflated balloon model
③ through a triangular-shaped piece of glass
④ with concave lens telescope

38 Which of the following is true?

① Bell and Hewish contacted with an alien civilization in the galaxy.
② A star can be enlarged to a gigantic size and become a black hole.
③ The existence of black holes was fully known in 1967.
④ A black hole can exercise a gravitational force on nearby matters.

[39-40] 한국외대 2017

> A new concern could be on the horizon for city dwellers, particularly those living in the more densely populated cities of the world, as a new study has found that certain particles found within pollution could enter the human brain by people breathing them in. The particles discovered, known as magnetite, commonly form inside engines and open fires. Magnetite is a mineral form of iron toxic to the human brain due to its ability to easily react and release other particles, which cause oxidative stress within brain cells, damaging and killing them in the process. Researchers found these particles inside the frontal cortex of the brain when they studied brain tissue samples from 37 people who lived in a large city. Unfortunately, magnetite particulates are always present in pollution. The particles go through the olfactory bulb located at the top of the nose, where there is no blood-brain barrier. Their minuscule size also reduces the chances of them being trapped by hairs and mucus that line your nose, further aiding them getting into your bloodstream and then your brain.

39 Why does the new finding raise special concern for city dwellers?

① The harmful agent exists in polluted city air.
② Dense buildings in a city trap the pollutants.
③ The pollutant becomes reactive in urban environments.
④ The harmful particle is formed by automobile exhaust.

40 Which of the following is NOT a feature of magnetite-derived pollutants?

① Their chemical reaction kills brain cells.
② They are too small to be filtered by nasal hairs.
③ They enter the human body through the nose.
④ They enter the body alongside all forms of iron intake.

[41-42] 항공대 2018

Up until the 1920s, everyone thought the universe was essentially static and unchanging in time. Then it was discovered that the universe was expanding. Distant galaxies were moving away from us. This meant they must have been closer together in the past. If we extrapolate back, we find we must have all been on top of each other about 15 billion years ago. This was the Big Bang, the beginning of the universe. But was there anything before the Big Bang? If not, what created the universe? Why did the universe emerge from the Big Bang the way it did? We used to think that the theory of the universe could be divided into two parts. First, there were the laws like Maxwell's equations and general relativity that determined the evolution of the universe, given its state over all of space at one time. And second, there was no question of the initial state of the universe. We have made good progress on the first part, and now have the knowledge of the laws of evolution in all but the most extreme conditions. But until recently, we have had little idea about the initial conditions for the universe. However, this division into laws of evolution and initial conditions depends on time and space being separate and distinct. Under extreme conditions, general relativity and quantum theory allow time to behave like another dimension of space. This removes the distinction between time and space, and means the laws of evolution can also determine the initial state. The universe can spontaneously create itself out of nothing. Moreover, we can calculate a probability that the universe was created in different states. These predictions are in excellent agreement with observations by the WMAP satellite of the cosmic microwave background, which is an imprint of the very early universe. We think we have solved _____. Maybe we should patent the universe and charge everyone royalties for their existence.

41 Choose the sentence that best fills in the blank.

① the chance of spreading out into space
② the mystery of creation
③ the future of the human race
④ the question of the universe through observation

42 Which of the following is true?

① It is undeniable that galaxies are moving closer to us.
② The evolutionary law cannot be applied to the initial state of the universe.
③ The distinction between time and space can disappear in an extreme condition.
④ The calculation of the age of the universe is not supported by any empirical observation.

[43-45] 한국외대 2016

Every day hundreds of discarded fishing nets drift through Pacific waters, twisting and turning with the currents. They stretch from several meters to 6 km, their plastic fibers indiscriminately trapping any marine life that gets in the way. These lethal damaged or abandoned "ghost nets" can, it's estimated, take up to 600 years to decay. Many eventually wash up on the beaches of Northern Australia. Twelve years ago, former fisherman Riki Gunn set about establishing a marine conservation group to patrol the beaches, pick up the nets, and free (A) _____. Today indigenous rangers from 40 different clans regularly scour 3,000 km of isolated coastline rescuing endangered turtles, dugongs, and other marine life. Within months of the rangers first beginning their work, piles of netting built up. With the help of Queensland artist Sue Ryan, Gunn set out to find solutions to help dispose of them. Ideas poured in through a national competition— to turn the plastic fibers into everything from guitar straps to bags and art installations.

Soon Ryan was organizing craft workshops with the Ghost Net Art Project. Ryan couldn't help but marvel at the variety of colors, weaves, and thicknesses of the fibers. "I was really excited because it was completely different from anything I'd ever worked with," she says. "It was also a great way of raising awareness about the ghost nets."

43 Which of the following is best supported by the passage?

① In Australia, a marine blight is being transformed into art.
② People's different tastes help create different art forms.
③ The future of the Australian art industry is promising.
④ The Ghost Net Art Project will be replicated by other countries.

44 Which of the following best fits into (A)?

① entangled creatures
② aquatic art
③ washed-up seaweed
④ trapped artifacts

45 Which of the following is true of the Ghost Net Art Project?

① It alerts the public to the dangers of technology.
② It aims to lead young people to appreciate art.
③ It develops solutions to reuse environmental hazards.
④ It makes the public recognize the importance of tradition.

[01-03] 한성대 2008

The behavior of chimpanzees has for a long time been a puzzle to those psychologists who have concerned themselves with these interesting beasts. The young chimpanzee is extraordinarily like a child, and clearly his equal or perhaps even his superior in intellectual matters. The animal psychologists have not been able to keep from wondering why a chimpanzee brought up in a human family and subject to the impact of human speech until the age of one or two, does not accept language as a mode of expression, and itself burst into baby talk.

The average animal psychologist is rather longingly hoping for that chimpanzee who will disgrace his simian ancestry by adhering to more human modes of conduct. The failure so far is not a matter of sheer bulk of intelligence, for ⓐ there are defective human animals whose brains would shame a chimpanzee. ⓑ It just does not belong to the nature of the beast to speak, or to want to speak.

01 밑줄 친 ⓐ와 가장 가까운 내용은?

① Some human animals are less intelligent than a chimpanzee.
② However defective human animals are, they are more intelligent than chimpanzees.
③ Human animals are so defective that they would shame a chimpanzee.
④ It's very shameful to compare human animals with a chimpanzee.

02 윗글의 내용과 일치하는 것은?

① Chimpanzees do not talk because they are less intelligent than human children.
② Chimpanzees would talk if they are brought up in a human family.
③ For a chimpanzee to fail in speaking is a matter of sheer bulk of intelligence.
④ For a chimpanzee not to speak is his nature.

03 밑줄 친 ⓑ It이 가리키는 것은?

① The failure
② Intelligence
③ A chimpanzee
④ To speak, or to want to speak

[04-05] 중앙대 2010

> Scientists haven't been able to measure elephants' intelligence precisely. Nevertheless, for decades, experts have observed the pachyderms' behavior and concluded that they rank among the smartest in the animal kingdom. That said, the theory of elephants never forgetting is an exaggeration, but doesn't stray terribly far from the truth. Elephants have the largest brains by mass of all mammals, weighing in at a hefty 4.7 kilograms for an adult. While we can't judge how effectively a brain works based solely on its size, it can offer a decent approximation and give us a hint as to the power of elephant memory. One conventional way of estimating an animal's intelligence is examining the encephalization quotient (EQ). The EQ compares the actual size of an animal's brain against the size scientists would project its brain to be based on body weight. To better understand this measurement, think of an apple and an avocado. Both fruits are relatively the same size, but an apple has tiny seeds, while an avocado's seed resembles a golf ball. The logic follows that the smaller the ratio of brain to body mass, the dumber the animal and vice versa. For instance, people have an average EQ above seven, while pigs have an EQ of around 0.27. Elephants score relatively high on this scale, coming in at a cross-species average of 1.88. For comparison, chimpanzees have an EQ of 2.5. Female elephants, the leaders of the herds, often have greater EQs than males. This is probably linked to the matriarchal social structure of elephant herds. Studies have also found that the elder female elephants exhibit signs of a superior memory, alerting the herd if a familiar danger arises or an old feeding site is recognized.

04 윗글에서 저자가 "an apple and an avocado"를 언급한 의도로 가장 적합한 것을 고르시오.

① to make a precise measurement of elephants' intelligence
② to calculate the size of the brain of an elephant
③ to explain the concept of the encephalization quotient
④ to compare elephants' memory with that of humans

05 윗글을 통해 알 수 있는 것으로 가장 적합한 것을 고르시오.

① Elder male elephants tend to have a better memory than young female ones.
② Chimpanzees on average tend to have lower intelligence than elephants.
③ The larger the ratio of brain to body mass, the dumber the animal.
④ Elephants have a relatively good memory because they have a higher encephalization quotient.

[06-07] 중앙대 2010

㉮ According to the Harlows, the basic quality of an infant's love for its mother is trust. If the infant is put into an unfamiliar playroom without its mother, the infant ignores the toys no matter how interesting they might be. It screeches in terror and curls up into a furry little ball. If its cloth mother is now introduced into the playroom, the infant rushes to the surrogate and clings to it for dear life. After a few minutes of contact comfort, it apparently begins to feel more secure. It then climbs down from the mother-substitute and begins tentatively to explore the toys, but often rushes back for a deep embrace as if to reassure itself that its mother is still there and that all is well. Bit by bit its fears of the novel environment are "desensitized" and it spends more and more time playing with the toys and less and less time clinging to its "mother."

㈏ Why is cloth preferable to bare wire? Something that the Harlows called contact comfort seems to be the answer, and a most powerful influence it is. Infant monkeys spend much of their time rubbing against their mothers' skins, putting themselves in as close contact with the parent as they can. Whenever the young animal is frightened, disturbed, or annoyed, it typically rushes to its mother and rubs itself against her body. Wire doesn't "rub" as well as does soft cloth. Prolonged "contact comfort" with a surrogate cloth mother appears to instill confidence in baby monkeys and is much more rewarding to them than is either warmth or milk. Infant monkeys also prefer a "rocking" surrogate to one that is stationary.

㈐ During the first two weeks of its life warmth is perhaps the most important psychological thing that a monkey mother has to give to its baby. The Harlows discovered this fact by offering infant monkeys a choice of two types of mother-surrogates—one wrapped in terry cloth and one that was made of bare wire. If the two artificial mothers were both the same temperature, the little monkeys always preferred the cloth mother. However, if the wire model was heated, while the cloth model was cool, for the first two weeks after birth the baby primates picked the warm wire mother-surrogates as their favorites. Thereafter they switched and spent most of their time on the more comfortable cloth mother.

06 윗글을 바른 순서대로 나열한 것으로 가장 적합한 것을 고르시오.

① ㈎ – ㈏ – ㈐
② ㈏ – ㈎ – ㈐
③ ㈐ – ㈏ – ㈎
④ ㈏ – ㈐ – ㈎

07 윗글을 통해 추론할 수 있는 것으로 가장 적합한 것을 고르시오.

① In the first two weeks of a monkey's life, contact comfort is more important than warmth.
② Contact comfort is determined by the warmth of the surface of the mother's body.
③ A baby primate finds comfort in familiar objects.
④ The love of an infant for its mother is primarily a response to certain stimuli that mother offers.

[08-09] 한양대 2010

Since 1960, worldwide production of meat has quadrupled to more than 280 million tons a year. Even if everyone in the rich nations swore off meat today, consumption would continue to soar. ㉮ For this reason, serious environmental planners have recently focused not on eliminating the meat industry but on turning it green. Making beef, pork, or chicken can be an environmentally devastating process. ㉯ And among animal proteins, to make a kilogram of beef takes seven times more farmland than is needed to produce a kilo of chicken, and 15 times the area needed for a kilo of pork. Yet scientist, herders, and green groups are convinced they can curb the damage by making adjustments all along the supply chain, changing the way we farm and feed livestock and building a cleaner cow through modern genetics. ㉰ When a cow eats, its stomach produces methane as a byproduct. Cows are pretty efficient at eating grass, but the soybeans and corn that most industrial livestock farms feed them make the bovine stomach rumble with excess gas. ㉱ To fight this, some farms found they could improve health and boost milk production in the herds, and reduce methane emissions, by eliminating soybean and corn-based feed. Instead, they give their cows old-fashioned alfalfa, which is packed with nutrients and benign fatty acids.

08 According to the passage, which of the following is true?

① People in the rich nations are trying to stop consuming meat today.
② Methane produced by cows is not environmentally harmful.
③ Cows' stomachs are efficient in digesting soybeans and corn.
④ To produce a kilo of meat, pork needs less farming area than beef or chicken.

09 Where does the following sentence fit best in the passage?

> The effort starts with the animals themselves.

① ㉮   ② ㉯
③ ㉰   ④ ㉱

[10-11] 한양대 2011

Contrary to widespread belief in China and South-East Asia, the rhinoceros horn has no proven medicinal or aphrodisiac qualities. Its effect, some scientists say, is the same as chewing your fingernails. It is made of the same stuff, agglutinated hair. Yet rhino horn is currently worth more than gold, selling for up to 60,000 dollars a kilo. That is why a beast that has been on earth for some 60 million years is fighting for its existence. So far this year, at least 260 South African rhinos have been illegally killed. Almost all were shot for their horns; these days, few are taken for bush meat. South Africa is home to more than 90% of the world's white rhinos and around a third of the rarer black one. Until 1970 all had been reasonably well. ㉮ _____, oil prices soared, resulting in a sevenfold increase in income per head in Yemen, where elaborately carved rhino-horn dagger handles are prized as a sign of status and wealth. Yemenis rapidly became the world's biggest importers of rhino horn. By 1980 half the world's rhinos, by some estimates, had disappeared.

10 What is most appropriate for blank ㉮?

① Then
② However
③ Therefore
④ Nevertheless

11 According to this passage, which is true?

① Unlike rhino horn, rhino meat has medical qualities.
② More than 40% of black rhinos live in South Africa.
③ The income of Yemenis has increased thanks to the rhino horn trade.
④ The oil price surge has caused the increase in rhino horn consumption in Yemen.

[12-14]

A plant is carnivorous if it attracts, captures, and kills animal life forms. It must also digest and absorb the nutrients from prey to qualify as a carnivorous plant. There are many noncarnivorous plants that do some, but not all, of these things. For example, flowers attract pollinators (insects, birds, and other creatures, even humans). Some plants temporarily trap insect pollinators to ensure pollen transfer. Plants such as members of the American genera Ibicella and Proboscidea trap and kill insects by their sticky leaves but do not digest the prey. All plants absorb nutrients either through their roots or leaves. However, even though these plants do some of the things that carnivorous plants do, they do not fulfill all of the criteria necessary to qualify as a carnivorous plant.

In recent years people have been realizing that nature is not quite as black and white as we would like. Some plants are neither completely carnivorous nor completely noncarnivorous. For example, there are sticky plants which harbor bugs on them. These bugs crawl freely on the plant and eat the insects trapped by the sticky leaves. The bugs excrete on the leaves, and the plant absorbs nutrients from the poop. Other plants rely on bacterial decomposition to break down their captured prey.

12 What is the purpose of the first paragraph?

① To describe various types of plants
② To compare the characteristics of carnivorous and noncarnivorous plants
③ To define which plants are true carnivorous plants
④ To inform about noncarnivorous plants

13 Why does the author mention sticky plants in paragraph 2?

① To give detailed characteristics of noncarnivorous plants
② To explain that carnivorous and noncarnivorous are not totally distinct from each other
③ To explain the relationship between sticky plants and harbor bugs
④ To illustrate that the plants must fulfill all of the criteria necessary to qualify as a carnivorous plant

14 What is the best title for the whole passage?

① The classification of carnivorous and noncarnivorous plants
② The criteria for distinguishing plants
③ Why do some noncarnivorous plants have the features of carnivorous plants?
④ Carnivorous plants' strategy for seizing their prey

[15-18]

The cosmos is one of a genus of tropical herbs, numbering about twenty species. It is a tall, graceful, late-flowering annual or perennial, of many different varieties and feathery foliage. The word "cosmos" is derived from the Greek term, cosmos, and signifies "an ornament or beautiful thing." And after seeing the lovely graceful cosmos in bloom, one feels that this flower has indeed been rightly named. It is native to tropical and semitropical America. Its American ancestors are said to have come from the warmer uplands of Mexico. The early kinds grown in the U.S. could not stand cold, for the cosmos glories in the sun. Often frost killed the plants before their seeds had ripened. However, new ones have been developed that now make the cosmos a fall as well as a summer flower.

The fact that the cosmos flowers late, when many other plants have completed their work, makes it of more value to gardeners and flower lovers. For it truly comes into its own at the first frosts. This late, aster-like blossom, with its filmy leaves, not only is most attractive in garden beds or against walls but the cut flowers make beautiful bouquets for indoor decorations.

The most commonly cultivated type in the U.S. may grow to heights of from 7 to 10 feet, though some are not so tall. It has smooth stems, and its brightly rayed, showy flowers have yellow disks. The rays are in a variety of colors including white, pink, red, purple, shell, yellow, orange — in fact, almost any hue except blue. The early primitive kinds had flowers only about an inch across. But various breeders have worked with this desirable plant, and have in some cases shortened the stems and increased the size of the blooms, some of which grow singly, other in clusters.

15 Which of the following cannot be inferred about the "cosmos"?

① The meaning of its name seems to suit the flower well.
② The origins of the ones found in the U.S. can be traced to Mexico.
③ It was originally a fall flower but now has developed into a summer one.
④ Some types live for a few growing seasons.

16 Choose the one closest in meaning to the underlined part.

① the cosmos grows better at the time of the first frosts
② the cosmos has developed skills to cope with frosts on its own
③ when the first frosts come, the cosmos blooms to its fullest
④ the first frosts are not conducive in making the cosmos grow

17 According to the passage, which of the following is not true about the appearance of the cosmos?

① The color of the rays varies widely but does not include blue.
② Not all blooms are found in clusters.
③ The stems are smooth and all flowers have yellow disks.
④ The average height is 7-10 feet with some types growing taller.

18 According to the passage, which aspect is associated with why the cosmos is valued?

① It is pleasing to look at when planted in garden beds.
② It is easy to cultivate since it does not need much water to grow.
③ It is a rare flower that cannot be found in warmer climates.
④ It lasts a longer time than other kinds of cut flowers.

[19-21] 한국외대 2010

Reefs are home to millions of animals. These underwater worlds are so ㉮ _____ that they've become known as the rain forests of the sea. But just as rain forests are in trouble on land, all is not well beneath the waves. Worldwide, half of all reefs have vanished, and the rest could be extinct by mid-century. If reefs disappear, we lose a source of extraordinary beauty and biodiversity. We also lose an underwater buffer that holds back waves during hurricanes; a nursery for fish that feed a billion people and provide 200 million jobs in the fishing industry; a home for plants and animals used to treat cancer, HIV, and other illnesses; and an estimated $105 billion a year from tourist revenue in the Caribbean alone. The threat to coral is a threat to all of us. So researchers are trying to save the coral: They are involved in a hopeful attempt at reseeding it. In Hawaii, for example, scientists and students have started the annual spawning of the coral. They boat out to the reef at sunset, gather up bundles of fertilized eggs, and then place them in collecting tanks.

19 Which of the following is the main topic of the passage?

① Degradation and restoration of coral reefs
② Investigation of a natural disaster
③ Annual coral spawning in Hawaiian reefs
④ Clearance of tropical rain forests
⑤ Exploitation of marine natural resources

20 Which of the following best fits into ㉮?

① barren
② achromatic
③ tranquil
④ lush
⑤ chaotic

21 Which of the following is NOT mentioned as a result of the disappearance of the coral?

① Job market shrinking in the fishing industry
② More frequent natural disasters
③ Decrease of tourists to marine attractions
④ Lack of medicine for some diseases
⑤ Cuts in funding for marine biological research

[22-24] 숭실대 2008

The word inheritance refers to the transmission, from parents to offspring, of structural and functional patterns characteristic of each species. In living cells, hereditary instructions are encoded in molecules of DNA. Hereditary instructions ensure that offspring will resemble their parents, but they also permit variations on the basic plan. For example, some humans are born with six fingers on each hand instead of five. The variations arise through mutations, which are changes in the structure of the number of DNA molecules.

Most mutations are harmful, for the separate bits of information in DNA are part of a coordinated whole. For example, a single mutation in a tiny bit of human DNA may lead to hemophilia or some other genetic disorder. ⓐ _____ some mutations may prove to be harmless, even beneficial, under prevailing conditions. One type of mutation in light-colored moths leads to dark-colored offspring. When a dark moth rests on a soot-covered tree, bird predators do not see it. Where most trees are soot-covered, as in industrial regions, light moths are more likely to be seen and eaten so the dark form has a better chance of surviving and reproducing. Under such conditions, ⓑ <u>the mutant form</u> is more adaptive.

22 Choose the word which would fit best in ⓐ.

① Therefore   ② Yet
③ Moreover   ④ For

23 According to the passage, which of the following statements is NOT true?

① DNA is the molecule of inheritance in all living organisms.
② Mutations introduce variations in heritable traits.
③ Some mutations are beneficial because they may turn out to be more adaptive.
④ Humans cannot have six fingers on each hand due to hereditary instructions.

24 Which of the following does ⓑ the mutant form refer to?

① a dark moth
② a bird predator
③ a soot-covered tree
④ a light moth

[25-28]

If the perennial culture war between science and fundamentalist Christianity about evolution seems insoluble, the reason is that it is insoluble. The fault line, which affects conservative belief not just in Christianity but in almost all other religions around the world, can be found along the outer edge of biology. On one side is the acceptance of evolution of all life independently of God, a view held by a small minority of Americans. On the other lies a spread of beliefs, from ⓐ _____ that evolution ever occurred to ⓑ _____ that it did, but under the direction of God. This gap, opened by Charles Darwin in his 1859 *On the Origin of Species*, has not been narrowed by the endless debates that ensued. Quite the contrary, it has been steadily widened by the growth of science. Modern biology has arrived at two major principles that are supported by so much interlocking evidence as to rank as virtual laws of nature. The first is that all biological elements and processes are ultimately obedient to the laws of physics and chemistry. The second principle is that all life has evolved by ⓒ random mutation and natural selection. Although as many as half of Americans choose not to believe it, evolution, including the origin of species, is an undeniable fact. Furthermore, the evidence supporting the principle of natural selection has improved year by year, and it is accepted with virtual ⓓ unanimity by the biologists who have put it to the test.

25 빈칸 ⓐ와 ⓑ에 들어갈 가장 적절한 표현은?

① denial – acceptance
② acceptance – denial
③ proof – theory
④ theory – proof

26 밑줄 친 ⓒ random mutation and natural selection을 우리말로 가장 적절히 옮긴 것은?

① 먹이사슬과 적자생존
② 적자생존과 돌연변이
③ 돌연변이와 자연도태
④ 먹이사슬과 자연도태

27 밑줄 친 ⓓ unanimity와 가장 유사한 의미를 가진 것은?

① hospitality
② hostility
③ commitment
④ consensus

28 이 글의 내용과 일치하는 것은?

① A majority of American people believe in the evolution of all life.
② *On the Origin of Species* narrowed the gap between science and Christianity.
③ All biological elements obey the laws of physics and chemistry.
④ The evidence indicating the principle of natural selection is difficult to find.

[29-31]

In evolutionary biology, an organism is said to behave altruistically when its behaviour benefits other organisms, at a cost to itself. The costs and benefits are measured in terms of reproductive fitness, or expected number of offspring. So by behaving altruistically, an organism reduces the number of offspring it is likely to produce itself, but boosts the number that other organisms are likely to produce. This biological notion of altruism is not identical to the everyday concept. In everyday parlance, an action would only be called "altruistic" if it was done with the conscious intention of helping another. But in the biological sense _____. For the biologist, it is the consequences of an action for reproductive fitness that determine whether the action counts as altruistic, not the intentions, if any, with which the action is performed. Altruistic behaviour is common throughout the animal kingdom, particularly in species with complex social structures. For example, in social insect colonies (e.g., ants and bees), sterile workers devote their whole lives to caring for the queen, which is maximally altruistic. From a Darwinian viewpoint, the existence of altruism in nature is at first sight puzzling. Natural selection leads us to expect animals to behave in ways that increase their own chances of survival and reproduction, not those of others. But by behaving altruistically an animal reduces its own fitness, so should be at a selective disadvantage vis-a-vis one which behaves selfishly.

29 What is the main idea of the passage?

① The number of offsprings an organism produces is a measure of altruism.
② The Darwinian theory of natural selection has been proven wrong by altruism in insects.
③ For some organisms, altruism is at odds with increasing their chance of survival.
④ Altruism is a concept usually reserved for humans who have emotions.

30 Which of the following best fills in the blank?

① it is completely logical
② there is no such requirement
③ this is a strong tendency
④ the action is accidental

31 Which of the following cannot be inferred from the passage?

① Biologists consider altruism to be actions that are an extension of intentions.
② For biologists, the notion of altruism involves some degree of self-sacrifice.
③ Altruistic organisms are more inclined to assist in other's reproduction rather than their own.
④ The biological view of altruism somewhat contradicts Darwin's theory of natural selection.

[32-33] 성균관대 2012

There have been several cases in which well-meaning boffins have introduced a new species to overcome one problem only to _____. After Australia brought the cane toad from Hawaii to control a beetle that eats sugar cane, the amphibian spread like a plague. The import of African bees to Brazil to increase honey yields set off swarms of "killer" bees throughout the Americas. And so it is with the moose in Newfoundland.

The moose may be a Canadian icon, but in the island of Newfoundland it is an alien, introduced a century ago when local leaders reckoned their presence would attract hunters and tourists to what was a struggling British colony. Unlike in the rest of Canada, the moose has no natural predators on the island, where the native wolf went extinct. There are now around 150,000 of the lumbering giants in Newfoundland. That has drawn hunters. But the habit of the moose to wander across highways in the dark has made it a road hazard responsible for around 700 collisions a year.

32 Which one would be most appropriate for the blank?

① lead to failure   ② create another
③ be criticized   ④ find none
⑤ waste the money

33 What does the underlined "what was a struggling British colony" mean?

① Canada
② America
③ Australia
④ Brazil
⑤ Newfoundland

[34-36]

At a distance a fish school resembles a large organism. Its members, numbering anywhere from two or three into the millions, swim in tight formations, wheeling and reversing in near unison. Either dominance systems do not exist or they are so weak as to have little or no influence on the dynamics of the school as a whole. There is, moreover, _____. When the school turns to the right or left, individuals formerly on the flank assume the lead. The average school size varies according to species, as does the spacing of its members, its average velocity, and its three-dimensional shape. Although the fish are usually aligned with military precision while the group is on the move, they assume a more nearly random orientation while resting or feeding. Their alignments also shift in particular ways when the fish are attacked by predators. Spacing within the moving school is evidently determined to a large extent by hydrodynamic force. Individual fish tend to seek positions in which they can be as close as possible to their neighbors without suffering serious loss of efficiency due to turbulence created by the other fish.

34 According to the passage, what does not influence school size?

① the direction of the fish
② the proximity of the fish
③ the type of the fish
④ the speed of the fish

35 Choose the one that best fills in the blank.

① an opportunity to swim solo
② no consistent leadership
③ little room for autonomy
④ a strong sense to diverge

36 Which of the following cannot be inferred about a "fish school"?

① Its main role is to provide safety to its members.
② Predators affect the alignment of the fish.
③ It refers to a group of more than two fish.
④ Feeding is an exception to uniform formation.

[37-39] 성균관대 2013

While the size of the brain certainly has some relation to smarts, much more can be learned from its structure. Higher thinking takes place in the cerebral cortex, the most evolved region of the brain and one many animals lack. Mammals are members of the cerebral-cortex club, and as a rule, the bigger and more complex that brain region is, the more intelligent the animal. But it's not the only route to creative thinking. Consider tool use. Humans are magicians with tools, apes dabble in them, and otters have mastered the task of smashing mollusks with rocks to get the meat inside—which, though primitive, counts. But if creativity lives in the cerebral cortex, why are corvids, the class of birds that includes crows and jays, better tool users than nearly all nonhuman species?

Crows, for example, have proved themselves adept at bending wire to create a hook so they can fish a basket of food from the bottom of a plastic tube. More remarkably, last year a zoologist at the University of Cambridge—the aptly named Christopher Bird—found that the rook, a member of the crow family, could reason through how to drop stones into a pitcher partly filled with water in order to raise the level high enough to drink from it. _____, the rooks selected the largest stones first, apparently realizing they would raise the level faster. Aesop wrote a tale about a bird that managed just such a task more than 2,500 years ago, but it took 21st century scientists to show that the feat is no fable.

37 According to the passage, many animals are not intelligent because they _____.

① live a simple life
② have a very small brain
③ didn't have to use the tools
④ were never trained to use their brain
⑤ don't have cerebral cortex

38 Which is most appropriate for the blank?

① On the contrary
② Nevertheless
③ What's more
④ Ironically
⑤ On the one hand

39 What does the underlined "the feat" mean?

① animals' use of language
② otters' use of rocks
③ chimpanzee's mastery of sign language
④ Christopher bird's reasoning
⑤ birds' use of tools to achieve their goal

[40-42] 성균관대 2014

The wolf prowls through stories as the embodiment of evil. In a way, it is odd that the wolf should be mankind's worst enemy. Bears, which get a far better press, are more dangerous. Disturb a bear and it may turn on you; disturb a wolf and it will run away. Presumably competition explains this ancient hatred. Once people took to raising animals, wolves competed with them more directly than any other creature. A pack of wolves will happily kill hundreds of sheep in an hour. In communities whose livelihood goes about on four legs, wolves and people are not compatible. This rivalry has spawned awful cruelty, and in the early 19th century America, killing wolves was regarded it as fine entertainment. (가) _____ around the middle of the 20th century sentiment started to change. First came a shift in conservationist thinking, illustrated by the life and writings of Aldo Leopold, father of the American environmental movement. In the early 20th centuries environmentalists believed that because predators killed other animals, conservation was best served by killing them. (나) _____ Mr Leopold grew concerned about the consequences of this campaign. In "*A Sand County Almanac*" first published in 1949 and probably the bestselling environmentalist book ever, he wrote, "I have watched the face of many a newly wolfless mountain, and seen the south-facing slopes wrinkle with a maze of new deer trails. I have seen every edible bush and seedling browsed, first to anaemic desuetude, and then to death."

40 According to the passage, wolves and people are incompatible because _____.

① wolves do the irreversible damages to the ecosystem
② wolves are the antithesis of human civilization
③ wolves are the violent creatures that breed and spread fast
④ wolves competed with people more directly than any other creature
⑤ original settler had no previous experience of wolves

41 Which of the following would be best for the blanks (가) and (나)?

	(가)	(나)
①	Yet	But
②	There	But
③	But	Moreover
④	Consequently	Indeed
⑤	Moreover	Therefore

42 According to the passage, which of the following is true?

① Mankind's ancient resentment of the wolf is completely groundless.
② The conservationists in the early 20th century emphasized that humans were responsible for the extinction of wolves.
③ Mr Leopold argued that the campaign to destroy wolves was destroying America's landscape.
④ Compared with wolves bears are more adaptable.
⑤ People could not domesticate wolves because they were natural predators.

[43-45] 서울여대 2018

It's a common belief that cows are unable to walk down stairs. Many people think that you can get a cow up stairs but getting it back down isn't going to happen without getting pretty creative. But is there actually any truth to this? To put it simply: it is very difficult for cows to walk down stairs. Although at first the notion may seem ridiculous, cows' inability to complete this seemingly simple feat actually makes quite a bit of sense.

Cows struggle with walking down stairs because the incline and structure of stairs are not found in nature and are tailored for human leg proportions. The average slope of a staircase is 35 degrees, so we humans can walk down it without a second thought.

Cows, on the other hand, have a much different weight distribution and bone structure than we do, so it is difficult for them to move in the same manner. When you think about it, anything as massive as a cow would have difficulty going downhill at a slope of 35 degrees. With the average cow weighing anywhere from 1,600 to 2,400 pounds (based on gender and breed), the animal's fear of walking down stairs seems pretty rational. Cows' necks are also far less mobile than ours, so when tilted that far forward it becomes difficult to see straight ahead—something that they instinctively want to avoid. While cows won't walk down stairs on their own, it has been proven that cows will walk down stairs if you force them to. So, yes, cows can walk down stairs. They just avoid the situation as much as possible, as they are not evolutionarily prepared for such steep slopes and foreign leg movements.

43 Which of the following is NOT relevant to cows' struggle with walking down stairs?

① Their breed
② Their weight
③ Their emotion
④ Their bone structure

44 According to the passage, which of the following is true?

① Cows' leg proportions are not the same as humans'.
② Cows cannot walk down stairs even if forced to do so.
③ Cows cannot see straight ahead whenever going down a slope.
④ The incline and structure of stairs are not rare in natural surroundings.

45 Which of the following would best describe the intention of the writer?

① To alarm us against cows' downward movement
② To persuade us into doing something for cows
③ To give us a moral lesson regarding animal life
④ To give us information on cows' characteristics

[46-50] 세종대 2018

Beavers are famously busy, and they turn their talents to reengineering the landscape as few other animals can. When sites are available, beavers burrow in the banks of rivers and lakes. But they also transform less suitable habitats by building dams. Felling and gnawing trees with their strong teeth and powerful jaws, they create massive log, branch, and mud structures to block streams and turn fields and forests into the large ponds that beavers love. [1]

Domelike beaver homes, called lodges, are also constructed of branches and mud. They are often (A) _____ located in the middle of ponds and can only be reached by underwater entrances. These dwellings are home to extended families of monogamous parents, young kids, and the yearlings born in the previous spring. [2]

Beavers are among the largest of rodents. They are herbivores and prefer to eat leaves, bark, twigs, roots, and aquatic plants.

These large rodents move with an ungainly waddle on land but are graceful in the water, where they use their large, webbed rear feet like swimming fins, and their paddle-shaped tails like rudders. [3] They can remain underwater for 15 minutes without surfacing, and have a set of transparent eyelids that function much like goggles. Their fur is naturally oily and waterproof.

Beavers are known for their danger signal which a beaver makes when the beaver is startled or frightened. A swimming beaver will rapidly dive while forcefully slapping the water with its broad tail. This means that the beaver creates a loud slapping noise, which can be heard over large distances above and below water. This beaver warning noise serves as a warning to beavers in the area. [4] Once a beaver has made this danger signal, nearby beavers dive and may not come back up for some time.

There are two species of beavers, which are found in the forests of North America, Europe, and Asia. These animals are active all winter, swimming and foraging in their ponds even when a layer of ice covers the surface.

46 Which of the following is most appropriate for the passage to appear in?

① a wildlife magazine
② a financial report
③ an environment pamphlet
④ a paper on omnivores

47 Which of the following is most likely to be the author's attitude toward beavers?

① indignant
② sympathetic
③ uninterested
④ adoring

48 Which is the most appropriate place for the sentence below?

> These attributes allow beavers to swim at speeds of up to five miles an hour.

① [1]
② [2]
③ [3]
④ [4]

49 Which of the following is most suitable for the blank (A)?

① inalienably
② strategically
③ indiscreetly
④ indescribably

50 According to the passage, which of the following is true?

① Beavers are mid-sized rodents that eat all plants and roots.
② Beavers can create a loud slapping noise by using their paddle-shaped tails.
③ Yearlings of beavers leave their lodges permanently in the spring.
④ Beavers do not swim when the surface of their ponds is covered with ice.

CHAPTER 04 인간

[01-02] 한국외대 2007

In a series of brain-scanning experiments, Christian Keysers, neuroscientist at the University of Groningen in the Netherlands, and his team identified a set of neurons in the premotor cortex that lit up when volunteers heard someone munching on potato chips or ripping paper. The same neurons flashed when the subjects performed similar actions themselves. People who displayed particularly strong activity in response to the sound cues alone scored higher on a questionnaire gauging their ability to put themselves in another person's shoes. Mirror neurons "transform what you see or hear other people do into what you would do yourself," Keysers says. "You start to really feel what it feels like to do a similar action." Mirror neurons also respond to the written word, according to researchers at UCLA. Simply reading a phrase like 'biting the peach' triggered the same premotor circuit in subjects as did watching a video of someone chomping on the fruit. It's as if the brain itself simulates the action while grasping the meaning of the words, says a neuroscientist who led the study. Scientists and philosophers traditionally place our higher cognitive powers in a realm distinct from that of our senses and actions, but, the neuroscientist observes, the faculties "are intrinsically tied to the flesh."

01 Judging from the passage, which of the following is most likely to happen when you hear another person open a can of soda?

① You take off your shoes and socks.
② You start to utilize your cognitive powers.
③ You find it difficult to stay awake.
④ You feel like opening a can.
⑤ You are tempted to tear paper.

02 Which of the following is NOT stated or implied in the passage?

① Mirror neurons stop operating when you move.
② Mirror neurons can respond to a variety of different stimuli.
③ Mirror neurons are activated when you see another person chomping on a peach.
④ The studies offer clues about how you understand others when you hear them speak.
⑤ The studies report that some people empathize with others just by knowing what they are doing.

[03-04] 인하대 2015

Most of us are aware that a positive attitude can improve health and speed recovery from illness, but does this also work the other way around? 'Embodied cognition' is a term used by psychologists to describe how the way we move affects the way we think and feel. An early study in this fascinating field demonstrated that holding a pencil horizontally between your teeth activates the same muscles used for smiling, thus sending pleasure signals to our brain, while people who have Botox injected to reduce laughter lines are less happy afterwards. If you've ever cried during a massage you will know that muscles are not simply an amalgamation of tissue and fibers. They contain delicate traces of our emotional lives and have the capacity to engender feelings without the executive influence of the mind. Our body can be _____ of feeling and a powerful co-creator of our emotional experience and there's research to prove it.

03 Which of the following is most appropriate for the blank?

① a mirror   ② a master
③ a reservoir   ④ an originator

04 Which of the following is NOT a proper example for the main idea of the passage?

① Open your arms when you feel timid.
② Recall happy memories when you feel bad.
③ Have a hot bath when you're feeling lonely.
④ Take a dance lesson when you need to be creative.

[05-07] 한국외대 2009

While you sleep your sense of hearing is diminished but still working. This becomes painfully obvious each morning when your alarm goes off. There is a much more subtle way to demonstrate that we are not only aware of sounds while we sleep but actually process some of their meanings. To see this, we can take a sleeping person as a test subject. First, make two or three chiming noises, for example, by tapping a spoon against an empty glass. These sounds should be neither loud nor soft but at about the same level of loudness that you might encounter in everyday speech. In most instances the sleeper will show little or no reaction to these test sounds. Now lean over near the sleeper's ear and quietly say his or her name two or three times. ⓐ _____ the sound of your whisper may only be half as loud as the chiming sound you used before, many sleepers will now awaken or will at least show signs of activity. Our names are very special personal stimuli that we are always on the lookout for. For example, if our names are uttered by someone in a group next to the person we are conversing with, we pick up our names without fail. Even in our sleep we detect the special sound stimuli from all of the other noises in the world and give ⓑ <u>them</u> special processing and attention.

05 What is the major theme of the passage?

① Sleeping person in general cannot hear alarms very well.
② Sleeping persons show signs of activity to clear chimes.
③ Some alarm sounds are more effective than others in waking people.
④ People can process some of what they hear while sleeping.
⑤ Testing the hearing of a sleeper requires a delicate procedure.

06 Which of the following best fits into ⓐ?

① Because
② However
③ Although
④ Therefore
⑤ On the other hand

07 To which of the following does ⓑ refer?

① Our names uttered
② Private conversations
③ Terms of endearment whispered
④ Snoring sounds of someone next to us
⑤ Chiming sounds from empty glasses

[08-10] 숙명여대 2009

> Euthanasia is the deliberate killing of a person for the benefit of that person. In most cases, it is carried out because the person who dies asks for it, but there are other instances of euthanasia where the patient can't make such a request.
>
> Euthanasia raises ⓐ <u>agonizing</u> moral questions such as 'is it ever right for another person to end the life of a terminally ill patient who is in severe pain?' or 'if euthanasia is sometimes right, under what circumstances is it right?' At the heart of the ethical and religious arguments over euthanasia are the different ideas that people have of the meaning and value of human existence, and of whether human beings have the right to decide issues of life and death for themselves. Some people think that euthanasia shouldn't be allowed even if it was morally right, because it would be abused and used as a cover for murder.

08 According to the passage, which of the following statements is true?

① Euthanasia needs to be prohibited.
② More considerations should be given to euthanasia.
③ Euthanasia should be left to the decision by a patient.
④ Family members should not be allowed in the decision process.
⑤ Governments should legalize euthanasia for the benefit of patients.

09 Which of the following can best replace the underlined ⓐ?

① carefree
② tormenting
③ unconscious
④ optimistic
⑤ straightforward

10 Which title does best describe the passage above?

① Illegalization of euthanasia
② Opposing perspectives regarding euthanasia
③ Importance of human free will
④ Crime and punishment
⑤ Development of medical technology

[11-13] 숭실대 2009

> GH or growth hormone has very broad influences, activating many tissues. It stimulates growth by promoting the uptake of amino acids into cells, thereby accelerating protein synthesis. In addition, GH stimulates the release of fats from fatty tissues, in effect shifting the body more towards the metabolism of fats as an energy source.
> Proper levels of GH in the body are essential to normal growth. This becomes painfully obvious when something goes wrong. Excessive secretion during the early years can produce giantism (pituitary giants), Many people with this condition range from seven to nine feet tall. ⓐ _____, in young people, an underactive pituitary with lower than normal GH levels produces pituitary dwarfs, often called midgets. There are several thousand pituitary dwarfs in the United States today. Until recently, treatment for growth deficiencies was difficult and expensive. Stimulating growth in even one pituitary dwarf required a daily injection of all the GH that could be isolated from several human bodies.

But since GH is a protein, new sources are now available through recombinant DNA technology.

ⓑ (GH levels, rise, should) suddenly in an adult human, the resulting condition is known as acromegaly. In this abnormality, growth that has stopped on time mysteriously resumes, but it is restricted to areas where cartilage persists, such as hands, feet, jaw, nose, and some internal organs.

*pituitary: 뇌하수체 *cartilage: 연골

11 Choose the word that would fit best in ⓐ.

① However
② Therefore
③ Incidentally
④ Conversely

12 Which order is correct for ⓑ?

① GH levels should rise
② Should GH levels rise
③ Should rise GH levels
④ Rise GH levels should

13 According to the passage, which of the following statements is true?

① Excessive levels of GH are responsible for pituitary dwarfs.
② There are thousands of GH deficiency patients in the US.
③ An adult human could resume growing with falling levels of GH.
④ One healthy person could help several GH deficiency patients.

[14-17] 이화여대 2009

One set of ethical ⓐ _____ about human clones involves the risks and uncertainties associated with the current state of cloning technology. This technology has not yet been tested with human subjects, and scientists cannot rule out the possibility of mutation or other biological damage. The ethical issues of greatest importance in the cloning debate, however, do not involve possible failures of cloning technology, but rather the consequences of its ⓑ _____. Assuming that scientists were able to clone human beings without incurring the risks mentioned above, what ⓒ _____ might there be about the welfare of clones?

Some ⓓ _____ of cloning believe that such individuals would be wronged in morally significant ways. Many of these wrongs involve the denial of what Joel Feinberg has called "the right to an open future." For example, a child might be constantly compared to the adult from whom he was cloned, and thereby burdened with oppressive expectations. Even worse, the parents might actually limit the child's opportunities for growth and development: a child cloned from a basketball player, for instance, might be denied any educational opportunities that were not in line with a career in basketball. Finally, regardless of his parents' conduct or attitudes, a child might be burdened by the thought that he is a copy and not an "original." The child's sense of ⓔ _____, so some have argued, would thus be difficult to sustain.

14 What can be a likely title of the passage?

① Technological Risks of Human Cloning
② The Oppressive Expectations for Human Clones
③ The Ethical Aspect of Human Cloning
④ The Right to an Open Future

15 Which of the following is not suitable for ⓐ and ⓒ?

① concerns   ② apprehension
③ trepidation   ④ dilapidation

16 Which of the following pair of words best fits in ⓑ and ⓓ?

① failure – supporters
② builder – contenders
③ accomplishment – advocates
④ success – opponents

17 Which of the following does not fit in ⓔ?

① privacy
② individuality
③ dignity
④ self-worth

[18-20] 단국대 2013

There is often a genetic inclination toward one type of addiction or another. This is not to say that heredity alone is sufficient to cause an addiction, but that the specific nature of the addiction may well be influenced by genetics. For instance, an alcoholic often has alcoholic parents or grandparents and may also have an unusually strong "positive" response to alcohol. Trauma can also shape and foster addiction. Chemical substance abusers may have a history of emotional trauma in childhood, or post-traumatic stress, such as that found among war veterans. Another important factor in addiction is shame. Shame is a very powerful feeling that we have when we feel that we don't measure up to certain standards. It often masquerades as other feelings, but it is commonly found in addicts both as a cause and a result of the addiction. Shame spirals upward as an addiction progresses. One last contributor to addiction is anxious depression, the type of depression in which pressure makes the next two hours seem like the most important time of your life. It is a(n) _____ feeling, very different from the melancholy depression that causes a person to sit in bed all day unable to get up or get dressed.

18 What would be the best title for the passage?

① Key Elements of Chemical Addiction
② Recovery from Any Addiction
③ Factors That Influence Addiction
④ Emotional Instability without Addiction

19 Which of the following is most appropriate for the blank?

① agitated
② sedate
③ humiliated
④ amicable

20 Which of the following is true according to the passage?

① Genetic factors play a trivial role in the development of alcoholism.
② Both of the anxious and melancholy depressions lead to addiction.
③ Shameful feelings have a positive correlation with addiction.
④ Getting used to a drug makes people have an inert emotional reaction.

[21-22] 한국외대 2013

Scientists are interested in how the brain grows and ages. Before a child is two years old, there is a surge in brain growth and development. During these early years, billions of new neurons are added to the body. Each one is connected to thousands of others, making trillions of connections. However, after the age of three, a new process begins. The connections that are used a lot remain strong and survive. Connections that are not used a lot become weak and are lost. For example, one child who is given books to read at an early age may learn to read by the age of four. On the other hand, a child who is not given any books to read at an early age may have trouble learning to read. This process continues, and our brains remain sensitive to stimulation and experience into old age. Older people who stay physically and mentally active can still make and keep neural connections.

21 Which of the following would be the best topic of the passage?

① Brain function
② Brain damages
③ Brain development
④ Brain activities

22 Which of the following is true of the passage?

① Aging can make neural connections stronger.
② An aged person cannot make new neural connections.
③ Brain development does not occur at uniform rate.
④ Neural connections begin to form robustly after the age of three.

[23-24] 성균관대 2013

Over the past 50 years, researchers who study human judgment have realized that we rely on emotions to make decisions about risk. We can't possibly mull over every new piece of data our brains collect, so our emotions give us shortcuts, helping us make split-second judgments about that information. The more uncertainty, the more shortcuts we use. This is a good thing. People who have suffered brain damage that removes emotions from their calculations cannot function. They can't make decisions, even simple ones. So we need our emotions to make sense of the world. _____ our emotions also can lead us astray—particularly when we encounter an exception to a lifetime's worth of rules. The brain's shortcuts come with certain predictable biases. In experiments, people reliably overestimate the chances of something happening if they can vividly imagine it. If we see something new, we try to fit it into a box that we understand.

23 The best title of the passage would be _____.

① Limitations in Human Judgement
② How We Manage Risk
③ How We Cope with Human Errors
④ Reason over Emotion in Decision-Making
⑤ Risks in the Information Age

24 Which of the following would be best for the blank?

① Similarly
② Logically
③ But
④ Moreover
⑤ Therefore

[25-26] 한양대 2013

Researchers have identified two phenomena that in previous literature were confounded under the category of nightmares. On the one hand, there is the true nightmare, which is an actual, detailed dream. On the other there is the "night terror," from which the sleeper, often a child, suddenly awakes in great fright with no memory of a dream, often screaming and sometimes going off in a sleepwalking trance. Night terrors are seldom of serious consequence, no matter how horrifying they may appear to anxious parents. Outside of taking commonsense precautions such as making sure a sleepwalker does not go to bed near an open window or on a balcony—there is nothing much to do about them. A child's night terrors can be reduced somewhat with a consistent sleep schedule and by avoiding excessive fatigue. Excessive concern or medication should usually be avoided.

25 윗글의 내용을 읽고 추론할 때 빈칸에 들어갈 가장 알맞은 것을 고르시오.

> The parents of children who experience night terrors _____.

① tend to dismiss them as inconsequential
② should consult a doctor as soon as possible
③ also suffered them when they were children
④ find them as frightening as their children themselves do

26 밑줄 친 "confounded"가 의미하는 것으로 가장 알맞은 것을 고르시오.

① confused
② explained
③ developed
④ unappreciated

[27-28] 서울여대 2014

After learning a new physical skill, such as riding a bike, it takes six hours to permanently store the memory in the brain. But interrupt the storage process by learning another new skill and that first lesson may be erased, according to research into memory and the mind. "We've shown that time itself is a very powerful component of learning," said Dr. Henry Holcomb, a psychiatrist who heads a Johns Hopkins University group that studies how people remember. "It is not enough to simply practice something. You have to allow time to pass for the brain to encode the new skill." The researchers used a device that measures blood flow in the brain. They concluded it takes five to six hours for the memory of a new skill to move from a temporary storage site in the front of the brain to a permanent storage site at the back. During those six hours, Holcomb said, there is a neural "window of vulnerability" when that new skill can be easily eroded from memory if the person attempts to learn a second new skill. "If you were performing a piano piece for the first time and then immediately started practicing something else, then that will cause problems in retention of the initial piece that you practiced," Holcomb said. It would be better, he said, if the first practice session were followed by five to six hours of routine activity that required no new learning.

27 According to the passage, which of the following is true?

① The researchers found a neural "window of vulnerability" by measuring blood pressure in the brain.
② You should practice new learning for more than six hours in order to remember the newly learned skill.
③ You'd better wait for five or six hours to learn riding a bike after playing a piano piece for the first time.
④ You'd better learn two different physical skills at the same time in order to retain both skills.

28 A neural "window of vulnerability" is a neurological phenomenon _____.

① which proves that the memory of a new skill can be immediately stored in a permanent storage site
② which explains why the routine activity of riding a bike does not require new learning
③ which shows the decoding process of the memories of old skills stored in the front of the brain
④ which takes place during five to six hours after a new physical skill is first learned

[29-30] 항공대 2017

As important as visual input is for a pilot, _____. For example, when flying above a cloud deck, there is a natural tendency to perceive any relatively straight line in the visual field as a horizon, which can lead to very undesirable results in a fast-moving aircraft. False horizons are everywhere around you in the clouds. Your aircraft's attitude may seem level, even if you are tilted and in a turn. Mountain ridges might lead you astray as well, and at night the combination of clouds, stars, mountains and lights on the ground can produce impossibly confusing percepts that lead the aircraft away from the safety of true straight and level flight. Don't think that you are safe from your own perception, however, just because you are flying above water on a clear day. A fixed horizon can still put you in the drink. Consider what may happen if you approach the beach from over the horizon. You may line up the beach in your sights and then keep it there in anticipation of flying from over sea to over land but if so you will never reach land: the beach is fixed, unlike a true horizon, and the only way to keep it stationary in your sight is to point your aircraft progressively downward. One might think that objective information from instruments is the logical solution to subjective sensory illusions. The proliferation of instrumentation is part of the problem, however, because of mounting attentional demands on the pilots, which cause cognitive overload during combat and other stressful flight scenarios. This kind of mental distress is an important contributor to spatial disorientation. New avionics are designed with simplicity, not complexity, in mind, and pilots learn how to scan their instruments at just the right times, under conditions of simulated duress.

29 Choose the most appropriate one for the blank.

① pilots are omnipotent
② the inner ear will compensate
③ aural reception matters
④ eyes can lie

30 Which of the following is true?

① Scanning complex instruments for objective information lessens the pilots' attentional demands.
② The beach can be a false horizon when the pilots fly from over sea to over land.
③ Spatial disorientation during a flight makes the pilots crave liquids.
④ Without the clouds, the pilots would be free from spatial disorientation.

[31-33] 한국외대 2016 A형

Can training to become ambidextrous improve brain function? Neuroscientists say that although teaching people to become ambidextrous has been popular for centuries, this practice does not appear to improve brain function, and it may even harm our neural development. Calls for ambidexterity were especially prominent in the late 19th and early 20th centuries. This hype died down in the mid-20th century as the purported benefits of being ambidextrous failed to materialize. Recent evidence even associates being ambidextrous from birth with developmental problems, including reading disability and stuttering. A study revealed that ambidextrous children and adults both performed worse than left-or right-handers on a range of skills, especially in math, memory retrieval, and logical reasoning. The risks of training to become ambidextrous may cause similar difficulties. The two hemispheres of the brain are not interchangeable. The left hemisphere, for example, is typically responsible for language processing, whereas the right hemisphere often handles nonverbal activities. These asymmetries probably evolved to allow the two sides of the brain to specialize. To attempt to undo or tamper with (A) <u>this efficient setup</u> may invite psychological problems. It is possible to train your non-dominant hand to become more proficient. A concert pianist demonstrates superb skill with both hands, but this mastery is complementary rather than competitive. The visual arts may enhance right-brain function, though not at the expense of verbal specialization in the left hemisphere. It seems, therefore, that a cooperative brain seems to work better than one in which the two sides (B) _____.

31 Which of the following is the main theme of the passage?

① Neuroscientists find evidence in favor of ambidexterity.
② Brain specialization is innate and universal.
③ Training to become ambidextrous can be harmful.
④ Ambidextrous individuals are at risk of brain damage.

32 Which of the following is closest what (A) refers to?

① Differential specialization
② Physiological symmetry
③ Evolution of human handedness
④ Interchangeability of brain hemispheres

33 Which of the following best fits into (B)?

① are separated
② consolidate
③ are interconnected
④ compete

[34-35] 중앙대 2017

In the late 1890s two German psychologists, Georg Müller and Alfons Pilzecker, found out that it takes an hour or so for memories to become fixed, or "consolidated", in the brain. Subsequent studies confirmed the existence of short-term and long-term forms of memory and provided further evidence of the importance of the consolidation phase during which the former are turned into the latter. In the 1960s, University of Pennsylvania neurologist Louis Flexner made a particularly intriguing discovery. After injecting mice with an antibiotic drug that prevented their cells from producing proteins, he found that the animals were unable to form long-term memories but could continue to store short-term ones. The implication was clear: long-term memories are not just stronger forms of short-term memories. (A) Storing long-term memories requires the synthesis of new proteins. Storing short-term memories does not. More recent research turned to the issue of the physical workings of both short-term and long-term memory. (B) The results demonstrated that the more times an experience is repeated, the longer the memory of the experience lasts. Repetition encourages consolidation. Particularly, when researchers examined the physiological effects of repetition on neuronal signals, they discovered something amazing. (C) Not only did the concentration of neurotransmitters in synapses change, altering the strength of the existing connections between neurons, but the neurons grew entirely new synaptic terminals. The formation of long-term memories, in other words, involves not only biochemical changes but anatomical ones. (D) That explains why memory consolidation requires new proteins. Proteins play an essential role in producing structural changes in cells.

34 아래의 문장이 들어갈 위치로 가장 적합한 곳을 고르시오.

> The two types of memory entail different biological processes.

① (A)
② (B)
③ (C)
④ (D)

35 윗글을 통해 추론할 수 있는 것으로 가장 적합한 것을 고르시오.

① Use of antibiotic drugs prevents humans from recalling even quite recent experiences.
② Short-term memory is a key predictor for how long we can hold consolidated information in mind in an active manner.
③ Relatively fewer neurotransmitters are expected to be released in the brain synapses when long-term memory is formed.
④ Retaining information in the brain for a longer period is most likely to be accompanied by anatomical changes of synapses.

CHAPTER 05 의학·건강

[01-02] 한국외대 2010

Most women should start regular breast cancer screening at age 50, not 40, according to new guidelines released by an influential medical research group. The new recommendations, which do not apply to a small group of women with unusual risk factors for breast cancer, reverse longstanding guidelines, and are aimed at reducing harm from overtreatment. The group said that women between 50 and 74 should have mammograms less frequently—every two years. Just seven years ago, the same group, with different members, recommended that women have mammograms every year starting at age 40.

The new guidelines, which are different from those of some professionals and advocacy organizations, are likely to touch off yet another round of controversy over the benefits of screening for breast cancer. While many women do not think a screening test can be harmful, medical experts say the risks are real. A test can prompt unnecessary further tests that can create extreme anxiety, and mammograms can find cancers that grow so slowly that they would never be noticed in a woman's lifetime, resulting in unnecessary treatment.

01 Which of the following do the new guidelines for breast cancer warn about?

① Risks from excessive treatment
② Extreme anxiety caused by treatment
③ Excessive medical expenses
④ Harm from maltreatment
⑤ Potential risks of irregular checkups

02 According to the passage, which of the following is NOT true?

① The new guidelines recommend that women have mammograms every other year.
② Some breast cancers develop so slowly that they do not cause a serious problem.
③ The new guidelines suggest that women start screening for breast cancer at 50.
④ There is a group of women who are at unusually increased risk for breast cancer.
⑤ Medical experts agree that women should receive tests for breast cancer less frequently.

[03-04] 한국외대 2009

If you often feel angry and overwhelmed, like when the stress in your life is spinning out of control, then you may be hurting your heart. And if you don't want to break your own heart, you need to learn to take charge of the areas of your life you can—and recognize that there are many things beyond your control. (A) _____ people activate their fight-or-flight response more intensely and more frequently during the course of everyday life than other people do. They respond to (B) _____ annoyances like supermarket lines, traffic jams and children who don't clean up their rooms as though they were a threat to life. Much research has found that high levels of anger are associated with greater risk for heart disease and poor immune responses. Men with high anger scores are three times more likely to develop heart disease than calmer people. And in women, arguments with spouses raise hormone levels and lower immunity—a real problem, since lower immune response may boost women's risk of cancer.

03 Which of the following is the author's main purpose in writing this passage?

① To criticize some research findings about anger
② To explain how harmful anger is to our body
③ To compare two theories about anger management
④ To discuss how to control one's anger
⑤ To voice an opinion on anger management

04 Which of the following best fits into (A) and (B)?

① Hostile – petty
② Amiable – trivial
③ Ill-natured – weighty
④ Intolerant – considerable
⑤ Congenial – negligible

[05-09] 세종대 2011

Schizophrenia is a mental disorder characterized by a disintegration of the process of thinking and of emotional responsiveness. It most commonly manifests as auditory hallucinations, paranoid or bizarre delusions, or disorganized speech and thinking, and it is accompanied by significant social or occupational dysfunction. Schizophrenia behavior is generally characterized by illogical thought patterns and withdrawal from reality such as families and friends. Schizophrenia often live in a fantasy world where they hear voices that other cannot hear. The disorder is thought mainly to affect cognition, but it also usually contributes to chronic problems with behavior and emotion. People with schizophrenia are likely to have additional conditions, including major depression and anxiety disorders. Social problems, such as long-term unemployment, poverty, and homelessness, are common. Furthermore, the average life expectancy of people with the disorder is 10 to 12 years less than those without, due to increased physical health problems and a higher suicide rate.

The onset of symptoms typically occurs during the late teen years or early twenties, with a global lifetime prevalence of around 1.5%. According to World Health Organization, schizophrenia is a serious form of mental illness affecting about 7 per thousand of the adult population, mostly in the age group 15-35 years. Despite the etymology of the term from the Greek roots skhizein ("to split") and phren ("mind"), schizophrenia does not imply a "split mind" and it is not the same as disorder—also known as "multiple personality disorder" or "split personality"—a condition with which it is often confused in public perception. Schizophrenia is considerably more common than multiple personality disorder.

05 According to the passage, which of the following is NOT true about schizophrenia and dissociative identity disorder?

① The etymology of the term "dissociative identity disorder" implies a "split mind".
② Schizophrenia commonly manifests as auditory hallucinations while dissociative identity disorder involves a division into separate personalities.
③ Many people mistake schizophrenia for dissociative identity disorder.
④ Dissociative identity disorder does not occur more often than schizophrenia.

06
Which of the following is closest in meaning to "disorder" in the passage?

① malignancy
② disease
③ misalignment
④ decrease

07
Which of the following can be inferred about schizophrenics?

① They communicate openly with their families.
② They have enhanced logical ability.
③ Their lifespan is longer than average.
④ They often feel remote from their families.

08
Which of the following CANNOT be inferred about schizophrenia?

① Schizophrenics usually have a fixed belief that is either false, fanciful or derived from deception.
② It is characterized by separate and distinct personalities.
③ Schizophrenics have difficulty in getting a job.
④ Its victims tend to hear imaginary voices.

09
According to the passage, which of the following is NOT true about dissociative identity disorder?

① It affects more than 0.7% of the adult population.
② It involves a division into separate personalities.
③ It is different from schizophrenia.
④ It is also called multiple personality disorder.

[10-11] 한성대 2006

Scurvy was a well-known scourge during the age of the seafaring explorers. During a long voyage, the fresh foods that contained vitamin C were eaten in the early weeks, but after months on a diet of salt pork, sailors developed scurvy. An account given of Jacques Cartier's expedition to Newfoundland in 1535 describes scurvy sufferers in terrifying terms: "Their mouths became stinking, their gums so rotten that all the flesh did rot off, even to the roots of their teeth, which almost all fell out."

This account goes on to note that while on land, a crew member was cured of scurvy by drinking sassafras tea. With the help of the scientific method, this knowledge might have led to an understanding of the disease.

Instead, the cure for scurvy continued to elude people. The idea of isolating effects by experiment was not yet appreciated. So when a sailor was cured of scurvy while on land, it was frequently attributed to "the air of the land" and not to the eating of fresh fruits and vegetables.

10 Which is true according to the passage?

① Sassafras tea was a proven medicine to cure scurvy sufferers.
② Sometimes it was believed that the air of the land cured a sailor of scurvy.
③ Scurvy sufferers were cured by eating salt pork while on land.
④ Sailors did not suffer from scurvy with fresh air during a long voyage.

11 Which was NOT a symptom of scurvy?

① Almost all the teeth fell out.
② All the flesh of the mouth rotted off.
③ The mouth became stinking.
④ Gums of the mouth got numb.

[12-14] 숭실대 2006

In Lithuania, rear-end auto collisions happen as they do in the rest of the world; bumpers crumple, tempers flare. But drivers there do not seem to suffer the complaints so common in other countries, the headaches and lingering neck pains known as "whiplash syndrome." Dr. Schrader and colleagues in Norway, without disclosing the purpose of their study, gave health questionnaires to 202 Lithuanian drivers whose cars had been struck from behind one to three years earlier in accidents of varying severity. The drivers' reports of their symptoms were compared to the reports of a control group (of the same size, same ages, and same home towns) of drivers who had not been in an accident. Thirty-five percent of the accident victims reported neck pain, but so did 33% of the controls; 53% of those who had been in an accident had headaches, but so did 50% of those in the control group. The researchers concluded: "No one in the study group had disabling or persistent symptoms as a result of the car accident." What then can account for the explosion of whiplash cases elsewhere in the world? Drivers in the Lithuanian study did not carry personal injury insurance at the time of the study, and people there very infrequently sue one another. Most medical bills are paid by the government, and at the time of the study there were no claims to be filed, no money to be won, and nothing to be gained from a diagnosis of chronic whiplash. Chronic whiplash syndrome, the Norwegian researchers concluded, "_____."

12 According to the passage, which of the following statements is true regarding a comparison of the study and control groups?

① More members in the control group suffered whiplash.
② Several members of the study group had disabling symptoms.
③ More members in the study group experienced headaches.
④ A few members of the control group sustained crippling injuries.

13 Which of the following statements fits best in the blank as a conclusion?

① has questionable liability
② has little validity
③ has persuasive reliability
④ has characteristic severity

14 Which of the following is NOT a probable reason why whiplash cases are more common outside of Lithuania?

① More people in other countries have personal injury insurance policies.
② People in other countries go to court more frequently against one another.
③ More governments in other countries don't pay the medical bills of their citizens.
④ Auto injuries happen far more often in other countries.

[15-17] 한양대 2007

The past thirty to forty years have seen a huge increase in the number of children who suffer from allergies, and scientists are still looking for the explanation. Some have blamed increased air pollution, but it has also been found that allergies are common not only among children in the city but also among children in the countryside, where pollution is typically much lower. [A] A currently popular explanation for the rise in allergies is so-called "hygiene hypothesis." The basic idea is that young children brought up in an environment which is too clean are most at risk of developing allergies. Nowadays, people bathe and wash their clothes more frequently than in the past, and thanks to vacuum cleaners homes are less dusty, too. [B] One result of all these changes is that in their early lives children are exposed to fewer allergens—substances that can cause allergies— and this means that their bodies cannot build up natural immunity to them. [C] The trend towards smaller families also means that young children encounter fewer allergens in the home. In fact, it is known that children who have older brothers and sisters are more resistant to allergies. The same is true of children who share their home with a pet. Such children are much less likely to develop the very common allergy to cat or dog hair. Scientists agree that being exposed to a wider range of allergens early in life helps children to develop greater immunity. There is, however, also some data suggesting that genetics, family income, and even the parents' level of education may play a part in how likely a child is to suffer from allergies. [D] Thus, although the hygiene hypothesis is an important area for research, we cannot yet be sure that too much attention to cleanliness is the only explanation for the enormous rise in the number of allergy victims.

15 이 글의 제목으로 가장 적절한 것은?

① Allergies and Children
② Allergies and Pollution
③ How Allergies Develop
④ Causes of Allergies

16 이 글의 흐름상 다음 문장이 들어갈 가장 적절한 곳은?

> Simply put, exposure to allergy-causing substances is necessary for natural protection against them to develop.

① [A]
② [B]
③ [C]
④ [D]

17 다음 중 이 글의 내용과 일치하지 않는 것은?

① Allergies are also common among children in the countryside.
② Air pollution used to be considered as the main cause of allergies.
③ It is important for children to be exposed to fewer allergens to develop more immunity.
④ Children who do not have older brothers or sisters tend to be less resistant to allergies than those who have.

[18-20] 숭실대 2006

[A] The placebo effect is the measurable, observable, or felt improvement in health not attributable to treatment. This effect is believed by many people to be due to the placebo itself in some mysterious way. A placebo is a medication or treatment believed by the administrator of the treatment to be inert or innocuous. Placebos may be sugar pills or starch pills. Even "fake" surgery and "fake" psychotherapy are considered placebos. [B] Researchers and medical doctors sometimes give placebos to patients. Anecdotal evidence for the placebo effect is garnered in this way. Those who believe there is scientific evidence for the placebo effect point to clinical studies, many of which use a control group treated with a placebo. Why an inert substance, or a fake surgery or therapy, would be effective is not known. [C] "The critical factor," says Psychologist Irving Kirsch, "is our beliefs about what's going to happen to us. You don't have to rely on drugs to see profound transformation." He analyzed 39 studies, done between 1974 and 1995, and again 19 studies done in 1998, of depressed patients treated with drugs, psychotherapy, or a combination of both. He found that 50% of the drug effect is due to the placebo response. [D]

18 According to the passage, which of the following statements is true?

① A placebo is more effective if a patient lacks a strong faith.
② A placebo is ineffective if a patient follows the rules set up by doctors.
③ A placebo contains both neurological and biochemical components.
④ A placebo could be either a harmless drug or a phony treatment.

19 Where would be the best location for the following sentence?

> Some believe, however, the placebo effect is all in a person's head, due to a belief in the treatment or to a subjective feeling of improvement.

① [A]　　　　② [B]
③ [C]　　　　④ [D]

20 According to the passage, which of the following words is NOT descriptive of the placebo effect?

① mysterious
② therapeutic
③ theological
④ psychological

[21-23] 성균관대 2006

This _____ is more than meets the eye. For example, the brain can mysteriously make you itch, without an external cause to scratch or swat. And emotional stress can interfere with the protective functions of the epidermis or can activate immune or inflammatory reactions deeper within. The skin is also a critical outpost of the immune system, laden with specialized white cells that gobble up invading microbes and trigger a bodywide immunologic response. So effective is the skin in this way that researchers are challenging the age-old practice of vaccinating people with a needle directly into muscle—which lacks this immunologic power—proposing instead a far less painful prick of the skin, more akin to a tuberculosis test. ⓐ It seems to do the job as well or better—at a fraction of the dose. ⓑ Skin is gender-sensitive as well. ⓒ Though men and women have similar skin, some sex differences leave women at a distinct disadvantage. ⓓ Perhaps in an evolutionary throwback to a time when women nested while their hunter-gathering men braved the outdoors, women's skin is less prepared to brace the elements, being thinner than men's and less oily. ⓔ Since thinner, drier skin is more prone to damage from the sun or the smoke of cigarettes, women so exposed are more apt to wrinkle. Women also sweat less than men do and are thus more likely to suffer heat stroke. Indeed, the frilly parasols of heavily clad Victorian ladies did double duty by imparting a cooling shade as well as sun relief.

21 Which is most appropriate for the blank?

① critical outpost
② hideous symptom
③ sensitive reaction of the skin
④ placebo effect
⑤ mind-skin interchange

22 If the above passage is divided into two, which would be the boundary?

① ⓐ
② ⓑ
③ ⓒ
④ ⓓ
⑤ ⓔ

23 Which is NOT true of the above passage?

① You can feel itchy without any external cause.
② Skin's white cells defend the invading germs.
③ Emotional stress can weaken the immune system.
④ Smoking has nothing to do with skin aging.
⑤ Women are more likely to have skin problems than men.

[24-27] 성균관대 2008

These critics, all academic researchers outside the medical community, do not dispute surveys that find the obese fraction of the population to have roughly doubled in the United States and many parts of Europe since 1980. And they acknowledge that obesity, especially in its extreme forms, does seem to be a factor in some illness and premature deaths.

They allege, however, that ⓐ experts are blowing hot air when they warn that overweight and obesity are causing a massive, and worsening, health crisis. They scoff, for example, at the 2003 assertion by ⓑ Juile L. Gerberding, director of the Centers for Disease Control and Prevention, that "if you looked at any epidemic—whether it's influenza or plague from the Middle Ages—they are not as serious as the epidemic of obesity in terms of the health impact on our country and our society." (An epidemic of influenza killed forty million people world-wide between 1918 and 1919, including 675,000 in the United States.)

What is really going on, asserts ⓒ Oliver, a political scientist at the University of Chicago, is that "ⓓ a relatively small group of scientists and doctors, many directly funded by the weight-loss industry, have created an arbitrary and unscientific definition of overweight and obesity. They have inflated claims and distorted statistics on the consequences of our growing weights, and they have largely ignored the complicated health realities associated with being fat."

One of those complicated realities, concurs Campos, a professor of law at the University of Colorado at Boulder, is the widely accepted evidence that genetic differences account for 50 to 80 percent of the variation in fatness within a population. Because no safe and widely practical methods have been shown to induce long-term loss of more than about 5 percent of body weight, Campos says, "ⓔ health authorities are giving people advice—maintain a body mass index in the 'health weight' range—that is literally impossible for many of them to follow." Body mass index, or BMI, is a weight-to-height ratio.

24 What does the underlined "blowing hot air" mean?

① assuming it to be true
② exaggerating the fact
③ hoping for the worse
④ deceiving common people
⑤ doing a trick

25 Which one is NOT true?

① The number of fat people has doubled in the United States since 1980.
② Obesity sometimes leads to premature death.
③ Genetic factors play a critical role for being obese.
④ Many doctors are funded from the companies selling weight-loss products.
⑤ The obesity is the most serious source of adult diseases.

26 Who has the different opinion on obesity?

① ⓐ ② ⓑ
③ ⓒ ④ ⓓ
⑤ ⓔ

27 Which one is NOT the problem of doctors and scientists aided by weight-loss industry?

① They wrongly define the notion of overweight.
② They overstate the problems of obesity.
③ They change the facts.
④ They ignore other facts to explain some health problems.
⑤ They suggest too practical criteria on BMI.

[28-31] 한양대 2008

> Anorexia nervosa literally means "loss of appetite for nervous reasons." It is characterized by weight loss. However, anorexia nervosa sufferers have not lost their appetite. They have lost weight because they are suppressing their urge to eat. Most anorexia sufferers cannot easily suppress the feeling that they are fat or at risk of becoming fat if they fail to keep their eating in control. Such feelings are usually quite (ⓐ) their actual weight. This is referred to as having a distorted body image. There is also a strong cultural component. Anorexia nervosa is more common in Western post-industrialized nations, and, in the United States, whites are more affected than African Americans or Hispanic Americans. While the culture of thinness in which we live is certainly an influential factor in the development of anorexia, it is by no means the sole cause.

Anorexia is a response to a complex mix of cultural, social, familial, psychological and biological influences unique to each person. Some possibilities are discussed below. One ⓑ plausible theory is that people develop anorexia because they seek control over themselves and their lives. Food and weight can be controlled when other aspects of life cannot. Restricting food intake while in the presence of enticing foods (ⓒ) feelings of accomplishment. A high percentage of people struggling with anorexia have a history of abuse, neglect, or other traumatic experiences, and develop anorexia as a coping mechanism. Losing weight provides a concrete way to cope with difficult circumstances because it serves to distract the sufferer from the pain. The following two features seem to be characteristic of many sufferers. First, most have low self-esteem. The second feature is that they find it difficult to deal openly with problematic emotions. This may have something to do with their personality. For instance, they may be obsessional and perfectionist. In general, eating disorders seem to arise in the midst of the difficult business of growing up and developing as a person.

28 Which of the following is the best title for the passage?

① Food and Anorexia Nervosa
② Emotional Aspects of Anorexia Nervosa
③ Causes and Symptoms of Anorexia Nervosa
④ Influence of the Culture of Thinness on Nervosa Anorexia

29 Which of the following best fits into (ⓐ) and (ⓒ)?

① free from – prohibits
② irrelevant to – controls
③ dependent on – provokes
④ independent of – evokes

30 Which is closest in meaning to ⓑ?

① feasible
② incredible
③ valuable
④ comparable

31 According to the passage, which of the following statements is true?

① Anorexia nervosa sufferers have doubts about their own worth and competence.
② People suffering from anorexia nervosa gain a sense of accomplishment by controlling their eating.
③ Anorexia nervosa is more common in the developing countries than in advanced technological societies.
④ Anorexia nervosa helps the sufferers forget about pain-filled experience and survive.

[32-34] 서강대 2012

Scientists haven't yet found all the reasons for a hangover, but they have proposed various causes. One is withdrawal, which would bring on the tremors and also sweating. A second factor may be dehydration. Alcohol interferes with the secretion of the hormone that inhibits urination. Hence the heavy traffic to the rest rooms at bars and parties. While that is going on, the alcohol may also be inducing hypoglycemia (low blood sugar), which converts into dizziness and muscle weakness, the feeling that one's bones have turned to jello. Meanwhile, the body, to break down the alcohol, is releasing chemicals that may be more toxic than alcohol itself; these would result in nausea and other symptoms. Finally, the alcohol has produced inflammation, which in turn causes the white blood cells to flood the bloodstream with molecules called cytokines. Apparently, cytokines are the source of the aches and pains and lethargy that, when our bodies are attacked by a flu virus—and likewise, perhaps, by alcohol—encourage us to stay in bed rather than go to work, thereby freeing up the body's energy for use by the white cells in combatting the invader.

[A] The hangover is a preventable malady: don't drink. Nevertheless, people throughout time have found what seemed to them good reason for recourse to alcohol. [B] One attraction is alcohol's power to disinhibit—to allow us, at last, to tell off our neighbor. [C] Alcohol may also persuade us that we have found the truth about life, a comforting experience rarely available in the sober hour. Through the lens of alcohol, the world seems nicer. [D] For all these reasons, drinking cheers people up.

32 Which of the four blanks in the passage is the most appropriate place for the following sentence?

> "I drink to make other people interesting," the theatre critic George Jean Nathan used to say.

① [A]   ② [B]
③ [C]   ④ [D]

33 Which of the following is true according to the passage?

① What triggers a hangover has been medically determined.
② Your body may be harming you more than the alcohol does when you are drunk.
③ Alcohol induces hypoglycemia, which helps to produce white blood cells called cytokines.
④ Alcohol has an inhibiting effect on your mind.

34 Which of the following would NOT happen due to a hangover according to the passage?

① getting thirsty   ② feeling queasy
③ catching a cold   ④ feeling sore and swollen

[35-37] 성균관대 2012

Falling asleep at the wheel could account for more than 20 percent of accidents on dull, monotonous roads such as motorways, according to recent medical report. Typically, these involve running off the road or into the back of another vehicle, and are more likely to cause serious injury owing to the sleepy driver's failure to break. (A) Of course it is a fact that the body's biological clock has a major influence, as these accidents peak at times when sleepiness is naturally higher. (B) Men under 30 are the most vulnerable, as they are the drivers most typically out on the roads in the early hours. Apparently, they take more risks in driving while sleepy. (C) In contrast, older people suffer from an early afternoon 'dip,' when they are more at risk. Time-of-day was found to be as important as the length of the drive, yet practical advice to drivers often concentrates more on the length of the drive than its timing. (D) Devices are now being marketed as in-car monitors of driver sleepiness, ostensibly to warn drivers, but doubts are being raised about these devices. (E) What is the use of alerting drivers already aware that they are sleepy but who still persist in driving? What is more, these devices are of unproven reliability and may simply encourage drivers to _____. (F) Not only does driving motivate tired drivers into putting more effort into remaining awake, but, in this kind of situation, sleep onset can be delayed and distorted. The best advice is either to find some reason not to drive at night, or to get the car off the road as soon as possible, if you're not feeling too bright and breezy!

35 When the above passage can be divided into three paragraphs, which would be the best boundaries?

① (A) and (E)
② (B) and (C)
③ (B) and (F)
④ (C) and (D)
⑤ (A) and (D)

36 Which of the following is most appropriate for the blank?

① stop driving immediately
② take further risks
③ be more careful
④ direct more attention to other vehicles
⑤ be more relaxed

37 According to the passage, which of the following is true?

① Younger drivers are at more risk because they are proud of their driving skill.
② Busy interchanges are far more dangerous to sleepy drivers than motorways.
③ Driving during the afternoon can be dangerous to older drivers.
④ Anti-sleep driving devices tend to work better for older drivers than younger ones.
⑤ Most drivers believe the length of the drive is less critical than the timing of the drive.

[38-40] 성균관대 2013

The existing formula is simple. When vaccinating against influenza, inoculate those most susceptible to the disease's wrath. Such vulnerable types include the elderly and infants. This seems a reasonable policy, and it is the one that has long been promulgated by America's Centres for Disease Control (CDC). Only recently has it been extended to include children up to the age of 18, on the basis that they are more likely than other people to catch flu in the first place—even though they are at little risk of dying from it. However, vaccinating those most at risk of bad effects is not the right way to deal with the disease. In a report published this week in *Science*, Dr. John Medlock argue that even with the extension of vaccination to school-age children, the existing policy of protecting the individual is still playing down the real public-health value of vaccines—namely that they create a so-called herd immunity which helps to break the disease's chain of transmission. He argue that it would be better to concentrate on vaccinating those _____ —both schoolchildren and people between the ages of 30 and 40, who are likely to be the parents of those children, and who are, at the moment, at the bottom of the vaccination priority list. That, at least, is the outcome of their mathematical model of how influenza spreads. As model epidemics they chose those of 1918 and 1957. Yet no matter which outcome was looked at, nor which pattern of epidemic was chosen, the result was the same. The best approach to influenza is to vaccinate young people and their parents, not infants and the elderly. Moreover, it is a cheaper and more efficient option. Around 85m doses of vaccine are distributed in the United States in normal years. Dr. Medlock reckons that if his approach were followed, that might be cut to just over 60m.

38 The best title of the passage would be _____.

① Overdependence on Flu Vaccination
② How to Stop the Spread of Flu Virus
③ How to Deal with Different Types of Flu
④ Need for New Flu Vaccines
⑤ Economic Cost of Vaccinating

39 Which of the following is most appropriate for the blank?

① young and careless
② old and weak
③ most likely to catch the virus
④ most likely to spread the virus
⑤ at risk of death

40 According to the passages, Dr. Medlock's mathematical model suggests _____.

① effective way to calculate different types of flu
② effective treatments for different ages
③ a marketing strategy for vaccines
④ a new way to make vaccines
⑤ a new way to allocate vaccines

[41-44] 서강대 2018

Until recently, pioneers of Ⓐ _____ health innovation had remained at the margins of our biomedical research and regulatory establishment. Yet in the last two months alone, two individuals widely shared videos in which they injected themselves with unregulated gene therapies. Josiah Zayner is one of the self-experimenters and the CEO of the Odin, a start-up that sells gene-editing kits for home use. (A) Is self-experimentation with gene-editing techniques something we should herald as a new form of "permission less" innovation? Or will self-proclaimed biohackers, by testing the regulatory framework, harm the emerging ecosystem of citizens who contribute to biomedical innovation? (B) Ⓑ _____ banning the sale of gene-editing kits is only a weak, temporary solution. What we need is to foster an ethos of responsible innovation outside of traditional research institutions. We must recognize the urgent need to build legitimacy, but also tailored regulatory support for new forms of health research. (C) The path forward is not to promote radical, unregulated science, but to develop engagement channels that force citizens, patients, ethicists and regulators to rethink and design an adaptive oversight system. (D)

41 Choose the words that fit best for blanks Ⓐ and Ⓑ.

① transnational – Furthermore
② democratized – Yet
③ ecological – For instance
④ optimal – Nevertheless

42 The author's presentation is most like that of a _____.

① researcher offering a scholarly analysis
② daily journalist reporting on a news story
③ motivational speaker giving an inspiring talk
④ public intellectual presenting an opinion on an ethical dilemma

43 Which of the following cannot be inferred from the passage?

① Biotechnologies have progressed to a point where individuals can experiment with gene therapies at home.
② The U.S. government recently approved self-experimentation by a practitioner outside of a traditional research institution.
③ A recent development in health research involves entrepreneurship.
④ Despite the potential for citizens to take a proactive role outside of medical practices, many ethical issues remain unresolved.

44 Which would be the best place for the following sentence?

> Self-experimentation with gene therapies raises troubling safety and ethical questions, from the potential for infections and immunological reactions to lack of understanding of the risks involved and unrealistic expectations from patients.

① (A)   ② (B)
③ (C)   ④ (D)

[45-47] 국민대 2016

Not so long ago, we thought our brains had reached their peak by the time we hit adulthood and everything was simply downhill from there. But now we know that's not true—scientists have identified a process dubbed "neuroplasticity," which acknowledges our brains are capable of growing and Ⓐ making new connections as we age. Giving our brains a regular mental workout can ⓐ _____ the risk of mild cognitive decline by as much as 40%, says Dr. Nicole Kochan. And a recent study conducted by the Mayo Clinic in the U.S. Ⓑ confirming that elderly people who'd kept up a hobby—such as arts and crafts, social activities or computer use—since middle age Ⓒ were less likely to be affected by dementia. It's due to a phenomenon called "cognitive reserve"—or the mind's resistance to damage of the brain. When we start developing dementia—usually several decades before we notice symptoms—certain regions of the brain start to shrink. However, complex activities boost new brain cells and improve the connections between them, which means less atrophy and shrinkage. We also know that what's good for the body is good for the brain, says Suha AN, risk reduction manager at Alzheimer's Australia. So there's another reason to exercise regularly. And being social Ⓓ gives our brains a boost too: spending time with others and having fun can contribute to brain reserve.

45 Which best fits into the blank ⓐ?

① cause ② reduce
③ predict ④ accelerate

46 Which is grammatically INCORRECT?

① Ⓐ ② Ⓑ
③ Ⓒ ④ Ⓓ

47 Which best describe the main idea of passage?

① Scientists identified ways to cure dementia.
② The number of brain cells decreases with age.
③ Regular computer use improves brain function.
④ You can promote brain health with some activities.

[48-50] 홍익대 2018

Forensic science helps us understand the past, whether in terms of studying the spread of a disease or investigating the site of an ancient massacre. And, of course, it is important to the legal system when it comes to solving crimes. Across all of these fields, the microscope is an important tool, used to help reconstruct past events. Microscopes are essential for many investigative purposes, because they can magnify an object to such great detail.

Forensic epidemiology investigates how diseases spread usually for legal reasons. For example, forensic epidemiologists may be assigned to discover the source of dangerous bacteria, such as E. coli or salmonella. To do so, they will use microscopes to study food for contamination. Under a microscope, the presence of certain strains of bacteria may point a scientist to the source of contamination. This can prove pivotal in stopping more people from being infected as well as pinpointing the individuals or group responsible for the outbreak.

In forensic anthropology, microscopes are used to study tissue, bone or other remains to determine factors of a death. For example, scanning electron microscopes can be used to identify the long-liquified remains of a person that have left behind a deposit in the soil. Microscopes in this field are additionally used in looking at the residue found on the teeth. Tissue, cells or other remains may coat the teeth after death, helping researchers determine a person's habits, ailments or even cause of death.

Forensic pathologists are responsible for determining the manner in which a person has died. If the person died from a certain disease, forensic pathologists may use a microscope to identify the deadly bacteria or virus. A microscope may be beneficial when it comes to more closely examining the tissue around a wound and determining what sort of object—be it a bullet, a knife or something else—caused the damage.

48 What would make the best title for the passage?

① Forensic Science and Its Legal Backgrounds
② Uses of Microscopes in Forensic Science
③ Early Development of Forensic Science
④ Needs for Forensic Science in the Future

49 According to the passage, which of the following CANNOT be inferred?

① Forensic science deals with understanding of the past by reconstructing past events.
② Forensic epidemiology contributes to stopping the spread of dangerous diseases.
③ Remains on teeth of the dead body can hint at the person's habit.
④ Deadly bacteria and virus cause difficulties in forensic pathologists' examining tissues.

50 Which of the following is closest to the way in which the passage is organized?

① Spatial order
② Chronological order
③ Question and answer
④ Main idea with supporting lists

에듀윌 편입영어 **기출심화 완성 독해**

PART 03

인문학

CHAPTER 01   역사 · 고고학
CHAPTER 02   철학 · 종교
CHAPTER 03   문학
CHAPTER 04   언어
CHAPTER 05   심리

CHAPTER 01 역사 · 고고학

[01-03]

The second point is the more familiar one of the historian's need of imaginative understanding for the minds of the people with whom he is dealing, for the thought behind their acts: I say "imaginative understanding," not "sympathy," lest sympathy should be supposed to imply agreement. Take Burckhardt's censorious remark about the Thirty Years' War: "It is scandalous for a creed, no matter whether it is Catholic or Protestant, to place its salvation above the integrity of the nation." It was extremely difficult for a nineteenth-century liberal historian brought up to believe that it is right and praiseworthy to kill in defense of one's country, but wicked and wrong-headed to kill in defense of one's religion, to enter into the state of mind of those who fought the Thirty Years War. Much of what has been written in English-speaking countries in the last ten years about the Soviet Union, and in the Soviet Union about the English-speaking countries, has been ⓐ vitiated by this inability to achieve even the most elementary measure of imaginative understanding of what goes on in the mind of the other party.

01 According to the passage, why do historians need imaginative understanding?

① To handle the enemy more effectively
② To better understand the mind of the people they meet in their ordinary life
③ To elicit more agreements easily
④ To get the idea of why people behaved in a certain way

02 Which is true about Burckhardt according to the author?

① He failed to understand the mind of the people during the War.
② He believed that it was right to kill people in defense of one's religion.
③ He thought that it was horrible to kill people in defense of one's country.
④ He was a historian who interpreted the War with imaginative understanding.

03 Choose the answer that is closest in meaning to the underlined word ⓐ in the passage.

① criticized
② impaired
③ manifested
④ obscured

[04-07] 성균관대 2007 B형

> History, like the drama and the novel, grew out of mythology, a primitive form of interpretation and expression—as in fairy tales listened to by children or in dreams dreamt by sophisticated adults—in which the line between fact and fiction is left undrawn. It has, (가), been said of the Illiad that anyone who starts reading it as history will find that it is full of fiction, but, equally, anyone who starts reading it as (나) will find that it is full of (다). All histories resemble the Illiad to this extent, that they cannot entirely dispense with the fictional element. The mere selection, arrangement and presentation of facts is a technique belonging to the field of fiction, and popular opinion is right in its insistence that no historian can be "great" if he is not also a great artist; that the Gibbons and Macaulays are greater historians than the Dryasdusts (a name coined by Sir Walter Scott—himself a great historian in some of his novels than in any of his histories) who have avoided <u>their more inspired colleagues'</u> factual inaccuracies.

04 Which of the following is best for (가)?

① however
② consequently
③ on the other hand
④ ironically
⑤ for example

05 Which of the following is the best for the pair of blanks (나) and (다)?

① history – fiction
② fiction – history
③ fiction – fiction
④ history – history
⑤ interpretation – expression

06 The main theme of the passage is _____.

① Mythology and history: What they share
② Historical elements in the Illiad
③ History: An interplay of fact and fiction
④ Fictional elements in history
⑤ How to be a great historian

07 The underlined "their more inspired colleagues" refer to _____.

① artists like Sir Walter Scott
② the Gibbons and the Macaulays
③ Dryasdusts
④ sophisticated adults
⑤ mythologists

[08-10]

History is necessary because it helps to explain current events. How do cultures rise and how do they fall? History will not give us the answers, but it will certainly help to focus our questions and our understanding of the forces at work in the world today. Of course history is easily manipulated, though that made it even more important for us to know what actually happened. We need a knowledge of history to spot the delusions of leaders and the media. As voters and citizens, we have to be able to see through these dangerous distortions. Besides, history is—or should be—interesting. The chain of cause and effect is fascinating, as are the details. _____, many teachers who lack historical training themselves are naturally defensive fearing that their subject may be boring to their pupils.

I would never argue that historians or history teachers have a moral role. Their main obligation is to understand the mentality of the time and to pass on that understanding. Nor should they simplify for moral effect. History offers the richest imaginable source of moral examples and moral dilemmas, which are themselves the essence of great fiction, great drama, and life itself. Without an understanding of history, we are politically, culturally and socially impoverished.

08 Which of the following cannot be inferred from the passage?

① Understanding history helps us resist untruths propagated by power.
② Morals of past events should be diluted through history education.
③ Some teachers today do not seem confident about the appeal of history.
④ History enables us to form a perspective required for understanding the present.

09 Choose the one that best fills in the blank.

① Repulsed by this
② Motivated by this
③ In concordance with this
④ Shying away from this

10 What is the best title for the passage?

① Pitfalls of History
② Competing Interpretations of History
③ What History Tells
④ Historical Insights for the Future

[11-12] 한국외대 2007

One of the aspects of the spirit of inquiry fostered by the Renaissance was the desire to provide a systematic classification of all areas of knowledge. This eventually extended to the arrangement of many of the collections that were later absorbed into Europe's major museums. Foremost among these was the British Museum, which was founded by Act of Parliament in 1753 to house the collections of Sir Hans Sloane. A physician by profession, Sloane's lucrative practice enabled him to indulge his great passion for natural science and collecting. He became a Fellow of the Royal Society in 1685, and in 1727 its President in succession to Sir Isaac Newton. On his death, he left some 80,000 objects, which included coins, medals, books, prints, drawings and manuscripts. ⓐ <u>The same impulse to expand the frontiers of knowledge</u>, allied to the trading interests of the European courts, supplied the incentive for geographical exploration; the establishment of additional trade routes and contact with hitherto unknown continents introduced new materials and imagery that had an immediate impact on European culture.

11 Which of the following is NOT true of Sloane?

① He was very interested in natural science.
② He was succeeded by Newton as the President of the Royal Society.
③ He had a profitable job.
④ His collections were displayed in the British Museum after he died.
⑤ He was a member of the Royal Society.

12 Judging from the passage, which of the following is closest in meaning to the underlined expression ⓐ?

① The extinction of the Renaissance
② A great passion for medical service
③ A systematic classification of knowledge
④ The desire for unknown ores
⑤ The spirit of inquiry

[13-14] 건국대 2007

The great heroes of history are tragic figures. They embody the new idea, purely and uncompromisingly. They arise in sunlike splendor. Their real significance goes unnoticed at first, until the old way of life senses its danger and gathers all its forces to destroy the new in the form of its outstanding representative. Whether Socrates or Julius Caesar, the first victorious protagonist of the new principle becomes, at the same time, the victim at the border of two eras. The old is justified in asserting itself, for it still functions. The new is justified also, but it is not yet protected by an established social order and culture. For the time being it is still functioning in a vacuum. But it is only the hero, the first great figure of the new way of life, whom the old, in a last frantic _____ of all its forces, can destroy.

13 Which is the most appropriate theme of the passage?

① The great heroes of history are not always victorious.
② The new tradition fights against and then replaces the old tradition.
③ The great heroes sacrifice themselves, creating a new way of life.
④ The war breaks out at the border of the old and the new.
⑤ Each of the old and the new strives toward justifying itself.

14 Which best fits in the blank?

① despair
② rally
③ rage
④ antagonism
⑤ dissent

[15-17] 숙명여대 2010

The discovery of the American continent had nothing to do with intellectual curiosity or even <u>unfathomable</u> human courage. It was almost entirely about one thing: money. And it was a mistake. The Portuguese throughout the sixteenth century ruthlessly and aggressively built a monopoly in the spice trade from the east by dominating the trade routes around the continent of Africa. Spain, on the other hand, began thinking of ways to get around this monopoly by developing a western route to the eastern countries. The problem was that this route was infinitely longer than the trip around Africa, and it lay across such a vast ocean. It was Christopher Columbus who convinced the Spanish Queen to _____ a western expedition to the eastern countries. Europeans also had a good idea as to the circumference of the earth; this circumference, in fact, had been accurately calculated in the second century B.C. The general view, then, was that a western voyage to India would be a disaster, for the ship would have to travel thousands of miles over open ocean. But Columbus believed that the world was considerably smaller than was imagined in the general view. He was, of course, completely mistaken and had not America gotten in his way, he and his men would have starved or died of dehydration. But fortunately for Columbus, America did get in the way.

15 Choose the word that could best replace the underlined <u>unfathomable</u>.

① profound
② audacious
③ curious
④ noble
⑤ mundane

16 According to the passage, which of the following statements is true?

① The expedition to the eastern countries was related to territorial expansion.
② It was Columbus who calculated the longer circumference of the earth.
③ Columbus proved that a western voyage to India was shorter than the eastern route.
④ Spanish Queen wanted to monopolize the spice trade from the west.
⑤ The discovery of America saved Columbus' crew members from being starved to death.

17 What would be the most appropriate word to fill in the blank?

① forfeit
② underwrite
③ abhor
④ imagine
⑤ inherit

[18-19] 항공대 2017

The facts of history never come to us pure, since they do not and cannot exist in a pure form: they are always refracted through the mind of the recorder. It follows that when we take up a work of history, our first concern should be not with the facts which it contains but with the historian who wrote it. Let me take as an example the great historian in whose honour and in whose name these lectures were founded. G. M. Trevelyan, as he tells us in his autobiography, was brought up at home on a somewhat exuberantly Whig tradition; and he would not, I hope, disclaim the title if I described him as the last and not the least of the great English liberal historians of the Whig tradition. It is not for nothing that he traces back his family tree, through the great Whig historian George Otto Trevelyan, to Macaulay, incomparably the greatest of the Whig historians. Trevelyan's finest and maturest work, *England under Queen Anne*, was written against that background, and will yield its full meaning and significance to the reader only when read against that background.

18 It can be inferred from the passage that _____.

① History is inseparable from a historian
② History means the collection of a series of pure facts
③ History requires an objective truth based upon solid facts
④ Historians are required to have the obligation of writing objective scissors-and-paste history without meaning or significance

19 Which of the following statements is true?

① G. M. Trevelyan fully understood the significance of pure history.
② G. M. Trevelyan's book is an outcome of an objective compilation of fact.
③ G. M. Trevelyan's book has the trace of this family background.
④ G. M. Trevelyan's family fought ferociously against the Whig tradition.

[20-22] 성균관대 2006

Just before Christmas 1887, a young Dutch doctor with an un-Dutch name, Marie Eugene Francois Thomas Dubois, arrived in Sumatra, in the Dutch East Indies, with the intention of finding the earliest human remains on Earth. Several things were extraordinary about this. To begin with, no-one had ever gone looking for ancient human bones before. Everything that had been found to this point had been found accidentally, and nothing in Dubois' background suggested that he was the ideal candidate to make the process intentional. He was an anatomist by training with no background in paleontology. Nor was there any special reason to suppose that the East Indies would hold early human remains. Logic dictated that if ancient people were to be found at all, it would be on a large and long-populated land mass, not in the comparative fastness of an archipelago. Dubois was driven to the East Indies on nothing stronger than a hunch, the availability of employment and the knowledge that Sumatra was full of caves, the environment in which most of the important hominid fossils had so far been found. What is most extraordinary in all this—nearly miraculous, really—is that he found what he was looking for.

20 What made Dubois go to Sumatra to find the hominid fossils?

① his experience
② earlier findings
③ the presence of human remains in Sumatra
④ his knowledge as an anatomist
⑤ many caves in Sumatra

21 Which is NOT true of Dubois?

① He was a doctor without any knowledge of paleontology.
② He was interested in the anatomy of ancient humans.
③ He knew that there were many caves in Sumatra.
④ He assumed that hominid fossils would be found in caves.
⑤ He found the early human bones in Sumatra.

22 Which was NOT regarded as extraordinary by the author?

① Dubois' intention to find out the earlier human remains
② Dubois' career, a doctor not a paleontologist
③ Sumatra as a candidate to hold the hominid fossils
④ Ancient people found in the long-populated cities
⑤ Dubois' success in finding the earlier human remains

[23-25] 숭실대 2013

The Western assumption is that nomadic hunter-gatherers, especially those who are still functional today (numbering in the tens of millions), would love to be free of their "subsistence" economy. But Marshall Sahlins argues that these people have clearly chosen their lifestyle. Even when neighboring tribes convert themselves from hunter-gatherers into stable agricultural communities, sometimes using "advanced technological tools," many hunter-gatherer communities refuse that choice on the ground that it would require them to work harder. Richard Lee quotes the Bushmen: "Why should we plant when there are so many mongomongo nuts in the world?"

Hunter-gatherers are often called "culturally inferior" for failing to produce a surplus that could protect them from the whims of nature. Sahlins suggests four reasons why they eschew surpluses. First, they are optimists. When there is food they tend to eat it all, even gorging themselves. The attitude seems to be that since food is abundant in nature, ⓐ _____ is not necessary; nature itself stores food here and there in the plants and animals, if you know where to find it. So even when storms or accidents deprive a community of food for a period of days or weeks, the results are rarely disastrous and you can always move on to the next place. Second, hunter-gatherers are nomadic by choice. If they stored or carried food they would be tied to a specific place, or have their movements seriously slowed. For nomadic hunter-gatherers, "It is truly sad that his wealth is a burden," says Sahlins. The fact of movement "rapidly depreciates the satisfactions of property." Third, an economy based on ⓑ _____ would increase the Bushmen's impact on the environment beyond the present-day ethic of underuse. Surplus would also lead to population growth, which would threaten the community's mobility and increase vulnerability to natural calamities. Fourth, the hunter's self-esteem is based on hunting. To accumulate surplus would diminish the cultural and psychological importance of the hunter. ⓒ _____.

23 Which of the following fits best in both ⓐ and ⓑ?

① barter
② farming
③ storage
④ competition

24 According to the passage, which of the following explains the nomadic hunter-gatherers' unwillingness to produce a surplus?

① They are educated from childhood not to produce more than they need.
② They strongly believe in the rich abundance and goodness of nature.
③ Surplus would inevitably increase conflicts between tribes.
④ Surplus would demoralize young minds and corrupt the society.

25 Which of the following fits best in ⓒ?

① It might also downplay the training of the young and produce a lazier society with fewer skills
② The majority of native peoples on the earth do not wish to climb onto the Western economic machine
③ So dancing, fishing, games, sleep, and ritual seem to occupy the greater part of one's time
④ The hunter might want to keep only the number of animals needed for his immediate family

[26-27] 한양대 2013

When archaeologists started to excavate a limestone cave on the Indonesian island of Flores, they weren't prepared for what they found: the tiny skeleton of an entirely new species of human, Homo floresiensis, that lived as recently as 18,000 years ago. "I would have been less surprised if someone had uncovered an alien," says Peter Brown, an anthropologist from the University of New England in Armidale, New South Wales.

Among the stone tools and bones of seven individuals found by the Indonesian and Australian team in the Liang Bua cave were the skull and incomplete skeleton of an adult whose shape suggests that it was female. It had long arms and its legs were light and apparently chimpanzee-like, but it walked upright. Its brain capacity was far smaller than any other known human species. Since the bones are not fossilized, they may contain DNA and answer questions about _____.

26 윗글의 내용과 일치하는 것을 고르시오.

① Archaeologist proved that the skeleton was that of a chimpanzee.
② The bones excavated were the remains of a grown-up woman who walked erect.
③ Archaeologists expected that a new species of human was buried in an Indonesian cave.
④ Peter Brown was surprised when he excavated an alien in a limestone cave on an Indonesian island.

27 윗글의 내용상 밑줄 친 곳에 들어갈 가장 알맞은 것을 고르시오.

① the shape of their skeleton
② what stone tools they used
③ where their remains were found
④ their genetic links with Homo sapiens

[28-29] 한양대 2013

> We historians have a responsibility to historical facts in general, and for criticizing the abuse of history in particular. I need say little about the first of these responsibilities. I would not have to say anything, but for two developments. One is the current fashion for novelist to base their plots on recorded reality rather than inventing them, thus _____. The other is the rise of "postmodernist" intellectual fashions in universities, particularly in departments of literature and anthropology, which imply that all "facts" claiming objective existence are simply intellectual constructions—in short, that there is no clear difference between fact and fiction. But there is. And for historians, the ability to distinguish between the two is absolutely fundamental. We cannot invent our facts. Either Elvis Presley is dead or he isn't. The question can be answered unambiguously on the basis of evidence, in so far as reliable evidence is available.

28 빈칸에 들어갈 가장 알맞은 것을 고르시오.

① coming up with a new term, "historical novel"
② bridging the gap between history and literature
③ fudging the border between historical fact and fiction
④ proving that literary imagination is better than historical facts

29 윗글의 내용으로부터 유추할 수 없는 것을 고르시오.

① The author does not like reading novels.
② The author is not favorable to postmodernism.
③ The author is certain that Elvis Presley is dead.
④ The author believes that historical facts can never be an intellectual construction.

[30-32] 성균관대 2014

The ancient stone statues at San Agustin are among the most mysterious pre-Columbian archaeological artefacts. So far archaeologists have discovered 40 large burial mounds containing 600 likenesses of mythical animals, gods and chieftains in what is South America's largest complex of megalithic statues. Like other sites in the region, San Agustín has suffered plunder. Konrad Preuss, a German anthropologist who led the first European excavations there, shipped 35 statues that he found to a museum in Berlin, where they remain. This history has made the local inhabitants, who live from tourist visits to the site, suspicious. So it proved with a plan by the national museum to take 20 of the statues to the capital, Bogotá, a ten-hour drive away, for a three-month exhibition to mark the centenary of Preuss' discovery of the site. Aware of the sensitivity of removing the statues even temporarily, anthropologists from the Colombian Institute of Anthropology held town meetings to explain the importance of allowing them to be seen by a wider public. But the locals said they worried that the objects would not return, or would be swapped for replicas. As the date for the exhibition neared, they began making demands, such as asking for a new drinking-water system for the town in exchange for letting the statues go. No deal was agreed. On the day last month when the sculptures, carefully wrapped and crated, were to travel to Bogotá, locals blockaded the road and prevented workers from loading the trucks. The museum has adopted its own form of protest. The exhibition opened, minus statues, on November 28th. Light is projected where the statues would have been; guides use a virtual-reality program and tablet computers to show visitors a 3D image of what was meant to be there. The museum has taken a robust position: the opening display invites visitors to consider "the emptiness and silence that emerge when a few people claim exclusive right over our heritage, trampling the cultural liberties of all Colombians."

30 The best title of the passage would be _____.

① Whose Statues?: An Exhibitions of Mistrust
② Return of Colombian Statues in Berlin
③ History and Politics of Arts Funding
④ Mysteries and Myths of Statues in Colombia
⑤ Preservation of Cultural Artefacts in Colombia

31 The local inhabitants were worried most about _____.

① foreign anthropologists excavating the town's artefacts
② reckless excavation destroying the infrastructure of the town
③ the museum displaying the statues without their permission
④ not retrieving their statues
⑤ not getting money for lending the statues

32 The national museum eventually _____.

① went ahead to display the statues
② opened the exhibition without the statues
③ purchased the statues with a large sum of money
④ cancelled the exhibition as a sign of protest
⑤ postponed the exhibition

[33-35] 성균관대 2017

> Technology has driven the two camps farther apart. Scientific advances mean that archaeologists, once content simply to examine pots or tombs, are paying much more attention to where they're found. Chemical analysis of any residue left on an artifact can offer clues about what it contained—or the people who used it. Dealers, for their part, question archaeology's obsession with context. "To say that an object is worthless when it's out of context is a lie, and a dangerous one," says Joan Lande, head of antiquities at the London-based auctioneer Bonham & Brooks.
>
> The demolition of the Bamiyan Buddhas blurred the debate between collectors and preservationists. Keeping the national heritage in place, some preservationists concede, doesn't always safeguard it. And removing artifacts can save them; Mr Dietschi says he plans to return the contents of his museum to Afghanistan when things calm down. Meanwhile, the black market continues to thrive: last month chunks of the Bamiyan Buddhas began showing up in Pakistan bazaars, where dealers have been fielding calls from European and Asian collectors desperate to own a piece.

33 What does the underlined "it's out of context" imply?

① it's not clear who made it
② it appears out of the blue
③ it lost its history
④ it's found in the unexpected area
⑤ it's taken out from the original place

34 Archaeologists are likely to be classified as _____.

① preservationists
② collectors
③ dealers
④ destroyers
⑤ auctioneers

35 Dealers would argue that to save Bamiyan Buddhas from demolition, they should have _____.

① reconstructed the statues
② removed them from their site
③ abandoned the demolished treasures
④ built more Buddha temples
⑤ stopped the war breakout

[36-40] 아주대 2017

[A] Prior to 1914 the dominant mood in Europe was one of pride in the accomplishments of Western civilization and confidence in its future progress. Advances in science and technology, the rising standard of living, the spread of democratic institutions and the expansion of social reforms all contributed to a sense of optimism. Another reason for optimism was that since the defeat of Napoleon, Europe had avoided a general war, and that since the Franco-Prussian War, the Great Powers had not fought each other.

[B] Few people recognized that these achievements masked an inner turbulence that was propelling Western civilization toward a cataclysm. The European state system was failing. ❶ In the early nineteenth century, liberals had believed that the redrawing of the political map of Europe on the basis of nationality would promote peaceful relations among nations. But quite the reverse occurred. ❷ By 1914, national states, answering to no higher power, were fueled by an explosive nationalism, and were grouped into alliances that faced each other with ever-mounting hostility. Nationalist thinkers propagated pseudoscientific racial and Social Darwinist doctrines that glorified conflict and justified the subjugation of other peoples. Committed to enhancing national power, statesmen lost sight of Europe as a community of nations sharing a common civilization. Ⓐ <u>Caution and restraint gave way to belligerency in foreign relations.</u>

[C] A cultural crisis also occurred. ❸ Many European intellectuals attacked the rational tradition of the Enlightenment and celebrated the primitive, the instinctual, and the irrational. Increasingly young people grew attracted to philosophies of action that ridiculed liberal bourgeois values and viewed war as a purifying and ennobling experience. ❹ These "splendid" little wars helped fashion an attitude that made war acceptable, if not laudable. Yearning to break loose from their ordinary lives and to embrace heroic values, Ⓑ _____.

[D] While Europe was seemingly progressing in the art of civilization, the mythic power of nationalism and the primitive appeal of conflict were driving European civilization to the abyss. ❺ Few people recognized the potential crisis, including the statesmen whose blunders and recklessness allowed the Continent to stumble into war.

36 What is the best title for the above passage?

① the West in despair
② the drift toward war
③ the European system of alliances
④ the downside of Western civilization
⑤ the failure of the European state system

37 Which of the following is NOT relevant to the proposition Ⓐ in paragraph [B]?

① Nationalism prevailed in most European states.
② The idea of glorifying conflict was spread by nationalists.
③ Politicians revised the European map based on nationality.
④ Groups of European nations stood in opposition to each other.
⑤ Political leaders abandoned the idea of Europe as a single community.

38 In paragraph [C], which of the following would best fit in the blank ⓑ?

① people found heightened agitation among the several nationalities, which created terrible anxiety among political leaders
② most thinkers emphasized their concern for individual liberty and social reform
③ many Europeans regarded violent conflict as the highest expression of individual and national life
④ scientists expected the advance of science and technology to make mankind richer
⑤ people tried to solve the problem of the irrational in a scientific manner

39 According to the passage, which of the following did NOT contribute to the sense of optimism in Europe before 1914?

① the increase of social reforms
② the awareness of the lack of wars
③ the progress in science and technology
④ the improvement in the standard of living
⑤ the avoidance of general wars and conflicts

40 The following is removed from the passage. In which parts may it be inserted to support the argument made by the author?

> Colonial wars, colorfully portrayed in the popular press, ignited the imagination of bored factory workers and daydreaming students and reinforced a sense of duty and an urge for gallantry among soldiers.

① ❶
② ❷
③ ❸
④ ❹
⑤ ❺

CHAPTER 02 철학·종교

[01-03] 한성대 2010

Mark Twain called the times in which he lived, and in particular the late 1800s, the Gilded Age. Twain wanted to point out that despite its outward showiness, American society was inwardly corrupt. But wealthy industrialists in the United States certainly did not see themselves in this way, and Social Darwinism helped ㉮ them believe that the accumulation of riches by a few was the "natural order."

Herbert Spencer, an English philosopher, was the person whom US industrialists turned to for the philosophical justification of their pursuit of wealth. Social Darwinism, the theory developed by Spencer, was in part an application of Charles Darwin's evolutionary theories to human societies. Spencer, who coined the expression "survival of the fittest," argued that those members of society who were "naturally" superior were meant to climb to the top and should not be ㉯ _____. In addition, Spencer warned that those who were at the bottom, by their very natures, were unfit to survive, and therefore, charity was meaningless.

01 밑줄 친 ㉮ them이 지칭하는 것은?

① believers in Social Darwinism
② general American people
③ American wealthy industrialists
④ theorists of Social Darwinism

02 빈칸 ㉯에 적절하지 않은 것은?

① admitted
② hindered
③ impeded
④ obstructed

03 윗글의 내용과 일치하지 않는 것은?

① Social Darwinism was based on Darwin's evolutionary theories.
② American industrialists relied on Spencer's theory to justify themselves.
③ The expression "survival of the fittest" was created by Darwin.
④ Spencer thought that the poor were naturally hopeless.

[04-05] 중앙대 2011

Rene Descartes was a French philosopher, mathematician, physicist, and writer. He has been dubbed the "Father of Modern Philosophy," and much of subsequent Western philosophy is a response to his writings, which have been studied closely to this day. In particular, his *Meditations on First Philosophy* continues to be a standard text at most university philosophy departments. In addition, *Discourse on the Method* became and remains one of the most influential books in all philosophy. In Part IV of that book, Descartes proposed the famous philosophical statement "Cogito ergo sum," meaning "I think, therefore I am." Another phrase, "de omnibus dubitandum" (we must doubt everything) often used by Descartes, also well expresses the crux of the Cartesian method. This statement may seem strangely ㉮ _____ advice from a religious man; and, indeed, it did not make him popular with the clergy of his day. Yet, when Descartes used the method of doubt, he reached a religious position somewhat by paradox. His aim in using the method was always clear. Unlike Michel de Montaigne and other skeptics against whom he wrote, Descartes had no interest in a modish attitude of doubt for the sake of doubting. His aim was by way of doubt to reach down to what can be shown with ㉯ _____. This was essentially the scientific procedure of seventeenth-century physics, in which doubt played a constant part: 'to accept nothing as true' until it was established, as far as possible, beyond doubt.

04 밑줄 친 ㉮와 ㉯에 들어가기에 가장 적합한 것을 고르시오.

① cynical – certainty
② skeptical – coercion
③ rational – deduction
④ sagacious – disbelief

05 윗글의 내용과 일치하는 것으로 가장 적합한 것을 고르시오.

① Descartes had many staunch supporters among religious men.
② Descartes's philosophical statements sometimes convey paradoxical messages.
③ Descartes and Montaigne were different in their attitude toward the method of doubt.
④ Descartes made an even bigger contribution to the field of mathematics than to that of physics.

[06-07] 숙명여대 2012

Arguments can be ambiguous. For example, there is one involving the phrase "have faith in" that helps to make faith look respectable. When a man says that he has faith in the president, he is assuming that it is obvious and known to everybody that there is a president, that the president exists, and he is asserting his confidence that the president will do good work on the whole. But, if a man says he has faith in telepathy, he does not mean that he is confident that telepathy will do good work on the whole, but that he believes that telepathy really occurs sometimes, that telepathy exists. Thus the phrase "to have faith in X" sometimes means to be confident that good work will be done by X, who is assumed or known to exist, but at other times means to believe that X exists. Which does it mean in the phrase "have faith in God"? It means ambiguously both; and the self-evidence of what it means in the one sense insinuates what it means in the other sense. If there is a perfectly powerful and good god, it is self-evidently reasonable to believe that he will do good.

06 _____ arguments are not always fallacious.

① Coherent   ② Convincing
③ Divine   ④ Equivocal
⑤ Precocious

07 Which of the following can best replace the underlined insinuates?

① clarifies   ② entangles
③ implies   ④ invokes
⑤ necessitates

[08-10]

Ordinary language tends to conflate envy and jealousy. The philosophical consensus is that these are distinct emotions. While it is linguistically acceptable to say that one is jealous upon hearing about another's vacation, say, it has been plausibly argued that one is feeling envy, if either, in such a case. Both envy and jealousy are three-place relations; but this superficial similarity conceals an important difference. Jealousy involves three parties, the subject, the rival, and the beloved, and the jealous person's real locus of concern is the beloved—the person whose affection he is losing or fears losing—not his rival. Whereas envy is a two party relation, with a third relatum that is a good (albeit a good that could be a particular person's affections); and the envious person's locus of concern is the rival. Hence, even if the good that the rival has is the affection of another person, there is a difference between envy and jealousy. Roughly, for the jealous person <u>the rival is fungible</u> and the beloved is not fungible. So he would be equally bothered if the beloved were consorting with someone else, and would not be bothered if the rival were. Whereas in envy it is the other way around. Because envy is centrally focused on competition with the rival, the subject might well be equally bothered if the rival were consorting with a different (appealing) person, but would not be bothered if the 'good' had gone to someone else (with whom the subject was not in competition). Whatever the ordinary meaning of the terms 'envy' and 'jealousy,' these considerations demonstrate that these two distinct syndromes _____.

08 Choose the one closest in meaning to the underlined "<u>the rival is fungible</u>".

① the rival should be condemned
② there is competition with the rival
③ it doesn't matter who the rival is
④ what the rival has done is unacceptable

09 Choose the one the best fills in the blank.

① are indeed near equivalents
② need to be distinguished
③ can have overlapping meanings
④ should be synthesized

10 Which of the following cannot be inferred from the passage?

① Ordinarily, jealousy and envy can be clearly distinguished.
② A good can be a thing or an emotion.
③ The number of parties involved are different for jealousy and envy.
④ The jealous person is not mainly concerned with his rival.

[11-12] 중앙대 2010

The key concept that Bourdieu employs in developing his approach is that of habitus. The term is a very old one, of Aristotelian and scholastic origins, but Bourdieu uses it in a distinctive and quite specific way. The habitus is a set of dispositions which incline agents to act and react in certain ways. The dispositions generate practices, perceptions and attitudes which are 'regular' without being consciously coordinated or governed by any 'rule.' The dispositions which constitute the habitus deserve a brief explanation. Dispositions are acquired through a gradual process of inculcation in which early childhood experiences are particularly important. Through _____ of training and learning, such as those involved in the inculcation of table manners ('sit up straight', 'don't eat with your mouth full', etc.), the individual acquires a set of dispositions which literally mould the body and become second nature. The dispositions produced thereby are also structured in the sense that they unavoidably reflect the social conditions within which they were acquired. An individual from a working-class background, for instance, will have acquired dispositions which are different in certain respects from those acquired by individuals who were brought up in a middle-class milieu. In other words, the similarities and differences that characterize the social conditions of existence of individuals will be reflected in the habitus, which may be relatively homogeneous across individuals from similar backgrounds. Structured dispositions are also durable: they are ingrained in the body in such a way that they endure through the life history of the individual, operating in a way that is pre-conscious and hence not readily amenable to conscious reflection and modification. Finally, the dispositions are generative and transposable in the sense that they are capable of generating a multiplicity of practices and perceptions in fields other than those in which they were originally acquired.

11 밑줄 친 빈칸에 들어가기에 가장 적합한 것을 고르시오.

① a myriad of mundane processes
② a collection of intimate vicissitudes
③ a scarcity of cognitive experiences
④ a throng of corporeal progressions

12 "habitus"의 특성을 윗글에 제시된 순서대로 요약한 것으로 가장 적합한 것을 고르시오.

① operating, reflective, mandatory, disposable
② regulated, conscious, homogeneous, harmonized
③ educated, organized, persistent, engendering
④ autonomous, constituting, enduring, productive

[13-16] 성균관대 2007

What the Japanese statesmen in the seventeenth century feared was that their countrymen whom these foreign missionaries were converting to Western Christianity would imbibe their adopted religion's fanatical spirit, and that, under this demoralizing influence, they would allow themselves to be used as what, in the West today, we should call "a fifth column." If this <u>suspected design</u> were to succeed, then Portuguese or Spaniards, who in themselves were not a serious menace to Japan's independence, might eventually contrive to conquer Japan through the arms of _____ traitors. In fact, the Japanese Government outlawed and repressed Christianity from the same motive that today is moving twentieth-century Western governments to outlaw and repress Communism.

13 The underlined "suspected design" means _____.

① to imbibe the foreign spirit
② to foster the demoralizing attitude
③ to bring in a "fifth column" against foreigners
④ to drink the foreign spirit and get drunk
⑤ to Christianize natives in order to use them later as agents

14 Which of the following is the best for the blank?

① Japanese
② Portuguese and Spanish
③ foreign
④ Western
⑤ intoxicated

15 What did the Japanese statesmen in the 17th century fear most?

① Superior foreign arms
② The spreading of Communism
③ Western missionaries
④ Their own people converted to Christianity
⑤ A conflict between Christianity and their native religion

16 The main theme of the passage is _____.

① Fanaticism of Christianity in Japan
② Unwarranted fear of Christianity in Japan
③ Christianity and communism: Where they meet
④ How to conquer Japan without arms
⑤ Japan's fear of Christianity and its adverse effects on the people

[17-18] 국민대 2013

In the 17th century the French philosopher René Descartes formally proposed the best-known dualist theory. Known as Cartesian dualism, this is the idea that the mind and the brain consist of different substances. According to Descartes, the mind is nonphysical and non-extended (i.e. it takes up no space or has no position), while the body and the rest of the physical world are made of physical, or extended, substance. The trouble with this is obvious. How do the two interact?

This problem of interaction bedevils any attempt to build a dualist theory, ⓐ which is probably why most philosophers and scientists completely reject all forms of dualism in favour of some kind of monism; but the options are few and also problematic. Idealists make mind fundamental but must then explain why and how there appears to be a consistent physical world. Neutral monists reject dualism but disagree about the fundamental nature of the world and how to unify it. A third option is materialism and this is by far the most popular among scientists today. Materialists take matter as fundamental, but they must then face the question how a physical brain, made purely of material substances, can give rise to conscious experience.

17 What does the underlined ⓐ refer to?

① this problem of interaction
② any attempt to build a dualist theory
③ to bedevil any attempt to build a dualist theory
④ this problem of interaction bedevils any attempt to build a dualist theory

18 Which is NOT true according to the passage?

① Idealists have difficulty in demonstrating the existence of the physical world.
② René Descartes thought that the mind was completely separated from the body.
③ What poses serious problems to materialists is the question of human consciousness
④ Monism is more adequate than dualism in explaining the question of human consciousness.

[19-21] 서울여대 2013

The fundamental aim of Descartes was, obviously enough, to attain philosophical truth by the use of reason. "I wished to give myself entirely to the search after truth." But what he was seeking was not to discover a multiplicity of isolated truths but to develop a system of true propositions, in which nothing would be presupposed which was not self-evident and indubitable. There would then be an organic connection between all the parts of the system, and the whole edifice would rest on a sure foundation. It would thus be impervious to the corroding and destructive effect of scepticism.

What did Descartes understand by philosophy? "Philosophy means the study of wisdom, and by wisdom we understand not only prudence in affairs but also a perfect knowledge of all things which man can know both for the conduct of his life and for the conservation of his health and the invention of all the arts." Under the general heading of philosophy, therefore, Descartes included not only metaphysics but also physics or natural philosophy, the latter standing to the former as trunk to roots. And the branches issuing from this trunk are the other sciences, the three principal ones being medicine, mechanics and morals. By morals "I mean the highest and most perfect moral science which, presupposing a complete knowledge of the other sciences, is the last degree of wisdom."

19 What is the main theme of this passage?

① The artistic implications of Descartes' philosophy
② The basic characteristics of Descartes' philosophical truth
③ Descartes' influence on contemporary philosophy
④ The role of philosophy in Descartes' age

20 What does "this trunk" refer to?

① Metaphysics
② Natural philosophy
③ Mechanics
④ Moral science

21 According to the passage, which of the following is true?

① Descartes was pursuing a multiplicity of individual truths.
② Descartes' philosophy is so well-organized that its parts are related with the whole.
③ Descartes did not insist on the practical value of philosophy from time to time.
④ Descartes did not rely on reason as much as other philosophers.

[22-25] 홍익대 2014

Philosophy, like all other studies, aims primarily at knowledge. The knowledge it aims at is the kind of knowledge which gives unity and system to the body of the sciences, and the kind which results from a critical examination of the grounds of our convictions, prejudices, and beliefs. But it cannot be maintained that philosophy has had any very great measure of success in its attempts to provide definite answers to its questions. If you ask a mathematician, a mineralogist, a historian, or any other man of learning, what definite body of truths has been ascertained by his science, his answer will last as long as you are willing to listen. But if you put the same question to a philosopher, he will, if he is (A) candid have to confess that his study has not achieved positive results such as those achieved by other sciences. It is true that (B) this is partly accounted for by the fact that, as soon as definite knowledge concerning any subject becomes possible, this subject ceases to be called philosophy and becomes a separate science. The whole study of the heavens, which now belongs to astronomy, was once included in philosophy; Newton's great work was called 'the mathematical principles of natural philosophy'. (C) _____ the study of the human mind, which was a part of philosophy, has now been separated from philosophy and has become the science of psychology. Thus, to a great extent, the uncertainty of philosophy is more apparent than real: those questions which are already capable of definite answers are placed in the sciences, while those only to which, at present, no definite answer can be given, remain to form the residue which is called philosophy.

22 The main topic of this passage is _____.

① the difficulty in defining the goal and the object of philosophy
② the relation between astronomy, psychology and philosophy
③ the joy and happiness of investigating knowledge in philosophy
④ the measure of successful investigation in philosophy

23 Which can be used instead of (A)?

① terrific
② insincere
③ discontented
④ forthright

24 What is (B) this referring to?

① The critical investigation of the grounds of our prejudices, convictions, and beliefs made by philosophy
② The definite body of truths ascertained by various types of sciences including philosophy
③ The lack of definite answers to the knowledge philosophy aims at
④ The fact that subjects with concrete answers become a separate science such as astronomy and psychology

25 Which is most suitable for (C)?

① In contrast
② Similarly
③ Therefore
④ Nevertheless

[26-27] 서강대 2014

In rapidly modernizing societies, if the traditional religion is unable to adapt to the requirements of modernization, the potential exists for the spread of Western Christianity and Islam. In these societies, the most successful protagonists of Western culture are not neo-classical economists or crusading democrats or multinational corporation executives. They are and most likely will continue to be Christian missionaries. Neither Adam Smith nor Thomas Jefferson will meet the psychological, emotional, moral, and social needs of urban migrants and first-generation secondary school graduates. Jesus Christ may not meet them either, but He is likely to have a better chance. In the long run, however, Mohammed wins out. Christianity spreads primarily by conversion, Islam by conversion and _____. The percentage of Christians in the world peaked at about 30 percent in the 1980s, leveled off, is now declining, and will probably approximate about 25 percent of the world's population by 2025. As a result of their extremely high rates of population growth, the proportion of Muslims in the world will continue to increase dramatically, amounting to 20 percent of the world's population about the turn of the century, surpassing the number of Christians some years later, and probably accounting for about 30 percent of the world's population by 2025.

26 Choose the one that best fills in the blank.

① modernization
② degeneration
③ education
④ reproduction

27 Which of the following CANNOT be inferred according to the passage above?

① Christianity and Islam are likely to play an important role in rapidly modernizing societies.
② The social needs of urban migrants will probably be met by multinational corporation executives.
③ The percentage of Christians in the world was higher in the 1980's than in the 2000's.
④ By 2025, the number of Muslims in the world will have surpassed that of Christians.

[28-29] 가톨릭대 2016

> In the fifth century B.C., the Greek philosophers tried to overcome the sharp contrast between the views of Parmenides and Heraclitus. In order to reconcile the idea of unchangeable Being of Parmenides with that of eternal Becoming of Heraclitus, they assumed that the Being is manifest in certain invariable substances, the mixture and separation of which gives rise to the changes in the world. This led to the concept of the atom, the smallest invisible unit of matter, which found its clearest expression in the philosophy of Democritus. The Greek atomists drew a clear line between spirit and matter, picturing matter as being made of several basic building blocks. These were purely passive and intrinsically dead particles moving in the void. The cause of their motion was not explained, but was often associated with external forces which were assumed to be of spiritual origin and fundamentally different from matter. In subsequent centuries, this image became an essential element of Western thought, of dualism between mind and matter, between body and soul.

28 What is the passage mainly about?

① The origin of Western dualism
② The main problem of Western thought
③ The relationship between spirit and matter
④ The uncanny world of the Greek philosophers

29 Which of the following is NOT true, according to the passage?

① Parmenides and Heraclitus were two opposing poles of the Greek thought.
② Parmenides and Heraclitus once worked together to reconcile their ideas.
③ The Greek atomists believed in the two different worlds of spirit and matter.
④ The tradition of Western thought has been largely embedded in the dualistic world view.

[30-32] 한국외대 2017

What makes people do things that are wrong? This question has puzzled philosophers since Plato who famously asked: If you found a magic ring that let you do whatever you wanted: rob a bank, take over the world, or enslave your enemies, would you? Plato postulated that if the price of exploiting this ring, doing something wrong, was not worth the reward, morality would be vindicated. Plato assumed that people stray from (A) the straight and narrow path due to temptation for personal gain. However, there is another school of thought that hypothesizes the inverse: people act immorally because they want to conform to society, even when it opposes their own core values. In other words, people (B) _____. For most people, doing the wrong thing is not embezzling millions of dollars or usurping political power in a coup. It is joining in when a person is being disparaged or laughing at a racist joke. We do this because we do not want any trouble. Immanuel Kant calls this sort of excessively deferential attitude 'servility.' Rather than downgrading the values and commitments of others, servility involves downgrading your own values and commitments relative to those of others. The servile person is thus the mirror image of the conventional, self-interested immoral person found in Plato. To Kant, servile people deny themselves the same moral equality and respect as anyone else. They do this so as not to appear arrogant, untoward, or rude and thereby allow themselves to be socialized into conformity and into doing the wrong thing.

30 According to the passage, which of the following is closest in meaning to (A)?

① A road that does not bend
② Behaving honestly and ethically
③ Working towards an academic goal
④ The shortest path to your destination

31 Which of the following best fits into (B)?

① think conforming to others is an evil behavior
② try too hard to reject society and promote their values
③ are too concerned about how others view them
④ become obsessed with doing the right thing

32 According to the passage, which of the following is NOT true?

① Plato thought that people did wrong acts for personal gain.
② Kant thought servile people act immorally because they want to conform.
③ Plato felt morality would be vindicated if immorality's cost was too high.
④ Kant felt that servile people often usurped political power.

[33-34] 항공대 2018

According to Fromm, the awareness of a disunited human existence is a source of guilt and shame, and the solution to this existential dichotomy is found in the development of one's uniquely human powers of love and reason. However, Fromm distinguished his concept of love from unreflective popular notions as well as Freudian paradoxical love. Fromm considered love to be an interpersonal creative capacity rather than an emotion, and he distinguished this creative capacity from what he considered to be various forms of narcissistic neuroses and sado-masochistic tendencies that are commonly held out as proof of true love. Indeed, Fromm viewed the experience of falling in love as evidence of one's failure to understand the true nature of love, which he believed always had the common elements of care, responsibility, respect, and knowledge. Fromm also asserted that few people in modern society had respect for the autonomy of their fellow human beings, much less the objective knowledge of what other people truly wanted and needed. Fromm believed that freedom was an aspect of human nature that we either embrace or escape. He observed that embracing our freedom of will was healthy, whereas escaping freedom through the use of escape mechanisms was the root of psychological conflicts. Fromm outlined three of the most common escape mechanisms: automaton conformity, authoritarianism, and destructiveness. Automaton conformity is changing one's ideal self to conform to a perception of society's preferred type of personality, losing one's true self in the process. Automaton conformity displaces the burden of choice from self to society. Authoritarianism is giving control of oneself to another. By submitting one's freedom to someone else, this act removes the freedom of choice almost entirely. Lastly, destructiveness is any process which attempts to eliminate others or the world as a whole, all to escape freedom. Fromm said that "the destruction of the world is the last, almost desperate attempt to save myself from being crushed by it."

33 Which of the following statement is NOT true?

① Fromm suggests love as the solution to existential problems.
② Fromm condemns authoritarianism.
③ Automaton conformity contributes to harmonizing self with society.
④ Fromm does not support the idea of falling in love.

34 It can be inferred from the passage that _____.

① Fromm's love is based upon an immediate feeling rather than a conscious effort
② escape from freedom significantly contributes to the establishment of the true self
③ falling in love can be an ultimate answer to deal with our unbearable feeling of loneliness and isolation
④ man devises some psychological mechanism to get rid of burden of freedom

[35-37] 홍익대 2018

At the start of it all there is He: the classical ideal of 'Man', formulated first by Protagoras as 'the measure of all things', later renewed in the Italian Renaissance as a universal model and represented in Leonardo da Vinci's Vitruvian Man. An ideal of bodily perfection which, in keeping with the classical dictum *mens sana in corpore sano**, doubles up as a set of mental, discursive and spiritual values. Together they uphold a specific view of what is 'human' about humanity. Moreover, they assert with unshakable certainty the almost boundless capacity of humans to pursue their individual and collective perfectibility. That iconic image is the emblem of Humanism as a doctrine that combines the biological, discursive and moral expansion of human capabilities into an idea of teleologically ordained, rational progress. Faith in the unique, self-regulating and intrinsically moral powers of human reason forms an integral part of this high-humanistic creed, which was essentially predicated on eighteenth- and nineteenth-century renditions of classical Antiquity and Italian Renaissance ideals.

This model sets standards not only for individuals, but also for their cultures. Humanism historically developed into a civilizational model, which shaped a certain idea of Europe as coinciding with the universalizing powers of self-reflexive reason. The mutation of the Humanistic ideal into a hegemonic cultural model was canonized by Hegel's philosophy of history. This self-aggrandizing vision assumes that Europe is not just a geo-political location, but rather a universal attribute of the human mind that can lend its quality to any suitable object. This is the view espoused by Edmund Husserl in his celebrated essay "The Crisis of European Sciences", which is a passionate defence of the universal powers of reason against the intellectual and moral decline symbolized by the rising threat of European fascism in the 1930s. In Husserl's view, Europe announces itself as the site of origin of critical reason and self-reflexivity, both qualities resting on the Humanistic norm.

*a sound mind in a sound body: 건강한 신체에 건강한 정신이 깃든다.

35 Which of the following is NOT associated with the other three views of humanity?

① a doctrine that asserts the boundless human capabilities
② the Vitruvian Man
③ the measure of all things
④ the moral decline symbolized by the threat of fascism

36 Why does the author mention Edmund Husserl's essay in the passage?

① To argue that he is the last successor to European humanism
② To illustrate the influence of the classical ideals on a modern standard
③ To provide an example of the qualities of critical reason and self-reflexivity
④ To give an explanation for an iconic image of humanism

37 According to the passage, which of the following is true?

① Leonardo da Vinci inherited a universal model of 'Man' from classical antiquity.
② Italian Renaissance ideas are opposed to classical antiquity.
③ Hegel is not related to the mutation of the Humanistic ideal into a hegemonic model.
④ Humanism has nothing to do with the universalist norms.

[38-40] 숭실대 2018

Since the dawn of the 20th century, the philosophy of Nietzsche has had great intellectual and political influence around the world. Nietzsche applied himself to such topics as morality, religion, epistemology, psychology, ontology, and social criticism. Because of Nietzsche's evocative style and his often outrageous claims, his philosophy generates passionate reactions running from love to disgust. Nietzsche noted in his autobiographical *Ecce Homo* that his philosophy developed over time, so interpreters have found it difficult to relate concepts central to one work to those central to another, for example, the thought of the eternal recurrence features heavily in *Also Sprach Zarathustra (Thus Spoke Zarathustra)*, but is almost entirely absent from his next book, *Beyond Good and Evil*. Added to this challenge is the fact that Nietzsche did not seem concerned to develop his thought into a system, even going so far as to disparage the attempt in *Beyond Good and Evil*.

Nietzsche saw nihilism as the outcome of repeated frustrations in the search for meaning. He diagnosed nihilism as a latent presence within the very foundations of European culture, and saw it as a necessary and approaching destiny. The religious worldview had already suffered a number of challenges from contrary perspectives grounded in philosophical skepticism, and in modern science's evolutionary and heliocentric theory. Nietzsche saw this intellectual condition as a new challenge to European culture, which had extended itself beyond a sort of point-of-no-return. Nietzsche conceptualizes this with the famous statement "God is dead," which first appeared in his work in section 108 of *The Gay Science*, again in section 125 with the parable of "*The Madman*," and even more famously in *Thus Spoke Zarathustra*. The statement, typically placed in quotation marks, accentuated the crisis that Nietzsche argued that Western culture must face and transcend in the wake of the irreparable dissolution of its traditional foundations, moored largely in classical Greek philosophy and Christianity. In aphorisms 55 and 56 of *Beyond Good and Evil*, Nietzsche talks about the ladder of religious cruelty that suggests how Nihilism emerged from the intellectual conscience of Christianity. Nihilism is sacrificing the meaning "God" brings into our lives, for "matter and motion," physics, "objective truth." In aphorism 56, he explains how to emerge from the utter meaninglessness of life by reaffirming it through the Nietzsche's ideal of Eternal Return.

38 Which of the following would be best for the title?

① Nietzsche's Influence on Modern Intellectuals
② The Search for Central Concepts in Nietzsche
③ Classical Greek Philosophy As the Cause of Nihilism
④ Religious Cruelty in Traditional Christianity

39 Which of the following is NOT what makes it hard to interpret Nietzsche's works?

① provocative and outrageous style
② development of ideas over time
③ lack of a central idea in his works
④ his own attitude to do away systematic thoughts

40 Which of the following is NOT true?

① Nihilism resulted from the failure of the search for meaning.
② The traditional religious worldview was supported by modern science.
③ Conscientious Christians caused the emergence of nihilism.
④ The ideal of Eternal Return was proposed as a cure for nihilism.

CHAPTER 03 문학

[01-02] 한양대 2007

Somewhere between 1860 and 1890, the dominant emphasis in American literature was radically changed. But it is obvious that this change was not necessarily a matter of conscious concern to all writers. In fact, many writers may seem to have been actually unaware of the shifting emphasis. Moreover, it is not possible to trace the steady march of the realistic emphasis from the first feeble notes to its dominant trumpet-note of unquestioned leadership. The progress of realism is, to change the figure, rather that of a small stream, receiving accessions from its tributaries at unequal points along its course, its progress now and then checked by the sand bars of opposition or the diffusing marshes of error and compromise. Again it is apparent that any attempts to classify rigidly, as romanticists or realists, the writers of this period are _____, since it is not by virtue of the writer's conscious espousal of the romantic or realistic creed that he does much of his best work, but by virtue of the writer's sincere surrender to the atmosphere of the subject.

01 이 글의 흐름상 빈칸에 들어갈 가장 알맞은 것은?

① doomed to failure
② welcomed by critics
③ against our taste
④ considered reasonable

02 이 글의 내용과 일치하지 않는 것은?

① There was a radical change in American literature between 1860 and 1890.
② Most writers were conscious of the movement toward realism from the beginning.
③ Realism could move forward while undergoing resistance and mistakes.
④ Writers achieved their best works by yielding themselves to the age's mood.

[03-05] 국민대 2018

I do not believe that genius is an entirely different thing from talent. I am not even sure that it depends on any great difference in the artist's natural gifts. For example, I do not think that Cervantes had an exceptional gift for writing; few people would deny him genius. Nor would it be easy in English literature to find a poet with a happier gift than Herrick and yet no one would claim that he had more than delightful talent. It seems to me that what makes genius is the combination of natural gifts for creation with an idiosyncrasy that enables its possessor to see the world personally in the highest degree and yet with such Ⓐ _____ that his appeal is not to this type of man or to that type, but to all men. His private world is that of common men, but ampler and more pithy. He is supremely normal. By a happy accident of nature seeing life with immense vivacity, he sees it, with its infinite diversity, in the healthy way that mankind at large sees it. In other words, he sees life vigorously and sees it Ⓑ _____.

03 Which best fits into the blank Ⓐ?

① opacity
② frivolity
③ depravity
④ catholicity

04 Which best fits into the blank Ⓑ?

① askew
② whole
③ offhand
④ tentatively

05 Which is true according to the passage?

① Everyone believes Herrick is a genius with a charming talent for poetry.
② Most people agree that Cervantes is an unusually gifted writer, but not a genius.
③ A genius sees the world very personally but appeals to all kinds of men.
④ A genius does not need natural gifts but a strong, unique personality of the highest degree.

[06-08]

Can personality change occur ㉮ _____? Literature certainly offers numerous examples, such as Charles Dickens's Ebenezer Scrooge, the old miser whose stingy personality changes dramatically in a single night. But does reality mirror fiction? Do people really undergo sudden and dramatic personality changes? Almost one hundred years ago, the psychologist William James identified what he called 'twice-born souls.' What James had in mind were people who ㉯ _____, in the midst of intense emotional turmoil, underwent a startling transformation. In fact, James counted himself among the twice-born souls he described in his book *The Varieties of Religious Experience*. More recently, researchers Miller and DeBeca located fifty-five individuals who reported that they had undergone a sudden and major change in personality. According to them, all fifty-five individuals claimed that ㉰ _____. They also claimed that one particular 'focal incident' had precipitated the personality change. Scrooge's focal incident, of course, would have been the appearance of the three ghosts.

06 빈칸 ㉮와 ㉯에 공통으로 들어갈 가장 적절한 단어는?

① intentionally ② suddenly
③ voluntarily ④ vicariously

07 문맥상 빈칸 ㉰에 들어갈 가장 적절한 문장은?

① these changes were usually preceded by a period of intense emotional distress
② these changes were usually delayed by a period of strong mental distress
③ these changes were sudden but not so dramatic as scientists had predicted
④ these changes were dramatic but not so sudden as scientists had predicted

08 윗글의 내용과 일치하는 것은?

① 연구에 따르면 일생 동안 성격 변화를 두 번씩 겪는 사람들이 많이 있다.
② 스크루지는 상상의 인물일 뿐 현실에서는 그와 같은 성격 변화를 볼 수 없다.
③ 연구에 따르면 하나의 중요한 'focal incident'에 의해 성격 변화가 촉발된다.
④ 윌리엄 제임스는 종교를 통해서 성격 변화를 겪었지만 밀러는 그렇지 않다.

[09-10] 중앙대 2010

Coleridge and Wordsworth helped each other to establish the Romantic School of poetry _____. Instead of finding a hidden meaning in common things, Coleridge transports us to a world of ㉮ <u>ethereal beauty</u>, not the familiar scenes of sky and earth but an imagined world of enchantment and gorgeous visions. The poets were both lovers of nature, but Coleridge observed more delicately the aspects of nature that he loved, such as the apple-green color in an evening sky. Wordsworth's romance lay essentially in breaking the eighteenth century poetic tradition in order to find new fields of truth and beauty. The spirit of romance which strives to escape from the bonds of every common-sense life had never found a purer expression than in Coleridge's masterpieces. Both poets could rise to a perfect expression of their ideas, but Wordsworth often lapses into ㉯ <u>the prosaic</u>, while Coleridge's verse flows on with a rhythm that haunts us for days, so subtly does it harmonize with the pictures and mood of the poem. Wordsworth was ㉰ <u>impulsive</u>; he liked to write of emotions recollected in tranquility, often long after the original joy or pain had been experienced. Coleridge was ㉱ <u>intoxicated</u> by poetry; his imagination worked at a white heat while the inspiration was still fresh and vigorous.

09 밑줄 친 빈칸에 들어갈 가장 적합한 것을 고르시오.

① because they were to make the supernatural seem natural
② but Coleridge's poems are quite unlike Wordsworth's
③ in that the revolt of Wordsworth and Coleridge has generally been archaic
④ and Coleridge was influenced by Wordsworth

10 윗글에서 논지의 흐름상 가장 적합하지 않은 것을 고르시오.

① ㉮   ② ㉯
③ ㉰   ④ ㉱

[11-12] 중앙대 2010

The material which Stevenson put into his stories was essentially the same as Scott's: Strange situations and striking adventure. Yet his romances can never be mistaken for Scott's. The intervening period of realistic fiction had made readers more critical of the way events are narrated. Even the reader of a romance wished to accept it as ㉮ <u>true</u>, at least while he was racing through it. He therefore came to demand more of the look of truth found in Defoe than Scott had provided. This requirement Stevenson meets. For one thing, his narrative method is much more ㉯ <u>lengthy</u> than Scott's. His stories fill one volume, whereas Scott's were written to fill three. Stevenson's pages are not peopled with peasants and high-born folk, lovers and humorous characters, as Scott's are, sometimes in bewildering numbers. ㉰ <u>On the contrary</u>, only those characters are introduced that are necessary to the swiftly-moving adventure. Often our interest in them is heightened by sharp contrast—as the dispassionate Long John Silver is set over against the ㉱ <u>impulsive</u> Jim Hawkins. In presenting these relatively few characters Stevenson used to the full the command of truth-giving details that a half-century of realistic fiction-writing had given to novelists.

11 윗글에서 논지의 흐름상 가장 적합하지 않은 것을 고르시오.

① ㉮ ② ㉯
③ ㉰ ④ ㉱

12 윗글의 제목으로 가장 적합한 것을 고르시오.

① Stevenson's Romantic Life
② The Contrast Between Scott and Stevenson
③ The Era of Realism and Stevenson
④ The Nature of Stevenson's Characters

[13-14] 서울여대 2011

Many gods in classical Greece were female—not least Athena herself. But ideas about women, sex and gender were very different from now and women played almost no role in public life. They were not full citizens, so had no direct part in politics, they owned no property, and they belonged to their fathers until marriage, after which they were the property of their husbands. If a woman's father died, she became the property of his next male kin. When a husband went out at night to attend symposia—fashionable dinners with serious conversation—his wife stayed at home: female company was provided by hetairai, cultured women brought in expressly. Aristotle was just one ancient Greek who believed that women were inferior to men. One scholar has claimed that the Greek masculine world was nervous about women, as a "defiling element" who, in the plays of Aeschylus, Sophocles, Euripides and Aristophanes, are put there to "subvert the orderliness of male society." In recent years there has been a vast amount of scholarship on gender in ancient Greece. The overall message appears to be that there was a tension between the idea of home-loving, child-bearing woman and the wild, unrestrained emotional woman (like Media).

13 Which of the following is true according to the passage?

① In ancient Greece no woman was allowed to attend symposia.
② Aristotle was the only Greek scholar who believed that women were inferior to men.
③ In the plays of Aeschylus and Sophocles women characters often try to subvert the male order.
④ In ancient Greece there were many female gods because women played major roles in public life.

14 What kind of woman is Media for ancient Greeks?

① a hetairai
② a Greek goddess
③ a defiling woman
④ a home-loving woman

[15-16] 단국대 2018

Three passions, simple but overwhelmingly strong, have governed my life: the longing for love, the search for knowledge, and unbearable pity for the suffering of mankind. These passions, like great winds, have blown me hither and thither, in a wayward course, over a deep ocean of anguish, reaching to the very verge of despair.

I have sought love, first, because it brings ecstasy. I have sought it, next, because it relieves loneliness—that terrible loneliness in which one shivering consciousness looks over the rim of the world into the cold unfathomable lifeless abyss.

With equal passion I have sought knowledge. I have wished to understand the hearts of men. I have wished to know why the stars shine. And I have tried to apprehend the Pythagorean power by which number holds sway above the flux. A little of this, but not much, I have achieved.

Love and knowledge, so far as they were possible, led upward toward the heavens. _____ always pity brought me back to earth. Echoes of cries of pain reverberate in my heart. Children in famine, victims tortured by oppressors, helpless old people who can be a hated burden to their sons, and the whole world of loneliness, poverty, and pain make a mockery of what human life should be. I long to alleviate the evil, but I cannot, and I too suffer.

15 Which is the most appropriate for the blank?

① But
② In particular
③ So far as
④ In case

16 According to the passage, which is true?

① Love is the virtue which gives us the knowledge of the world.
② Helpless old people are always a hated burden to their sons.
③ The apprehension of the Pythagorean power lets us understand why the stars shine.
④ Terrible loneliness can be relieved by love.

[17-19] 숙명여대 2010

Mary Shelley herself was the first to point to her immersion in the literary and scientific revolutions of her day as the source of her novel *Frankenstein*. Her extreme youth, as well as her sex, have contributed to the generally held opinion that she was not so much an author in her own right as a transparent medium through which the ideas of those around her passed. "All Mrs. Shelley did," writes Mario Praz, "was to provide a passive reflection of some of the wild fantasies living in the air about her." Passive reflections, however, do not produce original works of literature, and *Frankenstein*, if not a great novel, was unquestionably an original one. The major Romantic and minor Gothic traditions to which it should have belonged was the literature of the overreacher: the superman who breaks through normal human limitations to defy the rules of society and infringe upon the realm of God. From Faust through Byron's heroes to Prometheus, all are overreachers punished by their own excesses of sensation, of experience, of knowledge and, most typically, by the doom of eternal life. But Mary Shelley's overreacher is different. Frankenstein's exploration of the forbidden boundaries of human science does not cause the extension of his own life, but the creation of a new one. He defies mortality not by living forever, but by giving birth.

17 The primary purpose of the passage is to _____.

① discount Mary Shelley's contribution to the realm of fantastic literature
② trace Mary Shelley's familiarity with the scientific and literary theories of her day
③ reclaim Mary Shelley's reputation by stressing the innovative qualities in her work
④ clarify the nature of the literary tradition to which Frankenstein belonged
⑤ demonstrate the influence of Shelley's Frankenstein on other examples of the genre

18 The author quotes Mario Praz primarily to _____.

① support her own perception of Mary Shelley's uniqueness
② illustrate recent changes in scholarly opinions of Shelley
③ demonstrate Praz's unfamiliarity with Shelley's Frankenstein
④ provide an example of the predominant critical view of Shelley
⑤ contrast Praz's statement about Shelley with Shelley's own self-appraisal

19 According to the passage, which of the following is true about Mary Shelley?

① She was unaware of the literary and mythological traditions of the overreacher.
② She intentionally parodied the scientific and literary discoveries of her time.
③ She was exposed to radical literary and scientific concepts that influenced her work.
④ She was not so much an author in her own right as an imitator of the literary works of others.
⑤ She was away from the Romantic and Gothic traditions of her days.

[20-21] 한국외대 2010

All the best novels contain boring passages. A novel which sparkles from the first page to the last is pretty sure not to be a great book. Nor have lives of great men been exciting except at a few great moments. Socrates could enjoy a banquet now and again, and must have derived considerable satisfaction from his conversations while the hemlock was taking effect, but most of his life he lived quietly with Xantippe, taking a walk in the afternoon, and perhaps meeting few friends on the way. Kant is said never to have been more than ten miles from Konigsberg in his life. Marx, after stirring up a few revolutions, decided to spend the remainder of his days in the British museum. Altogether it will be found that ㉮ _____, and that their pleasures have not been of the sort that would look exciting to the outward eye.

20 Which of the following best fits into ㉮?

① pleasure is the major driving force for human actions
② great men have great ideas and aspirations
③ greatness is only momentary and evanescent
④ a quiet life is characteristic of great men
⑤ we need to be cautious when attributing greatness to others

21 Which of the following is NOT stated or implied in the passage?

① Great things often contain trivial things in them.
② Great people are bound to have vices and weaknesses.
③ The ordinary daily life of Socrates was largely uneventful.
④ Marx spent much of the latter part of his life visiting a museum.
⑤ Great books are not regarded as such because they are good throughout.

[22-23] 중앙대 2009

> What do I love best about the novels of E. L. Doctorow? The answer to that is simple. I love the way he mixes up fact and fiction to create something new and magical. Take *Ragtime*, for example. In *Ragtime* he throws together Emma Goldman, the anarchist; Harry Houdini, the "escapologist"; Sigmund Freud, the father of psychoanalysis; Carl Jung, another important psychologist, and Henry Ford, the father of the Model T, turning these historical figures into characters in a novel. Freud and Jung actually went to Coney Island on their visit to America together. That the historians can document. Did they take a ride through the Tunnel of Love, as in the novel? Who knows? But _____. Doctorow employed the facts, showing his creativity to the fullest.

22 밑줄 친 빈칸에 들어가기에 가장 적합한 것을 고르시오.

① money talks
② the historical details do not ring true
③ what a fantastic idea
④ the reading public stole the show

23 What is the author's purpose of mentioning Freud and Jung's ride through the Tunnel of Love?

① To evoke a sense of nostalgia
② To take issue with Doctorow's disregard for facts
③ To document a historic encounter
④ To commend a happy invention

[24-25]

A Christmas Carol remains one of the rare novels to have infiltrated popular culture, leaving the impress of its characters and language even on those who have never read it. Christmas offered a means for its author, Charles Dickens, to redeem the despair and the terrors of his childhood. After a series of financial embarrassments that left his family insolvent, the 12-year-old Dickens, his schooling interrupted, was sent to work at a shoe blacking factory in a quixotic attempt to remedy his family's plight.

Because Dickens's tribulations were not particular to him but emblematic of the Industrial Revolution, the concerns that inform his fiction were shared by millions of potential readers. Dickens intended to make the sufferings of the most vulnerable of the underclass so pungently real to his readers that they could not continue to ignore their need, not so much for charity as for the means to save themselves: education. At least this was his conscious purpose. In a sense, replacing the slippery Holy Ghost with anthropomorphized spirits, the infant Christ with a crippled child whose salvation waits on man's—not God's—generosity, Dickens laid claim to a religious festival, handing it over to the gathering forces of secular humanism.

24 Which of the following cannot be inferred from the passage?

① *A Christmas Carol* may not have been written had Dickens not faced difficulties in his youth.
② Dickens attempted to enlighten the public through religious renderings of a secular society.
③ The enduring popularity of *A Christmas Carol* stems from its universally appealing story.
④ Dickens upheld the ideal that education could be the salvation of the underprivileged.

25 What is the best title for the passage?

① Dickens's Humanistic Take on Christmas
② A Portrait of the Underclass in Dickens's Novel
③ How Poverty Shaped the Life of Dickens
④ Dickens's Christmas Theme of Spiritual Redemption

[26-28] 숭실대 2013

Please Look After Mom is the most moving and accomplished, and often startling, novel in translation I've read in many seasons. We watch the same story unfold through the eyes of the family's eldest daughter (a writer), the eldest son, the husband and, finally, the lost mother herself. Ms. Shin's careful, unflinching descriptions of a woman in "blue plastic sandals"—with three of the sections delivered in a plaintive, almost accusatory second-person voice ("You all blamed each other for Mom's going missing, and you all felt wounded")—achieve an emotional clarity and directness that speak straight to the heart.

Every sentence is saturated in detail. While tending to her family in the village, "Mom" is shown mashing frogs to feed her chickens and "making yeast with a soiled towel wrapped around her head." Even as she regularly goes to Catholic church, she gives money to passing Buddhist monks and believes that ancestors come back to dwell among the living, disguised as birds. The food stuffs that permeate the pages—fatsia pancakes and "dough-flake soup," wild-strawberry juice and "mung-bean porridge"—speak of a traditional woman's work in the fields, her home life in the kitchen and a connection between the two that her children, in their weightless urban lives, have lost. *Please Look After Mom* is full of quiet anger about a time when women had to give up everything to protect their ⓐ _____ and to walk behind their husbands. But it's also clear-eyed about a modern age in which some women don't know how to do anything for their ⓑ _____ —or even have ⓒ _____ to do anything for. It would be easy to say that Ms. Shin has given us an unforgettable East Asian mother out of Amy Tan in a globalized world we recognize from Jhumpa Lahiri. But the author's first novel to appear in English does something more than that. It tells an almost unbearably affecting story of remorse and belated wisdom that reminds us how globalism—at the human level—can tear souls apart and leave them uncertain of where to turn.

26 Which of the following is true about *"Please Look After Mom"*?

① It is the author's first successful novel.
② It has multiple points of view on the same story.
③ It shows troubled religious orientation in Korean society.
④ It has nothing to do with globalism.

27 Which of the following CANNOT be inferred from the passage?

① The book is favorably reviewed and appreciated.
② A woman in "blue plastic sandals" is the emotional center of the novel.
③ Amy Tan and Jhumpa Lahiri may be writers.
④ The reviewer's knowledge of Korean history is profound.

28 Which of the following fits best in ⓐ, ⓑ, and ⓒ?

① husbands
② families
③ ancestors
④ countries

[29-31] 한양대 2008

It must be admitted that in the beginning I was far too shocked to have any real reaction. If I reacted at all, I reacted by trying to be pleasant—it being a great part of the American Negro's education (long before he goes to school) that he must make people "like" him. This (A) routine worked about as well in this situation as it had in the situation for which it was designed, which is to say that it did not work at all. No one, after all, can be liked whose skin color cannot be, or has not been, admitted. My smile was simply another unheard-of phenomenon which allowed them to see my teeth—they did not, really, see my smile and I began to think that, even if I should snarl, no one would notice any difference. All of the physical characteristics of the Negro which had caused me, in America, a very different and almost forgotten pain were nothing less than miraculous in the eyes of the village people. Some thought that my hair was the color of tar and it had the texture of cotton. It was (B) jocularly suggested that I might let it all grow long and make myself a winter coat. While there was certainly no element of intentional unkindness, there was yet no suggestion that I was human: I was simply a living wonder.

29 Which of the following is most suitable for (A)?

① work-while-it-is-day
② out-of-sight-out-of-mind
③ a-stitch-in-time-saves-nine
④ smile-and-the-world-smiles-with-you

30 Which is closest in meaning to (B)?

① playfully
② joyfully
③ regrettably
④ unconsciously

31 According to the passage, which of the following is true?

① The villagers thought that the author was snarling when he smiled.
② The author thought that the villagers were intentionally kind to him.
③ The author was not shocked at the curiosities shown by the villagers in the beginning.
④ The lesson that the author had received worked neither in America nor in the village.

[32-34]

In fan fiction, stories and novels make use of the characters and settings from other people's professional creative work. Fan fiction is what literature might look like if it were reinvented from scratch after a nuclear apocalypse by a band of brilliant pop-culture junkies trapped in a sealed bunker. They do not do it for money. That is not what it is about. The writers write it and put it up online just for the satisfaction. They are fans, but they are not silent, couchbound consumers of media. The culture talks to them, and they talk back to the culture in its own language. Right now fan fiction is still the cultural equivalent of dark matter: it is largely invisible to the mainstream, but at the same time, it is unbelievably massive. Fan fiction predates the Internet, but the Web has made it exponentially easier to talk and be heard, and it holds hundreds of millions of words of fan fiction. There is fan fiction based on books, movies, TV shows, video games, plays, musicals, rock bands and board games. There is fan fiction based on the Bible. In most cases, the quantity of fan fiction generated by a given work is volumetrically larger than the work itself; in some cases, the quality is higher than that of the original too.

32 Choose the one closest in meaning to the underlined "from scratch".

① begin with modifications
② mark with major changes
③ discard irrelevant factors
④ start from a blank slate

33 According to the passage, which of the following is not true about writers of fan fiction?

① They actively participate in culture through their own ways.
② They make their work public but write for personal satisfaction.
③ They are addicted to certain characters and settings.
④ They are not paid for their work.

34 Which of the following can be inferred about "fan fiction"?

① It was introduced along with the advent of the Internet.
② There are no limits to what subjects can be written about.
③ It has gained more respect as a genre because of the Internet.
④ Its quality always exceeds that of the work it is about.

[35-36] 단국대 2013

Many critics of Emily Brontë's novel *Wuthering Heights* see its second part as a counterpoint that comments on, if it does not reverse, the first part, where a romantic reading receives more confirmation. Seeing the two parts as a whole is encouraged by the novel's sophisticated structure, revealed in its complex use of narrators and time shifts. Granted that the presence of these elements need not argue for an authorial awareness of novelistic construction, their presence does encourage attempts to unify the novel's heterogeneous parts. However, any interpretation that seeks to unify all of the novel's diverse elements is bound to be somewhat unconvincing. This is not because such an interpretation necessarily stiffens into a thesis (although rigidity in any interpretation of this or of any novel is always a danger), but because *Wuthering Heights* has recalcitrant elements of undeniable power that, ultimately, resist inclusion in an all-encompassing interpretation. In this respect, *Wuthering Heights* shares a feature of *Hamlet*.

35 According to the passage, which of the following is true about the second part of *Wuthering Heights*?

① It annuls the sophisticated structure of the novel.
② It strengthens the force of the first part.
③ It provides less substantiation for a romantic reading.
④ It unifies the complex elements in the novel.

36 According to the passage, the author would be most likely to agree that critics should _____.

① try to claim for an authorial awareness of novelistic construction
② not be inflexible when they analyze the novel's diverse elements
③ blindly accept the interpretations of other critics
④ not argue that the complex use of narrators or of time shifts indicates a sophisticated structure

[37-40] 가톨릭대 2016

One can think of literature less as some inherent quality or set of qualities displayed by certain kinds of writing than as a number of ways in which people relate themselves to writing. It would not be easy to isolate, from all that has been variously called 'literature', some constant set of inherent features. In fact, it would be as impossible as trying to identify the single distinguishing feature which all games have in common. There is no 'essence' of literature whatsoever. Any bit of writing may be read 'non-pragmatically', if that is what reading a text as literature means, just as any writing may be read 'poetically'. If I pore over the railway timetable not to discover a train connection but to stimulate in myself general reflections on the speed and complexity of modern existence, then I might be said to be reading it as literature. 'Literature' operates rather like the word 'weed'; weeds are not particular kinds of plant, but just any kind of plant which for some reason or another gardener does not want around. Perhaps 'literature' means something like the opposite: any kind of writing which for some reason or another somebody values highly. As the philosophers might say, 'literature' and 'weed' are functional rather than ontological terms: _____. 'Literature' is in this sense a purely formal, empty sort of definition. In any case, it is far from clear that we can discriminate neatly between 'practical' and 'non-practical' ways of relating ourselves to language. Reading a novel for pleasure obviously differs from reading a road sign for information, but how about reading a biology textbook to improve your mind? Is that a 'pragmatic' treatment of language or not? In many societies, 'literature' has served highly practical functions such as religious ones; distinguishing sharply between 'practical' and 'non-practical' may only be possible in a society like ours, where literature has ceased to have much practical function at all.

37 What would be the best title of the passage?

① What Is Literature?
② How to Read Literature
③ The Uses and Misuses of Literature
④ Significance of Literature

38 Choose the best expression for the blank.

① it is impossible to compare them from a linguistic point of view
② they operate as an index with which people gauge the meaning of life
③ they tell us about what we do, not about the fixed being of things
④ we cannot have direct access to their existence, regardless of their usefulness

39 According to the author, science textbooks can be read as literature when _____.

① they serve practical means of human life
② they give us valuable knowledge about the world
③ they are written in eloquent language
④ we treat them with a feeling of awe

40 Which of the following is NOT true, according to the passage?

① To some travellers, a railway timetable can be read as literature.
② Any bit of writing can be read pragmatically as well as non-pragmatically.
③ With proper efforts, the essence of literature can easily come out in the course of reading.
④ Literature has functioned differently from society to society.

[41-42] 성균관대 2016

For centuries the idea of two men facing each other in a duel has seemed anachronistic. Guy de Maupassant, a 19th-century writer, declared it to be "the last of our unreasonable customs". Two centuries before that Louis XIV, king of France, tried to outlaw it as a feudal archaism. Yet despite this, the literature of the 19th and even the early 20th century is peppered with accounts of swashbuckling men. Why? In the early 18th century many writers depicted men who fought duels as hot-headed. By the 19th century, although it still seemed to spring from an older, medieval age, duelling was regarded as quite glamorous. In "The Memoirs of Barry Lyndon, Esq"(1844) by William Makepeace Thackeray the hero rails against "cowardly pistols" and harks back to the "honourable and manly weapon of gentlemen". <u>And compared with the burgeoning violence at the start of the 20th century, duels could also seem remarkably measured</u>. A character in a G.K. Chesterton novel from 1908 prevents a suspected anarchist from exploding a bomb by challenging him to a duel. After two world wars, though, the glamour had begun to fade. In Evelyn Waugh's "Officers and Gentlemen"(1955) one character admits he would laugh if he was challenged to a duel.

41 The best title of the passage would be _____.

① Modern Parallels to Duel
② Duel in Literature
③ Origin of Duel
④ Duel as an Old-fashioned Folly
⑤ History of Violence

42 The underlined expression implies that the duel _____.

① has been legalized
② has almost disappeared
③ is a random act of anarchism
④ is a lower form of aggression
⑤ is a form of ordered violence

[43-45] 한국외대 2015

> Irish writer George Orwell's life and literature can be summarized by his faith in one thing: human decency. Although the definition can be ambiguous, it does contain a sense of fundamental dignity, and above all, honesty and tolerance. Orwell was opposed to dogma, ideological political doctrines, planned social reformation, and religious absolutism. He instead preferred to support the individual's right of expression, particularly the rights of minorities, and the freedom of press.
>
> Orwell's sense of human decency was based on the idea of liberation and expression. It was not something that could be enjoyed passively, but must be worked for and sought after. The phrase "The secret of freedom is courage" implies that people have an obligation to be brave in their speech and courageous in their tolerance of other opinions. For Orwell, decency meant, above all else, communality, common sense, and respect for the common man. He was adamantly opposed to Marxism, which dictates that freedom is denied by equality. He believed true socialism was possible not by Ⓐ _____ power but by Ⓑ _____ fair and open discussions.
>
> Orwell loathed abstract theories such as communism, which necessitated ideology. This can be seen in his anti-totalitarian work Animal Farm and his dystopia classic 1984, in which he pursues an anti-dictatorial, anti-class, and anti-discriminatory society. Orwell believed that it was the obligation of human beings to fight against these systems not just for the sake of society, but for the progression of a society.

43 Which of the following is the passage mainly about?

① Literary techniques and craftsmanship of Orwell
② Philosophical viewpoints of Orwell's literature
③ Critical review of Orwell's personality
④ Development of Orwell's literary career

44 Which of the following is LEAST likely to be opposed to by Orwell?

① Need to limit the powers of government
② Choice of equality over freedom
③ Adherence to political ideology
④ Belief in religion without any doubts

45 From the context, which of the following ordered pairs best fits into Ⓐ and Ⓑ?

① relinquishing – encouraging
② seizing – guaranteeing
③ capturing – restraining
④ renouncing – suppressing

[46-47] 서강대 2017

Sentimentality, notoriously, is entirely compatible with a taste for brutality and worse. (Recall the canonical example of the Auschwitz commandant returning home in the evening, embracing his wife and children, and sitting at the piano to play some Schubert before dinner.) People don't become inured to what they are shown—if that's the right way to describe what happens—because of the quantity of images dumped on them. It is passivity that dulls feeling. The states described as Ⓐ _____, moral or emotional anesthesia, are full of feelings; the feelings are rage and frustration. But if we consider what emotions would be desirable, it seems too simple to elect sympathy. The imaginary proximity to the suffering inflicted on others that is granted by images suggests a link between the far-away sufferers—seen close-up on the television screen—and the privileged viewer that is simply untrue, that is yet one more mystification of our real relations to power. So far as we feel sympathy, we feel we are not accomplices to what caused the suffering. Our sympathy proclaims our innocence as well as our impotence. To that extent, it can be (for all our good intentions) an impertinent—if not an inappropriate—response. To set aside the sympathy we extend to others beset by war and murderous politics for a reflection on how our privileges are located on the same map as their suffering, and may—in ways we might prefer not to imagine—be linked to their suffering, as the wealth of some may imply the destitution of others, is a task for which the painful, stirring images supply only an initial spark.

46 Choose the best word for blank Ⓐ.

① pathos
② sympathy
③ apathy
④ inertia

47 Choose the statement most consistent with the passage.

① The author calls for sympathy for the suffering caused by war and murderous politics.
② An innate tropism toward the gruesome is as natural to human beings as is sympathy.
③ The increase of information in media about calamities taking place in another country makes the spectator a better citizen of the world.
④ Journalism driven by mercantile values and its hunt for more dramatic images is a quintessential feature of modern experience.

[48-50] 한국외대 2017

Human Acts is a book that could easily founder under the weight of its subject matter. Neither inviting nor shying away from modern-day parallels, Han Kang neatly unpacks the social and political catalysts behind the massacre and maps its lengthy, toxic fallout. But what is remarkable is how she accomplishes this while still making it a novel of blood and bone. The characters frequently address themselves to an unnamed 'You.' Sometimes 'You' is the dead, occasionally it is the reader but often, and most disturbingly, Ⓐ "You" is who people were before the violence and have now become irrevocably exiled from. This sense of Ⓑ _____ is most obvious when a dead boy's soul converses with his own rotting flesh; it is here that the language comes closest to the gothic lyricism of Han's previous book, *The vegetarian*. At least the boy possesses a soul. Many of the other victims are no longer certain that they do, and their shame at having survived is palpable. By choosing the novel as her form, then allowing it to do what it does best, take readers to the very center of a life that is not their own, Han prepares us for one of the most important questions of our times: "What is humanity? What do we have to do to keep humanity as one thing and not another?" She never answers, but this act of unflinching Ⓒ _____ seems as good a place to start as any.

48 Which of the following is closest in meaning to Ⓐ?

① 'You' is the offspring of violent confrontation.
② 'You' is transformed into previous selves.
③ 'You' is characters prior to a permanent change.
④ 'You' is an exiled refugee in another country.

49 Which one of the following ordered pairs best fits into Ⓑ and Ⓒ.

① confirmation – withdrawal
② engagement – attestation
③ dislocation – witness
④ compatibility – spectacle

50 Which of the following is NOT true of the passage?

① The passage is a critical review of a literary work.
② The subject matter of the work is rather serious and disturbing.
③ In this novel, Han keeps the grotesque and poetic style of the earlier one.
④ Han focuses on analyzing an event and clearly answers an important question.

CHAPTER 04 언어

[01-02] 광운대 2015

The use of audiovisual materials has been integrated into language learning for many years. In fact, technology to listen to target language audio and record oneself has been commonly available in language classrooms since the 1970s. Despite countless innovations and technologies made available in language learning since then, the cassette recorder is the single piece of technology that has affected language learning the most. Audio material has been readily available online, either as streamed or downloadable files, since the 1990s. With the arrival of Web 2.0 tools, audio can be distributed by individuals or institutions while being Ⓐ _____ other content. 'Podcast' has made the transition from technical to commonplace in a very short time. The impact and penetration of podcasting has been wide-ranging, far-reaching, and arguably much faster than that of the world wide web. This impact can be Ⓑ _____ the fact that the uses of podcasting are varied, from entertainment to politics to education, and can appeal to a mass audience.

01 윗글의 주제로 가장 적절한 것은?

① The advantages and disadvantages of diverse audiovisual materials
② The substantial effect of the cassette recorder in language education
③ The introduction of streamed or downloadable files in language education
④ The evolution of audiovisual materials in language education and the emergence of podcasting
⑤ The prevalence of audiovisual materials and dependence on podcasting in various areas in the society

02 윗글에 주어진 빈칸 Ⓐ-Ⓑ에 들어갈 가장 적절한 표현을 순서대로 나열한 것은?

① replaced by – translated into
② separated from – argued against
③ restricted to – substantial with
④ interested in – liable to
⑤ combined with – attributed to

[03-04] 한양대 2011

When the military uses the phrase "self-injurious behavior incidents" regarding detainees at Guantanamo Bay, it means what most of us call "attempted suicides." In fact, when the word "detainees" is used, it means what most of us call "prisoners." "Water boarding" sounds at first like something you'd expect to see young people doing on a California beach, not a torture technique that involves forced simulated drowning. Less remarkable, perhaps, but possibly more relevant for most of us, we've heard the term "downsized" used when someone is fired or laid off. "Ethnic cleansing" covers everything from deportation to genocide. What we have to say may be important, but the words we choose to say it with can be equally important. The examples just given are cases of an attempt to get us to adopt a particular attitude toward a subject that, if described differently, would seem less attractive to us. Words have tremendous persuasive power, or what we have called their rhetorical force or emotive meaning—their power to express and ㉮ _____ rhetorical images, feelings, and emotional associations, thereby affecting people's attitudes, opinions, and behavior.

03 What is most appropriate for blank ㉮?

① elicit
② extort
③ instigate
④ surrogate

04 What is the best title of this passage?

① The Arbitrariness of Language
② How to Beat Around the Bush
③ Linguistic Etiquette in Everyday Life
④ Rhetorical Dimensions of Linguistic Coercion

[05-07] 한국외대 2006

French cognitive scientist Franck Ramus and his colleagues discovered that human infants raised in French-speaking households could distinguish between other languages ⓐ they heard over a loudspeaker. Ramus used the rate at which the babies sucked on their pacifiers as evidence of their level of interest, and found that after listening to sentences spoken in Dutch, ⓑ they recognized a change in language had occurred when the loudspeaker switched to Japanese. But the startling finding was that ⓒ they could not make this distinction if the recordings were played backwards. In other words, the babies understood certain properties of language that the backward sentences lacked, and ⓓ they measured differences in the two languages accordingly. An even more startling fact is that Marc Hauser got exactly the same results with tamarin monkeys that Ramus had found for human infants, using the same procedures. The monkeys distinguished Dutch from Japanese when the same sentences Ramus had used were played forward, but could not make the distinction when they were played backward. Of course neither the monkeys nor the babies understood the languages themselves, but the results indicate that ⓔ they parse out a new language based on its sound combinations and rhythms.

05 Which of the following is the major theme of the passage?

① Systematic differences across human languages
② Potential abilities of monkeys to learn human language
③ Fundamental differences between humans and monkeys
④ Language discrimination by human infants and monkeys
⑤ Importance of sound combinations and rhythms in language

06 Among ⓐ, ⓑ, ⓒ, ⓓ, and ⓔ, which one differs from the others in what they refer to?

① ⓐ
② ⓑ
③ ⓒ
④ ⓓ
⑤ ⓔ

07 According to the passage, which of the following is NOT among the findings from the experiments mentioned?

① Infants could perceive the differences between Dutch and Japanese.
② Infants attend to sound combinations and rhythms in language.
③ Infants distinguished the syntactic differences in different languages.
④ Monkeys exhibited the same language discrimination abilities as human infants.
⑤ Monkeys couldn't distinguish different languages when sentences were played backwards.

[08-09] 중앙대 2008

> Experts on language—the real ones, not those of us who merely use it—are having an intense debate about which species can talk. On one side are those who believe that only humans converse. On another side are those who say, what about dolphins and whales and certainly the amazing Koko, the gorilla? Koko has a sign language vocabulary of at least 1,000 words. She can recognize about 2,000 spoken words. In a new book called *The First Word*, Christine Kenneally catalogs the complex debate over language and includes one particularly revealing experiment in which scientists put two male apes who knew sign language together. One might have expected these guys to start grousing about their keepers. But, no, they started madly signing at each other, a manual shouting match, and in the end, neither appeared to actually listen to the other. So, are two creatures actually conversing if they're both talking and nobody is listening? Where does talking-without-listening put one in the animal brain chain? Let's see, talking without listening. Many wives can think of someone who might qualify. Teen-agers do, easily. And parents of teenagers. Also, a lot of successful politicians and talk show hosts. With a long political season ahead, we might venture that what really separates humans from ape is the ⓐ _____ capacity to ⓑ _____.

08 밑줄 친 ⓐ와 ⓑ에 들어가기에 가장 적합한 말을 고르시오.

① underused – listen   ② overused – listen
③ underused – talk   ④ overused – talk

09 다음 중 윗글의 내용과 가장 일치하는 것을 고르시오.

① Two male apes in the experiment did not know sign language.
② Two male apes in the experiment did not complain about their keepers.
③ No other creatures, except for humans, have sign language vocabularies.
④ No other creatures, except for humans, can recognize more than 1,000 spoken words.

[10-11] 한국외대 2011

In the first year of life, infants go through three stages generally thought to have nothing directly to do with the acquisition of language. The crying stage lasts from birth to around 2 months. The cooing stage, characterized by vowel-like sounds, lasts from about 2 months to 5 months. And the babbling stage, characterized by syllable-like consonant-vowel sounds, lasts from about 5 months to 12 months. Note that these sounds are described as language-like; they are not generally thought to be either an early form of language or necessary prerequisites to language acquisition. For example, even babies born deaf babble as infants, but they cease after about 6 months. The fact that deaf babies babble just as hearing infants do suggests that such behavior is not "practice" for language acquisition. However, the linguistic status of these stages is still best regarded as an open question for the present time.

If, however, language-like behaviors such as cooing and babbling are not actually practice for language, what are they? One hypothesis is that they are simple genetically-determined stages that the human organism goes through as it matures. In fact, there is evidence that much of what appears to be "practice" for a specific skill is actually just a genetically-encoded stage and may not be necessary for the acquisition of that skill. For example, young birds go through a stage of flapping their wings before they actually begin to fly. Years ago a scientist decided to test the hypothesis that wing flapping is practice for flying.

10 Which of the following questions CANNOT be answered on the basis of the passage?

① What is the probable age of a baby who starts making sounds such as 'ba-ba'?
② When can we identify if a baby is deaf or not?
③ Which sound should a baby be able to pronounce first: 'pa' or 'a'?
④ What role does babbling play in the process of language acquisition?

11 What will be most likely to follow this passage?

① How the scientist verified the similarity between language acquisition and flying skill acquisition
② How the scientist designed a test to verify how early birds start wing flapping
③ How the scientist designed a test to verify or falsify the hypothesis
④ How the scientist verified the relation between practice for a specific skill and language acquisition

[12-13]

Though subtle, notions of men's and women's language use abound: men are said to swear a lot, to be more coarse and casual; women know more color terms and men know tool names; women use more qualifiers and diminutives; and in meetings or other professional contexts, men are said to speak more than women and interrupt them more often. Clearly, these stereotypes aren't very trustworthy. It's probably not so much gender as gender roles that influence linguistic behavior. As gender roles change, gender differences in speech frequently disappear. Women who work as mechanics know the names of tools, and men who paint and decorate have to know their color terms. Gender roles change, but they may not disappear. For example, although the taboo against women swearing has eased, both men and women students still report some degree of discomfort when women swear in mixed company.

12 According to the passage, which of the following is not an example of "stereotypes"?

① Women must not use offensive language.
② Men know more color names than women.
③ Men speak more than women in a conference.
④ Women use adjectives or adverbs more than men.

13 According to the passage, the different language use between men and women is influenced by _____.

① gender
② gender differences in speech
③ gender roles
④ the taboo against women swearing

[14-15]

It has been particularly important to bring to light language that reinforces the dominant culture's views of disability. A useful step in that process has been the construction of the terms ableist and ableism, which can be used to organize ideas about the centering and domination of the non-disabled experience and point of view. Ableism has recently landed in the *Reader's Digest Oxford Wordfinder*, where it is defined as "discrimination in favor of the able-bodied." I would add, extrapolating from the definitions of racism and sexism, that ableism also includes the idea that a person's abilities or characteristics are determined by disability or that people with disabilities as a group are ⓐ _____ to non-disabled people. Although there is probably greater consensus among the general public on what could be labeled racist or sexist language than there is on what might be considered ableist, that may be because the nature of the oppression of disabled people is not yet as widely understood.

14 장애자의 차별에 대한 서술자의 입장을 가장 잘 표현한 것은?

① critical
② satirical
③ flexible
④ imaginative

15 글의 흐름상 빈칸 ⓐ에 알맞은 것은?

① exceptional
② inferior
③ parasitic
④ extraneous

[16-17] 서강대 2011

It is 400 years since Galileo published his *Sidereus Nuncius*, the starry messenger or astronomical message, a book which gravely downgraded humanity's place in the universe and at the same time revealed to it some of the mysteries previously hidden by the blindfold of doctrine. In that small volume he showed that the firmament was crowded with stars invisible to the naked eye, that the moon was rugged rather than the smooth, ludicrously perfect object of the churchmen, and that the Earth was not unique in having a moon and had therefore become a candidate for demotion from its cosmic egotism. The explosive little volume was the only book Galileo wrote in Latin. Everything else was in Tuscan. In his wittily challenging *Galileo: Watcher of the skies*, David Wootton argues that Galileo was (or said he was) primarily concerned with what his fellow Florentines thought about him. And when his works came to be banned, Galileo feared they would be forgotten in Italy, whether or not they were being read in Latin elsewhere in Europe. Tuscan was a language which could be read by the educated laity throughout northern Italy; Latin was the language of the Universities, where Aristotelian thinking ruled.

16 Which of the following would best replace the underlined word in the passage?

① diversion
② relegation
③ accretion
④ rudiment

17 Which of the following CANNOT be inferred from the above passage?

① *Sidereus Nuncius* debunked the idea of human supremacy in the universe.
② Galileo was afraid of being overlooked by his contemporary Florentines.
③ The publication of *Sidereus Nuncius* rejuvenated the Aristotelian conceptions of the universe.
④ Latin was the primary medium of scholarly research and writing in Galileo's age.

[18-20] 성균관대 2006

In every language there seem to be certain "unmentionables"—words of such strong affective connotations that they cannot be used in polite discourse. In English, the first of these to come to mind are, of course, words dealing with excretion and sex. Money is another subject about which communication is in some ways inhibited. When creditors send bills, they practically never mention money, although that is what they are writing about. The fear of death carries over, quite understandably in view of the widespread confusion of symbols with things symbolized, into fear of the words having to do with death. Many people, therefore, instead of saying "died," substitute such expressions as _____. Some of our verbal reticences, especially religious ones, have the authority of the Bible. It appears that there is a feeling that names of the gods are too holy, and the names of evil spirits too terrifying, to be spoken lightly. It could be true that verbal taboos also produce serious problems since they prevent frank discussion of sexual matters. The stronger verbal taboos have, however, a genuine social value. When we are extremely angry and we feel the need of expressing our anger in violence, the uttering of these forbidden words provides us with a relatively harmless verbal substitute for going berserk.

18 According to the passage, creditors seldom talk about money when sending bills because mentioning money _____.

① is immoral
② is a taboo
③ is inhabited by law
④ is not professional
⑤ is conventional

19 Which of the following is NOT appropriate for the blank?

① "passed away"
② "departed"
③ "cut the corners"
④ "gone to his reward"
⑤ "gone west"

20 According to the passage, verbal taboos _____.

① are used only by men
② serve as a safety valve in our moments of crisis
③ may promote friendly communication
④ are an imaginative way of understanding things
⑤ can encourage constructive debates on sex

[21-22] 중앙대 2010

Among all the countries where English is spoken as a major first language, the situation of English in South Africa is unique. English is only in fifth place in terms of the population of native speakers: it is the language of a minority within a white minority, while the majority (three-quarters) of South African citizens are black. Although English is the home language of less than 10 percent of the population, it is dominant in government at higher levels, business, technology, higher education and the media. ㉮ Most South Africans speak a language of the Bantu family of languages, but it has been estimated that one out of two South Africans know some English. Afrikaans is the mother tongue or second language for several million people in Southern Africa. ㉯ There are different reasons for the success story of English in South Africa. One reason is that there has been a positive shift in the attitude toward English. ㉰ No language is singled out for special status, although in practice English is institutionally entrenched and widely used as a lingua franca. Another reason for the support of English is the fact that using it avoids the potential divisiveness of using any particular African language. Ethnicity and linguistic identity are strongly linked, so that a politician using Xhosa would lose Zulu support—English can be resorted to as a neutral option. Furthermore, to the linguistically diverse black majority, Afrikaans has been perceived as the language of oppression. Yet the popularity of English among black Africans is hardly based on enthusiastic feelings for the language or for the culture it represents. ㉱ Rather, it is based on a wish to realize their dreams of a better future. It is ironic that here, as in so many other countries, the colonial language, English, tends to stand somehow for liberation and a window on the world.

21 윗글에서 논지의 흐름상 가장 불필요한 것을 고르시오.
① ㉮ ② ㉯
③ ㉰ ④ ㉱

22 윗글을 통해 추론할 수 있는 것으로 가장 적합한 것을 고르시오.
① Xhosa is not a mother tongue of Zulu people in South Africa.
② English is a dominant language in terms of the population of native speakers in South Africa.
③ English and Xhosa are the most frequently used languages in South Africa.
④ In many other countries except for South Africa, English is considered as a symbol for liberation.

[23-27] 서강대 2009

> Cultural imperialism is much more subtle than economic imperialism, which is itself less tangible than political and military imperialism, whose excesses are obvious and easy to denounce. It would be wrong to say that the world domination of English is something deliberately organized and supported by Anglo-Saxon powers, hand in glove with political initiatives or the penetration of the world economy by their transnational firms. The "language war" had very seldom been regarded as a war and has never, anywhere, been declared. The military, diplomatic, political and economic strategies of the major powers can be studied and criticized, but linguistic strategies seem to be ⓐ inconspicuous and tacit, even innocent or nonexistent. Will countries stand ㉮ _____ domination by a single language?

23 Which of the following best describes the main subject of the passage?

① the world economy and transnational firm
② the domination of English in the world
③ the role of English in international relations
④ Anglo-Saxon powers

24 The main idea of passage is mainly supported by _____.

① comparison   ② examples
③ cause and effect   ④ an anecdote

25 Which of the following is true according to the passage?

① The military and diplomatic imperialism of major powers is hard to criticize publicly.
② The human civilization has never experienced a linguistic war.
③ Economic policies are more obvious than linguistic policies.
④ The growing importance of English is part of a plan by English-speaking nations for global economic domination.

26 Which is the closest in meaning to ⓐ inconspicuous?

① unusual
② incredulous
③ indecent
④ unnoticeable

27 Which is the most suitable word for blank ㉮?

① for
② by
③ up to
④ up for

[28-29] 한국외대 2007

Neal Armstrong's famous first words from the moon in 1969 were heard as "That's one small step for man, one giant leap for mankind." But was that what he said? Grammarians have long been annoyed that such a world-famous moment was marred by bad grammar, arguing there should have been an 'a' in front of 'man'. Armstrong has long asserted that he did, in fact, say the 'a', although [A] the acoustic record begged to differ. To set the record straight, Peter Shann Ford, a Sydney-based computer programmer, conducted his own high-tech detective work, By analysing the NASA recording with advanced nerve-based voice analysis software usually used for people who are paralysed, Ford found the missing word. Armstrong did indeed say, "One small step for a man ...", but according to Ford, the 'a' lasted a total of only 35 milliseconds. Roger Launius, who chairs the space history division at the Air and Space Museum in Washington, said, "in the overall scheme of world history, it's probably not significant. But it's nice to know that what he thought he said, he actually did say, and that because of the nature of the electronic and communications systems of the time, it [B] _____."

28 Which one of the following is closest in meaning to the underlined expression [A] the acoustic record begged to differ?

① He asked permission to use the acoustic record in a different way.
② What he claimed was different from what the grammarians asserted.
③ His assertion did not agree with what the acoustic record seemed to indicate.
④ The acoustic record was not clear enough to identify his words.
⑤ The acoustic record was considered to be incorrect by the grammarians.

29 According to the context, which of the following best fits into [B]?

① just did not get through
② turned out to be nothing
③ was well worth waiting for
④ did not matter to us anyhow
⑤ was decided to accept his assertion

[30-31] 서강대 2017

Sound system of a language is broadly divided into two categories: consonant and vowel sounds (known as the segmental features) and more global aspects such as stress, rhythm, and intonation (known as suprasegmental features or prosody). Traditionally, the sound system has been described and taught in a building-block fashion: sounds > syllables > words > phrase > sentences > extended discourse. Although this makes sense from an analytical point of view, this is usually not how the language learners experience language. As speakers, we usually do not think about what we are saying sound by sound, or even syllable by syllable, Ⓐ _____ communication breaks down. So the bottom-up approach of mastering one sound at a time and eventually stringing sounds together has been replaced by a bit more top-down approach in which the sound system is addressed in the stream of speech.

30 Choose the best words or phrases for blank Ⓐ.

① lest
② unless
③ provided
④ as

31 Choose the statement LEAST consistent with the passage.

① Prosody is judged more important than segmental features in natural speech.
② Consonants and vowels are building blocks in the analytical view of sounds.
③ Language description and language learning are considerably disparate.
④ Communication breakdown demonstrates the analytical nature of language.

[32-34] 한국외대 2013

Now, consider: *gray, wrinkled, bingo, Florida*. If you were now to get up from your chair and walk to your kitchen, you would do so more slowly having read these words than if you hadn't read them. "Gray", "wrinkled", "bingo", and "Florida" are all part of the stereotype of elderly people. When John Bargh, a social psychologist at New York University presented participants with these words and others, embedded in scrambled sentences, something quite remarkable happened. After scrambling the sentences containing elderly stereotype words, participants were told that the study was over and they could leave. In fact, the study wasn't quite over yet. The experimenters surreptitiously timed participants as they walked from the experiment room to a nearby elevator. In one of the most fascinating findings in the past couple of decades of social psychology research, Bargh found that participants exposed to the elderly stereotype took significantly longer to reach the elevator than did those in a control condition, who unscrambled sentences containing neutral words.

This effect, just like the one presented earlier, is another example of priming. When people are exposed to words like *Florida* and *wrinkled*, activation spreads from these to other,

related concepts that are linked because they are part of the elderly stereotype. What happened in Bargh's study was that exposure to the elderly stereotype primed the concept "slow," and this activation leaked out into behavior, _____.
So just thinking about slowness, and not even intentionally, can impact the way we act.

32 Which of the following would be the best topic of the passage?

① How research participants should be controlled in experiments
② How language processing works in sentence-scrambling experiments
③ Why certain words are grouped together in the brain
④ How viewing stereotype words affects behavior

33 According to the context, the text preceding the above passage is most likely to be about _____.

① an example illustrating the 'priming' effect
② different stereotypes about the elderly
③ a profile of Professor John Bargh
④ the design of John Bargh's experiment

34 According to the context, which of the following best fits into the blank?

① exposing participants to prejudice
② slowing participants down
③ intensifying the stereotype even further
④ making participants ponder old age

[35-36] 한국외대 2014

Although English is the official language in the Philippines, Spanish is still perceived as an elite language for its historical and cultural importance, much more than English. In fact, Mestizo families and young students continue to use Spanish, especially in the provinces of Cebu, Zamboanga, and Bacolod. This is a consequence of the Spanish roots left in the Filipino language throughout the colonial period, from 1565, when the Spanish language was first introduced, up to the beginning of the twentieth century, when the American hegemony started. In 1990 there were about 2,700 Spanish speakers in the country. This number does not include the 1,200,000 natives who speak Chavacano, one of the 170 languages of the Philippines and the most similar one to Spanish. Currently in the Philippines there are many borrowings from Spanish. Because of the cultural basis and for historical reasons, the country supports the use of Spanish in legal documents and in court. However, Spanish has not been the official language since 1973, and from the 1980s it has no longer been a compulsory subject in schools.

35 Which of the following is the best title of the passage?

① Dominance of Spanish in the Philippines
② Spanish Threatening Filipino National Identity
③ Status of Spanish in the Philippines
④ Spanish Revitalization Among Filipino People

36 Which of the following is true of the passage?

① Spanish is spoken in certain Mestizo families in the Philippines.
② Spanish loanwords are rare in the Philippines.
③ Spanish was prohibited during the American hegemony.
④ Spanish is excluded from the courtrooms of the Philippines.

[37-38] 한양대 2015

Pidgins and creoles are the outcome of the need of people not sharing a language to communicate. They differ from national and international languages in that a pidgin does not begin as an already existing language or dialect selected to serve this purpose; it is rather a particular combination of two languages. Loreto Todd has the following to say about pidgins and creoles:

A pidgin is a marginal language which arises to fulfil certain restricted communication needs among people who have no common language. In the initial stages of contact the communication is often limited to transactions where a detailed exchange of ideas is not required and where a small vocabulary, drawn almost exclusively from one language, suffices. The syntactic structure of the pidgin is less complex and less flexible than the structures of the language that were in contact, and though many pidgin features clearly reflect usages in the contact languages, others are unique to the pidgin.

A creole arises when a pidgin becomes the mother tongue of a speech community. The simple structure that characterized the pidgin is carried over into the creole but since a creole, as a mother tongue, must be capable of expressing the whole range of human experience, the lexicon is expanded, and frequently a more elaborate syntactic system evolves.

Since creoles are often not regarded as "real" languages and consequently considered as inferior, it is worth noting that, for example, both French and English may be the outcome of pidgins—in the first case through contact between native Gauls and occupying Romans, and in the second through contact between the native Anglo-Saxons and the Danes who settled on the east coast of England.

37 윗글의 내용으로 추론할 수 있는 것은?

① French is possibly a creole.
② English is possibly a pidgin.
③ Pidgins develop to promote the exchange of philosophical ideas.
④ A creole becomes a pidgin when a speech community accepts it as its mother tongue.

38 윗글의 내용과 일치하지 않는 것은?

① A pidgin usually develops from two different languages.
② The vocabulary of the pidgin is typically drawn from the two languages that were in contact.
③ A creole can usually express a wider range of human experiences than a pidgin.
④ The structures of the languages that were in contact are generally more flexible than the structure of the pidgin.

[39-40] 성균관대 2016

The idea which people seem to find very hard to grasp is that languages cannot possess good or bad qualities; no language system can ever be shown to be clearer or more logical (or more beautiful or more ugly) than any other language system. Where differences of clarity and logic are to be found is not in the language itself but in the abilities of different user of the language to handle it effectively. Some French speakers produce utterances which are marvellous in their lucidity, while others can always be relied upon to produce impenetrable gibberish—but it is the speakers who deserve our praise or blame, not the language.

How is it that so obviously mythical an idea as the logicality of French has taken such strong root in France and to some extent among her neighbors? The external perceptions of French are not too hard to explain—they seem to be bound up with the _____ which developed in Europe a century ago and which are sadly still around today. Italian became a 'musical language', no doubt because of its association with Italian opera; German became a 'harsh, guttural language' because of Prussian militarism; Spanish became 'a romantic language' because of bull-fighters and flamenco dancing; French almost inevitably became a 'logical language' thanks to prestigious philosophers like Descartes, whose mode of thinking was felt to contrast sharply with that of the 'pragmatic English'.

39 The most appropriate expression for the blank would be _____.

① leader's vision
② national stereotypes
③ people's imagination
④ national economy
⑤ people's wish

40 According to the author, an English man _____.

① cannot be a romantic guy
② may not be so practical
③ doesn't sing in the opera
④ cannot speak French
⑤ is not logical

CHAPTER 05 심리

[01-04] 성균관대 2008

> Research on the psychology of happiness has borne out the curmudgeons. Kahneman and Tversky give an everyday example. You open your paycheck and are delighted to find you have been given a five percent raise—until you learn that your co-workers have been given a ten percent raise. According to legend, the diva Maria Callas stipulated that any opera house she sang in had to pay her one dollar more than the next highest paid singer in the company.
>
> People today are safer, healthier, better fed, and longer-lived than at any time in history. Yet we don't spend our lives walking on air, and presumably our ancestors were not chronically glum. It is not reactionary to point out that many of the poor in today's Western nations live in conditions that yesterday's aristocrats could not have dreamed of. People in different classes and countries are often content with their lot until they compare themselves to the more affluent. The amount of violence in a society is more closely related to its (가) _____ than to its (나) _____. In the second half of the twentieth century, the discontent of the Third World, and later the Second, have been attributed to their glimpses through the mass media of the First.

01 According to the passage, men can be happy only if _____.

① they don't have anybody to compare with
② they achieve something for which they have worked
③ they want everything
④ they have nothing to lose
⑤ they fall in love with someone

02 Which one describes the different notion of happiness?

① How bitter a thing it is to look into happiness through another man's eye!
② Happiness is an agreeable sensation arising from contemplating the misery of others.
③ It is not enough to succeed. Others must fail.
④ Anything you're good at contributes to happiness.
⑤ When does a hunchback rejoice? When he sees one with a larger hump.

03 Choose the one which is most appropriate for the blanks (가) and (나)?

① poverty – dictatorship
② dictatorship – atrocity
③ inequality – poverty
④ atrocity – politics
⑤ politics – inequality

04 According to the passage, development of mass media would _____.

① destroy the private lives of common people
② result in the equal society
③ make the entertaining businesses prosper
④ calm down the complaints of the Third World
⑤ produce more unhappy people

[05-07] 한국외대 2008

Probably the most frequently used attention device in public speaking is what is known as the 'common ground' technique. The speaker begins by identifying similarities that she and her audience possess in political or religious background, place of birth, ethnic heritage, or interest in certain sports. When Princess Margaret of the United Kingdom visited the Kentucky Derby and was asked to present a cup to the owner of the winning thoroughbred, she began her presentation speech by recalling the similarities between the Kentucky Derby and English Derby. ⓐ _____, she was deemphasizing her uniqueness as a princess from a foreign country and highlighting the interest in racing that she shared with her audience. This kind of 'recognition of sameness' between the speaker and listeners is an often-used method for ensuring audience attention. If there is little that is really common to both to which the speaker can honestly refer, she would be wise to choose another attention device. For a speaker to imply that she has had certain experiences which she actually has not had in order to establish common ground is not only a dangerous practice—it is also unethical.

05 Which of the following is not answered by the author?

① What are the ways of showing similarities between speakers and listeners?
② What technique did Princess Margaret use in her speech at the Kentucky Derby?
③ What is the aim of using the method of 'recognition of sameness'?
④ What is the name of a form of dishonest public speaking?
⑤ What is the purpose of the 'common ground' technique?

06 Which of the following is the title of the passage?

① How to get Audience Attention
② Types of Audience Reactions
③ How to Arrange Speech Topics
④ Practical Use of Ethical Topics
⑤ How to Conclude Public Speech

07 Which of the following best fits into ⓐ?

① At last
② For example
③ By doing this
④ On the other hand
⑤ Unfortunately

[08-10]

> The typical extrovert is sociable, likes parties, has many friends, needs to have people to talk to, and does not like reading or studying by himself. He craves excitement, takes chances, often sticks his neck out, acts on the spur of the moment, and is generally an impulsive individual. He is fond of practical jokes, always has a ready answer, and generally likes change; he is carefree, easy-going, optimistic, and likes to "laugh and be merry." He prefers to keep moving and doing things, tends to be aggressive and lose his temper quickly; altogether his feelings are not kept under tight control, and he is not always a reliable person. The typical introvert is a quiet retiring sort of person, introspective, fond of books rather than people; he is reserved and distant except to intimate friends. He tends to plan ahead, "looks before he leaps," and distrusts the impulse of the moment. He does not like excitement, takes matters of everyday life with proper seriousness, and likes a well-ordered mode of life. He keeps his feelings under close control, seldom behaves in an aggressive manner, and does not lose his temper easily. He is reliable, somewhat pessimistic, and places great value on ethical standards.

08 Which of the following cannot be inferred from the passage?

① Introverts are not as dynamic as extroverts.
② Extroverts tend to be more cautious than introverts.
③ Compared to introverts, extroverts are spontaneous.
④ If extroverts have many friends, introverts have few.

09 What is the author's purpose in the passage?

① to state that the definitions of extroverts and introverts are rather abstract
② to suggest that extroverts have better personalities than introverts
③ to imply that introverts and extroverts show almost polar characteristics
④ to argue that people are a combination of introversion and extroversion

10 Which of the following is not a characteristic of an introvert?

① He is gregarious.
② He is responsible.
③ He rarely displays emotion.
④ He is a moral person.

[11-13]

The brain structure that processes perceptions and thoughts and tags them with the warning "Be afraid, be very afraid!" is the amygdala. Located near the brain's center, this almond-shaped bundle of neurons evolved long before the neocortex, the seat of conscious awareness. There is good reason for the fear circuitry to be laid down first.
Any proto-humans who lacked a well-honed fear response did not survive long enough to evolve higher-order thinking: unable to react quickly and intuitively to rustling bushes or advancing shadows, they instead became some carnivore's dinner. Specifically, fear evolved because it promotes survival by triggering an individual to respond instantly to a threat—that is, without cogitating on it until the tiger has pounced. Human brains that detect fear and act on it behave in ways that are ultimately in our interest. They lead us to protect ourselves and our family. The evolutionary primacy of the brain's fear circuitry makes it more powerful than the brain's reasoning faculties. Fear tends to ⓐ _____, as the amygdala hobbles our logic and reasoning circuits. That makes fear far more powerful than reason. It evolved as a mechanism to protect us from life-threatening situations, and from an evolutionary standpoint there's nothing more important than that.

11 윗글의 제목으로 가장 적절한 것은?

① The Power of Brain
② The Power of Fear
③ The Fever of Fear
④ Fear Is Against Us

12 윗글의 내용과 일치하지 않는 것은?

① The amygdala was laid down long before the neocortex, the seat of conscious awareness.
② Fear response is a brain mechanism to protect us from life-threatening dangers.
③ Fear is far more powerful than reason because it is more destructive and carnivorous.
④ Fear promotes survival by triggering an individual to respond instantly to a threat.

13 빈칸 ⓐ에 들어갈 가장 적절한 단어는?

① enhance
② deliver
③ guide
④ overrule

[14-16] 숭실대 2013

When we remember our past selves, they seem quite different. We know how much our personalities and tastes have changed over the years. But when we look ahead, somehow we expect ourselves to stay the same, a team of psychologists said Thursday, describing research they conducted of people's self-perceptions.

They called this phenomenon the "end of history illusion," in which people tend to "underestimate how much they will change in the future." According to their research, which involved more than 19,000 people ages 18 to 68, the illusion persists from teenage years into retirement.

"Middle-aged people—like me—often look back on our teenage selves with some mixture of amusement and disappointment," said one of the authors, Daniel T. Gilbert, a psychologist at Harvard. "What we never seem to realize is that our future selves will look back and think the very same thing about us. At every age we think (1) we're having the last word, and at every age we're wrong."

Other psychologists said they were intrigued by the findings, published Thursday in the journal *Science*, and were impressed with the amount of supporting evidence.

Participants were asked about their personality traits and preferences—their favorite foods, vacations, hobbies and bands—in years past and present, and then asked to make predictions for the future. Not surprisingly, the younger people in the study reported more change in the previous decade than did the older respondents.

But when asked to predict what their personalities and tastes would be like in 10 years, people of all ages consistently (2) _____ the potential changes ahead.

Thus, the typical 20-year-old woman's predictions for her next decade were not nearly as radical as the typical 30-year-old woman's recollection of how much she had changed in her 20s. This sort of discrepancy persisted among respondents all the way into their 60s.

14 Which of the following best paraphrases (1)?

① Our future will never be the same.
② Our future will not change much.
③ The best is yet to come to our future.
④ We will be the ultimate winners of life.

15 Which of the following fits best in (2)?

① fantasized about
② overestimated
③ worried about
④ played down

16 According to the passage, which of the following is NOT true?

① It is easy to recall the past.
② It is hard to predict the future.
③ We remember both positive and negative parts of life.
④ Life will be almost the same after 50.

[17-18] 중앙대 2013

To study social conformity, Philip Zimbardo and Craig Haney (1977) advertised in newspapers for volunteers to take part in a mock prison experiment. The volunteers were randomly assigned roles as "prisoners" and "guards." Both groups were placed in the basement of the Stanford University psychology building and given minimal instructions; they were told to assume their assigned roles and that the guards' job was to "maintain law and order." In only a few hours, the behavior of one group became sharply differentiated from the behavior of the other group. The guards adopted the behavior patterns and attitudes that are typical of guards in maximum security prisons, with most of them becoming abusive and aggressive. Most of the prisoners became passive, dependent, and depressed, although some became enraged at the guards. Suffering among the prisoners was so great that one had to be released in less than thirty-six hours;

several other prisoners also had to be released before the intended two-week experiment was ended after six days.

Stereotypical social norms controlled the behavior of both groups. The guards adopted a manner they believed was necessary to simulate their role and maintain order. The prisoners, who were the targets of the guards' abuse, assumed attitudes that accorded with their image of prison life. As the groups became antagonistic, each reinforced the other's behavior. The prisoners expected the guards to be mean and vicious and treated them accordingly. The guards expected the prisoners to be rebellious and acted so as to prevent unruly behavior. A situation of pretense, by virtue of the participants' perceptions, had real effects on the feelings and behavior of everyone involved. As this experiment shows, conformity to social norms is not simply the result of social pressures from one's own group; the influence of other groups in society magnifies the pressure to conform.

17 윗글의 제목으로 가장 적합한 것을 고르시오.

① Psychological Insecurity of Inmates
② Efficacy of Stereotypical Social Norms
③ Behavior Change in a New Environment
④ Influence of Conformity on Social Behavior

18 윗글의 내용과 일치하는 것을 고르시오.

① Conformity prevented the situation from getting worse.
② The participants behaved according to stereotypical social norms.
③ The prisoner group pretended to be passive because of the instructions.
④ Social pressure to conform within a group is mitigated by contact with other groups.

[19-20] 한국외대 2007

The more resonant the images, the more difficult they are to forget. But even meaningful information is hard to remember when there's a lot of it. That's why competitive memorizers place their images along an imaginary route. That technique, known as the loci method, reportedly originated in 447 BC with the Greek poet Simonides of Ceos. Simonides was the sole survivor of a roof collapse that killed all the other guests at a royal banquet. The bodies were mangled beyond recognition, but Simonides was able to reconstruct the guest list by closing his eyes and recalling each individual around the dinner table. What he had discovered was that our brains are exceptionally good at remembering image and spatial information. Evolutionary psychologists have offered an explanation: Presumably our ancestors found it important to recall ⓐ _____. After Simonides' discovery, the loci method became popular across ancient Greece as a trick for memorizing speeches and texts. Aristotle wrote about it, and later a number of treatises on the art of memory were published in Rome. Before printed books, the art of memory was considered a staple of classical education, on a par with grammar, logic, and rhetoric.

19 Which of the following best fits into ⓐ?

① how they responded to the stimuli passively
② how to keep raw materials in a safe place
③ where they found their last meal or the way back to the cave
④ where they wanted the dinner table, and when they wanted to eat
⑤ how they reacted with smiles to hugging from their mothers

20 Which of the following is NOT stated or implied in the passage?

① Simonides could store mental snapshots and recall them with considerable fidelity.
② The brain's right hemisphere is known to be involved in visual memory and spatial information.
③ Some people can use visual imagery and spatial information to activate their memory.
④ Aristotle used the loci method to retain parts of speeches.
⑤ People used the loci method at schools in Rome before printed books.

[21-24] 이화여대 2009

The drop in self-esteem in adolescence was no surprise to Richard Robins, a psychology professor, who ⓐ <u>spearheaded</u> the study, but "the drop in old age is ⓑ _____," he said. Specifically, Robins was intrigued by the similarities in self-esteem levels between those entering adolescence and old age. "There is an accumulation of losses occurring all at once both in old age and adolescence," he suggested. "There is a critical mass of transition going on." Everybody is an individual, Robins stressed, so self-esteem can be affected by a number of things that are biological, social, and situational, but there are certain passages that all of us face—and each passage can have a powerful effect on your sense of self. "With kids, their feelings about themselves are often based on ⓒ _____," Robins explained. "As we get older, we base our self-esteem on actual achievements and feedback from other people."

21 Which of the following may replace ⓐ?

① analyzed
② contemplated
③ criticized
④ organized

22 Which of the following may best fit in ⓑ?

① dour
② sickening
③ novel
④ exploitative

23 Which of the following best fits in ⓒ?

① statistical evidence
② superficial information
③ peer responses
④ particular results

24 Which writing strategy is not adopted by the author?

① quotation ② comparison and contrast
③ anecdote ④ cause and effect

[25-27] 숭실대 2009

> The hallmarks of adolescence are self-consciousness, self-awareness and self-centeredness. Coupled with these is an inner conflict that seems to be a prerequisite of growing up. A stubborn determination to assert independence conflicts with a continuing need to rely on adult support in both emotional and financial aspects of life. The typical adolescent demands the right to question and criticize parental behavior and standards and resents parental efforts to shape and control his or her own behavior.
>
> Adolescent children are unlikely to reject their parents' values completely, but they will not completely accept them either. Quiet, cooperative teenagers often have as much inner conflict as their outwardly rebellious brothers or sisters, and they may have underlying disorders or developmental problems. Some clashes between parents and normal teenage children are inevitable.
>
> Teenagers are often moody and sullen. They tend to act as if they know everything, to reject advice from their elders, and to see situations from only their own viewpoint. Yet, they are inwardly much less confident ⓐ _____. For instance, they tend to attach extreme importance to outward appearance. Their adoption of outrageous fashions or ⓑ 'in' hair styles may seem to their elders to be an unpleasant flouting of convention. In fact, however, it is more likely to be an acceptance of the conventions of their peers. Lacking the self-confidence to be themselves, most teenagers need the security of dressing and behaving like the rest of their group.

25 Choose the expression that would fit best in ⓐ.

① as they seem ② than they seem
③ as they are ④ than they are

26 According to the passage, which of the following is NOT true?

① Adolescence is the time of self-confidence
② Adolescents are determined to assert independence.
③ Teenagers do not easily accept their parents' advice.
④ Teenagers need to rely on adults emotionally and financially.

27 Which of the following usages of 'in' is the same as ⓑ '<u>in</u>'?

① My roommate was <u>in</u> at the time.
② Simpson looked at them <u>in</u> surprise.
③ A few years ago jogging was the <u>in</u> thing.
④ The young Raphael painted <u>in</u> the style of Leonardo.

[28-29] 한양대 2007

Aristotle distinguished three types of friendship in *The Nicomanchean Ethics*: "friendship based on utility", such as businessmen cultivating each other for benefit; "friendship based on pleasure", like young people interested in partying; and "perfect friendship." The first two categories Aristotle calls "qualified and superficial friendships", because they are founded on circumstances that could easily change; the last, which is based on admiration for another's good character, is more permanent, but also rarer, because good men "are few." Cicero, who wrote perhaps the best treatise on friendship, also insisted that what brings true friends together is "a mutual belief in each other's goodness." This insistence on virtue as a precondition for true friendship may strike us as impossibly demanding: who, after all, feels himself good nowadays? And yet, if I am honest, I must admit that the friendships of mine which have lasted longest have been with those whose integrity, or humanity, or strength to bear their troubles I continue to admire. _____, when I lost respect for someone, however winning he otherwise remained, the friendship petered away almost immediately. "Remove respect from friendship", said Cicero, "and you have taken away the most splendid ornament it possesses."

28 이 글의 흐름상 빈칸에 들어갈 가장 알맞은 것은?

① Finally
② Conversely
③ Admittedly
④ Accordingly

29 이 글의 내용과 일치하는 것은?

① Aristotle views "friendship based on pleasure" as an exceptional one.
② Aristotle denies that perfect friendship is based on a good relationship.
③ Cicero believes that friendship should be based on reciprocal trust.
④ The author judges that Cicero valued the way of revealing rare friendship.

[30-32]

People taking part in a computer game ㉮ design to explore certain impulses in human nature consistently robbed from players assigned the most money while giving money to those with the least, scientists said. The experiment was carried out in a computer lab using 120 student volunteers. Once randomly placed into a group of four, each person was assigned an amount of money and was told how much money the other three members were given. The players then had the chance to spend some of their own money in order to ㉯ _____ or decrease the amount the others possessed, but their actions provided no financial gain for themselves. They played the game five times, but never with anyone from a previous group. This was to eliminate the possibility of players trying to establish a reputation for themselves or taking revenge on others who might have taken money from them. About 70 percent of participants ㉰ _____ or added to another person's money, most often by taking from the richest players or by donating to the poorest players, the study found.

30 According to the passage, what did the experiment reveal?

① Human beings are infinitely adaptable.
② There are egalitarian impulses in human nature.
③ Computer games ultimately could impair human nature.
④ Humans are often taking a pretty selfish attitude over money.

31 What is the right form of the underlined word ㉠ design in the context of the sentence?

① design
② designing
③ designed
④ have designed

32 Which of the following best fills in the blanks ㉡ and ㉢?

① increase – reduced
② minimize – increased
③ increase – expanded
④ minimize – reduced

[33-34] 덕성여대 2011

Keeping a commitment or a promise is a major deposit; breaking one is a major withdrawal. In fact, there's probably not a more massive withdrawal than to make a promise that's important to someone and then not to come through. The next time a promise is made, they won't believe it. People tend to build their hopes around promises, particularly promises about their basic livelihood.

I've tried to adopt a philosophy as a parent never to make a promise I don't keep. I therefore try to make them very carefully, very sparingly, and to be aware of as many variables and contingencies as possible so that something doesn't suddenly come up to keep me from fulfilling it.

Occasionally, despite all my effort, the unexpected does come up, creating a situation where it would be unwise or impossible to keep a promise I've made. But I value that promise. I either keep it anyway, or explain the situation thoroughly to the person involved and ask to be released from the promise.

I believe that if you cultivate the habit of always keeping the promises you make, you build bridges of trust that span the gaps of understanding between you and your child. Then, when your child wants to do something you don't want him to do, and out of your maturity you can see consequences that the child cannot see, you can say, "Son, if you do this, I promise you that this will be the result." If that child has cultivated trust in your word, in your promises, he will act on your counsel.

33 Which of the following states the author's main idea?

① Keeping promises enables you to build bridges of trust.
② Children are as negatively affected by broken promises as for parents.
③ Keeping promises to one's children is particularly important for parents.
④ The worst thing a person can do is break a promise because the other person will not trust you the next time.

34 Which of the following does not relate to keeping commitments in your everyday life?

① Keeping promises should be part of your philosophy.
② You should teach your children never to make promises until they are mature enough to understand the results.
③ You should think about all possible unexpected variables which might prevent you from keeping promises.
④ You should carefully make promises but if you can't keep them, you should give a thorough explanation.

[35-37] 광운대 2007

A serious study by Dr. David Weeks has discovered some very positive information for people society labels "eccentric." The report, which has also been made into a book, concludes that eccentrics live five to ten years longer than average, and that they are usually happier, healthier, and more intelligent than the rest of us. According to this report, some typical traits of eccentrics are that they are creative, nonconforming, strongly obsessed by curiosity, obsessed with one or more hobbies, intelligent, opinionated, and "convinced that he or she is right and the rest of the world is out of step." Eccentric people are sometimes mistakenly viewed as being mildly insane. But, actually, eccentrics choose to behave in an outlandish manner because it gives them positive pleasure. Dr. Weeks explains, "Eccentrics are healthier because they are happier. Stated simply, eccentrics experience much lower levels of stress because they do not feel the need to conform, and lower stress levels mean their immune systems can function more efficiently." So if you feel like walking around in a raincoat on the hottest day of the year or shaving half of your beard off while studying underwater basket-weaving, ⓐ _____! You are not crazy, you are eccentric, which, in turn, is very healthy indeed!

35 윗글의 제목으로 가장 적절한 것을 고르시오.

① Eccentric People Are Mildly Insane
② Embrace Your Eccentricity
③ Eccentrics Are Opinionated
④ Every Individual Is Eccentric

36 윗글의 ⓐ에 가장 적절한 표현을 고르시오.

① consult your friend
② give it a second thought
③ go for it
④ be patient

37 What is the author's attitude toward eccentricity?

① skeptical
② indifferent
③ affirmative
④ negative

[38-40] 한국외대 2012

> Our conceptions of human nature affect every aspect of our lives, from the way we raise our children to the political movements we embrace. Yet just as science is bringing us into a golden age of understanding of human nature, many people are hostile to the very idea. They fear that discoveries about innate patterns of thinking and feeling may be used to justify inequality, to subvert social change, to dissolve personal responsibility, and to strip life of meaning and purpose.
>
> In *The Blank Slate*, Steven Pinker explores the idea of human nature and its moral, emotional, and political colorings. He shows how many intellectuals have denied the existence of human nature by embracing three linked dogmas: The Blank Slate (the mind has no innate traits), the Noble Savage (people are born good and corrupted by society),

and the Ghost in the Machine (each of us has a soul that makes choices free from biology). Each dogma carries a moral burden, so their defenders have engaged in desperate tactics to discredit the scientists who are now challenging them.

Pinker injects calm and rationality into these debates by showing that equality, progress, responsibility, and purpose have nothing to fear from discoveries about a rich human nature. He disarms even the most menacing threats with clear thinking, common sense, and pertinent facts from science and history. Despite its popularity among intellectuals during much of the twentieth century, he argues, the doctrine of the Blank Slate may have done more harm than good.

38 Why do many people disapprove of scientific efforts to understand human nature?

① They want their theories to contribute to new scientific discoveries.
② They feel science is not adequate to explore the human mind.
③ They believe the human mind is something to be studied more rigorously.
④ They worry that the results of such endeavors may be abused.

39 Pinker believes that _____.

① the mind has no innate traits
② people are born good and corrupted by society
③ the doctrine of the Ghost in the Machine is correct
④ science deepens our understanding of human nature

40 Which of the following is NOT stated or implied in the passage?

① The way we rear children depends on our idea of human nature.
② We now have a better understanding of the innate patterns of thinking.
③ Some thinkers believe that people are born bad and improved through education.
④ The Blank Slate is a theory of the human mind which was influential in the 20th century.

[41-43] 홍익대 2012

> Like Madonna, Barbie has developed both a posse of devoted fans and a gang of hostile critics. For millions of children and adults in the United States and around the world, she is the most popular, most enduring of all toys—the doll that children and collectors most love to consume. For others—wary parents and feminist scholars in particular—Barbie is a dangerous weapon against womankind—the icon of idealized femininity they most love to hate or at least interrogate, deconstruct if not destruct. The doll's exaggerated proportions and the standard set by her morbidly thin form have been the center of controversy. (If life-size, her measurements would be something like 36-18-33, depending on who's calculating, and she wouldn't have enough body fat to menstruate regularly.) Indeed, read by many as a metaphor for young women often described pathologically as empty-headed, self-absorbed, anorexic material girls, Barbie has long attracted the ire of feminists, who revile her as yet another manifestation of the damaging myths of female beauty and the feminine body that patriarchy thrusts upon girls and women.

41 Which of the following is NOT true?

① Barbie is popular not only with children but also among adults.
② Parents are wary of feminist scholars' hatred against the icon of idealized femininity.
③ Feminists warn that Barbie can do harm to girls and women themselves.
④ Barbie's exaggerated proportions are associated with the image of anorexic material girls.

42 Which of the following can be inferred from the above passage?

① Feminist scholars are often antagonistic to toy industry.
② People's response to Barbie is split into more than two.
③ Madonna was one of the fans who were attracted to Barbie's measurements.
④ Patriarchy is not free from the charge of reproducing some myths of female beauty.

43. Which attitude does the author assume toward the Barbie controversy?

① analytical
② determined
③ ambivalent
④ aloof

[44-45] 성균관대 2015

Researchers have long been intrigued as to whether an ability to avoid, or defer, gratification is related to outcomes in life. The best-known test is the "marshmallow" experiment, in which children who could refrain from eating the confection for 15 minutes were given a second one. Children who could not wait tended to have lower incomes and poorer health as adults. Dr David Lindahl of Stockholm University used data from a Swedish survey in which more than 13,000 children aged 13 were asked whether they would prefer to receive $140 now or $1,400 in five year's time. About four-fifths of them said they were prepared to wait. Unlike previous researchers, Dr Lindahl was able to track all the children and account for their parental background and cognitive ability. He found that the 13-year-olds who wanted the smaller sum of money at once were 32% more likely to be convicted of a crime during the next 18 years than those children who said they would rather wait for the bigger reward. Individuals who are impatient, he believes, prefer instant benefits and are therefore less likely to be deterred by potential punishments. But those who fret that a person's criminal path is set already as a teenager should not despair. Dr Lindahl offers a remedy. When the respondents' education was included in the analysis, he found that higher educational attainment was linked to a preference for delayed gratification. "I therefore suspect that schooling can deter people from crime by making them value the future more", explains Dr Lindahl.

44. The best title of the above passage would be _____.

① Temptation and Punishment
② Human Behavior and legal Loopholes
③ How to Educate Impatient Children
④ Time Preferences and Criminal Behavior
⑤ Limitations of Higher Education

45 According to the passage, Dr Lindahl's research argues _____.

① educational background and patience are not related
② the "marshmallow" test does not serve any longer as an effective measure of children's self-control
③ kids who delay rewards are more likely to become criminals later
④ patience is not always a virtue
⑤ schooling could make people more likely to postpone rewards

[46-47] 한국외대 2013

> To forgive may be divine, but no one ever said it was easy. When someone has deeply hurt you, it can be extremely difficult to let go of your grudge. But forgiveness is possible—and it can be surprisingly beneficial to your physical and mental health. "People who forgive show less depression, anger and stress and more hopefulness," says Frederic Luskin, Ph.D., author of *Forgive for Good*. "So it can help save on (A) the wear and tear on our organs, reduce the wearing-out of the immune system, and allow people to feel more vital." If you want to begin the healing process, this is what you need to do first: Calm yourself. To defuse your anger, try a simple stress-management technique. Take a couple of breaths and think of something that gives you pleasure: a beautiful scene in nature, someone you love.

46 Which of the following is closest in meaning to (A)?

① Abuse
② Blemish
③ Damage
④ Disfigurement

47 Which of the following is NOT true of the passage?

① Forgiving can help restore our health from impairment.
② Healing through forgiveness requires peace of mind first.
③ Forgiving is sometimes amazingly simple and easy.
④ Getting rid of resentment is difficult to achieve.

[48-49] 성균관대 2013

An uninterrupted night of sleep is a rare commodity—what with TVs blaring, toilets flushing and the occasional plane flying overhead. The sleeping brain is designed to tune out these auditory distractions, but some people's brains do so a lot better than others'. Now researchers have the first clues to understand why.

Scientists at Massachusetts General Hospital analyzed the brain waves of 12 self-described healthy sleepers during a three-night study in a sleep lab. The volunteers were given cozy beds, but throughout the night they were assaulted with 14 sounds—including car traffic, airplane noise and slamming doors—piped through speakers at varying volumes.

It turned out that those who dozed through the loudest noises were those whose brains recorded the most "sleep spindles" on an EEG. Scientists say the spindles, produced by activity in the thalamus (a region deep in the brain that processes incoming stimuli), can be used as a measure of how well the brain blocks out sound during sleep. And some day, they say, they may be able to manipulate spindle activity to help light sleepers catch more zzz.

48 According to the passage, some people sleep better because they _____.

① hear the less noise
② have quiet neighbors
③ work hard in the daytime
④ sleep on the comfortable beds
⑤ dream more than others

49 According to the passage, the more spindles would mean _____.

① the more noise
② the more dream
③ the better sleep
④ the more stimuli
⑤ the longer sleep

[50-51] 단국대 2016

Although psychology was not recognized as its own field until the late nineteenth century, its early roots can be traced to the ancient Greeks. Plato and Aristotle, for instance, were philosophers concerned with the nature of the human mind. In the seventeenth century, René Descartes distinguished between the mind and body as aspects that interact to create human experience, thus paving the way for modern psychology. While philosophers relied on observation and logic to draw their conclusions, psychologists began to use scientific methods to study human thought and behavior. A German physiologist, Wilhelm Wundt, opened the world's first psychology laboratory at the University of Leipzig in 1879. He used experimental methods to study mental processes, such as reaction times. This research is regarded as marking the beginning of psychology as a separate field. The term psychiatry was first used by a German physician, Johann Reil, in 1808. Ⓐ _____, psychiatry as a field did not become popular until Sigmund Freud proposed a new theory of personality that focused on the role of the unconscious. Ⓑ _____, psychologists were concerned primarily with the conscious aspects of the mind, including perceptions, thoughts, memories, and fantasies of which a person is aware.

50 According to the passage, which is true?

① Plato had an interest in understanding the mind.
② Sigmund Freud paved the way for modern psychology.
③ Modern philosophers began to use scientific methods to study human thought.
④ Johann Reil proposed a new theory of personality that focused on the role of the unconscious.

51 Which is the most appropriate for the blanks Ⓐ and Ⓑ?

① For example – In the meantime
② Otherwise – At the same time
③ As a result – After that time
④ However – Before that time

[52-53] 성균관대 2016

A recent paper by Uma Karmarkar of Harvard Business School and Bryan Bollinger of Duke Fuqua School of Business finds that shoppers who bring their own bags when they buy groceries like to reward themselves for it. For two years the authors tracked transactions at a supermarket in America. Perhaps unsurprisingly, shoppers who brought their own bags bought more green products than those who used the store's bags. But the eco-shoppers were also more likely to buy sweets, ice cream and crisps.

Psychologists call this sort of behaviour "moral licensing." Although this example may seem harmless, the results can be perverse. A study from 2011 on water-conservation in Massachusetts, shows how. In the experiment, some 150 apartments were divided into two groups. Half received water-saving tips and weekly estimates of their usage; the other half served as a control. The households that were urged to use less water did so: their consumption fell by an average of 6% compared with the control group. The hitch was that their electricity consumption rose by 5.6%. The moral licensing was so strong, in other words, that it more or less outweighed the original act of virtue.

Moral licensing seems to occur when _____. In one study, participants imagined themselves doing community service. Then they were asked to pick between two rewards: an indulgent one (a pair of designer jeans) and a practical one (a vacuum cleaner). If they were told to imagine that they had been sentenced to community service for a driving violation, they were much less likely to choose the jeans than if they pictured themselves as volunteers.

52 The underlined expression, "moral licensing" means a tendency _____.

① to act morally in front of others
② to feel morally superior to others
③ to indulge yourself for doing something good
④ to give yourself permission to do something virtuous
⑤ to punish yourself for doing something bad

53 Which of the following is most appropriate for the blank?

① people feel bad about others
② people violate the laws
③ people are not willing to make sacrifices
④ virtuous conduct is not obligatory
⑤ the consumption patterns change

[54-55] 한양대 2017

It is suggested that moods perform an adaptive function. Positive mood indicates that the situation is safe and familiar, and that existing knowledge can be relied upon. In contrast, negative mood functions like a mild alarm signal, indicating that the situation is novel and unfamiliar, and that the careful monitoring of new, external information is required. There is supporting evidence suggesting that positive affect increases, and negative affect decreases—the tendency to rely on internal knowledge rather than external information in cognitive tasks, resulting in a selective memory bias for self-generated information. The theory thus predicts both positive and negative mood can produce processing advantages, albeit in response to different situations requiring different processing styles. Given the almost exclusive emphasis on the benefits of positive affect in our culture, this is an important message with some intriguing real-life implications. Numerous studies now suggests that negative mood can produce definite processing advantages in situations when _____ is required.

54 문맥상 밑줄 친 "adaptive"가 의미하는 것으로 가장 적절한 것은?

① protecting us from a flood of information
② helping us to develop a general-purpose cognitive skill
③ enabling us to change gradually over a long period of time
④ preparing us to respond to different environmental challenges

55 빈칸에 들어갈 가장 적절한 것은?

① the effort-minimizing skill
② the self-generated information
③ the careful monitoring of new, external information
④ the analysis of cognitive, psychological consequences

[56-58] 한국외대 2018

In 1996, the psychologist Roy Baumeister conducted an experiment showing that our willpower is a resource that can be depleted. In the first part of the study, the participants were tested in a room where a batch of freshly baked chocolate chip cookies was invitingly laid out. Not all the participants were allowed to eat the cookies, however. Half of the participants were given permission to indulge their sweet tooth, but the other half were given a batch of radishes to eat instead. In the second part of the study, all the participants were presented with a persistence-testing puzzle, that could only be solved with their utmost concentration after numerous attempts. The performance of the two groups of participants on this puzzle was strikingly contrastive. The participants who were given radishes to eat made far fewer attempts, gave up faster, and, on average, were less successful at solving the puzzle than the participants who had been given cookies. Baumeister concluded that self-control and willpower are resources that we can use across a wide range of tasks, but are ones that may be depleted with excessive use. The participants who had to resist the sweets in the first part of the experiment had depleted their pool of resources and no longer had enough to focus on the puzzle. These results contradicted previous views of self-control and willpower, which thought of self-control as a skill which could be mastered and executed with little consequence. Baumeister's study shows that self-regulation is more like using a muscle. After exercising it strenuously, it is (A) _____. The good news is, like a muscle, willpower may also be strengthened with regular practice and training.

56 According to the passage, why were the participants who ate radishes less successful at solving the puzzle?

① They had spent too much time eating the unsavory radishes.
② They had higher levels of intelligence than the other group.
③ They were angry because they did not get to eat the cookies.
④ They had used up their willpower trying not to eat the cookies.

57 According to the passage, which of the following is true?

① The participants who ate the cookies made more attempts to solve the puzzle.
② Self-control is an innate part of an individual's character.
③ Previously, self-regulation was viewed as a muscle which could be strengthened.
④ People with strong willpower remain persistent without exercise.

58 Which of the following best fits into (A)?
① liable to permanent injuries
② likely to become fatigued
③ replenished quickly
④ easier to use it the next time

[59-60] 한국외대 2017

A recent study examined three areas of father-daughter relationships: engagement, accessibility, and responsibility, within the context of daughter's self-esteem and life satisfaction. Ⓐ The researchers defined engagement as a father's direct interaction with his child, accessibility as his physical or psychological availability, and responsibility as his provision for the care of the child. Each of these types of involvement directly relates to a child's well-being, the researchers assumed. "What most heavily affects children's current and future behavior is the long term parent 'residue' within the children that is encapsulated within the children's retrospective perceptions of their parents," the authors wrote. Ⓑ For the study, female participants between the ages of 18 and 21 were recruited and completed an in-depth psychological questionnaire. Ⓒ Overall, results supported the prediction that the retrospective perceptions of a father's involvement have a moderately strong positive relationship with the self-esteem of emerging adult daughters. When emerging adult daughters' retrospective perceptions of father involvement during adolescence are higher, the self-esteem of daughters is also higher. Ⓓ Likewise, there was a positive relationship between perceived levels of father involvement and the life satisfaction level of their daughters.

59 Which of the following is the best place for the sentence below?

> What is unique about this study, then, is that it is all about a daughter's *perception* of her father's involvement and not the *facts* of his involvement.

① Ⓐ
② Ⓑ
③ Ⓒ
④ Ⓓ

60 According to the passage, which of the following is true?

① Accessibility is defined as a father's direct interaction with his child.
② The researchers used thorough questionnaires completed by emerging adults.
③ The researchers' assumption on the topic belies the result.
④ Father's engagement is not fundamental to a daughter's well-being.

에듀윌 편입영어 **기출심화 완성 독해**

PART 04

문화 · 예술

CHAPTER 01   문화
CHAPTER 02   정보 · 기술
CHAPTER 03   지역 · 지리
CHAPTER 04   음악 · 미술
CHAPTER 05   영화 · 스포츠

CHAPTER 01 문화

[01-03] 이화여대 2009

Theories of culture often end by seeing individuals as completely enclosed by a set of pre-existing values to which they must (A) _____. For some conservative critics, this leads to a (B) <u>reduction</u> in individual moral responsibility. To others, it results in a (C) _____ and (D) _____ image of culture as an immoveable burden that leaves us no freedom for dissent, negotiation and subversion. American anthropologist and cultural critic James Clifford has written: 'Since the mid-nineteenth century, ideas of culture have gathered up those elements that seem to give continuity and depth to collective experience, seeing it whole rather than disputed, torn, intertextual, or syncretic.' According to Clifford, we do need a term like culture to explain patterns in human behaviour that are neither generically human nor specific to the individual. Yet we also need to recognize cultures as internally unstable and riven, with perimeters that are unmappable and contested.

01 Which is the most appropriate in (A)?

① overcome
② exceed
③ become subordinate
④ become disengaged

02 Which word can be replaced with (B)?

① reanimation
② diminishment
③ aggrandizement
④ retardation

03 Which words are the most fitting in (C) and (D)?

① fatalistic — pessimistic
② existential — inevitable
③ penultimate — dismissive
④ egalitarian — humanitarian

[04-06] 숭실대 2006

People from different cultures often misinterpret each other's signals. In the conversations of Athabaskan Indians, a pause of up to about one and a half seconds does not necessarily indicate the end of a turn, and Athabaskans often pause that long within a turn. In contrast, most European Americans consider a pause of more than one second sufficient to signal the end of a turn (although there may be social variation). When Athabaskan Indians and European Americans interact with each other, the latter often misinterpret the Athabaskans' midturn pauses as end-of-turn signals and feel free to claim the floor. From the Athabaskans' perspective, the European Americans' claim of the floor at this point constitutes an interruption. With the same situation occurring time and again in interactions between the two groups, negative stereotypes arise. Athabaskans find European American rude, pushy, and uncontrollably talkative, while European Americans find Athabaskans conversationally uncooperative, sullen, and incapable of carrying on a coherent conversation. Unwittingly carrying those stereotypes into a classroom, European-American teachers may judge Athabaskan students to be unresponsive or unintelligent, because the teachers' unspoken ⓐ _____ are for students to speak up, interact, and be quick in their responses. While these tend to be the actions of children in mainstream European-American culture, Athabaskan children, honoring the norms of their own culture, tend not to behave in that manner. Though most people are unaware of such subtle cross-cultural differences, ⓑ _____.

04 Which of the following words fits best in blank ⓐ?

① cultural expectations
② personal intuitions
③ racial attitudes
④ social proficiencies

05 According to the passage, which of the following statements is INCORRECT regarding cross-cultural linguistic behavior?

① European-American teachers regard their Athabaskan students as reticent.
② Athabaskans regard European Americans as impolite.
③ European-American speakers yield the floor more frequently than Athabaskan speakers do.
④ Athabaskan students are labeled by their European-American teachers as incoherent.

06 Which of the following statements fits best in blank ⓑ as a conclusion?

① they can result in better interpersonal skills
② they can have profound social consequences
③ they can be used to enhance people's reputations
④ they can develop into a monolingual society

[07-09] 한국외대 2010

For more than a century, Western philosophers and psychologists have based their discussions of mental life on a cardinal assumption—that the same basic processes underlie all human thought. Cultural differences might dictate what people thought about. But western scholars assumed that the habits of thought—the strategies people adopted in processing information and making sense of the world around them—were ㉮ _____ for everyone: logical reasoning, categorization, and understanding events in linear terms of cause and effect.

Recent work by a social psychologist at the University of Michigan, however, is turning this long-held view of mental functioning upside down. In a series of studies comparing European Americans to East Asians, Dr. Richard Nisbett and his colleagues have found that people who grow up in different cultures do not just think about different things, they think differently. "We used to think that everybody uses categories in the same way, that logic plays the same kind of role for everyone in the understanding of everyday life, and that memory, perception, and so on are the same," Dr. Nisbett said. "But we're now arguing that cognitive processes themselves are far more different from ㉯ what mainstream psychology assumed."

07 Which of the following is the best title of the passage?

① Cultural Influences on Mainstream Western Philosophy
② Changes of Western Philosopher's Notion of Common Sense
③ Diverse Views in Psychology on Logical Reasoning
④ Long-held Views in Western Philosophy and Psychology
⑤ Newly Found Cultural Influence on Thinking Processes

08 Which of the following best fits into ㉮?

① peculiar
② ingrained
③ identical
④ inherited
⑤ manipulable

09 Which of the following does ㉯ refer to?

① That thinking processes are basically the same in all cultures
② That the ways of logical reasoning are dependant upon different generations
③ That our everyday life is governed by logical thinking
④ That people comprehend events in a circular way to identify cause and effect
⑤ That the method people use for calculation is affected by how they think

[10-12] 숭실대 2008

Taboo is the prohibition or avoidance in any society of behavior believed to be harmful to its members in that it would cause them anxiety, embarrassment, or shame. Consequently, so far as language is concerned, certain things are not to be said or certain objects can be referred to only in certain circumstances, only by certain people, or through deliberate circumlocutions, i.e., euphemistically. Of course, there are always those who are prepared to break the (A) in an attempt to show their own freedom from such social constraints or to expose the (B) as irrational and unjustified, as in certain movements for 'free speech.' Tabooed subjects can vary widely: sex, death, excretion, bodily functions, religious matters, and politics. Tabooed objects that must be avoided or used carefully can include your mother-in-law, certain game animals, and use of your left hand (the origin of 'sinister'). English has its (C), and most people who speak English know what these are and observe the 'rules.' When someone breaks the rules, that rupture may arouse considerable comment, although not perhaps quite as much today as formerly, as when Shaw's use of 'bloody' in *Pygmalion* or the use of 'damn' in the movie *Gone with the Wind* aroused widespread public (D). Standards and norms change.

10 Among (A), (B), (C), and (D), which one CANNOT be properly filled with the word taboo(s)?

① (A) ② (B)
③ (C) ④ (D)

11 According to the passage, which of the following does NOT count as a tabooed subject?

① Why do you believe in God?
② Did you vote for the Labor Party this time?
③ How much did you pay for your new home?
④ How often do you urinate a day?

12 According to the passage, which of the following is true?

① Taboos are strictly obeyed.
② Taboos become more important these days.
③ People break taboos for no obvious reasons.
④ Judgment about taboos changes over time.

[13-15] 명지대 2008

One of the most notable features of the Blue Mosque in Istanbul is visible from far away: its six minarets. This is very unique, as most mosques have four, two or just one minaret. According to one account, the Sultan directed his architect to make gold (altin) minarets, which was misunderstood as six (alti) minarets. Whatever the origins of the unique feature, the six minarets caused quite a scandal, as the mosque in Mecca also had six minarets. The problem was solved by adding a seventh minaret to Mecca's mosque. The main, west entrance is beautifully decorated and should not be missed. However, to preserve the mosque's sanctity, non-worshippers are required to use the north entrance, off the Hippodrome. Hanging from this gate are symbolic chains that encourage everyone, even the sultan on horseback, to bow his or her head upon entering. The interior's high ceiling is lined with about 20,000 blue tiles that give the mosque its popular name.

13 윗글의 내용과 다른 것은?

① Only Moslems are allowed to use the west entrance.
② Both entrances have symbolic chains hung low to make people bow upon entering.
③ The decoration of the main entrance is very beautiful.
④ The minarets of the Blue Mosque are visible from far away.

14 현재 메카에 있는 이슬람 사원의 첨탑 수는 몇 개인가?

① four ② five
③ six   ④ seven

15 이스탄불에 있는 이슬람 사원이 지금의 명칭을 갖게 된 이유는?

① The color of the main entrance
② The color of the minarets
③ The color of the symbolic chains hanging from the gate
④ The color of the tiles lined around the interior's high ceiling

[16-17] 한국외대 2007

When the British discuss migration, they usually mean foreigners coming to take their jobs and council flats. Much less notice is taken of the increasing stream of people heading the other way. That is because no one really knows how many Britons live abroad. No proper data on the subject have been gathered since the 19th century. Recent reports reveal that almost 200,000 Britons left the country in 2006 with no plans to return, and 5.5 million people now make their home abroad.

Why do people leave? Better jobs and a better life, say most of those who have already gone, and a quarter of those who are still flirting with the idea cite the high cost of living in Britain. Expensive houses are another reason: they enable home owners to sell their home and buy a bigger place abroad, and push the young and houseless to consider a move. Most leave because other countries sound better: a nicer climate, a higher quality of life. And who can blame them? Real disposable incomes barely rose between 2003 and 2005, and the quality of life is mediocre.

16 According to the passage, what makes the British focus on immigration rather than emigration, when it comes to migration in Britain?

① Data manipulation
② Lack of statistics
③ Government policies
④ Europe's unification
⑤ Financial problems

17 According to the passage, which of the following is true?

① Recently, emigrants outnumbered immigrants in Britain.
② The low pension in Britain is the main reason for leaving.
③ The national traits of the British discourage them from moving overseas.
④ Higher quality life is one main reason for considering emigration.
⑤ Young people feel less likely to leave Britain than their elders.

[18-19] 가톨릭 2013

Culture shock is precipitated by the anxiety that results from losing all familiar signs and symbols of social intercourse. These signs are the numerous ways in which we orient ourselves to the situations of daily life: when to shake hands, what to say when we meet people, etc. These signs, which may be words, gestures, facial expressions, customs, or norms, are acquired by all of us in the course of growing up and are as much a part of our culture as the language we speak or the beliefs we accept.

When an individual enters a strange culture, all or most of these familiar cues are removed. He or she is like _____. No matter how broad-minded or full of good will he may be, a series of props have been knocked from under him. (A) This is followed by a feeling of frustration and anxiety. People react to the frustration in much the same way. First they reject the environment which causes the discomfort: "the ways of the host country are bad because they make us feel bad." (B) Another phase of culture shock is regression. (C) The home environment suddenly assumes tremendous importance. (D) All difficulties and problems are forgotten and only the good things back home are remembered. It usually takes a trip home to bring one back to reality.

18 빈칸에 들어갈 가장 적절한 표현을 고르시오.

① a needle in a haystack
② a fish out of water
③ a castle in the sky
④ a cart before the horse

19 다음 문장이 들어갈 가장 적절한 곳을 고르시오.

> Everything becomes irrationally glorified.

① (A)
② (B)
③ (C)
④ (D)

[20-21] 단국대 2013

So many of the metaphors that once brought us together in shared wonder have lost their hold on us. The movies no longer grip the majority of us. Even team sports, which seemed unassailable, are growing more controversial as they grow more prosperous and we gain more sophistication about the way they exploit participants. And, in any event, familiarity, due in part to media overexposure, breeds restlessness, if not contempt, with the old metaphors. Looking for something fresh, untainted, we push hopefully into areas that were previously the provinces of buffs and aficionados. We are looking for novelty, of course, but praying as well for a certain purity, the kind that can only develop away from the distorting pressures of the celebrity system. The circus, once a form of mass entertainment, now a quiet backwater to which we take our children out of a sense of obligation to our own past and in hopes of getting them to share our possibly false nostalgia, is such a place— innocent, unworldly, a living anachronism.

20 Which of the following can be inferred from the passage?

① Technologies have grown a sense of nostalgia toward the past.
② People have changed their tastes in entertainment over time.
③ Generations have the same perspectives regarding the traditional metaphors.
④ Movies and sports are the provinces only buffs and maniacs can enjoy.

21 According to the author, the circus is an anachronism in that it _____.

① is a show of animals in groups
② brings joy and excitement to children
③ reflects the celebrity system
④ fails to share the values of today

[22-24] 명지대 2013

In one study of 50 Western American mothers and 48 Chinese immigrant mothers, almost 70% of the Western mothers said either that "stressing academic success is not good for children" or that "parents need to foster the idea that learning is fun." By contrast, roughly 0% of the Chinese mothers felt the same way. Instead, the vast majority of the Chinese mothers said that they believe their children can be "the best" students, that "academic achievement reflects successful parenting," and that if ① they did not excel at school then there was "a problem" and parents "were not doing their job."

Other studies indicate that compared to Western parents, Chinese parents spend approximately ten times as long every day drilling academic activities with their children. By contrast, Western kids are more likely to participate in various sports activities. This brings me to my final point. Some might think that the American sports parent is a(an) (A) _____ to the Chinese mother. This is so wrong. Unlike your typical Western over-scheduling soccer mom, ② they believe that schoolwork always comes first; an A-minus is a bad grade; your children must be two years ahead of their classmates in math; you must never compliment your children in public; if your child ever disagrees with a teacher or coach, you must always take the side of the teacher or coach; the only activities your children should be permitted to do are those in which ③ they can eventually win a medal; and that medal must be gold.

Asian mothers are often portrayed as scheming, callous, overdriven people indifferent to their kids' true interests. For their part, quite a few Chinese mothers secretly believe that they care more about ④ them and are willing to sacrifice much more for them than their Westerner counterparts. I think it's a misunderstanding on both sides. All decent parents want to do what's best for their children. The Chinese just have a totally different idea of how to do that.

22 Choose the most appropriate word for blank (A).

① analogue ② supplement
③ surrogate ④ antithesis

23 Choose the one that is not true according to the passage above.

① A study was conducted on Western & Chinese mothers' attitude towards parenting.
② Chinese mothers do not regard near perfect grades as satisfactory.
③ The author endorses the Chinese mothers' views over those of the Western mothers.
④ Western mothers tend not to overly emphasize their kids' academic achievement.

24 Choose the one that does not refer to the same as the rest.

① they
② they
③ they
④ them

[25-27]

If you read through the arguments and Op-Eds over the past few years about the impact of _____, you'll find that the debate keeps cycling back to two refrains: the impact of blogging on traditional journalism and the impact of Wikipedia on traditional scholarship. In both cases, a trained, institutionally accredited elite has been challenged by what the blogger Glenn Reynolds called an "army of Davids," with much triumphalism, derision and defensiveness on both sides. This is a perfectly legitimate debate to have, since bloggers and Wikipedians are likely to do some things better than their professional equivalents and some things much worse, and we may as well figure out which is which. The problem with spending so much time hashing out these issues is that it overstates the importance of amateur journalism and encyclopedia authoring in the vast marketplace of ideas that the Web has opened up. The fact is that most user-created content on the Web is not challenging the authority of a traditional expert. It's working in a zone where there are no experts or where the users themselves are the experts.

25 Choose the one closest in meaning to the underlined "army of Davids."

① people who have authority
② people who have military inclinations
③ people who are ordinary
④ people who are adventurous

26 Choose the one that best fills in the blank.

① Internet addiction
② Web surfing
③ Internet access
④ Web amateurism

27 What is the purpose of the passage?

① to contrast different types of writing venues on the Web
② to suggest that the Web is an uninhibited sphere of activity
③ to argue that expertise on the Web should be fostered more
④ to persuade people to refrain from posting false information

[28-29] 이화여대 2013

The merging of regional differences through the mixture of the population has been promoted by a certain mobility that characterizes the American people. It has been said that it is unusual to find adult Americans living in the place in which they were born, and while this is an obvious exaggeration, it is nevertheless true that change of [A] _____ is distinctly common. The very extensiveness of the country, moreover, tends to create an attitude of mind that may almost be said to diminish space. Americans are so accustomed to distance that they disregard it. Witness the willingness of the westerner to make trips of five hundred or a thousand miles upon slight occasions, or to drive across the continent for a vacation. In the past Americans have had to reckon with the influence of Webster's spelling book and Lindley Murray's grammar, and at all times public education in America has been a standardizing influence. We respect in language the authority of those who are supposed to know; it is part of our faith in specialists, whether in surgeons or "publicity experts." And [B] _____.

28 Which expression may not replace [A]?

① abode
② habitation
③ dwelling
④ residence
⑤ abatement

29 Which best completes [B]?

① the common pronunciation approximates to that of the well educated class of London and its vicinity
② the uniformity of American English seems to have been something generally recognized at the beginning of the nineteenth century
③ we must not forget the American instinct of conformity and the fact that they readily accept standardization in linguistic matters as in houses, automobiles, and other things
④ as a nation we have paid more attention to the Americanization process than to the self-maintenance process
⑤ these different cultural settings are reflected in the subsequent history of the English language in the region

[30-32] 광운대 2006

Today many people say they do not have heroes. Political figures in today's world of leaders rarely, if ever, appear larger than life to us. In today's world of prying journalists and a television-age public, it seems difficult for anyone to attain _____.
What is worse, we now dredge up information about our past heroes, only to take away their heroism: we now know that John Kennedy ran around with other women; there appears to be evidence that Martin Luther King did, too. And today, more and more of our heroes have been forced to abdicate their hero status as new discoveries of their real lives have been made.

With the loss of our heroes, then, what is left for us to look up to? The buzzword in today's language is "role model," someone whose behavior is "imitated," but not necessarily "courageous" or "heroic." Sports players continue to be regarded as role models by their fans and by the baseball team owners, who have an interest in "selling" the heroic quality of their players. But even being a role model in today's world is not easy. Much of the public, critical of their poor behavior and drug use, has rejected ballplayers as role models. Players' unions, who represent the rights of ballplayers to be treated fairly and paid equitable salaries, will argue that baseball players are just normal people like everybody else, denying any special treatment of them.

If our heroes have died and our role models are scrutinized, what can be said about our society? Perhaps the crux of the issue lies in the fact that Americans have always looked to heroes and role models to exemplify traditional American values. Yet today's public has become ungrateful and ungenerous toward its public figures. It doesn't want to let them get away with having fame and fortune if they are not perfect human beings.

30 Which is implied in the passage?

① Our heroes can be like gods.
② Ballplayers are used too much as role models by the unions.
③ People should be more generous toward their public figures.
④ Ballplayers, in spite of their flaws, should be considered heroes.

31 Why is it hard to become a hero in today's world?

① Because people do not value heroism.
② Because people prefer role models to heroes.
③ Because people deny any special treatment of heroes.
④ Because people dig into other people's private lives.

32 Choose the best phrase for the underlined part.

① heroic stature
② freedom of speech
③ fame and fortune
④ the status as a role model

[33-34] 서울여대 2009

Forty years ago a young, radical journalist helped ignite the War on Poverty with his pioneering book *The Other America*. In its pages, Michael Harrington warned that the recently proclaimed age of affluence was a mirage, that beneath the surface of U.S. prosperity lay tens of millions of people stuck in hopeless poverty that only massive government intervention could help. Today, a new generation of journalists is straining to duplicate Harrington's feat—to convince contemporary America that its economic system doesn't work for millions and that only government can lift them out of poverty. These new journalists face a tougher task than Harrington's though, because all levels of government have spent about $10 trillion on poverty programs since his book appeared, with disappointing, even counterproductive, results. And over the last four decades, millions of poor people, immigrants and native-born alike, have risen from poverty, without recourse to the government programs that Harrington inspired.

33 Which of the following is NOT true according to the passage?

① Michael Harrington was a journalist who called for governmental intervention in poverty.
② According to *The Other America*, many Americans suffered from poverty.
③ The contemporary journalists have been influenced by Harrington's claim.
④ Governmental poverty programs have helped millions of poor people escape from poverty.

34 Which of the following is most likely to follow the passage?

① The achievements of Harrington's strong conviction
② The re-evaluation of Harrington's argument
③ Successful examples of the U.S. governmental efforts to help the poor
④ The positive effects of the U.S. governmental efforts on economy

[35-37] 한국외대 2010

The three great American vices seem to be efficiency, punctuality and the desire for achievement and success. They are the things that make Americans very unhappy and nervous. They steal from them their inalienable right of loafing and cheat them of many a good, idle and beautiful afternoon. One must start out with a belief that there are no catastrophes in this world, and that besides the noble art of getting things done, there is a nobler art of ㉮ _____. On the whole, if you answer letters promptly, the result is about as good or as bad as if you had never answered them at all. If you keep them in your drawer for three months and then read them, you might realize what a waste of time it would have been to answer them all. Writing letters turns our writers into fine promotion salesmen and our college professors into good efficient business executives. In this sense, I can understand Thoreau's ㉯ _____ for Americans who always go to the post office.

35 Which of the following does the author prize the most?

① pursuing excellence
② maintaining motivation
③ slowing down the pace
④ thinking much before acting
⑤ acknowledging the futility of life

36 Which of the following best completes ㉮?

① leaving things undone
② making things organized
③ getting things done perfectly
④ appreciating work done well
⑤ preparing things to work on them

37 Which of the following best completes ㉮?

① praise
② neglect
③ sanction
④ contempt
⑤ sympathy

[38-40] 덕성여대 2011

As befits a nation made up of immigrants from all over the Christian world, Americans have no distinctive Christmas symbols, but we have taken the symbols of all the nations and made them our own. The Christmas tree, the exchange of gifts, the myth of Santa Claus, and the carols of all nations are all elements in the American Christmas of the mid-twentieth century. Though we have no Christmas symbols of our own, the American Christmas still has a distinctive aura by virtue of two characteristic elements.

The first of these is that, as might be expected in a nation as dedicated to the carrying on of business as the American nation, the dominant role of the Christmas festivities has become to serve as a stimulus to retail business. The themes of Christmas advertising begin to appear as early as September, and the open season on Christmas shopping begins in November. Fifty years ago, Thanksgiving Day was regarded as the opening day of the season for Christmas shopping; today, the season opens immediately after Halloween. Thus, virtually a whole month has been added to the Christmas season—for shopping purposes.

Second, the Christmas season of festivities has insensibly combined with the New Year's celebration into one lengthened period of Saturnalia. This starts with the "office parties" a few days before Christmas. It continues on Christmas Eve, now the occasion in America of one of two large-scale revels that mark the season—save that the Christmas Eve revels are often punctuated by a visit to one of the larger churches for midnight Mass, which has increasingly tended to become blended into a part of the entertainment aspect of the season—and continues in spirited euphoria until New Year's Eve, the second of the large-scale revels. New Year's Day is spent resting, possibly regretting one's excesses, watching a football "bowl" game, and indulging in the lenitive of one's choice.

38 Which of the following can best be inferred from the passage?

① The great waves of immigrants from many countries in the late 1800's and early 1900's had a significant effect on the American celebration of Christmas.
② The traditions on which American Christmas celebrations are based were brought primarily by the earliest settlers.
③ The Saturnalia of Christmas week is a release from the hard work of the Christmas shopping season.
④ New Year's Day is indistinguishable from Christmas Eve at this point.

39 Which of the following does the author find to be distinctive to the American Christmas season?

① The exchange of Christmas gifts
② Eating and drinking in celebration
③ Attending religious services on early Christmas morning
④ The dedication to commerce

40 According to the passage, the American celebration of the Christmas season has _____.

① demonstrated great symbolic originality
② little justification for existing
③ departed completely from the example of early settlers
④ borrowed extensively from the traditions of other countries

[41-43] 숙명여대 2017

The origin of the veil in Saudi Arabia is unknown. The most accepted theory about the specific veiling practices in Saudi Arabia is that when the eastern coastal areas were under Turkish control, women of high social standing wore veils, probably to protect their complexion against the brutality of the desert sun. Another theory is that when Bedouin tribes made war on each other and raided the livestock of the rival tribe, the women were veiled so that the beautiful ones would not be carried off with the goats. Others said Bedouin women were such fierce fighters in these raids that, by a code of desert chivalry, women were veiled as a form of identity and kept out of battle so the intrepid men were spared the risk of fighting them. Regardless of the veil's origins, today few Saudi women are allowed by their men outside the house without a veil. The rule applies to women in all social classes. In public, women lose all personality and individuality to become so many black blobs gliding down the street. Each is covered in black, her face masked behind impenetrable black gauze. In the eyes of a Westerner, the veil is starkly symbolic of a woman's subservience to man in all areas of Saudi life. It sets the tone of a woman's confinement and states her total dependence on the male members of her family, who regulate her ability to function as a member of society.

41 What would be the best title for the above passage?

① "The Theoretical History of Saudi Arabian Women"
② "The Veil in Saudi Arabia: Myth and Reality"
③ "The Origin of the Veil for Saudi Arabian Women"
④ "The Mystery of Veil"
⑤ "Various Theories of the Veil in Saudi Arabia"

42 Which can best replace the underlined intrepid?

① respectful
② dominating
③ involuntary
④ chivalrous
⑤ fearless

43 Whose point of view is represented in the underlined sentence in the concluding section of the above passage?

① Saudi women's
② Saudi men's
③ Asian men's
④ Westerners'
⑤ All of the above

[44-45] 성균관대 2016

England has long been the jurisdiction of choice for wives who have the luxury of being able to choose where they divorce. English law tries to balance lifelong need and fairness. The poorer partner—typically a wife bringing up children—can expect housing and many years of income, especially if she has sacrificed her career for the marriage. A court ruling on February 23rd has nonetheless continued a recent trend of tilting the balance a little towards husbands. Tracey Wright objected to her ex-husband's bid to cut her £75,000 annual maintenance, awarded after an 11-year marriage failed in 2008. She argued that she was too busy with the two children even to look for work. She lost, on appeal. Lord justice Pitchford said Mr Wright's payments should taper off as he neared retirement and that his ex-wife should get a job. The ruling is a legal landmark chiefly because _____. As David Hodson, a specialist lawyer, notes, that principle has long applied to poor women when it comes to claiming welfare benefits. But an ex-wife will still be able to argue that no suitable work is available for her and that she needs her ex-husband's help in order to keep up her own and her children's living standards. Such arguments would cut little ice in most other countries. The ruling will not dent London's attraction as a global centre for divorce. English divorce law, with its bespoke solutions reached after costly legal wrangling, is also likely to remain a luxury service, out of reach to all but the very rich.

44 Which of the following is most appropriate for the blank?

① it sets out a father's obligation to pay welfare benefits
② it sets out a mother's duty to have to seek a job
③ it recognizes husbands as the poorer partner for the first time
④ it recognizes ex-wives with children as the poorer partner
⑤ it recognizes the children's rights to choose between their parents

45 According to the passage, _____.

① England became a slightly worse place for idle ex-wives
② England became a better place for housewives
③ most other countries became better places than England for jobless ex-wives
④ most countries are bad places for retired ex-husbands
⑤ in most other countries husbands are ineligible for welfare benefits

[46-47] 한국외대 2018

F. Scott Fitzgerald was the most famous chronicler of 1920s America, an era he dubbed 'the Jazz Age'. Written in 1925, *The Great Gatsby* is one of the greatest literary documents of this period, in which the American economy soared, bringing unprecedented levels of prosperity to the nation. Prohibition, the ban on the sale and consumption of alcohol, made millionaires out of bootleggers, and an underground culture of revelry sprang up. Sprawling private parties escaped police notice, and secret clubs that sold liquor thrived. The chaos and violence of World War I left America in a state of shock, and the generation that fought the war turned to wild and extravagant living to compensate. Money, opulence, and exuberance became the order of the day. Like Nick in *The Great Gatsby*, Fitzgerald found this new lifestyle seductive and exciting and, like Gatsby, he had always idolized the very rich. Now he found himself in an era in which unrestrained materialism set the tone of society. Even so, Fitzgerald saw through the glitter of the Jazz Age to the moral emptiness and hypocrisy beneath, and part of him longed for this (A) _____ moral center. In many ways, *The Great Gatsby* represents Fitzgerald's attempt to confront his (B) _____ feelings about the Jazz Age.

46 Which one of the following ordered pairs best fits into (A) and (B)?

① absent — conflicting
② vacuous — generous
③ fixed — vague
④ persistent — cynical

47 According to the passage, which of the following is NOT true?

① Fitzgerald's book is an excellent chronicle of the Jazz Age.
② Alcohol was illegal during the 1920s except in private parties.
③ After World War I hedonism became the new way of life.
④ Nick and Gatsby embody Fitzgerald's attitude toward the 1920s.

[48-50] 서강대 2010

> Every culture feels the call of conscience—the voice of internal self-criticism. ㉮ But Western Christian culture has conscience on steroids, so to speak. Our sense of guilt is comparatively extreme, and, with our culture of original sin and fallen status, we feel guilty about our very existence. In the belly of Western culture is the feeling that we're not worthy. Why is this feeling there?
> All this internalized self-loathing is the cost we pay for being civilized. In a very well-organized society that protects the interests of many, we have to refrain daily from our natural instincts. We have to repress our own selfish, aggressive urges all the time, and we are so accustomed to it as adults that we don't always notice it. But if I was in the habit of acting on my impulses, I would regularly kill people in front of me at coffee shops who order elaborate whipped-cream mocha ㉯ concoctions. In fact, I wouldn't bother to line up in a queue, but would just storm the counter and muscle people out of my way. But there is a small wrestling match that happens inside my psyche that keeps me from such natural aggression. And that's just morning coffee—think about how many times you'd like to strangle somebody on public transportation.

48 Which of the following expression refers to the concept of conscience?

① natural instinct
② selfish, aggressive urges
③ internalized self-loathing
④ impulses

49 What does the underlined sentence ㉮ suggest?

① We repress our conscience at all times.
② Western culture overemphasizes a sense of guilt.
③ Humans often have no conscience in their daily thoughts.
④ Humans naturally have criminal instincts.

50 What does the underlined word ㉯ mean?

① blends   ② glades
③ convolutions   ④ droves

CHAPTER 02 정보·기술

[01-03] 경희대 2011

In 1993 a memorable cartoon in *The New York Times* explained that "on the internet, nobody knows you're a dog"; in 2010 anonymity is on the way to being abolished. At the Techonomy conference on 4 August 2010, Google's CEO Eric Schmidt said: "Show us 14 photos of yourself and we can identify who you are. You think you don't have 14 photos of yourself on the internet? You've got Facebook photos!" This state of affairs was not only irrevocable but also, in his eyes, necessary: "In a world of asymmetric threats, true anonymity is too dangerous... You need a name service for humans... governments are going to require it."

Although it is still possible to cheat, it will be increasingly difficult to do so in the future. The world's most powerful online architects and its political leaders plan to "civilise" the free internet, which they still see as a lawless zone. If they succeed in ㉮ _____ the internet, stating your real identity will be the price you have to pay in order to enjoy full access. The word "web" was originally an image used to describe a decentralised system of interconnected information networks. Nobody imagined that a spider would actually take up residence at its centre and start spying on the activities of all internet users.

01 윗글의 첫 문단에서 1993년으로부터 2010년까지라는 세월의 경과가 갖는 의미는?

① Over the years, the rising influence of the Internet has revolutionized how we carry out daily activities.
② The social authority formerly enjoyed by newspapers like *The New York Times* has passed on to the CEOs of IT companies like Google.
③ The aspect of the Internet which was once considered its positive asset is nowadays considered by some influential people as a serious threat to the society.
④ Politicians are envious of the growing social influence of people like Eric Schmidt.

02 빈칸 ㉮에 알맞은 단어는?

① domesticating
② inundating
③ scandalizing
④ mollifying

03 두 번째 문단에서 가장 핵심적으로 대비되는 한 쌍의 이미지는?

① decentralized system vs. law-governed zone
② architects vs. spider
③ politicians vs. CEOs of IT companies
④ off-line identity vs. on-line identity

[04-06] 숙명여대 2011

The Internet has brought countless benefits to mankind, but as we see now, it also creates incalculable potential for mischief: it amplifies the threats of schoolyard bullies, empowers terrorists and fringe groups, and opens up huge new spaces to technologically savvy criminals. Now that data can be shared, linked, and exploited with near-instantaneous ease, the risks entailed by the publication of information develop very quickly out of all recognition; there is simply no way that any editor, however well-meaning, can make an informed judgement about the potential repercussions entailed by the release of vast amounts of confidential data of this sort. But this is where we are, and I wonder whether preaching restraint can have much effect. The technology has outpaced the _____.

Advocates of total information freedom might object that I am overlooking the fact that the tug-of-war between journalists and governments remains a deeply lopsided one. They might contend that government bureaucracies, with their enormous resources and closed cultures, still have far more power to control information than any one who leaks the secret information. The Web's guerrilla leakers are merely trying to <u>even</u> the playing field.

04 What would be the most appropriate expression to fill in the blank?

① conscience
② ethics
③ generation
④ justice
⑤ law

05 Which of the following can best replace the underlined even?

① disrupt
② invalidate
③ level
④ organize
⑤ show

06 The author of the passage is _____ about the total information release in the Internet.

① skeptical
② solemn
③ convinced
④ playful
⑤ optimistic

[07-08] 한양대 2013

Smart cars create problems as well. One problem is how to control all this automotive technology. More buttons take more of the drivers' attention. Even voice controls are distracting for drivers. A recent study showed that drivers talking on handheld cell phones were four times more likely to be involved in accidents as drivers who were not. In fact, drivers using cell phones were almost as likely to be involved in accidents as those who were legally intoxicated. Using voice controls, even a hands-free system, might prove to be as distracting as chatting on the phone. Nevertheless, the auto industry's answer to the control problem so far has been voice control. When it comes to simple tasks—changing channels on the radio or opening the trunk—voice controls work well enough. But it is probably not the best method for directing more difficult operations such as navigating the Internet or controlling the car itself. Engine noise, highway noise, and the music on the stereo tend to garble instructions, and voice recognition system often cannot decipher strong accents.

07 윗글의 바로 앞에 나올 내용으로 가장 알맞은 것을 고르시오.

① Electronic defects of smart cars
② Virtues and vices of smart cars
③ Smart features of modern cars
④ Mechanic malfunctions of smart cars

08 윗글의 내용과 일치하는 것을 고르시오.

① Driving using cell phones is as dangerous as drunk driving.
② Voice control are efficient enough to overcome various noises.
③ New technology reduces the number of buttons necessary for car control.
④ Voice controls might be employed to lessen the car accidents dramatically.

[09-10] 성균관대 2014

Cars that need no driver are just around the corner according to Google, which has been testing vehicles bristling with aerials and cameras on public roads in America. But Google does not make cars (yet), so it will be up to firms that do to bring the technology to market. And carmakers are a conservative bunch. Still, slowly and steadily the autonomous car will arrive, with the help of an increasing number of automated driving aids. Volvo recently demonstrated one such feature: a car that really does park itself. Some cars already have systems that assist with parking, but these are _____. They can identify an empty parallel-parking space and steer into it while the driver uses the brake. The Volvo system, however, lets the driver get out and use a smartphone application to instruct the vehicle to park. The car then trundles off, manoeuvres into a parking place and sends a message to the driver to inform him where it is. The driver can collect the car in person or use his phone to call it back to where he dropped it off. Autonomous parking could thus be provided at places like shopping centers and airports, which are controlled areas in which automated vehicles can be managed more easily than on open highways.

09 Which of the following most appropriate for the blank.

① not safe enough
② not much different from non-autonomous vehicles
③ not on sale yet
④ too expensive
⑤ not completely autonomous

10 According to the passage, which of the following is true?

① Car manufacturers are quick to commercialize new technology.
② Driverless cars have a problem with communicating with one another.
③ Supported by Google's software applications, Volvo developed automatic valet parking system.
④ Self-driving cars will not be permitted on public roads in the near future because of safety issues.
⑤ Autonomous parking is comparatively easier in controlled areas.

[11-12] 명지대 2014

Tape is the oldest computer storage medium still in use. It was first put to work on a UNIVAC computer in 1951. Alberto Pace, head of data and storage at CERN, says that tape has four advantages over hard disks for the long-term preservation of data. The first is (A) _____. Although it takes about 40 seconds for an archive robot to select the right tape and put it in a reader, once it has loaded, extracting data from that tape is about four times as fast as reading from a hard disk. The second advantage is reliability. When a tape snaps, it can be spliced back together. The loss is rarely more than a few hundred megabytes. When a terabyte hard disk fails, by contrast, all the data on it may be lost. The third benefit of tape is that it does not need power to preserve data held on it. The fourth benefit is (B) _____. If a hacker with a grudge managed to break into CERN's data centre, he could delete all 50 petabytes of the disk-based data in minutes. To delete the same amount from the organisation's tape would take years. Tape has two other benefits. It is cheaper than disks, and it lasts longer. Tapes can still be read reliably after three decades, against five years for disks.

11 Choose the one that is not true according to the passage.

① Tape was first used as a computer storage medium in 1951.
② It takes less time to delete data from tapes than from hard disks.
③ Data preservation on tape does not need power.
④ Tape is cheaper and lasts longer than hard disks.

12 Choose the pair that best fills blanks (A) and (B).

① durability — stability
② manageability — protection
③ speed — security
④ readability — durability

[13-15] 한국외대 2014

In 1938, thousands of Americans famously mistook a radio adaptation of the H.G. Wells novel "War of the Worlds" for a genuine news broadcast. Police stations were flooded with calls from citizens who believed the US had been invaded by Martians. It is difficult to imagine a radio play causing such a misunderstanding in the Internet era. But the Internet, like radio in 1938, is a relatively young medium. It is conceivable that a misleading post on social media could spark a comparable panic. We can think of this possibility as a "digital wildfire." In a hyperconnected world, information can travel with unprecedented speed and reach. Social media can rapidly spread information that is either intentionally or unintentionally misleading or provocative.

Concern about such a situation has fanned the flames of a wider debate about regulation of the Internet, though it seems unlikely that an acceptable legal restriction on online speech will ever be arrived at. If a digital wildfire is to be avoided or contained, it seems that the responsibility lies mainly with users and consumers of social media. Paradoxically, one of the most effective ways to deal with a digital wildfire turns out to be use of the same social media avenues to set the record straight. It remains to be seen whether the metaphor will be extended to describe this self-correction as something like a "digital rainfall."

13 Why does the author mention "War of the Worlds"?

① To illustrate how to regulate digital information exchange
② To show an example of false information spreading fast
③ To highlight the responsibility of mass media for the public
④ To exemplify the fundamental role of commercial social media

14 According to the author, which of the following groups is mainly responsible for a "digital rainfall"?

① Policy makers
② Internet users
③ Service providers
④ Cyber-rights activists

15 Which of the following best characterizes the relation between "digital wildfire" and "digital rainfall"?

① Cause — Effect
② Inquiry — Response
③ Source — Outcome
④ Problem — Solution

[16-17] 단국대 2017

What do 'neural network,' 'machine learning,' and 'deep learning' actually mean? These are the three terms you're most likely to have heard lately. Neural networks are a type of computer architecture onto which artificial intelligence is built. These networks are a way of structuring a computer so that it looks like a cartoon of the brain, comprised of neuron-like nodes connected together in a web. Individually these nodes are dumb, answering extremely basic questions, but collectively they can tackle difficult problems. More importantly, with the right algorithms, they can be taught. Machine learning is a program you might run on a neural network, training computers to look for certain answers in pots of data. Deep learning is a particular type of machine learning that's only become popular over the past decade, largely thanks to two new resources: cheap processing power and abundant data (otherwise known as the internet). If a deep learning system is looking at a picture, each layer is essentially tackling a different magnification. The bottom layer might look at just a 5 x 5 grids of pixels, answering simply "yes" or "no" as to whether something shows up in that grid. If it answers yes, then the layer above looks to see how this grid fits into a larger pattern. Is this the beginning of a line, for example, or a corner? <u>This process gradually builds up, allowing the software to understand even the most complicated data by breaking it down into constituent parts.</u>

16 According to the passage, which is true?

① In a deep learning system, the most complicated data can be understood from the bottom layer.
② Deep learning is a type of computer architecture which makes machine learning possible.
③ Cheap processing power and abundant data enabled a neural network system to be developed.
④ In a neural network system, individual nodes collectively tackle difficult problems.

17 Which is indicated by the underlined part?

① processing complicated data at the bottom layer
② collectively tackling difficult problems
③ answering simple questions at the lower layer
④ breaking complicated data into constituent parts

[18-20] 이화여대 2017

Life might be about to get a lot shorter, if the AI-related fears of Stephen Hawking, Bill Gates, Elon Musk, Nick Bostrom and a host of other giant scientific minds are realised. Concerns range from unchecked AGI (Artificial General Intelligence) weaponry to an "intelligence explosion" in which a machine becomes capable of recursive [A] _____, and in doing so [B] _____ the intellectual capacity of the human brain and our ability to control it. Should a super-intelligence disaster loom, history is not exactly a reliable indicator that we'll have had the foresight to withdraw from the AI arms race before it's too late. "When you see something that is technically sweet," Robert Oppenheimer once observed, "you go ahead and do it, and you argue about what to do about it only after you have had your technical success." "If there is a way of guaranteeing that superior artificial intellects will never harm human beings," Bostrom noted, decades later, "then such intellects will be created. If there is no way to have such a guarantee, then they will probably be created nevertheless." "Success in creating AI," Hawking neatly summarized most recently, would be "the biggest event in human history. Unfortunately, it might also be the last."

"Well, I hope not," Demis Hassabis, the CEO of DeepMind deadpans. On the super-intelligence questions, he says: "We need to make sure the goals are correctly specified, and that there's nothing ambiguous in there and that they're stable over time. In all our systems, the top level goal will still be specified by its designers. AGI might come up with its own ways to get to that goal, but it doesn't create its own goal." His tone is relentlessly reassuring. "Look, these are all interesting and difficult challenges. As with all new powerful technologies, this has to be used ethically and responsibly, and that's why we're actively calling for debate and researching the issues now, so that when the time comes, [C] _____."

18 Which pair best fits [A] and [B]?

① self-reflection — underpins
② self-critique — dissolves
③ self-improvement — surpasses
④ self-illusion — diverts
⑤ self-recovery — objectifies

19 Which statement can be best inferred from the passage above?

① Hawking's remark celebrates the creation of AI as the best achievement in human history.
② According to Oppenheimer, there won't be any room for human intervention once highly advanced AIs are created.
③ Bostrom assures that superior artificial intellects cannot be created no matter what.
④ Hassabis informs that AIs will make ethical decisions.
⑤ According to Hassabis, the ambiguous goals assigned to AIs might not guarantee positive effects.

20 Which expression best completes [C]?

① we'll be well prepared
② AIs should function autonomously
③ scientific success can be achieved
④ human beings should hire AIs
⑤ the human brain should function as potently as AI's

[21-22] 성균관대 2016

> The technology to track our online life started with the humble cookie. A cookie is a small chunk of data a website sends to your browser that remembers where you've been. In the early days of the web, cookies helped e-commerce companies tag who you are. If you log into a service, put items in an online shopping cart or send an encrypted credit card number, it's cookies that tell the website it's still you doing the transacting.
>
> "The easiest way to understand a cookie is to compare it to a wrist band," says online entrepreneur Sam Oh. "When you attend a concert, it lets security know who you are and lets you re-enter without disruption."
>
> But e-marketers soon realized cookies could also tell them what else you've been doing. As I prefer to make my own decisions about what I share online, I've got into the habit of regularly deleting my cookies and browser history.
>
> However, it's _____. Culling these records covers my tracks but it means I have to repeatedly log into services I use often, plus those sites have no record of what I've bought in the past, and I can't store items in wishlists and shopping carts to come back later.

21 The most appropriate expression for the blank is _____.

① a double-edged sword
② a high-tech gadget
③ a hot potato
④ a pain in my neck
⑤ Big Brother

22 An advantage of using a cookie is that _____.

① you don't need to buy a new computer
② your computer is updated regularly
③ you can send your idea to anybody online
④ you don't have to relog into your favorite website
⑤ your record of internet surfing is deleted automatically

[23-25] 한국외대 2017

When it comes to automotive technology, self-driving cars are all the rage. These cars will be safer, cleaner, and more fuel-efficient than their human-driven counterparts. And yet, they can never be totally safe, raising an impossible ethical dilemma of algorithmic morality. How should the car be programmed to act in the event of an unavoidable accident? Should it minimize the loss of life, even if it means sacrificing the occupants, or should it protect the occupants at all costs? Who would buy a car programmed to sacrifice the owner? Some scientists set out to discover the public's opinion using the new science of experimental ethics. This involves posing ethical dilemmas to a large number of people to see how they respond. Ⓐ <u>The results of their experiments are interesting, if predictable.</u> In general people are comfortable with the idea that self-driving vehicles should be programmed to minimize the death toll. This utilitarian approach is certainly laudable but the participants were willing to go only so far. Participants were not as confident that autonomous vehicles would be programmed that way in reality and for a good reason: they actually wished others to cruise in utilitarian autonomous vehicles, more than they wanted to buy utilitarian autonomous vehicles themselves. And therein lies the paradox. People are in favor of cars that sacrifice the occupant to save the other lives—as long they do not have to drive one themselves.

23 Which of the following is the main topic of the passage?

① Pros and cons of autonomous automobiles
② Defective algorithms of self-driving vehicle
③ Ethical dilemmas of autonomous vehicles
④ Ethically programmed vehicles for non-ethical users

24 Which of the following is implied by Ⓐ?

① People respond tactfully to experimenters.
② People have accustomized to a computerized world.
③ People have become increasingly utilitarian recently.
④ People hesitate to sacrifice themselves to save others.

25 Which of the following describes the paradox of a utilitarian self-driving car?

① Others should drive it, but not me.
② It saves lives but costs money.
③ I want to drive it, but not buy it.
④ No one else can ride in it, only me.

[26-27] 가톨릭대 2018

Phantom traffic jams, in which cars suddenly screech to a dead stop on highways for no apparent reason, have long annoyed drivers. Interestingly, MIT researchers have recently offered a solution to help alleviate this stop-and-go driving. The logic is rather simple: The problem is inherent in our way of driving a car. If one car suddenly brakes, the car behind it has to brake and the car behind it has to brake. Ⓐ The braking increases with distance until a car actually stops. Ⓑ Dr. Hornstein, professor at MIT's Computer Science and Artificial Intelligence Laboratory, proposes redesigning the cruise control feature on our car to consider the space in front and behind the vehicle. Ⓒ To be sure, there are advanced cruise control systems on the market today that will adapt to the speed of a lead vehicle in order to maintain a steady following distance. Ⓓ Keeping the same distance between the vehicle in front and the vehicle trailing a car would prevent traffic jams. The technical name proposed for the traffic-busting technology is bilateral control.

26 What is inferred from the passage?

① Traffic jams could be solved by redesigned cruise control.
② Undesirable driving habits often cause highway traffic jams.
③ Research results show that highway traffic is beyond our control.
④ Traditional cruise control may increase vehicle crashes.

27 Choose the best place where the following sentence should be put.

> But the gap between the vehicle and a trailing car isn't considered.

① Ⓐ
② Ⓑ
③ Ⓒ
④ Ⓓ

[28-30] 숭실대 2017

Jason Zook started every morning by scrolling through Twitter, Instagram, Vine, his blog and Facebook. It started to have an effect on the 33-year-old entrepreneur's mental health. The San Diego resident was stressed, distracted and feeling like he could never fulfill the expectations he created in his digital world, where he amassed more than 33,000 followers. "You start your day looking at yourself compared to other people," he says. "You feel behind, and you have other people's opinions pressed upon you before you have a chance to have your own."

So (A) he went cold turkey, going on a 30-day social-media detox. It was a smart move: A recent study from the University of Pittsburgh's Center for Research on Media, Technology, and Health found that using multiple social-media platforms may put you at increased risk of depression and anxiety. The study found that people who use anywhere from seven to 10 social-media platforms are three times more likely to be depressed or anxious, compared to those using no more than two. Those who reported such symptoms were overwhelmed by the multitasking needed to manage their profiles—and the more profiles they had, the more the pressure added up.

Though it's on the high end, maintaining seven social-media profiles is possible with the bevy of options available to users today. "People compare themselves to the posts they see, and then feel inadequate," says Nicole Amesbury, head of clinical development at online-therapy company Talkspace. "Another reason is biology-based. Each time they open a social-media app and see a positive response, they get a small amount of dopamine released in the brain. When someone doesn't get enough 'likes' or dopamine hits, they feel the loss."

Social-media consultant and Queens resident Josh Springer, 35, recommends limiting usage to three platforms. Still, for Zook, the break was much needed. "After 30 days, my head felt like it just cleared, like the fog lifted," he says. "I had all this mental space back."

28 Which of the following best rephrases (A)?

① he went to the rural farm and made friends with turkeys
② he had to drink some iced drinks to keep calm
③ he stopped checking his social-media posts at once
④ he became incurably addicted to social-media networking

29 Which of the following is NOT true about Mr. Zook?

① He runs a business based on a social-media platform.
② He has more than 30 thousand followers in social-media network.
③ He felt some depression and anxiety from social-media networking.
④ He kept from social-media networking for 30 days.

30 Which of the following is NOT true?

① Mr. Zook's case warns us about the potential risk of social-media addiction.
② You should limit the number of social-media platforms if necessary.
③ You may get depression and anxiety if you spend too much time on social media.
④ Mr. Zook's case is exceptional since he has too many followers.

CHAPTER 03 지역·지리

[01-03] 한국외대 2016 C형

Home to a traumatic but rich history, stunning scenery, and some of the continent's most welcoming people, Colombia is Ⓐ a natural draw for travellers to South America. Despite its four-decade-long civil war, improved security conditions have led to a sharp increase in tourism. Foreigners and Colombians alike are now far more able to explore this thrilling paradise of cloud-forested mountains, palm-fringed beaches, and gorgeous colonial cities. The only country in South America to border both the Pacific and the Caribbean, Colombia offers a huge range of ecosystems, from the Amazon rainforest to snowcapped mountains to tropical islands. From gilded Caribbean coasts and cobblestoned colonial charm to clusters of coffee plantations, Colombia encapsulates Latin America in a single country. Don't miss the rejuvenated metropolis, Gabriel Garcia Marquez's magical Cartagena. Even more shrouded in mystery is San Agustin, where more than 500 life-sized ancient sculpted statues dot the surrounding countryside. Colombia's varied terrain is fertile ground for outdoor adventurers to dive, climb, raft, and trek. Some of South America's most iconic trekking is here. Ciudad Perdida is a multiday jungle walk to the ancient ruins of the Tayrona civilization, while numerous ascents inside national parks place fearless hikers on the highest reaches of the Andes. Providencia's world-class reef spells aquatic heaven for scuba divers, and whale-watchers on the Pacific coast can see majestic humpback whales in the wild.

01 Which of the following is NOT an example of Ⓐ?

① Four-decade-long civil war
② A cluster of coffee plantations
③ The Amazon rainforest
④ A jungle walk to ancient ruins

02 Which of the following is the passage mainly about?

① Natural history of Colombia
② Places to visit in Colombia
③ Colombian national security
④ Sporting opportunities in Colombia

03 Which of the following is NOT stated or implied by the passage?

① Colombia used to be an unsafe place to travel.
② Colombia has little in common with its neighbors.
③ You can hike up to the top of the Andes.
④ Colombia is both a Caribbean and Pacific country.

[04-05] 한국외대 2010

Sociologist Edwin Burgess's concentric zonal hypothesis explains that cities in the United States grow from the center to the periphery through a series of circular zones. Each zone has distinct social and housing features. Different land users—owners of single-family homes, apartment buildings, stores, factories, and warehouses—sort themselves out through the slow but constant ecological processes of competition, segregation, invasion, and succession, in such a way that similar-use zones arise. The zones reflect ecological competition, especially economic costs, rather than planning, zoning, or the efforts of government. Thus, downtown land usage went to the department stores and business offices that were most willing to pay the costs in terms of money, congestion, and pollution. Burgess also noted that each zone had distinctive social characteristics, with different kinds of social problems. Crime, mental illness, family breakdown, and other social problems were non-randomly distributed throughout the metropolitan area. The Burgess hypothesis explains why ㉠ _____.

04 Which of the following best fits into ㉮?

① most American cities look so similar
② people living in cities adapt to their zones rapidly
③ downtown shares characteristics with all the other zones
④ some metropolitan cities are more polluted than others
⑤ downtown areas have been developed slowly

05 Which of the following is NOT suggested by the Burgess hypothesis?

① Metropolitan area expanded from center to periphery.
② Each zone has its distinctive social problems.
③ Different land users reside in different zones.
④ Cities grow through circular zones as planned by the government.
⑤ Apartment buildings and warehouses are located in different zones.

[06-07] 한양대 2010

Why is the Dead Sea so salty? The body of water that lies along the Great Rift Valley has long fascinated tourists who come to drift effortlessly in its tranquil waters. Yet few know why they are able to float so easily in this giant saline pool. Although the Dead Sea is fed by the Jordan River and a number of smaller tributaries, the sea has no outlet. Therefore, any water that flows into the Dead Sea stays in the Dead Sea, at least until the process of evaporation takes effect. The heat of the region causes the water to evaporate at a high rate. Any mineral deposits remain behind, and as a result, the liquid turns brackish. No marine life or vegetation can survive in this salty concoction. In fact, the only living creatures that can be found in the Dead Sea are swimmers who are buoyed by the mineral salts that increase the density of the water.

06 What does the underlined word "tranquil" mean?

① deep
② calm
③ fresh
④ transparent

07 What is the purpose of the passage?

① to probe a unique phenomenon
② to introduce an irksome concept
③ to challenge a long held assumption
④ to question a misunderstood fact

[08-10] 광운대 2011

Suriname is the smallest independent country on South America. Its geographical size is just under 165,000, and it has an estimated population of approximately 470,000, most of whom live on the country's north coast, where the capital Paramaribo is located. Situated on the Guiana Shield, the country can be divided into two main geographic regions. The northern, coastal lowland has been cultivated, and most of the population lives here. The southern part consists of tropical rainforest and sparsely inhabited savanna along the southern border with Brazil, covering about 80% of Suriname's land surface, and the northern border with the Atlantic coast. Suriname has a very hot tropical climate, and temperatures do not vary much throughout the year. The year has two wet seasons, from April to August and from November to February. It also has two dry seasons, from August to November and February to April.

The economy of Suriname is dominated by the aluminum industry, which accounts for more that 15% of GDP and 70% of export earnings. Other main export products include rice, bananas and shrimp. Suriname has recently started exploiting some of its sizeable oil and gold reserves. About a quarter of the people work in the agricultural sector. The Suriname economy is very dependent on commerce, its main trade partners being the Netherlands, the United States, Canada and Caribbean countries.

08 윗글의 내용과 일치하지 않는 것을 고르시오.

① The population of Suriname exceeds one million, and they live near the capital city Paramaribo.
② Most population lives in the northern coast, while the southern part has a low density of population.
③ Most land surface is covered with tropical rainforest and nearly uninhabited savanna.
④ The climate of Suriname is very humid, and the temperature remains similar all year around.
⑤ Suriname has begun to make use of abundant natural resources such as oil and gold.

09 윗글에서 **Suriname**의 경제에 대하여 옳게 설명한 것을 고르시오.

① The aluminum export covers 15% of earnings and 70% of GDP for the nation.
② The export of rice, bananas and shrimp does not play a significant role for earnings.
③ The export of oil and gold also produces substantial earnings for the nation.
④ About 25% of the population is employed in the agricultural division.
⑤ The Netherlands, the U.S., Canada and Caribbean countries provide Suriname with economic aids.

10 윗글의 제목으로 가장 적합한 것을 고르시오.

① The Geography of Suriname
② The Climate of Suriname
③ The Introduction to Suriname
④ The Population of Suriname
⑤ The Economy of Suriname

[11-13] 경희대 2012

Once the world's fourth largest lake, the mighty Aral Sea is now in its death throes. Starved of its lifeblood of the waters of the Syur Darya and the Amu Darya rivers, the sea has been shrinking for the last 40 years. From the 1930s, the former Soviet Union started building large scale diversion canals to irrigate vast cotton fields in a grand plan to make cotton great export earner. This was achieved, and even today Uzbekistan is still a large exporter of cotton. But the cost in ecological and human health terms have been astronomical.

By 1960, 25 to 50 cubic kilometers of river water was being diverted annually for irrigation, and naturally enough, the shoreline began to recede. The mean sea level dropped 20cm(8") per year for 10 years, then the drop rate accelerated to 60 cm/year in the 70s, then to almost a metre per year in the 80s. By 1990, as a result of the continuing water diversion and evaporation, the shrinking Aral divided in two and its salinity increased from 10 grams per litre to 45. In some parts of the south Aral, salinity tops out at 98 g/litre (2001). Average seawater salinity is 33 g/litre. The once thriving fishing industry has been destroyed along with the fish and most the flora and ⓐ _____. Salt pans and contaminated runoff lakes have appeared, and winters have become harsher and longer, summer hotter and shorter.

11 윗글의 제목으로 가장 적당한 것은?

① Aral, the Dying Sea
② Salinity of Aral Sea
③ Diversion Project of Aral Sea
④ Rebirth of Aral Sea

12 윗글의 빈칸 ⓐ에 들어갈 단어로 가장 적당한 것은?

① fauna
② vegetation
③ foliage
④ insects

13 윗글에서 과거의 대형 사업이 Aral Sea에 미친 영향으로 언급되지 않은 것은?

① increased salinity of the sea
② increased cotton production
③ change in bio-diversity
④ change in climate

[14-15] 한양대 2013

Sierra Leone is regarded as a model of post-conflict reconstruction. All 11-year civil war that left some 50,000 dead by 2002 was overcome with the help of blue-hatted UN peacekeepers. In 2007 power changed hands in fair elections for only the second time in the country's history and this November citizens will once again go to the polls. But all is not well. Sierra Leone's president, Ernest Bai Koroma, has forced the UN mission chief out of his job in order to improve his re-election chances. Michael von der Schulenburg was abruptly moved on the orders of UN bosses in New York following appeals from the president. Foreign diplomats confirm that in September the president asked the UN to have Mr. von der Schulenburg removed, possibly questioning his impartiality. Two months later he repeated the request in writing, though he now denies this.

Mr. von der Schulenburg is deemed to have done a good job. He vastly reduced the UN presence in Sierra Leone—a rare achievement in an organization often unwilling to put itself out of business. He also acted as a valued mediator between political parties in an environment where disputes can still easily turn violent. He met opposition leaders but did not favor them. Yet his (A) _____ alone seems to have been enough to incur the wrath of the president. That the UN agreed to move Mr. von der Schulenburg establishes a bad precedent. Given how much blood and treasure it has expended in Sierra Leone, the episode damages its credibility. It also (B) _____.

14 밑줄 친 (A)에 들어갈 가장 알맞은 것을 고르시오.

① lightheadedness
② strongheadedness
③ even-handedness
④ heavy-handedness

15 문맥상 밑줄 친 (B)에 들어갈 가장 알맞은 것을 고르시오.

① bodes ill for the coming election
② reinforces the UN's international leadership
③ compromises the president's chance for re-eletion
④ paves the way for the country's burgeoning democracy

[16-17] 한국외대 2016

Iceland enjoys a much milder climate than its name and location adjacent to the Arctic circle would imply. A branch of the Gulf Stream flows along the southern and the western coasts greatly moderating the climate. However, this brings mild Atlantic air in contact with colder Arctic air resulting in a climate that is marked by frequent changes in weather and storminess. Furthermore, this leads to more rainfall in the southern and western parts than in the northern part of the island. The summer tourist season is from late May to early September. During this period, the sun stays above the horizon for 24 hours, and the interplay of light and shadows on mountains, lava fields, and glaciers yields an ever-changing landscape. The winter season is the abode of long nights and severe winter storms. However, the serenity of the frozen expanse and the dance of the aurora borealis, the so-called northern lights, on a clear night sky draw an increasing number of tourists.

16 Which of the following makes the Icelandic climate warmer than might be expected?

① The Gulf Stream
② Arctic air
③ Lava fields
④ Northern lights

17 Which of the following is true of Iceland?

① Winter travel to Iceland is decreasing in popularity.
② Rainfall is equally distributed across the country.
③ The weather in Iceland is highly changeable.
④ Summer tourists can watch the sun sink below the horizon.

[18-20] 국민대 2016

Tuscany, Italy, may be one of the best-known places in the world. Its beautiful landscape has become familiar to us through Renaissance paintings and Italian novels and movies. It really appeals to many tourists as paradise on earth. More than 32 million tourists visit Tuscany every year and return home to rave about its charms. Of course, advertisers and photographers are interested in the region, too. "We chose this region for its beauty," says Linda Fabris, who works for a large advertising agency. "No other place can really compare."

But residents are afraid of losing their heritage, the region that has remained virtually untouched since the Middle Ages. Tuscans have come up with a proposal to copyright their landscape to Ⓐ _____ the way the countryside is used for advertising. "We are trying to stop non-Tuscan brand names from advertising here," said Robert DiTommaso, a Tuscan businessman. "We have to protect the landscape that we have enjoyed for centuries. This is our heritage." At the same time, there is a voluntary trademark, "Made in Tuscany," to guarantee the quality of the olive oils, cheese, and wines that come from the district. The aim is to show people that many of the products, especially foods, that use the name Tuscany, do not actually come from that region.

18 Which best fits into the blank in the following sentence according to the passage?

> Tuscany first became well-known to us thanks to _____.

① works of art that portray the Tuscan landscape
② Tuscan residents who insist on their own trademark
③ advertising agencies that are interested in a Tuscan paradise
④ tourists who send the Tuscan pictures to people in their home

19 Which best fits into the blank Ⓐ?

① devise
② restrict
③ expand
④ establish

20 Which is true according to the passage?

① Tuscan people are prohibited from advertising their products in other countries.
② The trademark "Made in Tuscany" is used to increase advertising in the region.
③ Residents in Tuscany have had a trouble with too many tourists since the Middle Ages.
④ The residents want to copyright their landscape in order to keep their heritage.

CHAPTER 04 음악·미술

[01-03] 단국대 2006

It might seem logical to believe that our appreciation of music is ⓐ _____ —that nurture, not nature, determines this. However, it is now clear that nature also plays a role; recent studies indicate that the human brain is "wired" for music. At the University of Toronto, Canada, psychologists have been studying infants aged 6-9 months. These babies smile when researchers play ⓑ _____ music, but they appear to hate ⓒ _____ music. As adults, most people can remember only a few poems or pieces of prose but have the capacity to remember at least dozens of musical tunes and to recognize hundreds more. Even more interesting, perhaps, is the possibility that music might actually improve some forms of intelligence. A 1999 study proves that music can help children do better at math—not, oddly, other subjects, just math. It is probably not surprising that much of the brain activity that involves music takes place in the temporal lobes. Researchers at Beth Israel Deaconess Medical Center in Boston have also discovered that the front part of the corpus callosum is actually larger in musicians than in non-musicians.

01 Which of the following can be inferred from the passage?

① Since music is the result of education alone, it might help children do better at math.
② The corpus callosum might also be connected with the brain activity that involves music.
③ Children who are exposed to very little music might remember only a few poems or pieces of prose.
④ Brain activity that involves music might have nothing to do with the maturation of the corpus callosum.

02 Which is the most suitable to the blank ⓐ?

① learned
② endowed
③ controlled
④ preserved

03 Which is the most suitable pair to the blanks ⓑ and ⓒ?

① consonant — pleasant
② pleasant — consonant
③ dissonant — consonant
④ consonant — dissonant

[04-07] 서강대 2009

> Every day more than 100 million people hear the sound of background music. They hear it while they are working in offices, shopping in stores, and eating in restaurants. They even hear it while they are sitting in the dentist's chair. Why is background music layed in so many places? The answer is easy. Music is such a powerful force that it can affect people's behavior.
>
> Studies show that background music can affect the sales of business. Ronald Milliman, a marketing professor, measured the effects that fast music, slow music, and no music had on customers in a supermarket. He found that fast music did not affect sales very much when compared with no music.
>
> However, slow music made a big difference. Listening to music played slowly made shoppers move more slowly. When slow music was played, shoppers bought more and sales increased 38 percent.
>
> Milliman also found that restaurant owners can use music to their advantage. In the evening, playing slow music (A) the amount of time customers spend in the restaurant. At lunch time, restaurants want people to eat more quickly so that they can serve more customers. Playing lively music at lunchtime encourages customers to eat quickly and leave.

04 Which is the most suitable word for blank (A)?

① truncates
② shortens
③ lengthens
④ elongates

05 Who is Ronald Milliman?

① A marketing executive at a supermarket chain
② A psychologist interested in the effect of music on diet
③ A regular customer who enjoys music with his meals
④ A marketing expert who studied the effect of music

06 If you were an owner of a fast food restaurant, what kind of music would you play based on the given information?

① soul music
② exciting music
③ soothing music
④ irritating music

07 Which statement best expresses the main idea of the passage?

① Ronald Milliman has discovered the effect of music on human behavior.
② When slow music is played, supermarket sales increase.
③ Background music can help or hurt a store's sales.
④ Music encourages customers to eat more and spend more.

[08-10] 서울여대 2012

On October 10, 1919, the opera *Die Frau ohne Schatten*, meaning "The Woman without a Shadow," premiered at the Vienna State Opera. The music was composed by Richard Strauss, and the libretto, or text, was written by the poet Hugo von Hofmannsthal. The idea for the opera had come eight years earlier. For some time Hofmannsthal and Strauss had been searching for a subject about which to make their next opera. They wanted it to be a twentieth-century parallel for Mozart's *The Magic Flute*. On March 3, 1911, Hofmannsthal wrote a letter to Strauss suggesting an idea for a new opera. "It is a magic fairy tale ... and for one of the women your wife might well, in all discretion, be taken as a model." Hofmannsthal went on to propose a character based on Strauss's wife, Pauline. "She is a bizarre woman with a very beautiful soul," Hofmannsthal said of the character, "strange, moody, domineering, and yet at the same time likeable."

Strauss might well have taken offense at the suggestion that _____. He and Hofmannsthal had a famously contentious working relationship, sometimes likened to a cat trying to live in harmony with a dog. Strauss, however, did not take offense, probably because he knew there was some truth to the characterization. Pauline Strauss, a renowned opera singer, was often described as odd. She was known to be verbally combative in public, and was generally a force to be reckoned with.

08 Which of the following would best fit in the blank?

① his wife was bizarre
② the poet was attracted to his wife
③ his wife should be taken as a model
④ the poet might take the lead in composition

09 Strauss did not take offense at Hofmannsthal's suggestion because _____.

① he believed the poet was wiser than himself
② he did not want to talk about his wife any more
③ he knew his wife was a somewhat likeable opera singer
④ he thought his wife was rather strange, moody, and domineering

10 Which of the following is true according to the passage?

① Hofmannsthal did not know Pauline Strauss until March 3, 1911.
② Strauss and Hofmannsthal considered each other professional rivals.
③ *The Magic Flute* was modelled on *Die Frau ohne Schatten* in characterization.
④ *Die Frau ohne Schatten* was first produced eight years after its first conception.

[11-12] 서강대 2011

Almost everyone thinks "Greensleeves" is a sad song—but why? Apart from the melancholy lyrics, it's because the melody prominently features a musical construct called the minor third, which musicians have used to express sadness since at least the 17th century. The minor third's emotional sway is closely related to the popular idea that, at least for Western music, songs written in a major key (like "Happy Birthday") are generally upbeat, while those in a minor key (think of The Beatles' "Eleanor Rigby") tend towards the doleful.

While there might be a loose correlation—reinforced by our particular musical tradition—between minor scales and "sadness," it's a mistake to think that the moods evoked by music can be confidently reduced to tonality in and of itself. Think of Jonathan Richman's "Egyptian Reggae," the humor of which partly seems to spring from the exotic, vaguely Egyptian associations that its minor key melody mysteriously evokes in Western listener. A song's emotional valence cannot be simply reducible to its minor tonality. Indeed, those recalcitrant minor key songs that defy generalization about the link between tonality and mood may tell us something more important about music than the ones that conform.

11 Which of the following would be the main point of the passage?

① Musicians have used the minor third to express sadness and unhappy feeling.
② Unlike Oriental traditions, Western music has been reluctant to employ the minor keys.
③ The emotional effects of music may not be reduced to the tonality of minor keys.
④ Minor key songs prove particularly efficacious for the doleful moods.

12 Which of the following songs is different from the others in the context of discussion?

① Greensleeves
② Happy Birthday
③ Eleanor Rigby
④ Egyptian Reggae

[13-14] 숙명여대 2012

It is extraordinary how little musicians discuss among themselves Toscanini's rightness or wrongness about matters of speed and rhythm and the tonal amenities. Like other musicians, he is frequently apt about these and frequently in error as well. What seems to be more important is his unvarying ability to put over a piece. He quite shamelessly whips up the tempo and sacrifices clarity and _____ a basic rhythm, just making the music, like his baton, go round and round, if he finds his audience's attention tending to waver. No piece has to mean anything specific; every piece has to provoke from its hearers a spontaneous acceptance. This is what I call the "wow technique."

13 What would be the most appropriate expression in the blank?

① feigns
② follows
③ gets into
④ ignores
⑤ raises

14 According to the author, what is the most important element in Toscanini's "wow technique"?

① authenticity
② improvisation
③ lyrical colorations
④ musical rigour
⑤ practice

[15-17] 숭실대 2012

Actually, the story about Franz Schubert's the *Great* C-major Symphony is so great that we just have to tell it. When discussing Schubert's symphonic works, we cannot avoid mentioning the touching desperation with which musicologists have approached the numbering of his symphonies. Anyone trying to understand this must be prepared for a tough lesson with mathematics, as the choice of the numbers generally assigned to Schubert's symphonies may well cause some confusion. For instance, the *Great* Symphony has been thought to be his No. 9 in the line-up for those who are not familiar with the history of Schubert's symphonies. However, this symphony is also at times referred to as No. 8. There is a highly chaotic story behind this anomaly.

Up until the *Little* C-major Symphony No. 6 dating from 1818, all is clear: Schubert's first six completed symphonies all received a number in chronological order. The confusion begins subsequently. After having completed his Symphony No. 6, Schubert composed two additional movements, which were linked together at a much later date to create the well-known *Unfinished* Symphony. As these two movements were not discovered until much later, the symphony subsequent to his sixth—the *Great* Symphony, thus entitled so as to distinguish it from his other symphony in C-major, the *Little* Symphony No. 6—became known as his No. 7. After the discovery of Schubert's *Unfinished* Symphony, a new edition of his symphonies was prepared. It was then decided to call ⓐ this one his No. 8, and the *Great* Symphony was advanced to become his No. 9. If you have been reading carefully, you will have noticed that this left the number seven as a blank; a numeric hiatus for which as yet no elegant solution has been found. Thus, Schubert's (non-existent) Symphony No. 7 has likely become the best-known phantom composition in the history of music.

15 Which of the following would be best for the title?

① The Complexity of Numbering Symphonic Works
② The Inconsistency of Naming Schubert's Symphonies
③ The Importance of Schubert's Missing Symphony
④ The Numbering of Schubert's Symphonies

16 According to the passage, which of the following is true?

① Musicologists were rather at ease in dealing with Schubert's works.
② Schubert composed a symphony nicknamed as the *Phantom*.
③ Schubert's *Unfinished* was discovered much later than the *Great*
④ Schubert was said to care little about numbering his symphonies.

17 According to the passage, which of the following refers to ⓐ this one?

① the *Little* C-major Symphony
② the *Great* C-major Symphony
③ the *Unfinished* Symphony
④ the Phantom Symphony

[18-20] 가천대 2007

[1] Most grafftists may think they have some right like free speech to express their individualism or artistic ability. But graffiti is not an art form, which should be creation of beautiful things and requires a skill acquired by study or practice. Graffitists just take a spray can and draw their names or strange pictures on buildings, streets and even trains in cities. Graffiti reduces property values and instantly makes an area look ugly and rundown. So I think graffiti _____.

[2] Graffiti can be beautiful and creative and a non-violent way for people to express themselves. The practices of graffiti are generally related to a sub-culture that rebels against social authorities. It is considered one of the elements of the Hip Hop Culture. We can learn about elements of society which are otherwise unavailable. Moreover, graffiti artists strive to improve their skill, which is constantly progressing. Some cities have set aside particular community walls or areas to do legal graffiti. This encourages the artists to produce great art.

18 윗글 [1], [2]의 핵심 쟁점으로 가장 적절한 것은?

① ways to improve graffiti skills
② the role of graffiti artists
③ graffiti paintings as an art
④ areas to paint legal graffiti

19 윗글 [1]의 빈칸에 들어갈 말로 가장 적절한 것은?

① is used as an act of self expression
② is not an acceptable part of urban culture
③ tends to be less popular in poor districts
④ has not progressed for thousands of years

20 윗글의 내용과 맞지 않는 것은?

① Graffitists mean the graffiti artists.
② To rebel against social authorities is one of the elements of Hip Hop Culture.
③ Some cities allow graffiti partly.
④ Graffitists have rights to express their art anywhere.

[21-23] 한양대 2007

If the chief end of all art is delight, there is small blame to be attached to most of us in that we are glad to take our pleasure carelessly and to give little thought to the means whereby we have been moved. Properly enough, the enjoyment of most of us is unthinking; and in the appreciation of the masterpieces of the several arts few of us are wont to consider curiously the craftsmanship of the men who wrought these marvels, their skill of hand, their familiarity with the mechanics of their art, their perfect knowledge of technique. Our regard is centered rather on the larger aspects of the masterwork, on its meaning and on its truthfulness, on its intellectual elevation and on its moral appeal. No doubt this is the best, for it is only by its possession of these nobler qualities that a work of art endures. On the other hand, these nobler qualities by themselves will not suffice to confer immortality, if they are not sustained by the devices of the skillful craftsman.

21 밑줄 친 wont와 뜻이 가장 가까운 것은?

① able
② forced
③ delighted
④ inclined

22 이 글에 나타난 우리들의 일반적 예술 작품 감상의 태도는?

① 예술가의 장인 정신을 깊이 있게 헤아려 본다.
② 깊은 생각 없이 다만 작품에서 즐거움을 찾는다.
③ 작품의 진실성이나 의미에 대하여 많이 고려하지 않는다.
④ 우리를 감동시키는 것이 무엇인가에 대하여 깊이 생각한다.

23 이 글의 요지를 가장 잘 나타낸 것은?

① 예술 작품은 내용뿐만 아니라 기교도 중요하다.
② 예술 작품의 성공 여부는 예술가의 성품에 달려 있다.
③ 예술가의 완벽한 기교만이 최고의 예술품을 창조한다.
④ 예술 작품에서 즐거움을 찾는다고 해서 비난받을 수는 없다.

[24-28] 서강대 2009

Henri Matisse and Marc Chagall were both famous artists. The two men painted in France in the early twentieth century. Their paintings influenced many other artists of their time. Henri Matisse was born in a small town in France in 1869. He grew up in a wealthy family and showed no early interest in art. Then, while recovering from a surgery in 1890, he began to pass the time by painting. From then on, he considered himself a painter.

In his paintings, Matisse used color in a way that no artist had before. His bold and unusual use of color let the viewer see the world in a new way. When he grew ill and could no longer paint, Matisse did not give up being an artist. He cut out large and colorful paper shapes and arranged them on a canvas. In this way, he was able to create beautiful art until the end of his life.

Marc Chagall was born in a small Russian town in 1887. His family was poor, but young Chagall begged his parents to let him study art. After working for some time as an artist, Chagall decided to go to Paris. He studied and worked there for four years before returning to Russia, where he met and married his wife. Eventually, he moved his family to Paris, where he stayed for most of his remaining years. His later work included murals and stained-glass windows.

Chagall's paintings remind people of scenes they might see in a dream. Animals and people float in the air. Wonderfully unusual colors add to the dream-like quality. Chagall used ideas from Russian fairy tales and Jewish folk tales in many of his works.

Matisse and Chagall each used art and color to show ideas in new and unusual ways. Today their paintings hang in fine museums all over the world. Along with artists like Monet and Picasso, they are considered pioneers of modern art.

24 What is common between Matisse and Chagall?

① Both lived in Russia and moved to Paris.
② Both came from wealthy families.
③ Both painted dream-like scenes all their lives.
④ Both painted in France in the early twentieth century.

25 What similarities do Chagall's paintings have with those of Matisse?

① They include fairy tale scenes.
② They present colors in unusual ways.
③ They are mostly portraits.
④ They are made of cut-out shapes.

26 What did young Matisse and young Chagall have in common?

① Both had large families.
② Both grew up in a small town.
③ Both had an early interest in art.
④ Both grew up in France.

27 How did Chagall and Matisse differ toward the end of their lives?

① Matisse made cut-outs, while Chagall created murals.
② Matisse painted fairy tale scenes, while Chagall painted portraits.
③ Matisse worked in France, while Chagall worked in Russia.
④ Matisse discovered the effect of black and white, while Chagall used bolder color.

28 According to the author, what do Matisse and Chagall have in common with Monet and Picasso?

① They all painted until the end of their lives.
② They all stopped painting to work on other types of art.
③ They were all pioneers of modern art.
④ They all discovered a love for art early in their lives.

[29-30] 한국외대 2006

[1] The Renaissance painter Giotto imitated nature so accurately that his teacher swatted at a painted fly on one of Giotto's works. Is this not a superb artistic achievement? If so, the artist's object was mimesis. Beginning during the Renaissance, mimesis was considered the pinnacle of artistic achievement. However, modern art focuses on depicting not only the world of surfaces but also the inner world of abstract thoughts and feelings. Modern art focuses on the way the elements in the work of art interact and what feelings these elements evoke. A quick glance at art produced over the past century reveals that mimesis has been abandoned by the vast majority of artists.

[2] From around 1880 to the outbreak of World War I, a series of sweeping changes in technology and culture created distinctive new modes of thinking about and experiencing time and space. Such radical inventions as the telephone, automobile, airplane, X-Ray machine, cinema, and standard Greenwich time forced people to reconsider perceptions of the world that had been in place for centuries. Distances

seemed to shrink. Time grew more particularized and less subject to nature. Artists responded in kind. Intent on representing the shifting sands of reality, painters and novelists abandoned verisimilitude and forged new art forms that explored man's new relationship with his environment.

29 위의 두 지문에서 알게 된 내용으로 가장 적합한 것을 고르시오.

① Art before the Renaissance was propelled by its desire for mimetic representation.
② Modern art turned its attention away from producing a mimetic depiction of the world.
③ Modern technological inventions had little to do with the changes in modern art.
④ Changes in society from around 1880 to 1914 were characterized by speed.

30 Unlike the author of [1], the author of [2] _____.

① laments the loss of traditional modes of thought
② points to the cultural factors that led to a shift in artistic style
③ fixes the exact moment of a major shift in perspective
④ mentions a revolution in the forms art has taken

[31-33] 가톨릭대 2011

A friend told me he once took a copy of a Leonardo da Vinci painting to a museum and showed it to the curator. The curator took one look and correctly told him not only when it was painted, but also the nationality of the copyist.

"How did you do that?" my friend asked, thinking he had run across the world's greatest ㉮ parlour trick. It turned out to be something more than that. "We're all prisoners of our times," the curator said, "especially a copyist, whose powers of imagination are, by definition, (㉯). The choice of a subject to copy, the brush strokes and the emphasis all reflect the tastes and styles in vogue in the time and place he made this copy. The clues track behind him like muddy boots; they shriek from this canvas. How could anyone expect he would be able to escape his own skin?"

31 윗글의 내용과 일치하는 것은?

① The curator did not realize that the da Vinci painting was a fraud.
② Almost all of the copyists were confined in their time and place.
③ The copyist's imagination sometimes goes beyond the original painter's.
④ The curator found the trace of muddy boots from the canvas.

32 ㉮가 구체적으로 의미하는 것은?

① 다빈치 모조 기술
② 모조품 식별 기술
③ 미술관 관리 기법
④ 미술품 복원 기법

33 빈칸 ㉯에 가장 적절한 것은?

① limited
② potent
③ flexible
④ endurable

[34-37]

A combination of geometric regularity and keen observation of nature is characteristic of all Egyptian art. We can study it best in the reliefs and paintings that adorned the walls of tombs. The word "adorned," it is true, may hardly fit an art which was meant to be seen by no one but the dead man's soul. In fact, these works were not intended to be enjoyed. They, too, were meant to "keep alive." Once, in a grim distant past, it had been the custom when a powerful man died to let his servants accompany him into the grave. Later, these horrors were considered either too cruel or too costly, and art came to the rescue. Instead of real servants, the great ones of this earth were given images as substitutes. The pictures and models found in Egyptian tombs were connected with the idea of providing the soul with helpmates in the other world.
To us these reliefs and wall-paintings provide an extraordinarily vivid picture of life as it

was lived in Egypt thousands of years ago. And yet, looking at them for the first time, one may find them rather bewildering. The reason is that the Egyptian painters had quite a different way from ours of representing real life. Perhaps this is connected with the different purpose their paintings had to serve. What mattered most was not prettiness but _____. It was the artists' task to preserve everything as clearly and permanently as possible. So they did not set out to sketch nature as it appeared to them from any fortuitous angle. They drew from memory, according to strict rules which ensured that everything that had to go into the picture would stand out in perfect clarity. Their method, in fact, resembled that of the map-maker rather than that of the painter.

34 Choose the one that best fills in the blank.

① craftsmanship
② decoration
③ completeness
④ opaqueness

35 Which of the following can be inferred about "Egyptian tombs"?

① The art on their walls did not have to be aesthetically pleasing.
② The deceased commissioned the art work on them before he died.
③ The largest chamber was reserved for the deceased.
④ There are many more to be excavated in the desert.

36 According to the passage, what was the function of artwork in tombs?

① to keep the memory of the deceased alive for future generations
② to provide a means to purify the soul of the deceased
③ to uphold the belief that the deceased could be accompanied by others after death
④ to record the life history of the deceased and his family

37 According to the passage, why are Egyptian artists compared to map-makers?

① They had to take nature into consideration.
② They made efforts to record details in a precise way.
③ They learned drawing techniques from map-makers.
④ They had to revise their paintings every few years.

[38-40] 단국대 2012

> Camille Claudel (1864-1943) was a French sculptor who worked as an apprentice to artist Auguste Rodin, creator of the famous sculpture *The Kiss*. She served as Rodin's model and assistant, and as his mistress she bore him two children; yet Claudel also managed to produce quite a few of her own marble and bronze sculptures. These creations have won Claudel posthumous critical acclaim from many of today's art critics and historians. However, few of her own contemporaries appreciated her work. Some art historians argue that Claudel's talent was eclipsed by that of her mentor and lover. They note that the respected and popular Rodin occupied a prominent place in French culture, and even though Claudel tried to establish her own reputation, she never managed to emerge from his shadow. She was openly dismissed as deranged when she claimed that Rodin had stolen some of her ideas. Other historians and critics claim that Claudel's lack of success can be attributed to her gender; female artists of the nineteenth century were seldom taken seriously, _____. While studying nude models with Rodin, Claudel developed a deep admiration for the human form, and both artists created sculptures that reflected this admiration. Claudel's *The Age of Maturity*, for instance, portrays a nude woman on her knees pleading with a departing man. The public and the press at the time, however, rejected her sculptures as inappropriately lewd and unsuitable for display.

38 What would be the primary purpose of the passage?

① To persuade the reader to support female sculptors in need
② To inform how women artists were treated in the past
③ To illustrate how Claudel had developed her artistic imagination
④ To demonstrate some of the difficulties women artists are facing

39 Which of the following is most suitable for the blank?

① showing you an example
② but that was not the only reason
③ which was also the case for male artists
④ nor were they given equal opportunities

40 Which of the following best explains the underlined word posthumous?

① successful
② after-death
③ hardly possible
④ single-handed

[41-43] 동덕여대 2012

Dada artists showed their disapproval of and contempt for traditional culture and artistic conventions and continually tried to undermine them. A striking example of this is Marcel Duchamp's infamous act of drawing a mustache on a reproduction of Leonardo da Vinci's *Mona Lisa*, an act which the art establishment considered irreverent and ill-conceived. Dada sought to represent the opposite of whatever art stood for. If conventional art had at least an implied message, Dada was to have no meaning. Thus, the interpretation of Dada works depended wholly on the viewer.

Dada opened up and explored whole new approaches to creativity. No longer constrained by artistic traditions, Dada artists found themselves free to experiment with the creative process. For example, the painter Jean Arp took sheets of paper and tore them roughly into squares, which he then dropped unto a sheet of paper on the floor, gluing them wherever they landed. Arp was so pleased with the randomness and improvisation of this method that he used it to create one of his best known works, *Collage Arranged According to the Laws of Chance*.

Marcel Duchamp, perhaps the most influential of the Dada artists, was famous for his ready-mades, which were intended to be an overt criticism of the strictly conventional use of mediums within art. Ⓐ These were common mass-produced objects, such as soup cans and bottle racks, that the artists modified in some way or combined with other objects. Ⓑ The artist conferred the status of art upon them simply by exhibiting them in a gallery. Ⓒ Duchamp's most outrageous ready-made sculpture, Fountain, was simply a porcelain urinal. Ⓓ

41 According to paragraph 1, which of the following is true of Dada artists?

① They used classical art styles in their works.
② They were at odds with the established art world.
③ They attempted to destroy famous works of art.
④ The artists' messages are implied in their art.

42 Which of the following can be inferred from the passage about Jean Arp?

① He was the first to invent the technique of collage.
② He did not think it necessary to have control over his art.
③ He preferred to create art with a minimum effort.
④ He thought it important to apply scientific knowledge to his art.

43 Where would the sentence below best fit? Choose the blank where the sentence should be added to the passage.

> It was signed and dated as any work of art would be.

① Ⓐ ② Ⓑ
③ Ⓒ ④ Ⓓ

[44-45] 인하대 2014

Patience Webb learned long ago that the way to encourage a child in art is to find out what makes him tick. Webb, who has taught art for twenty-seven years in Massachusetts schools, tells the story of seven-year-old Chuckie who thought he couldn't do anything right in art class. So he wouldn't even try. But then Webb discovered he loved cheetahs. So she asked him to do a study of them. He spent weeks on his drawing and was so proud of it, he used it for the cover of a school report he did on the big cats. Figure out what _____ your child, says Webb, even on an unconscious level. What colors does he like? What does he collect? What are the constant themes of his life? Use what he likes as the basis for an art project. It takes some thinking: Does he love cars and like to draw? Make a map together of a town with roads for his toy cars. Whether you have a hesitant artist or a kid who already loves art, he or she can benefit from your thoughtful direction on occasional projects.

44 What is the best title of the passage?

① How to Make Children Creative
② Reduce Learning Anxieties of Children
③ Home as a Starting Point for Art Education
④ Tailor Art Projects to Children's Excitements

45 Which of the following is most appropriate for the blank?

① interests
② worries
③ enervates
④ celebrates

[46-47] 한국외대 2017

Robert Allen Zimmerman, music's own poet laureate, better known as Bob Dylan, has won the Nobel Prize for Literature. His influence still pervades music genres from rock and pop to folk and soul, while his stunning lyrical ability remains the pinnacle, inspiring a host of singer-songwriters hoping to make an impact of their own. Dylan's career has spanned more than five decades. His poignant, powerful, fiery, heartbreaking, and often witty way with words arguably sparks more admiration than his distinctive, gravelly drawl and proves that a skillful command of language really can change the world. The man himself has kept the meaning of many of his songs a mystery, once telling an interviewer that he did not know what they were about. He said, "Some are about four minutes long, some are about five," eluding probing and remaining a fascinating, complex (A) _____.

46 According to the passage, what did Dylan's way with words demonstrate?

① A five-decade music career
② The power of a skillful command of language
③ The secret meaning of his songs
④ More admiration for his musical skills

47 Which of the following best fits into (A)?

① parody ② ascetic
③ enigma ④ belief

[48-50] 중앙대 2017

Perhaps you've seen the painting: a pipe, depicted with photographic realism, floats above a line of careful script (A) <u>that reads</u> "Ceci n'est pas une pipe"—"This is not a pipe." René Magritte painted *The Treachery of Images* in the 1920s, and people have been talking ever since about what it means.

Did Magritte intend to remind us that a representation is not the object it depicts—that his painting is "only" a painting and not a pipe? Such an interpretation is widely taught to college students, but if it is true, Magritte went to an awful lot of trouble—carefully selecting a dress-finish pipe of particularly elegant design, making dozens of sketches of it, taking it apart to familiarize himself with its anatomy, then painting its portrait with great care and skill—just to tell us something we already knew. In another canvas, *The Two Mysteries*, Magritte is even more insistent: the original pipe painting, complete with caption, is depicted as sitting on an easel that rests on a plank floor, but above that painting, to the left, hovers a *second* pipe, larger (or closer) than the painted canvas and its frame. What we have here is a painting of a paradox. Obviously the smaller pipe is a painting and not a pipe. But what is the second pipe, the one that looms outside the represented canvas? And if (B) <u>that too</u> is but a painting, then where does the painting end?

It seems to me that the roots of the paradox reside in the concept of the frame. When we look at a realistic painting—a portrait of a historical figure—we accept (C) <u>by convention</u> that the portrait represents a real person and actual objects. When that convention is denied, as in Magritte's pipe paintings, the point is not to remind us that paintings are not real. That much is true but trivial. The point is to challenge the belief that everything outside the frame is real.

The enemy of artists like Magritte is naïve realism—the dogged assumption that the human sensory apparatus accurately records the one and only real world, (D) <u>which</u> the human brain can make but one accurate model. The truth, of course, is that nobody can grasp reality whole, that each person's universe is to some extent unique, and that this circumstance makes it impossible for us to prove that there is but one true reality.

48 윗글에서 어법상 가장 적합하지 않은 것을 고르시오.

① (A) ② (B)
③ (C) ④ (D)

49 윗글을 통해 추론할 수 있는 것으로 가장 적합한 것을 고르시오.

① Magritte's paintings are not familiar to many college students.
② Magritte exerted unnecessary efforts in drawing *The Treachery of Images*.
③ Magritte's two paintings convey different messages.
④ Magritte's intention of drawing the pipe paintings is often misunderstood.

50 윗글의 요지로 가장 적합한 것을 고르시오.

① Our understanding of reality is limited and variegated.
② Modern paintings are open to multiple interpretations.
③ The ultimate goal of modern artists is to portray the paradox residing in reality.
④ We can reach true reality only by collaborative efforts.

CHAPTER 05 영화·스포츠

[01-04] 삼육대 2007

West Side Story is a musical tragedy based on William Shakespeare's timeless love story, *Romeo and Juliet*. It is set in the early 1950s, when gang warfare in big cities led to injuries and even death. *West Side Story* transformed the Montagues and Capulets of Shakespeare's play into rival street gangs, the Jets and the Sharks. The Sharks were newly arrived Puerto Ricans, the Jets native born New Yorkers. The plot tells the story of Maria, a Puerto Rican whose brother Bernardo is the leader of the Sharks, and of Tony, a member of Jets. As the opposing gangs battle in the streets of New York, these two fall in love. While attempting to stop a street fight, Tony inadvertently kills Maria's brother Bernardo and is ultimately killed himself.

West Side Story featured the talents of a trio of theatrical legends. Leonard Bernstein, who composed the brilliant score, was a classical composer and the conductor of the New York Philharmonic. Stephen Sondheim, making his Broadway debut, revealed a remarkable talent for writing lyrics. Among the hit songs of the play are "Tonight," "Maria," "America," "Gee Officer Krupke," and "I Feel Pretty." Jerome Robbins' electrifying choreography broke new ground for musical theater in the 1950s. Before *West Side Story*, no one thought that dance could be as integral to a narrative as the music and the lyrics. But the dances in *West Side Story* are among the most thrilling elements of the play.

The play opened on September 26, 1957. It ran for 734 performances, toured for 10 months, and then returned to New York for an additional 246 performances. The classic motion picture starring Natalie Wood was released in 1961. It garnered ten Academy Awards, including ones for Best Picture and Best Director. The play was successfully revived in New York in 1980 and then again in 1995, almost forty years after its premier performance.

01 According to the passage, when does the action of the play *West Side Story* take place?

① In Shakespeare's play
② In the early 1950s
③ In 1957
④ In 1980

02 It can be inferred from the passage that the Capulets and Montagues _____.

① were families in Shakespeare's play
② were 1950s street gangs
③ fought against the Jets and Sharks
④ were groups of actors, dancers, and singers

03 What can be inferred from the passage about musical plays produced before *West Side Story*?

① They involved fewer songs.
② Dance was not such an important feature in them.
③ They depended on dance and song more than on plot.
④ Legendary talents did not help create them.

04 During its initial appearance in New York, how many times was *West Side Story* performed?

① 10
② 26
③ 246
④ 734

[05-07] 성균관대 2012

The camera is the means by which we stamp ourselves on everything we see, under cover of recording the Wonders of the World already wonderfully recorded by professionals and on sale at every corner bookshop and newsagent. But what use to us an illustrated book of perfect photographs? What use to show our friends, back home, postcards of the Taj Mahal, the Coliseum, the Leaning Tower of Pisa since _____? No temple is of interest without our faces beside it, grinning. Most amateur photographers show no interest in the world as it is, only in the world as it ideally should be. For example, you want a picture of the Real Morocco—a scene as old as time. Unfortunately for you a glassy modern building edges up to the mosque; behind the minaret television aerials spike the sky; beside the camel two Moroccans in unsuitable Western suits stand discussing business. So you must stand and twist your camera, hold it up sideways, shift your position so that the little yellow lines just clear the building, just cut out the aerials and the telegraph wires, just exclude the business men while retaining the rest. And when all these alien elements have, for a precious moment, been obliterated, click. There, the Real Morocco. That is the summit of the amateur photographer's art—total unreality. The World As It Isn't.

05 What is the tone of the passage?

① informative
② sentimental
③ apologetic
④ satirical
⑤ gloomy

06 Which of the following would be best for the blank?

① our pictures are out of focus
② we don't visit the real places
③ we are not in the picture
④ we forget to bring the cameras
⑤ we are not the professional photographers

07 According to the passage, which of the following is true?

① In Morocco, it is very hard to find the real Moroccans.
② The poor skill of amateur photographers often distorts the reality.
③ Tourists tend to prefer modern Morocco to old-fashioned one.
④ Travelling with camera encourages tourist to experience the unexpected things.
⑤ Travelling with camera often narrows the minds of tourists.

[08-10] 단국대 2006

I can't think of anything more exciting than watching a well-crafted, really scary, suspenseful movie. I write horror fiction myself and love the suspension of reality that accompanies the experience. For ninety minutes or so, I have no problems, no dishes or laundry to do and no bills to pay. I have always been attracted to this genre, although I am not sure why. Perhaps it concerns hostile feelings that find a harmless vent in this way. In any case, a good scary movie or murder mystery is always my cup of tea.

To those who claim that horror films have no redeeming value, I would ask if they themselves think they have any. Movies are an art form and should be done well. If they are true to their genre, then it all becomes a matter of personal choice. Blue isn't necessarily better than red; it's just different. The English take the horror genre more seriously than American filmmakers. Christopher Lee and Peter Cushing both portrayed psychopaths and moody monsters with purpose and dignity. The English seem to have it all in that regard, except for maybe Vincent Price, whose spirit belongs exclusively to the American horror cinema scene.

Science fiction, suspense and horror films all have their place in the modern cinema. Do dead men walk our city streets? Perhaps they do. Maybe they're just looking for a good movie. As Rodney Dangerfield used to say, "a little respect," let's give it to them.

08 What is the main purpose of the passage?

① To promote one of the famous horror movies
② To argue that watching horror films is harmless
③ To assert that scary films have their own merits
④ To chronicle the history of English horror movies

09 What is the author's attitude toward movies?

① Horror movies should be restricted to adult viewers.
② Movies are movies, and people should take them lightly.
③ Some valuable lessons should be included in the movies.
④ Preference for certain movies is a matter of personal choice.

10 The author says that blue isn't necessarily better than red, because _____.

① they do not belong to the same colors
② s/he has a personal preference to red color
③ s/he implies that there are various kinds of movies
④ black and white movies are as good as color movies

[11-12] 중앙대 2006

Up until 1915, the movies were little more than the cheap amusements. Technically crude, poorly made, and generally plotless, they were most certainly not considered art. Then along came D. W. Griffith's *Birth of a Nation*. Practically overnight, moving pictures became respectable. Griffith introduced technical novelties like the close-up. Griffith's film also told a story. It even showcased actors and actresses who conveyed genuine emotion. In other words, they could act. A runway hit almost immediately, *Birth of a Nation* was nevertheless far from a complete triumph. It was racist to the core. The film reveled in crude and cruel stereotypes of African Americans. It actually presented members of the Ku Klux Klan as the movie's heroes. Outraged, the newly formed NAACP (National Association for the Advancement of Colored People) picketed movie theaters where *Birth of a Nation* was showing. Some concerned citizens, like social worker Jane Addams, wrote letters of protest. Unfortunately, the protests only stimulated interest in the film. To see what all the fuss was about, _____.

11 윗글의 빈칸에 들어가기에 가장 적당한 것을 고르시오.

① administrators had to shut down movie theaters
② moviegoers bought tickets in droves
③ legislators decided to stop showing the movie
④ many people wrote letters of protest

12 윗글의 내용과 일치하지 않는 것을 고르시오.

① Early movies before 1915 were not considered art because they were plotless and technically crude.
② *Birth of a Nation* was a racist film because it portrayed cruel stereotypes of black people.
③ Jane Addams formed NAACP to protest racism in *Birth of a Nation*.
④ Paradoxically, the fuss over *Birth of a Nation* stimulated interest in the film.

[13-14] 명지대 2009

Characterization in a play is based almost entirely on action and dialogue. Action can include such subtle devices as a gesture or a change of expression, and dialogue can include a monologue that resembles the expression of thoughts and feelings. In a play, the role of costuming is also important. But the major impression of a character on stage is made by what that character does and what he or she says to others. Compare this with the devices available in fiction. In that more flexible genre you as author can use the character's own thoughts, the thoughts of others, quick glimpses into the past through flashbacks, and direct exposition. Since the devices available to the dramatist are more limited, the tendency is to use them more boldly. Audiences are used to this. Just as the makeup is heavier, the voice louder, characterization is applied more bluntly in a play. It seems natural to use the word 'theatrical' to describe individuals whose personalities are vivid and striking.

13 윗글의 제목으로 가장 적절한 것은?

① The History of the Development of the Theatre
② The Merits of Fiction Writing
③ The Nature of Characterization in Drama
④ The Relationship between the Author and His Audience

14 윗글의 내용과 일치하지 않는 것은?

① Fiction provides the author with much more flexibility than does drama.
② Monologue is one of the ways in which the playwright deals with characterization.
③ The novelist often uses flashbacks and direct expositions, devices that are not readily available to the dramatist.
④ It is often the audience who complains most about the heavy makeup actors must wear on stage.

[15-18]

We go see a horror movie to re-establish our feelings of essential normality; _____. It urges us to put away our more civilized and adult penchant for analysis and to become children again, seeing things in pure blacks and whites. And we go to have fun. This is where the ground starts to slope away, because this is a very peculiar sort of fun. The fun comes from seeing others menaced—sometimes killed. A critic has suggested that the horror film has become the modern version of the public lynching.

The potential lyncher is in almost all of us, and every now and then, he has to be let loose. Our emotions and our fears form their own body, and we recognize that it demands its own exercise to maintain proper muscle tone. Certain of these emotional muscles are accepted, even exalted, in civilized society. Love, friendship, loyalty, kindness—these are the emotions that we applaud. When we exhibit these emotions, society showers us with positive reinforcement. But anticivilization emotions don't go away, and they demand periodic exercise. The horror movie has a dirty job to do. It deliberately appeals to all that is worst in us. It is morbidity unchained, our most abject instincts let free, our nastiest fantasies realized. The most aggressive of horror films lifts a trap door in the civilized forebrain and throws a basket of raw meat to the hungry alligators swimming around in that subterranean river beneath. It keeps them from getting out. It keeps them down there and me up here.

15 Choose the one that best fills in the blank.

① the horror movie transforms moral standards
② the horror movie is innately conventional
③ the horror movie disavows antisocial desires
④ the horror movie is traumatic for children

16 Which of the following cannot be inferred from the passage?

① We tend to use horror movies as an outlet for socially unacceptable emotions.
② The simplicity of a horror movie can provide psychic relief to a degree.
③ A periodic lapse into irrationality enables us to eradicate our fears.
④ What makes us recoil may at the same time satisfy our unconscious desire.

17 What is the purpose of the passage?

① to explain why people crave horror movies
② to analyze various types of insanity
③ to prove everyone is prone to violence
④ to persuade people to view horror movies

18 What is the tone of the passage?

① accusatory
② analytical
③ inspirational
④ judgmental

[19-21] 국민대 2013

Superheroes are extraordinarily powerful people who have both strengths and weaknesses. They typically have superpowers, such as the ability to fly or leap over tall buildings. (A) Superheroes must possess a noble character that guides them into worthy achievements. They may have dark thoughts, just like any human being, but that darkness must be constrained by their desire to do the right thing. (B) So, not every costumed crime fighter is necessarily a hero, and not every character that has superpowers is necessarily a superhero. The image of the superhero is inspirational and aspirational. (C) In stories and movies, superheroes present us with something we can all aspire to. Plato believed that good is inherently attractive. That's why superheroes are depicted as moral forces, forces for what is good and right. (D) They remind us of the importance of self-discipline, self-sacrifice, and using our lives for something good and noble. In short, our favorite superheroes teach us lessons while also ⓐ _____ us.

19 Which is the best place for the following sentence?

> But while the "super" parts are certainly impressive, we should never forget the "hero" element as well.

① (A) ② (B)
③ (C) ④ (D)

20 Which best fits into the blank ⓐ?

① mitigating ② preempting
③ disapproving ④ entertaining

21 Which is NOT true according to the passage?

① Plato argued for superheroes' moral perfection.
② Superheroes control their weaknesses to act morally.
③ We are inspired by superheroes to better ourselves.
④ Superpower is not the only thing required of superheroes.

[22-24] 명지대 2013

In 1968, Paramount had optioned a draft of the novel *The Godfather* by New York writer Mario Puzo, but had let the novel sit dormant until it became a bestseller. By 1970, Paramount executives were seeking a director to make a movie based on Puzo's book. After a number of film-makers rejected the project, Ⓐ the studio turned to Francis Ford Coppola, a man with experience in the industry but no hit to his name.

[A] Throughout the production of the film, Coppola reportedly believed he had failed at every aspect of his job. He had won small victories along the way, though—among them persuading Paramount to cast Al Pacino and Marlon Brando, and getting Ⓑ the studio to finance location shoots in New York City and Sicily. When production wrapped up in September 1971, Coppola again sailed for Europe expecting to leave his troubles behind.

[B] *The Godfather* opened in Manhattan on March 15, 1972, and people stood six abreast in block-long lines. The movie was an unmitigated commercial and critical success. By mid-April, it was bringing in $1 million a day. After its first run, it had taken in $86.2 million, making it the highest grossing movie in history. By the end of its second run, *The Godfather* had earned over $150 million—establishing Coppola as Hollywood's most lucrative and powerful director.

[C] Ⓒ The studio figured that as an Italian-American, Coppola would have an innate feel for the movie's subject and thus lend authenticity to the plot and production. Coppola, although reluctant to accept the assignment, had recently failed to finance his own studio, named Ⓓ Zoetrope, and needed money to repay his Hollywood lenders. He accepted the job while on a cruise across the Atlantic and set to work by literally breaking the book down into sections and taping them to the windows of one of the ship's rooms.

22 Choose the best order of the paragraphs after the one given in the box.

① [A] — [B] — [C] ② [B] — [A] — [C]
③ [B] — [C] — [A] ④ [C] — [A] — [B]

23 Choose the best title for the passage above.

① Stories Untold about Coppola and *The Godfather*
② The Sole Secret of The Godfather's Success
③ *The Godfather*. A Movie Before a Novel
④ *The Godfather* Still Haunts Hollywood

24 Choose the one that does not refer to the same as the rest.

① Ⓐ the studio
② Ⓑ the studio
③ Ⓒ the studio
④ Ⓓ Zoetrope

[25-26] 명지대 2009

The origins of baseball date back to 1839 when Abner Doubleday laid out a diamond-shaped field at Coopertown, and attempted to standardize the rules governing the game. By the end of the Civil War, over 200 teams or clubs existed, and were constantly on the road competing with one another. They belonged to a national association of "Baseball Players." These teams were amateurs, but as the game waxed in popularity, it offered opportunities for profit, and the first professional team, the Cincinnati Red Stockings, appeared in 1869. Other cities soon fielded professional teams, and in 1876 the present National League was organized chiefly by Albert Spalding. Soon a rival league appeared, the American Association. Competition between the two was intense, and in 1883 they played a post-season contest, the first "World's Series." The American Association eventually collapsed, but in 1900 the American League was organized.

25 1869년 이전의 야구선수들의 특성과 일치하지 않는 것은?

① They traveled extensively.
② They belonged to a handful of clubs.
③ They played by agreed rules.
④ They were not professional.

26 다음 중 National League에 대한 설명으로 옳지 않은 것은?

① Its first professional team was the Red Stockings.
② The organization did not exist prior to 1876.
③ Albert Spalding was instrumental in its establishment.
④ It was eventually superceded by the American League.

[27-28] 중앙대 2009

How and why did studying the career trajectories of star football players give you a window on better management of business organizations and careers? As research on the National Football League(NFL) reveals, sometimes the specific nature of a job determines whether a great performer at one company can replicate that performance at another. Sports teams are organizations much like many others, subject to the errors that are common elsewhere. But their successes and failures are highly visible and amplified by the fact that they perform in a zero-sum world. In order for one team to win, another team has to lose. As a result, their focus is especially performance-oriented. Teams hire stars on the basis of talent—as do many organizations. Thus, if a star's performance is measured into highly accurate statistical data, they allow researchers to examine whether performance is as (A) portable in a new environment as many in the NFL believe. For business managers, the fact that the star's performance is portable for some positions and not portable for others is necessary to know.

27 밑줄 친 (A)의 문맥상의 의미로 가장 적합한 것을 고르시오.

① distinguishable
② measurable
③ replicable
④ tangible

28 위의 지문의 내용과 가장 일치하는 것을 고르시오.

① Assigning a proper position is important for star performers' portability.
② Star performers are at their best in any organizations.
③ It is very difficult for star performers to survive in a new organization.
④ NFL research finally concludes that star performers should be chosen on the basis of their talent.

[29-30] 숙명여대 2012

> One oarsman on his own cannot win the Oxford and Cambridge boat race. He needs eight colleagues. Each one is a specialist who always sits in a particular part of the boat—bow or stroke or cox etc. Rowing the boat is a cooperative venture, but some men are nevertheless better at it than others. Suppose a coach has to choose his ideal crew from a pool of candidates, some specializing in the bow position, others specializing as cox, and so on. Suppose that he makes his selection as follows. Every day he puts together three new trial crews, by random shuffling of the candidates for each position, and he makes the three crews race against each other. _____ some weeks of this it will start to emerge that the winning boat often tends to contain the same individual men. These are marked up as good oarsmen. Other individuals seem consistently to be found in slower crews, and these are eventually rejected. But even an outstandingly good oarsman might sometimes be a member of a slow crew, either because of the inferiority of the other members, or because of bad luck—say a strong adverse wind.

29 What would be the most appropriate expression to fill in the blank?

① After
② Before
③ In spite of
④ Into
⑤ Out of

30 It is only _____ that the best men tend to be in the winning boat.

① in the know
② on average
③ on a lark
④ out of action
⑤ out of necessity

[31-33] 한국외대 2014

U.S. audiences devour Western films. In the United States, it is easy to see why Anglos might like Westerns, for it is they who are portrayed as heroes who tame the savage wilderness and defend themselves from cruel, barbaric Indians who are intent on destruction. But why would Indians like Westerns? Intrigued, sociologist JoEllen Shively decided to investigate the matter by showing a Western movie to adult Native Americans and Anglos. She found something surprising: All Native Americans and Anglos identified with the cowboys; none identified with the Indians. The ways in which Anglos and Native Americans identified with the cowboys, however, were _____. While Anglos saw the movie as an actual portrayal of the Old West and a justification of their own status in society, Native Americans saw it as embodying a free, natural way of life. What appears to make Westerns meaningful to Indians is the fantasy of being free and independent like the cowboys. Indians find a fantasy in the cowboy story in which the important parts of their ways of life triumph and are morally good, validating their own cultural group in the context of a dramatically satisfying story. "Values, not ethnicity, are the central issue," says Shively. If a Native American film industry were to portray Indians with the same values that the Anglo movie industry projects onto cowboys, then Native Americans would identify with their own group.

31 Which of the following statements is best supported by this passage?

① People of different ethnicities can share similar values.
② People's taste in movies has to do with their ethnicity.
③ Westerners are prejudiced against Native Americans.
④ Native Americans were portrayed variously in Westerns.

32 According to the passage, Native Americans identify with cowboys because _____.

① cowboys represent a way of life they envision
② cowboys justify the status of the Indians
③ cowboys portray the Wild West
④ cowboys are always victorious

33 Which of the following best fits into the blank?

① fairly practical
② quite different
③ highly effective
④ rather groundless

[34-35] 에리카 2018

Baseball is one of the most widely watched and played sports in the world, ranking with soccer and basketball in terms of the number of countries in which it is played and the number of people who take part in the game. The game — originally known as "townball" — developed in the early nineteenth century in the northeastern United States. It borrowed from the English games of cricket and rounders, and from children's games such as "one old cat." In the 1840s, Alexander Cartwright _____ the field dimensions in use today. In 1858, sportswriter Henry Chadwick wrote the first rule book. Union soldiers helped spread the popularity of the game during the Civil War(1861-1865). Then, in 1869, baseball's first professional team, the Cincinnati Red Stockings, was organized. The National league was established in 1876, and the rival American league in 1901. The first World Series was played between the Pittsburgh Pirates, the champions of the National league, and the Boston Pilgrims, American league champions, in 1903. Baseball had become "the national pastime" of the United States.

34 빈칸에 들어갈 가장 알맞은 것을 고르시오.

① increased
② diversified
③ temporized
④ standardized

35 윗글의 내용과 맞지 않는 것을 고르시오.

① Baseball was influenced by English games such as cricket and rounders.
② The American league was established much earlier than the National league.
③ Baseball was originally known as townball in the early nineteenth century in the United States.
④ The first World Series was played between the Pittsburgh Pirates and the Boston Pilgrims.

[36-38] 명지대 2017

Many people enjoy benefits from sports without ever paying the team or event organizer. They bask in civic pride because they live in a major league city, or they bask in national pride when their nation's athletes win Olympic medals. They line the streets of Manhattan for tickertape parades when the Yankees win the World Series, or pack Trafalgar Square in London and the beaches of Rio de Janeiro to celebrate their cities' being awarded the Olympic Games.

This complicates benefit-cost analysis of government policies supporting sports. In principle, measuring the benefits from ticket purchases and cable subscriptions is easy. Market data on ticket prices and sales, for instance, allow estimation of demand functions, and consumer and producer surplus. Such methods use revealed preference data, so called because people's purchases reveal their preferences for sports over alternative goods and services.

But no markets exist for tickertape parades and office conversations about last night's game. No league or team collects statistics measuring national pride or the value fans place on checking the highlights at ESPN.com or the league standings in their local newspapers. Crompton calls such benefits 'psychic income' and says they are perhaps the greatest _____ benefits produced by sports.

In this respect, sport resembles the environment. Both produce important benefits in the nature of non-rival and non-excludable public goods. No one disputes that many people value public goods such as scenic vistas, survival of endangered species, and clean air. But no one has to go to the corner shop or to an online seller to buy them. In other words, as in sports, many of the benefits are difficult to value because there are no revealed preference data with which to estimate demand and consumer surplus. Fortunately for sports economists, environmental economists have developed a method to measure the benefits of non-traded public goods.

36 Choose the one that would best fill in the blank.

① intangible
② pervasive
③ flamboyant
④ succulent

37 Which of the following is not mentioned?

① where Londoners gather for celebrations
② a definition of 'revealed preference data'
③ reasons for fans checking their team's league standings
④ an analogy between sport and the environment

38 What is the most likely purpose of this passage?

① to introduce a method to measure 'psychic income'
② to criticize government subsidization of sport teams
③ to emphasize the importance of government sports policies
④ to illustrate hidden benefits of sporting events

[39-40] 성균관대 2017

The depiction of a Polynesian character in a Disney film has prompted anger across the Pacific islands, with one New Zealand MP saying the portrayal of the god Maui as obese was "not acceptable." Jenny Salesa, who is of Tongan heritage, said Disney's rendering of Maui in the film *Moana* resembled a creature that was "half pig, half hippo."

In Polynesian mythology Maui is a heroic figure who created the Pacific Islands by fishing them out of the sea. Will Illolahia told Waatea News that Disney's version of Maui did not fit with his heroic endeavors in Pacific creation myths. "He is depicted in the stories, especially in my culture, as a person of strength and magnitude, a person of a godly nature," Illolahia said. "This depiction of Maui being obese is typical American stereotyping. Obesity is a new phenomenon because of the first world food that's been stuffed down our throat."

However, many people have commented on social media that Disney's Maui looks strong and powerful, and that his physique is not unusual among Polynesian men. Isoa Kavakimotu, a Tongan New Zealand man who identifies with being "a pretty big guy" created a YouTube video on the controversy, saying he had no problem with Disney's Maui. "I am fine with it," he said. "He doesn't look fat to me, he looks like a powerhouse who could do extraordinary labours. He is big for that reason. In the film they are sailing on a traditional waka, it is set before colonization, I highly doubt <u>a take-away store will pop up in the film</u>. To me, he looks ready for action."

39 The underlined "a take-away store will pop up in the film" means _____.

① the film uses speculative, fictional science-based depictions
② the time setting of the film is the modern period after colonization
③ the realistic depiction is strongly apparent in the film
④ the film focuses on everyday common life
⑤ the film is exploring the racial issue of a colony

40 According to the passage, which of the following is NOT correct?

① Most of Polynesian people are not overweight at present.
② Some expressed their approval of Disney's portrayal of Maui.
③ Portrayal of Maui prompted debate over stereotypes of Polynesian men on screen.
④ Disney's depiction of obese Polynesian god in the film sparked anger among Polynesian People.
⑤ The physical attributes of Maui were indicative of character in the Disney film.

여러분의 작은 소리
에듀윌은 크게 듣겠습니다.

본 교재에 대한 여러분의 목소리를 들려주세요.
공부하시면서 어려웠던 점, 궁금한 점,
칭찬하고 싶은 점, 개선할 점, 어떤 것이라도 좋습니다.

에듀윌은 여러분께서 나누어 주신 의견을
통해 끊임없이 발전하고 있습니다.

에듀윌 도서몰 book.eduwill.net
- 부가학습자료 및 정오표: 에듀윌 도서몰 → 도서자료실
- 교재 문의: 에듀윌 도서몰 → 문의하기 → 교재(내용, 출간) / 주문 및 배송

에듀윌 편입영어 기출심화 완성 독해

발 행 일	2022년 9월 8일 초판 ｜ 2022년 11월 30일 2쇄
편 저 자	에듀윌 편입 컨텐츠연구소, 홍준기 공저
펴 낸 이	권대호, 김재환
펴 낸 곳	(주)에듀윌
등록번호	제25100-2002-000052호
주 소	08378 서울특별시 구로구 디지털로34길 55 코오롱싸이언스밸리 2차 3층

* 이 책의 무단 인용·전재·복제를 금합니다.

www.eduwill.net
대표전화 1600-6700

꿈을 현실로 만드는
에듀윌

고객의 꿈, 직원의 꿈,
지역사회의 꿈을 실현한다

취업, 공무원, 자격증 시험준비의 흐름을 바꾼 화제작!
에듀윌 히트교재 시리즈

에듀윌 교육출판연구소가 만든 히트교재 시리즈!
YES24, 교보문고, 알라딘, 인터파크, 영풍문고 등 전국 유명 온/오프라인 서점에서 절찬 판매 중!

공인중개사 기초입문서/기본서/핵심요약집/문제집/기출문제집/실전모의고사 외 다수

주택관리사 기초서/기본서/핵심요약집/문제집/기출문제집/실전모의고사/네컷회계

7·9급공무원 기본서/단원별 문제집/기출문제집/기출팩/오답률TOP100/실전, 봉투모의고사

공무원 국어 한자/문법/독해/영어 단어·문법·독해/한국사/행정학·행정법 노트/행정법·헌법 판례집/면접

7급공무원 PSAT 기본서/기출문제집

계리직공무원 기본서/문제집/기출문제집

군무원 기출문제집/봉투모의고사

경찰공무원 기본서/기출문제집/모의고사/판례집/면접

소방공무원 기본서/기출팩/단원별 기출/실전, 봉투 모의고사

뷰티 미용사/맞춤형화장품

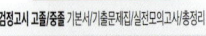

검정고시 고졸/중졸 기본서/기출문제집/실전모의고사/총정리

사회복지사(1급) 기본서/기출문제집/핵심요약집

직업상담사(2급) 기본서/기출문제집

경비 기본서/기출/1차 한권끝장/2차 모의고사

전기기사 필기/실기/기출문제집

전기기능사 필기/실기

※ YES24 수험서 자격증 공인중개사 베스트셀러 1위 (2011년 12월, 2012년 1월, 12월, 2013년 1월~5월, 8월~12월, 2014년 1월~5월, 7월~8월, 12월, 2015년 2월~4월, 2016년 2월, 4월, 6월, 12월, 2017년 1월~12월, 2018년 1월~12월, 2019년 1월~12월, 2020년 1월~12월, 2021년 1월~12월, 2022년 1월~11월 월별 베스트, 매월 1위 교재는 다름)
※ YES24 국내도서 해당분야 월별, 주별 베스트 기준

| 한국사능력검정시험 기본서/2주끝장/기출/우선순위50/초등 | 조리기능사 필기/실기 | 제과제빵기능사 필기/실기 | SMAT 모듈A/B/C | ERP정보관리사 회계/인사/물류/생산(1, 2급) | 전산세무회계 기초서/기본서/기출문제집 |

| 무역영어 1급 | 국제무역사 1급 | KBS한국어능력시험 | ToKL | 한국실용글쓰기 | 매경TEST 기본서/문제집/2주끝장 | TESAT 기본서/문제집/기출문제집 | 운전면허 1종·2종 |

| 스포츠지도사 필기/실기구술 한권끝장 | 산업안전기사 | 산업안전산업기사 | 위험물산업기사 | 위험물기능사 | 토익 입문서 | 실전서 | 종합서 | 컴퓨터활용능력 | 워드프로세서 | 정보처리기사 |

| 월간시사상식 | 일반상식 | 월간NCS | 매1N | NCS 통합 | 모듈형 | 피듈형 | PSAT형 NCS 수문끝 | PSAT 기출완성 | 6대 출제사 | 10개 영역 찐기출 | 한국철도공사 | 서울교통공사 | 부산교통공사 |

| 국민건강보험공단 | 한국전력공사 | 한수원 | 수자원 | 토지주택공사 | 행과연형 | 휴노형 | 기업은행 | 인국공 | 대기업 인적성 통합 | GSAT | LG | SKCT | CJ | L-TAB | ROTC·학사장교 | 부사관 |

※ YES24 수험서 자격증 주택관리사 베스트셀러 1위 (2010년 12월, 2011년 3월, 9월, 12월, 2012년 1월, 3월~12월, 2013년 1월~5월, 8월~11월, 2014년 2월~8월, 10월~12월, 2015년 1월~5월, 7월~12월, 2016년 1월~12월, 2017년 1월~12월, 2018년 1월~12월, 2019년 1월~12월, 2020년 1월~7월, 9월~12월, 2021년 1월~12월, 2022년 1월~11월 월별 베스트, 매월 1위 교재는 다름)
※ YES24, 알라딘 국내도서 해당분야 월별, 주별 베스트 기준

꿈을 현실로 만드는
에듀윌

공무원 교육
- 선호도 1위, 인지도 1위! 브랜드만족도 1위!
- 합격자 수 1,800% 폭등시킨 독한 커리큘럼

자격증 교육
- 6년간 아무도 깨지 못한 기록 합격자 수 1위
- 가장 많은 합격자를 배출한 최고의 합격 시스템

직영학원
- 직영학원 수 1위, 수강생 규모 1위!
- 표준화된 커리큘럼과 호텔급 시설 자랑하는 전국 53개 학원

종합출판
- 4대 온라인서점 베스트셀러 1위!
- 출제위원급 전문 교수진이 직접 집필한 합격 교재

어학 교육
- 토익 베스트셀러 1위
- 토익 동영상 강의 무료 제공
- 업계 최초 '토익 공식' 추천 AI 앱 서비스

콘텐츠 제휴 · B2B 교육
- 고객 맞춤형 위탁 교육 서비스 제공
- 기업, 기관, 대학 등 각 단체에 최적화된 고객 맞춤형 교육 및 제휴 서비스

부동산 아카데미
- 부동산 실무 교육 1위!
- 상위 1% 고소득 창업/취업 비법
- 부동산 실전 재테크 성공 비법

공기업 · 대기업 취업 교육
- 취업 교육 1위!
- 공기업 NCS, 대기업 직무적성, 자소서, 면접

학점은행제
- 97.6%의 과목이수율
- 14년 연속 교육부 평가 인정 기관 선정

대학 편입
- 편입 교육 1위!
- 업계 유일 500% 환급 상품 서비스

국비무료 교육
- '5년우수훈련기관' 선정
- K-디지털, 4차 산업 등 특화 훈련과정

IT 아카데미
- 1:1 밀착형 실전/실무 교육
- 화이트 해커/코딩 개발자 양성 과정

에듀윌 교육서비스 **공무원 교육** 9급공무원/7급공무원/경찰공무원/소방공무원/계리직공무원/기술직공무원/군무원 **자격증 교육** 공인중개사/주택관리사/전기기사/세무사/전산세무회계/경비지도사/검정고시/소방설비기사/소방시설관리사/사회복지사1급/건축기사/토목기사/직업상담사/전기기능사/산업안전기사/위험물산업기사/위험물기능사/ERP정보관리사/재경관리사/도로교통사고감정사/유통관리사/물류관리사/행정사/한국사능력검정/한경TESAT/매경TEST/KBS한국어능력시험/실용글쓰기/IT자격증/국제무역사/무역영어 **어학 교육** 토익 교재/토익 동영상 강의/인공지능 토익 앱 **대학 편입** 편입 교재/편입 영어·수학/경찰대/의치대/편입 컨설팅/면접 **공기업·대기업 취업 교육** 공기업 NCS·전공·상식/대기업 직무적성/자소서·면접 **직영학원** 공무원 학원/기술직공무원 학원/군무원학원/경찰학원/소방학원/공무원 면접학원/공인중개사 학원/주택관리사 학원/전기기사학원/취업아카데미/경영아카데미 **종합출판** 공무원·자격증 수험교재 및 단행본/월간지(시사상식) **학점은행제** 교육부 평가인정기관 원격평생교육원(사회복지사2급/경영학/CPA)/교육부 평가인정기관 원격사회교육원(사회복지사2급/심리학) **콘텐츠 제휴·B2B 교육** 교육 콘텐츠 제휴/기업 맞춤 자격증 교육/대학 취업역량 강화 교육 **부동산 아카데미** 부동산 창업CEO과정/실전 경매 과정/디벨로퍼 과정 **국비무료 교육(국비교육원)** 전기기능사/전기(산업)기사/소방설비(산업)기사/IT(빅데이터/자바프로그램/파이썬)/게임그래픽/3D프린터/실내건축디자인/웹퍼블리셔/그래픽디자인/영상편집(유튜브) 디자인/온라인 쇼핑몰광고 및 제작(쿠팡, 스마트스토어)/전산세무회계/컴퓨터활용능력/ITQ/GTQ/직업상담사 **IT 아카데미** 화이트 해커/코딩

교육문의 1600-6700 www.eduwill.net

- 한국리서치 '교육기관 브랜드 인지도 조사' (2015년 8월) • 2022 대한민국 브랜드만족도 공무원·자격증·취업·학원·편입·부동산 실무 교육 1위 (한경비즈니스) • 2017/2021 에듀윌 공무원 과정 최종 환급자 수 기준 • 2022년 공인중개사 직영학원 기준 • YES24 공인중개사 부문, 2022 에듀윌 공인중개사 1차 7일끝장 회차별 기출문제집(2022년 11월 월별 베스트) 그 외 다수 교보문고 취업/수험서 부문, 2020 에듀윌 농협은행 6급 NCS 직무능력평가+실전모의고사 4회 (2020년 1월 27일~2월 5일, 인터넷 주간 베스트) 그 외 다수 알라딘 월간 이슈&상식 부문, 월간최신 취업에 강한 에듀윌 시사상식 (2017년 8월~2022년 10월 월간 베스트)그 외 다수 인터파크 자격서/수험서 부문, 에듀윌 한국사능력검정시험 2주끝장 심화 (1, 2, 3급) (2020년 6~8월 월간 베스트) 그 외 다수 • YES24 국어 외국어 사전 영어 토익/TOEIC 기출문제/모의고사 분야 베스트셀러 1위 (에듀윌 토익 READING RC 4주끝장 리딩 종합서, 2022년 9월 4주 주별 베스트) • 에듀윌 토익 교재 입문~실전 인강 무료 제공 (2022년 최신 강좌 기준/109강) • 2021년 종강한 학기 중 모든 평가항목 정상 참여자 과목 이수율 기준 • A사, B사 최대 200% 환급 서비스 (2022년 6월 기준) • 에듀윌 국비교육원 구로센터 고용노동부 지정 "5년우수훈련기관" 선정(2023~2027) • KRI 한국기록원 2016, 2017, 2019년 공인중개사 최다 합격자 배출 공식 인증 (2022년 현재까지 업계 최고 기록)

에듀윌
편입영어

기출심화 완성

독해

정답과 해설

에듀윌 편입영어 **기출심화 완성 독해**

PART 01

사회과학

CHAPTER 01 법학 · 정치
CHAPTER 02 사회
CHAPTER 03 언론 · 광고
CHAPTER 04 교육
CHAPTER 05 경제 · 경영

CHAPTER 01 법학·정치

01	②	02	③	03	①	04	①	05	②	06	④	07	②	08	③	09	①	10	④
11	③	12	①	13	④	14	①	15	⑤	16	②	17	③	18	④	19	①	20	②
21	②	22	②	23	②	24	③	25	②	26	①	27	②	28	②	29	④	30	④

[01-02] 한양대 2016

유권자 여론조사는 부정확한 것으로 인식되거나 공중파 뉴스가 시청률을 높이기 위해 오용하는 관계로 종종 폄하의 대상이 된다. 하지만 선거용 유권자 여론조사의 신빙성을 의심하려는 사람들은 몇 가지 사실을 간과한다. 첫 번째로 선거 1~2주 전은 악평이 자자할 만큼 변덕스럽다. 유권자는 이 시기가 되어야 최종적으로 투표를 할지 말지를 결정하고, 결심이 서지 않은 유권자들은 자신들이 표를 줄 후보자가 누구인지 마음을 먹는다. 이는, 즉 선거 전 너무 일찍 앞서서 시행된 여론조사는 선거 결과를 정확하게 예측할 수 없음을 의미한다. 두 번째로, 출구 조사는 대부분의 다른 형태의 과학적 여론조사와는 다르며, 주된 이유는 투표장소가 분산되어 출구조사원들이 보통의 표본 추출 방법을 사용할 수 없기 때문이다. 하지만 유권자 여론조사가 정확한지 여부를 놓고 논쟁을 벌이는 것은 논점에서 벗어난 일이다. 유권자 여론조사는 승자와 패자를 예측하려는 의도에서 진행되는 것이 아니다. 유권자 여론조사는 대중의 폭넓은 의견을 묘사하고, 유권자들이 실제 어떤 생각을 갖고 있는지를 설명하고, 유권자들에게 어떤 정책이 가장 중요한지를 설명하고자 고안되었다. 실제로 우리가 유권자의 행동 및 정책 선호도에 대해 우리가 알고 있는 것 가운데 대부분은 선거 관련 과거의 여론조사를 통해 획득한 것이다.

01 빈칸에 들어갈 가장 알맞은 것은?
① 까다로운
② 변덕스러운
③ 고상한
④ 평온한

| 정답 | ②

| 해설 | 빈칸 다음을 보면 유권자는 선거 1~2주 전이 되어야 최종적으로 투표 여부 및 누구에게 표를 던질지를 결정함을 알 수 있다. 이를 근거로 선거 1~2주 전은 유권자의 선택이 매우 '변덕스러운' 시기임을 유추할 수 있다. 바로 이 때문에 선거 전에 너무 일찍 시행된 여론조사는 선거 결과를 제대로 예측하지 못하는 것이다. 따라서 답은 ②이다.

02 윗글의 내용과 가장 거리가 먼 것은?
① 매스컴은 종종 시청자 수를 늘리기 위해 유권자 의견을 오용하는 것으로 여겨진다.
② 너무 이르게 진행된 유권자 여론조사는 선거 결과를 정확히 예측할 수 없다.
③ 유권자 여론조사의 가치는 승자와 패자를 예측하는 데 있다.
④ 출구조사와 다른 형태의 여론조사 간에 차이가 생긴 이유는 대체로 출구조사가 보통의 표본 추출 방법을 사용하지 않기 때문이다.

| 정답 | ③

| 해설 | "유권자 여론조사는 승자와 패자를 예측하려는 의도에서 진행되는 것이 아니다(Voter polls are not intended to forecast winners and losers)." 따라서 답은 ③이다. "유권자 여론조사는 부정확한 것으로 인식되거나 공중파 뉴스가 시청률을 높이기 위해 오용하는 관계로 종종 폄하의 대상이 된다(Voter opinion polls are often disparaged because they are seen as inaccurate or misused by network news shows eager to boost ratings)"는 ①에 해당된다. "이는, 즉 선거 전 너무 일찍 앞서서 시행된 여론조사는 선거 결과를 정확하게 예측할 수 없음을 의미한다(This means that polls taken too far in advance of an election cannot possibly forecast with precision the outcome of that election)"는 ②에 해당된다. 마지막으로 "두 번째로, 출구조사는 대부분의 다른 형태의 과학적 여론조사와는 다르며, 주된 이유는 투표장소가 분산되어 출구조사원들이 보통의 표본 추출 방법을 사용할 수 없기 때문이다(Second, exit polls differ from most other types of scientific polling, mainly because dispersed polling places preclude exit pollsters from using normal sampling methods)."는 ④에 해당된다.

| 어휘 | opinion poll – 여론조사
network ⓐ 지상파의, 공중파의
discredit ⓥ 신용하지[믿지] 않다, 의심하다
volatile ⓐ 변덕스러운
with precision – 정확하게
preclude ⓥ 못하게 하다, 불가능하게 하다
sampling ⓝ 표본[견본/샘플] 추출, 표본화
miss the point – 핵심[논점]에서 벗어나다, 의도를 잘못 이해하다
intended ⓐ 의도한, 겨냥한
elucidate ⓥ 설명하다
fussy ⓐ 안달복달하는, 까다로운
tranquil ⓐ 고요한, 평온한
viewership ⓝ 시청자
discrepancy ⓝ 차이, 불일치
disparage ⓥ 폄하하다, 비난하다
rating ⓝ 시청률
overlook ⓥ 간과하다
in advance – 미리, 앞서
dispersed ⓐ 흩어진, 분산된
pollster ⓝ 여론조사원
spectrum ⓝ 범위, 폭
preference ⓝ 선호(도)
elevated ⓐ 높은, 고상한
media outlet – 매스컴
reside in – ~에 있다

[03-05] 동국대 2006

평등에 대한 일반적 개념에 공감하는 사람들 사이에서 소위 평등사회를 이루는 가장 좋은 방법은 어떤 것인지를 두고 논쟁이 벌어지고 있다. 여기서 평등사회란 사회 정의에 대한 평등주의적 개념을 달성한 사회를 말한다. 우리가 소위 "분배적" 개념이라고 부르는 이 견해는 Cohen이 잘 설명하고 있다. "정의(justice)로 인해서 사람들이 반드시 똑같은 양을 소유해야 하는 그 어떤 것이 존재한다는 것을 나는 당연하게 생각한다"고 밝힌 바 있다. 이런 관점에서 보면 평등사회는 사람들이 부, 행복, 생활수준 등과 같은 어떤 것을 동일한 양만큼 갖고 있는 사회를 말한다. 이의 대안적 개념으로 "사회적" 개념이 있는데, 이는 평등사회란 무엇인가 같은 양을 갖고 있는 것이 아니라 개인들 사이의 사회적 관계라는 특별한 형식에 달려 있다고 생각한다. 이 관점에서 보면 평등의 적(enemy)은 불평등한 분배가 아니라 우월의식이나 노예근성 등과 같은 것이다. 사회적 평등에 대해 초창기 시절 옹호한 내용은 영국 사회학자 Tawney의 저서인 〈평등(Equality)〉에서 찾아 볼 수 있고, 보다 최근의 내용은 David Miller와 Richard Norman의 저서에서 찾아볼 수 있다. 분배적 평등과 사회적 평등의 일반적인 접근법에 공감하는 것은 어렵지 않지만, 그와 동시에 극단적인 내용들은 무엇인가가 빠져 있는 것처럼 보인다는 생각도 어렵지 않게 하게 된다.

03

다음 중 저자가 본문을 쓴 주요 목적은 무엇인가?
① 평등에 관한 2가지 관점을 소개하기 위해
② 평등의 사회적 관점이 분배의 관점보다 더 좋다는 것을 보이기 위해
③ 사회적 평등은 많은 학자들이 지지해 온 것이라는 사실을 알리기 위해
④ 평등에 대한 개념에 공감하는 것이 어렵지 않은 이유가 무엇인지를 설명하기 위해

| 정답 | ①

| 해설 | 저자는 본문에서 평등에 대한 분배적 개념과 사회적 개념을 간략히 소개하고 있으며, 이 두 관점 모두에 대해 쉽게 공감할 수 있다고 지적하면서도, 극단적인 형태에는 쉽게 공감할 수 없다고 말하고 있다. 그런 의미에서 정답은 ①이 되며, ②와 같이 특정한 것이 더 좋다는 것은 아니다. ③은 글의 후반부에만 해당되는 내용이므로 전체를 포괄할 수 없으며, ④에서와 같은 이유에 대해서는 구체적으로 밝히고 있지 않다.

04

다음 중 분배적 개념과 관련된 것이 아닌 것은?
① 계층
② 소유물
③ 복지
④ 삶의 즐거움

| 정답 | ①

| 해설 | 분배의 개념에서는 부와 행복, 생활수준에 있어서 평등하게 분배된 것을 의미한다고 했으므로 ②는 부에 해당하고, ③은 생활수준에, ④는 행복과 연결될 수 있다. 하지만 ①의 계층 관계는 분배적 개념이 아닌 사회적 개념에 해당한다.

05

다음 중 본문의 내용에 부합하는 것은?
① 평등의 2가지 형식에 대한 일반적인 접근법에 반대하는 것이 어렵지 않다.
② Tawney와 Miller, Norman은 분배적 개념을 지지하지 않는 학자들이다.
③ 사회적 평등의 극단적인 형태는 분배적 평등의 그것보다 더 많은 단점을 가지고 있다.
④ 사회적 개념에서는 평등하지 않은 분배가 노예 상태보다 더 심각하다고 생각한다.

| 정답 | ②

| 해설 | ①의 경우 반대(object to)가 아닌 공감할 수 있다(sympathetic)고 했으며, ③의 경우 특정 개념의 극단적인 형태가 아닌 두 개념 모두를 포괄하고 있으므로 본문에 부합하지 않는다. ④의 경우 본문의 "the enemy of equality is not so much unequal division but, for example, snobbery and servility"를 통해 본문과 정반대되는 내용이라는 것을 알 수 있다. 정답은 ②로, Tawney와 Miller, Norman은 분배적 평등이 아닌 사회적 평등을 지지한 학자들이라고 본문에서 밝히고 있다.

| 어휘 |
sympathetic ⓐ 동정적인, 동정어린
take place – 일어나다
distributive ⓐ 분배의
take something for granted – ~을 당연하게 여기다
standard of living – 생활수준
consist in – (주요 특징 등이) ~에 있다
equality ⓝ 평등
egalitarian ⓐ 평등주의(자)의
put ⓥ 말하다
alternative ⓐ 대체 가능한, 대안이 되는
not so much A but B – A가 아니라 B이다

снобbery ⓝ 속물근성, 우월의식
approach ⓝ 접근 방식
advocate ⓥ 옹호하다
possession ⓝ 소유물, 재산
object to – ~에 반대하다
servitude ⓝ 노예 상태

servility ⓝ 노예 상태
extreme ⓐ 극도의, 극단적인
hierarchy ⓝ 계층, 체계
welfare ⓝ 복지
drawback ⓝ 결점, 문제점

[06-07] 한양대 2008

여러분이 내면의 공포로 고통을 받고 있고, 여러분이 이 세상에서 "쓸모없는 존재"라는 퇴보적 의식에 대항해 부단히 싸우고 있다면, 그렇다면 여러분은 우리가 왜 기다릴 수 없다고 생각하는지 이해할 수 있을 것입니다. 인내의 잔이 차고 넘쳐흐르게 된 시점이 온 것입니다. 그리고 사람들은 더 이상 좌절을 경험하게 되는 불의의 심연에 빠져드는 것을 기꺼이 거부하고 있는 것입니다. 여러분들이야말로 우리의 이 물러설 수 없는 인내의 한계를 이해해 주길 바랍니다. 여러분은 우리가 어떻게 해서든 법을 어기려고 하는데 대해 많은 우려를 표명하고 있습니다. 당연히 그런 걱정은 정당한 것입니다. 우리가 그렇게도 열심을 다해 사람들에게 공립학교에서 인종차별을 금지한 1954년 연방 대법원 판결을 존중해 달라고 사람들에게 촉구하고 있기 때문에, 의도적으로 법을 어기려는 우리들의 모습이 다소 이상하고 모순되게 보일 수 있습니다. "어떻게 어떤 법은 따르지 않을 것을 옹호하면서, 어떤 법은 지킬 것을 옹호하느냐?"고 묻는 사람도 있을 것입니다. 이 질문에 대한 답은 법에는 두 종류의 법, 즉 공정한 법과 불공정한 법이 있다는 사실에서 찾을 수 있습니다. 저는 정의로운 법을 따르는 일에 대해서라면 그 어느 누구보다도 더 큰 지지를 보낼 것입니다. 우리는 정의로운 법을 따라야 하는 법적일 뿐 아니라 도의적인 책임도 지고 있기 때문입니다. 하지만 저는 정의롭지 못한 법은 결코 법이 아니라는 성 아우구스티누스의 주장에도 동감합니다.

06 다음 중 ⓐ의 뜻으로 가장 적절한 것은?

① 사람들이 정의에 만족하는 시점
② 사람들이 인내를 잔에 쏟는 시점
③ 컵이 인내로 가득 찬 시점
④ 사람들이 더 이상 지연되는 것을 참을 수 없는 시점

| 정답 | ④

| 해설 | "인내의 잔이 가득 차서 넘쳐흐른다"는 표현은 인내심이 바닥이 낮다는 의미로, 더 이상 참을 수 없다는 ④와 같은 말이다.

07 다음 중 ⓑ에 들어갈 것으로 가장 적절한 것은?

① 본질적으로 모든 법은 불공정하다.
② 불공정한 법은 결코 법이라고 할 수 없다.
③ 불공정한 법이라도 언제나 법은 법인 것이다.
④ 공정한 법과 불공정한 법을 구분하는 것은 의미 없는 일이다.

| 정답 | ②

| 해설 | 앞에서 저자는 법에는 공정한 법과 불공정한 법, 두 가지가 있다고 했고, 공정한 법은 앞장서서 지킬 것이라고 했으므로, 불공정한 법은 저항하겠다는 것을 추론할 수 있다. 따라서 정답은 ②가 된다.

| 어휘 | plague ⓥ 괴롭히다, 성가시게 하다
degenerate ⓥ (도덕적·육체적·정신적으로) 악화되다
endurance ⓝ 인내심
plunge ⓥ 뛰어들다, 급락하다
abyss ⓝ 심연
frustration ⓝ 좌절
impatience ⓝ 성급함, 조급, 안달, 초조, 조바심
Supreme Court – 대법원
outlaw ⓥ 불법화하다, 금하다
paradoxical ⓐ 역설적인
advocate ⓥ 옹호하다

be plagued with – ~에 시달리다, ~의 괴롭힘을 당하다
be willing to – 기꺼이 ~하다
be plunged into – ~에 빠지게 되다, 돌입하다
injustice ⓝ 불평등, 부당함, 부당성
unavoidable ⓐ 피할 수 없는
a great deal of – 다량의, 많은
legitimate ⓐ 정당한
segregation ⓝ 인종차별
may well – (~하는 것도) 당연하다, 무리가 아니다
brim with – ~으로 가득 차다

[08-11] 성균관대 2007

사형 반대론자들은 사형 집행이 범죄를 억제하고 범죄자들에게 적절한 처벌을 가하는 데 반드시 필요한 것은 아니라고 주장했다. 대신, 투옥과 같은 대체 방식의 형벌이 잠재적 범죄자들의 범행을 보다 효과적으로 억제할 수 있다는 것이다. 이러한 논리에 따르면, 처벌의 가혹함보다는 처벌의 확실성이 보다 나은 억제 수단이 될 수 있다는 것이다. 사형 찬성론자들은 개인의 자유를 단순히 구속하는 것보다는 죽음이 훨씬 더 두려운 형벌이기 때문에 사형이 보다 많은 범죄를 예방하는 것은 자명하다고 주장했다. 사형 찬성론자들과 반대론자들의 사형 실효성 논쟁은 지금까지 계속되고 있다. 사회 과학자들은 관할 구역에서 사형 제도를 폐지한 이전과 이후의 살인 범죄 추이에 관한 통계 자료를 수집해 왔다. 또한 이들은 사형이 있는 지역과 없는 지역의 살인 범죄율을 비교해 왔다. 이들 통계 비교 수치의 대다수는 사형 제도의 유무가 살인 범죄율에 가시적일 만큼의 큰 영향을 주는 것은 아니라는 사실을 보여준다. 사형 반대론자들은 이러한 연구 결과는 사형이 범죄를 억제할 수 있다는 주장을 반박하는 것이라고 주장한다. 많은 사형 반대론자들은 범죄 억제 수단으로서의 사형은 이미 용도 폐기됐다고 생각하며, 더 이상 논쟁거리가 될 수 없다고 생각한다. 하지만 사형 찬성론자들은 사형은 가장 흉악한 살인 사건에 대해 가해지는 형벌이기 때문에, 그 같은 흉악 범죄에 대한 사형의 억제 효과는 일반적인 살인 범죄율의 자료에는 분명히 나타나지 않을 수도 있다는 점을 주목하고 있다.

08 위 지문을 두 개의 문단으로 나눌 경우, 어느 부분에서 나누는 것이 가장 적절한가?
① ⓐ
② ⓑ
③ ⓒ
④ ⓓ
⑤ ⓔ

| 정답 | ③

| 해설 | 지문 전반부는 사형 제도에 대한 찬반의 입장에 대해 다루고 있고, 후반부는 이를 통계적으로 입증하기 위한 연구와 이 결과에 대한 양측의 의견이 소개되어 있으므로 정답은 ③이 된다.

09 다음 중 빈칸 (가)와 (나)에 들어갈 가장 적절한 단어로 짝지어진 것은?
① 확실성 – 가혹함
② 가혹함 – 확실성
③ 존재함 – 존재하지 않음
④ 존재하지 않음 – 향상
⑤ 증거 – 자료

| 정답 | ①

| 해설 | 문장의 시작이 'According to this logic'으로 되어 있으므로, 바로 앞에서 언급한 사형 반대론자들의 주장을 다시 언급하고 있다는 것을 알 수 있다. 사형 반대론자들의 주장에 따르면, 범죄자들에게 사형이라는 극한(severity) 형벌을 주는 것보다 범죄를 저질렀을 때는 반드시 처벌을 받는다(certainty)는 것을 주지시키는 것으로도 범죄 억제 효과가 있다는 내용이므로, 정답은 ①이 적합하다.

10 다음 중 빈칸 (다)에 들어갈 단어로 가장 적절한 것은?
① 기원　　　　　　② 도덕성
③ 객관성　　　　　④ 실효성
⑤ 비용

| 정답 | ④

| 해설 | 사형 제도라는 것이 과연 범죄 억제 효과가 있는 것인가에 대한 효과성이나 실효성(effectiveness)에 대한 논쟁이므로 정답은 ④가 된다.

11 본문의 문맥을 고려할 경우, 다음 중 빈칸 (라)에 들어갈 가장 적절한 것은?
① 사형 제도가 범죄를 증가시킨다
② 사형 제도는 범죄를 예방하지 못한다
③ 사형 제도가 범죄를 억제한다
④ 사형 제도는 범죄와 무관하다
⑤ 대체 형벌이 범죄를 억제한다

| 정답 | ③

| 해설 | 사형 제도의 유무가 살인 범죄율에 영향을 주지 않는다는 내용을 통해, 사형 반대론자들이 반대편 주장을 반박(refute)하는 내용이므로, 빈칸에는 사형 찬성론자들의 주장이 들어가야 한다. 따라서 정답은 ③이 된다.

| 어휘 |
opponent ⓝ 반대자
inflict ⓥ (고통을) 주다, 입히다, 가하다
alternative ⓐ 대체의, 대안의
deter ⓥ 단념시키다, 방해하다
deterrent ⓝ 억제 수단
self-evidently ⓐⓓ 그 자체로 자명하게
homicide ⓝ 살인
abolish ⓥ 폐지하다
execution ⓝ 처형, 실행
negated ⓐ 무효화된
be reserved for - ~을 위해 남겨지다
apparent ⓐ 명백한

capital punishment - 사형(=death penalty)
wrongdoer ⓝ 범죄자, 가해자
imprisonment ⓝ 구속
potential ⓐ 잠재적인
contend ⓥ 주장하다
restriction ⓝ 제한
urisdiction ⓝ 사법 관할 구역
statistical ⓐ 통계의
refute ⓥ 반박하다
advocate ⓝ 찬성론자, 지지자
aggravated ⓐ 악화된

[12-13] 단국대 2011

동서를 막론하고 불법 마약류의 광범위한 판매 및 사용은 각국 정부에 어려운 과제임이 틀림없다. 마약과의 전쟁에서, 싱가포르를 포함한 몇몇 나라들은 마약 밀매나 소지자에 대해 "무관용 정책(zero tolerance)"을 시행해 왔다. 싱가포르에서는 1975년부터 불법으로 마약을 밀매하다 붙잡힌 모든 이들에게 사형을 선고하고 있다. 사형에 처해지기 위해서는 피의자가 일정 분량 이상의 마약을 소지한 채로 검거되어야만 한다. 마약거래에 대한 가혹한 처벌과 더불어, 싱가포르 법에서는 일정량 이상의 마약을 소지한 모든 이들에게 장차 마약 밀매업자가 될 수도 있다는 "고의 추정(presumption of intent)"의 원칙을 부여하고 있다. 여기서 고의 추정이 법적으로 작용하는 바를 이해하려면 피의자는 "명백한 유죄가 입증되기 전까지는 무죄"라는 무죄추정의 원칙을 먼저 생각해봐야 한다. 일반적으로 무죄추정의 원칙에서는 다음 두 가지 사항이 반드시 밝혀져야 한다. 첫째 피의자가 물리적으로 그 범죄를 저질렀다는 증거와 둘째 그럴 의도가 있었다는 증거가 그것이다.

12 다음 중 밑줄 친 imposes와 가장 의미가 가까운 것은?
① (해를) 가하다 ② 비난하다
③ 확장하다 ④ 분리 독립하다

| 정답 | ①

| 해설 | impose는 의무나 벌, 세금 등을 지우는 것을 의미한다. 본문에서는 고의 추정의 원칙(presumption of intent)을 부과한다는 뜻이 된다. 보기에서 ① inflict는 '해를 가하다'라는 뜻이므로 정답이 된다.

13 다음 중 본문의 내용과 다른 것은?
① 싱가포르는 불법 마약류를 용인하지 않는다.
② 싱가포르에서 마약밀매는 사형에 처해진다.
③ 싱가포르는 마약밀매에 관하여 가장 강경한 조치들을 취하는 나라이다.
④ "고의 추정" 원칙은 더 이상 마약밀매 사건에서는 유효하지 않다.

| 정답 | ④

| 해설 | 싱가포르는 마약밀매에 대해 강경한 조치인 사형을 시행하고 있는 나라이며, 이에 더해 일정량 이상의 마약을 소지하고 있는 이들에게 '무죄 추정의 원칙'이 아닌 '고의 추정의 원칙'을 적용하고 있는 나라라고 했으므로, 더 이상 고의 추정의 원칙이 유효하지 않다고 말한 ④가 정답이 된다.

| 어휘 | **A pose a challenge/threat to B** – A가 B에게 어려움/위협을 가하다
throughout the world – 동서를 막론하고
zero tolerance – 무관용 정책 (범법자에 대한 처벌을 대단히 엄격하게 가하는 정책)
drug trafficking – 마약밀매   **drug trafficker** – 마약밀매자
incur ⓥ 초래하다, 처하게 되다   **the accused** – 피의자, 피고인
harsh ⓐ 가혹한   **impose** ⓥ 부과하다, 강제하다
presumption ⓝ 추정   **intent** ⓝ 목적, 계획
commit ⓥ 저지르다   **inflict** ⓥ 가하다, 안기다
reproach ⓥ 비난하다   **dilate** ⓥ 확장하다, 넓어지다
secede ⓥ 분리 독립하다, 탈퇴하다   **tolerate** ⓥ 용인하다
provoke ⓥ 유발하다; 화나게 하다   **measure** ⓝ 방법, 조치

[14-17] 숙명여대 2008

'연방정부'는 통치 시스템의 한 형태로, 지방 정부에게 상당한 정도의 자치권을 보장해 주는 방식으로 헌법에 의해 권력이 중앙 정부와 지방 정부로 나뉘는 것을 지칭하는 용어이다. 연방제의 특징은 지방 정부와 중앙 정부의 권력이 헌법에 의해 명확히 구분되어 있다는 것이다. 아무리 중앙집권화 돼 있다고 하더라도, 모든 시스템에 지방 정부가 존재하며, 이 지방 정부가 박물관에서나 볼 수 있는 쓸모없는 것은 아니기 때문에 항상 일정한 정도의 권한을 가진다. 연방제에서 주요 지방 정부의 권한은 헌법에 의해 보장된다. 전 세계 대부분의 통치 체제는 그 기본 구성이 단일 중앙 집권제이지 연방제를 택하고 있지는 않다. 중앙 집권제에서는 주요 지방 정부의 권한이 중앙 정부에 의해 제한을 받으며, 전자(지방 정부)의 허락이나 동의 없이 후자(중앙 정부)에 의해 확대되거나 축소될 수도 있다. 반면 연방제에서 지방 정부는 그 명칭과는 무관하게(미국에서는 'state', 캐나다는 'province'라고 지칭함) 자국의 기본법인 헌법에 의해 보장된 일정 정도의 권한을 보유한다.

14 다음 중 연방제에서 주요 지방 정부의 권한은 어떠하다고 할 수 있는가?
① 자동적으로 부여되지 않는다.
② 자치권을 갖는다.
③ 중앙 정부의 권한과 동일하게 보장받는다.
④ 헌법으로 보장받는다.
⑤ 허가 없이 정부에 의해 확대되거나 축소된다.

| 정답 | ④

| 해설 | 본문 중간 부분에 "In a federal system the powers of the principal local governments are constitutionally guaranteed to them."을 통해 정답이 ④임을 알 수 있다.

15 다음 중 전 세계 대부분의 통치 체제는 어떤 것인가?
① 민주적이다   ② 기본적이다
③ 영역이 보장되어 있다   ④ 연방제이다
⑤ 단일 중앙 집권제이다

| 정답 | ⑤

| 해설 | 본문의 "Most governmental systems of the world are unitary and not federal in their basic patterns of organization" 부분을 통해 대부분의 나라가 연방제가 아닌 중앙 집권제를 선택하고 있음을 알 수 있으므로 정답은 ⑤가 된다.

16 다음 중 밑줄 친 "museum pieces"가 의미하는 것은?
① 매우 가치 있는   ② 권한이 부족한
③ 낡은 성질   ④ 장점이 없는 것이 아닌
⑤ 작지만 강력한

| 정답 | ③

| 해설 | 'museum pieces'는 '박물관에 진열할 만한 가치가 있는 것' 혹은 '시대에 뒤떨어진 것[사람]'이란 뜻으로 본문에서는 후자로 사용되었다. 지방 정부가 명목상의 구실을 하는 것이 아니라는 뜻으로 실제 권한을 갖고 있다는 의미이다.

17

다음 중 연방제에서의 지방 정부에 대한 설명으로 바르지 않은 것은?

① 상당한 정도까지 자치권을 갖는다.
② 헌법에 의해 보장된 권한을 갖는다.
③ 중앙 정부의 결정을 반대할 권한을 갖는다.
④ 헌법에 의해 지방 정부와 중앙 정부의 권한이 구별된다.
⑤ 어느 정도의 권한을 갖는다.

| 정답 | ③

| 해설 | ①과 ⑤는 비슷한 내용으로 본문에서 여러 차례 언급되어 있다. 그리고 지방 정부의 권한은 헌법으로 보장받는다고 했으므로 ②도 맞는 내용이며, ④도 이와 비슷한데 본문에서는 'constitutionally distinguished'라는 말을 사용하고 있다. 정답은 ③으로, 본문에서는 언급하고 있지 않으므로 알 수 없는 내용이 된다.

| 어휘 |
federal ⓐ 연방의
constitution ⓝ 헌법
considerable ⓐ 상당한
autonomy ⓝ 자치권
distinguish ⓥ 구별하다, 구별 짓다, 차이를 보이다
museum piece – 박물관에 진열할 만한 가치가 있는 것, 시대에 뒤떨어진 것[사람]
authority ⓝ 권한
unitary ⓐ 통합된, 일원화된
expand ⓥ 확대되다
the latter – 후자
the former – 전자
fundamental ⓐ 근본적인
invaluable ⓐ 매우 유용한, 귀중한
not without merit – 전혀 장점이 없는 것은 아닌
refer to – ~을 지칭하다
in a fashion – ~한 방식으로
measure ⓝ (꽤 많은) 양[정도]
hallmark ⓝ 특징
guarantee ⓥ 보증하다, 보장하다
be subject to – ~받기 쉽다, ~의 대상이다
contract ⓥ 축소되다
concurrence ⓝ 동의, 의견 일치
block out – 스케치하다, 대강의 계획을 세우다
autonomous ⓐ 자치의
archaic ⓐ 낡은, 폐물이 된

[18-20] 이화여대 2010

정부의 권위는, 비록 내가 기꺼이 순종하려는 정부의 권위일지라도 아직까지는 순수하지 못하다. 엄정하게 말하면, 정부는 피통치자의 허락과 동의를 받아야 한다. 정부는 내가 허용해 준 부분 이외에는 나의 신체나 재산에 대해서 순수한 권리를 가질 수 없다. 전제군주제에서 입헌군주제로, 입헌군주제에서 민주주의로 진보해 온 것은 개인에 대한 진정한 존중을 향해 온 진보이다. 중국의 철학자조차도 개인을 제국의 근본으로 볼 만큼 현명했다. 국가가 개인을 보다 커다란 독립된 힘으로 보고 국가의 권력과 권위는 이러한 개인의 힘으로부터 나온 것임을 인정하고, 이에 알맞은 대접을 개인에게 해 줄 때까지는 진정으로 자유롭고 개화된 국가는 나올 수 없다. 나는 마침내 모든 사람을 공정하게 대할 수 있고 개인을 한 이웃으로 존경할 수 있는 국가를 상상하는 즐거움을 가져 본다. 그런 국가는, 일부 소수의 사람들이 국가에 대해 초연하며 국가에 대해 참견하지도 않고 살더라도 동포에 대한 의무를 다하는 한 그들이 국가의 안녕을 해치는 자들이라고 생각하지는 않을 것이다.

18

다음 중 ㉠에 가장 잘 맞는 것은 무엇인가?

① 논쟁과 의심
② 지지와 의구심
③ 교양과 신뢰성
④ 허락과 동의

| 정답 | ④

| 해설 | 저자가 바라보는 정부에 대한 관점은 "It can have no pure right over my person and property but what I concede to it(정부는 내가 허용해 준 부분 이외에는 나의 신체나 재산에 대해서 순수한 권리를 가질 수 없다)"이다. 이를 바탕으로 볼 때 정부가 "must have(가져야 할 것)"은 바로 "the governed(피지배자)"의 '허락'이나 '동의'가 될 것이다. 따라서 답은 ④가 된다.

19 다음 중 ㉮에 가장 잘 맞는 것은 무엇인가?

① 모든 사람을 공정하게 대할 수 있고 개인을 한 이웃으로 존경할 수 있는
② 개인을 외부의 위협으로부터 보호해야만 하는
③ 개인을 사회의 규칙에 따르도록 강요해야만 하는
④ 개인에게 국가의 높은 이상을 제시하는

| 정답 | ①

| 해설 | 저자는 "a really free and enlightened State(진정으로 자유롭고 개화된 국가)"를 이루기 위해서는 국가가 "recognize the individual as a higher and independent power, from which all its own power and authority are derived, and treats him accordingly(개인을 보다 커다란 독립된 힘으로 보고 국가의 권력과 권위는 이러한 개인의 힘으로부터 나온 것임을 인정하고, 이에 알맞은 대접을 개인에게 해 줘야)" 한다고 생각한다. 이로 미루어 볼 때 저자가 "please myself with imagining(상상하는 즐거움)"을 갖는 국가, 즉 저자가 바라는 이상적인 국가란 바로 ①의 '모든 사람을 공정하게 대할 수 있고 개인을 한 이웃으로 존경할 수 있는' 국가이다. 따라서 답은 ①이다.

20 다음 중 저자의 요점을 나타낸 것은 무엇인가?

① 개인이 국가에 도전하는 것은 언제나 정당한 행위이다.
② 최고의 정부는 개인의 권리를 존중하는 정부이다.
③ 정부의 힘은 민주적 지도자들에 의해 정당화가 이루어진다.
④ 개인은 사회로부터 소외되는 경우가 거의 없다.

| 정답 | ②

| 해설 | "it must have the sanction and consent of the governed(정부는 피통치자의 허락과 동의를 받아야 하고)", "a State which can be just to all men and treat the individual with respect(모든 사람을 공정하게 대할 수 있고 개인을 한 이웃으로 존경할 수 있는 국가)"가 저자가 생각하는 바람직한 국가임을 알 수 있다. 보기 중에서 국민 개개인을 국가의 중심에 놓는 이러한 국가의 성격과 가장 잘 맞는 것은 ②의 '개인의 권리를 존중하는 정부'이다. 따라서 답은 ②가 된다.

| 어휘 | sanction ⓝ 허락
submit to – ~에 따르다, 순종하다
monarchy ⓝ 군주제
accordingly ⓐⓓ 부응해서, ~에 맞춰서
repose ⓝ 안녕, 휴식
meddle with – ~에 간섭하다, 참견하다
reservation ⓝ 의구심
force A to do – A에게 ~하도록 강요하다
esteem ⓥ 존중하다, 존경하다

consent ⓝ 동의
concede to – ~을 허용하다, 인정하다
enlightened ⓐ 개화된
inconsistent ⓐ 모순되는, 규범에 부합하지 않는
aloof ⓐ 냉담한, 초연한
disobedience ⓝ 불복종
external ⓐ 외부의
legitimate ⓐ 정당한
alienate ⓥ ~을 멀리하다, 소원하게 하다

[21-23] 가천대 2017

우리 모두는 "악의 평범성(banality of evil)"이라는 말을 들어 봤을 것이며, 어떤 정치이론가가 그런 용어를 만들었는지 아는 사람도 있을 것이다. 1961년 한나 아렌트(Hannah Arendt)는 〈뉴요커(The New Yorker)〉라는 잡지사의 요청을 받고 아돌프 아이히만(Adolf Eichmann)의 재판을 취재하기 위해 예루살렘으로 향했다. 아돌프 아이히만은 그보다 1년 전 이스라엘의 보안 부대에 의해 붙잡혔던 인물이다. 1963년 아렌트가 쓴 기사들이 더욱 보완되어 〈예루살렘의 아이히만: 악의 평범성에 대한 보고서〉가 출판되었다. 그 책에서 아렌트는 히틀러의 "마지막 해결책"의 "아버지"로 알려진 아이히만이 사실은 악마와 같은 괴물이 아니라 명령을 따르고 승진하기 위해 힘쓰는 평범한 관료였다고 지적했다. 그녀는 한발 더 나아가 유대인 대학살이라는 사악함은 평범한 무관심에서 유래했다고 주장하며, 평범한 사람이 자신의 행동에 책임을 지지 않는 것을 비난했다. 이런 상태를 그녀는 "악의 평범성"이라고 지칭했다. 뿐만 아니라 나치 지배로 타락한 환경에서 나치에 의해 임명된 지역 유대교 연합회도, 일부 균열이 있었지만 나치와 동맹 관계에 있었기 때문에, 일정 부분 6백만 명의 죽음에 책임이 있다고도 시사했다. 아렌트의 이 같은 주장은 격렬한 항의를 불러 일으켰다. 그녀의 책에 대한 신랄한 논평과 비판이 쏟아졌다. 이 책은 오늘날에도 여전히 그녀의 가장 도발적인 저작으로 간주되고 있다.

21 다음 중 빈칸 (A)에 들어갈 것으로 가장 적합한 것은?
① 히틀러의 폭력적인 정책들
② 평범한 무관심
③ 눈에 띄는 협조
④ 인간의 사악한 본성

| 정답 | ②

| 해설 | 빈칸 뒤에서 평범한 사람이 자신의 책임을 다하지 않는 것이 문제라고 지적했으며, 앞에서는 악의 평범성에 대해 지적하고 있으므로 이와 유사한 ② '평범한 무관심'이 정답이 된다.

22 다음 중 빈칸 (B)에 들어갈 것으로 가장 적합한 것은?
① 경쟁
② 충돌
③ 환멸
④ 동맹

| 정답 | ④

| 해설 | because of를 이용해 빈칸 때문에 나치가 임명한 유대인 연합회도 유대인 대학살에 일부 책임이 있다고 했기 때문에, 나치와의 '협조'에 해당하는 단어가 와야 한다. 따라서 보기 중 ④가 이에 가장 적합하다.

23 다음 중 본문의 내용과 일치하지 않는 것은?
① 아이히만은 1960년에 체포되었다.
② 아렌트에 따르면, 아이히만은 사악한 인물이 아니라 자신이 속한 관료 조직에서 승진하기 원했던 그저 평범한 사람이었다.
③ 유대인 대학살은 나치의 잔악성을 충분히 인식했던 지역 유대인 연합회에 의해 주로 자행된 것이다.
④ 아렌트는 평범한 사람이 자신의 행위에 대한 책임을 포기할 때 사악함이 발생할 수 있다고 주장한다.

| 정답 | ③

| 해설 | ①의 경우, 아렌트가 예루살렘으로 취재를 위해 갔던 해가 1961년이고, 아이히만은 그보다 1년 전에 체포되었다고 했으므로, 1960년에 체포된 것이다. ②의 경우 "was actually not so much a monster as just a regular guy" 부분을 통해 설명하고 있다. ④는 "she blamed ordinary people for not taking responsibility for their actions"에서 밝히고 있는 내용이다. 정답은 ③으로 아렌트는 유대인 연합회가 홀로코스트에 부분적(in part) 책임이 있다고 했으므로 전적인 책임이 있다는 ③은 본문과 일치하지 않는다.

| 어휘 | banality of evil – 악의 평범성
coin ⓥ (신조어를) 만들다
Hannah Arendt – 한나 아렌트(1906~75 미국의 유대계 여성 정치 철학자)
trial ⓝ 재판
bureaucratic ⓐ 관료주의의
holocaust ⓝ 홀로코스트(1930~40년대 나치에 의한 유대인 대학살)
stem from – ~로부터 유래하다
in part – 부분적으로
fractured ⓐ 파열된, 골절된
outcry ⓝ (대중들의) 격렬한 반응[항의]
censure ⓝ 비난, 견책, 불신임 ⓥ 비난하다
commonplace ⓐ 아주 흔한
disillusionment ⓝ 환멸
relinquish ⓥ 포기하다
theorist ⓝ 이론가
not so much A as B – A가 아니라 B인
term ⓝ 용어 ⓥ (특정한 이름·용어로) 칭하다[일컫다]
albeit ⓒⓞⓝ 비록 ~일지라도
assertion ⓝ 주장, 단언
scathing ⓐ (비판이) 준열한[통렬한/가차 없는]
provocative ⓐ 도발적인, 화[부아]를 돋우려는
inattentiveness ⓝ 부주의; 무뚝뚝함
alliance ⓝ 동맹, 연합

[24-25] 국민대 2014

법의 본질에 대한 의문은 법실증주의자와 자연법 이론가 간의 전형적인 논쟁에 의해 오랫동안 주도되었다. 실증주의자들은 법이 특정한 사회에서 존재할 수 있을지의 여부 그리고 만일 존재한다면 특정한 법적인 의문에 대해 해당 사회 내에서의 답이 무엇인지는 권력이 해당 사회 내에서 어떻게 행사되는지에 대한 사실 문제라고 간주했다. 자연법 법률가들은 법이란 우선 현 상황에 구현된 일련의 도덕적 규범이라고 생각한다. 이들은 법을 정의와 권리의 객관적 원칙과 결부시켰고, 이는 인간 권력의 행사를 판단하기 위한 기준으로 활용될 수 있다. 따라서 자연법 이론에 따르면 우리는 어떤 특정 사회 내에서 시행된 포고령의 경우 객관적 권리로서 특정한 경계를 넘을 수 있을지 여부를 고려하지 않고서는 해당 포고령이 법의 자격을 부여받을 수 있을지 여부를 말할 수 없으며, 반면에 법실증주의에 따르면 무언가를 법으로 판단하는 행위는 우리로 하여금 전혀 그런 평가를 내리지 않게 하는 사회적 사실의 판단이다.

24 다음 문장이 들어가기에 가장 적합한 위치는 어디인가?

> 그들은 법을 정의와 권리의 객관적 원칙과 결부했고, 이는 인간 권력의 행사를 판단하기 위한 기준으로 활용될 수 있다.

① A ② B ③ C ④ D

| 정답 | ③

| 해설 | 주어진 문장에 따르면 법은 "정의와 권리의 객관적 원칙(objective principles of justice and right)" 역할을 한다. '객관성'을 감안하면 법을 '도덕적 규범'으로 보는 것과(C 앞 문장의 내용), 법을 '객관적 권리'로 보면서 특정 경계를

넘을 수 있을지 여부에 따라 법의 자격을 부여한다는 것(ⓒ 뒤 문장의 내용) 모두 뜻이 통한다. 또한 주어진 문장의 주어인 They가 누구일지 생각해 보면, 실증주의자(ⓑ) 또는 자연법 법률가(ⓒ) 이 둘 중 하나인데 주어진 문장의 내용은 법실증주의보다는 자연법 변호사와 연계되어 있으므로 ⓑ는 답이 될 수 없다. 따라서 글의 흐름상 주어진 문장은 ⓒ에 와야 한다.

25

본문에 따르면 다음 중 사실은 무엇인가?
① 법실증주의와 자연법 이론 둘 중 그 어느 것도 법의 윤리적 측면과 관련이 없다.
② 실증주의자의 관점에 따르면 법적 정의의 개념은 사회적 산물이다.
③ 법실증주의와 자연법 이론 모두 법은 객관적 기준에 근거한다고 주장한다.
④ 자연법 이론에 따르면 특정 사회의 법은 자연법으로부터 선천적으로 벗어난 것이다.

| 정답 | ②

| 해설 | "반면에 법실증주의에 따르면 무언가를 법으로 판단하는 행위는 우리로 하여금 전혀 그런 평가를 내리지 않게 하는 사회적 사실의 판단이다(whereas according to legal positivism, the judgment that something is the law is a judgment of social fact which commits us to no such evaluation)." 여기서 무언가를 법으로 판단한다는 것은 법적인 정의를 규정하는 것을 의미한다. 즉, 법적 정의는 사회적 사실의 판단에 따른 것이자 '사회적 산물'임을 의미한다. 따라서 답은 ②이다.

| 어휘 | dominate ⓥ 지배하다, 통치하다, 주도하다
positivist ⓝ 실증주의자
given ⓐ 특정한, 주어진
in the first instance – 우선, 먼저
embody ⓥ 구체화하다, 구현하다, 상징하다
associate A with B – A와 B를 결부[연관]짓다, A에서 B를 연상하다
edict ⓝ 포고령, 칙령
status ⓝ 상태; 지위, 자격
objective ⓐ 객관적인
concern ⓥ 관련되다, ~에 관한 것이다
inherently ⓐⓓ 선천적으로, 타고나서

dispute ⓝ 토론, 논의, 논쟁
hold ⓥ (무엇이 사실이라고) 간주[생각]하다
particular ⓐ 특별한, 특유한, 특정한
norm ⓝ 기준, 규범
the way things are – 현 상황[상태]
enforce ⓥ (법률 등을) 실시하다, 집행하다, 강제하다
threshold ⓝ 경계, 한계; 발단
evaluation ⓝ 평가
maintain ⓥ 주장하다; 유지하다
deviant ⓐ 벗어난, 일탈적인

[26-28] 단국대 2018

전체주의 방식의 일방적 의견 표출에 대한 민주주의 방식의 대안이 각각의 임시 연단을 한 줄로 세우는 것이라면, 나는 그와 같은 대안이 실행 가능하지 않고, 불합리하며, 인간적으로 매력이 없다고 말하고 싶다. 무엇보다 그것은 잘못된 대안이다. 자유라고 하는 것이 누구든지 (자신의 의견을 표명하기 위해) 임시 연단을 자유롭게 세울 수 있고, 자신의 주장을 기꺼이 들어줄 사람들에게 자신의 의견을 설명할 수 있는 홀을 자유롭게 대관할 수 있는 문명인들 사이에서 생겨났다는 것은 사실이 아니다. 그러기는커녕 동일한 홀에서 동일한 대중들을 상대로 서로 다른 의견을 설명할 수 있도록 했을 때에야 비로소 언론의 자유가 그 본질적 목적을 달성하도록 정착되는 것이다. 말을 할 수 있는 권리가 자유의 시작일 수 있지만, 경청의 필요성이 그 권리를 의미 있게 만드는 것이기 때문이다. 중요한 것은 의견의 표출이 아니다. 중요한 것은 토론을 통해 의견이 서로 대립되도록 하는 것이다. 모든 바보가 자신이 좋아하는 것을 말할 수 있어야 한다는 사실을 온전히 좋아할 사람은 없기 때문이다.

26

다음 중 밑줄 친 (A)와 의미상 가장 가까운 것은?

① 개인의 의견을 말하는 것
② 자신의 작은 공간을 만드는 것
③ 자신의 세계를 만드는 것
④ 자신의 극장을 만드는 것

| 정답 | ①

| 해설 | 밑줄 친 'to set up a soapbox'란 즉석연설을 할 수 있도록 임시 연단을 세우는 것을 말한다. 따라서 개인의 의견을 말하는 ①이 정답이 된다.

27

다음 중 밑줄 친 (B)를 통해 추론할 수 있는 것은?

① 모든 바보가 존경받아야 한다.
② 서로 다른 의견을 논의하는 것이 모든 의견을 듣는 것보다 더 중요하다.
③ 모든 사람은 자신이 좋아하는 것을 말할 권리를 가진다.
④ 아무도 바보들의 의견을 좋아하지 않는다.

| 정답 | ②

| 해설 | 밑줄 친 부분은 모든 사람의 의견을 듣는 것이 중요한 것이 아니라고 말하고 있다. 바로 앞에서 밝힌 서로 대립되는 의견을 토론을 통해 들을 수 있는 것이 중요하다는 점을 돌려 말하고 있으므로, 정답은 ②가 된다. ④는 밑줄 친 부분의 표면적 의미만을 나타내므로 정답이 될 수 없다.

28

다음 중 본문의 내용과 일치하는 것은?

① 전체주의 방식의 의사소통에 대한 실제적 대안은 존재하지 않는다.
② 언론의 자유를 얻기 위해서는, 서로 다른 의견이 같은 조건에서 노출될 수 있어야 한다.
③ 별도의 임시 연단이 전체주의에 대한 대안이다.
④ 자기 자신의 의견을 말할 수 있는 자유를 허용하는 것이 가장 중요한 것이다.

| 정답 | ②

| 해설 | 본문에서 On the contrary 이하에 주제문이 제시되어 있다. 본문의 "freedom of speech is established ... only when different opinions are expounded in the same hall to the same audience" 부분을 ②로 재진술한 것이므로, 정답은 ②가 된다.

| 어휘 | **democratic** ⓐ 민주적인, (조직의 운영이) 평등주의에 입각한, 평등한
alternative ⓝ 대안, 양자택일 ⓐ 대안적인, 대체의 **totalitarian** ⓐ 전체주의의
one-way ⓐ 일방적인, 일방통행의 **a row of** – 한 줄로 늘어선
soapbox ⓝ 임시[가두] 연단 **submit** ⓥ 말하다, 진술[제안]하다; 굴복하다; 제출하다
unworkable ⓐ 실행 불가능한 **unreasonable** ⓐ 불합리한, 부당한
above all – 무엇보다도, 특히 **civilized** ⓐ (문화·생활양식 등이) 문명화된
set up a soapbox – (즉석연설을 할 수 있도록) 임시 연단을 세우다
expound ⓥ 자세히 설명하다
on the contrary – 그와는 반대로; ~하기는커녕, ~는 고사하고

freedom of speech - 언론의 자유
utterance ⓝ 발언
do not care - 좋아하지 않다, 염두에 두지 않다, 안중에 없다
profoundly ⓐ (영향 등을) 깊이
matter ⓥ 중요하다
confrontation ⓝ 직면, 조우, 대결, 대치

[29-30] 국민대 2016

기후변화에 대한 태도는 정치 노선에 따라 급격하게 양극화되어 있는 것으로 보인다. 적어도 미국에서는 이런 현상이 두드러진다. 2013년 대규모 조사에 따르면, 민주당(진보) 유권자의 70%가 최근 기상 패턴에서 인재에 의한 기후 변화의 증거를 보았다고 답했으나(기후변화가 인간에 의해 인위적으로 발생했다고 보는 비율을 의미함), 공화당(보수) 유권자는 이렇게 응답한 비율이 19%에 그쳤다. 보수주의자들이 무지하다는 것이 아니다. 과학에 대한 지식은 기후 변화에 대한 사람들의 믿음에 큰 차이를 가져오지 않는다. (지식이 많으면 많을수록) 그들이 믿는 것에 대해 더 확신하게 만든다는 점만 다르다. 과학 지식이 풍부한 공화당원들은 지식이 부족한 공화당원보다 지구온난화에 대해 더 회의적이다.

이런 격차를 설명할 수 있는 가장 좋은 방법은 기후변화에 대한 사람들의 믿음이 정치 집단과의 동질감에 의해 결정된다는 것이다. 기후 변화에 대한 견해를 묻는 질문을 받을 경우 사람들은 이 질문을 더 넓은 질문, 즉 '당신은 어느 편에 속해 있는가'로 해석하는 것처럼 보인다. 기후변화라는 문제가 민주당원들과 연관지어져 왔기 때문에, 보수주의자들은 이와 반대로 자신의 입장을 고수해 왔다. 이와 같은 (진보주의자들과 보수주의자들 사이의) 격차는 향후 몇 년 내에 해결될 것으로 보이지 않는다.

29 다음 중 본문의 주제로 가장 적합한 것은?
① 정치적 보수주의자들은 일반적으로 낙관적이다.
② 지구 온난화의 진전은 아직 논란의 여지가 있다.
③ 과학적 지식은 사람들의 신념과 아무런 관련이 없다.
④ 기후변화에 대한 사람들의 견해는 사실보다는 정치적 지향성에 더 의존한다.

| 정답 | ④

| 해설 | 본문의 주제문 첫 번째 문장에 잘 나타나 있다. 즉, "Attitudes to climate change seems to have been sharply polarized along political lines at least in America" 내용을 통해, 기후변화에 대한 진보주의자들과 보수주의자들의 극명한 입장 차이를 설명하고 있는 글이므로, 정답은 ④가 된다.

30 다음 중 보수주의자들이 지구온난화에 대해 보다 회의적인 시각을 갖는 이유로 본문의 내용과 가장 일치하는 것은?
① 과학 지식은 항상 제한적이며 위조될 수 있다.
② 보수주의자들은 일반적으로 자신들이 믿는 바에 대해 더 확신한다.
③ 최근의 기후 패턴에는 인간이 초래한 변화는 많지 않다.
④ 민주당 지지자들은 보수주의자들보다 기후변화에 대해 더 많은 걱정을 한다.

| 정답 | ④

| 해설 | 보수주의자들이 지구온난화에 회의적인 시각을 갖는 이유를 본문 후반부의 "The issue has become associated with Democrats, causing conservatives to dig in against it."에서 잘 보여주고 있다. 지구온난화 문제는 진보주의자들의 문제로 인식이 되면서, 보수주의자들은 이들과 반대편의 입장을 고수했다고 말하고 있다. 이를 달리 말하면 진보주의자들은 지구온난화가 인재에 의한 결과로 많은 우려를 표명하고 있으며, 보수주의자들은 지구온난화가 큰 문제라는 사실에 의심의 눈길로 바라본다는 내용이 된다.

| 어휘 | **climate change** – 기후 변동[변화] (기상 이변·지구온난화 등)
polarize ⓥ 양극화되다, 양극화를 초래하다
along political lines – 정치 노선에 따라
survey ⓝ 여론 조사
Democratic ⓐ 민주당의
man-made ⓐ 인공의
Republican ⓐ 공화당의
conservative ⓝ 보수주의자
ignorant ⓐ 무지한
make little difference – 큰 차이가 없다
skeptical ⓐ 의심 많은, 회의적인
gap ⓝ 격차
identification ⓝ 신원 확인, 신분 증명; 식별
translate A into B – A를 B로 해석하다, A를 B로 바꾸다[옮기다]
be associated with – ~와 관련되다
dig in – 꾹 참고 기다리다[견디다]; (명령문의 형태로) 먹어라[먹기 시작해라]
divide ⓝ 격차
resolve ⓥ 해결하다
have nothing to do with – ~와 서로 관계가 없다
political orientation – 정치성향
falsify ⓥ (문서를) 위조[변조/조작]하다

CHAPTER 02 사회

01	①	02	②	03	④	04	④	05	①	06	④	07	②	08	④	09	②	10	④
11	①	12	③	13	②	14	①	15	④	16	②	17	④	18	④	19	②	20	④
21	①	22	①	23	②	24	③	25	①	26	①	27	④	28	②	29	④	30	②

[01-03] 숭실대 2012

한국의 융통성 없는 사회적 모델은 극단적인 인구학적 문제를 악화시킨다. 한국 여성들은 국가가 미래에 필요한 노동력을 공급할 수 있을 만큼의 아이를 낳는 것을 멈췄다.

수없이 많은 한국 여성들이 노동력을 제공하기 시작하면서 아이를 가질 경우의 기회비용이 급격히 상승했다. 직장에서는 여성이 직무 휴직을 원하더라도 이를 거의 허용하지 않고 있다. 만일 여성이 직무 경력을 밟고 있다가 경로에서 (육아 문제로) 수년 동안 벗어나게 될 경우 한국 기업들은 서양 기업에 비해 여성의 복귀를 환영할 가능성이 훨씬 낮다. 그리고 만일 기업이 직장에 다니는 어머니의 복귀를 받아들이더라도, 어머니는 출세 가도에서 벗어날 것인가 아니면 탄력적으로 바꿀 수도 없는 오랜 시간 동안 근무를 할 것인지를 두고 냉혹한 선택을 해야 한다.

탄력 근무 및 재택근무는 좋게 받아들여지지 않는다. 이로 인해 일과 육아를 결합하는 일이 충격적일 만큼 힘들게 되었다. 특히 한국의 어머니들은 자녀가 뛰어난 학업 능력을 보이도록 해야 할 전적인 책임을 지는 것으로 기대되기 때문에 더욱 그러하다.

지극히 중요한 시험을 통과할 수 있는 자녀를 키우는 데 드는 직접적인 비용 또한 엄청나게 크다. 자녀 한 명을 월 수업료 천 달러에 달하는 학원에 보내는 것도 힘든데, 학원 세 곳에 보내는 일은 죽을 만큼 끔찍한 일이다. 부모는 교육비 경쟁에 참여하고 있다. 자녀가 하나뿐인 가정은 더 높은 교육비를 감당할 수 있고 그래서 최고의 학원에 보내기 위한 비용이 증가한다. 이는 다른 부모 입장에서도 아이를 덜 가질 수밖에 없는 동기가 된다.

1960년부터 한국의 출산율은 세계의 거의 모든 지역에 비해 빠르게 하강하여, 여성 1인당 6명의 자녀였던 출산율이 2009년에는 1.15명이 되었다. 이는 인구학적 붕괴를 가져올 수밖에 없다. 만일 한국 여성이 오직 한 명의 아이만 낳을 경우, 매 세대는 이전 세대에 비해 인구가 반씩 줄 것이다. 한국은 노쇠화가 진행되면서 전 세계적으로 별 비중 없는 국가로 축소될 것이다.

01 다음 중 밑줄 친 (1)을 다른 말로 가장 잘 풀어쓴 것은 무엇인가?

① 따라서 부모는 최고의 교육을 제공하기 위해 지출을 기꺼이 늘릴 것이다.
② 따라서 부모는 최저 가격을 지불하기 위해 경매에 참여할 것이다.
③ 따라서 부모는 자녀를 위해 직무 휴직을 취할 것이다.
④ 따라서 부모는 가능한 돈을 적게 지불할 것이다.

| 정답 | ①

| 해설 | (1)을 해석하면 "그래서 최고의 학원에 보내기 위한 비용이 증가한다"이다. 최고의 학원에 보낸다는 것은 그만큼 돈이 많이 들어간다는 의미이므로 보기 중에서 "교육에 들어갈 지출이 증가한다"는 의미의 ①이 답으로 가장 적합하다.

02

다음 중 빈칸 (2)에 가장 알맞은 것은 무엇인가?
① 두 배
② 반
③ 덜
④ 4분의 1

| 정답 | ②

| 해설 | 여성이 자녀를 한 명씩만 낳을 경우, 남녀 두 사람이 자녀를 하나만 낳는 셈이니 산술적으로 자녀 세대엔 인구가 반으로 줄 수밖에 없다. 따라서 답은 ②이다.

03

본문에 따르면 다음 중 사실이 아닌 것은 무엇인가?
① 한국은 매우 낮은 수준의 출생률과 함께 심각한 노령화 문제에 직면해 있다.
② 2009년 가구당 평균 자녀 수는 1.15명이었으나 1960년대에는 이보다 다섯 배 많았다.
③ 한국 여성은 자녀를 낳은 후 직장에 복귀하기가 대체로 힘들다.
④ 한국 여성은 현재로서는 노동력을 충분히 제공할 수 있을 만큼의 자녀를 낳고 있지만, 곧 이는 불가능해질 것이다.

| 정답 | ④

| 해설 | 2009년 한국 여성의 출산율은 1.15명이며 "이는 인구학적 붕괴를 가져올 수밖에 없다(That is a recipe for demographic collapse)." 즉, 지금 수준으로도 이미 한국 여성은 충분한 노동력을 제공할 수 있을 만큼 자녀를 낳지 못하고 있다. 따라서 답은 ④이다. 참고로 ①과 ②는 본문 마지막 단락에서 근거를 찾을 수 있고, ③은 본문 두 번째 단락의 내용과 일치한다.

| 어휘 | rigid ⓐ 엄격한, 융통성 없는   aggravate ⓥ 악화시키다
       demographic ⓐ 인구학의   stark choice – 냉혹한 선택
       fast track – 출세 가도   frown on – ~을 못마땅해하다
       staggeringly ⓐⓓ 충격적으로, 비틀거리며   hefty ⓐ 장대한, 크고 무거운
       bid up – ~의 값을 올리다   recipe ⓝ 방안, 비책
       irrelevance ⓝ 무관함, 중요하지 않음

[04-06] 단국대 2011

가장 최신 자료에서는 수명이 더 이상 늘어나고 있지 않다는 것을 암시한다. 또한 새로운 연구결과에 따르면, 우리는 불과 10년 전보다도 더 많은 시간을 질병으로 고통받으며 보낼 것이라고 한다. 최근의 연구 결과에서는 건강하게 장수하는 인류의 목표가 대부분의 사람들에게는 가능하지 않을지도 모른다는 것을 시사한다.

자료의 분석에 따르면, 이환율(이환율이란 심각한 질병에 걸리거나 신체의 기능적 움직임이 제한되는 기간을 말함)의 평균 기간은 지난 20년간 꾸준히 증가해 왔다. 예를 들어, 1998년에는 20세의 남성이 심장병, 암 또는 당뇨와 같은 질병을 전혀 앓지 않고도 45년을 더 살 수 있을 것으로 기대됐다. 하지만 2006년에는 이것이 43.8년으로 줄어들었다. "우리는 지금까지 노화와 연관 있는 질병이나 생리적 변화들을 늦추거나 없애는 데 거의 아무것도 이룬 것이 없다는 것에 상당한 증거도 있다"고 연구 저자들은 말한다. "우리는 언제나 다음 세대가 이전 세대보다 건강하고, 또 더 오래 살 것이라고 추정해 왔다. 하지만 만성비만과 고혈압의 증가 그리고 노년에 접어든 사람들의 혈중 콜레스테롤 증가 등은 건강이라는 것이 매 세대 간 반드시 발전하는 것만은 아니라는 것을 보여주는 신호이다. 우리가 질병이나 기능손실, 장애 등을 겪지 않고 늙어갈 수 있는 그런 세상을 향해 가고 있는 것은 아닌 것 같다."고 이들은 덧붙였다.

04

본문의 제목으로 가장 적절한 것은?
① 오래 사는 것의 중요성
② 장수의 비밀
③ 노인들의 건강 비결
④ 길고 건강하지 못한 인생

| 정답 | ④

| 해설 | 장수라는 것은 오래 사는 것도 중요하지만 아프지 않고 건강하게 오래 사는 것이 더 중요하다. 하지만 최근의 연구에서는 인류가 오래 살지만 건강하게 사는 기간은 오히려 줄었다는 내용을 본문에서 다루고 있기 때문에, 장수와 더불어 이런 내용에 초점이 맞춰진 제목을 선택해야 한다. 그런 의미에서 정답은 ④가 된다.

05

다음 중 빈칸에 들어갈 가장 적절한 것은?
① 이환율
② 사망률
③ 겸손
④ 노령

| 정답 | ①

| 해설 | 빈칸 바로 뒤에 정의가 나온다. 정의에 따르면 아프거나 다치지 않고 사는 기간을 의미한다고 말하고 있으므로, 정답은 ① morbidity가 된다.

06

다음 중 지문을 통해 유추할 수 있는 내용과 가장 거리가 먼 것은?
① 인류는 심각한 질병에 걸린 채 더 오래 살고 있으며, 기대수명조차 더 이상 늘어나지 않을 것으로 생각된다.
② 대부분의 인류에게는 건강하게 장수하는 것이 불가능할지 모른다.
③ 계단을 올라갈 수 없다든지, 0.5마일도 제대로 걸을 수 없는 등의 신체적 장애를 가진 사람들의 수가 증가하고 있다.
④ 주요 질병의 치료법들이 발달되고 백신이나 좀 더 나은 치료법에 의해 전염병이 줄어들고 있는 가운데, 기대수명은 곤두박질치고 있다.

| 정답 | ④

| 해설 | ①의 경우 첫 번째 문장에 대한 설명(The most recent data hint that life span is no longer growing.)이며, ②의 경우 전반부에 나오는 본문의 내용을 그대로 사용하고 있다. ③의 경우 두 번째 문장에 나오는 이환율에 대한 내용을 예를 들어 설명하고 있다. ④에서는 기대수명이 급격히 떨어지고 있다(plummet)고 했지만, 본문에서는 기대수명이 더 이상은 늘지 않을 것 같다고 했으므로, 본문의 내용과 부합하지 않아서 ④가 정답이 된다.

| 어휘 | hint ⓥ 넌지시 알려주다
humanity ⓝ 인류
substantial ⓐ 상당한
obesity ⓝ 비만
cohort ⓝ 집단
longevity ⓝ 장수
fatality ⓝ 사망률
life expectancy – 기대수명
be quelled by – ~에 의해 진압되다
life span – 수명
analysis ⓝ 분석
assume ⓥ 추정하다
hypertension ⓝ 고혈압
significance ⓝ 중요성
morbidity ⓝ 이환율, 병이 생길 확률
senility ⓝ 노쇠, 노망
plummet ⓥ 곤두박질치다

[07-09] 동국대 2011

급속히 발전 중인 동아시아 국가들은 수년간 세계의 부러움의 대상이었지만, 한 가지 결정적인 분야의 부족함, 즉 아이의 부족함이 과거의 호랑이를 이빨 빠진 호랑이로 만들어 버릴 조짐을 보인다. 세계 최저의 출산율로 인해 싱가포르·한국·대만의 노동력은 대폭 줄기 시작된 것으로 보이며, 이들 국가는 앞으로 줄어든 노동력으로 더 많은 은퇴자를 부양할 뿐만 아니라 급격히 증가 중인 은퇴자들을 위한 보건과 연금비용도 지탱하게 되었다. 이들 국가와 함께 고령화의 선봉에서 발을 이끌며 걷고 있는 국가로 일본을 들 수 있다. 일본의 인구는 3년 전부터 서서히 줄기 시작했으며, 인구 4분의 1 가량이 65세 이상인데 반해 아이들은 (전체 인구의) 13%에 불과하다. 현재 추세로는 일본의 현재 1억 2,700만의 인구는 2055년경에는 9,000만으로 줄 것이며, 이는 일본이 전후 호경기에 접어들던 1955년의 수준이다. 아시아의 인구 대국인 중국은 아직은 (인구의) 절정기에 거의 근접한 상황이며, 젊은 농민공들이 무리지어 공장으로 몰려들고 있다. 하지만 30년 가량 지속된 한 자녀 정책 덕분에 중국의 인구학적 시한폭탄 또한 폭발을 향해 똑딱이고 있다.

07
밑줄 친 문장 ㉮는 감소하는 출산율이 '아시아 경제를 약화시킬 것이다'와 가장 가까운 의미이다.
① 아시아에 사는 호랑이를 위협한다
② 아시아 경제를 약화시킬 것이다
③ 아시아의 신흥 경제국을 끌어올릴 수 있다
④ 아시아 국가들을 과열 위험에 빠뜨린다

| 정답 | ②

| 해설 | 밑줄 친 문장 ㉮의 해석은 '한 가지 결정적인 분야의 부족함, 즉 아이 부족이 과거의 호랑이를 이빨 빠진 호랑이로 만들어 버릴 조짐을 보인다'이며, 이는 호랑이로 불릴 만한 힘을 보여준 아시아의 신흥 경제국들이 출산율 저하로 인해 힘(이빨)이 빠진 호랑이 꼴이 될 수 있음을 의미한다. 따라서 답은 ②이다.

08
다음 중 빈칸 ㉯에 들어갈 가장 알맞은 것은 무엇일까?
① 그럼에도 불구하고
② ~의 이전에
③ ~와는 반대로
④ ~의 덕분에

| 정답 | ④

| 해설 | 중국에서 30년간 한 자녀 정책을 지속했다면 신생아의 수는 줄어들 것임을 유추할 수 있다. 본문은 신생아 감소로 인해 동아시아 여러 나라가 많은 문제에 봉착하게 될 것임을 말하고 있으며, 중국의 경우는 이를 시한폭탄이 똑딱이다 터지는 것에 비유하고 있다. 따라서 빈칸에는 '~으로 인해' 또는 '~ 때문에'에 해당하는 단어가 와야 할 것이다. 보기 중에서 이에 해당하는 것은 ④이다.

09
본문에 따르면 다음 중 사실인 것은?
① 대만에서는 비숙련 노동력의 수요가 증가한다.
② 싱가포르는 젊은이들이 무거운 연금 부담을 떠맡을 것이다.
③ 일본의 전후 호황은 2055년에 끝이 난다.
④ 중국의 인구 증가는 앞으로 수십 년 동안 (출산율 감소로 인한) 중대 사태를 무시할 수 있을 정도이다.

| 정답 | ②

| 해설 | 본문에 따르면 싱가포르는 대만이나 한국처럼 출산율 저하로 인해 "앞으로 줄어든 노동력으로 더 많은 은퇴자를 부양할 뿐만 아니라 급격히 증가 중인 은퇴자들을 위한 보건과 연금비용도 지탱할(fewer workers will support

more retirees and their ballooning health care and pension costs)" 상황에 처해 있다. 이는, 즉 지금의 젊은 층이나 앞으로 태어날 세대가 그 윗세대를 부양해야 할 부담이 점점 커질 것임을 의미한다. 따라서 답은 ②이다. ①의 경우는, 본문의 내용과 상관이 없다. ③의 경우는, 일본의 인구가 2055년에 줄어든다는 내용은 있지만 전후 세대가 끝날 것이라는 내용은 담겨 있지 않다. 따라서 답으로 볼 수 없다. ④의 경우는, 보기를 해석하면 앞으로 수십 년간 중국은 다른 동아시아 국가들이 출산율 감소로 인해 겪는 문제를 겪지 않을 것이라는 의미를 갖는다. 하지만 이는 본문과는 동떨어진 의미이다. 따라서 답으로 볼 수 없다.

| 어휘 | booming ⓐ 급속히 발전 중인
threaten ⓥ 위협하다, (좋지 않은) 조짐을 보이다
set to – 착수하다, 시작하다
retiree ⓝ 은퇴자, 퇴직자
shuffle along – 발을 이끌며 가다
shrink ⓥ 줄다
kick off – 개시하다
prime ⓝ 전성기, 한창때
demographic ⓐ 인구(학)의
drive up – ~을 들어 올리다
assume ⓥ (권력·책임 등을) 떠맡다
defy ⓥ 거역하다, 무시하다, 견디다, 설명하기 불가능하다
gravity ⓝ 중력; 중대한 사태, 심상치 않은 문제

shortfall ⓝ 부족함
render ⓥ (어떤 상태)가 되게 하다
slash ⓥ 베다, 대폭 줄이다
balloon ⓥ 급격히 증가하다
at the vanguard of – ~의 선봉에서
make up – ~을 구성하다
post-war ⓐ 전후의(특히 제2차 대전 이후의)
flock to – ~로 밀려들다
tick ⓥ 시계 등이 째깍[똑딱]거리다
prior to – ~에 앞서

[10-12] 성균관대 2011

1798년 영국의 성직자이자 경제학자인 Thomas Malthus는 자신의 일반 인구 법칙을 발표했다. 여기서 그는 전쟁·질병·기근이 도래해 사람의 수를 줄이기 전까지는 필연적으로 인구가 식량 공급의 증가보다 빠르게 증가할 것이라고 주장했다. 이미 드러난 바대로 전 세계 인구의 감소를 불러일으킬 정도의 대규모 전염병의 확산은 Malthus가 글을 작성했던 당시의 이전에 이미 벌어진 바 있었다. 역사가들은 14세기 대흑사병 시기 이후로 세계 인구가 감소한 적은 없었던 것으로 생각한다.
Malthus가 인구가 계속 증가할 수는 없다고 선언한 지 2세기가 지난 지금, 인구는 그대로 계속 증가했다. 이 같은 증가 과정은 발표 당시에도 발전 중이었고 현재는 우리가 선진국으로 부르는 국가에서 시작되었다. 옥수수와 감자 같은 신세계에서 난 작물의 확산과 여기에 덧붙인 화학비료의 발견은 유럽에서 기아를 몰아내는 데 도움이 되었다. 성장하는 도시는 처음에는 온갖 질병의 도가니였지만, 19세기 중반부터는 하수도가 인간의 노폐물을 식수에서 떨어진 곳으로 보내기 시작했고, 노폐물은 (떨어진 곳으로 보내진 다음) 여과된 후에 염소처리가 되었다. 이는 콜레라와 발진티푸스의 확산을 크게 줄였다.
게다가 Malthus가 자신의 비관적인 소책자를 발표한 바로 그해인 1798년에는 그와 같은 영국인인 Edward Jenner가 천연두 백신에 관해 최초로 서술했는데, 이 천연두 백신은 영양 및 위생의 개선과 함께 공업국의 기대수명을 35세에서 오늘날의 77세로 두 배로 늘린 (일등공신인) 일련의 백신과 항생제 중에서 최초이자 가장 중요한 것이었다.

10 밑줄 친 '인구는 그대로 계속 증가했다'가 의미하는 것은 무엇인가?
① 인구수가 크게 줄었다
② 너무 많은 사람들이 세계대전에서 살해되었다
③ 사람들이 전보다 오래 살기 시작했다
④ 세계 인구가 계속 빠르게 증가했다
⑤ 모든 것이 그가 예측한 대로 진행되었다

| 정답 | ④

| 해설 | 밑줄 친 문장 뒤의 내용은 모두 왜 Malthus의 법칙이 나온 이후에 세계 인구가 줄지 않고 늘었는지를 말하고 있다. 열거해 보면 신대륙이 원산지인 작물의 확산, 화학비료의 발견, 하수도, 정수시설 등과 같은 "영양 및 위생의 개선(better nutrition and sanitation)"에 덧붙여 백신의 발견 등을 들 수 있다. 이 같은 요소가 '기대수명을 35세에서 오늘날의 77세로 두 배로 늘린(double life expectancy in the industrializing countries, from 35 years to 77 today)' 것을 알 수 있다. 따라서 밑줄 친 표현이 의미하는 것은 ④임을 유추할 수 있다.

11

Malthus의 일반 인구 법칙은 거짓임이 드러났다. 그 이유는 무엇이었는가?
① 현대의 발전을 생각하지 못했다
② 정확한 인구수를 몰랐다
③ 그의 소책자를 너무 늦게 출판했다
④ 성경에서 글의 발상을 얻었다
⑤ 세계대전은 계산에 넣지 않았다

| 정답 | ①

| 해설 | 인구론이 발표된 이후 지속적인 발전 덕분에 세계의 인구는 인구 상승이 정체되거나 인구가 줄기는커녕 계속 증가했다. 따라서 Malthus의 일반 인구 법칙이 잘못인 이유는 ①임을 쉽게 유추할 수 있다.

12

다음 중 인구 증가에 기여하지 않은 것은 무엇인가?
① 백신　　　　　　　　　　② 화학비료
③ 성장하는 도시　　　　　　④ 하수도
⑤ 미국산 작물

| 정답 | ③

| 해설 | 본문에서 언급되지 않은 것은 ③뿐이다. 참고로 ⑤에서 미국 또한 신세계의 일부이므로 미국산 작물 역시 인구 확산에 기여했다.

| 어휘 | enunciate ⓥ 말하다, 밝히다　　　　　general law – 일반 법칙
plague ⓝ 전염병　　　　　　　　　　dent ⓝ 움푹 들어간 곳, 감소
Black Death – 흑사병(14세기 대유행한 흑사병은 대흑사병이라 부름)
banish ⓥ 몰아내다　　　　　　　　　starvation ⓝ 기아
cesspool ⓝ 오수 구덩이, 불결한 장소　channel ⓥ ~을 통해 보내다
chlorinate ⓥ 염소화하다　　　　　　typhus ⓝ 발진티푸스
dyspeptic ⓐ 비관적인; 소화불량의　　tract ⓝ 글, 소책자
compatriot ⓝ 동포　　　　　　　　　antibiotic ⓝ 항생제
sanitation ⓝ 위생　　　　　　　　　life expectancy – 기대수명
turn out to be – ~임이 드러나다　　count ⓥ 계산에 넣다, 간주하다

[13-15] 한국외대 2006

많은 이들이 미국의 시민권 운동은 1955년 12월 1일 시작됐다고 생각한다. 이 날은 Rosa Parks라는 흑인 여성이 앨라배마 주 몽고메리 시가 운영하는 버스에서 백인 남성에게 자신의 자리를 양보하길 거부했던 날이다. 당시만 하더라도 지역 법상으로 흑인들은 하급 시민으로 부당한 처우를 받았다. 남부지역 전역에 걸쳐 많은 호텔과 식당, 심지어 식수대조차 백인들만을 위한 것이었다. 또한 앨라배마 주도인 몽고메리에서도, 다른 남부지역과 마찬가지로, 시내버스가 백인과 흑인이 앉는 구역이 구별되어 있었다. 앞 좌석 10개는 백인들을 위한 좌석이고, 흑인 승객들은 뒷자리에서 타고 가야 했다.

흑인 전용 좌석에 앉아야 한다는 것을 모욕적인 처사로 생각했기 때문에 Rosa Parks는 직장에서 집까지 주로 걸어서 퇴근했다. 하지만 1955년 12월 1일 겨울 저녁, Parks는 피로감을 느끼고 버스를 타고 집에 가기로 마음 먹었다. 집으로 향하는 동안 얼마 되지 않아 앞의 10좌석이 모두 백인 승객들로 채워졌고, 이후 또 다른 백인 남성이 버스에 탔을 때, 기사는 백인 전용 좌석을 더 넓히고자 Parks와 다른 세 명의 흑인들에게 자리 양보를 요구했다. 세 명의 흑인들은 자신들의 자리를 양보했지만, Parks는 거부하고 움직이지 않았다. 기사는 경찰을 불렀고, 경찰에 의해 그녀는 구금됐다.

13 Rosa Parks는 퇴근할 때 주로 버스를 타지 않았다. 그 이유는 무엇이었는가?
① 어떤 민족인지에 따라 버스 좌석을 구분하는 것은 불법이라고 생각했기 때문에
② 유색 인종을 위해 지정된 좌석에 앉는다는 사실이 굴욕적이라고 생각했기 때문에
③ 비용을 아끼기 위해서 퇴근 때는 걸어왔기 때문에
④ 백인들만 편한 자리에 앉는 것은 부적절하다고 믿었기 때문에
⑤ 피부색으로 버스 좌석을 구분하는 것은 효율적이지 못하다고 믿었기 때문에

| 정답 | ②

| 해설 | 둘째 문단 첫 부분인 "Because she found it degrading to have to sit in the 'Colored' section of the bus,"를 통해 버스를 타지 않았던 이유를 알 수 있다. 본문의 degrading과 보기 ②의 humiliating은 비슷한 뜻의 단어이므로 정답은 ②가 된다.

14 문제가 됐던 버스 앞의 10개 좌석에서 몇 명의 흑인이 앉아 있었는가?
① 0   ② 1
③ 2   ④ 3
⑤ 4

| 정답 | ①

| 해설 | 둘째 문단에 보면 앞좌석은 모두 백인들로 차 있었는데, 그 이후 추가로 백인이 올라타자, 버스기사가 백인용 자리를 더 넓히기(extend) 위해 흑인들에게 자리 양보를 요구했다고 했으므로, 앞좌석에 앉아 있던 흑인은 없었다는 것을 알 수 있다.

15

다음 중 본문에 나와 있거나 추론할 수 있는 내용은?

① 미국의 시민권 운동은 교통사고로 촉발됐다.
② 1950년대 피부색을 기준으로 사람들을 차별하는 것은 앨라배마 주에서는 불법이었다.
③ 당시 미국 대부분의 호텔과 식당은 백인들만이 사용할 수 있었다.
④ Rosa Parks는 특정 기간 동안 경찰서에 구금됐다.
⑤ 몽고메리의 흑인들이 높은 버스비를 이유로 시내버스 탑승을 보이콧했다.

| 정답 | ④

| 해설 | ①과 ⑤의 내용은 본문에 등장하지 않는다. ②의 경우 본문과 반대로 서술하고 있으며, ③의 경우 본문에서는 미국 전역이 아닌 남부 지역에서 그런 곳이 많았다고 서술하고 있으므로 정답이 될 수 없다. 정답은 ④로, 본문에서 경찰이 'took her into custody'했다는 내용을 통해 그녀가 경찰서에 구금됐었다는 것을 알 수 있다.

| 어휘 | Civil Rights Movement – 시민권 운동
local ⓐ 지방의, 지역의
drinking fountain – 식수대
segregated ⓐ 분리된, 격리된, 인종차별의
take a person into custody – ~을 구금하다
designated ⓐ 지정된
refuse ⓥ 거부하다
unjustly ⓐⓓ 부당하게
state capital – 주도
degrading ⓐ 품위를 떨어뜨리는, 창피한
humiliating ⓐ 굴욕적인, 치욕적인
detain ⓥ 구금하다

[16-18] 홍익대 2016

하지만 미국 북부에 거주하던 대부분의 유대인들은 자신들의 지위에 대해 불안감을 매우 심하게 느낀 나머지 한결같은 방식으로 흑인들에게 이타적인 행동을 할 수가 없었다. 이들은 대신 서로 상반된 태도가 격렬히 공존하는 행동 패턴을 보이게 되었는데, 한편으로는 백인으로서 자신의 사회적 우월성을 지속적으로 옹호했지만, 다른 한편으로는 자신들의 지위 유지에 문제가 되지 않을 경우엔 흑인들을 걱정하고 흑인들의 처지에 공감했다. 거주지 분리 문제가 이와 관련하여 유익한 사례를 제시한다. 유대인들은 뉴욕 및 시카고에서 동네에 설립된 "보호" 협회를 지지했지만, 유대인 언론은 종종 이러한 움직임을 비난하는 것이 타당함을 깨닫기도 했다. 하지만 (주간지인) "미국의 히브리인(American Hebrew)" 편집인들은 결국에는 자신들이 속한 지위를 많이 의식하는 유대인들이 직면한 딜레마를 이해하고 있었다. 편집인들은 유대인들이 분명히 "흑인들이 자기 동네가 아닌 다른 지역에서 흑인들이 발전하는 한" 흑인 사회의 발전과 교육 및 자족을 권장할 것이라고 생각했다. 과도기적 동네에서 거주하던 여러 유대인들은 거주지역의 제한이라는 불편한 의문을 전적으로 회피했고, 대신 집을 흑인들에게 팔고 이사를 가는 편을 선호했다. 이런 식으로 유대인들은 스스로를 변화 중인 동네와 거리를 두면서 인종 분리 노력에 직접적으로 참여하지 않으려 했던 모순적인 욕구를 충족시킬 수 있었다. 이러한 이중적 충동이 작용했던 사례로 1919년 시카고의 (유대교 회당인) 템플 이사야(Temple Isaiah) 구성원들이 투표를 통해 자신들이 있는 지역으로 침범해 들어 오던 "흑인 밀집 지대"로부터 벗어나 이전하기로 결정했지만 미국 흑인 교회 신도들에게 판매를 하지 말라는 하이드 파크-켄우드 어소시에이션(Hyde Park-Kenwood Association)의 간청을 무시했던 일을 들 수 있다.

16

위 본문에 따르면 다음 중 사실이 아닌 것은 무엇인가?

① 미국 북부에서 유대인의 사회적 지위는 충분히 안정되어 있지 않았다.
② 거주지역의 제한이라는 문제는 유대계 미국인들이 이타적인 사람들이었음을 나타낸다.
③ 유대인들은 미국 흑인들의 교육 및 사회적 지위 향상을 지지했다.
④ 인종 관계에 있어 유대계 미국인들의 태도는 서로 상반된 태도가 공존하는 모습이었다.

| 정답 | ②

| 해설 | 본문 처음부터 "거주지 분리 문제가 이와 관련하여 유익한 사례를 제시한다(The issue of residential segregation provides an instructive example)"까지의 내용을 간단히 살피면, 미국 북부의 유대인들은 미국 사회 내에서 자신들의 지위를 불안하게 여겼고 때문에 같은 소수집단인 흑인들에게 한결같이 이타적인 태도를 보일 수 없었고 대신 서로 상반된 태도가 공존하는 모습을 보였다. 거주지 분리 문제는 이에 대한 좋은 사례가 된다. 즉, ②에서 말하는 것과는 달리 한결같이 이타적인 태도를 보일 수는 없었다. 따라서 답은 ②이다.

17 다음 중 (A) but과 의미상 가장 가까운 것은 무엇인가?
① 하지만
② 오로지
③ 여전히
④ ~을 제외하고

| 정답 | ④

| 해설 | (A) but은 문맥상 '~을 제외하고, ~ 외에' 등을 의미하며, 따라서 ④가 답이 된다.

18 다음 중 위 본문으로부터 유추할 수 있는 것은 무엇인가?
① 유대인들은 동네를 백인 중심으로 유지하는 방식을 통해 자신들이 백인임을 강조했다.
② 유대인들은 미국 흑인들에 대한 행동에 일관성이 있었다.
③ 거주지역과 관련된 문제가 종종 유대인들의 지위에 의문을 던졌다.
④ 유대인들은 종종 포함되고 싶다는 충동과 독특한 존재가 되고 싶다는 충동 사이에서 괴로워했다.

| 정답 | ④

| 해설 | 본문에 따르면 유대인들은 미국 사회 내에서 자신의 지위를 강하게 의식하며 살았고 사회의 일원으로 포함되고 싶다는 욕구를 강하게 보였으며 흑백 분리 같은 차별 행동에 적극적으로 참여하려는 생각은 없었지만, 동시에 과도기적 동네에서 흑인들의 비중이 많아지면 이사를 가는 식으로 흑인들과는 거리를 두려고도 했다. 즉, 내가 사는 동네가 아닌 다른 곳에서 흑인들의 발전을 지원한 것이다. 이를 본문에서는 딜레마로 표현한 바 있다. 따라서 답은 ④이다.
참고로 유대인들은 흑인들이 많아지면 집을 팔고 떠났지 흑인들의 진입을 금지하지는 않았으므로 ①은 답이 될 수 없다. 일관성이 없었다는 것이 본문에 제시되므로 ②도 답이 될 수 없다. 거주지역과 관련된 문제는 자신이 흑인들과는 다른 존재임을 인식하면서도 적극적으로 인종 분리에 참여하지는 않는 양면적이고 모순된 모습을 드러내었지 유대인들의 사회 내 지위에 어떤 의문을 제기한 것은 아니었다. 따라서 ③도 답이 될 수 없다.

| 어휘 |
insecure ⓐ 불안감을 느끼는, 자신이 없는
altruistically ⓐd 이타적으로
consistent ⓐ 한결같은, 일관된
fall into - ~에 빠지다, ~하게 되다
ambivalent ⓐ 서로 상반된 감정이[태도가] 공존하는, 애증이 엇갈리는
assert ⓥ 주장하다, 옹호하다
superiority ⓝ 우월성, 우월함
bring ~ into question - ~에 의문을 던지다, ~을 문제 삼다
residential ⓐ 거주지의, 주택지의
segregation ⓝ 분리, 차별
instructive ⓐ 유익한
protective ⓐ 보호하는, 보호용의
association ⓝ 협회, 연합
Hebrew ⓝ 히브리인, 유대인
ultimately ⓐd 결국, 궁극적으로
conscious ⓐ 의식하는, 자각하는

self-sufficiency ⓝ 자족, 자급자족	but ⓟ ~ 외에, ~을 제외하고
transitional ⓐ 변천하는, 과도적인	in this manner - 이런 식으로
dual ⓐ 이중의	impulse ⓝ 충동, 충격
at work - 작용한, ~을 하고 있는	relocate ⓥ 이전하다
encroach ⓥ 침해하다, 잠식하다	the Black Belt - (미국 남부의) 흑인 (밀집) 지대
congregation ⓝ (특정 교회의) 신자[신도]들	indicate ⓥ 나타내다, 보여주다
uplift ⓝ 사회적 지위의 향상	torn between - ~ 사이에서 괴로운[망설이는]
inclusion ⓝ 포함	distinctiveness ⓝ 독특함, 특수함

[19-21] 가톨릭대 2016

페미니즘 사상의 주요 주장 중 하나는 생물학적 '성(sex)'은 문화적 관습의 영역인 '사회적 성(gender)'과는 별개의 존재라는 것이다. '남성성'과 '여성성'이 어떤 특성을 수반하는지에 관한 생각은 사회마다 차이가 있다. 어떤 맥락에서는 '여성적인' 행동이라 여겨지는 것이 다른 맥락에서는 '남성적인' 행동에 더욱 가까운 것으로 여겨질 수 있다. 사람들은 자신들이 속한 사회적 맥락에 의해 결정된 '남성적 행동'과 '여성적 행동'에 관한 문화적 규범을 준수한다. 사람들은 출생 시점부터 줄곧 사회화를 통해 해당 문화적 규범을 무의식적으로 수용하고 이를 기반으로 행동한다. 성장의 주요 요소 중 하나는 '남성'이 되는 법이나 '여성'이 되는 법을 학습하는 것과 관련이 있다. 대체로 이러한 학습 과정은 무의식적 및 반의식적 심리 단계에서 벌어진다. 그리고 인간은 스스로의 모습을 형성한 문화적으로 파생된 사회적 성(gender)의 규범을 실제로는 자연스러운 것이자 불변의 것으로 인식하게 된다. 이런 식으로, 우리가 자연적으로 '여성적'이거나 '남성적'이라고 사고하고 행동하는 방식이라고 우리가 생각하는 경향이 있는 것들은 실제로는 문화적으로 특정한 행동을 해야 한다는 요구사항이 머릿속에 주입된 결과물이다.

그 결과, 우리는 사회적 성에 따른 문화적 규범은 사람이 성장하면서 사고방식 측면에서뿐만 아니라 육체적으로 존재한다는 측면, 즉 몸을 움직이고 경험한다는 측면에서 사람에게 영향을 미칠 것으로 생각할 수 있다. 대부분의 사회에서 남성은 여성에 비해 권세 있는 지위를 더 많이 차지하는 경향이 있다. 가부장적 사회구조에서 하나의 집단으로서의 남성은 여성에 비해 더 많은 권세를 누리며 또한 여성을 지배하는 권세를 누린다. 이런 사회에서 문화적 영향력은 이러한 상황을 반영하면서 동시에 정당화하는 경향이 있다. 남성은 여성에 비해 왠지 자연적으로 우월한 존재로 인식된다. 이러한 우월성은 마치 삶의 불변의 진리인양 받아들여진다. 가부장적 사회의 특성이 되는 사회적 성의 규범은 자연적인 본질이 아니라 문화적으로 꾸며낸 것에 불과한 '여성성'의 본질을 창조하게 된다. '여성성'은 대체로 부정적인 방향으로 정의되며, 이 과정에서 여성은 심리적으로 그리고 신체적으로 열등한 존재임이 강조된다.

19 빈칸에 가장 알맞은 것을 고르시오.
① 언어학적 표현
② 역사적 사건
③ 사회적 변화
④ 문화적으로 꾸며낸 것

| 정답 | ④

| 해설 | 페미니즘 사상에 따르면 생물학적 성과 사회적 성은 서로 다른 개념이며, 사회적 성은 문화적 관습 및 규범의 영역이다. 즉, 어떤 것이 남성적이고 어떤 것이 여성적인지를 규정하는 것은 문화적으로 우리가 어떠한 행동을 해야 한다는 요구사항에 따른 결과일 뿐 자연스럽거나 선천적인 것은 아니다. 때문에 가부장적 사회와 같이 준수해야 할 특정 문화적 관습 및 규범이 존재하는 사회에서 '여성성'이니 '남성성'이니 하는 것들은 모두 자연적인 것이 아니라 문화적으로 규정된 것, 즉 만들어지고 "꾸며낸 것"이다. 따라서 답은 ④이다.

20 다음의 문장이 들어가기에 가장 알맞은 장소를 고르시오.

> 대체로 이러한 학습 과정은 무의식적 및 반의식적 심리 단계에서 벌어진다.

① Ⓐ　　　② Ⓑ　　　③ Ⓒ　　　④ Ⓓ

| 정답 | ②

| 해설 | 주어진 문장의 "이러한 학습 과정(these learning processes)"은 문맥상 남성과 여성에게 사회적 성을 주입하는 과정, 즉 어떤 것이 남성적인 행동이고 여성적인 행동인지를 문화적 규범 및 관습에 따라 개개인에게 주입하는 과정을 의미한다. 때문에 주어진 문장은 해당 학습 과정이 언급된 뒤에 위치해야 한다. 학습 과정은 Ⓐ 뒤에 언급되어 있으므로 Ⓐ는 답이 될 수 없다. 그리고 Ⓒ 앞을 보면, 인간은 이러한 학습의 결과 사회적 성의 개념을 학습된 것임에도 불구하고 마치 자연스러운 것이자 불변의 것인 양 받아들이게 됨을 알 수 있다. 여기서 본문의 흐름이 Ⓐ 뒤에 학습에 관한 사항이 등장하고 ⇨ 주어진 문장이 삽입되고 ⇨ 그 결과 사람들 사이에서 학습된 개념이 마치 당연한 것인 양 받아들여지게 되는 것으로 이어짐을 유추할 수 있다. 즉, 주어진 문장은 Ⓐ 뒤 Ⓒ 앞에 위치해야 한다. 따라서 답은 ②이다.

21 다음 중 본문에 따르면 사실이 아닌 것은 무엇인가?
① 대부분의 사회에서 문화적 규범은 사물이 실제 존재하는 모습을 반영하고 자연적인 것으로 받아들여진다.
② 문화는 우리의 사고방식뿐만 아니라 우리가 신체를 사용하는 방식에도 영향을 미친다.
③ 가부장적 사회에서 여성에 대한 남성의 우월성은 삶의 불변의 진리인 것으로 여겨진다.
④ 여성성이나 남성성을 이루는 것이 무엇인가에 대한 생각은 모든 사회 조직에서 동일하게 나타나지 않는다.

| 정답 | ①

| 해설 | 페미니스트들의 주장에 따르면 사회적 성은 어디까지나 문화적 규범에 따른 학습에 의한 개념이며, 불변의 것이나 자연적인 것은 아니다. 여기서 문화적 규범은 실제와는 거리가 있는 인위적 개념임을 유추할 수 있다. 따라서 답은 ①이다.

| 어휘 |
biological ⓐ 생물학의
as to – ~에 관해
masculinity ⓝ 남성성
conform to – ~에 따르다, ~을 준수하다
onwards ⓐⓓ 계속, 줄곧
unconsciously ⓐⓓ 무의식적으로
derived ⓐ 유래된, 파생된
expectations ⓝ (어떤 일을 꼭 하기를 바라는) 기대[요구]
corporeality ⓝ 유형[유체]인 성질[상태]; 육체로서의 존재
patriarchal ⓐ 가부장제의, 가부장적인
superiority ⓝ 우월성
fabrication ⓝ 꾸며낸 것, 거짓말
constitute ⓥ ~을 구성하다, ~을 이루다
convention ⓝ 관습
trait ⓝ 특성
femininity ⓝ 여성성
norm ⓝ 규범
socialize ⓥ 사회화시키다
semi-conscious ⓐ 반(半)의식적인
inculcation ⓝ 머릿속에 심어줌, 주입함
simultaneously ⓐⓓ 동시에, 일제히
characteristic ⓐ 특유의, 독특한
inferiority ⓝ 열등함

[22-23] 한양대 2018

뒤르켐(Durkheim)의 주요 관심사 중 하나는 무엇이 사회를 하나로 묶는지에 대한 것이다. 이러한 사회적 결속을 촉진하고 유지하는 데 법이 결정적인 역할을 하고 있다고 그는 지적한다. 사회가 정교일치에서 세속주의로 발전하고, 집단주의에서 개인주의로 발전하면서, 법이 처벌보다는 보상에 더 관여한다는 것을 그는 제시한다. 그러나 처벌은 사회적 연대가 유지되도록 하는 집단적 도덕관을 표출하는 데 중요한 역할을 수행한다. 그는 소위 기계적 연대와 유기적 연대라는 용어로 이를 구별한다. 전자는 가치관의 통일성을 지니고 있고 대규모의 노동 분업을 찾아볼 수 없는 단순하고 동질적인 사회에서 존재한다. 이러한 단순한 공동체들은 사실상 집단적인 경향이 있다. 그러나 노동의 분업이 존재하는 진보된 사회에서는 높은 수준의 상호의존성이 존재한다. (둘 사이에는) 상당한 차이가 존재하고, 집단주의는 개인주의로 대체된다. 그는 이런 형태의 사회적 연대가 법에 반영된 것이라고 주장한다. 다양한 법을 분류해 보면 그 법에 상응하는 다양한 사회적 연대를 발견할 수 있다는 것이다. 뒤르켐에 따르면, 기계적 연대는 전통적이고 소규모의 사회에서 작동하며, 유기적 연대는 개인들이 특정 과제를 수행하기 위한 서로가 서로에게 의존하는 것에서 비롯된다.

22 윗글의 제목으로 가장 적절한 것은?
① 사회적 연대의 유형, 사회의 유형
② 법과 처벌, 다시 원점으로 돌아온 것인가?
③ 노동 분업, 사회가 발전해 온 방식
④ 연대 및 개인주의, 타협의 여지 만들기

| 정답 | ①

| 해설 | 본문에서는 뒤르켐의 관심사였던 사회적 결속(연대)에 대해 말하고 있고, 사회에 따라 기계적 결속과 유기적 결속으로 나뉜다고 보고 있다. 따라서 이러한 연대와 사회의 유형에 대해 말한 ①이 정답으로 적합하다.

23 빈칸에 들어갈 가장 적절한 것은?
① 유대 - 다양성
② 응집력 - 상호의존성
③ 연대 - 집단주의
④ 동질성 - 특수성

| 정답 | ②

| 해설 | 첫 번째 빈칸은 바로 앞의 'what holds societies together'를 받고 있는 단어이므로, 결속이나 연대를 나타내는 bond, cohesion, solidarity가 적합하다. ④의 homogeneity는 동질성을 나타내는 단어로, 사회가 동질의 사람들로 구성되어 있다고 해서 반드시 결속력이 좋은 것은 아니므로, 정답에서 제외된다. 두 번째 빈칸의 경우 기계적 결속이 나타나는 집단주의와 대비되는 유기적 결속이 나타나는 개인주의에 대해 서술하고 있다. 그리고 이러한 개인들이 마지막 문장의 'individuals' reliance on each other'에서와 같이 서로가 서로에게 의존하면서 분업화된 사회를 이루고, 이런 사회에서 유기적 연대가 나타난다고 서술하고 있으므로, '상호의존성'을 뜻하는 'interdepence'가 정답이 된다. collectivism은 개인주의에 반대되는 개념이며, diversity는 homogeneity와 반대되는 개념이지 집단주의에 반대되는 개념이 아니므로 유의한다.

| 어휘 | **preoccupation** ⓝ 집착; 선입견, 편견
crucial ⓐ 중대한, 결정적인
collectivism ⓝ 집단주의, 집산주의 (모든 농장이나 산업을 정부나 집단이 소유하는 정치 제도)
individualism ⓝ 개성, 개인주의
compensation ⓝ 보상; 보수, 급료
organic ⓐ 유기적인
homogeneous ⓐ 동종의, 균질의
Durkheim - 뒤르켐 (프랑스의 사회학자이자 교육자)
secularism ⓝ 세속주의, 비종교주의
be concerned with - ~에 관계가 있다, 관심이 있다
solidarity ⓝ 연대
the former - 전자
uniformity ⓝ 균일성, 획일

division of labour – 분업
substantial ⓐ 상당한, 많은, 비중 있는
classify ⓥ 분류하다
reliance ⓝ 의존
come full circle – (한 바퀴 돌아, 여러 가지 변화를 거쳐) 제자리로 되돌아오다
bond ⓝ 유대; 굴레, 속박; 합의, 계약
cohesion ⓝ 응집력
homogeneity ⓝ 동종, 동질성, 균질

uncomplicated ⓐ 복잡하지 않은, 단순한
differentiation ⓝ 구별, 차별
correspond to – ~에 일치하다, 들어맞다

diversity ⓝ 다양성, 차이
interdependence ⓝ 상호 의존
distinctiveness ⓝ 특수성

[24-25] 성균관대 2013

왕따에 관한 단일한 정의가 존재하지 않기 때문에 연구진은 왕따가 얼마나 빈번하게 벌어지는지를 측정하는 데 어려움을 겪고 있다. 말로만 이루어지는 것을 왕따라 할 수 있을까 아니면 신체적인 행위가 있어야만 왕따라고 할 수 있을까? 만일 당신이 운동장에서 놀리는 소리를 들었고, 이를 어떻게 하면 무시하고 넘어갈 수 있는지를 알고 있다면, 당신은 왕따의 표적이 된 것으로 봐야 하는가 아니면 단지 짜증나는 일에 불과하다고 할 수 있는가? 반복되어 벌어져야만 왕따로 간주할 수 있는가 아니면 한 번만 벌어진 것도 왕따로 간주할 수 있는가? 반 전체에 지장을 줘야 왕따라 하는가 아니면 한 두 명의 아이들만이 피해를 입어도 왕따라 하는가? 왕따 예방에 관한 법을 연구하고 제정하는 사람들에게는 이런 여러 사항 가운데 명확하게 드러난 사항은 하나도 없다. 대부분의 주의법은 괴롭힘이 벌어진 사례를 왕따라고 간주하기 위해 필요한 정확한 동기와 결과에 대해 서로 다른 입장을 취한다. 만일 한 명의 12세 소년이 다른 아이를 놀릴 경우, 만일 희생자가 (최소한 심리적으로라도) 상처를 받는 것 같은 입증 가능한 피해를 입었으며 입증 가능한 의도가 있었을 경우가 아닌 이상은, 대부분의 주에서는 그런 놀림을 왕따라고는 하지 않으려 한다. 다른 말로 하자면, 그냥 남의 고통에 무신경한 아이를 남을 괴롭히는 왕따 주동자로는 부를 수 없다. 진짜 주동자가 되려면 그 아이는 자신의 급우를 다치게 만들기를 원하는 아이여야 한다.

24 빈칸 (A)에 가장 알맞은 것은 무엇인가?
① 왕따에는 여러 종류의 패턴이 존재한다.
② 미국 내 모든 학교를 점검하는 것은 불가능하다.
③ 단일한 정의가 존재하지 않는다.
④ 대학생들 사이에서는 흔한 일은 아니다.
⑤ 인간의 마음을 이해하는 것은 불가능하다.

| 정답 | ③

| 해설 | 빈칸 (A) 다음부터는 왕따를 명확히 정의하기가 힘들다는 것이 제시되고 있으므로 ③이 답으로 보기 가장 적합하다

25 빈칸 (B)에 가장 알맞은 것은 무엇인가?
① 다른 말로 하자면   ② 반대로
③ 반면에   ④ 이와는 대조적으로
⑤ 어떤 수를 써서든

| 정답 | ①

| 해설 | 빈칸 (B) 앞에서는 "입증 가능한 피해와 의도(demonstrable harm and demonstrable intent)"가 있어야만 왕따로 분류된다는 점을 말하고 있으며, 빈칸 뒤에서는 앞에서 설명한 내용을 부연설명하고 있다. 따라서 ①이 가장 적합하다.

| 어휘 | schoolyard ⓝ 운동장
brush off – 무시하다
disrupt ⓥ 지장을 주다, 방해하다
harassing ⓐ 괴롭히는, 괴로움을 주는
insensitive ⓐ (남의 기분에) 둔감한, 무신경한
taunt ⓝ 놀림, 비웃음 ⓥ 놀리다, 비웃다
count as – ~이라 간주되다[간주하다]
precise ⓐ 정확한
demonstrable ⓐ 보여줄 수 있는, 입증할 수 있는
by all means – 기어코, 어떤 수를 써서든

[26-28] 한국외대 2013

뉴욕타임즈/CBS 뉴스 여론조사에 따르면, 코네티컷 주 뉴타운에 위치한 한 초등학교에서 벌어진 아동 대학살 사건은 미국인들의 총에 대한 시각을 엄청나게 변화시켰고, 근 10년 만에 더욱 엄격한 총기규제 법안에 대한 가장 폭넓은 지지를 갑작스럽게 이끌어 냈다. 이번 여론조사에 따르면 미국인 가운데 다수인 54%가 총기 규제가 강화되어야 한다는 생각을 갖고 있으며, 이는 더욱 엄격한 법을 지지하는 사람의 비율이 39%에 불과했던 지난 4월의 CBS 뉴스 여론조사에 비해 현저하게 증가한 수치이다. 엄격한 총기규제 법안에 대한 지지세 증가는 당파에 상관없이 전체적으로 나타나며, 심지어 공화당 지지자들 사이에서도 18% 포인트의 증가가 이루어졌다. 무당파 중에서도 다수는 더욱 엄격한 총기 규제 법안을 지지한다. 스무 명의 1학년 학생과 여섯 명의 어른이 사망한 뉴타운 총기사건이 대중의 의견에 장기간의 영향을 미칠지 여부는 광란이 벌어진 지 한 달이 막 된 시점에서는 가늠하기 쉽지 않다. 하지만 투손에서 하원의원 개브리엘 기퍼즈에게 심각한 부상을 입힌 2011년의 총기난사 사건 이후를 포함해, 다른 총기난사 사건 직후에 총기 규제에 대한 지지가 약간 올랐던 것과는 달리, 가장 최근에 벌어진 여론조사 결과는 더 깊고 어쩌면 더욱 반향이 큰 변화가 일어날지 모른다는 느낌을 전하고 있다.

26

다음 중 본문에 따르면 사실인 것은 무엇인가?
① 더욱 엄격한 총기규제 법안을 지지하는 공화당원의 수가 증가하고 있다.
② 총기규제 법안에 대한 최근 두 번의 여론조사는 모순되는 결과를 드러냈다.
③ 최근의 총기난사 사건은 총기에 대한 미국인들의 시각에 영구적인 변화를 가져왔다.
④ 미국인들은 총기난사 사건에 영향을 받지 않았다.

| 정답 | ①

| 해설 | 본문에 따르면, 최근의 총기난사 사건으로 인해 더욱 엄격한 총기 규제를 원하는 목소리가 증가했으며 "공화당 지지자들 사이에서도 18% 포인트의 증가가 이루어졌다(an 18-point increase among Republicans)." 따라서 답은 ①이다.

27 다음 중 밑줄 친 (A)를 통해 언급되는 것은 무엇인가?
① 공화당원들 사이의 더욱 엄격한 총기규제 법안을 요구하는 긴급한 목소리
② 자위를 위한 총기 구매의 기록적 증가
③ 보수주의자들 사이의 총기 규제에 대한 과반수가 넘는 지지
④ 더욱 엄격한 총기 규제 법안에 대한 전국적인 급격한 지지 증가

| 정답 | ④

| 해설 | 밑줄 친 (A)는 "미국인들의 총에 대한 시각을 엄청나게 변화시켰다"이며, 본문을 읽어 보면 여기서 말하는 변화는 총기 규제 강화를 지지하는 목소리임을 알 수 있다. 따라서 답은 ④이다.

28 문맥상 다음 중 빈칸 (B)에 가장 알맞은 것은 무엇인가?
① 때문에　　　　　　　　　② ~와는 달리
③ 마치 ~같은　　　　　　　④ 게다가

| 정답 | ②

| 해설 | 기존에는 2011년의 사례와 같은 대량 총기학살 사건 이후에는 총기 규제를 지지하는 목소리가 그리 높이 올라가지 않았지만, 이번 사건으로 인해서는 지지하는 목소리가 대폭 증가했다. 때문에 빈칸이 들어간 문장은 서로 상반되는 내용을 담을 것으로 볼 수 있다. 따라서 빈칸에 가장 적합한 것은 ②이다.

| 어휘 | **massacre** ⓝ 대학살　　　　　　　　　　　**profound** ⓐ 엄청난, 깊은
galvanize ⓥ 충격 요법을 쓰다, 갑자기 기운[활기]을 내게 하다
markedly ⓐⓓ 현저하게, 두드러지게　　　　**stretch** ⓥ 펼쳐지다, 이어지다
political line – 당파　　　　　　　　　　**rampage** ⓝ 광란
assess ⓥ 가늠하다, 평가하다　　　　　　**mass shooting** – 총기난사 사건
resonate ⓥ 반향을 불러일으키다; ~을 상기시키다
contradictory ⓐ 모순되는　　　　　　　　**permanently** ⓐⓓ 영구히, 불변으로
urgent ⓐ 다급한, 긴급한　　　　　　　　**record-breaking** ⓐ 신기록을 수립한, 기록을 깨는
owing to – ~ 때문에

[29-30] 항공대 2018

경제학자들은 종종 시장을 타성적인 존재로 가정하며, 시장은 시장에서 거래되는 재화를 건드리거나 오염시키지 않는다고 가정한다. 경제학자들은 시장교환은 시장에서 교환되는 재화의 의미나 가치를 변화시키지는 않는다고 가정한다. 이는 만일 우리가 유형재화에 관해 논하고 있을 경우에는 충분히 사실일지도 모른다. 만일 당신이 내게 평면 TV를 하나 팔거나 평면 TV 하나를 내게 선물로 제공했을 경우, 이 평면 TV는 동일한 재화이다. 이렇게 동일한 재화는 판 것이든 선물한 것이든 똑같이 작동할 것이다. 하지만 이는 무형재화와 교수와 학습 또는 시민적 생활에 함께 참여하는 것 등의 사회적 관행에 관해 논할 경우엔 사실이 아닐 수 있다. 이러한 영역에서 시장적 메커니즘과 현금 인센티브를 제공해 주는 것은 관심을 기울일 만한 가치가 있는 비시장적 가치와 태도를 약화시키거나 밀어낼 수 있다. 물리적 영역을 넘어 확장되는 시장과 상업이 교수와 학습의 사례에서와 마찬가지로 재화 그 자체의 성격을 바꾸는 것을 알게 되면, 그리고 사회적 관행의 의미를 바꾸는 것을 알게 되면, 우리는 시장이 어디에 속해 있으며 어디에 속해 있지 않은지를 물어야 하고 관심을 기울일 만한 가치와 태도를 실제 어디에서 약화시키게 되는지를 물어야 한다. 하지만 이러한 논쟁을 하기 위해서는 우리는 우리가 그다지 익숙하지 못한 일을 해야 한다. 바로 우리의 신체에서 출발하여 가정생활과 개인 관계, 건강, 교수와 학습 그리고 시민적 생활에 이르기까지 우리가 귀중하게 여기는 사회적 관행의 가치와 의미에 관해 함께 공개적으로 판단하는 일 말이다. 이제 이러한 일은 논란의 여지가 있는 문제이며 따라서 우리는 이러한 문제에 대해 몸을 사리는 경향이 있다. 실제로, 시장논리와 시장주의적 사고가 점차 힘을 얻고 위신을 획득해 왔던 지난 30년 동안 우리들의 대중 담론은 더 큰 도덕적 의미가 사라진 속 빈 강정이 되었다. 의견의 불일치를 두려워한 나머지 이러한 의문을 꺼려 하고 있다. 하지만 시장이 재화의 성격을 변화시킨다는 사실을 알게 된 다음에 우리는 서로 재화의 가치를 어떻게 평가할 것인지에 관한 더 큰 의문을 두고 토의를 해야 한다. 모든 일에 가격을 책정하는 것으로 인해 야기된 가장 유해한 영향 중 하나는 우리 모두가 함께 한다는 의미인 '공통성'에 미치는 영향이다. 증가하는 불평등을 배경으로 삶의 모든 측면을 사유 시장화하는 것은 부유한 사람과 수입이 변변치 않은 사람이 서로 각자의 삶을 사는 상황으로 이어진다. 우리는 서로 다른 곳에서 살고, 일하고, 쇼핑하며 논다. 우리의 아이들은 서로 다른 학교에 다닌다. 이는 민주주의 입장에서 좋은 일이 아니며, 남들보다 앞서 나갈 수 있을 만한 돈을 보유한 사람들 입장에서도 만족스러운 삶의 방식이 아니다. 이유는 다음과 같다. 민주주의는 완벽한 평등을 필요로 하지 않는다. 하지만 민주주의가 필요로 하는 것은 공통의 삶을 공유하는 시민들이다. 각기 다른 사회적 배경과 계급을 갖춘 사람들이 서로 만나고 일반적인 삶의 과정에서 서로 마주하는 일이 중요한데, 왜냐하면 이를 통해 우리가 협상하는 법과 서로의 차이점을 감수하는 법을 배우기 때문이다. 그리고 이를 통해 우리는 공공의 이익에 주의를 기울이게 된다.

29 다음 중 사실이 아닌 것은 무엇인가?

① 우리는 재화의 가치를 어떻게 평가할 것인지에 관한 더 큰 의문을 두고 서로 토의해야 한다.
② 시장의 역할과 영향권에 대한 진지한 토론은 우리의 삶 속에서 대체로 부재한 상황이다.
③ 우리는 모든 것들이 판매 대상이 되는 사회로 점차 나아가고 있음을 우려하고 있다.
④ 최근 시장논리는 시장교환에 의해 대체되었다.

| 정답 | ④

| 해설 | 본문에 따르면 시장교환은 유형재화에 관해 논하고 있을 경우는 사실일지도 모르지만 무형재화의 경우에는 사실이 아닐 수 있다. 그리고 시장논리는 지난 30년 동안 점차 힘을 얻고 있다. 시장교환과 시장논리에 관해 본문에서 언급된 사항은 이 정도이며, 그 외에 시장논리가 시장교환에 의해 대체되었다는 내용은 본문에 존재하지 않는다. 따라서 답은 ④이다. "하지만 시장이 재화의 성격을 변화시킨다는 사실을 알게 된 다음에 우리는 서로 재화의 가치를 어떻게 평가할 것인지에 관한 더 큰 의문을 두고 토의를 해야 한다(But once we see that markets change the character of goods, we have to debate among ourselves these bigger questions about how to value goods)." 이는 보기 ①의 내용과 일치하며 따라서 ①은 답이 될 수 없다. "실제로, 시장논리와 시장주의적 사고가 점차 힘을 얻고 위신을 획득해 왔던 지난 30년 동안 우리들의 대중 담론은 더 큰 도덕적 의미가 사라진 속 빈

강정이 되었다. 의견의 불일치를 두려워한 나머지 이러한 의문을 꺼려 하고 있다(In fact, during the past three decades, when market reasoning and market thinking have gathered force and gained prestige, our public discourse during this time has become hollowed out, empty of larger moral meaning. For fear of disagreement, we shrink from these questions)"는 보기 ②의 내용과 일맥상통하며 따라서 ②는 답이 될 수 없다. "모든 일에 가격을 책정하는 것으로 인해 야기된 가장 유해한 영향 중 하나는 우리 모두가 함께한다는 의미인 '공통성'에 미치는 영향이다. 증가하는 불평등을 배경으로 삶의 모든 측면을 사유 시장화하는 것은 부유한 사람과 수입이 변변치 않은 사람이 서로 각자의 삶을 사는 상황으로 이어진다. … 이는 민주주의 입장에서 좋은 일이 아니며, 남들보다 앞서 나갈 수 있을 만한 돈을 보유한 사람들 입장에서도 만족스러운 삶의 방식이 아니다(One of the most corrosive effects of putting a price on everything is on commonality, the sense that we are all in it together. Against the background of rising inequality, marketizing every aspect of life leads to a condition where those who are affluent and those who are of modest means increasingly live separate lives. … This isn't good for democracy, nor is it a satisfying way to live, even for those of us who can afford to buy our way to the head of the line)." 즉, 우리는 모든 것들이 판매 대상이 되는 사회에 살고 있고, 이는 상당히 우려스러운 일로 ③의 내용과도 일치한다. 따라서 ③은 답이 될 수 없다.

30

본문에서 유추할 수 있는 것은 무엇인가?
① 공정한 사회의 건설을 위해 효용성의 극대화를 원칙으로 삼아야 한다.
② 사회는 올바른 삶에 관해 함께 추론하는 행위를 수반해야 한다.
③ 가장 높은 수준의 도덕성은 행복을 극대화한다.
④ 시장의 규범보다는 무조건적인 또는 정언적인 명령을 따라야 한다.

| 정답 | ②

| 해설 | 본문은 유형재화만이 아니라 무형재화까지 모든 것에 가격이 책정되고 상업화되는 상황에서 재화의 가치를 어떻게 판단할 것인지 사회 내에서 토론이 있어야 한다고 주장하고 있다. 왜냐하면 이러한 사회는 불평등을 야기하고, 불평등은 각기 다른 사회적 배경을 지닌 사람들이 서로 마주하는 일을 막게 된다. 각기 다른 사회적 배경과 계급을 갖춘 사람들이 서로 만나고 일반적인 삶의 과정에서 서로 마주해야만 우리는 협상하는 법과 서로의 차이점을 감수하는 법을 배우고 결과적으로 공공의 이익에 주의를 기울이게 된다. 그렇지 못하게 되면 사회적으로 부정적인 결과에 직면하게 된다. 즉, 우리에게 필요한 것은 사람들끼리 올바른 삶이 무엇일지 서로 토의하고 추론하는 것이다. 따라서 답은 ②이다.

| 어휘 | inert ⓐ 타성적인, 활발하지 못한   taint ⓥ 더럽히다, 오염시키다
material goods – 물적재, 유형재화   non-material goods – 비물적재, 무형재화
domain ⓝ 영역, 분야   undermine ⓥ 약화시키다
crowd out – ~을 밀어내다   reason ⓥ 추론하다, 판단하다
prize ⓥ 소중하게[귀하게] 여기다   shrink from – ~을 꺼리다, ~에 몸을 사리다
prestige ⓝ 위신, 명망   discourse ⓝ 담화, 담론
hollow out – ~의 속을 비우다   empty of – ~이 없는
corrosive ⓐ 좀먹는, 유해한   commonality ⓝ 공통성
against the background – ~을 배경으로 하여
marketize ⓥ 자유 시장 경제로 전환하다, 사유 시장화하다
affluent ⓐ 부유한   modest ⓐ 보통의, 수수한

means ⓝ 재력, 수입
encounter ⓥ 접하다, 마주하다
abide ⓥ 참다, 감수하다
utility ⓝ 유용성, 효용
categorical ⓐ 정언적인
norm ⓝ 규범, 규준

walk of life - 사회적 계급, 신분
bump up against - ~을 마주하다, 직면하다
reach ⓝ 영향권, 범위
unconditional ⓐ 무조건적인
imperative ⓝ 명령

CHAPTER 03 언론·광고

01	③	02	④	03	②	04	③	05	②	06	②	07	③	08	①	09	③	10	②
11	②	12	④	13	②	14	③	15	④	16	①	17	②	18	④	19	②	20	③
21	②	22	④	23	③	24	③	25	②	26	②	27	①	28	④	29	②	30	④

[01-02] 단국대 2016

필리핀에서 TV는 친구, 교사, 연인, 어머니의 입장에서 모든 사람들의 비위를 맞춰 주는 존재가 되었다. 필리핀 현지의 영화 생산이 감소하는 상황에서 시청자들은 이제 필리핀 영화계의 가장 인기 많은 스타들을 매일 가정에서 접하고 있다. 필리핀에서 가장 큰 두 곳의 TV 방송국은 자신들을 "kapuso(한마음)", "kampamilya(한가족)"이라 광고하면서 시청자들과 개인적으로 친밀한 관계를 맺고 있음을 강조한다. 뉴스 앵커들은 그날의 뉴스를 그저 읽는 것에 그치지 않고 잘못을 저지른 정부 관료들을 맹비난하는데, 종종 아무런 조사도 이루어지지 않은 채 비난을 가한다. 방송사는 의료지원에서 장학금 및 (겉보기엔 기본적 필수품으로 보이는) 노래방 기기에 이르기까지 모든 것을 제공하는 공공 서비스 프로그램을 진행한다.

인구의 대략 절반가량이 가난 속에 지내는 국가에서 TV는 가장 손쉬운 도피 수단이다. TV는 버라이어티 쇼, 연속극, 슈퍼히어로 판타지물 등을 제공할 뿐만 아니라 각종 게임쇼 및 콘텐츠를 통해 엄청난 규모의 돈을 현금으로 나눠주고 있다. 물론 궁극적인 도피는 새로 등장한 "아메리칸 아이돌(American Idol)" 스타일의 TV쇼를 통해 이루어지는데, 시청자들은 문자메시지를 통한 투표로 우승자를 선정한다. 이것이 바로 여과되지 않은 채 즉각적으로 기능하는 민주주의의 현장이다.

01

본문에 따르면 사실인 것은 무엇인가?
① 시청자들은 고액의 상금을 따내기 위해 문자메시지를 보내야 한다.
② 필리핀에서 TV 수상기 구매는 가난을 극복하기 위한 가장 쉬운 방법이다.
③ 뉴스 앵커는 종종 불충분한 증거만으로 부패한 정부 관료들을 비난한다.
④ 필리핀에서 TV 방송국은 국산 영화 산업을 촉진시키기 위해 자주 영화를 방영한다.

| 정답 | ③

| 해설 | "뉴스 앵커들은 그날의 뉴스를 그저 읽는 것에 그치지 않고 잘못을 저지른 정부 관료들을 맹비난하는데, 종종 아무런 조사도 이루어지지 않은 채 비난을 가한다(News anchors don't just read the day's news, they also blast erring government officials, often without benefit of any investigation)." 이는, 즉 뉴스 앵커들은 조사를 통해 증거가 충분히 확립되지 않은 상태에서도 비난을 가한다는 의미이다. 따라서 답은 ③이다. 상금을 따는 쪽은 시청자가 아니라 우승자이므로 ①은 답이 될 수 없으며, 필리핀에서 TV는 가난 극복 수단이 아니라 도피 수단으로 나와 있으므로 ②는 답이 될 수 없고, 필리핀의 국산 영화 생산 규모는 감소 중에 있고 방송국에서 국산 영화를 방영한다는 내용은 본문에 없기 때문에 ④도 답이 될 수 없다.

02

밑줄 친 부분을 통해 암시되는 것은 무엇인가?

① 신뢰할 만한 변명
② 최종 목적지
③ 안전한 화재 대피구
④ 부자가 되는 것

| 정답 | ④

| 해설 | 두 번째 단락의 내용은 필리핀에서 TV는 일종의 현실을 잊기 위한 도피 수단으로 쓰인다는 것이다. 단순히 정신적인 도피가 아닌 '궁극적인 도피'가 무엇일지 생각해 보면 문자메시지를 통해 가장 많은 표를 얻은 우승자가 엄청난 돈과 명성을 얻게 될 것임을 생각해 보면 우승자가 하게 될 '궁극적인 도피'는 가난으로부터의 도피로 볼 수 있다. 따라서 답은 ④이다.

| 어휘 | be all things to all people/men – 모든 사람의 비위를 다 맞추려 들다, 누구에게나 마음에 들도록 행동하다
underscore ⓥ 강조하다
blast ⓥ 혹평[맹비난]하다
host ⓥ 진행하다, 주최하다
necessity ⓝ 필수품
in action – 활동하는, 기능하는
instantaneous ⓐ 즉각적인, 순간적인
insufficient ⓐ 불충분한
intimate ⓐ 친밀한
erring ⓐ 잘못을 저지른, 부정한
apparently ⓐⓓ 겉보기로는, 외상 보니
avenue ⓝ 방안, 수단
unfiltered ⓐ 여과되지 않은
corrupted ⓐ 부패한, 타락한
promote ⓥ 촉진[고취]하다, 홍보하다

[03-05] 한국외대 2010

미디어 업계의 거물 Rupert Murdoch은 뉴스 콘텐츠를 온라인에서 무료로 제공하는 지금의 신문의 사업모델이 "제 기능을 다 하지 못한다"고 언급했다. 수익이 나는 구독 기반의 웹사이트를 보유한 희귀한 신문사중 하나인 Wall Street Journal을 보유한 Murdoch은 자신이 보유한 사이트 중에서 콘텐츠에 비용을 부과하는 사이트의 수를 늘리는 방식으로 자신의 디지털 자산을 통한 수익력을 높이겠다고 단언했다. 다른 출판업자들도 뉴스를 공짜로 얻는 것에 익숙해진 소비자들에게 온라인 신문과 잡지의 구독을 따내는 것은 힘든 일이 될 것이지만, 소비자들은 자신의 주목을 끈 글마다 몇 페니에서 수 달러까지 약간의 돈을 기꺼이 지불할 것임을 시사하고 있다.

물론 출판업자들만이 최초로 소액 전자 지불을 디지털상의 콘텐츠를 통한 가능성 있는 수익원으로 본 것은 아니나. 애플의 iTunes 스토어는 곡을 99센트씩에 팔아서 수십억 달러 규모의 산업을 창출하는 것이 가능하다는 것을 보여줬다. 또한, 비록 많은 분석가들은 출판업자들이 무료에서 유료로의 전환을 할 수 있을지 의심하고 있지만, 현재 유사한 전환을 하고 있는 또 다른 산업이 있으니 이는 온라인게임 산업이다.

다중 사용자 온라인 롤플레잉 게임이나 소셜게임은 현재 온라인 세계에서 가장 빠르게 성장하는 분야 중 두 가지인데, 현재 소규모 온라인 결제를 통해 점차적으로 상당한 수익을 거두고 있다. 원래 이들은 주로 구독을 통한 수익에 의존했다. 하지만 현재의 경향은 'freemium'으로 불리는 무료 플레이 모델이다. 이 시스템하에서, 게이머들은 비용을 지불하지 않고 게임을 할 수 있지만, 일반적으로는 소액의 비용을 지불하면 게임이 더욱 재밌어짐을 알게 된다.

03

다음 중 ㉮에 가장 알맞은 것은 무엇인가?

① 뉴스를 온라인상에서 구입하기 쉬운
② 뉴스를 공짜로 얻는 것에 익숙해진
③ 뉴스를 읽고 싶어 하는
④ 다른 경우라면 매우 관대한
⑤ 종이신문을 읽는 성향이 있는

| 정답 | ②

| 해설 | 우선 루퍼트 머독은 지금의 무료 기반 온라인 뉴스서비스가 제 기능을 못한다고 언급한 다음 자신은 유료 기반의 온라인 콘텐츠를 늘릴 것이라고 천명했는데, 이것이 그만의 입장은 아니고 다른 업체의 입장이기도 하다는 것이 본문 전반부의 내용이다. 우선 빈칸 뒤를 보면 업계는 기사가 재미있다면 소비자들이 "might be willing to pay small fees(약간의 돈을 기꺼이 지불할 수도 있다)"고 판단하고 있음을 알 수 있는데, 여기서 중요한 것은 "pay" 즉 돈을 지불한다는 의미의 단어가 쓰인 점이다. 이를 역으로 생각해 보면 소비자들이 기사를 보는 데 돈을 내지 않았을 것임을 추론할 수 있다. 그렇다면 "subscriptions to online newspapers and magazines might be a tough sell(소비자들에게 온라인 신문과 잡지의 구독을 따내는 것이 힘든)" 이유는 결국 지금까지 소비자들이 "accustomed to getting their news for free(뉴스를 공짜로 얻는 것에 익숙하기)" 때문인 것으로 유추해 볼 수 있다. 공짜로 뉴스를 볼 수 있다면 소비자가 굳이 돈을 내고 구독할 이유는 없고, 따라서 구독을 따내는 일이 힘든 것이다. 따라서 보기 중에서 빈칸에 들어갈 가장 알맞은 것은 ②가 된다.

04 다음 중 본문에서 언급되거나 암시되지 않은 것은 무엇인가?
① 대부분의 온라인 신문은 수익이 나는 구독 기반 웹사이트를 갖고 있지 못하다.
② 몇몇 디지털 콘텐츠 제공업체들은 이미 상당한 양의 돈을 벌었다.
③ 미디어 기업들은 온라인 서비스에서 해결책을 찾았다.
④ 많은 전문가들은 뉴스기사에 요금을 부과하는 것에 회의적인 반응을 보였다.
⑤ 온라인 게이머들은 공짜로 즐기거나 재미를 얻기 위해 즐긴다.

| 정답 | ③

| 해설 | 우선 ③만 놓고 보면 다른 서비스가 아닌 온라인 서비스가 해결책으로 떠오른 것이 된다. 그러나 온라인 서비스는 이미 시행 중에 있으나 수익을 거두지 못해 고민거리였고, 미디어 기업들이 결국 수익을 거두기 위해 찾은 해결책은 무료 기반의 단순한 온라인 서비스가 아니라 구독료를 받는 온라인 서비스라는 것이 본문의 내용이다. 때문에 ③은 본문에서 언급되거나 암시된 것으로는 보기 힘들다. 따라서 ③이 답이 된다.
①의 경우, 본문에는 Wall Street Journal을 제외하면 거의 수익을 거두지 못한다고 나와 있으므로 답이 될 수 없다. ②의 경우, 실례로 iTunes 서비스를 들고 있으므로 답으로 볼 수 없다. ④의 경우, "doubt publishers can make the switch from free to fee(출판업자들이 무료에서 유료로의 전환을 할 수 있을지 의심하고)" 있다고 나와 있기 때문에 ④도 답이 될 수는 없다. ⑤의 경우, "find the games are more entertaining when pay small fees(소액의 비용을 지불하면 게임이 더욱 재미있어짐을 발견한다)"는 문장을 미루어 볼 때 공짜로 하다가도 더 재미를 얻고 싶다면 돈을 투자하는 것이 현재 온라인게이머의 성향임을 알 수 있다. 따라서 ⑤도 답이 될 수 없다.

05 온라인 출판업자들이 게임 산업을 벤치마크하고 나서 가장 할 가능성이 높은 일은 무엇인가?
① 온라인 신문의 구독료를 높일 가능성이 크다.
② 독자의 시선을 잡는 이야기에 약간의 비용을 부과할 가능성이 크다.
③ 온라인 저널을 확대하기 위해 오프라인 뉴스업체를 판매할 가능성이 크다.
④ 게임업계의 수익성 있는 사업모델 때문에 게임 산업으로 뛰어들 가능성이 크다.
⑤ 온라인 신문의 구독료를 낮출 가능성이 크다.

| 정답 | ②

| 해설 | 본문에 따르면 게임 산업이 돈을 버는 구조는 부분유료화이다. 기본적으로는 "can play for no cost(비용을 지불하

지 않고 게임을 할 수 있다)." 그러나 "the games are more entertaining when pay small fees(소액의 비용을 지불하면 게임이 더욱 재밌어지는)"이 현재 게임 산업의 수익구조이다. 이로 미루어 볼 때 온라인 출판업자들은 이를 벤치마크해서 전체가 아니라 일부 "grabs their attention(시선을 사로잡는)" 이야기에 비용을 부과하도록 할 것이다. 따라서 답은 ②가 된다. 다른 보기는 게임 산업의 사례와 연계했을 때 연관성이 떨어지기 때문에 답으로 보기 힘들다.

| 어휘 | tycoon ⓝ 실업계의 거물
profitable ⓐ 수익을 거두는, 유익한
-based ⓐ ~에 기반을 둔
property ⓝ 재산, 자산
a tough sell – 먹히기 힘든 것, 팔리기 힘든 것
grab one's attention – ~의 주목을 끌다, 시선을 사로잡다
micropayment ⓝ 소액전자지불
transition ⓝ 전환, 이동
transaction ⓝ 거래
generous ⓐ 관대한
be inclined to – ~하는 성향이 있다
skeptical ⓐ 회의적인

malfunction ⓥ 제 기능을 다하지 못한다
subscription ⓝ 구독
vow ⓥ 단언하다
charge ⓥ 대금을 청구하다

potential ⓐ 가망성이 있는, 유망한
segment ⓝ 단편, 부분
be accustomed to – ~에 익숙하다
otherwise ⓐⓓ 그렇지 않았더라면 ~인
way out – 출구, 해결책
subscription fee – 구독료

[06-08] 성균관대 2008

지금 시대의 선전 문구 중에서 가장 뛰어난 것은 여전히 광고업계의 창조물 속에서 발견 가능하다. 물론 광고업계는 심리학과 행동주의를 활용해 설득의 기술을 유사 과학의 영역으로 처음으로 변화시킨 분야이다. 유행어를 통해 거둔 성공은 국가 재정 적자액도 비교해 보면 사소해 보일 만큼 거대한 소매 판매액 수치를 보면 확인이 가능하다. 더 정확하게 말하자면, 누구든 머릿속을 이리저리 굴리면 "지금 (비행기를) 타시고 요금은 나중에 내시면 됩니다", "여러분은 이제 안전합니다", "꽃으로 고백하세요", "다이아몬드는 영원히" 같은 선전 문구가 떠오른다는 사실을 통해 업계가 내놓은 최고의 선전 문구가 어느 정도로 마음속에 강하게 붙어 있는지 확인 가능하다. 이러한 사례는 끝도 없이 제시될 수 있다. 사실 이러한 상황을 통해 현재 쏟아져 나오는 선전 문구에 번뜩이는 재미가 사라진 "선전 문구에 질려 버린 현상"의 원인을 설명할 수 있을 것이다. 기묘한 새로운 형태의 과잉 현상을 목격하고 있는 것일까? 돈의 과잉 공급이 통화의 가치를 떨어뜨리는 것처럼, 선전 문구의 과잉이 유행어의 유행성을 약화시키고 대중을 유행어가 지닌 마법으로부터 풀어 주는 역할을 하는 것일까?

물론 선전 문구를 내놓는 행위가 완전히 사라지길 바라는 사람도 있다. 선전 문구라는 기술은 감정에 호소하기 때문에, 일부 이상주의자들과 지적 순수주의자들은 차분하고 합리적인 문구를 선호하는 대신 선전 문구는 경멸한다. 이런 사람들은 분명히 대중의 매우 강력한 추세를 거부하고 정반대로 헤엄쳐 나가는 사람들이다. 또한 이 사람들은 리더십과 인간적 딜레마라는 두 가지 문제에 관해 모르는 사람들이다. 사람들이 문제 때문에 뭔가를 할 것인지 생각해 본 적은 없다. 사람들은 어려움 때문에 행동을 취하게 된다. 아주 오래전부터 지도자들은 가장 좋은 방법은 좋은 일이든 나쁜 일이든 "여러분, 선전 문구 중심으로 모여 힘을 합칩시다"라고 말하는 것임을 깨달았다.

06 본문의 제목으로 가장 알맞은 것은 무엇인가?
① 선전 문구의 역사
② 현대 사회에서의 선전 문구의 과도한 사용
③ 선전 문구의 경제적 이득
④ 선전 문구 및 공교육
⑤ 현대 사회에서의 선전 문구의 완연한 감소

| 정답 | ②

| 해설 | 본문은 선전 문구의 과잉으로 인해 선전 문구 자체가 지루해진 현상에 관해 말하고 있다. 따라서 답은 ②이다. 참고로 선전 문구 자체가 감소한 것이 아니라 선전 문구가 지루해진 것이 문제이므로 ⑤는 답이 될 수 없다.

07 저자에 따르면 "선전 문구에 질려 버린 현상"의 원인은 무엇인가?
① 대중의 불신
② 경제적 인플레이션
③ 선전 문구의 과잉 공급
④ 약한 리더십
⑤ 광고에서 심리학의 과도한 사용

| 정답 | ③

| 해설 | "돈의 과잉 공급이 통화의 가치를 떨어뜨리는 것처럼, 선전 문구의 과잉이 유행어의 유행성을 약화시키고 대중을 유행어가 지닌 마법으로부터 풀어주는 역할을 하는 것일까?(Is it conceivable that just as an oversupply of money drives down the value of currency, an excess of sloganizing diminishes the catchiness of catchwords and the public's vulnerability to their magic?)" 본문의 이 부분을 통해 선전 문구에 사람들이 질려 버리게 된 원인이 선전문구의 과도한 사용에 있음을 알 수 있다. 따라서 답은 ③이다.

08 본문에 따르면 저자가 말하는 바는 무엇인가?
① 선전 문구의 주된 목적은 대중에게 행동하도록 유도하는 것이다
② 선전 문구를 내놓는 행위는 미래에 사라질 것이다
③ 선전 문구의 언어는 더욱 지적으로 변화해야 한다
④ 국가 경제는 선전 문구의 미래와 깊은 연관이 있다
⑤ 선전 문구는 인간의 약점을 이용하기 위해 사용된다

| 정답 | ①

| 해설 | "아주 오래전부터 지도자들은 가장 좋은 방법은 좋은 일이든 나쁜 일이든 '여러분, 선전 문구 중심으로 모여 힘을 합칩시다'라고 말하는 것임을 깨달았다(From time immemorial, leaders have found that one of the best ways, for good or ill, is to say, 'Rally round the slogan, folks.')." 이 문장을 통해 선전 문구의 역할은 사람들에게 행동을 취할 것을 유도하는 것임을 유추할 수 있다. 따라서 답은 ①이다.

| 어휘 | the cream of the crop – 가장 좋은 것, 알짜
slogan ⓝ 구호, 선전 문구
psychology ⓝ 심리학
persuasion ⓝ 설득
turn A into B – A를 B로 변화시키다
confirm ⓥ 사실임을 확인하다, 증명하다
figure ⓝ 수치
trifle ⓐ 사소한, 약간의
scavenge ⓥ 뒤지다, 찾다
output ⓝ 산출량
contemporary ⓐ 동시대의, 현대의
exploit ⓥ 이용하다
behaviorism ⓝ 행동주의
quasi-science ⓝ 유사 과학
catchword ⓝ 유행어
retail sales – 소매 판매
deficit ⓝ 적자
more to the point – 더 중요한 것은
diminish ⓥ 줄어들다, 약해지다
weird ⓐ 기묘한

conceivable ⓐ 가능한, 상상할 수 있는
vulnerability ⓝ 취약함, 약함
disdain ⓥ 업신여기다, 무시하다
be out of touch with – ~을 모르다
rally around – 힘을 합치다, 한데 모이다

oversupply ⓝ 공급 과잉
precisely ⓐd 바로, 꼭
rational ⓐ 합리적인
immemorial ⓐ 먼 옛날의
distrust ⓝ 불신

[09-10] 한양대 2016

어느 기업은 뛰어난 제품을 보유했고 자연스럽게 고객들이 해당 제품을 자신들이 구매할 수 있는 최상의 제품으로 여기기를 원했다. 따라서 그 기업의 마케팅 팀은 왜 해당 제품이 경쟁 제품에 비해 특징 및 가격 측면에서 더 우월한지를 보여주는 광고 캠페인을 개시했고 이는 활발한 매출을 통해 보답받았다. 하지만 그 기업은 이러한 성공을 누리는 대신에 수많은 불평을 듣고 제품 환불을 많이 받게 되었다. 분명히 말하자면 전략이 역효과를 낳은 것이다. 왜 그런 결과를 낳게 된 것일까? 비교 광고 및 "저희 제품은 최고입니다!" 식의 제품 포지셔닝은 소비자들 사이에서 '최고를 지향하는 심리'로 알려진 현상을 촉발시키며, 이는 소비자들로 하여금 완벽하지 못하다고 여겨지는 것들을 돈 낭비로 인식하게끔 한다. 우리의 연구를 통해 드러난 점은, 비록 어떤 이들은 천성적으로 "최고를 지향하는 사람들"이고 다른 이들은 "그 정도면 괜찮다"고 자족하는 경향이 있는 사람들이지만, 이러한 태도가 변치 않는 것은 아니라는 점이다. 최고를 지향하는 심리는 사람들로 하여금 비교를 통해 최상의 것을 찾도록 권장하는 상황을 통해 유발될 수 있다. 마케팅 메시지가 무심코 이러한 심리를 유발할 경우, 구매 이후 후회하면서 약간이나마 실망할 조짐이 보이면 바로 브랜드를 갈아타는 결과를 낳을 수 있다.

09 빈칸에 들어갈 표현으로 가장 적절한 것은?

	(A)	(B)
①	실패하다	역경
②	움츠러들다	개선
③	역효과를 낳다	실망
④	허우적거리다	만족감

| 정답 | ③

| 해설 | (A): 최고의 제품을 만들었다고 자신 있게 광고했지만 반품과 불평이 이어졌다. 이는, 즉 광고 전략이 "실패하였고", "역효과를 낳은" 것이다. 따라서 빈칸에는 failed 또는 backfired가 적합하다.

(B): 최상의 것만을 취하려는 심리하에서 소비자는 제품이 최상에 미치지 못했다는 약간의 "실망"만으로 바로 "브랜드를 갈아타는(brand switching)" 행위를 할 것이다. 따라서 빈칸에는 disappointment가 적합하다.

이러한 점들을 감안했을 때 답으로 가장 적합한 것은 ③이다.

10 윗글의 내용과 거리가 먼 것은?

① 비교 광고가 항상 성과를 올리는 것은 아니다.
② 최고를 지향하는 사람들은 다른 이들이 비교하도록 유인하는 경향이 있다.
③ 최고를 지향하는 심리는 상황에 따라 좌우된다.
④ 최고를 지향하는 심리를 지닌 소비자는 최상의 것을 추구하는 경향이 있다.

| 정답 | ②

| 해설 | 최고를 지향하는 사람들이 비교하는 것은 제품이며, 본문 어디에도 최고를 지향하는 사람들이 다른 이들이 비교를 하도록 유도한다는 내용은 실려 있지 않다. 따라서 답은 ②이다.

전반부 역효과에 관한 사항은 ①에 해당된다. "우리의 연구를 통해 드러난 점은, 비록 어떤 이들은 천성적으로 '최고를 지향하는 사람들'이고 다른 이들은 '그 정도면 괜찮다'고 자족하는 경향이 있는 사람들이지만, 이러한 태도가 변치 않는 것은 아니라는 점이다(Our research has found that although some people are 'maximizers' by nature, and others tend to be content with 'good enough,' those attitude aren't fixed)"에서 변치 않는다는 말은, 즉 상황에 따라 변할 수 있음을 의미한다. 이는 ③에 해당된다. "비교 광고 및 '저희 제품은 최고입니다!' 식의 제품 포지셔닝은 소비자들 사이에서 '최고를 지향하는 심리'로 알려진 현상을 촉발시키며, 이는 소비자로 하여금 완벽하지 못하다고 여겨지는 것들을 돈 낭비로 인식하게끔 한다(It turns out that comparative ads and 'Ours is the best!' product positioning activate something known as the maximizing mind-set, which leads people to regard anything that's less than perfect as a waste of money)"는 ④에 해당된다.

| 어휘 |
roll out – 출시하다, (선전을) 개시하다
in terms of – ~면에서, ~에 관하여
sales ⓝ 매출
backfire ⓥ 역효과를 낳다
comparative ⓐ – 비교 광고
positioning ⓝ 포지셔닝(소비자의 마음속에 어떤 자리를 차지하게끔 위치를 각인시키는 마케팅 기법)
activate ⓥ 활성화시키다, 촉발시키다
by nature – 선천적으로, 천성적으로
fixed ⓐ 고정된, 변치 않는
inadvertently ⓐⓓ 무심코, 우연히
adversity ⓝ 역경
flounder ⓥ (곤경에 처해) 허우적거리다
pay off – 성과를 올리다
contingent ⓐ ~여하에 달린, ~의 여부에 따라
advertising campaign – 광고 캠페인
robust ⓐ 굳건한, 활발한
bask in – (관심·칭찬 등을) 누리다
turn out – ~인 것으로 드러나다[밝혀지다]
maximizing ⓐ 최고를 지향하는, 최대한도에 미치는
content ⓐ 만족하는, 자족하는
induce ⓥ 유도하다, 유발[초래]하다
hint ⓝ 징후, 조짐
recoil ⓥ 움츠러들다, 움찔하다
gratification ⓝ 만족감, 희열
entice ⓥ 유도하다, 유인하다
inclined ⓐ ~하는 경향이 있는, ~할 것 같은

[11-13] 성균관대 2010

마케팅의 세계는 소비자가 색에 보이는 반응에 대한 속설로 가득 차 있다. 색 선호도는 종종 일시적 유행과 문화적 관습이 혼합된 것으로 들리며, 특히 프랑스인들이 회색의 통조림 완두콩과 콩을 먹고, 반면에 영국인은 그렇지 않을 때 그리고 우리가 미국의 광택이 나는 붉은색 사과보다 녹색 사과를 더 선호할 때 더욱 그러하다. [I] 하지만 색에는 보이는 것 이상의 것이 있다. 색이 신경계에 영향을 줄 수 있다는 생각은 주위가 붉으면 혈압이 오르고 파랗다면 혈압이 내려간다는 것이 실험에 기록되었다는 사실을 통해 어느 정도 힘을 얻는 것으로 보인다. [II] 붉은색은 에너지와 배고픔의 증가라는 주관적 반응을 불러일으키고, 파란색은 고요함과 긴장이 풀리는 느낌을 불러일으킨다. 의도적이든 그렇지 않든, 붉은색을 봄으로서 생기는 효과는 패스트푸드 체인에 의해 영리하게 이용되어 왔다. [III] 사람들을 배고프게 하는 것 이외에도, 붉은색과 그와 가까운 색인 오렌지색은 사람들에게 서두르는 느낌을 주게 한다. 이러한 색들을 사용하여, 맥도날드 같은 곳에서는 식욕을 증가시키면서도 교묘하게 고객들이 오랫동안 머무르지 않게 하는 환경을 만든다. [IV] 색은 또한 소비자용 제품을 마케팅 하는 데 있어 두드러진 영향을 끼치는 것에도 익숙해 왔다. 가정주부 한 그룹은 노란색, 파란색, 노란색과 파란색의 혼합 등 이렇게 세 가지 다른 박스에 담긴 동일한 가루비누의 샘플을 시험해 볼 것을 요청받았다. [V] 놀라운 결과가 뒤따랐는데, 노란색 통에 담긴 가루비누는 가루비누가 옷을 상하게 했다고 일부가 말할 정도로 강력한 것으로 판단되었는데 반해, 파란색 통에 담긴 것은 가루비누가 얼룩을 남겼다고 말할 정도로 약했다는 말이 나왔고, 두 색이 혼합된 통에 담긴 것이 딱 맞는 것으로 평가받았다. 하지만 유일한 차이점은 용기의 색의 차이일 뿐이었다.

11 위의 본문이 세 단락으로 나뉠 때, 각 문장의 시작으로 가장 알맞은 것은 무엇인가?
① [I] and [III]
② [I] and [IV]
③ [II] and [III]
④ [III] and [IV]
⑤ [III] and [V]

| 정답 | ②

| 해설 | 본문은 크게 셋으로 나눌 수 있다. 첫째 '특정 색의 선호에는 과학적 근거가 있다기보다 문화적 관습, 일시적 유행, 속설 등이 혼합된 것으로 보인다.' 둘째 '하지만 실제로 실험에 따라 특정 색이 사람에게 어떤 반응을 불러일으킨다는 것이 기록되었고, 이 사실을 활용하고 있는 곳이 패스트푸드점이다.' 셋째 '색깔을 달리한 세제통의 실험에서도 알 수 있듯이, 제품 마케팅에도 색이 두드러진 영향을 끼칠 수 있다.' 따라서 답은 ②가 된다.

12 다음 중 빈칸 ㉮에 가장 알맞은 것은 무엇인가?
① 평화로운
② 관대한
③ 초조한
④ 서두르는
⑤ 편안한

| 정답 | ④

| 해설 | 맥도날드에서는 붉은색과 오렌지색을 활용해 "create an atmosphere which increases the appetite but subtly dissuades the customer from hanging around for very long(식욕을 돋워 고객들을 배고프게 만들고 교묘하게 고객들이 오랫동안 머무르지 않게 하는 환경을 만든다)." 이를 근거로 그 두 색의 특성을 한 단어로 압축하면, 빈칸에 알맞은 것은 ④가 된다. ③의 '초조한'을 답으로 보고 '손님들이 초조해서 빨리 나간다'라고 주장할 수도 있겠지만, 여기서 '초조하다'는 실상 "easily worried or frightened, anxious about or afraid of(불안해하는, 신경이 과민한)"의 의미이기 때문에 음식점에서 활용하기에 적합한 이미지는 아닐 것이다. 따라서 ③은 답이 될 수 없다.

13 다음 중 빈칸 ㉯에 가장 알맞은 것은 무엇인가?
① 가루비누의 색
② 통의 색
③ 옷의 색
④ 가루비누의 품질
⑤ 통의 품질

| 정답 | ②

| 해설 | "samples of identical soap powder in three different boxes(세 가지 다른 박스에 담긴 동일한 가루비누의 샘플)"을 가지고 가정주부들을 대상으로 실험을 했는데, 가루비누가 동일하다면 세탁 결과 역시 동일해야 하지만 주부들은 그렇게 느끼지 않았고, 따라서 본문은 이를 "extraordinary results(놀라운 결과)"로 묘사하고 있다. 비록 가정주부들의 반응은 상이했지만, 색깔이 다른 통에 담긴 가루비누는 "identical(동일한)" 것이라고 본문에 명확히 묘사되어 있으므로 답은 ②가 되어야 한다.

| 어휘 | folklore ⓝ 민속; 속설　　preference ⓝ 선호(도)
fad ⓝ (일시적) 유행　　especially ⓐⓓ 특히
tinned ⓐ 통조림에 담긴　　prefer A to B – B보다 A를 선호하다
glossy ⓐ 광택이 나는
there's more to A than meets the eye – A에는 보이는 것 이상의 것이 있다

nervous system – 신경계	experiment ⓝ 실험
record ⓥ 기록하다, (특정 수치가) 나오다	blood pressure – 혈압
surroundings ⓝ 주변, 배경	evoke ⓥ ~을 불러일으키다
subjective ⓐ 주관적인	tranquility ⓝ 고요, 평온
knowingly ⓐⓓ 의도적으로, 고의로	otherwise ⓐⓓ (만약) 그렇지 않으면
exploit ⓥ ~을 (최대한 잘) 활용하다; 착취하다	subtly ⓐⓓ 미묘하게, 교묘하게
dissuade ⓥ (…을 하지 않도록) ~을 설득[만류]하다	
hang around – 서성이다, 배회하다	be used to ~ing – ~에 익숙하다
striking ⓐ 두드러진, 눈에 띄는	identical ⓐ 동일한
extraordinary ⓐ 놀라운, 기이한	ensue ⓥ (어떤 일·결과가) 뒤따르다
packet ⓝ (종이·마분지로 된 상품 포장용) 통[갑/곽], 용기	
stain ⓝ 얼룩	assess ⓥ 평가하다
just right – 딱 맞는	generous ⓐ 관대한
nervous ⓐ 초조한, 불안해하는	hurried ⓐ 서두르는

[14-15] 한양대 2008

기자는 이러한 객관적인 세상에 대한 자신의 신념을 공언하지만, 그러한 세상을 인식할 수 있는 능력이 자신에게 있는지에 대해서는 거의 자신하지 못한다. 따라서 "객관적인" 보도라는 규범에 따르면 사건의 진실성과는 관계없이 해당 사건의 "양 측면"을 보도하게 된다. 그러므로 우리는 조직적으로 사실을 입증하려는 기자, 즉 어떤 사실이 더 정확한지 말하려는 기자가 어느 한쪽보다 다른 한쪽을 선호하게 되면서 자신의 객관성을 포기했다는 비난을 듣는 위험을 무릅쓰게 된다는 가슴 아픈 아이러니에 직면하게 된다. 흥미로운 점은 객관적 보도는 특정한 이념을 조장하는 경향이 있다는 사실이다. 진실은 어디에 있는가에 대한 구체적인 철학적 추정이 이 특정 이념 내에 암약하고 있다. 객관적인 보도는 양측이 언제나 진실의 일부만을 말한다고 가정하는 경향이 있기 때문에, 완전한 진실은 그 중간 어디에 있다고 추론하기 쉽다.

14 본문의 제목으로 가장 알맞은 것은 무엇인가?
① 이념과 언론
② 진실의 입증
③ 객관적 보도로 인해 빠지기 쉬운 함정
④ 객관적 보도의 규범

| 정답 | ③

| 해설 | 본문은 객관적 보도 행위가 사건의 실체적 진실을 파헤치기보다 "진실성과는 관계없는(regardless of their veracity)" 기계적인 진실에 치중하게 될 위험성에 대해 말하고 있다. 또한 객관적 보도가 오히려 "특정한 이념을 조장하는(promote a specific ideology)" 결과를 낳을 수 있음을 말하고 있다. 즉, 객관적 보도가 지닌 악영향에 관해 말하고 있다. 따라서 답은 ③이다.

15 다음 중 빈칸 (A)에 가장 알맞은 것은 무엇인가?
① 완전한 진실은 우리에게 있다
② 완전한 진실은 우리 가까이에 있다
③ 완전한 진실은 저 너머에 있다
④ 완전한 진실은 그 중간 어디에 있다

| 정답 | ④

| 해설 | "객관적인 보도는 양측이 언제나 진실의 일부만을 말한다고 가정하는 경향이 있다(the objective reporting tends to assume that both sides will always be speaking partial truth)." 즉, 진실을 말하는 쪽은 없고 모두 자기 쪽에 유리한 말만 한다. 그렇다면 진실은 어느 한쪽에 있는 것이 아니라 그 중간에 있는 것이라는 유추가 가능하다. 따라서 답은 ④이다.

| 어휘 | **profess** ⓥ 주장하다, 공언하다
norm ⓝ 규범, 규준
poignant ⓐ 통렬한, 마음 아픈
promote ⓥ 고취하다, 조장하다
specific ⓐ 구체적인, 특정한
faith ⓝ 신념
veracity ⓝ 진실성
systematically ⓐⓓ 조직적으로, 질서 정연하게
lurk ⓥ 도사리다, 암약하다
pitfall ⓝ 위험, 함정

[16-17] 한양대 2014

19세기 초부터 미국 신문에서 중추적 역할을 하던 정치풍자 만화는 그래픽 아트를 활용해 독자들에게 정보와 즐거움을 제공하고, 독자를 도발하거나 짜증나게 하고, 독자를 설득하는 방향으로 시사 문제에 관해 논평을 남긴다. 정치 풍자 만화는 한 칸의 솜씨 좋게 그려진 이미지에다 당대의 주요 문제와 지도자들을 소재로 삼아, 위선적이거나 부패한 정치인들을 날카롭게 비판하고, 주요 사건의 터무니없거나 역설적인 또는 진지한 측면을 묘사한다. 정치풍자 만화는 혹여 메시지 전달을 위해 말을 사용하더라도 거의 사용하지 않는 거나 마찬가지 수준으로 사용한다. 일부는 만화가 유명인사들을 풍자하기 위해 이들의 특징을 과장하여 표현하는 기법인 캐리커처를 활용한다. 정치풍자 만화에는 독자들로부터 감정적 반응을 이끌어 낼 수 있는 능력을 갖고 있으므로 대중의 의견을 뒤흔들기 위한 수단으로서 기능하며 개혁에 기여할 수 있다. 19세기 후반부의 걸출한 정치풍자 만화가인 토머스 네스트(1840-1902)는 자신의 기술을 활용해 뉴욕시의 부패 집단인 보스 트위드 집단을 멸망시켰고, 이를 통해 자신이 지닌 매체의 힘을 증명했다. 그가 그린 이미지는 아직도 통용되고 있는데, 그는 최초로 태머니 홀을 상징하기 위해 호랑이를, 공화당을 상징하기 위해 코끼리를, 민주당을 상징하기 위해 당나귀를 창조한 사람이다. 신문과 같이 하루 단위로 구성되는 형태의 매체는 마감이 촉박하며 이런 상황에서 창조되는 정치풍자 만화는 여전히 영향력을 갖고 있다. 비록 정치풍자 만화가 당대의 주요 문제와 지도자들을 다루고 있지만, 종종 미래 세대를 위해 생생한 역사적 상황을 제공하기도 한다.

16 빈칸에 들어갈 가장 알맞은 것을 고르시오.

(A)	(B)
① 풍자하다	하루 단위의
② 경멸하다	순식간의
③ 비난하다	부수적인
④ 우세하다	즉흥적인

| 정답 | ①

| 해설 | 빈칸 (A)의 경우를 보면, 정치풍자 만화에서 사용되는 캐리커처는 유명인사들의 특징을 과장하여 표현하는 기법이며, 정치풍자 만화의 목적을 생각하면 이는 "풍자(make fun of)"를 위한 것이다. 그렇다고 "경멸(look down on)"을 위한 것으로 보는 것은 무리가 있다. 빈칸 (B)의 경우를 보면, 신문은 "하루 단위로(ephemeral)" 발행되는 매체이므로 당연히 "마감이 촉박(tight deadline)"할 것이다. 이러한 점들을 고려했을 때 답은 ①이다.

17 윗글의 내용과 가장 어울리는 견해를 고르시오.
① 정치풍자 만화는 비열해질수록 효과가 커진다.
② 정치풍자 만화는 대중에게 영향력을 행사하기 위한 강력한 수단이다.
③ 정치풍자 만화는 논란이 되는 주제에 대해 객관성을 유지해야 한다.
④ 정치풍자 만화는 시사문제와 관련이 있기 때문에 역사적 문건으로는 적합하다고 보기 힘들다.

| 정답 | ②

| 해설 | 정치풍자 만화는 신문에서 중추적 역할을 하며, 정보와 즐거움을 제공하고, 독자를 화나게도 하지만 독자를 설득하기도 한다. 또한 "정치풍자 만화에는 독자들로부터 감정적 반응을 이끌어 낼 수 있는 능력을 갖고 있으므로 대중의 의견을 뒤흔들기 위한 수단으로서 기능하며 개혁에 기여할 수 있다(Because they have the ability to evoke an emotional response in readers, political cartoons can serve as a vehicle for swaying public opinion and can contribute to reform)." 즉, 정치풍자 만화는 대중에게 상당한 영향력을 미칠 수 있다. 따라서 답은 ②이다.

| 어휘 | mainstay ⓝ 중심, 중추
poke ⓥ 찌르다, 쑤시다
hypocritical ⓐ 위선적인
sway ⓥ 동요시키다, 흔들다
ring ⓝ 불법[비밀] 집단
Tammany Hall – 태머니 홀(19세기에서 20세기 초까지 뉴욕에서 강력한 영향력을 행사하던 부정한 정치 조직)
ephemeral ⓐ 수명이 짧은, 하루 뿐의
look down on – ~을 경멸하다[낮춰보다]
collateral ⓐ 부수적인, 부차적인
improvise ⓥ 즉흥으로 처리하다
objectivity ⓝ 객관성

provoke ⓥ 도발하다
skewer ⓥ 날카롭게 비판하다
deftly ⓐⓓ 솜씨 좋게
preeminent ⓐ 탁월한, 걸출한

picture ⓝ 상황
fleeting ⓐ 순식간의, 잠깐 동안의
get the upper hand of – ~보다 우세하다
mean-spirited ⓐ 비열한
serve ⓥ 적합하다, 특정 용도로 쓰이다

[18-20] 이화여대 2017

컨버전스(convergence)에 대한 산업계 담론은 대부분 내가 블랙박스의 오류(black box fallacy)라고 부르는 것으로 시작해서 그것으로 끝난다. 블랙박스의 오류란 조만간 모든 미디어가 우리 거실에 단 하나의 블랙박스를 통해 전달될 것이며, 우리가 해야 할 일은 그것이 어떤 블랙박스일지 알아내는 것이 전부라는 생각이다. 미디어 컨버전스는 마지막 종점이 아니다. 오히려 그것은 미디어 기술, 산업계, 콘텐츠, 수용자 사이의 다양한 교차점에서 발생하는 지속적 과정이다. 채널의 확산과 점점 더 흔히 볼 수 있는 컴퓨터와 이동통신의 특성 덕분에, 미디어가 어디에나 있고 모든 종류의 미디어를 서로 연관지어 사용할 수 있는 시대로 접어들고 있다.
미디어 컨버전스는 기술 변화 이상의 의미를 지닌다. 그것은 기존의 기술, 산업, 시장, 장르, 수용자 사이의 관계를 변화시킨다. 이런 미디어 변화의 초기 파장이 불안정적 영향을 발산하며, 그 결과 환호와 공황 사이의 계속되는 휘청거림이 발생한다. 하지만 미디어 컨버전스는 대중문화 거의 모든 부문에서 창의적 혁신 또한 일으키고 있다. 현재 우리의 미디어 환경은 다양성의 확산에 의해 특징지어진다.

18 다음 중 본문의 제목으로 가장 적합한 것은?
① 블랙박스의 오류: 미디어 컨버전스의 시작과 끝
② 블랙박스의 오류와 기술적 변화
③ 미디어 컨버전스와 그것의 불안정적 영향
④ 미디어 컨버전스와 변화하는 환경
⑤ 미디어와 컨버전스 오류의 교차점

| 정답 | ④

| 해설 | '블랙박스의 오류'는 기존의 잘못된 생각에 대해 저자가 이름 붙인 것이므로 글의 주제에 해당하지 않고 제목으로도 부적합하다. 본문은 미디어 컨버전스가 대중문화에 어떤 영향을 주고 있는지에 대해 서술하고 있다. 본문 후반부에 미디어 컨버전스로 인해 환희와 패닉이 동반되는 불안정적 영향을 주고 있는 것도 사실이지만, 그것 이외에도 대중 문화에 창의적 혁신을 불러오고 있다고 서술하고 있다. 따라서 한 가지 측면만 강조한 ③ 또한 정답이 될 수 없다. 정답은 ④로 '미디어 컨버전스와 변화하는 환경'이 제목으로 적합하다.

19 다음 중 빈칸 [A]에 올 수 있는 가장 적합한 것은?
① 그것은 블랙박스의 오류를 뒤엎었다
② 그것은 발생하고 있는 지속적 과정이다
③ 그것은 발생하고 있는 붕괴되는 상황이다
④ 그것은 수용자를 혼란스럽게 만들었다
⑤ 그것은 산업계를 오도했다

| 정답 | ②

| 해설 | 'not A rather B'는 'A라기보다는 B이다'를 의미하며, A와 B는 대조를 보인다. 여기서 A는 endpoint가 되므로, B는 '끝'이 아니라 '지속적 과정'이라고 설명한 ②가 정답으로 적합하다.

20 다음 중 빈칸 [B]와 [C]에 올 수 있는 가장 적합한 것은?
① 증식 – 상반되는 감정을 가진
② 사유화 – 선조치하는
③ 확산 – 도처에 있는
④ 발산 – 제한된
⑤ 분산 – 추방된

| 정답 | ③

| 해설 | 미디어 컨버전스에 대해 설명하면서, [B]와 [C] 때문에 미디어가 어디에나 있고 모든 종류의 미디어를 서로 연관시켜 사용할 수 있는 시대로 접어들고 있다고 말하고 있다. 먼저 미디어를 접할 수 있는 채널(통로)이 '많아야' 뒤의 내용이 가능하므로, '많다'에 해당하는 증식(multiplication)이나 확산(proliferation)이 적합하다. diffusion이나 dispersion은 중심 지점에서 다른 지점으로 뻗어가는 발산이나 분산을 의미하므로 적합하지 않다. [C]의 경우 본문의 'be everywhere'와 유사한 '도처에 있는, 편재하는'을 의미하는 ubiquitous가 적합하므로, 정답은 ③이 된다.

| 어휘 | discourse ⓝ 담론, 담화   convergence ⓝ 한 곳으로 모임(집합), 통합, 융합
fallacy ⓝ 오류
black box fallacy – 블랙박스의 오류 [MIT 인문학부 교수인 헨리 젠킨스(Henry Jenkins)가 만든 용어로, 미래

에 모든 미디어 콘텐츠가 하나의 블랙박스를 통해 우리 거실로 유통될 것이라고 믿었던 때도 있었지만 젠킨스는 이러한 예측이 빗나갔다면서, 이를 가리켜 '블랙박스의 오류'라고 지칭했음]

endpoint ⓝ 종점
rather ⓐⓓ 오히려, 차라리(앞에 말한 내용과 다르거나 반대되는 말을 도입할 때)
intersection ⓝ 교차로, 교차 지점   **era** ⓝ 시대, 시기; 중대한 사건
alter ⓥ 바꾸다, 변경하다   **existing** ⓐ 기존의
initial ⓐ 처음의, 시초의 ⓝ 머리글자
exert ⓥ (권력·영향력을) 가하다[행사하다]; 열심히 노력하다
destabilizing ⓐ 불안정한, 불안정하게 만드는   **result in** - (결과적으로) ~을 낳다[야기하다]
lurch ⓝ 휘청함; 요동침 ⓥ (갑자기) 휘청하다[휘청거리다]
exhilaration ⓝ 흥분, 유쾌한 기분   **spark** ⓥ 불붙이다, 촉발하다
innovation ⓝ 혁신, 쇄신   **be marked by** - ~에 의해 특징 지어지다
proliferation ⓝ 증식, 확산   **overturn** ⓥ 뒤집다, 전복시키다 ⓝ 전복, 붕괴
disintegrating ⓐ 분해되는, 해체되는, 산산조각 나는
mislead ⓥ 잘못된 길로 이끌다, 오도하다, 호도하다
multiplication ⓝ 곱셈; 증식
ambivalent ⓐ 상반(모순)되는 감정을 가진, 양면 가치적인, 이중 의식의
privatization ⓝ 민영화, 사유화   **proactive** ⓐ 선조치하는, 사전 대책을 강구하는
proliferation ⓝ 증식, 확산   **ubiquitous** ⓐ 도처에 있는, 편재하는
diffusion ⓝ 보급, 확산   **circumscribed** ⓐ ~에 의해 제한된, 국한된
dispersion ⓝ 확산, 분산   **displaced** ⓐ 추방된, 유민[난민]의

[21-24] 동국대 2008

미국 사회에는 미디어 폭력을 비판하는 오랜 전통이 있다. 19세기에는, 교육자를 위시한 많은 사람들이 잔인한 내용의 3류 소설과 범죄 기사들이 청소년에게 미치는 영향에 대해 경고했다. 20세기 초반에는, 영화와 라디오가 모두 심각한 사회적 위협으로 간주되었다. 오늘날엔, 컴퓨터 게임과 대중음악, 인터넷상의 폭력이 우려의 대상이다. 미디어 기술은 계속 발전했지만, 근본적인 질문은 그대로이다. 미디어 폭력이 현실의 폭력에 영향을 미치는가? 1950년대 이후로, TV는 미디어 폭력 논란의 중심에 있다. 논란이 TV에 집중된 데는 몇 가지 이유가 있다. TV는 널리 보급된 매체이고 그렇기 때문에 과다 시청된다. 게다가 TV 프로그램은 보통 폭력적이었다. 1982년, 한 연구에 따르면 180시간 분량의 프로그램을 분석한 결과 1,846건의 폭력 장면을 발견했다. TV의 대중성과 폭력적인 콘텐츠 때문에, 결국 평균적인 미국 아동은 초등학교를 졸업할 때까지 총 8,000건의 살인과 10만 건의 그 폭력 장면들을 보게 된다. 그 정도로 많은 폭력 장면에 노출되면 아이들에게 해롭고 현실의 폭력에도 영향을 미친다고 주장하는 사람들이 많다. 특히, TV 속 폭력은 아이들에게 폭력을 정당한 문제 해결책으로 가르치고, 시청자들에게 세상이 실제보다 더 폭력적이라는 착각을 일으키면서 현실 세계를 두려워하는 태도를 조장한다는 것이다.

21 밑줄 친 ⓐlurid와 의미가 가장 비슷한 것은 _____이다.
① 더러운   ② 끔찍한
③ 터무니없는   ④ 지루한

| 정답 | ②

| 해설 | lurid(끔찍한, 충격적인)=grisly(끔찍한, 처참한)

22

이 글의 제목으로 가장 적절한 것은?
① 미국 사회의 미디어 폭력의 역사
② TV 폭력보다 심각한 인터넷 폭력
③ 미디어 기술의 발전적 변화
④ TV 폭력이 미국 청소년에게 미치는 영향

| 정답 | ④

| 해설 | 지엽적인 사실만으로는 제목이 될 수 없다는 점에 유의한다. 주제문 "Many argue that exposure to such quantities of violent depictions damages children and contributes to violence in real life."를 참조하면, 이 글의 소재는 'TV 폭력'이고, 주제는 "TV 폭력이 청소년에게 영향을 미친다(실제 폭력을 조장한다)"는 것이다. ①, ③은 첫 단락에 언급되었으나 지엽적 내용이므로 선택하지 않도록 주의한다.

23

지문에 따르면, 다음 중 사실은?
① 미국 사회는 오랫동안 폭력에 시달려 왔다.
② 라디오와 신문 모두 오늘날 사회구조에 여전히 심각한 위협이 된다.
③ 20세기 중반 이후, 미국인들은 TV를 미디어 폭력의 온상이라고 비난해 왔다.
④ 1982년 연구는, 미디어 폭력이 직접적으로 폭력을 조장한다는 주장을 반박한다.

| 정답 | ③

| 해설 | "Since the 1950s, television has been at the center of the debate over media violence. There are several reasons for the focus on television."에서 '20세기 중반 이후, TV가 미디어 폭력 논쟁의 중심, 즉 비난의 대상이 되었음'을 알 수 있다. 보기 ①은 선택하지 않도록 주의한다. 미국 사회를 괴롭힌 것은 현실 세계의 폭력(acts of violence)이 아니라 미디어 폭력(media violence)이다.

24

다음 중 TV가 논란의 초점이 된 이유로 언급되지 않은 것은?
① TV는 광범위하게 보급되어 있다.
② TV는 매우 대중적이다.
③ TV는 가증스럽다.
④ TV 콘텐츠는 폭력적이다.

| 정답 | ③

| 해설 | "There are several reasons for the focus on television. It is pervasive and thus it is heavily watched. More worse, television shows are frequently violent."를 참조하면, TV가 논란의 초점이 된 이유는 세 가지(광범위한 보급, 과다 시청을 통한 대중성, 콘텐츠의 폭력성)이다. 보기 ③ It is scandalous(TV는 가증스럽다).는 언급되지 않았을 뿐 아니라 비약이다.

| 어휘 |
long-standing ⓐ 오래된
dime novel - 3류 소설
significant ⓐ 중요한
concern ⓝ 우려; 관심
fundamental ⓐ 근본적인
lurid ⓐ 끔찍한
motion picture - 영화
threat ⓝ 위협
evolving ⓐ 발전하는
depiction ⓝ 묘사

contribute to – ~에 영향을 미치다, 기여하다	pervasive ⓐ 만연한, 보편적인
analyze ⓥ 분석하다	witness ⓥ 목격하다
net result – 궁극적[최종적] 결과	elementary school – 초등학교
exposure ⓝ 노출	quantity ⓝ 양
claim ⓥ 주장하다	acceptable ⓐ 타당한, 옳은
foster ⓥ 조장하다	fearful ⓐ 두려워하는, 소심한
grisly ⓐ 끔찍한, 처참한(주로 죽음, 폭력과 관련)	ludicrous ⓐ 터무니없는, 어리석은

[25-26] 성균관대 2012

언론매체가 인간복제와 관련해 과장된 수사를 남발하는 것이 지닌 가장 두드러진 문제점은 아마도 인간이 단순히 유전자의 산물일 뿐이라고 쉽사리 가정하는 것이다. 이러한 시각은 일반적으로 "유전자 본질주의"로 불린다. TV쇼 진행자나 라디오 진행자들은 마이클 조단의 복제인간으로 농구 팀 전체를 채우는 것이 가능한지를 묻곤 한다. 철학자, 신학자, 그 외 전문가들은 이에 대응해 비록 인간의 행동에는 명백하게 유전적 요소가 존재하긴 하지만 그 외 자궁 내 환경·가족 역동성·사회적 환경·식단·그 외 개인적 내력 등 다수의 여러 요소들이 개인 발달에 중요한 영향을 끼친다고 물릴 정도로 강조해서 말해 왔다. 그 결과로 뛰어난 운동선수의 DNA를 통해 만들어진 복제인간이 스포츠에 별 관심을 갖지 않을 수도 있는 것이다. 게다가 인간복제 문제는 대중매체가 기술 및 과학 결정론을 어떤 식으로 조장하는지 드러내는데, 바로 과학적 '진보'는 멈춰져서는 안 된다는 생각을 대중매체가 은연중에 풍기고 있는 것이다. 물론 많은 과학자들 역시 이 같은 시각을 공유하고 있으며, 인간이 고통받는 데 한몫할 수도 있는 연구에 참여함으로써 지게 될 도덕적 책임을 받아들이기를 거부하는 사례도 빈번하다.

25 본문의 제목으로 가장 알맞은 것은 <u>언론매체와 인간복제 윤리</u>이다.
① 과학 발전의 혜택
② 언론매체와 인간복제 윤리
③ 반 인간복제 운동에 대한 언론의 기여
④ 스포츠와 과학 결정론
⑤ 법을 통한 인간복제 규제

| 정답 | ②

| 해설 | 본문은 언론매체가 어떤 방식으로 인간복제 문제를 다루고 있는지를 전반적으로 비판적 논조로 설명하고 있다. 따라서 답은 ②이다.

26 본문에 따르면 다음 중 사실은 무엇인가?
① 과학자들은 도덕적 논란에 객관적인 태도를 취할 자격이 있다.
② 언론매체는 DNA를 운명으로 바라보는 시각에 사로잡혀 있다.
③ 대부분의 과학자들은 인간복제 연구에 제한을 둬야 한다고 인정한다.
④ 대부분의 신학자들은 과학에 대한 지식이 거의 없다.
⑤ 언론매체는 인간 복제에 관해 너무 부정적인 시각을 보여 왔다.

| 정답 | ②

| 해설 | 언론매체가 인간복제에 대해 품고 있는 생각은 "유전자 본질주의(genetic essentialism)"이며, 이를 풀어서 설명하면 "인간이 단순히 유전자의 산물일 뿐(humans simply are a product of their genes)" 또는 인간은 유전자에서 벗어날 수 없는 존재라는 의미이다. 이처럼 유전자를 운명과 같이 바라보는 시각은 보기 ②의 내용과 같으며, 따라서 ②가 답이 된다.

| 어휘 |
hyperbole ⓝ 과장(법)
essentialism ⓝ 본질주의
stock ⓥ 채우다, 갖추다
theologian ⓝ 신학자
wearily ⓐⓓ 질릴 정도로, 지쳐서
a host of – 다수의, 수많은
consequently ⓐⓓ 그 결과, 따라서
foster ⓥ 조장하다, 발전시키다
imply ⓥ 은연중 풍기다, 암시하다
contribute to – ~에 기여하다
be entitled to – ~할 자격이 있다, ~할 권리가 있다
objective ⓐ 객관적인

concerning ⓟⓡⓔⓟ ~에 관하여
personality ⓝ 저명인사, 쇼 진행자
in response – 이에 대응하여
reiterate ⓥ 반복하다, 되풀이하다
undeniably ⓐⓓ 명백하게, 틀림없이
uterine ⓐ 자궁의
outstanding ⓐ 뛰어난
determinism ⓝ 결정론, 결정주의
halt ⓥ 멈추다, 중단시키다
ethics ⓝ 윤리, 윤리학
be obsessed with – ~에 푹 빠지다, ~에 사로잡히다

[27-30] 숙명여대 2017

대중매체는 여성이 섭식장애를 경험하는 문화적 맥락에서 중요한 역할을 수행한다. 섭식장애의 폐해는 무리한 다이어트, 과도한 운동이나 구토를 통해 신체에 손해를 끼칠 뿐만 아니라 자신의 정서적 건강에도 손해를 끼친다. 섭식장애를 앓고 있는 여성은 자신을 무가치하게 여기거나 낮은 자존감에 빠지게 되며, 이런 감정들이 자신의 몸에 대한 통제권을 갖기 위해 훨씬 더 살을 빼도록 그들을 부추긴다. 연구 결과에 따르면 개인의 미디어 노출량과 신체의 불만족 사이에는 상관관계가 존재한다. 연구는 종종 이룰 수 없는 문화적 이상에 대한 언론의 묘사가 자신의 신체에 대한 여성의 자기 인식에 부정적인 영향을 줄 뿐만 아니라 여성들의 자존감을 깎아내린다고 지적한다. 낮아진 자존감과 가족 관계나 다른 1차 집단을 통해 주입되었을 수 있는 완벽주의적 가치관의 결합으로 인해 일부 여성들은 자신의 신체를 부정확하게 인식한다. 이와 같은 비현실적인 신체 모델로부터 이익을 얻는 많은 산업이 존재한다. 성형수술 업계는 사상 최고의 수익을 기록하고 있다. 여성들은 순수하게 성형수술에만 60억 달러가 넘는 금액을 지불하고 있다. 많은 여성은 엄청난 돈을 들여 불필요한 수술을 받고 있으며, 이런 수술은 마취제와 장기간의 회복 시간을 필요로 하는 침습 수술이 종종 사용된다. 우리 사회가 가지고 있는 문화적 이상과 더 닮아 보이기 위해 이런 수술이 행해진다. 하지만 우리 사회의 이상적 신체 모델은 의학계의 신체 모델에 따르면 건강한 체중보다 훨씬 더 낮다.

27

다음 중 빈칸 [A]와 [B]에 올 수 있는 가장 적합한 것은?
① 부정적인 – 끌어내리다
② 압도적인 – 지지하다
③ 부적격의 – 고조시키다
④ 막대한 – 요구하다
⑤ 나쁜 – 비난하다

| 정답 | ①

| 해설 | 사회가 제시하는 이상적 신체의 모습을 갖기 위해 여성들은 성형수술을 마다하지 않는다는 내용으로, 대중매체도 이런 현상에 일조한다고 설명하고 있다. 첫 번째 빈칸의 경우, TV와 같은 미디어에서 비현실적인 이상적 신체를 묘사하는 것이 자신의 신체에 대한 여성들의 인식에 부정적인(negative, bad) 영향을 줄 것이다. 두 번째 빈칸의 경

우, 앞에서의 상황으로 여성들의 자존감은 떨어질 것이므로, 자존감을 끌어내린다는 'pulling down'이 어울린다. 참고로 빈칸 앞부분에서 섭식장애를 앓고 있는 여성들이 느끼는 감정을 "feelings of unworthiness and low self-esteem"으로 묘사하고 있는 것과도 연결시킬 수 있다.

28 다음 중 성형수술에서 마취제 사용의 부작용으로 지적된 것은?
① 마취제 사용이 성형수술을 불필요하게 만든다.
② 마취제 사용은 여성들이 막대한 돈을 사용하도록 끌어들인다.
③ 마취제 사용은 섭식장애를 일으킨다.
④ 마취제 사용은 수술 후 회복 시간이 길어지게 만든다.
⑤ 마취제 사용은 TV에 나온 닮고 싶은 대상을 닮을 수 있는 대안적 방법을 찾도록 만들어 준다.

| 정답 | ④

| 해설 | 본문 후반의 "the use of anesthetics and oftentimes invasive procedures that require long recovery times"를 통해 마취제를 사용하고 메스를 사용해 봉합이 필요한 침습 수술을 받게 되면 수술 후 회복 기간이 길어진다고 했으므로 정답은 ④가 적합하다.

29 다음 중 본문의 섭식장애 여성에 대한 내용과 일치하지 않는 것은?
① 그들은 보통 과도한 다이어트를 실시한다.
② 그들은 자신의 신체 이미지를 자율적으로, 그리고 다차원적으로 만들어 낸다.
③ 그들은 불필요한 성형수술을 위해 많은 돈을 지출하고 있다.
④ 그들은 외부에서 주입된 완벽주의적 가치관을 통해 자기 자신의 이미지를 인식할 것이다.
⑤ 위의 어느 것도 해당되지 않는다.

| 정답 | ②

| 해설 | 섭식장애 여성들은 스스로를 비만으로 생각하므로 ① 과도한 다이어트를 하며, ③ 불필요한 성형수술을 받는다. 그리고 자신의 신체에 대한 인식이 외부에 의해 주입된 것이라고 "perfectionist values that may have been instilled through familial relations or other primary groups."에서 말하고 있다. 정답은 ②로, 섭식장애 여성을 자신의 신체를 자율(독립)적으로 보지 못하며, 완벽한 신체적 모형이 존재한다는 1차원적인 관점에서 스스로를 바라보기 때문에 "autonomously and multidimensionally"라는 설명이 일치하지 않는 부분이다. 참고로 ⑤는 ①부터 ④의 설명이 모두 섭식장애 여성에 대한 올바른 설명이란 뜻이므로 정답에서 제외된다.

30 다음 중 본문의 내용과 일치하지 않는 것은?
① 자신의 신체 모습에 만족하지 않는 여성은 대게 운동을 과도하게 한다.
② 성형수술 업계는 요즘 높은 수익을 올리고 있다.
③ 대중매체는 있을 것 같지 않은 여성 신체 유형을 광고한다.
④ 여성의 섭식장애는 현 시대에 상당히 자연스러운 것이다.
⑤ 위의 어느 것도 해당되지 않는다.

| 정답 | ④

| 해설 | 여성의 섭식장애는 대중매체의 영향을 받은 의학적으로는 매우 저체중에 해당하는 비현실적인 신체 모델에 기인한 것이므로 결코 자연스러운 현상이라고 할 수 없으므로 정답은 ④가 된다.

| 어휘 |
- **serve as** – ~의 역할을 하다
- **consequence** ⓝ 결과; 중대성
- **purge** ⓥ 숙청하다, 추방하다, 제거하다
- **unworthiness** ⓝ 가치 없음, 하찮음
- **correlation** ⓝ 연관성, 상관관계
- **unattainable** ⓐ 달성할 수 없는, 이루기 힘든
- **dualistic** ⓐ 이원적인, 이원론의
- **perfectionist** ⓝ 완벽주의자 ⓐ 완벽주의의
- **familial** ⓐ 가족의
- **cosmetic surgery** – 성형수술
- **extraordinary** ⓐ 비범한, 기이한, 놀라운
- **invasive** ⓐ 급속히 퍼지는, 침습성의
- **uphold** ⓥ 지지하다; (판결을) 확정하다, 확인하다, 인용하다
- **ineligible** ⓐ 자격이 없는, 부적격의
- **summon** ⓥ 소환하다, 소집하다; 요청하다
- **inculcate** ⓥ 심어 주다
- **eating disorder** – 섭식장애
- **strenuous** ⓐ 정력적인, 활발한, 분투적인
- **be caught up** – ~에 휘말리다
- **low self-esteem** – 낮은 자존감
- **portrayal** ⓝ 묘사
- **self-perception** ⓝ 자아 인식, 자각
- **combination** ⓝ 조합
- **instill** ⓥ 주입시키다, (방울방울) 떨어뜨리다
- **profit off of** – ~로부터 이익을 얻어내다
- **all-time high** – 사상 최고치
- **anesthetic** ⓝ 마취제
- **overwhelming** ⓐ 압도적인
- **condemn** ⓥ 비난하다
- **autonomously** ⓐⓓ 자체적으로; 독자적으로

CHAPTER 04 교육

01	④	02	②	03	①	04	②	05	④	06	①	07	④	08	③	09	①	10	④
11	②	12	②	13	④	14	①	15	①	16	③	17	③	18	②	19	④	20	④
21	④	22	③	23	②	24	④	25	②	26	③	27	④	28	①	29	①	30	②

[01-03] 숭실대 2006

만약 "x가 y에 대한 필요조건이다"고 말한다면, 이것은 x를 갖지 않았다면 y도 갖지 않을 것임을 의미한다. 다르게 말하면, x가 없다면 y도 갖지 못할 것이라는 말이다. 하지만 x가 y에 대한 필요조건이라고 해서 x가 y를 보장한다는 것을 의미하지는 않는다. 만약 "x가 y에 대한 충분조건이다"고 말하면 이는 x를 가지면 y가 반드시 뒤따른다는 것을 우리가 알고 있다는 말이다. 다시 말해, x가 y를 보장한다는 것이다. 예를 들어, 일부 교육자들은 공립학교 학생들의 학업성적 향상(SAT로 측정된 것을 의미함)과 학교에 대한 주정부 지출비용 사이에 인과관계가 있다고 주장한다. 즉, 지출비용이 많으면 많을수록 더 나은 학습이 유발된다는 것이다. 이 같은 주장은 다음 몇 가지 예를 주장하는 이들로 인해 일정 정도 신빙성이 떨어진다. 예를 들어 1992~1993년 동안 교사의 급여가 가장 높은 5개 주 가운데서 그 어떤 주도 SAT 최고 점수를 받은 상위 15개 주에 들지 못했다는 사실과, 학생 1인당 지출되는 비용이 가장 높은 상위 10개의 주 가운데 오직 한 주(위스콘신주)만 SAT 점수가 가장 높은 상위 10개 주에 들었다는 사실, 그리고 학생 1인당 교육비 지출이 가장 많은 뉴저지주는 SAT 점수 순위에서 39위를 차지했다는 사실이다. 이는 높은 비용지출이 모두 학생들의 학업성적 향상으로 이어지는 충분조건은 아니라는 것을 보여주는 증거이다. 하지만 학생 1인당 비용지출이 가장 낮은 하위 10개 주 가운데 SAT 점수가 가장 높은 상위 10개 주에 속한 주가 4곳(노스다코타, 사우스다코타, 테네시, 유타)이나 포함되어 있으며, 노스다코타주는 비용지출이 44위임에도 불구하고 SAT 점수는 2위였다는 사실과, 사우스다코타주의 경우 교사 급여는 최하위를 기록했지만 SAT 점수는 3위를 기록했다는 사실에 주목할 필요가 있다. 이는 높은 비용지출이 학생들의 학업성적에 대한 필요조건 또한 아니라는 점을 보여주는 증거이다.

01 본문에 따르면, 다음 중 1992~1993년에 걸쳐 수집된 데이터가 보여주는 것은?
① 일부 학자들은 주들이 교육에 더 많은 비용을 사용해야 한다고 주장한다.
② 더 많은 비용이 교육에 사용된다면 학생들의 학업성적은 예외 없이 향상될 것이다.
③ 충분조건보다는 필요조건이 학교의 성과 향상에 더 중요하다.
④ 교육에 사용된 비용이 학생들의 학업성적을 반드시 더 높여주는 것은 아니라는 것이다.

| 정답 | ④

| 해설 | 자료를 보면 교육비 지출과 학생들의 성적 향상이 반드시 일치하는 것은 아니라는 것을 보여주고 있으므로 정답은 ④가 된다.

02

본문에 따르면, 다음 중 어떤 주가 높은 교육비 지출이 반드시 높은 학업 성적을 이끌어 내는 것은 아니라는 사실을 가장 잘 보여주고 있는가?

① 테네시주
② 뉴저지주
③ 위스콘신주
④ 사우스다코다주

| 정답 | ②

| 해설 | 테네시주와 사우스다코다주는 학생 1인당 비용지출이 가장 낮은 하위 10개 주에 속하기 때문에 질문과 맞지 않으며, 위스콘신주는 교육비 지출이 높은 주이면서 동시에 학생들의 성적도 높았던 곳이므로 마찬가지로 질문과 맞지 않다. 정답은 ②의 뉴저지주로 "학생 1인당 교육비 지출이 가장 많은 뉴저지주는 SAT점수 순위에서 39위를 차지했다"고 했으므로 문제의 지문과 부합한다는 것을 알 수 있다.

03

다음 중 빈칸 ⓐ와 ⓑ에 들어갈 가장 알맞은 단어의 짝은?

	ⓐ	ⓑ
①	충분한	필요한
②	필요한	필요한
③	필요한	충분한
④	충분한	충분한

| 정답 | ①

| 해설 | 본문 서두에서 필요조건(a necessary condition)과 충분조건(a sufficient condition)의 차이점을 설명하고 있다. 먼저 x가 y의 필요조건이라면, x는 y를 하기 위해 꼭 필요한 것이지만, x를 했다고 반드시 y가 된다는 보장은 없다고 설명하고 있다. 반면 x가 y의 충분조건이라면, x는 y를 하는 데 충분한 것으로, x를 했다고 하면 반드시 y도 된다는 보장을 받는다. 본문에서 설명한 교육비 지출 증가와 성적 향상 간의 관계를 생각해 보면, 교육비 지출을 증가했다고 해서 반드시 성적 향상으로 이어지지 않는다는 것을 ⓐ의 앞부분에서 설명하고 있다. '교육비 지출 증가'라는 x가 '성적 향상'이라는 y를 보장하는 데 충분하다면 이는 '충분' 조건이 되어야 하는데, 그렇지 않다는 것이므로 이 경우 '충분' 조건이 와야 한다. 마찬가지로 ⓑ의 앞부분에서는 교육비 지출이 감소했다고 해서 반드시 성적 하락으로 이어지지 않는다는 것을 설명하고 있다. '교육비 지출 감소'라는 x가 '성적 하락'이라는 y를 보장했다면 이도 역시 '충분' 조건이 되어야 하겠지만, 여기서는 주어가 '교육비 지출 감소'가 아닌 ⓐ와 같은 '교육비 지출 증가'이기 때문에 '충분' 조건이 적절하지 않게 된다. '교육비 지출 감소'도 '성적 향상'으로 이어질 수 있다는, 다시 말하면, '교육비 지출 증가'가 반드시 '성적 향상'에 필요한 것은 아니라는 설명이 되어, 이 경우는 '필요' 조건이 된다.

| 어휘 | a necessary condition – 필요조건
guarantee ⓥ 보장[약속]하다
illustrate ⓥ 설명하다, 보여주다
performance ⓝ 성적, 실적, 성과
expenditure ⓝ 지출, 소비
yield ⓥ (수익·결과·농작물 등을) 내다[산출/생산하다]
in some degree – 어느 정도

put differently – 다르게 말하면
a sufficient condition – 충분조건
a casual connection – 인과관계
public school – 공립학교

undermine ⓥ 약화시키다

[04-06] 이화여대 2013

교육은 대중을 향상시키는 것을 목표로 할 것인가 아니면 가장 큰 잠재력을 지니고 있음을 입증한 사람들을 육성하는 것을 목표로 할 것인가는 바로 재능 있는 사람들을 어떻게 대우해야 할지에 영향을 미치는 주요 철학적 문제이다. 이 문제는 엘리트주의와 민주적 평등 사이의 이분법 형태로 제시된다. 또 다른 관점은 동등한 지능을 갖추지 못한 사람들에게 동등한 가르침을 제공하는 민주적 관행, 즉 똑똑한 사람과 멍청한 사람에게 동일한 기대와 표준을 적용하는 행위는 평등에 대한 개념을 그릇되게 잡은 것으로, 범용함을 낳고 재능을 낭비하게 만든다. 그보다 진정한 평등은 각 개개인에게 "지능에 맞는 교육을 제공하여 이득을 볼 수 있는 기회를 동등하게" 제공하는 데 있다. (쓴첸, 1961). 인류 역사에 걸쳐 기회의 평등과 관련한 지배적인 철학은 재능이 있는 개개인을 대우하는 방식을 통해 드러난다.

시간이 흐르면서 사회에서 가치 있게 여기는 것 또한 어떤 사람을 재능이 있는 사람으로 규정하고 이들을 어떻게 식별할 것인지 규정하는 데 도움을 제공해 왔다. 예를 들어 르네상스 시기의 유럽과 같이 시각 예술이 존중받던 시절에 사회는 예술적으로 재능을 보유한 사람들을 찾아내어 지원했다. 전시나 기근 같은 긴급한 상황으로 인한 긴급한 필요와 오랜 시간에 걸쳐 존재하는 만성적인 필요 모두 사회가 재능 있는 개개인을 식별하는 행위에 영향을 미쳤다. 예를 들어 고대 스파르타의 전시 사회에서는 군사적 기량을 갖춘 사람들을 필요로 했고 따라서 그런 사람들을 육성했다.

04 위 본문에서 유추할 수 있는 것을 고르시오.
① 재능이 있는 아동의 부모는 종종 과도하게 적극적이다.
② 재능이 있는 사람은 능력에 맞는 교육을 받아야 한다.
③ 어떤 사람을 재능이 있는 사람으로 정의해야 할지의 기준은 세월이 흘러서도 변하지 않고 있다.
④ 재능이 있는 아동의 부모는 가정에서 자극을 불러일으키는 자료를 제공해야 한다.
⑤ 경제적 차이가 자녀를 양육하는 습성에 영향을 줄 수 있다.

| 정답 | ②

| 해설 | 본문의 첫 번째 단락에서는 재능을 가진 사람과 그렇지 못한 사람에게 동일한 기준을 적용하여 재능 있는 사람들이 자신의 능력을 꽃피우지 못하게 하는 것보다는, 개인의 능력과 지능에 맞는 교육을 제공하여 각자의 재능을 발휘하게 도울 것을 강조하고 있다. 이는 보기 ②의 내용과 일맥상통한다.
참고로 "시간이 흐르면서 사회에서 가치 있게 여기는 것 또한 어떤 사람을 재능이 있는 사람으로 규정하고 이들을 어떻게 식별할 것인지 규정하는 데 도움을 제공해 왔다(What society values has also helped determine the definition and identification of gifted individuals over time)." 이 말은, 즉 어떤 사람을 재능이 있는 사람으로 규정하는 기준은 세월이 흐를수록 바뀌었다는 의미이며 ③과는 반대된다. 그리고 ①, ④, ⑤는 본문에 딱히 언급된 바 없다.

05 빈칸 [A]와 [B]에 가장 알맞은 것은 무엇인가?
① 우월성 – 능숙함
② 파벌 – 업적
③ 찌꺼기 – 보통
④ 엘리트주의 – 범용함
⑤ 추출물 – 숙달

| 정답 | ④

| 해설 | "교육은 대중을 향상시키는 것을 목표로 할 것인가 아니면 가장 큰 잠재력을 지니고 있음을 입증한 사람들을 육성하는 것을 목표로 할 것인가(whether education should be aimed at elevating the masses or at nurturing those who evidence the greatest potential)"는 교육을 둘러싼 "이분법(dichotomy)"적 태도를 일컬으며 문맥상 전자는 "민주적 평등(democratic equality)"을 의미하고 후자는 빈칸 [A]를 일컫는다. '민주적 평등'과 [A]가 서로 대조적인 의미를 갖고 있으므로, 보기 중에서 평등과는 정반대되는 '엘리트주의'가 [A]에 적합하다.

[B]의 경우를 보면, "동등한 지능을 갖추지 못한 사람들에게 동등한 가르침을 제공하는 민주적 관행, 즉 똑똑한 사람과 멍청한 사람에게 동일한 기대와 표준을 적용하는 행위(the democratic practice of educating equally individuals of unequal intelligence – that is, having the same expectations and standards for the bright and the dull –)"라는 말의 의미는 똑똑한 사람이 자신의 재능을 살려주는 교육을 받지 못해 결국 "범용(mediocrity)"한 존재가 된다는 의미이다. 이러한 점들을 감안했을 때 답으로 가장 적합한 것은 ④이다.

06 인용문인 [C]에 가장 알맞은 것은 무엇인가?
① 지능에 맞는 교육을 제공하여 이득을 볼 수 있는 동등한 기회
② 전문화된 자원과 집중적인 교육을 위한 노력
③ 개인적인 헌신과 뛰어난 교육 그리고 지원을 아끼지 않는 가정환경
④ 가정에서 자극을 불러일으키는 자료
⑤ 더욱 정교한 말, 설명, 추론, 칭찬, 구체적인 피드백

| 정답 | ①

| 해설 | 빈칸 앞의 내용을 보면, 서로 다른 재능을 보유한 사람들에게 동등한 교육을 제공하는 것은 그릇된 개념에 기반한 것이라 하고 있다. 그리고 빈칸 뒤에서는 "기회의 평등(equality of opportunity)"에 관해 논하고 있다. 즉, 빈칸에 적합한 내용은 그릇된 개념에 기반하지 않은 '각 개인의 지능별 수준에 맞는 학습'에 관한 사항과 '기회의 평등'에 관한 내용이 들어있어야 한다. 따라서 답은 ①이다.

| 어휘 | gifted ⓐ 재능이 있는
the masses – 대중
dichotomy ⓝ 양분, 이분
mediocrity ⓝ 범용함, 평범함
manifest ⓥ 나타내다, 드러내 보이다
acute ⓐ 긴급한, 급성의
prowess ⓝ 기량, 솜씨
assertive ⓐ 적극적인, 확신에 찬
superiority ⓝ 우월성
clique ⓝ 파벌, 패거리
dregs ⓝ 앙금, 찌꺼기
extract ⓝ 추출물
intensive ⓐ 집중적인
elaborate ⓐ 정교한

elevate ⓥ 승격시키다, 향상시키다
evidence ⓥ 입증하다, ~의 증거가 되다
expectation ⓝ 기대, 요구
prevailing ⓐ 우세한, 지배적인
prize ⓥ 귀하게 여기다, 존중하다
chronic ⓐ 만성적인
overly ⓐⓓ 몹시, 과도하게
stimulating ⓐ 자극이 되는, 고무적인
competence ⓝ 능숙함, 능숙도
achievement ⓝ 업적
ordinariness ⓝ 평상 상태, 보통
skillfulness ⓝ 숙달
supportive ⓐ 지원하는, 힘을 주는

[07-09] 경희대 2012

재택학습은 아이들이 동급생이나 다른 어른과 관계를 수립하는 데 영향을 미치며 그 이유는 아이가 부모와 오랫동안 시간을 보내기 때문이라고 교육학자들은 주장해 왔다. 학계 대부분은 앞으로의 교육이 점차 가정을 중심으로 이루어질 것임을 수긍하고 있으며, 아이들은 점차 고립되고 내향적으로 변할 것임을 두려워하고 있다. 런던 대학교 교육연구대학원 소속의 마이클 바버 교수는 절충안으로 학생들이 집에서 보내는 시간 반, 학교에서 보내는 시간 반으로 할 수도 있음을 언급했다. 그에 따르면 집에서 이루어지는 수업은 앞으로 아이들의 교육에 있어 점차 중요한 역할을 할 것이다. 그는 다음과 같이 덧붙였다. "저는 아이들이 학교를 다니는 경험을 할 필요가 있음을 확신합니다. 학생들이 기본적인 사항을 배우고 평가받도록 하는 데 있어 품질관리 문제가 존재합니다. 아이들은 또한 동급생들과 함께 민주사회에서 행해야 할 일의 규칙을 배우고 부모 이외의 어른과의 관계에 대처하는 방법도 배워야 합니다." 고돌핀 엔 레티머 스쿨(Godolphin and Latymer School)의 교장인 마거릿 러드런드는 이들이 동급생과 어울리면서 야단법석을 떠는 것도 경험해 볼 필요가 있다고 말했다.

07 윗글의 주제로 가장 알맞은 것은?
① 아이들이 동급생 및 어른과 맺는 관계
② 교육에 있어 재택학습의 역할
③ 가정은 교육의 중심이다
④ 재택학습의 위험성

| 정답 | ④

| 해설 | 본문은 재택학습을 받는 아이가 경험할 수 있는 여러 부정적 사례와 함께 전통적인 의미의 학교에서 벌어지는 학습의 필요성에 관해 말하고 있다. 따라서 답은 ④이다.

08 윗글로부터 알 수 없는 것은?
① 어떤 사람들은 재택학습을 받는 아이들을 동급생과 격리하는 것이 위험할 수 있다고 생각한다.
② 재택학습은 아이들이 동급생과 보내는 시간이 별로 없기 때문에 아이들의 사회화 기술에 영향을 미칠 수 있다.
③ 일부 교육가들은 전통적인 의미의 학교가 미래에는 더 이상 존재하지 않을 것이라고 생각한다.
④ 대부분의 전문가들은 미래 교육의 중심이 집에 있을 것이라고 생각한다.

| 정답 | ③

| 해설 | "학계 대부분은 앞으로의 교육이 점차 가정을 중심으로 이루어질 것임을 수긍(Most academics concede that education will in the future be increasingly centered around the home)"하고는 있지만, 그렇다고 전통적인 의미의 학교가 완전히 사라질 것이라는 언급은 본문에 존재하지 않는다. 따라서 답은 ③이다.

09 ⓐ rough and tumble이 의미하는 것은?
① 어렵거나 힘든 측면　　　　　　　② 운동
③ 경쟁심　　　　　　　　　　　　④ 다른 동급생과의 대화

| 정답 | ①

| 해설 | ⓐ의 rough and tumble은 "소란, 야단법석; 원하는 것을 얻기 위한 드잡이질" 등을 의미하며, 본문의 문맥상 학교에서 아이들이 서로 부대끼며 어렵거나 힘든 일을 겪는다는 의미로 봐야 한다. 따라서 답은 ①이다.

| 어휘 | prolonged ⓐ 오래 계속되는, 장기간의 concede ⓥ 인정하다, 수긍하다
withdrawn ⓐ 내성적인, 내향적인 compromise ⓝ 절충, 타협
tuition ⓝ 수업
rough and tumble – 소란, 야단법석; 원하는 것을 얻기 위한 드잡이질
socialization ⓝ 사회화 demanding ⓐ 힘든, 부담이 큰

[10-11] 성균관대 2012

모든 시험 응시자의 악몽 깊은 곳에는 공들여 쓴 시험지 사방에 붉은 색 잉크를 흘리고는 사악하게 웃는 두꺼비 같은 채점관이 도사리고 있다. 하지만 채점관은 매우 참을성이 있는 사람이다. 그들 모두는 자신들이 잘 본 시험을 찾길 원하고 떨어뜨리기보다는 통과시키려고 한다는 것을 강조한다. 하지만 아무리 우호적인 채점관이라도 짜증나게 만들 것이 확실한 것들이 있다. 한 총 감독관은 "아무렇게나 제출된 시험지는 애초에 실패한 것이다. 우리가 쓴 것을 읽을 수도 없는 상황에서 그런 시험지를 제출한 응시자에게 우리가 공정하게 대할 수 있겠는가?"라고 언급한다. 모든 채점관들을 가장 화나게 하는 것은 총제적인 관점으로 문제를 바라보고 답을 하지 못하는 경우이다. 일부 응시자는 질문에서 단어 하나나 두 개를 고른 다음에 '아, 나 이거 무슨 말인지 기억나'라고 생각하고선 수업시간에 했던 것들을 단순하게 쏟아내기만 한다. 한 시간 시험시간 중 첫 15분 동안 응시자 아무도 펜을 들어서는 안 된다고 법으로 정해야 할 판이다. 응시자는 문제가 원하는 것이 무엇인지 확실히 이해한 다음에 답을 어떻게 쓸지 계획하는 것만으로 그 15분을 보내야 한다. 일부 학생들은 자기가 알맹이 없는 말을 늘어놓을 수 있는 능력을 가진 것에 자랑스러워한다. 하지만 다른 사람보다 시험지에 길게 쓴 것만으로 상을 받지는 못하니까 쓸데없는 말을 추가하지는 말라. 반면에 질문에 빈칸을 남겨놓는 것보다는 알맹이 없는 말을 늘어놓는 행위에 의지하는 편이 더 낫다.

10 다음 중 빈칸에 가장 알맞은 것은 무엇인가?

① 필기도구를 잊는 경우
② 한 문제를 푸는 데 너무 많은 시간을 보내는 경우
③ 시험에 늦는 경우
④ 총제적인 관점으로 문제를 바라보고 답을 하지 못하는 경우
⑤ 시험지를 제때 제출하지 않는 경우

| 정답 | ④

| 해설 | 빈칸 뒷부분을 보면 빈칸에 들어갈 내용, 즉 "모든 채점관들을 가장 화나게 하는 것(The one thing that most infuriates them all)"이 무엇인지 알 수 있다. 바로 "질문에서 단어 하나나 두 개를 고른 다음에(pick out one or two words in the written question)" "수업시간에 했던 것들을 단순하게 쏟아내기(just pour out what they did in class)"이다. 이를 간단히 줄여 말하면 출제자의 의도와 상관없는 "알맹이 없는 말을 늘어놓기(waffle)"이다. 때문에 저자는 "한 시간 시험시간 중 첫 15분 동안 응시자 아무도 펜을 들어서는 안 된다고 법으로 정해야 할 판이다. 응시자는 문제가 원하는 것이 무엇인지 확실히 이해한 다음에 답을 어떻게 쓸지 계획하는 것만으로 그 15분을 보내야 한다(It should be statutory that no exam candidate is allowed to pick up a pen for the first quarter of an hour. They should spend that time just making sure they understand what's wanted and then planning answers)"고 말하고 있다. 즉, 출제자의 의도를 이해하고 문제를 총제적인 관점에서 보기 전까지 문제를 섣불리 풀어서는 안 된다고 말하고 있다. 따라서 답은 ④이다.

11 본문에 따르면 다음 중 사실은 무엇인가?

① 일부 학생들은 자존심이 너무 강해서 자신이 시험에 떨어졌다고 인정하지 못한다.
② 일부 시험 응시자들은 답에 불필요한 것들을 집어넣는 성향이 있다.
③ 시험 채점관의 최악의 악몽은 시험 응시자의 무례한 태도이다.
④ 엄청 길게 답을 적는 것은 시험에서 좋은 점수를 받기 위한 최고의 방법이다.
⑤ 시험 채점관들은 시험 응시자의 악필에 영향을 거의 받지 않는다

| 정답 | ②

| 해설 | 본문 후반부에서 제시된 시험 채점관들을 화나게 하는 행위는 바로 시험지에 제대로 된 답을 쓰는 것이 아니라 '알맹이 없는 말을 늘어놓는 일'이다. 따라서 답은 ②이다.
①과 ③은 본문에 언급이 되지 않은 사항이며, ④는 좋은 점수를 받는 행위가 아니라 오히려 채점관들을 화나게 하는 행동이기 때문에 절대 답으로 볼 수 없고, ⑤는 "우리가 쓴 것을 읽을 수도 없는 상황에서 그런 시험지를 제출한 응시자에게 우리가 공정하게 대할 수 있겠는가?(How can we be fair to someone if we can't read what they have written?)"에서 답이 될 수 없음을 알 수 있다.

| 어휘 | exam candidate – 시험 응시자
toad ⓝ 두꺼비, 기분 나쁜 사람을 지칭
painfully ⓐd 공들여서, 극도로 노력을 기울여서
fiendishly ⓐd 사악하게
guaranteed ⓐ 확실한
start off – (처음에는) ~이다
pour out – 쏟아져 나오다
waffle ⓥ 알맹이 없는 말을 늘어놓다
resort to – ~에 기대다, ~에 의지하다
lurk ⓥ 도사리다
examiner ⓝ 시험 채점관
exam script – 시험지
stress ⓥ 강조하다
irritate ⓥ 짜증나게 하다
infuriate ⓥ 화나게 만들다
statutory ⓐ 법으로 정한
pad ⓥ (문장에 군말을 추가해) 길게 만들다

[12-13] 중앙대 2015

최초 동기가 무엇이었든 간에 기독교 근본주의자들은 지난 세기 초반 수십 년 동안 남부 및 남서부 지역에서 진화론에 반대하는 목표를 추구하는 과정에서 이따금 성공을 거두었다. 1920년대 말이 되면 기독교 근본주의자들은 다수의 미국 주 의회에 진화론에 반대하는 내용의 법안을 제출했으며, 이 가운데 일부는 남부의 몇몇 주에서 통과되었다. 어쩌면 진화론과 성경에 따른 창조설 간의 대립 가운데 가장 유명한 것은 학교 교사인 존 스코프스(John Scopes)에 대한 1925년의 재판일 것이다. 스코프스는 테네시 주의 학교에서 진화론 교육을 금지하는 금지령을 무시한 죄로 유죄판결을 받았다.

많은 생물학자들은 스코프스 재판이 본질적으로는 창조설 신봉자들이 지닌 견해의 지적 타당성을 근본적으로 무력화했다고 생각했지만, 겉보기에는 창조설 신봉자들은 이들 지역에서 입지가 거의 약해지지 않았고 남부 및 남서부 지역을 넘어 다른 곳의 공공 교육에 어렵사리 영향력을 행사하는 데 성공했다. 넬킨(Nelkin)이 지적한 바와 같이 창조설 신봉자들은 미국 내 여러 지방 및 주 교육 위원회에서 진행되는 교과서 선정 절차에 영향을 끼친 결과 오랫동안 성공적으로 중등학교 교과서에서 진화론에 따른 설명이 등장하는 것을 최소화할 수 있었다.

미국의 중등학교에서 진화론 교육이 증가하게 된 원동력은 바로 1950년대 말과 1960년대 초에 진행된 과학 교육과정 혁신 운동의 결과였다. 당시 미국은 자국의 과학 교육과정이 다른 국가에 비해 뒤떨어졌고, 특히 최초의 인공위성인 스푸트닉을 발사한 소련에 비해 뒤떨어진다는 사실을 깨달았다. 당시 이루어진 혁신 가운데에는 생물학 및 사회과학 고등학교 교과서에서 진화를 논하고 인간의 사회적 관계 변화를 분석한 것을 들 수 있다. 1960년대 말이 되면 진화론에 반대하는 법안은 폐지되거나 위헌으로 선언되었다. 지난 10년 동안 창조과학과 지적설계를 선전하기 위해 기독교 근본주의자들이 설립한 다수의 협회 및 기관이 과학 교육과정에 창조설을 포함시키겠다는 목표를 품고 이를 둘러싼 설전에 가담하였다. 창조과학은 과학이라는 이름을 달고 있지만 과학에 해당된다고 인식할 수 있는 요소가 (설사 있다 하더라도) 거의 존재하지 않는다. 상당한 양의 문건이 진화론에 대한 창조론 신봉자들의 공격을 다루고 있지만, 과학적 증거를 받아들이기를 거부하는 기독교 근본주의 창조설 신봉자들의 모습을 보면 문제가 해결될 가망이 보이지 않는다.

12 윗글을 통해 추론할 수 있는 것으로 가장 적합한 것을 고르시오.
① 진화론 교육이 확대된 결과 일반 대중은 창조설 신봉자들이 과학 교육의 질을 떨어뜨렸다는 믿음을 갖게 되었다.
② 본문의 저자는 근본주의자들이 제시한 지적설계에 의거한 주장에 관해 회의적이다.
③ 기독교 근본주의자들은 1920년대 미국의 모든 주를 대상으로 창조론에 반대하는 법안을 성공적으로 제출했다.
④ 기독교 근본주의자들의 핵심 주장은 진화 생물학의 전제에 기반을 둔다.

| 정답 | ②

| 해석 | "창조과학은 과학이라는 이름을 달고 있지만 과학에 해당된다고 인식할 수 있는 요소가 (설사 있다 한들) 거의 존재하지 않는다. 상당한 양의 문건이 진화론에 대한 창조론 신봉자들의 공격을 다루고 있지만, 과학적 증거를 받아들이기를 거부하는 기독교 근본주의 창조설 신봉자들의 모습을 보면 문제가 해결될 가망이 보이지 않는다[Despite the name, there is little (if any) recognizable science in creation science. Although considerable literature deals with creationist attacks on evolution, the refusal of fundamentalist creationists to accept the scientific evidence shows no promise of ever being resolved]." 본문 마지막에 해당되는 이 부분을 보면 저자가 창조과학과 지적설계에 대해 회의적인 견해를 갖고 있음을 알 수 있다. 따라서 답은 ②이다.

13 윗글의 제목으로 가장 적합한 것을 고르시오.
① 과학교육이 우주과학의 발달에 기여한 점
② 미국 중등학교에서의 과학 교육과정의 개혁
③ 창조설의 선전에 대한 찬사
④ 미국 과학교육에서의 창조설 신봉자와 진화론자 간의 갈등

| 정답 | ④

| 해설 | 본문은 미국의 과학교육 과정에서 창조설과 진화론 간의 갈등의 역사를 기술하고 있다. 따라서 답은 ④이다.

| 어휘 | motivation ⓝ 동기
fundamentalist ⓝ 근본주의 신자, 원리주의자
occasionally ⓐ 가끔, 이따금
introduce ⓥ 법안을 제출하다
bill ⓝ 법안
legislature ⓝ 입법부, 의회
confrontation ⓝ 대립
creationism ⓝ 창조설
be convicted of – ~로 유죄판결을 받다
ban ⓝ 금지령
biologist ⓝ 생물학자
essentially ⓐ 근본적으로, 본질적으로
validity ⓝ 유효함, 타당성
creationist ⓝ 창조설 신봉자
position ⓝ 입장, 견해
apparently ⓐ 겉보기에는
school board – 교육 위원회, 학교 이사회
impetus ⓝ 자극, 원동력
curriculum ⓝ 교육과정
lag behind – 뒤떨어지다
repeal ⓥ (법률을) 폐지하다
unconstitutional ⓐ 헌법에 위배되는, 위헌의
society ⓝ 학회, 협회
propagation ⓝ 선전, 보급
creation science – 창조과학
intelligent design – 지적설계
enter the fray – 설전에 가담하다
recognizable ⓐ 알아볼 수 있는, 인식 가능한
considerable ⓐ 상당한, 많은
literature ⓝ 문헌, 문건
deteriorate ⓥ 악화시키다, 더 나쁘게 하다
skeptical ⓐ 의심 많은, 회의적인
premise ⓝ (주장의) 전제
eulogy ⓝ 찬사

[14-17] 경희대 2013

예일 대학의 기원을 찾고자 한다면 이 신성시되는 미국의 고등 교육 기관이 위치한 뉴잉글랜드 지역 코네티컷 주 뉴헤이븐 시로 이동할 필요는 없다. 대신 인도 센네이에 위치한 포트 세인트 조지라는 이름의 오래된 영국의 보루로 향해야 한다. 바로 이곳에서 17세기 엘리후 예일이라는 인물이 동인도회사의 고위 관리로서 큰 부를 거머쥐었다. 그는 벌어들인 부를 활용해 1718년 마침내 대양을 건너 식민지 지역이었던 코네티컷 주에 있던 잘 알려져 있지 않던 학교에 한 상자의 책과 직물을 기부했다. 이들 물품은 결국 합계 562파운드라는 엄청난 금액에 팔렸고 이제 막 설립된 학교를 지탱하는 데 도움을 제공했으며, 이로 인해 학교는 그의 이름을 따게 되었다. 예일 대학은 이후 다섯 명의 대통령, 수많은 세계 지도자들, 여기에 수 세대에 걸친 미국의 전문가 집단을 배출했지만 만일 아시아와의 관계가 없었더라면 지금의 위상을 얻지 못했을 수도 있다. 거의 300년의 세월이 흘러 예일 대학과 동양과의 관계는 다시금 캠퍼스에서 벌어지는 여러 일들을 지배하고 있다. 동인도회사가 만들어 낸 또 하나의 결과물인 싱가포르와의 논란 많은 모험적 사업이 빠른 속도로 진행 중에 있다. 2013년 8월에 예일-싱가포르 국립대(NUS) 교양대학이 곧 학생들의 입학을 받을 예정이다. 예일 대학교의 운영진은 예일-NUS 교양대학을 아시아 최고의 교양대학이자 "비판적 사고와 교실 내 상호 작용"을 강조하는 교육기관으로 홍보했다. 작년 예일 대학 학장인 리차드 레빈은 다음과 같이 말했다. "19세기에 예일 대학이 미국 내 교양교육의 형태를 확립했던 것처럼 새로 설립된 예일-NUS 교양대학이 앞으로 수십 년 동안 아시아에서 설립될 수많은 교양대학들의 형태를 확립하는 데 있어 핵심적인 역할을 할 것임을 믿습니다."

14

윗글의 제목으로 적절한 것은?

① 예일 대학과 동양과의 연결고리
② 엘리후 예일이 부를 얻은 방식
③ 예일-NUS 교양대학
④ 필수 교양 과목 교육의 중요성

| 정답 | ①

| 해설 | 본문은 예일 대학이 과거 지금의 이름을 얻게 된 계기와 현재 예일-NUS 교양대학 설립에 관한 내용을 중심으로, 과거와 현재의 예일 대학과 동양과의 관계에 관해 논하고 있다. 따라서 답은 ①이다.

15

밑줄 친 ⓒ에 들어갈 알맞은 표현은?

① 만일 아시아와의 관계가 없었더라면
② 아시아와 관계를 맺고 있었기 때문에
③ 아시아와 관계를 맺고 있지 않기 때문에
④ 비문

| 정답 | ①

| 해설 | ⓒ 앞 주절에 조동사 would가 사용되었으면서 현재를 나타내는 what it is today란 표현이 쓰였음을 감안하면, ⓒ가 들어간 문장은 가정법 과거임을 유추할 수 있다. 따라서 ⓒ에는 가정법 과거의 조건절 문장이 들어가야 한다. "~이 없었더라면"의 의미를 지닌 if it were not for ~에서 도치가 일어난 것이 ①의 were it not for ~이다. 따라서 답은 ①이다.

16

밑줄 친 ⓐ hallowed, ⓑ fledgling, ⓓ pivotal의 가장 적절한 의미의 조합은?

① 신성한 – 급상승하는 – 주요한
② 신성한 – 치솟는 – 중요한
③ 신성시된 – 어린 – 주요한
④ 신성시된 – 저명한 – 주요한

| 정답 | ③

| 해설 | ⓐ의 hallowed는 '소중한, 신성시되는' 등의 의미를 가지며, '신성한'의 의미를 지닌 sacred 및 '(종교적 목적에 따라) 바쳐진[봉헌된], 신성시된'의 의미를 지닌 consecrated와 유사하다.
ⓑ의 fledgling은 '미숙한, 갓 태어난' 등의 의미를 가지며, 보기 중에서 이와 의미상 가장 유사한 것은 young뿐이다.
ⓓ의 pivotal은 '중심이 되는, 핵심적인' 등의 의미를 가지며, 보기에 제시된 네 단어 모두와 의미가 유사하다.
이런 사항들을 전부 조합해 보면, 보기 중에서 답으로 가장 적절한 것은 ③이다.

17

윗글의 내용과 일치하는 것은?

① 예일 대학교는 인도에서 처음으로 개교하였다.
② 예일 대학교는 처음부터 세계적으로 유명했다.
③ 예일-싱가포르 국립대의 교양대학은 논란이 되고 있다.
④ 예일 대학교는 영국의 동인도회사에 의해 설립되었다.

| 정답 | ③

| 해설 | 예일–NUS 교양대학은 본문에서 "싱가포르와의 논란 많은 모험적 사업(A controversial venture into Singapore)"으로 지칭된다. 따라서 답은 ③이다. 예일 대학은 식민지 시절 미국에 설립된 대학이며, 엘리후 예일의 기부 당시엔 잘 알려져 있지 못한 대학이었고, 본문에 영국의 동인도회사에 의해 설립되었다고 명시된 것은 싱가포르이다. 따라서 ①, ②, ④ 모두 답이 될 수 없다.

| 어휘 | hallowed ⓐ 소중한, 신성시되는
a carton of - 한 통, 한 상자
shore up - 강화하다, 지주를 받치다
fledgling ⓝ 풋내기, 갓 태어난 것 ⓐ 미숙한, 갓 태어난
myriad ⓐ 무수히 많은
apace ⓐⓓ 빠른 속도로, 빨리
tout ⓥ 광고하다, 홍보하다
sacred ⓐ 성스러운, 신성한
skyrocketing ⓐ 치솟는, 급상승하는
consecrated ⓐ (종교적 목적에 따라) 바쳐진[봉헌된], 신성시된

redoubt ⓝ 보루
obscure ⓐ 잘 알려지지 않은, 무명의
cognoscenti ⓝ 전문가
proceed ⓥ 진행되다
pivotal ⓐ 중심이 되는, 핵심적인
soaring ⓐ 급상승하는

[18-19] 중앙대 2013

미국에서는 1890년대에 고등교육의 지도가 완전히 변했다. 진화론 이후의 과학관에 맞춰 학습 구성을 조직해야 한다는 압박이 증가하고 자연진화에 대한 수용도가 높아지면서, 신의 개입이 제외된 인간의 작용에 대한 믿음이 신속하게 커졌다. 이는 과학적 탐구 및 설명을 위해 선호되던 방식을 바꿔놓았다. 점차 혁신과 진보가 전문화 및 실험과 연계되기 시작했으며, 하나의 결과가 새로운 학문 분야를 증대시켰다. 이러한 발전 상황에 도전을 받게 된 철학은 전면적인 변화를 겪게 된다. 한때는 성직자로서 훈련을 받은 사람만의 독점적인 영역이었던 철학은 이제는 세속적인 학문 분야가 되었다. 게다가 범위가 광활하면서 심지어 포괄적이기까지 했던 철학은 이제는 초점이 더 좁혀졌다. 자연철학이 이전에 다양한 자연과학으로 발달한 것처럼 이제는 도덕철학도 다양한 사회과학으로 발달했다. 실험실에서 연구되던 심리학 가운데 이러한 측면도 별도의 학문으로 정의가 내려지게 되었다. 20세기가 시작되기 전에 심리학자들은 의사소통을 촉진시키고 새로 생긴 자신들만의 공동체의 자율성을 드러내기 위해 자체적인 전문 협회 및 학술지를 개발했다. 철학에서 심리학을 분리한 것은 교육 차원에서도 중요한 결과를 낳았는데, 당시는 교육이 대학의 연구 분야로 새로 수용되기 시작되던 시점이었다. 심리학이 정신적 기능 및 구조에 대한 연구도 포함하기 때문에 교육과의 연관성 또한 분명했다. 게다가 추상적인 가치나 신학적 믿음의 지도를 받아 진리를 추구하는 학문 분야인 철학과는 달리 심리학은 실증적인 연구가 포함된다. 교육에 과학적 기반을 제공하는 것으로 보이는 심리학은 교육에 관심을 지닌 교사와 개혁가들 사이에서 인기 있는 주제가 되었다.

18 논지의 흐름상 빈칸에 들어가기에 가장 적합한 것을 고르시오.
① 혁신적인 운동에도 불구하고 철학은 워싱턴의 엘리트층 사이에서 흠잡을 곳이 없었다.
② 이러한 발전 상황에 도전을 받은 철학은 전면적인 변화를 겪었다.
③ 패러다임 변화로 인해 동기를 부여받은 철학은 다양한 분야로부터의 반박을 수용했다.
④ 드러난 것처럼 철학은 자연과학으로부터의 객관적인 연구 차원의 접근을 피했다.

| 정답 | ②

| 해설 | 빈칸 앞에서 "새로운 학문 분야를 증대시켰다(new disciplines multiplied)"는 "이러한 발전 상황(these developments)"을 가리키는 것으로 볼 수 있으며, 빈칸 뒤의 철학이 겪은 변화는 "철학은 전면적인 변화를 겪었다(philosophy underwent a thoroughgoing transformation)"로 표현한 것으로 볼 수 있다. 따라서 답은 ②이다.

19
아래의 문장이 들어갈 위치로 가장 적합한 곳을 고르시오.

> 이는 철학에게는 없는 "객관적 과학"의 분위기를 심리학에 부여했다.

① (A) ② (B) ③ (C) ④ (D)

| 정답 | ④

| 해설 | (D) 앞의 "심리학은 실증적인 연구가 포함된다(psychology involved empirical research)"에서 '실증적'이란 '객관적 방법을 통한 증명'을 의미하며, 주어진 문장의 this가 가리키는 대상으로 볼 수 있다. 즉, 이런 실증적 연구를 통해 철학이 '객관적 과학'의 분위기를 지니게 된 것이다. 따라서 답은 ④이다.

| 어휘 | higher learning – 고등교육
mount ⓥ (서서히) 증가하다
agency ⓝ 힘, 작용
grow apace – 빨리 자라다
thoroughgoing ⓐ 전면적인, 완전한
province ⓝ 분야, 영역
secular ⓐ 세속적인
comprehensive ⓐ 포괄적인, 종합적인
association ⓝ 협회
mark ⓥ 특징짓다, 드러내다
empirical ⓐ 실증적인
inside the Beltway – 워싱턴의 엘리트층[특권층] 사이에서
contradiction ⓝ 모순, 반박
lend ⓥ 주다, 부여하다
profoundly ⓐⓓ 완전히
around ⓟⓡⓔⓟ ~에 맞춰
apart from – ~을 제외한, ~ 외에도
discipline ⓝ 학문 분야
exclusively ⓐⓓ 배타적으로, 독점적으로
ministerial ⓐ 각의의; 성직자의
expansive ⓐ 광활한
mental philosophy – 심리학
autonomy ⓝ 자율성, 자주성
theological ⓐ 신학의
impeccable ⓐ 흠잡을 데 없는, 결점이 없는
shun ⓥ 피하다

[20-21] 중앙대 2013

난독증은 전통적으로 배타적인 범주에 따라 정의되어 왔다. 이 용어는 아이가 딱히 분명히 드러나는 이유 없이 효과적인 읽기 기술을 습득하는 데 매우 어려움을 겪는 상황을 묘사하기 위해 사용된다. 감각이나 지능 또는 신경의 장애, 말 및 언어 장애, 정서 또는 행동 장애, 교육 기회의 부재 등은 이러한 어려움의 원인이라 할 수는 없다. "특정 읽기 장애" 또는 "읽기 장애" 등의 용어가 이러한 상태를 가리키기 위해 바꿔 가면서 사용된다. 난독증에 대한 이러한 배타적인 정의는 아직 증명되지 않은 추정으로 가득하다. 평균적인 지적 능력을 갖추었지만 읽기에 어려움을 겪는 (즉, 읽기 불일치 범주에 속하는) 아이들은 지능이 낮은 것에 비례하여 읽기에 어려움을 겪는 아이들과는 다른 유형의 어려움을 겪고 있다.

연구진이 주장하는 바에 따르면, 이러한 가설을 입증할 만한 일관성 있는 증거는 거의 존재하지 않는다. 예를 들어 난독증을 앓고 있는 것으로 진단된 아이는 낮은 지적 능력과 일치하여 읽기에 어려움을 겪는 아이와 매우 유사한 이해 과정을 보여주었다. 대규모의 발달 연구에 따르면 읽기 능력은 갖추고 있지만 언어적 지적 능력에 차이를 보이는 두 집단의 아동의 경우 다수의 소리 인지 과업을 수행한 결과에 차이를 보이지 않았다. 게다가 지능검사의 타당성에 전반적으로 의문이 제시될 뿐 아니라 지능검사와 읽기에 어려움을 겪는 사람들 간의 관계에도 문제가 제기되며, 그 이유는 이러한 지능검사에는 읽기 경험이 있는 것만으로도 성과가 향상될 수 있는 검사가 들어있기 때문이다. 하지만 현저하게 뛰어난 지적 능력을 갖춘 사람에게도 난독증이 있을 수 있다는 것이 밝혀져 있다. 토마스 에디슨, 알베르트 아인슈타인, 오귀스트 로댕 등은 효과적인 읽기 또는 쓰기 능력을 습득하기 위해 애를 쓴 "명성 높은 사람들"의 예이다.

20 빈칸에 들어가기에 가장 적합한 것을 고르시오.
① ~와 매우 다른 행동 패턴을 보여주었다
② ~와 매우 유사한 회복력을 드러냈다
③ ~와 매우 다른 지적 능력을 보여주었다
④ ~와 매우 유사한 이해 과정을 보여주었다

| 정답 | ④

| 해설 | 본문을 보면 지적 능력이 낮은 아이들은 어찌 보면 읽기에 어려움을 겪는 것이 당연하다 볼 수 있지만, 지적 능력은 평균 수준임에도 읽기에 어려움을 겪는 아이들도 있음을 알 수 있고 이런 아이들이 난독증의 범주에 속함을 알 수 있다. 즉, 난독증을 겪는 아이들은 지적 능력이 떨어지는 아이와는 다른 유형의 어려움을 겪고 있는 것이다. 문제는 과연 무엇을 난독증이라 할지 가설을 세워도 이를 입증할 수 있는 일관성 있는 증거가 존재하지 않는 것이다. 따라서 "난독증을 앓고 있는 것으로 진단된 아이(children diagnosed as having dyslexia)"와 "낮은 지적 능력과 일치하여 읽기에 어려움을 겪는 아이(children whose reading difficulties were consistent with their lower intellectual abilities)"가 서로 "매우 유사한 이해 과정을 보여주고" 있으므로, 겉으로는 둘 다 읽기를 잘못하는 것으로 보이고, 난독증이라 할 만한 일관성 있는 증거가 없으므로 어느 쪽을 난독증이라 할지 문제가 되는 것이다. 따라서 답은 ④이다.

21 윗글을 통해 추론할 수 있는 것으로 가장 적합한 것을 고르시오.
① 대체로 지능이 낮은 아이들은 지능이 높은 아이들에 비해 읽기 능력을 습득하는 데 있어 어려움을 겪을 가능성이 더 높다.
② 발달 연구의 결과는 아이의 지능검사 점수와 아이가 읽기에 어려움을 겪는 것 간에는 양의 상관관계가 있음을 설명하는 데 크게 쓸모가 있다.
③ 아이가 읽기 능력에 큰 어려움을 겪는 원인으로 다수의 요인을 들 수 있지만, 말 및 언어 장애가 가장 결정적인 것이다.
④ 아이들은 소리 인지 능력에 차이가 없더라도 읽기 능력을 쉽게 획득할 수 있을지 여부에는 서로 차이가 존재할 수 있다.

| 정답 | ④

| 해설 | "대규모의 발달 연구에 따르면 읽기 능력은 갖추고 있지만 언어적 지적 능력에 차이를 보이는 두 집단의 아동의 경우 다수의 소리 인지 과업을 수행한 결과에 차이를 보이지 않았다(A large-scale developmental study demonstrated that the performance of two groups of young children with reading ability, who also demonstrated differing levels of verbal intellectual ability, did not differ on a number of sound awareness tasks)." 이를 역으로 말하면, 소리 인지 과업 수행 결과는 차이가 없더라도 언어적 지적 능력 또는 읽기 능력에는 차이가 발생할 수 있다. 따라서 답은 ④이다. 참고로 본문에는 지능 차이에 따른 읽기 능력의 차이가 구체적으로 나와 있지 않으므로 ①은 답이 될 수 없다.

| 어휘 | dyslexia ⓝ 난독증
attribute A to B - A를 B의 결과로[덕분으로] 보다
neurological ⓐ 신경의
be fraught with - ~ 투성이다, ~로 가득하다
be commensurate with - ~에 비례하다, ~에 어울리다
validate ⓥ 입증하다
decode ⓥ 해독하다, 이해하다
exclusionary ⓐ 배타적인, 제외적인
impairment ⓝ 장애
hypothesis ⓝ 가설, 추정
validity ⓝ 유효함, 타당성

foster ⓥ 조성하다, 발전시키다
eminence ⓝ 명성, 탁월함
account for – ~을 설명하다
markedly ⓐⓓ 현저하게, 두드러지게
resilience ⓝ 회복력, 탄력
positive correlation – 양의 상관관계

[22-24] 성균관대 2017

우리는 '단과대학(college)'과 '종합대학(university)'이라는 용어를 서로 혼용해서 쓴다. 우리는 "그녀는 미시간에 다녔다."라고 말하거나 "그는 오벌린에 다닌다."라고 말한다. 마치 college와 university가 같은 의미가 있는 것처럼 이름 뒤에 오는 명사는 그다지 신경을 쓰지 않는다. 두 용어는 같지 않다. 확실히 두 용어는 서로 연관성이 있으며, college는 university 내에 학부로 존재할 수 있다. 하지만 college와 university는 서로 다른 목적을 가지고 있다. A 전자인 college는 과거의 지식을 학부생들에게 전달해 주기 위한 것으로, 학부생들은 이것을 미래를 살아갈 자원으로 활용할 수 있다. 후자인 university는 과거를 대체할 새로운 지식을 창조하려는 목표로 교수진과 대학원생들이 수행하는 다수의 연구 활동이 주를 이룬다. B 이 둘은 모두 가치 있는 목표이며, college에 다니는 학부생이 최첨단 연구나 획기적인 연구를 수행하는 학자나 과학자와 협업하는 경우 두 목표가 서로 만나기도 한다. 하지만 명성의 사다리를 타고 위로 올라가는 경우(더 수준 높은 연구를 진행하게 되는 경우) 이 둘의 목표는, 갈등까지는 아니더라도, 경쟁 관계에 놓이게 된다. C 세계에서 가장 우수한 종합대학 중 하나인 캘리포니아 대학교의 설립자는 "뛰어난 교수일수록 학부생의 수업에 대한 관심이 낮아질 수 있다."라고 이례적으로 솔직하게 시인한 바 있다. D (캘리포니아 대학교 총장인) 클라크 커(Clark kerr)가 거의 50년 전에 이러한 '잔인한 역설(cruel paradox)'을 우리가 당면한 보다 긴박한 문제라고 확인했다. 오늘날 이 문제는 그 어느 때보다 더 긴박하다. E 하지만 정확히 단과대학(college)에서 문제가 되는 것은 무엇이고, 그곳에서 얼마나 많은 일이 혹은 얼마나 적은 일이 진행되고 있느냐 하는 것이 중요한 이유는 무엇일까? F 본질적으로 단과대학은 젊은 사람들이 청소년기와 성인기 사이에 놓인 지형을 통과하는 데 도움이 될 수 있는 곳이어야 한다. 그곳은 자기 인식을 향해 나아가는 여정에서 험난한 지형을 건너기 위해 노력하는 대학생들에게 강요가 아닌 안내를 제공해 주는 곳이어야 한다. 그곳은 사색적인 시민을 위해 필요한 특정한 정신과 마음의 자질을 기르는 것을 도와주는 곳이어야 한다.

22 다음 중 밑줄 친 "Both of these"가 지칭하는 것은?
① 단과대학과 종합대학
② 대학원생과 학부생
③ 교육과 연구
④ 과거와 미래
⑤ 전통과 최첨단 과학

| 정답 | ③

| 해설 | 밑줄 친 부분이 포함된 전체 문장이 "Both of these are worthy aims"이므로, 주어인 'Both of these'는 앞에 제시된 목표(aims)를 지칭하는 것으로 ①과 같이 대학을 지칭하고 있는 것이 아니다. 앞에서 단과대학의 목표는 '과거의 지식 전수'라고 했고, 종합대학의 목표는 과거의 지식을 대체할 '새로운 지식의 창출'이라고 했다. '과거의 지식 전수'는 '교육'을 의미하고, '새로운 지식의 창출'은 '연구'를 의미하므로, 정답은 ③이 된다.

23 다음 중 밑줄 친 "cruel paradox"가 의미하는 것은?
① 단과대학이 종합대학보다 더 나을 수 있다
② 위대한 학자가 꼭 위대한 스승인 것은 아니다
③ 단과대학의 졸업장이 좋은 직장을 보장해 주지 않는다
④ 종합대학 교수가 단과대학 교수보다 더 잘 가르칠 수 있다
⑤ 학생들의 대학 생활을 통해 많은 것을 배우지 못한다

| 정답 | ②

| 해설 | 밑줄 친 '잔인한 역설'이란 캘리포니아 대학교 설립자가 말한 "a superior faculty results in an inferior concern for undergraduate teaching"을 의미한다. 뛰어난 교수(superior faculty)라도 학부생의 수업에 대한 관심은 뛰어나지 않을 수(inferior) 있다는 말이므로, 상호 모순에 해당하는 역설적인 말이 되어, '위대한 학자가 꼭 위대한 스승인 것은 아니다'는 ②와 비슷한 의미를 지니게 된다.

24

본문을 세 개의 문단으로 나눌 경우 가장 적합한 지점은 어느 곳인가?
① A C ② A D
③ B D ④ B E
⑤ C F

| 정답 | ④

| 해설 | 첫 문단은 B 앞까지로, 단과대학과 종합대학이 각각 지향하는 목표의 차이에 대해 서술하고 있다. 두 번째 문단은 B부터 E까지로, 앞에서 말한 두 목표의 차이가 일치하기도 하고 가끔은 경쟁하기도 한다고 설명하면서, 역설적인 상황에 놓이기도 한다고 설명하는 대목이다. 마지막 문단은 E 이후로, 단과대학이 지향해야 할 목표에 대해 서술하고 있다.

| 어휘 | term ⓝ 용어; 임기
not bother with – ~에 신경 쓰지 않다
to be sure – 틀림없이
division ⓝ (조직의) 분과
transmit ⓥ 보내다, 송달하다, 전하다
draw upon – ~을 이용하다, ~에 의지하다
an array of – 다수의
graduate student – 대학원생
supersede ⓥ 대신하다
cutting-edge ⓐ 최첨단의
come into competition – 경쟁하다
ladder ⓝ 사다리
paradox ⓝ 역설
at stake – 성패가 달려 있는, 위태로운
navigate ⓥ 나아가다, 항해하다, 길을 찾다
adolescence ⓝ 청소년기, 사춘기
guidance ⓝ 지도, 안내
treacherous ⓐ 배반하는, 반역하는, (특히 겉보기와 달리) 위험한
terrain ⓝ 지형, 지역
reflective ⓐ 생각이 깊은, 사색적인
decent ⓐ 꽤 좋은, 만족할 만한; 예의 바른, 점잖은
interchangeably ⓐⓓ 상호 교환해서
noun ⓝ 명사
interconnect ⓥ 서로 연결하다[관련되다]
the former – 전자
undergraduate student – 학부생
the latter – 후자
faculty ⓝ 교수진; 능력
with the aim of ~ing – ~을 지향하여, ~을 목표로
converge ⓥ 모이다, 모아지다
groundbreaking ⓐ 신기원을 이룬, 획기적인
if not – [정도의 대조] ~까지는 아니라 하더라도
prestige ⓝ 명성, 위신
pressing ⓐ 긴급한, 중요한
matter ⓥ 중요하다
territory ⓝ 지역, 영토
adulthood ⓝ 성인, 성년
coercion ⓝ 강요
requisite ⓐ 필요한
diploma ⓝ 학위, 졸업장

[25-27] 홍익대 2018

로렌스 콜버그(Lawrence Kohlberg)의 도덕 발달 단계는 엄청난 영향력을 지니고 있으며 널리 받아들여지고 있다. 콜버그는 피아제의 연구를 기반으로 삼았으며, 아이들과 청년들, 어른들이 도덕적 추론을 이용해 해결책을 제시하는 과정을 살펴보기 위해 일련의 딜레마를 만들어 냈다. 그는 도덕 발달이 세 가지 단계로 이루어진다고 결론을 짓고, 이를 전관습적 단계(6∼13세), 관습적 단계(13∼16세), 후관습적 단계(16세 이상)로 구분했다.

전관습적 단계에서는 아이들이 자신만의 도덕적 추론에 의해 이끌리지 않고, 그들의 부모와 보호자를 따른다. 아이들은 보상을 구하거나 처벌을 피하기 위해 이런 일들을 수행한다. 처벌과 복종을 통해 아이들은 자신의 행동이 낳은 결과를 살펴봄으로써 무엇이 옳고 그른지를 알아낸다. 개인주의와 도구적 목적은 아이들이 어떤 행동과 행위가 보상을 받는지 배우는 결과를 낳는다. 그 아이는 또한 처벌을 의미할 수 있는 행동을 기피하는 법을 배운다. 전관습적 단계가 끝날 때쯤 아이는 사람들을 돕는 것을 즐기기 시작하고, "내가 너를 도와주면, 너도 나를 도울 수 있을 거야"라는 접근방식을 배우게 된다.

관습적 단계는 집단행동에 대한 인식과 사회에서 받아들여질 수 있는 것과 그렇지 않은 것에 대한 사고 등으로 구성된다. 이 단계에서 아이들은 서로간의 상호적 기대, 관계, 그리고 순응을 인식하게 된다. 아이들은 좋은 행동이 다른 사람들, 예를 들어 부모, 친구, 교사를 기쁘게 한다고 믿게 된다. 그들은 또한 "그가 일부러 그것을 떨어뜨린 것이 아니야. 그는 도와주려고 했던 거야."와 같이 동기의 요인을 인식하게 된다. 또한 그들은 사회의 필요와 관심을 더 잘 인식하게 되고, 사회가 옳거나 그른 것으로 간주하는 것을 더 잘 인식하게 된다. 그들은 규정과 법을 더 잘 지키려고 한다.

25 다음 중 글을 쓴 목적으로 가장 적합한 것은?
① 어린 시절의 도덕 발달을 설명하기 위해서
② 아동의 연령과 정신적 성장을 기술하기 위해서
③ 어릴 때 부모의 중요성을 설득하기 위해서
④ 지적 발달을 위한 사례를 제공하기 위해서

| 정답 | ②

| 해설 | 이 글은 개인의 도덕 발달(moral development)이 어떤 식으로 이뤄지는지에 대해 연구한 로렌스 콜버그의 이론을 소개하는 글이며, 개인의 도덕 발달이 세 가지 단계를 거쳐 발전한다고 제시하면서 그중 앞의 두 단계를 설명하고 있다. ①이 정답으로 적합하지만 '유아기(early childhood)'의 아이만 대상으로 한 것이 아니므로 오답이 된다. 정답은 ②로, '도덕의 발달'을 정신이 성장해 가는 것으로 표현한 것이다.

26 다음 중 본문의 내용과 일치하는 것은?
① 14세의 아이는 전근대적 단계의 도덕 발달을 보인다.
② 피아제는 콜버그의 연구를 비판했으며, 세 단계로 구성된 아동 발달을 제시했다.
③ 13∼16세의 아이들은 인간 행동의 기저에 위치한 동기를 이해하기 시작한다.
④ 도덕 발달에서, 관습적 단계 이후 전관습적 단계가 그 뒤를 따른다.

| 정답 | ③

| 해설 | ① 14세의 아이는 관습적 단계(13∼16세)의 도덕 발달을 보인다. ② 세 단계로 구성된 아동의 도덕 발달을 제시한 사람은 피아제가 아니라 콜버그였다. 또한 콜버그는 피아제의 연구를 바탕으로 자신의 연구를 제안한 것이므로, 서로의 연구에 대해 비판적 입장을 취하지 않는다. ④ 순서가 서로 바뀐 것으로 관습적 단계 이후에는 후관습적 단계가 이어져야 한다. 정답은 ③으로, 본문의 'They are also becoming aware of the motive factor' 부분을 재진술한 것이다.

27 다음 중 본문 이후 이어질 내용으로 가장 적합한 것은?
① 피아제 연구에 대한 콜버그의 비판적 논평
② 우정이 도덕 발달에 미치는 영향
③ 도덕 발달과 인지 발달에 대한 이유
④ 아이들의 후관습적 도덕 발달

| 정답 | ④

| 해설 | 첫 번째 문단 후반부에서 도덕 발달이 세 가지 단계로 이루어진다고 했고, 이를 각각 전관습적, 관습적, 후관습적 단계로 구분했다. 그 이후 전관습적 단계와 관습적 단계에 대해 각각 소개했으므로, 본문 이후에는 후관습적 단계를 소개하는 내용이 이어져야 한다. 따라서 정답은 ④가 된다.

| 어휘 | moral development – 도덕 발달
be widely accepted – 일반적으로 받아들여지다
build on – ~을 기반으로 하다, ~의 위에 쌓다
Piaget ⓝ 피아제(1896–1980 스위스의 아동 심리학자)
dilemma ⓝ 딜레마, 진퇴양난
consist of – ~로 구성되다
consequence ⓝ 결과, 중대성
instrumental ⓐ [심리학] 도구적인, 포상을 조건으로 하는, 시행착오적인
result in – (결과적으로) ~을 낳다[야기하다]
acceptable ⓐ (사회적으로) 용인되는[받아들여지는]
be aware of – ~을 알다, 의식하다
interpersonal ⓐ 대인관계에 관련된
motive factor – 동기 요인
deem ⓥ ~로 여기다, 생각하다
regulation ⓝ 규정
cognitive ⓐ 인지의, 인식적인
influential ⓐ 영향력 있는
moral reasoning – 도덕 추론
obedience ⓝ 순종, 복종, 충실
individualism ⓝ 개성, 개인주의
awareness ⓝ 의식, 관심
mutual ⓐ 서로의, 상호관계가 있는
conformity ⓝ 순응
not mean to – 의도한 것은 아니다
be keen to – ~하고 싶어 하다, ~에 열중해 있다
be followed by – 뒤이어 ~가 계속되다

[28-30] 국민대 2016

미국 전역의 어린 아이들이 매년 8월 말 또는 9월 초에 방학을 마치고 학교로 돌아간다. 그러나 모턴(Moton) 초등학교 학생들은 여름방학이 7월 10일에 끝났다. 그 날, 아이들은 3년 차에 접어든 시범 프로그램을 위해 학교로 돌아갔다. 이 프로그램으로 인해 일반적으로 180일인 한 학년도에 40일의 수업일수가 더 추가되게 된다. 그들은 긴 여름방학이라는 미국의 오랜 전통을 깨고 있었다. 여름방학이 긴 것은 늦여름 수확을 위해 가족의 노동력이 절실했던 시절로 거슬러 올라가며, 긴 여름방학으로 인해 미국은 다른 산업 국가 중에서 가장 짧은 학년도를 갖는 국가 중 하나가 됐다. 여름방학이 길어서 학년도의 수업일수가 다른 공업국에 비해 적다는 특징과 미국 학생들의 학업 성취도가 형편없는 것은 다른 국가의 학생들과 비교할 때 분명한 연관성이 있다. 점점 더 많은 미국인들이 이 아이디어를 지지한다. 갤럽이 이런 주제에 대해 지난 1958년 이래 계속 조사한 바에 따르면 지난 주 처음으로 표본 응답자의 대다수가 더 긴 학년도를 선호한다는 것을 발견했다. 모턴 초등학교의 대부분의 학부모는 또한 학교 수업시간이 길어지는 것을 강력히 지지하며, 이전 시스템으로 복귀하는 것에 대해 걱정하고 있다. 더 긴 학년도에 대해 주의 깊게 들여다 볼 시간이 왔다. 우리가 교육에 대해 얼마나 진지한지를 판단할 시금석이 될 것이다. 요즘 미국이 수확해야 하는 여름철의 수확은 농장에 있는 것이 아니라 아이들의 두뇌 속에 담겨 있다.

28

다음 중 본문의 제목으로 가장 적합한 것은?

① 더 긴 학년도에 대한 필요성
② 방학에 대한 아이들의 기대
③ 낡은 학업 시스템으로의 회귀
④ 미국과 다른 나라들의 농장 수확

| 정답 | ①

| 해설 | 미국 학생들의 학업 성취도가 낮은 이유가 1년 중 수업일수가 부족해서라고 설명하고 있다. 그리고 이렇게 수업일수가 부족한 이유로 긴 여름방학을 들고 있다. 하지만 이제 여름방학이 줄어들면서 수업일수가 늘어가고 있고 사람들의 인식 또한 변하고 있다고 설명하는 글이다. 따라서 이 글은 1년 중 수업일수가 증가해야 한다는 내용을 담은 ①이 제목으로 적합하다.

29

다음 중 밑줄 친 Ⓐ dismal과 가장 가까운 단어는?

① 비참한　　　　　　　② 지속적인
③ 향상된　　　　　　　③ 아주 뛰어난

| 정답 | ①

| 해설 | Ⓐ의 dismal은 '음울한, 울적하게 하는'이라는 뜻을 가진 단어이므로 ①의 miserable(비참한)과 비슷한 뜻을 지닌다.

30

다음 중 본문의 내용과 일치하는 것은?

① 모든 초등학교 학부모들은 교육에 대해 진지하지 않다.
② 우리는 다른 대부분의 산업 국가가 미국보다 더 긴 학년도를 갖는다는 것을 알 수 있다.
③ 모든 초등학교는 작년부터 더 긴 학년 일수를 갖기 시작했다.
④ 학년도에 관한 두 번째 갤럽 조사는 첫 번째 조사가 실시된 지 오랜 시간이 흐른 이후 실시됐다.

| 정답 | ②

| 해설 | 본문의 "They were breaking a long-standing American tradition of summer vacation ... that gives the U.S. one of the shortest school years in the industrialized world." 부분을 통해 ②의 내용을 확인할 수 있다.

| 어휘 | troop ⓥ 무리를 지어 걸어가다　　　　youngster ⓝ 젊은이, 청소년
　　　　long-standing ⓐ 오래 지속되는, 오랜　　date back to – (시기 따위가) ~까지 거슬러 올라가다
　　　　vital ⓐ 중요한　　　　　　　　　　　dismal ⓐ 음울한, 울적하게 하는
　　　　academic performance – 학업 성적　　peer ⓝ 동료
　　　　poll ⓥ 여론 조사를 실시하다　　　　favor ⓥ 선호하다
　　　　litmus test – 리트머스 시험; 그것만 보면 사태[본질]가 분명해지는 일; 시금석
　　　　reap ⓥ (특히 좋은 결과 등을) 거두다[수확하다]

CHAPTER 05 경제·경영

01	①	02	①	03	④	04	①	05	④	06	④	07	②	08	③	09	④	10	③
11	②	12	①	13	④	14	①	15	③	16	④	17	④	18	③	19	④	20	③
21	④	22	④	23	②	24	②	25	①	26	②	27	④	28	②	29	②	30	②
31	②	32	②	33	④	34	②	35	②	36	①	37	②	38	④	39	①	40	②
41	②	42	④	43	①	44	②	45	④	46	①	47	②	48	③	49	⑤	50	②

[01-02] 중앙대 2008

인구증가가 저개발국가의 경제성장을 방해한다는 여러 주장들이 제기되고 있다. 먼저 그런 국가의 경제는 의존도가 높은 부담을 갖게 된다. 무슨 말이냐면 아이들의 수가 이들을 부양해야 하는 근로자의 수에 비해 상대적으로 많다는 뜻이다. 인구가 증가한다는 것은 아이들의 수가 증가하는 것을 의미하기 때문에, 이런 부담이 늘어나게 되는 것이다. 이렇게 되면 아이들을 부양하는 일에 더 많은 노동력이 어쩔 수 없이 묶이게 되는 것을 의미한다. 게다가 투자목적을 위해 사용될 수 있는 자원이 현재 소비량을 충족시키는 데 사용된다. 이와 관련하여, 근로자 1인당 벌어들이는 자본형성량을 증가시키는 데 사용될 수 있는 자금(이것이 생산자본 혹은 사회간접자본이든 간에)이 대신 현존 시설물을 늘리는 데 필요하게 된다. 인구증가의 속도가 더 빨라질수록 근로자 1인당 자본형성량을 일정하게 유지하기 위해서 그만큼 더 많은 투자가 필요하다는 것이 입증되고 있다. 수치적으로 보면, 인구가 매년 1% 증가할 경우 근로자 1인당 노동장비량을 일정하게 유지하는 데만도 국민소득의 2.5~5%가 필요한 것으로 추산된다.

01 윗글에서 다음 문장이 들어갈 곳으로 가장 적합한 것을 고르시오.

> 이렇게 되면 아이들을 부양하는 일에 더 많은 노동력이 어쩔 수 없이 묶이게 되는 것을 의미한다.

① ⓐ   ② ⓑ   ③ ⓒ   ④ ⓓ

| 정답 | ①

| 해설 | 문제에서 제시된 them은 'caring for'를 통해 'children'을 지칭한다는 것을 알 수 있다. 보다 더 많은 노동력이 아이들을 부양하는 데 묶이게 될 수 있다고 했으므로, 바로 앞에 아이들의 수가 증가하는 내용이 등장하는 ⓐ가 답이 된다. 즉, 인구가 늘어난다는 것은 아이들이 늘어난다는 것이고, 아이들이 늘어나면 경제성장을 위해 쓰여야 하는 노동력이 아이들을 부양하는 데 쓰이게 되어 경제성장에 저해된다는 뜻이 된다.

02 윗글에 제시된 내용과 가장 일치하는 것을 고르시오.

① 저개발국가의 인구성장은 투자 목적을 위해 자원이 사용되는 것을 방해한다.
② 저개발국가의 인구성장은 노동비용의 감소로 이어진다.
③ 저개발국가의 인구성장은 노동력의 증가로 바로 이어진다.
④ 저개발국가의 인구성장은 경제성장과 양립할 수 있다.

| 정답 | ①

| 해설 | 저개발국가에서 인구가 증가하면, 아이들을 부양해야 하는 이유로 인해 노동력이 감소하고, 현재의 소비를 유지하는 데 추가 비용이 들어가는 등, 경제성장과 인구성장은 양립할 수 없다고 설명하고 있다. 본문에서 "resources that might have been used for investment purposes will be needed to satisfy current consumption"이라고 한 부분에서 투자목적으로 쓰일 수 있는 자원이 오히려 현재의 상태를 유지하는 데 쓰인다고 했으므로 이는 ①의 내용과 일치함을 알 수 있다.

| 어휘 | **bring forward** – 의견을 내다, 제기하다
underdeveloped ⓐ 저개발의, 후진국의
relative to – ~에 관하여; ~에 비례하여
the amount of capital per worker – 근로자 1인당 자본형성량
duplicate ⓥ 두 배로 하다, 이중으로 하다
numerical ⓐ 수의, 수와 관련된
per annum – (라틴어에서) 1년에
the amount of equipment per worker – 근로자 1인당 노동장비량
hinder ⓥ 방해하다, 훼방하다
dependency ⓝ 의존, 종속
consumption ⓝ 소비
social overhead capital – 사회간접자본(SOC)
reckon ⓥ 판단하다, 생각하다

[03-05] 한국외대 2016

2008년 금융위기 이래 달러화의 종말을 예견하는 목소리는 반복적으로 들리고 있다. 미국 경제가 불황에 빠지면서 달러화가 오랫동안 누려온 세계 제1의 준비통화로서의 지위를 계속 유지할 수 있을지에 관한 확신 또한 가라앉고 있었다. 하지만 이제 지금 상황을 보면, 금융위기 이후 여러 해가 지난 지금 달러화가 얼마나 대단한 통화인지가 여실히 드러나고 있다. 다른 통화와 비교하여 달러화의 가치를 측정하는 지표인 달러 인덱스는 최근 지난 4년 만의 최고치를 기록했다. 그리고 달러화에 비난을 가하던 정책입안자들은 달러 투매에 거의 관심을 보이지 않는다. 달러화의 부양은 미국이 세계 주요 경제대국 가운데 드물게도 상황이 좋은 국가임을 반영한다. 3분기 미국의 연간 국내총생산(GDP)은 3.5% 성장했으며 이는 다른 대부분의 선진국들이 발표한 것보다 훨씬 높다. 진정한 의미에서 달러화에 비할 만한 통화는 달리 존재하지 않는 것 또한 여전히 사실이다. 유로화의 안정성은 불확실하고 이는 여러 해 동안 진행된 국가 채무 위기와 이에 뒤이어 유럽의 지도자들이 보인 혼란스러운 반응을 통해 드러났다. 달러화의 독주가 얼마나 진행될지는 앞으로의 미국 GDP의 성장률에서부터 세계 경제의 건전성에 이르기까지 온갖 요소에 달려 있다. 장기적으로 달러화를 약화시킬 요소는 여럿 존재한다. 러시아와 중국은 양국 간의 거래를 점차 많이 루블화와 위안화로 결제하고 있다. 만일 다른 경제대국들이 러시아와 중국의 뒤를 따를 경우, 이는 점차적으로 달러화의 유용성을 낮추게 될 것이다. 하지만 지금 시점에서는 그럴 가능성은 매우 낮다.

03

문맥상 다음 중 빈칸 (A)와 (B)에 가장 적합한 것은 무엇인가?
① 대단히 귀중한 – 없애다
② 개연성이 낮은 – 보충하다
③ 민감한 – 이기다
④ 대단한 – ~에 비할 만하다

| 정답 | ④

| 해설 | (A): 빈칸 뒤를 보면 금융위기 이후 한때는 세계 제1의 준비통화로서의 달러의 위상에 의문을 가하던 목소리가 있었지만, 지금에 와서는 달러의 영향력은 결코 줄지 않고 오히려 증가하고 있음을 알 수 있다. 즉, 달러는 지금도 "대단한" 통화이다. 따라서 빈칸에는 almighty가 적합하다.
(B): 빈칸 뒤를 보면 달러화의 대항마로 여겨진 유로화 또한 달러에 비해 불안정한 통화임을 알 수 있다. 때문에 달

러화가 독주하고 있다는 표현도 등장한 것이며, 이에 비해 유로화는 달러화에 '비할 바가' 못 된다. 따라서 빈칸에는 rival이 적합하다.

이러한 점들을 감안했을 때 답으로 가장 적합한 것은 ④이다.

04 다음 중 (C)를 통해 암시되는 것은 무엇인가?
① 달러화의 안정성은 한동안 지속될 것이다.
② 다른 경제 대국들은 더 많이 달러화로 거래할 것이다.
③ 세계 경제의 건전성은 계속 약화된 상태일 것이다.
④ 러시아와 중국은 달러화의 유용성을 위협할지도 모른다.

| 정답 | ①

| 해설 | (C)를 해석하면 '하지만 지금 시점에서는 그럴 가능성은 매우 낮다'이다. 여기서 말하는 '그럴 가능성'이란 달러화 이외의 통화를 활용한 국제 거래의 규모가 증가하면서 달러화의 유용성이 떨어지는 사태를 의미한다. 하지만 그럴 가능성이 매우 낮다는 것, 즉 한동안 달러화의 안정성은 지속될 것임을 의미한다. 따라서 답은 ①이다.

05 다음 중 본문과 일치하지 않는 것은 무엇인가?
① 사람들은 미국 통화의 몰락을 예측해 왔다.
② 루블화 및 위안화 같은 다른 통화가 달러화에 도전할 가능성이 존재한다.
③ 미국의 GDP 성장률은 최근 다른 경쟁국의 GDP 성장률을 능가하고 있다.
④ 유럽의 부채에도 불구하고 유로화의 유용성은 여전히 강력한 채이다.

| 정답 | ④

| 해설 | "유로화의 안정성은 불확실하고 이는 여러 해 동안 진행된 국가 채무 위기와 이에 뒤이어 유럽의 지도자들이 보인 혼란스러운 반응을 통해 드러났다(The uncertain stability of the euro was exposed by its multiyear sovereign-debt crisis and the chaotic response that followed from Europe's leaders)." 여기서 답은 ④임을 알 수 있다.

"2008년 금융위기 이래 달러화의 종말을 예견하는 목소리는 반복적으로 들리고 있다(Ever since the 2008 financial crisis, predictions of the dollar's demise have come repeatedly)"는 ①에 해당되는 내용이며, "러시아와 중국은 양국 간의 거래를 점차 많이 루블화와 위안화로 결제하고 있다(Russia and China are settling more trade between the two nations in rubles and yuan)"는 ②에 해당되는 내용이고, "3분기 미국의 연간 국내총생산(GDP)은 3.5% 성장했으며 이는 다른 대부분의 선진국들이 발표한 것보다 훨씬 높다(American GDP in the third quarter grew an annualized 3.5% – far higher than what most other industrialized economies have been posting)"는 ③에 해당되는 내용이다.

| 어휘 | prediction ⓝ 예측, 예견　　　　demise ⓝ 종말, 죽음
recession ⓝ 불경기, 불황　　　　greenback ⓝ 미국 달러화 지폐
long-held ⓐ 오랫동안 간직해 온　　premier ⓐ 최고의, 제1의
reserve currency – 준비통화　　　almighty ⓐ 전능한, 대단한
dollar index – 달러 인덱스(세계 주요 6개국 통화에 대한 달러화의 평균적인 가치를 한눈에 보여주는 지표)

currency ⓝ 통화	dump ⓥ 투매하다, 덤핑하다
buoyancy ⓝ 부양, 시세가 오를 기미[경향]	annualized ⓐ 연간으로 환산한
post ⓥ 발표하다	rival ⓥ (~에) 필적하다[비할 만하다]
sovereign debt – 국가 부채[채무]	health ⓝ 건강[건전]성
undercut ⓥ 약화시키다	settle ⓥ 정산하다, 결제하다
powerhouse ⓝ 강국, 대국	follow suit – 뒤를 따르다, 선례를 따르다
chip away at – ~을 조금씩 갉아먹다[깎다]	utility ⓝ 효용성, 유용성
that's a big if – 가능성이 높지 않다, 가능성이 낮다	
priceless ⓐ 대단히 귀중한	eliminate ⓥ 없애다
improbable ⓐ 있을 수 없는, 개연성이 낮은	supplement ⓥ 보충하다, 추가하다
beat ⓥ 이기다; 억제하다	potential ⓝ 가능성
outstrip ⓥ 앞지르다, 능가하다	

[06-07] 광운대 2007

수년 전 내가 하버드 경영 대학원에서 경험이 많지 않던 조교수로 있던 시절에, 나는 경영상의 지도력을 발전시킬 수 있는 핵심은 순전히 지적 능력에 달려 있다고 생각했다. 나는 경영 대학원의 역할은 기업의 다양한 기능을 통달하고 있는 미래의 경영자들을 육성하는 것으로, 이들에게 문제를 간단명료하게 규정할 수 있는 방안과, 이들 문제를 분석할 수 있는 방안과, 대안을 논리적으로 분명하게 식별할 수 있는 방안을 알려주고, 마침내는 현명한 판단을 내릴 수 있도록 알려주는 것이라고 생각했다. 내 생각은 미국 밖에서 거주하고 일하면서 그리고 대학 학장으로 7년을 일하면서 차차 단련되었다. 나는 뱁슨 대학의 학장으로 일하면서 좋은 경영자라면 응당 갖춰야 할 자질 및 기술을 추가로 덧붙이게 되었다. 첫 번째는 스스로를 분명하고 뚜렷하게 표현할 수 있는 능력이다. 훌륭한 화법 및 글쓰기를 통한 의사소통 기술은 효과적인 경영자가 되려면 반드시 필수적인 기술이다. 두 번째는 지도력 기술이라 불리는 일련의 무형 자질을 보유해야 한다는 점이다. 좋은 지도자가 되려면 사람을 이해하고 사람의 기분을 헤아리는 데 세심해야 하고, 사람들에게 공동의 목표를 달성할 수 있도록 영감을 줄 수 있어야 한다. 세 번째는 내가 내린 결론에 따르면 효과적인 경영자는 업계에 대한 이해뿐 아니라 삶과 사회에 대한 문화, 사회, 정치, 역사, 그리고 특히 국제적 측면에 대한 감각을 지닌 지식이 넓은 인간이 되어야 한다. 이는 모든 경영자를 위한 교육 과정에 교양 과목 및 인문학을 다루는 과정이 들어가야 한다는 점을 나타낸다.

06 글쓴이의 주장이 아닌 것을 고르시오.
① 경영자는 사람들을 이해하고 이들에게 영감을 불어넣을 수 있어야 한다.
② 경영자는 훌륭한 의사소통 기술을 갖춰야 한다.
③ 저자는 경영자가 폭넓은 지식을 갖춰야 한다고 생각한다.
④ 경영자는 청렴한 사람이어야 한다.

| 정답 | ④

| 해설 | "좋은 지도자가 되려면 사람을 이해하고 사람의 기분을 헤아리는 데 세심해야 하고, 사람들에게 공동의 목표를 달성할 수 있도록 영감을 줄 수 있어야 한다(To be a good leader one must understand and be sensitive to people and be able to inspire them toward the achievement of common goals)"는 보기 ①의 근거로 볼 수 있으며, "훌륭한 화법 및 글쓰기를 통한 의사소통 기술은 효과적인 경영자가 되려면 반드시 필수적인 기술이다(Good oral and written communication skills are absolutely essential if one is to be an effective manager)"는 보기 ②의 근거로 볼 수 있고, "효과적인 경영자는 업계에 대한 이해뿐 아니라 삶과 사회에 대한 문

화, 사회, 정치, 역사, 그리고 특히 국제적 측면에 대한 감각을 지닌 지식이 넓은 인간이 되어야 한다(effective managers must be broad human beings who not only understand the world of business but also have a sense of the cultural, social, political, historical and, particularly, the international aspects of life and society)"는 보기 ③의 근거로 볼 수 있다. 하지만 보기 ④는 본문에 제시된 바 없으므로 답은 ④이다.

07

윗글의 ⓐ에 들어갈 수 있는 가장 적절한 표현을 고르시오.
① 둔한
② 뚜렷한
③ 지루한
④ 까다로운

| 정답 | ②

| 해설 | 빈칸 앞 쉼표를 통해 빈칸에 들어갈 말은 앞에 등장한 "분명한(clear)"과 유사한 의미의 단어임을 유추할 수 있다. 따라서 답은 ②이다. 만약 ②가 아닌 보기의 다른 단어를 대입할 경우 바로 뒤의 "좋은 지도자가 되려면 사람을 이해하고 사람의 기분을 헤아리는 데 세심해야 하고, 사람들에게 공동의 목표를 달성할 수 있도록 영감을 줄 수 있어야 한다"와 의미상 연결이 어색할 것이다.

| 어휘 |
assistant professor – 조교수
lie in – ~에 있다, ~에 위치하다
fashion ⓝ 방안, 방식
trait ⓝ 특성, 자질
intangible ⓐ 무형의
liberal arts – 교양 과목
exposure ⓝ 다룸(← 노출, 폭로)
blunt ⓐ 둔한
perplexing ⓐ 난처하게 하는, 까다로운

managerial ⓐ 경영의
succinctly ⓐⓓ 간단명료하게
temper ⓥ 단련하다
articulate ⓐ 뚜렷한, 분명한
sensitive ⓐ (남의 기분을 헤아리는 데) 세심한
humanities ⓝ 인문학
a man of integrity – 강직한 사람, 청렴한 사람
lengthy ⓐ 장황한, 지루한

[08-10] 항공대 2017

맬서스(Malthus)와 리카도(Ricardo)의 진정한 차이는 공급 과잉, 지대, 보호(무역주의)에 있지 않고, 오히려 (그것을 논증하는) 방법에 있었다. 두 사람은 모두 과학적 발견의 시대에 살았다. 그리고 두 사람 모두 (모든 경제 현상을) 인과관계로 설명하고자 했다. 그들은 이런 인과관계를 통해 미래에 무슨 일이 일어날지 예측했다. 하지만 리카도는 그 과정에 연이어져 있는 복잡한 단계들에 대해 매우 집중했다. 맬서스는 일반적 원리를 찾아내고 그것을 세상에 적용하는 것에 만족해하는 것 같았다. 앞서 리카도가 정체된 세상에 이르는 7단계 경로를 자세하게 분석했던 것을 떠올려 보자. 맬서스는 그런 엄격한 모델을 구성하지 않았다. 제임스 밀(James Mill)의 지도를 받았던 리카도는 긴 연역적 추리를 시도했다. 그는 유클리드 기하학 또는 뉴턴 역학만큼 분명한 경제의 명제들을 추론해 내고 싶어 했다. 때로는 그의 가설이나 제1전제가 완전히 잘못된 경우도 있었다. 하지만 그런 (확고한) 전제들을 세웠을 경우, 그의 이론은 상당히 견고하고 치밀했다. 논리가 견고하고 치밀한 것이 좋을 수는 있지만, 그렇다고 그것이 반드시 유용한 것은 아니다. 조지프 슘페터(Joseph Schumpeter)는 리카도가 자신이 의도하는 결과를 보장해 주는 가정이나 사례들만 선택하였다고 비난했다. 슘페터는 이것을 '리카도의 악행'이라고 불렀다.

08 다음 중 빈칸에 올 수 있는 가장 적합한 것은?

① 맬서스의 함정
② 리카도의 미덕
③ 리카도의 악행
④ 슘페터의 창조적 파괴

| 정답 | ③

| 해설 | 앞에서 "슘페터는 리카도가 자신이 의도하는 결과를 보장해 주는 가정이나 사례들만 선택하였다고 비난했다"는 내용을 통해, 슘페터가 리카도에 대해 그의 잘못이나 문제점을 지적한 내용이 와야 하므로, 정답은 ③이 적합하다.

09 다음 중 본문을 통해 추론할 수 있는 것은?

① 맬서스와 리카도는 고전 경제학의 주요 개념인 원인을 거의 동일하게 정의했다.
② 제임스 밀이 리카도의 방법론적 사고에 미친 영향은 미미하다.
③ 리카도는 그가 경험과 사례를 경시한 것에 대해 결코 비난받지 않았다.
④ 리카도는 경제가 수학과 같은 엄격한 과학이라고 믿었다.

| 정답 | ④

| 해설 | 본문에서 리카도는 "유클리드 기하학 또는 뉴턴 역학만큼 분명한 경제의 명제들을 추론해 내고 싶어 했다"는 내용을 통해, 경제학도 수학처럼 엄밀한 과학이라고 믿었다는 ④가 본문을 통해 추론할 수 있는 내용이 된다.

10 다음 중 본문의 내용과 일치하는 것은?

① 맬서스는 자신의 이론을 설명하기 위해 그 어떤 모델도 구성하지 않았다.
② 리카도의 이론은 모든 상황에서 유용했다.
③ 리카도와 맬서스를 나눈 중요한 사항 중 하나는 리카도가 경제 원칙을 도출하기 위한 단계를 중시했다는 점이다.
④ 리카도의 가정과 전제는 확고부동했다.

| 정답 | ③

| 해설 | ① 본문에서 "맬서스는 그런 엄격한 모델을 구성하지 않았다."는 내용은 모델 자체를 구성하지 않았다는 내용은 아니므로 적합하지 않다. ② "논리가 견고하고 치밀한 것이 좋을 수는 있지만, 그렇다고 그것이 반드시 유용한 것은 아니다."고 했으므로, 모든 상황에서 유용하다고 할 수는 없다. ④ 리카도의 전제가 완전히 틀린 경우도 있었다고 했으며, "그런 (확고한) 전제들을 세웠을 경우, 그의 이론은 상당히 견고하고 치밀했다"고 했으므로, 리카도의 가정과 전제는 항상 확고부동했다고 볼 수 없다. 정답은 ③으로, 맬서스와 리카도의 차이점은 방법론에 있다고 하면서, "Ricardo focuses more intensely on the intricate sequence of steps along the way."에서 경제 원칙을 도출하기 위한 단계를 중시했다고 말하고 있다.

| 어휘 | **revolve around** – ~의 주위를 돌다
glut ⓝ (공급) 과잉, 과다, 과식 ⓥ 과식시키다, 물리게 하다
rent ⓝ 지대, 임차료   **cause-and-effect** ⓐ 인과 관계의
intricate ⓐ 뒤얽힌, 복잡한
sequence ⓥ (유전자·분자의) 배열 순서를 밝히다; 차례로 배열하다

stationary ⓐ 움직이지 않는, 고정된
deductive ⓐ 연역적인
proposition ⓝ 제안, 계획; 명제
mechanics ⓝ 역학
impregnable ⓐ 난공불락의, (신념이) 확고한
vice ⓝ 악, 악덕, 비행, 범죄
inconsiderable ⓐ 적은; 중요치 않은, 하찮은, 사소한
methodological ⓐ 방법론의, 방법론적인
rigorous ⓐ 엄격한, 철저한
derive ⓥ 끌어내다, ~을 얻다
geometry ⓝ 기하학
premise ⓝ 전제; (pl.) 구내, 경내
virtue ⓝ 미덕
classical economics – 고전 경제학
invincible ⓐ 천하무적의, 아무도 꺾을[바꿀] 수 없는

[11-13] 경희대 2009

최근의 경제적 통계 수치가 미국뿐만 아니라 전 세계에서 두려움을 불러일으키는 것이 사실이다. 특히 제조업의 경우 어디서든 추락하고 있다. 은행에서는 더 이상 대출을 하지 않고 있으며, 기업과 소비자는 돈을 쓰지 않는다. 솔직히 까놓고 말하자면 현 상황은 2차 경제 대공황의 시작이라 해도 무방할 정도로 끔찍하다.

우리는 이런 상황에 처해서는 안 되었다. 오랜 시간 동안 대부분의 경제학자들은 또 다른 경제 대공황이 닥치지 못하게 막는 일은 쉬울 것이라 믿었다. 2003년 시카고 대학의 경제학자 로버트 루카스는 미국 경제학 협회에서 한 회장단 연설에서 불황 예방에 있어 주요 문제점들은 사실상 해결되었고, 실제로도 수십 년 동안 해결되어 왔다고 선언했다.

특히 밀턴 프리드먼은 연방준비제도 이사회라면 은행들에게 유동성을 제공하는 방식으로 즉각 대공황을 막을 수 있었을 것이고, 이를 통해 통화 공급량이 급격하게 떨어지는 일은 막았을 것이라고 수많은 경제학자들을 납득시켰다. 연방준비제도 이사회의 의장인 벤 버냉키는 연준위를 대신해 프리드먼에게 다음과 같은 유명한 사과의 말을 남겼다. "프리드먼 당신이 옳았습니다. 우리가 그랬습니다. 정말 죄송합니다. 하지만 덕분에 더 이상 그러지는 않을 것입니다."

하지만 불황을 예방하기란 전혀 쉬운 일이 아님이 드러났다. 버냉키의 지도하에서 연준위는 사방에서 경보가 울려 퍼지는 화재를 진압하려는 엔진실 승무원처럼 유동성을 공급했고, 통화 공급량은 급격히 증가했다. 하지만 신용은 여전히 부족하고, 경제는 아직도 자유 낙하 중이다.

통화정책이 경제 대공황을 예방할 수 있었다는 프리드먼의 주장은 불황일 때 통화정책은 효과가 없고 대량 실업에 맞서려면 정부의 대규모 적자 지출 같은 재정정책이 필요하다고 주장한 존 메이너드 케인스의 분석을 반박하려는 시도였다. 현재의 위기 상황에서 통화정책의 실패는 케인스가 애초에 옳았다는 것을 나타낸다.

11 본문에 따르면 프리드먼의 이론을 지지하는 많은 경제학자들은 경제 위기를 줄이기 위한 방법으로 통화 정책을 선호한다.
① 경제 불황에 맞서 효과적인 예방책을 고안했다
② 경제 위기를 줄이기 위한 방법으로 통화정책을 선호한다
③ 경제 대공황의 원인을 예측하는 데 성공적이었다
④ 경제 공황을 막기 위해 대규모의 지출 계획을 제공했다

| 정답 | ②

| 해설 | 프리드먼은 "통화정책이 경제 대공황을 예방할 수 있었다(monetary policy could have prevented the Great Depression)"는 주장을 편다. 따라서 답은 ②이다.

12

> 밑줄 친 부분은 연방준비제도 이사회 의장인 버냉키는 현재의 경제 정책을 신뢰하며 정책 방향을 바꾸지 않을 것임을 나타낸다.
> ① 현재의 경제 정책을 신뢰하며 정책 방향을 바꾸지 않을 것이다
> ② 추가적 고용을 위한 소비는 더 이상 권장해서는 안 된다는 점에 동의한다
> ③ 프리드먼의 시장 중심적 경제 정책에 문제가 있음을 인정했다
> ④ 돈을 부유한 사람보다 가난한 사람에게 빌려줘야 한다고 생각하는 프리드먼에 동의하지 않는다

| 정답 | ①

| 해설 | 버냉키의 사과는 과거 프리드만이 주장하는 방식을 따르지 않았기 때문에 대공황이 일어난 것에 대한 사과이며, 덕분에 이제는 더 이상 그렇지 않을 것임을 의미한다. 즉, 현재의 유동성 공급 위주 정책을 신뢰하고 있으며 앞으로도 변경하는 일 없이 계속 지속하겠다는 의미 표명이다. 따라서 답은 ①이다.

13

> 케인스주의 경제학자들에 관해 사실인 것은 무엇인가?
> ① 이들은 자유 시장을 위해 정부의 규제를 덜 요구한다.
> ② 이들은 경제 위기 동안에는 정부의 개입이 더욱 효과적이라고 생각한다.
> ③ 이들은 신용 부도를 막기 위해 무제한적인 은행 대출 및 기타 통화정책을 원한다.
> ④ 이들은 실직자를 위한 재정정책을 제공하는 작은 정부에 대해 반대하는 주장을 펼친다.

| 정답 | ②

| 해설 | "불황일 때 통화정책은 효과가 없고 대량 실업에 맞서려면 정부의 대규모 적자 지출 같은 재정정책이 필요하다 (monetary policy is ineffective under depression conditions and that fiscal policy—large-scale deficit spending by the government—is needed to fight mass unemployment)"는 것은 케인스의 주장이다. 따라서 답은 ②이다.

| 어휘 | plunge ⓥ 급락하다, 추락하다
for practical purposes – 사실상
in one's tracks – 그 자리에서, 즉각
on one's behalf – ~을 대신하여
monetary policy – 통화정책
fiscal policy – 재정정책
curtail ⓥ 단축하다, 줄이다
argue against – ~에 반대론을 펼치다
not mince one's words – 까놓고 솔직히 말하다
Federal Reserve – 연방준비제도 이사회
liquidity ⓝ 유동성
turn out – ~인 것으로 드러나다[밝혀지다]
refute ⓥ 반박하다
in favor of – 찬성하는, 지지하는
market-oriented ⓐ 시장 지향의, 시장 중심적인

[14-15]

바닥으로의 질주는 사회경제적 개념으로 국가들 간에 발생하는 것이다. 특정 무역 및 제품 분야에서 국가들 간의 경쟁이 치열해지면, 각국은 현재 존재하는 규제 기준을 폐지해야 할 동기가 더 커진다. 각국이 자유 무역이란 방향으로 나아가는 상황에서 노동력은 이제 바닥으로의 질주라는 모델의 영향을 매우 받기 쉽다. 전 세계적으로 이용 가능한 노동력은 넘쳐나고 자본을 이동할 수 있는 능력은 사실상 제한을 받지 않는 상황에서 다국적 기업들은 이제 자유로이 사업체를 나라에서 나라로 가장 가격이 맞는 노동력을 따라 옮겨 다닐 수 있다. 이는 결국 최저임금이나 시간외 수당을 의무화하는 것이 저임금 노동에 있어 엄청난 장애물로 작용하게 되는 개도국 같은 국가에서는 특히나 노동법에 영향을 주게 된다. 따라서 바닥으로의 질주는 더 많은 국가들 (다시 말하지만 특히 개도국에서) 노동법을 폐기하는 데 영향을 준다.

14 다음 중 본문에서 유추할 수 있는 것은 무엇인가?
① 바닥으로의 질주 모델은 노동법에 변화를 야기한다.
② 국제 무역은 개도국으로의 자본 흐름을 제한한다.
③ 값싼 노동력은 개도국보다 선진국에 집중된다.
④ 아웃소싱은 다국적 기업에게선 덜 일반적이다.

| 정답 | ①

| 해설 | "따라서 바닥으로의 질주는 더 많은 국가들(다시 말하지만 특히 개도국에서) 노동법을 폐기하는 데 영향을 준다[The race to the bottom therefore, dictates that more and more nations (again, particularly in the developing world) will eliminate their labor laws]." 여기서 답이 ①임을 유추할 수 있다.

15 빈칸에 가장 알맞은 것을 고르시오.
① 철저히 제한하다
② 영향을 전혀 받지 않는다
③ 영향을 매우 받기 쉽다
④ 필요한지 여부를 놓고 논쟁 중이다

| 정답 | ③

| 해설 | 노동 관련 법안이 자국의 노동을 보호하는 방향으로 나갈 경우 자본이 다른 곳으로 빠져나갈 위험이 있다는 것이 빈칸 뒤의 내용이다. 즉, 노동 문제는 바닥으로의 질주에 큰 영향을 받는다는 의미이다. 따라서 답은 ③이다.

| 어휘 | socioeconomic ⓐ 사회경제적인　　dismantle ⓥ 해체하다, 폐지하다
susceptible to – ~의 영향을 받기 쉬운, ~의 여지가 있는
pool ⓝ 이용 가능 인력　　virtually ⓐⓓ 사실상, 거의
unrestricted ⓐ 제한 받지 않는, 구속 받지 않는　　operation ⓝ 기업, 사업체
affordable ⓐ 감당 가능한, 가격이 맞는　　in turn – 결국, 결과적으로
dictate ⓥ ~을 좌우하다, ~에 영향을 주다　　concentrate ⓥ 집중하다
outsourcing ⓝ 아웃 소싱, 외부 위탁　　thoroughly ⓐⓓ 완전히, 철저히
immune to – ~에 영향을 받지 않는

[16-17] 중앙대 2009

증거금 계정은 모르는 사람에겐 불가사의하게 들린다. 실제로는 주식 중개인이 여러분의 주식을 담보 삼아 여러분에게 해 주는 대출에 불과하다. 증거금 계정이 어떤 방식으로 작동되는지 설명하자면 다음과 같다. 3천 달러를 예치하여 증거금 계좌를 개설했다고 가정해 보자. (모든 주식 중개인들은 증거금 계정 개설 시 최소한도의 예치 금액을 요구하며, 연방 준비제도 이사회에서는 구매 주식의 가치의 50%를 최초 증거금률로 규정하고 있다.) 그 다음에 ABC의 주식을 주당 50달러의 비용으로 100주 사들였다 치자. 이렇게 되면 3천 달러의 예치금을 가지고 수수료는 제외하고 5천 달러 상당의 주식을 구매한 것이다. 여기서 2천 달러는 분명히 중개인으로부터 온 금액이다. 아 만약에 주식의 가치가 오르거나 내리면 어떻게 될까? 오른다면 별 문제는 없다. 원하는 때면 언제든지 주식을 팔고 2천 달러에 이자를 더한 금액을 지불한 다음에 차액을 챙기면 된다. 만약에 내린다면, 손실은 모두 여러분의 몫이라는 간단한 사실을 기억해 두면 된다. 여러분은 손실을 중개인과 공유할 일은 없다. 때문에 ABC의 주식이 주당 30달러로 떨어진 다음에 판다면, 중개인은 그래도 이자 포함 2천 달러를 손에 쥐고, 여러분은 남은 금액을 얻게 된다. 이 경우엔 천 달러가 된다. 여러분은 2천 달러를 잃게 되며, 이는 주당 20달러에 100주를 곱한 금액이다.

16 저자는 증거금 계정을 어떻게 정의하고 있는가?
① 주식에 투자하여 잃은 것
② 주식에 투자하여 얻은 것
③ 주식 중개인이 여러분에게 지불한 것
④ 주식 중개인이 여러분에게 빌려준 것

| 정답 | ④

| 해설 | 본문에서는 증거금 계정을 "주식 중개인이 여러분의 주식을 담보 삼아 여러분에게 해 주는 대출에 불과하다(it is nothing more than a loan the stockbroker makes to you using your securities as collateral to support the loan)"라고 정의하고 있다. 따라서 답은 ④이다.

17 밑줄 친 ⓐ와 ⓑ에 들어가기에 가장 적합한 것을 고르시오.
① 30 – 50
② 30 – 100
③ 50 – 50
④ 50 – 100

| 정답 | ④

| 해설 | ABC사의 주식을 100주 사들인 가격이 5천 달러이므로 한 주당 가격은 50달러가 된다. 따라서 빈칸 ⓐ에 들어갈 숫자는 50이다. 손실금이 2천 달러인데 주당 가격이 20달러이므로 주식의 수는 100주가 된다. 따라서 빈칸 ⓑ에 들어갈 숫자는 100이다.

| 어휘 | margin account – 증거금 계정
nothing more than – ~에 불과한
collateral ⓝ 담보
margin requirement – 증거금률
pocket ⓥ (얼마의 돈을) 벌다
uninformed ⓐ 지식이 없는, 모르는
securities ⓝ 증권, 주식
deposit ⓥ 예치하다
commission ⓝ 수수료

[18-20] 숭실대 2010

수년간 미국 교육자들은 "지식경제"의 부상을 홍보해 왔고 육체적 직업에 집중하기보다는, 10대들에게 아마도 다가올 후기산업화 시대에 대처하여 4년간의 대학과정을 밟을 것을 권장했다. 동시에 사무직은 점차적으로 제조업의 전철을 밟을 것이라고 보았으며, 그 이유는 기업들이 무선 연결을 통해 전달이 가능한 업무는 아웃소싱하기 때문이다. 게다가 경제위기 덕분에 이 같은 일자리 유출은 가속화될 가능성이 높다. 따라서 지금은 아마도 남은 세기 동안 직업의 미래가 어디로 향하는지 돌아볼 시간이 되었다. 이 주제는 점차 관심을 끌고 있으며, 처음에는 Princeton 대학의 경제학자인 Alan Blinder의 글에서 시작되어 가장 최근에는 철학자인 (그리고 오토바이 수리공인) Matthew Crawford가 쓴 Shop Class as Soul-craft(영혼을 가꾸는 기술수업)이라는 기발한 책에서 논의된다.

Crawford는 독립적 사고, 자기 의존, 스스로의 힘으로 일하기 사이의 연결고리에 관해 설득력 있는 의견을 제시한다. 그 관계는 새로운 것은 아니다. 고대 그리스의 '지식(sophia)'에 관한 관념과 '솜씨 있음(techne)'에 관한 관념은 손재주가 있음을 시사한다. (아테나 여신은 지혜와 솜씨 있음을 후원하는 여신이었다.) 그리고 Heidegger는 인간을 근본적으로 도구를 사용하는 동물로 보았다. Blinder는 일은 곧 대인 접촉을 요하는 '개인 서비스'와 그렇지 않기 때문에 외국으로 보내질 '비개인적 서비스'로 구분될 것으로 예측했다. 그는 비개인적 서비스를 제공하는 직업을 가진 사람이 3천만에서 4천만에 달할 것으로 보고 있으며, 화이트칼라 노동자들에게 닥칠 경제적 격변은 막 시작되었을 뿐으로 보았다. 그러나 육체노동의 경우 그는 봉급이 오르고 수요가 증가할 것임을 시사했다.

18 본문에 따르면 다음 중 맞는 것은 무엇인가?
① 교육자들은 "지식경제"의 도래를 비판적으로 바라봤다.
② 육체노동의 인기는 고대 그리스 시대부터 지속되었다.
③ 기술적 진보는 노동시장의 변화에 기여한다.
④ Crawford와 Blinder는 사무직이 미래에는 육체노동으로 변환될 것으로 예측했다.

| 정답 | ③

| 해설 | 본문의 "corporations outsource any task that can be delivered over a wireless connection(기업들이 무선 연결을 통해 전달이 가능한 업무는 아웃소싱한다)"는 말은, 기술이 발전하여 무선통신을 통해 전달이 가능한 것들은 직접 하기보다 아웃소싱을 할 것이라는 의미이다. 이는 미국 기업들이 콜센터 업무를 직접 미국 내에서 하는 대신에 인도에 맡기는 것처럼 기술발전이 노동시장의 변화를 가져온다는 의미이다. 따라서 답은 ③이 된다. ①의 경우, 미국의 교육자들은 "touting the rise of the 'knowledge economy'('지식경제'의 부상을 홍보)"해 왔기 때문에 비판적으로 바라본 것과는 거리가 멀다. 따라서 ①은 답이 될 수 없다. ②의 경우, 고대 그리스 시대의 사례를 들긴 했으나 인기가 그때부터 지속되었다는 말은 본문에 나오지 않기 때문에 답으로 보기 힘들다. ④의 경우, Crawford와 Blinder가 말한 것은 "where the future of work is headed(직업의 미래가 어디로 향하는지)"에 관한 것이지 미래에는 사무직이 육체노동으로 변화할 것이라고 논의했다고는 본문에 나오지 않으므로 답으로 보기엔 무리가 있다.

19 ㉮의 사무직은 점차적으로 제조업의 전철을 밟을 것이다가 의미하는 것은 무엇인가?
① 사무직의 수요가 늘어난다.
② 사무직은 제조업으로 전환된다.
③ 사무직의 과정은 제조업의 과정과 유사하다.
④ 사무직은 점차 사라지고 있다.

| 정답 | ④

| 해설 | "cubicle jobs"는 "(큰 방 한쪽을 칸막이 해 만든) 좁은 방에서 일하는 직업"을 의미하며, 이는 즉 일반 사무직이나 콜센터 같이 정해진 공간에 앉아 컴퓨터를 조작하거나 모니터를 보면서 하는 일을 의미한다. 그런데 이들 직업이 "제조업의 전철을 밟는다"는 것은 제조업 일자리가 해외로 빠져나간 것처럼 "corporations outsource any task that can be delivered over a wireless connection(기업들이 무선 연결을 통해 전달이 가능한 업무는 아웃소싱)"해서 콜센터 업무 같은 "cubicle jobs"가 해외로 빠져나가게 되었음을 의미한다. 따라서 답은 ④가 된다.

20

㉯의 '개인 서비스'와 ㉰의 '비개인적 서비스' 간의 좋은 예로 각각 들 수 있는 것은 무엇인가?
① ㉯ 요리사 — ㉰ 수리공
② ㉯ 방사선 전문의 — ㉰ 인테리어 디자이너
③ ㉯ 간호사 — ㉰ 출판인
④ ㉯ 타이피스트 — ㉰ 고객 서비스 직원

| 정답 | ③

| 해설 | "personal service(개인 서비스)"와 "impersonal service(비개인적 서비스)"가 의미하는 것은 각각 '직접 개인을 1:1로 상대하는 서비스'와 '직접 개인을 대면하여 상대하는 대신에 불특정 다수를 상대하는 서비스'를 의미한다. 따라서 보기 중에서 이러한 서비스의 예로 가장 잘 설명이 된 것은 ③이다.

| 어휘 |
tout ⓥ 장점을 내세우다, 홍보하다
trade ⓝ 무역, 직업
cubicle ⓝ (큰 방 한쪽을 칸막이 해 만든) 좁은 방, 좁은 사무실
cubicle job – 좁은 공간에서 일하는 직업, 즉 사무직이나 콜센터 같은 직업을 의미함
drain ⓝ 배수관; 유출, 고갈
traction ⓝ 견인; 매력; 영향력
self-reliance ⓝ 자기 의존
dexterity ⓝ 재주
advent ⓝ 도래, 출현
manual ⓐ 손의, 육체의
supposedly ⓐⓓ 아마, 추정상
unfold ⓥ 펼치다, 밝혀지다
shop class – (학교에서 학과목으로 배우는) 기술
craftiness ⓝ 교활함; 솜씨 있음
upheaval ⓝ 격변

[21-22] 한양대 2015

공식적 경제 모델이 실제 정책에 얼마나 적절한지 여부는 오랫동안 논란거리였다. 경제학자 R. D. Norton과 S. Y. Rhee는 이러한 모델을 14년 동안 한국 경제에 소급 적용하는 데 있어 일부 성공을 맛보았다. 즉, 해당 모델에서 생산량, 가격, 그 외 변수에 해당되는 수치들을 실제 통계와 면밀하게 조합했다. 하지만 해당 모델의 정책적 측면에서의 값은 이보다는 덜 분명했다. Norton과 Rhee는 장기적 요인은 일정하게 유지하면서 단기적 정책 변화가 미치는 영향을 정확히 집어낼 수 있도록 시뮬레이션을 수행했다. 이들의 모델에 따르면 수입 원유의 가격이 상승하면 인플레이션이 올라가며, 수출이 5% 감소되면 GDP는 내려가고 인플레이션은 올라가며, 통화 공급량의 상승을 늦추면 인플레이션이 약간 올라가는 것이 나타났다. 이러한 연구 결과는 다소 놀라운 것이었다. 많은 경제학자들은 수출을 줄이면 인플레이션이 강화되는 것이 아니라 약화될 것이라 주장했다. 그리고 대부분은 높아지는 원유가격이 인플레이션을 유발하는 것으로 보고 있지만, 통화 공급량의 상승을 늦추는 것도 인플레이션을 유발할 것이라 생각하는 사람은 거의 없었다. Norton과 Rhee의 모델은 어쩌면 실제 정책의 적절성을 대가로 희생하면서 통계적인 "적합도"를 강조하는 형식주의적 접근법이 빠지기 쉬운 함정을 나타내는 것으로 볼 수 있다.

21

윗글의 목적으로 가장 알맞은 것은?

① 새로운 유형의 결제 분석을 제안하기
② 한국의 인플레이션에 대한 설명을 제시하기
③ Norton과 Rhee의 분석의 정확도를 밝히기
④ 공식적 경제 모델의 한계를 기술하기

| 정답 | ④

| 해설 | 본문 첫 번째 문장에서는 공식적 경제 모델이 실제 정책에 얼마나 적절하게 적용되는지를 묻고 있다. 그리고 이를 파악하기 위해 두 명의 학자가 시뮬레이션을 수행해 봤는데, 그 결과 생각했던 것과는 다른 결과가 나왔다. 즉, 공식적 경제 모델을 수립하고 통계학적으로 여기에 맞는 결과가 나오는 것, 즉 '적합도'를 강조하는 형식주의적 접근법은 실제와는 맞지 않음을 두 학자가 보여준 것이다. 따라서 본문은 공식적 경제 모델이 보여주는 한계를 기술한 것으로 볼 수 있으며, 따라서 답은 ④이다.

22

빈칸에 들어갈 가장 알맞은 것은?

	(A)	(B)
①	소급하여	놀라운
②	반사적으로	유망한
③	장래에 관하여	예상하는
④	강하게	실망스러운

| 정답 | ①

| 해설 | 빈칸 (A)의 경우, 두 학자는 공식적 경제 모델을 실제 한국 경제의 수치에 적용한 다음 시뮬레이션을 수행하여 어떤 영향이 나타나는지를 확인했다. 실제 경제 수치라는 말은, 즉 과거의 경제 수치를 의미하며, 14년 동안의 수치에 적응했다는 말은 모델을 '소급' 적용했다는 의미이다.

빈칸 (B)의 경우, 모델을 통해 시뮬레이션을 돌린 결과 예상치 못한 결과가 나왔기 때문에 '놀라운' 결과가 나온 것으로 볼 수 있다.

이러한 점들을 고려했을 때 답으로 가장 적합한 것은 ①이다.

| 어휘 | relevance ⓝ 적절, 타당성
clear-cut ⓐ 명쾌한, 분명한
startling ⓐ 놀라운, 특이한
pitfall ⓝ 위험, 함정
goodness of fit – 적합도
reflectively ⓐⓓ 반사적으로, 반영하여
prospectively ⓐⓓ 장래에 관하여
retrospectively ⓐⓓ 과거로 거슬러 올라가, 소급하여
pinpoint ⓥ 정확히 집어내다, 정확히 기술하다
escalate ⓥ 증가시키다, 확대시키다
formalist ⓐ 형식주의의
at the expense of – ~을 훼손시키면서, ~을 대가로
promising ⓐ 유망한, 촉망되는
intensively ⓐⓓ 강하게, 철저하게

[23-25] 경희대 2013

일본인들은 자신들이 "구조적인 비관주의"라 부르는 경제적 질환에 시달리고 있다고 말한다. 또한 비록 11월 14일에 발표한 수치에 따르면 일본 경제는 3분기에 3월에 일어난 쓰나미와 원전사고에서 빠르게 반등하여 연간 환산 수치로 6% 성장했음에도 불구하고 해외에서는 일본을 유로존과 미국 경제가 처하게 될 불행한 운명을 미리 나타내 보여주는 전조로 보는 경향이 있다. 하지만 지난 10년 동안 일본의 경제적 성과를 냉정하게 바라보면, 첫 번째 잃어버린 10년은 부적절한 명칭이라 할 수 없겠지만 "두 번째 잃어버린 10년"은 부적절한 명칭이다. 일본의 이미지를 더럽히는 것 가운데 상당 부분은 인구 변동에 기인하는데, 현재 일본 인구 가운데 반 이상이 45세 이상이다. 전체적으로 2001년에서 2010년 사이에 일본 경제의 발전 속도는 미국 경제 발전 속도의 절반이었다. 간단히 말해 일본의 경제는 젊은 층보다 중년 및 노년층에 더 적합하다. 그렇지만 일본 경제는 아직 위기 상황에 처하지 않았고 경제학자들은 일본이 잠재 성장률을 높이기 위해 할 수 있는 일이 많이 존재한다고 말한다. 문제는 비관적인 이야기가 깊이 뿌리박혀 있다는 점이다. 현재 일본을 이끄는 정치인, 관료, 사업가 무리의 나이는 중년을 훌쩍 넘었다. 웨인스타인에 따르면, 이들은 중국의 경제적 부상을 불안하게 바라보면서 "힘 빠진 거인 증후군"에 시달리고 있다.

23 문맥상 밑줄 친 ⓐ structural pessimism과 관계가 없는 것은?
① 종말이 우려되는 일본의 사회적 환경
② 일본의 경제적 성취
③ 일본인들 사이의 부정적 자아상에 관한 이야기
④ 일본인들의 상실감

| 정답 | ②

| 해설 | '구조적인 비관주의'란 말에서 유추할 수 있듯이 보기 중에서 ②를 제외하면 모두 일본 경제 상황에 대한 일본인들의 비관적이고 부정적인 인식을 의미한다. 따라서 답은 ②이다.

24 빈칸 ⓑ _____ 에 들어갈 가장 알맞은 어구는?
① GDP 비율에 따른 일본의 순 채무는 OECD 회원국 가운데 가장 높은 수준에 속한다.
② 일본의 실업률은 2000년보다 높다.
③ 대부분의 일본인은 지난 10년 동안 더 부유해졌다.
④ 현재 일본 인구 가운데 반 이상이 45세 이상이다.

| 정답 | ④

| 해설 | ⓑ 앞에서 일본이 인구 문제 때문에 이미지가 훼손되고 있음을 언급하고 있으므로 ⓑ에는 인구 문제와 관련된 사항이 등장해야 한다. 또한 ⓑ 뒤에 일본 경제가 젊은 층보다 중년 및 노년층에 적합하고 일본을 이끄는 사람들의 연령대가 중년임이 언급되어 있다. 따라서 답은 ④이다.

25 윗글의 내용과 맞지 않는 것은?
① 일본은 경제 성장 측면에서 유럽의 경쟁국에 비해 뒤떨어진다.
② 일본은 경제적 재앙과 자연재해에서 빠르게 회복했다.
③ 경제 위기에 처한 일본을 바라보는 국제적 이미지는 실제 수치와 상반된다.
④ 일본이 처한 진정한 위기는 일본인들의 마음에 사기가 영향을 미치고 있다는 점이다.

| 정답 | ①

| 해설 | 본문 어디에도 일본의 경제 성장률이 유럽 국가들에게 비해 뒤떨어진다는 내용은 등장하지 않는다. 따라서 답은 ①이다. 본문에는 일본이 쓰나미와 원전사고에서 빠르게 회복하고 있으며 잃어버린 10년을 다시 맞이하고 있다는 표현은 적합하지 않다고 명시되어 있으며 이는 ②의 내용과 일맥상통하다. 해외에서는 현재 일본이 앞으로 유로존과 미국 경제가 처하게 될 모습을 미리 보여주고 있다고 생각하지만 실제로 일본의 경제 성장 추세는 그렇게 나쁘지는 않다고 본문에 언급되어 있으므로 ③도 답이 될 수 없다. 마지막으로 현재 일본의 문제는 수치상의 문제라기보다는 "비관적인 이야기가 깊이 뿌리박혀 있다(the downbeat narrative is deeply ingrained)"는 말처럼 심리적이며 정신적인 문제라 할 수 있으므로 ④ 또한 답이 될 수 없다.

| 어휘 | **structural** ⓐ 구조적인
tendency ⓝ 성향, 경향
doom ⓥ 불행한 운명[결말]을 맞게 하다
annualized ⓐ 연간으로 환산한
misnomer ⓝ 부적절한 명칭
demography ⓝ 인구 통계학, 인구 변동
downbeat ⓐ 침울한, 비관적인
ingrained ⓐ 뿌리 깊은, 몸에 밴
milieu ⓝ 환경
psyche ⓝ 마음, 정신

pessimism ⓝ 비관주의
harbinger ⓝ 징조, 선구자
rebound ⓥ 반등하다
dispassionately ⓐⓓ 냉정하게, 공정하게
tarnish ⓥ 더럽히다, 손상시키다
in aggregate – 전체적으로
narrative ⓝ 묘사, 이야기
crop ⓝ 무리, 집단
contradict ⓥ 반박하다; 모순되다

[26-28] 숭실대 2011

갈등이라는 단어는 부정적, 긍정적 의미를 동시에 지니고 있다. 갈등이라는 단어에 부정적인 태도를 지닌 사람들은 상대방을 적으로 보는 경향이 있다. 이런 사람들에게 갈등은 공격, 폭력, 파괴적 경쟁 등을 시사한다. 극심한 갈등이 편향된 인식과 현실의 중대한 왜곡을 가져오는 것은 사실이다. 이런 상황이 심화되면 우리는 종종 자신의 의견을 주장하는 데만 정신이 팔려서 다른 사람의 욕구나 관점을 무시하게 된다. 서로 간에 유익한 해결책을 내놓는 것 보다 상대를 꺾는 것이 더 중요해진다. 따라서 개인의 부정적인 감정은 갈등을 유발한 문제를 타당하게 해결하는 데 지장을 준다.

조직 내의 갈등은 경영진이 상호의존적인 개인이나 단체가 서로 경쟁하길 기대할 때 파괴적일 수 있다. 이러한 상황에서는 한 사람 또는 한 단체의 성공은 다른 사람이나 단체의 희생을 대가로 이루어진다. 수시로 고강도의 갈등에 말려든 직원들은 스트레스를 겪으며, (스트레스받는) 상황에서 벗어나는 식으로 대응한다. 직원들의 불편함은 (무관심과 무심함을 통해) 심리적으로 또는 (지각, 결근 또는 이직 등을 통해) 육체적으로 표현될 것이다. 매우 극단적인 경우에는 직원들은 회사의 자산을 훔치거나 파괴하는 등의 공격적이고 적대적인 행동으로 반응할 것이다.

일부 경영자들은 조직 내 어떤 형태이든 갈등은 바람직하지 않은 것으로 여긴다. 이들은 신중한 인원 선정, 훈련, 자세한 직무 분석표, 정교한 규칙, 인센티브제도 등을 통해 갈등을 줄이거나 척결하려 시도한다. 이 같은 수단은 바람직하지 않은 갈등을 예방하기엔 도움이 되지만 완전한 답은 될 수 없다.

갈등에 좀 더 긍정적 태도를 보이는 경영자들은 갈등이 일어나는 상황을 흥분되고, 흥미롭고, 도전적인 상황으로 바라본다. 의사결정의 측면에서 살펴보면, 사람들이 점수를 따고 서로를 물리치는 상황에서 생기는 갈등이 아니라면 갈등이 더 나은 선택을 낳을 수 있다. 대신 갈등은 상충하는 의견의 원인을 탐색하고 의견 충돌을 해결할 방법을 탐색하려는 노력을 활성화시킬 수 있다. 이 같은 긍정적 접근법은 혁신과 변화를 이끌어 내는 경향이 있다. 갈등은 경영자들에게 조직 활동에 관한 정보를 제공함으로써 (잘못을) 수정하기 위한 행동이 어느 곳에 필요할지를 드러낸다.

26

다음 중 본문의 제목으로 가장 적합한 것은 무엇인가?
① 왜 경영자들은 갈등을 즐기는가
② 갈등에 대한 다른 태도
③ 갈등과 경쟁
④ 갈등의 이점

| 정답 | ②

| 해설 | 본문은 조직 내에서 갈등의 부정적 요소와 긍정적 요소에 관해 말하는 글이므로, 가장 첫 문장인 "갈등이라는 단어는 부정적, 긍정적 의미를 동시에 지니고 있다(The word conflict has both negative and positive connotations)"는 본문 전체의 내용을 포괄하는 문장임을 알 수 있다. 따라서 ②를 본문의 제목으로 가장 잘 어울리는 것으로 볼 수 있다.

27

본문에 따르면 다음 중 사실인 것은 무엇인가?
① 갈등은 문제의 공정한 해결로 이어지지 않는다.
② 부정적인 사람에게는 서로 이익이 되는 해결책이 승리보다 중요하다.
③ 조직 내 갈등은 어떤 것이든 바람직하지 않으며 따라서 우리는 갈등을 줄여야 한다.
④ 갈등에 대한 긍정적 태도는 혁신과 변화로 이어진다.

| 정답 | ④

| 해설 | 문제 해결을 위한 핵심 문장은 "긍정적 접근법은 혁신과 변화를 이끌어 내는 경향이 있다(The positive approach tends to lead to innovation and change)"이다. 여기서 말하는 '긍정적 접근법'은 갈등에 대한 긍정적 접근법을 의미한다. 따라서 갈등에 대한 긍정적 접근법이 혁신과 변화를 낳을 수 있음이 본문에서 주장하는 바임을 알 수 있으며, 이는 ④의 내용과 일맥상통한다.

28

㉮의 connotations와 ㉯의 distortions의 의미로 가장 가까운 것을 고르시오.
① 결심 – 의미
② 결심 – 왜곡
③ 의미 – 왜곡
④ 의미 – 결심

| 정답 | ③

| 해설 | ㉮의 connotation은 '의미'를 뜻하며, ㉯의 distortion은 '왜곡'을 뜻한다. 따라서 답은 ③이 된다.

| 어휘 | connotation ⓝ 의미
biased ⓐ 편향된, 왜곡된
gross ⓐ 끔찍한, 중대한
in the heat of – ~이 한창일 때
come up with – (해답 등) 내놓다, 찾아내다
apathy ⓝ 무관심
tardiness ⓝ 지각
turnover ⓝ 이직
undesirable ⓐ 바람직하지 않은, 원하지 않는
opposing party – 상대방
perception ⓝ 인식, 개념
distortion ⓝ 왜곡
make one's own point – 자신의 의견을 확실히 밝히다
at the expense of – ~을 희생하며
indifference ⓝ 무관심
absenteeism ⓝ 결근
property ⓝ 재산, 소유물
job description – 직무 분석표

elaborate ⓐ 정교한	intriguing ⓐ 아주 흥미로운
decision-making ⓝ 의사결정	standpoint ⓝ 관점
take place – 일어나다, 발생하다	viewpoint ⓝ 관점
disagreement ⓝ 의견 충돌	implication ⓝ 의미
twist ⓝ 왜곡, 예상치 못한 전개	perversion ⓝ 왜곡, 변태적 행동

[29-31] 경희대 2012

심리학자들 및 행동경제학자들은 돈을 쓰는 사람과 저축하는 사람을 구분 짓는 성격 유형과 기타 특성을 찾아 보고 있으며, 여기서 돈을 잘 아끼지 않는 사람이 멍청하거나 비이성적인 것은 아니고 그보다는 종종 돈을 아끼지 않았을 경우 결과를 정확히 예측할 수 없을 뿐임이 나타났다. (돈을 아끼고) 나중에 받을 보상에 기쁨을 찾도록 뇌를 재구성하면 여러분이 진실로 원하는 미래로 향하는 길을 걷게 될 것이다.

뉴욕대학의 신경경제학자 폴 글림처는 한 실험에서 사람이 기꺼이 만족감을 늦추려 한다면 무엇이 필요할지를 보고 싶었다. 그는 십여 명의 사람들에게 선택지를 제공했는데, 한 달 뒤 21달러를 받겠다는 사람이 있었다. 단 1달러의 이득을 보려고 본질적으로 한 달을 기다리겠다는 뜻이다. 경제학 용어로 말하자면 이런 사람은 '균일 할인 기능'을 가졌다. 이는 내일을 거의 오늘 만큼 중시하기 때문에 만족하는 시점을 미룰 수 있다는 의미이다. 다른 쪽의 극단적인 예로는 68달러를 받게 될 경우에만 한 달을 기다리겠다는 사람이었다. 원래 제안한 20달러에서 48달러를 상여금으로 받겠다는 것이었다. 경제학자들은 이런 부류를 '대폭 할인자'라고 부른다. 이는 미래(그리고 나중에 돈을 갖는다는 것)에 부여하는 가치가 현재에 부여하는 가치보다 크게 낮다는 의미이다. 무엇을 원하면 즉시 해결되기를 바라는 부류다. 21달러를 선택한 사람은 바로 의과학박사 과정 학생이었다. 그 점이 시사하는 바가 많다. "대학원을 8년 동안 다니겠다고 결심한 사람이라면 만족을 기꺼이 미룰 수 있다"고 글림처가 말했다.

29 윗글의 주제로 알맞은 것은?
① 20달러로 재테크를 시작하는 방법
② 두 가지 유형의 돈을 소비하는 성격
③ 대학원에 가기 위해 준비하는 방법
④ 소비 욕구를 억누르는 효과적인 방법

|정답| ②

|해설| 본문은 한 실험을 통해 왜 어떤 사람은 "돈을 쓰는 사람(spender)"이 되고 다른 사람은 "돈을 저축하는 사람(saver)"이 되는지를 탐구하고 있다. 따라서 답은 ②이다.

30 글의 흐름상 빈칸 ⓐ에 들어갈 표현으로 알맞은 것은?
① 다시 ② 옛날에
③ 나중에 ④ 지금

|정답| ④

|해설| "이는 미래(그리고 나중에 돈을 갖는다는 것)에 부여하는 가치가 현재에 부여하는 가치보다 크게 낮다는 의미이다 [he puts on the future (and having money then) is dramatically less than value he places on today]."

이들은 '돈을 쓰는 사람들'이며 나중에 돈을 받을 것이라는 생각보다 지금 돈을 받겠다고 생각하는 사람이므로 "무엇을 원하면(when he wants something)" 바로 '지금' 원하는 사람일 것이다. 따라서 답은 ④이다.

31

윗글에 사용된 표현 중에서 빈칸 ⓑ에 가장 알맞은 것은?
① 결과
② 만족감
③ 가치
④ 상여금

| 정답 | ②

| 해설 | 빈칸이 들어간 문장에서 설명하는 사람은 의과학박사 과정을 밟는 사람들로 "대학원을 8년 동안 다니겠다고 결심한 사람(get to grad school for eight years)"이다. 즉, 이들은 '돈을 저축하는 사람들'이며, 미래를 위해 '빈칸의 것'을 "기꺼이 미룰 수 있는(really willing to delay)" 사람이다. 보기의 것을 빈칸에 대입해 보면 답으로 가장 적절한 것은 '미래를 위해 지금의 만족을 미룬다'는 의미에서 ②가 된다.

| 어휘 | **psychologist** ⓝ 심리학자 **behavioral economist** – 행동경제학자
personality ⓝ 성격 **trait** ⓝ 특성
irrational ⓐ 비이성적인 **foresee** ⓥ 예측하다
consequence ⓝ 결과 **rewire** ⓥ 배선을 바꾸다
neuroeconomist ⓝ 신경경제학자 **willingly** ⓐⓓ 자진해서, 기꺼이
gratification ⓝ 만족감 **essentially** ⓐⓓ 본질적으로
premium ⓝ 보너스, 상여금 **tellingly** ⓐⓓ 명확히 드러내는
M.D.-Ph.D. – 의과학 박사(의사로서 기초과학 연구 능력까지 갖춰야 하기 때문에 미국에선 8년이 걸림)
grad school – 대학원 **suppress** ⓥ 억누르다, 진압하다

[32-33] 숭실대 2012

2012년 초입에 폭스바겐에 성원을 보내자. 독일의 자동차 회사인 폭스바겐은 자사 노동자 협의체의 요청에 화답하여 블랙베리를 사용하는 직원들의 교대조 근무 시간이 끝난 지 30분 후에 이메일 서버를 차단하고 다음날 업무 시작 30분 전에 차단을 복구하기로 합의했다.

이러한 합의는 독일에서 근무하는 19만이 넘는 폭스바겐 직원 가운데 1,150명에만 해당되지만, 이는 기기의 스위치를 끄고, 몇 분 간격으로 이메일을 살펴보기 위해 안절부절못하면서 반사적 반응을 보이는 일이 없도록 하면서, 깜빡이는 붉은 빛에 정신이 팔리는 대신 가족이나 더 큰 세상 같이 주변을 돌아볼 것을 직원들에게 권유하기 위한 움직임이 이제 시작되었음을 의미한다.

물론 나는 우리 모두 성인이고 기기 전원을 끄는 일 정도는 충분히 간단히 결심할 수 있다고 생각하지만, 실제로는 블랙베리나 기타 휴대용 기기의 중독성은 강한 데다가 중독자가 도움 없이 올바른 약을 스스로 투여할 수 있을 것으로 예상하는 사람은 아무도 없다. 폭스바겐의 이번 결정은 근로자가 노동생활과 사생활을 분리할 수 없게 된 실태와 연계하여 근로자가 극도의 피로감을 느끼고 있다는 증거가 축적되고 있는 상황을 반영하며, 그 이유는 선진국 사회는 폭발적으로 증가한 통신망과 하루 온종일 연결된 삶을 살고 있기 때문이다.

직원이 극도의 피로감을 느끼는 실태는 사회적 의식의 수준이 높은 독일에서 이미 문젯거리가 되어 왔으며, 이는 저명한 분데스리가 소속 샬케 팀의 감독이었으나 스스로가 탈진 상태에 빠졌음을 호소하며 9월에 사임한 랄프 랑닉과 관련한 슈피겔 지의 표지 기사의 주제이기도 했다. 볼프스부르크에 위치한 폭스바겐의 대변인은 폭스바겐은 직원들과 24시간 내내 접촉했을 경우 얻을 수 있는 혜택과 직원의 사생활을 보호할 경우의 혜택 간에 균형을 취해야 했다고 블룸버그 뉴스에 밝혔다.

32

다음 중 독일 사회에서 긴급한 문제는 무엇인가?

① 노동자 협의체
② 직원이 극도의 피로감을 느낌
③ 가족과의 삶의 가치
④ 슈피겔 지의 표지 기사

| 정답 | ②

| 해설 | "직원이 극도의 피로감을 느끼는 실태는 사회적 의식의 수준이 높은 독일에서 이미 문젯거리가 되어 왔으며(Employee burnout has become an issue on socially conscious Germany) …" 여기서 답이 ②임을 알 수 있다.

33

다음 중 (1) switching off의 혜택이 아닌 것은 무엇인가?

① 직장 밖에서 근무시간을 줄이기
② 근로자의 불안감을 덜어 주기
③ 가족에게 시간을 내기
④ 직원의 의지를 강화하기

| 정답 | ④

| 해설 | (1)의 switching off는 통신기기의 전원을 끄는 것을 의미한다. 이를 통해 직원들은 가족과 더 많은 시간을 보내고, 근무시간이 아닐 때 일에 더 이상 신경을 쓰지 않아도 되고, 일과 사생활을 분리할 수 있게 되면서 극도의 피로감을 느끼지 않고 안절부절못하지 않아도 된다. 하지만 본문에 ④에 관한 내용은 존재하지 않는다. 따라서 답은 ④이다.

| 어휘 | let's hear it for – ~에 성원을 보냅시다
shift ⓝ 교대조
twitchy ⓐ 불안해하는, 초조해하는
distraction ⓝ 집중을 방해하는 것, 정신이 팔리는 일
administer ⓥ (약을) 투여하다
tied to – ~와 관련이 있는, ~와 연계된
socially conscious – 사회적으로 의식이 있는

works council – 노동자 협의체
curb ⓥ 억제하다, 제한하다
reflex ⓝ 반사 작용, 반사적인 동작[반응]
burnout ⓝ 심신의 소모, 극도의 피로
paroxysm ⓝ 발작, 폭발
round-the-clock ⓐ 밤낮 없이[24시간 동안] 지속되는

[34-36] 이화여대 2012

패스트푸드 식당은 엄격한 계열화를 통해 대량으로 제품을 쏟아낼 수 있게 되었다. 그 결과 처리량이 증가했다. 또한 이로 인해 패스트푸드 업체는 직원들을 대상으로 상당한 권한을 휘두를 수 있게 되었다. 사회학자 로빈 라이드너는 다음과 같이 언급했다. "경영진은 모든 업무가 어떤 식으로 정확히 이루어져야 할지를 결정하고 … 또한 속도·생산량·품질·기술 등에 관해 자체적인 규칙을 강요합니다. 그 결과 직원들은 점차 대체 가능한 존재가 되고 있습니다." 경영진은 더 이상 직원의 재능이나 기술에 의존하지 않는다. 재능이나 기술 같은 것들은 운영체제와 기계 안에 포함되어 있다. "숙련도를 요하지 않는" 일자리는 값싸게 충원될 수 있다. 직원 개개인을 용이하게 대체할 수 있다는 점 때문에 직원을 유지할 필요성은 크게 줄어들었다.

오랫동안 10대 청소년들은 패스트푸드 업계의 노동력 가운데 대부분을 차지해 왔다. 패스트푸드 업계의 빠른 성장은 베이비 붐 연령대가 급속히 성장했던 것과 일치한다. 10대 청소년들은 많은 점에서 패스트푸드 같은 저임금 일자리의 이상적인 후보군이다. 대부분의 10대 청소년들은 여전히 집에서 살기 때문에 성인을 부양하기엔 너무 낮은 임금으로도 일할 여유가 있고, 최근까지도 이들은 제한적인 기술만 보유하고 있으므로 패스트푸드 업계 이외의 고용주들의 관심을 거의 끌지 못하고 있다. 패스트푸드 업계의 근무 기간은 유동적이기 때문에 추가적인 가계 소득을 필요로 하는 가정주부들의 관심도 끌고 있다. 베이비 붐 세대에 속한 10대 청소년의 수가 줄어들면서 패스트푸드 체인점은 최근에 이주한 이민자·노인·장애인 같이 10대 청소년 및 가정주부 이외의 소외계층에 소속된 근로자들을 고용하기 시작했다.

현재 패스트푸드 업계는 사회적으로 가장 혜택을 받지 못한 구성원들 가운데 일부를 고용하고 있다. 또한 제시간에 직장에 도착하는 것 같은 기본적인 업무 기술을 삶이 혼란스럽기 그지없거나 주류로부터 배척된 사람들인 거의 문맹이나 다름없는 사람들에게 가르쳐 주고 있다. 각 프랜차이즈 업계는 소속 근로자들의 안녕에 관해 진심으로 신경을 쏟고 있다. 하지만 직원 교육·최저 임금·노동조합·시간외 근무 같은 문제에 관해 패스트푸드 업계가 취하는 입장을 보면, 이들이 젊은 사람·가난한 사람·장애인 등을 고용하려는 동기는 이타적인 것으로 보기가 힘들다는 점이 강하게 시사된다.

34 다음 중 패스트푸드 업계가 "처리량"이란 단어를 사용하는 방식에서 유추할 수 있는 것은 무엇인가?

① 식당을 자주 찾는 고객을 위한 편안함과 친밀함을 창조하고자 사교적인 식사 분위기를 만듦
② 주어진 시간 안에 더 많은 것을 생산하고자 조합 시간을 높이고 모든 단계가 빠르게 진행되도록 함
③ 고객이 식당 안에서 식사를 섭취하는 시간을 줄이며 따라서 고객의 회전율을 더 빠르게 하면서 높은 이득을 거두게 함
④ 식당 메뉴에 수록된 항목을 최소화하여 식품을 조합하는 데 필요한 보유 직원 수를 늘림
⑤ 광고 활동과 판촉 거래 수립을 통해 고객의 수를 증대시킴

| 정답 | ②

| 해설 | "패스트푸드 식당은 엄격한 계열화를 통해 대량으로 제품을 쏟아낼 수 있게 되었다. 그 결과 처리량이 증가했다(The strict systematization at fast food restaurants creates mass products. It raises the throughput.)." 여기서 "대량으로 제품을 쏟아내다"는 표현을 통해 처리량은 패스트푸드 식당이 생산하는 제품, 즉 음식의 양을 의미함을 알 수 있다. 햄버거를 만드는 과정을 생각하면 패스트푸드 식당에서는 본사에서 공급한 재료를 재빨리 조합하여 내놓기만 하면 되므로, 처리량의 증가는 정해진 시간 안에 재빨리 조합하여 내놓는 양이 늘었음을 의미한다. 따라서 답은 ②이다.

35 위 본문의 저자가 궁극적으로 강조하고자 하는 패스트푸드 식당 및 이를 운영하는 사람들의 두 개의 주요 특징은 무엇인가?

① 경력상의 기회와 부가 혜택
② 친근함과 익숙함
③ 조직화와 표준화
④ 합리적인 가격과 고객 만족
⑤ 조합 라인의 정신과 건강에 좋은 요리

| 정답 | ③

| 해설 | 첫 번째 단락을 보면 패스트푸드 업계는 누가 들어와 일하든 아무 상관이 없도록 모든 과정을 계열화하고 조직화했음을 알 수 있다. 이런 체제하에서는 직원은 짜여진 대로만 정확히 일하면 되는 부품에 불과하며, 직원의 숙련도 같은 것들은 필요하지 않다. 따라서 답은 ③이다.

36

위 본문의 어조로 미루어 봤을 때 빈칸 [A]에 가장 알맞은 것은 무엇인가?
① 이타적인
② 착취하는
③ 수익성이 좋은
④ 달래는
⑤ 악의에 찬

| 정답 | ①

| 해설 | 패스트푸드 업계는 젊은이, 가정주부, 장애인과 같이 별다른 지식이나 기술을 갖추지 못한 사람들을 고용한다. 이는 언뜻 보면 이들에게 돈을 벌 기회를 제공하는 것이므로 이타적인 행위로 볼 수 있지만, 사실은 패스트푸드 매장에서의 일은 별다른 숙련도나 기술이 없이도 주어진 단순 반복 작업만 하면 되고, 그만큼 할 수 있는 사람도 많기 때문에 인력 충원이 용이하며, 돈을 많이 주지 않아도 된다. 이런 패스트푸드 업계의 관행을 '이타적'으로 보기에는 무리가 있다. 따라서 답은 ①이다.

| 어휘 | systematization ⓝ 계열화, 조직화   throughput ⓝ 처리량
interchangeable ⓐ 교체[대체] 가능한   coincide with – ~와 동시에 일어나다[일치하다]
marginalize ⓥ 사회에서 소외하다, 사회적으로 무시하다
disadvantaged ⓐ 사회적으로 혜택을 받지 못한, 빈곤한
stance ⓝ 입장, 태도   altruistic ⓐ 이타적인
sociable ⓐ 사교적인, 붙임성 있는   frequent ⓥ 자주 다니다
turnover ⓝ 회전율   augment ⓥ 늘리다, 증가시키다
fringe benefit – 부가 혜택   regimentation ⓝ 조직화, 획일화
ethos ⓝ 기풍, 정신   salubrious ⓐ 건강에 좋은
exploitative ⓐ 착취하는   lucrative ⓐ 수익성이 좋은
conciliatory ⓐ 달래는, 회유하기 위한   malignant ⓐ 악성의, 악의에 찬

[37-38] 중앙대 2012

2007년 마이클 블룸버그는 시험 점수가 상승한 학교의 교사들에게 현금으로 보너스를 지불하겠다는 내용의 교원 노조와의 합의 사항을 발표했을 당시 다음과 같이 말했다. "민간분야에서 현금 형태의 유인책을 제공하는 행위는 성과를 내는 데 있어 효과가 입증된 동기유발 요인입니다. 가장 좋은 성과를 낸 직원은 더 열심히 일을 하고, 다른 사람들도 마찬가지로 어떻게 해야 성과를 향상시킬 것인지 파악하기 위해 노력합니다." 자신의 재단을 활용해 교사들을 대상으로 장려금을 제공하는 계획을 추진하는 엘리 브로드는 다음과 같이 덧붙였다. "교육 분야 이외의 거의 모든 업계에서는 성과에 따라 직원에게 보상을 제공합니다. 우리는 다른 산업 및 분야로부터 획득한 경험을 통해 성과와 보상을 연계시키는 것이 강력한 유인책임을 알고 있습니다." 이러한 주장은 민간부문에 속한 기업이 직원들에게 어떻게 동기를 부여하는지 제대로 전하고 있지 못하다. 비록 장려금 제공 시스템은 널리 존재하고 있지만, 전문가들의 질적인 성과를 측정한 수치만을 배타적으로 또는 주로 근거로 삼아 장려금을 제공하는 경우는 거의 존재하지 않는다. 실제로 민간부문에서 성과별 장려금을 지급받은 근로자의 규모는 증가하고 있지만, 숫자로 표현된 성과 척도에 근거하여 성과별 장려금을 지급받은 근로자의 수는 감소하고 있다. 요즘의 경영 관련 문헌은 사람들을 호도하여 질적인 척도보다는 양적인 척도에 대한 의존도가 매우 높은 유인책에 관한 경고를 수용하게 만든다. 직원들 대부분이 오직 양적인 유인책만을 용이하게 달성한다는 점 때문에 민간부문 책임 시스템 가운데 대부분은 양적인 척도와 질적인 척도를 혼합하면서 후자(질적인 척도)를 가장 많이 강조한다. 이러한 방법은 비교적 직급이 낮거나 높은 직원들이 맡는 책임의 특성을 설명한다. 예를 들어 맥도날드에서는 판매량이나 수익성만을 가지고 매장 책임자를 평가하지 않는다. 대신에 책임자 및 책임자의 관리자는 판매량 및 비용 같은 쉽게 정량화가 가능한 척도를 목표로 삼는 동시에 제품의 품질, 서비스, 청결, 직원 훈련 같은 요소도 목표로 삼으며, 그 이유는 이러한 요소들이 다른 매장의 평판(그러므로 수익성)뿐만 아니라 장기적인 수익성에 영향을 줄 수 있기 때문이다. 분명히 말하자면, 직원에 대한 감독 평가는 매장 전체의 매출(또는 학생의 시험 점수) 같은 숫자로 표현된 성과 척도보다는 신뢰성이 떨어진다. 감독 평가는 어쩌면 편애, 편견, 부풀리거나 간략화하기(평가 범위를 좁혀 처벌을 회피하거나 너무 많은 직원들에게 포상을 제공하는 행위), 심지어는 뇌물이나 기타 부패행위 같은 것들로 인해 더럽혀질 수 있다. 그렇지만 이러한 결점에도 불구하고 주관적 평가가 경영 차원에서 널리 활용되고 있는 실태는 다음의 인사관리 비평에서 결론 내려진 바와 같다. "무관한 것들을 완벽하게 측정하는 것보다 관련 있는 요인을 불완전하게나마 측정하는 편이 낫다."

37 윗글에서 논지의 흐름상 가장 적합하지 않은 것을 고르시오.
① (A) ② (B)
③ (C) ④ (D)

| 정답 | ②

| 해설 | 최근 일부 교육계에서 교사가 담당하는 학생의 성적 같은 수량화가 가능한 평가 기준에 따라 보너스 같은 보상을 지급하는 시스템을 도입하면서 이를 민간부문의 직원 평가 기준을 도입한 것으로 표현했다. 하지만 실제로는 민간 부문의 직원 평가 기준은 양적 평가와 질적 평가를 혼합하여 사용하지 수치화할 수 있는 양적 평가만 중심으로 하지는 않는다. 따라서 (B)의 "질적인(qualitative)"은 "양적인(quantitative)"으로 바뀌어야 한다.

38 윗글의 제목으로 가장 적합한 것을 고르시오.
① 직원들을 대상으로 권한 부여를 촉진시키는 방안
② 교사들에게 올바른 봉급을 제공할 수 있도록 교사의 자질을 측정하는 방안
③ 중대한 딜레마: 직원들을 평가할 수 있는 사람은 누구인가?
④ 직원들의 성과를 측정하기 위한 믿을 만한 방법

| 정답 | ④

| 해설 | 본문은 직원의 평가 기준은 수치화할 수 있는 양적인 방안에 의존하는 것보다 질적인 방안과 양적인 방안을 조합하되 질적인 방안을 더욱 강조하는 것이 현재 추세이며, 그 이유는 질적인 방안도 나름의 결점은 있으나 불완전하게나마 감안하여 측정하는 것이 양적인 수치만을 기준으로 삼는 것보다 더 신뢰할 수 있는 평가가 이루어지기 때문이라고 말하고 있다. 즉, 본문은 직원들의 성과를 측정할 수 있는 믿을 만한 방법이 무엇인지 논하고 있다. 따라서 답은 ④이다.

| 어휘 | motivator ⓝ 동기를 부여하는 것, 동기유발 요인   compensate ⓥ 보상하다
misrepresent ⓥ 잘못[불완전하게] 전하다[표현하다]
exclusively ⓐⓓ 배타적으로, 독점적으로   primarily ⓐⓓ 주로
qualitative ⓐ 질적인   output ⓝ 산출량, 생산량
numerical ⓐ 수의, 수와 관련된   literature ⓝ 문헌
mislead ⓥ 오도하다, 호도하다   quantitative ⓐ 양적인
accountability ⓝ 책임, 의무
characterize ⓥ ~의 특성을 설명하다, ~의 특성을 나타내다
profitability ⓝ 수익성, 이윤율   quantifiable ⓐ 정량화할 수 있는
supervisory ⓐ 감독의, 관리의   taint ⓥ 더럽히다, 오염시키다
favoritism ⓝ 편애, 편파   kickback ⓝ 뇌물, 리베이트
personnel management – 인사관리   dimension ⓝ 요인, 요소
empowerment ⓝ 권한 부여, 권한 이양   accountable ⓐ 설명할 수 있는, 책임 있는

[39-40] 한국외대 2012

타타 자동차가 내놓은 저가형 자동차 나노의 판매는 차의 설계 형태에 대한 일반 대중의 인식과 차이가 생긴 결과 한계에 봉착했다. 2007년 발표되어 "국민차"라는 별명이 붙었던 나노는 세계에서 가장 싼 자동차로 대서특필되었다. 나노는 인도에서 오토바이나 모패드에 네 명 이상씩 올라타서 이동하는 수백만에 달하는 가정을 위한 안전한 업그레이드 수단이 되겠다는 취지에서 제작되었다.

하지만 언론의 관심이 컸던 탓에 취지와 다른 유형의 고객들이 나노를 구매하기 시작했다. 나노는 오토바이에서 한 단계 개선된 것으로 인식되기보다 값싼 자동차로 알려졌고, 세 번째 자동차나 뭔가 새로운 것으로 취급되어 구매되었다. 2륜구동 차량에서 업그레이드를 한 사람들은 비 내리는 우기에는 안전함과 편안함을 느꼈지만 도시에서 오토바이를 쉽게 주차할 수 있기 때문에 느꼈던 편안함은 포기해야 했다. 또한 최고 속도가 시간당 105km이었기 때문에 나노는 국도에서 장거리를 운행하는 사람들에겐 제한적인 매력을 지녔다.

마지막으로, 인도의 자동차 시장은 입문 단계 가격대의 소형 차량이 지배하고 있으며 현재 나노는 과거만큼 가격이 낮지는 않다. 저가 자동차와 25% 비싸지만 "제대로 된 자동차" 사이에서 선택을 해야 한다면, 사람들은 후자를 선택할 것이다. 계층 피라미드 가장 밑바닥에 위치한 구매자들 입장에서도 자동차는 출세 지향적인 성격을 지니고 있기 때문에 이들도 자신이 소유한 자동차가 인도에서 가장 값싼 자동차로 불리는 상황을 원하지 않는다.

39 다음 중 나노가 판매 목표를 달성하지 못한 이유를 가장 잘 설명한 것은 무엇인가?
① 마케팅 전략이 목표 소비자를 정확히 식별하지 못했다.
② 최고 속도가 시간당 105km에 불과했다.
③ 현재 나노는 최고급 모델이자 시장에 출시된 다른 차와 비교해 너무 비싼 것으로 여겨진다.
④ 나노를 뭔가 새로운 것으로 구매하려는 사람들의 수는 제한적이다.

| 정답 | ①

| 해설 | 나노가 제대로 팔리지 않은 가장 큰 원인은 원래 나노를 사야 할 유형의 사람들이 아니라 엉뚱한 유형의 사람들이 구매하고 나서 실망했기 때문이다. 그리고 이는 과도한 언론의 관심 때문에 원래 용도가 제대로 알려지지 않고 왜곡된 탓이 크다. 타타 자동차는 이런 상황이 발생하지 않도록 마케팅을 할 때 목표 소비자층을 잡고 이들에게 메시지를 정확히 전달했어야 했지만, 그렇지 못한 관계로 결국 실패하게 된 것이다. 따라서 답은 ①이다.

40 밑줄 친 부분을 가장 잘 해석한 것은 무엇인가?

① 부유한 사람들은 "인도에서 가장 값싼 자동차"로 알려진 자동차를 운전하는 모습을 보이고 싶어 하지 않는다.
② 구매자들은 입수 가능한 가장 값싼 모델을 원하며 다른 사람들이 자신이 얼마나 돈을 적게 지불했는지 알기를 원하지 않는다.
③ 가난한 사람들은 자동차를 구매할 때 자신의 사회적 지위를 높이길 원하며, 이 때문에 자동차의 평판에 민감하게 반응한다.
④ 인도 소비자들은 가격보다 품질을 더 높게 여기며 좋은 자동차에 기꺼이 돈을 더 많이 지불하려 한다.

| 정답 | ③

| 해설 | 밑줄 친 부분은, 사회적 지위가 낮은 사람들 입장에서는 차가 일종의 자신의 신분을 높이는 수단이기 때문에 자신들이 구매한 차가 싸구려 취급을 받는 것은 덩달아 자신들도 싸구려 취급을 받는 것으로 생각할 것이며 결국 그런 자동차를 구매하는 것을 꺼리게 될 것임을 의미한다. 즉, 이들은 자동차가 세상에서 받는 평판에 민감하게 반응할 수밖에 없다. 따라서 답은 ③이다.

| 어휘 | perception ⓝ 인식, 자각
dub ⓥ 별명을 붙이다
moped ⓝ 모페드(모터 달린 자전거)
entry-level ⓐ 입문 단계의, 초보자용의
reputation ⓝ 평판, 명성
unveil ⓥ 발표하다
make headline – 대서특필되다
novelty ⓝ 새로운 것
aspirational ⓐ 출세 지향적인, 열망하는

[41-43] 경희대 2013

뉴욕 타임즈의 컬럼니스트 토마스 프리드먼의 주장에 따르면 세계화는 "기업이 전 세계 곳곳으로 더 멀리, 빠르게, 값싸게, 깊게 도달할 수 있도록 하며" "세계가 이전에 볼 수 없었던 수준의 부와 기술적 혁신이 꽃피울 수 있도록" 조장한다. 전직 포드 재단 임원이자 현재는 저명한 세계화 비판가인 데이비드 코텐에게 있어 세계화는 "암과 같이 지구 전역으로 손을 뻗으면서, 지구상의 생활공간을 점점 식민지화하고, 사람들의 생계를 파괴하고, 사람들을 살던 곳에서 쫓아내고, 돈에 대한 끝없는 추구 끝에 생명을 잡아먹으며 살아가는 시장의 폭압"이다. 이제는 친숙해진 이러한 논란을 주의 깊게 들은 사람은 실제로 눈에 띌 만한 합의점을 파악할 수 있다. 간단히 말해, 찬성 반대 양측 모두 전 지구를 무대로 진행되는 사업이 미래의 대세가 될 것임을 상정하고 있지만, 한쪽은 이를 희열 섞인 눈으로 상정하고 다른 한쪽은 공포심을 품으며 상정하고 있다. 하지만 다국적 기업이 국가 규모 기업이나 지역 기반 기업에 비해 경쟁력 있는 상품을 내놓을 능력이 떨어진다는 증거도 점차 증가하고 있다. 경제학과 1학년 학생이라면 누구든지 기업은 확장을 통해 평균 비용을 낮출 수 있지만, 어디까지나 일정 시점까지만 가능하다는 점을 배우게 된다. 해당 시점을 넘어서게 되면 (규모에 대한 수익감소 법칙에 의거해), 복잡성·고장·비능률 등이 평균 비용을 다시 올려 버린다. 구소련에서 대규모의 국경기업이 붕괴한 사례나 크라이슬러 및 뉴욕시의 파산은 우리가 공룡으로부터 받아들여야 했던 교훈을 다시금 주목할 수 있게 상기시켜 줬다. 즉, 크다고 항상 좋은 것은 아니라는 점이다.

41

윗글의 내용과 맞지 않는 것은?

① 경쟁력이 떨어지는 제품을 생산하는 다국적 기업
② 대규모 마케팅을 통한 제한 없는 비용 감축
③ 거대한 기업의 몰락에 대한 역사적 사례
④ 세계적 기업에 대한 두 가지 상반된 시각

| 정답 | ②

| 해설 | 본문은 세계화 또는 전 지구적 차원에서 진행되는 기업 활동을 바라보는 부정적 시선과 긍정적 시선에 관해 언급한 다음, 다국적 기업같이 규모가 큰 기업이 반드시 성공한다는 보장도 없음을 언급하고 있다. 본문에서 이를 잘 나타낸 말이 "경제학과 1학년 학생이라면 누구든지 기업은 확장을 통해 평균 비용을 낮출 수 있지만, 어디까지나 일정 시점까지만 가능하다는 점을 배우게 된다(Any first-year economics student learns that firms can lower average costs by expanding, but only up to a point)"이다. 따라서 ③은 본문의 내용과 맞지 않음을 알 수 있다. 참고로, "하지만 다국적 기업이 국가 규모 기업이나 지역 기반 기업에 비해 경쟁력 있는 상품을 내놓을 능력이 떨어진다는 증거도 점차 증가하고 있다(Yet there's mounting evidence that multinational firms may be less capable of delivering competitive products than national or local firms)"는 ①과 일치하며, "구소련에서 대규모의 국경기업이 붕괴한 사례나 크라이슬러 및 뉴욕시의 파산(The collapse of massive state-owned enterprises in the old Soviet Union and the bankruptcies of Chrysler and New York City)"은 ③을 잘 나타내는 사례이다. 그리고 토마스 프리드먼과 데이비드 코텐은 ④에 대한 예시라 할 수 있다.

42

빈칸 ⓐ _____ 에 들어갈 어구 중 적합하지 않은 것은?

① 지구상의 생활공간을 점점 식민지화함
② 사람들의 생계를 파괴함
③ 사람들을 살던 곳에서 쫓아냄
④ 민주적 기관이 활동할 수 있게끔 함

| 정답 | ④

| 해설 | ④를 제외하면 모두 세계화로 인한 부정적 사례에 속한다. 그리고 ④는 민주주의에 관한 내용인데, 본문 어디에도 민주주의에 관한 내용은 언급되지 않는다. 따라서 답은 ④이다.

43

다음 문장이 삽입될 본문의 가장 적합한 곳을 고르시오.

간단히 말해, 찬성 반대 양측 모두 전 지구를 무대로 진행되는 기업 활동이 미래의 대세가 될 것임을 상정하고 있지만, 한쪽은 이를 희열 섞인 눈으로 상정하고 다른 한쪽은 공포심을 품으며 상정하고 있다.

① ⓑ ② ⓒ
③ ⓓ ④ ⓔ

| 정답 | ①

| 해설 | 주어진 문장은 '전 지구를 무대로 진행되는 기업 활동이 미래의 대세가 될 것'이라는 합의점이 존재함을 언급하고 있다. ⓑ 앞의 "합의점(agreement)"이 바로 이를 가리킨다. 그리고 ⓑ 앞에서는 세계화와 다국적 기업에 대한 긍정적 시각과 부정적 시각을 토마스 프리드먼과 데이비드 코텐의 입을 빌어 제시하고 있는데, 주어진 문장은 이를 하나로 요약한 것으로 볼 수 있다. 따라서 주어진 문장의 위치는 ⓑ가 되어야 한다.

| 어휘 | foster ⓥ 조장하다, 발전시키다
displace ⓥ (살던 곳에서) 쫓아내다
discern ⓥ 파악하다, 알아차리다
euphoria ⓝ 희열
complexity ⓝ 복잡성
inefficiency ⓝ 비능률
reminder ⓝ 상기시키는 것
downfall ⓝ 몰락

tyranny ⓝ 압제, 폭압
insatiable ⓐ 만족할 줄 모르는, 끝없는
striking ⓐ 눈에 띄는, 두드러진
mounting ⓐ 증가하는
breakdown ⓝ 고장
notable ⓐ 주목할 만한
colossal ⓐ 거대한, 엄청난
render ⓥ (어떤 상태가 되게) 만들다

[44-46] 숭실대 2014

오늘날 세계에는 자신이 태어난 곳 밖의 나라에서 살고 있는 사람은 대략 1억 9천만 명 가량 되며, 이 중 근 60%는 부국에서 살고 있다(3,600만 명은 유럽에서 살며 3,800만 명은 미국에 살고 있다). 사람들은 주로 경제적 이유 때문에 이주하지만, 일부는 정치적 탄압과 종교적 탄압을 피해 이주한다. 미국에 살고 있는 3,800만 명의 외국 태생 인물들은 미국 전체 인구의 12.6%를 나타낸다. 이들 중 근 30%인 1,100만 명은 미국에 불법으로 입국했다. 대부분의 국가는 미숙련 인구의 유입을 줄이고자 이민에 제한을 가한다(반면에 고숙련 기술직 인구의 이민을 권장하는 경우는 종종 있다). 대체로 상품·서비스·자본의 국제적인 흐름에 비해 이주에 제약 및 규제를 가하는 경우가 더 많다.

대체로 자본은 사람에 비해 국경을 넘어 더욱 자유롭게 흐른다. 금융자본 또는 (은행 대출 및 채권 같은) 포트폴리오자본은 대체로 금리가 높은 시장 및 국가로 흐르며, 공장 및 기업을 대상으로 한 외국의 직접 투자는 예상 수익이 높은 곳으로 흐른다. 이를 통해 자본의 더욱 효율적인 활용이 이루어지며 대체로 채권자 및 채무자 모두에게 이득이 된다. 1970년대에 중동 국가들은 석유를 팔아 거둔 엄청난 규모의 수익을 뉴욕 및 런던의 은행들에 예치했고, 그러자 뉴욕 및 런던의 은행들은 이렇게 예치된 금액을 라틴아메리카와 아시아의 정부와 기업에 대출(재순환)했다. 1980년대에 일본은 엄청난 규모의 수출 이익 가운데 상당한 액수를 금융자산 및 부동산에 투자하고 미국에 기업의 자회사를 설립했다.

1980년대 중반부터 미국은 생산에 비해 소비가 초과하고 있는 상황을 감당하고자 전 세계의 다른 모든 국가로부터 점차로 많은 돈을 빌리는 순 채무국이 되었다. 세계적인 은행들은 전 세계에 위치한 중요 국제 금융 센터에 지점을 설립하였고, 국제 금융센터에서는 24시간 내내 거래를 통해 3조 달러에 달하는 외국 통화가 교환되고 있으며, 새로 설립된 국부 펀드 (중동의 석유수출국, 싱가포르, 중국, 러시아, 브라질 등이 보유한 금융 기관)에서는 전 세계를 무대로 엄청난 규모로 온갖 것들에 투자를 하고 있다. 금융시장은 과거 전례 없는 수준으로 세계화가 진행되어 있다. 이로 인한 단점은 금융위기가 한 나라에 닥칠 경우 다른 나라로 재빨리 확산된다는 점이다.

44 다음 중 제목으로 가장 적합한 것은 무엇인가?
① 국제 무역의 현대적 측면
② 이민자의 세계화
③ 노동과 자본의 국제적인 흐름
④ 세계 금융 시장에서 미국의 역할

| 정답 | ③

| 해설 | 본문 첫 번째 단락은 노동의 국제적인 이동에 관해 그리고 두 번째 및 세 번째 단락은 자본과 금융의 국제적인 이동에 관해 논하고 있다. 따라서 이 모두를 포괄하는 제목으로 가장 적합한 것은 ③이다.

45

다음 중 사실이 아닌 것은 무엇인가?

① 이민의 주된 이유는 경제적인 이유이다.
② 돈보다는 사람들이 이동할 기회가 더 적다.
③ 돈은 수익이 큰 쪽으로 이동한다.
④ 미국은 1980년대부터 최대 채권국이 되었다.

| 정답 | ④

| 해설 | "1980년대 중반부터 미국은 생산에 비해 소비가 초과하고 있는 상황을 감당하고자 전 세계의 다른 모든 국가로부터 점차로 많은 돈을 빌리는 순 채무국이 되었다(Since the mid-1980s, the United States has become an increasingly large net borrower from the rest of the world to cover its excess of spending over production)." 따라서 답은 ④이다.

46

다음 중 세계화된 시장에 관해 사실인 것은 무엇인가?

① 돈이 바로 주된 매개체이다.
② 이주 노동자에 주로 의존한다.
③ 외국 투자는 안전상의 이유로 낮은 금리를 요구한다.
④ 돈의 자유로운 흐름은 금융위기에 대응하기 위한 방어기제이다.

| 정답 | ①

| 해설 | 자본이 국경을 넘어 자유롭게 흐르게 된 이유는 더 높은 수익을 창출하기 위해서였고, 이 과정에서 금융시장의 세계화가 이루어진 것이다. 즉, 세계화는 돈이 주된 매개체가 되어 이루어진 것이다. 따라서 답은 ①이다.

| 어휘 | migrate ⓥ 이주하다, 이동하다
oppression ⓝ 압박, 압제, 억압, 탄압
illegally ⓐⓓ 불법으로, 비합법적으로
impose ⓥ (새로운 법률·세금 등을) 도입[시행]하다, (힘들거나 불쾌한 것을) 부과하다[지우다]
restriction ⓝ 제한, 제약
inflow ⓝ 유입
technical ⓐ 과학 기술의, 기술적인, 전문적인
restricted ⓐ 제한된, 한정된, 제약된
in general - 대체로, 일반적으로
portfolio ⓝ 유가 증권 명세표, 포트폴리오, 자산 구성(각종 금융 자산의 집합)
deposit ⓥ (돈 따위를) 맡기다, 예금[예치]하다
recycle ⓥ 재생 이용하다, 재순환시키다, (차관·투자 등의 형태로) 환류시키다
chunk ⓝ 큰 덩어리, 상당한 양[액수]
set up - ~을 건립하다, 설립하다
net ⓐ (에누리 없는) 정(正)~, 순(純)~; 최종적인
branch ⓝ 지점, 분과, 부문
around-the-clock ⓐ 24시간 연속의, 쉴 새 없이 계속되는
sovereign ⓐ 주권을 갖는, 자주적인, 독립된
downside ⓝ 불리한[덜 긍정적인] 면, 단점

primarily ⓐⓓ 주로
foreign-born ⓐ 외국 태생의
immigration ⓝ 이주, 이민, 이민자 수
low-skilled ⓐ 미숙련의
migration ⓝ 이주, 이동
regulated ⓐ 통제된, 규제된
petroleum ⓝ 석유
export earnings - 수출 이익
subsidiary ⓝ 자회사
excess ⓝ 과잉, 초과
monetary ⓐ 통화[화폐]의, 금융의
sovereign fund - 국부 펀드
agency ⓝ 매개, 대리(권), 중개

[47-48] 성균관대 2018

아날로그 시대에서는 자신들의 비즈니스 모델의 유익한 선례를 찾을 수 없는 소수의 거대 기업들의 성장은 자본주의 경제가 작동하는 방식에 대한 재평가를 강요한다. 세계에서 가장 높은 가치를 보유한 7대 기업은 모두 기술 분야에 속한다. (구글을 소유한) 알파벳과 페이스북 같은 거대 기업들은 3차원 공간에 존재하지 않는 제품을 전문적으로 취급한다. 애플과 아마존은 개념뿐만 아니라 현실 세계의 제품도 판매하지만, 그들의 막대한 부와 시장 지배력은 모델, 브랜드, 알고리즘과 같은 모호한 개념을 토대로 구축된 것이다.

부는 더 이상 공장이나 파이프라인, 할인 매장에 있는 것이 아니다. 그들의 자본은 특정 분야에 고정되어 있지 않다. 그것이 그들을 규제하기 어렵게 만들고 세금을 부과하기 어렵게 한다. 이런 것들은 디지털 혁명을 선행하는 경제적 세계화(economic globalization)의 패턴이다. 소프트웨어 및 데이터 같은 일부 무형의 것은 컴퓨터에 크게 의존하지만, 다른 것은 그렇지 않다. 예를 들어 브랜드가 그러하다.

새로운 시대를 다르게 만드는 것은 가치가 유형의 것에서 분리되는 정도와, 이에 상응하는 사회적, 경제적 결과에 있다. 이것은 조너선 하스켈(Jonathan Haskell)과 스티언 웨스틀레이크(Stian Westlake)가 '자본 없는 자본주의(capitalism without capital)'라고 언급한 역학적 관계를 말한다. 이것을 제목으로 한 책에서, 저자들은 무형의 규모가 시장 경제의 익숙한 메커니즘을 변형시키고 있는 방식을 밝히고 있다.

47 다음 중 밑줄 친 "capitalism without capital"이 의미하는 것은?
① 자본주의 경제의 붕괴
② 무형의 자본을 지닌 자본주의
③ 비즈니스에서 글로벌 네트워크의 중요성
④ 자본주의에서 부의 불평등
⑤ 자본주의에서 유형 자산의 전 세계적 확장

| 정답 | ②

| 해설 | 본문에서 밝히고 있는 것과 같이 '자본 없는 자본주의'란 자본주의가 유형의 것으로 작동하는 것을 넘어 오히려 지금은 무형의 것(모델, 브랜드, 알고리즘)이 자본주의 작동에 더 큰 영향을 주고 있다는 사실을 지칭하는 용어이다. 따라서 '무형의 자본을 지닌 자본주의'라는 ②가 가장 비슷한 의미가 된다.

48 다음 중 글의 제목으로 가장 적합한 것은?
① 자본주의에서 세계화의 필요성
② 자본주의의 세계화
③ 무형 자산의 증가
④ 자본주의의 본질적 변화
⑤ 새로운 시대의 성공을 위한 지침

| 정답 | ③

| 해설 | 본문은 자본주의 작동 방식이 유형 자산에서 무형 자산 위주로 변화하고 있는 것을 다루고 있으므로, 무형의 자산이 늘어나는 방식으로 자본주의가 변화하고 있다는 의미에서 ③이 제목으로 적합하다.

| 어휘 | a handful of – 소수의

corporate ⓐ 기업[회사]의; (그룹 구성원을 다 포함하는) 공동의
powerhouse ⓝ 강국, 유력[실세] 집단[기관]
precedent ⓝ 선례, 전례, 판례
specialize in − ~을 전공하다, ~을 전문적으로 다루다
market dominance − 시장 점유
retail outlet − 할인 매장, 대형 매장
regulate ⓥ 조정하다, 통제하다, 규제하다, 단속하다
pre-date ⓥ 선행하다
intangible ⓝ 만질 수 없는 것, 무형 자산 ⓐ 만질 수 없는, 무형의
detached ⓐ 분리된, 고립된
tangible ⓝ 만질 수 있는 것, 유형 자산 ⓐ 분명히 실재하는, 유형의
dynamic ⓝ 역학

instructive ⓐ 유익한
reappraisal ⓝ 재평가, 재검토
nebulous ⓐ 성운의, 흐린, 애매한
be anchored to − ~에 고정되다

deform ⓥ 변형시키다, 기형으로 만들다

[49-50] 광운대 2018

비트코인 열풍이 역사적으로 가장 큰 거품 붕괴로 변할 것인가? 가상화폐인 비트코인의 막대한 가격 상승(올해만 1,400% 이상 상승했다)은 엄청난 투기적 거품의 특성을 모두 갖추고 있다고 워렌 버핏(Warren Buffett)과 같은 사람들은 말한다. 그리고 비트코인의 거품이 꺼진다면 그 결과는 굉장할 것으로 예상된다. "비트코인이 어떻게 막을 내릴지 거품의 역사를 보면 흐지부지 끝나는 것이 아니라 '펑'하는 소리와 함께 폭발적으로 끝날 것을 암시한다."라고 ANZ의 경제학자인 샤론 졸러(Sharon Zoller)는 말했다. "이번에는 다를 것이라는 그 어떤 이유도 떠올리기 어렵다."라고 덧붙였다. 앞으로 어떤 일이 놓여 있을지 더 잘 이해하기 위해, 역사적으로 유명한 금융 거품인 '튤립 파동'의 내막을 살펴보자. 17세기 초 네덜란드에서는 투기로 인해 튤립 구근의 가치가 이전에는 생각지도 못했던 가격까지 치솟았다. 터키에서 새로 수입된 튤립은 당시 아주 신기한 것이었다. 당시의 구체적인 자료가 부족하기 때문에 가격이 얼마나 올랐는지 정확히 판단하기는 어렵다. 하지만 사람들은 (튤립을 사들이기 위해) 자신의 집을 담보로 내놓았다. 많은 거품과 마찬가지로 튤립의 가격은 탐욕이나 좋은 기회를 나 혼자만 놓칠 것 같은 생각에 따라 움직였다. 투기꾼들은 향후 더 높은 가격에 튤립을 팔 수 있다는 희망에서 튤립을 사모았다. 그러나 그것은 오래 가지 않았다. 튤립을 팔아 치우려는 광풍이 도미노 효과를 일으켰고, 가격은 무너져 내렸다. 외환거래 전문업체 오안다(Oanda)의 아시아 지역 매매 담당자인 스티븐 이네스(Stephen Innes)는 비트코인 거품도 같은 길을 갈 수 있다고 생각한다. "가격이 일반인들이 살 수 없을 정도로 높아지면서 결국에는 수요가 점차 줄어들 것"이라고 말했다.

49

다음 주어진 표현이 들어갈 가장 적절한 위치는?

외환거래 전문업체 오안다(Oanda)의 아시아 지역 매매 담당자인 스티븐 이네스(Stephen Innes)는 비트코인 거품도 같은 길을 갈 수 있다고 생각한다.

① (A) ② (B)
③ (C) ④ (D)
⑤ (E)

| 정답 | ⑤

| 해설 | 제시문의 'bitcoin bubble could go the same way' 내용을 통해 앞에서는 비트코인과 유사한 튤립 거품의 결과

가 와야 하고, 뒤에서는 비트코인의 결과가 와야 한다는 것을 알 수 있다. 그런 점에서 제시문은 (E)에 들어가야 한다. (E) 앞에서는 어떻게 튤립의 가격이 폭락했는지 설명하고 있으며, 뒤에서는 앞으로 비트코인의 수요가 감소하면서 폭락할 수 있다는 내용을 '미래시제'를 이용해 제시하고 있다.

50 빈칸 ⓐ, ⓑ, ⓒ에 들어갈 가장 적절한 모둠은?
① 부족한, 불충분한 – 투기적인 – 굉장한, 극적인
② 투기적인 – 굉장한, 극적인 – 부족한, 불충분한
③ 부족한, 불충분한 – 투기적인 – 부족한, 불충분한
④ 투기적인 – 부족한, 불충분한 – 굉장한, 극적인
⑤ 굉장한, 극적인 – 부족한, 불충분한 – 투기적인

| 정답 | ②

| 해설 | ⓐ는 '투기의 거품'을 설명하는 내용이므로 speculative가 적합하다. ⓑ의 경우, 비트코인이 어떻게 끝날 것인지 설명하는 내용으로 뒤에 나오는 'A rather than B'에서 A에 해당하는 'with a bang'과 동일한 내용이 ⓑ에 와야 한다. 따라서 투기의 끝이 '펑'하고 터지는 것 같이 엄청나게 폭발적으로 끝날 것이라는 의미에서 spectacular가 적합하다. 마지막 ⓒ의 경우, 바로 뒤 결과를 의미하는 접속사 so 이하의 내용을 통해 정확히 가격이 얼마까지 폭등했는지 측정하기 어려운 근거는 객관적인 자료(hard data)가 부족하기 때문이라는 의미에서 scarce가 와야 한다. 따라서 정답은 ②가 된다.

| 어휘 | boom ⓝ (사업·경제의) 붐, 호황 ⓥ 호황을 누리다, 번창[성공]하다
be about to – 막 ~하려는 참이다
bust ⓝ 실패, 파산 ⓥ 부수다, 파멸시키다
massive ⓐ 거대한, 엄청나게 큰
hallmark ⓝ 특징, 특질
in terms of – ~에 관하여
(end) with a whimper – 흐지부지 끝나다, 훌쩍이며 끝나다
lie ahead – 앞에 놓여 있다, 앞으로 전개될 것이다
lowdown ⓝ 실정, 진상, 내막
speculation ⓝ 투기; 추측
unheard of – 전례가 없는, 아주 유별난
hard data – 확실한 데이터
soar ⓥ 급증하다, (허공으로) 솟구치다
collateral ⓝ 담보물 ⓐ 부차적인
fear of missing out – (신조어) 좋은 기회를 놓치고 싶지 않은 마음(약어로 FOMO라고 함)
speculator ⓝ 투기꾼, 투기자
last ⓥ 지속되다
domino effect – 도미노 효과(하나의 사건이 비슷한 사건들의 연쇄적인 발생을 초래하는 효과)
collapse ⓝ (계획의) 좌절, 붕괴, 와해 ⓥ 무너지다, 붕괴하다
fade ⓥ 바래다, 희미해지다, 서서히 사라지다
spectacular ⓐ 굉장한, 극적인
turn into – ~으로 변하다
currency ⓝ 통화, 통용; 유행
surge ⓝ 급증 ⓥ 밀려들다
burst ⓥ 터지다, 파열하다
with a bang – 쾅[쿵, 펑]하고; 멋지게, 성공적으로
tulip mania – 튤립 파동
tulip bulb – 튤립 구근
novelty ⓝ 새로움, 신기함 ⓐ 색다른, 진기한
gauge ⓥ 측정하다
put up A as collateral – A를 담보물로 제공하다
greed ⓝ 탐욕
in the hope that – ~라는 희망을 가지고
a flurry of – 갑작스럽게 몰아치는, 일진의
scarce ⓐ 부족한, 불충분한
speculative ⓐ 투기적인; 추측에 근거한

에듀윌 편입영어 **기출심화 완성 독해**

PART 02

자연과학

CHAPTER 01　기초 과학
CHAPTER 02　지구 · 환경
CHAPTER 03　생물
CHAPTER 04　인간
CHAPTER 05　의학 · 건강

CHAPTER 01 기초 과학

01	②	02	④	03	①	04	③	05	③	06	②	07	③	08	①	09	④	10	②
11	①	12	③	13	②	14	③	15	①	16	①	17	①	18	②	19	①	20	④
21	②	22	①	23	②	24	②	25	①	26	④	27	①	28	④	29	①	30	②

[01-05] 경기대 2010

Thomas Kuhn은 과학적 변화의 전반적인 방향에 대해 몇 가지 논쟁적인 주장을 펼쳤다. 일반적인 시각에서는 과학은 진실을 향해 선형으로, 즉 낡고 부정확한 사고가 더 새롭고 더 정확한 사고로 대체되는 방식으로 진보한다고 보고 있다. 따라서 나중의 이론들이 객관적으로 그 전의 이론보다 우월하다고 할 수 있다. 이런 누적적인 과학 개념이 일반인이나 과학자들 사이에 대중적이었으나, Kuhn은 이는 역사적으로도 부정확할 뿐만 아니라 철학적으로는 순진한 생각이라고 주장한다. 예를 들면, 그는 아인슈타인의 상대성이론이 어떤 면에서는 뉴턴의 이론보다는 아리스토텔레스의 이론과 더 유사하므로 역학의 역사는 틀린 것에서 바른 것으로의 단순한 선형의 진보는 아니라는 것이다. 게다가, 객관적 진실이라는 개념이 맞는 말인지에 대해 의문을 제기했다. 그가 생각하기에 어느 특정한 패러다임과는 독립적인, 세상에 관한 확고부동한 일련의 사실들이 존재할 것이라는 생각은 일관성 면에서 의심스러웠다. 그는 급진적인 대안을 제시했다. 바로 세상에 대한 사실들은 패러다임에 상대적이며, 따라서 변한다는 것이다. 만약 이 주장이 옳다면, 어떤 이론이 있는 그대로의 사실과 부합하는지를 묻는 것도 이치에 맞지 않으며, 따라서 그것이 객관적으로 진실인지의 여부를 묻는 것도 모두 이치에 닿지 않는다는 것이다.

01 다음 중 빈칸 ㉮에 가장 적절한 문장은 무엇인가?
① 그러나 초기의 이론이 후기의 이론보다 본질적으로 낫다.
② 따라서 나중의 이론들이 객관적으로 그 전의 이론보다 우월하다.
③ 그래서 전과 후의 이론 모두 나란히 존재한다.
④ 그래서 나중의 이론들이 전의 이론들보다 반드시 우월한 것은 아니다.

| 정답 | ②

| 해설 | 빈칸 앞뒤의 내용을 살펴보자. 먼저 앞의 내용에는 linear라는 단어가 등장한다. 과학적 진실의 진보가 선형적(linear)임을 말하고 있다. 빈칸 바로 뒤에는 'this cumulative conception'이란 표현이 나오는데, 여기서 cumulative(누적되는)가 바로 앞에 나왔던 linear라는 단어와 동의어임을 알 수 있다. 왜냐하면 과학적 사실이 시간적으로 차곡차곡 쌓여서(cumulative) 형성된다는 말은 선형적으로 진보가 이루어진다는 말의 다른 표현이기 때문이다. 따라서 빈칸에는 앞뒤의 내용과 같은 맥락이 이어져야 한다. ①은 역접의 but을 사용했으므로 탈락된다. ③은 옛 이론과 새로운 이론은 나란히 존재하는 것이 아니라 대체된다(be replaced)고 했으므로 본문의 내용과 맞지 않게 된다. ④의 경우는 앞서 등장하는 말을 뒤엎고 있다. 'not necessarily'는 '반드시 ~한 것은 아니다'라는 뜻이기 때문이다. 따라서 답은 ②로 빈칸 앞뒤의 내용을 잘 이어주고 있다.

02

다음 중 빈칸 ㉯에 가장 적절한 것을 고르시오.
① 반면에
② 그럼에도 불구하고
③ 역설적이게도
④ 게다가

| 정답 | ④

| 해설 | 적절한 연결어구(transition)를 묻는 문제이다. 빈칸의 앞뒤 문맥을 따져 보아 순접인지 아니면 역접의 흐름인지 살피는 것이 중요하다. 빈칸 앞의 내용을 보면 아인슈타인의 상대성이론은 과학의 진보가 선형적이라면 시기적으로 가까운 뉴턴의 이론과 비슷해야 하지만, 그렇지 않고 시기적으로 보다 먼 아리스토텔레스의 이론과 유사하다는 점을 강조하고 있다. 빈칸 뒤의 내용을 보면 객관적인 진실(objective truth)에 대한 개념 자체에 회의적인 시각을 보이고 있다. 이 모든 것은 앞서 말한 일반적으로 사실로 받아들여지는 것들에 대한 의구심이라고 할 수 있다. 따라서 빈칸 앞뒤의 내용이 모두 같은 내용임을 알 수 있고, 순접의 관계로 묶여 있는 것을 알 수 있다. 따라서 답은 ④가 된다.

03

다음 중 밑줄 친 "dubious"라는 단어와 뜻이 가장 유사한 것을 고르시오.
① 의심스러운
② 믿을 만한
③ 끈기 있는
④ 간헐적인

| 정답 | ①

| 해설 | dubious는 '의심스러운'이란 뜻이므로 ① questionable이 정답이 된다. 참고로 questionable은 '의심스러운, 의문을 제기할 수 있는'이란 뜻이다.

04

다음 중 빈칸 ㉰에 가장 적절한 것은?
① 효력이 있다, 사실이다
② 매우 중요하다
③ 이치에 닿지 않다
④ 커다란 차이를 가져오다

| 정답 | ③

| 해설 | 이 문제는 빈칸의 앞뒤 문맥을 통해 파악해야 한다. 앞서의 제안(suggestion)에서는 사실(facts)은 패러다임과 상대적(paradigm-relative)이라고 했으므로, 각각의 사실은 상대적이라는 말이 되며, 이 말은 고정된(fixed) 절대적인 사실이란 존재하지 않는다는 것을 의미한다. 따라서 앞의 제안이 사실이라면 to 이하를 물어보는 것(to ask whether a given ... 혹은 to ask whether it is objectively true)은 말이 되지 않는 어불성설이 된다고 보는 것이 문맥의 흐름과 일치한다. 따라서 답은 ③이 된다. 참고로 ①, ②, ④는 모두 긍정의 뜻을 지니고 있다는 점도 고려해 볼 만하다.

05

본문에 따르면, 다음 중 사실이 아닌 것은?
① Kuhn 이전 사람들은 일반적으로 과학의 역사는 진실을 향해 똑바로 진보하는 것이라고 믿었다.
② Kuhn은 객관적 진실이라는 개념이 유효한가에 대해 의심했다.
③ Kuhn은 어느 특정한 패러다임에도 속하지 않은 세상에 대한 일련의 고정된 사실을 찾을 수 있다고 믿었다.
④ Kuhn은 아인슈타인의 상대성이론이 아리스토텔레스의 이론과 공통점을 가진다고 믿었다.

| 정답 | ③

| 해설 | ①의 경우 본문에 나오는 "According to a widely-held view, science progresses towards the truth in a linear fashion"이라는 문장을 바꾸어 쓴 것이다. ②의 경우 "Kuhn questioned whether the concept of objective truth actually makes sense at all"의 문장을 보고 사실임을 알 수 있다. ③은 본문에서 "The idea that there is a fixed set of facts about the world … was of dubious coherence"라고 했으므로 이에 대해 의심했다는 것을 알 수 있으며, 따라서 ③이 정답이 된다. ④의 경우 "(Kuhn) noted that Einstein's theory of relativity is … more similar to Aristotelian"이라는 문장을 통해 사실임을 알 수 있다.

| 어휘 |
controversial ⓐ 논란의 여지가 있는, 논쟁적인　claim ⓝ 주장
overall ⓐ 총체적인, 종합적인　widely-held ⓐ 보편적으로 사람들이 생각하는
progress ⓥ 나아가다, 진보하다　linear ⓐ 일직선으로 늘어선, 직선의; 선 모양의
in a linear fashion – 선형적인 방식으로　cumulative ⓐ 누적하는, 누증적인
conception ⓝ 개념　layman ⓝ (전문가와 대비되는) 일반인, 아마추어, 문외한
A and B alike – A와 B 모두　naive ⓐ 순진한, 단순한, 고지식한
theory of relativity – (아인슈타인의) 상대성 이론
in some respects – 어떤 면에서는　mechanics ⓝ 역학
question ⓥ 의문을 제기하다　objective ⓐ 객관적인 (cf. subjective ⓐ 주관적인)
make sense – 이치에 닿다, 뜻이 통하다　fixed ⓐ 고정된
a set of – 일련의　(be) independent of – 독립적인
paradigm ⓝ 패러다임, 이론적 틀　dubious ⓐ 의심스러운
coherence ⓝ 통일, 일관성, 긴밀성, 결합력　of coherence (=coherent) – 일관성이 있는
of dubious coherence (=dubiously coherent) – 일관성이 의심스러운
radical ⓐ 과격한, 급진적인, 급격한　alternative ⓝ 대안, 다른 방도
paradigm-relative ⓐ 패러다임에 상대적인　correspond to – ~에 일치하다, 부합하다
subjectively ⓐⓓ 주관적으로, 본질적으로　objectively ⓐⓓ 객관적으로
side by side – 나란히; 협력하여　thus ⓐⓓ 그러므로, 따라서, 요컨대
questionable ⓐ 의심나는(doubtful), 미심쩍은　trustworthy ⓐ 신뢰할 수 있는, 믿을 수 있는
enduring ⓐ 참을성 있는; 영속하는, 영구적인(lasting)
intermittent ⓐ 때때로 중단되는, 간헐적인　hold good – 효력이 있다
makes a difference – 차이가 생기다, 효과가 있다; 중요하다
vital ⓐ 극히 중대한, 절대 필요한, 불가결한　be of importance (=important) – 중요한
straightforward ⓐ 똑바른; 정직한, 솔직한　valid ⓐ 유효한, 효과적인
A have something in common with B – A와 B는 서로 공통점이 있다

[06-08] 숭실대 2009

케플러의 법칙은 지구가 태양 주위의 궤도에 따라 움직이는 방식을 설명한다. 복합적 운동 법칙과 가속 운동 방정식 같은 갈릴레오의 발견들은 물체가 여기 지구 위의 실험실에서 움직이는 방식을 설명한다. 그러나 이 두 종류의 법칙들 중 어느 것에도 행성이 포탄(갈릴레오가 피사의 사탑 실험에서 사용한 공)과 비슷할 수 있다거나, 지구에서 작용하는 법칙이 우주에서도 작용할 것이라는 암시는 없다. 다시 말해서, 케플러와 갈릴레오의 연구가 완성된 후에 물리학과 천문학은 완전히 별개의 과학 분야가 되었다는 것이다. 지구에서 일어나는 일들은 우주 어디에서나 일어나는 일들과 전혀 다르지 않다는 것을 보여준 최초의 인물은 바로 아이작 뉴턴(1642~1727)이다.

지금까지의 과학자들 중 아마도 가장 뛰어난 과학자인 뉴턴은 갈릴레오와 다른 과학자들의 연구를 통합해, 별과 행성에서 구름, 포탄, 인체의 근육에 이르기까지 우주 만물의 운동을 지배하는 기본 법칙들을 완성했다. 이 연구결과가 뉴턴의 운동법칙이다. 뉴턴의 운동법칙은 너무 간단하고 자명해서 이 법칙이 수 세기에 걸친 실험과 관찰의 결과라는 것을 깨닫기 어려울 뿐 아니라, 이 법칙이 과학 발전에 얼마나 중요한 영향을 미쳤는지 인식하기는 더 어렵다. 뉴턴 운동법칙은 세 가지 기본법칙으로 이루어진다.

06 지문에 따르면 다음 중 사실이 아닌 것은?
① 뉴턴의 운동법칙은 수 세기에 걸친 연구 결과에 기초한다.
② 뉴턴은 오랫동안 케플러의 연구를 모방했다.
③ 뉴턴 덕분에 천문학과 물리학은 밀접하게 연관되었다.
④ 운동법칙은 우주에서 이동하는 모든 물체에 적용할 수 있다.

| 정답 | ②

| 해설 | "Newton ~ synthesized the work of Galileo and others into a statement of the basic principles that govern the motion of everything in the universe"를 참조하면, 뉴턴의 업적은 케플러와 갈릴레오의 법칙을 통합한 것이지 어느 한쪽을 모방한 것이 아니다.

07 다음 중 이어지는 단락의 화제로 적절한 것은?
① 뉴턴의 전기적인 일화
② 갈릴레오의 발견의 중요성
③ 뉴턴의 세 가지 운동법칙에 대한 자세한 설명
④ 케플러의 법칙에 대한 간단한 소개

| 정답 | ③

| 해설 | 마지막 문장에 뉴턴 이론의 핵심이 세 가지 기본법칙(Three basic laws formed the centerpiece of Newton's description of motion.)이라는 언급이 있으므로 다음 단락은 이 세 가지 기본법칙에 대한 내용이 이어지는 것이 논리적이다.

08 다음 중 이 지문이 실렸을 책은 무엇인가?
① 물리학 입문서
② Galileo Galilei의 전기
③ 은하계에 대한 책
④ 영화 가이드북

| 정답 | ①

| 해설 | 이 글은 뉴턴 물리학을 간략하게 소개하는 글이다. 따라서 ① "물리학 입문서"에 실릴 글임을 알 수 있다. 지문의 소재는 뉴턴의 물리학이지 우주 그 자체가 아니므로 ③은 틀린 보기이다.

| 어휘 |
describe ⓥ 설명하다, 묘사하다
orbit ⓝ 궤도
compound ⓐ 복합의
accelerated motion – 가속운동
laboratory ⓝ 실험실
suggestion ⓝ 암시; 주장
operate ⓥ 작동하다, 작용하다
in other words – 즉, 다른 말로
separate ⓐ 별개의, 분리된
synthesize ⓥ 합성하다, 통합하다
principle ⓝ 법칙, 원리
muscle ⓝ 근육
experiment ⓝ 실험
appreciate ⓥ (진가를) 이해하다, 평가하다
effect ⓝ 영향, 결과
planet ⓝ 행성
discovery ⓝ 발견
equation ⓝ 방정식
object ⓝ 물체
surface ⓝ 표면
cannonball ⓝ 포탄
heaven ⓝ 하늘
astronomy ⓝ 천문학
unconnected ⓐ 서로 상관없는
statement ⓝ 진술, 서술
govern ⓥ 지배하다
represent ⓥ 나타내다, 상징하다
observation ⓝ 관찰
extraordinary ⓐ 탁월한
centerpiece ⓝ 중심 항목

[09-11] 한국외대 2006

수학의 정리는 논리적 과정을 따른다. 그리고 일단 증명이 되면 영원히 참이다. 수학적 증명은 절대적이기 때문이다. 수학적 증명의 가치를 이해하기 위해서는 그보다 빈약한 과학적 증명과 비교해 보아야 한다. 과학에서는 물리 현상을 설명하기 위해 가설을 세운다. 관찰된 현상이 가설과 부합할 경우, 이것은 가설을 지지하는 증거가 된다. 가설의 예측 가능성을 테스트하기 위해서 실험을 할 수 있다. 실험이 계속해서 성공하면 이것은 가설을 뒷받침하는 훨씬 더 강력한 증거가 된다. 결국 증거가 압도적으로 많아지면 가설은 과학 이론으로 인정된다.

그러나 과학 이론은 수학정리와 같은 수준의 절대적 증명이 불가능하다. 과학 이론은 그저 현재 있는 증거에 기초해 참일 확률이 매우 높은 정도에 지나지 않는다. 과학적 증거가 의존하는 관찰과 지각은 모두 오류 가능성이 있고 진실에 가까운 근삿값일 뿐이다. 과학혁명은 이러한 과학적 증거의 약점으로 인해 일어나는데, 과거에 참으로 간주되었던 이론은 단지 더 개선된 후속 이론으로 대체되거나 완전히 모순되는 이론으로 대체된다.

09 빈칸 ⓐ에 가장 적절한 것은?

① 설명
② 모방
③ 부정
④ 근삿값
⑤ 반례

| 정답 | ④

| 해설 | 빈칸 앞부분에서 언급된 관찰과 지각이 틀릴 수 있다는 것은 관찰과 지각이 참이 아니라 진실에 가까운 "근삿값"에 불과하다는 뜻이다. 참이 아니라는 내용을 완성하는 보기는 ④뿐이다.

10 다음 중 지문에서 주로 다루고 있는 것은?
① 가설을 입증하는 가장 좋은 방법으로서의 실험
② 수학 정리와는 다른 과학 이론
③ 과학적 증명의 믿을 만한 증거
④ 과학 혁명의 모순들
⑤ 과학과 수학에서의 실험의 중요성

| 정답 | ②

| 해설 | 첫 단락에 수학이론의 특징이, 두 번째 단락에 수학이론과 다른 과학이론의 특징이 대조적으로 상술되고 있으므로 글의 전체 소재는 ②가 적절하다.

11 다음 중 지문에 언급되어 있거나 유추할 수 있는 것은?
① 한때는 확실히 참으로 여겨지던 과학이론이 다음에는 오류로 판명될 수 있다.
② 수학이론과 마찬가지로 과학이론도 절대적이며 의심의 여지가 없다.
③ 수학에는 실험적 증거나 완벽한 논리가 매우 중요하다.
④ 과학적 증명은 수학적 증명만큼이나 강력하고 확실하다.
⑤ 과학이론과 수학정리 모두 상대적 현상에 대한 충분한 관찰이 필요하다.

| 정답 | ①

| 해설 | 지문의 "This weakness in scientific proof leads to scientific revolutions in which a theory that was assumed to be correct is replaced with another theory"를 이해하는지 묻는 문제이다. "과학증명의 오류 가능성 때문에 과거 참이던 이론이 이후 다른 이론으로 대체된다"는 내용은 ①에 가장 잘 paraphrasing되어 있다.

| 어휘 | mathematical ⓐ 수학의 theorem ⓝ 정리
logical ⓐ 논리적인 proof ⓝ 증명, 증거
absolute ⓐ 절대적인 appreciate ⓥ (진가 등을) 알아보다, 인정하다
compare ⓥ 비교하다
poor relation – 가난한 친척(같은 종류이지만 열등한 대상에 대한 비유)
hypothesis ⓝ 가설 put forward – 제시하다
physical ⓐ 물리적인 phenomenon ⓝ 현상
observation ⓝ 관찰 in favor of – ~에 유리한, 호의적인
back ⓥ 지지하다 overwhelming ⓐ 압도적인
merely ⓐⓓ 그저, 단순히 perception ⓝ 지각, 인식
fallible ⓐ 오류 가능성이 있는 scientific revolution – 과학혁명
assume ⓥ 가정하다 replace ⓥ 대체하다
refinement ⓝ 개선, 정제, 세련됨 contradiction ⓝ 모순; 반박

[12-14]

이와 같은 동시다발적인 발견, 즉 과학사학자들이 "멀티플스(multiples)"라 부르는, 현상은 아주 흔한 것임이 드러났다. 과학과 철학에서 아주 중요한 법칙인 에너지 보존의 법칙은 줄, 톰슨, 콜딩, 헬므호르쯔 등에 의해 1847년에 네 번이나 개별적으로 형성되었다. 그리고 1842년에는 로버트 메이어에 의해 예측된 바 있다.

멀티플스의 수만 봐도 단 한 가지 점이 나타난다. 바로 과학적 발견은 어떤 의미로는 필연적인 것이 틀림없다는 것이다. 과학적 발견은 불확실한 것으로, 특정 시기 및 장소의 지적 환경의 결과인 것이 분명하다. 그래서 미적분이 역사상 동일한 순간에 두 사람에 의해 창조된 것은 놀랄 일이 아니다. 라이프니츠와 뉴턴은 같이 실제로 앉은 적도 없을 것이고 상세하게 자신들의 연구를 공유한 적도 없을 것이다. 하지만 이들은 동일한 지적 환경에서 살았었다.

물론 이는 뉴턴이 본 방식과는 달랐다. 그는 자신의 미적분 연구를 1660년대 중반에 실시했지만, 출판한 적은 없었다. 그리고 라이프니츠가 자신만의 미적분을 들고 나온 1680년대 이후에, 뉴턴이 속한 학계의 사람들은 라이프니츠가 뉴턴의 연구를 훔쳤다고 비난했고, 이로 인해 17세기의 가장 큰 과학적 스캔들을 촉발시켰다. 이는 어쩔 수 없는 인간적 반응이다. 우리는 위대한 발견은 불확실한 것이라는 점을 믿기를 주저한다. 우리는 위대한 발견은 우리의 머릿속에 있다고 믿고 싶다.

12 빈칸에 가장 알맞은 것을 고르시오.
① 적절히 타이밍이 맞은
② 당황스러울 정도로 신비에 싸인
③ 아주 흔한
④ 절대적으로 새로운

| 정답 | ③

| 해설 | 빈칸 뒤에서는 소위 '멀티플스'가 희귀한 일도 아니라 자주 일어난 일임을 설명하고 있다. 따라서 답은 ③이다.

13 다음 중 "멀티플스"에 관해 유추할 수 있는 것은 무엇인가?
① 시간과 공간을 뛰어넘지 못한다.
② 서로 사전에 알지 못하더라도 발생된다.
③ 발견자의 명성을 드높인다.
④ 이미 발견된 것에 중요성을 더한다.

| 정답 | ②

| 해설 | 라이프니츠와 뉴턴은 서로 만난 적도 연구를 공유한 적도 없었지만, 결국 미적분의 멀티플스 현상을 야기했다. 따라서 답은 ②이다.

14 본문의 주제는 무엇인가?
① 생각의 표절은 라이벌 간에 만연하다.
② 동일한 발견을 한 여러 과학자들을 인정해야 한다.
③ 멀티플스는 과학적 발견이 미리 정해진 것임을 나타내는 증거이다.
④ 과학사학자들은 멀티플스를 객관적으로 기록해야 한다.

| 정답 | ③

| 해설 | 저자에 따르면 "과학적 발견은 어떤 의미로는 필연적인 것이 틀림없다(scientific discoveries must, in some sense, be inevitable)" 그리고 과학적 발견은 "특정 시기 및 장소의 지적 환경의 결과(products of the intellectual

climate of a specific time and place)"이다. 즉, 어떤 시대가 되면 필연적으로 특정 과학적 발견이 이루어질 수밖에 없는 환경이 조성되며 이 과정에서 멀티플스가 등장한다는 것이 저자의 의견이다. 따라서 답은 ③이다.

| 어휘 | simultaneous ⓐ 동시의
sheer ⓐ (크기·정도·양을 강조하여) 순전한
inevitable ⓐ 필연적인
up in the air - 아직 미정인, 불확실한
calculus ⓝ 미적분
milieu ⓝ 환경
reluctant ⓐ 꺼리는, 마지못한
bafflingly ⓐⓓ 당황스럽게
transcend ⓥ 초월하다
plagiarism ⓝ 표절
rampant ⓐ 만연한
credit ⓝ 칭찬, 인정
predestinate ⓥ 예정하다, 미리 정하다 ⓐ 예정된, 미리 정해진

[15-17] 국민대 2013

당신은 우선 공리를 선언한 다음 온갖 추론을 제시하는 유클리드 기하학과 같은 방식으로 첫 페이지에 기본 법칙에 관해 설명한 다음 가능한 모든 상황에서 기본 법칙이 어떻게 작용하는지를 보여주는 식으로 물리학을 가르치는 것이 왜 불가능한지 묻고 싶을 것이다. (그래서 4년 안에 물리학을 배우는 것에 만족하지 못한 채 4분 안에 물리학을 배우기를 원하는 것인가?) 우리는 두 가지 이유로 인해 이런 식으로는 물리학을 배울 수 없다. 첫 번째로 우리는 아직 기본 법칙을 전부 알지 못하는데, 무지의 경계는 점차 넓어만 가고 있기 때문이다. 두번째로 물리법칙을 정확히 서술하려면 묘사하는 데만 고도의 수학적 지식을 요하는 아주 낯선 개념을 알아야 하기 때문이다. 심지어 말의 의미를 파악하는 데만 상당한 분량의 준비 훈련이 필요하다. 따라서 그런 방식으로 물리학을 가르치는 것은 불가능하다. 우리는 물리학을 한 부분씩 서서히 배울 수밖에 없다. 자연 전체의 한 부분 또는 일부는 완전한 진실의 근사치에 불과하며, 어쩌면 우리가 완전한 진실이라고 알고 있는 것의 근사치에 불과할 수도 있다. 사실 우리가 알고 있는 모든 것들은 단지 이런 근사치에 불과한데, 그 이유는 우리는 아직 모든 법칙을 알지 못하기 때문이다. 따라서 우리는 뭔가를 열심히 배워야 하지만 배운 것들을 잊어먹어 다시 배워야 하거나, 이보다 더 가능성이 높은 상황인, 잘못된 내용을 배운 탓에 수정해야 할 뿐이다.

15 다음 중 본문의 유형을 가장 잘 설명한 것은 무엇인가?
① 강의 원고
② 학술 논문
③ 신문 기사
④ 물리학 교과서

| 정답 | ①

| 해설 | 본문은 왜 우리는 물리학을 유클리드 기하학과 같은 방식으로 가르치는 것이 불가능한지를 설명하는 글이다. 저자가 you라는 인칭대명사를 사용한 것을 보면, 저자가 사람들을 눈 앞에 두고서 강의하는 것임을 유추할 수 있다. 따라서 답은 ①이다.

16 본문에 따르면 다음 중 사실이 아닌 것은 무엇인가?
① 지식이 늘어날수록, 무지는 줄어든다.
② 우리가 무언가에 관해 배운 것은 결코 궁극적인 진리가 될 수 없다.
③ 유클리드 기하학을 가르치는 방식으로 물리학을 가르치는 것은 불가능하다.
④ 물리학 법칙은 고도의 수학적 지식을 통해서만 올바른 서술이 가능하다.

| 정답 | ①

| 해설 | "첫 번째로 우리는 아직 기본 법칙을 전부 알지 못하는데, 무지의 경계는 점차 넓어만 가고 있기 때문이다(First, we do not yet know all the basic laws: there is an expanding frontier of ignorance)." 이 말은 우리는 더 많은 것을 알수록 모르는 것도 늘어나며 때문에 무지는 지식이 늘어난다고 줄기는커녕 오히려 늘어난다는 의미이다. 따라서 답은 ①이다.

참고로, "우리가 알고 있는 모든 것들은 단지 이런 근사치에 불과하다(everything we know is only some kind of approximation)."는 ②에 해당되며, ③은 저자가 서두에서 주장하는 바이며, "두 번째로 물리법칙을 정확히 서술하려면 묘사하는 데만 고도의 수학적 지식을 요하는 아주 낯선 개념을 알아야 하기 때문이다(Second, the correct statement of the laws of physics involves some very unfamiliar ideas which require advanced mathematics for their description)."는 ④에 해당된다.

17
밑줄 친 ⓐ는 무엇을 가리키는가?
① 물리학을 가르치기
② 기본법칙을 전부 아는 것
③ 말의 의미를 파악하는 것
④ 물리 법칙에 관한 정확한 서술

| 정답 | ①

| 해설 | 우선 ⓐ 앞에서 저자가 생각하는 물리학을 유클리드 기하학과 같은 방식으로 가르칠 수 없는 두 가지 이유가 나와 있다. ⓐ가 들어간 문장을 직역하면 "따라서 그런 방식으로 그것을 하는 것은 불가능하다"이며, '그런 방식'이 유클리드 기하학과 같은 방식을 의미하므로 '그것'은 '물리학을 가르치는 것'을 의미한다. 따라서 답은 ①이다.

| 어휘 | geometry ⓝ 기하학   axiom ⓝ 자명한 이치, 공리
        deduction ⓝ 추론, 연역   frontier ⓝ 경계, 한계
        preparatory ⓐ 준비의   approximation ⓝ 근사치, 비슷한 것

[18-20] 홍익대 2013

과학이 지닌 또 다른 가치는 지적 즐거움으로 불리는 재미이며, 일부는 과학에 관해 읽고, 배우고, 생각하는 과정에서 지적 즐거움을 얻고 다른 이들은 과학 분야에 속해 연구하면서 얻게 된다. 이는 매우 현실적이면서 중요한 점이며, 과학이 사회에 미치는 영향에 관해 심사숙고하는 것이 우리의 사회적 책임이라고 말하는 사람들이 충분히 고려하지 않는 점이다.

단순한 개인적인 즐거움은 사회 전체적으로 가치 있는 것이라 할 수 있는가? 그렇지 않다. 하지만 사회 그 자체의 가치를 고려하는 것 또한 책임이다. 그것은 결국에 여러 가지 것들을 정리하여 사람들이 이를 누릴 수 있도록 하는 것인가? 만일 그렇다면 과학을 통한 즐거움은 다른 어떤 것들과 마찬가지로 중요한 일이다.

하지만 나는 과학적 노력의 결과인 세계관의 가치를 과소평가하지 않고 싶다. 우리는 과거의 시인들이나 몽상가들이 상상하는 것보다 더 놀라운 온갖 것들을 무한히 상상할 수 있도록 인도되어 왔다. 이는 자연의 상상력이 인간의 상상력보다 정말로 훨씬 더 위대하다는 것을 보여준다. 예를 들어 우리 모두가 바닥이 보이지 않는 바다를 헤엄치는 거북이가 떠받치는 코끼리의 등에 타고 있다는 것보다는, 신비한 인력 덕분에 우주 속에서 곡선을 그리며 빙 돌고 있는 자전하는 공에 붙어 있고 그중 반은 거꾸로 붙어 있다는 사실은 얼마나 놀라운 일이겠는가.

18

다음 중 (A)에 가장 적합한 것은 무엇인가?

① as
② to
③ off
④ up

| 정답 | ②

| 해설 | 문장 구조를 잘 살펴보면 (A)에 들어갈 전치사는 수동형 표현인 to be stuck과 연결되어 '~에 붙어 있다'는 의미를 지닌 to be stuck to가 됨을 알 수 있다. 이후 문장 전체를 해석해 보면 자전하는 공, 즉 지구에 '붙어 있다'는 의미에서 다른 보기를 대입했을 때와 달리 의미에 어색함이 없다. 따라서 답은 ②이다.

19

다음 중 본문에서 유추할 수 없는 것은 무엇인가?

① 바닥이 보이지 않는 바다를 헤엄치는 거북이가 떠받치는 코끼리의 등에 타고 있는 모습은 자연의 상상력의 한 가지 예이다.
② 사람들은 과학 분야에 속해 연구를 하면서 즐거움을 얻을 뿐만 아니라 과학에 관해 읽고 배우는 것에서 재미를 느낀다.
③ 자연의 상상력은 과거 시인들 및 몽상가들의 상상력보다 훨씬 더 위대하다.
④ 저자는 과학에서 얻는 지적 즐거움은 중요하다고 생각한다.

| 정답 | ①

| 해설 | ①은 자연의 상상력이 아니라 인간의 상상력이고, 자연의 상상력은 '신비한 인력 덕분에 우주 속에서 곡선을 그리며 빙 돌고 있는 자전하는 공'으로 지구를 묘사한 것이다. 따라서 답은 ①이다.

20

위 본문의 주제는 무엇인가?

① 지적 즐거움을 얻는 법
② 시적 상상력의 위대함
③ 독특한 세계관의 중요성
④ 과학의 가치

| 정답 | ④

| 해설 | 본문은 "과학이 지닌 또 다른 가치(Another value of science)"인 "지적 즐거움으로 불리는 재미(the fun called intellectual enjoyment)"에 관해 말하고 있다. 즉, 본문은 과학이 지닌 여러 가치 가운데 재미에 관해 말하고 있으며, another 덕분에 본문 앞 문장에서는 재미 이외의 과학의 가치에 관해 언급했을 것으로 추측이 가능하다. 따라서 답은 ④이다.

| 어휘 | in the last analysis – 결국
attraction ⓝ 인력, 끌어당기는 힘
underestimate ⓥ 과소평가하다
apart from – 뿐만 아니라

[21-22] 중앙대 2014

일부 사람들은 수학을 어렵고 지루한 과목이며 선명하고 논리적인 방식으로만 추구되어야 하는 과목으로 여긴다. 이러한 믿음이 영속적으로 자리 잡은 것은 수많은 교과서에서 수학이 제시된 방식 때문이다. 종종 수학은 일련의 정의, 다양한 유형의 문제를 해결하기 위한 방법, 정리 등으로 간추려진다. 정리는 연역적 추론과 증명을 통해 참임이 입증되는 서술을 말한다. 이는 수학에 있어 증명의 중요성을 최소화하기 위한 것이 아니며, 그 이유는 수학의 힘은 증명에 있기 때문이다. 하지만 상상력의 힘은 연역적 추론의 힘만큼이나 모든 면에서 중요하다.

개념이 발전해 온 기나긴 역사나 초기 수학자들이 취한 생산적이지 못한 접근법이 수학 과정에서 항상 다뤄지는 것은 아니다. 사실 수학자들은 간단한 사례 속에서 관계를 찾아내고, 패턴을 찾으며, 그 이후에만 일반화를 시도한다. 일반화한 것이 증명되어 실제 교과서에 수록되는 것은 훨씬 나중의 일인 경우가 종종 있다.

우리가 수학에 관해 많은 것을 배울 수 있으며 동시에 이 과정에서 즐거움을 찾을 수 있는 한 가지 방법은 특이한 패턴을 드러내는 숫자들의 관계를 연구하는 것이다. 예를 들어, 어린 아이들은 곱셈표에 있는 숫자들이 드러내는 패턴을 탐구하면서 곱셈표를 쉽게 익힐 수 있다. 복잡한 연산 문제도 때로는 패턴을 활용해 해결할 수 있다. 까다로운 문제가 주어지면 수학자는 비슷하면서 더 간단한 문제를 풀려고 한다. 우선 패턴을 관찰한 다음에 더 복잡한 문제의 답을 예측하는 이러한 형태의 추론은 귀납적인 추론의 한 예이다. 이 방법은 특정한 사실이나 개별 사례에서 추론을 통해 사실일 수 있는 일반적인 진술을 추론하는 것을 수반한다. 관찰된 개별적 경우가 점점 더 많아질수록 일반화를 더 정확하게 할 수 있게 된다. 예를 들어 우리는 매일 해가 뜨고 지는 시간을 정확하게 예측할 수 있다. 따라서 이 예측이 성공할 가능성 또한 매우 높다.

21 윗글의 제목으로 가장 적합한 것을 고르시오.
① 인습에 얽매이지 않는 수학적 추론
② 수학 연구에 있어 귀납적 추론
③ 일반화의 발전 패턴
④ 복잡한 문제에 있어 수학 정리의 힘

| 정답 | ②

| 해설 | 본문은 수학 문제를 해결하는 데 있어 연역적 추론과 증명뿐만 아니라 패턴을 활용한 귀납적 추론 또한 중요하다는 점을 논하고 있다. 따라서 답은 ②이다.

22 윗글에서 빈칸에 들어가기에 가장 적합한 것을 고르시오.
① 복잡한 연산 문제도 때로는 패턴을 활용해 해결할 수 있다.
② 대부분의 학령기 아동은 연산 문제를 까다롭다고 여긴다.
③ 아동의 연산 능력은 일련의 까다로운 문제를 해결하면서 향상된다.
④ 수학적 논쟁은 예측이 불가능한 사고 궤도를 따른다.

| 정답 | ①

| 해설 | 우선 빈칸 앞 문장인 "어린 아이들은 곱셈표에 있는 숫자들이 드러내는 패턴을 탐구하면서 곱셈표를 쉽게 익힐 수 있다(children may find it easier to learn their multiplication tables by exploring the patterns that the numbers display)."를 통해 수학 문제 해결에 있어 패턴 파악의 중요성을 제시하고 있다. 여기의 문제는 "간단한" 문제이며, 빈칸 뒤 문장을 보면 "까다로운 문제가 주어지면 수학자는 비슷하면서 더 간단한 문제를 풀려고 한다. 우

선 패턴을 관찰한 다음에 더 복잡한 문제의 답을 예측하는 이러한 형태의 추론은 귀납적인 추론의 한 예이다(Given a difficult problem, a mathematician will often try to solve a simpler, but similar, problem. This type of reasoning – first observing patterns and then predicting answers in complicated problems – is an example of inductive reasoning)"라고 말하는 것을 통해 "복잡한 문제가 등장하더라도 패턴을 활용해 해결이 가능하다"는 것을 알 수 있다. 즉, 빈칸에는 우선 간단한 문제도 패턴을 통해 해결이 가능하다 ⇨ 어려운 문제도 패턴을 통해 해결이 가능하다와 같이 논리적 흐름이 이어지는 것으로 봤을 때 ①이 적합하다.

| 어휘 | clear-cut ⓐ 선명한, 명쾌한   perpetuate ⓥ 영구화하다, 영속시키다
reduce A to B – A를 (더 단순한 형태인) B로 간추리다[정리하다]
theorem ⓝ 정리   deductive ⓐ 연역적인
reasoning ⓝ 추론, 추리   proof ⓝ 증명
generalize ⓥ 일반화하다   numerical ⓐ 숫자의
multiplication table – 곱셈표   arithmetic ⓝ 산수, 연산
inductive ⓐ 귀납적인   unconventionality ⓝ 자유로움, 인습에 얽매이지 않음
trajectory ⓝ 궤적, 궤도

[23-25] 항공대 2017

자연적 과정에는 우연의 요소가 많이 내재되어 있다. 예를 들어, 숲 속 나무들 간격은 무작위적이다. 모든 나무들이 동일한 간격으로 위치해 있는 숲을 발견했다면, 당신은 누군가가 나무를 심은 숲이라는 결론을 내릴 것이다. <u>마찬가지로, 나뭇잎들도 무작위적인 배열로 땅에 떨어진다.</u> 그 나뭇잎들이 완전히 일직선으로 줄지어 배열되어 있는 것을 발견할 가능성은 거의 없다. 만일 자연법칙이 외부의 간섭 없이 작용할 수 있도록 허용된다면, 우리는 그러한 관찰의 결과를 무질서한 배열이 질서 정연한 배열보다 훨씬 더 개연성이 높다는 말로 표현할 수 있을 것이다. 엔트로피는 원래 열역학에서 유래한 개념이었지만, 통계역학이 발전하면서 그 중요성이 크게 높아졌다. 이런 분석적 접근 방식에서는 엔트로피에 대한 다른 해석을 사용한다. 통계역학에서 물질의 운동은 물질에 내포되어 있는 원자와 분자의 통계적 운동으로 기술된다. 통계역학적 접근법의 주요 결론 중 하나는, 고립계가 더 큰 무질서를 향해 나아가는 경향이 있으며, 엔트로피는 그러한 무질서를 측정하는 한 척도라고 설명한다. 모든 계들이 한데 결합하여 우주를 형성할 때, 우주의 엔트로피는 항상 증가할 것이다. 궁극적으로 우주의 엔트로피는 최댓값에 도달하게 될 것이다. 그렇게 되면 우주는 온도와 밀도가 균일한 상태에 도달할 것이다. 완벽한 무질서 상태란 일을 수행하는 데 이용할 수 있는 에너지가 더 이상 없다는 것을 의미하기 때문에, 이때의 경우 모든 물리적, 화학적, 생물학적 과정이 중단되게 될 것이다.

23 다음 중 제시된 문장이 들어갈 가장 적합한 장소는?

마찬가지로, 나뭇잎들도 무작위적인 배열로 땅에 떨어진다.

① (A)   ② (B)
③ (C)   ④ (D)

| 정답 | ②

| 해설 | 제시문의 '비슷하게'라는 뜻의 'Likewise'를 통해, 앞의 내용도 제시문과 비슷한 내용이 와야 한다는 것을 알 수 있다. 따라서 제시문은 나무들이 무작위적인 간격으로 숲에 배열되어 있다는 내용인 (B) 이후에 와야 하므로, 정답은 ②가 된다.

24 다음 중 본문의 내용과 일치하는 것은?
① 엔트로피라는 개념은 원래 통계역학에서 시작되었으며, 이후 열역학에 적용되었다.
② 엔트로피에 대한 분석적 접근법은 원자와 분자의 통계적 운동을 설명해 준다.
③ 모든 자연적 과정에서 우주의 엔트로피는 줄어든다.
④ 모든 계는 자연적으로 무질서 상태에서 질서 상태로 이동하는 경향이 있다.

| 정답 | ②

| 해설 | ① 본문의 "Entropy originally found its place in thermodynamics, but its importance grew tremendously as the field of statistical mechanics developed."를 통해, 엔트로피는 열역학에서 시작되었다고 통계역학에 많이 적용됐음을 알 수 있다. ③ "isolated systems tend toward greater disorder, and entropy is a measure of that disorder" 부분을 통해 우주의 계는 무질서가 증가하는 방향을 향하므로, 우주의 엔트로피는 자연적 과정에서 늘어나게 된다. ④ "a disorderly arrangement is much more probable than an orderly one" 부분을 통해, 무질서 상태가 질서 상태보다 개연성이 있기 때문에, 자연계는 자연적으로 질서 상태에서 무질서 상태를 향해 이동한다는 것을 알 수 있다. 정답은 ②로, 본문 중반의 "In statistical mechanics, the behavior of a substance is described by the statistical behavior of the atoms and molecules contained in it." 부분, 즉 엔트로피에 대한 분석적 접근법인 통계역학에서는 '물질의 운동은 물질에 내포되어 있는 원자와 분자의 통계적 운동으로 기술된다'고 한 부분을 통해 ②가 본문의 내용과 일치한다는 것을 알 수 있다.

25 다음 중 본문의 제목으로 가장 적합한 것은?
① 엔트로피와 무질서
② 엔트로피와 신진대사
③ 엔트로피의 가역적 영향
④ 자연 상태의 엔트로피와 인공적 엔트로피의 차이점

| 정답 | ①

| 해설 | 본문에서는 자연 상태의 무질서를 언급한 이후, 이를 통계역학에서 무질서를 측정하는 척도로 사용하는 엔트로피를 통해 무질서를 해석하고 있으므로, '엔트로피와 무질서'라는 ①이 제목으로 적합하다.

| 어휘 | inherent ⓐ 고유한, 선천적인
disorderly ⓐ 무질서한, 난동을 부리는
interference ⓝ 방해, 간섭
entropy ⓝ 엔트로피(열역학상으로 존재하는 추상적인 에너지의 양을 나타내는 척도)
thermodynamics ⓝ 열역학
statistical ⓐ 통계의
employ ⓥ 고용하다; 사용하다
interpretation ⓝ 해석, 이해, 설명; 통역
maximum ⓐ 최대의 ⓝ 최대
imply ⓥ 암시하다
reversible ⓐ 되돌릴 수 있는

row ⓝ 열, 줄
arrangement ⓝ 합의; 정리, 배열
tremendously ⓐⓓ 엄청나게
analytical ⓐ 분석적인
alternate ⓐ 번갈아 하는 ⓥ 교대하다
molecule ⓝ 분자
cease ⓥ 그만두다, 중지하다
metabolism ⓝ 신진대사
artificial ⓐ 인공의, 인조의

[26-27] 인하대 2018

열은 어디에나 존재한다. 열은 자연 상태의 에너지로, 물질의 이동으로 귀결된다. 우리 자신을 포함해 우리 주변의 모든 것을 구성하고 있는 기본 요소인 원자와 분자들은 끊임없이 그리고 무작위로 이동한다. 이들이 빠르게 움직이면 움직일수록, 이들은 더 뜨거운 물질을 구성하게 된다. 아무리 차갑게 보이는 물체라도 이 세상의 모든 물체는 열을 일부 포함하고 있다. 심지어 얼음물이 담긴 주전자조차 너무도 많은 분자 운동을 포함하고 있기 때문에 만약 표면에 가볍게 잉크 한 방울을 떨어뜨리면 그 잉크는 몇 시간 안에 물 전체에 고르게 퍼질 것이다. 실제로 1월에 눈 덮인 스키 슬로프에 포함된 모든 열에너지를 당신이 추출해서 저장할 수 있다면, 그 열에너지를 이용해 며칠 동안 집을 난방할 수 있다. 과학자들은 적어도 이론상으로는 모든 운동이(따라서 모든 열이) 작동을 멈추는 절대온도라 불리는 지점이 있다는 사실을 밝혀냈다. 하지만 그 절대온도는 화씨 마이너스 460도로 도달하기에는 불가능한 수준의 차가운 상태이다.

열은 항상 온도를 일정하게 만드는 방향으로 이동한다. 즉, 열에너지가 높은 지역과 상대적으로 따뜻한 지역에서 추운 지역으로 이동한다. 충분한 열을 한 곳에 모아 놓으면, 원자와 분자 사이의 서로 끌어당기는 인력을 뛰어넘을 수 있을 것이고, 고체에서 액체나 액체에서 기체로 상태 변화를 일으킬 수 있을 것이다. 그러한 변화는 잠열이라 불리는 에너지를 추가로 필요로 하는데, 이것은 물질의 온도를 높이는 것이 아니라 단지 상태를 바꾸기 위해서만 필요하다. 따라서 물 1쿼트를 화씨 210도에서 220도로 올리는 것이 온도를 화씨 85도에서 95도로 올리는 것보다 더 많은 에너지를 필요로 한다.

26
다음 중 본문의 내용과 일치하지 않는 것은?
① 열은 더 차가운 곳으로 이동한다.
② 차가운 물에도 열에너지가 있다.
③ 절대 온도를 경험한 사람은 없다.
④ 겨울철 스키 슬로프에는 열에너지가 없다.
⑤ 얼음물 표면에 떨어진 잉크 한 방울은 물 전체로 퍼져 나간다.

| 정답 | ④

| 해설 | 첫 번째 문단의 "In fact, if you could extract and store all the thermal energy contained in a single snowy ski slope in January, you could heat your house with it for days."의 내용을 보면, 차가운 겨울철 스키 슬로프에도 많은 열이 포함되어 있다고 설명하고 있으므로, 반대로 설명한 보기 ④는 본문과 일치하지 않음을 알 수 있다.

27
다음 중 빈칸에 가장 적합한 것은?
① 더 많은 에너지가 든다
② 더 위험해진다
③ 더 적은 열을 필요로 한다
④ 덜 비싸진다
⑤ 더 잘 지각할 수 있게 된다

| 정답 | ①

| 해설 | 동일한 온도라고 하더라도 물질의 상태가 변할 때 에너지가 필요하다는 내용의 예시로 부연 설명하고 있는 부분이다. 따라서 동일 상태에서 10도 올리는 것보다 상이한 상태에서 10도 올리는 것이 더 많은 에너지가 요구된다. 따라서 정답은 ①이 적합하다.

| 어휘 | raw ⓐ 익히지 않은, 날것의, 가공하지 않은　　boil down to – ~로 귀결되다
atom ⓝ 원자　　molecule ⓝ 분자
building block – 구성요소, 기초 단위; (장난감) 집짓기 블록
frigid ⓐ 몹시 추운
jug ⓝ (액체를 담아 부을 수 있게 주둥이가 있고 손잡이가 달린) 주전자
harbor ⓥ 정박하다; (생각 등을) 마음에 품다 ⓝ 항구; 피난처
diffuse ⓥ 퍼뜨리다, 발산하다, 유포하다　　extract ⓥ 추출하다
thermal energy – 열에너지　　in theory – 이론상으로
absolute zero – 절대영도　　cease ⓥ 그만두다, 중지하다
unattainably ⓐⓓ 도달할 수 없게; 얻을 수 없게　　equalize ⓥ 동등하게 하다, 대등하게 하다
force of attraction – 인력　　solid ⓐ 입체의; 견고한
liquid ⓝ 액체　　latent heat – 잠열
quart ⓝ 쿼트(액량의 단위)

[28-30] 가톨릭대 2017

빵 한 조각을 소화할 때, 우리는 탄수화물을 단당(simple sugars)으로 분해하고 단백질을 아미노산으로 분해한다. 이와 동시에 우리는 피부, 근육, 뼈의 단백질을 분해하고 재생성한다. 모든 유기체는 고분자를 끊임없이 분해하고 구성요소(building blocks)를 끊임없이 재사용한다.

유기체는 고분자를 쉽게 조립하고 분해할 수 있어야 한다. 고분자를 묶고 있는 결합은 고분자가 떨어져 나가지 않을 만큼 충분히 강해야 한다. 그러나 그 결합이 너무 강해서 유기체가 필요할 때 고분자를 쉽게 분리해 낼 수 없어서도 안 된다. 어린아이들이 가지고 노는 팝비즈나 레고 블록과 같이, 생명의 구성요소는 쉽게 결합하고 쉽게 분리된다.

놀랍게도 생물학적 구성요소는 모두 같은 방식으로 결합한다. 모든 주요 고분자의 구성요소는 동일한 방식의 간단한 화학반응으로 결합한다. 모든 경우에 효소(화학 결합을 만들고 끊는 데 도움이 되는 분자)가 구성요소의 쌍 사이에서 2개의 수소 원자와 1개의 산소 원자를 제거하여 결합을 형성한다. 2개의 수소 원자와 1개의 산소 원자(이것은 물 분자 하나에 해당한다)를 제거하는 것은 하나의 물 분자가 제거되기 때문에 탈수축합반응(dehydration condensation reaction)이라고 한다.

고분자를 분리하기 위해서는 유기체가 탈수축합반응을 반대로 시행하며, 각각의 구성요소에 하나의 물 분자를 추가한다. 효소는 물 분자를 추가함으로써 고분자에서 각각의 작은 분자를 분리하는데, 이 과정을 가수분해(hydrolysis)라 고 한다. (고대 그리스어로 물을 의미하는 'hydro'와 분해를 의미하는 'lysis'가 결합되어 만들어진 단어이다.)

모든 구성요소가 유사한 탈수축합반응으로 결합하지만, 형성되는 정확한 결합은 각각의 경우마다 다르다. 예를 들어 설탕은 글리코사이드(glycosidic) 결합을 형성하는 반면, 아미노산은 펩티드(peptide) 결합을 형성한다.

28 다음 중 글의 주제로 적합한 것은?

① 유기체가 에너지를 저장하고 소모하는 방식
② 효소에 의해 형성되는 화학 결합의 종류
③ 고분자를 묶어 두고 있는 결합의 복잡한 구조
④ 생명의 구성요소의 메커니즘에서 효소가 수행하는 역할

| 정답 | ④

| 해설 | 본문은 유기체가 고분자를 분해하고, 분해된 각각의 구성요소가 다시 결합되는 과정을 설명하고 있는 글이다. 이때 분해 및 결합되는 과정에서 효소가 2개의 수소 원자와 1개의 산소 원자를 추가하거나 제거하는 역할을 담당한다. 따라서 이 글의 주제는 '생명의 구성요소의 메커니즘에서 효소가 수행하는 역할'이라는 ④가 적합하다. ②의 경우 효소에 의해 형성(결합)되는 것만 설명하고 있으므로 두 가지 과정을 모두 포함하고 있지 않아 정답에서 제외된다.

29

본문을 근거로 다음 문장의 빈칸에 올 수 있는 가장 적합한 것은?

- 효소는 하나의 물 분자에 상당하는 것을 제거해 두 구성요소를 결합시킨다.
- 효소는 하나의 물 분자를 추가해 긴 체인을 두 개의 단일 구성요소로 분해한다.

① 제거하다 – 분해하다
② 제거하다 – 형성하다
③ 추가하다 – 분해하다
④ 추가하다 – 형성하다

| 정답 | ①

| 해설 | 첫 번째 문장은 본문의 탈수축합반응(dehydration condensation reaction)을 설명한 것으로, 물 분자 하나를 '제거'해 각 구성요소가 '결합'한다. 두 번째 문장은 가수분해(hydrolysis)를 설명한 것으로 탈수축합반응의 반대에 해당한다. 물 분자 하나를 '추가(add)'해 각각의 구성요소로 '분해'하는 것을 의미한다. 따라서 정답은 ①이 된다.

30

다음 중 본문의 내용과 일치하지 않는 것은?
① 인간을 포함한 모든 생명체는 끊임없이 고분자를 분해한다.
② 고분자의 결합은 매우 강력해 구성요소가 분리되지 않는다.
③ 생물학적 구성요소가 서로 결합되어 있는 방식은 모든 주요 분자에 대해 동일하다.
④ 탈수로부터 형성되는 결합은 각각의 경우 다르다.

| 정답 | ②

| 해설 | ①은 첫 번째 문단의 "All organisms continually break down macromolecules and reuse the building blocks."를 통해 알 수 있다. ③은 세 번째 문단의 "The building blocks of all the major macromolecules join by the same simple chemical reaction"을 재진술한 내용이다. ④는 마지막 문단에 제시되어 있다. 정답은 ②로, 고분자의 결합은 분리되지 않을 만큼 강력해야 하지만 필요할 때도 분리되지 않을 만큼 강력해서는 안 된다고 두 번째 문단에서 서술하고 있다. 따라서 본문의 "the building blocks of life easily snap together and easily snap apart."와 같이 고분자의 결합은 쉽게 결합되고 쉽게 분리되는 것이므로, ②가 정답이 된다.

| 어휘 | **digest** ⓥ 소화하다; 요약하다 ⓝ 요약, 적요   **carbohydrate** ⓝ 탄수화물 (식품)
protein ⓝ 단백질   **amino acid** ⓝ 아미노산
break down – 부수다, 분해하다; 나누다, 분류하다
muscle ⓝ 근육   **macromolecule** ⓝ 고분자
building block – 구성요소, 기초 단위; (장난감) 집짓기 블록
assemble ⓥ 모으다, 조립하다   **disassemble** ⓥ 분해[해체]하다

fall apart – 부서지다
take apart – ~을 분해하다
pop beads – 팝비즈(팔찌나 목걸이를 만드는 데 사용되는 작은 구슬들을 의미함)
snap together – 딱 소리가 나며 맞물리다
snap apart – 딱 소리가 나며 맞물림이 풀리다
chemical reaction – 화학 반응
enzyme ⓝ (생물) 효소
chemical bond – 화학 결합
hydrogen ⓝ 수소
atom ⓝ 원자
oxygen ⓝ 산소
equivalent ⓝ 등가물, 상당어구 ⓐ 동등한, 같은 가치의
dehydration ⓝ 탈수, 건조; [의학] 탈수증
condensation ⓝ 응축, 응결
dehydration condensation reaction – 탈수축합반응
reverse ⓥ (정반대로) 뒤바꾸다, 반전[역전]시키다
hydrolysis ⓝ 가수분해
glycosidic bond – 글리코사이드 결합
peptide bond – 펩티드 결합

CHAPTER 02 지구·환경

01	③	02	③	03	①	04	④	05	②	06	④	07	③	08	②	09	④	10	④
11	①	12	①	13	③	14	①	15	④	16	④	17	⑤	18	①	19	④	20	④
21	①	22	②	23	②	24	①	25	①	26	②	27	④	28	①	29	②	30	①
31	②	32	①	33	②	34	②	35	②	36	②	37	①	38	④	39	①	40	②
41	②	42	③	43	①	44	②	45	③										

[01-03] 숭실대 2010

물의 주목할 만한 많은 특성 중 하나는 기온이 매우 다른 물의 덩어리끼리는 한데 섞이지 않으려고 하는 현상이다. 이러한 특성은 담수호에서 변온층으로 알려진 현상의 형성을 야기하며, 이 현상은 호수의 여름 생태에 있어 중요한 역할을 한다. 미국 남부의 전형적인 수심이 깊은 인공호에서 1년간의 기온 변동을 생각해 보자. 늦겨울에는 호수 표면에 예전에 형성되었던 얼음은 무엇이든지 간에 녹게 되고, 물의 온도는 한결같이 38~42도를 기록한다. 호수 표면에서는 파도가 물속으로 산소를 섞고 기온이 한결같기 때문에 용해된 산소가 모든 깊이에 다 도달하게 된다. 산소가 충분해지면 포식자이든 피식자이든 저수지의 물고기의 대다수는 물의 층 전체에 걸쳐 발견된다.

초여름의 화창한 날에는 표면 온도는 증가하여 물이 팽창한다. 50도의 물이 40도의 물보다는 가볍기 때문에, 따뜻한 물의 층이 호수의 표면에 형성되고, 아래쪽의 많은 양의 차가운 물 위에서 베개처럼 위치한다. 베개같은 따뜻한 표면의 물은 천천히 그 두께가 증가하는데, 제한적으로 파도가 치면서 열을 섞는 작용을 해서 열이 물속 깊은 곳으로 전달되기 때문이다. 초여름에는 상당한 계층화가 일어나고, 뚜렷한 경계가 만들어지면서 호수 내의 물을 두 개의 구별되는 덩어리로 분리시킨다. 온도 변화의 경계는 변온층으로 불리고, 변온층은 산소가 차가운 깊은 물에 더 이상 섞이지 않도록 막는 장벽 역할을 한다. 이러한 온도 장벽은 산소가 표면에서 순환하여 물고기나 죽어가는 동물성 플랑크톤에 의해 소비되는 산소를 대체하지 못하게 막는다. 살아남기 위해 물고기는 위를 향해서 변온층과 표면 사이의 비교적 좁은 지역으로 올라가도록 강요받는다. 가을의 추운 밤은 이 같은 추세를 거꾸로 뒤집는다.

01 본문에 따르면 다음 중 사실이 아닌 것은?

① 표면의 따뜻한 물의 증가는 물속 깊은 곳의 산소 부족을 야기한다.
② 산소는 늦겨울 호수의 모든 부분에 충분히 공급된다.
③ 변온층은 뜨거운 온도에 의해 따뜻한 표면에서 형성된다.
④ 온도 장벽은 물과 산소의 이동을 제한한다.

| 정답 | ③

| 해설 | 우선 초여름이 되면 "the surface temperature increases and water expands(표면 온도는 증가하여 물이 팽창하며)", "a layer of warmer water builds at the surface of the lake, resting like a pillow on the mass of colder water below(따뜻한 물의 층이 호수의 표면에 형성되고, 아래쪽의 많은 양의 차가운 물 위에서 베개처럼 위치한다)." 그 결과 "the pillow of warm surface water slowly increases in thickness, as heat is transferred into the depths by the limited stirring of wave action(베개 같은 따뜻한 표면의 물은 천천히 그 두께가 증가하는데, 제한적으로 파도가 치면서 열을 섞는 작용을 해서 열이 물속 깊은 곳으로 전달되기 때문이다)"라고 본문

은 설명하고 있다. 이는, 즉 날씨가 따뜻해지면서 표면의 물도 따뜻해지고, 열기는 점차 호수 깊은 곳으로 내려가면서 따뜻한 물의 층이 점차 두꺼워진다는 의미이다. 이렇게 되면 따뜻한 표면과 그렇지 않은 호수 속끼리 온도 차가 나게 되며 그 결과 "a remarkable stratification has occurred, and a sharp boundary separates two independent bodies of water(상당한 계층화가 일어나고, 뚜렷한 경계가 만들어지면서 호수 내의 물을 두 개의 구별되는 덩어리로 분리시킨다)." 이러한 경계를 변온층이라 부르며, 이를 통해 변온층은 표면이 아니라 물속 깊은 곳에서 형성됨을 알 수 있다. 따라서 답은 ③이 된다.

①의 경우는, 따듯한 물이 증가하여 생긴 온도 차로 인한 "the temperature barrier prevents oxygen from circulating from the surface to replace the oxygen consumed by fish and dying zooplankton(온도 장벽은 산소가 표면에서 순환하여 물고기나 죽어가는 동물성 플랑크톤에 의해 소비되는 산소를 대체하지 못하게 막는다)." 따라서 ①은 답이 될 수 없다. ②의 경우, "Wave action stirs oxygen into the water at the lake's surface, and the temperature uniformity allows distribution of this dissolved oxygen to all depths(호수 표면에서는 파도가 물속으로 산소를 섞고 기온이 한결같기 때문에 용해된 산소가 모든 깊이에 다 도달하게 된다)." 따라서 ②도 답이 될 수 없다. ④의 경우, ①과 같은 맥락에서 답이 될 수 없다.

02

㉮에 가장 알맞은 단어를 고르시오.
① 뒤로   ② 아래로
③ 위로   ④ 앞으로

| 정답 | ③

| 해설 | 앞 문제의 해설과 연계해서 살펴보면, 아래쪽에 온도 장벽이 생겼기 때문에 물고기는 호흡을 하기 위해서는 표면으로 '올라가야' 한다. 따라서 ㉮에 들어갈 가장 알맞은 것은 ③이 된다.

03

㉯의 가을의 추운 밤은 이 같은 추세를 거꾸로 뒤집는다에 따르면, 가을에는 어떤 일이 일어나는가?
① 온도 장벽이 점차 얇아진다.
② 표면의 차가운 물이 물속 깊은 곳으로 급격히 내려간다.
③ 물속 깊은 곳은 이전보다 산소를 덜 포함한다.
④ 표면은 더욱 빠르고 두껍게 확장된다.

| 정답 | ①

| 해설 | 날씨가 따뜻해서 온도 장벽이 생겼으므로, 가을의 추운 밤이라면 당연히 온도 장벽이 점차 얇아짐을 추측할 수 있다. 또한 첫 번째 단락에서는 날씨가 추워지는 늦가을이 되면 산소가 고루 퍼진다고 설명하고 있는데, 이를 역으로 생각하면 산소의 흐름을 막는 온도 장벽이 얇아졌음을 유추할 수 있다. 따라서 답은 ①이 된다.

| 어휘 | body ⓝ ~의 덩어리, 많은 양   fresh water lake – 담수호
        thermocline ⓝ [호소(湖沼)의 수온이 급격히 변하는] 변온층, (수온) 약층(躍層)
        ecology ⓝ 생태(계)   impoundment ⓝ 인공호
        fluctuation ⓝ 변동   measure ⓥ (치수가) ~이다
        uniform ⓐ 한결같은   stir ⓥ 섞다, 젓다
        distribution ⓝ 분배, 배포   dissolve ⓥ 용해하다
        reservoir ⓝ 저수지   predator ⓝ 포식자

forage ⓝ 사료, 먹이
mass of – 양이 많은
sharp ⓐ 선명한, 뚜렷한
zooplankton ⓝ 동물성 플랑크톤
column ⓝ 원주; 세로줄
stratification ⓝ 계층화
gradient ⓝ (두 지역 간 온도·기압 등의) 변화도[증감률]
plunge ⓥ 급격히 내려가다

[04-05]

일식은 지구가 태양을 마주하는 쪽으로 달이 이동한 삭월(new moon phase: 태양, 달, 지구가 일직선상에 있는 위상)에만 일어난다. 그러나 달은 지구를 약간 비스듬한 각도로 공전하기 때문에, 이 세 천체는 주기적으로 일직선상에 위치해 일식이 발생하게 되어 있다. 흥미롭게도, 개기일식(total eclipse)을 지구에서만 볼 수 있는 것은 뜻밖의 우연이다. 즉, 달의 지름과 지구로부터의 거리 덕분에 달의 상대적 크기는 태양을 가릴 정도로 크다. 달이 조금이라도 더 작았거나, 더 멀었다면, 지구에서는 부분 일식만 볼 수 있을 것이다. 실제로, 약 십억 년 후에는 달이 지구로부터 너무 멀리 떨어져서 공전하기 때문에 더 이상은 일식을 볼 수 없게 된다. 또 다른 유형의 일식인 금환일식(annular eclipse: 달이 태양을 모두 가리지 못하고 가장자리가 링 형태로 빛나는 현상)은 달이 타원 궤도상 지구로부터 너무 멀리 떨어져서 그 상대적 크기가 너무 작아 태양을 완전히 가리지 못할 때 일어난다. 이런 경우, 일식은 가장자리가 빛나는 검은 원형으로 보인다. 개기일식은 1~2년마다 일어나지만 개기일식과 부분일식을 합치면 평균적으로 연 2.5회 정도 일어난다. 그러나 일식은 매번 지구상의 극히 일부 지역에서만 볼 수 있기 때문에, 한 지역에서 더군다나 개기일식을 볼 확률은 평생에 한 번도 되지 않는다.

04 빈칸에 적절한 것을 고르시오.
① 가설상의 예
② 체계적인 착각
③ 파괴적인 상호작용
④ 뜻밖의 우연

| 정답 | ④

| 해설 | 빈칸 다음에 이어지는 상술과 같은 내용으로 빈칸을 완성한다. 달의 지름과 지구로부터의 거리가 우연히도 태양을 가릴 정도로 적당하기 때문에 일식이 발생한다. 이 천체현상의 조건은 가설이거나 착각이거나 상호작용의 결과물이 아니므로 ①, ②, ③을 선택하지 않도록 주의한다. 이어지는 문징에서 조금이라도 거리가 더 가깝거나 멀다면 일식은 일어나지 않는다는 부연 설명이 있으므로, 일식은 우연의 결과물임을 알 수 있다. 따라서 정답은 ④이다.

05 다음 중 지문에서 유추할 수 있는 것은?
① 미세하게 기울어진 태양의 각도 때문에, 지구와 달이 일직선상에 있을 때 태양이 가려진다.
② 달과 지구 간의 거리가 멀어지면 결국엔 일식이 사라진다.
③ 오늘날, 개기일식은 부분일식보다 자주 관찰된다.
④ 금환일식은 부분일식 중에서도 이례적이고 가장 드문 일식이다.

| 정답 | ②

| 해설 | "However, because the moon orbits Earth at a slight angle, the three bodies will only periodically line up on the same plane to create an eclipse."를 참조하면, 태양이 가려지는(일식) 이유는 태양이 아니라 달의 공전 궤도가 미세하게 기울었기 때문이므로 ①은 본문 내용과 일치하지 않는다. 개기일식은 1~2년에 한 번씩 발

생하지만 부분일식까지 합치면 연 2.5회 발생하므로 부분일식이 개기일식보다 자주 일어난다. ③을 선택하지 않도록 주의한다. 금환일식은 부분일식이고 개기일식보다 자주 발생하는 일반적인 일식이므로 ④는 본문 내용과 일치하지 않는다. ②는 "In fact, in a billion years or so, the moon will have drifted so far from Earth that solar eclipses will no longer occur."에서 유추할 수 있다.

| 어휘 | eclipse ⓝ 일식, 월식
phase ⓝ 달의 위상
orbit ⓥ 궤도를 돌다
body ⓝ 천체
line up – 정렬하다
total eclipse – 개기일식
relative ⓐ 상대적인
partial eclipse – 부분일식
drift from ~ – ~로부터 떠내려가다
no longer – 더 이상 ~않다
annular eclipse – 금환일식
block ⓥ 가리다, 막다
circle ⓝ 원형
incidence ⓝ 발생(률)
chance ⓝ 가능성, 확률; 우연
single ⓐ 하나의
lifetime ⓝ 평생

new moon – 삭월
face ⓥ 마주하다
at an angle – 비스듬히
periodically – 주기적으로, 주기상으로
plane ⓝ 면, 수평면
diameter ⓝ 지름
cover ⓥ 가리다, 덮다
billion ⓝ 십억
solar ⓐ 태양의
occur ⓥ 발생하다
elliptical orbit – 타원궤도
blacken ⓥ 검게 만들다
rim ⓝ 가장자리(테두리) ⓥ 가장자리를 두르다
visible ⓐ 보이는
observe ⓥ 관찰하다
spot ⓝ 지역

[06-07] 성균관대 2009

오늘날 대부분의 과학자들은 우주가 150~200억 년 전 화구(fireball: 원시화구. 초고온 초고밀도의 우주탄생 이전의 상태)의 거대한 폭발로 순식간에 탄생했다는 이론을 인정한다. 그러나 소위 말하는 이 빅뱅이론에는 일부 과학자들에게 매우 꺼림칙한 부분이 있다. 즉, 과학의 모든 결과에는 원인이 있다. 그러나 빅뱅이론에 따르면, 우주의 탄생은 원인이 없는 결과이다. 한편, 이 이론은 신성한 지적 존재가 무로부터(ex nihilo) 만물을 창조했다고 믿는 많은 종교인들에게는 확신의 기쁨을 가져다주었다. 이성의 힘에 대한 신념을 지켜 온 과학자에게는, 이 이야기는 악몽으로 끝난다. 그가 험난한 무지의 산을 올라 가장 높은 정상을 정복하려는 순간, 마지막 바위를 넘어 몸을 앞으로 내미는 바로 그 순간에, 수 세기 동안 그 자리에 앉아 있던 신학자들이 그를 맞이하는 형국이다.

06 밑줄 친 (가) "this story"가 의미하는 것은 _____ .

① "이성의 힘"에 대한 과학의 신념은 무너졌다
② 신학자들은 과학이 입증한 것들을 이미 그 전에 예견했다
③ 과학은 우주의 탄생을 증명하지 못했다
④ 우주는 신이 무로부터 창조했다
⑤ 과학자들은 마침내 빅뱅이론을 받아들였다

| 정답 | ④

| 해설 | 밑줄 친 부분은 문맥상 바로 앞 문장에 상술된 종교인들의 믿음, 신이 만물을 창조했다는 창조론을 의미하므로 ④가 적절하다.

07

지문의 주제는 _____ 이다.
① 신학보다 우위에 선 과학
② 과학과 신학의 갈등
③ 과학과 신학이 만나는 곳
④ 신학이 실패한 곳에서 과학이 성공을 거두었다
⑤ 빅뱅이론: 우주의 기원에 대한 성서적 설명

| 정답 | ③

| 해설 | 지문의 주제는 마지막 부분의 "산 위에서 만난 과학자와 신학자들" 비유에 압축되어 있다. 빅뱅이론은 과학 이론인 동시에 역설적으로 창조론의 근거가 되기도 하므로 과학과 종교가 만나는 접합점이다. 따라서 ③이 적절하다. 빅뱅이론에 대한 과학계와 종교계의 서로 다른 해석을 과학과 종교의 갈등으로 비약하지 않도록 주의한다.

| 어휘 |
accept ⓥ 인정하다, 받아들이다
instant ⓝ 순식간
vast ⓐ 거대한
explosion ⓝ 폭발
acutely ⓐⓓ 몹시, 날카롭게
uncaused ⓐ 원인 없는
ignite ⓥ 점화하다
thrill ⓝ 흥분, 설렘, 전율
divine ⓐ 신성한, 신의
will ⓥ 의지력을 발휘하다, 애쓰다
live by – ~에 따라 살다
reason ⓝ 이성
ignorance ⓝ 무지, 무식
conquer ⓥ 정복하다
greet ⓥ 환영하다, 맞이하다
theologian ⓝ 신학자

universe ⓝ 우주
creation ⓝ 창조
fireball ⓝ 화구
Big Bang theory – 빅뱅이론
uncomfortable ⓐ 불편한, 언짢은
on the other hand – 반면에, 한편
mind ⓝ 지성인
confirmation ⓝ 확인
intellect ⓝ 지적인 존재
ex nihilo – 무(無)에서
faith ⓝ 신앙, 믿음
scale ⓥ (가파르고 험난한 곳을) 오르다
be about to – 막 ~하려 하다
peak ⓝ 정상
a band of – 여러 명의, 한 무리의

[08-10] 서강대 2008

운석을 연구하는 과학자들은 구체적인 방식으로 운석을 연구한다. 그들은 연구 대상을 멀리서 관찰하지 않는다. 대신 항성들의 산물이자 흩어진 행성들의 잔재인 운석을 실제로 갖고 연구한다. 우주로부터 온 이 암석들 안에는 태양계의 작은 조각들이 들어 있다. 이 조각들은 태양계 행성들보다도 먼저 생겼다. 수십만 개의 운석들이 세계 곳곳에서 수집되었다. 우주로부터 온 이 암석들은 수십 가지 방식으로 분류할 수 있지만 운석학자들은 운석을 크게 두 가지 범주로 나눈다. 미세한 입자들이 모여 행성 크기의 천체를 형성했던 태양계 성운의 기록을 보존한 운석과 화산작용, 내부 융해, 충돌, 균열 등 이후의 행성 과정을 보존한 운석이 있다.

08 다음 중 괄호에 가장 적절한 단어는 무엇인가?

① 단순한 ② 구체적인
③ 화려한 ④ 과학적인

| 정답 | ②

| 해설 | 두 번째 문장에 괄호를 완성할 수 있는 운석 연구 방식이 상술되어 있다. 일반적인 천문학 연구처럼 멀리서 관찰하는 것이 아니라 실제 운석을 가지고 연구하므로 "구체적인(specific)" 방식으로 연구한다는 것을 알 수 있다. 따라서 정답으로 ②가 적절하다. 두 번째 문장은 운석 연구 방식의 과학성을 강조하는 상술이 아니므로 ④를 선택하지 않도록 주의한다.

09 다음 중 지칭하는 것이 나머지와 다른 단어는?

① 운석 ② 태양계의 작은 조각들
③ 우주로부터 온 암석 ④ 미세한 입자들

| 정답 | ④

| 해설 | ①, ②, ③은 문맥상 우주의 탄생과 천체 형성, 파괴에 이르기까지 우주의 역사의 흔적을 포괄적으로 담은 운석을 지칭하지만, ④는 태양계 형성 당시 천체를 구성한 미세한 물질만을 지칭한다.

10 지문에 따르면, 다음 중 사실이 아닌 것은?

① 운석은 태양계 형성의 증거이다.
② 운석은 화산 활동의 증거를 보여준다.
③ 운석학자들은 운석을 통해서 행성 과정을 연구한다.
④ 태양계는 대부분 행성들이 형성되기 훨씬 이전에 존재했다.

| 정답 | ④

| 해설 | "Locked within these rocks from space are tiny pieces of the solar system that predate even the planets."를 참조하면, 행성들보다 먼저 존재한 것은 태양계가 아니라 태양계를 떠돌던 조각들(운석)이다. 이 사실만으로 태양계가 행성 형성 이전에 존재했다는 유추는 비약이다.

| 어휘 | meteorite ⓝ 운석
object ⓝ 물체, 대상
remnant ⓝ 잔여물
classify ⓥ 분류하다
preserve ⓥ 보존하다
microscopic ⓐ 미세한
subsequent ⓐ 후속의, 이어지는
impact ⓝ 충돌

tangible ⓐ 만질 수 있는, 유형의
from afar — 멀리서
predate ⓥ ~보다 앞서다
dozens of — 수십 개의
solar nebula — 태양계 성운
grain ⓝ 알갱이, 입자
volcanism ⓝ 화산활동
fragmentation ⓝ 균열, 분열, 파편화

[11-12] 중앙대 2010

지구상의 생명체는 20개의 아미노산을 사용해 수천 개의 서로 다른 단백질 위에 또 다른 수천 개의 단백질을 축적한다. (이 단백질들은 매우 다양한 세포 기능을 수행한다.) ㉮ 우주생물학자들은 생명이 어디로부터 왔는지 이해하기 위해 종종 아미노산의 기원에 중점을 둔다. 원시대기 상태의 재현과 그 화학작용을 알아보기 위해 실행한 초기 실험들 중 하나로 1953년 Stanley Miller에 의해 시행된 실험을 들 수 있다. 그는 목성과 같은 메탄올, 암모니아, 물로 구성된 환원성 대기에서 번개와 비슷한 전기 충격을 일으켜 아미노산을 합성하는 데 성공했다. 그의 선구적인 실험이 있었던 이후 과학자들은 초기 지구의 대기상태는 주로 질소와 이산화탄소를 포함하고 있는 보다 더 산성 대기였을 것이라고 생각하게 되었다. 그러나 Emily Blank 박사는 "이 같은 환원성 대기가 없는 경우라면, Miller가 제시한 방식은 아미노산을 만들기에는 효율적이지 않다."고 다른 견해를 제시했다. ㉯ 이 문제를 우회해서 해결할 수 있는 방법은 우주에서 아미노산을 만들어 혜성이나 운석에 실어서 충돌시키는 것이다. 그리고 운석이 아미노산을 운반한다는 매우 많은 증거가 존재한다. 또한 최근에 NASA 우주선 Stardust가 가져온 혜성의 물질에서 아미노산이 발견되기도 했다. Blank와 그녀의 동료들은 아미노산을 실은 "우주캡슐", 즉 혜성이나 운석이 지구와 충돌할 때 이 아미노산에 무슨 일이 일어날지에 대해 궁금증을 가졌다. ㉰ 연구팀은 운석보다는 혜성에 초점을 맞춰 일을 진행했다. 비록 내태양계(inner solar system)에 혜성이 운석보다 더 널리 퍼져 있는 것은 아니지만, 혜성은 건조하며 바위투성이인 운석보다 행성에 생물학적으로 연관성 있는 물질을 운송해 주는 데 더 많은 장점을 가지고 있다. 먼저, 혜성은 운석보다 밀도가 낮은 편이어서, 혜성의 충돌이 운석의 충돌보다 더 낮은 충격을 주며, 이는 혜성의 충격으로 인해 더 낮은 온도와 압력을 생성한다는 것을 의미한다. Blank는 혜성이 경사지게 충돌할 경우 그 충격이 훨씬 더 완화될 수 있다고 말한다. ㉱ 두 번째 장점은 혜성이 생명을 탄생시키는 화학작용의 열쇠인 물을 지니고 있다는 것이다. 혜성이 충돌하는 순간 혜성의 얼음이 녹아 충돌 지점에 작은 웅덩이가 생긴다. "혜성은 (생명 탄생에 필요한) 모든 재료를 제공해 주는, 일종의 소형 진화 세트와 같다."고 Blank는 말한다.

11 아래의 문장이 들어갈 위치로 가장 적합한 곳을 고르시오.

우주생물학자들은 생명이 어디로부터 왔는지 이해하기 위해 종종 아미노산의 기원에 중점을 둔다.

① ㉮   ② ㉯
③ ㉰   ④ ㉱

| 정답 | ①

| 해설 | 이 문제에서 주어진 문장의 내용이 아미노산의 기원에 대한 내용임을 생각하며 다시 본문에서 보기에 해당하는 부분에 대입시켜 보도록 한다. ㉮의 바로 앞 내용을 보면 '생명체는 단백질 생성을 위해 아미노산이 필요'하다고 언급하고 있으며, 바로 이어 '아미노산 생성에 관한 최초의 실험'이 있었다고 말하고 있는데, 이때 문제에서 제시된 문장인 '이런 아미노산은 어디로부터 기원'했는지에 대한 과학자들의 의문에 대해 말하고 있으므로 중간 흐름에 잘 어울린다. 따라서 답은 ①이 된다.

12 윗글을 통해 추론할 수 있는 것으로 가장 적합한 것을 고르시오.
① 행성 충돌은 지구 생명체의 탄생을 유발하는 데 일조했다.
② 아미노산은 지구상의 생명체가 살아가는 데 선택적 요소이다.
③ 유성의 충돌은 혜성의 충돌보다 비교적 낮은 압력을 생성한다.
④ 전기 충격은 아미노산을 생성하는 데 (비용이 적게 드는) 경제적인 수단이다.

| 정답 | ①

| 해설 | ②와 ③은 본문 내용과 반대로 서술하고 있으며, ④의 전기 충격 실험이 본문 전반부에 등장하지만 경제적 이유로 수행한 것은 아니다. 답은 ①로 혜성 출동이 지구 생명체 출현의 직접적인 영향을 주지는 않았더라도 이에 일조(help)했다는 내용을 담고 있다.

| 어휘 |
build up A upon B – A 위에 B를 쌓아 올리다
a myriad of – 무수히 많은
primordial ⓐ 원시의
synthesize ⓥ 합성하다
pioneering ⓐ 선구적인, 최초의
state ⓥ 진술하다 ⓝ 국가; 상태
on-board ⓐ (기내에) 탑재한, 적재한; 태워서, 실어서
meteorite ⓝ 운석
biomolecular ⓝ 생체분자
meteor ⓝ 유성
rocky ⓐ 바위투성이의; 불확실한, 불안정한
counterpart ⓝ 대응하는 사람이나 사물, 한 쌍의 한쪽, 상대방, 등가물
when it comes to sth – ~에 대해서라면
impact ⓝ 충돌
blow ⓝ 강타, 타격; 바람
beget ⓥ 탄생시키다
astrobiologist ⓝ 우주생물학자
in order to – ~하기 위해서
optional ⓐ 선택적인

myriad ⓐ 무수한
aim ⓥ 겨누다, 향하다
undertake ⓥ 맡다, 착수하다
reducing atmosphere – 환원성 대기
oxidative ⓐ 산화의, 산화력이 있는
get around sth – 돌아가다, 우회하다
comet ⓝ 혜성
smack ⓥ 찰싹 때리다, 충돌하다
prevalent ⓐ 널리 퍼져 있는, 우세한
relevant ⓐ 상응하는, 관련된
dense ⓐ 밀도가 높은, 빽빽한, 밀집한
oblique ⓐ 사선의, 비스듬한
ingredient ⓝ 성분, 구성요소
focus on – ~에 초점을 맞추다, ~에 중점을 두다
spark ⓥ 유발하다; 불꽃이 튀다 ⓝ 불꽃
means ⓝ 방법

[13-15] 덕성여대 2007

다른 모든 날씨처럼, 허리케인도 열, 즉 햇볕이 내리쬐는 열대 바다의 열에 의해 생긴다. 이 열은 마치 굴뚝 위로 솟아오르는 연기처럼, 따뜻하고 습한 공기를 대기의 차가운 상층부로 내뿜으면서 허리케인을 발생시킨다. 주변의 공기는 허리케인의 중심부로 빨려 들어가고, 지구의 자전에 의해 회전력을 얻어서 소용돌이치는 강우대가 된다. 채찍 꼬리 모양의 이 뇌우는, 회전하며 상승하는 회오리 안에 구름이 없는 태풍의 눈 주위를 둘러싼 태풍의 눈 벽(eyewall: 태풍의 눈을 둘러싼 두꺼운 적란운층)을 형성하는 곳에서 가장 강력하다. 허리케인(서태평양에서는 타이푼, 인도양에서는 열대 사이클론으로 불린다.)은 고도 50,000미터 이상까지 상승할 수 있다. 그 고도에 이르면 상승하는 공기는 마침내 권운(새털구름)의 소용돌이 모양 분출구로 빠져나간다. 역사상 가장 거대한 허리케인인 1997년 태평양 타이푼 Tip이 일으킨 강풍은 650마일 이상을 휩쓸었다. 평범한 허리케인조차도 풍력이 약 1.5조 와트에 달하는데 이것은 전 세계 전력 생산량의 약 절반에 해당한다.

13 허리케인이 형성되기 위해서는 _____.
① 습한 공기가 대기 상층부에 있어야 한다
② 태양이 눈부신 화창한 날씨여야 한다
③ 바다가 충분히 데워져야 한다
④ 구름이 열대 바다 위를 가려야 한다

| 정답 | ③

| 해설 | 첫 문장 "Like all weather, hurricanes are fueled by heat—the heat of heat of sun-drenched tropical seas,"를 참조하면, 허리케인이 형성되기 위한 동력은 "열(heat)"임을 알 수 있으므로 ③이 적절하다. 열대의 눈부신 태양은 바다가 데워지는 원인일 뿐, 허리케인 형성의 직접적 원동력이 아니다. ②를 선택하지 않도록 주의한다.

14

> 허리케인 뇌우는 _____에서 가장 강력하다.
> ① 태풍의 눈 벽   ② 태풍의 눈
> ③ 소용돌이치는 공기   ④ 강우대

| 정답 | ①

| 해설 | "These whip-tails of thunderstorm activity are strongest where they convey in a ring of rising, spinning air, the eyewall, which encloses the cloud-free eye."를 참조하면, 허리케인의 뇌우는 태풍의 눈 벽(eyewall)에서 가장 강력하다는 것을 알 수 있으므로 ①이 적절하다. 태풍의 눈은 태풍의 눈 벽으로 둘러싸인 구름 없는 지역이므로 ②를 선택하지 않도록 주의한다.

15

> 일반적인 허리케인의 풍력은 _____.
> ① 약 15조 와트이다.
> ② 솟아오르는 공기가 빠져나가게 한다.
> ③ 파도가 50,000피트 이상 솟구치게 한다.
> ④ 전 세계 전력 생산량을 초과하지 않는다.

| 정답 | ④

| 해설 | 마지막 문장 "Even an average hurricane packs some 1.5 trillion watts of power in its wind—equivalent to about half the world's entire electrical generating capacity.(평범한 허리케인조차도 풍력이 약 1.5조 와트에 달하는데 이것은 전 세계 전력 생산량의 약 절반에 해당한다.)"에 착안한 문제이다. 일반적인 허리케인이 풍력인 1.5와트는 전 세계 전력 생산량의 절반 정도이므로 ④가 적절하다.

| 어휘 | fuel ⓥ 연료[동력]를 공급하다   sun-drenched ⓐ 햇볕이 내리쬐는
rush ⓥ 돌진하다   frigid ⓐ 냉랭한, 매우 추운
atmosphere ⓝ 공기, 대기   suck in – 빨아들이다
base ⓝ 기저, 바닥, 근거   rotation ⓝ 자전
twist ⓝ 비틀기, 전환   whorl ⓝ 소용돌이무늬
rain band ⓝ 강우대   whip-tail ⓝ (길고 가느다란 꼬리가 있는) 채찍 모양
thunderstorm ⓝ 뇌우   converge ⓥ 모여들다, 집중하다
spinning ⓐ 회전하는   eyewall ⓝ 태풍의 눈 벽
enclose ⓥ 에워싸다, 포위하다   propel ⓥ 추진하다
altitude ⓝ 고도   vent itself – 새어 나오다
spiraling ⓐ 소용돌이치는, 상승하는   exhaust ⓝ 배기가스, 배기관
jet ⓝ 분사, 분출, 분출구   gale-force ⓐ 강풍급의
pack ⓥ 지니다, 채우다   equivalent to – ~와 동등한

[16-18] 아주대 2016

[A] 지구를 둘러싼 대기는 다섯 개의 층으로 나누어진다. 대기는 지표 근처에서 가장 밀도가 높고, 고도가 높아질수록 대기가 희박해지다 결국 우주와 합쳐지게 된다. 오존은 대류권과 성층권인 두 가지 대기권에서 발견된다. 전자에 속한 오존은 지상 수준의 오존으로, 인간의 건강을 자극하는 물질이자 스모그를 구성하는 물질이며, 후자는 대다수의 대기 오존을 구성하는 오존으로, 태양으로부터 방출되는 자외선을 흡수하여 인간의 건강을 지켜 주며, 이로써 태양의 자외선이 지구 표면을 타격하지 못하도록 하며, 자외선과 같은 생명체에 위협이 되는 방사선으로부터 생명체에 피해가 가지 않도록 막아 준다.

[B] '오존 구멍'이라는 용어는 이러한 보호 역할을 하는 성층권의 오존이 극지방에서 최근 들어 고갈되고 있는 것을 의미한다. 오존 구멍 아래에 살고 있는 사람과 동식물은 이제 지구 표면까지 도달하는 태양의 방사선에 의해 피해를 입고 있으며, 눈 손상에서 피부암에 이르는 건강상의 문제가 나타나고 있다.

[C] 과학자들은 성층권 하부에서 오존층이 줄어들고 있으며, 남극 지방의 봄철에 특히 극적으로 오존층이 줄어드는 '오존 구멍' 현상이 진행되고 있음을 발견했다. 이것은 프레온(CFC) 가스라고 불리는 성층권에서 오존을 파괴하는 화학 물질의 농도가 증가함에 따라 발생한 것으로, 프레온 가스는 수십 년에서 길게는 100년 넘게 대기 중에 머무른다. 극지방의 봄에 태양이 다시 나타나고, 이때 얼음 입자가 녹으면서 오존층을 파괴하는 분자를 방출하며, 이는 다시 자외선을 흡수하는 오존의 분자 결합을 깨뜨리는 지저분한 일을 하게 된다.

[D] 그러나 오존 구멍은 지구온난화의 메커니즘이 아니다. 자외선 복사는 태양으로부터 나오는 에너지의 1% 미만을 나타내며, 이는 인간의 활동으로 인한 과도한 열의 원인이 되기에는 충분하지 않다. 지구온난화는 석탄과 석유 같은 화석 연료를 연소해 전기를 생산하거나 차량을 구동하는 과정에서 대기로 너무 많은 탄소가 방출되어 발생한다. 이 가스들은 담요처럼 지구 주변으로 확산되며, 우주로 복사될 수 있는 태양열을 붙잡고 있게 된다.

[E] 그러나 이러한 환경 문제는 모두 공통된 원인, 즉 대기로 가스를 방출하여 대기가 변화되는 인간의 활동을 그 원인이라는 공통의 원인을 가지고 있다. 오존층 파괴는 이전에는 에어로졸 스프레이 캔이나 냉매에서 발견된 프레온 가스가 대기 중으로 방출될 때 발생한다. 이러한 가스는 여러 화학 반응을 통해 오존 분자를 분해시키며, 오존의 자외선 복사 흡수 능력을 감소시킨다. 지구의 대기는 하나로 연결된 시스템이기 때문에 오존층 파괴와 지구온난화가 다른 어떤 방식으로 관련이 있다는 것은 놀라운 일이 아니다. 예를 들면, 기후 변화가 보호 역할을 하는 오존층을 얇게 하는 데 기여할 수 있다는 증거가 있다.

16 다음 중 본문의 내용을 통해 답변할 수 있는 것이 아닌 것은?

① 오존 구멍이란 무엇인가?
② 무엇이 오존 구멍을 만들어 내는가?
③ 오존 구멍은 사람들에게 어떤 영향을 미치는가?
④ 오존 구멍은 어떻게 지구온난화에 기여하고 있는가?
⑤ 기후 변화가 성층권의 오존층에 영향을 미치는가?

| 정답 | ④

| 해설 | [D] 문단의 첫 번째 문장인 "The ozone hole, however, is not the mechanism of global warming."에서 오존 구멍이 지구온난화를 일으키는 것은 아니라고 설명한다. 오존 구멍을 통해 지상에 도달하는 자외선 복사는 태양 에너지의 1%가 되지 않아서 지구의 온도를 올리는 데 별다른 기여를 하지 않는다고 설명한다. 따라서 ④의 내용은 사실이 아니며, 그에 대한 답변도 불가능하다. ①은 [B] 문단의 첫 번째 문장에서 찾을 수 있고, ②의 경우 [B] 문단에서, ③은 [B] 문단의 두 번째 문장에서 답을 찾을 수 있다. ⑤의 경우 이어진 문제에 제시된 글에서 해답을 찾을 수 있다.

17

아래 내용은 본문에서 추출된 부분이다. 저자의 주장을 뒷받침할 수 있도록 다음의 내용을 ❶ – ❺ 중에 삽입할 때 적합한 위치는?

> 지구의 대기는 하나로 연결된 시스템이기 때문에 오존층 파괴와 지구온난화가 다른 어떤 방식으로 관련이 있다는 것은 놀라운 일이 아니다. 예를 들면, 기후변화가 보호 역할을 하는 오존층을 얇게 하는 데 기여할 수 있다는 증거가 있다.

① ❶
② ❷
③ ❸
④ ❹
⑤ ❺

| 정답 | ⑤

| 해설 | 제시된 글에서 주목할 부분은 오존층 파괴와 지구온난화라는 두 가지 문제가 서로 연결되어 있다는 내용이다. 하지만 [D] 문단의 서두에서 오존층의 파괴가 지구온난화의 원인은 아니라고 설명하고 있으므로 ❹에 들어가는 것은 적절하지 않다. [E] 문단의 서두에서 말한 두 가지 환경 문제가 바로 오존층의 파괴와 지구온난화이며, 이 두 문제는 인간의 행위라는 공동의 원인을 가지고 있다고 말한다. 따라서 ❺에 제시문을 놓게 되면 두 가지 문제에 대한 내용이 설명이 되며, 서로 연관 가능성이 있을 수 있다는 흐름도 설명이 가능해진다.

18

다음 중 본문의 내용과 일치하지 않는 것은?

① 대류권의 '오존 구멍'은 인간과 동물에 해를 끼친다.
② 지구온난화로 인해 오존층을 파괴하는 분자가 얼음 입자에서 방출된다.
③ 인간이 개발한 합성물인 프레온 가스는 상당히 파괴적이며, 대기 중에 오랫동안 머무른다.
④ 극지방 성층권의 오존층이 두껍다는 것은 대기에 의한 오존층의 보호 기능이 온전히 작동하고 있다는 것을 보여준다.
⑤ 탄소 화학물질과 열을 가두는 다른 가스들이 대기 중에 올라가 지구 주위로 확산되면, 지구 주위에서 열을 가두고 있는 담요처럼 역할을 한다.

| 정답 | ①

| 해설 | [B] 문단의 "The term 'ozone hole' refers to recent depletion of this protective layer of stratospheric ozone over the polar regions." 부분을 통해 오존 구멍은 대류권이 아닌 성층권에서 발생한다는 것을 알 수 있으므로, 정답은 ①이 된다.

| 어휘 | atmosphere ⓝ 대기
thin out – 옅어지다, (수가) 줄어들다
troposphere ⓝ 대류권
the former – 전자
irritant ⓝ (피부를 따갑게 하거나 하는) 자극물
ultraviolet ⓝ 자외선(UV)
depletion ⓝ (자원 등의) 고갈, 소모
concentration ⓝ 농도; 집중, 정신 집중
chlorofluorocarbon ⓝ 클로로플루오르카본, 프레온 가스(CFC)
molecular ⓐ 분자의

layer ⓝ 층
merge with – ~와 통합[합병]되다
stratosphere ⓝ 성층권
the latter – 후자
account for – ~을 설명하다, 차지하다
radiation ⓝ 방사선, 복사
Antarctic ⓝ 남극 지역
ozone-depleting ⓐ 오존층을 파괴하는

global warming – 지구온난화

carbon ⓝ 탄소
refrigerant ⓝ 냉각제, 냉동제
do harm – 해를 끼치다
intact ⓐ (하나도 손상되지 않고) 온전한, 전혀 다치지 않은
blanket ⓝ 담요
chemical reaction – 화학 반응
compound ⓝ 합성물

[19-21] 단국대 2017

현대의 기상 예측 방법은 단기 예측에는 상당히 정확하지만, 예측이 장기화되면 될수록 예측이 정확하지 않을 가능성이 더 커진다. 수학적으로 기상조건을 계산하는 현재의 방법은 날씨의 카오스적인 특성으로 인해 정확한 예측은 5일 앞까지로 제한된다. 기상학자들은 전산 자료 수집 방법의 결과를 현재 발생하고 있는 실제 대기 조건과 결합한다. 다양한 높이의 온도, 이슬점, 바람에 관한 최신 정보가 전 세계 곳곳에서 수집되어 과거 조건을 기반으로 한 컴퓨터 모델과 비교되며, 이를 통해 예상되는 기후 패턴을 찾아낸다. 하지만 기상학 방법의 과학 및 방법론이 향상된 것은 사실이지만, 대기 및 날씨 관련 활동에 대한 이해에는 여전히 큰 격차가 존재한다. 결과적으로 매우 다양한 기상조건을 경험하고 그런 기상조건이 만들어 낼 수 있는 변화무쌍함에 대해 잘 알고 있는 풍부한 경험을 가진 기상학자가 미래의 기상조건을 정확히 예측할 수 있는 확률은 컴퓨터에 의해 생성된 수치예보모델의 예측 확률과 거의 비슷할 가능성이 크다.

19 다음 중 밑줄 친 부분과 가장 가까운 의미에 해당하는 것은?
① 변화
② 정도
③ 속도
④ 고도

| 정답 | ④

| 해설 | level의 뜻 중에 '높이'가 있으므로, '고도'를 뜻하는 ④ elevation이 동의어가 된다.

20 다음 중 아래 내용이 들어갈 가장 적절한 위치를 본문에서 고르시오.

> 하지만 기상학 방법의 과학 및 방법론이 향상된 것은 사실이지만, 대기 및 날씨 관련 활동에 대한 이해에는 여전히 큰 격차가 존재한다.

① (A)
② (B)
③ (C)
④ (D)

| 정답 | ④

| 해설 | 제시된 문장의 내용을 통해, 앞 내용은 기상 예측의 과학적 향상이 와야 하고, 뒤에 이어지는 내용은 그런 향상에도 불구하고 실제와 큰 격차(large gaps)를 보이는 기상 예측, 즉 기상 예측의 '한계'에 대해서 서술된 내용이 나와야 한다. 정답은 ④로, (D) 이후의 내용이 슈퍼컴퓨터를 이용한 수치예보모델의 정확한 기상 예측 가능성이 숙련된 사람의 수준과 비슷하다는 내용이므로, 현대 기상 예측의 한계를 우회적으로 설명한 것에 해당한다.

21 다음 중 본문의 내용과 일치하지 않는 것은?

① 컴퓨터에 의해 생성된 수치예보모델은 장기간의 기상 패턴을 예측하는 데 상당히 신뢰할 만하다.
② 경험이 풍부한 기상학자는 컴퓨터에 의해 생성된 수치예보모델만큼 정확하게 예측할 수 있다.
③ 날씨가 급격히 변하기 때문에 가까운 미래에 대해서만 정확한 기상 예측이 가능하다.
④ 현대 기상 예측은 온도, 습도, 바람의 패턴 등을 고려해 미래의 기상 패턴을 결정한다.

| 정답 | ①

| 해설 | 본문 서두의 "the longer the forecast, the more chances there are that the forecasts are going to be incorrect."에서 기상 예측은 단기에만 정확하고, 장기 예측은 부정확할 확률이 커진다고 했으므로, 장기간의 기상 패턴을 예측하는 데 상당히 신뢰할 만하다는 ①의 내용은 본문과 일치하지 않는다.

| 어휘 |
accurate ⓐ 정확한
short-range ⓐ 단기의, 단거리의
in advance – 미리[앞서], 사전에
meteorologist ⓝ 기상학자, 기상 전문 기자
atmospheric ⓐ 대기의
dew point – 이슬점(대기 중의 수증기가 엉겨 물방울이 되는 온도)
clue ⓝ 실마리, 단서
shift ⓝ 변화, 교대 ⓥ 이동시키다, 바꾸다, 옮기다
elevation ⓝ 해발 높이, 고도; 승진, 승격
take ~ into account – ~을 고려하다, 참작하다, 계산에 넣다
humidity ⓝ 습도

when it comes to – ~에 관하여
confine ⓥ 감금하다, 가둬놓다, 제한하다 ⓝ 한계, 범위
chaotic ⓐ 혼돈[혼란] 상태인
combine A with B – A를 B와 합치다
concerning ⓟ ~에 관한
come up with – (아이디어를) 생각해 내다
stand a chance – (~을 할) 가능성이 있다
meteorological ⓐ 기상의, 기상학상의

[22-25]

열점은 전 세계의 화산활동이 활발한 여러 지역 가운데 바위가 거대한 가마솥처럼 지하에 용해된 지점을 일컫는다. 옐로스톤 국립공원의 증기를 뿜는 간헐 온천, 온천수가 흐르는 물웅덩이, 머드 포트 등은 이런 열점 덕분에 존재하게 되었다.
매년 옐로스톤 국립공원에서는 200개가 넘는 간헐 온천이 솟아오르며, 덕분에 옐로스톤은 지질학자들에게 세계에서 가장 흥미로운 곳 중 하나이다. 세계에서 가장 유명한 간헐 온천인 올드 페이스풀 부근 1평방마일 정도 크기의 어퍼 가이저 베이슨에는 100개가 넘는 간헐 온천이 존재한다. 옐로스톤 열점은 대략 천만 년 전에 형성되었고, 국립공원의 중심에서는 아직도 화산활동이 활발히 이루어지며, 지표에서 단지 1~2마일 깊이에 용해된 바위가 존재한다.
비와 녹은 눈이 지표의 작은 갈라진 틈 사이로 스며들어 가면, 물은 결국에 용암으로 달궈진 바위로 만들어진 공간에 도달한다. 바위는 물을 뜨겁게 만들고, 끓는 물과 증기가 종종 간헐 온천, 온천수가 흐르는 물웅덩이, 머드포트 등의 형태로 지표로 거슬러 올라가 분출된다.
간헐 온천의 경우, 지하 공간에 갇힌 물은 끓는점 이상으로 가열되어 증기를 형성한다. 증기는 물보다 최대 1,500배의 공간을 차지하므로, 압력이 축적되면서, 결국에는 과열된 물이 간헐 온천의 형태로 지표로 터지듯 분출된다. 온천수가 흐르는 물웅덩이는 열점으로부터 나온 물이 냉각되기 전에 지표에 도달할 때 형성된다. 만일 물이 지면에 끝까지 도달하지 못할 경우, 증기와 가스가 바위를 녹여 거품이 나오는 머드 포트가 대신 형성된다.

22

열점이 형성되는 지점은 어디인가?
① 적도 주변 암석이 많은 지역
② 활화산 부근 지표면 아래
③ 화산 분화구로부터 대략 1마일 위
④ 고대 화산 중심부

| 정답 | ②

| 해설 | "열점은 전 세계의 화산활동이 활발한 여러 지역 가운데 바위가 거대한 가마솥처럼 지하에 용해된 지점을 일컫는다(A hot spot is a giant underground caldron of molten rock in one of the world's many volcanically active areas)." 따라서 답은 ②이다.

23

본문에 따르면 옐로스톤 국립공원이 지질학자들에게 흥미로운 지역인 이유는 무엇인가?
① 100평방마일의 열점이 존재한다.
② 매년 200개가 넘는 간헐 온천이 솟아오른다.
③ 간헐 온천의 종류가 100개가 넘는다.
④ 발견되는 바위 종류가 200개가 넘는다.

| 정답 | ②

| 해설 | "매년 옐로스톤 국립공원에서는 200개가 넘는 간헐 온천이 솟아오르며, 덕분에 옐로스톤은 지질학자들에게 세계에서 가장 흥미로운 곳 중 하나이다(Annually, more than 200 geysers erupt in Yellowstone, making this one of the most interesting places in the world for geologists)." 따라서 답은 ②이다.

24

열점은 어떻게 간헐 온천의 형성에 기여하는가?
① 열점은 화산 분화구에 떨어지는 눈을 전부 녹인다.
② 물이 지하 공간에 갇혀서 결코 밖으로 빠져나가지 못한다.
③ 뜨거운 바위로 인해 지하에서 물이 끓고, 증기랑 압력이 형성된다.
④ 열점에서 나온 물이 식기 전에 지표로 분출된다.

| 정답 | ③

| 해설 | "간헐 온천의 경우, 지하 공간에 갇힌 물은 끓는점 이상으로 가열되어 증기를 형성한다. 증기는 물보다 최대 1,500배의 공간을 차지하므로, 압력이 축적되면서, 결국에는 과열된 물이 간헐 온천의 형태로 지표로 터지듯 분출된다(In a geyser, water trapped in an underground chamber heats up beyond the boiling point and forms steam. Since steam takes up 1,500 times more space than water, pressure builds up, eventually forcing the superheated water to burst to the surface as a geyser)." 따라서 답은 ③이다.

25

머드 포트는 언제 형성되는가?
① 증기랑 가스가 지표 주변의 바위를 녹일 때
② 지하수가 끓는점을 초과할 때
③ 눈이 옐로스톤 국립공원의 간헐 온천 지대에서 녹을 때
④ 과열된 물이 지표로 터지듯 분출될 때

| 정답 | ①

| 해설 | "만일 물이 지면에 끝까지 도달하지 못할 경우, 증기와 가스가 바위를 녹여 거품이 나오는 머드 포트가 대신 형성된다(If the water does not make it all the way to the surface, steam and gases may dissolve rocks and form a bubbling mud pot instead)." 따라서 답은 ①이다.

| 어휘 | caldron ⓝ 가마솥, 큰 냄비
molten ⓐ 녹은, 용해된
geyser ⓝ 간헐 온천
thermal ⓐ 온천수가 나는
mud pot – 머드 포트(뜨겁고, 대개는 부글부글 끓어오르고 있는, 진흙이 가득 찬 움푹 파인 곳)
owe A to B – A는 B 덕분이다
geologist ⓝ 지질학자
seep ⓥ 스미다, 배다
lava ⓝ 용암
dissolve ⓥ 녹이다, 용해시키다
active volcano – 활화산

[26-28] 서울여대 2013

찰스 햅굿이 자신의 저서인 "지구의 지각 이동: 지구과학의 일부 기본적 문제에 대한 해결책"에서 암시한 이론은 1908년 미국의 아마추어 지질학자인 프랭크 버슬리 테일러가 처음 제시한 것이었다. 부유한 집안 출신인 테일러는 재력과 함께 학문적 제약에서 벗어날 수 있는 자유도 갖추고 있었고, 덕분에 기존과는 다른 계통의 연구 분야를 추구할 수 있었다. 그는 아프리카와 남아메리카가 서로 마주하고 있는 해안선의 모양이 비슷하다는 생각을 가진 사람 중 하나였고, 관찰을 통해 과거 여러 대륙이 미끄러지듯 이리저리 이동했다는 생각을 고안했다. 그는 여러 대륙이 서로 부서지는 소리를 내며 충돌하는 과정에서 전 세계의 산맥이 밀쳐지듯 올라갔다는 의견을 제시했다. 하지만 그는 증거라고 할 만한 것을 많이 제시하지 못했고 그의 이론은 제대로 된 관심을 받기엔 터무니없는 것으로 취급되었다.

하지만 독일에서 테일러의 이론은 마르부르크 대학 기상학자이자 이론가인 알프레트 배게너에 의해 발견되었고 그는 이 이론을 사실상 도용하였다. 배게너는 표준적인 지구 역사 모델에 아무 문제없이 들어맞지 않는 이례적인 식물과 화석들을 다수 조사했고, 이 중 거의 대부분은 전통적인 방법으로 해석할 경우 이치에 맞지 않는다는 사실을 깨달았다. 대양의 양쪽 반대 지역은 헤엄쳐 가기엔 분명히 너무 먼 거리에 있지만 동물 화석이 양쪽에서 반복적으로 등장했다. 그는 어떻게 유대목 동물이 남아메리카 대륙에서 호주로 이동할 수 있었는지 그리고 어떻게 동일한 달팽이가 스칸디나비아 지역과 뉴잉글랜드에서 나타날 수 있는지를 궁금해했다. 그리고 그런 점에 있어, 어떻게 노르웨이 북쪽 400마일 지점의 스피츠베르겐 같은 몹시 추운 지역에서 탄층과 그 외 아열대지방의 흔적이 존재하는 이유가 무엇인지 설명할 수 있는 방법은, 따뜻한 곳에서 추운 곳으로 어떻게든 이동했기 때문이라고 말하는 것을 제외하고 달리 무엇이 있을까?

26 본문 첫 줄의 "이론"은 무엇인가?

① 빅뱅이론
② 구운 사과 이론
③ 대륙이동설
④ 진화론

| 정답 | ③

| 해설 | 본문은 과거 한 덩어리로 뭉쳐져 있던 대륙이 이동하면서 갈라지고 지금의 모양을 갖추게 되었다는 대륙이동설의 기원에 관해 말하고 있다. 따라서 첫 줄의 "이론(The theory)"은 대륙이동설을 의미한다.

27 다음 중 프랭크 버슬리 테일러에 관해 사실이 아닌 것은 무엇인가?
① 그의 이론은 찰스 햅굿의 지질 연구에 영향을 미쳤다.
② 그는 자신의 지리 연구 분야에 제약을 가하지 않을 만큼 재력이 있었다.
③ 그는 세상의 산맥은 대륙의 이동을 통해 형성되었다고 주장했다.
④ 그는 여러 대륙이 미끄러지듯 이리저리 이동했다는 자신의 이론을 증명했다.

| 정답 | ④

| 해설 | "하지만 그는 증거라고 할 만한 것을 많이 제시하지 못했고 그의 이론은 제대로 된 관심을 받기엔 터무니없는 것으로 취급되었다(He failed, however, to produce much in the way of evidence, and the theory was considered too crackpot to merit serious attention)." 즉, 테일러의 주장은 결국에는 증명되지 못한 채 터무니없는 헛소리로 치부되었다. 따라서 답은 ④이다.

28 다음 중 배게너가 자신의 이론을 증명하기 위해 사용한 것이 아닌 것은 무엇인가?
① 그가 있던 당시의 기상학적 연구
② 남아메리카와 호주에서 발견된 유대목 동물의 화석
③ 지하에서 발견된 석탄층
④ 스칸디나비아 지역과 뉴잉글랜드에서 발견된 달팽이

| 정답 | ①

| 해설 | "그는 어떻게 유대목 동물이 남아메리카 대륙에서 호주로 이동할 수 있었는지 그리고 어떻게 동일한 달팽이가 스칸디나비아 지역과 뉴잉글랜드에서 나타날 수 있는지를 궁금해했다(How, he wondered, did marsupials travel from South America to Australia? How did identical snails turn up in Scandinavia and New England?)." 그리고 어떻게 "노르웨이 북쪽 400마일 지점의 스피츠베르겐같은 몹시 추운 지역에서 탄층과 그 외 아열대지방의 흔적이 존재하는(coal seams and other semi-tropical remnants in frigid spots like Spitsbergen, four hundred miles north of Norway)" 것이 가능한지 궁금해했다. 그리고 이들은 만일 그의 이론이 증명된다면 충분히 설명이 가능한 사례들이다. 하지만 본문에 따르면 배게너는 기상학자이긴 했으나 자신의 대륙이동설을 증명하는 데 기상학적 연구는 수행한 바 없다. 따라서 답은 ①이다.

| 어휘 | allude ⓥ 암시하다, 시사하다
crust ⓝ 지각
constraint ⓝ 제약
strike ⓥ 생각이 떠오르다[들다]
thrust ⓥ 밀치다
crackpot ⓐ 터무니없는
pick up – 알아채다, 발견하다
appropriate ⓥ 자기 것으로 하다, 도용하다
comfortably ⓐⓓ 수월하게, 아무 문제없이
come to that – 그런 점은 (바로 앞에 한 말과 관련된 내용을 덧붙일 때 씀)
coal seam – 탄층
frigid ⓐ 몹시 추운
entitled ⓐ ~라는 제목의
propound ⓥ 제기하다
line ⓝ 유형, 계통
crunch ⓥ 아삭아삭 깨물다, 바삭바삭 밟으며 나아가다
in the way of – ~라고 할 만한 것이
merit ⓥ (칭찬·관심 등을) 받을 만하다
effectively ⓐⓓ 실질적으로
anomaly ⓝ 변칙, 이례
marsupial ⓝ 유대목 동물
remnant ⓝ 자취, 남은 물건
clime ⓝ 기후, 풍토; 지방

[29-30] 인하대 2013

M. 케리 오베니언 박사와 그의 연구팀에 따르면 미래 화성으로 긴 여행을 떠나는 우주인들은 어쩌면 걱정할 것이 더 생겼을지도 모른다. 오베니언 박사는 다음과 같이 말했다. "우주에 있을 때 생길 수 있는 잠재적인 위험으로 이미 알려진 것들은 암이나 백내장이 있는데, 여기에 더해 신경병성 질환이 악화될 가능성도 위험으로 존재합니다." 연구진은 실험 쥐를 높은 단계의 우주선에 노출시켰는데, 노출된 양은 우주인이 화성에 도달하기까지 걸리는 시간인 3년이 넘는 기간 동안 노출되는 것과 동일하다. 연구진은 쥐가 알츠하이머병의 징후를 보이기 시작했음을 발견했다. 오베이언 박사는 현재의 우주선 기술은 태양 복사는 충분히 막을 수 있지만, 지구 궤도 밖에서 발견되는 높은 수준의 우주방사선을 차단할 수 있게끔 설계되어 있지는 않다고 밝혔다. 오베니언 박사는 다음과 같이 말했다. "은하 우주방사선은 속도가 매우 빠르고 질량도 매우 큰 하전입자입니다. 이들 입자는 기존의 물질로는 차단하기가 매우 까다롭습니다. 물이나 콘크리트 또는 납을 매우 두껍게 깔아야 합니다. 제가 이해하기로는 현재 우리는 이러한 경우에 대응해 우주선을 효과적으로 보호할 수 있는 기술을 갖고 있지 못하며, 그 이유는 물이나 콘크리트 또는 납 등의 물질을 그렇게나 많이 실을 수 없기 때문입니다." 오베니언 박사는 앞으로 수년 동안 연구진이 이런 방사성 입자를 차단할 수 있는 방법을 개발하여 미래에 우주인은 우주선에 노출되는 일은 걱정할 필요 없이 임무에만 집중할 수 있게 보장할 것이라고 확신하고 있다.

29 다음 중 빈칸에 가장 알맞은 것은 무엇인가?
① 태양 복사
② 우주방사선
③ 기존의 물질
④ 암 및 백내장에 걸릴 잠재적 위험

| 정답 | ②

| 해설 | 본문에 따르면 우주인은 우주에 장시간 있게 되면 우주방사선에 노출되면서 암이나 백내장뿐만 아니라 신경병성 질환의 악화 같은 새로운 부작용을 경험할 가능성이 존재한다. 따라서 우주인들은 장기간 우주에 머무르기 위해서 우주방사선에 노출되지 않아야 한다. 본문 마지막 문장을 보면, 연구진의 목표는 우주인들이 임무에 집중하게 만드는 것이고 '빈칸'에 걱정하지 않도록 하는 것이다. 빈칸이 무엇인지 유추해 보면 '우주인들이 임무에 집중할 수 있도록 우주방사선에 노출될 걱정을 하지 않게 한다'는 의미에서 ②가 가장 적합하다.

30 본문에 따르면 다음 중 사실인 것은 무엇인가?
① 우주인이 화성에 도달하기까지는 3년이 넘게 걸릴 것이다.
② 우주인이 화성으로 여행을 하는 동안 겪게 될 위험은 존재하지 않는다.
③ 실험에서 쥐는 알츠하이머병의 징후를 보이지 않았다.
④ 연구진은 우주에서 발생하는 방사성 입자를 차단할 수 있는 방안을 개발했다.

| 정답 | ①

| 해설 | "노출된 양은 우주인이 화성에 도달하기까지 걸리는 시간인 3년이 넘는 기간 동안 노출되는 것과 동일하다(the same amount an astronaut would be exposed to over the three years it would take to get to Mars)." 여기서 화성에 도달하기까지 3년이 넘게 걸림을 알 수 있다. 따라서 답은 ①이다.
참고로, 우주인은 화성으로 여행하는 도중에 우주선에 의해 신경병성 질환이 악화될 수 있으므로 ②는 답이 될 수 없고, 쥐가 알츠하이머병의 징후를 보이기 시작했다고 명시되어 있으므로 ③도 답이 될 수 없고, 아직 방안은 발견하지 못했지만 곧 발견할 것임을 확신하고 있으므로 ④도 답이 될 수 없다.

| 어휘 | **cataract** ⓝ 백내장   **exacerbate** ⓥ 악화시키다

neurodegenerative ⓐ 신경병성의
solar radiation - 태양 복사
charged particle - 하전입자
cosmic radiation - 우주선(우주방사선)
galactic ⓐ 은하의

[31-32] 중앙대 2013

아스완 하이 댐은 러시아의 지원을 받아 이집트에 건설된 댐으로 수력 발전 및 예측이 불가능한 나일강을 제어하여 이집트의 식량 공급을 증대시킬 목적으로 만들어졌다. 이 댐 건설 계획이 의미하는 것은 경작을 위해 수몰된 지역의 물이 빠져나가고 그 결과 위대한 예술적 보물은 물에 잠기게 되었다는 것이다. 하지만 댐의 건설 기간 동안에 증가한 이집트 인구 1인당 이용 가능한 토지는 10분의 1 에이커에 불과했다. 댐 건설의 결과 중 하나는 나일강의 삼각주 농지가 더 이상 매년 범람되지 않는다는 점이다. 나일강 삼각주는 매년 침수로 인해 토사가 침전되어 다시 토지가 비옥해지곤 했었다. 그러나 이제는 더 이상 홍수가 일어나지 않게 되면서 농지의 지력이 감소하게 되었다. 또한 아스완 하이 댐은 매년 홍수와 함께 지중해로 쓸려 내려가던 영양분을 차단하는 결과를 낳았다. 이 때문에 또는 댐으로 인해 바다의 염도가 변화했기 때문에 정어리 어획량은 연간 18,000톤에서 500톤으로 급감했다. 댐에 의해 형성된 호수가 안정화되자 수생 달팽이들이 번창하게 되었다. 이들 달팽이는 인간을 뚫고 들어와 주혈흡충병이라는 무서운 질병을 야기하는 주혈흡충의 중간 숙주 역할을 한다. 아스완 하이 댐의 건설은 당시엔 정치적으로 중요한 의미를 함축한다.

31

밑줄 친 (A), (B)에 들어가기에 가장 적합한 것을 고르시오.
① 따라서 – 때문에
② 그러나 – 때문에
③ 결국 – 그럼에도 불구하고
④ 그럼에도 불구하고 – 따라서

| 정답 | ②

| 해설 | 빈칸 (A) 앞은 위대한 유산들이 댐의 수몰로 인해 없어졌음을 말하고 있으며, 뒤에서는 댐을 건설했으나 실제 얻은 것은 크지 않았음을 말하고 있다. 즉, 희생에 비해 대가가 그리 크지 않음을 말하고 있다. 따라서 (A)는 서로 상반된 내용의 문장을 연결 짓는 however나 nonetheless가 답으로 적합하다. 빈칸 (B) 앞은 댐으로 인해 "지중해로 쓸려 내려가던 영양분을 차단(cut off the nutrients that had been washed to the Mediterranean Sea)"했다는 내용을 담고 있으며, 뒤에서는 영양분 차단 또는 염도 변화로 인한 피해를 정어리의 예를 들어 설명하고 있다. 따라서 빈칸에는 인과 관계를 나타내는 because of나 due to가 적합하다. 이 모든 사항을 종합해 봤을 때 답은 ②이다.

32

윗글의 제목으로 가장 적합한 것을 고르시오.
① 아스완 하이 댐으로 인해 발생한 환경 문제
② 이집트의 아스완 하이 댐이 미치는 경제적 영향
③ 나일강에 벌어지는 홍수가 주는 혜택과 문제점
④ 아스완 하이 댐 건설에 정치가 미친 영향

| 정답 | ①

| 해설 | 본문은 아스완 하이 댐이 건설되고 나서 환경적으로 어떤 악영향이 발생했는지를 논하고 있다. 따라서 답은 ①이다.

| 어휘 | hydroelectric power – 수력 발전
drain ⓥ 물을 빼내다
deposited ⓐ 침전된, 퇴적된
cut off – 중단시키다, 차단시키다
sardine ⓝ 정어리
aquatic snail – 수생 달팽이
blood fluke – 주혈흡충
schistosomiasis ⓝ 주혈흡충병

submerged ⓐ 수몰된, 침수된
delta ⓝ 삼각주
silt ⓝ 토사, 침니
salinity ⓝ 염분, 염도
catch ⓝ 잡은 양
intermediate host – 중간 숙주
bore ⓥ 구멍을 뚫다
implication ⓝ 암시, 함축

[33-35] 한국외대 2014

쓰나미는 외해의 깊은 물을 벗어나 해안가의 덜 깊은 물로 이동하면서 변화한다. 쓰나미가 이동하는 속도는 물의 깊이와 관련이 있으며, 따라서 물의 깊이가 낮아질수록 쓰나미의 속도도 늦춰진다. 쓰나미의 에너지 유량은 파도의 속도와 파도의 높이에 달려 있다. 쓰나미는 덜 깊은 물로 이동할수록 높이가 높아진다. 이를 천수라 부른다. 이러한 천수 효과 때문에 바다에서는 눈에 띄지 않는 쓰나미가 해안가에서는 수 미터 이상의 높이로 커지곤 한다. 쓰나미는 마침내 해안에 도달하게 되면 급격하게 오르내리는 조류로도, 연쇄적으로 진행되는 쇄파로도, 심지어는 해일로도 보인다. 다른 물결과 마찬가지로 쓰나미는 해안으로 쇄도해 들어오면서 에너지를 잃게 된다. 조류 에너지의 일부는 바다 쪽으로 되돌아가며, 해안으로 전파되는 조류 에너지는 해저 마찰과 난류로 인해 소멸하게 된다. 이처럼 에너지가 사라지더라도 쓰나미는 여전히 엄청난 에너지를 품고 해안에 도달하게 된다. 쓰나미의 침식력은 상당히 커서 축적되기까지 수년이 걸린 해안의 모래를 쓸어가 버리고 나무와 해안에 심어진 초목의 기반 부분을 약화시킨다. 평소에 수위가 가장 높을 때와 비교해 지상 방향으로 수백 미터에 달하는 지역을 침수시키거나 물에 잠기게 할 가능성이 있기 때문에, 밀려들어 오는 쓰나미와 함께 연계되어 빠른 속도로 물이 이동하게 되면 집뿐만 아니라 해안가의 다른 구조물이 파괴된다. 추가로 이렇게 빠른 속도로 움직이는 쓰나미의 파괴력은 엄청나고 대양 분지 전체에 영향을 미칠 수 있다.

33 다음 중 본문의 주제는 무엇인가?
① 쓰나미는 태풍과 어떻게 유사한가
② 쓰나미는 대양 분지에 어떻게 영향을 미치는가
③ 쓰나미는 육지로 밀려들면서 어떻게 변모하는가
④ 쓰나미가 닥칠 때 어떻게 대피하는가

| 정답 | ③

| 해설 | 본문은 쓰나미가 육지로 밀려들어 오면서 어떻게 "변화(transform)"하고 해안 지역에 어떤 영향을 미치는지를 설명하고 있다. 따라서 답은 ③이다.

34 다음 중 (A)와 관련해 사실인 것은 무엇인가?
① 파도가 높을수록 쓰나미의 속도는 빨라진다.
② 쓰나미는 속도가 줄수록 높이가 낮아진다.
③ 쓰나미의 높이는 속도가 줄수록 올라간다.
④ 쓰나미의 에너지는 파도의 속도 및 높이와 관련이 없다.

| 정답 | ③

| 해설 | "쓰나미가 이동하는 속도는 물의 깊이와 관련이 있으며, 따라서 물의 깊이가 낮아질수록 쓰나미의 속도도 늦춰진다(A tsunami travels at a speed that is related to the water depth—hence, as the water depth decreases, the tsunami slows)." "쓰나미는 덜 깊은 물로 이동할수록 높이가 높아진다. 이를 천수라 부른다(As it travels into shallower water, its height grows. This is called shoaling)." 이 두 가지를 조합해 보면, 쓰나미는 물의 깊이가 낮을수록 속도는 줄고 높이는 높아진다. 따라서 답은 ③이다.

35 다음 중 본문과 일치하는 것은 무엇인가?
① 쓰나미는 해안에서 멀리 떨어진 곳에서 모여들 가능성이 높다.
② 쓰나미의 에너지는 해안에 도달하면서 감소한다.
③ 쓰나미는 깊은 대양에서 쉽게 감지될 수 있다.
④ 쓰나미의 영향력은 해안 지역으로 국한된다.

| 정답 | ②

| 해설 | "다른 물결과 마찬가지로 쓰나미는 해안으로 쇄도해 들어오면서 에너지를 잃게 된다(Just like other water waves, tsunamis begin to lose energy as they rush onshore)." 따라서 답은 ②이다.

| 어휘 | open ocean – 외해
shoaling ⓝ 천수
bore ⓝ 강한 해류, 해일
dissipate ⓥ 소멸하다
erosion ⓝ 부식, 침식
ocean basin – 대양 분지
association ⓝ 연계, 관련
energy flux – 에너지 유량
breaking wave – 쇄파
propagate ⓥ 전파하다, 증식하다
turbulence ⓝ 난류
inundate ⓥ 침수시키다
evacuate ⓥ 대피하다
converge ⓥ 모여들다

[36-38] 항공대 2016

1967년 캠브리지 대학 소속 연구생이었던 조셀린 벨 버넬(Jocelyn Bell-Burnell)이 하늘에서 전파의 파동을 정기적으로 내뿜는 물체를 발견하면서 블랙홀이 존재한다는 주장이 더욱 힘을 받게 되었다. 처음에는 벨과 지도 교수인 앤터니 휴이시(Antony Hewish)는 자신들이 우주의 외계 문명과 접촉을 하게 된 것일지도 모른다고 생각했다. 하지만 이들은 펄사란 명칭을 갖게 된 이들 물체가 사실은 자기장과 주변 물질 간의 복잡한 상호작용 때문에 전파의 파동을 내뿜는 자전하는 중성자별이라는 낭만적이지 못한 결론을 내렸다. 이는 우주를 무대로 한 서부극의 작가들에게는 좋지 못한 소식이지만 당시 블랙홀의 존재를 믿고 있던 우리 같은 소수의 사람들에게는 매우 희망적인 소식이었다. 왜냐하면 그것은 중성자별이 존재한다는 최초의 결정적 증거였기 때문이다. 중성자별은 반지름이 약 10마일인데, 이는 별이 블랙홀로 변하는 임계 반지름의 고작 몇 배에 불과하다. 별이 이 정도 크기로 붕괴했다면, 다른 별이 이보다 더 작은 크기로 붕괴하여 블랙홀이 될 것이라고 예측하는 것은 합리적인 추론이다. 정의에 따르면 빛을 전혀 내뿜지 않는 별인 블랙홀을 어떻게 발견하리라 기대할 수 있을까? 이는 어느 정도는 마치 지하 석탄 저장고에서 검은 고양이를 찾는 것과 같을지도 모른다. 다행스럽게도 한 가지 방법이 존재한다. 존 미첼(John Michell)이 1783년에 발표한 선구적 논문에서 지적했다시피 블랙홀은 주변 물체에 계속하여 중력을 가한다.

36

본문의 주제는 무엇인가?

① 블랙홀의 유산　　　　　　　　　② 블랙홀의 기능
③ 블랙홀의 발견　　　　　　　　　④ 블랙홀의 잠재력

| 정답 | ③

| 해설 | 본문은 펄사의 발견과 함께 블랙홀이 존재할지도 모른다는 의견이 힘을 얻게 되었음을 언급하면서 그 외에도 블랙홀을 찾아낼 수 있는 방법이 존재함을 언급하고 있다. 즉, 본문은 블랙홀의 '발견'을 주제로 작성된 글이다. 따라서 답은 ③이다.

37

빈칸에 가장 알맞은 것을 고르시오.

① 석탄 저장고에서
② 팽창 풍선 모델에서
③ 삼각형 모양의 유리 조각을 통해
④ 오목렌즈 망원경을 가지고

| 정답 | ①

| 해설 | 빈칸 앞에서 "정의에 따르면 빛을 전혀 내뿜지 않는 별인 블랙홀을 어떻게 발견하리라 기대할 수 있을까(How could we hope to detect a black hole, as by its very definition it does not emit any light)"라고 나와 있는데, 우주도 검고 블랙홀도 검기 때문에 우주공간에서 검은 무언가를 찾는다는 것은 마치 "지하 석탄 저장고에서 검은 고양이를 찾는 것"과 같을 것으로 유추 가능하다. 따라서 답은 ①이다.

38

다음 중 사실인 것은 무엇인가?

① 벨과 휴이시는 우주의 외계 문명과 접촉했다.
② 별은 거대한 크기로 확대된 후 블랙홀이 될 수 있다.
③ 1967년에 블랙홀의 존재가 완전히 알려지게 되었다.
④ 블랙홀은 주변 물체에 중력을 가할 수 있다.

| 정답 | ④

| 해설 | "존 미첼(John Michell)이 1783년에 발표한 선구적 논문에서 지적했다시피 블랙홀은 주변 물체에 계속하여 중력을 가한다(As John Michell pointed out in his pioneering paper in 1783, a black hole still exerts a gravitational force on nearby objects)." 따라서 답은 ④이다.
　벨과 휴이시는 외계 문명과 접촉했을지도 모른다고 생각은 했지만 실제 접촉하지는 않았다. 따라서 ①은 답이 될 수 없다. 블랙홀이 되기 전에는 별이 붕괴하지 확대되지 않는다. 따라서 ②는 답이 될 수 없다. 1967년의 펄사의 발견은 블랙홀의 존재를 밝히기 위한 실마리일 뿐이며, 본문 어디에도 펄사로 인해 블랙홀의 존재가 완전히 알려지게 되었다는 내용은 존재하지 않는다. 따라서 ③은 답이 될 수 없다.

| 어휘 | emit ⓥ 내다, 내뿜다　　　　　　　　　　　pulse ⓝ (광선·음향 따위의) 진동[파동]; (전기의) 펄스
　　　pulsar ⓝ 펄서, 맥동전파원; 고도로 자기화된, 관측 가능한 전파의 형태로 전자기파의 광선을 뿜는, 자전하는 중성자별

rotate ⓥ 자전하다
magnetic field – 자기장
radius ⓝ 반경, 반지름
coal cellar – 지하 석탄 저장고
exert ⓥ 가하다, 행사하다
latent ⓐ 잠재하는
gigantic ⓐ 거대한

neutron star – 중성자별
positive ⓐ 결정적인, 분명한
critical radius – 임계 반지름
pioneering ⓐ 선구적인, 개척적인
gravitational force – 중력
concave lens – 오목렌즈

[39-40] 한국외대 2017

도시 거주자들, 특히 세계에서 인구 밀도가 높은 도시에 살고 있는 사람들에게, 새로운 걱정거리가 떠오르고 있다. 새로운 연구에 따르면, 오염 물질 내부에서 발견된 특정 입자가 호흡 기관을 통해 인간의 뇌로 들어올 수 있다는 사실이 밝혀졌다. 자철석(magnetite)이라고 알려진 이 입자들은 일반적으로 엔진과 덮개 없는 불 내부에서 형성된다. 자철석은 미네랄 형태의 산화철로 인간의 뇌에 치명적이다. 왜냐하면 자철석이 쉽게 화학반응을 일으키며, 다른 물질을 내놓기 때문인데, 이때 나온 다른 물질들은 뇌세포 내에서 산화 스트레스(oxidative stress)를 유발하며, 이 과정에서 뇌세포를 손상시키고 파괴한다. 연구자들은 대도시에 살았던 37명의 사람들로부터 뇌조직 샘플을 받아 연구했는데, 이 입자가 뇌의 전두엽 피질 안에 있다는 사실을 발견했다. 불행하게도, 자철석 미립자는 오염 물질 내부에 항상 존재한다. 이 입자는 혈액뇌장벽(blood-brain barrier)이 없는 코의 윗부분에 위치한 후각신경구(olfactory bulb)를 관통한다. 입자의 극소한 크기로 인해 코털과 코의 점액질에 의해 걸러질 가능성이 줄어들며, 이로 인해 혈관 및 뇌로 들어가는 것이 용이해진다.

39 새로 발견된 연구 결과가 도시 거주자들에게 특별한 걱정거리를 불러일으키는 이유로 적합한 것은?
① 오염된 도시 공기에 해로운 물질이 존재하기 때문에
② 도시의 밀집된 빌딩들에 오염물질이 갇히기 때문에
③ 오염물질이 도시 환경에서 반응하기 때문에
④ 해로운 입자가 자동차 배기가스에 의해 형성되기 때문에

| 정답 | ①

| 해설 | ①과 ④가 도시 거주자들에게 걱정을 주는 내용이다. 하지만 둘 중에서 보다 직접적인 원인은 ①이 된다. 매연이 심한 도시의 대기오염이 직접적인 이유가 되며, 자동차 배기가스는 오염 물질이 만들어지는 여러 이유 중 하나에 해당하기 때문이다.

40 다음 중 자철석에 의해 유발된 오염물질의 특징이 아닌 것은?
① 오염물질의 화학반응이 뇌세포를 파괴한다.
② 오염물질이 너무 작아 코털로 걸러지지 않는다.
③ 오염물질이 코를 통해 몸으로 들어간다.
④ 오염물질이 모든 종류의 철분 섭취와 함께 몸에 들어간다.

| 정답 | ④

| 해설 | 본문의 "damaging and killing them in the process" 부분을 통해 ①을 알 수 있다. ②의 경우 후반부의 "Their minuscule size also reduces the chances of them being trapped by hairs" 부분을 통해 알 수 있다. ③의 경우 "enter the human brain by people breathing them in"을 통해 확인 가능하다. 정답은 ④로 본문에 등장하지 않는 내용이다.

| 어휘 | be on the horizon – 곧 일어날 듯한
magnetite ⓝ 자철석
oxidative ⓐ 산화의, 산화력이 있는
particulate ⓝ 미립자 ⓐ 미립자의
minuscule ⓐ 극소의
automobile exhaust – 자동차 배기가스
densely populated – 인구 밀도가 높은
open fire – 덮개 없는 불
frontal cortex – 전두 피질
olfactory ⓐ 후각의
mucus ⓝ 점액

[41-42] 항공대 2018

1920년대까지 모든 사람들은 우주가 근본적으로 고정되어 있으며 시간에 따라 변하지 않는다고 생각했다. 그러다가 우주가 팽창하고 있다는 사실이 발견되었다. 멀리 떨어진 은하는 우리에게서 멀어지고 있다. 이는, 즉 지금은 멀리 떨어진 은하가 과거에는 더욱 가까이 위치해 있었음이 분명하다는 의미이다. 이를 되짚어 다시 추론할 경우, 약 150억 년 전에는 우리 모두가 서로 중첩되어 있음이 분명함을 알 수 있다. 이것이 바로 우주의 시작, 빅뱅이었다. 그렇지만 빅뱅 이전에는 무엇이 있었을까? 만일 아무것도 없더라면 우주를 창조한 것은 무엇일까? 왜 우주는 빅뱅에서부터 그런 식으로 생겨났던 것일까? 과거 우리는 우주에 대한 이론이 두 부분으로 나뉠 수 있다고 생각했다. 첫 번째는 맥스웰 방정식이나 일반 상대성 이론 같은 법칙이다. 이들 법칙은 어느 시기에 우주 전체에서 상태에 따라 우주의 진화를 결정짓는다. 두 번째로, 우주의 초기 상태에 대해서는 의문의 여지가 없다. 첫 번째 부분의 경우 우리는 상당한 진전을 보았고 이제는 가장 극단적인 상황을 제외하면 진화의 법칙에 대해 모든 지식을 얻게 되었다. 하지만 최근까지 우리는 우주의 최초 상태에 대해서는 거의 아는 바가 없다. 그렇지만 위와 같이 우주에 대한 이론을 진화의 법칙과 초기 조건 이 둘로 나누는 것은 서로 별개로 동떨어져 존재하는 시간과 공간에 좌우된다. 극단적인 상황에서 일반 상대성 이론과 양자론은 시간이 마치 공간의 다른 차원과 같이 작용하게끔 한다. 이는 시간과 공간의 구분을 없애며 진화의 법칙이 초기 상태를 결정할 수 있음을 의미한다. 우주는 무에서 자연스럽게 스스로를 창조할 수 있다. 게다가 우리는 우주가 다른 상태에서 창조될 수 있었던 확률을 계산할 수 있다. 이러한 예측은 극초창기 우주의 흔적인 우주배경복사를 WMAP 위성으로 관측한 결과와 아주 잘 들어맞고 있다. 우리는 우리가 우주 창조의 신비를 해결했다고 생각한다. 어쩌면 우리는 우주에 대해 특허를 취득하고 우주에 존재하는 온갖 것들에 대해 모두를 상대로 저작권 사용료를 부과해야 할지도 모른다.

41

빈칸에 들어갈 올바른 문장은?
① 우주로 확산될 기회
② 우주 창조의 신비
③ 인류의 미래
④ 관측을 통한 우주의 문제

| 정답 | ②

| 해설 | 빈칸 앞에 제시된 일반 상대성 이론과 양자론, '우주는 무에서 자연스럽게 스스로를 창조할 수 있다'는 결론, '우주가 다른 상태에서 창조될 수 있었던 확률' 등은 모두 우주 탄생과 관련된 일이고, 이들을 계산하고 파악한다는 것은 '우주 창조의 신비'를 해결할 수 있었음을 나타낸다. 여기서 ②가 답임을 유추할 수 있다.

42 다음 중 사실인 것은 무엇인가?

① 우주가 우리를 향해 접근하고 있다는 것은 명백한 사실이다.
② 진화의 법칙은 우주의 초기 상태에 대해서는 적용할 수 없다.
③ 시간과 공간의 구분은 극단적인 상황에서는 사라질 수 있다.
④ 우주 나이의 계산은 경험적 관측을 통해서는 뒷받침되지 못한다.

| 정답 | ③

| 해설 | "극단적인 상황에서 일반 상대성 이론과 양자론은 시간이 마치 공간의 다른 차원과 같이 작용하게끔 한다. 이는 시간과 공간의 구분을 없애며 진화의 법칙이 초기 상태를 결정할 수 있음을 의미한다(Under extreme conditions, general relativity and quantum theory allow time to behave like another dimension of space. This removes the distinction between time and space, and means the laws of evolution can also determine the initial state)." 이 말은 극단적인 상황에서는 시간과 공간의 구분이 없어진다는, 즉 사라진다는 내용의 ③과 일치한다. 따라서 답은 ③이다.

우주는 팽창하고 있고 멀리 떨어진 은하는 우리로부터 멀어지고 있으므로 ①은 답이 될 수 없다. 앞서 언급한 바대로 진화의 법칙은 우주의 초기 상태를 결정할 수 있으며 이는 진화의 법칙이 우주의 초기 상태에 적용할 수 없다는 ②의 내용과는 상반된다. 때문에 ②는 답이 될 수 없다. 마지막으로 우주배경복사를 WMAP 위성으로 관측하는 행위는 ④에서 말하는 '경험적 관측'에 해당되며, 따라서 ④는 본문의 내용과는 상반된다.

| 어휘 | essentially @ 근본적으로, 기본적으로
extrapolate ⓥ 추론하다, 추정하다
equation ⓝ 방정식
make good progress – 상당한 진전을 보다
quantum theory – 양자론
behave ⓥ (어떤 조건이나 환경에 대하여) 반응을 나타내다, 작용하다
spontaneously @ 자발적으로, 자연스럽게
prediction ⓝ 예측
cosmic microwave background – 우주배경복사, 우주 마이크로파 배경
imprint ⓝ 흔적
royalty ⓝ 저작권 사용료, 인세
undeniable @ 부인할 수 없는, 명백한

static @ 정적인, 고정된
on top of – ~의 아주 가까이에, ~의 위에 (중첩된)
general relativity – 일반 상대성
distinct @ 별개의

probability ⓝ 확률
observation ⓝ 관찰, 관측

patent ⓥ 특허를 취득하다
existence ⓝ (온갖) 존재하는 것, 실재물
empirical @ 경험[실험]에 의거한, 실증적인

[43-45] 한국외대 2016

매일 수백 개의 버려진 어망이 태평양 위에 표류하고 있고, 해류를 따라 이리저리 뒤틀리고 뒤집어지고 있다. 버려진 어망은 크기가 몇 미터에서 6킬로미터까지 늘어나며, 어망을 구성하는 플라스틱 섬유는 표류 중인 어망의 길을 가로막은 모든 해양 생물을 무차별적으로 가둬 버린다. 이처럼 치명적인 피해를 입히는 손상된 또는 버려진 "유령 어망"은 추정치에 따르면 부식되기까지 600년이나 걸린다. 다수는 결국에 오스트레일리아 북부 해안가로 쓸려 올라온다. 12년 전 전직 어부였던 리키 건(Riki Gunn)은 해변을 순찰하고, 어망을 수거하며, 어망에 얽힌 생명체를 구출하기 위해 해양 보존 단체를 설립하는 일에 착수했다. 현재 40개 씨족 출신 현지 경비대원들이 정기적으로 3,000킬로미터 거리의 외딴 해안가를 샅샅이 뒤지면서 위험에 처한 거북이와 듀공 및 기타 해양 생물체를 구조하고 있다. 경비대원들이 업무를 시작한지 몇 개월 만에 어망이 차곡차곡 무더기로 쌓이게 되었다. 퀸즐랜드 출신 예술가인 수 라이언(Sue Ryan)의 도움을 통해 건은 어망을 처리하는 데 도움을 얻기 위한 해결책을 찾기 시작했다. 전국적인 경진대회를 통해 플라스틱 섬유를 기타 스트랩에서 가방 및 설치미술로 변환하는 것처럼 온갖 아이디어가 쏟아져 들어왔다. 얼마 지나지 않아 라이언은 "고스트 넷 아트 프로젝트(Ghost Net Art Project; 유령 어망 예술 프로젝트)"란 명칭으로 공방을 조직했다. 라이언은 플라스틱 섬유가 다양한 색과 무늬 및 두께를 지니고 있음에 경탄하지 않을 수 없었다. 라이언은 다음과 같이 말했다. "제가 지금까지 작업했던 것과는 근본적으로 달라서 정말 흥미로웠습니다. 또한 이는 유령 어망에 대한 사람들의 관심을 일깨울 수 있는 매우 좋은 방법이기도 합니다."

43 다음 중 본문을 가장 잘 뒷받침하는 것은 무엇인가?
① 오스트레일리아에서 해양 생물을 파괴하던 것이 예술 작품으로 탈바꿈했다.
② 사람들의 다양한 취향이 다양한 예술 양식을 창조하는 데 기여한다.
③ 오스트레일리아 예술 산업이 미래는 밝다.
④ "고스트 넷 아트 프로젝트"는 다른 국가에서도 되풀이될 것이다.

| 정답 | ①

| 해설 | 본문은 환경을 파괴하던 버려진 어망이 예술 프로젝트를 통해 수거되어 예술 작품으로 탈바꿈되었음을 말하고 있다. 따라서 답은 ①이다.

44 다음 중 빈칸 (A)에 가장 알맞은 것은 무엇인가?
① 어망에 얽힌 생명체
② 수중 예술
③ 해안으로 쓸려 올라온 해초
④ 어망에 걸린 인공물

| 정답 | ①

| 해설 | 리키 건이 설립한 해양 보존 단체는 "해변을 순찰하고(patrol the beaches)" "어망을 수거하는(pick up the nets)" 등의 일을 했고, 나머지 빈칸에 해당되는 일이 무엇인지 유추하기 위해 보기의 표현을 빈칸에 대입해 보면 가장 적합한 것은 '어망에 얽힌 생명체를 구출'한다는 의미에서 ①임을 알 수 있다.

45 다음 중 "고스트 넷 아트 프로젝트"에 관해 맞는 것은 무엇인가?
① 대중에게 기술의 위험성을 알렸다.
② 젊은이들이 예술의 진가를 알아보도록 유도하는 것이 목표이다.
③ 환경적으로 해악이 되던 것들을 재사용할 수 있는 해결책을 고안한다.
④ 대중이 전통의 중요성을 인식하도록 한다.

| 정답 | ③

| 해설 | 버려진 어망은 그냥 놔두면 환경을 오염시키고 특히 해양 생명체에 피해를 입힌다. "고스트 넷 아트 프로젝트"는 이러한 어망을 수거하여 예술작품으로 재활용하는 운동이다. 즉, "고스트 넷 아트 프로젝트"는 환경에 피해를 입히던 것들을 재사용하기 위한 하나의 해결책으로 볼 수 있다. 따라서 답은 ③이다.

| 어휘 |
discard ⓥ 버리다, 폐기하다
current ⓝ 해류
indiscriminately ⓐⓓ 마구잡이로, 무차별적으로
in the way – (~의[를]) 길을 막는[방해하는]
up to – (특정한 수·정도 등)까지
eventually ⓐⓓ 결국, 종내
set about – ~을 착수하다[시작하다]
patrol ⓥ 순찰하다
indigenous ⓐ (어떤 지역) 원산의[토착의], (그 지역) 고유의
ranger ⓝ 공원[삼림/자연] 관리원[경비대원]
scour ⓥ 샅샅이 뒤지다
endangered ⓐ 위험[위기]에 처한
build up – (~이 되도록) 점점 커지다
dispose of – ~을 처분[처리]하다
craft workshop – 공방
marvel ⓥ 경이로워하다, 경탄하다
weave ⓝ (직물의) 무늬, 짜는 방식
blight ⓝ (사기·희망 따위를) 꺾는 사람[것], 망치는[파괴하는] 것
transform ⓥ 변형시키다, 탈바꿈시키다
replicate ⓥ 모사[복제]하다; 되풀이하다
seaweed ⓝ 해초
alert ⓥ (위험 등을) 알리다, 경보를 발하다
reuse ⓥ 재사용하다

drift ⓥ 표류하다, 부유하다
stretch ⓥ 늘이다, 늘어나다
marine ⓐ 바다의, 해양의
lethal ⓐ 치명적인
decay ⓥ 부패하다, 부식하다
wash up – (육지로) ~을 쓸고[싣고] 오다
conservation ⓝ 보존, 보호
entangled ⓐ 얽힌, 뒤엉킨
clan ⓝ 씨족
isolated ⓐ 외딴, 외떨어진
pile ⓝ (차곡차곡 쌓은) 무더기[더미]
set out – 착수하다, 시작하다
art installation – 설치미술
cannot help but – ~하지 않을 수 없다
variety ⓝ 다양함, 다양성
awareness ⓝ 의식, 관심
promising ⓐ 유망한, 미래가 밝은
aquatic ⓐ 수중의, 물과 관련된
artifact ⓝ 인공물; 공예품
appreciate ⓥ 진가를 알아보다[인정하다]
hazard ⓝ 위험(요소), 해악

CHAPTER 03 생물

01	①	02	④	03	④	04	③	05	④	06	③	07	④	08	④	09	③	10	①
11	④	12	③	13	②	14	①	15	③	16	③	17	④	18	①	19	①	20	④
21	⑤	22	②	23	②	24	①	25	②	26	②	27	④	28	②	29	③	30	②
31	①	32	②	33	⑤	34	①	35	②	36	②	37	⑤	38	③	39	⑤	40	④
41	①	42	③	43	②	44	①	45	④	46	①	47	②	48	②	49	②	50	②

[01-03] 한성대 2008

침팬지의 행동은 이 흥미로운 동물에 관심을 가졌던 심리학자들에게 오랫동안 미스터리였다. 어린 침팬지는 인지적인 측면에 있어서 인간 아이와 매우 흡사한데, 인간 아이와 동등하거나 심지어 더 탁월할 수도 있다. 그런데도 1~2세까지 인간 가정에서 키워지고 인간의 언어를 들으며 자란 침팬지가 왜 언어를 표현 수단으로 사용하지 않는지, 옹알이(언어 발달의 초기 과정)를 하지 못하는지에 대해 동물심리학자들은 의문을 품지 않을 수 없었다.

일반적인 동물심리학자들은 침팬지가 인간과 더 닮은 행동 방식을 고수함으로써 유인원 조상을 부끄럽게 할 침팬지를 오랫동안 기다려 왔다. 지금까지의 실패(인간과 닮은 행동 방식, 즉 언어를 사용하는 침팬지를 만나지 못한 것)는 침팬지의 지능 수준의 문제가 아니다. 침팬지에게 민망할 정도로 지능이 낮은 인간도 있기 때문이다.(=인간보다 지능이 높은 침팬지도 있다.) (결론적으로) 말을 하거나 말을 하고 싶어 하는 것은 침팬지의 본성이 아닐 뿐이다.

01 밑줄 친 ⓐ와 가장 가까운 내용은?
① 일부 인간들은 침팬지보다 지능이 낮다.
② 아무리 결함 있는 인간이라도 침팬지보다 지능이 높다.
③ 인간은 결함이 심해서 침팬지를 부끄럽게 만들 정도이다.
④ 인간을 침팬지와 비교하는 것은 정말 수치스러운 일이다.

| 정답 | ①

| 해설 | 'shame'은 '~을 부끄럽게 하다'는 뜻이다. 그러나 shame의 1차적 의미에만 의존하지 말고 문맥을 확인해야 한다. 두 번째 문장에 인간보다 지능이 높은 침팬지도 있다고 했으므로, ② "아무리 결함 있는 인간이라고 해도 침팬지보다 지능이 높다."는 '모든 인간은 침팬지보다 지능이 높다는 의미'이므로 두 번째 문장의 내용과 모순되므로 ②를 선택하지 않도록 주의한다. 밑줄이 위치한 문장은 "지능이 높은 침팬지도 언어를 사용하지 않는 것을 보면 침팬지가 언어를 사용하지 않는 것은 지능과 무관하다."는 주제를 완성해야 한다. 따라서 밑줄은 "인간보다 지능이 높은 침팬지도 있다." 혹은 "침팬지보다 지능이 낮은 인간도 있다."라는 내용으로 해석하는 것이 문맥에 맞는다. ex. Behaviour that would shame chimpanzees is on display in the state's legislature.[침팬지도 부끄러워할(=침팬지보다 더한) 행태가 주 의회에서 벌어지고 있다.] 따라서 ①이 적절하다.

02

윗글의 내용과 일치하는 것은?
① 침팬지는 인간 아이보다 지능이 낮기 때문에 언어를 사용하지 못한다.
② 침팬지가 인간의 가정에서 키워진다면 언어를 사용할 것이다.
③ 침팬지가 언어를 사용하지 못하는 것은 순전히 지능 수준의 문제이다.
④ 침팬지가 언어를 사용하지 않는 것은 본성이다.

| 정답 | ④

| 해설 | 마지막 문장에 힌트가 있다. 말을 하거나 하고 싶어 하는 것은 침팬지의 본성이 아니라고 했으므로 ④가 사실과 일치한다. "It just does not belong to the nature of the beast to speak, or to want to speak."를 참조하면, 침팬지가 말을 못하는 것은 지능 수준의 문제가 아니라고 했으므로 ①이나 ③을 선택하지 않도록 주의한다.

03

밑줄 친 ⓑ It이 가리키는 것은?
① 그 실패　　　　　　　　　　　② 지능
③ 침팬지　　　　　　　　　　　④ 말을 하거나 하고 싶어 하는 것

| 정답 | ④

| 해설 | 문맥상 It은 to부정사를 대신하는 가주어이다. 따라서 진주어인 ④가 정답이다.

| 어휘 |
puzzle ⓝ 당황스러운 문제
extraordinarily ⓐⓓ 예외적으로, 탁월하게
superior ⓝ 우월한 것
keep from ~ing – ~을 막다, 중단하다
bring up – ~을 키우다
impact ⓝ 영향
baby talk – 옹알이
simian ⓝ 유인원 ⓐ 유인원의
adhere to – ~에 집착하다
sheer ⓐ 순전한(양이나 규모를 강조하는 표현)
intelligence ⓝ 지능
shame ⓥ 부끄럽게 하다
nature ⓝ 본성

concern oneself with – ~에 관심이 있다
equal ⓝ 동등한 것
intellectual ⓐ 지적인
wonder ⓥ 궁금하게 여기다
be subject to – ~에 영향을 받다, 종속되다
burst into – ~을 터뜨리다
disgrace ⓥ 치욕을 주다, 망신시키다
ancestry ⓝ 조상
conduct ⓝ 행동, 행실
bulk ⓝ 양
defective ⓐ 결함 있는
belong to – ~에 속하다

[04-05] 중앙대 2010

과학자들은 코끼리의 지능을 여태껏 정확히 측정할 수 없었다. 그럼에도 불구하고 지난 수십 년간 전문가들은 코끼리의 행동을 관찰한 후 그들이 동물의 왕국에서 가장 똑똑한 축에 속한다는 결론을 내렸다. 그렇다고 해도 코끼리가 절대 잊어버리지 않는다는 학설은 과장이라 할 수 있지만, 완전히 틀린 말도 아니다. 코끼리는 포유류 중에 무게로 따졌을 경우 가장 큰 뇌를 가졌으며, 성인 코끼리의 뇌 무게는 무려 4.7킬로그램에 육박한다. 뇌의 크기 하나만 가지고 뇌가 얼마나 효과적으로 작동하는지 판단할 수는 없다 할지라도, 상당히 좋은 근사치를 제공해 주며 코끼리 기억력에 대한 힌트를 제공해 준다. 동물의 지능을 측정하는 가장 일반적인 방법은 EQ(대뇌화 지수)를 측정하는 것이다. EQ는 동물의 실제 뇌 무게를 몸무게를 바탕으로 추정되는 뇌의 무게와 비교하는 것이다. 이 측정을 보다 더 잘 이해하기 위해, 사과와 아보카도를 생각해 보자.

이 두 과일은 크기는 서로 비슷하지만 골프공만한 씨를 가진 아보카도에 비해 사과는 상대적으로 작은 씨를 가졌다. 이 논리에 따르면, 몸집에 비해 뇌의 비율이 낮으면 낮을수록 그 동물은 더 지능이 낮으며, 그 반대의 경우도 마찬가지라고 할 수 있다. 예를 들어 사람의 평균 EQ는 7이며, 돼지의 EQ는 0.27이다. 코끼리는 여기서 상대적으로 높은 EQ 수치를 나타내며, 모든 종을 통틀어 평균 1.88을 나타낸다. 이와 비교해, 침팬지는 2.5 정도의 EQ를 나타낸다. 그룹의 우두머리인 암 코끼리들은 종종 수컷보다도 더 높은 EQ를 보인다. 이것은 아마도 모계 중심 사회를 이루는 코끼리 무리 구조와 관계가 깊은 것으로 생각된다. 또한 늙은 암 코끼리의 경우, 익숙한 위험이 발생하거나 이전 취식지를 다시 발견해 무리에게 알리는 경우, 놀라울 정도로 우수한 기억력을 가진 정황들을 보인다는 연구 결과도 나온 바 있다.

04 윗글에서 저자가 "an apple and an avocado"를 언급한 의도로 가장 적합한 것을 고르시오.
① 코끼리의 지능을 정확히 측정하기 위해
② 코끼리의 뇌 크기를 측정하기 위해
③ EQ의 개념을 설명하기 위해
④ 인간과 코끼리의 기억력을 비교하기 위해

| 정답 | ③

| 해설 | 사과와 아보카도는 크기가 비슷하지만 속의 씨는 크기가 각각 다르다고 했다. 즉, 속의 씨를 뇌로 보아 EQ의 개념을 좀 더 이해하기 쉽게 설명하고 있으므로 정답은 ③이 된다.

05 윗글을 통해 알 수 있는 것으로 가장 적합한 것을 고르시오.
① 늙은 수 코끼리는 젊은 암 코끼리보다 기억력이 좋은 편이다.
② 침팬지는 평균적으로 코끼리보다 지능이 낮은 편이다.
③ 동물은 체중에 비해 뇌가 크면 클수록, 더 아둔하다.
④ 코끼리는 높은 EQ를 가져서 비교적 좋은 기억력을 가지고 있다.

| 정답 | ④

| 해설 | ④를 제외한 나머지 보기는 모두 사실과 다르거나 반대로 기술하고 있어서 답이 될 수 없다. ①의 경우 암 코끼리가 수컷에 비해 지능이 좋은 편이라고 했으며, 늙은 암 코끼리가 이전 기억과 관련된 일에 매우 우수한 기억력을 보인다고 했으므로, 주어진 보기는 본문 외의 내용으로 사실 판단을 할 수 없는 문장이다. ②는 침팬지가 코끼리보다 EQ가 더 높기 때문에 본문의 내용과 반대로 설명한 문장이 되며, ③ 또한 반대로 설명하고 있다.

| 어휘 | intelligence ⓝ 지능, 지성   precisely ⓐ 정확히, 정밀하게, 꼼꼼하게

nevertheless ⓐ 그럼에도 불구하고
expert ⓝ 전문가
pachyderm ⓝ 후피동물, 코끼리(pachy[thick] +derm[skinned]은 후피동물로 가죽이 두꺼운 동물을 의미한다.)
that said - 그렇다고는 해도(= having said that, that being said)
exaggeration ⓝ 과장, 과장된 이야기
stray far from the truth - 진실에서 많이 벗어나다
hefty ⓐ 무거운, 살찐
solely ⓐ 혼자서, 단독으로; 단지, 오직
approximation ⓝ 근사치, 접근
encephalization quotient(EQ) - 대뇌화 지수
resemble ⓥ 닮다, 비기다
ratio ⓝ 비, 비율
matriarch ⓝ 여자 가장, 여성 지도자
alert ⓥ ~에게 경계 태세를 취하게 하다 ⓐ 빈틈없는, 조심성 있는
precise ⓐ 정확한

decade ⓝ 10년

stray ⓥ 벗어나다, 길을 잃다, 탈선하다

weigh in at - 무게가 ~만큼 나가다
decent ⓐ 좋은, 상당한; 점잖은
conventional ⓐ 전통적인; 상투적인
relatively ⓐ 비교적, 상대적으로
logic ⓝ 논리, 논리학
dumb ⓐ 지능이 낮은
herd ⓝ (가축의) 무리

[06-07] 중앙대 2010

㉮ Harlow 부부에 따르면, 새끼 원숭이가 어미 원숭이에게 느끼는 사랑의 기본 성질은 신뢰라고 한다. 만약 새끼가 어미 원숭이가 없는 낯선 놀이 공간에 놓인다면 새끼는 아무리 흥미로운 장난감이 있다 하더라도 그것을 무시한다. 그리고 공포에 휩싸여 비명을 지르게 되며, 털로 뒤덮인 공처럼 몸을 웅크리게 된다. 만약 여기서 헝겊 대리모를 놀이 공간에 놓아 둔다면 새끼는 죽을힘을 다해 대리모에게 달려와 매달릴 것이다. 몇 분간의 접촉 위안(contact comfort)을 느낀 후에는 좀 더 안정된 모습을 보이게 된다. 그리고 대리모에게서 내려와 일시적으로 장난감을 이리저리 만지기 시작한다. 그러나 엄마가 아직 그곳에 있고 모든 것이 다 괜찮은지 확인하려는 듯 자꾸 대리모에게 달려와 깊은 포옹을 한다. 조금씩 새로운 환경에 대한 두려움은 "무뎌지며", 더 많은 시간을 장난감과 보내고 "엄마"에게 매달리는 시간은 짧아진다.

㉯ 왜 헝겊을 철사보다 더 선호하는 것일까? 아마도 Harlow 부부가 지칭한 접촉 위안(contact comfort)이라는 용어가 그 해답이 될 수 있을 것이며, 사실 가장 강력한 영향력을 행사하는 것이기도 하다. 새끼 원숭이는 대부분의 시간을 어미 원숭이의 피부에 비비며, 최대한 엄마와 가까이서 지내려고 한다. 새끼 원숭이는 놀라거나, 불안하거나, 괴롭힘을 당할 때면 일반적으로 엄마에게 달려가 몸을 비벼댄다. 철사는 부드러운 헝겊처럼 "비벼지지" 않는다. 지속적인 헝겊 대리모와의 "접촉 위안"은 새끼원숭이에게 서서히 자신감을 불어넣어 주고, 따뜻함이나 우유보다 훨씬 더 많은 보상을 가져다준다. 새끼 원숭이는 또한 움직이지 않는 대리모 보다는 흔들의자처럼 "흔들림이 있는" 대리모를 더 선호한다.

㉰ 생후 첫 2주 동안에는 따뜻함이야말로 어미 원숭이가 새끼 원숭이에게 제공해야 하는 심리학적으로 가장 중요한 것이라 할 수 있다. Harlow 부부는 새끼 원숭이에게 두 종류의 대리모(하나는 보풀코 헝겊으로 둘러싸인 대리모 모형이고, 다른 하나는 앙상한 철사로 만든 대리모 모형)를 보여주는 실험을 통해 이런 사실을 발견했다. 두 종류의 대리모 모형을 같은 온도로 유지시켰을 때, 새끼 원숭이는 언제나 헝겊 대리모를 선호했다. 하지만 헝겊 모형을 차갑게 한 상태에서 철사 모형을 따뜻하게 했을 때는 새끼 원숭이가 생후 첫 2주 동안은 따뜻한 철사 대리모를 선호했다. 그 이후에는 대부분의 시간을 좀 더 편안한 헝겊 대리모와 보냈다.

06 윗글을 바른 순서대로 나열한 것으로 가장 적합한 것을 고르시오.

① ㉮ – ㉯ – ㉰
② ㉯ – ㉮ – ㉰
③ ㉰ – ㉯ – ㉮
④ ㉯ – ㉰ – ㉮

| 정답 | ③

| 해설 | ㉯ 문단에서 천과 철사 중에 하나를 선호하는 이유를 묻고 있으므로, 이 문단에 앞서 천이나 철사 중 하나를 선호했다는 사실을 담고 있는 ㉰ 문단이 ㉯ 문단 앞에 놓여야 한다. 이런 순서를 보이는 보기는 ③밖에 없다. 또한 "contact comfort(접촉 위안)"이라는 용어가 등장하는 순서를 통해서도 추론할 수 있다. 이 용어는 ㉮와 ㉯ 문단에 등장하는데, ㉯ 문단 도입부의 'Something that the Harlows called contact comfort'라는 표현을 통해 'contact comfort'가 처음 사용됨을 알 수 있다. 따라서 ㉯ 문단이 ㉮ 문단 앞에 위치해야 한다.

07 윗글을 통해 추론할 수 있는 것으로 가장 적합한 것을 고르시오.

① 원숭이의 생후 첫 2주 동안에는, 접촉 위안이 따뜻함보다 중요하다.
② 접촉 위안은 어미 원숭이의 몸 표면에서 오는 따뜻함으로 결정된다.
③ 새끼 원숭이는 친숙한 사물에서 편안함을 느낀다.
④ 어미 원숭이에 대해 새끼 원숭이가 느끼는 사랑의 감정이란 사실 어미 원숭이가 주는 특정 자극에 대한 반응인 것이다.

| 정답 | ④

| 해설 | ①은 본문의 글과 반대로 기술했다. 생후 첫 2주 동안은 따뜻함이 촉감보다 더 중요하다고 했다. ②의 경우, 접촉 위안은 물체의 따뜻함이 아닌 촉감에 의해 결정된다고 해야 옳다. ③은 친근한 물체에서 위안을 찾는 것이 아니라, 친근한 물체와의 체온이나 접촉을 통해서 위안을 찾는다고 해야 옳다. 답은 ④로 본문 전체 내용을 요약한 글이라고 할 수 있다. 새끼 원숭이는 실제 어미 원숭이에게 애정을 보이는 것이 아니라, 천이나 철사로 된 모형이라 하더라도 그것이 새끼 원숭이가 원하는 따뜻함이나 부드러운 촉감(어미 원숭이가 주는 특정 자극)을 줄 때 그 대상에 애정(이 자극에 대한 반응)을 보이게 된다.

| 어휘 |
screech ⓥ 비명을 지르다 ⓝ 외마디 소리, 날카로운 외침
curl up – 몸을 웅크리다, ~을 감아올리다
surrogate ⓝ 대리모
for dear life – 죽을힘을 다해
substitute ⓝ 대리인, 대역, 대용품
reassure ⓥ 자신감을 되찾게 하다
desensitize ⓥ 무뎌지다, 감도를 줄이다, 민감성을 줄이다
frighten ⓥ 놀라게 하다
annoy ⓥ 짜증나게 하다, 괴롭히다
contact comfort ⓝ 접촉 위안
rewarding ⓐ 가치가 있는, 보람이 있는
psychological ⓐ 심리학의, 심리학적인
artificial ⓐ 모조의, 인조의
determine ⓥ 결정하다
furry ⓐ 털이 덮인
cling to – ~에 달라붙다, 매달리다
apparently ⓐⓓ 겉보기에는, 외관상으로
tentatively ⓐⓓ 실험적인; 일시적인, 임시의
novel ⓐ 새로운 ⓝ 소설
disturb ⓥ 방해하다, 혼란시키다, 불안하게 하다
prolong ⓥ 연장하다, 늘이다
instill ⓥ 주입하다, 서서히 불어넣다
stationary ⓐ 움직이지 않는, 정지한
terry ⓝ 테리직물 (보풀코 모양의 두꺼운 직물)
primate ⓝ 영장류
stimulus ⓝ 자극 (pl. stimuli)

[08-09] 한양대 2010

1960년부터 전 세계 육류 생산은 연간 2억 8천만 톤으로 4배 이상 증가했다. 부유한 국가의 모든 사람이 오늘 고기를 그만 먹겠다고 맹세하더라도 (육류) 소비는 계속 증가할 것이다. 이 때문에 생각 있는 환경 계획 입안자들은 최근에 육류 산업을 없애는 것이 아니라 육류 산업을 친환경화하는 것에 집중하기 시작했다. 소고기, 돼지고기, 또는 닭고기를 만드는 것은 환경적으로 재앙을 불러오는 과정이 될 수 있다. 그리고 동물성 단백질 중에서도 1kg의 소고기를 만들기 위해서는 닭고기 1kg을 만들기 위해 필요한 것보다 7배나 많은 농지가 필요하고, 돼지고기 1kg을 만들기 위해 필요한 것보다 15배나 많은 농지가 필요하다. 하지만 과학자, 농장주, 환경단체 등은 우리가 가축을 사육하고 먹이는 방식을 바꾸고 현재의 유전학을 통해 소를 더 깨끗하게 만들어서 육류 공급망 전체에 조정을 가하는 방식으로 이 같은 피해를 억제할 수 있다고 확신한다. 이러한 노력은 가축들에서부터 시작된다. 소가 먹이를 먹을 때 소의 위는 메탄을 부산물로 생산한다. 소는 풀을 섭취하는 데 있어선 꽤 효율적이지만, 대부분 산업 형태의 가축 농장에서 소에게 먹이는 콩이나 옥수수는 소의 위가 과도한 가스로 울렁이게 만든다. 이에 대처하기 위해, 콩 및 옥수수로 된 먹이를 없앰으로써 소 무리들의 건강을 향상시키고 우유 생산을 증진시키며 메탄가스 발생을 줄일 수 있음을 몇몇 농장에서는 발견했다. 그 대신에, 농장에서는 옛날 방식으로 소에게 영양소와 무해한 지방산이 가득한 알팔파를 먹이로 준다.

08 본문에 따르면 다음 중 옳은 것은 무엇인가?
① 부유한 국가의 사람들은 이제 고기 섭취를 중단하기 위해 노력하고 있다.
② 소가 생산하는 메탄은 환경에 해를 끼치지 않는다.
③ 소의 위는 콩과 옥수수를 소화하기에 효율적이다.
④ 1kg의 고기를 생산하기 위해서는, 돼지고기는 소고기나 닭고기보다 더 적은 면적이 필요하다.

| 정답 | ④

| 해설 | 본문에 따르면 "to make a kilogram of beef takes seven times more farmland than is needed to produce a kilo of chicken, and 15 times the area needed for a kilo of pork(1kg의 소고기를 만들기 위해서는 닭고기 1kg을 만들기 위해 필요한 것보다 7배나 많은 농지가 필요하고, 돼지고기 1kg을 만들기 위해 필요한 것보다 15배나 많은 농지가 필요하다)"는 사실을 알 수 있다. 이는 보기 ④의 내용과 일치하기 때문에 ④를 답으로 봐야 한다. ①의 경우, "even if", 즉 가정을 말하는 것이기 때문에 실제 섭취를 중단하기 위해 노력하는 것은 아니며 따라서 답으로 볼 수 없다. ②의 경우, 본문에서 메탄이 어떤 해를 끼치는지는 구체적으로 나와 있지는 않지만 메탄가스 발생을 줄이기 위해 노력한다는 내용으로 미루어 보건대 최소한 메탄가스가 이로운 것이 아님은 알 수 있다. 따라서 ②는 답이 아니다. ③의 경우, 소의 위는 풀을 효율적으로 섭취할 수 있게 만들어졌지만 소가 콩이나 옥수수를 섭취하면 "make the bovine stomach rumble with excess gas(소의 위가 과도한 가스로 울렁이게)" 할 정도의 과도한 메탄가스가 발생된다는 점을 알 수 있다. 따라서 소의 위는 콩이나 옥수수의 섭취에 그다지 효율적이지 않음을 유추할 수 있으므로 ③은 답이 아니다.

09 다음 문장이 들어가기에 가장 적절한 곳은?

이러한 노력은 가축들에서부터 시작된다.

① ㉮ ② ㉯
③ ㉰ ④ ㉱

| 정답 | ③

| 해설 | 늘어만 가는 육류 생산을 완전히 멈추는 것보다 친환경으로 생산 과정을 전환하자는 것이 본문의 주장이다. 이 문제에서 말하는 "the effort(노력)"은 '친환경을 위한 노력'을 의미한다. 그리고 친환경을 위한 노력이 "starts with the animals themselves(가축들에서부터 시작된다)"는 것은 본문에서 가축의 예로 든 소를 키우는 방식을 친환경적으로 변화시키는 노력이 진행 중이라는 의미이다. 그리고 본문에서 친환경 조치의 일환으로 소의 먹이를 바꾸는 것을 예로 들고 있기 때문에, 소에 관한 내용이 시작되기 전 부분에 문제에서 주어진 문장이 들어가야 글의 전체적인 논리적 흐름이 맞는다. 따라서 답은 ③ 아니면 ④가 된다. ④의 경우, 바로 다음 문장이 "to fight this(이에 대처하기 위해)"라고 시작되는데, "이러한 노력은 가축들에서부터 시작된다"라는 문장과 연결시키면 'this'가 의미하는 것이 '이러한 노력'이 되면서 "이러한 노력은 가축들에서부터 시작된다. 노력에 대처하기 위해, 콩 및 옥수수로 된 먹이를 없앰으로서…"라고 해석이 된다. 그러나 글을 계속 읽으면 알 수 있지만 'this'가 의미하는 것은 "excessive gas(과도한 가스)"의 발생이며 이로 인한 "methane emissions(메탄가스 발생)"이지 '이러한 노력'이 아니기 때문에 ④에 주어진 문장을 삽입하는 것은 논리적으로 맞지 않는 일임을 알 수 있다.

따라서 답은 ④가 아니라 ③이다.

| 어휘 | quadruple ⓥ 4배가 되다 swear off – (술 등을) 맹세하고 끊다
soar ⓥ 치솟다, 증가하다 serious ⓐ 진지한, 생각 있는
green ⓐ 친환경적인 take ⓥ ~을 필요로 하다
herder ⓝ 목동; 농장경영자 curb ⓥ ~을 억제하다
adjustment ⓝ 조정, 조절 all along – 내내, 처음부터, 죽
supply chain – 공급망 genetics ⓝ 유전학
byproduct ⓝ 부산물 bovine ⓐ 소의
rumble ⓥ 우르르 울리다 excess ⓐ 과도한
herd ⓝ 무리, 떼 be packed with – ~로 가득하다
fatty acid – 지방산 digest ⓥ 소화하다

[10-11] 한양대 2011

중국과 동남아시아에 널리 퍼진 믿음과는 달리 코뿔소의 뿔에는 약효나 정력제와 관련된 증명된 특성이 전혀 존재하지 않는다. 일부 과학자들은 코뿔소 뿔의 효능이 손톱을 씹는 것과 다를 바 없다고 말한다. 코뿔소 뿔은 손톱과 같은 물질로 이루어졌으며, 이는 즉 (손톱처럼 뿔은) 털이 접합된 것이라는 의미이다. 하지만 코뿔소의 뿔은 현재 금보다 더 가치가 있는데, 1kg당 최고 6만 달러에 팔린다. 이것이 바로 지구상에 6천만 년 동안 존재해 온 한 짐승(코뿔소)이 생존을 위한 투쟁을 하는 이유이다. 올해만 해도 남아프리카 공화국에서 최대 260마리의 코뿔소가 불법적으로 밀렵되었다. 그들 중 대부분은 뿔 때문에 총에 맞았으며, 고기를 얻고자 잡힌 경우는 거의 없다. 남아프리카 공화국에는 전 세계 흰 코뿔소의 90%와 희귀한 검은 코뿔소 3분의 1이 서식한다. 1970년까지는 모든 것들이 꽤 괜찮았다. 그러다가 석유 값이 치솟으면서 예멘의 1인당 소득이 7배로 증가하는 결과가 나왔는데, 예멘은 정교하게 조각된 코뿔소 뿔로 된 단검 손잡이가 지위와 부의 상징으로 귀히 여겨지는 곳이다. 예멘인들은 급격히 세계 제1의 코뿔소 뿔 수입국이 되었다. 1980년에 이르러서는 일부 추정에 따르면 전 세계 코뿔소의 반이 사라졌다.

10 빈칸 ㉮에 가장 알맞은 것은 무엇인가?

① 그러다가 ② 그러나
③ 그러므로 ④ 그럼에도 불구하고

| 정답 | ①

| 해설 | 언뜻 생각하면 ②를 답으로 볼 수 있다. 그런데 however는 두 문장이 서로 대조가 되는 상황을 나타낼 때 사용하며, then은 앞서 어떤 일이 있은 뒤에 이어지는 다음을 말할 때 사용한다. 빈칸 ㉮의 앞뒤 문장의 관계를 보면, 대조 관계로 보기는 힘들고 시간 순서대로 있은 일을 열거한 것이므로 however보다는 then이 더 답에 가깝다. 따라서 답은 ②가 아니라 ①이다.

11

본문에 따르면 다음 중 사실은 무엇인가?
① 코뿔소 뿔과는 달리 코뿔소의 고기에는 의학적 특성이 있다.
② 40%가 넘는 검은 코뿔소가 남아프리카 공화국에 산다.
③ 예멘인들의 소득은 코뿔소 뿔 무역 덕분에 증가했다.
④ 석유 값의 상승이 예멘에서의 코뿔소 뿔 소비의 증가를 가져왔다.

| 정답 | ④

| 해설 | 석유 값이 오르면서 예멘사람들의 1인당 소득이 7배나 증가했고, 소득이 늘면서 부의 상징인 코뿔소 뿔로 만든 단검 손잡이를 가지려는 사람들이 증가했다. 따라서 석유 값의 상승이 예멘에서 코뿔소 뿔 소비를 늘린 것으로 볼 수 있으므로 ④가 정답이다. ①의 경우, 본문에는 코뿔소 고기에 관해 약효가 있다거나 정력에 효력이 있다는 언급이 전혀 없으므로 답으로 볼 수 없다. ②의 경우, 남아프리카 공화국에는 "희귀한 검은 코뿔소 3분의 1가량(around a third of the rarer black one)"이 살고 있지 40% 이상 사는 것은 아니므로 답으로 볼 수 없다. ③의 경우, 예멘사람들의 소득이 늘어 간 것은 "석유 값이 치솟으면서 예멘의 1인당 소득이 7배로 증가(oil prices soared, resulting in a sevenfold increase in income per head in Yemen)"했기 때문이지 코뿔소 뿔 무역 때문은 아니므로 답으로 볼 수 없다.

| 어휘 | **medicinal** ⓐ 약효가 있는
quality ⓝ 특성, 성질
bush meat – 야생 동물의 고기
soar ⓥ 급증하다
-fold ⓐ ~배의
elaborately ⓐd 정교하게, 공들여서
then ⓐd 그러고 나서, 그 후에
aphrodisiac ⓝ 정력제
agglutinated ⓐ 접합된, 교착성의
reasonably ⓐd 꽤, 상당히
result in – ~라는 결과를 낳다, ~하는 결과를 야기하다
income per head – 1인당 소득
prize ⓥ 귀하게 여기다
nevertheless ⓐd 그럼에도 불구하고

[12-14]

동물을 유혹하고 잡아먹는 식물은 육식성이다. 또한 먹이의 영양분을 소화하고 흡수해야 육식 식물이라 할 수 있다. 이런 행태의 전부가 아닌 일부만 보이는 비육식성 식물들이 많다. 예를 들어 꽃들은 꽃가루 매개체(곤충이나 새, 그 외 생물들, 심지어 인간)를 끌어들인다. 어떤 식물들은 꽃가루 매개체를 잠시 가두어서 확실히 수분되도록 한다. American 속(屬) Ibicella와 Proboscidea는 곤충을 가둬서 끈적끈적한 잎으로 죽이지만 소화시키지는 않는다. 모든 식물은 뿌리나 잎으로 영양분을 흡수한다. 그러나 이런 식물들이 육식 식물들이 하는 행동들 중 일부를 하기는 하지만 육식 식물이기 위한 모든 조건을 충족시키지는 않는다.

최근에 사람들은 자연에는 우리가 좋아하는 이분법적 논리가 전혀 통하지 않는다는 것을 깨달았다. 어떤 식물들은 완전한 육식성도 완전한 초식성도 아니다. 예를 들어, 어떤 끈끈이 식물들 안에는 벌레가 있다. 이 벌레들은 그 식물 위를 마음대로 기어다니고 끈적거리는 잎에 갇힌 곤충을 잡아먹는다. 이들이 잎 위에 배설하면 식물은 그 배설물의 영양분을 흡수한다. 또 다른 식물들은 갇힌 먹이를 녹이는 박테리아 분해에 의존하기도 한다.

12

첫 번째 단락의 목적은 무엇인가?
① 다양한 종류의 식물들을 묘사하는 것
② 육식 식물과 비육식 식물의 특징을 비교하는 것
③ 육식 식물을 엄밀하게 정의하는 것
④ 비육식 식물에 대해 알려주는 것

| 정답 | ③

| 해설 | 첫 문장과 두 번째 문장이 엄밀한 의미의 육식 식물을 정의하는 핵심 문장이다. 그 뒤로 예시를 통해 육식동물의 정의를 구체화하고 있다. 따라서 ③이 적절하다.

13

필자가 두 번째 단락에서 끈끈이 식물을 언급하는 이유는 무엇인가?
① 비육식 식물의 특징을 상술하기 위해서
② 육식성과 비육식성이 완전히 뚜렷하게 구별되지는 않는다는 것을 설명하기 위해
③ 끈끈이 식물과 그 안에 사는 벌레들의 관계를 설명하기 위해서
④ 필요한 기준들을 모두 충족시켜야 육식 식물로 간주될 수 있다는 것을 예시하기 위해서

| 정답 | ②

| 해설 | "Some plants are neither completely carnivorous nor completely noncarnivorous."가 정답의 힌트이다. 끈끈이 식물은 완전히 육식성도 아니고 완전히 비육식성도 아닌 식물이므로 육식성과 비육식성의 구분이 뚜렷하지 않다는 것을 보여주기 위한 적절한 예시이다. 따라서 정답은 ②이다. 예시에 언급된 끈끈이 식물과 벌레의 관계는 지엽적인 내용이므로 ③을 선택하지 않도록 주의한다.

14

지문의 가장 적절한 제목은 무엇인가?
① 육식 식물과 비육식 식물의 분류
② 식물 분류의 기준
③ 왜 비육식 식물들에게 육식 식물의 특징이 있는가?
④ 육식 식물들이 먹이를 잡는 방법

| 정답 | ①

| 해설 | 육식 식물을 정의하고 비육식 식물과의 차이를 상술하는 글이므로 ①이 제목으로 적절하다. ②는 지나치게 포괄적이고 ③은 언급되지 않았으며 ④는 지엽적이다.

| 어휘 | carnivorous ⓐ 육식의
absorb ⓥ 흡수하다
prey ⓝ 먹이
pollinator ⓝ 꽃가루 매개체
ensure ⓥ 반드시 ~하게 하다
genera (genus의 복수) ⓝ 속(屬)

digest ⓥ 소화시키다
nutrient ⓝ 영양분
qualify ⓥ 자격을 주다[얻다]
temporarily ⓐⓓ 일시적으로
transfer ⓥ 옮기다, 전학[전근]하다, 전염시키다
sticky ⓐ 끈적끈적한

fulfill ⓥ 완료하다, 달성하다
black and white – 이분법(의), 흑백논리(의)
excrete ⓥ 배설[분비]하다
break down – 무너뜨리다, 고장 나다
criteria ⓝ 기준, 규격
harbour ⓥ 지니다, 품다
decomposition ⓝ 분해

[15-18]

코스모스는 열대 초본 식물의 한 속이며, 대략 20개 종이 속해 있다. 코스모스는 키 크고 우아하며 가을에 꽃이 피는 일년생 혹은 다년생 식물이고, 다양한 품종이 존재하며, 깃털과도 같은 잎이 난다. "코스모스"라는 말은 그리스어 "cosmos"에서 유래하며 "장신구 혹은 아름다운 것"을 의미한다. 활짝 핀 코스모스의 사랑스럽고 우아한 자태를 보면, 코스모스란 이름이 정말 제대로 지어졌다는 생각이 들 것이다. 코스모스의 원산지는 열대 및 아열대 미주 지역이다. 코스모스의 미주 쪽 조상은 멕시코의 따뜻한 고지대로부터 왔다고 한다. 초창기에 미국에서 자란 코스모스는 추위를 견디지 못했는데, 원래 코스모스는 태양빛을 흠뻑 받으며 크는 식물이었기 때문이다. 종종 서리가 내려서 씨앗이 여물기 전에 코스모스가 죽기도 했다. 하지만 새로운 종이 개발되어 코스모스는 이제 여름뿐 아니라 가을에도 피는 꽃이 되었다.

코스모스가 다른 꽃들은 이미 다 피우고 시들 무렵인 가을에 피는 식물이라는 점은 정원사나 꽃 애호가들에게 코스모스가 더욱 가치 있는 꽃이 되게 했다. 왜냐하면 코스모스는 첫 서리가 내릴 때 진가를 발휘하기 때문이다. 가을에 별 모양의 꽃이 피고 비칠 정도로 얇은 잎이 달린 코스모스는 정원 화단이나 벽 가까이에서 필 때 가장 매력적일 뿐 아니라 잘라낸 코스모스는 실내 장식을 위한 아름다운 꽃다발이 된다.

미국에서 가장 흔히 재배되는 코스모스의 종류는 7피트에서 10피트 높이까지 자라며, 그렇게까지 높지 않은 것도 있다. 코스모스의 줄기는 부드러우며, 밝게 빛나고 방사형으로 뻗어 나가며 현란한 색깔을 지닌 코스모스 꽃의 중심에는 노란색 원반이 달려 있다. 방사형으로 뻗은 꽃잎은 흰색, 분홍색, 붉은색, 자주색, 아이보리색, 노란색, 오렌지색 등 다양한 색을 띠는데, 사실 푸른색을 제외하면 거의 모든 색을 띤다. 초기 원시적인 코스모스 종은 꽃의 크기가 직경 1인치 정도밖에 되지 않았다. 하지만 여러 육종가들이 이 호감 가는 식물을 대상으로 연구한 끝에 몇몇 경우에서 줄기를 짧게 줄이고 꽃의 크기를 키울 수 있었다. 그 중 일부는 따로따로 자라고, 다른 일부는 무리를 이루어 자란다.

15 다음 중 "코스모스"로부터 유추할 수 없는 것은 무엇인가?
① 이름의 의미가 꽃과 잘 어울리는 것으로 보인다.
② 미국에서 발견되는 코스모스의 기원은 멕시코로 거슬러 올라간다.
③ 원래는 가을꽃인데 현재는 여름꽃으로 발달했다.
④ 일부 종은 짧은 생장기에만 생존한다.

| 정답 | ③

| 해설 | 원래 열대 및 아열대 지방이 원산지인 코스모스는 태양 볕을 받으며 크는 식물이라서 서리가 내리면 죽기도 했었다. 그러다가 새 품종이 개발되면서 이제는 여름뿐 아니라 가을에도 피고 지는 꽃이 되었다. 이는 원래 가을에 피고 지는 꽃이었다가 여름에도 피고 지는 꽃이 되었다는 ③의 내용과는 정반대되는 내용이므로 답은 ③이다.

16
밑줄 친 것과 의미상 가장 가까운 것을 고르시오.
① 코스모스는 첫 서리가 내릴 때 더 잘 자란다.
② 코스모스는 자체적으로 서리에 대처할 수 있는 기술을 개발했다.
③ 첫 서리가 내릴 때, 코스모스는 가장 활짝 핀다.
④ 첫 서리는 코스모스가 자라도록 하기에 좋지 않다.

| 정답 | ③

| 해설 | 'come into its own'은 '진가를 발휘하다'라는 의미를 가지며, 밑줄 친 부분의 의미는 "코스모스는 첫 서리가 내릴 때 진가를 발휘한다"이다. 풀어서 설명하면 첫 서리가 내릴 때 코스모스가 활짝 핀다는 의미이다. 따라서 답은 ③이다.

17
본문에 따르면 다음 중 코스모스의 의견에 관해 사실이 아닌 것은 무엇인가?
① 꽃잎의 색은 매우 다양하지만 푸른색은 없다.
② 모든 꽃이 무리지어 피는 것은 아니다.
③ 줄기는 부드럽고 모든 꽃에는 노란색 원반이 달려 있다.
④ 평균 높이는 7에서 10피트이고 그보다 더 높이 자라는 종류도 있다.

| 정답 | ④

| 해설 | 본문에 따르면 코스모스는 7에서 10피트까지 자라지만, 그보다 더 높은 것은 없다고 나와 있다. 10피트가 넘는 코스모스 종이 있다는 의미의 ④는 코스모스의 외양을 묘사한 것 중에서 사실로 볼 수 없으며, 따라서 답은 ④이다.

18
본문에 따르면 어떤 측면에서 코스모스가 가치 있게 여겨지는가?
① 정원 화단에서 심은 모습을 보면 즐겁다.
② 자라는 데 물을 많이 필요로 하지 않으므로 키우기 쉽다.
③ 따뜻한 기후에서는 발견할 수 없는 희귀한 꽃이다.
④ 다른 절화 종류보다 오래간다.

| 정답 | ①

| 해설 | 코스모스는 다른 꽃이 다 시드는 가을철에 꽃을 피우므로 정원사나 꽃을 사랑하는 사람들에게는 매력적인 꽃이다. 또한 본문에서는 코스모스를 우아하고 아름다운 것으로 묘사하고 있으며, 당연히 코스모스를 관상하는 것은 즐거운 일일 것이다. 따라서 답은 ①로 봐야 한다. 본문에서 코스모스를 키우는 데 물이 많이 필요하다는 언급은 없었으니 ②는 답이 될 수 없고, 코스모스는 따뜻한 지역이 원산지인 꽃이므로 ③은 답이 될 수 없고, 다른 절화보다 잘라낸 코스모스 꽃이 더 오래간다는 언급도 본문에 없으므로 ④도 답이 될 수 없다.

| 어휘 | genus ⓝ (생물 분류상의) 속(屬)　　　　number ⓥ (합한 수가) 총 ~이 되다
late-flowering ⓐ 가을에 꽃이 피는; 만기 개화성의
perennial ⓐ 다년생의　　　　　　　　　　feathery ⓐ 깃털과도 같은
foliage ⓝ 나뭇잎　　　　　　　　　　　　signify ⓥ 의미하다, 뜻하다
ornament ⓝ 장신구　　　　　　　　　　　semitropical ⓐ 아열대의

upland ⓝ 고지대	glory in – ~을 즐기다, 누리다
come into one's own – 평가를 받다; 진가를 발휘하다	
aster ⓐ 별의	filmy ⓐ 얇은
garden bed – 정원지(화단 등)	cut flower – 절화, 자른 꽃
bouquet ⓝ 부케, 꽃다발	ray ⓝ 방사형으로 뻗은 꽃의 꽃잎
hue ⓝ 색조, 빛깔	breeders ⓝ 육종가, 사육가
stem ⓝ 줄기	in clusters – 무리를 이룬
suit ⓥ 어울리다	trace to – ~로 거슬러 가다
growing season – 생육기, 생장 시기	conducive ⓐ ~에 좋은

[19-21] 한국외대 2010

산호초는 수백만 마리의 동물이 사는 곳이다. 물속의 세상인 산호초에는 수상 생물이 매우 무성하여 산호초는 바다의 열대우림으로 알려지게 되었다. 하지만 지상의 열대우림이 어려움을 겪는 것처럼, 파도 밑에 위치한 산호초도 상황이 좋지 못하다. 전 세계적으로 산호초가 반이 넘게 사라졌고, 남은 것들도 이번 세기 중반에 멸종할 수 있다. 만약 산호초가 사라지면, 우리는 보기 드문 아름다움과 생물다양성의 원천을 잃는 것이다. 우리는 또한 허리케인이 불 때 파도를 억제하는 물 밑의 완충지대를 잃고, 10억의 사람들에게 먹이를 제공하고 2억 개의 수산업 일자리를 창출하는 물고기의 생육 환경을 잃고, 암ㆍHIVㆍ그 외 다른 질병을 치료하는 데 사용되는 식물과 동물의 서식지를 잃고, 카리브해에서만 관광 수익으로 1년에 1,050억 달러를 잃는다. 산호에 가해지는 위협은 우리 모두에게 가해지는 위협이다. 따라서 연구원들은 산호를 보호하기 위해 노력하고 있다. 연구원들은 산호에 다시 씨를 뿌리는 희망 섞인 시도에 참여하고 있다. 예를 들어 하와이에서는 과학자들과 학생들이 매년 산호의 산란 작업에 착수하기 시작했다. 이들은 해질녘에 산호초로 보트를 타고 나가서, 수정된 알을 한 다발 모은 다음에, 수집 탱크에 넣는다.

19 다음 중 본문의 주제는 무엇인가?
① 산호초의 붕괴와 복원
② 자연재해의 조사
③ 하와이 산호초에서의 매년 있는 산호의 산란
④ 열대우림의 벌채
⑤ 해양자원의 착취

| 정답 | ①

| 해설 | 본문 전체를 한 문장으로 요약해 보면, '자원의 보고인 산호가 사라져 가고 있는 상황에서 복원을 위한 노력이 이루어지고 있다'가 될 것이다. 보기 중에서 이에 가장 흡사한 것은 ①이고, 따라서 답은 ①이다. 본문은 산호초와 관련된 내용이므로 ②, ④는 답이 될 수 없다. ③은 산호초 복원을 위한 노력 중 하나로 본문 막바지에서 제시될 뿐 본문 전체를 포괄하는 내용은 아니므로 답으로 볼 수 없다. ⑤는 본문에는 산호초가 자원의 보고라는 말은 나와 있으나, 그 외 해양자원 전체가 나온 내용은 아니므로 역시 답으로 보기 힘들다.

20 ㉠에 가장 잘 알맞은 것은 무엇인가?
① 불모의
② 무색의
③ 고요한
④ 무성한
⑤ 혼돈된

| 정답 | ④

| 해설 | '너무 ~해서 …하다'는 뜻의 'so ~ that …' 용법에서 'that 이하' 부분은 산호를 "rain forests of the sea(바다의 열대우림)"으로 묘사하고 있고, 따라서 'so' 다음에 올 형용사는 최소한 식물과 관련되면서 뭔가 열대우림이 연상되는 뜻의 단어가 와야 할 것이다. 보기 중에서 그에 가장 흡사한 것은 ④가 된다.

21

다음 중 산호가 사라지는 결과로 언급되지 않은 것은 무엇인가?
① 어업에서의 고용시장 위축
② 더 빈번한 자연재해
③ 해양의 관광 명소로 오는 관광객의 감소
④ 몇몇 질병에 대한 약품의 부족
⑤ 해양의 생물학적 연구에 대한 자금 삭감

| 정답 | ⑤

| 해설 | ①, ②, ③, ④ 모두 본문의 중간 부분에 언급된 사항이다. "200 million jobs in the fishing industry(2억 개의 수산업 일자리)", "underwater buffer that holds back waves(파도를 억제하는 물 밑의 완충지대)", "관광 수익 1년 1,050억 달러(an estimated $105 billion a year from tourist revenue)", "암·HIV·그 외 다른 질병을 치료하는 데 사용되는 식물과 동물의 서식지(a home for plants and animals used to treat cancer, HIV, and other illnesses)" 등이 모두 산호초가 사라지면서 없어질 것들이다. 따라서 보기 중에서 언급되지 않은 ⑤가 답이 된다.

| 어휘 | reef ⓝ 암초
in trouble – 곤란에 처한, 어려운
vanish ⓥ 사라지다
extinct ⓝ 멸종하다
biodiversity ⓝ 생물다양성
hold back – ~을 억제하다
feed ⓥ ~에게 먹이를 주다
treat ⓥ 치료하다
revenue ⓝ 수익
spawn ⓥ 알을 낳다, 산란하다, ~을 생기게 하다
fertilize ⓥ 수정시키다
restoration ⓝ 복원
exploitation ⓝ 개척, 착취
achromatic ⓐ 무색의, 수색성(收色性)의
lush ⓐ 무성한, 우거진
job market – 고용시장
attraction ⓝ 볼거리, 명소

coral reef – 산호초
all is well – 상황이 좋다
the rest – 나머지
extraordinary ⓐ 보기 드문, 특별한
buffer ⓝ 완충기, 완충장치
nursery ⓝ 탁아소, ~의 생육환경
home ⓝ 서식지
estimated ⓐ 추정되는, 추정치의
reseed ⓥ ~에 다시[새로] 씨를 뿌리다, 자생하다
bundle of – 묶음, 다발
degradation ⓝ 붕괴
clearance ⓝ 벌채
barren ⓐ 불모의, 황량한
tranquil ⓐ 고요한, 평온한
chaotic ⓐ 혼돈된
shrink ⓥ 축소되다, 줄다
funding ⓝ 자금 제공

[22-24] 숭실대 2008

유전이란 한 종의 구조적, 기능적 특질이 부모에게서 자손에게로 전달되는 것을 의미한다. 유전 정보는 살아 있는 세포 안의 DNA 분자에 암호화되어 있다. 유전 정보에 의해 자손은 부모를 닮지만 동시에 기본 틀 내에서 변이가 생기기도 한다. 예를 들어, 어떤 사람들은 다섯 손가락이 아닌 여섯 손가락으로 태어난다. 변이는 DNA 분자 구조의 변화인 돌연변이에 의해 발생한다.

대부분의 돌연변이는 위험하다. DNA의 개별 정보들은 조화로운 전체의 일부이기 때문이다. 예를 들어, 인간 DNA의 매우 작은 부분의 돌연변이 하나도 혈우병이나 다른 유전병을 초래할 수 있다. 그러나 일부 돌연변이는 무해할 수도 있고, 특정한 상황에서는 심지어 이로울 수도 있다. 밝은 색 나방이 돌연변이를 일으키면 자손은 짙은 색 나방으로 태어난다. 짙은 색 나방이 검댕 묻은 나무 위에 앉으면 포식자인 새에게 보이지 않는다. 산업 지대처럼 대부분의 나무가 검댕으로 뒤덮인 곳에서는, 밝은 색 나방은 더 눈에 잘 띄어서 잡아먹히기 쉽다. 따라서 짙은 색 나방이 살아남아 번식할 가능성이 더 많다. 이런 상황에서는 돌연변이한 종이 더 잘 적응하는 것이다.

---

22 빈칸 ⓐ에 적절한 단어를 고르시오.

① 그러므로　　② 그러나
③ 게다가　　　④ 왜냐하면

| 정답 | ②

| 해설 | 빈칸 앞 문장은 돌연변이가 해로운 예를, 빈칸 뒤 문장은 돌연변이가 이로운 예를 대비하고 있으므로 역접을 나타내는 ②가 적절하다.

---

23 지문에 따르면 다음 중 사실이 아닌 것은?

① DNA는 모든 살아 있는 유기체 안에 있는 유전 분자이다.
② 돌연변이는 유전적 특질에 변화를 초래한다.
③ 일부 돌연변이는 더 적응력이 있으므로 이롭다.
④ 인간은 유전 정보 때문에 여섯 손가락을 가질 수 없다.

| 정답 | ④

| 해설 | 첫 문단의 "어떤 사람들은 여섯 손가락으로 태어난다."는 내용이 있으므로 보기 ④는 틀린 진술이다.

---

24 다음 중 밑줄 친 ⓑ the mutant form이 지칭하는 것은?

① 짙은 색 나방　　② 포식자 새
③ 검댕 묻은 나무　④ 밝은 색 나방

| 정답 | ①

| 해설 | 두 번째 단락에서 생존에 유리한 돌연변이의 예로서 밝은 색 나방의 돌연변이인 짙은 색 나방을 들고 있다. "When a dark moth rests on a soot-covered tree, bird predators do not see it."에 착안해 짙은 색 나방이 환경에 더 잘 적응한다는 것을 유추할 수 있다. 따라서 정답은 ①이다.

| 어휘 | inheritance ⓝ 유전
transmission ⓝ 전달, 전염
characteristic of – ~의 특징(성질)인
hereditary instruction – 유전 정보
molecule ⓝ 분자
resemble ⓥ 닮다
variation ⓝ 변형, (양, 정도의) 변화
mutation ⓝ 돌연변이
coordinated ⓐ 조화를 이루는
hemophilia ⓝ 혈우병
under prevailing conditions – 정해진 조건에서, 특정한 상황에서
moth ⓝ 나방
predator ⓝ 포식자
reproduce ⓥ 번식하다

refer to – ~을 가리키다; 언급하다; 참고하다
offspring ⓝ 자손
species ⓝ 생물종
encode ⓥ 암호화하다
ensure ⓥ 보장하다, 확실하게 하다
permit ⓥ 허락하다
arise ⓥ 발생하다
separate ⓐ 분리된, 별개의
a bit of – 약간의
genetic disorder – 유전병
soot ⓝ 검댕, 그을음
be likely to – ~ 하기 쉽다, ~할 가능성이 있다
adaptive ⓐ 적응의, 적응력이 있는

[25-28]

진화를 둘러싼 과학과 근본주의 기독교 간의 계속되는 문화 전쟁이 해결될 수 없는 것이라면, 그 이유는 그 전쟁은 해결될 수 없기 때문이다. 기독교뿐 아니라 전 세계 거의 모든 종교의 보수적 믿음을 미치는 그 단층선(좁힐 수 없는 차이)은 생물학의 가장자리를 따라 형성되어 있다. 한쪽에는 모든 생명체가 신과 무관하게 진화해 왔음을 인정하는 입장이 있다. 이 입장은 소수의 미국인의 입장이다. 반대쪽에는, 진화가 발생했다는 사실 자체에 대한 (적극적인) 부정에서부터 진화가 일어나기는 했지만 신의 뜻에 따라서 일어났다는 (소극적인) 진화의 인정에 이르기까지, 종교적 믿음이 자리하고 있다. 1859년 출간된 다윈의 On the Origin of Species에 의해 벌어진 이 간극은 그 후에 끝없이 이어진 논쟁을 통해서도 좁혀지지 않았다. 오히려 반대로, 그 간극은 과학이 발전함에 따라 점차 더 벌어졌다. 현대 생물학이 도달한 두 가지 대원칙은 너무나 견고한 증거에 의해 뒷받침되기 때문에, 사실상 자연의 법칙이 되었다. 첫 번째 원칙은, 생물학적 요소들과 과정들은 궁극적으로는 물리학적, 화학적 법칙의 지배를 받는다는 것이다. 두 번째 원칙은, 모든 생명체는 우연한 돌연변이와 자연선택을 통해 진화해 왔다는 것이다. 미국인 중 절반이나 되는 사람들이 진화를 믿으려 하지 않지만, 종의 기원을 비롯한 진화는 부인할 수 없는 사실이다. 뿐만 아니라, 자연선택의 법칙을 뒷받침하는 증거는 매년 확실해지고 있으며, 증거를 테스트했던 생물학자들은 진화를 사실상 만장일치로 인정하고 있다.

25 빈칸 ⓐ과 ⓑ에 들어갈 가장 적절한 표현은?

① 부인 – 인정 ② 인정 – 부인
③ 증거 – 이론 ④ 이론 – 증거

| 정답 | ①

| 해설 | 진화를 바라보는 보수적 종교의 관점은 정도의 차이가 있을 뿐 진화를 부인하는 것이다. 따라서 그 부인의 정도가 가장 적극적인 것에서 가장 소극적인 것까지의 정도의 범위를 나타내야 한다. 진화 자체를 부정하는 것은 적극적인 부인이고, 진화는 인정하지만 신이 의도한 진화라는 입장은 생물학적 진화에 대한 소극적 부인이다. 따라서 ①이 문맥에 적절하다.

26 밑줄 친 ⓒ random mutation and natural selection을 우리말로 가장 적절히 옮긴 것은?
① 먹이사슬과 적자생존
② 적자생존과 돌연변이
③ 돌연변이와 자연도태
④ 먹이사슬과 자연도태

| 정답 | ③

| 해설 | 'random mutation'은 '우연한 돌연변이'라는 뜻이고 'natural selection'는 '자연선택(자연도태)'라는 뜻이다. 따라서 정답은 ③이다.

27 밑줄 친 ⓓ unanimity와 가장 유사한 의미를 가진 것은?
① 환대
② 적대
③ 헌신
④ 의견 일치

| 정답 | ④

| 해설 | 'unanimity'는 '만장일치'라는 뜻이다. 따라서 ④ consensus(의견 일치)가 유의어이다.

28 이 글의 내용과 일치하는 것은?
① 대다수의 미국인들은 생물의 진화를 믿는다.
② "종의 기원"은 과학과 기독교 간의 간극을 좁혔다.
③ 모든 생물학적 요소들은 물리학과 화학 법칙을 따른다.
④ 자연선택 원리를 보여주는 증거는 찾기 어렵다.

| 정답 | ③

| 해설 | 현대 생물학이 도달한 두 가지 대원칙을 이해했는지 묻는 문제이다. 첫 번째가 "모든 생물학적 요소와 과정들은 물리학과 화학 법칙을 따른다."는 것이므로 ③이 내용과 일치한다. 자연선택 원리를 보여주는 증거가 매년 확실해지고 있다는 언급이 있으므로 ④를 선택하지 않도록 주의한다.

| 어휘 | perennial ⓐ 다년생의, 영원한
evolution ⓝ 진화
fault line – 단층선; 극명한 차이
edge ⓝ 가장자리
hold a view – 관점을 지니다
gap ⓝ 간극, 차이
ensue ⓥ 뒤따르다, 이어지다
widen ⓥ 넓히다
interlocking ⓐ 상호 연결된
obedient ⓐ 복종하는
mutation ⓝ 돌연변이
origin ⓝ 기원
unanimity ⓝ 만장일치
fundamentalist ⓝ 근본주의자
insoluble ⓐ 해결되지 않는
conservative ⓐ 보수적인
acceptance ⓝ 수용, 인정
occur ⓥ 발생하다, 일어나다
narrow ⓥ 좁히다
steadily ⓐⓓ 점차, 꾸준히
support ⓥ 지지하다
virtual ⓐ 사실상의
random ⓐ 임의의
natural selection – 자연선택
undeniable ⓐ 부인할 수 없는
put ~ to test – ~을 테스트하다

[29-31]

진화생물학에서는, 개체가 자신을 희생해서 다른 개체들에게 이로운 행동을 할 때 이타적으로 행동한다고 한다. 이타적 행동의 득과 실은 번식 적합성의 관점으로, 즉 예상되는 자손의 수로 평가한다. 따라서 개체가 이타적으로 행동하면, 자신이 낳을 수 있는 자손의 수는 줄어드는 대신 다른 개체가 낳을 수 있는 자손의 수는 늘어난다. 이러한 생물학적 이타주의의 개념은 일상적인 이타주의의 개념과는 다르다. 일상적인 언어에서는, 남을 도우려는 의식적인 의도가 있어야만 어떤 행동을 "이타적"이라고 한다. 그러나 생물학적 관점에서는 그럴 필요가 없다. 생물학적으로 어떤 행동이 이타적인지를 결정하는 것은 그 행동의 결과이지, 혹시 있을지도 모르는 의도가 아니기 때문이다. 이타적 행동은 동물 세계, 특히 복잡한 사회구조를 갖춘 생물종들에게 흔하다. 예를 들어 개미와 벌같은 사회적인 곤충 집단에서는, 번식을 하지 않는 일개미(일벌)가 평생 동안 여왕개미(여왕벌)를 돌보는 것이 최대로 이타적인 행동이다. 그러나 진화론적 관점에서는, 자연 상태에 이타주의가 존재한다는 것은 납득하기 어려운 일이다. 자연선택의 원리에 따르면 동물들은 다른 개체가 아닌 자신의 생존과 번식 가능성을 높이는 쪽으로 행동하게 되어 있기 때문이다. 그러나 동물이 이타적으로 행동하면 적합성이 낮아지기 때문에, 결국 이기적으로 행동하는 개체에 비해 자연선택에 있어서 더 불리하다.

29 지문의 요지는 무엇인가?
① 이타주의의 기준은 개체가 낳는 자손의 수이다.
② 자연선택이라는 진화이론은 곤충들의 이타주의에 의해 틀린 것으로 판명되었다.
③ 이타주의는 어떤 개체들에게는 생존 가능성을 높이는 데 방해가 된다.
④ 이타주의는 일반적으로는 감정을 지닌 인간에게만 해당되는 개념이다.

| 정답 | ③

| 해설 | 지문의 첫 단락에 상술된 생물학적 이타주의의 정의는 도입이지 주제가 아니다. "But by behaving altruistically an animal reduces its own fitness, so should be at a selective disadvantage vis-a-vis one which behaves selfishly."를 참조하면, 세 번째 단락에 "이타적인 개체는 생존 경쟁에서 불리하다."라는 요지가 담겨 있다. 이에 보기 ③이 지문의 요지를 적절하게 요약하고 있다. 보기 ①은 사실이지만 지문의 내용을 포괄하는 요지는 아니므로 선택하지 않도록 주의한다.

30 다음 중 빈칸에 적절한 것은 무엇인가?
① 그것은 분명 논리적이다.　　② 그럴 필요가 없다.
③ 이런 경향은 강하다.　　　　④ 그것은 우연한 행동이다.

| 정답 | ②

| 해설 | But을 중심으로 대조의 논리를 완성한다. 일상 어법에서의 이타주의에는 남을 도우려는 의식적 '의도'가 있다. ↔ 생물학적 이타주의에는 남을 도우려는 의식적 '의도'가 없다. 따라서 답은 ②이다.

31 다음 중 지문에서 유추할 수 없는 것은?
① 생물학자들은 이타주의를 의도가 확장된 행위로 정의한다.
② 생물학적 관점에서, 이타주의 개념은 약간의 자기희생을 수반한다.
③ 이타적 개체들은 자신의 번식보다는 다른 개체의 번식을 돕는 경향이 더 있다.
④ 이타주의에 대한 생물학적 관점은 자연선택이라는 진화론과 모순되는 부분이 있다.

| 정답 | ①

| 해설 | 첫 문단에 상술된 일상적 의미의 이타주의와 생물학적 이타주의의 차이에 주목한다. 일상적 의미의 이타주의는 의도에서 시작되는 행위인 반면, 생물학적 이타주의는 의도가 없는 행위이다. 따라서 ①은 잘못된 유추이다. 마지막 문장에서 생물학적 이타주의는 진화론의 관점에서는 납득하기 어렵다는 내용이 있으므로 "생물학적 이타주의는 자연선택이라는 진화론과는 모순되는 부분이 있다."는 것을 유추할 수 있다. ④를 선택하지 않도록 주의한다.

| 어휘 |
evolutionary biology - 진화생물학
behave ⓥ 행동하다
benefit ⓥ 이득을 주다
measure ⓥ 측정하다, 계산하다
reproductive fitness - 번식 적합성
reduce ⓥ 줄이다
boost ⓥ 증가시키다, 강화하다
identical ⓐ 동일한, 똑같은
parlance ⓝ 용어, 어법
intention ⓝ 의도
determine ⓥ 결정하다, 좌우하다
perform ⓥ 수행(실행)하다
complex ⓐ 복잡한
colony ⓝ 군집, 집단
devote A to B - A를 B에 바치다(헌신하다)
maximally ⓐⓓ 최대한으로
puzzling ⓐ 당황스럽게 하는, 이해하기 어려운
chance ⓝ 가능성, 확률
vis-a-vis ~ - ~와 비교해서, ~와의 관계에서, 마주보고
selfishly ⓐⓓ 이기적으로

organism ⓝ 생명체
altruistically ⓐⓓ 이타적으로
costs and benefits - 득과 실, 비용과 이득
in terms of - ~의 관점에서
offspring ⓝ 자손
be likely to - ~할 가능성이 있는, ~하기 쉬운
notion ⓝ 개념
concept ⓝ 개념
conscious ⓐ 의식적인
consequence ⓝ 결과
count as - ~로 간주되다
common ⓐ 흔한, 공통적인
insect ⓝ 곤충
sterile ⓐ 불임의, 무성의
care for - ~을 돌보다
viewpoint ⓝ 관점
natural selection - 자연선택
be at disadvantage - 불리하다

[32-33] 성균관대 2012

한 가지 문제점을 극복하기 위해 과학자들이 선의로 하나의 종을 도입했지만 단지 또 다른 문제를 야기했던 사례가 여럿 존재한다. 오스트레일리아가 사탕수수를 잡아먹는 딱정벌레를 퇴치하기 위해 하와이로부터 캐인 토드를 들여온 이후, 이 양서류는 마치 전염병처럼 확산되었다. 꿀 산출량을 늘리기 위해 아프리카 꿀벌을 브라질에서 들여온 결과 미주 대륙 전체에 "살인마" 벌이 떼로 몰려다니게 되었다. 뉴펀들랜드의 무스도 마찬가지이다.

무스는 캐나다의 상징일지 모르지만 뉴펀들랜드 섬에서는 외래종으로, 한 세기 전 당시 뉴펀들랜드 섬의 지도자들은 무스가 있다면 영국의 식민지로 어려움을 겪던 그곳에 사냥꾼과 관광객을 끌어당길 수 있을 것이라고 생각했었다. 캐나다의 여타 다른 지역과는 달리 그 섬에서는 무스의 천적은 존재하지 않았고, 토착 늑대종은 멸종한 상태였다. 현재 뉴펀들랜드 섬에는 15만 마리의 무스가 육중한 덩치를 자랑하면서 느릿느릿 돌아다니고 있다. 이 덕분에 사냥꾼들이 몰려들고는 있지만, 어두울 때 고속도로를 가로질러 배회하는 습성을 지닌 탓에 무스는 연간 700건의 차량과의 충돌사고를 유발하는 도로의 위험요소가 되었다.

32

다음 중 빈칸에 가장 알맞은 것은 무엇인가?

① 실패로 이어졌다
② 또 다른 문제를 야기하다
③ 비판받다
④ 아무것도 발견하지 못하다
⑤ 돈을 낭비하다

| 정답 | ②

| 해설 | 빈칸 뒤 제시된 사례는 모두 어떤 문제를 해결하려다 또 다른 문제가 도입된 사례로 볼 수 있다. 따라서 답은 '또 다른 문제'를 의미하는 ②가 적합하다.

33

밑줄 친 "영국의 식민지로 어려움을 겪던 그곳"은 무엇을 지칭하는가?

① 캐나다
② 미국
③ 오스트레일리아
④ 브라질
⑤ 뉴펀들랜드

| 정답 | ⑤

| 해설 | 밑줄이 들어간 단락 전체가 뉴펀들랜드 섬을 가리키고 있으므로 답은 ⑤이다.

| 어휘 | **well-meaning** ⓐ 선의로 한
cane toad – 캐인 토드(독두꺼비의 일종)
reckon ⓥ 생각하다
lumbering ⓐ (육중한 덩치로) 느릿느릿 움직이는
boffin ⓝ 과학자
amphibian ⓝ 양서류
struggling ⓐ 고생하는, 어려운

[34-36]

밀리서 보면 물고기 떼는 한 마리 큰 생물로 보인다. 물고기 떼 속 물고기는 두세 마리에서 많게는 수백만 마리에 이르는데 대형을 단단히 갖추고 헤엄을 치며, 거의 일치된 동작으로 선회하고 반전한다. 어느 하나가 물고기 떼 내에서 우위를 차지하지 못하는 체제를 보유하고 있거나 아니면 물고기가 너무 약해서 물고기 떼 전체의 역학에 거의 또는 아무 영향을 주지 못하는 것이다. 덧붙여 한결같은 리더십도 존재하지 않는다. 물고기 떼가 왼쪽이나 오른쪽으로 돌면, 측면에 있던 물고기들이 앞장선다. 물고기 떼의 평균 크기는 종에 따라 다른데, 물고기마다의 간격이나 평균 속도나, 3차원적 모습 또한 각기 다르다. 물고기 떼는 이동 중에는 마치 군대에서나 볼 수 있는 정확성으로 정렬되어 있지만, 쉬는 중이나 음식을 먹을 때는 거의 무작위로 방향을 잡고 있다. 정렬된 물고기들은 포식자로부터 공격을 받으면 특정한 방식으로 방향을 바꾼다. 움직이는 물고기 떼 안에서의 간격 조정은 대체로 유체 역학적 힘에 의해 결정되는 것이 분명하다. 물고기 각각은 다른 물고기로 인해 생기는 난류로 효율성에 심각한 손상이 가해지는 일이 없도록 이웃한 물고기들과 가능한 한 가까이 있을 수 있는 위치를 찾으려 한다.

34

본문에 따르면 물고기 떼의 크기에 영향을 주지 못하는 것은 무엇인가?

① 물고기의 방향
② 물고기끼리의 가까움
③ 물고기의 종류
④ 물고기의 속도

| 정답 | ①

| 해설 | "물고기 떼의 평균 크기는 종에 따라 다른데(The average school size varies according to species)"는 ③의 근거가 되고, "물고기마다의 간격이나 평균 속도, 3차원적 모습 또한 각기 다르다(as does the spacing of its members, its average velocity, its average velocity, and its three-dimensional shape)"는 ②와 ④의 근거가 된다. 그러나 본문에 ①의 근거인 것은 존재하지 않으므로 답은 ①이다.

35

빈칸에 가장 알맞은 것을 고르시오.
① 홀로 헤엄칠 수 있는 기회
② 확고한 리더십이 없음
③ 자율성이 들어갈 공간이 없음
④ 갈라지고자 하는 강한 의식

| 정답 | ②

| 해설 | "물고기 떼가 왼쪽이나 오른쪽으로 돌면, 측면에 있던 물고기 들이 앞장선다(When the school turns to the right or left, individuals formerly on the flank assume the lead)"를 통해, 물고기 떼에는 특정한 우두머리가 있는 것이 아니고 아무것이나 상황에 따라 우두머리가 될 수 있음을 알 수 있다. 따라서 답은 ②이다.

36

다음 중 "물고기 떼"에서 유추할 수 없는 것은 무엇인가?
① 물고기 떼의 주된 역할은 구성원들에게 안전함을 제공해 주는 것이다.
② 포식자들은 물고기의 정렬된 모습에 영향을 준다.
③ 물고기 떼는 두 마리가 넘는 물고기의 무리를 의미한다.
④ 식사할 때는 한결같은 대형 형성의 예외가 된다.

| 정답 | ①

| 해설 | "물고기 떼는 이동 중에는 마치 군대에서나 볼 수 있는 정확성으로 정렬되어 있지만, 쉬는 중이나 음식을 먹을 때는 거의 무작위로 방향을 잡고 있다. 정렬된 물고기들은 포식자로부터 공격을 받으면 특정한 방식으로 방향을 바꾼다(Although the fish are usually aligned with military precision while the group is on the move, they assume a more nearly random orientation while resting or feeding. Their alignments also shift in particular ways when the fish are attacked by predators)." 여기서 ②, ③, ④의 근거를 모두 찾을 수 있으나, ①은 찾을 수 없고 본문 어디에도 ①의 근거는 보이지 않는다. 따라서 답은 ①이다.

| 어휘 | **fish school** – 물고기 떼
wheel ⓥ 선회하다
in unison – 일제히
consistent ⓝ 한결같은, 확고한
spacing ⓝ 공간, 간격
align ⓥ 가지런하게 만들다, 조정하다
orientation ⓝ 방향
evidently ⓐⓓ 분명히, 눈에 띄게
turbulence ⓝ 난류
diverge ⓥ 갈라지다

organism ⓝ 생물
reverse ⓥ 반전하다
dynamics ⓝ 원동력, 역학
flank ⓝ 측면
velocity ⓝ 속도
precision ⓝ 정밀, 정확
alignment ⓝ 가지런함, 정렬됨
hydrodynamic ⓐ 유체 역학의
proximity ⓝ 가까움, 인접함

[37-39] 성균관대 2013

뇌의 크기가 지능과 어느 정도 연관이 있는 것은 분명하지만, 뇌의 구조로부터 더 많은 것을 배울 수 있다. 고차원적 사고는 뇌의 가장 진화된 영역이자 수많은 동물은 보유하지 못한 부위인 대뇌 피질에서 벌어진다. 포유동물은 대뇌 피질을 보유한 동물군에 속하고, 대체로 대뇌 피질이 더 크고 복잡할수록 동물의 지능은 더욱 높아진다. 하지만 대뇌 피질이 창조적 사고로 이어지는 유일한 경로는 아니다. 도구 활용에 관해 생각해 보자. 인간은 도구의 마술사이며, 유인원은 잠깐 손대는 수준으로만 도구를 다루며, 수달은 연체동물을 바위로 깨서 속살을 획득하는 방법을 터득했는데, 이는 원시적이긴 해도 통하는 방법이다. 하지만 만일 창의력이 대뇌 피질에서 나오는 것이라면, 까마귀와 어치 등을 포함해 동일 부류의 새를 지칭하는 까마귀과 새들은 어떻게 인간을 제외한 거의 모든 동물종보다 도구를 더 잘 사용할 수 있는 것일까?

예를 들어 까마귀는 플라스틱 관 밑바닥에 있는 음식 바구니를 낚기 위해 능숙하게 철사를 구부려 고리를 만들 수 있다는 것을 보여줬다. 이보다 더 놀라운 점은, 크리스토퍼 "버드"라는 적절한 이름을 지닌 캠브리지 대학의 동물학자가 작년에 까마귀과에 속하는 새인 떼까마귀가 일부만 물이 잠긴 물 주전자에서 물을 마실 수 있도록 수면을 높이기 위해 돌을 떨어뜨리는 방법을 추론할 수 있다는 것을 발견했다. 게다가, 떼까마귀는 가장 크기가 큰 돌을 먼저 골랐는데, 이는 떼까마귀는 큰 돌이 수면을 빨리 상승시킬 수 있을 것임을 아는 것으로 보였다. 이솝은 2,500년 전에 이런 과업을 수행해 낸 새에 관한 이야기를 창작했지만, 21세기가 돼서야 이런 솜씨가 단지 우화에 불과한 것은 아니라는 것이 드러났다.

37 본문에 따르면 많은 동물들은 <u>대뇌 피질이 없기</u> 때문에 똑똑하지 않다.

① 단순한 삶을 살다
② 뇌가 매우 작다
③ 도구를 사용할 필요가 없다
④ 뇌를 활용하는 방법을 훈련받지 못했다
⑤ 대뇌 피질이 없다

| 정답 | ⑤

| 해설 | "고차원적 사고는 뇌의 가장 진화된 영역이자 수많은 동물은 보유하지 못한 부위인 대뇌 피질에서 벌어진다(Higher thinking takes place in the cerebral cortex, the most evolved region of the brain and one many animals lack)." 여기서 대뇌 피질이 없는 동물은 고차원적 사고를 할 수 없음을 즉 똑똑하지 않음을 알 수 있다.

38 빈칸에 가장 알맞은 것은 무엇인가?

① 반대로
② 그럼에도 불구하고
③ 게다가
④ 얄궂게도
⑤ 반면에

| 정답 | ③

| 해설 | 빈칸 앞에서는 떼까마귀는 돌을 넣어 수면을 높일 수 있다는 것을 알 수 있고, 빈칸 뒤에서는 떼까마귀가 아무 돌을 넣는 것이 아니라 무거운 것을 먼저 넣는 것이 좋다는 것을 알 수 있을 만큼 지능을 갖고 있음을 보여준다. 즉, 빈칸 뒤 내용은 떼까마귀의 지능에 관해 빈칸 앞 내용에 더해 더 상세한 사항을 다루고 있다. 따라서 답은 ③이다.

39

밑줄 친 "이런 솜씨"는 무엇을 의미하는가?

① 동물의 언어 사용
② 수달의 바위 사용
③ 침팬지의 몸짓 언어 숙달
④ 크리스토퍼 버드의 추론
⑤ 새가 목표 달성을 위해 도구를 사용한 것

| 정답 | ⑤

| 해설 | feat는 '솜씨'를 의미하며, 문맥상 새가 물을 마시기 위해 물 주전자에 돌을 넣어 물의 수위를 높인 것을 뜻한다. 따라서 답은 ⑤이다.

| 어휘 |
smarts ⓝ 지능
as a rule – 대체로
otter ⓝ 수달
corvid ⓝ 까마귀과 새
adept at – ~에 능숙한
aptly ⓐⓓ 적절히
rook ⓝ 떼까마귀
apparently ⓐⓓ 분명히, 겉보기에
mastery ⓝ 숙달
cerebral cortex – 대뇌 피질
dabble in – 조금 해 보다, 잠깐 손대다
mollusk ⓝ 연체동물
jay ⓝ 어치
remarkably ⓐⓓ 주목할 만하게, 놀랍게
zoologist ⓝ 동물학자
family ⓝ 과
feat ⓝ 위업; 솜씨

[40-42] 성균관대 2014

늑대는 악의 화신인양 이야기 속을 배회하며 등장한다. 어떤 면에서 보면 늑대가 인류 최악의 적이라고 하는 것은 이상한 일이다. 늑대에 비하면 호평을 받는 곰이 늑대보다 더 위험하다. 곰은 건드리면 달려들지만 늑대는 건드리면 도망간다. 아마도 고대부터 내려온 늑대에 대한 이러한 증오는 경쟁으로 설명할 수 있을 것이다. 과거 인간이 동물을 기르기 시작하던 시기에 늑대는 다른 생명체와 비교하면 인간과 더욱 직접적인 경쟁을 했다. 한 무리의 늑대는 한 시간 안에 수백 마리의 양을 기꺼이 죽일 것이다. 생계가 네발 달린 동물에 좌우되는 공동체의 경우, 사람과 늑대는 양립이 불가능하다. 이러한 라이벌 관계는 끔찍한 잔인함을 낳게 되고, 19세기 초 미국의 경우 늑대를 죽이는 것이 괜찮은 오락거리로 간주되었다. 하지만 20세기 중반 경에 정서가 변하기 시작했다. 처음에는 환경보호론적 사고에 변화가 있었고, 이는 미국 환경운동의 아버지인 알도 레오폴드의 삶과 저작을 통해 잘 드러났다. 20세기 초에 환경 운동가들은 포식자가 다른 동물을 죽이기 때문에 포식자를 죽이는 것이 환경 보호에 가장 크게 기여할 수 있다고 생각했다. 하지만 레오폴드는 이러한 운동이 낳을 결과에 점차 우려의 뜻을 표했다. 1949년에 초판이 출간되었으며 아마도 가장 많이 팔린 환경운동 관련 서적인 "모래군의 열두달(A Sand County Almanac)"에서 레오폴드는 다음과 같은 글을 남겼다. "나는 최근에 늑대가 더 이상 살지 않게 된 산의 모습을 봤고 남쪽을 향해 나 있는 경사면이 미로처럼 복잡하게 새로 생긴 사슴길로 인해 어지럽게 된 모습을 봤다. 나는 사슴이 먹을 수 있는 관목과 묘목이 뜯어 먹히면서 처음에는 활기 없이 시들어가다가 죽는 모습을 봤다."

40

본문에 따르면 늑대와 사람이 양립 불가능한 이유는 무엇인가?

① 늑대는 생태계에 되돌릴 수 없는 피해를 입힌다.
② 늑대는 인간 문명과 대조 관계에 있다.
③ 늑대는 빨리 번식하고 확산하는 폭력적인 생물이다.
④ 늑대는 다른 생물에 비해 인간과 더욱 직접적으로 경쟁했다.
⑤ 초창기 정착민들은 이전에 늑대를 경험한 적이 없다.

| 정답 | ④

| 해설 | "아마도 고대부터 내려온 늑대에 대한 이러한 증오는 경쟁으로 설명할 수 있을 것이다. 과거 인간이 동물을 기르기 시작하던 시기에 늑대는 다른 생명체와 비교하면 인간과 더욱 직접적인 경쟁을 했다(Presumably competition explains this ancient hatred. Once people took to raising animals, wolves competed with them more directly than any other creature)." 그리고 "한 무리의 늑대는 한 시간 안에 수백 마리의 양을 기꺼이 죽일 것이다. 생계가 네발 달린 동물에 좌우되는 공동체의 경우, 사람과 늑대는 양립이 불가능하다(A pack of wolves will happily kill hundreds of sheep in an hour. In communities whose livelihood goes about on four legs, wolves and people are not compatible)." 즉, 늑대와 인간은 라이벌 관계이자 직접적인 경쟁을 하는 관계이기 때문에 양립이 불가능한 것이다. 따라서 답은 ④이다.

41 다음 중 빈칸 (가)와 (나)에 가장 알맞은 것은 무엇인가?

(가)	(나)
① 하지만	하지만
② 거기서	하지만
③ 하지만	게다가
④ 결국	실제로는
⑤ 게다가	그러므로

| 정답 | ①

| 해설 | (가)의 앞까지는 늑대를 죽이는 것이 오락거리로 치부될 만큼 흔하게 벌어진 일이었지만, 그 다음부터는 환경보호 차원에서 늑대를 죽이는 것에 대한 정서가 변화하기 시작했음을 알 수 있다. 즉, (가)를 기준으로 서로 대조적인 내용이 실리고 있다.
(나)의 앞까지는 포식자를 죽이는 것이 환경보호에 기여할 것이라는 생각이 있었지만, 그 다음부터는 레오폴드가 그러한 움직임에 우려의 뜻을 표했음을 알 수 있다. 즉, (나) 역시 서로 대조적인 내용이 실려 있는 것이다.
이러한 점들을 감안했을 때 답으로 가장 적절한 것은 ①이다.

42 본문에 따르면 다음 중 사실인 것은 무엇인가?
① 인류가 고대에 늑대를 대상으로 품은 증오는 전혀 근거가 없는 것이다.
② 20세기 초 환경보호론자들은 인간이 늑대의 멸종에 책임이 있다고 강조했다.
③ 레오폴드는 늑대를 죽이자는 운동이 미국의 풍경을 파괴하고 있다고 주장했다.
④ 늑대와 비교하면 곰의 적응력이 더 뛰어나다.
⑤ 늑대는 자연의 포식자이기 때문에 인간이 늑대를 길들일 수는 없었다.

| 정답 | ③

| 해설 | 본문 마지막 부분에서 레오폴드는 늑대가 다 사라지고 사슴만 남은 산에 어떤 일이 있는지를 설명하고 있다. 그중에서도 "나는 사슴이 먹을 수 있는 관목과 묘목이 뜯어 먹히면서 처음에는 활기 없이 시들어 가다가 죽는 모습을 봤다(I have seen every edible bush and seedling browsed, first to anaemic desuetude, and then to death)"를 보면, 포식자가 사라진 나머지 사슴이 풀을 다 먹어 버린 바람에 산이 황폐화되었음을 알 수 있다. 따라서 답은 ③이다.

| 어휘 | prowl ⓥ 돌아다니다, 배회하다
in a way – 어느 정도는, 어떤 면에서
turn on – 공격하다, 달려들다
take to – ~하기 시작하다
compatible ⓐ 호환이 가능한, 양립할 수 있는
conservationist ⓝ 환경보호론자
serve ⓥ 기여하다, 도움이 되다
seedling ⓝ 묘목
anaemic ⓐ 활기 없는, 빈혈이 있는
irreversible ⓐ 되돌릴 수 없는
groundless ⓐ 근거 없는
adaptable ⓐ 적응할 수 있는

embodiment ⓝ 전형, 화신
better press – 호평, 호의적인 소개
presumably ⓐ 아마, 짐작건대
livelihood ⓝ 생계
spawn ⓥ (어떤 결과·상황을) 낳다
illustrate ⓥ 보여주다, 드러내다
slope ⓝ 비탈, 경사면
browse ⓥ (높이 자란 잎 등을) 뜯어먹다
desuetude ⓝ 폐지, 소용없음, 무용
antithesis ⓝ 반대, 대조
extinction ⓝ 멸종, 소멸
domesticate ⓥ 길들이다, 사육하다

[43-45] 서울여대 2018

사람들은 일반적으로 소들은 계단을 걸어 내려올 수 없다고 생각한다. 소가 계단을 걸어 올라가게 할 수는 있어도 내려오게 하는 것은 꽤 창의적인 방법 없이는 불가능할 것이라고 많은 사람들이 생각한다. 하지만 실제로 이런 생각은 어느 정도까지 사실일까? 간단히 말하자면, 소들이 계단을 내려가게 하는 것은 매우 어렵다. 처음에는 그런 생각이 터무니없게 느껴질 수도 있지만, 겉보기에 매우 단순해 보이는 그런 일을 소들이 할 수 없다는 것은 실제로 상당히 이치에 맞는 것이기도 하다.

소들이 계단 내려오는 것을 힘겨워하는 것은 계단의 경사와 구조가 자연 상태에서는 발견할 수 없고 계단이 인간의 다리 비율에 맞춰 만들어졌기 때문이다. 계단의 평균 경사는 35도로 우리 인간은 더 생각할 것 없이 내려올 수 있다. 반면 소들은 우리와는 무척 다른 체중 분포와 골격을 지니고 있어서 소들이 사람과 같은 방식으로 움직이는 것이 쉽지 않다. 생각해 보면 소처럼 육중한 것은 어떤 것이든 35도 경사를 내려오는 데 힘겨워할 수밖에 없다. (성별 및 종에 따라) 보통의 소는 체중이 1,600~2,400파운드가 나가기 때문에, 소가 계단을 내려올 때 느끼는 공포는 상당히 합리적으로 보인다. 그리고 소의 목은 사람의 목보다는 움직일 수 있는 범위가 훨씬 제한적이다. 그래서 앞쪽을 향해 그 정도까지 기울어져 있을 경우 앞을 똑바로 보는 것이 어렵게 된다. 그것이 소가 본능적으로 계단을 내려오는 것을 회피하는 이유일 것이다. 소는 혼자서는 계단을 내려가지 않으려고 하지만, 만약 억지로 내려가게 시키면 소도 계단을 내려간다는 것이 (실험을 통해) 입증되어 있다. 그래서 소도 계단을 내려갈 수 있는 것이다. 단지 가능하면 그런 상황을 피하려고 하는 것이다. 왜냐하면 소들은 진화적으로 그런 가파른 경사와 어색한(이질적인) 발 움직임에 대해 준비가 되어 있지 않기 때문이다.

43

다음 중 소가 계단을 내려올 때 힘겨워하는 것과 관련이 없는 것은?
① 소의 종
② 소의 체중
③ 소의 감정
④ 소의 골격

| 정답 | ①

| 해설 | 소의 육중한 체중, 계단을 내려갈 때 느끼는 소의 공포감이라는 감정, 사람과는 다른 소의 골격 구조 등이 소가 계단을 내려가기 어렵게 만드는 원인들이 된다. 정답은 ①로, 소의 품종에 따라 어떤 품종은 계단을 잘 내려가고 다른 품종은 계단을 잘 내려가지 못하는 것이 아니므로, 종은 체중과 관련이 있지 계단을 내려가는 것과의 연관성은 본문에 등장하지 않았다.

44

다음 중 본문의 내용과 일치하는 것은?

① 소의 다리 비율은 인간의 다리 비율과 같지 않다.
② 소는 계단을 내려가도록 강요받는다고 해도 계단을 내려갈 수 없다.
③ 소는 경사면을 내려갈 때는 항상 앞을 똑바로 볼 수 없다.
④ 계단의 경사와 구조는 자연환경에서 흔하게 볼 수 없는 것은 아니다.

| 정답 | ①

| 해설 | ② 본문 후반부에서 소는 혼자서는 계단을 내려가지 않으려고 하지만, 만약 억지로 내려가게 시키면 소도 계단을 내려간다는 것이 입증되어 있다고 했다. ③ 소가 경사면을 내려갈 때 앞을 절대 볼 수 없는 것이 아니라, 구조상 앞을 보는 것이 힘들다고 했다. ④ 계단의 경사와 구조는 자연환경에서 '흔하게 볼 수 없는 것은 아니다'는 이중부정을 통해 흔히 볼 수 있다고 했으므로, 이는 본문과 반대의 내용이 된다. 정답은 ①로, 소가 계단을 잘 내려가지 못하는 이유는 계단이 '인간의 다리 비율에 맞춰' 제작되었고, 소는 '우리와는 무척 다른 체중 분포와 골격을 지니고' 있다고 했으므로, 소의 다리 비율은 인간의 다리 비율과 같지 않다는 것을 알 수 있다.

45

다음 중 저자의 의도를 가장 잘 기술한 것은?

① 소가 아래로 내려가는 움직임을 보이면 안 된다는 것을 경고하기 위해서
② 우리를 설득해 소를 위해 무엇인가를 하게 만들기 위해서
③ 동물의 삶에 대한 도덕적 교훈을 우리에게 주기 위해서
④ 소의 특성에 대한 정보를 우리에게 제공하기 위해서

| 정답 | ④

| 해설 | 일반인들이 소에 대해 갖고 있는 '소는 계단을 내려갈 수 없다'는 사실이 맞는지를 서술하고 있는 글이므로, 우리에게 소의 특성에 대한 정보를 제공하고 있다고 볼 수 있으므로, 정답은 ④가 된다.

| 어휘 |
walk down stairs – 계단을 내려가다
notion ⓝ 생각, 관념
feat ⓝ 위업, 개가; (뛰어난) 솜씨[재주]
incline ⓝ 경사 ⓥ (마음이) ~쪽으로 기울다, 기울어지게 하다
tailor ⓥ (특정한 목적·사람 등에) 맞추다, 조정하다 ⓝ 재단사
proportion ⓝ 비율
without a second thought – 데[두 번] 생각할 것도 없이 바로
on the other hand – 다른 한편으로는
in the same manner – 마찬가지로
have difficulty ~ing – ~하는 데 어려움을 겪다
rational ⓐ 이성적인, 합리적인
tilted ⓐ 경사진
evolutionary ⓐ 진화의
steep ⓐ 가파른, 비탈진; 급격한 ⓥ 담그다, 적시다; 몰두시키다
foreign ⓐ 이질적인, ~과 맞지 않는
breed ⓝ (사람의) 유형, (특히 개·고양이·가축의) 품종
to put it simply – 간단히 말하면
ridiculous ⓐ 웃기는, 말도 안 되는, 터무니없는
make sense – 이치에 맞다, 의미가 통하다[이해가 되다]
slope ⓝ 경사
weight distribution – 무게 분포
massive ⓐ 거대한, 엄청나게 큰
go downhill – 아래로 내려가다, 언덕을 내려가다
mobile ⓐ 움직이기 쉬운, 유동하는 ⓝ 이동전화
instinctively ⓐⓓ 본능적으로

[46-50] 세종대 2018

비버는 잘 알려진 대로 바쁜 동물이고 자신의 재능을 활용하여 다른 동물들이라면 거의 불가능한 방식으로 주변 풍경을 탈바꿈시킨다. 비버는 가능한 장소만 있으면 강과 호수의 둑에 굴을 판다. 하지만 비버는 또한 댐을 건설하여 거주에 덜 적합한 서식지를 탈바꿈한다. 튼튼한 이빨과 강력한 아래턱으로 나무를 베어 넘어뜨리고 갉아먹은 다음에 거대한 크기의 통나무와 나뭇가지 그리고 진흙으로 구조물을 만들어 물줄기를 막고 들판과 숲을 자신들이 매우 좋아하는 거대한 연못으로 바꿔놓는다.

돔 형태의 비버의 집은 롯지(lodge)라는 명칭으로 불리며 나뭇가지와 진흙으로 지어진다. 롯지는 흔히 전략적으로 연못의 중앙에 위치하며 수중의 입구를 통해서만 도달할 수 있다. 이러한 비버의 주택은 일자일웅인 부모 비버와 어린 새끼 그리고 작년 봄에 태어난 한 살배기 새끼들이 사는 집이다.

비버는 가장 큰 설치류 중 하나이다. 비버는 초식동물이며 잎, 나무껍질, 잔가지, 뿌리, 수생식물을 먹는 것을 선호한다.

이들 대형 설치류는 육지에서는 볼품없게 뒤뚱거리며 움직이지만 물속에서는 우아하게 움직인다. 물속에서 비버는 물갈퀴가 달린 큰 뒷발을 마치 발갈퀴처럼 활용하며 노처럼 생긴 꼬리를 키와 같이 활용한다. 이러한 특질 덕분에 비버는 시간당 최대 5마일의 속력으로 수영할 수 있다. 비버는 수면으로 올라가지 않은 채 15분 동안 물속에 머무를 수 있고 마치 보호 안경처럼 기능하는 투명한 눈꺼풀을 갖고 있다. 비버의 모피는 천연적으로 기름기에 덮여 있으며 방수이다.

비버는 놀라거나 겁을 먹었을 때 보내는 위험 신호로 유명하다. 수영을 하던 비버는 갑작스럽게 잠수를 하며 그 와중에 널찍한 꼬리로 물을 격렬하게 두드린다. 이를 통해 비버는 물 표면을 철썩 때리는 소리를 매우 크게 낼 수 있고, 이 소리는 멀리 떨어진 물 밖에서 그리고 물속에서 들린다. 비버의 이러한 경고음은 지역 내의 다른 비버에게 경고로서 작용한다. 비버 한 마리가 이러한 경고 신호를 보내면 부근의 비버들은 물속으로 잠수하고 한동안 돌아오지 않을 수 있다.

현재 두 가지 종의 비버가 존재하며, 북미와 유럽 및 아시아의 숲 속에서 비버를 발견할 수 있다. 비버는 얼음층이 연못 표면을 덮을지라도 겨울 내내 활발하게 활동하면서 연못에서 수영을 하고 먹이를 찾아다닌다.

46
다음 중 위 본문의 글의 유형으로 가장 적합한 것은 무엇인가?
① 야생동물 잡지
② 재무 보고서
③ 환경에 대한 팸플릿
④ 잡식동물에 대한 논문

| 정답 | ①

| 해설 | 본문은 초식동물인 비버의 생태에 관해 전반적인 정보를 제공하고 있으며, 때문에 야생동물에 관한 내용을 다루는 잡지에 수록된 것으로 볼 수 있다.

47
다음 중 비버를 향한 저자의 태도와 가장 가까운 것은 무엇인가?
① 분개한
② 동정적인
③ 무심한
④ 흠모하는

| 정답 | ④

| 해설 | 저자는 비버에 대해 어떤 감정을 가지기보다는 비버의 특성이나 성향에 대해 객관적으로 서술하고 있다. 하지만 비버에 대한 서술들이 비버에 대해 긍정적으로 언급하고 있으므로 보기 중에서 정답의 가능성이 있는 것은 ④뿐이다.

48 아래 문장이 들어가기에 가장 알맞은 장소는 어디인가?

> 이러한 특질 덕분에 비버는 시간당 최대 5마일의 속력으로 수영할 수 있다.

① [1]　　　　　　　　　　　　② [2]
③ [3]　　　　　　　　　　　　④ [4]

| 정답 | ③

| 해설 | 주어진 문장 앞에서는 "이러한 특질"에 관한 설명이 있을 것이며, "이러한 특질"은 수영과 관련이 있을 것임을 유추할 수 있다. 이를 감안하고 주어진 문장을 대입해 보면, 뒷발과 꼬리의 형태를 묘사하면서 이것들이 비버의 수영 능력과 관련이 있을 것임을 유추할 수 있는 [3]에 주어진 문장이 들어가야 함을 알 수 있다.

49 빈칸 (A)에 가장 알맞은 것은 무엇인가?

① 양도할 수 없게　　　　　　② 전략적으로
③ 무분별하게　　　　　　　　④ 형언할 수 없게

| 정답 | ②

| 해설 | 빈칸이 들어간 문장을 보면, 비버의 집인 롯지가 연못에 중앙에 위치해 있고 수중으로 헤엄쳐 들어가는 것 이외에는 롯지에 도달할 수 있는 방법이 없음을 알 수 있다. 이는 위험 회피를 위한 '전략적인' 위치 선정의 결과로 유추할 수 있다. 따라서 답은 ②이다.

50 본문에 따르면 다음 중 사실인 것은 무엇인가?

① 비버는 중간 크기의 설치류로 모든 종류의 식물과 뿌리를 먹는다.
② 비버는 노 형태의 꼬리를 사용하여 물 표면을 철썩 때리는 소리를 매우 크게 낼 수 있다.
③ 비버의 한 살배기 새끼들은 봄에 롯지를 영구히 떠난다.
④ 비버는 연못의 표면이 얼음으로 뒤덮였을 때는 수영을 하지 않는다.

| 정답 | ②

| 해설 | "수영을 하던 비버는 갑작스럽게 잠수를 하며 그 와중에 널찍한 꼬리로 물을 격렬하게 두드린다. 이를 통해 비버는 물 표면을 철썩 때리는 소리를 매우 크게 낼 수 있고, 이 소리는 멀리 떨어진 물 밖에서 그리고 물속에서 들린다(A swimming beaver will rapidly dive while forcefully slapping the water with its broad tail. This means that the beaver creates a loud slapping noise, which can be heard over large distances above and below water)." 여기서 답이 ②임을 쉽게 알 수 있다.
비버는 대형 설치류이기 때문에 ①은 답이 될 수 없다. 비버의 한 살배기 새끼들이 봄에 롯지를 영구히 떠난다는 내용은 본문에 등장하지 않으며, 따라서 ③은 답이 될 수 없다. "비버는 얼음 층이 연못 표면을 덮을지라도 겨울 내내 활발하게 활동하면서 연못에서 수영을 하고 먹이를 찾아다닌다(These animals are active all winter, swimming and foraging in their ponds even when a layer of ice covers the surface)." 이는 연못의 표면이 얼음으로 뒤덮였을 때는 수영을 하지 않는다는 ④의 내용과는 상반된 것이며, 따라서 ④는 답이 될 수 없다.

| 어휘 |
turn ⓥ (~한 상태로) 변하게[~되게] 만들다
burrow ⓥ 파고든다, 굴을 판다
suitable ⓐ 적합한, 알맞은
fell ⓥ (나무를) 베어 넘어뜨리다
lodge ⓝ 롯지; 비버의 굴[집]
extended family – 대가족
yearling ⓝ 한 살배기 동물
herbivore ⓝ 초식동물
twig ⓝ 잔가지
waddle ⓝ 뒤뚱거림
paddle ⓝ (배의) 노
attribute ⓝ 속성, 특질
startled ⓐ 놀란
forcefully ⓐⓓ 격렬하게
forage ⓥ 먹이를 찾다
omnivore ⓐ 잡식동물
sympathetic ⓐ 동정적인, 동정 어린
adoring ⓐ 흠모하는
indiscreetly ⓐⓓ 무분별하게
permanently ⓐⓓ 영구히

reengineer ⓥ 재설계하다, 재조직하다
bank ⓝ 둑, 제방
habitat ⓝ 서식지
gnaw ⓥ 갉아먹다, 물어뜯다
dwelling ⓝ 주거지, 주택
monogamous ⓐ 일부일처의, 일자일웅(一雌一雄)의
rodent ⓝ 설치류
bark ⓝ 나무껍질
ungainly ⓐ 어색한, 볼품없는
webbed ⓐ 물갈퀴가 있는
rudder ⓝ (배의) 키
surface ⓥ 수면으로 올라오다
frightened ⓐ 겁먹은
slap ⓥ 철썩 때리다[치다]
pamphlet ⓝ 팸플릿, 소논문
indignant ⓐ 분개한, 분해 하는
uninterested ⓐ 무(관)심한
inalienably ⓐⓓ 양도할 수 없게, 이양할 수 없게
indescribably ⓐⓓ 형언할 수 없게, 말로 다 할 수 없게

CHAPTER 04 인간

01	④	02	①	03	④	04	②	05	④	06	③	07	①	08	②	09	②	10	②
11	④	12	②	13	②	14	③	15	④	16	④	17	①	18	③	19	①	20	③
21	③	22	③	23	②	24	③	25	④	26	①	27	③	28	④	29	④	30	②
31	③	32	①	33	④	34	①	35	④										

[01-02] 한국외대 2007

일련의 뇌 스캐닝 실험에서 네덜란드 Groningen 대학의 신경과학자 Christian Keysers가 이끄는 연구팀은 피험자들의 전운동 피질(premotor cortex)에서 누군가 감자 칩을 먹거나 종이를 찢는 소리를 들었을 때 반응하는 뉴런들을 발견했다. 이 뉴런들은 피험자가 직접 비슷한 행동을 할 때도 반응했다. 소리만으로도 매우 강한 반응을 보인 사람들은 공감 능력을 측정하는 설문조사에서 더 높은 점수를 받았다. 거울 뉴런은 "당신이 보거나 듣는 타인의 행동을 당신이 직접 할 것처럼 만듭니다."라고 Keysers는 말한다. "비슷한 행동을 할 때 어떤 기분일지 정말 느끼게 되는 거죠." UCLA 연구진들에 따르면, 거울 뉴런은 글자에도 반응한다. 피험자들은 '복숭아를 한 입 물다.' 같은 문구를 읽기만 해도, 누군가 과일을 먹는 비디오를 시청했을 때와 같은 전운동피질 신경회로가 반응했다. 연구를 이끈 신경과학자들은 그것은 마치 뇌가 글자의 의미를 이해하면서 그 행동을 모방하는 것 같다고 말한다. 전통적으로, 과학자와 철학자들은 인간의 고등한 인지능력이 속하는 영역은 감각과 행동의 영역과는 다르다고 생각해 왔다. 그러나 신경과학자들이 발견한 것은, 그 능력은 본질적으로 육체와 연관되어 있다는 것이다.

01 지문에 따르면, 당신이 누군가 음료 캔을 따는 소리를 들었을 때 일어날 일로 다음 중 가장 적절한 것은?
① 당신은 신발과 양말을 벗는다.
② 당신은 인지 능력을 발휘하기 시작한다.
③ 당신은 깨어 있기 쉽지 않다는 것을 깨닫는다.
④ 당신은 캔을 따고 싶어진다.
⑤ 당신은 종이를 찢고 싶어진다.

| 정답 | ④

| 해설 | 지문의 주제인 거울 뉴런의 역할을 알고 있는지 묻는 문제이다. 거울 뉴런은 타인의 행동을 자신의 행동처럼 경험하고, 그 행동을 모방하고 싶도록 만든다. (Mirror neurons "transform what you see or hear other people do into what you would do yourself," Keysers says. 참조.) 따라서 ④가 적절하다.

02 다음 중 지문에서 알 수 없거나 유추할 수 없는 것은?

① 움직이면 거울 뉴런은 활동을 멈춘다.
② 거울 뉴런은 다양한 자극에 반응한다.
③ 누군가 복숭아를 베어 무는 소리가 들리면 당신의 거울 뉴런이 활성화된다.
④ 연구는 당신이 다른 사람들이 말하는 것을 들었을 때 어떻게 그들을 이해하는지에 대한 단서를 제공한다.
⑤ 연구에 따르면 어떤 사람들은 타인의 행동을 보는 것만으로도 그들에게 공감할 수 있다.

| 정답 | ①

| 해설 | 거울 뉴런은 소리와 행동뿐 아니라 글자에도 반응하므로 ②는 옳은 진술이다. 복숭아를 한입 무는 소리를 들었을 때 거울 뉴런이 반응했다는 내용이 있으므로 ③은 옳은 진술이다. 거울 뉴런의 반응이 강한 피험자들은 공감 능력이 탁월하다는 언급이 있으므로 ④, ⑤는 옳은 유추이다. 지문의 내용과 무관한 것은 ①이다.

| 어휘 |
a series of – 일련의
neuroscientist ⓝ 신경과학자
premotor cortex – 전운동피질
munch ⓥ 우적우적 먹다
flash ⓥ 번쩍이다, 신호를 보내다
display ⓥ 보이다, 전시하다
cue ⓝ 힌트, 암시
questionary ⓝ 질문지
put oneself in another person's shoes – 타인의 처지를 이해하다, 공감하다
mirror neuron – 거울 뉴런
trigger ⓥ 촉발하다, 일으키다
chomp ⓥ 쩝쩝 먹다
grasp ⓥ 파악하다, 움켜쥐다
sense ⓝ 감각, 지각, 의식
intrinsically ⓐⓓ 본질적으로, 내재적으로
flesh ⓝ 육체, 살

experiment ⓝ 실험
identify ⓥ 알아내다, 확인하다
light up – 불을 켜다, 환해지다, (신경이) 활동하다
rip ⓥ 찢다
subject ⓝ 피험자
in response to – ~에 대한 반응으로
score ⓥ 점수를 내다
gauge ⓥ 측정하다
transform ⓥ 바꾸다
circuit ⓝ 회로, 신경회로
simulate ⓥ ~인 척하다, 모의실험하다
cognitive ⓐ 인지의
faculty ⓝ 능력, 교수진
be tied to – ~와 연관되다

[03-04] 인하대 2015

우리 가운데 대부분은 긍정적 태도가 건강을 향상시키고 질병으로부터의 회복 속도를 높인다는 사실을 알고 있다. 하지만 이것이 과연 반대로도 작용할까? "체화된 인지"는 우리가 행동하는 방식이 어떻게 우리가 사고하는 방식과 느끼는 방식에 영향을 미치는지 기술하기 위해 심리학자들이 사용하는 용어이다. 이 매력적인 분야에 관한 초창기 연구를 보면, 이로 연필을 수평으로 물고 있으면 미소를 짓는 데 사용되는 근육이 활성화되기 때문에 우리의 뇌에 쾌락 신호를 보내게 되는 반면에 잔주름을 펴기 위해 보톡스 주사를 맞은 사람들은 시술 후 행복감을 더 느끼게 된다는 것이 입증되었다. 만일 마사지를 받는 동안 울어 본 경험이 있다면 근육이 단순히 조직과 섬유질이 합해진 것은 아님을 알게 될 것이다. 근육에는 우리의 정서적 삶에 대한 섬세한 흔적이 담겨 있으며 정신의 작용을 통한 영향력 없이도 감정을 불러일으킬 수 있는 역량이 존재한다. 우리의 몸은 감정의 시초가 되며 정서적 경험의 강력한 공동 창조자가 될 수 있다. 그리고 이를 입증하는 연구도 존재한다.

03

다음 중 빈칸에 가장 적합한 것은 무엇인가?

① 거울
② 주인
③ 저장소
④ 시초

| 정답 | ④

| 해설 | 본문의 핵심은 "마음이 몸에 영향을 주는 것처럼 몸도 마음에 영향을 준다"이다. 이를 감안하고 문제를 보면, 빈칸에는 "우리의 몸은 감정이 생겨나게 만드는 역할을 할 수 있다"는 취지에서 ④가 적합하다.

04

다음 중 본문의 주제에 대한 적절한 예가 아닌 것은 무엇인가?

① 용기가 없을 때는 팔을 활짝 펴라.
② 기분이 좋지 않을 때는 행복한 추억을 떠올려라.
③ 외롭다는 기분이 들면 뜨거운 물로 목욕하라.
④ 창의성을 발휘해야겠다면 춤 강습을 받아라.

| 정답 | ②

| 해설 | 본문은 마음이 몸에 영향을 주고 몸도 마음에 영향을 미친다는 내용을 담고 있다. 이를 감안하고 보기를 보면, ②는 몸과는 관계없이 정신적인 내용만을 다루고 있지만, 나머지는 몸을 통해 정신적 효과를 얻는 내용을 다루고 있다. 따라서 답은 ②이다.

| 어휘 |
the other way around – 반대로, 거꾸로
fascinating ⓐ 대단히 흥미로운, 매력적인
laughter lines – 잔주름
delicate ⓐ 섬세한, 미묘한
executive ⓐ 집행의, 운영의
reservoir ⓝ 저수지, 저장소
embodied cognition – 체화된 인지
horizontally ⓐⓓ 수평으로
amalgamation ⓝ 합동, 합병
engender ⓥ 낳다, 불러일으키다
originator ⓝ 시초, 창시자
timid ⓐ 소심한, 용기가 없는

[05-07] 한국외대 2009

당신이 잠든 사이, 청각은 약해지기는 해도 여전히 작동하고 있다. 이 사실은 매일 아침 알람이 울릴 때 너무도 분명해진다. 우리가 자는 동안에도 소리를 인식할 뿐 아니라 그 소리의 의미를 정보 처리한다는 것을 보여주는 훨씬 더 정교한 방법이 있다. 이 사실을 확인하기 위해 잠든 사람을 대상으로 테스트해 볼 수 있다. 먼저, 스푼으로 빈 잔을 두드려서 종소리를 두세 번 낸다. 이 소리들은 너무 시끄럽지도 너무 조용하지도 않고 평상시 대화에서 들을 수 있을 정도의 소음이다. 대부분의 경우, 잠든 사람은 이 테스트 소리에 거의, 혹은 전혀 반응하지 않을 것이다. 이번에는 잠든 사람의 귀에 대고 조용히 그의 이름을 두세 번 부른다. 이 속삭임은 좀 전의 종소리에 비하면 반 정도의 소음이지만, 많은 피험자들이 깨거나 최소한 반응하는 움직임을 보일 것이다. 이름은 우리가 항상 귀 기울이는 매우 특별하고 개인적인 자극이다. 예를 들어 우리가 대화하고 있는 사람 주변에서 누군가가 우리 이름을 말할 때도 분명히 들을 수 있다. 잠들어 있을 때도, 우리는 주변의 모든 소음들 가운데서 그 특별한 소리 자극을 인지할 수 있고 그 자극들을 특별하게 정보 처리하고 주의를 기울인다.

05

지문의 주제는 무엇인가?

① 잠든 사람은 보통 알람 소리를 잘 듣지 못한다.
② 잠든 사람은 분명한 종소리에 반응하는 움직임을 보인다.
③ 사람을 깨울 때 다른 알람 소리보다 더 효과적인 알람 소리가 있다.
④ 사람들은 잠들어 있을 때도 특정한 소리를 정보 처리한다.
⑤ 잠든 사람의 청각을 테스트하기 위해서는 정교한 방법이 필요하다.

| 정답 | ④

| 해설 | 첫 문장이 주제문이다. "While you sleep your sense of hearing is diminished but still working."를 참조하면, 잠든 동안에도 소리를 인식할 수 있다는 주제를 적절하게 요약한 것은 보기 ④이다.

06

다음 중 빈칸 ⓐ에 가장 적절한 것은?

① 왜냐하면
② 그러나
③ ~에도 불구하고
④ 그래서
⑤ 반면에

| 정답 | ③

| 해설 | 이름을 부르는 소리가 크지 않았는데도 잠든 사람들은 소리에 반응했다. 문맥상 양보 접속사가 필요하다. 보기 ②, ④, ⑤는 모두 부사이므로 선택하지 않도록 주의한다. 따라서 ③이 정답이다.

07

다음 중 밑줄 ⓑ가 지칭하는 것은?

① 불린 이름
② 사적인 대화
③ 애정을 담아 속삭인 말
④ 옆 사람의 코 고는 소리
⑤ 빈 잔의 종소리

| 정답 | ①

| 해설 | 문맥상 앞부분의 "the special sound stimuli", "our names are uttered", 즉 이름을 부르는 소리를 지칭한다. 따라서 ①이 정답이다.

| 어휘 | sense of hearing – 청각
painfully ⓐd 극명하게, 고통스럽게
go off – (종소리, 경보음 등이) 울리다
demonstrate ⓥ 보여주다, 시연하다
process ⓥ (정보)처리하다
chiming ⓝ 종소리
tap ⓥ 두드리다
encounter ⓥ 만나다, 마주치다
instance ⓝ 예, 경우
whisper ⓥ 속삭이다

diminish ⓥ 줄이다
obvious ⓐ 명백한
subtle ⓐ 섬세한, 정교한
be aware of – ~을 인식하다, 알다
subject ⓝ 피험자
noise ⓝ 소음
loudness ⓝ 큰 목소리, 소란스러움
speech ⓝ 말, 연설
reaction ⓝ 반응
awaken ⓥ 깨다, 각성하다

sign ⓝ 신호, 조짐
stimuli ⓝ 자극들
utter ⓥ 말하다, 언급하다
pick up – ~을 알아채다
attention ⓝ 관심, 주목

personal ⓐ 개인적인
be on the lookout for – ~을 주의 깊게 살피다
converse with – ~와 대화하다
detect ⓥ 알아채다, 추적하다

[08-10] 숙명여대 2009

안락사란 환자의 이익을 위해 환자를 고의로 죽이는 행위이다. 대부분의 경우에는, 죽어가는 환자의 요구가 있을 때 안락사가 집행되지만 환자가 그러한 요구를 할 수 없는 경우의 안락사도 있다.

안락사는 고통스러운 도덕적 문제들을 제기한다. 예를 들어 "극심한 고통에 시달리는 말기 환자의 생명을 다른 사람이 끝내는 것이 정말 옳은 일일까?", "때로는 안락사가 옳다면, 어떤 상황에서 옳은 걸까?" 안락사에 대한 윤리적, 종교적 논쟁의 중심에는 인간 존재의 의미와 가치에 대한, 인간에게 삶과 죽음의 문제를 스스로 결정할 권리가 있는지에 대한 서로 다른 생각들이 있다. 일부에서는 안락사가 도덕적으로 옳다고 해도 결코 허용되어서는 안 된다고 생각한다. 안락사가 남용될 뿐 아니라 살인을 은폐하는 수단으로도 악용될 수 있기 때문이다.

08
지문에 따르면 다음 중 사실은 무엇인가?
① 안락사는 금지되어야 한다.
② 안락사 문제에 대해서는 더 많은 고민이 필요하다.
③ 안락사 시행 여부는 부모의 결정에 맡겨야 한다.
④ 안락사 결정 과정에 가족은 결코 개입해서는 안 된다.
⑤ 정부는 환자를 위해 안락사를 합법화해야 한다.

| 정답 | ②

| 해설 | 안락사를 둘러싼 윤리적, 종교적 갈등이 지문의 주제이므로 ②가 적절하다. 지문은 찬반의 입장을 객관적으로 상술하고 있으므로 찬반 중 어느 한쪽의 입장에 치우친 내용의 보기는 선택하지 않도록 주의한다.

09
다음 중 밑줄 친 ⓐ를 가장 잘 대체할 수 있는 것은?
① 낙천적인
② 괴로운
③ 무의식적인
④ 낙관적인
⑤ 간단한

| 정답 | ②

| 해설 | 'agonizing'은 '고통스러운'의 뜻이므로 '괴로운, 성가신'의 의미인 'tormenting'과 가장 의미가 비슷하다. ②는 문맥상 안락사는 윤리적, 종교적 고민과 갈등을 불러일으켰다는 내용에 부합한다.

10 다음 중 지문의 제목으로 가장 적절할 것은?
① 안락사 금지
② 안락사에 대한 상반된 견해들
③ 인간의 자유의지의 중요성
④ 범죄와 처벌
⑤ 의학 기술의 발전

| 정답 | ②

| 해설 | 지문은 안락사를 둘러싼 상반된 입장들을 상술하고 있으므로 ②가 제목으로 적절하다. 보기 ①은 안락사 반대 입장만을 요약한 지엽적 제목이므로 선택하지 않도록 주의한다.

| 어휘 | euthanasia ⓝ 안락사
benefit ⓝ 이익, 이해
ask for – ~을 부탁하다
make a request – 요청하다
agonizing ⓐ 고통스러운
terminally ill patient – 말기 환자
circumstance ⓝ 상황
religious ⓐ 종교적인
existence ⓝ 존재
for oneself – 스스로
abuse ⓥ 남용[오용]하다, 욕설하다

deliberate ⓐ 고의적인, 의도적인
carry out – ~을 집행[수행]하다, 실시하다
instance ⓝ 예, 경우
raise a question – 질문을 제기하다
moral ⓐ 도덕적인
severe ⓐ 극심한, 가혹한
ethical ⓐ 윤리적인
argument ⓝ 논쟁, 말다툼
issue ⓝ 문제, 사안
allow ⓥ 허용하다
cover ⓝ 은폐, 위장

[11-13] 숭실대 2009

성장 호르몬, 일명 GH는 많은 세포조직을 활성화하며 매우 폭넓은 영향을 미친다. GH는 세포의 아미노산 흡수를 도와 단백질 합성을 활성화함으로써 성장을 촉진한다. 또한 지방조직의 지방 분비를 촉진해서, 지방이 에너지원으로 이용될 수 있도록 신진대사를 활성화한다.

적절한 체내 GH 수치는 정상적인 성장에 필수적이다. 이 사실은 몸에 문제가 생겼을 때 극명하게 드러난다. 어릴 때 GH가 과도하게 분비되면 거인증(뇌하수체 호르몬 과다분비로 인한 거인)이 생긴다. 이 병이 있는 사람들은 키가 7피트에서 9피트에 달한다. 반대로, 어릴 때 뇌하수체 기능 저하로 GH가 정상 수치보다 적게 분비될 경우, 흔히 소인으로 불리는 뇌하수체성 난쟁이가 된다. 미국에는 수천 명의 뇌하수체성 난쟁이가 있다. 최근까지도, 성장 호르몬 결핍증의 치료는 어렵고 비쌌다. 뇌하수체성 난쟁이 한 명의 성장을 촉진하기 위해서는 여러 명의 몸에서 추출한 모든 GH를 매일 주사해야 했다. 그러나 GH는 단백질이기 때문에, 이제는 DNA 재조합 기술을 통해 새로운 방식으로 GH를 만들 수 있다.

성인의 GH 수치가 갑자기 증가하면, 말단비대증이라는 병이 생긴다. 이 기형 질환은 정상적인 시점에서 멈췄던 성장이 이상하게도 다시 시작되는 병이다. 그러나 이 성장은 손, 발, 턱, 코, 일부 체내 기관 등 연골이 남아 있는 곳에서만 일어난다.

11 빈칸 ⓐ에 적절한 단어를 고르시오.
① 그러나
② 그러므로
③ 말하자면, 그건 그렇고
④ 반대로

| 정답 | ④

| 해설 | 빈칸 앞은 GH 과다분비, 빈칸 뒤는 GH 과소분비에 대한 설명이므로 대조 연결사 Conversely가 적절하다. 보기 ①의 However는 역접 연결사이기는 하지만 완전한 대조를 표현하지는 않으므로 선택하지 않도록 주의한다. 정답은 ④이다.

12

다음 중 밑줄 친 ⓑ의 바른 순서는?
① GH levels should rise
② Should GH levels rise
③ Should rise GH levels
④ Rise GH levels should

| 정답 | ②

| 해설 | 가정(조건)절의 if가 생략될 때는 주어 동사가 도치된다. 'If GH levels should rise' ⇨ 'Should GH levels rise' 따라서 ②가 정답이다.

13

지문에 따르면 다음 중 사실은 무엇인가?
① GH 과다수치는 뇌하수체성 난쟁이의 원인이다.
② 미국에는 수천 명의 GH 결핍 환자들이 있다.
③ 성인은 GH 수치가 감소하면서 다시 성장이 시작될 수도 있다.
④ 건강한 한 명이 여러 명의 GH 결핍 환자들을 도울 수 있다.

| 정답 | ②

| 해설 | "There are several thousand pituitary dwarfs in the United States today."를 참조하면, 미국에는 수천 명의 뇌하수체성 난쟁이가 있다는 구체적인 언급이 지문에 있으므로 ②가 정답이다. 보기 ④의 경우, 한 명의 GH 결핍 환자를 돕기 위해 여러 명의 몸에서 추출한 GH가 필요하다는 지문의 내용과 상반되므로 선택하지 않도록 주의한다.

| 어휘 | growth hormone – 성장 호르몬
activate ⓥ 활성화하다
stimulate ⓥ 자극하다
uptake ⓝ 흡수
accelerate ⓥ 가속화하다
in addition – 게다가
in effect – 사실상
metabolism ⓝ 신진대사
normal ⓐ 정상적인
excessive ⓐ 과도한, 지나친
giantism ⓝ 거인증
range A from B – 범위가 A에서 B에 이르다
midget ⓝ 소인
require ⓥ 필요로 하다, 요구하다
be isolated from – ~에서 추출되다
broad ⓐ 폭넓은, 일반적인
tissue ⓝ 세포조직
promote ⓥ 촉진하다
amino acid – 아미노산
protein synthesis – 단백질 합성
release ⓝ 분비
shift ⓥ 바꾸다
proper ⓐ 적절한
obvious ⓐ 명백한
secretion ⓝ 분비
condition ⓝ 질병, 상태
dwarf ⓝ 난쟁이
deficiency ⓝ 결핍(증)
injection ⓝ 주사, 투약
protein ⓝ 단백질

recombinant ⓐ 재조합의
on time – 시간을 어기지 않고 정각에, 제때
restrict ⓥ 제한하다
jaw ⓝ 턱

acromegaly ⓝ 말단비대증
resume ⓥ 다시 시작되다(하다)
persist ⓥ 지속하다, 고집하다
internal organ – 체내 기관

[14-17] 이화여대 2009

인간 복제에 대한 윤리적 우려들 중 하나는 현재의 복제 기술 현황과 관련된 위험과 불확실성이다. 복제 기술은 아직 인간을 대상으로 테스트되지 않았기 때문에 과학자들은 돌연변이나 기타 생물학적 부작용의 가능성을 배재하지 못한다. 그러나 복제 논쟁에서 가장 중요한 윤리적 문제들은 복제의 실패 가능성이 아니라 복제 성공의 결과에 대한 것이다. 과학자들이 앞서 언급했듯 위험 없이 인간을 복제할 수 있다고 가정한다면, 복제 인간의 건강과 행복에 관해 어떤 우려가 생길까?

복제에 반대하는 일부는 복제 인간들이 도덕적으로 매우 부당한 취급을 받을 것이라고 생각한다. 이러한 부당한 대우는 대부분 Joel Feinberg가 "열린 미래에 대한 권리"라고 부른 것들을 인정하기를 거부하는 것이다. 예를 들어, 복제된 아이는 자신이 복제된 성인과 끊임없이 비교될 것이고 따라서 지나친 기대에 억눌릴 것이다. 더 심각한 경우, 부모는 아이가 성장하고 발전할 수 있는 기회마저 제한할 수 있다. 예를 들어, 야구선수를 복제한 아이에게는 야구선수라는 직업과 상관없는 교육적 기회는 주어지지 않을 수도 있다. 결국 부모의 행동이나 태도와는 상관없이, 아이는 자신은 복제물이지 "진짜(original)"가 아니라는 생각에 시달리게 될 것이고 일부의 주장처럼 자존감이나 개성, 존엄성을 지키기 어려울 것이다.

14 지문의 제목으로 적절한 것은 무엇인가?
① 인간 복제의 기술적 위험성
② 복제 인간에 대한 억압적인 기대
③ 인간 복제의 윤리적 측면
④ 열린 미래에 대한 권리

| 정답 | ③

| 해설 | 세 번째 문장이 주제문이다. 인간 복제 논쟁의 핵심은 기술의 위험성이 아니라 윤리적 우려이다. 두 번째 문단은 복제 인간이 겪게 될 대우의 비윤리성과 그 부정적 결과를 상술하고 있다. 따라서 ③이 정답이다.

15 다음 중 빈칸 ⓐ과 ⓒ에 적절하지 않은 것은?
① 우려
② 두려움
③ 당황
④ 황폐화

| 정답 | ④

| 해설 | 보기에는 문맥상 인간 복제에 관한 '우려, 두려움' 등이 필요하다. '황폐함'을 뜻하는 보기 ④는 문맥에 맞지 않는다.

16 다음 중 빈칸 ⓑ와 ⓓ에 적절한 단어는 무엇인가?
① 실패 – 지지자
② 창시자 – 도전자
③ 성취 – 옹호하다
④ 성공 – 반대자

| 정답 | ④

| 해설 | 보기 ②는 'not A but B'의 대조 논리를 완성하는 단어로 채운다. 인간 복제에 대한 윤리적 우려는 복제의 '실패'가 아니라 복제의 '성공'에 대한 것이다. 보기 ④는 that절의 주장을 펼칠 만한 사람들로 빈칸을 완성한다. 복제 인간들이 부당한 대우를 받게 될 것이라고 걱정하는 사람들은 복제 기술에 '반대'하는 사람들일 것이다. 따라서 ④가 정답이다.

17 다음 중 빈칸 ⓔ에 적절하지 않은 것은?
① 사생활
② 개성
③ 존엄성
④ 자존감

| 정답 | ①

| 해설 | 빈칸은 인과의 논리로 완성한다. 아이가 자신을 'original'이 아닌 복제물에 불과하다고 생각하면 그 결과 '자존감, 개성, 존엄성'을 지킬 수 없을 것이다. 빈칸에 적절한 단어들은 'original'과 관련된 속성이므로 "privacy(사생활)"는 적절치 않다. 따라서 ①이 정답이다.

| 어휘 |
ethical ⓐ 윤리적인
involve ⓥ 포함하다
uncertainty ⓝ 불확실성
current state – 현황
rule out – ~을 배제하다, 제거하다
biological ⓐ 생물학적인
consequence ⓝ 결과, 중요성
incur ⓥ 수반하다, 초래하다
welfare ⓝ 건강과 행복, 복지
morally ⓐⓓ 도덕적으로
denial ⓝ 부인, 거부
compare ⓥ 비교하다
be burden with – ~를 짐으로 지다, 부담에 시달리다
oppressive ⓐ 억압적인, 숨 막히게 하는
limit ⓥ 제한하다
regardless of – ~와 상관없이
attitude ⓝ 태도, 관점
self-worth ⓝ 자존감
dignity ⓝ 존엄성

human clone – 인간 복제
risk ⓝ 위험(성)
be associated with – ~와 관련 있다
subject ⓝ 피실험자, 실험 대상
mutation ⓝ 돌연변이
debate ⓝ 논쟁, 논란
assume ⓥ 추정하다, ~인 척하다
mentioned above – 위에서 언급한
wrong ⓥ 부당하게 대우하다
significant ⓐ 상당한, 중요한
constantly ⓐⓓ 계속해서
thereby ⓐⓓ 그렇기 때문에, 그로 인해서
expectation ⓝ 기대
be in line with – ~와 어울리다, 일치하다
conduct ⓝ 행동, 행실
copy ⓝ 복제(본)
individuality ⓝ 개성
sustain ⓥ 지탱하다, 유지하다

[18-20] 단국대 2013

종종 유전적 원인으로 인해 이런저런 중독에 걸리는 경향이 존재한다. 물론 이는 오직 유전만이 중독을 유발하기에 충분한 원인이 된다는 말은 아니며, 중독이 지닌 특정한 속성은 유전적인 영향을 받기도 한다는 의미이다. 예를 들어 알코올 중독자는 부모나 조부모가 알코올 중독에 걸렸을 가능성이 있으며 알코올에 대해 대단히 강한 "양성" 반응을 보일 수 있다. 정신적 외상 또한 중독을 형성하고 이를 조장할 수 있다. 화학 물질을 남용하는 사람들은 어린 시절에 정서적인 외상에 시달린 이력을 보유했을 수 있으며 아니면 참전군인들 사이에서 발견되는 것과 같은 외상 후 스트레스 이력을 보유했을 수 있다. 중독과 관련하여 또 한 가지 중요한 요소로는 수치심을 들 수 있다. 수치심은 우리가 특정한 기준에 미치지 못했다는 생각이 들 때 갖게 되는 매우 강력한 감정이다. 수치심은 종종 다른 감정으로 가장하여 나타나지만 일반적으로는 중독자들 사이에서 중독의 원인이자 결과로 나타난다. 수치심은 중독이 진행되면서 급증한다. 중독을 야기하는 마지막 하나의 원인 제공 요인은 불안 우울증으로, 압박으로 인해 앞으로 두 시간이 인생에서 가장 중요한 시기인 마냥 느껴지는 것과 같은 유형의 우울증이다. 불안 우울증에 걸리면 마음이 불안해지는 기분이 들며, 사람을 하루 종일 침대에 누워 있게 만들어 일어나거나 옷을 입는 것조차도 못하게 만드는 낙담 우울증과는 큰 차이가 있다.

18 본문의 제목으로 가장 알맞은 것은 무엇인가?
① 화학 중독의 핵심 요소
② 중독으로부터의 회복
③ 중독에 영향을 미치는 요소
④ 중독 상태가 아닐 때의 정서불안

| 정답 | ③

| 해설 | 본문은 유전 · 정신적 외상 · 수치심 · 불안 우울증 등 중독을 야기하는 요인들을 열거하고 있다. 따라서 답은 ③이다.

19 다음 중 빈칸에 가장 알맞은 것은 무엇인가?
① 불안한
② 차분한
③ 굴욕감을 느끼는
④ 우호적인

| 정답 | ①

| 해설 | 빈칸이 들어간 문장은 문맥상 불안 우울증을 수식하는 말이며, 따라서 빈칸의 단어는 '불안'과 의미상 비슷해야 한다. 그러므로 답은 ①이다.

20 다음 중 본문에 따르면 사실인 것은 무엇인가?
① 유전적 요인은 알코올 중독 증상의 형성에 사소한 역할을 한다.
② 불안 우울증 및 낙담 우울증 모두 중독으로 이어진다.
③ 부끄러운 감정은 중독과 결정적인 상관관계가 있다.
④ 약물에 익숙해지면 힘 빠진 감정적 반응을 보이게 된다.

| 정답 | ③

| 해설 | "수치심은 종종 다른 감정으로 가장하여 나타나지만 일반적으로는 중독자들 사이에서 중독의 원인이자 결과로 나타난다(It often masquerades as other feelings, but it is commonly found in addicts both as a cause and a result of the addiction)." 따라서 답은 ③이다.

유전적 요인은 알코올 중독 발현의 중요 요인으로 제시되어 있으며 결코 사소한 요인 정도에 그치지 않으므로 ①은 답이 될 수 없고, 불안 우울증은 중독과 상관관계가 깊지만 낙담 우울증과의 관계에 관해서는 본문에 언급된 바 없으므로 ② 또한 답이 될 수 없다. 마지막으로 ④는 본문에 언급된 바 없다.

| 어휘 | inclination ⓝ 성향, 경향
sufficient ⓐ 충분한
masquerade ⓥ 가장하다
contributor ⓝ 원인 제공자
sedate ⓐ 차분한
amicable ⓐ 우호적인, 원만한
positive ⓐ 결정적인

heredity ⓝ 유전
foster ⓥ 조장하다, 조성하다
spiral upward - 급등하다, 급증하다
agitated ⓐ 불안해하는, 동요된
humiliate ⓥ 굴욕감을 주다
trivial ⓐ 사소한
inert ⓐ 기력이 없는, 힘 빠진

[21-22] 한국외대 2013

과학자들은 뇌의 성장과 노화 방식에 관심을 갖고 있다. 아이가 두 살이 되기 전에 뇌가 갑작스럽게 성장 및 발전하는 시기가 있다. 이 초기 성장 및 발달 시기에는 신체에 수십억 개의 신경세포가 새로 생성된다. 각각의 신경세포는 수천 개의 다른 신경세포에 연결되면서 수조 개의 연결이 이루어진다. 하지만 세 살 이후엔 새로운 과정이 시작된다. 연결 가운데 많이 사용된 것이 더욱 강해지고 살아남는다. 많이 사용되지 않은 연결은 약해지고 상실된다. 예를 들어 어렸을 때 읽으라고 책을 받은 아이는 네 살이 되면 책을 읽는 법을 배울 수 있다. 반면에 어렸을 때 읽으라고 책을 받지 않은 아이는 책을 읽는 데 어려움을 겪을 수 있다. 이러한 과정은 지속되며 우리의 뇌는 나이가 들 때까지 자극과 경험에 민감해진다. 신체 및 정신적으로 활동적인 노인들은 여전히 신경 연결을 새로 만들고 유지할 수 있다.

21 다음 중 본문의 주제로 가장 알맞은 것은 무엇인가?
① 뇌의 기능
② 뇌의 손상
③ 뇌의 발달
④ 뇌의 활동

| 정답 | ③

| 해설 | 본문은 뇌가 어떻게 성장하고, 발달하며, 노화하는지를 말하고 있다. 따라서 답으로 가장 적합한 것은 ③이다.

22 다음 중 본문에 따르면 사실인 것은 무엇인가?
① 노화는 신경 연결을 강하게 만들 수 있다.
② 노인은 새로운 신경 연결을 만들 수 없다.
③ 뇌의 발달은 균일한 비율로 이루어지지 않는다.
④ 신경 연결은 세 살 이후 왕성하게 벌어지기 시작한다.

| 정답 | ③

| 해설 | 본문에 따르면 태어나서 두 살 때까지는 뇌가 갑작스럽게 성장 및 발달하다가, 세 살 이후에는 많이 사용한 것은 발달하고 그렇지 않은 것은 쇠퇴하게 된다. 그 결과 뇌의 발달에 개인차가 생길 수밖에 없다. 따라서 답은 ③이다.

| 어휘 | surge ⓝ 급증, 급등
stimulation ⓝ 자극
uniform ⓐ 균일한, 한결같은
sensitive ⓐ 민감한
neural ⓐ 신경의
robustly ⓐⓓ 원기 왕성하게, 튼튼하게

[23-24] 성균관대 2013

지난 50년 동안 인간의 판단력을 연구하는 연구자들은 우리가 위험에 관한 판단을 내릴 때 감정에 의존한다는 사실을 점차 깨닫게 되었다. 우리는 두뇌가 수집하는 새로운 정보를 일일이 전부 다 곰곰이 생각할 수는 없다. 따라서 우리의 감정은 우리에게 지름길 역할을 하며, 수집한 정보에 관해 눈 깜짝할 사이에 결정을 내리도록 돕는다. 불확실성이 높을수록 우리는 이러한 지름길을 더 많이 사용한다. 이는 우리에겐 좋은 일이다. 신중한 사고로부터 감정을 제거하는 뇌 손상을 입은 사람들은 제 기능을 다 하지 못한다. 그런 사람들은 심지어 간단한 결정조차도 내리지 못한다. 따라서 우리는 세상을 이해하기 위해서 감정을 필요로 한다. 하지만 우리의 감정은 또한 우리를 타락시킬 수 있다. 특히 평생 지켜야 할 가치가 있는 규칙의 예외에 마주했을 때 더욱 그러하다. 두뇌가 취하는 지름길은 어느 정도는 예측 가능한 편견을 수반한다. 실험에 따르면 사람들은 자신이 생생하게 상상할 수 있는 일이 벌어질 기회를 확실히 과대평가한다. 만일 우리가 새로운 것을 보게 되면 우리는 우리가 이해할 수 있는 생각의 틀 내에 그것을 맞춰 넣으려 한다.

23

본문의 제목으로 가장 알맞은 것은 "위험 관리법"이다.
① 인간 판단의 한계
② 위험 관리법
③ 인간의 실수에 대응하는 방법
④ 결정을 내리는 과정에서 감정보다 이성이 앞서는 현상
⑤ 정보화 시대의 위험 요소

| 정답 | ②

| 해설 | 우리 인간은 위험에 관한 판단을 내릴 때 감정에 의존하며, 이를 통해 위기 상황이 닥쳐도 모든 것들을 세심하게 살필 필요 없이 바로 판단을 내려 위기를 회피할 수 있도록 되어 있다. 하지만 이런 감정 때문에 오히려 편견에 빠져 판단을 그르칠 수 있다.
즉, 본문은 위험을 회피하고 관리하기 위해 감정을 어떻게 활용하는지를 설명하고 있다. 따라서 답은 ②이다.

24

다음 중 빈칸에 가장 알맞은 것은 무엇인가?
① 비슷하게   ② 논리적으로
③ 하지만   ④ 게다가
⑤ 따라서

| 정답 | ③

| 해설 | 빈칸 앞까지의 본문 내용은 위험 판단을 위한 감정의 필요성에 관해 논하고 있지만, 빈칸 뒤에서부터는 감정의 위험성에 관해 논하고 있다. 즉, 빈칸을 경계로 앞과 뒤 내용이 서로 상반된다. 따라서 답은 서로 상반된 사항을 이어 주는 ③이다.

| 어휘 | rely on – ~에 의존하다
shortcut ⓝ 지름길
calculation ⓝ 계산, 숙고, 신중한 사고
lead ~ astray – ~을 잘못된 방향으로 이끌다, ~을 타락시키다
encounter ⓥ 마주하다, 접하다
reliably ⓐⓓ 확실하게
vividly ⓐⓓ 선명하게, 생생하게
logically ⓐⓓ 논리적으로

mull over – ~에 대해 숙고하다, 곰곰이 생각하다
split-second ⓐ 순식간의, 눈 깜짝할 사이의

exception ⓝ 예외
overestimate ⓥ 과대평가하다
similarly ⓐⓓ 비슷하게, 유사하게

[25-26] 한양대 2013

연구진은 과거 문헌에서 악몽의 범주에 속하는 것으로 분류되었지만 서로 혼동되는 두 가지 현상을 확인했다. 한편으로는 진짜로 악몽을 꾸는 경우, 즉 실제로 구체적인 내용의 꿈을 꾸는 현상을 들 수 있다. 다른 한편으로는 "야경증"을 들 수 있는데, (어린아이인 경우를 종종 포함해) 사람이 자다가 갑자기 무척 두려워하면서 깨는데 꿈을 꾼 기억도 없고 때로는 소리를 지르거나 무아지경 상태에서 몽유병 환자처럼 자리를 뜨곤 하는 현상이다. 야경증은 불안해하는 부모의 눈에는 아무리 무섭게 비추더라도, 실제로는 심각하게 위험한 경우가 거의 없다. 몽유병자가 열려 있는 창문에 가까이 있는 침대에서 잠을 자거나 발코니에 위치한 침대에서 잠을 자지 않도록 하는 것과 같이 상식적인 예방 조치를 취하는 것 이외에는 야경증에 대해 딱히 어떻게 할 수 있는 것은 없다. 아이의 야경증은 어느 정도는 일관성 있는 수면 일정을 준수하고 과도한 피로에 시달리지 않도록 하면 감소한다. 보통은 과도한 염려나 약물 치료는 피해야 한다.

25

윗글의 내용을 읽고 추론할 때 빈칸에 들어갈 가장 알맞은 것을 고르시오.

> 야경증을 겪는 아이의 부모는 아이들이 겁내는 것만큼이나 겁을 낸다.

① 야경증을 중요하지 않은 것으로 일축하는 경향이 있다.
② 가능한 한 빨리 의사의 진찰을 받아야 한다.
③ 어렸을 때 아이와 마찬가지로 고생했다.
④ 아이들이 겁내는 것만큼이나 부모도 겁을 낸다.

| 정답 | ④

| 해설 | 우선 "사람이 자다가 갑자기 무척 두려워하면서 깨는데 꿈을 꾼 기억도 없고 때로는 소리를 지르거나 무아지경 상태에서 몽유병 환자처럼 자리를 뜨곤 하는 경우(the sleeper, often a child, suddenly awakes in great fright with no memory of a dream, often screaming and sometimes going off in a sleepwalking trance)"를 보면 아이가 야경증을 두려워한다는 것을 알 수 있고, "불안해하는 부모의 눈에는 아무리 무섭게 비추더라도(no matter how horrifying they may appear to anxious parents)"를 보면 부모도 아이만큼이나 야경증을 두려워하고 있음을 알 수 있다. 따라서 답은 ④이다.

26

밑줄 친 "confounded"가 의미하는 것으로 가장 알맞은 것을 고르시오.
① 혼란스러운
② 설명된
③ 개발된
④ 인정받지 못하는

| 정답 | ①

| 해설 | 밑줄 친 'confounded'는 '혼동되는, 혼란을 일으키는' 등의 의미를 지니며, 보기 중에서 이와 의미상 가장 가까운 것은 '혼란스러운' 등의 의미를 가진 ①의 confused이다.

| 어휘 | literature ⓝ 문헌
confound ⓥ 혼동하다, 혼란시키다
night terror – 야간 공포, 야경증
fright ⓝ 놀람, 두려움
go off – 자리를 뜨다
trance ⓝ 가수면 상태, 무아지경
commonsense ⓐ 상식적인
precaution ⓝ 예방책, 예방 조치
consistent ⓐ 일관성 있는, 한결같은
excessive ⓐ 지나친, 과도한
dismiss ⓥ 일축하다, 묵살하다
inconsequential ⓐ 중요하지 않은, 하찮은
unappreciated ⓐ 인정받지 못하는

[27-28] 서울여대 2014

자전거를 타는 것과 같이 새로운 신체적 기술을 학습하고 나면 뇌 속에 해당 신체적 기술의 기억이 영구적으로 저장되기까지는 여섯 시간이 걸린다. 하지만 기억과 정신에 대한 연구 결과에 따르면 위와는 다른 새로운 기술을 학습하게 되면 이러한 저장 과정이 방해받게 되면서 먼저 배웠던 것이 없어지게 된다. 인간의 기억법에 관해 연구하는 존스 홉킨스 대학 소속 연구 팀을 이끄는 정신의학 전문의 헨리 홀컴(Henry Holcomb) 박사는 다음과 같이 말했다. "저희는 시간 그 자체가 학습에 있어 매우 강력한 구성요소임을 발견했습니다. 단순히 뭔가를 연습하는 것으로는 충분하지 않습니다. 뇌가 새로운 기술을 암호화할 수 있을 만큼의 시간이 흐르게 해야 합니다." 연구진은 뇌 안의 혈류를 측정하는 기기를 활용했다. 연구진은 새로운 기술에 대한 기억이 뇌의 앞쪽에 위치한 임시 저장 공간에서 뇌의 뒤쪽에 위치한 영구 저장 공간으로 이동하기까지 다섯 시간에서 여섯 시간이 걸린다는 결론을 내렸다. 홀컴 박사의 말에 따르면 이와 같은 여섯 시간 동안 신경계에 "깨지기 쉬운 창"이 형성되는데, 이 시점에서 만일 사람이 두 번째의 새로운 기술을 학습하려 할 경우 앞서 새로 배운 첫 번째 기술이 기억 속에서 쉽게 침식된다. 홀컴 박사는 다음과 말했다. "만일 피아노곡 하나를 처음으로 연주한 다음에 바로 다른 것을 연습하기 시작할 경우, 처음 연습한 곡의 기억에 문제가 생깁니다." 그의 말에 따르면, 첫 번째로 연습 시간을 가진 후에 새로운 것을 학습하는 일 없이 다섯 시간에서 여섯 시간 동안 반복 활동을 하는 편이 더 낫다.

27

본문에 따르면 다음 중 사실인 것은 무엇인가?

① 연구진은 뇌 속 혈압을 측정하여 신경계의 "깨지기 쉬운 창"이 존재함을 발견했다.
② 새로 학습한 기술을 기억하려면 여섯 시간 이상 새로 배운 것을 연습해야 한다.
③ 피아노곡을 처음으로 연주한 다음에 자전거 타는 법을 배우려면 다섯 시간에서 여섯 시간을 기다리는 편이 좋다.
④ 두 개의 신체적 기술을 잊지 않고 계속 간직하려면 동시에 이 두 가지를 배우는 편이 좋다.

| 정답 | ③

| 해설 | 새로 학습한 것이 영구적으로 기억 속에 저장되기까지는 5~6시간이 걸리는데, 만일 도중에 다른 것을 또 새로 배우게 되면 이전에 배운 것을 까먹게 될 수 있으며, 따라서 "첫 번째로 연습 시간을 가진 후에 새로운 것을 학습하는 일 없이 다섯 시간에서 여섯 시간 동안 반복 활동을 하는 편이 더 낫다(It would be better ... if the first practice session were followed by five to six hours of routine activity that required no new learning)." 즉, 일단 뭔가를 새로 배운 후에는 다른 것을 배우지 않고 이미 배운 것을 계속 반복하면 영구적으로 기억할 수 있다는 의미이다. 이는 보기 ③의 내용과 일치하며, 따라서 답은 ③이다.

28 신경계의 "깨지기 쉬운 창"은 신경 현상으로 다음의 특징을 지닌다.
① 새로운 기술의 기억은 영구 저장 공간에 즉시 저장된다는 것을 증명했다.
② 자전거를 타는 반복적 활동이 새로운 학습을 요하지 않는지를 설명한다.
③ 뇌의 앞쪽에 위치한 예전에 배운 기술에 대한 기억을 해독하는 과정을 보여준다.
④ 새로운 신체적 기술을 처음으로 학습한 후 다섯 시간에서 여섯 시간 동안 벌어진다.

| 정답 | ④

| 해설 | "깨지기 쉬운 창"은 뭔가를 배운 후 이를 완전히 기억하기까지 걸리는 시간인 5~6시간 존재하는 신경 현상으로, 만일 또 다른 새로운 것을 배우려 할 경우 깨지면서 이전에 배운 것을 잊게 만드는 것이다. 따라서 답은 ④이다.

| 어휘 |
physical ⓐ 신체적인, 육체적인
store ⓥ 저장하다
erase ⓥ 지우다, 없애다
psychiatrist ⓝ 정신과 의사
encode ⓥ 암호화하다, 부호화하다
measure ⓥ 측정하다
vulnerability ⓝ 취약성, 상체[비난]받기 쉬움
retention ⓝ 기억(력)
retain ⓥ (계속) 함유[간직]하다
decode ⓥ (암호를) 해독하다, 복호화하다
permanently ⓐⓓ 영구적으로
interrupt ⓥ 가로막다, 방해하다
component ⓝ 성분, 구성요소
head ⓥ 이끌다, 지도하다
device ⓝ 장치, 기기
neural ⓐ 신경(계통)의, 신경 중추의
erode ⓥ 서서히 파괴하다, 침식하다
initial ⓐ 처음의, 초기의
neurological ⓐ 신경의, 신경학의

[29-30] 항공대 2017

시각적 입력이 조종사에게 아주 중요한 것이긴 해도, 눈은 거짓말을 할 수 있다. 예를 들어, 구름 마루 위를 비행할 경우, 시야에 비교적 직선을 이루는 것을 수평선인 것으로 자연스럽게 인식하는 경향이 있는데, 이는 빠른 속도로 비행하는 항공기에서는 매우 바람직하지 못한 결과를 초래할 수 있다. 구름 속에 있을 경우 사방에 가짜 수평선들이 존재한다. 실제로는 기울어진 상태이거나 선회하고 있는 상황에서도 항공기의 자세가 수평을 이룬 것처럼 보일 수 있다. 당신은 산등성이로 인해 길을 잃을 수도 있을 것이다. 밤에는 구름, 별, 산, 지방의 조명으로 인해 항공기가 실제 비행하는 수준에서 벗어난 것으로 인식하는 혼란스러운 개념이 생길 수 있다. 하지만 구름 없는 맑은 날 수면 위를 날고 있다는 이유만으로 당신이 인식한 것을 근거로 안전하다고 생각해서는 안 된다. 고정된 수평선도 당신을 바다에 빠뜨릴 수 있다. 수평선 위를 날아 해변으로 접근하고 있는 상황에서 무슨 일이 일어날지 생각해 보자. 당신은 시야에 해변을 확보하고, 그 상태를 유지하면서 바다 위를 지나 육지 위로 날아갈 수 있다고 생각하겠지만, 만약 그럴 경우 당신은 결코 육지에 다다를 수 없다. 진짜 수평선과는 달리, 해변은 고정된 것이기 때문에, 해변을 당신의 시야에 정지한 상태로 붙들어 두는 유일한 방법은 항공기를 점점 하강시키는 것뿐이다. 계기판에서 얻는 객관적 정보가 주관적인 감각의 착각을 해결해 줄 수 있는 논리적으로 타당한 해결책이라고 생각할 수 있다. 하지만 계기판을 통해 해야 할 일이 늘어나면 이는 조종사에게 더 많은 주의집중을 요구하기 때문에 문제가 될 수 있으며, 이것은 전투나 기타 스트레스가 가해지는 비행 시나리오의 경우 인지적 과부하를 초래한다. 이러한 정신적 고통이 공간적 방향감각 상실의 중요한 원인 제공자이다. 새로운 항공 전자공학은 복잡함이 아닌 단순함을 염두에 두고 설계되며, 조종사들은 시뮬레이션을 통한 가상으로 압박을 받는 상황에서 적시에 계기판을 보는 법을 배우게 된다.

29

다음 중 빈칸에 올 수 있는 가장 적합한 것은?
① 조종사들은 전능하다
② 내이가 보완할 것이다
③ 청각적 수용은 중요하다
④ 눈은 거짓말을 할 수 있다

| 정답 | ④

| 해설 | 빈칸 이하의 내용은 비행 중 일어날 수 있는 시각적 착각에 대해 말하고 있다. 구름 속에서 일직선처럼 보이는 것을 수평선으로 인식한다든지, 고정된 해변을 수평선으로 인식해 사고가 발생할 수 있다는 사실들에 대해 언급하고 있으므로, 빈칸은 '눈은 거짓말을 할 수 있다', 즉 시각적으로 착각할 수 있다는 ①이 정답이 된다.

30

다음 중 본문의 내용과 일치하는 것은?
① 객관적 정보를 얻기 위해 복잡한 계기판을 훑어보는 것은 조종사의 주의 집중에 대한 요구를 줄여준다.
② 조종사가 바다 위를 지나 육지 위로 날아갈 때 해변은 거짓 수평선이 될 수 있다.
③ 비행 중 공간적 방향감각 상실은 조종사가 액체를 갈구하게 만든다.
④ 구름이 없다면 조종사는 공간적 방향감각 상실을 겪지 않을 것이다.

| 정답 | ②

| 해설 | 본문 중반의 "진짜 수평선과는 달리, 해변은 고정된 것이기 때문에, 해변을 당신의 시야에 정지한 상태로 붙들어 두는 유일한 방법은 항공기를 점점 하강시키는 것뿐이다."는 내용을 통해 해변은 진짜 수평선이 될 수 없는 거짓 수평선이며, 이를 수평선으로 믿고 비행하다가는 큰 사고로 이어질 수 있음을 경고하고 있으므로, 정답은 ②가 된다.

| 어휘 | cloud deck ⓝ [기상학] 구름 마루
level ⓐ 평평한, 반반한 ⓥ 평평하게 하다, ~을 동등하게 하다
tilt ⓥ 기울이다 ⓝ 경사, 기울기
line up – ~을 마련하다, 확보하다; ~을 한 줄로 세우다
stationary ⓐ 움직이지 않는, 고정된
sensory ⓐ 감각의
mount ⓥ (산·단상·왕위에) 오르다, (계단·사다리 따위를) 올라가다 ⓝ 야산, 구릉
cognitive overload – 인지 과부하
spatial ⓐ 공간의, 우주의
avionics ⓝ 항공 전자공학
omnipotent ⓐ 전능한
crave ⓥ 열망하다, 간청하다
attitude ⓝ 자세, 태도
put ~ in the drink – ~을 물속에 빠뜨리다
progressively ⓐⓓ (꾸준히) 계속해서
proliferation ⓝ 증식, 확산
distress ⓝ (정신적) 고통, 괴로움
disorientation ⓝ 방향감각 상실; 혼미
duress ⓝ 협박, 압력; 구속, 감금
aural ⓐ 청각의
liquid ⓝ 액체

[31-33] 한국외대 2016 A형

양손잡이가 되기 위한 훈련이 두뇌 기능을 향상시킬까? 신경과학자들의 말에 따르면 양손잡이가 되도록 사람들을 훈련시키는 행위는 지난 수 세기 동안 인기를 끌었지만 양손잡이가 되려는 연습이 두뇌 기능을 향상시키는 것으로는 보이지 않으며 오히려 신경 발달에 해를 끼칠 수 있다. 양손잡이를 요구하는 목소리는 19세기 말과 20세기 초에 특히나 두드러졌다. 하지만 이러한 과장된 선전은 20세기 중반에 양손잡이가 누릴 수 있다고 알려진 여러 혜택이 실제로 구체화되어 나타나지 않게 되면서 차차 사그라졌다. 심지어 최근 제시된 증거에 따르면 태어났을 때부터 양손잡이인 것은 읽기 장애와 말더듬 같은 발달장애와 서로 연관이 있는 것으로 보인다. 한 연구를 통해 드러난 점은 양손잡이인 아이와 어른 모두 왼손잡이나 오른손잡이에 비해 다양한 분야에서 기량이 떨어진다는 사실이며, 특히 수학·기억 인출·논리적 추론 등의 분야에서 더욱 그러했다. 양손잡이가 되기 위한 훈련이 지닌 위험성 또한 이러한 어려움을 야기할 수 있다. 뇌의 양쪽 반구는 서로 교환이 불가능하다. 예를 들어 좌반구는 보통 언어 처리를 관장하고 반면 우반구는 종종 비언어적 활동을 처리한다. 아마도 이러한 비대칭성이 진화하면서 양쪽 반구가 각기 분화된 기능을 갖게 되었을 것이다. 이처럼 효과적인 구성을 무효화하거나 조작하려는 시도는 정신적 문제를 초래할 수 있다. 주로 쓰지 않는 손을 능숙하게 사용할 수 있도록 훈련하는 것은 가능하다. 콘서트 피아노 연주자는 양손을 사용하여 대단히 훌륭한 기량을 발휘할 수 있지만, 이러한 숙달된 모습은 경쟁적이라기보다는 상호 보완적인 것이다. 시각 예술은 좌반구에 분화된 언어 기능을 희생하는 일 없이 우뇌의 기능을 향상시킬 수 있다. 따라서 좌뇌와 우뇌가 서로 경쟁하는 뇌보다는 서로 협력하는 뇌가 더 잘 기능하는 것으로 보인다.

31 다음 중 본문의 주제로 알맞은 것은 무엇인가?
① 신경과학자들은 양손잡이가 되는 것에 우호적인 증거를 발견했다.
② 두뇌 기능 분화는 선천적인 것이며 보편적인 것이다.
③ 양손잡이가 되도록 훈련하는 것은 해로울 수 있다.
④ 양손잡이는 두뇌 손상을 입을 위험이 있다.

| 정답 | ③

| 해설 | 본문은 과거와 달리 지금은 후천적으로 양손잡이가 되도록 훈련하는 것은 오히려 해로울 수 있다는 인식이 널리 퍼져 있음을 말하고 있으며, 그 이유는 뇌의 좌반구와 우반구 각기 서로 교체될 수 없는 전문화된 기능을 보유하고 있기 때문이다. 따라서 답은 ③으로 볼 수 있다. 참고로 본문에는 양손잡이인 것이 왼손이나 오른손잡이에 비해 기량이 떨어지는 것으로 보인다는 내용은 있지만 뇌 손상까지 언급된 것은 아니므로 ④는 답이 될 수 없다.

32 다음 중 (A)가 가리키는 것과 가장 가까운 것은 무엇인가?
① 차등적 분화
② 생리적 대칭
③ 인간이 오른손이나 왼손 가운데 어느 한쪽을 더 잘 쓰도록 진화한 모습
④ 뇌의 반구를 서로 교환할 수 있음

| 정답 | ①

| 해설 | (A)의 의미는 '이처럼 효과적인 구성'이며, 이 말은 '좌반구는 보통 언어 처리를 관장하고 반면 우반구는 종종 비언어적 활동을 처리'하는 식으로 좌반구와 우반구가 각기 분화되어 전문화된 기능을 발휘하도록 구성되었음을 나타낸다. 즉, 좌반구와 우반구는 서로 "비대칭성(asymmetries)"을 갖도록 진화했고 그 결과 각기 분화된 기능을 갖게 된 것이다("evolved to allow the two sides of the brain to specialize"). 따라서 답은 ①이 된다.

33

다음 중 빈칸 (B)에 가장 알맞은 것은 무엇인가?

① 분리되다　　　　　　　　　　　　② 통합되다
③ 서로 연결되다　　　　　　　　　　④ 경쟁하다

| 정답 | ④

| 해설 | better than 덕분에 빈칸이 들어간 문장이 비교 구문임을 알 수 있고, 빈칸의 비교대상이 cooperative이므로 빈칸에는 이와 대비되는 compete가 들어감을 알 수 있다. 따라서 답은 ④이다.

| 어휘 |
ambidextrous ⓐ 양손잡이의, 양손을 다 잘 쓰는
neural ⓐ 신경의
ambidexterity ⓝ 양손잡이, 양손을 다 잘 씀
hype ⓝ 과대[과장] 선전; 허위, 거짓말
purported ⓐ ~라고 알려진[진술된]
associate A with B – A와 B를 서로 연관[결부] 짓다
developmental problem – 발달장애
stuttering ⓝ 말더듬, 구음장애
retrieval ⓝ 인출, 회수
hemisphere ⓝ (뇌의) 반구
processing ⓝ 처리
handle ⓥ 처리하다
asymmetry ⓝ 비대칭, 불균형
undo ⓥ 무효화하다, 원상태로 되돌리다
setup ⓝ 구성, 배열
psychological ⓐ 정신[심리]의, 정신[심리]적인
demonstrate ⓥ 보여주다, 발휘하다
mastery ⓝ 숙련도, 통달, 숙달
enhance ⓥ 향상시키다
specialization ⓝ 전문화, 분화
differential ⓐ 서로 다른, 차등적인
symmetry ⓝ 대칭, 균형
handedness ⓝ 오른손이나 왼손 중 어느 한쪽을 다른 쪽 손보다 잘 쓰는 모습
consolidate ⓥ 통합하다[되다]
neuroscientist ⓝ 신경과학자
call for – ~에 대한 요청[요구]
prominent ⓐ 두드러진, 현저한
die down – 차츰 잦아들다, 사그라들다
materialize ⓥ 구체화되다, 실현되다
reading disability – 읽기 장애
a range of – 다양한
reasoning ⓝ 추론
interchangeable ⓐ 교체[교환]할 수 있는
whereas ⓒⓞⓝ 반면
nonverbal ⓐ 비언어적인, 말로 할 수 없는
specialize ⓥ 전문화하다, 분화하다
tamper with – 조작하다, 건드리다
invite ⓥ 자초하다, 초래하다
proficient ⓐ 능숙한, 능한
superb ⓐ 최고의, 대단히 훌륭한
complementary ⓐ 상호 보완적인
at the expense of – ~을 희생하면서, ~을 잃어 가며
innate ⓐ 선천적인, 타고난
physiological ⓐ 생리적인, 생리학의
interconnect ⓥ 서로 연결하다[관련되다]

[34-35] 중앙대 2017

1890년대 말 두 명의 독일 심리학자 게오르크 뮐러와 알폰스 필제커는 기억이 뇌에 고착되는, 다시 말해 기억이 '공고화되는(consolidated)' 데 대략 한 시간이 걸리는 것을 발견했다. 후속 연구들은 단기 및 장기 형태의 기억이 존재하는 것을 확인했으며, 전자인 단기기억이 후자인 장기기억으로 변화하는 공고화 단계의 중요성을 추가적으로 보여주는 증거들을 제공했다. 1960년대 펜실베이니아 대학의 신경학자 루이스 플렉스너는 매우 흥미로운 발견을 했다. 쥐의 세포가 단백질을 생성하지 못하도록 방해하는 항생제를 쥐에 투여하면, 쥐들이 장기기억을 형성할 수는 없지만, 단기기억은 계속 저장할 수 있다는 사실을 그는 발견했다. 이 연구의 함의는 분명했다. 장기기억은 단순히 단기기억의 강력한 형태만은 아니라는 것이다. 두 종류의 기억이 서로 다른 생물학적 과정을 수반한다. 장기기억을 저장하려면 새로운 단백질을 합성하는 것이 필요하다. 단기기억을 저장하는 것은 그렇지 않다. 좀 더 최근의 연구는 단기 및 장기기억 모두의 물리적 작동 문제에 초점을 맞추었다. 그 결과 경험이 여러 번 반복되면 될수록 경험의 기억이 더 오래 지속된다는 사실이 밝혀졌다. 반복은 공고화를 장려한다. 특히 반복이 뉴런의 신호에 미치는 생리적 영향을 연구자들이 조사했을 때, 그들은 놀라운 사실을 발견했다. 시냅스의 신경전달물질의 농도가 변화해 뉴런 사이의 기존 연결 강도가 변경되었을 뿐만 아니라 뉴런이 완전히 새로운 시냅스 말단을 성장시켰다. 다시 말하면 장기기억의 형성은 생화학적 변화뿐만 아니라 해부학적 변화도 포함한다. 이것은 기억의 공고화가 왜 새로운 단백질을 필요로 하는지를 설명해 준다. 단백질은 세포의 구조적 변화를 일으키는 데 필수적인 역할을 수행한다.

34 아래의 문장이 들어갈 위치로 가장 적합한 곳을 고르시오.

두 종류의 기억이 서로 다른 생물학적 과정을 수반한다.

① (A) ② (B)
③ (C) ④ (D)

| 정답 | ①

| 해설 | (A) 앞부분에서 실험 결과인 단백질 생성의 의미에 대해 설명하고 있다. 장기기억은 단기기억의 더 강화된 형태만은 아니라고 설명한다. 〈not only A but also B〉에서 A만 진술되어 있으므로, 더 중요한 내용인 B에 해당하는 내용이 필요하며, 그 내용이 주어진 문장이 된다. 따라서 주어진 문장이 들어갈 적합한 위치는 ①이 된다. 장기기억은 단기기억과는 다른 생물학적 과정을 수반한다고 주제문을 제시한 후, 이후 내용을 통해 어떻게 다른지 제시하고 있다.

35 윗글을 통해 추론할 수 있는 것으로 가장 적합한 것을 고르시오.
① 항생제 사용은 인간이 아주 최근의 경험조차 떠올리지 못하게 방해한다.
② 단기기억은 우리가 공고화된 정보를 적극적 방식으로 얼마나 오랫동안 기억할 수 있는지를 예측하게 해 주는 중요한 지표이다.
③ 장기기억이 형성될 때 뇌의 시냅스에서 비교적 적은 수의 신경전달물질이 방출될 것으로 예상된다.
④ 뇌에서 장기간 정보를 유지하는 것은 시냅스의 해부학적 변화를 동반할 가능성이 매우 높다.

| 정답 | ④

| 해설 | 본문 후반에서 "장기기억의 형성은 생화학적 변화뿐만 아니라 '해부학적' 변화도 포함한다(The formation of long-term memories involves not only biochemical changes but anatomical ones)"고 설명하고 있다. 따라서 뇌에서 장기간 정보를 유지하는 장기기억은 "시냅스 말단이 새로 생기는 등(the neurons grew entirely new synaptic terminals)" 시냅스의 '해부학적' 변화를 동반한다고 볼 수 있으므로 정답은 ④가 된다.

| 어휘 |

psychologist ⓝ 심리학자
subsequent ⓐ 차후의, 뒤의, 후속적인
short-term ⓐ 단기의, 단기적인
consolidation ⓝ 통합, 규합, 합병
the latter - 후자
intriguing ⓐ 아주 흥미로운, 음모를 꾸미는
antibiotic ⓝ 항생제, 항생물질
implication ⓝ 내포, 암시
repetition ⓝ 반복, 되풀이
neuronal ⓐ 뉴런의
synapse ⓝ 신경 접합부, 시냅스
biochemical ⓐ 생화학의, 생화학적인
memory consolidation - 기억 공고화, 기억 강화
entail ⓥ 의미하다; 수반하다
accompany ⓥ 동반하다, 수반하다

consolidated ⓐ 통합된, 강화된
confirm ⓥ 확인하다, 확증하다
long-term ⓐ 장기적인
the former - 전자
neurologist ⓝ 신경학자, 신경과 전문의
inject ⓥ 주입하다, 주사하다
protein ⓝ 단백질
synthesis ⓝ 종합, 합성
physiological ⓐ 생리학의, 생리적인
neurotransmitter ⓝ 신경전달물질
synaptic ⓐ 시냅스의
anatomical ⓐ 해부학상의, 해부의

retain ⓥ 보유하다, 유지하다, 기억하다; 보류하다

CHAPTER 05 의학·건강

01	①	02	⑤	03	②	04	①	05	①	06	②	07	④	08	②	09	①	10	②
11	④	12	③	13	②	14	④	15	④	16	④	17	③	18	④	19	③	20	③
21	⑤	22	②	23	④	24	②	25	②	26	②	27	⑤	28	③	29	③	30	①
31	②	32	④	33	②	34	②	35	②	36	②	37	②	38	②	39	②	40	⑤
41	②	42	④	43	②	44	②	45	②	46	②	47	④	48	②	49	④	50	④

[01-02] 한국외대 2010

영향력 있는 의학 연구 기관에 의해 발표된 새로운 지침에 따르면, 대부분의 여성들은 40세가 아니라 50세부터 정기 유방암 검진을 받기 시작해야 한다. 유방암에 대한 흔치 않은 위험 요소를 가진 소규모의 여성들에게 적용되지 않는 이 새로운 권고안은, 오래 지속되어 온 지침을 뒤집는 것이고, 과도한 치료로 인한 피해를 줄이는 데 목적이 있다. 이 기관은 50세에서 74세 사이의 여성은 유방조영상을 덜 자주, 즉 2년에 한 번 받아야 한다고 말했다. 바로 7년 전에는 구성원은 달랐지만 같은 기관에서 여성은 유방조영상을 40세부터 매년 한 번 받아야 한다고 권고했었다.

새 지침은 몇몇 전문가나 검진을 옹호하는 기관의 지침과는 다른 것이라 유방암 검진의 혜택에 관한 또 다른 논란을 촉발할 가능성이 높다. 많은 여성들은 검진이 해로울 것이라고는 생각하지 않는 반면에, 의학 전문가들은 검진으로 인한 위험이 실제 있다고 말한다. 검진은 불필요한 추가 검진을 야기해 극도의 긴장감을 유발할 수 있으며, 유방조영상은 너무 느리게 자라서 여성의 일생 동안 절대 눈에 띄지 않는 암도 발견할 수 있어서, 불필요한 치료를 받게 하는 결과를 낳을 수 있다.

01 다음 중 유방암에 대한 새로운 지침이 경고하는 것은 무엇인가?
① 과도한 치료로 인한 위험
② 치료로 인한 극도의 긴장
③ 과도한 의료비
④ 영양실조로 인한 해
⑤ 불규칙한 건강 진단으로 인해 생길 수 있는 잠재적인 위험

| 정답 | ①

| 해설 | 본문은 이번에 새로 나온 지침은 "are aimed at reducing harm from overtreatment(과도한 치료로 인한 피해를 줄이는 데 목적)"이 있음을 말하고 있다. 그리고 "While many women do not think a screening test can be harmful, medical experts say the risks are real(많은 여성들은 검진이 해로울 것이라고는 생각하지 않으나, 의학 전문가들은 검진으로 인한 위험이 실제 있다고 말한다)"는 사실을 인지할 수 있다. 따라서 이번에 치료를 과도하게 받는 것이 오히려 위험할 수 있음을 감안하여 새로운 지침을 내놓은 것으로 볼 수 있다. 이를 통해 보기 중에서 답에 해당되는 것은 ①임을 알 수 있다.
②는 ①의 '과도한 치료로 인한 위험'에 포함되는 것이므로 ①이 답인 이상 ②를 답으로 보기는 힘들다. ③은 유추는 가능하나 직접적으로 언급된 내용은 아니므로 답으로 볼 수 없다. ④, ⑤는 본문의 내용과 관련이 없으므로 답이 될 수 없다.

02 본문에 따르면 다음 중 사실이 아닌 것은?

① 새로운 지침은 여성들이 2년마다 유방조영상을 받을 것을 권고한다.
② 몇몇 유방암은 너무 느리게 자라서 심각한 문제를 야기하지 않는다.
③ 새로운 지침은 여성이 유방암 검진을 50세에 받을 것을 제안한다.
④ 유방암에 걸릴 위험이 몹시 높은 여성들이 있다.
⑤ 의학 전문가들은 여성은 덜 자주 유방암 검진을 받아야 한다는 데 동의한다.

| 정답 | ⑤

| 해설 | "The new guidelines, which are different from those of some professionals and advocacy organizations, are likely to touch off yet another round of controversy over the benefits of screening for breast cancer(새 지침은 몇몇 전문가나 검진 옹호기관의 지침과는 다른 것이라 유방암 검진의 혜택에 관한 또 다른 논란을 촉발할 가능성이 높다)"고 본문에 명시되어 있으며, 이는 "Medical experts agree that women should receive tests for breast cancer less frequently(의학 전문가들은 여성은 덜 자주 유방암 검진을 받아야 한다는 데 동의한다)"는 보기 ⑤의 내용과는 상충된다. 따라서 답은 ⑤가 된다. ①의 'every other year'는 '한해 걸러', 즉 '2년에 한 번'의 뜻이다. 본문에 따르면 새 지침은 검진을 덜 자주, 즉 "every two years(2년에 한 번)" 받을 것을 권고하고 있으며 이는 ①에 언급된 사항이므로 ①은 답이 될 수 없다. 본문의 "cancers that grow so slowly that they would never be noticed in a woman's lifetime(너무 느리게 자라서 여성의 일생 동안 절대 눈에 띄지 않는 암)"은 보기 ②의 "develop so slowly that they do not cause a serious problem(너무 느리게 자라서 심각한 문제를 야기하지 않는)" 유방암과 마찬가지 내용이다. "Most women should start regular breast cancer screening at age 50, not 40, according to new guidelines(새로운 지침에 따르면, 대부분의 여성들은 40세가 아니라 50세부터 정기 유방암 검진을 받기 시작해야 한다)"라고 본문에 명시되어 있는데, 이는 ③의 내용과 일치한다. 정기검진 권고안의 예외로 "a small group of women with unusual risk factors for breast cancer(흔치 않은 위험 요소를 가진 소규모의 여성들)"을 들고 있는데, 이들은 암에 걸릴 위험 요소가 커서 1년이나 2년에 한 번이라는 정기검진만 받다가는 조기에 암을 발견 못할 수 있기 때문에 더 많이 검진을 받아야 하는 예외가 된 것으로 유추할 수 있다. 즉 이들은 보기 ④의 "a group of women who are at unusually increased risk for breast cancer(유방암에 걸릴 위험이 몹시 높은 여성들)"도 볼 수 있다.

| 어휘 |
regular ⓐ 정기적인
screening ⓝ 검사, 검진
guideline ⓝ 지침
recommendation ⓝ 권고안, 추천
risk factor – 위험 요소
longstanding ⓐ 오래 계속되는, 다년간의
overtreatment ⓝ 과도한 치료
every two years – 2년에 한 번
touch off – ~을 유발[촉발]하다
controversy ⓝ 논란
prompt ⓥ ~을 촉발하다, 유도하다
extreme ⓐ 극도의
result in – ~라는 결과를 낳다
expense ⓝ 비용
irregular ⓐ 불규칙한

breast cancer – 유방암
according to – ~에 따르면
influential ⓐ 영향력 있는
apply to – ~에 적용된다
reverse ⓥ 뒤집다, 역전시키다
aim at – ~을 목표로 하다
mammogram ⓝ 유방조영상
advocacy ⓝ 옹호, 지지
round ⓝ (장기적으로 진행되는 일의) 한 차례
expert ⓝ 전문가
further ⓐ 추가적인
anxiety ⓝ 긴장
excessive ⓐ 과도한
maltreatment ⓝ 학대; 잘못된 치료
checkup ⓝ 점검, 건강진단

every other year＝every two years － 2년에 한 번
at risk － 위험에 처한

[03-04] 한국외대 2009

살면서 스트레스를 통제할 수 없을 때, 자주 화가 나고 감정을 주체할 수 없다면, 당신의 심장은 손상될 수도 있다. 심장을 망가뜨리고 싶지 않다면, 당신이 제어할 수 있는 문제들을 다루는 법을 배워야 하고 당신이 통제할 수 없는 것들이 많다는 것도 인정해야 한다. 괴팍한 사람들은 일상에서 "싸움－도주 반응(fight of flight response: 갑작스런 자극에 대하여 싸울 것인가 도주할 것인가를 결정하려는 본능적 반응으로서 혈압과 심장박동수가 높아지고 동공이 확대되는 등 스트레스에 대처하려는 극단적인 신체 반응이 나타난다.)"을 다른 사람들보다 더 강하게 더 자주 보인다. 그들은 슈퍼마켓의 긴 줄, 교통체증, 방을 치우지 않는 아이들 같은 사소한 짜증거리들이 삶에 위협이라도 되는 것처럼 반응한다. 많은 연구 결과들에 따르면, 높은 분노 수치는 심장질환 위험성의 증가, 면역 체계의 약화와 관련 있다. 분노 수치가 높은 남성들이 심장질환에 걸릴 가능성은 차분한 사람들에 비해 세 배이다. 여성의 경우, 남편과의 말다툼은 호르몬 수치를 증가시키고 면역력을 약화시킨다. 특히 면역저하야말로 심각한 문제이다. 면역반응이 약화되면 여성의 암 발병률이 증가하기 때문이다.

03 다음 중 필자가 이 글을 쓴 목적은 무엇인가?
① 분노에 관한 특정 연구 결과를 비판하기 위해서
② 분노가 우리 몸에 얼마나 해로운지를 설명하기 위해서
③ 분노 조절(anger management)에 관한 두 이론을 비교하기 위해서
④ 분노 조절 방법에 대해서 토론하기 위해서
⑤ 분노 조절에 대한 의견을 제시하기 위해서

| 정답 | ②

| 해설 | 분노는 심장 질환, 면역 저하, 암 발병 등 인체에 해로운 영향을 미친다는 것이 주제이므로 지문의 목적으로 적절한 것은 ② "분노가 우리 몸에 얼마나 해로운지를 설명하기 위해서"이다.

04 다음 중 빈칸 (A)와 (B)에 가장 적절한 것은?
① 적대적인 － 사소한
② 쾌활한 － 사소한
③ 괴팍한 － 중요한
④ 편협한 － 상당한
⑤ 다정한 － 사소한

| 정답 | ①

| 해설 | 화를 잘 내고 감정을 주체하지 못하는 사람들의 특징을 상술하는 문장들이다. 빈칸 (A)에는 '화를 잘 내는' 사람의 성격인 'hostile'이 적절하고, 빈칸 (B)에는 '사소한' 문제에도 화를 낸다는 내용을 완성하기 위해 'petty'가 적절하다. 보기 ③과 ④의 단어들은 빈칸 (A)에는 적절하지만 빈칸 (B)에 적절치 않으므로 선택하지 않도록 주의한다. 따라서 ①이 정답이다.

| 어휘 | **overwhelmed** ⓐ 압도된   **spin** ⓥ 돌다, 회전하다

out of control – 통제를 벗어난
break down – 고장 내다, 악화되다
recognize ⓥ 인식하다, 인정하다
activate ⓥ 활성화하다
intensely ⓐⓓ 강하게, 강렬하게
respond ⓥ 반응하다
annoyance ⓝ 짜증, 골칫거리
clean up – 청소하다
threat ⓝ 위협
heart disease – 심장질환
score ⓝ 점수, 수치
calm ⓐ 차분한
spouse ⓝ 배우자
cancer ⓝ 암

hurt ⓥ 다치게 하다
take charge of – ~을 책임지다
hostile ⓐ 적대적인
fight-or-flight response – 싸움-도주 반응
frequently ⓐⓓ 빈번하게, 자주
petty ⓐ 사소한
traffic jam – 교통체증
as though – 마치 ~인 것처럼
be associated with – ~와 연관되다
immune response – 면역반응
develop ⓥ 발병시키다
argument ⓝ 말다툼, 논쟁
boost ⓥ 급증시키다, 강화하다

[05-09] 세종대 2011

정신분열병은 사고 과정과 정서적 반응의 분열을 특징으로 삼는 정신질환이다. 정신분열병은 보통 환청, 편집증이나 기괴한 망상, 체계적이지 못한 언어와 사고 등의 형태로 드러나며 상당한 수준의 사회적 및 직업상의 기능장애가 동반된다. 정신분열병적 행동의 일반적 특징으로는 비논리적인 사고 유형과 가족과 친구 같은 현실로부터의 도피 등이 있다. 정신분열병 환자는 종종 다른 사람에겐 들리지 않는 목소리가 들리는 환상의 세계 속에서 산다. 이 정신질환은 주로 지각에 악영향을 주는 것으로 생각되나 행동과 감정의 고질적인 문제에도 기여한다. 정신분열병에 걸린 사람들은 심각한 우울증이나 불안 장애 같은 추가적인 질환에 걸리기 쉽다. (정신분열병에 걸린 사람들에겐) 장기간의 실업, 가난, 노숙 등의 사회적 문제가 흔하다. 게다가 정신분열병에 걸린 사람의 평균 기대수명은 걸리지 않은 사람의 수명보다 10년에서 12년이 짧으며, 그 이유는 육체 건강 관련 문제가 증가하고 자살율이 높기 때문이다.

증상의 발현은 10대 말이나 20대 초에 일반적으로 일어나고, 전 세계적인 평생 유병율은 대략 1.5%이다. 세계 보건기구에 따르면 정신분열병은 성인 인구 1,000명당 대략 7명에 영향을 주는 심각한 형태의 정신질환이고, 이들 중 대부분은 연령대가 15세에서 35세이다. 정신분열병의 어원은 그리스어 skhizein(분열시키다)와 phren(정신)을 기원으로 하지만, 정신분열병은 "분열된 정신"을 나타내는 것은 아니고 대중의 인식 속에서는 종종 정신분열병과 혼동되는 "다발성 인격장애", 다른 말로는 "다중 인격"으로 알려진 정신질환과도 동일하지 않다. 정신분열병은 다발성 인격장애보다는 훨씬 더 흔하다.

05

본문에 따르면 다음 중 정신분열병과 해리성 정체감 장애에 관해 사실이 아닌 것은 무엇인가?
① "해리성 정체감 장애"라는 용어의 어원은 "분열된 정신"을 나타낸다.
② 정신분열병은 보통 환청의 형태로 드러나며 해리성 정체감 장애는 별개의 인격들로 분열되는 것이 포함된다.
③ 많은 사람들은 정신분열병을 해리성 정체감 장애로 착각한다.
④ 해리성 정체감 장애는 정신분열병보다 자주 발생하지는 않는다.

| 정답 | ①

| 해설 | "정신분열병의 어원은 그리스어 skhizein(분열시키다)와 phren(정신)을 기원으로 하지만, 정신분열병은 '분열된 정신'을 나타내는 것은 아니다(Despite the etymology of the term from the Greek roots skhizein ("to split")

and phren ('mind'), schizophrenia does not imply a 'split mind')." 이 문장을 통해 '분열된 정신'은 정신분열병에 관한 것이지 해리성 정체감 장애와는 관련 없음을 알 수 있다. 따라서 답은 ①이다.

06

다음 중 본문의 "질환"과 의미상 가장 가까운 것은 무엇인가?
① 악성 종양
② 질병
③ 배열이 어긋남
④ 감소

| 정답 | ②

| 해설 | disorder는 '(신체 기능의) 장애, 이상'을 의미하며, 보기 중에서 의미상 가장 가까운 것은 ②이다.

07

다음 중 정신분열병 환자에 관해 추론할 수 있는 것은 무엇인가?
① 이들은 가족과 터놓고 대화한다.
② 이들은 강화된 논리력을 지녔다.
③ 이들의 수명은 평균보다 길다.
④ 이들은 종종 가족에게서 멀어진 느낌을 받는다.

| 정답 | ④

| 해설 | 정신분열병의 특징 중 하나로 "가족과 친구 같은 현실로부터의 도피(withdrawal from reality such as families and friends)"를 들고 있다. 이는 보기 ④의 내용과 일맥상통한다.

08

다음 중 정신분열병에 관해 추론할 수 없는 것은 무엇인가?
① 정신분열병 환자는 일반적으로 그릇되거나, 상상 속에서나 가능하거나, 기만에 기인한 고착화된 믿음을 갖고 있다.
② 정신분열병은 분리되고 개별적인 인격이 특징이다.
③ 정신분열병 환자는 직업을 얻는 데 어려움을 겪는다.
④ 정신분열병의 피해자는 상상속의 목소리를 듣기 쉽다.

| 정답 | ②

| 해설 | 본문에 따르면 정신분열병은 "대중의 인식 속에서는 종종 정신분열병과 혼동되는 '다발성 인격장애' 다른 말로는 '다중 인격'으로 알려진 정신질환과도 동일하지 않다(it is not the same as disorder—also known as 'multiple personality disorder' or 'split personality'—a condition with which it is often confused in public perception)"고 명시되어 있으며, 이는 '정신분열병은 분리되고 개별적인 인격이 특징'이라는 ②의 내용과는 정반대이다. 따라서 답은 ②가 된다.

09

본문에 따르면 다음 중 해리성 정체감 장애에 관해 사실이 아닌 것은 무엇인가?
① 해리성 정체감 장애는 성인 인구 0.7% 이상에 영향을 준다.
② 해리성 정체감 장애는 별개의 인격들로 분열되는 것이 포함된다.
③ 해리성 정체감 장애는 정신분열병과는 다르다.
④ 해리성 정체감 장애는 다발성 인격장애라고도 불린다.

| 정답 | ①

| 해설 | 본문에는 해리성 정체감 장애의 유병율이 구체적으로 나와 있지는 않다. "전 세계적인 평생 유병율이 대략 1.5%(with a global lifetime prevalence of around 1.5%)"이면서 "성인 인구 1,000명당 대략 7명(about 7 per thousand of the adult population)", 달리 말하면 0.7%에 영향을 주는 질병이라고 구체적 수치가 나온 것은 해리성 정체감 장애가 아니라 정신분열병이다. 따라서 답은 ①이다.

| 어휘 |
schizophrenia ⓝ 정신분열병
disintegration ⓝ 분열, 붕괴
manifest ⓥ 드러내 보이다, 나타나다
hallucination ⓝ 환각
bizarre ⓐ 기괴한, 기이한
disorganized ⓐ 혼란스러운, 체계적이지 못한
affect ⓥ ~에 영향을 미치다, 악영향을 주다
contribute to – ~에 기여하다
condition ⓝ 질환
average life expectancy – 평균 기대수명
lifetime prevalence – 평생 유병율; 한 개인의 평생 동안 어느 질환이 발현할 확률
etymology ⓝ 어원
multiple personality disorder – 다발성 인격장애(=해리성 정체감 장애)
split personality – 다중 인격
considerably ⓐⓓ 훨씬, 상당히
mistake A for B – A를 B로 착각하다
misalignment ⓝ 배열이 어긋남
enhanced ⓐ 강화된, 향상된
fanciful ⓐ 상상 속의

mental disorder – 정신병, 정신질환
emotional responsiveness – 정서적 반응
auditory ⓐ 청각의
paranoid ⓝ 편집증
delusion ⓝ 망상
dysfunction ⓝ 장애, 기능 장애
cognition ⓝ 지각, 인지
chronic ⓐ 만성적인, 고질적인
anxiety disorder – 불안 장애
onset ⓝ 시작, 발현
perception ⓝ 인식, 개념
dissociative identity disorder – 해리성 정체감 장애
malignancy ⓝ 악성 종양
schizophrenic ⓝ 정신분열병 환자
lifespan ⓝ 수명
deception ⓝ 속임수

[10-11] 한성대 2006

괴혈병은 해상 탐험가들의 시대에 널리 알려진 천형 같은 병이었다. 오랜 항해 중에, 선원들은 처음 몇 주는 비타민 C를 함유한 신선한 음식을 먹지만 그 이후 수개월간 가염 돼지고기를 주로 먹다가 괴혈병에 걸렸다. 1935 Jacques Cartier의 Newfoundland 탐험 기록은 괴혈병 환자들을 끔찍하게 표현하고 있다. "입에선 악취가 났는데 잇몸은 완전히 썩어서 살점이 모두 떨어져 나가고 치근까지 드러나 이가 거의 빠졌다."
이 기록은 계속 이어져, 육지에서 사사프라스 차를 마시고 괴혈병이 나은 선원의 이야기를 전하고 있다. 과학의 도움이 있었다면, 이 사실을 통해 괴혈병을 이해할 수 있었을 것이다.
그러나 여전히 괴혈병 치료법은 알 수가 없었다. 실험을 통해서 (치료의) 효과를 분리할 수 있다는 생각은 아직 못했기 때문이다. 그래서 선원이 육지에 있을 때 괴혈병이 나으면 그 원인은 "그 땅의 공기" 때문이지 신선한 과일과 야채를 먹었기 때문이라고는 생각하지 않았다.

10 지문에 따르면 다음 중 사실인 것은?
① 사사프라스 차는 괴혈병 환자 치료 효과가 검증된 약이다.
② 때로는, 그 땅의 공기가 선원의 괴혈병을 치료했다고 믿기도 했다.
③ 괴혈병 환자는 육지에서 가염 돼지고기를 먹고 나았다.
④ 오랜 항해 동안 선원들은 맑은 공기를 쐬면 괴혈병에 걸리지 않았다.

| 정답 | ②

| 해설 | 두 번째 단락 마지막 문장 "So when a sailor was cured of scurvy while on land, it was frequently attributed to "the air of the land" and not to the eating of fresh fruits and vegetables."를 참조하면, "사람들은 괴혈병 치료의 원인을 신선한 음식이 아니라 그 땅의 공기라고 생각했다."는 언급이 있으므로 ②가 적절하다. 괴혈병 환자가 사사프라스 차를 마시고 괴혈병이 낫기는 했지만 과학적 방식을 통해 사사프라스 차의 효능이 검증되지는 않았으므로 ①은 오답이다.

11 괴혈병의 증상이 아닌 것은?
① 이가 거의 빠진다.
② 입안의 살이 썩는다.
③ 입에서 지독한 냄새가 난다.
④ 잇몸이 마비된다.

| 정답 | ④

| 해설 | 첫 단락 마지막 문장에 괴혈병의 증상이 상술되었다. "There mouths became stinking, their gums so rotten that all the flesh did rot off, even to the roots of their teeth, which almost all fell out."를 참조하면, 잇몸이 썩는다고는 했지만 마비된다는 언급은 없으므로 ④가 정답이다.

| 어휘 | well-known ⓐ 잘 알려진, 유명한
explore ⓝ 탐험가
on a diet of – ~을 주식으로
scurvy ⓝ 괴혈병
expedition ⓝ 탐험, 원정
term ⓝ 용어
rotten ⓐ 썩은
go on – 계속하다
disease ⓝ 질병
elude ⓥ 피하다, 빠져나가다, 이해되지 않다, 받아들이지 않다
isolate ⓥ (복합물에서 순수한 물질, 성분을) 분리하다
appreciate ⓥ 이해하다, 인정하다

seafaring ⓐ 해상의
voyage ⓝ 항해, 여행
develop ⓥ 발병하다
account ⓝ 설명
sufferer ⓝ 환자
stink ⓥ 악취가 나다
fall out – 떨어지다
cure ⓥ 치료하다

attribute A to B – A의 원인을 B라고 생각하다

[12-14] 숭실대 2006

리투아니아에서도 전 세계 어느 곳에서나 마찬가지로 자동차 추돌 사고가 난다. 범퍼는 일그러지고 화가 치솟는다. 그러나 그곳의 운전자들은 다른 나라에서는 너무나 흔한 통증인 두통과 지속적인 경부통(neck pain), 즉 휘플래시 증후군(whiplash syndrome)을 겪지 않는다. Norway의 Dr. Schrader와 연구진들은 연구 목적을 밝히지 않고, 1년에서 3년 전 사이에 자동차 추돌사고를 당했고, 사고의 정도도 다양했던 202명의 리투아니아 운전자들을 대상으로 건강 설문조사를 했다. 이 운전자들의 증상에 대한 응답은 사고를 당하지 않은 대조 집단(같은 체격, 같은 나이, 같은 지역 출신)의 응답과 비교 연구되었다. 조사 집단의 35%가 경부통이 있었다고 밝혔으나 대조집단도 33%가 경부통이 있었다. 조사 집단의 53%가 두통이 있다고 밝혔으나 대조 집단의 50%도 두통이 있었다. 설문 결과 "조사 집단의 피험자들 중 누구도 자동차 사고로 장애 증상이나 영구적 증상을 보이지 않았다." 그렇다면 전 세계의 나머지 국가들에서 휘플래시 증후군 환자가 급증하는 이유는 무엇일까? 리투아니아 운전자들을 대상으로 한 조사 당시, 운전자들은 개인상해보험이 없었다. 그리고 그곳에서는 서로에게 소송을 거는 일도 매우 드물다. 대부분의 의료 비용은 정부에서 지급한다. 따라서 조사 당시에 추돌 사고에 대한 소송도 없었고, 지급받을 손해배상금도 없었다. 즉, 만성적인 휘플래시 증후군 진단으로 얻어낼 것은 아무것도 없었던 것이다. 노르웨이 연구자들은 만성적 휘플래시 증후군은 "진단적 타당성이 거의 없다. (실제 증상으로 보기 어렵다.)"는 결론을 내렸다.

12 지문에 언급된 조사 집단과 대조 집단의 비교가 옳은 것은?
① 대조 집단에서 더 많은 사람들이 휘플래시 증후군을 보였다.
② 조사 집단의 몇몇은 장애 증상이 있었다.
③ 조사 집단에서 더 많은 사람들이 두통을 경험했다.
④ 대조 집단의 몇몇은 심한 부상을 입었다.

| 정답 | ③

| 해설 | 지문의 후반부에 조사 집단과 대조 집단의 증상이 비교 서술되고 있다. "53% of those who had been in an accident had headaches, but so did 50% of those in the control group."를 참조하면, 조사 집단은 53%가 대조 집단은 50%가 두통을 보고했으므로 미미한 차이나마 조사 집단에서 더 많은 사람들이 두통을 경험했다는 ③이 정답이다. 연구 결과 조사 집단은 장애 증상이나 영구적 증상을 보이지 않았으므로 ②를 선택하지 않도록 주의한다.

13 다음 중 결론으로서 빈칸을 완성하기에 가장 적절한 것은?
① 의심스러운 책임이 있다
② 타당성이 거의 없다
③ 확실히 신뢰할 수 있다
④ 특유의 통증이 있다

| 정답 | ②

| 해설 | 연구는 보험과 소송, 피해배상금이 없을 때는 휘플래시 증후군이 나타나지 않는다는 것을 보여준다. 이것은 휘플래시 증후군은 실제 증상이 아니라는 것을 의미한다. "증상으로서는 신뢰할 수 없다."는 결론으로서는 보기 ②가 적절하다.

14

다음 중 휘플래시 증후군 환자가 리투아니아 외의 국가들에서 더 흔한 이유가 아닌 것은?

① 다른 국가에서는 개인상해보험에 가입한 사람들이 더 많다.
② 다른 국가에서는 서로 소송하는 일이 더 잦다.
③ 다른 국가에서는 국민의 의료비를 지급하지 않는 정부들이 더 많다.
④ 다른 국가에서는 자동차 상해가 더 자주 발생한다.

| 정답 | ④

| 해설 | 정부가 의료 비용을 지급하기 때문에 개인상해보험이 필요 없고 소송을 거의 하지 않는 리투아니아 특유의 문화적, 사회적 특징 때문에 휘플래시 증후군이 나타나지 않는다. 따라서 이와는 대조적인 특징이 휘플래시 증후군의 원인임을 유추할 수 있다. ①, ②, ③은 리투아니아의 문화적, 사회적 특징과 대조되는 특징이지만 ④는 이 대조와 무관하다.

| 어휘 |
rear-end collision – 추돌
temper ⓝ 화
complaint ⓝ 통증, 질환, 불평
disclose ⓥ 밝히다, 공개하다
varying ⓐ 다양한
control group – 대조군, 대조 집단
persistent ⓐ 영구적인
explosion ⓝ 급증, 폭발
sue ⓥ 고소하다
file a claim – 소송을 제기[신청]하다
diagnosis ⓝ 진단
validity ⓝ 타당성, 유효성, 신뢰성
crumple ⓥ 일그러지다, 구겨지다
flare ⓥ 불길처럼 치솟다
linger ⓥ 지속하다, 남아 있다
questionnaires ⓝ 설문지
severity ⓝ 심각성
disabling ⓐ 장애를 만드는
symptom ⓝ 증상
injury insurance – 상해보험
medical bill – 의료비 청구서
gain ⓥ 얻다
chronic ⓐ 만성적인

[15-17] 한양대 2007

지난 30~40년간 알레르기에 시달리는 아이들이 크게 늘었고 과학자들은 그 현상을 설명하기 위해 계속 노력 중이다. 일부 과학자들은 대기오염의 증가를 탓하지만 도시에 사는 아이들뿐 아니라 공해가 훨씬 적은 시골에 사는 아이들에게도 알레르기가 흔하다는 것이 밝혀졌다. 알레르기 증가에 대한 최근의 일반적인 설명은 일명 "위생 가설"이다. 이 가설의 핵심은, 지나치게 깨끗한 환경에서 자란 아이들에게 알레르기가 생기기 가장 쉽다는 것이다. 오늘날, 사람들은 목욕과 빨래를 예전보다 더 자주 한다. 진공청소기 덕분에 집에는 먼지도 덜하다. 이러한 변화로 인해, 아이들은 어릴 때 알레르기를 유발하는 알레르겐(알레르기 항원)에 덜 노출되고 따라서 신체는 알레르기에 대한 면역을 기를 수 없다. 간단히 말하자면, 알레르기 유발 물질에 노출되는 것은 알레르기에 대한 자연적 방어력(면역력)을 생성하는 데 꼭 필요하다. 핵가족화는 아이들이 집에서 노출되는 알레르겐이 더 적다는 것을 의미한다. 사실, 형이나 누나(오빠나 언니)가 있는 아이들은 알레르기에 대한 면역이 더 강하다고 한다. 집에 애완 동물이 있는 아이들도 마찬가지이다. 이 아이들은 매우 흔한 알레르기인 고양이나 개털 알레르기가 생길 가능성이 훨씬 적다. 과학자들은 어릴 때 다양한 알레르겐에 노출될수록 알레르기에 대한 면역력이 강해진다는 데 동의한다. 그러나 유전, 가정 소득, 심지어는 부모의 교육 수준이, 아이에게 알레르기가 생길 가능성에 영향을 미칠 수 있음을 시사하는 자료도 있다. 따라서 알레르기 연구에서 위생 가설이 차지하는 역할이 중요하기는 하지만, 지나친 위생 관념이 알레르기 환자 급증의 유일한 원인이라고 속단할 수는 없다.

15

이 글의 제목으로 가장 적절한 것은?

① 알레르기와 아이들
② 알레르기와 공해
③ 알레르기 발생 과정
④ 알레르기의 원인들

| 정답 | ④

| 해설 | 공해, 지나친 위생, 유전, 가정환경 등 알레르기 급증의 다양한 원인을 설명하는 글이므로 ④가 적절하다. 알레르기 발생의 과정이 아닌 원인에 초점이 맞추어진 글이므로 ③을 선택하지 않도록 주의한다.

16

이 글의 흐름상 다음 문장이 들어갈 가장 적절한 곳은?

> 간단히 말하자면, 알레르기 유발 물질에 노출되는 것은 알레르기에 대한 자연적 방어력(면역력)을 생성하는 데 꼭 필요하다.

① [A]
② [B]
③ [C]
④ [D]

| 정답 | ③

| 해설 | 삽입 문장은 위생 가설에 대한 요약이므로 위생 가설에 대해 구체적으로 설명하는 문장 다음인 [C]에 위치하는 것이 글의 흐름상 논리적이다. 따라서 ③이 정답이다.

17

다음 중 이 글의 내용과 일치하지 않는 것은?

① 알레르기는 시골에 사는 아이들에게도 흔하다.
② 예전에는 공해가 알레르기의 주원인이라고 생각했다.
③ 아이들의 면역이 강해지기 위해서는 알레르겐에 덜 노출되어야 한다.
④ 형이나 누나(오빠나 언니)가 없는 아이들은 있는 아이들보다 알레르기에 대한 면역력이 약하다.

| 정답 | ③

| 해설 | ③은 "어릴 때 알레르겐에 더 많이 노출되어야 면역이 강해진다."는 위생 가설의 주장에 반대되므로 내용과 일치하지 않는다. 지문 전반부의 '공해가 알레르기의 원인'이라는 설명은 시골에 사는 아이들에게도 알레르기가 흔하다는 사실로 인해 반박되었음을 알 수 있다. 따라서 오늘날에는 유효하지 않은 과거의 이론이므로 ②도 내용과 일치한다.

| 어휘 | suffer from – ~을 앓다, ~에 시달리다
blame ⓥ 탓하다, 비난하다
allergy ⓝ 알레르기
hygiene hypotheses – 위생 가설
vacuum cleaner – 진공청소기
be exposed to – ~에 노출되다
substance ⓝ 물질
look for – ~을 찾다
air pollution – 대기오염
common ⓐ 흔한, 일반적인
bring up – ~을 양육하다
dusty ⓐ 먼지가 많은
allergen ⓝ 알레르기를 유발하는 항원
build up – ~을 강화하다

immunity ⓝ 면역(력)
be resistant to – ~에 저항력(면역력)이 있다
genetics ⓝ 유전, 유전학
play a part – 역할을 하다
enormous ⓐ 거대한, 막대한
victim ⓝ 환자

encounter ⓥ 마주치다
a wide range of – 다양한
income ⓝ 소득
attention ⓝ 집중, 관심
rise ⓝ 증가

[18-20] 숭실대 2006

플라시보 효과(위약 효과)는 실제로는 치료를 하지 않았는데도 측정, 관찰할 수 있거나 자각될 수 있는 건강상의 치료 효과를 뜻한다. 많은 사람들이 이 효과는 위약 그 자체가 알 수 없는 방식으로 작용했기 때문이라고 생각한다. 위약이란 치료를 하는 의료 행위자가 비활성이거나 무해하다고 생각하는 약이나 치료법이다. 위약은 설탕 성분의 알약일 수도 있고 전분 성분의 알약일 수도 있다. 심지어는 "가짜" 수술과 "가짜" 심리요법도 위약이 될 수 있다. 연구자들과 의사들은 가끔 환자에게 위약을 준다. 위약의 일화적 증거(anecdotal evidence: 일회적인 사건이나 주관적 에피소드에서 얻는 증거로서 과학적이거나 체계적이지 않다.)는 이런 식으로 얻어진 것들이다. 위약 효과에는 과학적 근거가 있다고 생각하는 사람들은, 위약 치료를 받는 대조군을 이용한 임상 연구를 근거로 삼는다. 왜 비활성 물질, 가짜 수술이나 치료 요법이 효과가 있는지는 밝혀지지 않았다. [그러나 일부 사람들은 위약 효과는 머릿속에 있다고 생각한다. 즉, 이 효과는 치료될 수 있다는 믿음이나 회복되고 있다는 주관적 느낌 때문에 생긴다는 것이다.] 심리학자 Irving Kirsch은 "중요한 것은, 자신에게 어떤 일이 일어날지에 대한 자신의 믿음입니다. 중요한 변화를 얻기 위해서 반드시 약에 의존할 필요는 없습니다."라고 말한다. 그는 약물치료, 심리 치료 혹은 병행치료를 받은 우울증 환자에 대한 1972년부터 1995년 사이의 연구 38건과 1998년의 연구 19건을 분석했다. 분석 결과, 약물치료 효과의 50%는 플라시보 효과였다.

18 지문에 따르면 사실인 것은?
① 환자에게 강한 신념이 없을 때, 위약은 더 효과적이다.
② 환자가 의사의 지시를 잘 따를 때, 위약은 효과가 없다.
③ 위약에는 신경학적 성분과 생화학적 성분이 모두 들어 있다.
④ 위약은 무해한 약이거나 가짜 치료일 수 있다.

| 정답 | ④

| 해설 | "Even 'fake' surgery and 'fake' psychotherapy are considered placebos."를 참조하면, 위약에는 설탕 성분이나 전분 성분의 알약뿐 아니라 가짜 수술, 가짜 심리요법까지 포함된다. 따라서 답은 ④이다. 위약 효과는 치료에 대한 주관적 믿음 때문에 생긴다는 것이 중요한 논지이므로 ①을 선택하지 않도록 주의한다.

19 다음 문장의 위치로 가장 적절한 것은?

그러나 일부 사람들은 위약 효과는 머릿속에 있다고 생각한다. 즉, 이 효과는 치료될 수 있다는 믿음이나 회복되고 있다는 주관적 느낌 때문에 생긴다는 것이다.

① [A] ② [B]
③ [C] ④ [D]

| 정답 | ③

| 해설 | however에 주의한다. 앞 문장과 대조적인 내용의 문장임을 알 수 있다. 위약 효과의 정확한 원인은 밝혀지지 않았다는 내용("Why an inert substance, or a fake surgery or therapy, would be effective is not known") 뒤에서 글의 흐름을 전환시켜야 하므로 ③이 논리적으로 적절한 위치이다.

20

지문에 따르면, 다음 중 위약 효과에 대한 묘사가 아닌 것은?
① 알 수 없는
② 치료적인
③ 신학적인
④ 심리적인

| 정답 | ③

| 해설 | 위약 효과는 아직 그 원인이 확실히 규명되지 않았다(mysterious). 실제 치료와 상관없이 치료 효과가 나타나므로 치료적(therapeutic)이다. 위약 효과는 치료에 대한 믿음이나 회복에 대한 신념의 결과이므로 심리적(psychological)이다. 지문에 사용된 단어 'belief'는 주관적 신념이지 종교적 믿음이 아니므로 ③은 위약 효과에 대한 묘사가 아니다.

| 어휘 |
placebo effect – 위약 효과
observable ⓐ 관찰 가능한
attributable to – ~ 때문인
treatment ⓝ 치료, 치료제
inert ⓐ 비활성의
pill ⓝ 알약
fake ⓐ 가짜의 ⓝ 가짜
anecdotal ⓐ 일화적인
point to – ~을 가리키다
effective ⓐ 효과가 있는
rely on – ~에 의존하다
transformation ⓝ 변화
depressed patient – 우울증 환자
due to – ~ 때문에
measurable ⓐ 측정 가능한
improvement ⓝ 개선, 향상
medication ⓝ 약, 약물
administrator ⓝ 집행자, 관리자
innocuous ⓐ 무해한
starch ⓝ 전분
psychotherapy ⓝ 심리요법
garner ⓥ 수집하다, 모으다
substance ⓝ 물질
critical ⓐ 중요한, 중대한, 결정적인
profound ⓐ 근본적인, 심오한
analyze ⓥ 분석하다
combination ⓝ 결합, 조합
response ⓝ 반응

[21-23] 성균관대 2006

이러한 정신과 피부의 상호 교류는 눈에 보이는 것 이상이다. 예를 들어 긁거나 때리는 외부의 자극 없이도 뇌는 신비하게도 당신을 가렵게 할 수 있다. 정서적 스트레스는 표피의 보호 기능을 방해하거나 면역력을 활성화하거나 피부 안쪽에 염증을 일으킬 수 있다. 피부는 또한 면역체계의 중요한 전초기지로서, 그 안에 가득한 백혈구는 체내로 침입한 세균을 먹어 치우며 몸 전체에 면역 반응을 일으키도록 특성화되어 있다. 피부는 이처럼 매우 효과적이기 때문에, 연구자들은 예방 접종 시 이런 면역력이 없는 근육에 직접 주사바늘을 주사하는 오래된 방식 대신에, 결핵 테스트와 유사한 훨씬 덜 아픈 피부 주사를 제안하고 있다. 피부 주사는 매우 소량만으로도 근육주사만큼의 또 그 이상의 효과를 나타내는 것으로 보인다. 피부는 성별에 따라서도 다르다. 남성과 여성의 피부는 비슷하지만, 몇몇 성적 차이로 인해 여성들은 분명히 불리한 점이 있다. 아마도 여성들은 집을 지키고 남성들은 용감히 밖으로 나가 수렵 채집하던 진화적 과거에는 여성의 피부는 더 얇고 덜 지성이어서 비바람을 견디는 데 덜 적합했다. 피부가 얇고 건성일수록 태양이나 담배 연기에 손상되기 더 쉽기 때문에, 그런 환경에 노출된 여성들은 주름이 더 잘 생긴다. 게다가 여성은 남성에 비해 땀을 덜 흘리기 때문에 열사병에 걸리기 더 쉽다. 실제로, 옷을 겹겹이 껴입은 빅토리아 시대 여성들이 항상 쓰고 다니던 프릴 장식 양산은 태양 빛을 차단해 주는 동시에 시원한 그늘을 제공하는 두 가지 기능을 했다.

21 다음 중 빈칸에 적절한 것은?
① 중요한 전초기지
② 흉측한 증세
③ 피부의 예민한 반응
④ 위약 효과
⑤ 정신과 피부의 상호 교류

| 정답 | ⑤

| 해설 | 빈칸이 위치한 문장 다음에 신체적 자극 없이도 뇌가 피부 반응을 일으키는 예시가 이어지므로 정신(뇌)과 피부가 밀접하게 연관되어 있음을 알 수 있다. 정신과 피부의 밀접한 관계를 나타나는 ⑤가 빈칸에 적절하다.

22 지문을 둘로 나눈다면 다음 중 어느 곳에서 나누어야 하는가?
① ⓐ
② ⓑ
③ ⓒ
④ ⓓ
⑤ ⓔ

| 정답 | ②

| 해설 | ⓑ 앞까지는 피부의 효과적인 역할들이, ⓑ 뒤부터는 성별에 따른 피부의 차이가 언급되므로 내용이 바뀌는 경계선인 ⓑ에서 단락을 나누는 것이 좋다.

23 지문에 따르면, 다음 중 사실이 아닌 것은?
① 외부적 원인 없이도 가려움을 느낄 수 있다.
② 피부의 백혈구는 인체에 침입한 세균으로부터 방어한다.
③ 정서적 스트레스는 면역체계를 약화시킬 수 있다.
④ 흡연은 피부노화와 아무 관련이 없다.
⑤ 여성들은 남성들보다 피부 트러블이 생기기 더 쉽다.

| 정답 | ④

| 해설 | "Since thinner, drier skin is more prone to damage from the sun or the smoke of cigarettes, women so exposed are more apt to wrinkle."를 참조하면, 남성의 피부보다 더 얇고 건성인 여성의 피부는 태양빛이나 담배 연기에 손상되기 쉽다는 것은 피부 트러블이 더 잘 생긴다는 뜻이다. 따라서 정답은 ④이다.

| 어휘 |
interchange ⓝ (정보, 생각 등의) 상호 교류
external ⓐ 외부의
swat ⓝ 찰싹 때리기
epidermis ⓝ 표피
immune ⓐ 면역의
outpost ⓝ 전초기지
specialized ⓐ 특성화된
gobble up – 먹어 치우다
trigger ⓥ 유발하다
vaccinate ⓥ 예방 접종하다
akin to – ~와 비슷한
fraction ⓝ 소량
distinctive ⓐ 분명한
hunter-gathering ⓐ 수렵채집(하는)
oily ⓐ 기름기가 있는
expose ⓥ 노출하다
sweat ⓥ 땀 흘리다
frilly ⓐ 프릴 장식이 달린
heavily clad – 옷을 두껍게 껴입은
impart ⓥ 전해 주다

itch ⓝ 가려움
scratch ⓝ 긁기
protective function – 보호기능
activate ⓥ 활성화하다
inflammatory ⓐ 염증의
laden with – ~이 가득한
white cell – 백혈구
microbe ⓝ 세균
immunologic response – 면역 반응
muscle ⓝ 근육
tuberculosis ⓝ 결핵
dose ⓝ 투여량
throwback ⓝ 과거의 것
elements ⓝ 비바람, 폭풍우
be prone to – ~하는 경향이 있다, ~하기 쉽다
be apt to – ~하는 경향이 있다, ~하기 쉽다
heat stroke – 열사병
parasol ⓝ 양산
duty ⓝ 임무, 의무
shade ⓝ 그늘

[24-27] 성균관대 2008

의학계 외의 모든 학계 연구자들인 이 비판가들은 1980년대 이후로 미국과 유럽 여러 국가에서 인구 비만율이 거의 두 배가 되었다는 조사 결과는 반박하지 않는다. 또한 비만, 특히 심각한 비만은 일부 질병과 조기 사망의 원인일 수 있다는 것도 인정한다. 그러나 그들은 과체중과 비만이 매우 심각하고 악화되는 건강 문제를 일으킬 수 있다는 전문가들의 경고는 과장된 것이라고 주장한다. 예를 들어 그들은 2003년 질병 통제 및 예방 센터(Centers for Disease Control and Prevention) 소장 Juile L. Gerberding의 "독감과 중세의 흑사병을 망라해 그 어떤 전염병도 국가와 사회에 미치는 영향 면에서 오늘날의 대대적안 비만 현상만큼 심각하지 않다"는 주장을 비웃었다. (1918년~1919년 사이에 전 세계를 휩쓴 독감은 미국에서만 675,000명을 전 세계적으로 4천만 명의 인명을 앗아갔다.)
시카고 대학의 정책과학자인 Oliver의 주장에 따르면, 사실은 현재 "상당수가 다이어트 산업으로부터 연구비 지원을 받고 있는 소수의 과학자들과 의사들이 과체중과 비만에 대한 임의적이고 비과학적인 정의를 내리고 있다. 그들은 체중 증가에 대한 주장들을 과장하고 통계를 조작한다. 게다가 비만과 관련된 건강의 복잡한 현실들을 대부분 간과하고 있다."
Boulder의 콜라라도 대학 법학 교수인 Campos도 같은 의견이다. 그에 따르면 이 복잡한 현실들 중 하나는 한 집단에서 나타나는 비만도의 차이는 50~80%는 유전적 차이 때문이라는, 널리 인정되는 증거이다. 체중의 5% 이상을 장기적으로 감량시킬 수 있다고 입증된 안전하고 실용적인 방법은 없기 때문에, "보건 당국의 권고, 즉 '적정 체중' 범위 내로 체질량지수를 유지하는 것은 이를 따르려는 대다수의 사람들에게 정말 불가능하다." BMI로 표기하는 체질량지수는 체중 대 신장의 비율이다.

24

다음 중 밑줄 친 "blowing hot air"의 뜻은 무엇인가?

① 사실인 척하다
② 사실을 과장하다
③ 비관적이다
④ 일반 사람들을 속이다
⑤ 속임수를 쓰다

| 정답 | ②

| 해설 | 'hot air'는 '대단해 보이지만 실제로는 실속 없는 장담, 허풍'을 의미한다. 따라서 ②가 답이다.

25

다음 중 사실이 아닌 것은?

① 비만 인구의 수는 1980년 이후로 두 배로 증가했다.
② 비만은 때로 조기 사망에 이를 수 있다.
③ 비만에는 유전적 요인이 중요한 역할을 한다.
④ 다이어트 제품을 파는 기업들로부터 연구 지원을 받는 의사들이 많다.
⑤ 비만은 성인병의 가장 큰 원인이다.

| 정답 | ⑤

| 해설 | 첫 단락에 "비만이 일부 질병의 원인이 될 수는 있다"는 언급이 있지만 "성인병의 가장 주요한 원인"이라는 언급은 없다. ⑤는 비약이므로 사실이 아니다.

26

비만에 대해 다른 의견을 가진 사람은 누구인가?

① ⓐ experts
② ⓑ Juile L. Gerberding
③ ⓒ Oliver
④ ⓓ a relatively small group of scientists and doctors
⑤ ⓔ health authorities

| 정답 | ③

| 해설 | Oliver를 제외한 인물들은 비만을 심각한 질병으로 정의한다. Oliver는 비만을 심각한 질병으로 정의하는 이들의 입장에 반대하면서, 다이어트 산업의 지원을 받은 일부 과학자와 의사들이 비만을 임의적이고 비과학적으로 정의한다고 비판하고 있다. 따라서 ③이 정답이다.

27

다음 중 다이어트 산업의 지원을 받는 의사와 과학자들의 문제가 아닌 것은?

① 그들은 과체중을 잘못 정의한다.
② 그들은 비만의 위험성을 과장한다.
③ 그들은 사실을 조작한다.
④ 그들은 몇 가지 건강 문제들을 설명하기 위해 다른 사실들을 간과한다.
⑤ 그들은 지나치게 현실적인 BMI 기준을 제시한다.

| 정답 | ⑤

| 해설 | 세 번째 단락에는 다이어트 산업으로부터 연구지원을 받는 의사들의 문제점이 상술되어 있다. 'BMI에 대해 지나치게 현실적인 기준'을 제시한다는 내용은 없다. 따라서 ⑤가 정답이다.

| 어휘 |
critic ⓝ 비평가, 비판가
obese ⓐ 비만한
roughly ⓐⓓ 대략; 거칠게
extreme ⓐ 극단적인
premature death – 조기 사망
overweight ⓝ 과체중
massive ⓐ 심각한; 대량의, 엄청난
assertion ⓝ 주장
influenza ⓝ 독감
in terms of – ~의 관점에서
political scientist – 정책과학자
arbitrary ⓐ 임의적인
inflate ⓥ 과장하다, 부풀리다
statistics ⓝ 통계
complicated ⓐ 복잡한
account for – ~을 차지하다, 설명하다
long-term ⓐ 장기적인
maintain ⓥ 유지하다
literally ⓐⓓ 말 그대로, 완전히

dispute ⓥ 반박하다
fraction ⓝ 일부, 소수
acknowledge ⓥ 인정하다, 시인하다
factor ⓝ 요소, 원인
blow hot air – 과장하다, 허풍떨다
obesity ⓝ 비만
scoff ⓥ 비웃다, 조롱하다
epidemic ⓝ 전염병, 대대적인 유행
plague ⓝ 흑사병
impact ⓝ 영향, 충돌
fund ⓥ 자금(기금)을 대다
definition ⓝ 정의
distort ⓥ 왜곡하다
ignore ⓥ 무시하다
genetic difference – 유전적 차이
induce ⓥ 유도하다
authorities ⓝ 관계 당국
body mass index – 체질량지수(BMI)
ratio ⓝ 비율

[28-31] 한양대 2008

신경성 식욕 부진(Anorexia nervosa: 거식증)은 말 그대로 "과민으로 인한 식욕 상실"이고 체중 감소가 그 특징이다. 그러나 거식증 환자는 식욕을 잃는 것이 아니라, 식욕의 억제를 통해 체중을 잃는다. 대부분의 거식증 환자는 자신이 뚱뚱하다거나 식사를 조절하지 못하면 뚱뚱해질 수도 있다는 생각에 시달린다. 이런 생각은 보통 자신의 실제 체중과 무관하다. 이것을 신체 이미지가 왜곡되었다고 한다. 그리고 이 현상에는 뚜렷한 문화적 요인도 있다. 거식증은 서구의 후기 산업국가에서 더 흔하고, 미국에서는 흑인이나 히스패닉보다 백인들에게서 더 많이 나타난다. 우리가 살고 있는 마른 체형의 문화는 분명 거식증에 영향을 미치는 요인이기는 하지만 유일한 원인은 아니다.

거식증은 개인의 고유한 문화, 사회, 가족, 심리, 생물학적 요인들의 복합적 결과물이다. 가능한 이론은 다음과 같다. 설득력 있는 한 이론에 따르면, 자신과 자신의 삶을 통제하려는 사람들이 거식증에 걸린다는 것이다. 삶의 다른 측면들은 그렇지 않지만 음식과 체중은 통제할 수 있다. 음식의 유혹 앞에서 먹는 것을 자제하면 성취감이 생긴다. 거식증 환자 상당수가 과거에 학대, 방치, 기타 정신적 외상을 경험했고, 그에 대한 대처기제(cope mechanism)로 거식증이 생긴다. 체중 감소는 어려움을 극복하는 구체적인 방법이다. 고통으로부터 주의를 돌리는 데 도움이 되기 때문이다. 많은 거식증 환자들이 다음의 두 가지 특징을 보인다. 첫째, 대부분이 자존감이 낮다. 둘째, 감정적 문제를 솔직하게 드러내는 것을 어려워한다. 이것은 성격과도 관련 있다. 예를 들어, 이들은 강박적이거나 완벽주의자일 수 있다. 대체로, 섭식장애는 주체적 인간으로 성장하고 성숙하는 과정의 어려움 속에서 나타난다.

28

다음 중 지문의 제목으로 가장 적절한 것은?

① 음식과 거식증
② 거식증의 정서적 양상
③ 거식증의 원인과 증상
④ 마른 체형 문화가 거식증에 미치는 영향

| 정답 | ③

| 해설 | 첫 단락에 거식증의 증상, 두 번째 단락에 거식증의 복합적 원인들이 상술되었으므로 ③이 적절하다. ①, ②, ④는 언급되기는 했지만 지엽적인 내용이므로 선택하지 않도록 주의한다.

29

ⓐ와 ⓒ에 들어갈 말은?

① ~이 없는 – 금지하다
② ~와 무관한 – 억제하다
③ ~에 좌우되는 – 유발하다
④ ~의 영향을 받지 않는 – 불러일으키다

| 정답 | ④

| 해설 | 빈칸 ⓐ가 위치한 문장과 그 다음 문장이 부연의 논리구조이다. 왜곡된 신체 이미지란 자신의 실제 체중과 무관하게 (independent of) 자신이 뚱뚱하다는 착각이다. 빈칸 ⓒ가 위치한 문장과 그 앞 문장은 인과의 논리구조이다. 거식증 환자들은 삶을 통제하고 싶어하므로, 음식 섭취를 자제(통제)했을 때, 성취감이 생길(evoke) 것이다. 따라서 ④가 정답이다.

30

ⓑ와 비슷한 의미의 단어는?

① 실현 가능한
② 믿기 힘든
③ 가치 있는
④ 비슷한

| 정답 | ①

| 해설 | plausible은 '이치에 맞는, 그럴듯한, 타당해 보이는'의 뜻이므로 feasible(실현 가능한, 현실적인)과 의미가 비슷하다. 앞 문장 "Some possibilities are discussed below.[가능성 (있는 이론)은 다음과 같다.]"에서 plausible의 의미가 feasible과 가깝다는 것을 유추할 수 있다. 따라서 ①이 정답이다.

31

지문에 따르면, 다음 중 사실인 것은?

① 거식증 환자들은 자신의 가치와 능력을 의심한다.
② 거식증 환자들은 음식 섭취를 억제하면서 성취감을 얻는다.
③ 거식증은 선진국보다 개발도상국에서 더 흔하다.
④ 거식증은 환자가 고통스러운 기억을 잊고 살아가는 데 도움이 된다.

| 정답 | ②

| 해설 | ②는 문장 "Restricting food intake while in the presence of enticing foods evokes feelings of accomplishment.(음식의 유혹 앞에서 먹는 것을 자제하면 성취감이 생긴다.)"의 내용과 일치한다. 거식증 환자들

의 낮은 자존감은 자신의 가치와 능력에 대한 의심이 아니라 신체 이미지와 관련된 자신감의 결여를 의미하므로 ①을 선택하지 않도록 주의한다. 거식증은 환자가 고통스러운 기억으로부터 주의를 돌리는 대응 기제일 뿐이므로 ④는 비약이다.

| 어휘 |
anorexia nervosa – 신경성 식욕 부진, 거식증
appetite ⓝ 식욕
suppress ⓥ 억제하다
keep ~ in control – ~을 통제하다
refer to A as B – A를 B라고 부르다
component ⓝ 요소
thinness ⓝ 수척함, 빈약
by no means – 결코 ~가 아닌
response ⓝ 반응, 대응
restrict ⓥ 제한하다, 자제하다
enticing ⓐ 유혹적인
abuse ⓝ 학대
traumatic ⓐ 정신적 외상의
concrete ⓐ 구체적인
serve to – ~에 도움이 되다
feature ⓝ 특징
problematic ⓐ 문제가 있는
personality ⓝ 성격, 개성
eating disorder – 섭식 장애
grow up – 성장하다

literally ⓐⓓ 문자 그대로
nervous ⓐ 예민한, 불안한
urge ⓝ 충동, 욕구
independent of – ~와 무관한
distorted ⓐ 왜곡된
affect ⓥ 병이 나게 하다, 영향을 미치다
factor ⓝ 요인, 요소
sole ⓐ 유일한
plausible ⓐ 그럴듯한, 타당성이 있을 듯한
intake ⓝ 섭취
accomplishment ⓝ 성취
neglect ⓝ 방치
coping mechanism – 대처기제
cope with – 대처하다
distract ⓥ 주의를 돌리다
deal with – ~에 대처하다, ~을 처리하다
have something to do with – ~와 관련 있다
obsessional ⓐ 강박적인
arise ⓥ 발생하다

[32-34] 서강대 2012

과학자들은 아직 숙취의 이유를 전부 파악하지는 못했으나 다양한 원인을 제시한 바 있다. 한 가지 원인은 금단 증상으로, 떨림과 함께 땀을 흘리게 만든다. 두 번째 요소는 탈수일 것으로 보인다. 알코올은 배뇨 작용을 억제하는 호르몬의 분비를 방해한다. 따라서 술집과 파티장에서 화장실에 사람이 몰리는 결과를 낳는다. 이 와중에 알코올은 저혈당 현상을 유발하기도 하며, 이로 인해 현기증과 함께 뼈가 젤리로 변한 것 같은 느낌을 주는 근력저하 현상이 발생한다. 이와 동시에 신체는 알코올을 분해하기 위해 알코올 그 자체보다 독성이 더 강할 수 있는 화학 물질을 분비한다. 이로 인해 메스꺼움 및 기타 여러 증상이 발생한다. 마지막으로, 알코올은 염증을 유발하며, 이는 결과적으로 백혈구가 사이토카인이라 불리는 분자를 혈류에 넘쳐날 정도로 과잉 생성하는 결과를 낳는다. 분명히 말하자면 사이토카인은 통증과 고통 그리고 무기력 발생의 원인이며, 이런 증세로 인해 우리의 신체는 독감 바이러스의 공격을 받았을 경우, 그리고 마찬가지로 어쩌면 알코올의 공격을 받았을 경우, 일을 하게 되기보다 침대에 누워 있게 되며, 이를 통해 백혈구는 신체 에너지를 활용하여 침입자와 싸우도록 에너지를 해방시킨다.

숙취는 예방 가능한 질병이다: 술을 안마시면 된다. 그럼에도 불구하고 사람들은 언제나 자신들이 생각하기에 알코올에 의존하게 될 좋은 이유를 찾아 왔다. 알코올이 지닌 한 가지 매력은 알코올에는 소심함을 덜어 주어 결국에는 우리가 이웃에게 호통을 칠 수 있게 하는 힘이 있다는 점이다. 알코올은 우리로 하여금 삶의 진리를 발견했다는 생각이 들도록 설득시키는 힘이 있고, 이는 위로가 되는 경험이자 술에 취하지 않았을 때는 거의 할 수 없는 경험이다. 알코올이라는 렌즈를 통해 세상을 보면 세상은 좀 더 멋져 보인다. 연극 비평가인 조지 진 네이션은 "술을 마시면 다른 사람들이 재밌어 보인다"고 말했다. 이런 모든 이유 때문에 음주는 사람들에게 힘을 준다.

32

본문 빈칸 가운데 다음 문장이 들어갈 위치로 가장 적합한 것은 무엇인가?

> 연극 비평가인 조지 진 네이선은 "술을 마시면 다른 사람들이 재밌어 보인다"고 말했다.

① [A]
② [B]
③ [C]
④ [D]

| 정답 | ④

| 해설 | 마지막 단락에서는 사람들이 숙취에도 불구하고 알코올을 섭취하는 이유에 관해 말하고 있다. [B] 다음 문장은 그 첫 번째 이유를 설명하고 있고, [C] 다음 문장은 그 두 번째 이유를 설명하고 있다. 그리고 주어진 문장은 "다른 사람들이 재밌어 보인다", 즉 "세상이 즐거워 보이고 멋져 보인다"는 내용을 담고 있다. 이는 [D] 앞 문장인 "알코올이라는 렌즈를 통해 세상을 보면 세상은 좀 더 멋져 보인다(Through the lens of alcohol, the world seems nicer)"와 통하는 내용이다. 따라서 주어진 문장은 [D]에 들어가야 하며, 답은 ④가 된다.

33

다음 중 본문에 따르면 사실인 것은 무엇인가?

① 숙취를 유발하는 것은 의학적으로 밝혀졌다.
② 술에 취했을 때 알코올이 여러분에게 해를 끼치는 것보다 신체가 해를 더 많이 끼친다.
③ 알코올은 저혈당을 유발하며, 저혈당은 사이토카인이라 불리는 백혈구 세포의 생성을 돕는다.
④ 알코올은 정신을 억제하는 효과를 낳는다.

| 정답 | ②

| 해설 | "이와 동시에 신체는 알코올을 분해하기 위해 알코올 그 자체보다 독성이 더 강할 수 있는 화학 물질을 분비한다(Meanwhile, the body, to break down the alcohol, is releasing chemicals that may be more toxic than alcohol itself)" 이는 보기 중에서 ②와 일치하는 내용이다. 따라서 답은 ②이다. 참고로, 본문 첫 문장은 ①과 정반대되는 내용이며, 알코올이 저혈당 현상을 유발하는 것은 맞지만 사이토카인은 백혈구와 관련이 있지 저혈당과는 관계가 없으므로 ③은 답이 될 수 없고, 본문 마지막 단락에서 알코올은 소심함을 덜어 주지 정신을 억제하는 효과는 낳지 않으므로 ④도 답이 될 수 없다.

34

다음 중 본문에 따르면 숙취가 원인인 것이 아닌 것은 무엇인가?

① 갈증
② 메스꺼움
③ 감기
④ 따갑고 부어오름

| 정답 | ③

| 해설 | "두 번째 요소는 탈수일 것으로 보인다(A second factor may be dehydration)"에서 술을 마시면 탈수 현상이 일어나며 탈수 현상은 갈증을 유발한다(①). "이로 인해 메스꺼움 및 기타 여러 증상이 발생한다(these would result in nausea and other symptoms)"에서 메스꺼움은 ②에 해당된다. "알코올은 염증을 유발하며(the alcohol has produced inflammation)"에서 염증이 발생했다는 말은 따갑고 부어오르는 증상이 발생했다는 의미이기도 하다(④). 그러나 본문은 숙취 때문에 누워 있는 것을 독감 때문에 누워 있는 것에 비유하고 있으나, 숙취 때문에 독감이

나 감기에 걸린다는 주장은 하고 있지 않다. 따라서 답은 ③이다.

| 어휘 | hangover ⓝ 숙취
tremor ⓝ 떨림
secretion ⓝ 분비
hypoglycemia ⓝ 저혈(당)
muscle weakness – 근력저하
inflammation ⓝ 염증
bloodstream ⓝ 혈류
apparently ⓐⓓ 외견상으로는, 명백히, 분명히
thereby ⓐⓓ 그렇게 함으로써, 그것 때문에
recourse ⓝ 의지, 의존
tell off – 호통치다, 야단치다
sober ⓐ 술에 취하지 않은
induce ⓥ 유발하다
queasy ⓐ 메스꺼운

withdrawal ⓝ 금단
dehydration ⓝ 탈수
urination ⓝ 배뇨 (작용)
convert into – ~로 바꾸다[변화하다]
jello ⓝ 젤리
flood A with B – B가 A에 넘쳐나게[범람하게] 하다
cytokine ⓝ 사이토카인
lethargy ⓝ 무기력
malady ⓝ 질병, 심각한 문제
disinhibit ⓥ 소심함을 덜어 주다
comforting ⓐ 위로가 되는
determine ⓥ 밝히다
inhibit ⓥ 억제하다, 저항하다

[35-37] 성균관대 2013

최근의 의학 보고서에 따르면 졸음운전은 고속도로 같은 지루하고 단조로운 도로상에서 벌어지는 사고의 20% 이상을 차지한다. 보통 이런 사고의 경우 도로 밖으로 벗어나기, 다른 차의 뒤를 들이박기 등이 있고 졸고 있는 운전자가 브레이크를 제때 밟지 못해 심각한 부상을 야기할 가능성도 크다. (A) 물론 신체의 생체 시계가 주된 영향을 미치는 것도 사실인데, 이는 졸음운전 사고는 자연적으로 졸음이 닥칠 확률이 높을 때 최고조에 달하기 때문이다. (B) 30세 미만의 남성이 가장 취약하며 그 이유는 이들 운전자가 가장 보통 이른 시간에 도로에 나서기 때문이다. 명백히 이들 운전자가 졸면서도 운전을 하는 위험을 더 많이 무릅쓴다. (C) 이와는 달리 나이 든 사람들은 오후 일찍 찾아오는 '졸음' 때문에 고생하며, 이 시간대에 가장 위험하다. 운전 당시의 시간도 총 운전 시간만큼 중요하다는 것이 드러났지만 운전자에게 제공되는 실질적인 조언은 종종 운전 당시의 시간보다는 총 운전 시간에 집중한다. (D) 차량 탑재형 졸음운전 감시 모니터 같은 장비가 표면적으로는 운전자에게 경고할 목적으로 광고되고 있으나, 이들 장비에 관한 의문이 제기되고 있다. (E) 이미 자기가 졸리다는 것을 알고 있으면서도 운전을 고집하는 운전자에게 경고를 준다는 것이 무슨 의미가 있는가? 게다가 이들 장비의 신뢰성은 증명되지 않았고 어쩌면 운전자들이 <u>더 큰 위험을 무릅쓰도록 조장할지도 모른다</u>. (F) 운전은 피곤한 운전자들에게 계속 깨어 있도록 노력을 기울이게 자극할 뿐 아니라, 이런 상황에서는 졸음의 시작이 늦춰지거나 시작되지 못할 수도 있다. 가장 좋은 조언은 밤에 운전할 이유를 찾지 않는 것이고 아니면 만약 활기가 넘치는 것 같지 않다면 가능하면 차를 도로 밖으로 빨리 빼는 것이다.

35 위 본문이 세 부분으로 나뉘게 된다면 경계선으로 삼기 가장 좋은 부분은 어디인가?
① (A) and (E)　　② (B) and (C)
③ (B) and (F)　　④ (C) and (D)
⑤ (A) and (D)

| 정답 | ⑤

| 해설 | 본문 처음부터 (A)까지의 내용은 졸음운전이 전체 사고에 차지하는 비중과 졸음운전의 위험성에 대해 말하고 있다. (A)에서부터 (D)까지는 졸음운전의 경우 생체시계의 측면을 포함하여 운전하는 시간뿐 아니라 운전 당시의 시간과도 관계가 있음을 말하고 있다. 마지막으로 (D) 이하는 새로운 장비를 소개하며, 단점을 서술하고 졸음운전을 하지 않기 위한 조언을 담고 있다. 이 문제는 1995년 The Guardian 기사로 원문에는 (A)와 (D)로 구분되어 있는데, 보기가 제대로 복원이 안 된 것 같아 저자가 ⑤번 보기를 수정하였다.

36

다음 중 빈칸에 가장 알맞은 것은 무엇인가?
① 즉시 운전을 멈춘다
② 더 큰 위험을 무릅쓰도록 조장한다
③ 더 조심한다
④ 다른 차량에 더 많은 주의를 돌린다
⑤ 더 편안해하다

| 정답 | ②

| 해설 | 운전자가 졸음운전을 하면 경고하는 장비가 판매되고 있는데, (E) 단락에서는 과연 그러한 장비가 효용성이 있을지 의문을 표하고 있다. "이미 자기가 졸리다는 것을 알고 있으면서도 운전을 고집하는 운전자에게 경고를 준다는 것이 무슨 의미가 있는가?(What is the use of alerting drivers already aware that they are sleepy but who still persist in driving?)"라고 저자는 의문을 표하고 있으며, "게다가(What is more)"라는 접속사가 들어가 있으므로 그 다음 문장에서도 마찬가지로 효용성에 의문을 표하는 내용이 들어갈 것임을 유추할 수 있다. 이러한 점을 고려해 보면 보기 중에서 빈칸에 대입했을 때 가장 적합한 것은 '장비로 인해 오히려 위험을 무릅쓰려 한다'는 의미의 ②이다.

37

본문에 따르면 다음 중 사실은 무엇인가?
① 젊은 운전자들은 자신의 운전 기술을 자랑스러워하기 때문에 더 큰 위험을 무릅쓴다.
② 혼잡한 분기점은 고속도로보다 졸리운 운전자들에게 훨씬 더 위험하다.
③ 오후에 운전하는 것은 나이 든 운전자들에게 위험할 수 있다.
④ 졸음을 쫓는 운전 장비는 젊은이보다 나이 든 사람들에게 더 잘 먹히는 경향이 있다.
⑤ 대부분의 운전자들은 운전 당시의 시간보다는 총 운전 시간이 덜 중요하다고 믿는다.

| 정답 | ③

| 해설 | "나이 든 사람들은 오후 일찍 찾아오는 '졸음' 때문에 고생한다(older people suffer from an early afternoon 'dip')." 따라서 답은 ③이다.
①, ②, ④는 본문과 별 관계 없는 내용이며 ⑤의 경우는 본문에 "운전자에게 제공되는 실질적인 조언은 종종 운전 당시의 시간보다는 총 운전 시간에 집중한다(practical advice to drivers often concentrates more on the length of the drive than its timing)"는 내용은 있지만 운전자들이 이에 집중한다는 내용은 없다. 따라서 ⑤ 역시 답으로 볼 수 없다.

| 어휘 | wheel ⓝ 운전대 motorway ⓝ 고속도로
account for – (부분·비율을) 차지하다 typically ⓐⓓ 보통, 일반적으로

biological clock – 생체시계
vulnerable ⓐ 취약한
time of day – 시계가 가리키는 시각
what is the use of – ~이 무슨 소용이 있는가
unproven ⓐ 증명되지 않은
motivate ⓥ ~에게 동기를 주다, 자극하다
distort ⓥ 왜곡하다, 일그러뜨리다
immediately ⓐⓓ 즉시
interchange ⓝ (고속도로의) 분기점

peak ⓥ 최고조에 달하다
apparently ⓐⓓ 명백히
ostensibly ⓐⓓ 표면적으로
persist in – ~을 고집하다
reliability ⓝ 신뢰도, 신뢰성
onset ⓝ 시작, 징후
bright and breezy – 쾌활한, 활기가 넘치는
relaxed ⓐ 느긋한, 편안한

[38-40] 성균관대 2013

기존의 공식은 간단하다. 독감예방접종 시에는 독감의 노여움으로 인해 가장 큰 피해를 받게 될 사람들을 우선적으로 접종한다. 이렇게 취약한 유형의 사람들로는 노인 및 갓난아이들을 들 수 있다. 이는 이치에 맞는 정책으로 보이며, 미국의 질병통제센터에서 오랫동안 보급해 온 정책이기도 하다. 최근에 와서야 우선 접종 대상이 18세까지의 청소년으로 확대되었으며, 이는 비록 청소년들이 독감으로 인해 사망할 위험은 거의 없지만 독감에 걸릴 가능성은 다른 사람들에 비해 높다는 것을 근거로 한다. 하지만 안 좋은 영향을 받을 가능성이 가장 높은 이들에게 예방접종을 하는 것이 독감에 대처하기 위한 올바른 방법은 아니다. 이번 주 "사이언스"지에 발표된 한 논문에 따르면, 존 매드락 박사는 예방접종의 범위를 학령기 아동들까지 확대하더라도, 개인 보호에 집중하는 기존의 정책은, 독감의 확산 고리를 끊는 데 도움이 되는 소위 집단면역을 창조하는, 예방접종이 지닌 진정한 보건적 가치를 여전히 폄하하고 있다고 주장한다. 매드락 박사는 독감 바이러스를 확산시킬 가능성이 가장 높은 사람, 즉 학령기 아동 및 이들의 부모일 가능성이 가장 높은 사람들이지만 현재 시점에서는 예방접종 우선순위에서 가장 밀리는 연령대인 30~40대를 대상으로 한 예방접종에 집중하는 것이 낫다고 주장한다. 이는 적어도 독감 확산 방식을 수학적으로 모델화한 결과이다. 이들은 1918년과 1957년의 독감 확산 사례를 수학적 모델로 삼았다. 하지만 어떤 결과를 살펴보았든지 그리고 어떤 독감 확산 패턴을 살펴보았든지 간에 결과는 항상 같았다. 독감에 대한 최선의 접근법은 갓난아이와 노인에게 예방접종을 하는 것이 아니라 어린아이 및 아이의 부모에게 예방접종을 하는 것이었다. 게다가 이 방법이 비용도 적게 들고 더 효율적인 방법이다. 평상시에는 한 해에 미국에서 대략 8,500만 개의 백신이 보급된다. 매드락 박사는 만약 자신의 접근법을 따를 경우, 보급량이 6,000만 개로 줄어들 수 있다고 추정했다.

38 본문의 제목으로 가장 알맞은 것은 "독감 바이러스 확산을 막는 방법"이다.
① 독감예방접종에 대한 과도한 의존
② 독감 바이러스 확산을 막는 방법
③ 다양한 유형의 독감에 대처하는 방법
④ 새로운 독감 백신의 필요성
⑤ 예방접종의 경제적 비용

| 정답 | ②

| 해설 | 본문은 독감 바이러스 확산을 막기 위해 기존과는 다른 접근법을 취할 것을 주장하고 있다. 따라서 답은 ②이다.

39

다음 중 빈칸에 가장 적합한 것은 무엇인가?

① 젊고 부주의한 사람
② 나이 들고 약한 사람
③ 독감 바이러스에 옮을 가능성이 가장 높은 사람
④ 독감 바이러스를 확산시킬 가능성이 가장 높은 사람
⑤ 사망할 가능성이 있는 사람

| 정답 | ④

| 해설 | 매드락 박사는 독감의 확산 고리를 끊기 위해 우선적으로 접종해야 할 사람들이 30~40대라고 주장했다. 이는 역으로 말하면, 이 연령대의 사람들이 "독감 바이러스를 확산시킬 가능성이 가장 높은 사람들"이기 때문에 이들로부터 바이러스가 확산되지 못하도록 우선적으로 접종을 시켜야 한다는 의미가 된다. 따라서 답은 ④이다.

40

본문에 따르면 매드락 박사의 수학적 모델은 백신 분배에 대한 새로운 방법을 제시한다.

① 다른 유형의 백신을 추산하기 위한 효과적인 방법
② 다른 연령대에 맞는 효과적인 치료법
③ 백신의 마케팅 전략
④ 백신 제조에 대한 새로운 방법
⑤ 백신 분배에 대한 새로운 방법

| 정답 | ⑤

| 해설 | 매드락 박사의 수학적 모델을 통해 기존의 주 접종 대상이 아니라 30~40대의 사람들에게 접종이 먼저 이루어져야 한다는 사실을 알 수 있었다. 즉 백신을 어떻게 분배해야 할지에 관해 새로운 방안이 제시된 것이다. 따라서 답은 ⑤이다.

| 어휘 | inoculate ⓥ 접종하다
wrath ⓝ 분노, 노여움
transmission ⓝ 전염, 확산
reckon ⓥ 추정하다

susceptible to – ~에 영향 받기 쉬운, ~에 걸리기 쉬운
promulgate ⓥ 널리 알리다, 보급하다
herd immunity – 집단면역
calculate ⓥ 추산하다, 예측하다

[41-44] 서강대 2018

최근까지만 하더라도 대중화된 의료 혁신의 선구자들이 오늘날 바이오 연구 및 규제 기관의 주변부에 머물러 왔다. 하지만 불과 지난 두 달 동안 허가받지 않은 유전자 치료제를 자신의 몸속에 주입한 비디오를 공개한 사람들이 2명에 달했다. 자가 실험자 2명 중 하나인 조시아 제이너(Josiah Zayner)는 가정용 유전자 편집 키트를 판매하는 신생 기업인 디 오딘(the Odin)의 CEO이다. 유전자 편집 기술을 이용한 자가 실험이 새로운 형태의 '허가가 필요 없는(permission less)' 혁신으로 불려야 할까? 아니면 자칭 바이오 해커들이 기존의 규제 체계를 시험해 봄으로써 생체의학 혁신에 일조하는 사람들의 신생 생태계를 해칠 것으로 봐야 하는가? 유전자 치료를 이용한 자가 실험, 감염의 위험과 면역체계 부작용에서부터 관련 위험에 대한 이해의 부족과 환자들의 비현실적 기대에 이르기까지, 안전성과 윤리적 측면에서 골치 아픈 의문을 제기한다. 하지만 유전자 편집 키트의 판매를 금지하는 것은 빈약하고 임시적인 해결책에 불과하다. 우리에게 필요한 것은 기존의 연구 체계 외부에 '사회에 책임지는 혁신(responsible innovation)'의 풍토를 조성하는 것이다. 우리는 합법성을 구축하는 것 외에도 새로운 형태의 의료 연구에 대해 맞춤형 규제 지원을 구축하는 것도 시급히 필요하다는 것을 인식해야 한다. 앞으로 나아가야 할 길은 규제되지 않는 급진 과학을 촉진하는 것이 아니라 시민, 환자, 윤리학자, 규제감시관 등이 함께 참여해 맞춤형 규제 체계(adaptive oversight system)에 대해 재고하고 설계할 수 있도록 하는 참여 채널을 발전시키는 것이다.

41 다음 중 빈칸 Ⓐ와 Ⓑ에 들어갈 가장 적합한 것은?

	Ⓐ	Ⓑ
①	초국가적인	뿐만 아니라
②	대중화된	하지만
③	생태계의	예를 들어
④	최적의	그럼에도 불구하고

| 정답 | ②

| 해설 | Ⓐ의 경우 최근 발견한 의료 혁신을 사유화하지 않고 대중들에게 공개했다는 'widely shared videos' 부분을 통해, '대중화시키다, 민주화시키다'라는 의미에서 democratized가 와야 한다. Ⓑ의 경우, 앞 내용이 바이오 해커들이 의료 혁신에 해를 가져올 수 있다는 내용이고, 뒤에는 유전자 편집 키트의 판매와 같은 바이오 해커들의 행위를 금지하는 것이 해결책이 되지 못한다는 내용이므로, 역접을 나타내는 Yet, Nevertheless가 올 수 있다. 따라서 정답은 ②가 된다.

42 다음 중 저자의 설명 방식과 가장 유사한 설명 방식은?

① 학술적 분석을 제공하는 연구원
② 뉴스 기사를 보도하는 일간신문 기자
③ 감동적인 강연을 들려주는 동기부여 연설가
④ 윤리적 딜레마에 대해 의견을 제공하는 대중 참여 지식인

| 정답 | ④

| 해설 | 본문은 의료계 외부에 위치한 최근의 의학적 혁신을 어떻게 다룰 것인지에 대해 설명하고 있다. 이에 권장해서도 안 되지만 무조건 금지해서도 안 된다고 말하면서, 마지막 문장에서와 같이 여러 이해당사자들이 참여하는 소통의 공간

을 통해 맞춤형 규제 체계를 고안해 내자는 것이므로, 지식인이 특정 문제에 대해 자신의 사적 견해를 밝히고 있다는 측면에서 ④가 적합하다.

43

다음 중 본문을 통해 추론할 수 있는 것이 아닌 것은?

① 생명공학은 개인이 집에서 유전자 치료를 시험할 수 있는 수준까지 발전했다.
② 미국 정부는 최근 기존의 연구 기관에 소속되어 있지 않은 이들의 자가 실험을 허용했다.
③ 최근 전개되고 있는 의료 연구에는 신생 기업의 창업이 포함된다.
④ 기존의 의료체계에 소속되지 않은 시민들이 선조치적 역할을 취할 잠재력을 가지고 있지만, 아직 많은 윤리적 문제가 해결되지 않은 채 남아 있다.

| 정답 | ②

| 해설 | 본문의 주요 내용이 현 의료체계의 제도권 밖에 있는 이들이 행하는 의학적 혁신에 대해 어떤 태도를 가져야 하는지 논의하고 있다. 또한 필자는 "We must recognize the urgent need to build legitimacy, but also tailored regulatory support for new forms of health research." 부분에서 그들에 대해 합법성을 부여하고 맞춤형 규제 제도를 갖추는 것이 필요하다고 역설하고 있으므로, 아직 그들은 정부의 정식 허가를 받지 못했음을 알 수 있다. 따라서 정답은 정부가 그들에 대해 허가를 해 주었다고 말한 ②가 사실과 다른 내용이 되어 정답이 된다.

44

다음 중 아래 문장이 위치할 가장 적합한 곳은?

유전자 치료를 이용한 자가 실험은, 감염의 위험과 면역체계 부작용에서부터 관련 위험에 대한 이해의 부족과 환자들의 비현실적 기대에 이르기까지, 안전성과 윤리적 측면에서 골치 아픈 의문을 제기한다.

① (A) ② (B)
③ (C) ④ (D)

| 정답 | ②

| 해설 | (A)와 (B) 사이에서 '유전자 치료를 이용한 자가 실험'을 혁신이라고 할 수 있는지, 아니면 기존의 의학적 혁신의 생태계를 파괴하는 것인지에 대해 의문을 던지고 있다. 제시문은 '유전자 치료를 이용한 자가 실험'이 여러 문제를 안고 있다는 내용이므로 (A)에 위치할 수 없다. 여러 문제를 안고 있다고 말한 이후 이것을 과연 혁신이라고 볼 수 있는지 묻는 것은 부적절하기 때문이다. 따라서 정답은 (B)에 위치해야 하고, 여러 문제를 안고 있지만 단순히 금지하는 것이 최선은 아니라고 언급하는 다음 문장과 좋은 호응 관계를 보인다. 그런 후 이에 대한 저자의 주장을 제시하는 방식으로 글이 이어지고 있다.

| 어휘 | **pioneer** ⓝ 개척자, 선구자 ⓥ 개척하다
margin ⓝ 가장자리; 여유; 판매 수익, 이문
unregulated ⓐ 규제되지 않은
start-up ⓝ 신규 업체(특히 인터넷 기업)
permission-less ⓐ 허가가 필요 없는
biohacker ⓝ DNA 등 유전학 관련 내용을 취미로 실험하는 사람
innovation ⓝ 혁신, 쇄신
establishment ⓝ 지배층, 기득권층, 기성 체제
gene therapy – 유전자 치료(법)
herald ⓥ 알리다, 발표하다
self-proclaimed ⓐ 자기 혼자 주장하는, 자칭의

regulatory framework – 규제 체계
ethos ⓝ (특정 집단·사회의) 기풍[정신]
tailored ⓐ 맞춤의
radical ⓐ 근본(기본)적인, 기초의; 타고난, 본래의; 철저한; 과격한
ethicist ⓝ 윤리학자, 도덕가
oversight ⓝ 관리, 감독; 실수, 간과
democratized ⓐ 대중화된, 민주화된
optimal ⓐ 최적의, 이상적인
public intellectual – 공공 지식인, 사회 참여 지식인
entrepreneurship ⓝ 기업가 정신
medical practice – 의료 업무
troubling ⓐ 골치가 아픈, 괴롭히는

foster ⓥ 기르다, 육성하다, 촉진하다; 마음에 품다
legitimacy ⓝ 합법성, 적법, 타당성

adaptive ⓐ 조정의; 적응할 수 있는
transnational ⓐ 초국가적인, 다국적 기업의
ecological ⓐ 생태학적인
motivational speaker – 동기부여 연설가

proactive ⓐ 선조치하는, 사전 대책을 강구하는
raise questions – 의문을 제기하다
immunological ⓐ 면역의

[45-47] 국민대 2016

우리는 얼마 전까지만 해도 우리 뇌가 성인이 될 때 최고조에 다다르고, 그 이후 모든 것이 그저 내리막길을 걷게 된다고 생각했다. 그러나 이제 우리는 그것이 사실이 아니라는 것을 알고 있다. 과학자들은 우리가 나이를 먹으면서도 뇌가 계속 성장할 수 있으며, 새로운 연결 고리를 만들어 낼 수 있다는 것을 보여주는 "신경가소성(neuroplasticity)"이라는 과정을 밝혀냈다. 우리의 두뇌에 정기적인 정신 운동을 실시하면 가벼운 인지능력 감소 위험을 40%까지 줄일 수 있다고 니콜 코칸(Nicole Kochan) 박사는 말한다. 최근 메이요 클리닉(Mayo Clinic)이 미국에서 실시한 조사에 따르면, 중년 이후로 예술이나 공예, 사회 활동 또는 컴퓨터 사용과 같은 취미 생활을 유지하는 노인들이 치매의 영향을 덜 받게 된다는 사실이 확인됐다. 그것은 "인지적 비축(cognitive reserve)"이라고 불리는 현상, 즉 뇌의 손상에 대한 정신의 저항 때문이다. 우리가 치매 증상에 주목하기 전에 보통 수십 년 동안 치매가 발병하기 시작하면서 뇌의 특정 영역이 줄어들기 시작한다. 그러나 복잡한 활동으로 인해 새로운 뇌세포가 활성화되고, 뇌세포들 간의 연결성이 개선되어 뇌의 쇠퇴와 수축이 줄어든다. 우리는 또한 신체에 좋은 것이 뇌에도 좋다는 것을 알 수 있다고 알츠하이머 오스트레일리아(Alzheimer's Australia)의 위험감소 관리자인 수하 알리(Suha Ali)는 말한다. 그래서 규칙적인 운동을 해야 하는 또 다른 이유가 있는 것이다. 친목 활동을 하는 것도 우리의 뇌에 도움이 된다. 다른 사람들과 시간을 보내고 재미있게 노는 것이 인지 비축에 기여할 수 있다.

45 다음 중 빈칸 ⓐ에 들어갈 가장 적합한 것은?

① 일으키다 ② 줄이다
③ 예상하다 ④ 가속화하다

| 정답 | ②

| 해설 | 빈칸에서는 규칙적인 정신 운동(뇌 운동)과 가벼운 인지능력 감소 위험 간의 관계를 묻고 있다. 빈칸 다음 문장에서 뇌 운동에 해당하는 여러 취미활동을 유지할 경우 치매에 걸릴 가능성이 더 적다고 했으므로, 이를 토대로 앞의 빈칸에도 더 줄어든다는 ②가 정답이 된다.

46

다음 중 문법적으로 올바르지 않은 것은?

① Ⓐ ② Ⓑ
③ Ⓒ ④ Ⓓ

| 정답 | ②

| 해설 | Ⓑ가 들어간 문장에서 'a recent study'가 주어이며 'conducted by the Mayo Clinic in the U.S.'는 과거분사로 앞의 주어를 수식하고 있다. 따라서 Ⓑ가 동사가 되면서 뒤에 that 명사절을 이끌어야 하기 때문에, 이를 동사인 confirmed로 수정해야 한다.

47

다음 중 본문의 주제로 가장 적절한 것은?

① 과학자들이 치매를 완치할 수 있는 방법을 밝혀냈다.
② 나이가 들면서 뇌세포의 수가 줄어든다.
③ 규칙적인 컴퓨터 사용이 두뇌의 기능을 향상시킨다.
④ 당신은 여러 활동을 통해 뇌의 건강을 향상시킬 수 있다.

| 정답 | ④

| 해설 | ① 치매를 완치(cure)할 수 있다는 내용은 등장하지 않는다. ② 나이가 들면서 뇌세포의 수가 줄어드는 것은 맞지만 이 내용이 주제문은 아니다. ③ 본문의 내용과 무관하며, ④가 주제문이 되며, 본문의 "elderly people who'd kept up a hobby ... since middle age were less likely to be affected by dementia"를 통해 확인할 수 있다.

| 어휘 | **reach one's peak** – 절정에 다다르다 **hit adulthood** – 성인이 되다
downhill ⓐ 비탈[내리막]을 내려가는 ⓐⓓ 비탈[내리막] 아래로
identify ⓥ (신원 등을) 확인하다[알아보다] **neuroplasticity** ⓝ 신경가소성
mental workout – 정신 운동 **cognitive decline** – 인지력 감퇴
keep up a hobby – 취미를 유지하다 **craft** ⓝ (수)공예
dementia ⓝ 치매 **cognitive reserve** – 인지 비축, 예비 인지능력
shrink ⓥ 줄어들다[오그라지다] **atrophy** ⓝ (혈액 부족으로 인한 신체 부위의) 위축(증)

[48-50] 홍익대 2018

법의학(forensic science)은 우리가 과거를 이해하는 데 도움을 준다. 질병의 확산을 연구하거나 오래전 발생했던 대학살의 현장을 조사하는 것이 그 예가 될 수 있다. 그리고 당연하게도 법의학은 범죄를 해결하는 데 있어 법률 제도에 중요하다. 이 모든 분야에서 현미경은 과거의 사건들을 재구성하는 것을 돕기 위해 사용되는 중요한 도구이다. 현미경은 물체를 매우 세밀하게 확대할 수 있으므로 조사를 위한 많은 목적에 필수적이다.

법의학 역학(forensic epidemiology)은 법적인 이유로 질병이 어떻게 확산되는지를 조사한다. 예를 들어, 대장균이나 살모넬라 같은 위험성 박테리아의 출처를 밝혀내기 위해 법의학 전염병학자들이 배정될 수 있다. 작업을 수행하기 위해서, 그들은 현미경을 사용해 음식의 오염 여부를 살펴볼 것이다. 현미경 아래 특정 종류의 박테리아가 존재할 경우, 이는 과학자들을 오염의 출처로 안내하게 된다. 이것은 더 많은 사람들이 감염되는 것을 막고, 발병의 원인이 되는 개인이나 단체를 정확히 지적하는 데 있어 매우 중요한 것으로 드러날 수 있다.

법의학 인류학(forensic anthropology)에서는 사망 원인을 특정하기 위해 현미경을 사용해 조직이나 뼈, 또는 다른 유해 등을 살펴본다. 예를 들어, 전자 현미경을 이용해 땅에 퇴적물로 남겨진 오래된 액화 상태의 유해의 신원을 확인할 수 있다. 이 분야에서는 현미경이 치아에서 발견된 잔여물을 관찰하는 데에도 사용된다. 조직이나 세포, 혹은 다른 잔해들이 사후의 치아에 막을 형성하고 있을 수 있으며, 연구자들이 그 사람의 습관, 질병, 심지어 사망 원인까지 알아내는 데 도움을 준다.

법의학 병리학자들(forensic pathologists)은 어떤 사람이 어떻게 사망했는지 특정해야 할 책임이 있다. 만약 그 사람이 특정 질병으로 사망했다면, 법의학 병리학자들은 그 치명적인 박테리아나 바이러스를 확인하기 위해 현미경을 사용할 수 있다. 현미경은 상처 주위의 조직을 좀 더 면밀히 조사하고, 총알이든, 칼이든, 다른 것이든 손상을 일으킨 물체가 어떤 것인지 결정할 때 유용할 수 있다.

48
다음 중 본문의 제목으로 가장 적합한 것은?
① 법의학과 그 법적 배경
② 법의학에서 이뤄지는 현미경의 사용
③ 법의학의 초기 발전
④ 미래 법의학의 필요성

| 정답 | ②

| 해설 | 본문은 법의학의 여러 분야에서 현미경이 매우 중요하게 사용되고 있다는 것을 서술하고 있으므로, '법의학에서 이뤄지는 현미경의 사용'이라는 ②가 글의 제목으로 가장 적합하다.

49
다음 중 본문을 통해 추론할 수 있는 것이 아닌 것은?
① 법의학은 과거의 사건을 재구성하여 과거를 이해하도록 하는 것과 관련이 있다.
② 법의학 역학은 위험한 질병의 확산을 막는 데 기여한다.
③ 사체의 치아에 남아 있는 유해가 사망자의 생전의 습관에 힌트를 제공해 줄 수 있다.
④ 치명적인 박테리아와 바이러스는 법의학 병리학자들의 조직 검사에 어려움을 초래한다

| 정답 | ④

| 해설 | ①은 첫 번째 문단에 등장하는 내용이다. ②는 두 번째 문단의 '법의학 역학'과 관련된 내용에 등장한다. ③의 경우 세 번째 문단 후반부에 등장한다. 정답은 ④로, 마지막 문단의 "forensic pathologists may use a microscope to identify the deadly bacteria or virus"에서 "법의학 병리학자들은 그 치명적인 박테리아나 바이러스를 확인하기 위해 현미경을 사용할 수 있다"고만 밝히고 있고, ④와 관련한 내용은 등장하지 않는다.

50

다음 중 본문의 구성 방식과 가장 밀접한 관련이 있는 것은?
① 공간적 순서
② 시간적 순서
③ 질문 및 응답
④ 주제 및 부연 목록

| 정답 | ④

| 해설 | 첫 번째 문단에서는 법의학에 현미경이 중요한 도구라는 주제를 밝히고 있고, 뒤이은 세 문단을 통해 각각의 분야에서 현미경이 어떻게 사용되는지를 밝히고 있다. 따라서 주제와 이 뒤를 이은 부연 설명이 목록처럼 나열되어 있다는 ④가 정답이 된다.

| 어휘 |
forensic science – 법의학, 과학수사
when it comes to – ~에 관하여
essential ⓐ 필수의, 근본적인
magnify ⓥ 확대하다
epidemiologist ⓝ 역학자, 유행병학자
contamination ⓝ 오염
strain ⓝ 종, 종류
stop ⓥ (어떤 일이나 행동을) 막다
pinpoint ⓥ 정확히 집어내다, 찾아내다
anthropology ⓝ 인류학
remains ⓝ 나머지; 유적, 유해
identify ⓥ 찾다, 지목하다; 확인하다, 인식하다; 동일시하다
leave behind – 뒤에 남기다
soil ⓝ 토양, 흙
coat ⓥ (막 같은 것을) 덮다, 입히다
pathologist ⓝ 병리학자
beneficial ⓐ 유익한, 이익을 가져오는
chronological ⓐ 연대순의

massacre ⓝ 대량 학살 ⓥ 대량으로 학살하다
microscope ⓝ 현미경
investigative ⓐ 조사의, 수사의
epidemiology ⓝ 역학, 전염병학
be assigned to – ~에 배정되다
presence ⓝ 존재, 참석
pivotal ⓐ 중추의, 중요한
infect ⓥ 감염시키다
outbreak ⓝ 발생, 발발
tissue ⓝ (세포들로 이뤄진) 조직
deposit ⓝ 퇴적물, 침전물
residue ⓝ 나머지, 잔여
ailment ⓝ 질병
manner ⓝ (일의) 방식, (사람의) 태도
spatial ⓐ 공간의

에듀윌 편입영어 **기출심화 완성 독해**

PART 03

인문학

CHAPTER 01 　역사·고고학

CHAPTER 02 　철학·종교

CHAPTER 03 　문학

CHAPTER 04 　언어

CHAPTER 05 　심리

CHAPTER 01 역사·고고학

01	④	02	①	03	②	04	⑤	05	②	06	③	07	②	08	②	09	④	10	③
11	②	12	⑤	13	③	14	②	15	①	16	⑤	17	②	18	①	19	③	20	⑤
21	②	22	④	23	③	24	②	25	①	26	②	27	④	28	③	29	①	30	①
31	④	32	③	33	⑤	34	①	35	②	36	②	37	③	38	③	39	②	40	④

[01-03]

두 번째 지적할 점은 좀 더 이해하기 쉬운 것으로 역사가는 자신이 상대하는 사람들의 마음, 즉 그 사람들의 행위의 배후에 있는 생각을 상상을 통해 이해할 필요가 있다는 점이다. 내가 "공감"이라 하지 않고 "상상을 통한 이해"라고 한 것은 공감이 동의를 의미하는 것으로 비치지 않기 위함이다. 30년 전쟁에 관한 Burckhardt의 매우 비판적 견해를 예로 들어 보자. "천주교이든 개신교이든 국가의 안녕보다 종교적 신념을 통한 구원을 우선시하는 것은 가증스러운 일일 뿐이다." 국가를 수호하기 위해 살인을 행하는 것이 정당하고 칭송받을 만한 일이지만 종교를 수호하기 위해 살인을 행하는 것은 사악하고 잘못된 것이라고 믿도록 자라 온 19세기 자유주의 사학자의 입장에선 30년 전쟁에서 싸운 사람들의 정신 상태에 공감하기란 매우 어려웠을 것이다. 지난 10년간 소련에 관해 영어권 국가에서 저술된 것들과, 영어권 국가에 관해 소련에서 저술된 것 중 상당수는 이처럼 상대방의 마음속에 무슨 일이 일어나는지를 상상을 통해 이해할 수 있도록 해 주는 가장 기본적인 수단조차도 획득할 수 없는 무능함 때문에 가치가 상실되었다.

01 본문에 따르면 왜 역사가에게는 상상을 통한 이해가 필요한가?
① 적을 더 효과적으로 상대하기 위해
② 일상생활에서 만나는 사람들의 마음을 더 잘 이해하기 위해
③ 합의를 더 쉽게 이끌어 내기 위해
④ 왜 사람들이 어떤 특정한 방식으로 행동하는지 이해하기 위해

| 정답 | ④

| 해설 | 본문에 따르면 역사가에게는 "자신이 상대하는 사람들의 마음, 즉 그 사람들의 행위의 배후에 있는 생각을 상상을 통해 이해할 필요(need of imaginative understanding for the minds of the people with whom he is dealing, for the thought behind their acts)"가 있다. 즉, 사람들의 행동 양식과 그 이유를 이해할 필요가 있다는 의미이다. 이는 보기 중에서 ④의 내용과 일맥상통한다.

02 저자에 따르면 다음 중 Burckhardt에 관해 맞는 것은 무엇인가?
① 그는 30년 전쟁 기간 중의 사람들의 마음을 이해하는 데 실패했다.
② 그는 종교 수호를 위해 사람을 죽이는 것이 정당하다고 믿었다.
③ 그는 국가 수호를 위해 사람을 죽이는 것이 끔찍하다고 생각했다.
④ 그는 상상을 통한 이해를 활용해 30년 전쟁을 해석한 역사가이다.

| 정답 | ①

| 해설 | 본문에 따르면 Burckhardt는 "국가를 수호하기 위해 살인을 행하는 것이 정당하고 칭송받을 만한 일이지만 종교를 수호하기 위해 살인을 행하는 것은 사악하고 잘못된 것이라고 믿도록 자라 온 19세기 자유주의 사학자(a nineteenth-century liberal historian brought up to believe that it is right and praiseworthy to kill in defense of one's country, but wicked and wrong-headed to kill in defense of one's religion)"이다. 따라서 그는 "30년 전쟁에서 싸운 사람들의 정신 상태에 공감(to enter into the state of mind of those who fought the Thirty Years War)"하기가 "매우 어려웠다(extremely difficult)." 이는 보기 ①의 내용과 통한다.

03

본문의 밑줄 친 단어 ⓐ와 의미상 가장 가까운 것을 고르시오.
① 비판하다
② 손상시키다
③ 분명해지다
④ 모호해지다

| 정답 | ②

| 해설 | 본문의 vitiate는 '손상시키다, ~의 가치를 떨어뜨리다'의 뜻이며 보기 중에서 '가치를 손상시키다, 해치게 하다'는 의미인 ②의 impair와 가장 의미가 흡사하다. 따라서 답은 ②이다.

| 어휘 | imaginative ⓐ 상상의, 상상력이 풍부한
lest ~ should … – …하지 않도록
censorious ⓐ 매우 비판적인
creed ⓝ 종교적 신념, 교의
integrity ⓝ 온전함, 본래의 상태임
bring up – ~을 기르다, 양육하다
wicked ⓐ 사악한
enter into – (감정, 생각 등을) 이해하다, 공감하다
vitiate ⓥ ~의 가치를 떨어뜨리다, 손상시키다
elicit ⓥ 이끌어 내다, 유도해 내다
impair ⓥ 가치를 손상시키다, 해치게 하다
obscure ⓥ 이해하기 어렵게 하다, 모호하게 하다
sympathy ⓝ 공감
imply ⓥ 암시하다, 의미하다
scandalous ⓐ 가증스러운; 언어도단의
salvation ⓝ (기독교적) 구원
liberal ⓐ 자유적인, 진보적인
praiseworthy ⓐ 칭찬할 만한
wrong-headed ⓐ 생각이 잘못된
what goes on – 현재 일어나는 일[상황]
get the idea – 이해하다
manifest ⓥ 나타나다, 분명해지다

[04-07] 성균관대 2007 B형

드라마와 소설처럼 역사도 신화에서 생겨났다. 신화는 어린이들이 듣는 동화나 지적인 어른들이 꾸는 꿈처럼 현실과 가상의 경계선이 모호하게 나뉜 해석과 표현의 원시적인 형태이다. 예를 들어 일리아드의 경우를 보면 일리아드를 역사인 줄 알고 읽기 시작한 사람은 그 작품이 허구로 가득 차 있음을 알게 된다고 한다. 하지만 마찬가지로 일리아드를 허구로 알고 읽기 시작한 사람은 그 작품이 역사로 가득 차 있음을 알게 된다고 한다. 모든 역사는 이렇듯 허구적 요소를 완전히 없앨 수 없다는 점에서 일리아드와 흡사하다. 단순한 사실의 선정·배열·제시는 소설 분야에 속하는 기교이며, 그래서 역사가는 동시에 "위대한" 작가가 아니라면 위대한 역사가가 될 수 없다는 일반 대중의 주장도 정당하며, 기번이나 매컬리 같은 역사가들이 '학구적이고 지루한 역사가'(the Dryasdusts; 자신이 저술한 역사서를 통해서라기보다 소설을 통해서 더 뛰어난 역사가로 여겨진 바로 그 월터 스콧 경이 창조한 단어), 즉 자신보다 더 뛰어난 창조적 영감 속에서 글을 쓴 동료 역사가들이 남긴 역사적으로 부정확한 서술은 회피해 온 '학구적이고 지루한 역사가들'보다 위대한 역사가라는 주장도 정당하다.

04

(가)에 가장 알맞은 것은 다음 중 무엇인가?
① 그러나 ② 결국
③ 반면에 ④ 얄궂게도
⑤ 예를 들어

| 정답 | ⑤

| 해설 | 본문에서는 "모든 역사는 이렇듯 허구적 요소를 완전히 없앨 수 없다는 점에서 일리아드와 흡사하다.(All histories resemble the Illiad to this extent, that they cannot entirely dispense with the fictional element.)"고 설명되어 있다. 또한 일리아드는 '허구로 가득한 역사이자 역사로 가득한 허구'이다. 즉, 일리아드는 '현실과 가상의 경계선이 모호하게 나뉜(the line between fact and fiction is left undrawn)' 것의 예로 볼 수 있다. 따라서 답은 ⑤이다.

05

다음 중 두 빈칸 (나)와 (다)에 가장 알맞은 것은 무엇인가?
① 역사 – 허구 ② 허구 – 역사
③ 허구 – 허구 ④ 역사 – 역사
⑤ 해석 – 표현

| 정답 | ②

| 해설 | 우선 "일리아드를 역사인 줄 알고 읽기 시작한 사람은 그 작품이 허구로 가득 차 있음을 알게 된다(anyone who starts reading it as history will find that it is full of fiction)." 그런데 그 다음 문장은 역접의 접속사 but과 동등함을 나타내는 부사 equally가 등장한다. 따라서 빈칸에 들어갈 말은 앞 문장과 구조는 동일(equally)하면서 의미가 반대(but)가 됨을 유추할 수 있다. 즉, '일리아드를 허구로 알고 읽기 시작한 사람은 그 작품이 역사로 가득 차 있음을 알게 된다'가 올바른 문장으로 답은 ②이다.

06

본문의 주제는 '역사는 사실과 허구의 상호작용'이다.
① 신화와 역사, 이 둘이 공유하는 것 ② 일리아드 속의 역사적 요소
③ 역사는 사실과 허구의 상호작용 ④ 역사상의 허구적 요소
⑤ 위대한 역사가가 되는 방법

| 정답 | ③

| 해설 | 본문의 전반적인 내용은 일리아드의 예를 들면서 역사와 허구의 경계는 칼로 베듯이 나뉠 수 없으며 위대한 역사가는 동시에 위대한 작가이기도 하다는 것이다. 즉, 역사를 사실과 허구가 서로 공존하면서 상호작용을 일으키는 것으로 간주하고 있다. 따라서 답은 ③이다.

07

밑줄 친 "자신보다 창조적 영감을 받아 글을 쓴 동료 역사가들"이 나타내는 대상은 기번이나 매컬리 같은 역사가이다.
① 월터 스콧 경 같은 작가 ② 기번이나 매컬리 같은 역사가
③ 학구적이고 지루한 역사가 ④ 지적인 어른
⑤ 신화학자

| 정답 | ②

| 해설 | 본문의 "자신보다 창조적 영감을 받아 글을 쓴 동료 역사가들(their more inspired colleagues)"은 학구적이고 지루한 역사가의 눈에는 "역사적으로 부정확한 서술(factual inaccuracies)을 하는" 사람들인데, 여기서 말하는 역사적으로 부정확한 서술이란 바로 역사적인 허구와 사실의 공존을 의미한다. 이는 허구나 소설을 쓸 때 작용하는 '창조적 영감'이라는 표현을 통해서도 유추 가능하다. 따라서 '자신보다 더 뛰어난 창조적 영감 속에서 글을 쓴 동료 역사가들'은 학구적이고 지루한 역사가들보다 '위대한' 역사가인 기번이나 매컬리 같은 역사가를 의미하며, 답은 ②이다.

| 어휘 |
mythology ⓝ 신화
interpretation ⓝ 해석, 설명
undrawn ⓐ 그려진 것이 아닌
insistence ⓝ 주장
Gibbon – 로마제국 쇠망사를 저술한 영국 역사가(Edward Gibbon)
Dryasdust ⓝ dry as dust에서 파생된 말로 너무 학구적이어서 지루한 역사가를 의미
coin ⓥ 새로운 말을 만들다
factual ⓐ 사실의
interplay ⓝ 상호작용
grow out of – ~에서 생겨나다
primitive ⓐ 원시의; 본원적인
sophisticated ⓐ 지적인, 세련된
dispense with – ~을 없애다
inspired ⓐ 창조적 영감을 받은
inaccuracy ⓝ 부정확함

[08-10]

역사가 필요한 이유는 역사가 현재 벌어지는 상황들을 설명하는 데 도움을 주기 때문이다. 문화들이 어떻게 흥하고 쇠하는가? 역사가 우리에게 정답을 주는 것은 아니지만, 확실히 역사는 현재 전 세계에서 영향력을 행사하고 있는 힘들에 대해 우리의 물음과 이해를 집중하도록 하는 데 일조한다.

물론 역사는 쉽게 조작된다. 하지만 그렇기 때문에 더더욱 실제 어떤 일이 벌어졌는지 우리가 아는 것이 중요하다. 우리는 역사 지식을 통해 지도자들과 언론이 만들어 낸 기만들을 포착할 수 있다. 유권자이자 시민으로서, 우리는 이런 위험한 왜곡들을 꿰뚫어 볼 수 있어야 한다. 게다가, 역사는 흥미롭고 또한 흥미로워야 한다. 역사의 인과관계 사슬은 매혹적이며, 역사의 세부적인 사항들 또한 그러하다. (하지만) 이렇게 하지 못하고, 스스로 역사 수업 훈련이 부족한 많은 교사들이 역사 과목이 학생들에게 지루할 것이라고 두려워한 나머지 자연스럽게 방어적인 태도를 보인다.

나는 역사학자들이나 역사 교사들이 도덕적 역할을 수행해야 한다고 주장하는 것이 결코 아니다. 그들의 주요 임무는 시대정신을 이해하고 이를 후대에 물려주는 것이다. 그렇다고 그들이 도덕적 영향에 대해 단순화시켜서도 안 된다. 역사는 상상할 수 있는 가장 풍부한 도덕적 모범 사례와 도덕적 딜레마를 제공하며, 이는 그 자체로 훌륭한 픽션과 훌륭한 드라마이자 인생 그 자체의 정수라고 할 수 있다. 역사의 이해가 없이는 우리는 정치적으로, 문화적으로, 사회적으로 빈곤하게 된다.

08 다음 본문에서 유추할 수 없는 것은 무엇인가?
① 역사를 이해하는 일은 우리가 권력에 의해 선전된 거짓에 저항하도록 돕는다.
② 과거 사건의 도덕률은 역사 교육을 통해 희석되어야 한다.
③ 오늘날 일부 교사들은 역사의 매력에 확신을 갖지 못한 것 같다.
④ 역사는 우리로 하여금 현재를 이해하기 위해 필요한 관점을 형성하도록 한다.

| 정답 | ②

| 해설 | 본문에서 delusion에 관한 대목이 보기 ①에 해당한다. 본문 중간에 등장하는 역사 교사들이 defensive한 입장을

취한다는 대목이 보기 ③에 해당하며, 본문 첫 번째 줄이 ④에 해당한다. ②의 경우 본문에서 "그렇다고 그들이 도덕적 영향에 대해 단순화시켜서도 안 된다(Nor should they simplify for moral effect)"라고 했으므로 'should be'가 아니라 'should not be'가 되어야 한다. 따라서 정답은 ②가 된다.

09

빈칸에 가장 알맞은 것을 고르시오.
① 이에 혐오감을 받아
② 이를 통해 동기를 부여받아
③ 이에 따라
④ 이렇게 하지 못하고

| 정답 | ④

| 해설 | 보기 ①과 같이 "혐오감에 하지 않는 것이 아니라(repulsed by this)", 역사를 싫어할 것이라는 두려움으로 역사 수업이 흥미롭고 매혹적인 수업이 되도록 시도하는 것을 역사 교사들이 꺼린다는 것을 의미하므로 답은 ④가 된다. 참고로 'shy away from'은 '회피하다(avoid having to deal with some unpleasant task)'라는 뜻을 지닌다.

10

본문의 제목으로 가장 알맞은 것은 무엇인가?
① 역사의 함정
② 서로 경쟁하듯 다른 역사 해석
③ 역사가 우리에게 말하는 것
④ 미래를 위한 역사적 통찰력

| 정답 | ③

| 해설 | 본문의 필자는 역사가 우리들에게 매우 중요한 과목이라는 점을 계속 주지시키고 있다. 역사가 지닌 함정을 말하거나, 역사에 대한 서로 다른 해석을 말하려는 것이 아니므로 보기 ①, ②는 답이 될 수 없다. ④도 답이 될 수 있을 것 같지만 필자는 미래를 위해 역사적 통찰력을 갖추어야 한다고 주장한 부분은 본문에 등장하지 않는다. 다만 실제 역사적으로 무슨 일이 벌어졌는지 아는 것을 통해 역사적 현혹들에 휘둘리지 말아야 한다고 주장한다. 여기에 가장 적절한 보기가 ③이라고 할 수 있다. 역사가 우리에게 말하는 것, 바로 시대정신을 이해하는 것과도 일맥상통한다.

| 어휘 | manipulate ⓥ 조작하다
delusion ⓝ 망상; 기만
obligation ⓝ 임무, 의무
essence ⓝ 정수, 핵심
untruth ⓝ 거짓, 허위
dilute ⓥ 희석시키다; 약화시키다
perspective ⓝ 관점
motivate ⓥ 동기를 부여하다, (행동의) 이유가 되다
in concordance with – ~에 따라, ~와 일치하여
shy away – 회피하다
insight ⓝ 통찰력

spot ⓥ 포착하다
distortion ⓝ 왜곡, 곡해
mentality ⓝ 사고방식
impoverished ⓐ 빈곤한
propagate ⓥ 전파하다, 선전하다
appeal ⓝ 매력
repulse ⓥ 혐오감을 주다; 격퇴하다
pitfall ⓝ 위험, 함정

[11-12] 한국외대 2007

르네상스 시대 조성된 탐구정신의 여러 측면 중 하나로는 지식의 모든 분야를 체계적으로 분류해 제공하려는 욕구를 들 수 있다. 이 욕구는 결과적으로 수많은 소장품을 정리하는 것으로 확대되었고, 이들 소장품은 차후 유럽의 주요 박물관으로 흡수되었다. 이 같은 박물관 중에서 최고봉으로 꼽히는 것은 영국박물관으로, Hans Sloane 경의 소장품을 수용하기 위해 1753년 의회법에 의거 설립되었다. 전문 외과의였던 Sloane 경은 벌이가 좋은 개업의 생활을 하면서 획득한 많은 돈을 통해 자연 과학과 수집에 가지고 있던 엄청난 열정을 마음껏 충족시킬 수 있었다. Sloane 경은 1685년 영국 학술원의 회원이 되었고, 1727년에는 Isaac Newton 경의 뒤를 이어 학술원장이 되었다. 사망했을 때 Sloane 경은 약 8만 건의 수집품을 남겼는데 그중에는 동전, 메달, 책, 판화, 회화, 필사본 등이 있었다. Sloane 경의 경우처럼 지식의 한계를 뛰어넘고자 하는 자극이 유럽 궁정의 무역 이권과 결탁하여 지리적 탐험을 추구하려는 유인책으로 작용했다. 추가적인 무역로의 확립이나 그때까지 알려지지 않은 대륙과의 접촉은 새로운 물질과 심상을 도입하게 해 주었고, 이는 유럽 문화에 즉각적인 영향을 끼쳤다.

11 다음 중 Sloane 경에 대해 사실이 아닌 것은?
① 그는 자연과학에 매우 관심이 많았다.
② 그의 뒤를 이어 Newton이 영국 학술원의 원장이 되었다.
③ 그는 벌이가 좋은 직업을 갖고 있었다.
④ 그의 수집품은 그의 사망 후 영국박물관에 전시되었다.
⑤ 그는 영국 학술원의 회원이었다.

| 정답 | ②

| 해설 | Sloane 경이 "Isaac Newton 경의 뒤를 이어(in succession to Sir Isaac Newton)" 학술원 원장이 되었지, ②에서 말하는 것처럼 Sloane 경의 뒤를 이어 Newton 경이 학술원 원장이 된 것은 아니다.

12 본문을 통해 판단해 보건대, 다음 중 밑줄 친 ⓐ의 표현과 의미상 가장 가까운 것은 무엇인가?
① 르네상스의 소멸　　② 의료 서비스를 향한 크나큰 열정
③ 지식의 체계적인 분류　　④ 알려지지 않은 광물에 대한 욕구
⑤ 탐구정신

| 정답 | ⑤

| 해설 | 본문에서 핵심이 되는 문장은 "르네상스 시대 조성된 탐구정신의 여러 측면 중 하나로는 지식의 모든 분야를 체계적으로 분류해 제공하려는 욕구를 들 수 있다(One of the aspects of the spirit of inquiry fostered by the Renaissance was the desire to provide a systematic classification of all areas of knowledge)."이다. 탐구 정신의 여러 측면 중 하나가 지식의 체계적 분류이고, 이러한 분류를 향한 욕구가 지식의 한계를 넘으려는 자극으로 이어진 것이다. 따라서 답은 ⑤이다.

| 어휘 | spirit ⓝ 정신　　　　　　　　　foster ⓥ 조성하다, 발전시키다
systematic ⓐ 체계적인　　　　　classification ⓝ 분류
extend ⓥ 확대하다, 포괄하다　　arrangement ⓝ 정리, 배열
absorb ⓥ 흡수하다　　　　　　　foremost ⓐ 가장 중요한
lucrative ⓐ 수익성이 좋은　　　　practice ⓝ (의사·변호사 등의) 업무[사무실]
indulge ⓥ (욕구를) 채우다, 마음껏 하다　print ⓝ 판화

impulse ⓝ 충동, 자극
ally ⓥ 결합하다, 제휴하다
hitherto ⓐ 지금까지, 그때까지
extinction ⓝ 멸종, 소멸
frontier ⓝ (영역·지식의) 한계
exploration ⓝ 탐험
imagery ⓝ (예술 작품에서의) 형상화[이미지], 심상

[13-14] 건국대 2007

역사 속 위대한 영웅들은 비극적인 인물들이다. 그들은 새로운 사상을 순수하고 단호히 구현한다. 그들은 태양과 같은 광휘를 받으며 부상한다. 그들의 진정한 중요성은 처음에는 관심받지 못하지만, 낡은 삶의 방식이 (새로운 방식으로 인한) 위험을 감지하고서 걸출한 대행자의 모습을 빌어 등장한 새로운 방식을 파괴하기 위해 자신의 모든 힘을 동원할 때 관심받게 된다. 소크라테스든 율리우스 카이사르든, 새로운 원칙을 최초로 주창한 승리의 주역은 동시에 (한 시대에서 다른 시대로 넘어가는) 두 시대의 경계에서 희생양이 된다. 낡은 방식은 여전히 제 기능을 하고 있으므로 당연히 단호하게 스스로를 내세울 수 있다. 새로운 방식 또한 당연히 단호하게 스스로를 내세우지만 이미 자리를 잡은 사회질서나 문화에 의한 보호를 아직 받지 못한다. 당분간 새로운 방식은 외부와 단절된 상태에서 기능을 한다. 하지만 낡은 방식이 자신의 모든 힘을 규합하여 최후의 발악 끝에 파괴할 수 있는 것은 단지 새로운 삶의 방식을 연 최초의 위대한 인물인 영웅밖에 없다.

13 본문의 주제로 가장 알맞은 것은 무엇인가?
① 역사상 위대한 영웅들이 항상 승리를 거둔 것은 아니다.
② 새로운 전통은 낡은 전통과의 투쟁 끝에 낡은 전통을 교체한다.
③ 위대한 영웅들은 자신을 희생하여 새로운 삶의 방식을 창조한다.
④ 전쟁은 낡은 것과 새로운 것의 경계에서 발발한다.
⑤ 낡은 것이든 새로운 것이든 자신을 정당화하기 위해 분투한다.

| 정답 | ③

| 해설 | 본문의 핵심이 될 만한 문장을 몇 개 선정해 보면, "역사 속 위대한 영웅들은 비극적인 인물들이다(The great heroes of history are tragic figures)", "새로운 원칙을 최초로 주창한 승리의 주역은 동시에 (한 시대에서 다른 시대로 넘어가는) 두 시대의 경계에서 희생양이 된다(the first victorious protagonist of the new principle becomes, at the same time, the victim at the border of two eras)", "낡은 방식이 파괴할 수 있는 것은 영웅밖에 없다(it is only the hero ... whom the old ... can destroy)." 등이 있다. 이를 통해 본문의 핵심을 유추해 보면 "새로운 시대를 여는 영웅들은 과거의 낡은 방식에 의해 탄압받고 희생양이 되지만, 낡은 방식의 탄압은 오로지 시대에 뒤처진 자들의 최후의 발악일 뿐이고 결국에는 영웅들의 희생을 밑거름으로 하여 새로운 시대가 열린다."이다. 따라서 답은 ③이다.

14 빈칸에 가장 알맞은 것은 무엇인가?
① 절망
② 규합
③ 분노
④ 적의
⑤ 반대

| 정답 | ②

| 해설 | 낡은 방식이 "최후의 발악(last frantic)" 끝에 "자신의 모든 힘(all its forces)"을 '동원'한다는 의미의 단어가 빈칸에 들어가는 것이 문맥상 가장 적합하다. 이 부분은 본문의 "새로운 방식을 파괴하기 위해 자신의 모든 힘을 동원(gathers all its forces to destroy the new)"한다는 표현과 의미상 통한다. 따라서 gather와 의미상 흡사한 ② rally(규합)이 답으로 적합하다.

| 어휘 | figure ⓝ 인물
uncompromisingly ⓐⓓ 단호하게
splendor ⓝ 탁월함, 빛남, 광휘
go unnoticed – 주목받지 못하다, 간과되다
outstanding ⓐ 뛰어난, 탁월한, 걸출한
victorious ⓐ 승리한, 승리를 거둔
border ⓝ 경계
assert oneself – 스스로를 내세우다
in a vacuum – 외부와 단절된
replace ⓥ 교체하다, 대체하다
despair ⓝ 절망
rage ⓝ 분노
dissent ⓝ 반대

embody ⓥ 구현하다, 담다
arise ⓥ 떠오르다, 부상하다
significance ⓝ 중요성, 의의
sense ⓥ 느끼다, 감지하다
representative ⓝ 대표(자), 대리인
protagonist ⓝ 주인공
justified ⓐ 당연한, 정당한
established ⓐ 자리를 잡은, 인정받은
frantic ⓐ 미친 듯이 서두르는, (두려움으로) 제정신이 아닌
strive ⓥ 분투하다
rally ⓝ 재집결, 규합
antagonism ⓝ 적의

[15-17] 숙명여대 2010

아메리카 대륙의 발견은 지적 호기심이나 심오한 인간의 용기와는 아무 관련이 없었다. 이는 거의 전적으로 한 가지와 관련이 있었는데, 이는 바로 돈이었다. 그리고 이는 실수에 의한 것이었다. 16세기를 통틀어 포르투갈 인들은 동방으로부터의 향료 무역에서 아프리카 대륙을 돌아가는 무역로를 지배함으로써 거침없고 공격적으로 독점을 이뤘다. 반면에 스페인은 동방 국가까지의 서쪽 항로를 개발함으로써 이 독점을 회피하는 방법을 생각해 내기 시작했다. 문제는 이 항로는 아프리카 대륙을 둘러 가는 여행보다 훨씬 길고 광대한 대양을 가로질러 놓여 있다는 것이다. 스페인 여왕에게 동방 국가로 가는 서쪽 원정 비용을 지원해 줄 것을 설득한 것은 Christopher Columbus였다. 유럽인들은 지구 둘레 길이에 대해 상당한 지식이 있었다. 이 원주는 사실상 기원전 2세기에 정확하게 계산되어진 바 있다. 그 당시의 일반적인 시각으로는 배가 공해 위로 수천 마일을 항해해야 했으므로 인도를 향한 서쪽으로의 항해는 재앙이 될 것이라는 것이었다. 그러나 Columbus는 세상이 일반인들이 생각하는 것보다 훨씬 작을 것이라고 믿었다. 물론 이는 그가 완벽하게 잘못 판단한 것이었으며, 아메리카 대륙이 그를 막아서지 않았더라면 그와 그의 부하들은 굶거나 탈수로 목숨을 잃었을 것이다. 그러나 Columbus에게는 운이 좋게도 아메리카 대륙이 그들이 항해하는 길목에 있었다.

15 밑줄 친 unfathomable을 대신할 가장 적절한 단어를 고르시오
① 심오한
② 대담한
③ 호기심 많은
④ 고상한
⑤ 일상적인

| 정답 | ①

| 해설 | fathom은 명사로 물의 깊이를 측정하는 단위로 사용되며, 동사로는 '(깊이 등을) 헤아리거나 가늠하다'로 사용된다. 따라서 unfathomable이라고 하면 '측정하기 어려운, 심오한'이라는 뜻이 되어 답은 ①이 된다.

16

지문에 따르면 다음 중 옳은 설명은 무엇인가?
① 동방 국가로의 원정은 영토 확장과 관계가 있었다.
② 지구의 더 긴 원주를 계산한 것은 바로 Columbus였다.
③ Columbus는 인도로의 서쪽 항로가 동쪽 항로보다 짧다는 것을 증명했다.
④ 스페인 여왕은 서쪽으로부터의 향료 무역을 독점하기 원했다.
⑤ 아메리카 대륙의 발견으로 Columbus의 선원들은 굶어 죽는 것을 피할 수 있었다.

| 정답 | ⑤

| 해설 | ①의 경우, 동방 국가로의 원정은 영토 확장이 아닌 돈과 관련이 있었다고 본문 서두에 나온다. ②의 내용은 본문에 등장하지 않으며, ③의 경우는 Columbus가 증명한 것이 아니라 실수(mistake)에 의한 것이라고 나온다. ④의 내용도 본문에 등장하지 않는다. 답은 ⑤로 본문 마지막 부분에 "had not America gotten in his way, he and his men would have starved ..."라는 문장을 통해 유추할 수 있다. if가 생략되어 도치된 문장이므로 if를 포함해 생각해 보면 "If America had not gotten in his way, he and his men would have starved ..."와 같으며, "아메리카 대륙이 그가 가는 길목에 없었더라면, 그와 그 선원들은 굶어 죽었을 수 있다"고 했으므로 보기 ⑤와 같은 뜻이 된다.

17

빈칸에 들어갈 가장 적절한 단어는 무엇인가?
① 몰수하다   ② 자금을 대다
③ 혐오하다   ④ 상상하다
⑤ 물려받다

| 정답 | ②

| 해설 | 빈칸이 들어간 문장은 'It was ~ who ...'로 강조구문이다. 스페인 여왕을 to~ 하도록 설득한 이는 바로 Columbus라는 뜻이 된다. Columbus는 스페인 여왕을 설득해 서방 원정을 지원해 달라고 설득했으므로 적절한 단어는 ② underwrite(영영 뜻: to support an activity, business plan with money, and to take financial responsibility if it fails)가 된다.

| 어휘 | A has nothing to do with B – A는 B와 관련이 없다
intellectual ⓐ 지적인
ruthlessly ⓐd 무자비하게
monopoly ⓝ 독점
get around – 우회하다, 돌아가다
convince ⓥ 설득하다, 확신시키다
as to – ~에 관한
accurately ⓐd 정확히
get in one's way – ~의 가는 길목에 있다, ~의 방해가 되다
profound ⓐ 심오한
noble ⓐ 고결한, 숭고한, 고매한
territorial ⓐ 영토의
forfeit ⓥ 잃다, 몰수당하다, 박탈당하다
underwrite ⓥ ~에 지불을 승인하다, 사업의 비용 부담을 동의하다
abhor ⓥ 혐오하다
unfathomable ⓐ 잴 수 없는, 깊이를 헤아릴 수 없는, 심오한
aggressively ⓐd 공격적으로
dominate ⓥ 지배하다, 군림하다
infinitely ⓐd 훨씬
expedition ⓝ 원정, 여행
circumference ⓝ 원주, 구의 둘레
audacious ⓐ 대담한
mundane ⓐ 재미없는, 일상적인, 세속적인
save A from B – A를 B로부터 막다, 보호하다

[18-19] 항공대 2017

역사적 사실들은 우리에게 결코 순수한 형태로 다가오지 않는다. 왜냐하면 역사적 사실들은 순수한 형태로 존재하지도 않고, 존재할 수도 없기 때문이다. 역사적 사실들은 언제나 기록한 사람의 정신을 통해 굴절(왜곡)된다. 따라서 우리가 역사적 기록물을 접할 때, 우리의 첫 번째 관심사는 그 기록물이 포함하고 있는 사실들이 아니라, 그것을 기술한 역사학자이어야 한다. 위대한 한 역사가를 예로 들어 보고자 한다. 이 강의는 그에게 경의를 표하기 위해, 그리고 그의 이름을 기리기 위해 개설되었다. 그의 이름은 G. M. 트리벨리언(G. M. Trevelyan)으로, 자신의 자서전에서 밝히고 있는 것과 같이, 그는 휘그당(Whig) 전통이 다소 강한 가정에서 자랐다. 내가 만약 그를 휘그당 전통의 영국의 마지막 위대한 자유주의 역사학자라고 기술한다고 하면, 바라건대, 그는 그러한 칭호를 부인하지 않을 것이다. 그가 자신의 가계도를 거슬러 올라가면서 위대한 휘그당 전통의 조지 오토 트리벨리언(George Otto Trevelyan)을 거쳐 비교가 안 될 정도로 가장 뛰어난 휘그당 역사학자인 매콜리(Macaulay)까지 언급한 것은 충분히 그럴만한 이유가 있는 것이다. 〈앤 여왕 치세의 영국(England under Queen Anne)〉이라는 트리벨리언의 가장 훌륭하고 원숙한 저서는 바로 이러한 배경에서 집필된 것으로, 이러한 배경에서 읽혀질 때에만 그 저서의 온전한 의미와 중요성이 도출될 수 있을 것이다.

18 다음 중 본문을 통해 추론할 수 있는 것은?
① 역사는 역사학자와 불가분의 관계에 있다.
② 역사는 일련의 순수한 사실들의 모음을 의미한다.
③ 역사는 확고한 사실에 기반을 둔 객관적인 사실을 요구한다.
④ 역사학자는 의미와 중요성을 배제한 객관적 역사를 짜깁기해서 집필해야 할 의무감을 가지고 있어야 한다.

| 정답 | ①

| 해설 | 역사적 사실들은 역사를 기록한 사람의 정신을 통해 굴절(왜곡)되기 때문에, 역사서를 읽을 때는 역사적 사실보다 역사가가 누구인지 관심을 가져야 한다고 본문 서두에서 지적하고 있다. 이것은 역사는 역사학자와 불가분의 관계에 있다는 ①을 의미하는 것이다.

19 다음 중 본문의 내용과 일치하는 것은?
① G. M. 트리벨리언은 순수한 역사의 중요성을 이해하고 있었다.
② G. M. 트리벨리언의 저서는 사실들을 객관적으로 편집한 결과이다.
③ G. M. 트리벨리언의 저서는 자신의 가문 배경의 자취를 간직하고 있다.
④ G. M. 트리벨리언의 가문은 휘그 전통에 대항해 맹렬히 싸웠다.

| 정답 | ③

| 해설 | 본문의 "자신의 가계도를 거슬러 올라가면서 위대한 휘그당 전통의 조지 오토 트리벨리언(George Otto Trevelyan)을 거쳐 비교가 안 될 정도로 가장 뛰어난 휘그당 역사학자인 매콜리(Macaulay)까지 언급한 것은 충분히 그럴만한 이유가 있는 것이다"라는 내용을 통해, G. M. 트리벨리언이 자신의 가문 배경을 언급했다고 했으므로, ③이 정답이 된다.

| 어휘 | **refract** ⓥ 굴절시키다; 왜곡하다
it follows that ~ - ~라는 결론이 뒤따르다, 결과적으로 ~이다
in one's honour - ~에게 경의를 표하여; ~을 기념하여
autobiography ⓝ 자서전
exuberantly ⓐⓓ 풍성하게; 생기에 가득 차게; 화려하게
Whig ⓝ 휘그당, 휘그당원(휘그당은 영국에서 자유주의자와 공화주의자들의 진영이었고, 왕당파인 토리(Tory)당은

절대주의를 찬성했으며 왕의 신적인 권리를 방어했음)

disclaim ⓥ 부인하다	liberal ⓐ 자유로운, 관대한; 진보적인, 진보주의의
it is not for nothing that ~ - ~하는 데는 충분한 이유가 있다, 괜히 ~한 것이 아니다	
incomparably ⓐⓓ 비교가 안 될 정도로, 빼어나게	inseparable ⓐ 불가분의, 갈라놓을 수 없는
objective ⓐ 객관적인 ⓝ 목적어	solid ⓐ 견고한
scissors-and-paste ⓐ 가위와 풀로 편집한(남의 책을 오려내어 편집하는), 독창성이 없는	
compilation ⓝ 모음집, 편집	ferociously ⓐⓓ 맹렬히, 격렬하게

[20-22] 성균관대 2006

> 1887년 크리스마스 직전에 이름은 네덜란드인 같지 않은 Marie Eugene Francois Thomas ubois라는 한 젊은 네덜란드 의사가 지구상에서 가장 오래된 인류의 유해를 찾고자 네덜란드령 동인도에 위치한 수마트라에 도착했다. 이 점에 있어 특이할 만한 사항이 몇 가지 있다. 우선 고대 인류의 뼈를 찾으러 떠난 사람은 이전에 아무도 없었다. 그 당시까지 발견된 고대 인류의 뼈는 전부 우연히 발견된 것이었고, Dubois의 배경만 놓고 보면 그를 그런 목적을 갖고 탐색을 진행할 만한 이상적인 후보자의 구석이 전혀 없었다. 그는 훈련을 쌓은 해부학자였지만 고생물학 분야의 배경이 전무했다. 그리고 네덜란드령 동인도에 초기 인류의 유해가 있으리라 가정할 만한 특별한 이유도 없었다. 논리적으로 따져 보면 어쨌든 만약 고대인들의 흔적이 발견된다면 오랫동안 사람들이 살아온 거대한 땅덩이에서 발견될 것이지 상대적으로 요새와 같은 군도에서 발견될 리는 없었다. Dubois가 네덜란드령 동인도에 이끌린 이유는 다름 아닌 예감과, 인력 고용 가능성, 그리고 인류의 주요 화석 대부분이 지금까지 발견된 환경인 동굴이 수마트라에는 가득하다는 지식 때문이었다. 이 모든 일 가운데 가장 특이하면서 진실로 기적과 같은 것은 그가 실제 자신이 찾던 것을 발견했다는 점이다.

20 무엇 때문에 Dubois는 인류의 화석을 찾고자 수마트라로 갔는가?
① 경험
② 이전의 발견
③ 수마트라에서의 인간 유해의 존재
④ 해부학자로서의 지식
⑤ 수마트라의 많은 동굴

| 정답 | ⑤

| 해설 | 본문 마지막에서 두 번째 문장을 보면 Dubois는 "예감과, 인력 고용 가능성, 그리고 중요한 인류의 화석 대부분이 지금까지 발견된 환경인 동굴이 수마트라에는 가득하다는 지식(a hunch, the availability of employment and the knowledge that Sumatra was full of caves, the environment in which most of the important hominid fossils had so far been found)" 때문에 수마트라로 향했음을 알 수 있다. 따라서 답은 ⑤가 된다.

21 Dubois에 관하여 사실이 아닌 것은?
① 그는 고생물학에 관한 지식이 없던 의사였다.
② 그는 고대인의 해부학적 구조에 관심이 있었다.
③ 그는 수마트라에 많은 동굴이 있음을 알고 있었다.
④ 그는 동굴에서 인류의 화석이 발견될 것이라고 생각했다.
⑤ 그는 수마트라에서 초기 인류의 뼈를 발견했다.

| 정답 | ②

| 해설 | Dubois는 "고생물학 분야의 배경이 전무(with no background in paleontology)"했으며, "동굴이 수마트라에는 가득하다는 지식(the knowledge that Sumatra was full of caves)"을 갖고 있었고, 동굴은 "인류의 주요 화석 대부분이 지금까지 발견된 환경(the environment in which most of the important hominid fossils had so far been found)"임을 인식하고 있었고, 결국 수마트라에서 "그가 실제 자신이 찾던 것을 발견(he found what he was looking for)", 즉 고대 인류의 화석을 발견했다. 모두 각각 ①, ③, ④, ⑤에 대응된다. 그러나 Dubois는 해부학자이긴 했지만 '고대인의 해부학적 구조에 관심이 있었는지 여부'는 알 수 없다. 따라서 답은 ②이다.

22 다음 중 저자가 특이하다고 여기지 않은 것은 무엇인가?
① 초창기 인간의 유해를 발견하려는 Dubois의 의도
② 의사였지만 고생물학자는 아니었던 Dubois의 경력
③ 인류 화석이 있을 만한 후보로 수마트라가 꼽힌 것
④ 오랫동안 사람이 살아온 도시에서 발견된 고대인(의 흔적)
⑤ Dubois의 초창기 인류의 유해 발견의 성공

| 정답 | ④

| 해설 | 본문의 'Logic dictated that ~'이란 표현은 '논리적으로 따져 보면'의 의미로, 저자가 논리적으로 생각하기에 합당한 것이 이 표현 뒤에 등장할 것임을 유추할 수 있다. 그리고 그 내용은 "만약 고대인들의 흔적이 발견된다면 오랫동안 사람들이 살아 온 거대한 땅덩이에서 발견될 것(if ancient people were to be found at all, it would be on a large and long-populated land mass)"이다. 즉, 저자는 오랫동안 사람이 살아온 곳에서 고대인의 흔적이 발견되는 것은 특이한 일이 아니라 당연한 것으로 여김을 알 수 있다. 따라서 답은 ④가 된다.

| 어휘 | **Dutch East Indies** – 네덜란드령 동인도
extraordinary ⓐ 특이한
intentional ⓐ 의도적인, 고의인
paleontology ⓝ 고생물학
land mass – 대륙
fastness ⓝ 요새
hunch ⓝ 예감
remains ⓝ 유적, 유해
accidentally ⓐ 우연히
anatomist ⓝ 해부학자
dictate ⓥ 지시하다, 명령하다
comparative ⓐ 상대적인, 비교적
archipelago ⓝ 다도해, 군도
hominid ⓝ 인류, 인류의 조상

[23-25] 숭실대 2013

서양에서 추정하기로는 유목 생활을 하는 수렵·채집인들은, 특히 오늘날에도 여전히 수렵·채집 기능을 수행하고 있는 사람들은 (그 수는 대략 수천만 정도임), "생존을 위한" 경제에 얽매이지 않고 벗어나고 싶어한다. 하지만 마셜 살린스의 주장에 따르면, 이들은 분명히 지금의 삶의 방식을 스스로 선택했다. 때로는 주변 부족이 "첨단 기술 도구"를 활용하여, 수렵·채집 공동체에서 안정적인 농업 공동체로 전환하더라도, 많은 수렵·채집 공동체는 농업 공동체로 전환 시 더 열심히 일해야 할 것이라는 점을 근거로 들어 이러한 선택을 거부한다. 리처드 리는 부시맨 종족의 말을 다음과 같이 인용했다. "세상에 몽고몽고 열매가 이렇게나 많은데 왜 굳이 뭔가를 심어야 하는가."

수렵·채집인들은 자연의 변덕으로부터 스스로를 보호해 줄 수 있는 잉여물을 생산하지 못한다는 이유로 "문화적으로 열등한" 존재로 불리는 경우가 종종 있다. 살린스는 왜 이들이 잉여물 생산을 삼가는지 네 가지 이유를 제시했다. 첫 번째로, 이들은 긍정적이다. 음식이 있으면 다 먹어 버리고, 심지어 잔뜩 먹어 버린다. 이러한 태도는 음식은 자연 속에서 풍부하게 존재하므로 보관은 불필요하다는 태도로 보인다. 자연은 자체적으로 음식을 식물과 동물 속에 이곳저곳 저장하며, 인간은 어디에 저장하는지를 알기만 하면 된다. 따라서 폭풍우나 사고로 인해 어느 한 공동체가 음식을 며칠 또는 몇 주 동안 접하지 못하게 되더라도, 처참한 결과를 낳는 경우는 거의 없고 다른 지역으로 이동하면 된다. 두 번째로, 수렵·채집인들은 유목 생활을 한다는 선택을 했다. 이들이 만일 음식을 저장하거나 가지고 다녔다면, 이들은 특정한 장소에 묶여 있거나 움직임이 매우 느려졌을 것이다. 유목 생활을 하는 수렵·채집인들에게 있어 "그의 부는 짐일 뿐이라는 것이 정말로 슬픈 일입니다"라고 살린스는 말했다. 이동을 해야 한다는 사실이 "재산에 대한 만족감을 급격하게 떨어뜨린다." 세 번째로, ⓐ저장에 기반을 둔 경제는 현재의 "덜 쓰기" 윤리가 미치는 수준을 넘어 부시맨 족이 환경에 미치는 영향을 증가시킬 것이다. 잉여물은 또한 인구 성장을 야기할 것이며, 이는 공동체의 이동성을 위협하며 자연재해에 대한 취약성을 증가시킬 것이다. 네번째로, 수렵인의 자부심은 수렵에 달려 있다. 잉여물을 축적하는 행위는 수렵인의 문화적 중요성과 심리적 중요성을 약화시킬 것이다. 이는 또한 젊은이들의 훈련을 경시하고 더 적은 기술만을 습득한 게으른 사회가 도래하게 만들 것이다.

23 다음 중 빈칸 ⓐ와 ⓑ에 적합한 것은 무엇인가?
① 물물교환
② 농업
③ 저장
④ 경쟁

| 정답 | ③

| 해설 | 빈칸 ⓐ의 경우, 식품이 풍부하고 자연 속에서 이곳저곳 저장된 식품을 찾는 것으로 충분하다면 굳이 '저장'을 할 필요는 없을 것이다. 빈칸 ⓑ의 경우, 부시맨들은 잉여물을 생산하기보다 덜 쓰는 것을 미덕으로 삼고 있는데 이와는 반대로 생산한 것을 쌓아 놓고 '저장'하게 되면 지금의 부시맨들보다 환경에 더 큰 영향을 줄 수밖에 없다. 이러한 점들을 고려했을 때 답으로 가장 적절한 것은 ③이다.

24 본문에 따르면 다음 중 유목 생활을 하는 수렵·채집인들이 잉여물을 생산하지 않으려 하는 이유를 설명한 것은 무엇인가?
① 이들은 어렸을 때부터 필요 이상으로 생산하지 말라는 가르침을 배웠다.
② 이들은 자연의 풍요로움과 선량함을 강하게 믿는다.
③ 잉여물은 필연적으로 종족 간의 갈등을 유발한다.
④ 잉여물은 젊은이들의 사기를 꺾고 사회를 타락시킨다.

| 정답 | ②

| 해설 | 유목생활을 하는 수렵·채집인들은 "긍정적이다. 음식이 있으면 다 먹어 버리고, 심지어 잔뜩 먹어 버린다. 이러한 태도는 음식은 자연 속에서 풍부하게 존재하므로 보관은 불필요하다는 태도로 보인다(optimists. When there is food they tend to eat it all, even gorging themselves. The attitude seems to be that since food is abundant in nature, storage is not necessary)." 즉, 수렵·채집인들 입장에서 자연은 자신들에게 언제나 음식을 제공하는 풍요롭고 선량한 존재이다. 따라서 답은 ②이다.

25 다음 중 빈칸 ⓒ에 가장 알맞은 것은 무엇인가?

① 이는 또한 젊은이들의 훈련을 경시하고 더 적은 기술만을 습득한 게으른 사회가 도래하게 만들 것이다.
② 지구상의 토착 민족 가운데 대다수는 서구 경제 장치에 올라타기를 원하지 않는다.
③ 그래서 춤추기, 낚시하기, 사냥, 잠, 의식 등이 인생 대부분을 차지하는 것으로 보인다.
④ 수렵인은 직계 가족들이 필요로 하는 수의 동물만 키우고 싶을 것이다.

| 정답 | ①

| 해설 | "잉여물을 축적하는 행위는 수렵인의 문화적 중요성과 심리적 중요성을 약화시킬 것이다(To accumulate surplus would diminish the cultural and psychological importance of the hunter)." 즉, 잉여물이 존재하는 상황에서 이를 저장해 놓으면 수렵을 해야 할 필요성이 떨어지고, 결과적으로 젊은이들은 수렵을 제대로 배우지도 못한 채 저장한 것만 활용하면 되니 게을러질 수밖에 없다. 따라서 답은 ①이다.

| 어휘 | **nomadic** ⓐ 유목의 **hunter-gatherer** ⓝ 수렵·채집인
functional ⓐ 가동 중인 **subsistence** ⓝ 최저 생활, 생존
whim ⓝ 변덕 **eschew** ⓥ 삼가다, 피하다
gorge oneself – 잔뜩 먹다 **depreciate** ⓥ 떨어뜨리다
calamity ⓝ 재앙, 재난 **downplay** ⓥ 폄하다, 경시하다
demoralize ⓥ 사기를 꺾다, 의기소침하게 만들다

[26-27] 한양대 2013

고고학자들은 인도네시아의 플로레스 섬에 위치한 석회암 동굴을 발굴하기 시작했을 때 자신들이 발견하게 될 것에 대한 준비가 되어 있지 않았다. 바로 호모 플로레시엔시스라는 이름이 붙었으며 18,000년 전에 살았던 완전히 새로운 인간 종의 자그마한 골격이었다. 뉴사우스웨일스주 아미데일에 위치한 뉴잉글랜드 대학의 인류학자인 피터 브라운은 다음과 같이 말했다. "누군가가 외계인을 발굴했다고 하더라도 이렇게 놀라지는 않았을 것입니다."
리앙부아 동굴에서 인도네시아인과 호주인으로 구성된 발굴단이 발견해 낸 석기와 7명의 골격 가운데는 여성일 것으로 짐작되는 형태를 지닌 성인의 두개골과 불완전한 골격이 있었다. 이 골격은 팔과 다리가 길고 가벼웠으며 겉보기에는 침팬지처럼 보였지만, 직립보행을 했다. 두개골의 뇌 용적은 지금까지 알려진 인간 종에 비해 훨씬 작았다. 뼈가 화석화되지 않았기 때문에 DNA가 담겨 있을 것으로 보이며 호모 사피엔스와의 유전적 연결고리에 대한 답이 나올지도 모른다.

26 윗글의 내용과 일치하는 것을 고르시오.

① 인류학자들은 그 골격이 침팬지의 것임을 증명했다.
② 발굴된 뼈는 직립보행을 한 성인 여성의 유해였다.
③ 고고학자들은 새로운 인간 종이 인도네시아의 동굴에 묻혀 있을 것이라고 예측했다.
④ 피터 브라운은 인도네시아의 한 섬에 위치한 석회암 동굴에서 외계인을 발굴하여 놀랐다.

| 정답 | ②

| 해설 | 세 번째 문단을 보면 발굴된 골격은 직립보행을 하는 여성의 것임을 알 수 있다. 따라서 답은 ②이다.

27 윗글의 내용상 밑줄 친 곳에 들어갈 가장 알맞은 것을 고르시오.
① 골격의 모양
② 이들이 어떤 석기를 사용했는가
③ 이들의 발견된 곳이 어디인가
④ 호모 사피엔스와의 유전적 연결 고리

| 정답 | ④

| 해설 | DNA가 '빈칸'에 해당하는 문제에 대한 답을 내 준다고 나와 있는데, DNA의 성격을 생각해 보면 보기 중에서 답으로 가장 적절한 것은 '유전'에 관한 내용인 ④이다.

| 어휘 | archaeologist ⓝ 고고학자   excavate ⓥ 발굴하다, 출토하다
limestone ⓝ 석회석, 석회암   anthropologist ⓝ 인류학자
remains ⓝ 유해

[28-29] 한양대 2013

우리 역사가들은 일반적으로 역사적 사실에 대해 책임이 있으며 특히 역사가 남용되는 것을 비판해야 할 책임이 있다. 나는 이들 책임 중 첫 번째에 관해서는 말할 필요가 없다. (하지만) 두 가지 전개된 사항에 대해서는 말해야 할 것 같다. 그중 하나는 소설가들이 현실을 창조하기보다 기록된 현실에 기반하여 줄거리를 작성하는 요즘의 시류로, 이로 인해 역사적 사실과 허구 간의 경계가 날조되고 있다. 다른 하나는 대학 그중에서도 특히 문학과와 인류학과에서의 "포스트모더니즘적" 지적 유행의 부각으로, 이는 즉 객관적 실재를 주장하는 모든 "사실"이 단순히 지적 구성에 불과하다는 것, 간단히 말하자면 사실과 허구 간의 경계가 분명하지 않다는 것을 시사한다. 하지만 경계는 분명히 존재한다. 그리고 역사가들에게 있어 양자를 분간하는 능력은 반드시 가장 기본이 되는 능력이다. 우리는 사실을 창조할 수 없다. 엘비스 프레슬리는 죽었을 수도 아닐 수도 있다. 이 의문은 믿을 수 있는 증거가 있다는 전제하에서 증거를 기반으로 분명하게 답할 수 있다.

28 빈칸에 들어갈 가장 알맞은 것을 고르시오.
① "역사 소설"이라는 신조어를 생각해 내다
② 역사와 문학 간의 격차를 메운다
③ 역사적 사실과 허구 간의 경계가 날조되고 있다
④ 문학적 상상은 역사적 사실보다 더 낫다는 것을 증명하다

| 정답 | ③

| 해설 | 소설의 줄거리가 완전히 허구에서 만들어진 것이라면 허구와 역사적 사실 간에는 분명한 경계가 존재하겠지만, "기록된 현실에 기반하여 줄거리를 작성할(base their plots on recorded reality)" 경우엔 그 경계가 흐려지게 된다. 따라서 답은 ③이 된다.

29

윗글의 내용으로부터 유추할 수 없는 것을 고르시오.

① 저자는 소설 읽기를 좋아하지 않는다.
② 저자는 포스트모더니즘에 호의적이지 않다.
③ 저자는 엘비스 프레슬리가 죽었다고 확신한다.
④ 저자는 역사적 사실이 지적 구성은 결코 아니라고 생각한다.

| 정답 | ①

| 해설 | 본문 어디에도 저자가 소설 읽기를 좋아하는 것인지 아닌지가 나와 있지 않으므로 ①이 답이 된다. 참고로 다른 보기를 보면, 우선 "포스트모더니즘"에서는 사실과 허구 간의 경계가 불분명하다고 말하지만, 저자는 경계가 분명히 존재한다고 말하므로 ②는 답이 될 수 없다. 그리고 포스트모더니즘적 관점에서는 허구와 사실을 구분하지 않으면서 모든 사실이 단순히 지적 구성에 불과하다고 하지만, 저자는 양자를 구분하는 것이 가장 기본적인 능력이라고 말하고 있다. 즉 역사적 사실을 양자 간의 구분이 없는 지적 구성이라고 할 수는 없는 것이다. 따라서 ④도 답이 아니다. 마지막으로 엘비스의 생존 여부는, 현재 시점에서는 엘비스가 사망한 것이 사실인데 이를 날조하여 사실을 만들 수는 없고, 그가 사망하지 않았다는 사실을 증명하는 신뢰할 만한 증거가 있지 않은 한은 사망한 것으로 봐야 한다. 따라서 ③도 답이 될 수 없다.

| 어휘 |
abuse ⓝ 남용
anthropology ⓝ 인류학
in so far as – ~인 한에 있어서는
fudge ⓥ 날조하다, 조작하다
unambiguously ⓐ 분명하게, 명료하게
come up with – ~을 생각해 내다, ~을 제시하다

[30-32] 성균관대 2014

산 아구스틴에 위치한 고대 석상은 콜롬비아 형성 이전의 가장 신비로운 고고학적 유물에 속한다. 고고학자들은 현재 기준으로 남아메리카 대륙에서 가장 큰 거대 석상 단지인 이 장소에서 40개의 봉분을 발견했고, 봉분에는 신비로운 동물·신·족장 등의 모습이 담긴 600개의 화상이 손재했다. 지역 내 다른 장소와 마찬가지로 산 아구스틴도 약탈로 고통받고 있다. 유럽 최초의 산 아구스틴 발굴단을 이끈 독일 인류학자인 콘라드 프루스는 베를린에 있는 박물관으로 자신이 발견한 35개의 석상을 실어 날랐고, 현재 그 석상은 지금도 그 박물관에 있다. 이러한 역사로 인해 현지에 방문하는 관광객들로 생계를 유지하는 현지 거주민들은 의심의 눈길을 보내고 있다. 현장에서 차로 10시간 거리에 위치한 수도 보고타의 국립 박물관에서 콘라드 푸루스의 현장 발견 100주년을 기념하기 위해 석상 가운데 20개를 가져가 전시하려는 계획을 세웠으나, 이 계획으로 인해 현지 거주민들이 의구심을 품고 있다는 사실이 입증되었다. 일시적으로라도 석상을 옮기는 문제가 민감한 일이라는 점을 인식하고 있던 콜롬비아 인류학 위원회 소속 인류학자들은 더 많은 관객에게 석상을 선보이도록 허용하는 것이 얼마나 중요한 결정인지를 설명하기 위해 마을 회의를 개최했다. 하지만 지역민들은 석상이 반환되지 않거나 복제품으로 바꿔치기 되지 않을지 우려한다고 밝혔다. 전시 일자가 가까워지면서 지역민들은 석상을 보내도록 허용하는 대가로 상수도 시스템을 새로 설치할 것을 요청하는 등의 요구를 하기 시작했다. 협상은 결렬되었다. 지난 달 조심스럽게 포장되어 상자에 담긴 석상이 보고타로 운송되던 날 지역민들은 길을 차단하고 인부들이 차에 석상을 싣지 못하게 막았다. 박물관은 자기 나름의 저항 방식을 채택했다. 석상이 놓이기로 된 장소에 빛을 쏜 다음 안내원들이 가상현실 프로그램과 태블릿 PC를 사용해 방문객들에게 원래 놓여 있기로 된 것의 3차원 이미지를 보여줬다. 박물관은 확고한 입장을 취했다. 개막식 영상은 방문객들에게 "소수의 사람들이 우리의 문화유산에 대한 독점적 권리를 주장하고 모든 콜롬비아인들의 문화적 자유를 짓밟은 결과 드러나는 공허함과 침묵"을 생각하게 했다.

30

본문의 제목으로 가장 알맞은 것은 무엇인가?

① 석상은 누구의 것인가? 불신의 전시
② 베를린에 있던 콜롬비아 석상의 반환
③ 예술 기금의 역사와 정치
④ 콜롬비아의 석상의 미스터리와 신화
⑤ 콜롬비아의 문화유적 보존

| 정답 | ①

| 해설 | 본문은 고대 석상이 위치한 지역의 주민과 석상을 일시 반출하여 박물관에 전시하려던 박물관 당국 간의 불신으로 인해 석상의 전시가 무산되었다는 내용을 담고 있다. 따라서 답으로는 ①이 가장 적합하다.

31

현지 거주민들은 무엇에 관해 가장 우려하고 있는가?

① 외국 인류학자들이 마을의 유물을 발굴하는 것
② 무분별한 발굴이 마을의 인프라를 파괴하는 것
③ 자신들의 허가 없이 박물관이 석상을 전시하는 것
④ 석상을 돌려받지 못하는 것
⑤ 석상의 대여 조건으로 돈을 받지 못하는 것

| 정답 | ④

| 해설 | "하지만 지역민들은 석상이 반환되지 않거나 복제품으로 바꿔치기 되지 않을지 우려한다고 밝혔다(But the locals said they worried that the objects would not return, or would be swapped for replicas)." 따라서 답은 ④이다.

32

국립박물관은 결국 석상 없이 전시회를 개최했다.

① 석상의 전시를 관철했다
② 석상 없이 전시회를 개최했다
③ 대량의 돈을 지불하여 석상을 구매했다
④ 항의의 의미로 전시회를 취소했다
⑤ 전시회를 연기했다

| 정답 | ②

| 해설 | "석상이 놓이기로 된 장소에 빛을 쏜 다음 안내원들이 가상현실 프로그램과 태블릿 PC를 사용해 방문객들에게 원래 놓여 있기로 된 것의 3차원 이미지를 보여줬다(Light is projected where the statues would have been; guides use a virtual-reality program and tablet computers to show visitors a 3D image of what was meant to be there)." 즉, 석상 없이 전시가 이루어진 것이다. 따라서 답은 ②이다.

| 어휘 | archaeological ⓐ 고고학의   artefact ⓝ 인공물, 가공물
burial mound – 봉분, 무덤   likeness ⓝ 화상, 닮은 것
chieftain ⓝ 족장   megalithic ⓐ 거석의

plunder ⓝ 약탈, 강탈
excavations ⓝ 발굴
sensitivity ⓝ 민감함
in exchange for - ~ 대신의
robust ⓐ 확고한
trample ⓥ 짓밟다

anthropologist ⓝ 인류학자
centenary ⓝ 100주년
replica ⓝ 복제품
crate ⓥ 상자에 담다
invite A to *do* - A의 마음을 끌어 ~하고 싶게 하다
reckless ⓐ 무모한, 무분별한

[33-35] 성균관대 2017

기술이 두 진영을 더 멀어지게 만들어 왔다. 과학적 진보로 인해, 이전에는 항아리나 무덤을 조사하는 것만으로도 만족했던 고고학자들이 지금은 유물을 발견한 위치에 더 많은 신경을 쓰고 있다. 유물에 남아 있을 수 있는 잔여물의 화학적 분석은 유물에 담겨 있던 것에 대한 단서를 제공해 주거나, 그것을 사용한 사람에 대한 단서도 제공해 준다. 중개인들 입장에서는 고고학이 주변 환경에 집착하는 것에 의문을 제기한다. "주변 환경과 동떨어진 유물은 가치가 없다고 말하는 것은 거짓말이자, 위험한 거짓말이다."라고 런던에 본사를 둔 경매회사 본햄 & 브룩스의 유물관리 실장인 조앤 랜드(Joan Lande)는 말한다.

바미안 석불의 파괴는 수집가들과 유물 보호주의자들 사이의 논쟁을 모호하게 만들었다. 일부 보호주의자들도 인정하듯이 국가 문화유산을 원래 자리에 둔다고 항상 유물이 안전하게 보호되는 것은 아니다. 그리고 유물을 제거하는(다른 곳으로 옮기는) 것도 유물을 지킬 수 있다. 디에취(Dietschi)는 자신의 박물관에 있는 유물을 (아프가니스탄의) 상황이 안정되면 아프가니스탄으로 반환할 계획이라고 말한다. 그러는 사이에 암시장은 계속 성장하고 있다. 지난달 많은 양의 바미안 석불이 파키스탄의 시장에 모습을 드러내기 시작했다. 그곳의 중개인들은 필사적으로 유물을 소유하길 원하는 유럽 및 아시아 수집가들의 요청에 응대해 왔다.

33

다음 중 밑줄 친 "it's out of context"가 의미하는 것은?
① 유물을 만든 사람이 누구인지 확실하지 않다
② 유물이 갑자기 나타나다
③ 유물이 역사를 잃어버렸다
④ 유물이 예상하지 못한 곳에서 발견되다
⑤ 유물이 원래 장소에서 다른 곳으로 옮겨지다

| 정답 | ⑤

| 해설 | 고고학자들은 유물이 발견된 장소(context)가 중요하다고 생각하고(keep artifacts in place), 중개인들은 그것은 거짓이라고 생각한다. 즉, 유물이 발견된 원래 장소에 있어야 하는 것은 아니라고 생각한다. 그런 관점에서 'out of context'란 발견한 유물을 원래 장소에서 다른 장소로 옮기는(remove artifacts) 것을 의미하므로, 정답은 ⑤가 적합하다.

34

다음 중 고고학자들을 분류하기에 적합한 것은?
① 유물 보호주의자
② 수집가
③ 중개인
④ 파괴자
⑤ 경매인

| 정답 | ①

| 해설 | 유물과 그 보존에 대한 고고학자와 중개인의 서로 다른 생각을 보여주고 있다. 고고학자는 유물이 발견된 자리에 보존되어야 한다고 생각하며, 중개인은 다른 곳으로 옮겨져도 된다고 생각한다. 이런 관점에서 고고학자들은 ①의 '유물 보호주의자'라고 할 수 있다.

35

다음 중 바미안 석불이 파괴되는 것을 막기 위해 중개인들이 해야 한다고 주장할 내용에 해당하는 것은?
① 불상을 재건했어야 했다
② 불상을 유적지에서 옮겼어야 했다
③ 파괴된 보물을 버렸어야 했다
④ 더 많은 절을 지었어야 했다
⑤ 전쟁이 발발하는 것을 막았어야 했다

| 정답 | ②

| 해설 | 중개인들은 바미안 석불을 구하려면 두 번째 문단의 'removing artifacts can save them'처럼 불상을 다른 곳으로 옮겼어야 한다고 생각하므로, 정답은 ②가 된다.

| 어휘 | archaeologist ⓝ 고고학자
examine ⓥ 시험하다, 검사하다, 조사하다
residue ⓝ 나머지, 잔여
clue ⓝ 실마리, 단서
question ⓥ 의문을 제기하다; 심문하다
out of context – 전후 관계[문맥, 정황]를 무시하고, 전후 관계와 분리하여
antiquity ⓝ 고대, 아주 오래됨
demolition ⓝ 파괴, 폭파, 분쇄
preservationist ⓝ 환경 보호[보존] 운동가
concede ⓥ 인정하다; 양보하다
thrive ⓥ 번창하다, 잘 자라다, 무성해지다
bazaar ⓝ 바자회; 상점가, 시장 거리
field ⓥ (질문·전화 등을) 능란하게 응대하다, 척척 처리하다
out of the blue – 갑자기, 난데없이

content ⓐ 만족한 ⓝ 만족감; 내용
pot ⓝ 단지, 항아리
artifact ⓝ 인공물, 공예품; (pl. 유사 이전 유물)
for one's part – 자기로서는, 자기에 관한 한
obsession ⓝ 강박관념, 사로잡혀 있기
auctioneer ⓝ 경매인
blur ⓥ 흐리게 하다
heritage ⓝ 세습 재산, 혈통, 전승
safeguard ⓥ 보호하다
show up – (갑자기) 나타나다, 등장하다

[36-40] 아주대 2017

[A] 1914년 이전 유럽의 지배적 분위기는 서구 문명의 성취에 대한 자부심과 미래의 발전에 대한 자신감으로 넘쳐났다. 과학 및 기술의 발전, 생활수준의 향상, 민주적 기관의 확산, 사회개혁의 확대, 이 모두가 낙관주의에 기여했다. 낙관주의에 대한 또 다른 이유로는, 나폴레옹의 패배 이후 유럽은 전면전을 회피했고, 보불전쟁(프랑스–프로이센 전쟁, Franco-Prussian War) 이후 강대국들은 서로 전쟁을 치르지 않았다.

[B] 이 같은 성취가 서구 문명을 대재앙으로 몰아넣고 있는 내부의 격변을 감추고 있다는 사실을 알아차린 사람은 많지 않았다. 유럽의 국가체제가 무너지고 있었다. 19세기 초반 자유주의자들은 민족을 바탕으로 유럽의 정치 지도를 다시 그리는 것이 국가 간의 평화적 관계를 촉진할 것이라고 믿었다. 하지만 정반대의 결과가 발생했다. 1914년이 되는 시기에, 민족 국가들은, 더 강력한 세력을 인정하지 않고, 폭발적인 민족주의에 힘입어 끊임없이 커져가는 적대감으로 서로 마주하는 동맹세력을 형성했다. 민족주의 사상가들은 갈등을 미화하고 다른 민족의 정복을 정당화하는 사이비 과학과 같은 인종적 교리 및 사회적 다윈주의 교리를 전파했다. 국력 강화에 여념이 없던 정치인들은 공통의 문명을 공유하는 국가 공동체로서의 유럽을 망각했다. 국제 관계에서 신중과 절제가 호전성에 자리를 내주었다.

[C] 문화적 위기도 발생했다. 많은 유럽 지식인들은 계몽주의의 합리적 전통을 공격하고, 원시적이고 본능적이며 비이성적인 것에 환호했다. 점차 젊은 사람들은 자유주의의 부르주아적 가치를 조롱하고, 전쟁을 인간을 정화시키고 고귀하게 만드는 체험으로 여기는 실천철학에 이끌렸다. ❹ [대중매체에서 다채롭게 묘사되는 식민지 전쟁은 지루한 공장 노동자들과 몽상에 잠긴 학생들의 상상력에 불을 붙였으며, 군인들에게는 의무감과 용맹성의 촉구를 강화시켰다.] 이런 "찬란한" 작은 전쟁들은 전쟁을 칭송할 정도는 아니더라도 용인할 수 있는 것으로 만들어주는 태도가 형성되는 데 일조했다. 일상의 생활에서 벗어나 영웅적 가치를 받아들이길 열망하면서, 많은 유럽인들은 폭력적 갈등(전쟁)을 개인과 국가의 삶에서 나타날 수 있는 최고의 발현으로 여겼다.

[D] 겉으로 보기에는 유럽의 문명이 진보하고 있는 것처럼 보였지만, 민족주의라는 신화적 힘과 갈등(전쟁)의 원시적 매력이 유럽 문명을 심연으로 몰아넣고 있었다. 실책과 무모함으로 유럽 대륙을 전쟁에 빠져들게 만든 정치인들을 포함해, 앞으로 닥친 위기를 알아차린 사람들은 거의 없었다.

36 다음 중 본문의 제목으로 가장 적합한 것은?
① 서구의 절망
② 전쟁으로의 표류
③ 동맹 체제를 맺은 유럽
④ 서구 문명의 단점
⑤ 유럽 국가체제의 실패

| 정답 | ②

| 해설 | 본문은 1914년에 일어난 1차 세계대전으로 빠져들어 가고 있는 전쟁 이전의 유럽 상황을 설명하고 있는 글이다. 아직 전쟁이 시작된 것은 아니고 낙관주의가 지배하는 시기이므로 ① '서구의 절망'은 적절하지 않다. ④ '서구 문명의 단점'은 주제에서 벗어난 내용이며, ③과 ⑤는 본문에서는 언급되어 있지만 세부적 내용에 해당하므로 제목에 적합하지 않다. ②는 '전쟁을 향해 표류해 가고 있는 유럽'을 나타내는 내용이므로, 제목에 적합하다.

37 다음 중 문단 [B]의 ④ 명제와 연관되어 있는 것이 아닌 것은?
① 대부분의 유럽 국가에서 민족주의가 만연했다.
② 민족주의자들에 의해 갈등을 미화하는 사상이 확산됐다.
③ 정치인들은 민족에 따라 유럽의 지도를 개정했다.
④ 유럽 국가들은 그룹으로 연합해 서로 대치했다.
⑤ 정치 지도자들은 하나의 공동체로서의 유럽의 개념을 포기했다.

| 정답 | ③

| 해설 | Ⓐ는 유럽의 '신중과 절제'가 '호전성'으로 바뀐 것을 설명하고 있다. ①은 "By 1914, national states ... were fueled by an explosive nationalism, and were grouped into alliances"를 통해 짐작할 수 있다. ②는 "Nationalist thinkers propagated pseudoscientific racial and Social Darwinist doctrines that glorified conflict"를 통해 알 수 있으며, ④는 "national states ... were grouped into alliances that faced each other with ever-mounting hostility"에서 드러난다. ⑤는 "statesmen lost sight of Europe as a community of nations sharing a common civilization"을 통해 알 수 있다. 정답은 ③으로, "In the early nineteenth century, liberals had believed that the redrawing of the political map of Europe on the basis of nationality would promote peaceful relations among nations. But quite the reverse occurred."에서, 정치인들은 민족에 따라 유럽의 지도를 개정하면 평화적 관계를 증진할 것으로 희망했다고 나온다. 실제로 유럽의 지도를 개정했는지는 알 수 없으므로, ③이 정답이 된다.

38 다음 중 [C] 문단의 빈칸 Ⓑ에 올 수 있는 가장 적합한 것은?
① 사람들은 몇몇 민족에서 불안감이 커지고 있는 것을 알게 되었고, 이것으로 인해 정치 지도자들은 엄청난 불안감을 느꼈다
② 대부분의 사상가는 개인의 자유와 사회의 개혁에 대한 자신들의 관심을 강조했다
③ 많은 유럽인은 폭력적 갈등을 개인과 국가의 삶에서 나타날 수 있는 최고의 발현으로 여겼다
④ 과학자들은 과학과 기술의 발전이 인류를 더 풍요롭게 만들어 줄 것이라고 기대했다
⑤ 사람들은 과학적 방식으로 비이성적 문제를 해결하려고 시도했다

| 정답 | ③

| 해설 | [C] 문단에서는 유럽 대륙이 전쟁의 소용돌이에 휘말려 들어가고 있는 과정을 문화적 측면에서 설명하고 있다. 전쟁은 미화되고 사람들은 이를 어느 정도 받아들일 수 있는 것으로 보았다고 서술하고 있다. 무료한 일상의 삶에서 벗어나 영웅적 가치를 받아들이기 갈망하는 주체는 청년들로 대변되는 대중들이 되어야 하며, 이런 대중들의 태도는 전쟁을 두려워하는 것이 아닌 전쟁을 선호하는 것이 되어야 하므로, 정답은 ③이 된다.

39 다음 중 1914년 이전 유럽의 낙관주의에 영향을 준 것이 아닌 것은?
① 사회 개혁의 증가
② 전쟁 부족에 대한 인식
③ 과학과 기술의 발달
④ 생활수준의 향상
⑤ 전면적 전쟁과 갈등의 회피

| 정답 | ②

| 해설 | 첫 번째 문단의 "Advances in science and technology, the rising standard of living, the spread of democratic institutions and the expansion of social reforms all contributed to a sense of optimism." 및 이후 내용을 통해 유럽의 낙관주의에 영향을 요인들을 파악할 수 있다. ①은 'expansion of social reforms'를, ③은 'Advances in science and technology'를, ④는 'the rising standard of living'을, ⑤는 또 다른 예로 언급한 'Europe had avoided a general war'를 지칭한다. 정답은 ②로, '전쟁이 그렇게 많이 일어나지는 않는다는 인식을 의미'하는데 본문에 서술된 내용과 뉘앙스에 차이가 있어 정답이 된다.

40

다음 문장은 본문에서 제거된 것이다. 저자가 제기한 주장을 뒷받침하기 위해 이 문장이 들어가기에 가장 적합한 곳은 어느 곳인가?

> 대중매체에서 다채롭게 묘사되는 식민지 전쟁은 지루한 공장 노동자들과 몽상에 잠긴 학생들의 상상력에 불을 붙였으며, 군인들에게는 의무감과 용맹성의 촉구를 강화시켰다.

① ❶
② ❷
③ ❸
④ ❹
⑤ ❺

| 정답 | ④

| 해설 | 정답은 ④로, 바로 뒤에 이어지는 문장에서 'These "splendid" little wars'가 지칭하는 대상이 없기 때문에 ❹에 제시된 문장이 삽입되어야 한다. 'These "splendid" little wars'는 'Colonial wars'를 지칭하며, 'splendid'는 'colorfully portrayed'를 의미한다.

| 어휘 |
prior to – ~에 앞서, ~보다 먼저
accomplishment ⓝ 성취, 업적
standard of living – 생활수준
democratic ⓐ 민주적인; (조직의 운영이) 평등주의에 입각한; 평등한
institution ⓝ 제도; 기관; 관례
optimism ⓝ 낙관주의
mask ⓥ 가리다[감추다]
propel ⓥ 나아가게 하다; 몰고 가다
European state system – 유럽 국가체제
promote ⓥ 향상시키다, 승진시키다; 홍보하다
nationalism ⓝ 민족주의
mounting ⓐ 증가하는[커져 가는]
propagate ⓥ 전파하다, 선전하다
Social Darwinist ⓐ 사회적 다원주의의 ⓝ 사회적 다윈주의자
doctrine ⓝ 교리
conflict ⓝ 갈등, 충돌
subjugation ⓝ 정복, 예속
enhance ⓥ 향상하다, 높이다
lose sight of – ~이 더 이상 안 보이게 되다
restraint ⓝ 제한, 자제
belligerency ⓝ 호전성; 교전 상태
rational ⓐ 이성적인, 합리적인
primitive ⓐ 원시의
irrational ⓐ 불합리한
bourgeois ⓐ 자본가 계급, 부르주아
ennoble ⓥ 작위를 내리다, 고귀하게 하다
acceptable ⓐ (사회적으로) 용인되는[받아들여지는]
if not – [정도의 대조] ~까지는 아니라 하더라도
dominant ⓐ 지배적인, 유력한, 주요한
civilization ⓝ 문명
contribute to – ~에 기여하다
general war ⓝ 전면전
turbulence ⓝ 난기류, 격동, 격변
cataclysm ⓝ 대재앙, 대격변, 대홍수
nationality ⓝ 국적, 민족
fuel ⓥ 부채질하다, 연료를 공급하다
alliance ⓝ 동맹, 결연, 연합, 제휴
hostility ⓝ 적의, 적개심
pseudoscientific ⓐ 사이비 과학의, 유사 과학의
glorify ⓥ 찬미하다, 찬양하다
justify ⓥ 정당화하다
be committed to – ~에 헌신하다, 전념하다
statesman ⓝ 정치인
caution ⓝ 조심, 경고[주의]
give way to – ~로 바뀌다, 대체되다
intellectual ⓝ 지식인 ⓐ 지적인, 지력이 뛰어난
the Enlightenment – 계몽주의
instinctual ⓐ 본능에 따른
ridicule ⓥ 조롱하다 ⓝ 비웃음
purify ⓥ 정화하다, 정제하다
fashion ⓥ 만들다, 형성하다; 맞추다
laudable ⓐ 칭찬할 만한, 훌륭한

yearn ⓥ 그리워하다, 갈망하다
break loose from – ~에서 탈출하다, 떨어져 나오다[독립하다]
embrace ⓥ 포옹하다; (생각을) 받아들이다[수용하다]

mythic ⓐ 신화적인	abyss ⓝ 심연, 나락
blunder ⓝ 큰 실수 ⓥ 실수하다, 서툰 짓을 하다	recklessness ⓝ 무모함
continent ⓝ 대륙 ⓐ 자제하는, 절제하는	stumble into – 우연히 ~에 관여하게 되다
despair ⓝ 절망	drift ⓝ 표류, (서서히 일어나는) 이동, 추이 ⓥ 표류하다
downside ⓝ 불리한 면; 하락세	prevail ⓥ 우세하다, 널리 보급되다, 유력하다
revise ⓥ 수정하다	agitation ⓝ 동요, 선동, 혼란
in a ~ manner – ~한 방식으로, ~한 태도로	gallantry ⓝ 용맹

CHAPTER 02 철학·종교

01	③	02	①	03	③	04	①	05	③	06	④	07	③	08	③	09	②	10	①
11	①	12	③	13	⑤	14	①	15	④	16	②	17	④	18	④	19	②	20	②
21	②	22	①	23	④	24	②	25	②	26	④	27	②	28	①	29	②	30	②
31	③	32	④	33	③	34	④	35	④	36	②	37	①	38	②	39	①	40	②

[01-03] 한성대 2010

Mark Twain은 자신이 살던 시기, 특히 1800년대 후반을 도금 시대(the Gilded Age)라고 불렀다. 이를 통해 Twain은 미국 사회가 외적 화려함에도 불구하고 내적으로 부패했음을 지적하고자 했다. 그러나 미국의 부유한 산업자본가들은 스스로를 이러한 방식으로 바라보지 않았으며, 사회 다윈주의는 그들에게 소수에 의한 부의 축적을 "자연의 질서(natural order)"라고 믿게 해 주었다. 영국의 철학자인 Herbert Spencer는, 미국 산업자본가들이 자신들의 부에 대한 추구를 철학적으로 정당화하기 위해 의존했던 인물이다. Spencer에 의해 발전한 이론인 사회 다윈주의는 Charles Darwin의 진화론을 인간 사회에 부분적으로 적용한 것이다. "적자생존(survival of the fittest)"이라는 표현을 만들어 낸 Spencer는 "자연적으로" 우수한 사회 구성원들은 최정상까지 오를 운명을 타고난 이들로 이들은 방해받아서는 안 된다고 주장했다. 게다가, Spencer는 타고난 습성으로 인해 사회의 밑바닥에 있는 사람들은 생존에 적합하지 않으며, 그렇기 때문에 이들에 대한 동정은 무의미하다고 경고했다.

01 밑줄 친 ㉮ them이 지칭하는 것은?
① 사회 다윈주의를 믿는 사람들
② 일반 미국인들
③ 미국의 부유한 산업자본가들
④ 사회 다윈주의의 이론가들

| 정답 | ③

| 해설 | ㉮의 them은 앞에 나오는 'wealthy industrialists in the United States'를 받는 말로, 이들은 사회 다윈주의를 통해 소수에 의한 부의 축척이 "자연의 질서(natural order)"라고 믿었다. 따라서 답은 ③이 된다.

02 빈칸 ㉯에 적절하지 않은 것은?
① 인정되다
② 방해되다
③ 방해되다
④ 방해되다

| 정답 | ①

| 해설 | 빈칸의 문장은 사회 다윈주의를 주장한 Herbert Spencer의 사상을 담고 있는 것으로, 그는 사회 다윈주의에서 '자연적으로' 우월한 존재가 정상에 오르는 것은 신의 섭리와도 같이 당연한 것으로, 이들이 정상에 오르는 것을 막거나 통제해서는 안 된다는 주장이 나와야 한다. 따라서 이에 해당하는 단어들로는 hindered / impeded / obstructed 등이 적당하며, 반대의 뜻을 지닌 ①의 admitted는 뜻이 반대가 되므로 빈칸에 올 수 없다.

03 윗글의 내용과 일치하지 않는 것은?

① 사회 다윈주의는 Darwin의 진화론에 기초를 두고 있다.
② 미국의 산업자본가들은 스스로를 정당화하기 위해 Spencer의 이론에 의존했다.
③ "적자생존"이라는 표현은 Darwin에 의해 만들어졌다.
④ Spencer는 가난한 사람들은 본래 가망이 없다고 생각했다.

| 정답 | ③

| 해설 | ①의 경우, 본문에서 "Social Darwinism ... was in part an application of Charles Darwin's evolutionary theories to human societies."라고 한 부분을 통해 유추할 수 있다. ②에 대한 설명도 본문에서 쉽게 찾아볼 수 있는데, 본문의 "Herbert Spencer ... was the person whom US industrialists turned to for the philosophical justification of their pursuit of wealth."라는 부분을 통해 알 수 있는 내용이다. ③의 경우는 본문의 "Spencer, who coined the expression 'survival of the fittest,' argued ..."라고 한 부분을 통해 '적자생존'이란 용어는 Darwin이 아닌 Spencer에 의해 만들어진 것임을 알 수 있다. 보기 ④에 대한 내용은 본문의 마지막 문장인 "those who were at the bottom ... were unfit to survive, and therefore, charity was meaningless"라는 부분을 통해 알 수 있다. 따라서 정답은 ③이다.

| 어휘 |
in particular – 특히, 그중에서도
point out – 지적하다
showiness ⓝ 화려함
corrupt ⓐ 부패한, 타락한
social Darwinism ⓝ 사회 다윈주의
turn to – ~에 의지하다
pursuit ⓝ 추구
coin ⓥ (새로운 용어를) 만들어 내다
by nature – 날 때부터, 본래, 천성적으로
theorist ⓝ 이론가
hinder ⓥ 방해하다
obstruct ⓥ 막다
the Gilded Age – 도금 시대
outward ⓐ 외부의
inwardly ⓐⓓ 내부에
industrialist ⓝ 산업자본가
accumulation ⓝ 축적
justification ⓝ 정당화
application ⓝ 적용
be meant to *do* – ~하기로 되어 있다
charity ⓝ 자애, 동정, 자선
admit ⓥ 인정하다, 수용하다
impede ⓥ 방해하다

[04-05] 중앙대 2011

르네 데카르트(René Descartes)는 프랑스의 철학자이자 수학자, 물리학자, 저술가였다. 그는 '근대 철학의 아버지'로 불리며, 이후 등장한 서양 철학의 대부분은 오늘날까지 면밀히 연구되고 있는 그의 저술에 대한 답변이라고 할 수 있다. 특히 그의 저서 〈성찰, Meditations on First Philosophy〉은 대부분의 대학 철학과의 주교재로 사용되고 있다. 뿐만 아니라 그의 다른 저서 〈방법서설, Discourse on the Method〉은 모든 철학을 통틀어 가장 영향력 있는 책 중 하나로 여겨지고 있다. 데카르트는 〈방법서설〉 4장에서 그의 유명한 철학적 명제인 "Cogito ergo sum(나는 생각한다. 고로 존재한다.)"이라는 말을 남겼다. 또 다른 유명한 말로는 데카르트가 종종 사용했던 "de omnibus dubitandum(우리는 모든 것을 의심해야 한다.)"로 이는 데카르트식 방법의 정수를 잘 표현해 주고 있다. 이 말은 성직자인 사람이 내놓은 의견치고는 이상하리만큼 냉소적인 면이 있다. 사실 이 때문에 당시 성직자들 사이에서 그는 인기 있는 사람이 아니었다. 하지만 데카르트는 의심의 방법을 사용해서 다소 역설적이게도 성직자의 위치에 이르렀다. 그가 이런 방법을 사용한 목적은 항상 명확했다. 미셸 몽테뉴(Michel de Montaigne)나 그가 비평의 글을 썼던 다른 회의론자들과는 달리, 데카르트는 당시 유행하는 의심을 위한 의심이라는 접근법에는 관심이 없었다. 그의 목적은 의심의 방법을 통해 확실하게 추론되는 것에 도달하는 것이었다. 이는 본질적으로 17세기 물리학의 과학적 접근법으로, 이때 의심은 항상 동일한 역할을 수행했다. 바로 가능한 모든 방법을 통해 의심의 여지없이 확립되기까지 "그 어떤 것도 사실로 받아들이지 않는 것"을 의미했기 때문이다.

04 밑줄 친 ㉮와 ㉯에 들어가기에 가장 적합한 것을 고르시오.
① 냉소적인 – 확실성
② 회의적인 – 강제
③ 이성적인 – 추론
④ 현명한 – 불신

| 정답 | ①

| 해설 | 성직자인 사람이 모든 것을 의심해야 한다고 말했으므로 ㉮에는 이성적이거나 현명한 충고라고 할 수는 없다. 상당히 냉소적이거나 회의론적인 충고라고 할 수 있으므로 ①과 ②로 정답의 범위를 줄일 수 있으며, ㉯에는 데카르트가 의심의 방법을 통해 이루고자 했던 것을 설명하고 있다. 즉 어떤 현상을 파헤쳐 확실하게 도출되거나 또는 추론을 통해 도출될 수 있는 것까지 도달하는 것이 그의 목적이라고 생각하는 것이 타당하므로 ㉯에는 ①과 ③이 가능하다. 따라서 두 가지 경우 모두 해당되는 ①이 정답이 된다.

05 윗글의 내용과 일치하는 것으로 가장 적합한 것을 고르시오.
① 신자들 중에 데카르트를 열성적으로 지지하는 사람이 많았다.
② 데카르트의 철학적 명제는 가끔 역설적인 메시지를 전한다.
③ 데카르트와 몽테뉴는 의심의 방법에 대한 태도 면에서 서로 달랐다.
④ 데카르트는 물리학보다 수학 분야에 더 큰 공헌을 했다.

| 정답 | ③

| 해설 | ①의 경우 신자들 사이에서 인기가 없었다고 나오므로 정답이 아니며, ②의 경우 역설적인 것은 신자인 데카르트가 의심의 방법을 통해 사물의 본질에 접근했다는 것이지, 역설적인 메시지를 전했다는 것은 사실이 아니다. ③의 경우 데카르트는 당시 유행하던 의심을 위한 의심의 방식에는 몽테뉴와 달리 관심이 없었다고 했으므로, 의심의 방법을 두 사람이 모두 사용했지만 방법적인 측면에서 서로 달랐다는 것을 알 수 있다. ④는 타당한 설명일 수 있지만 본문에는 등장하지 않기 때문에 정답이 될 수 없다.

| 어휘 | dub ⓥ ~라고 부르다
discourse ⓝ 담론, 담화
crux ⓝ 요점, 가장 중요한 부분
clergy ⓝ 성직자
skeptic ⓝ 회의론자
for the sake of – ~을 위해서
beyond doubt – 의심할 여지없이
deduction ⓝ 추론

meditation ⓝ 성찰, 명상
influential ⓐ 영향력 있는
Cartesian ⓐ 데카르트의
paradox ⓝ 역설
modish ⓐ 유행하는
essentially ⓐⓓ 본질적으로
coercion ⓝ 강제, 강압
staunch ⓐ 충실한, 견고한

[06-07] 숙명여대 2012

주장은 애매모호할 수 있다. 예를 들어 "~을 믿는다"는 구문이 포함된 주장은 "신뢰"가 지닌 영향력을 높인다. 어떤 사람이 자신은 대통령을 믿는다는 주장을 할 경우, 이 사람은 현재 대통령이란 직책이 존재하고 실제로 대통령이 존재한다는 것을 모든 사람이 분명히 알고 있다고 추정하고 있으며, 대통령이 대체로 일을 잘할 것임을 확신한다고 단언하고 있다. 그런데 만일 어떤 사람이 자신은 텔레파시를 믿는다는 주장을 할 경우, 이 사람은 자신이 텔레파시가 대체로 일을 잘할 것임을 확신한다는 의도로 주장한 것이 아니라 텔레파시가 실제 발생하는 경우도 있음을 믿는다는 의도로 주장한 것이며 실제로 텔레파시가 존재한다는 의도로 주장한 것이다. 따라서 "X를 믿는다"는 구문은 어떨 때는 실제 존재하리라 추정되거나 존재한다고 알려진 X가 일을 잘할 것이라고 확신한다는 의미를 갖기도 하지만, 어떤 경우엔 X가 존재한다고 믿는다는 의미를 갖기도 한다. 이는 "신을 믿는다"는 구문에 있어서는 어떤 의미일까? 모호하지만 양쪽 모두를 의미하며, 어느 한 의미를 통해 자명하게 의도된 것은 다른 의미에서 의도된 것을 암시하게 된다. 만일 완벽하게 강력하고 훌륭한 신이 존재한다면, 그 신이 일을 잘할 것으로 믿는 것은 명백히 합리적인 행위이다.

06 모호한 주장을 항상 틀린 것이라고는 볼 수 없다.
① 일관성 있는
② 설득력 있는
③ 신성한
④ 모호한
⑤ 조숙한

| 정답 | ④

| 해설 | 본문은 여러 가지 의미를 내포할 수 있는 모호한 주장에 관해 설명하고 있으며, 본문 어디에서 이런 모호한 주장이 틀린 주장이라는 언급은 없고, 단지 상황에 맞게 의미가 달라질 수 있음을 알아 둘 것을 언급할 뿐이다. 따라서 답은 ④이다.

07 다음 중 밑줄 친 "암시하다"를 가장 잘 대체할 수 있는 것은 무엇인가?
① 명확하게 하다
② 얽어매다
③ 암시하다
④ 들먹이다
⑤ 필요하게 만들다

| 정답 | ③

| 해설 | 밑줄 친 insinuate는 "암시하다"는 의미를 지니며 보기 중에서 이와 가장 가까운 것은 ③의 imply이다.

| 어휘 | ambiguous ⓐ 애매모호한
respectable ⓐ 존경할 만한, 품위 있는
self-evidently ⓐⅾ 명백하게
convincing ⓐ 설득력 있는, 확실한
equivocal ⓐ 모호한, 애매한
fallacious ⓐ 잘못된, 틀린
entangle ⓥ 얽어매다, 꼼짝 못하게 하다
necessitate ⓥ ~을 필요하게 만들다

have faith in – ~을 신뢰하다
insinuate ⓥ 암시하다
coherent ⓐ 일관성 있는
divine ⓐ 신성한
precocious ⓐ 조숙한
clarify ⓥ 명확하게 하다, 분명히 말하다
invoke ⓥ 들먹이다, 적용하다

[08-10]

일상 언어에는 시기와 질투가 하나로 섞여 사용되는 경향이 있다. 이 둘이 서로 다른 감정이라는 것은 철학 분야에서 일치된 의견이다. 이를테면 다른 사람이 휴가 간 것을 듣고 나서 질투를 느낀다고 말하는 것은 언어학적으로는 용인될 수 있지만, 이런 경우를 두고 느끼는 감정이 시기인지 질투인지 말한다면 시기를 느낀다고 말하는 것이 타당하다는 주장이 예전부터 있어 왔다. 시기와 질투는 3항 관계이다. 하지만 이런 피상적인 유사성에는 중요한 차이점이 숨어 있다. 질투에는 질투하는 주체, 질투의 경쟁자, 사랑하는 사람 이 세 당사자가 관련되며, 여기서 질투하는 주체가 진실로 중요하게 보는 대상은 질투의 경쟁자가 아니라 사랑하는 사람이다. 질투하는 주체는 사랑하는 이가 자신을 향한 애정을 거두고 있거나 거둘까 봐 두려워하고 있다. 반면에 시기는 (3항 관계이긴 하나 질투처럼 세 당사자 간의 관계가 아니라) 양자 간의 관계로, 제3의 관계항은 '좋은 일'이다. (비록 이 좋은 일은 어떤 특정인이 애착을 갖는 대상일 수도 있지만 말이다.) 그리고 시기하는 사람이 중요하게 보는 대상은 경쟁자이다. 따라서 비록 경쟁자가 좋은 일이 생겼고 이 좋은 일에 다른 이가 애착을 갖더라도, 시기와 질투에는 차이가 존재한다. 대략적으로 볼 때, 질투하는 사람에게 있어 경쟁자는 대체가 될 수 있지만 사랑하는 사람은 대체가 될 수 없다. 따라서 질투하는 이는 만약 사랑하는 사람이 (경쟁자가 아닌) 다른 누군가와 교제하고 있다면 (사랑하는 사람이 경쟁자와 사귀고 있을 때와) 마찬가지로 마음이 괴로울 것이고, 만약 경쟁자가 다른 누군가와 교제하고 있다면 마음이 괴로워지는 않을 것이다. 반면 시기의 경우는 이와 반대이다. 시기는 경쟁자와의 경쟁에 주로 초점이 맞춰져 있으므로, 시기의 주체는 만약 경쟁자가 (이전과는) 다른 (매력적인) 사람과 교제할 경우 마찬가지로 마음이 괴로웠겠지만, '좋은 일'이 (질투의 주체와 경쟁 대상이 아닌) 다른 이에게 가 버린다면 마음이 괴로워지는 않을 것이다. '시기'와 '질투'라는 용어가 일상에서 어떤 의미를 지니든지 간에, 이렇게 고려해 볼 점을 감안해 보면 시기와 질투라는 서로 다른 이 두 개의 행동 양식은 서로 구별될 필요가 있음이 잘 나타난다.

08 밑줄 친 "경쟁자는 대체가 될 수 있다"는 말과 의미상 가장 가까운 것을 고르시오.
① 경쟁자는 비난받아야 한다
② 경쟁자와의 경쟁이 존재한다
③ 경쟁자가 누구인지는 중요하지 않다
④ 경쟁자가 해 온 일은 용납될 수 없다

| 정답 | ③

| 해설 | "경쟁자는 대체가 될 수 있다"는 말은 경쟁자가 누구든 상관없다는 의미이다. 이를 잘 설명한 것은 본문의 "질투하는 이는 만약 사랑하는 사람이 (경쟁자가 아닌) 다른 누군가와 교제하고 있다면 (사랑하는 사람이 경쟁자와 사귀고 있을 때와) 마찬가지로 마음이 괴로울 것이고, 만약 경쟁자가 다른 누군가와 교제하고 있다면 마음이 괴로워지는 않을 것이다(he would be equally bothered if the beloved were consorting with someone else, and would not be

bothered if the rival were)"이다. 간단히 말하면 질투하는 사람은 사랑의 경쟁자가 누구든 경쟁자가 있는 것 자체만으로도 질투를 느낄 것이라는 의미이다. 따라서 답은 ③이다.

09

빈칸에 가장 알맞은 것을 고르시오.
① 실제로는 거의 동등한 것이다
② 구별될 필요가 있다
③ 중복된 의미를 가질 수 있다
④ 통합되어야 한다

| 정답 | ②

| 해설 | 본문의 주제는 질투와 시기는 일상에서는 서로 구분되지 않고 쓰일 수 있지만 엄연히 다른 감정이고 따라서 구분되어 쓰여야 한다는 것이다. 따라서 "서로 다른 이 두 개의 행동 양식(these two distinct syndromes)"은 구별되어 쓰여야 할 것이다. 따라서 답은 ②이다.

10

다음 중 본문에서 유추할 수 없는 것은 무엇인가?
① 원래 질투와 시기는 분명하게 구별이 가능하다.
② 본문의 '좋은 일'은 사물을 뜻할 수도 감정을 뜻할 수도 있다.
③ 질투와 시기는 연관된 당사자의 수에 차이가 있다.
④ 질투하는 사람은 경쟁자를 그다지 중요시하지 않는다.

| 정답 | ①

| 해설 | 본문 첫 문장의 "일상 언어에는 시기와 질투가 하나로 섞여 사용되는 경향이 있다(Ordinary language tends to conflate envy and jealousy)"는 말이 의미하는 것은 질투와 시기는 서로 구별이 힘들다는 것이다. 그렇기 때문에 사람들이 일상적으로는 서로 양자를 구분하지 않고 사용하는 것이다. 따라서 답은 ①이다.

| 어휘 | ordinary language - 일상 언어
consensus ⓝ 일치
linguistically ⓐⓓ 언어학적으로
three-place ⓐ 3항의(=ternary)
conceal ⓥ 숨기다
the beloved - 사랑하는 사람
albeit ⓒⓞⓝⓙ 비록 ~일지라도
roughly ⓐⓓ 대략, 개괄적으로
consort ⓥ 교제하다, 사귀다
syndrome ⓝ (감정·행동의) 징후, 양식
overlapping ⓐ 중복된, 서로 겹치는
ordinarily ⓐⓓ 원래, 본래

conflate ⓥ 융합하다, 섞다
distinct ⓐ 별개의, 다른
plausibly ⓐⓓ 그럴싸하게, 타당하게
superficial ⓐ 피상적인, 표면적인
subject ⓝ 주체
relatum ⓝ 관계항
locus ⓝ 중심지, 장소, 소재
fungible ⓐ 대용할 수 있는, 대체 가능한
the other way around - 반대로, 거꾸로
equivalent ⓝ 동등한 것, 등가물
synthesize ⓥ 합성하다, 통합시키다

[11-12] 중앙대 2010

Bourdieu가 그의 접근법을 전개하는 데 사용한 핵심 개념은 습관(habitus)이다. 이 용어는 아리스토텔레스학파와 스콜라학파에게서 기원을 찾을 수 있는 매우 오래된 용어이지만, Bourdieu는 이것을 특별한 방법으로 뚜렷이 구별되게 사용했다. 습관은 일련의 기질로서 행위자가 어떤 방식으로 행동하거나 반응하도록 만드는 경향이 있다. 기질은 의식적으로 조율되거나 어떤 특정 '규칙'에 지배되지 않는 '일반적(regular)' 형태의 행위와 지각, 태도 등을 만들어 낸다. 습관을 형성하는 기질에 대해 간단한 설명이 필요할 듯하다. 기질은 점진적인 습득 과정을 통해 얻어지며, 이런 습득의 과정에서 어린 시절의 경험은 특히 중요하게 작용한다. 예를 들어 식탁 예절(똑바로 앉아라, 먹으면서 얘기하지 마라 등등)의 습득 과정에 포함된 훈련과 습득의 수많은 일상적 과정을 통해서 개인은 일련의 기질을 습득하는데, 이런 기질들이 문자 그대로 틀을 갖추게 되고 제2의 천성으로 변모하게 된다. 또한 이런 식으로 생성된 기질은 구조화된다고 할 수 있는데, 이는 기질들이 당시의 사회현상을 필연적으로 반영하기 때문이다. 예를 들어, 노동자 집안 출신의 개인은 여러 면에서 중산층에서 자란 이들이 습득한 기질과는 다른 기질을 갖게 된다. 다시 말하면, 개인이 살던 당시 사회 환경을 특징짓는 유사점과 차이점이 습관에 반영되기 마련이며, 이는 비슷한 배경의 인물들 사이에서 상대적으로 동일하게 나타난다. 조직화된 기질은 또한 영속적인 측면이 있다. 기질들이 몸에 박혀 개인의 인생 전체에 걸쳐 남아 있게 되고, 의식보다 선행하며 그렇기에 의식적 성찰이나 의식적 변경에 바로 순응하는 식으로는 작동하지 않는다. 마지막으로 기질은 원래 이를 습득했던 영역 이외에서도 다양한 실행과 지각을 생산해 낼 수 있다는 점에서 재생력이 있고, 전위적인 특성을 지닌다고 할 수 있다.

11 밑줄 친 빈칸에 들어가기에 가장 적합한 것을 고르시오.
① 수많은 일상적 과정
② 수많은 본질적 변화
③ 인지적 경험의 부족
④ 수많은 신체상의 진보

| 정답 | ①

| 해설 | 빈칸의 앞부분 내용을 보면 습관(habitus)은 일련의 기질(disposition)이 모여서 생성된 것이며, 기질이 의미하는 것이 무엇인지에 대해 부연 설명하고 있다. 기질이란 '점진적인' 습득 과정(a gradual process of inculcation)을 통해 습득된다고 말하고 있으며, 예로 보통 부모님의 잔소리에 해당하는 식탁 예절(table manners)을 들고 있다. 이런 예와 잘 어울리는 말은 ①이다. mundane이란 단어를 영영사전에서 찾아보면 "something that is mundane is very ordinary and not at all interesting or unusual"이란 뜻으로 '너무 평범해서 전혀 특별하거나 흥미롭지 않은 것'을 뜻한다는 사실을 알 수 있다. 단순히 사전상의 '이승의, 이 세상의'란 말로는 접근하기 어렵다. 또한 ②에 등장하는 vicissitude의 영영 뜻풀이를 보면 "one of the sudden or unexpected changes or shifts often encountered in one's life, activities, or surroundings"라고 나와 있어, '인생에서 맞닥뜨리게 되는 갑작스러운 변화'라는 의미임을 알 수 있다. 따라서 ②는 점진적 변화와는 다른 '갑작스런 본질적인 변화'의 의미를 함축하고 있어서 정답이 될 수 없다.

12 "habitus"의 특성을 윗글에 제시된 순서대로 요약한 것으로 가장 적합한 것을 고르시오.
① operating(운영상의), reflective(반사적인), mandatory(필수적인), disposable(처분할 수 있는)
② regulated(규제받는), conscious(의식적인), homogeneous(동질의), harmonized(조화로운)
③ educated(교육을 받는), organized(조직화된), persistent(영속하는), engendering(생산적인)
④ autonomous(자발적인), constituting(구성하는), enduring(영속적인), productive(생산적인)

| 정답 | ③

| 해설 | 본문에 나와 있는 단어를 사용해서 구성해 보면, be acquired > structured > durable > generative (and transposable) 순으로 배열된다. 이 단어들과 가장 비슷한 의미의 단어들을 선택할 경우, 정답은 ③이 되며, ④의 답도 enduring과 productive는 사용될 수 있지만 앞부분의 autonomous가 자발적으로 습득한다는 의미이므로, 점진적인 학습을 통해 얻어진다(acquired)는 본문의 내용과 일치하지 않게 되어 답이 될 수 없다.

| 어휘 | **employ** ⓥ 사용하다, 쓰다; 고용하다
Aristotelian ⓐ 아리스토텔레스학파의 ⓝ 아리스토텔레스학파의 사람
scholastic ⓐ 스콜라학파의 ⓝ 스콜라학파의 사람　**distinctive** ⓐ 특유의
disposition ⓝ 기질, 성질, 배열　**incline A to B** – A가 B하려는 마음이 내키게 하다
coordinate ⓥ 조율하다　**constitute** ⓥ 구성하다
deserve ⓥ ~을 받을 가치가 있다　**gradual** ⓐ 점진적인, 점차적인
inculcation ⓝ 설득함, 터득시킴　**literally** ⓐⓓ 문자 그대로, 말 그대로
mould ⓥ 틀을 형성하다　**second nature** – 제2의 천성
unavoidably ⓐⓓ 필연적으로, 피할 수 없이　**reflect** ⓥ 반영하다, 반사하다, 비치다
in certain respects – 몇몇 관점에서　**milieu** ⓝ 환경
homogeneous ⓐ 동질의 (cf. **heterogeneous** ⓐ 이질적인)
durable ⓐ 영속성 있는, 항구성의; 오래 견디는, 튼튼한
be ingrained in – ~에 각인되다, 뿌리 깊게 자리를 잡다
pre-conscious ⓐ 의식에 앞서는　**readily** ⓐⓓ 쉽사리, 흔쾌히
amenable ⓐ 순종하는, 따르는　**reflection** ⓝ 심사숙고, 반성; 반사
modification ⓝ 변경　**generative** ⓐ 생식력이 있는
transposable ⓐ 전위의, 위치를 옮길 수 있는　**multiplicity** ⓝ 다수
originally ⓐⓓ 원래는　**a myriad of** – 무수히 많은, 수많은
mundane ⓐ 평범한, 일상적인, 지루한; (저승의 반대인) 이승의
intimate ⓐ 개인적인, 친밀한, 친근한, 본질적인　**vicissitude** ⓝ 변화, 추이
scarcity ⓝ 부족　**cognitive** ⓐ 인지의
a throng of – (무리나 떼) 수많은　**corporeal** ⓐ 신체상의
progression ⓝ 진보, 진행, 연속

[13-16] 성균관대 2007

17세기 일본의 정치인들이 두려워했던 것은 외국인 선교사들이 서양의 기독교로 개종시킨 자국민들이 자신들이 선택한 종교의 광신성을 받아들이리라는 점과, 일본 전래의 풍속을 어지럽히는 기독교의 영향력하에서 개종자들이 오늘날 서양에서 우리가 "제5열"이라 부르는 첩자로 이용당하기를 자처할 것이라는 점이었다. 이렇게 수상쩍은 음모가 성공할 경우, 그 자체로는 일본의 자주에 심각한 위협은 아니었던 포르투갈인이나 스페인들이 결국 일본인 반역자들의 무력을 통해 일본을 정복할지도 몰랐다. 실제로 일본 정부는 오늘날 20세기 서구국가들이 공산주의를 불법화하고 억압하도록 행동한 것과 동일한 동기하에서 기독교를 불법화하고 억압했다.

13

밑줄 친 "수상쩍은 음모"는 일본인들을 나중에 첩보원으로 이용하고자 기독교로 개종시키는 일을 의미한다.

① 이질적인 정신을 받아들이다
② 전래의 풍속을 어지럽히려는 태도를 조장하다
③ 외국인에 대항해 "제5열"을 들여오다
④ 외국산 술을 마시고 술에 취한다
⑤ 일본인들을 나중에 첩보원으로 이용하고자 기독교로 개종시킨다

| 정답 | ⑤

| 해설 | 앞서 언급된 것을 가리킬 때 사용하는 대명사 this가 있기 때문에 '수상쩍은 음모'는 바로 앞에서 언급된 내용을 가리킨다. 즉, 일본 내에 암약하는 첩자로 활동시키고자 일본인들을 기독교도로 개종하는 행위를 말한다. 따라서 답은 ⑤이다.

14

다음 중 빈칸에 가장 알맞은 것은 무엇인가?

① 일본인의
② 포르투갈인과 스페인 사람의
③ 외국의
④ 서양의
⑤ 술에 취한

| 정답 | ①

| 해설 | 빈칸 뒤 '반역자(traitor)'는 문맥상 기독교로 개종되어 서양 세력을 위해 일본 내에서 암약하는 일본인 기독교도를 의미한다. 따라서 반역자를 수식하는 단어인 '일본인(Japanese)'이 빈칸에 들어가야 할 것이다. 따라서 정답은 ①이다.

15

17세기 일본의 정치인이 가장 두려워했던 것은 무엇인가?

① 우월한 외국의 무기
② 공산주의의 확산
③ 서양 선교사
④ 기독교로 개종한 자국민
⑤ 기독교과 토착 종교 간의 갈등

| 정답 | ④

| 해설 | 본문에 따르면 17세기 일본의 정치인들이 가장 두려워했던 것은 "외국인 선교사들이 서양의 기독교로 개종시킨 자국민(their countrymen whom these foreign missionaries were converting to Western Christianity)"들이 서양 세력에 의해 "오늘날 서양에서 우리가 '제5열'이라 부르는 첩자로 이용당하기를 자처할 것(allow themselves to be used as what, in the West today, we should call 'a fifth column')"이었다. 따라서 당시 일본 정치인들은 기독교로 개종한 국민들을 가장 무서워했을 것이므로 답은 ④이다.

16

본문의 주제는 기독교에 대한 일본의 터무니없는 두려움이다.

① 일본의 광신적 기독교
② 기독교에 대한 일본의 터무니없는 두려움
③ 기독교와 공산주의 – 접점은 어디인가
④ 무기 없이 일본을 정복하는 법
⑤ 기독교에 대한 일본의 두려움과 그것이 일본인들에게 미치는 악영향

| 정답 | ②

| 해설 | 본문의 내용은 "일본 정치인들은 기독교로 개종한 국민들이 국가를 배반할 것이라는 근거 없는 두려움에 사로잡혀 있었다"이다. 따라서 답은 ②이다. 참고로 ⑤의 경우 '일본인들에게 미치는 악영향'에 관해 언급된 사항이 없기 때문에 답으로 볼 수 없다.

| 어휘 |
statesman ⓝ 정치가
missionary ⓝ 선교사
Christianity ⓝ 기독교 신앙
adopted ⓐ 채택한
demoralize ⓥ 풍속을 어지럽히다
a fifth column – 제5열; 첩자, 적국이나 적대 세력과 내통하는 내부의 적
suspected ⓐ 수상쩍은, 의심 가는
Portuguese ⓝ 포르투갈 사람
menace ⓝ 협박
eventually ⓐⓓ 결국
conquer ⓥ 정복하다
traitor ⓝ 배반자
repress ⓥ 억압하다
Communism ⓝ 공산주의
intoxicated ⓐ 술에 취한
unwarranted ⓐ 보증되지 않은, 터무니없는

countryman ⓝ 동포, 자국민
convert ⓥ 개종하다
imbibe ⓥ 받아들이다
fanatical ⓐ 광신적인
influence ⓝ 영향
design ⓝ 계획; 의도
Spaniard ⓝ 스페인 사람
Independence ⓝ 독립, 자주
contrive to(=manage to) – 용케 ~하다
arms ⓝ 무기
outlaw ⓥ 금지하다, 불법화하다
motive ⓝ 동기
spirit ⓝ 술, 증류주
fanaticism ⓝ 광신
adverse effects – 악영향

[17-18] 국민대 2013

17세기 프랑스 철학자 르네 데카르트는 널리 알려진 이원론을 정식으로 제의했다. 데카르트 이원론으로 알려진 이 이론은 정신과 뇌가 서로 다른 질료로 구성되어 있다는 사상이다. 데카르트에 따르면, 정신은 비물질적이면서 연장되어 있지 않다(즉, 정신은 공간을 차지하지 않으며 어떤 위치에도 있지 않다), 반면에 육체와 그 외 모든 물질세계는 물질적인 또는 연장되는 질료로 만들어진다. 이 이론은 명백한 문제점을 지닌다. 정신과 육체는 과연 어떻게 상호작용을 하는 것인가?

이러한 상호작용에 관한 문제는 이원론을 확립하려는 어떠한 시도도 힘들게 만들며, 아마도 이는 대부분의 철학자들과 과학자들이 몇몇 유형의 일원론은 선호하면서도 모든 유형의 이원론은 완전히 거부하게 된 이유일 것이다. 하지만 일원론에 따른 선택의 폭도 좁고 일원론도 마찬가지로 문제가 존재한다. 이상주의자들은 정신을 근본으로 보지만 그럴 경우 왜 그리고 어떻게 하여 물질세계가 변함없이 존재하는 것으로 보이는지를 설명할 수 있어야 한다. 중립적인 일원론자들은 이원론을 거부하지만 세계의 근본 성질에 관해서 그리고 세계를 통합하는 방안에 관해서는 서로 의견이 다르다. 일원론도 이원론도 아닌 제3의 선택지는 유물론이며, 현재까지는 오늘날 과학자들 사이에서 가장 인기 있는 이론이다. 유물론자들은 물질을 근본으로 보지만 그럴 경우 물질적인 질료로만 구성된 실체가 있는 뇌가 의식에 의한 경험을 어떻게 야기할 수 있는지에 대한 의문에 답해야만 한다.

17 밑줄 친 ⓐ가 가리키는 것은 무엇인가?
① 상호작용에 관한 문제
② 이원론을 구축하려는 어떠한 시도
③ 이원론을 구축하려는 어떠한 시도도 힘들게 만들다
④ 상호작용에 관한 문제는 이원론을 구축하려는 어떠한 시도도 힘들게 만든다

| 정답 | ④

| 해설 | 밑줄 친 which는 앞의 쉼표를 통해 봤을 때 계속적 용법으로 앞 문장 전체를 수식하는 것으로 볼 수 있다. 따라서 답은 ④이다.

18 다음 중 본문에 따르면 사실이 아닌 것은 무엇인가?
① 이상주의자들은 물질세계의 존재를 입증하는 데 어려움을 겪고 있다.
② 르네 데카르트는 정신과 육체가 완전히 분리되어 있다고 생각했다.
③ 인간 의식에 관한 문제는 유물론자들에게 심각한 문제를 제기한다.
④ 인간 의식에 관한 문제를 설명하는 데 있어 이원론보다 일원론이 더 적합하다.

| 정답 | ④

| 해설 | 본문 어디에서 인간 의식에 관한 문제를 설명하는 데 있어 어느 한쪽이 다른 한쪽보다 적합하다고 명시된 점은 존재하지 않는다. 따라서 답은 ④이다.
"이상주의자들은 정신을 근본으로 보지만 그럴 경우 왜 그리고 어떻게 하여 물질세계가 변함없이 존재하는 것으로 보이는지를 설명할 수 있어야 한다(Idealists make mind fundamental but must then explain why and how there appears to be a consistent physical world)"는 ①의 내용과 일치하며, ②는 데카르트가 주장한 이원론의 핵심이고, "유물론자들은 물질을 근본으로 보지만 그럴 경우 물질적인 질료로만 구성된 실체가 있는 뇌가 의식에 의한 경험을 어떻게 야기할 수 있는지에 대한 의문에 답해야만 한다(Materialists take matter as fundamental, but they must then face the question how a physical brain, made purely of material substances, can give rise to conscious experience)"는 ③의 내용과 일치한다.

| 어휘 | dualist theory – 이원론
bedevil ⓥ 몹시 괴롭히다
consistent ⓐ 일관된, 한결같은
consciousness ⓝ 의식, 자각
Cartesian ⓐ 데카르트의
monism ⓝ 일원론
materialism ⓝ 유물론

[19-21] 서울여대 2013

분명히 말하자면, 데카르트의 근본 목적은 이성을 활용해 철학적 진실을 획득하는 것이다. "나는 진실을 추구하는 일에 온전히 몰두하기를 바랐다." 하지만 그가 하는 말은 다수의 고립된 진실을 발견하는 것이 아니라 진정한 명제로 구성된 체제를 구축하는 것이며, 자명하고 명백하지 않은 것은 그 어떤 것도 전제로 삼지 않는 체제를 구축하는 것이다. 그 결과 체제를 구성하는 모든 요소 간에 유기적 연결이 형성되며, 전체 조직은 확고한 토대 하에 실립될 것이다. 따라서 마음을 좀먹고 파괴적인 영향을 미치는 회의론에 휘둘리지 않게 될 것이다.
데카르트는 철학을 무엇으로 이해했을까? "지혜를 연구하는 것을 철학이라 하며, 지혜라 함은 온갖 상황에서 신중함을 보이는 것뿐만 아니라 인간이 삶을 영위하고, 건강을 보존하고, 온갖 예술을 창조하는 과정에서 알 수 있는 모든 것들에 관한 완벽한 지식을 의미한다고 이해한다." 따라서 철학이라는 보편적인 주제하에서 데카르트는 형이상학뿐만 아니라 물리학이나 자연 철학도 포함했는데, 전자를 나무뿌리로 본다면 이에 대응해 후자는 줄기라 할 수 있다. 그리고 이러한 줄기에서 뻗는 가지를 철학 이외의 다른 학문 분야로 볼 수 있는데, 그중 가장 주요한 세 가지는 의학, 역학, 윤리학이다. 윤리학에 관해 말하자면, "나는 도덕학 중에서도 가장 숭고하고 완벽한 것이 윤리학이라고 본다. 윤리학은 다른 학문 분야에 대해 완벽한 지식을 갖출 것을 전제로 하며, 지혜의 최종 단계이다."

19
본문의 주제는 무엇인가?
① 데카르트 철학의 예술적 영향
② 데카르트가 말하는 철학적 진실의 기본적 특성
③ 현대 철학에 데카르트가 미친 영향
④ 데카르트 시대의 철학의 역할

| 정답 | ②

| 해설 | 본문은 데카르트 철학이 어떤 성격을 지니고 있는지 기본적인 사항을 제시하고 있다. 따라서 답은 ②이다.

20
"이러한 줄기"는 무엇을 가리키는가?
① 형이상학
② 자연철학
③ 역학
④ 도덕학

| 정답 | ②

| 해설 | 형이상학을 나무뿌리에 비유하고 있으며, 물리학이나 자연철학을 나무줄기에 비유하고 있다. "이러한 줄기"는 나무줄기를 의미하며 따라서 답은 ②이다.

21
본문에 따르면 다음 중 사실인 것은 무엇인가?
① 데카르트는 다수의 개별적인 진실을 추구했다.
② 데카르트 철학은 아주 잘 조직되어 있어서 부분과 전체가 서로 연관성을 갖는다.
③ 데카르트는 이따금 철학의 실용적 가치를 고집하지 않았다.
④ 데카르트는 다른 철학자들만큼 이성에 의존하지 않았다.

| 정답 | ②

| 해설 | "그 결과 체제를 구성하는 모든 요소 간에 유기적 연결이 형성되며, 전체 조직은 확고한 토대하에 설립될 것이다(There would then be an organic connection between all the parts of the system, and the whole edifice would rest on a sure foundation)." 따라서 답은 ②이다.

| 어휘 | give oneself to – ~에 몰두하다   multiplicity ⓝ 다수, 다양
proposition ⓝ 명제   presuppose ⓥ 예상하다, 전제로 하다
self-evident ⓐ 자명한   indubitable ⓐ 의심할 나위 없는, 명백한
edifice ⓝ 조직, 체계   impervious ⓐ ~에 영향 받지[휘둘리지] 않는
scepticism ⓝ 회의론   heading ⓝ 제목, 주제
metaphysics ⓝ 형이상학   standing ⓝ 지위, 신분
mechanics ⓝ 역학   moral science – 도덕학
implication ⓝ 영향; 암시

[22-25] 홍익대 2014

철학은 다른 모든 학문과 마찬가지로 지식의 성취를 주된 목표로 삼는다. 철학이 목표로 삼는 지식은 학문적 본질의 통합과 체계의 확립을 야기하는 그런 유형의 지식이며, 우리의 신념·선입관·믿음의 근간이 되는 요소를 비판적으로 검토한 후 이를 기반으로 생성된 유형의 지식이다. 하지만 철학이 의문에 대해 확고한 답을 제공하는 과정에서 매우 높은 성공률을 자랑한다고 단언할 수는 없다. 수학자나 광물학자 아니면 역사가 같은 학자에게 자신의 학문 분야를 통해 확인된 확고한 핵심적 진실이 무엇인지 묻는다면, 학자의 답은 여러분에게 듣고자 하려는 의지가 있는 한 지속될 것이다. 하지만 같은 질문을 철학자에게 던질 경우, 그 철학자는 솔직한 사람이라면 자신의 학문은 다른 학문 분야를 통해 이룩한 만큼의 긍정적 결과를 달성하지 못했다고 시인해야 할 것이다. 철학이 목표로 삼는 지식에 대한 확고한 답이 부재한 이유는 부분적으로는 어느 주제에 관하여 확고한 지식이 존재하게 되면 그 순간 해당 주제는 더 이상 철학이라 불리지 않게 되며 별도의 학문이 되기 때문이다. 하늘에 관해 연구하는 모든 학문은 현재는 천문학에 속해 있지만 과거에는 철학의 일부였다. 뉴턴이 저술한 위대한 저서의 명칭은 "자연철학의 수학적 이해"이다. 마찬가지로 인간 정신의 연구는 철학의 한 분야였지만 이제는 철학과 분리되어 심리학이 되었다. 따라서 대부분의 경우 철학의 불확실성은 실제보다 더욱 분명하게 나타난다. 확고한 답이 이미 가능한 질문은 학문의 분야에 속해 있으며 반면에 현재 시점에서 확고한 답이 나와 있지 않은 질문은 그 외의 아직 대답되지 않은 잔여물을 형성하게 되며, 이들 잔여물은 철학이라 불린다.

22 본문의 주제는 무엇인가?
① 철학의 목표와 주제를 정의하는 행위의 까다로움
② 천문학·심리학·철학 간의 관계
③ 철학에 있어 지식을 탐구하는 행위의 즐거움과 행복함
④ 철학에 있어 성공적 탐구를 위한 수단

| 정답 | ①

| 해설 | 본문은 우선 철학의 목표가 무엇인지 언급한 다음 여러 학문 분야 가운데 무엇을 철학으로 부를 수 있을지에 관해 논하고 있으며, 의문에 관해 확고한 답이 나오는 것은 학문이고 확고한 답이 제시되지 않는 그 외 나머지는 철학으로 분류되고 "철학이 목표로 삼는 지식에 대한 확고한 답이 부재한 이유는 부분적으로는 어느 주제에 관하여 확고한 지식이 존재하게 되면 그 순간 해당 주제는 더 이상 철학이라 불리지 않게 되며 별도의 학문이 되기 때문이다 (It is true that this is partly accounted for by the fact that, as soon as definite knowledge concerning any subject becomes possible, this subject ceases to be called philosophy and becomes a separate science.)"라고 언급하고 있다. 즉, 본문은 무엇이 철학의 목표이자 주제인지를 둘러싼 고민을 논하고 있다. 따라서 답은 ①이다.

23 (A) 대신에 사용 가능한 것은 무엇인가?
① 훌륭한
② 진실되지 못한
③ 불만스러워하는
④ 솔직 담백한

| 정답 | ④

| 해설 | (A)의 candid는 '솔직한' 등의 의미를 지니며 보기 중에서 대신 사용 가능한 것은 ④이다.

24

(B)가 가리키는 것은 무엇인가?

① 우리의 신념·선입관·믿음의 근간이 되는 요소의 비판적 검토
② 철학을 포함해 다양한 유형의 학문 분야를 통해 확인된 확고한 핵심적 진실
③ 철학이 목표로 삼는 지식에 대한 확고한 답이 부재함
④ 천문학 및 심리학처럼 구체적인 답을 지닌 주제가 별도의 학문 분야가 된다는 사실

| 정답 | ③

| 해설 | 특정 학문을 연구하는 학자에게 자신의 분야가 추구하는 진실이 무엇인지 묻는다면 나름의 대답을 얻을 수 있지만, 같은 질문을 철학자에게 하면 철학자는 그런 긍정적 결과를 얻지 못한다고 솔직하게 시인한다. 그리고 (B)의 this는 문맥상 바로 그 '철학이 목표로 삼는 지식에 대한 확고한 답이 부재함'을 가리키고, 이 부재의 원인이 this 뒤에 제시되어 있다. 따라서 답은 ③이다.

25

(C)에 가장 알맞은 것은 무엇인가?

① 대조적으로
② 마찬가지로
③ 따라서
④ 그럼에도 불구하고

| 정답 | ②

| 해설 | 뉴턴은 현대 기준으로 물리학자이자 수학자이지만 그의 책에는 '자연철학'이란 명칭이 들어가 있다. 이는 별도로 분리되기 전 철학에 편입되었던 학문의 한 사례이다. 그리고 빈칸 뒤에는 심리학이 또 다른 사례로 제시되어 있다. 따라서 빈칸에는 빈칸 앞과 빈칸 뒤의 내용이 유사함을 뒷받침하기 위해 ②가 가장 적합하다.

| 어휘 |

philosophy ⓝ 철학, 형이상학
body ⓝ 중심부, 본체
examination ⓝ 조사; 검사, 검토
prejudice ⓝ 편견, 선입관
maintain ⓥ 주장하다, 단언하다
mathematician ⓝ 수학자
ascertain ⓥ 확인하다, 확정하다; 규명하다
candid ⓐ 솔직한, 숨김없는
account for – ~의 이유가 되다
cease ⓥ 그치다, 그만두다, 중지하다
separate ⓐ 별도의, 개별적인, 단독의
mathematical ⓐ 수학의, 수리적인
uncertainty ⓝ 불확실성
residue ⓝ 잔여[잔류]물, 나머지
insincere ⓐ 진실되지 못한
forthright ⓐ 솔직 담백한

primarily ⓐⓓ 주로, 첫째로
science ⓝ 과학, 학문
conviction ⓝ 확신, 신념
belief ⓝ 믿음, 확신
measure ⓝ 기준, 정도
mineralogist ⓝ 광물학자
philosopher ⓝ 철학자
confess ⓥ 자백하다, 시인하다, 실토하다
concerning ⓟⓡⓔⓟ ~에 관한
the heavens – 하늘
astronomy ⓝ 천문학
to a great extent – 대부분은, 크게
apparent ⓐ 분명한
terrific ⓐ 아주 멋진, 훌륭한
discontented ⓐ 불만스러워하는

[26-27] 서강대 2014

급격하게 현대화된 사회에서 만일 전통 종교가 현대화의 요건에 적응하지 못했을 경우, 서양의 기독교와 이슬람교가 확산될 가능성이 존재한다. 이러한 사회의 경우, 서양 문화의 가장 성공적인 주역은 신고전주의파 경제학자들도 아니고, 혁신을 이끄는 민주주의자들도 아니고, 다국적 기업의 중역도 아닌, 기독교 선교사들이고 앞으로도 그럴 가능성이 높다. 아담 스미스도 토마스 제퍼슨도 도시 이주자들과 이민 후 최초 세대에 속하는 중등학교 졸업생들의 심리적, 정서적, 도덕적, 사회적 요건을 충족시켜 주지 못한다. 예수 그리스도 또한 이런 요건을 충족시켜 주지 못할 수 있지만, 그럴 수 있는 더 나은 가능성은 품고 있다. 하지만 장기적으로는 무함마드가 성공한다. 기독교는 주로 개종을 통해 확산되며 이슬람교는 개종과 번식을 통해 확산된다. 전 세계 기독교인들의 비율은 1980년대 대략 30%로 정점에 달했다가, 변동됨 없이 정체 상태에 머물렀고, 현재는 감소 중에 있으며, 2025년경에는 전 세계 인구의 대략 25%에 이를 것이다. 전 세계의 무슬림 비율은 인구 상승세가 극도로 강한 덕분에 급격히 증가할 것인데, 이번 세기에 접어들 무렵에 전 세계 인구의 20%에 달했고, 수년 후에는 기독교인의 수를 능가했고, 아마도 2025년에는 전 세계 인구의 대략 30%를 차지할 것이다.

26 빈칸에 가장 알맞은 것을 고르시오.
① 현대화 ② 타락
③ 교육 ④ 번식

| 정답 | ④

| 해설 | 빈칸 뒤 내용은 기독교도와 달리 이슬람교도는 아이를 많이 낳기 때문에 자녀들도 자연히 이슬람교를 믿게 되면서 더 많은 인구로 '포교'가 이루어진 덕분에 이슬람교 신자의 수가 기독교 신자의 수를 넘고 있음을 말하고 있다. 따라서 답은 '아이를 낳는다'는 의미에서 ④가 적합하다.

27 다음 중 위 본문에서 유추할 수 없는 것은 무엇인가?
① 기독교와 이슬람교는 빠르게 현대화되고 있는 사회에서 중요한 역할을 할 가능성이 높다.
② 도시 이주민들의 사회적 요건은 아마도 다국적 기업 중역들에 의해 충족될 것이다.
③ 전 세계의 기독교인들의 비율은 2000년대보다 1980년대에 더 높았다.
④ 2025년에는 전 세계의 무슬림 수는 기독교인 수를 능가할 것이다.

| 정답 | ②

| 해설 | "아담 스미스도 토마스 제퍼슨도 도시 이주자들과 이민 후 최초 세대에 속하는 중등학교 졸업생들의 심리적, 정서적, 도덕적, 사회적 요건을 충족시켜주지 못한다(Neither Adam Smith nor Thomas Jefferson will meet the psychological, emotional, moral, and social needs of urban migrants and first-generation secondary school graduates)." 아담 스미스는 경제학자 및 다국적 기업 중역을 상징하고 토마스 제퍼슨은 민주주의자를 상징한다. 즉, 도시 이주민들의 사회적 요건을 다국적 기업 중역들이 충족할 수는 없다는 의미이다. 따라서 답은 ②이다.

| 어휘 | adapt to – ~에 적응하다
crusade ⓥ 개혁[혁신] 운동에 참가하다
first-generation ⓐ 이민자의 자녀로 태어난, 이민 후 최초 세대의
secondary school – 중등학교
level off – 수평이 되다, 변동이 없다
account for – (부분·비율을) 차지하다
protagonist ⓝ 주인공, 주역
migrant ⓝ 이주자
reproduction ⓝ 번식
surpass ⓥ 능가하다
degeneration ⓝ 악화, 타락

[28-29] 가톨릭대 2016

기원전 5세기 고대 그리스 철학자들은 파르메니데스(Parmenides)와 헤라클레이토스(Heraclitus) 간에 뚜렷이 대비되는 입장차를 극복하기 위해 애썼다. 파르메니데스가 주장한 불변하는 존재(Being)론과 헤라클레이토스가 주장한 영원한 생성(Becoming)론을 조화시키기 위해 철학자들은 존재는 특정한 변치 않는 물체들을 통해 분명히 드러나며 이들 물체들을 혼합하고 분리하는 과정에서 세상의 변화가 발생한다고 추정했다. 이러한 추정은 원자에 대한 개념으로 이어졌는데, 원자란 눈으로 볼 수 있는 가장 작은 크기의 물질단위이며 데모크리토스(Democritus)의 철학에서 원자에 대한 표현이 가장 명확하게 등장했다. 고대 그리스의 원자론자들은 정신과 물질을 명확하게 구분했으며, 물질은 몇 가지 기본적인 구성요소로 이루어져 있다고 묘사했다. 여기서 말하는 구성요소는 순전히 수동적이며 본질적으로 빈 공간을 이동하는 생명 없는 입자였다. 입자의 이동 원인에 대해서는 설명되지 않았지만 이동 원인은 종종 외부의 힘과 종종 연계되었으며, 여기서 말하는 외부의 힘은 그 근원이 정신적인 것이며 근본적으로 물질과는 구분되는 것으로 추정되었다. 이후 수 세기 동안 이러한 개념은 정신과 물질을 구분하고 육체와 영혼을 구분하는 이원론적 서구 사상의 근본 요소가 되었다.

28 본문의 주제는 무엇인가?
① 서구 이원론의 기원
② 서구 사상의 주된 문제점
③ 정신과 물질 간의 관계
④ 고대 그리스 철학자들의 기묘한 세계

| 정답 | ①

| 해설 | 고대 그리스 철학자인 파르메니데스와 헤라클레이토스 간의 입장 차를 좁히는 과정에서 원자론이 생성되었고, 원자론에서는 정신과 물질을 명확히 구분하였는데, 이는 이후 서구 사상의 근본 요소인 육체와 영혼을 구분하는 이원론의 근간이 되었다는 것이 본문의 내용이다. 따라서 답은 ①이다.

29 본문에 따르면 다음 중 사실이 아닌 것은 무엇인가?
① 파르메니데스와 헤라클레이토스는 고대 그리스 사상의 서로 대조되는 양극이었다.
② 파르메니데스와 헤라클레이토스는 한때 자신들의 사상을 조화시키기 위해 협력했었다.
③ 고대 그리스의 원자론자들은 정신과 물질이라는 각기 다른 두 세계를 믿었다.
④ 서구 사상의 전통은 대체로 이원론적 세계관에 깊숙이 포함되어 있다.

| 정답 | ②

| 해설 | 파르메니데스와 헤라클레이토스가 서로 자신들의 입장 차를 좁히기 위해 노력했다는 내용은 본문에 존재하지 않으며 이 두 철학자 간의 입장 차를 좁히려 노력한 것은 다른 동료 철학자들이었다. 따라서 답은 ①이다.
"기원전 5세기 고대 그리스 철학자들은 파르메니데스(Parmenides)와 헤라클레이토스(Heraclitus) 간에 뚜렷이 대비되는 입장차를 극복하기 위해 애썼다(In the fifth century B.C., the Greek philosophers tried to overcome the sharp contrast between the views of Parmenides and Heraclitus)"는 ①에 해당되는 내용이며, "고대 그리스의 원자론자들은 정신과 물질을 명확하게 구분했으며(The Greek atomists drew a clear line between spirit and matter)"는 ③에 해당되는 내용이고, "이후 수 세기 동안 이러한 개념은 정신과 물질을 구분하고 육체와 영혼을 구분하는 이원론적 서구 사상의 근본 요소가 되었다(In subsequent centuries, this image became an essential element of Western thought, of dualism between mind and matter, between body and soul)"는 ④에 해당되는 내용이다.

| 어휘 | overcome ⓥ 극복하다
reconcile ⓥ 조화시키다, 화해시키다
manifest ⓐ 분명한, 명백한
substance ⓝ 물질, 실체
atomist ⓝ 원자론자
building block – 구성요소
particle ⓝ 입자, 미립자
associate ⓥ 연상하다, 결부[연관]짓다
subsequent ⓐ 그 다음의, 차후의
dualism ⓝ 이원론
pole ⓝ (서로 대조되는) 극

sharp ⓐ 선명한, 뚜렷한
assume ⓥ 추정하다
invariable ⓐ 변함없는, 변치 않는
separation ⓝ 분리, 구분
picture ⓥ 상상하다, 묘사하다
intrinsically ⓐⓓ 본질적으로
void ⓝ 빈 공간
spiritual ⓐ 정신의, 영의
image ⓝ 심상, 표상, 개념
uncanny ⓐ 이상한, 묘한
embed ⓥ 끼워 넣다, 깊이 간직하다

[30-32] 한국외대 2017

무엇 때문에 사람들은 바르지 못한 행동을 하는 것일까? 이 질문은 플라톤 이후 철학자들을 오랫동안 괴롭힌 질문이다. 플라톤은 다음과 같은 유명한 질문을 던진 적이 있다. 당신이 원하는 무엇이든 할 수 있게 해 주는 마법의 반지를 당신이 발견했다면, 예를 들어 은행을 털고, 세상을 지배하고, 원수를 노예로 삼을 수 있는 그런 반지를 발견했다면, 당신은 그렇게 하겠는가? 플라톤은 이 반지를 사용하는 대가, 즉 옳지 않은 일을 하는 대가가 보상보다 더 가치 있지 않다면, 도덕성이 정당함을 입증받을 것이라고 주장했다. 플라톤은 사람들이 곧고 좁은 길에서 벗어나는 이유는 개인적인 이득을 얻으려는 유혹 때문이라고 가정했다. 그러나 이와 반대되는 가설을 세우는 다른 학파가 있었다. 그들은 사람들이 부도덕한 행위를 하는 이유는 사회에 순응하길 원하기 때문이며, 그 행위가 자신들의 핵심적 가치관과 배치되는 경우에도 이런 일이 일어난다고 주장했다. 다시 말하면, 사람들은 다른 사람들이 자신을 어떻게 보는가에 대해 많은 신경을 쓰고 있다는 말이 된다. 대부분의 사람들의 경우, 올바르지 못한 일이라는 것이 수백만 달러를 횡령하거나 쿠데타로 정치권력을 빼앗는 것을 의미하지 않는다. 어떤 사람이 비난받고 있을 때, 인종 차별적 농담으로 비웃음을 받을 때 여기에 동참하는 것을 의미한다. 우리가 이런 행위를 하는 이유는 문제가 발생하는 것을 원하지 않기 때문이다. 임마누엘 칸트(Immanuel Kant)는 이런 종류의 과도한 경의의 태도를 '굴종(servility)'이라고 부른다. 다른 사람들의 가치와 헌신을 낮추는 것이 아니라, 자신의 가치와 헌신을 다른 사람보다 더 낮추는 것을 말한다. 그러므로 굴종의 모습을 보이는 사람은 플라톤에서 찾아볼 수 있는 전통적인 자기 이익을 추구하는 부도덕한 사람의 또 다른 모습인 것이다. 칸트에게 있어서, 굴종의 모습을 보이는 사람들은 다른 사람과 동일한 도덕적 평등과 존중을 스스로 부인한다. 그들이 이런 일을 하는 이유는 거만하게 보이거나, 다르게 보이거나, 무례하게 보이는 것을 원하지 않기 때문이며, 이를 통해 다른 사람들과 어울려 그들과 같은 일을 하고, 올바르지 못한 일을 하게 되는 것이다.

30

다음 중 (A)의 의미와 가장 가까운 것은?

① 굽어 있지 않은 길
② 정직하고 도덕적인 행동
③ 학업 목표를 향해 공부하는 것
④ 목적지로 가는 가장 짧은 길

| 정답 | ②

| 해설 | 도덕(morality)과 관련된 문제에 대해 다루고 있으며, 왜 사람들이 나쁜 짓을 저지르는가에 대해 다루고 있는 글이다. 사람들이 개인적인 이득을 위해 유혹에 빠지며, 그런 과정에서 (A)의 길에서 벗어난다고 했으므로 (A)는 도덕적으로 바른 길이라는 사실을 알 수 있다. 따라서 정답은 ②가 된다.

31 다음 중 빈칸 (B)에 가장 적합한 것은?
① 다른 사람들이 하는 일에 순응하는 것은 사악한 행동이라고 생각한다
② 사회를 거부하고 자신의 가치관을 증진하기 위해 부단히 노력한다
③ 다른 사람들이 자신을 어떻게 보는가에 대해 많은 신경을 쓰다
④ 올바른 일을 하는 것에 집착하다

| 정답 | ③

| 해설 | 'in other words'를 통해 바로 앞 내용을 다시 부연 설명을 하고 있다. 앞 문장에서 'conform to society'를 통해 비록 어떤 행위가 나의 가치관과 맞지 않는다고 해도 다른 사람들이 하는 행위를 그대로 '순응'해서 행한다는 내용이므로, 그 이유에 해당하는 ③이 정답이 된다.

32 다음 중 본문의 내용과 일치하지 않는 것은?
① 플라톤은 사람들이 개인적인 이익을 위해 잘못된 행동을 한다고 생각했다.
② 칸트는 사람들이 순응을 원하기 때문에 굴종의 모습을 보이는 사람들이 비도덕적 행위를 한다고 생각했다.
③ 플라톤은 부도덕의 비용이 너무 높다면 도덕성이 정당성을 입증받게 될 것이라고 생각했다.
④ 칸트는 굴종의 모습을 보이는 사람들이 종종 정치권력을 찬탈한다고 생각했다.

| 정답 | ④

| 해설 | 본문의 "doing the wrong thing is not embezzling millions of dollars or usurping political power in a coup" 부분을 통해 칸트가 말한 굴종의 모습이 횡령이나 쿠데타를 이용한 정치권력과 같은 거창한 행위가 아니라고 설명하므로 정답은 ④가 된다.

| 어휘 | **puzzle** ⓥ 어리둥절하게[이해할 수 없게] 만들다   **take over enslave** ⓥ 노예로 만들다
postulate ⓥ 가정하다, (이론 등의 근거로 삼기 위해 무엇이 사실이라고) 상정하다
morality ⓝ 도덕
vindicate ⓥ (특히 남들은 달리 생각할 때) ~의 정당성을 입증하다, 무죄를 입증하다
temptation ⓝ 유혹   **a school of thought** – 학파
hypothesize ⓥ 가설을 세우다   **inverse** ⓝ 정반대
conform to – ~에 순응하다   **embezzle** ⓥ 횡령하다
usurp ⓥ (왕좌·권좌 등을) 빼앗다[찬탈하다]   **disparage** ⓥ 폄하하다
deferential ⓐ 경의를 표하는, 공손한   **servility** ⓝ 노예근성, 비굴한 복종, 굴종
servile ⓐ 굽실거리는   **arrogant** ⓐ 오만한
untoward ⓐ (보통 좋지 못한 방향으로) 뜻밖의[별다른]

[33-34] 항공대 2018

프롬(Fromm)에 따르면 분열된 인간 존재에 대한 인식은 죄의식과 수치심의 원천이며, 이러한 실존주의적 이분에 대한 해결책은 인간 고유의 힘인 사랑과 이성의 힘을 발달시킴으로써 찾을 수 있다. 하지만 프롬은 자신의 사랑에 대한 개념을 프로이트의 역설적 사랑뿐만 아니라 경솔한 대중적 개념과도 구분 지었다. 프롬은 사랑을 감정이 아니라 대인 관계의 창조적 역량으로 간주했고, 이러한 창조적 역량을 진정한 사랑의 증거라고 일반적으로 제시되고 있지만 자신이 판단하기에는 다양한 형태의 자기도취적 신경증 및 SM적 경향에 불과한 것과는 구분 지었다. 실제로도 프롬은 사랑에 빠지는 경험을 사랑의 진정한 속성을 이해하지 못한 증거로 인식했다. 프롬은 사랑의 진정한 속성에는 보살핌, 책임, 존중, 지식이라는 공통된 요소가 항상 존재한다고 봤다. 프롬은 또한 현대 사회에서는 다른 사람들의 자율성을 존중해 주는 사람은 거의 존재하지 않으며, 하물며 다른 사람들이 진정 원하고 필요로 하는 것에 관해 객관적인 지식을 갖춘 사람은 그보다도 더 존재하지 않을 것이라고 주장했다. 프롬은 자유란 우리가 받아들이거나 도피하는 인간 본성의 한 측면이라고 생각했다. 프롬은 우리 인간의 자유의지를 받아들이는 것은 건강한 일이지만, 반면에 도피기제를 활용하여 자유로부터 도피하는 것은 심리적 갈등의 근원이라고 말했다. 프롬은 가장 일반적인 도피기제로 기계적 순종과 권위주의 그리고 파괴성 이 세 가지를 약술했다. 기계적 순종은 자신의 이상적 자아를 사회가 바라는 유형으로 인식되는 성격에 맞추기 위해 바꾸는 것을 의미하며, 이 과정에서 자신의 진정한 자아를 잃고 만다. 기계적 순종은 선택의 부담을 자아에서 사회로 대체한다. 권위주의는 자신에 대한 통제권을 타인에게 넘기는 것이다. 자신의 자유를 다른 누군가에게 넘김으로써 선택의 자유를 거의 완전히 없애 버린다. 마지막으로 파괴성은 자유로부터 도피하기 위해 타인이나 세상 전체를 제거하려 시도하는 모든 과정을 말한다. 프롬은 "세상의 파괴는 세상에 의해 짓밟히지 않으려고 스스로를 구원하기 위한 최후의 그리고 거의 자포자기식의 시도이다"라고 말했다.

33 다음 중 사실이 아닌 것은 무엇인가?
① 프롬은 사랑을 실존주의적 문제의 해결책으로 제시했다.
② 프롬은 권위주의를 비난했다.
③ 기계적 순종은 자아를 사회와 조화시키는 데 기여한다.
④ 프롬은 사랑에 빠진다는 생각을 지지하지 않았다.

| 정답 | ③

| 해설 | "기계적 순종은 자신의 이상적 자아를 사회가 바라는 유형으로 인식되는 성격에 맞추기 위해 바꾸는 것을 의미하며, 이 과정에서 자신의 진정한 자아를 잃고 만다(Automaton conformity is changing one's ideal self to conform to a perception of society's preferred type of personality, losing one's true self in the process)." 자신의 진정한 자아를 잃는 것은 ③에서 말하는 것처럼 자아와 사회를 조화시키는 것으로는 보기 힘들다. 따라서 답은 ③이다. "이러한 실존주의적 이분에 대한 해결책은 인간 고유의 힘인 사랑과 이성의 힘을 발달시킴으로써 찾을 수 있다(the solution to this existential dichotomy is found in the development of one's uniquely human powers of love and reason)." 여기서 프롬은 사랑을 실존주의적 문제의 해결책으로 제시했음을 알 수 있다. 따라서 ①은 답이 될 수 없다. 권위주의는 심리적 갈등의 원인인 세 가지 도피기제 가운데 하나로, "자신의 자유를 다른 누군가에게 넘김으로써 선택의 자유를 거의 완전히 없애 버리는(By submitting one's freedom to someone else, this act removes the freedom of choice almost entirely)" 행위이다. 때문에 프롬은 이를 비판적으로 바라봤을 것으로 유추 가능하며 따라서 ②는 답이 될 수 없다. "실제로도 프롬은 사랑에 빠지는 경험을 사랑의 진정한 속성을 이해하지 못한 증거로 인식했다(Indeed, Fromm viewed the experience of falling in love as evidence of one's failure to understand the true nature of love)"에서 프롬이 사랑에 빠지는 것을 지지하지 않았음을 알 수 있다. 따라서 ④는 답이 될 수 없다.

34 본문에서 유추할 수 있는 것은 무엇인가?

① 프롬의 사랑은 의식적인 노력보다는 즉각적인 감정에 기인한다.
② 자유로부터의 도피는 진정한 자아의 확립에 크게 기여한다.
③ 사랑에 빠지는 일은 외로움과 고독이라는 견디기 힘든 감정에 대처하기 위한 궁극적인 답이 될 수 있다.
④ 인간은 자유의 부담을 덜기 위해 일부 심리적 기제를 고안했다.

| 정답 | ④

| 해설 | "프롬은 자유란 우리가 받아들이거나 도피하는 인간 본성의 한 측면이라고 생각했다. 프롬은 우리 인간의 자유의 지를 받아들이는 것은 건강한 일이지만, 반면에 도피기제를 활용하여 자유로부터 도피하는 것은 심리적 갈등의 근원이라고 말했다(Fromm believed that freedom was an aspect of human nature that we either embrace or escape. He observed that embracing our freedom of will was healthy, whereas escaping freedom through the use of escape mechanisms was the root of psychological conflicts)." 여기서 자유는 인간에게 있어 부담이 될 수 있고 때문에 인간은 자유로부터 도피하기 위한 도피기제를 고안했음을 알 수 있다. 따라서 ④가 답이 된다.

프롬은 사랑은 빠지는 것이 아니라 보살핌, 책임, 존중, 지식 같이 즉각적인 감정이 아니라 의식적 노력을 기울여야 하는 것으로 보았다. 따라서 ①은 답이 될 수 없다. 기계적 순종과 권위주의 그리고 파괴성 같은 자유로부터의 도피 기제는 자신에 대한 통제권을 상실시키고, 선택의 자유를 짓밟고, 세상을 파괴하는 결과를 낳는다. 이는 진정한 자의 확립으로 보기는 힘들다. 따라서 ②는 답이 될 수 없다. 프롬이 사랑에 빠지는 일에 대해 갖고 있는 시각은 부정적이며 따라서 사랑에 빠지는 일이 견디기 힘든 감정에 대처하기 위한 궁극적인 답이라는 내용의 ③은 답으로 보기 힘들다.

| 어휘 | disunited ⓐ 분열된
dichotomy ⓝ 양분, 이분
unreflective ⓐ 무분별한, 경솔한
paradoxical ⓐ 역설의, 자기모순의
neurosis ⓝ 신경증, 노이로제(pl. neuroses)
assert ⓥ 주장하다
much less – ~은 더욱 아니다, ~은 더 말할 것도 없다
objective ⓐ 객관적인
observe ⓥ (발언·논평·의견을) 말하다
escape mechanism – 도피기제
automaton conformity – 기계적 순종
destructiveness ⓝ 파괴성
perception ⓝ 인식
eliminate ⓥ 없애다, 제거하다
condemn ⓥ 비난하다, 규탄하다
unbearable ⓐ 참을 수 없는, 견딜 수 없는

existential ⓐ 인간의 존재에 관한, 실존주의적인
distinguish A from B – A와 B를 구분하다
Freudian ⓐ 프로이트 학설의
narcissistic ⓐ 자기애의, 자기도취적인
hold out – ~을 내밀다, 제시하다
autonomy ⓝ 자주성, 자율성
aspect ⓝ 측면, 양상
freedom of will – 의지의 자유, 자유 의지
outline ⓥ ~에 관하여 간추려 말하다, 약술하다
authoritarianism ⓝ 권위주의
conform to – ~에 따르다, ~에 맞추다
displace ⓥ 대신하다, 대체하다
desperate ⓐ 필사적인, 자포자기한
conscious ⓐ 의식적인, 자각하는
isolation ⓝ 고립, 고독

[35-37] 홍익대 2018

그 모든 시작에 '그(He)'가 있다. 프로타고라스가 최초로 "모든 사물의 척도"로 공식화하였고, 나중에 이탈리아 르네상스에서 보편적 모델로 바뀌어 레오나르도 다 빈치의 비트루비우스적 인간(Vitruvian Man) 안에 표상된 고전적 이상인 '인간(Man)'이다. 건강한 신체에 건강한 정신이라는 고전적 격언에 발맞추어, 이상적 신체의 완벽함은 일련의 정신적, 담론적, 영적 가치들을 나타낸다. 이들이 함께 나타내는 것은 '인간성/휴머니티(humanity)'에서 '인간/휴먼(human)'이 무엇인가에 대한 특정한 견해다. 더 나아가 그들은 흔들림 없는 확신을 가지고 인간에게 개인적인 그리고 집단적인 완전성을 추구하는 거의 무한한 능력이 있다고 주장한다. 이런 상징적 이미지는 목적론적으로 인가된 합리적 진보 개념에 인간 능력의 생물학적, 담론적, 도덕적 확장을 결합시키는 교리인 '휴머니즘(Humanism)'을 상징한다. 유일무이하고, 자기규율적이며, 내재적으로 도덕적인 인간 이성의 힘에 대한 믿음이 이 고양된 휴머니즘적 신조의 주요한 부분을 형성하며, 이는 본질적으로 고대 고전주의와 이탈리아 르네상스의 이상들에 대한 18세기와 19세기의 재해석에 입각해 있다.

이 모델은 개인들을 위한 기준만이 아니라 문화의 기준도 제시한다. 휴머니즘이 역사적으로 문명화 모델로 발전하면서 유럽을 자기 성찰적 이성의 보편화시키는 힘과 일치시키는 개념이 형성되었다. 헤게모니적 문화 모델로 돌연변이를 일으킨 휴머니즘적 이상을 신성화한 것은 헤겔의 역사 철학이었다. 스스로를 확대하여 강화하는 이 전망은 유럽이 단지 하나의 지정학적 장소가 아니라 인간 정신의 보편적 속성이며, 그 특질은 적절한 어느 대상에게도 부여될 수 있다고 가정한다. 이는 에드문트 후설(Edmund Husserl)이 자신의 유명한 에세이 「유럽 학문의 위기(The Crisis of European Sciences)」에서 지지한 견해로서, 1930년대 유럽을 뒤덮은 파시즘의 위협이 상징하는 지적, 도덕적 쇠퇴에 대항하여 이성의 보편적 힘을 열정적으로 옹호했다. 후설의 견해에 따르면 유럽은 스스로를 비판적 이성과 자기성찰성의 기원적 터전으로 선언하였고, 이 두 자질은 모두 휴머니즘적 규범에 의존하고 있었다.

35 다음 휴머니티(humanity)의 견해 중 나머지 셋과 관련성이 없는 것은?
① 무한한 인간의 능력을 주장한 교리
② 비트루비우스적 인간
③ 모든 사물의 척도
④ 파시즘의 위협으로 상징되는 도덕적 쇠퇴

| 정답 | ④

| 해설 | 본문은 인본주의를 의미하는 휴머니즘(Humanism)이 어떻게 생성되었고, 유럽 사회에 어떤 영향을 주면서 휴머니즘의 개념이 진화했는지에 대해 서술하고 있다. 맨 처음 등장하는 ③ '모든 사물의 척도'와 ② "비트루비우스적 인간(Vitruvian Man)"은 모두 고전적 이상인 "인간(Man)"을 지칭하며, 이런 인간에게 완전성을 추구하는 거의 무한한 능력이 있다고 주장하는 ①의 내용도 뒤이어 등장한다. 이런 사상들이 휴머니즘의 토대가 되었다고 설명하고 있다. 후반부의 "a passionate defence of the universal powers of reason against the intellectual and moral decline symbolized by the rising threat of European fascism"에서 '파시즘의 위협으로 상징되는 도덕적 쇠퇴'에 대항하는 '이성의 보편적 힘'을 휴머니즘으로 바라봤으므로, ④는 휴머니즘과 정반대되는 개념이 된다.

36 다음 중 본문에서 저자가 에드문트 후설의 에세이를 언급한 이유에 해당하는 것은?
① 그가 유럽의 휴머니즘의 마지막 계승자라고 주장하기 위해서
② 고전적 이상이 현대 기준에 미친 영향을 설명하기 위해서
③ 비판적 이성과 자기성찰성의 특질에 대한 예를 제공하기 위해서
④ 휴머니즘의 상징적 이미지에 대한 설명을 제공하기 위해서

| 정답 | ②

| 해설 | '인간(Man)'이라는 고전적 이상이 현대의 휴머니즘이라는 개념에 어떤 영향을 주었는지에 대해 후설의 에세이를 통해 설명하고 있으므로, 정답은 ②가 적합하다. 본문 후반부에서 후설은 "1930년대 유럽을 뒤덮은 파시즘의 위협이 상징하는 지적, 도덕적 쇠퇴에 대항한 이성의 보편적 힘"으로써의 휴머니즘을 주장하며, 유럽이 비판적 이성과 자기성찰성의 기원적 터전이라고 주장했다. ①의 경우 후설이 유럽의 휴머니즘에 의미를 부여한 것이지, 그 자신이 휴머니즘의 계승자를 자처한 것이 아니기 때문에 본문의 내용과 맞지 않는다. ③ 비판적 이성과 자기성찰성이 휴머니즘의 예가 되므로, 본문과 반대되는 진술에 해당한다.

37

다음 중 본문의 내용과 일치하는 것은?
① 레오나르도 다 빈치는 고대 고전주의로부터 '인간(Man)'이라는 보편적 모델을 물려받았다.
② 이탈리아 르네상스 사상은 고대 고전주의와 반대된다.
③ 헤겔은 휴머니즘의 이상이 헤게모니적 모델로 변형된 것과 관련이 없다.
④ 휴머니즘은 보편적 규범과 관련이 없다.

| 정답 | ①

| 해설 | '인간'이라는 고전적 이상이 프로타고라스에서 르네상스로, 그리고 이후 레오나르도 다 빈치에게로 이어진 것이므로, ①의 설명과 같이 다 빈치는 고대 고전주의로부터 '인간(Man)'이라는 보편적 모델을 물려받았다고 볼 수 있다. ②의 경우 고대 고전주의에서 르네상스 사상이 이어진 것이므로 서로 대치되는 것이 아니다. ③의 경우 헤게모니적 문화 모델로 돌연변이를 일으킨 휴머니즘적 이상을 신성화한 것은 헤겔의 역사 철학이라고 설명하고 있다. ④ 첫 번째 문단과 두 번째 문단 모두에서 이성을 위시한 인본주의를 인류 보편적인 규범으로 바라보고 있다.

| 어휘 | formulate ⓥ (세심히) 만들어 내다, 표현하다, 진술하다
dictum ⓝ 언명, 격언 double up as – ~로서의 기능을 겸하다
discursive ⓐ 추론[논증]적인; (글이나 말이) 두서없는, 산만한
uphold ⓥ 지지하다; (판결을) 확정하다, 확인하다, 인용하다
assert ⓥ 단언하다, 주장하다 unshakable ⓐ 흔들리지 않는, 확고부동한
boundless ⓐ 무한한 pursue ⓥ 추구하다; 추적하다
collective ⓐ 집단의, 공동의, 공통의 perfectibility ⓝ 완전성
iconic ⓐ ~의 상징[아이콘]이 되는, 우상의 emblem ⓝ 엠블럼, 상징
doctrine ⓝ 교리 teleologically ⓐⓓ 목적론적으로
ordain ⓥ 명하다, (미리) 정하다; (성직자로) 임명하다
rational ⓐ 이성적인, 합리적인 intrinsically ⓐⓓ 본질적으로
integral ⓐ (전체를 구성하는 일부로서) 필수적인, 필요불가결한
creed ⓝ 신조, 신념
predicate ⓥ 근거를 두다, 입각하다; (사실이라고) 단정하다 ⓝ 술부
rendition ⓝ 표현, 번역, (노래·음악의) 연주; 용의자 인도[송환]
antiquity ⓝ 고대, 아주 오래됨 civilizational ⓐ 문명의, 세련된, 우아한
coincide with – ~와 일치하다 self-reflexive ⓐ 자아성찰적인
mutation ⓝ 돌연변이 hegemonic ⓐ 지배하는, 패권을 장악한
canonize ⓥ 인정하다, 찬양하다; 시성하다, 성자의 반열에 올리다
self-aggrandizing ⓐ 자기 강화적인 attribute ⓝ 속성, 특질

espouse ⓥ 신봉하다, 지지하다; 장가들다, 시집보내다
fascism ⓝ 파시즘(국수주의적, 권위주의적, 반공주의적 정치사상 및 운동을 의미함)
critical reason – 비판적 이성   **self-reflexivity** ⓝ 자기성찰성, 자기반영성
rest on – ~에 달려 있다[의지하다]   **norm** ⓝ 표준, 기준, 규범

[38-40] 숭실대 2018

20세기가 시작된 이래 니체(Nietzsche)의 철학은 전 세계에서 지성적·정치적 영향을 미쳐 왔다. 니체는 도덕, 종교, 인식론, 심리학, 존재론, 사회 비평과 같은 주제에 전념했다. 니체의 도발적 문체와 종종 드러내 보이는 난폭한 주장 때문에, 그의 철학은 사랑에서부터 혐오에 이르는 격한 반응을 불러일으킨다. 니체가 자서전적 저서인 「이 사람을 보라(Ecce Homo)」에서, 자신의 철학은 시간의 경과에 따라 형성된 것이어서, 결과적으로 해석자들이 한 연구의 중심 개념을 다른 연구의 중심 개념과 연관 맺는 것이 쉽지 않다고 말한 바 있다. 예를 들어, 영원 회귀(eternal recurrence) 사상은 「차라투스트라는 이렇게 말했다(Thus Spoke Zarathustra)」에서 빈번하게 등장하지만, 그의 다음 저서인 「선악의 저편(Beyond Good and Evil)」에서는 거의 등장하지 않는다. 이런 문제에 더해 니체는 자신의 사상을 하나의 체계로 만드는 것에 관심이 없어 보이며, 심지어 「선악의 저편」에서는 그러한 시도를 비방하기에 이른다.

니체는 허무주의(nihilism)를 의미를 탐색하는 과정에서 반복된 좌절의 결과로 보았다. 그는 허무주의가 유럽 문화의 근본 토대 안에 잠재되어 있는 존재로 진단했고, 허무주의를 필연적이고 앞으로 닥칠 운명으로 인식했다. 종교적 세계관은 이미 철학적 회의론 및 현대 과학의 진화론 지동설에 기반을 둔 반대되는 관점으로부터 무수한 도전을 겪어 왔다. 니체는 이러한 지성적 상황을 유럽 문화에 대한 새로운 도전으로 인식했으며, 유럽 문화는 이제 일종의 배수진에 해당하는 지점을 뛰어넘어서까지 확장되었다고 인식했다. 니체는 이것을 "신은 죽었다(God is dead)."라는 유명한 말로 개념화했으며, 이는 그의 저서 「즐거운 지식(The Gay Science)」의 108장에서 처음 등장했고, [광인(The Madman)]의 우화 125장에 다시 등장했으며, 훨씬 더 유명한 [차라투스트라는 이렇게 말했다]에 또 다시 등장했다. 일반적으로 인용 부호가 붙는 "신은 죽었다."라는 이 말은, 고대 그리스 철학과 기독교 사상에 대부분 기반을 두고 있는 서구 문화의 기존 토대가 이제는 회복할 수 없는 상태로 무너져 내린 상황에서, 이 같은 위기를 서구 문화가 직시해야 하고 뛰어넘어야 하는 것을 강조한 것이다. [선악의 저편]의 아포리즘 55절과 56절에서 니체는 어떻게 허무주의가 기독교의 지성적 양심으로부터 발생했는지 보여주는 종교적 잔혹성의 사다리(단계)에 대해 말한다. 허무주의는 '신'이 우리의 삶에 부여한 의미를 희생시키고 '물질과 운동', 물리학, '객관적 진리'를 얻으려고 한다. 아포리즘 56절에서 니체는 어떻게 하면 극도로 무의미한 삶으로부터 벗어날 수 있는지를 설명하는데, 그것은 니체의 영원 회귀 이상을 통해 극도로 무의미한 삶을 재차 강조함으로써 이를 설명한다.

38 다음 중 본문의 제목으로 가장 적합한 것은?
① 니체가 현대 지성인들에게 미친 영향
② 니체의 핵심 사상에 대한 탐구
③ 허무주의의 원인으로서의 고대 그리스 철학
④ 전통 기독교의 종교적 잔혹성

| 정답 | ②

| 해설 | 본문에서는 니체라는 철학자와 그의 저서 및 핵심 사상을 소개하고 있으므로, '니체의 핵심 사상에 대한 탐구'라는 ②가 정답이 된다.

39

다음 중 니체의 사상을 해석하기 어렵게 만드는 것이 아닌 것은?

① 도발적이고 무모한 스타일
② 시간에 따른 생각의 발전
③ 저서들에서 핵심 사상의 부재
④ 체계적 사고를 없애려는 그만의 태도

| 정답 | ①

| 해설 | 첫 번째 문단 중후반부에 니체의 저서를 해석하기 어렵게 만드는 것들이 나열되어 있다. 먼저 자신의 철학이 시간에 따라 발전했다는 내용이 등장하는데 이는 ②와 관련이 있다. 또한 한 저서의 중심 개념이 다른 저서에는 나오지 않을 수 있다는 것은 ③과 관련된다. 마지막으로 니체는 자신의 사상을 체계화하는 데 관심을 기울이지 않았으며, 심지어 그런 시도를 비난했다고 했으므로 이는 ④에 해당한다. 따라서 정답은 ①이 되며, 니체의 도발적이고 무모한 스타일로 인해 사랑에서 경멸까지 다양한 격한 반응을 대중들로부터 이끌어 냈다는 내용이 나오지만, 이는 니체의 사상을 해석하는 것과는 무관하므로 정답에 해당된다.

40

다음 중 본문의 내용과 일치하지 않는 것은?

① 허무주의는 의미의 탐색에 대한 실패에서 비롯됐다.
② 전통적인 종교의 세계관이 현대 과학에 의해 뒷받침됐다.
③ 양심적인 기독교인들이 허무주의의 출현을 야기했다.
④ 영원 회귀의 이상이 허무주의의 해결책으로 제시되었다.

| 정답 | ②

| 해설 | 두 번째 문단의 "종교적 세계관은 이미 철학적 회의론 및 현대 과학의 진화론 지동설에 기반을 둔 반대되는 관점으로부터 무수한 도전을 겪어 왔다." 부분을 통해 기존의 종교적 세계관과 현대 과학은 서로 대립적 관점을 지니고 있으며, 서로가 서로를 뒷받침하는 관계가 아님을 알 수 있다. 따라서 정답은 ②가 된다.

| 어휘 | dawn ⓝ 새벽, 여명, 동이 틀 무렵 ⓥ 밝다, 시작되다
apply oneself to – ~에 전념하다   morality ⓝ 도덕성
epistemology ⓝ 인식론   ontology ⓝ 존재론, 형이상학
evocative ⓐ 좋은 생각[기억]을 떠올리게 하는, ~을 환기시키는
outrageous ⓐ 난폭한   passionate ⓐ 정열적인
disgust ⓝ 혐오 ⓥ 혐오감을 유발하다, 역겹게 만들다
autobiographical ⓐ 자서전의   interpreter ⓝ 해설자; 통역사
eternal ⓐ 영원한, 불멸의   recurrence ⓝ 되풀이, 반복, 재발
go so far as to – (극단적으로, 또는 놀랍게도) ~하기까지 하다
disparage ⓥ 비방하다, 헐뜯다, 경시하다   nihilism ⓝ 허무주의
frustration ⓝ 좌절(감)   diagnose ⓥ 진단하다, 조사 분석하다
latent ⓐ 잠복성의   foundation ⓝ 재단
be grounded in – ~에 근거하다   skepticism ⓝ 회의, 회의적인 태도
heliocentric ⓐ 태양을 중심으로 하는
point-of-no-return (결정한 대로 계속 밀고 나가야지) 이미 뒤로 물러설 수 없는 단계

conceptualize ⓥ 개념화하다
accentuate ⓥ 강조하다
in the wake of - ~에 뒤이어, ~의 결과로서
dissolution ⓝ 파경, 해산
aphorism ⓝ 아포리즘, 금언, 격언
sacrifice A for B - B를 위해 A를 희생하다
Eternal Return 영원 회귀

parable ⓝ 우화, 비유
transcend ⓥ 초월하다, 능가하다, 탁월하다, ~보다 앞서다
irreparable ⓐ 고칠(돌이킬) 수 없는
moor ⓥ 정박하다
ladder ⓝ 수준, 단계; 사다리
objective ⓐ 객관적인

CHAPTER 03 문학

01	①	02	②	03	④	04	②	05	③	06	②	07	①	08	③	09	②	10	③
11	②	12	②	13	③	14	③	15	①	16	④	17	③	18	④	19	③	20	④
21	②	22	③	23	④	24	②	25	①	26	②	27	④	28	②	29	④	30	①
31	④	32	④	33	③	34	②	35	③	36	②	37	①	38	③	39	④	40	②
41	②	42	⑤	43	②	44	①	45	②	46	③	47	②	48	②	49	③	50	④

[01-02] 한양대 2007

1860년대와 1890년대 어느 시점에서 미국 문학이 주로 강조했던 점이 급격히 변했다. 그러나 이러한 변화가 필연적으로 모든 작가가 의식적으로 관심을 보였던 문제는 아니었다는 점은 분명하다. 사실, 많은 작가들은 이러한 변화의 중요성을 실제로 인식하지 못했던 것처럼 보인다. 더구나, 사실주의가 초기에 미약한 소리를 내다가 의심할 수 없는 지도력이란 주된 주도적 목소리를 내며 꾸준하게 발전한 것을 쫓는 것은 불가능하다. 사실주의의 발전은 전체적 그림을 바꾸어 생각해 본다면 다소 작은 하천의 발전과 같은데, 물길이 흐르는 길을 따라 불규칙한 지점의 지류에서 물이 유입되는 것을 얻는 것으로 그 과정이 때때로 반대편의 모래톱이나 여기저기 흩어져 있는 오류와 협상이라는 늪지대에 의해 방해를 받는다. 낭만주의자 또는 현실주의자와 같이 이 시기의 작가를 엄격하게 구별하는 어떠한 시도도 실패하게 되어 있는데, 이는 이것이 최고의 작품을 해야 한다는 낭만 또는 현실주의적인 신조를 작가가 의식적으로 따르는 것에 의해서가 아니라 그 주제의 분위기에 전적으로 포기하는 것에 의해서 이뤄지기 때문이다.

01 이 글의 흐름상 빈칸에 들어갈 가장 알맞은 것은?
① 반드시 실패할 운명의
② 비평가들에 의해서 환영을 받는
③ 우리의 취향과 반대의
④ 타당하게 간주되는

| 정답 | ①

| 해설 | 빈칸 바로 뒤에 이어지는 'since' 이후의 근거를 바탕으로 답을 이끌어 내야 한다. 본문은 낭만주의에서 사실주의로의 이행을 모든 작가가 의식적으로 직감할 수 있는 정도의 변화가 아니었다고 말하면서, 이를 작은 하천의 발전에 비유하고 있다. 이런 맥락에서 낭만주의인지 사실주의인지를 엄격하게 구별하는 일은 '실패할 수밖에 없다'는 보기 ①이 이 빈칸에 가장 적절한 표현이다.

02 이 글의 내용과 일치하지 않는 것은?
① 1860년대와 1890년대 사이 미국 문학에 급격한 변화가 있었다.
② 대부분의 작가는 초기부터 사실주의로의 운동을 인식했었다.
③ 사실주의는 저항과 실수를 경험하면서도 나아갈 수 있었다.
④ 작가는 자신을 시대의 분위기에 굴복함으로 자신의 최고의 작품을 이룰 수 있었다.

| 정답 | ②

| 해설 | 보기 ①의 경우 첫 번째 문장에서 파악할 수 있다. 보기 ②의 경우 "it is obvious that this change was not necessarily a matter of conscious concern to all writers. In fact, many writers may seem to have been actually unaware of the shifting emphasis."에서 알 수 있듯이 본문의 요지와 정반대의 내용이다. "by virtue of the writer's sincere surrender to the atmosphere of the subject" 부분을 통해 보기 ④를 확인할 수 있다.

| 어휘 |
dominant ⓐ 유력한, 지배적인
radically ⓐⓓ 급격하게, 과격하게
a matter of ― ~의 문제
concern ⓝ 관계, 중요성, 관심, 용건(복수형), 사업, 회사
unaware ⓐ 인식하지 못하는
steady ⓐ 꾸준한
feeble ⓐ 미약한
unquestioned ⓐ 문제되지 않는, 의심되지 않는, 의문의 여지가 없는
tributary ⓐ 공물을 바치는, 종속하는, 지류의 ⓝ 공물 (강의) 지류
diffusing ⓐ 흩뜨려져 있는
rigidly ⓐⓓ 엄격하게, 엄밀하게, 완고하게
realist ⓝ 사실주의자
creed ⓝ 신조, 교리, 교파

emphasis ⓝ 강조
obvious ⓐ 뻔한, 분명한
conscious ⓐ 의식적인, 의식의, 지각하고 있는, 알고 있는
shifting ⓐ 변화하는, 움직이는
realistic ⓐ 현실적인
marsh ⓝ 습지, 늪
romanticist ⓝ 낭만주의자
espousal ⓝ 지지, 옹호

[03-05] 국민대 2018

나는 천재성이 재능과 완전히 다르다고 생각하지 않는다. 예술가의 타고난 재능이 저마다 달라 그 차이에 의해 천재성이 좌우되는 것이라고는 더더욱 생각하지 않는다. 예를 들어, 나는 세르반테스(Cervantes)가 글을 쓰는 뛰어난 재능을 지녔다고 생각하지 않지만, 그런데도 그의 천재성을 부정하는 사람들은 거의 없을 것이다. 마찬가지로 영국 문학에서 헤릭(Herrick)만큼 즐거움을 선사하는 능력을 지닌 시인을 찾기도 쉽지 않지만, 아무도 그가 즐거움을 주는 재능 이상의 천재성을 지녔다고 말하지 않을 것이다. 내가 볼 때 천재성이란 타고난 창의적 능력에 개인의 특이성이 결합하여 만들어지는 것으로, 그 개인적 특이성 덕분에 그 특이성의 소유자는 세상을 극도로 개인적 관점에서 바라보면서도 동시에 극도의 보편성을 가지고 세상을 바라보기 때문에, 그의 매력은 이런저런 유형의 한정된 사람들에게만 호소하는 것이 아닌 모든 이들에게 호소하는 것이 된다. 그의 개인적 세계는 평범한 사람들의 세계이지만 더욱 풍성하고 더욱 함축적이다. 그는 극도로 평범하다. 세상을 극도로 왕성하게 바라보는 기질을 운 좋게 타고난 그는 세상을 무수히 다양한 측면에서 바라보며, 대다수의 사람들이 바라보는 건전한 방식으로 바라본다. 다시 말하면 그는 세상을 활기차게 바라보며 또 전체적으로 바라본다.

03 다음 중 빈칸 Ⓐ에 들어갈 가장 적합한 것은?
① 불투명함
② 경박함
③ 타락
④ 보편성

| 정답 | ④

| 해설 | 역접을 이루는 'and yet'를 통해, 앞의 "개인적인 관점에서(personally)"와 대조를 이루는 '보편적 관점'이라는 의미의 ④가 와야 한다. 천재들은 세상을 '자신만의' 관점에서 바라보면서도 동시에 '보편적' 관점에서 바라볼 수 있는 개인적 특성을 지닌 이들이라고 설명하는 대목이다.

04 다음 중 빈칸 Ⓑ에 들어갈 가장 적합한 것은?

① 삐딱하게 ② 전체적으로
③ 즉시 ④ 잠정적으로

| 정답 | ②

| 해설 | 천재들은 세상을 극도의 활발함(immense vivacity)으로 바라본다. 이것을 vigorously라는 부사로 다시 받고 있다. 따라서 빈칸에는 극도의 활발함과 대조를 이루는 무한한 다양성(infinite diversity)을 받을 수 있는 부사가 와야 한다. 세상을 다양한 관점에서 바라본다는 것은 세상을 전체적인 관점에서 조망할 수 있다는 것을 의미하므로 정답은 ②가 된다. 저자가 말한 천재들은 세상을 지치지 않고 끊임없이 활발하게 관찰하며, 동시에 그러면서도 세상의 다양한 부분을 놓치지 않고 전체적으로 조망할 수 있는 이들이라고 말하고 있다.

05 다음 중 본문의 내용과 일치하는 것은?

① 모든 사람이 헤릭은 매력적 재능을 지닌 천재라고 생각한다.
② 세르반테스는 비범한 재능을 지닌 작가이지만 천재는 아니라는 데 대부분의 사람이 동의한다.
③ 천재는 세상을 매우 개인적인 관점에서 바라보지만 모든 사람에게 매력을 호소한다.
④ 천재는 타고난 재능이 아닌 최고 수준의 강력하고 독특한 인격을 필요로 한다.

| 정답 | ③

| 해설 | 본문 중반의 "(천재는) 세상을 극도로 개인적 관점에서 바라보면서도 동시에 극도의 보편성을 가지고 세상을 바라보기 때문에, 그의 매력은 … 모든 이들에게 호소하는 것이 된다"는 내용이 ③과 일치함을 알 수 있다.

| 어휘 |
genius ⓝ 천재성, 천재
talent ⓝ 재능, 재주
exceptional ⓐ 극히 예외적인; 이례적일 정도로 우수한, 특출한
combination ⓝ 조합
idiosyncrasy ⓝ (한 개인 특유의) 특징, 개성, 특이 체질
possessor ⓝ 소유자, 주인
ample ⓐ 풍만한, 충분한
supremely ⓐⓓ 극도로, 지극히
vivacity ⓝ 생기, 활발, 쾌활
diversity ⓝ 다양성, 차이
vigorously ⓐⓓ 활기차게, 정력적으로
frivolity ⓝ 경박, 경솔, 천박함
catholicity ⓝ 보편성, 포용성, 너그러움
whole ⓐⓓ 전체적으로
tentatively ⓐⓓ 잠정적으로, 임시로, 시험적으로

entirely ⓐⓓ 전적으로, 완전히, 전부
natural gift – 타고난 재능
appeal ⓝ 항소; 매력, 호소, 간청 ⓥ 항소[상고]하다
pithy ⓐ (논평·글 등이) 간결하나 함축적인
happy accident – 예상치 못한 기쁜 일 혹은 상황
infinite ⓐ 무한한, 끝없는
mankind at large – 일반적인 인류
opacity ⓝ (유리·액체; 말·태도 등이) 불투명함
depravity ⓝ 타락, 부패
askew ⓐⓓ 비스듬히, 삐딱하게
offhand ⓐⓓ 즉시, 즉석에서

[06-08]

성격의 변화가 갑자기 일어날 수 있을까? 문학 작품에는 그런 예가 무수히 등장한다. 예를 들어 Charles Dickens의 Ebenezer Scrooge와 같이, 늙은 구두쇠의 인색한 성격은 하룻밤 사이에 극적으로 변화한다. 하지만 현실이 (문학 작품과 같은) 허구를 반영할까? 사람들은 정말 갑작스럽고, 극적인 성격 변화를 경험하는가? 거의 100여 년 전에, 심리학자인 William James는 소위 '두 번 태어난 영혼들'을 지목한 바 있다. James가 마음에 두고 있던 사람들은, 격렬한 감정적 혼란 속에서 갑자기 놀라운 변화를 겪은 사람들이었다. 사실 James는 그의 저서 'The Varieties of Religious Experience'에서 자신도 '두 번 태어난 영혼들'에 포함시켰다. 좀 더 최근에는, 연구원인 Miller와 DeBeca도 55명의 사람들을 지목했는데, 이들도 갑작스럽고도 극적인 성격의 변화를 겪었다고 한다. 연구원들에 따르면, 55명 전원은 이러한 변화들이 보통 극심한 감정적 고뇌의 시기에 뒤이어 왔다고 주장했다. 그리고 그들은 하나의 특별한 '중심 사건(focal incident)'이 성격의 변화를 촉진시켰다고 주장했다. Scrooge의 중심 사건은 당연히 세 유령의 등장이었을 것이다.

06 빈칸 ㉮와 ㉯에 공통으로 들어갈 가장 적절한 단어는?
① 고의적으로 ② 갑작스럽게
③ 자진해서   ④ 대신하여

| 정답 | ②

| 해설 | 위 문장은 스크루지 영감처럼 갑작스레 성격의 변화를 겪은 이들에 대해 말하고 있다. 그리고 실제로도 그런 사례가 있는지에 대해 말하고 있다. 따라서 빈칸에 알맞은 부사는 갑작스럽다는 뜻의 ② suddenly가 된다. 본문 중 힌트가 되는 표현으로는 "changes dramatically in a single night", "undergo sudden and dramatic personality changes", "underwent a startling transformation", "had undergone a sudden and major change", "precipitated the personality change" 등이 있다.

07 문맥상 빈칸 ㉰에 들어갈 가장 적절한 문장은?
① 이러한 변화들은 보통 극심한 감정적 고뇌의 시기에 뒤이어 왔다.
② 이러한 변화들은 보통 극심한 정식적 고뇌의 시기에 의해 지연되었다.
③ 이러한 변화들은 갑작스럽지만 과학자들이 예상했던 것과 같이 극적이지는 않았다.
④ 이러한 변화들은 극적이었지만 과학자들이 예상했던 것과 같이 갑작스럽지는 않았다.

| 정답 | ①

| 해설 | 빈칸 바로 앞에서 연구원들은 "they had undergone a sudden and major change in personality"라고 주장하며 갑작스럽고(sudden)도 주요한(major) 변화를 겪었다고 했으므로, 보기에서 ③과 ④는 답이 될 수 없다. 그리고 빈칸 뒤의 내용을 통해, 이런 성격상의 변화가 격렬한 정신적 고뇌의 시기에 의해 지연(delayed)되었다고 보기보다는 이런 고뇌의 시기가 먼저 찾아온 후(preceded) 성격상의 변화가 왔다고 보는 것이 합리적이다.

08 윗글의 내용과 일치하는 것은?

① 연구에 따르면 일생 동안 성격 변화를 두 번씩 겪는 사람들이 많이 있다.
② 스크루지는 상상의 인물일 뿐 현실에서는 그와 같은 성격 변화를 볼 수 없다.
③ 연구에 따르면 하나의 중요한 'focal incident'에 의해 성격 변화가 촉발된다.
④ 윌리엄 제임스는 종교를 통해서 성격 변화를 겪었지만 밀러는 그렇지 않다.

| 정답 | ③

| 해설 | 보기 ①의 내용은 본문의 내용과 다르다. 성격의 변화를 두 번씩 겪는 이들이 있다고 밝히고는 있으나 많이 있다는 내용은 본문에 등장하지 않는다. ②의 경우 본문의 내용 중에서 "But does reality mirror fiction?"이라고 언급한 후 뒤이어 이런 사례를 소설이 아닌 실제로 존재한다고 주장한 이들의 사례를 소개하고 있으므로 답이 될 수 없다. ③의 내용은 본문의 마지막 부분의 내용, 즉 "They also claimed that one particular 'focal incident' had precipitated the personality change."라고 한 부분을 해석해 놓은 것으로 정답이 된다. ④의 경우 윌리엄 제임스와 밀러라는 인물이 본문에 등장하지만 "종교를 통해서 성격 변화를 겪었다"는 내용은 본문에 전혀 언급되지 않는다.

| 어휘 |
personality ⓝ 성격
literature ⓝ 문학, 문헌
miser ⓝ 구두쇠
dramatically ⓐⓓ 극적으로
undergo ⓥ 겪다
in the midst of – ~의 와중에, ~의 한가운데에
startling ⓐ 깜짝 놀라게 하는, 놀라운
focal ⓐ 초점의
precipitate ⓥ 촉진시키다
voluntarily ⓐⓓ 스스로, 자진해서
A is preceded by B – B가 A에 앞서 일어나다
occur ⓥ 일어나다, 생기다
numerous ⓐ 다수의, 수많은
stingy ⓐ 인색한
mirror ⓥ 비추다, 반영하다
identify ⓥ 지목하다
turmoil ⓝ 소란, 혼란, 분투
count ⓥ 포함시키다, 세다
incident ⓝ 사건
intentionally ⓐⓓ 고의적으로
vicariously ⓐⓓ 대신하여
distress ⓝ 고민, 고뇌

[09-10] 중앙대 2010

Coleridge와 Wordsworth는 시의 낭만주의 학파를 확립시키기 위해 서로 도왔지만, Coleridge의 시는 Wordsworth의 작품과는 매우 다르다. Coleridge는 평범한 사물에서 숨은 의미를 찾기보다는 우리를 천상의 아름다운 세계로 인도한다. 이 세계는 하늘이나 대지의 친숙한 풍경이 아닌 매혹과 아름다운 광경이 있는 상상의 세계이다. 두 시인은 모두 자연을 사랑했지만, Coleridge는 저녁 하늘의 사과 빛 초록색 같은 그가 사랑한 자연의 면모를 섬세하게 관찰했다. Wordsworth의 낭만주의는 사실 아름다움과 신뢰의 새로운 장을 찾기 위해, 18세기의 시적 전통을 깨는 것이었다. 인생의 모든 일상적 감각의 속박으로부터 탈출하기 위한 낭만주의 정신을 Coleridge의 걸작이 아닌 다른 곳에서는 이보다 더 순화된 표현으로 찾아보기는 어려웠을 것이다. 두 시인 모두 자신들의 생각을 완벽한 표현으로 변모시킬 수도 있었을 것이다. 하지만 Wordsworth는 종종 산문체로 빠지는 반면, Coleridge의 운문은 며칠 동안 머릿속에서 떠나지 않는 리듬감을 타고 물 흐르듯 흘러간다. 그리고 이는 너무도 미묘해서 그의 시에 나오는 풍경 및 정서와 완벽한 조화를 이룬다. Wordsworth는 충동적이었다. 그는 기쁨이나 고통을 경험한 후 종종 오랜 시간이 지난 후 평온함 속에서 쌓였던 감정에 대해 글을 쓰는 것을 즐겼다. Coleridge는 시에 도취해 있었다. 그의 상상력은, 영감이 아직 생생하고 격렬할 때, 활활 타오르는 백열과 같은 상태에서 이루어졌다.

09 밑줄 친 빈칸에 들어갈 가장 적합한 것을 고르시오.

① 왜냐하면 그들은 초자연적인 현상을 자연스러운 것처럼 보이도록 만들었기 때문이다.
② 그러나 Coleridge의 시는 Wordsworth의 작품과는 매우 다르다.
③ Wordsworth와 Coleridge의 반란은 일반적으로 구식이 되었다는 점에서 그렇다.
④ Coleridge는 Wordsworth에게 영향을 받았다.

| 정답 | ②

| 해설 | 빈칸의 앞뒤 문맥을 먼저 파악하는 것이 우선되어야 한다. 앞의 내용은 이 두 사람이 낭만주의 학파의 터를 닦는 역할을 했다는 것이며, 빈칸 뒤의 내용은 두 사람의 방식이 달랐다는 내용이 주를 이룬다. 중반에서 후반으로 갈수록 두 사람이 모두 자연을 사랑했지만, 이를 표현하는 방식이 다르다는 데 초점을 두고 있다. 따라서 답은 ②이다. 참고로 ③과 ④는 지문에 아예 등장하지 않으며, ①은 이들이 초자연적인(supernatural) 현상을 노래했던 것은 아니라는 점에서 답이 될 수 없다. 대신 천상의 아름다움(ethereal beauty)이나 상상의 세계(imagined world)에 대해 노래했다는 말이 등장해서 혼동을 줄 수는 있다. 하지만 이는 마법이 등장하거나 이승과 저승을 오가는 등의 불가사의하며 신비적인(supernatural:that cannot be explained by the laws of science and that seems to involve gods or magic) 것과는 구분되어야 한다.

10 윗글에서 논지의 흐름상 가장 적합하지 않은 것을 고르시오.

① ㉮
② ㉯
③ ㉰
④ ㉱

| 정답 | ③

| 해설 | ①과 ②는 바로 앞뒤 문맥과 잘 일치하는 단어들이다. ③과 ④의 경우 각각 Wordsworth와 Coleridge를 묘사하는 단어이다. '충동적(impulsive)'이라는 뜻은 감정에 이끌려 앞뒤 가리지 않고 행동한다는 뜻인데, Wordsworth는 느끼는 감정을 곧바로 글로 옮기지 않고 오랜 시간이 지난 후 평온한 상태에서 글을 썼다고 했으므로 이 단어와 어울리지 않게 된다. ④의 '도취한(intoxicated)'이라는 뜻은 뒤에 나오는 영감이 살아 있고 격정적인 상태로 글을 썼다는 표현과 잘 어울린다. 즉 'impulsive'와 'intoxicated'는 비슷한 뜻으로 쓰였는데, 다른 성향의 두 인물을 비슷한 단어로 표현해서 흐름이 깨진 것이다. 따라서 답은 ③이 된다.

| 어휘 | school ⓝ (학문, 예술 등의) 학파
enchantment ⓝ 매력, 매혹
aspect ⓝ 관점, 면
bond ⓝ 속박
prosaic ⓐ 산문의, 산문적인
subtly ⓐⓓ 미묘하게
recollected ⓐ 생각난, 추억의
intoxicated ⓐ 술에 취한; 흥분된
inspiration ⓝ 영감
revolt ⓝ 반란
archaic ⓐ 낡은, 구식인, 고대의
ethereal ⓐ 천상의, 공기 같은, 아주 가벼운, 미묘한
delicately ⓐⓓ 우아하게, 섬세하게
strive ⓥ 노력하다
lapse into – ~에 빠지다
verse ⓝ 운문 (cf. prose ⓝ 산문)
impulsive ⓐ 충동적인
tranquility ⓝ 평온
white heat ⓝ 백열, 극도의 긴장, 격앙 상태
vigorous ⓐ 정력적인, 원기 왕성한, 활기 있는, 격렬한
in that – ~라는 점에서

[11-12] 중앙대 2010

Stevenson이 그의 소설에 사용했던 소재들은 본질적으로는 Scott의 것과 동일하다. 생소한 상황들과 인상적인 모험이 바로 그것이다. 하지만 Stevenson의 로맨스 소설은 Scott의 작품과 결코 헷갈릴 수 없다. 사실주의 소설이 만들어지던 조정기에 독자들은 소설이 전개되는 방식에 더욱 비판적으로 변모했다. 심지어 로맨스 소설을 읽는 독자들조차도 적어도 작품을 읽어 나가는 동안은 소설 내용을 사실로 받아들이고 싶어 했다. 그래서 독자들은 Scott이 내놓았던 것보다는 Defoe의 작품에서 발견되는 사실적 요소들을 더 요구하게 되었다. 바로 이런 요구 사항들을 Stevenson은 충족시킨 작가이다. 한 예로 그의 서술 방식은 Scott보다 훨씬 짧다. Stevenson의 소설이 책 한 권으로 끝나는 데 반해, Scott의 소설은 책 3권의 분량을 채운다. Stevenson의 소설에는 Scott의 소설에서와 같은 농부나 귀족, 연인들, 익살스러운 인물들로 채워지지 않는다. Scott의 소설에서는 종종 황당할 정도로 많은 인물들이 이런 부류로 채워진다. 이와는 대조적으로 극의 빠른 전개를 위해 꼭 필요한 인물들만 등장한다. 등장인물에 대한 관심은 종종 극명한 대조로 더 깊어진다. 예를 들어 (보물섬에 등장하는) 냉정한 성격의 실버 선장(Long John Silver)과 충동적인 성격의 주인공 소년 짐(Jim Hawkins)이 대비되어 작품에 등장하는 것을 볼 수 있다. 상대적으로 적은 등장인물을 내세우면서도, Stevenson은 사실적 묘사를 위해 세부적인 내용까지 상세히 묘사하는 방식(이 방식은 반세기에 걸쳐 사실주의 작품의 작가들이 사용했던 방식임)을 최대한 활용했다.

11 윗글에서 논지의 흐름상 가장 적합하지 않은 것을 고르시오.
① ㉮ ② ㉯
③ ㉰ ④ ㉱

| 정답 | ②

| 해설 | 보기 ㉯ 바로 다음 문장인 "His stories fill one volume, whereas Scott's were written to fill three."를 보면 Scott에 비해 Stevenson은 한 권 분량으로 짧게 쓴다는 것을 알 수 있으므로 ㉯ lengthy의 반의어인 abbreviated, curtailed, shortened 등의 단어로 변경되어야 한다. 따라서 정답은 ②이다.

12 윗글의 제목으로 가장 적합한 것을 고르시오.
① Stevenson의 낭만인 삶
② Scott과 Stevenson의 차이점
③ 사실주의 시대와 Stevenson
④ Stevenson 작품에 등장하는 인물들의 특성

| 정답 | ②

| 해설 | 제목을 고르는 문제는 제목이 글의 전체적인 내용을 함축할 수 있어야 한다는 전제로 시작한다. Stevenson의 로맨스 소설에 대해 초반부에 언급하지만 그의 삶이 로맨틱하다고 말한 것은 아니므로 ①은 답이 될 수 없다. 답은 ②로 본문의 내용은 시작부터 후반부까지 일관되게 두 작가를 대조적으로 비교하는 내용이기 때문이다. ③의 경우가 제목이 되려면 Stevenson과 사실주의 시대가 겹쳐서 나와야 하는데, 본문의 마지막 문장 중 끝부분의 "a half-century of realistic fiction-writing had given to novelists"를 보면 사실주의 시대는 Stevenson이 살았던 시대보다 앞섰던 것을 알 수 있다. 또한 Stevenson이 사실주의 기법에 영향을 받은 것은 사실이나 이런 내용을 사실주의 시대와 연결하는 것은 무리가 있다. ④는 본문과 맞는 내용이지만 지엽적인 내용으로 글 전체 내용을 담을 수 없다.

| 어휘 | **striking** ⓐ 인상적인, 주목할 만한, 현저한　　**A is mistaken for B** – A가 B로 오해받다
intervening ⓐ 중재하는, 사이에 일어나는(= intervenient)

narrate ⓥ 이야기하다, 서술하다
race through – ~을 지나 빠르게 나아가다(본문에서는 소설을 빠르게 읽어 가는 것을 의미한다)
whereas ⓒⓞⓝ 반면
peasant ⓝ 농부, 노동자
high-born folk – 명문가 출신의 사람들
bewildering ⓐ 당혹케 하는, 갈피를 못 잡게 하는
bewildering number – (눈이 휘둥그레질 정도로) 매우 많은 수
swiftly ⓐⓓ 신속하게, 빠르게
heighten ⓥ 끌어올리다, 높아지게 하다
dispassionate ⓐ 냉정한
impulsive ⓐ 충동적인
to the full – 최대한
era ⓝ (정치 및 역사상의) 시대, 시기, 연대

[13-14] 서울여대 2011

고대 그리스 신화 속에서는 아테나뿐 아니라, 많은 신이 여성이다. 그러나 당시의 여성, 성, 성별에 대한 생각들은 지금과 매우 달랐고 여성은 공적 생활에서 거의 어떤 역할도 하지 못했다. 여성은 완전한 시민이 아니었고, 따라서 정치에 직접 참여하지 못했고, 재산을 소유하지 못했으며, 결혼 전까지는 아버지의 소유였고 결혼한 후에는 남편의 소유였다. 여성의 아버지가 죽으면 계보에 따라 남자 친족의 소유가 되었다. 세련된 저녁 식사에 심도 있는 토론이 함께하는 저녁 모임인 symposia에 참석하려고 남편이 밤에 외출할 때 부인은 집에 있었다. 남편들과 동반하던 여자들은 hetairai라고 불리는데, 이들은 교양을 갖추도록 특별히 키워진 여성들이었다. Aristotle도 여성이 남성보다 열등하다고 믿은 고대 그리스 남자 중에 하나였다. 한 학자는 남성 우위인 그리스 세계는 여성을 불안하게 바라봤고, Aeschylus · Sophocles · Euripides · Aristophanes의 희곡에서 나타난 것처럼 여성을 "남성사회의 질서 정연함을 전복시키는", "부정한 존재"로 봤다. 최근 고대 그리스의 성에 관한 아주 많은 학문 연구가 이루어지고 있다. 연구에서 도출된 전체적인 메시지는 가정을 사랑하고 아이를 낳는 여성이라는 관념과(Media처럼) 거칠고 거리낌 없이 감정을 표출하는 여자라는 관념 사이에 긴장이 존재했던 것으로 보인다.

13 다음 중 본문과 일치하는 것은 무엇인가?
① 고대 그리스에서 여성은 누구도 symposia에 참석할 수 없었다.
② Aristotle는 여성이 남성보다 열등하다고 믿은 유일한 그리스 학자이다.
③ Aeschylus와 Sophocles의 희곡에서 여성 등장인물들은 종종 남성적 질서를 전복시키려 한다.
④ 고대 그리스에는 여성이 공적 생활에서 주요한 역할을 했기 때문에 많은 여신이 존재했다.

| 정답 | ③

| 해설 | 본문에 따르면 여성은 고대 그리스 희곡작가들의 작품 속에서 "남성 사회의 질서 정연함을 전복시키는(subvert the orderliness of male society)" 존재로 묘사되었음을 알 수 있다. 따라서 답은 ③이다. ①의 경우 hetairai라는 여성들이 참여할 수 있었음을 알 수 있으므로 답이 될 수 없고, Aristotle도 다른 그리스 남자들과 마찬가지였기 때문에 ②도 답이 될 수 없고, 여성은 공적 생활에서 거의 어떤 역할도 하지 못했으므로 ④ 역시 답이 될 수 없다.

14 고대 그리스에서 Media는 어떤 종류의 여성인가?
① hetairai
② 그리스 여신
③ 부정한 여성
④ 가정을 사랑하는 여성

| 정답 | ③

| 해설 | 가정을 사랑하고 아이를 낳는 여성과 정반대되는 여성의 예로 Media를 들고 있으므로, 그리스 남성이 가진 여성에

대한 부정적 시각을 함축한 '부정한 존재'라는 말이 바로 Media를 상징함을 알 수 있다. 따라서 답은 ③이 된다.

| 어휘 | not least – 특히
cultured ⓐ 교양 있는
masculine ⓐ 남성의, 남성 위주의
subvert ⓥ 타락시키다, 전복시키다
childbearing ⓐ 출산하는
property ⓝ 재산, 소유물
expressly ⓐⓓ 특별하게
defiling ⓐ 불결한, 모독적인, 부정한
orderliness ⓝ 질서 정연함
unrestrained ⓐ 억제되지 않은, 거리낌 없는

[15-16] 단국대 2018

단순하지만 극도로 강렬한 세 가지 열정이 내 인생을 지배해 왔다. 그것은 바로 사랑에 대한 갈망, 지식에 대한 탐구욕, 인류의 고통에 대한 참기 힘든 연민이었다. 이러한 열정들이 마치 거센 바람과도 같이 나를 이리저리 제멋대로 몰고 다니며, 깊은 고뇌의 대양 위로, 절망의 벼랑 끝으로 떠돌게 했다. 나는 사랑을 찾아 헤맸다.

그 첫째 이유는 사랑이 황홀함을 가져오기 때문이다. 내가 사랑을 찾아 헤맨 또 다른 이유는 사랑이 외로움을 덜어 주기 때문이다. 이 세상 언저리에서, 저 차갑고 깊이를 가늠할 수 없는 생명이 없는 심연을 들여다보며 몸서리치도록 만드는 그 지독한 외로움을 덜어 주기 때문이다.

동일한 열정으로 나는 지식을 찾아 헤맸다. 나는 사람들의 마음을 이해하고 싶었다. 하늘의 별이 왜 반짝이는지 알고 싶었다. 그리고 부단한 변천 너머에서 숫자가 지배력을 발휘한다고 말한 피타고라스 학설의 힘을 이해하려고 노력했다. 그리하여 나는 많지는 않으나 이 중에서 일부를 이룰 수 있었다.

사랑과 지식은 나름대로의 범위에서 천국으로 가는 길을 이끌어 주었다. 그러나 늘 연민이 나를 지상으로 되돌아오게 했다. 고통스러운 절규의 메아리들이 내 가슴에 울려 퍼진다. 굶주리는 아이들, 압제자에게 핍박받는 희생자들, 자식들에게 미운 짐이 되어 버린 의지할 데 없는 노인들, 외로움과 궁핍과 고통 가득한 이 세계 전체가 인간의 삶이 지향해야 할 바를 비웃고 있다. 고통이 덜어지기를 갈망하지만 그렇게 하지 못해 나 또한 고통을 받고 있다.

15 다음 중 빈칸에 들어갈 가장 적합한 것은?
① 하지만
② 특히
③ ~하는 한
④ ~할 경우에 대비해

| 정답 | ①

| 해설 | 본문은 저자의 삶을 이끌었던 세 가지 열정에 대해 소개하고 있다. 사랑에 대한 갈망, 지식에 대한 갈망, 고통을 당하는 이들에 대한 연민이 세 가지 열정에 해당한다. 빈칸 앞에서는 사랑과 지식에 대한 열정이 자신을 천상의 세계로 인도했다고 밝히고 있다. 하지만 연민은 자신을 지상의 세계로 인도했다고 밝히고 있으므로, 앞뒤 내용이 대조가 된다는 것을 알 수 있다. 따라서 역접을 이끄는 접속사인 ①이 정답이 된다.

16 다음 중 본문의 내용과 일치하는 것은?
① 사랑은 세상의 지식을 우리에게 주는 미덕이다.
② 의지할 데 없는 노인들은 항상 자식들에게 미운 짐이 된다.
③ 피타고라스 학설의 힘을 이해하면 우리는 별이 왜 빛나는지 이해할 수 있다.
④ 끔찍한 고독은 사랑을 통해 완화될 수 있다.

| 정답 | ④

| 해설 | 저자가 사랑을 갈망하는 이유를 설명하는 대목에서, "I have sought it, next, because it relieves loneliness"의 내용을 통해 ④의 내용을 알 수 있으므로, 정답은 ④가 된다.

| 어휘 |
overwhelmingly ⓐd 압도적으로, 불가항력적으로, 극도로
longing ⓝ 갈망, 동경 ⓐ 갈망하는, 동경하는
pity ⓝ 동정 ⓥ 불쌍히 여기다
wayward ⓐ 불규칙적인, 변덕스러운
verge ⓝ 가장자리, 아슬아슬한 순간
ecstasy ⓝ 황홀감, 황홀경
shivering ⓐ 몸을 떠는
unfathomable ⓐ 깊이를 잴 수 없는, 끝 모를
apprehend ⓥ 이해하다; 체포하다
hold sway – 지배하다
flux ⓝ 부단한 변화[변천], 확실성[목적, 방향성]이 없음; 흐름, 유동
reverberate ⓥ 반향하다, 울려 퍼지다
torture ⓥ 고문하다
burden ⓝ 부담, 짐
alleviate ⓥ 완화하다, 경감하다
unbearable ⓐ 참을[견딜] 수 없는
hither and thither – 여기저기[사방에]
anguish ⓝ 격통, 고민
despair ⓝ 절망
relieve ⓥ 경감하다, 완화시키다
rim ⓝ (둥근 물건의) 가장자리[테두리/테]
abyss ⓝ 심연, 나락
Pythagorean ⓐ 피타고라스의 ⓝ 피타고라스의 학설 신봉자
famine ⓝ 기근
oppressor ⓝ 압제자
mockery ⓝ 조롱, 조소

[17-19] 숙명여대 2010

자신의 소설 Frankenstein이 어디로부터 나오게 되었는지 그 원천을 처음 밝힌 사람은 바로 Mary Shelley 작가 자신으로, 자신이 살던 시대의 문학과 과학의 혁명적 변화에 깊게 빠져 있었기 때문에 Frankenstein과 같은 작품을 쓸 수 있었다고 밝힌 바 있다. 여성이라는 성별과 지극히 어린 나이(역자 주: 19세에 소설을 썼다고 한다)에 이 소설을 내놓았기 때문에, Mary Shelley는 자신의 소설에 대해 당당한 권리를 가진 작가라기보다는 그녀 주변 사람들의 생각들이 전해져 나오도록 한 투명한 매개체 구실을 담당했을 뿐이라는 일반인들의 생각이 굳어지게 되었다. 심지어 Mario Praz는 "그녀가 한 일이라고는 자신에 관해 여기저기 떠오르는 망상들을 수동적으로 반영한 것일 뿐"이라고 주장하고 있다. 그러나 수동적인 반영만으로는 독창적인 작품이 나올 수 없고, Frankenstein이 비록 위대한 작품은 아닐지라도 독창적인 작품인 것만은 분명하다. 이 작품의 모티브가 되었을 것으로 생각되는 주로는 낭만주의적이며, 부치적으로는 고딕적인 전통들은 바로 거대한 권력을 추구하는 오버리처(overreacher)의 문학이다. 정상적인 인간의 한계를 돌파하고 사회의 규범을 무시하면서 신의 영역을 침범하는 철인은 파우스트(Faust)부터 바이런(Byron)의 영웅들을 거쳐 프로메테우스(Prometheus)까지 모두 그들의 과도한 감각과 경험, 지식 때문에 형벌을 받으며, 가장 전형적으로는 영생이라는 저주로 인해 고통을 당하는 존재들이었다. 그러나 Mary Shelley의 오버리처는 이들과 다르다. Frankenstein이 인간 과학의 금지된 영역을 추구한 것으로 가져올 수 있었던 것은 자신의 생명 연장이 아니었다. 바로 새로운 생명을 창조한 것이었다. 그는 영원히 사는 것이 아닌 새로운 생명을 만드는 것으로 인간의 죽을 수밖에 없는 운명을 거역한 것이다.

17 이 지문의 주된 목적은 무엇인가?

① Mary Shelley의 판타지 문학에 대한 기여를 평가절하하기 위해
② Mary Shelley가 살았던 시대의 과학과 문학 이론에 그녀가 정통했다는 것을 뒤쫓아 밝히기 위해
③ Mary Shelley 작품의 혁신적 측면을 강조해서 그녀의 명성을 회복하기 위해
④ Frankenstein이 속한 문학적 전통의 본질을 명확히 밝히기 위해
⑤ Mary Shelley의 Frankenstein이 판타지 장르의 다른 예들에 어떤 영향을 미쳤는지 보여주기 위해

| 정답 | ③

| 해설 | Mary Shelley가 여성이자 어린 나이에 Frankenstein을 쓴 것을 두고, 사람들은 그녀가 자신의 생각을 쓴 것이 아니라 주변에서 들리는 이야기를 그저 생각 없이 수동적으로 전달한 것에 불과하다고 생각했다. 그래서 심지어 그녀를 작가라고 하지 않고 전달자(medium)의 역할을 했다고 비하하는 이들도 있었다고 본문 초반에 밝히고 있다. 하지만 후반부에서 필자는 그녀의 작품이 이전의 비슷한 작품과 어떻게 다른지 설명하면서 이 작품의 독창적인 부분을 강조하고 있다. 따라서 정답은 ③이 된다.

18 작가는 Mario Praz의 말을 인용한 주요 이유는 무엇인가?
① Mary Shelley의 독특함에 대해 Mario Praz가 갖고 있던 견해를 뒷받침하기 위해
② Mary Shelley에 대한 학자들의 견해가 최근 달라진 점을 보여주기 위해
③ Mary Shelley의 Frankenstein에 대해 Mario Praz가 잘 알지 못한다는 점을 보여주기 위해
④ Mary Shelley에 대한 사람들이 주로 하는 비평적 견해의 한 예를 보이기 위해
⑤ Mary Shelley가 자신에 대해 스스로 평가한 것과 Mario Praz가 Mary Shelley에 대해 언급한 것을 대조하기 위해

| 정답 | ④

| 해설 | Mary Shelley가 여성이자 어린 나이에 Frankenstein을 쓴 것을 두고, 사람들은 그녀가 자신의 생각을 쓴 것이 아니라 주변에서 들리는 이야기를 그저 생각 없이 수동적으로 전달한 것에 불과하다고 생각했다. 그래서 심지어 그녀를 작가라고 하지 않고 전달자(medium)의 역할을 했다고 비하하는 이들도 있었다고 나오는데, 심지어 Mario Praz 같은 인물은 "그녀가 한 일이라고는 자신에 관해 여기저기 떠오르는 망상들을 수동적으로 반영한 것일 뿐"이라고 까지 주장한다고 얘기하면서 Mary Shelley에 대한 세간의 좋지 않은 예를 보이고 있다. 따라서 답은 ④가 된다.

19 지문에 따르면, 다음 중 Mary Shelley에 대해 사실인 것은?
① 그녀는 문학과 신화적 오버리처(overreacher)에 관한 전통을 알지 못했다.
② 그녀는 의도적으로 당시의 과학적이고, 문학적인 발견을 풍자했다.
③ 그녀는 자신의 작품에 영향을 준 문학적이고 과학적인 급진적 개념들에 노출되어 있었다.
④ 그녀는 자신의 소설에 대해 당당한 권리를 가진 작가라기보다는 다른 이들의 문학 작품들을 모방하는 사람이었다.
⑤ 그녀는 당시의 낭만주의와 고딕 전통으로부터 멀리 있었다.

| 정답 | ③

| 해설 | ①의 경우, 본문에서 "The major Romantic and minor Gothic traditions to which it should have belonged was the literature of the overreacher"라고 말하면서 Frankenstein이라는 작품과 overreacher에 관한 문학을 연결시키고 있으므로, overreacher에 대해 알지 못했다는 것은 사실이 아니다. ②는 본문의 내용에 등장하지 않으며, ③의 경우 문장의 도입부에서 이를 유추할 수 있다. 문장의 도입부를 보면 "Mary Shelley herself was ... her immersion in the literary and scientific revolutions"라고 나오는데, 'immersion' 부분이 'be exposed to'에 해당하며, 'revolutions' 부분이 'radical concepts'에 해당한다. 따라서 답은 ③이 된다. ④의 경우 당시 살았던 사람들의 평가이지 사실이라고는 할 수 없으며, ⑤의 경우 Frankenstein이 ①에서와 같이 'Romantic and Gothic traditions'에 기반하고 있다고 했으므로 사실이 아니다.

| 어휘 | immersion ⓝ 열중, 골몰, 몰두　　　　　extreme ⓐ 과격한, 극단적인
not so much A as B – A가 아니라 B인(= not A but B)
transparent ⓐ 투명한　　　　　　　　　medium ⓝ 매개체, 전달자

passive ⓐ 수동적인, 활기 없는, 소극적인
unquestionably ⓐd 의심할 나위 없이, 분명히
overreacher ⓝ 오버리처(거대한 권력을 추구하는 인물을 의미한다)
defy ⓥ 무시하다, 도전하다
realm ⓝ 영역, 범위, 왕국
trace ⓥ 추적하다
reclaim ⓥ 되찾다, 회수하다
perception ⓝ 인식
scholarly ⓐ 학문적인, 학술적인
predominant ⓐ 지배적인
parody ⓥ 풍자하다, 서투르게 흉내내다
reflection ⓝ 반영, 투영, 영향
infringe upon – ~을 침해하다
discount ⓥ 무시하다
familiarity ⓝ 정통
innovative ⓐ 혁신적인
illustrate ⓥ 설명하다, 예증하다
be unfamiliar with – ~에 대한 생소한
contrast A with B – A와 B를 대조하다
be exposed to – ~에 노출되다, ~을 잘 알고 있다

[20-21] 한국외대 2010

모든 최고의 소설에는 지루한 문장이 담겨 있다. 첫 장부터 끝까지 재기 발랄한 소설은 위대한 책이 아닌 것이 거의 확실하고, 이는 위대한 사람의 삶이 몇몇 위대한 순간을 제외하고는 흥미롭지는 않은 것과 마찬가지이다. 소크라테스는 이따금 성찬을 즐길 수 있었을 것이고, 독미나리로부터 추출한 독약이 효력을 발휘하는 동안에는 자신이 나눈 대화 속에서 상당한 만족을 이끌어 낼 수 있었을 것이다. 하지만 그는 삶의 대부분 기간 동안 아내인 크산티페와 조용히 살면서, 오후에 산책을 하고, 아마도 산책 중에 몇몇 친구를 만나곤 했을 것이다. 칸트는 평생 그가 살던 쾨니히스베르크에서 10마일 밖을 벗어난 적이 없다고 한다. 마르크스는 몇몇 혁명을 선동한 이후에 자기 일생의 남은 기간을 대영박물관에서 보내기로 결정했다. 전체적으로, ㉮ 조용한 삶은 위대한 인물의 특성이라는 것을 알 수 있으며, 외부의 시선으로 보기에 흥미 있어 보이는 종류의 것들은 위대한 이들이 즐거워하던 일은 아니었다.

20 ㉮에 가장 알맞은 것은 다음 중 무엇인가?
① 기쁨은 인간 행동의 주요 원동력이다
② 위대한 인물은 위대한 사상과 포부를 갖고 있다
③ 위대함은 순간적이고 덧없을 뿐이다
④ 조용한 삶은 위대한 인물의 특성이다
⑤ 우리는 다른 사람을 위대하다고 할 때 조심해야 한다

| 정답 | ④

| 해설 | 본문의 핵심은 '흥미진진한 순간도 있었지만, 위대한 인물의 삶 대부분은 특별한 일이 없었다'는 것이다. 문장의 후반부에서 'altogether'란 표현을 사용해, 앞에 설명한 내용을 한마디로 표현하고자 하고 있기 때문에, 빈칸의 내용은 당연히 본문의 핵심을 담아야 한다. 따라서 보기 중에서 본문의 핵심과 의미상 가장 흡사한 것은 ④이다.

21 다음 중 본문에서 언급되거나 드러나지 않는 것은 무엇인가?
① 위대한 것들에는 종종 사소한 것들이 포함된다.
② 위대한 사람들은 결함과 약점을 갖게 되어 있다.
③ 소크라테스의 보통의 매일의 삶은 대체적으로 평온무사했다.
④ 마르크스는 그의 삶 후반부의 대부분을 박물관을 방문하면서 보냈다.
⑤ 위대한 책은 처음부터 끝까지 다 좋기 때문에 위대하다고 여겨지는 것이 아니다.

| 정답 | ②

| 해설 | ②의 경우, 본문에는 위대한 인물의 삶에 지루한 구석도 있었다고 말하고는 있지만 그 외에 '결함과 약점'에 관해 논한 부분은 없다. 따라서 ②를 답으로 볼 수 있다. ①의 경우, 책과 위대한 인물을 비교해 '위대한 책에 지루한 부분이 있듯이 위대한 사람의 삶도 지루할 때가 있다'고 말하고 있으므로 직접적이진 않으나 ①의 내용이 언급된다고 볼 수 있다. 따라서 ①은 답이 될 수 없다. ③의 경우, 소크라테스가 '만찬에 참가하거나 마지막 독배를 마시는 경우'를 제외하고는 그다지 별일 없이 살았다고 본문에 언급되어 있기 때문에 ③ 역시 답이 될 수 없다. ④의 경우, 유럽을 떠돌다 영국에 망명해 죽을 때까지 런던에 산 마르크스는 '자기 일생의 남은 기간을 대영박물관에서 보내기로 결정'했고, 실제로도 런던에서 대영박물관을 자료를 활용해 계속 연구를 하다 사망했다. 따라서 ④ 역시 답이 될 수 없다. ⑤의 경우, "위대한 소설에도 지루한 문장은 있고, 처음부터 끝까지 흥미진진한 소설은 위대한 책이 아닌 것이 거의 확실하다"라고 문장 가장 처음에 나와 있으며, 이를 뒤집으면 "위대한 소설을 위대하다 하는 이유는 처음부터 끝까지 책이 모두 다 좋아서라기보다 지루한 부분도 있지만 위대한 부분이 있기 때문이다"라고 유추할 수 있다. 따라서 ⑤ 역시 답으로 볼 수 없다.

| 어휘 | sparkle ⓥ 생기 넘치다, 재기 발랄하다
now and again – 이따금
hemlock ⓝ 독미나리
on the way – ~하는 와중에, 도중에
remainder ⓝ 나머지
of the sort – 그런, 그와 같은
the following – 다음의
aspiration ⓝ 포부
evanescent ⓐ 덧없는
attribute A to B – A를 B 덕분이라 하다, B가 A(성질)를 갖고 있다고 생각하다
imply ⓥ 암시하다, 드러내다
be bound to – ~하게 되어 있다
largely ⓐⓓ 대체적으로
the latter – 후반부
banquet ⓝ 공식 만찬, 성찬
derive ⓥ 끌어내다, 추출하다
take effect – 효력을 발휘하기 시작하다
stir up – 일으키다, 선동하다
altogether ⓐⓓ 전체적으로
outward ⓐ 외부의
driving force – 원동력
momentary ⓐ 순간적인
trivial ⓐ 사소한
vice ⓝ 결함
uneventful ⓐ 평온무사한, 특별한 사건이 없는
throughout ⓟⓡⓔⓟ – 쭉, 내내

[22-23] 중앙대 2009

내가 닥터로의 소설에서 가장 좋아하는 것은 무엇인가? 이에 대한 대답은 간단하다. 나는 닥터로(Doctorow)가 새롭고 신비로운 무언가를 창조하기 위해 사실과 허구를 혼합한 방식을 좋아한다. 랙타임(ragtime)을 예로 들어 보자. 랙타임에서 그는 무정부주의자인 Emma Goldman, 탈출 전문 곡예사인 Harry Houndini, 정신분석학의 창시자인 Sigmund Freud, 또 다른 중요한 심리학자인 Karl Jung, 그리고 모델 T를 생산한 Henry Ford와 같은 역사적인 인물들을 소설의 등장인물로 바꿔 놓았다. 프로이드와 융은 실제로 그들이 미국에 방문했을 때 코니아일랜드를 들른 적이 있다. 역사가들은 이를 기록할 수 있다. 그들이 소설에서처럼 사랑의 터널을 지나갔는가? 누가 알겠는가? 그렇지만 너무 멋진 상상이지 않은가? 닥터로는 사실을 이용해서, 자신의 창조적인 세상을 충만하게 보여주었다.

22

밑줄 친 빈칸에 들어갈 가장 적합한 것을 고르시오.

① 돈이면 다 된다
② 역사적인 세부 사실이 진짜처럼 들리지 않았다
③ 얼마나 멋진 생각인가
④ 독서계가 관심을 독차지했다

| 정답 | ③

| 해설 | 진짜 프로이드와 융이 사살의 터널을 지나갔는지는 알 수 없지만, 미국의 코니아일랜드에 방문한 것을 근거로 사실과 허구를 적절히 혼재해 그런 상상을 해냈다는 것이 얼마나 대단한지에 대하여 서술하고 있다. 바로 뒤의 '닥터로는 사실을 이용해서, 자신의 창조적인 세상을 충만하게 보여주었다'는 문장을 근거로도 충분히 끌어낼 수 있다. 따라서 정답은 ③이다.

23

저자가 프로이드와 융이 사랑의 터널을 지나갔는지를 언급한 목적은 무엇인가?

① 향수를 불러일으키기 위하여
② 닥터로의 사실에 대한 무시를 문제 삼기 위하여
③ 역사적인 만남을 기록하기 위하여
④ 행복한 창조임을 칭찬하려고

| 정답 | ④

| 해설 | 닥터로의 소설들이 이렇게 사실과 허구를 적절히 혼합하여 창조적인 멋진 세상을 그려 낸 것이 대단하다는 것을 알리고자 함이다. 따라서 정답은 ④이다.

| 어휘 | anarchist ⓝ 무정부주의자　　　　　escapologist ⓝ 탈출 전문 곡예사
money talks – 돈이면 다 된다　　　ring true – 진짜처럼 들리다
steal the show – 인기나 관심을 독차지하다　nostalgia ⓝ 향수
take issue – 대립하다, 의견이 맞지 않다

[24-25]

크리스마스 캐럴은 대중문화에 침투해 이 소설을 읽지 않은 사람에게조차 이 작품의 등장인물과 언어의 인상을 남긴 흔하지 않은 소설 중 하나로 여겨진다. 크리스마스는 작가인 찰스 디킨스가 자신의 어린 시절의 절망과 공포를 회복할 수 있는 도구를 제시했다. 일련의 경제적 곤란으로 가정이 파산하게 된 후, 12세의 디킨슨은 학교 공부를 마치지 못하고 가정의 곤궁함을 구제한다는 비현실적인 시도로 검정 구두약 공장의 일터로 보내진다.

디킨슨의 고난은 단지 자신에게만 특별히 적용되는 것이 아니라 산업혁명의 상징이었기 때문에, 그의 소설에서 드러난 관심사는 수백만의 잠재적 독자들과 공유되었다. 디킨슨은 최하층의 가장 취약한 사람들의 고통을 자신의 독자들에게 날카롭도록 현실적으로 다가오게 만드는 것을 의도하여 이들(독자)이 이들(최하층 사람)의 필요인, 구제가 아닌, 자신을 살릴 수 있는 수단으로서 교육을 계속적으로 무시하지 못하도록 만들었다. 적어도 이것은 바로 그가 의식적으로 의도했던 목적이었다. 어떤 의미에서 손에 잡히지 않는 영의 존재를 인간의 영혼으로, 자신의 구원을 위해 하나님의 관용이 아닌 인간의 관용을 기다리는 절름발이 아이를 아기 예수와 대체함으로 디킨슨은 더욱 힘을 얻어 가는 세속적 인본주의에 넘겨주면서 종교 축제(크리스마스)에 대한 권리를 주장했다.

24

본문에서 유추할 수 없는 것은?

① 크리스마스 캐롤은 만약 디킨스가 어린 시절 어려움을 직면하지 않았더라면 쓰여지지 않았을지도 모른다.
② 디킨스는 세속적 사회의 종교적 표현을 통해 대중을 교화하려고 시도했다.
③ 크리스마스 캐롤의 지속적인 인기는 보편적 호소를 담은 이야기에서 기인한다.
④ 디킨스는 교육이 비특권층을 구원할 수 있는 이상이라 지지했다.

| 정답 | ②

| 해설 | 본문 중반에 크리스마스의 캐롤의 배경으로 작용한 자신의 궁핍한 어린 시절이 그려져 있다. 보기 ①은 유추가 가능하며, 보기 ②는 디킨스가 크리스마스 캐롤을 통해서 전달하려는 요지와 정반대의 내용에 해당한다. "the concerns that inform his fiction were shared by millions of potential readers"에서 보기 ③의 내용은 잘 드러나 있다. 보기 ④의 내용은 "Dickens intended to make the sufferings of the most vulnerable of the underclass so pungently real to his readers that they could not continue to ignore their need, not so much for charity as for the means to save themselves: education."에서 유추할 수 있다.

25

본문의 제목은?

① 크리스마스에 대한 디킨스의 인본주의적 관점
② 디킨스 소설 속 하층 계급에 대한 묘사
③ 어떻게 시가 디킨스의 삶에 영향을 미쳤는가
④ 영적 구제라는 디킨스의 크리스마스 주제

| 정답 | ①

| 해설 | 본문 마지막에 글의 요지가 드러난다. 디킨스는 궁핍한 인간을 상징하는 'crippled child'를 실질적으로 구원할 손은 신으로부터가 아닌 인간의 관용에 의한 것임을 암시하면서 종교적 관점에서 '세속적 인본주의'를 강조하고 있다. 따라서 정답은 ①이다.

| 어휘 | infiltrate ⓥ 스며들게 하다, 침투시키다   impress ⓝ 흔적, 인상, 감명, 특징
despair ⓝ 절망, 절망의 원인   financial ⓐ 재정의, 금융의
embarrassment ⓝ 당황, 곤혹, (pl. 재정 곤란, 방해, 골칫거리)
insolvent ⓐ 지급불능의, 파산한   interrupt ⓥ 방해하다, 가로막다
quixotic ⓐ 비실제적인, 공상적인   plight ⓝ 곤경, 궁지, 어려운 입장
tribulation ⓝ 고난, 고생, 시련   emblematic ⓐ 상징의, 상징적인
the Industrial Revolution – 산업혁명   potential ⓐ 잠재적인
intend ⓥ ~할 작정이다, 의도하다   suffering ⓝ 괴로움, 고생, (pl. 재난, 피해)
vulnerable ⓐ 상처를 입기 쉬운, 비난받기 쉬운, 약점이 있는
pungently ⓐⓓ 날카로운, 신랄하게   charity ⓝ 자애, 자비 (pl. 자선, 자선사업)
slippery ⓐ 미끄러운, 붙잡기 힘든, 파악할 수 없는, 믿을 수 없는
anthropomorphized ⓐ 인격화된   crippled ⓐ 절름발이의
secular ⓐ 세속적인   humanism ⓝ 인문(인본)주의

[26-28] 숭실대 2013

"엄마를 부탁해"는 내가 여러 해 동안 읽은 번역 소설 가운데 가장 감동적이면서 세련된 그러면서도 어쩔 땐 가장 놀라운 작품이다. 우리는 같은 이야기가 가족의 큰딸(작가), 큰아들, 남편, 그리고 마지막으로 실종된 어머니의 시선을 통해 펼쳐지는 모습을 지켜본다. 신경숙 작가는 "파란 플라스틱 슬리퍼"를 신은 여성을 조심스러우면서도 단호히 묘사하였고, 소설 속 세 장에서 애처로우면서도 거의 비난조의 2인칭 시점을 빌려("서로 엄마의 실종이 네 탓이라고 비난했고 모두가 상처를 입었다") 글을 전개하였으며, 이를 통해 전달되는 정서적인 명료함과 단순명쾌함이 마음에 직접 닿는다.

모든 문장이 세세한 내용으로 가득하다. "엄마"는 마을에서 식구를 돌보는 동안 개구리를 으깨서 닭에게 먹였고 "머리에 때 묻은 수건을 질끈 동여매고 누룩을 빚었다." 엄마는 천주교 성당에 정기적으로 다니면서도 돌아다니던 중에게 시주를 했고 조상님께서 새의 모습을 빌려 산 자들 사이에서 살기 위해 돌아오신다고 믿었다. 두릅 부침개, "수제비", 산딸기 즙, "녹두죽" 등 매 페이지마다 가득한 음식 이야기는 전통적인 여성의 밭일, 부엌에서의 살림살이, 그리고 엄마의 자식들이 도시에서 비중 없는 삶을 살면서 잃게 되는 이 두 가지 사이의 관계 등에 관해 말해 준다. "엄마를 부탁해"는 여성이 가정을 지키기 위해 모든 것을 포기해야만 했고 남편의 뒤에서 걸어야만 했던 시대에 관한 조용한 분노로 가득하다. 하지만 일부 여성들이 자신의 가정을 위해 무엇을 해야 할지 모르고 있는, 아니면 무언가라도 해 줄 수 있는 가정을 가진, 현대 시대에 관해서 현실적인 시선을 던지고 있다. 신경숙 작가가 우리에게 줌파 라히리를 통해 인식하게 된 세계화된 세상에서 에이미 탄을 통해 알게 된 동아시아 어머니에 대한 잊을 수 없는 상을 제공했다고 말하는 것은 간단한 일이다. 하지만 저자의 첫 영어 번역본은 이보다 더 많은 일을 한다. 이 소설은 세계화가 인간의 눈높이에서 사람들의 영혼을 어떻게 찢어 버리고 어디로 향해야 할지 모르도록 내버려 두는지 우리에게 상기시켜 주는, 후회와 뒤늦은 지혜가 담긴 견딜 수 없을 만큼 충격적인 이야기이다.

26 다음 중 "엄마를 부탁해"에 관해 사실인 것은 무엇인가?

① 저자의 첫 베스트셀러이다.
② 같은 이야기를 두고 여러 가지 시점이 공존한다.
③ 한국 사회의 문제 많은 종교적 지향을 드러낸다.
④ 세계화와 아무 관련이 없다.

| 정답 | ②

| 해설 | "우리는 같은 이야기가 가족의 큰딸(작가), 큰아들, 남편, 그리고 마지막으로 실종된 어머니의 시선을 통해 펼쳐지는 모습을 지켜본다(We watch the same story unfold through the eyes of the family's eldest daughter(a writer), the eldest son, the husband and, finally, the lost mother herself)." 따라서 답은 ②이다.

27 본문에서 유추할 수 없는 것은 무엇인가?

① 이 책은 평이 좋고 인정받고 있다.
② "파란 플라스틱 슬리퍼"를 신은 여성은 소설 속에서 정서적 중심에 위치한다.
③ 에이미 탄과 줌파 라히리는 작가일 것이다.
④ 한국 역사에 관해 이 서평을 작성한 평론가는 풍부한 지식을 갖고 있다.

| 정답 | ④

| 해설 | 본문 어디에도 이 서평을 작성한 평론가가 한국 역사에 관해 풍부한 지식을 갖고 있는지 여부를 판단할 수 있는 근거가 존재하지 않는다. 따라서 답은 ④이다.

본문 전반적으로 소설에 호의적인 평을 내리고 있으며, 이는 ①의 근거가 된다. '파란 플라스틱 슬리퍼'를 신은 여성이 소설 속 '엄마'이며, 엄마는 바로 소설 속에서 등장인물들의 감정의 중심에 있다. 이는 ②의 근거가 된다. 마지막으로 줌파 라히리와 에이미 탄은 신경숙 작가처럼 세계화에 관해 그리고 어머니에 관해 어떠한 이미지를 전달해 주었고, 이미지 전달 수단이 무엇일지 생각해 보면 이 두 사람은 작가임을 유추할 수 있다.

28

다음 중 빈칸 ⓐ, ⓑ, ⓒ에 공통으로 들어가는 것은 무엇인가?
① 남편　　　　　　　　　　　② 가정
③ 조상　　　　　　　　　　　④ 국가

| 정답 | ②

| 해설 | 보기의 단어를 빈칸에 대입했을 때 가장 적합한 것은, 소설이 엄마와 엄마 주변의 가정을 중심으로 진행되고 있음을 감안했을 때 ②이다.

| 어휘 | accomplished ⓐ 기량이 뛰어난, 세련된　　　unfold ⓥ 펼쳐지다, 밝히다
unflinching ⓐ 단호한, 위축되지 않는　　　plaintive ⓐ 애처로운
accusatory ⓐ 비난하는　　　saturate ⓥ 포화시키다, 흠뻑 적시다
mash ⓥ 으깨다　　　permeate ⓥ 스며들다, 가득하다
fatsia ⓝ 두릅　　　weightless ⓐ 무중력의, 비중 없는
clear-eyed ⓐ 총명한; 현실적인　　　belated ⓐ 뒤늦은
unbearably ⓐⓓ 견딜 수 없게　　　affecting ⓐ 충격적인, 깊은 슬픔을 유발하는
orientation ⓝ 지향

[29-31] 한양대 2008

맨 처음 나는 너무도 큰 충격을 받아 사실상 어떠한 반응도 할 수 없었다. 만일 어떤 식으로든 반응을 보였다면, 그것은 내가 예의 바른 사람이라는 것을(즉, 나쁜 사람이 아니라는 것을) 보여주려는 의식적인 노력의 일환이었을 것이다. 미국의 흑인들은 어떤 상황에서도 사람들이 자신을 좋아하게끔 만들어야 한다는 말을 들으면서 자라는데, 이는 흑인들이 학교 교육을 받기 오래 전부터 주입된 가르침의 일부였다. '웃으면 온 세상이 같이 웃어 준다'는 틀에 박힌 공식은 의도적으로 이 공식이 만들어진 상황과 비슷한 결과를 가져왔다. 무슨 말이냐면, 전혀 효과가 없었다는 뜻이다. 생각해 보면, 남들에게 인정받을 수 없거나 인정받아 오지 못한 피부색을 가진 사람을 남들이 결코 좋아해 줄 수는 없는 일이다. (마을 사람들의 눈에 비친) 나의 미소는 나의 치아를 볼 수 있는, 한 번도 이전에 본 적 없는 그저 또 다른 기이한 현상이었던 것이다. 이들의 눈에는 실제로 내 미소가 보이지 않았던 것이다. 그래서 설사 내가 이를 드러내고 으르렁거린다고 하더라도 아무도 웃음과의 차이를 알아차리지 못할 것이란 생각까지 들었다. 미국에서는 내게 전혀 다른 종류의, 그리고 지금은 거의 잊혀진, 고통을 주었던 흑인의 신체적 특징 모두가 이곳 마을 사람들의 눈에는 그야말로 기적과도 같은 것으로 여겨졌다. 어떤 사람들은 나의 머리카락이 타르 색상을 갖고 있고, 솜과 같은 질감을 가졌다고 생각했다. 머리카락을 길게 길러 그것으로 겨울 코트를 만들 수도 있겠다는 말을 농담으로 제안하기도 했다. 의도적으로 악한 마음을 품고 말한 것이 아니라는 점은 어느 면으로 보나 확실했지만, 여전히 그 말 속에는 내가 사람이라는 것을 보여주는 면은 느낄 수 없었다. 그들에게 난 그저 살아 있는 기이한 어떤 것일 뿐이었다.

29

다음 중 (A)에 들어갈 말로 가장 적합한 것은?

① 해가 떠 있을 때 일하라 (일할 수 있을 때 열심히 일하라)
② 눈에서 멀어지면 마음도 멀어진다 (멀리 떨어져 있으면 마음도 멀어진다)
③ 제때 한 바늘을 꿰매면 나중에 아홉 바늘 할 수고를 덜 수 있다 (적시에 하는 것이 많은 수고를 던다)
④ 웃으면 온 세상이 같이 웃어 준다 (웃으면 복이 온다)

| 정답 | ④

| 해설 | 본문의 저자가 마을 사람들에게 미소를 지었다는 내용이 나오므로, 미소와 관련이 있으며 좋은 의도로 상대를 대하면 상대도 좋게 대한다는 내용의 ④가 적합하다.

30

다음 중 (B)와 가장 의미가 유사한 것은?

① 농담조로
② 기쁘게
③ 유감스럽게
④ 무의식적으로

| 정답 | ①

| 해설 | 마을 사람들이 농담으로 한 제안(솜털 같은 머리를 길게 길러 겨울용 코트로 사용하면 좋겠다)이라는 것을 알지만 그래도 저자에게는 큰 상처가 됐다는 내용이므로, 농담에 해당하는 ①이 정답이 된다.

31

본문의 내용에 따르면, 다음 중 사실인 것은?

① 저자가 웃을 때 마을 사람들은 저자가 이를 드러내고 으르렁거린다고 생각했다.
② 저자는 마을 사람들이 의도적으로 자신에게 친절하다고 생각했다.
③ 저자는 마을 사람들이 처음에 보인 호기심에 놀라지 않았다.
④ 저자가 이전부터 알고 있던 교훈이 미국에서도 그리고 마을에서도 모두 효과가 없었다.

| 정답 | ④

| 해설 | ①의 경우 미소를 짓는 자신을 보고도 마을 사람들이 기이하게 반응하는 것을 보고 저자가 혼자 상상한 내용이므로 본문과 다르다. ②는 본문과 무관하며, ③의 경우 저자는 사람들의 호기심 어린 반응에 너무 놀라 어떠한 반응 조차 할 수 없었다고 도입부에 밝히고 있다. 정답은 ④로 남들에게 좋은 인상을 주어 남들이 자신을 좋아하게 만들어야 한다는 가르침대로 했지만 미국에서와 마찬가지로 이 마을에서도 같은 결과를 가져왔다고 나온다.

| 어휘 | at all – 조금이라도
routine ⓝ 반복, 일상
unheard-of ⓐ 들어본 적 없는
snarl ⓥ 으르렁거리다
physical ⓐ 물리적인, 신체적인
nothing less than – 다름 아닌 바로
tar ⓝ (석탄을 건류할 때 생기는) 콜타르, 타르
jocularly ⓐⓓ 장난스럽게
pleasant ⓐ 상냥한, 예의 바른; 쾌적한, 즐거운
work ⓥ 효과가 있다
phenomenon ⓝ 현상
notice ⓥ 알아차리다
characteristic ⓝ 특징
miraculous ⓐ 기적 같은
texture ⓝ 직물, 질감
intentional ⓐ 의도적인

[32-34]

팬픽이란, 다른 이의 전문 창작물에서 빌려 온 등장인물이나 배경을 활용해 만들어진 이야기나 소설이다. 뉴클리어 아포칼립스 발발 이후 한 무리의 똑똑한 대중문화 마니아들이 봉쇄된 벙커 안에 갇힌 채 아무런 사전 지식 없이 문학작품을 재창조할 경우 갖게 될 문학의 모습이 바로 팬픽일 것이다. 이 마니아들은 돈 때문에 팬픽을 짓는 것이 아니다. 돈은 팬픽의 본질이 아니다. 팬픽 작가들은 자기만족을 위해 작품을 쓰고 인터넷에 올린다. 팬픽 작가들은 미디어의 팬이지만 단순히 소파에서 꼼짝도 안하고 아무 말 없이 미디어를 소비하는 사람들은 아니다. 문화가 그들에게 말을 걸면, 그들은 자신들만의 언어로 문화에게 화답한다. 현재 팬픽은 여전히 문화적 차원에서 보면 암흑 물질과 동등하게 여겨지는데, 주류의 눈에는 대체적으로 보이지 않지만, 동시에 믿을 수 없을 만큼 거대한 규모를 자랑하기 때문이다. 팬픽은 인터넷 이전부터 존재했지만, 웹 덕분에 팬픽에 관해 논의하고 팬픽을 접하기가 급격하게 쉬워졌으며, 인터넷에 올라온 팬픽 수만 따져도 수억에 달할 것이다. 팬픽은 책·영화·TV 쇼·비디오게임·연극·뮤지컬·록 밴드·보드게임 등에 기반을 둔다. 심지어 성경에 기반을 둔 팬픽도 있다. 대부분의 경우 어느 특정한 한 작품을 기반으로 만들어진 팬픽의 양은 작품 그 자체보다 용량으로 따졌을 때 더 크다. 일부는 원작보다 품질마저 뛰어난 경우도 있다.

32 본문에 밑줄 친 "아무런 사전 지식 없이"와 의미상 가장 가까운 것을 고르시오.
① 수정과 함께 시작하다
② 주요 변경 사항을 표시하다
③ 무관한 요소를 버리다
④ 백지상태에서 출발하다

| 정답 | ④

| 해설 | from scratch는 '아무런 사전 지식 없이, 밑바닥에서부터' 등의 의미를 지니며, 이는 보기 중 "백지상태에서 출발하다"는 의미의 ④ start from a blank slate와 의미상 가장 흡사하다.

33 본문에 따르면 다음 중 팬픽 작가들에 관해 사실이 아닌 것은 무엇인가?
① 팬픽 작가들은 자신들만의 방식으로 문화에 활발히 참가한다.
② 팬픽 작가들은 자신의 작품을 공개하되 어디까지나 개인적 만족을 위해 작품을 쓴다.
③ 팬픽 작가들은 어느 특정 인물이나 배경에 푹 빠져 있다.
④ 팬픽 작가들은 작품에 대한 돈을 받지 않는다.

| 정답 | ③

| 해설 | 팬픽 작가들은 "자신들만의 언어로 문화에게 화답하기(talk back to the culture in its own language)" 때문에 "자신들만의 방식으로 문화에 참가하는(actively participate in culture through their own ways)" 것으로 볼 수 있고, "돈 때문에 팬픽을 짓지 않기(do not do it for money)" 때문에 팬픽을 짓고 "작품에 대해 돈을 받지 않으며(are not paid for their work)", "자기만족을 위해 작품을 쓰고 인터넷에 올려(write it and put it up online just for the satisfaction)" 공개하기 때문에 "자신의 작품을 공개하되 어디까지나 개인적 만족을 위해 작품을 쓴다(make their work public but write for personal satisfaction)." 각각 보기 ①, ④, ②에 해당되며, 모두 답이 될 수 없다. ③에서 팬픽 작가들이 "어느 특정 인물이나 배경에 푹 빠져(are addicted to certain characters and settings)" 있다고 말하는 것은 어느 특정 작품에만 팬픽이 있다는 의미로도 해석이 가능하지만, 본문에는 팬픽이 어느 특정 작품에만 존재한다는 내용은 담겨 있지 않다. 따라서 답은 ③이다.

34

다음 중 "팬픽"에서 유추할 수 있는 것은 무엇인가?

① 인터넷의 도래와 함께 소개되었다.
② 팬픽을 작성하기 위한 소재에는 아무 제한이 존재하지 않는다.
③ 인터넷 덕분에 장르로서 더 많은 존중을 받게 되었다.
④ 팬픽의 품질은 팬픽의 대상이 되는 작품의 품질을 항상 뛰어넘는다.

| 정답 | ②

| 해설 | 본문의 "팬픽은 책·영화·TV 쇼·비디오게임·연극·뮤지컬·록 밴드·보드게임 등에 기반을 둔다. 심지어 성경에 기반을 둔 팬픽도 있다(There is fan fiction based on books, movies, TV shows, video games, plays, musicals, rock bands and board games. There is fan fiction based on the Bible)"라는 문장이 의미하는 것은, 성경을 포함해 모든 작품에는 팬픽이 존재한다는 것이고, 달리 말하면 심지어 성경까지 소재로 삼을 만큼 팬픽이 다루는 대상에는 제한이 없음을 의미한다. 따라서 답은 ②이다. 팬픽은 "인터넷 이전부터 존재(predates the Internet)" 했으므로 ①은 답이 될 수 없고, 본문에는 팬픽이 인터넷 덕분에 더 존중받게 되었다는 언급은 전혀 없으므로 ③은 답이 될 수 없으며, 원작의 품질을 팬픽이 뛰어넘는 경우는 어디까지나 "일부(in some cases)"일 따름이니 ④ 역시 답이 될 수는 없다.

| 어휘 | **fan fiction** – 팬픽(특정 드라마나 영화의 팬들이 자신들이 좋아하는 작품을 바탕으로 창작한 이야기)
reinvent ⓥ 재창조하다, 다른 모습을 고안하다
from scratch – 아무런 사전 지식 없이, 밑바닥에서부터
nuclear apocalypse – 뉴클리어 아포칼립스(핵전쟁으로 인해 대부분의 인류가 사멸하고, 생존자들이 지하 또는 지상에서 생존하는 이야기)
junkie ⓝ (마약) 중독자, 마니아, 광팬
couchbound ⓐ 소파에서 꼼짝도 안 하는
dark matter – 암흑 물질(우주에 존재하는 물질 중 아무런 빛을 내지 않는 물질)
the mainstream – 주류
massive ⓐ 거대한, 광범위한
exponentially ⓐⓓ 기하급수적으로, 급격하게
given ⓐ 특정한
modification ⓝ 수정, 변경
discard ⓥ 버리다, 폐기하다
start from a blank slate – 백지상태에서 출발하다
advent ⓝ 도래, 출현
sealed ⓐ 봉쇄된
equivalent ⓝ 동일한 것, 맞먹는 것
unbelievably ⓐⓓ 믿을 수 없을 정도로
predate ⓥ ~보다 앞서 오다
words ⓝ 이야기
volumetrically ⓐⓓ 용량으로 따져서
mark ⓥ 표시하다
irrelevant ⓐ 무관한

[35-36] 단국대 2013

많은 비평가들은 에밀리 브론테의 소설 "폭풍의 언덕"의 두 번째 부분은, 첫 번째 부분과 반대되는 구성을 갖춘 것은 아닐지라도, 첫 번째 부분에 관해 언급하면서 첫 번째 부분과 일종의 대조를 이루고 있는 것으로 판단하며, 첫 번째 부분의 경우 낭만적인 관점에서 읽는 것이 낫다는 확증을 더 많이 획득했다. 이 소설은 정교한 구성을 갖추고 있으므로 두 부분을 한데 묶어 하나로 바라볼 것이 권장되며, 이는 화자와 시간 변화를 복잡하게 활용하는 글의 구성을 통해 드러난다. 이들 요소의 존재를 소설의 구조에 대한 작가의 인식을 뒷받침해야 한다는 근거로는 볼 수 없더라도, 이들 요소의 존재는 소설 속 여러 다른 종류로 구성된 부분을 통합하려는 시도를 권장한다. 하지만 소설 속 다양한 요소를 전부 통합하고자 하는 어떠한 시도도 다소 설득력이 떨어질 수밖에 없다. 이는 이러한 해석이 학위 논문처럼 반드시 경직되기 때문은 아니고(비록 이 작품뿐만 아니라 다른 소설에서도 해석이 경직되는 것은 언제나 위험 요소이긴 하지만), "폭풍의 언덕"이란 작품은 부인할 수 없이 강력하고 다루기 힘든 요소를 보유하고 있으며, 결과적으로, 이들 요소는 한 번에 모든 것을 망라하는 식으로 해석될 수 없기 때문이다. 이러한 측면에서 "폭풍의 언덕"은 "햄릿"과 특징을 공유한다.

35

본문에 따르면 다음 중 "폭풍의 언덕"의 두 번째 부분에 관해 사실인 것은 무엇인가?
① 소설의 복잡한 구조를 무효화한다.
② 첫 번째 부분의 힘을 강화한다.
③ 낭만적인 시각에서 읽을 만한 것으로 볼 증거가 부족하다.
④ 소설의 복잡한 요소를 통합한다.

| 정답 | ③

| 해설 | 우선 첫 번째 부분과 두 번째 부분은 서로 대조를 이루고 있다. "첫 번째 부분의 경우 낭만적인 관점에서 읽는 것이 낫다는 확증을 더 많이 획득했다(the first part, where a romantic reading receives more confirmation)"는 말은 역으로 말하면 첫 번째 부분과 대조되는 두 번째 부분은 낭만적인 관점에서 읽을 편이 낫다는 확증을 주지 못한다는 의미이다. 따라서 답은 ③이다.

36

본문에 따르면 저자는 비평가들이 <u>소설의 다양한 요소를 분석할 때 유연함을 보여야 한다</u>는 사실에 동의할 가능성이 가장 높다.
① 소설의 구조에 대한 작가의 인식을 요구하도록 노력해야 한다
② 소설의 다양한 요소를 분석할 때 유연함을 보여야 한다
③ 다른 비평가들의 해석을 맹목적으로 수용해야 한다
④ 화자 및 시간 변화를 복잡하게 활용한다는 것이 정교한 구조를 나타낸다고 주장하지 말아야 한다

| 정답 | ②

| 해설 | "이 작품뿐만 아니라 다른 소설에서도 해석이 경직되는 것은 언제나 위험 요소이다(rigidity in any interpretation of this or of any novel is always a danger)"는 말은 즉 글의 저자는 소설의 분석에 있어 경직된 모습은 위험하고 이와 반대되는 유연함이 필요함을 말하고 있다. 따라서 답은 ②이다.

| 어휘 | counterpoint ⓝ 대위법, 대조 granted that – 설사 ~이라 할지라도[하더라도]
authorial ⓐ 작가의 heterogeneous ⓐ 여러 다른 종류로 이루어진
be bound to – 반드시 ~하다 unconvincing ⓐ 설득력이 없는
stiffen ⓥ 경직시키다, 뻣뻣하게 만들다 recalcitrant ⓐ 반항하는, 다루기 힘든

undeniable ⓐ 부인할 수 없는, 명백한   **annul** ⓥ 무효화하다, 취소하다
substantiation ⓝ 입증, 증거

[37-40] 가톨릭대 2016

어떤 이는 문학을 특정한 유형의 글을 통해 드러나는 고유의 특성이거나 일련의 특성으로 간주하기보다 사람이 스스로를 글과 결부시킬 수 있는 여러 방안으로 간주할 수 있다. '문학'이라고 다양하게 불린 온갖 것들로부터 일련의 고유한 불변의 특성을 구분하는 일은 쉽지 않을 것이다. 실제로도 이는 모든 게임들이 공통적으로 갖고 있는 하나의 독특한 특징을 식별하려 노력하는 것만큼이나 불가능할 것이다. 뭐든지 간에 문학의 '본질'이란 것은 존재하지 않는다. 어떤 글이든 '시적으로' 읽힐 수 있는 것과 마찬가지로 어떤 글이든 '비실용적으로' 읽힐 수 있다. 어떤 텍스트를 문학으로서 읽는다는 것이 이런 의미, 즉 글을 '비실용적으로' 읽는다는 의미라면 말이다. 만일 내가 열차 연결편을 찾기 위해서가 아니라 현대인으로서 생활이 얼마나 빠르게 그리고 복잡하게 진행되고 있는지를 전반적으로 숙고하는 행위를 마음속에서 촉진하기 위해 열차 시간표를 자세히 조사할 경우, 나는 시간표를 문학으로서 읽고 있다고 할 수 있다. '문학'이란 단어는 다소 '잡초'란 단어와 비슷하게 기능한다. 잡초는 어느 특정한 종류의 식물을 지칭하는 것이 아니라 어떤 종류든 간에 정원사가 무슨 이유에서든 주변에 두길 원하지 않는 식물을 지칭한다. 아마도 '문학'은 이와 정반대되는 의미를 지닐 것이다. 즉 문학은 어떤 종류든 간에 누군가가 무슨 이유에서든 높이 평가하는 글을 지칭한다. 철학자들이 말했듯이 '문학'과 '잡초'는 존재론적인 용어라기보다 기능적인 용어이다. 둘 다 어떤 고정된 존재에 관해 말하는 것이 아니라 우리의 행동에 관해 말한다. '문학'은 이러한 의미에서 순전히 형식적이고 공허한 유형의 정의이다. 어쨌든, 우리가 스스로를 언어와 결부시키기 위한 '실용적' 방안과 '비실용적' 방안을 깔끔하게 구별할 수 있을지는 분명치 않다. 즐거움을 위해 소설을 읽는 것은 정보를 얻기 위해 도로 표지를 읽는 것과는 확연한 차이가 있다. 하지만 정신 함양을 위해 생물학 교과서를 읽는 것은 어떠한가? 생물학 교과서를 읽는 것은 언어를 '실용적으로' 처리하는 행위인가 아니면 그렇지 않은가? 많은 사회에서 '문학'은 종교적 기능처럼 고도로 실용적인 기능을 수행해 왔다. '실용적인 것'과 '비실용적인 것'을 선명하게 구별하는 것은 문학이 실용적 기능을 더 이상 수행할 수 없게 된 우리 사회와 같은 사회에서만 가능할지도 모른다.

37 본문의 제목으로 가장 알맞은 것은 무엇인가?
① 문학은 무엇인가?
② 문학을 읽는 법
③ 문학의 올바른 사용과 잘못된 사용
④ 문학의 중요성

| 정답 | ①

| 해설 | 본문은 무엇을 문학이라 할 수 있을지에 관해 저자의 여러 생각들을 담은 글이다. 따라서 답은 ①이다.

38 빈칸에 가장 알맞은 것을 고르시오.
① 언어학적 관점에서 그것들을 비교하는 것은 불가능하다.
② 둘 다 사람들이 삶의 의미를 판단하기 위해 사용되는 지표로서 기능한다.
③ 둘 다 어떤 고정된 존재에 관해 말하는 것이 아니라 우리의 행동에 관해 말한다.
④ 우리는 둘 다 얼마만큼 유용한지와는 관계없이 둘의 존재에 대해 직접 접근할 수 없다.

| 정답 | ③

| 해설 | 빈칸 앞에서 '문학'과 '잡초'는 존재론적 용어가 아니라 기능적 용어라고 말하고 있다. 본문에 따르면 모든 문학에서 공통적으로 등장하는 문학의 '본질' 같은 것은 존재하지 않으며 결국은 우리가 무엇을 문학이라 할지 가치를 평가하고 내리는 것에 따라 문학의 정의가 달라진다. 즉 어떤 글이든 문학이라 생각하고 읽으면 문학이 되고 아니라고 생각

하면 문학이 아니게 되는 것이다. 여기서 본문에 제시된 잡초의 정의를 보면 "잡초는 어느 특정한 종류의 식물을 지칭하는 것이 아니라 어떤 종류든 간에 정원사가 무슨 이유에서든 주변에 두길 원하지 않는 식물을 지칭한다(weeds are not particular kinds of plant, but just any kind of plant which for some reason or another gardener does not want around)"고 나와 있는데, 이 말은 달리 보면 어떤 식물이 '잡초'라 불리는 것은 모든 잡초에 공통된 어떤 불변의 특징을 보유하기 때문이 아니라 정원사의 판단에 따라 잡초가 될 수도 있고 아닐 수도 있다는 소리이다. 즉, 두 단어 모두 어떤 '고정된 존재' 내지는 불변의 특징을 지칭하는 단어가 아니다. 그리고 '우리의 행동'이라 함은, 즉 우리가 무엇을 문학이라 할지 내지는 무엇을 잡초라고 할지 결정하는 것은 우리의 행동에 따른 결과임을 나타낸다. 따라서 답은 ③이다.

39

저자에 따르면 과학 교과서는 다음에 해당되는 경우 문학으로 읽힐 수 있다.
① 인간의 삶에 있어 실용적인 수단으로 기능함
② 세상에 대한 귀중한 정보를 제공함
③ 유창한 언어로 쓰여짐
④ 외경심을 품고서 과학 교과서를 다룸

| 정답 | ④

| 해설 | 열차 시간표를 본래의 기능에 맞게 읽는다면 문학으로 볼 수 없다. 하지만 열차 시간표를 현대인의 삶을 숙고하는 계기로 삼는다면 열차 시간표도 문학이 될 수 있다. 따라서 만일 과학 교과서를 본래 목적인 지식 전달의 용도가 아니라 "외경심", 즉 과학 교과서를 통해 뭔가를 공경하고 두려워할 수 있는 계기로 삼아 스스로를 성찰하게 된다면, 즉 "정신 함양(improve your mind)"을 하게 된다면 과학 교과서도 문학으로 볼 수 있다. 따라서 답은 ④이다.

40

다음 중 본문에 따르면 사실이 아닌 것은 무엇인가?
① 일부 여행자들에게 있어 열차 시간표는 문학으로 읽힐 수 있다.
② 글은 실용적으로도 비실용적으로도 읽힐 수 있다.
③ 제대로 노력하면 독서 중에 문학의 정수가 쉽게 모습을 드러낼 수 있다.
④ 문학은 사회마다 다른 방식으로 기능해 왔다.

| 정답 | ③

| 해설 | 본문에 따르면 문학에는 어떤 고정된 정수나 핵심 같은 것은 존재하지 않는다. 따라서 문학의 정수에 관해 말하는 ③은 답으로 볼 수 없다. 본문에 언급된 열차 시간표의 사례는 실용문도 문학으로 읽힐 수 있는 사례로 제시된 것이며 ①의 내용에 해당된다. "어떤 글이든 '시적으로' 읽힐 수 있는 것과 마찬가지로 어떤 글이든 '비실용적으로' 읽힐 수 있다(Any bit of writing may be read 'non-pragmatically', if that is what reading a text as literature means, just as any writing may be read 'poetically')." 이는 ②의 내용에 해당된다. 본문 마지막 부분을 읽어보면 과거에는 문학이 고도로 실용적 기능을 수행했음을 알 수 있고 현대 사회는 문학이 실용적 기능을 수행하지 않음을 알 수 있다. 이는 보기 ④에 해당된다.

| 어휘 | inherent ⓐ 내재하는, 고유한   quality ⓝ 자질, 특성
relate ⓥ 관련[결부]시키다   isolate ⓥ 분리하다, 구분하다
constant ⓐ 변치 않는, 불변의   distinguishing ⓐ 특색 있는, 독특한
whatsoever – whatever의 강조형   pragmatically ⓐⓓ 실용적으로
poetically ⓐⓓ 시적으로   pore over – ~을 자세히 조사하다
connection ⓝ (교통) 연결편

reflection ⓝ (특정 주제·화제에 대해 말·글에) 반영된 생각, 숙고, 의견
existence ⓝ 생활, 생존
formal ⓐ 형식적인, 형식상의
discriminate ⓥ 구별[식별]하다
obviously ⓐⓓ 분명히, 확연하게
gauge ⓥ 판단하다, 측정하다
awe ⓝ 경외감, 외경심
ontological ⓐ 존재론적인
in any case – 어쨌든
neatly ⓐⓓ 깔끔하게, 솜씨 있게
sharply ⓐⓓ (대조가) 선명하게[뚜렷이]
eloquent ⓐ 유창한, 웅변의

[41-42] 성균관대 2016

수 세기 동안 두 사람이 서로 마주보고 결투를 벌이는 것은 시대에 뒤떨어진 것처럼 보였다. 19세기 작가 모파상(Guy de Maupassant)은 이 같은 결투를 '비합리적인 관행의 최후의 잔재'라고 말했다. 그로부터 200년 전인 17세기에, 프랑스의 루이 14세(Louis XIV)는 이런 결투를 낡은 봉건시대의 유물이라고 지칭하며 불법화하려고 했다. 하지만 이런 노력들에도 불구하고, 19세기와 심지어 20세기 초의 문학작품에 이런 결투를 벌이는 남자들의 이야기가 도처에 가득 남아 있는 것은 무엇 때문일까? 18세기 초반의 많은 작가들은 결투를 벌이는 사람들을 성급한 인물로 묘사했다. 19세기에 이르러서는 결투가 여전히 옛날 중세시대에서 유래한 것으로 보였음에도 불구하고, 결투를 상당히 근사한 것으로 간주했다. 윌리엄 메이크피스 새커리(William Makepeace Thackeray)의 《배리 린든 님의 회고록(The Memoirs of Barry Lyndon, Esq)》에서 주인공은 '비겁한 권총'을 비난하며, '신사의 영예롭고 남자다운 무기'를 떠올린다. 20세기 초에 급증하는 폭력사건과 비교했을 때, 결투는 상당히 신중한 것처럼 보였을 수 있다. 1908년에 나온 길버트 케이스 체스터턴(G. K. Chesterton)의 소설 속 등장인물은 수상쩍은 무정부주의자가 폭탄을 터뜨리려는 것을 그에게 결투를 신청함으로써 저지한다. 하지만 두 차례의 세계대전 이후 결투의 빛이 바래기 시작했다. 에벌린 워(Evelyn Waugh)의 《사관과 신사(Officers and Gentlemen(1955))》에서 한 등장인물은 누군가가 자신에게 결투를 신청해 온다면 그는 그저 웃어넘길 것이라고 말한다.

41 이 글의 제목으로 가장 적합한 것은?
① 과거 결투에 필적하는 현대적인 대상들
② 문학에서의 결투
③ 결투의 기원
④ 구식의 어리석은 행위인 결투
⑤ 폭력의 역사

| 정답 | ②

| 해설 | 두 사람이 마주보고 싸우는 결투(duel)를 문학 작품에서 어떻게 묘사하고 있는지를 설명하고 있는 글이므로, ②가 글의 제목으로 적합하다.

42 본문의 밑줄 친 부분을 통해 대결은 _____ 하다는 사실을 함축하고 있다.
① 합법화되었다
② 거의 사라졌다
③ 무정부주의의 무분별한 행동이다
④ 공격의 저급한 형태이다
⑤ 질서 정연한 폭력의 형태이다

| 정답 | ⑤

| 해설 | 밑줄 친 부분은 결국 measured의 의미를 묻고 있는 것으로, 이 단어는 '신중한, 침착한'의 뜻을 지니며, 앞부분의 'burgeoning violence'와 대조를 보인다. 따라서 보기에서 '신중한'의 의미로 사용된 'ordered'가 들어 있는 ⑤가 정답이 된다.

| 어휘 | duel ⓝ 결투, (두 사람·집단 사이의) 다툼[싸움]   anachronistic ⓐ 시대착오의, 시대에 뒤진
outlaw ⓥ 불법화하다, 금하다   feudal ⓐ 봉건적인, 봉건 제도의
archaism ⓝ 고어, 고풍스러운 표현, 고풍스러운 습관
be peppered with – ~가 퍼부어진, ~가 많은
swashbuckling ⓐ (과거를 배경으로 모험·액션·칼싸움 등이) 넘치는, 허세 부리는
depict ⓥ 묘사하다   hot-headed ⓐ 성급한, 성마른
medieval ⓐ 중세의   glamorous ⓐ 화려한, 매력이 넘치는
memoir ⓝ (특히 유명인의) 회고록   rail against – ~을 욕하다
hark back to – ~을 상기하다[떠올리다]   burgeoning ⓐ 급증하는, 급성장하는
measured ⓐ 신중한, 침착한   anarchist ⓝ 무정부주의자
folly ⓝ 판단력 부족, 어리석음, 어리석은 행동[생각]
aggression ⓝ 공격성   ordered ⓐ 정돈된, (질서) 정연한

[43-45] 한국외대 2015

아일랜드 출신 작가인 조지 오웰(George Orwell)의 삶과 문학을 요약하면 그가 인간의 품위에 관해 믿음을 지녔음을 알 수 있다. 인간의 품위가 무엇인지 정의내리기는 애매모호하지만, 근원적인 존엄성 그리고 무엇보다도 정직함과 관용에 대한 인식을 포함하고 있다. 오웰은 독단적인 신조, 이념적이면서 정치적인 주의, 계획된 형태의 사회 개혁, 종교적 절대주의 등에 반대했다. 대신에 오웰은 개인의 표현의 권리, 특히 소수집단의 권리와 언론의 자유를 지지하는 것을 더욱 선호했다.

오웰이 인간의 품위에 관해 지녔던 감각은 해방과 표현에 대한 스스로의 생각에 기반을 둔다. 인간의 품위는 수동적으로 누려야 할 것이 아니라 이를 달성하기 위해 노력하고 추구해야 하는 것이다. "자유의 비결은 용기이다"라는 구절은 사람들에게는 말은 용기 있게 하면서 다른 의견에 대해서는 용기 있는 관용을 보여야 한다는 것을 암시한다. 조지 오웰에게 있어 품위란 다른 무엇보다도 공동체의 조화와 상식 그리고 상식 있는 사람들에 대한 존중 등을 의미한다. 오웰은 마르크스주의에 단호한 반대 입장을 보였으며 그 이유는 마르크스주의는 평등을 이유로 자유를 부인하도록 만들기 때문이다. 오웰은 진정한 사회주의는 권력을 장악함으로써 가능한 것이 아니라 공정하고 개방된 논의를 보장하는 것으로 가능하다고 생각했다.

오웰은 이념을 필요로 하는 공산주의 같은 추상적 이론을 혐오했다. 이는 전체주의에 반대하는 작품인 "동물농장"과 디스토피아적 세상을 그린 대표적 작품인 1984를 통해 잘 드러나 있다. 이들 작품을 통해 오웰은 독재에 반대하고, 계급에 반대하고, 차별에 반대하는 사회를 추구하고 있다. 오웰은 이러한 체제에 맞서 싸우는 것이 인간의 의무라고 생각했으며, 이는 사회를 위해서 뿐만이 아니라 사회의 진보를 위해서도 필요한 것으로 보았다.

43 다음 중 본문의 주제는 무엇인가?
① 오웰의 문학적 기법과 훌륭한 솜씨   ② 오웰의 문학에 대한 철학적 관점
③ 오웰의 성격에 대한 비판적 논평   ④ 오웰의 문필가로서의 경력의 발전

| 정답 | ②

| 해설 | 본문은 조지 오웰의 작품이 어떤 생각을 기반으로 하여 쓰였는지에 관해 논하고 있으며, 보기 중에서 이와 의미상 가장 가까운 것은 철학적 관점에 관해 논하는 ②이다.

44 다음 중 오웰이 반대했을 가능성이 가장 낮은 것은 무엇인가?
① 정부 권력을 제한할 필요성
② 자유보다 평등을 선택하기
③ 정치적 이념의 고수
④ 어떤 의심 없이 종교를 믿기

| 정답 | ①

| 해설 | "오웰은 독단적인 신조, 이념적이면서 정치적인 주의, 계획된 형태의 사회 개혁, 종교적 절대주의 등에 반대했다. 대신에 오웰은 개인의 표현의 권리, 특히 소수집단의 권리와 언론의 자유를 지지하는 것을 더욱 선호했다(Orwell was opposed to dogma, ideological political doctrines, planned social reformation, and religious absolutism. He instead preferred to support the individual's right of expression, particularly the rights of minorities, and the freedom of press)." 또한 "평등을 이유로 자유를 부인하도록 만들기 때문에(dictates that freedom is denied by equality)" 마르크스주의도 반대했다. "독재에 반대하고, 계급에 반대하고, 차별에 반대하는(anti-dictatorial, anti-class, and anti-discriminatory)" 그의 입장에서 보면 정부 권력은 개인을 억압하며 따라서 그는 정부 권력의 축소나 제한에 찬성했을 것이다. 따라서 답은 ①이다.

45 문맥에 따르면 다음 중 빈칸 Ⓐ와 Ⓑ에 가장 알맞은 것은 무엇인가?
① 포기하기 – 권장하기
② 장악하기 – 보장하기
③ 사로잡기 – 저지하기
④ 포기하기 – 진압하기

| 정답 | ②

| 해설 | 오웰은 사회주의의 한 분파인 마르크스주의를 반대했으며 그 이유는 마르크스주의는 평등을 이유로 자유를 부인하도록 만들기 때문이다. 즉, 오웰은 평등보다 자유를 더 중시했다. 자유는 "공정하고 개방된 논의(fair and open discussions)"를 보장(guaranteeing)하거나 권장(encouraging)하는 것을 자유라 볼 수 있으므로 Ⓑ에는 ①이나 ②가 적합하다. not A but B 구문이므로 Ⓐ에는 Ⓑ와 대조적인 개념이 들어가야 한다. Ⓑ의 자유를 옹호하는 개념과 반대되는 의미를 가지려면 Ⓐ는 ②의 권력의 "장악(seizing)"이나 ③의 "사로잡음(capturing)"이란 의미를 지니는 것이 적합하다. 이러한 점들을 모두 감안했을 때 가장 적합한 것은 ②이다.

| 어휘 | summarize ⓥ 요약하다
human decency – 인간의 품위
dignity ⓝ 존엄성, 품위
dogma ⓝ (독단적인) 신조, 도그마
reformation ⓝ 개혁, 개선
prefer to – ~을 더 선호하다
liberation ⓝ 해방
obligation ⓝ 의무
adamantly ⓐⓓ 단호하게, 굳세게
guarantee ⓥ 보장하다, 약속하다
necessitate ⓥ ~을 필요하게 만들다, 필요로 하다
totalitarian ⓐ 전체주의의
faith ⓝ 믿음, 신뢰
ambiguous ⓐ 애매모호한
tolerance ⓝ 용인, 관용
doctrine ⓝ 교리, 정책, 주의
absolutism ⓝ 절대론, 절대주의
minorities ⓝ 소수자, 소수집단
passively ⓐⓓ 수동적으로, 소극적으로
communality ⓝ 공동체의 일치[조화]
dictate ⓥ 요구하다, 지시하다
loathe ⓥ 혐오하다
classic ⓐ 전형적인, 대표적인

discriminatory ⓐ 차별의, 차별적인	**for the sake of** – ~을 위해서
progression ⓝ 진보	**craftsmanship** ⓝ (훌륭한) 솜씨
adherence ⓝ 고수, 집착	**relinquish** ⓥ 포기하다
restrain ⓥ 저지하다, 제지하다	**renounce** ⓥ 포기하다, 단념하다
suppress ⓥ 진압하다, 숨기다	

[46-47] 서강대 2017

감상적인 감정이 무자비함이나 그보다 더 나쁜 것을 즐기는 취향과 완벽히 양립할 수 있다는 것은 주지의 사실이다. (대표적인 예로, 저녁에 퇴근해 아내와 자식들을 포옹해 준 뒤 저녁 식사 전까지 피아노 앞에 앉아 슈베르트의 곡을 연주했다는 아우슈비츠 사령관의 사례를 떠올려 보라.) 사람들이 자신에게 보이는 것에 익숙해지는 것은 – 만약 익숙해진다는 표현이 이 상황을 기술하는 적절한 방식이라면 – 단지 그들에게 쏟아지는 이미지들의 양 때문은 아니다. 감정을 무디게 만드는 것은 다름 아닌 수동성이다. ⓐ냉담함, 도덕적 혹은 감정적 무감각증 등으로 묘사되는 이 상태는 사실 여러 감정으로 가득 차 있다. 그 감정은 분노와 좌절의 감정이다. 하지만 우리가 어떤 감정들이 바람직한 감정일까 생각해 볼 때, 동정심을 바람직한 감정으로 선택하는 것은 지나치게 단순한 생각일 수 있다. 이미지를 통해 제공되는, 타인이 겪는 고통에 대한 가상의 근접성은 멀리 떨어진 곳에서 고통을 받는 사람들(텔레비전 화면에 클로즈업되어 보이는 사람들)과 그 사람들을 볼 수 있는 특권을 지닌 시청자 사이에 일련의 연결고리가 있다는 사실을 암시해 준다. 하지만 이런 연결고리는 분명 허구적인 것이며, 우리의 실질적 권력 관계에 대한 또 하나의 신비화일 수 있다. 고통을 받고 있는 사람들에게 우리가 동정심을 느끼는 한, 우리는 그런 고통을 야기한 공범자가 아니라고 느끼는 것이다. 우리가 보여주는 동정심은 우리의 무능력함뿐만 아니라 우리의 무고함도 증명해 주는 셈이다. 따라서 (우리의 선한 의도에도 불구하고) 동정심은 부적절한 반응은 아니라고 할지라도 어느 정도는 뻔뻔스러운 반응일 수 있다. 전쟁과 악랄한 정치로 고통받는 이들에게 우리가 내미는 동정심을 한쪽으로 제쳐 두고, 우리가 누리는 특권이 그들이 받는 고통과 같은 지도상에 존재하며, 어떤 이들의 부가 다른 이들의 궁핍을 의미할 수도 있기에 우리의 특권이 우리가 상상하고 싶어 하지 않는 식으로 그들의 고통과 연결되어 있을지도 모른다는 사실을 숙고해 보는 것이 우리의 과제이며, 사람들의 마음을 휘저어 놓는 고통스러운 이미지들은 최초의 자극만을 제공할 뿐이다.

46 다음 중 빈칸 ⓐ에 올 수 있는 가장 적합한 것을 고르시오.

① 비애감
② 동정심
③ 무관심, 냉담
④ 무기력, 관성

| 정답 | ③

| 해설 | 빈칸 다음에 이어지는 'moral or emotional anesthesia'와 동격 관계이므로, anesthesia(무감각증)에 해당하는 ③ apathy(무관심, 냉담)가 가장 가까운 의미를 지니게 된다.

47 다음 중 본문의 내용과 가장 일치하는 것을 고르시오.

① 저자는 전쟁과 악랄한 정치로 야기된 고통에 대해 동정심을 보일 것을 촉구하고 있다.
② 섬뜩한 것을 지향하는 인간에 내재된 성향은 동정심과 마찬가지로 인간에게 자연스러운 것이다.
③ 다른 국가에서 벌어지고 있는 재난에 관한 언론의 정보가 늘어나면서 이를 지켜보는 청중들을 더 나은 세계 시민으로 만들어 주고 있다.
④ 상업적 가치 및 좀 더 자극적인 이미지의 추구로 작동되는 저널리즘은 현대적 경험의 본질적 특징에 해당한다.

| 정답 | ②

| 해설 | 본문은 전쟁과 같은 비극에 시달리는 이들에게 단지 동정심을 베푸는 것만으로는 충분하지 않다고 강조하고 있다. 동정심과 같은 감성적인 태도는 악인들도 보이는 것으로, 동정심의 이면에는 비극을 자신이 일으킨 것은 아니라는 결백과 비극에 자신이 할 수 있는 일이 별로 없다는 무능력을 보이는 일이라고 설명한다. 후반부에 그런 동정심을 제쳐 두고, 우리가 누리는 특권과 타인의 고통이 어떻게 같은 세상에서 발생할 수 있는지, 어떻게 누군가의 특권이 다른 이의 고통과 연결되어 있는지 고민하라고 강조하면서, 미디어에서 볼 수 있는 고통을 당하는 이들의 이미지는 그런 적극적 고민을 위한 도화선에 불과하다고 강조한다. 이런 관점에서 ① 이 글은 동정심을 촉구하는 글이 아니라는 것을 알 수 있다. ③ 미디어의 정보 증가로 미디어 시청자들이 세계 시민으로 변모하고 있다는 내용은 본문과 무관하다. ④ 저널리즘을 이끄는 것이 상업적 가치이며, 자극적 이미지라는 것 또한 본문의 내용과 무관한다. 정답은 ②로, 본문의 첫 문장의 "Sentimentality ... is entirely compatible with a taste for brutality and worse." 내용을 재진술한 것이다. 감상적인 감정(sympathy)이 무자비함을 즐기는 성향(innate tropism toward the gruesome)과 양립할 수 있다는 내용은, 이 두 가지가 인간에게 자연스러운 것이라는 보기 ②의 내용과 일치한다.

| 어휘 |
sentimentality ⓝ 감상적인 마음
compatible ⓐ 양립하는, 조화하는, 모순이 없는
canonical ⓐ 규범[표준]적인, 인정된; 정전으로 인정받는, 교회법으로 정해진
commandant ⓝ 사령관
be inured to - ~에 익숙하다, ~에 단련되다
passivity ⓝ 수동성
dull ⓥ 둔해지다, 약해지다 ⓐ (감각이) 무딘, 둔한, 어리석은, 우둔한
anesthesia ⓝ 마취, 무감각증
frustration ⓝ 좌절(감)
elect ⓥ 선출하다, 선택하다
imaginary ⓐ 가상적인
inflict ⓥ 고통을 주다, 형벌 등을 과하다, 괴롭히다
privileged ⓐ 특권을 가진
mystification ⓝ 신비화, 속임수
proclaim ⓥ 선포하다, 선언하다
impotence ⓝ 무기력
impertinent ⓐ 무례한, 버릇없는, 뻔뻔스러운; 적절하지 않은
if not [정도의 대조] - ~까지는 아니라 하더라도
set aside - (다시 필요할 때까지) ~을 한쪽으로 치워 놓다
beset ⓥ (위험, 유혹 등이) 괴롭히다, 포위하다, 봉쇄하다
destitution ⓝ 결핍
pathos ⓝ 연민의 정을 자아내게 하는 힘, 비애감
inertia ⓝ 관성; 무(기)력증
gruesome ⓐ 섬뜩한, 무시무시한
spectator ⓝ 관중
quintessential ⓐ 정수의, 본질적인

notoriously ⓐⓓ 악명 높게도; 주지의 사실로서
brutality ⓝ 잔인한 행위, 만행
embrace ⓥ 포옹하다; (생각을) 받아들이다[수용하다]
quantity ⓝ 양
rage ⓝ 격노, 분격
desirable ⓐ 바람직한, 호감 가는, 가치 있는
sympathy ⓝ 동정심, 연민
proximity ⓝ 근접성
grant ⓥ 주다, 인정하다, 허가하다
untrue ⓐ 사실이 아닌, 허위의
accomplice ⓝ 공범자
innocence ⓝ 결백, 무죄
inappropriate ⓐ 부적절한, 부적합한
stirring ⓐ 마음을 뒤흔드는
apathy ⓝ 냉담, 무관심
tropism ⓝ (생물의) 향성, (식물의) 굴성
calamity ⓝ 재앙, 재난
mercantile ⓐ 상업의

[48-50] 한국외대 2017

〈소년이 온다(Human Acts)〉는 주제의 중압감 때문에 쉽게 좌초될 수 있는 책이다. 오늘날의 유사한 사건들을 불러들이지도 그렇다고 회피하지도 않은 채, 소설가 한강은 대량 학살(1980년 5·18 광주 민주화운동 당시 행해졌던 무력 진압을 지칭함) 이면의 사회·정치적 촉매가 된 사건들을 깔끔하게 풀어 가면서, 그 사건이 가져온 오랜 기간의 해악적 결과를 그려 나간다. 하지만 주목할 점은 작가가 그것(대량 학살)을 피와 뼈의(폭력적) 소설로 만들고 있으면서도 이런 작품을 완성할 수 있었다는 데 있다. 작품 속 인물들은 종종 이름이 없는 '너'에게 말을 건넨다. 가끔 '너'는 죽은 사람이고, 또 때로는 독자이기도 하다. 하지만 빈번하게 그리고 매우 심란하게, '너'는 그 폭력 사태 이전의 사람들로, 이제는 돌이킬 수 없을 정도로 영영 추방된 사람들을 지칭한다. 이런 전위의 느낌이 가장 명확해지는 순간은 죽은 소년의 영혼이 자기의 썩어 가는 육신과 대화하는 장면에서다. 바로 이 장면에서 작품의 언어는 한강의 이전 소설인 〈채식주의자(The Vegetarian)〉의 고딕풍의 서정적 언어와 가장 가까워진다. 적어도 그 소년은 영혼을 지니고 있다. 다른 많은 희생자들은 자신에게 영혼이 있다는 사실을 더 이상 확신하지 못하며, 또한 자신들은 살아남았다는 수치심이 분명하게 느껴진다. 소설을 자신의 표현 형식으로 선택해, 소설이 가장 잘할 수 있는 일을 소설이 하도록 한 후, 독자들을 자신의 삶이 아닌 다른 사람의 삶의 한가운데로 데려가는 일을 하게 함으로써, 한강은 우리 시대의 가장 중요한 질문 중 하나를 우리에게 준비시킨다. 그것은 바로 "인간성이란 무엇인가? 인간성을 지키기 위해 우리가 해야 할 일은 무엇인가?"이다. 한강은 이 질문에 결코 답변을 내놓고 있지 않지만, 결코 위축되지 않는 증언의 행위가 가장 좋은 출발점으로 보인다.

48 다음 중 밑줄 친 Ⓐ의 의미와 가장 가까운 것은?

① '너'는 폭력적 대결이 낳은 자손이다.
② '너'는 이전의 자신들로 변화된 인물이다.
③ '너'는 영원한 변화 이전의 인물이다.
④ '너'는 다른 나라로 추방된 난민이다.

| 정답 | ②

| 해설 | 작품 속 '너'는 여러 의미로 사용되는데, 그 중에서 Ⓐ의 '너'는 "폭력 사태 이전의 사람들로, 이제는 돌이킬 수 없을 정도로 영영 추방된 사람들"이라고 지칭하고 있다. (광주에서 있었던) 대량 학살에 대해 타인으로서 슬퍼질지는 몰라도 주체로서 공감하며 아파하지 않는 것을 의미한다. 즉 대량 학살이라는 비극이 있기 전의 인물로 변화된, 그래서 광주의 문제에 대해 철저히 타자였던 우리를 지칭하고 있다. 정답은 ②이며, 이런 대중들의 모습을 바로 뒤에서 "dislocation(원래 있어야 할 자리에 있지 않는 상태인 전위를 의미함)"이라는 단어를 사용해 표현하고 있다.

49 다음 중 빈칸 Ⓑ와 Ⓒ에 올 수 있는 가장 적합한 것은?

① 확인 – 철회   ② 참여 – 증명
③ 전위 – 증언   ④ 공존 – 광경

| 정답 | ③

| 해설 | Ⓑ의 경우 "폭력 사태 이전의 사람들로, 이제는 돌이킬 수 없을 정도로 영영 추방된 사람들"을 지칭하는 단어가 온다. 대량 학살에 대해 주체가 아닌 타자로서의 모습을 의미하는 차원에서 "dislocation(원래 있어야 할 자리에 있지 않는 상태인 전위를 의미함)"이라는 단어가 적합하다. Ⓒ의 경우 작가가 특정 질문에 답을 하는 것이 아닌, 사건을 굽히지 않는 자세로 있는 그대로 서술하는, 즉 증언하는 행위를 통해 문제를 풀어 나가려고 한다는 뜻에서 'witness(증언)'이 적합하다.

50 다음 중 본문의 내용과 일치하지 않는 것은?

① 이 글은 문학 작품에 대한 비평문이다.
② 작품의 주제는 다소 심각하고 충격적이다.
③ 이 소설에서 한강은 이전 소설의 기괴하고 시적인 스타일을 지속하고 있다.
④ 한강은 하나의 사건을 분석하는 데 집중하며 중요한 질문에 명확하게 답하고 있다.

| 정답 | ④

| 해설 | 본문 마지막 부분에서 작가 자신이 질문에 결코 답변을 내놓고 있지는 않다고 했으므로, ④가 본문과 일치하지 않는다.

| 어휘 | founder ⓥ 실패하다[좌초되다]; 침몰하다 ⓝ 창립자, 창시자
under the weight of – ~의 중압을 받고, ~을 위해서
subject matter – (책·연설·그림 등의) 주제[소재]
invite ⓥ 초대하다; 요청하다; 불러들이다[자초하다]
shy away from – ~을 피하다   parallel ⓝ 유사점
neatly ⓐⓓ 깔끔하게, 말쑥하게   unpack ⓥ 꺼내다, (짐을) 풀다
catalyst ⓝ 촉매, 기폭제   massacre ⓝ 대량 학살 ⓥ 대량으로 학살하다
toxic ⓐ 독성의   fallout ⓝ 방사성 낙진, 부수적인 결과
address oneself to – ~에게 말을 걸다
disturbingly ⓐⓓ 걱정스러울 만큼, 동요시킬 만큼, 불안하게 할 정도로
irrevocably ⓐⓓ 변경할 수 없는   be exiled from – ~로부터 추방당하다
converse with – ~와 대화하다   rotting flesh – 썩어 가는 살덩이
gothic ⓐ 고딕양식의; 고트족의   lyricism ⓝ 서정적인 표현[서정성]
palpable ⓐ 만질 수 있는, 명백한   humanity ⓝ 인류, 인간, 인류애
unflinching ⓐ 변함없는, 굽히지 않는   offspring ⓝ 자식, 새끼
confrontation ⓝ 직면, 조우, 대결, 대치   refugee ⓝ 난민, 망명자
confirmation ⓝ 확인, 인준   withdrawal ⓝ 철회, 취소; 금단 현상
engagement ⓝ 교전; 참여; 약속, 업무; 약혼   attestation ⓝ 증명, 입증, 증거
dislocation ⓝ 탈구, 전위, 혼란   compatibility ⓝ 양립[공존] 가능성, 호환성
spectacle ⓝ 장관, (굉장히 인상적인) 광경   grotesque ⓐ 괴상한, 기괴한, 터무니없는

CHAPTER 04 언어

01	④	02	⑤	03	①	04	④	05	⑤	06	⑤	07	③	08	①	09	②	10	④
11	③	12	②	13	②	14	①	15	②	16	②	17	③	18	②	19	③	20	②
21	③	22	①	23	②	24	①	25	②	26	④	27	③	28	③	29	①	30	②
31	④	32	④	33	①	34	②	35	②	36	①	37	①	38	②	39	②	40	②

[01-02] 광운대 2015

여러 해 동안 언어 학습에 있어 시청각 자료의 활용이 통합되어 왔다. 사실 목표어의 청각 자료를 듣고 자신의 말을 녹음할 수 있는 기술은 1970년대부터 언어를 배우는 교실에서 널리 활용되고 있었다. 이후 언어 학습에 있어 수많은 혁신과 기술이 이루어져 왔지만, 카세트테이프 녹음기야말로 언어 학습에 가장 큰 영향을 미친 단일 기술이다. 청각 자료는 1990년대부터 온라인상에서 스트리밍 형태나 다운 가능한 파일의 형태로 쉽게 입수 가능하다. 웹 2.0 도구의 도입 이후 청각 자료는 다른 콘텐츠와 결합된 형태로 개인이나 기관을 통해 유통된다. 이처럼 기술적으로 까다로운 문제가 아주 흔한 일로 단시간에 이행된 것은 '팟캐스트' 덕분이다. 팟캐스팅의 영향력과 침투 범위는 광범위하며 매우 큰 영향을 야기하고 주장컨대 월드 와이드 웹에 비해 훨씬 더 빨리 이루어졌다. 이러한 영향은 팟캐스팅의 용도가 오락에서 정치 및 교육에 이르기까지 다양하며 일반 대중의 흥미를 끌 수 있다는 사실 덕분일 수 있다.

01 윗글의 주제로 가장 적절한 것은?

① 다양한 시청각 자료의 장단점
② 언어 교육에 있어 카세트테이프 녹음기가 미친 상당한 영향
③ 언어 교육에 있어 스트리밍 방식 또는 다운 가능한 파일 형태의 도입
④ 언어 교육에 있어 시청각 자료의 발전과 팟캐스팅의 출현
⑤ 시청각 자료의 보급과 사회 다양한 영역에 있어서 팟캐스팅에 대한 의존

| 정답 | ④

| 해설 | 본문의 전반부는 언어 학습을 위한 시청각 자료의 활용에 관해 말하고 있으며, 후반부는 팟캐스팅의 등장과 팟캐스팅이 미치게 될 영향에 관해 말하고 있다. 이 두 가지를 모두 포괄한 주제로는 ④가 가장 적합하다.

02 윗글에 주어진 빈칸 Ⓐ - Ⓑ에 들어갈 가장 적절한 표현을 순서대로 나열한 것은?

① ~에 의해 대체되다 – ~로 해석되다
② ~와 분리되다 – ~에 대해 반박이 이루어지다
③ ~로 제한되다 – ~에 있어 실질적인
④ ~에 관심이 있는 – ~의 영향을 받기 쉬운
⑤ ~와 결합된 – ~ 덕분이다

| 정답 | ⑤

| 해설 | ⓐ: 웹 2.0 도구의 등장과 함께 청각 자료가 다른 콘텐츠와 '결합된' 상태로 보급이 가능해졌다는 내용이 적합하다.
ⓑ: 빈칸 앞 문장에서는 팟캐스팅이 상당히 광범위하고 큰 영향력을 지니게 되었음을 말하고 있으며, 빈칸 뒤 문장에서는 어떻게 하여 그런 영향력을 지니고 있는지 말하고 있다. 따라서 빈칸에는 영향력을 지니게 된 것은 "~ 덕분이라"는 의미의 표현이 적합하다. 이러한 점들을 감안했을 때 답으로 가장 적합한 것은 ⑤이다.

| 어휘 | integrate ⓥ 통합시키다
target language ⓝ 목표어(외국어 학습에서 학습 대상이 되는 언어)
available ⓐ 이용 가능한, 입수 가능한
countless ⓐ 수많은, 무수히 많은
readily ⓐⓓ 손쉽게, 순조롭게
arrival ⓝ 도래, 도입
distribute ⓥ 유통시키다, 분배하다
combine ⓥ 결합하다
transition ⓝ 이행, 과도
technical ⓐ 기술적인, 전문적인
commonplace ⓐ 아주 흔한
impact ⓝ 영향
penetration ⓝ (세력) 침투, 확장
wide-ranging ⓐ 광범위한, 폭넓은
far-reaching ⓐ 지대한 영향을 가져오는
arguably ⓐⓓ 주장컨대, 거의 틀림없이
be attributed to - ~에 기인하다, ~ 덕분이다
entertainment ⓝ 오락
appeal to - ~의 관심[흥미]를 끌다
mass audience - 일반 대중
advantages and disadvantages - 장단점
substantial ⓐ 상당한; 실질적인
emergence ⓝ 출현
prevalence ⓝ 유행, 보급
replace ⓥ 대체하다, 대신하다
translate ⓥ 옮기다; 해석[이해]하다
separate ⓥ 분리하다, 나누다
argue against - ~에 대해 반대 의견을 말하다
restrict ⓥ 제한하다, 한정하다
liable to - ~의 영향을 받기[당하기] 쉬운

[03-04] 한양대 2011

군에서 관타나모 수용소의 수감자들과 관련해 "자해 행위"라는 표현을 사용하면, 이 표현은 우리 대부분이 "자살 시도"라고 부르는 것을 의미한다. 사실 "수감자"라는 단어가 사용되면, 이 표현은 우리 대부분이 "죄수"라고 부르는 것을 의미한다. "water boarding"이란 것은 처음에는 캘리포니아 해변에서 젊은이들이 하는 모습을 여러분이 지켜보는 어떤 것으로 들리지, 강제로 익사시키는 것과 유사한 상황을 만드는 고문 기술로는 들리지 않는다. 아마도 이보다는 덜 두드러질지 몰라도 우리 대부분에겐 가장 관련도가 높은 것을 들자면, 우리는 누군가 해고될 경우 "인원을 축소하다"라는 용어가 사용되었음을 듣는다. "인종 청소"는 추방에서 대량 학살까지를 포괄하는 말이다. 우리가 해야 하는 말 역시 중요하지만, 해야 할 말을 하기 위해 선택한 말 또한 마찬가지로 중요하다. 여기 주어진 예는 다른 방식으로 묘사된다면 우리가 별 매력을 느끼지 못할 것으로 보이는 주제에 관해 어떤 특정한 태도를 취하게 하려는 시도가 이루어진 사례이다. 말에는 상당한 설득력이 있으며, 또는 우리가 '수사적인 힘'이나 '감정을 표출시키는 의미'라고 부르는 힘을 가지고 있는데, 이들 '수사적인 힘'이나 '감정을 표출시키는 의미'를 풀어서 설명하면 수사적인 심상, 느낌, 감정적 연상 등을 표현하고 이끌어 내며 이를 통해 사람들의 태도, 의견, 행동에 영향을 주는 말의 힘을 말한다.

03 빈칸 ㉮에 가장 알맞은 것은 무엇인가?
① 이끌어 내다
② 갈취하다
③ 부추기다, 선동하다
④ ~의 대리 노릇을 하다

| 정답 | ①

| 해설 | 일반적으로 '(이미지, 심상 등을) 이끌어 내다'라는 의미로 elicit라는 동사를 사용한다. 그 외에의 extort나 instigate 등은 image, feeling, association 등의 단어와 같이 쓰이면 어색함을 준다. 따라서 답은 ①이 될 수밖에 없다.

04 본문에 가장 알맞은 제목은 무엇인가?
① 언어의 자의성
② 어떻게 말을 돌려서 표현할 것인가
③ 일상에서의 언어적 예의
④ 수사학적 측면에서 바라보는 언어를 통한 강압

| 정답 | ④

| 해설 | 본문에서 물고문을 water boarding이라고 부르는 것은 '고문'이라는 단어를 사용하면 거부감을 불러일으킬 수 있는 일에 직접적으로 '고문'이란 말을 쓰지 않음으로서 단어가 내포하는 의미를 흐리게 만들고 사람들에게도 실제보다 심각성을 낮춰 받아들이게 만드는 역할을 한다. 따라서 "여기 주어진 예는 다른 방식으로 묘사된다면 우리가 별 매력을 느끼지 못할 것으로 보이는 주제에 관해 어떤 특정한 태도를 취하게 하려는 시도가 이루어진 사례이다(The examples just given are cases of an attempt to get us to adopt a particular attitude toward a subject that, if described differently, would seem less attractive to us)."에서 '다른 방식으로 묘사'라 함은 고문을 고문으로 부르는 것을 말하고, '별 매력을 느끼지 못할 주제'라 함은 고문 같이 사람들에게 거부감을 불러일으키는 것을 뜻하며, '어떤 특정한 태도를 취하게 하려는 시도'라 함은 고문을 고문이라 부르지 않고 의미를 희석시키는 단어를 사용해 사람들이 심각성을 느끼지 못하게 하는 것을 의미한다. 이처럼 본질에서 벗어난 단어를 사용한 결과 사람들이 실제보다 심각성을 깨닫지 못하게 되는 것은 말에 '상당한 설득력(tremendous persuasive power)'이 있기 때문이며, 말이 사람의 사고를 규정하기 때문이다. ④에서 '언어를 통한 강압(linguistic coercion)'에서 coercion이란 단어가 사용된 이유는 바로 말이 지니고 있는 설득력이 강압적일 정도의 힘을 갖고 있기 때문이다. 그리고 '수사학적 측면(rhetorical dimension)'은 고문을 water boarding이라 하고 자살 시도를 자해 행위 정도로 말을 돌려 표현하는 것을 뜻한다. 본래 수사학이란 단어는 문장과 언어를 어떻게 활용해야 사상이나 감정을 효과적으로 전달할 수 있을지 연구하는 학문이지만, 의미가 변질되면 본질과 상관없는 미사여구를 뜻하게 되기도 한다. 즉, 보기 ④의 '수사학적 측면에서 바라보는 언어를 통한 강압'이 의미하는 것은 수사학적 표현을 활용해 다듬은 언어를 사용하여 사람의 사고를 본질에서 비껴가도록 특정 방향으로 강제하는 것을 의미한다. 따라서 본문의 제목으로 가장 적절한 것은 본문의 내용을 함축해 담고 있는 ④이다. ②의 경우 best around the bush가 의미하는 것은, 단도직입과 반대로 어떤 사항에 대해 말할 때 완곡하게 표현하거나 직접적으로 말을 못하고 빙빙 돌려말하는 것을 의미한다. 그런데 본문에서 자살 시도를 자해 행위로 부르고, 해고를 인원 축소로 부르는 것은 사실상 한글로 번역하면 차이를 느끼기가 쉽지 않지만 영어로 봤을 경우 해당 주제를 사람의 사고를 특정 방향으로 이끌기 위해 '다른 식으로 표현'한 것이다. 이는 '직접 언급하지 않기 위해 돌려서 표현'한 것과는 거리가 있다. 따라서 ②를 답으로 보기엔 무리가 있다.

| 어휘 | injurious ⓐ 손상을 주는　　　　　　　　detainee ⓝ 수감자, 억류자
water boarding – 물고문의 한 형태[판자(board)에 사람을 머리가 아래로 향하게 눕힌 다음 얼굴에 수건을 씌우고 수건에 물(water)을 부어 익사 직전까지 가게 하는 고문]
simulated ⓐ 모조의, 가장된
relevant ⓐ ~와 관련 있는　　　　　　　　downsize ⓥ (비용 절감을 위해) 인원을 축소하다
lay off – 해고하다　　　　　　　　　　　ethnic ⓐ 인종의
deportation ⓝ 추방　　　　　　　　　　genocide ⓝ 대량 학살
persuasive ⓐ 설득력 있는　　　　　　　rhetorical ⓐ 수사적인, 미사여구의

emotive ⓐ 감정을 표출시키는, 감정적인	**association** ⓝ 연상, 연관
elicit ⓥ 이끌어 내다	**extort** ⓥ 갈취하다
instigate ⓥ 부추기다, 선동하다	**surrogate** ⓥ ~의 대리 노릇을 하다
arbitrariness ⓝ 독단, 자의적임	**beat around the bush** – 에둘러 말하다
linguistic ⓐ 언어의	**etiquette** ⓝ 예의
dimension ⓝ 측면	**coercion** ⓝ 강압, 강제적 설득

[05-07] 한국외대 2006

프랑스 인지과학자 Franck Ramus와 그의 동료는 프랑스 가정에서 자란 아동은 확성기에서 들은 다른 언어를 구별할 수 있다는 점을 발견했다. Ramus는 흥미의 수준의 증거로 아이들이 공갈 젖꼭지는 빠는 속도를 사용해 네덜란드어의 문장을 들은 후 아이들이 확성기가 (네덜란드에서) 일본어로 전화했을 때 언어의 변화를 인식했다는 점을 발견했다. 그러나 놀라운 발견은 이들이 녹음을 거꾸로 틀 경우 이렇게 구별할 수 없었다는 점이었다. 다른 말로 하자면, 아이들은 거꾸로 튼 문장이 가지지 못하는 언어의 독특한 특성을 이해한다는 것이며, 이들은 그에 따라 두 언어의 차이점을 구별할 수 있다는 말이다. 더 놀라운 사실은 Marc Hause의 경우 Ramus가 인간의 아이에서 발견한 것을 동일한 절차를 사용하여 타마린 원숭이에게도 정확하게 같은 결과를 얻었다는 점이다. 원숭이들은 Ramus가 사용했던 동일한 문장을 들었을 때, 네덜란드어에서 일본어를 구별할 수 있었지만, 이것을 거꾸로 틀었을 경우 이러한 사항을 구별하지 못했다. 물론 원숭이와 아이 모두 언어 자체를 이해하지 못했지만, 이 결과는 이들이 소리의 조합과 리듬을 바탕으로 새로운 언어를 이해할 수 있다는 것을 드러낸다.

05
본문의 주제는 무엇인가?
① 인간 언어 간의 체계적 차이점
② 인간의 언어를 배울 수 있는 원숭이의 잠재된 능력
③ 인간과 원숭이의 근본적 차이점
④ 인간 아기와 원숭이의 언어 차별
⑤ 언어의 소리의 조합과 리듬의 중요성

| 정답 | ⑤

| 해설 | ⑤ 실험을 통해 드러난 내용을 바탕으로 글의 요지를 파악할 수 있다. 본문 마지막 문장인 "they(아이와 원숭이) parse out a new language based on its sound combinations and rhythms"에서 알 수 있듯이, 아이와 원숭이는 모두 소리의 조합과 리듬을 통해서 상이의 언어를 구별할 수 있다고 말하고 있다.

06
ⓐ, ⓑ, ⓒ, ⓓ, ⓔ 중에서 가리키는 것이 나머지와 다른 것은?
① ⓐ   ② ⓑ
③ ⓒ   ④ ⓓ
⑤ ⓔ

| 정답 | ⑤

| 해설 | 보기 ⓔ의 경우 인간 아이와 원숭이 모두를 지칭하는 반면, 나머지는 모두 인간 아이를 의미한다.

07 본문에 언급된 실험에서 발견된 결과가 아닌 것은?

① 유아는 네덜란드어와 일본어의 차이점을 인식할 수 있었다.
② 유아는 언어의 소리의 합성과 리듬에 주의를 기울인다.
③ 유아는 서로 다른 언어의 문법적 구조의 차이점을 구별했다.
④ 원숭이는 인간의 유아와 같은 동일한 언어 구별 능력을 보였다.
⑤ 원숭이는 문장을 거꾸로 틀 때, 서로 다른 언어를 구별할 수 없었다.

| 정답 | ③

| 해설 | 아이들은 소리의 조합과 리듬을 바탕으로 네덜란드어와 일본어를 구별했다고 언급되어 있으므로 보기 ①은 옳다. ①과 같은 맥락에서 보기 ②도 옳은 진술이다. 본문에서 아이들은 소리의 조합과 리듬에 대한 인식이 있음은 알 수 있지만, 여러 다른 언어의 문법적 구조를 구별할 수 있다는 내용은 없다. 보기 ③은 틀린 진술이다. 본문 마지막 부분에서 보기 ④의 내용도 확인할 수 있다. ⑤의 내용도 인간과 원숭이 모두에게 적용되는 내용으로 본문에 잘 드러나 있다.

| 어휘 | cognitive ⓐ 인식의　　　　　　　　　infant ⓝ 유아
　　　　loudspeaker ⓝ 확성기　　　　　　　　suck ⓥ 빨다
　　　　pacifier ⓝ 고무젖꼭지, 갓난아이에게 빨리는 장난감
　　　　startling ⓐ 놀라운, 깜짝 놀랄 만한　　　backward ⓐⓓ 거꾸로
　　　　lack ⓥ 부족하다　　　　　　　　　　procedure ⓝ 절차
　　　　parse ⓥ (문장을 문법적으로) 분석하다

[08-09] 중앙대 2008

언어 전문가들 — 단지 사용하는 우리와 같은 사람이 아니라 진짜 전문가 — 은 어느 종이 말을 할 수 있는지에 대한 열렬한 논의를 벌이고 있었다. 한쪽에선 단지 인간만이 대화를 할 수 있다고 믿는 쪽이다. 다른 한쪽이 말하길 그럼 돌고래와 고래 그리고 분명 놀라운 코코라는 고릴라는 어떤가? 코코는 적어도 1,000단어의 수화를 안다. 코코는 약 2,000 구어를 인식할 수 있다. The First Word라 불리는 새로운 책에서 Christine Kenneally는 언어에 대한 아주 복잡한 논의를 담고 있는데, 그 실험에서 과학자들은 수화를 알고 있는 두 마리의 수컷 원숭이를 함께 두었다. 사람들은 이 원숭이들이 자기 주인들에 대해 불평하기 시작할 것이라 기대했을 수도 있다. 그러나 아니었다. 그들은 미친 듯이 서로에게 그야말로 손으로 하는 고함치기 같은 수신호를 보내기 시작했는데, 결국에는 어느 편도 상대방의 말을 듣지 않는 것처럼 보였다. 그렇다면, 두 동물이 동시에 얘기하면서 상대방의 말을 듣고 있지 않다면 그들은 실제로 대화를 하고 있다고 할 수 있을까? 듣지 않고 말하는 것은 동물의 두뇌 신경망 어디에 속해 있다고 봐야 할 것인가? 듣지 않고 말하는 것에 대해 살펴보자. 많은 아내가 여기에 합당한 누군가를 생각할 수 있다. 10대들은 쉽게 듣지 않고 말한다. 그리고 10대의 부모도 그렇다. 또한 성공한 많은 정치인과 토크쇼 호스트도 마찬가지다. 우리는 앞으로 장시간 지속될 긴 정치 시즌을 앞두고 인간과 유인원을 구별하는 실질적인 요소는 듣는 능력이 덜 사용되는 능력이라고 과감히 말할 수 있을 것이다.

08 밑줄 친 ⓐ와 ⓑ에 들어가기에 가장 적합한 말을 고르시오.

① 잘 사용이 되지 않는 – 듣다
② 지나치게 사용되는 – 듣다
③ 잘 사용이 되지 않는 – 말하다
④ 지나치게 사용되는 – 말하다

| 정답 | ①

| 해설 | 실험에 등장하는 원숭이들은 상대방에 대한 언어 행위를 전혀 듣지 않는다. 이와 달리 인간들은 듣는 행위 자체는 가능하기 때문에 'capacity to listen'이라 표현하는 것이 옳다. 하지만 인간의 경우 이런 능력이 있음에도 다른 사람의 말에 경청하지 않으려 하므로 첫 번째 빈칸은 '덜 사용된 능력'의 'underused'가 가장 적절하다. 따라서 정답은 ①이다.

09 다음 중 윗글의 내용과 가장 일치하는 것을 고르시오.
① 실험에 참여한 두 남자 원숭이는 수화를 몰랐다.
② 실험에 참여한 두 남자 원숭이는 자신의 관리자에게 불평하지 않았다.
③ 인간을 제외한 다른 어떤 동물도 수화 어휘를 가지고 있지 않다.
④ 인간을 제외한 다른 어떤 동물도 천 개의 구어 어휘를 인식할 수 없다.

| 정답 | ②

| 해설 | "One might have expected these guys to start grousing about their keepers. But, no, they started madly signing at each other"에서 보기 ②는 본문과 일치하는 것을 확인할 수 있다. Koko의 예를 통해서 원숭이는 어느 정도 수화("Koko has a sign language vocabulary of at least 1,000 words. She can recognize about 2,000 spoken words")를 할 수 있다고 했으며, 본문에서 실험에 참여한 두 원숭이가 수화를 몰랐다는 내용은 없다. 나머지 보기는 모두 본문과 일치하지 않는다.

| 어휘 | intense ⓐ 강렬한, 치열한   debate ⓝ 토론, 의견, 논쟁거리
converse ⓥ 대화를 나누다   catalog ⓥ 목록을 작성하다, 목록에 싣다, 분류하다
reveal ⓥ 드러내다, 까발리다   ape ⓝ 유인원
grouse ⓥ 투덜거리다   keeper ⓝ 사육자

[10-11] 한국외대 2011

생후 첫해 동안 신생아들은 언어의 습득과는 직접적인 연관이 없을 것으로 생각되는 세 단계를 거친다. 우는 단계는 생후 2개월 정도까지 지속된다. 초기 옹알이 단계는 모음과 유사한 소리를 내는 것이 특징이며 생후 2개월부터 5개월까지 지속된다. 그리고 옹알이 단계는 음절과 유사하고 자음에 모음이 결합된 소리를 내는 것이 특징이며 생후 5개월부터 12개월까지 지속된다. 이러한 (아기들이 내는) 소리가 언어와 유사한 것이라고 묘사되는 점에 주목할 필요가 있다. 즉, 아기들이 내는 소리는 일반적으로는 언어의 초기 형태나 언어 습득을 위한 필수 전제 조건으로 생각되지는 않는다. 예를 들어 청각 장애를 지니고 태어난 아이도 옹알이를 하지만, 대략 생후 6개월 정도면 옹알이를 멈춘다. 청각 장애가 있는 아이가 장애가 없는 아이처럼 옹알이를 한다는 점은, 옹알이가 언어 습득을 위한 "연습"이 아님을 나타낸다. 하지만 이들 세 단계의 언어학적 위치는 현재로서는 여전히 잘 봐줘야 미해결된 문제로 취급된다.

하지만 초기 옹알이나 옹알이 같이 언어와 유사한 행동을 하는 것이 실제로 언어를 연습하는 것이 아니라면 대체 무엇인 걸까? 한 가지 가설은 인체가 성숙하면서 겪는 유전적으로 결정된 단계로 보는 것이다. 사실 특정 기술을 습득하기 위한 "연습"으로 보이는 것 중 상당수가 실제로는 유전적으로 부호화된 단계이며 그 특정 기술을 습득하기 위해 꼭 필요한 것은 아닐 수 있다는 증거도 있다. 예를 들어 어린 새들은 실제로 날기 전에 날개를 파닥이는 단계를 겪는다. 수년 전에 한 과학자는 날개 파닥임이 날기 위한 연습이라는 가설을 실험하기로 결정했다.

10 다음 중 본문을 근거로 삼아서는 해결될 수 없는 문제는 무엇인가?
① '바-바' 같은 소리를 내기 시작하는 아이의 대략적 나이는 몇인가?
② 아이에게 청각 장애가 있는지 없는지를 식별할 수 있는 시기는 언제인가?
③ '파'와 '아' 중에서 아이가 먼저 발음할 수 있는 것은 무엇인가?
④ 언어 습득 과정에서 옹알이는 어떤 역할을 하는가?

| 정답 | ④

| 해설 | 본문의 "아기들이 내는 소리는 일반적으로는 언어의 초기 형태나 언어 습득을 위한 필수 전제 조건으로 생각되지는 않는다(they are not generally thought to be either an early form of language or necessary prerequisites to language acquisition)"라는 말의 의미는, 아이의 언어 습득 과정에서 옹알이가 어떤 몫을 차지하고 있지 못하다는 의미이다. 따라서 답은 ④이다. ①의 경우, '바-바' 하는 소리는 자음과 모음이 결합된 소리이므로 생후 5개월에서 12개월 사이에 내는 소리이다. 이는 본문의 "그리고 옹알이 단계는 음절과 유사하고 자음에 모음이 결합된 소리를 내는 것이 특징이며 생후 5개월부터 12개월까지 지속된다(And the babbling stage, characterized by syllable-like consonant-vowed sounds, lasts from about 5 months to 12 months)"를 통해 유추할 수 있다. ②의 경우, 청각 장애가 있더라도 아이는 옹알이를 하다가 생후 6개월 정도엔 멈춘다. 따라서 6개월이 지나면 아이에게 청각 장애가 있는지를 알 수 있다. 이는 본문의 "청각 장애를 지니고 태어난 아이도 옹알이를 하지만, 대략 생후 6개월 정도면 옹알이를 멈춘다(even babies born deaf babble as infants, but they cease after about 6 months)"를 통해 유추할 수 있다. ③의 경우, '파'가 자음과 모음이 결합된 소리라면 '아'는 모음으로만 구성된 소리이다. 아이는 생후 2개월부터 5개월까지는 모음과 유사한 소리를 낸다. 이는 본문의 "초기 옹알이 단계는 모음과 유사한 소리를 내는 것이 특징이며 생후 2개월부터 5개월까지 지속된다(The cooing stage, characterized by vowel-like sounds, lasts from about 2 months to 5 months)"를 통해 유추할 수 있다.

11 본문 다음에 이어질 내용으로 가능성이 가장 높은 것은 무엇인가?
① 과학자들은 언어 습득과 비행 기술 습득의 유사성을 어떻게 입증했는가
② 과학자들은 일찍 일어나는 새들이 어떤 방법으로 날개를 퍼덕이기 시작하는지 입증하기 위한 실험을 어떻게 고안했는가
③ 과학자들은 이론을 입증하거나 이론의 거짓을 논파할 수 있는 실험을 어떻게 고안했는가
④ 과학자들은 특정 기술을 위한 연습과 언어 습득 간의 관계를 어떻게 입증했는가

| 정답 | ③

| 해설 | 본문 가장 마지막을 보면 한 과학자가 "날개 파닥임이 날기 위한 연습이라는 가설을 실험(to test the hypothesis that wing flapping is practice for flying)"하고자 했음을 알 수 있다. 즉, 가설이 수립되었고 이를 실험을 통해 증명하기로 했음을 의미한다. 따라서 이 다음에는 가설이 사실임이 입증되었다는 이야기 또는 가설이 거짓임이 입증되었다는 이야기 둘 중의 하나가 와야 한다. 그리고 가설이 사실인지 아닌지를 입증하려면 가설의 수립 여부를 증명할 수 있는 실험이 우선 확립되어야 한다. 따라서 답은 ③이 된다. ①의 경우, 본문에는 언어 습득과 비행기술 습득 간에 어떤 관계가 수립된 적이 없으므로 답으로 볼 수 없다. ②의 경우, 과학자가 증명하려 한 것은 '날개 퍼덕임은 날기 위한 연습'이라는 가설이지 ②에서 말하는 '일찍 일어나는 새들이 어떤 방법으로 날개를 퍼덕이기 시작하는지' 증명하려 한 것은 아니다. 따라서 답으로 볼 수 없다. ④의 경우, '특정 기술'이 무엇을 의미하는지 모호하며 직접적으로 본문과 관계된 내용도 아니다. 따라서 ④ 역시 답이 아니다.

| 어휘 | go through – ~을 거치다, 겪다　　　　acquisition ⓝ 습득
cooing ⓝ 초기 옹알이　　　　　　　 characterize ⓥ 특징짓다, ~의 특징이 되다
vowel ⓝ 모음　　　　　　　　　　　babbling ⓝ 옹알이
syllable ⓝ 음절　　　　　　　　　　consonant ⓝ 자음
prerequisite ⓝ 전제 조건　　　　　　cease ⓥ 멈추다, 그만두다
linguistic ⓐ 언어(학)의　　　　　　　open question – 미해결된 문제
hypothesis ⓝ 가설　　　　　　　　　determined ⓐ 결정된
human organism – 인체　　　　　　 encoded ⓐ 부호화된
flap ⓥ 날개를 파닥이다　　　　　　　probable ⓐ 개연성 있는, 사실일 것 같은
verify ⓥ 입증하다　　　　　　　　　falsify ⓥ 거짓임을 밝히다

[12-13]

비록 미묘하긴 해도, 남자와 여자의 언어 사용(의 차이)에 관한 생각은 많이 다양하다. 즉, 남자는 욕을 많이 하고 말할 때 세련미도 떨어지고 격식도 덜 차린다던가, 여자는 색 용어를 더 많이 알지만 남자는 도구 이름을 더 많이 안다든가, 여자는 수식어구와 약칭을 더 많이 쓰는 데 반해, 남자는 회의나 다른 직업적 사정에 따라서 여성보다 말을 더 많이 하고 여성들이 말하는 중간에 말을 더 많이 끊는다든지 등의 생각을 말한다. 분명히 말하면 이 같은 고정관념에는 믿을 만한 구석이 없다. 언어적 행동에 영향을 주는 요소는 성별이라기보다는 성 역할이다. 성 역할이 변화면서 언어의 성별 차이는 자주 사라진다. 기계공으로 일하는 여성은 도구의 이름을 알고 있으며, 꾸미고 그리는 일을 하는 남성은 색 용어를 알아야 한다. 성 역할은 변화하지만 사라지지는 않는다. 예를 들어 비록 여성은 욕해서는 안 된다는 금기는 완화되었지만, 여전히 남학생이나 여학생 모두 남녀 혼성 무리에서 여성이 욕을 할 때 어느 정도의 불편함을 느낀다고 보고한다.

12 본문에 따르면 다음 중 "고정관념"의 예가 아닌 것은?
① 여성은 불쾌한 말을 써서는 안 된다.
② 남성은 여성보다 색 이름을 많이 안다.
③ 남자는 회의에서 여자보다 말을 더 많이 한다.
④ 여성은 남자보다 형용사와 부사를 더 많이 사용한다.

| 정답 | ②

| 해설 | 본문에서 열거된 여러 고정관념 중에서 "여자는 색 용어를 더 많이 안다(women know more color terms)"는 부분은 보기 ②와 정반대이다. 따라서 답은 ②이다.

13 본문에 따르면 남성과 여성이 사용하는 언어의 차이는 '성 역할'에 의해 영향을 받는다.
① 성별　　　　　　　　　　　　　② 말할 때의 성별 차이
③ 성 역할　　　　　　　　　　　　④ 여성이 욕하면 안 된다는 금기

| 정답 | ③

| 해설 | 본문에 "언어적 행동에 영향을 주는 요소는 성별이라기보다 성 역할이다(It's probably not so much gender as

gender roles that influence linguistic behavior)"라고 명시되어 있으며, 이는 다시 풀어쓰면 남성과 여성이 쓰는 언어의 차이는 성 자체에 기인한 것이 아니라 성 역할에 기인한 것이라는 의미이다. 따라서 ③이 답이 된다.

| 어휘 | subtle ⓐ 미묘한
swear ⓥ 욕하다
qualifier ⓝ 수식어구
context ⓝ 맥락, 전후 사정
stereotype ⓝ 고정관념
not so much A as B – A라기보다는 B
gender role – 성 역할(개인이 속해 있는 문화 내에서 남성이냐, 여성이냐 하는 범주에 따라 주어지는 지위와 이에 따르는 행동 양식, 태도, 성격 특성을 의미하는 학습된 역할)
taboo ⓝ 금기
discomfort ⓝ 불편함
adjective ⓝ 형용사

abound ⓥ 많다, 풍부하다
coarse ⓐ 천한, 세련되지 않은
diminutive ⓝ 약칭
interrupt ⓥ 말을 중간에 끊다, 방해하다
trustworthy ⓐ 믿을 만한

ease ⓥ 덜다, 덜해지다
offensive ⓐ 모욕적인, 불쾌한
adverb ⓝ 부

[14-15]

장애에 대한 지배적인 문화의 시각을 강화해 주는 언어를 살펴보는 것이 중요한 일이었다. 이러한 과정에서 유용한 조치는 ableist와 ableism이란 용어를 확립하는 것이다. 이러한 용어를 사용함으로 비장애인의 경험과 시각이 중심이 되어 지배하는 것에 대한 생각들이 조직화될 수 있다. ableism은 최근에 리더스 다이제스트 옥스퍼드 워드파인더에 실렸으며, '비장애인을 선호함에 의해 생긴 차별'이라고 정의 내리고 있다. 인종차별과 성차별의 정의로부터 추론하여, 나는 ableism 또한 사람의 능력이나 인격은 장애에 의해 결정된다거나 혹은 집단으로 장애가 있는 사람들은 비장애인에 대하여 열등한 지위에 있다는 생각을 포함한다는 것을 더하고 싶다. 아마도 일반 대중들 사이에서는 장애인 차별주의자라고 여겨질 수 있는 것보다 인종 차별주의자나 성차별적 언어에 대하여는 더 많은 동의가 있지만, 그것은 아마도 장애인에 대한 억압의 본질이 아직까지 널리 이해되지 않았기 때문일 수도 있다.

14 장애인의 차별에 대한 서술자의 입장을 가장 잘 표현한 것은?
① 비판적인 ② 냉소적인
③ 유연한 ④ 상상력이 풍부한

| 정답 | ①

| 해설 | 장애인의 차별은 인종차별이나 성차별만큼 바람직하지 않은 것임에도 널리 알려지지 않아서 마치 없는 것처럼 느끼고 있지만, 실상은 그렇지 않으며 다른 차별만큼이나 심한 것이라는 것을 드러낸 글이다. 그러므로 장애인의 차별에 대해서는 반대하는 비판적 시각임을 알 수 있다. 따라서 답은 ①이다.

15 글의 흐름상 빈칸 ⓐ에 알맞은 것은?
① 예외적인 ② 열등한
③ 기생의 ④ (본질과) 무관한

| 정답 | ②

| 해설 | 인종차별은 백인을 흑인보다 우위에 두면서 차별하는 것이고, 성차별은 남성을 여성보다 우위에 두고 차별하는 것이다. 그렇다면 장애인의 차별은 비장애인를 장애인보다 우위에 놓는 것이라 할 수 있다. 따라서 답은 ②이다.

| 어휘 | bring to light – 드러내다, 밝히다
land ⓥ 실리다
consensus ⓝ (의견의) 일치, 조화
parasitic ⓐ 기생의, 기생하는
disability ⓝ 장애
extrapolate ⓥ 추론하다
satirical ⓐ 풍자의, 풍자적인
extraneous ⓐ (본질과) 무관한

[16-17] 서강대 2011

갈릴레오가 그의 저서 〈별에서 온 메신저(Sidereus Nuncius)〉를 출판한 지 400년이 지났다. 그의 책은 우주에서 인류의 지위를 심대하게 낮추었으며, 동시에 인류에게 이전에는 교리의 눈가리개로 감추어져 있던 신비의 일부를 펼쳐 보였다. 그토록 작은 책에 갈릴레오는 창공이 육안으로는 보이지 않는 별들로 가득함을 보였으며, 달은 성직자들이 주장하듯 매끈하고 말도 안 되게 완벽한 구형의 물체라기보다는 울퉁불퉁하다는 사실도 밝혔으며, 달을 가진 행성이 지구만이 아니며 그렇기에 지구를 우주적 자만으로부터 강등되어야 할 대상이 되도록 했다. 엄청난 파괴력을 지닌 이 작은 책은 갈릴레오가 라틴어로 기술한 유일한 책이다. 다른 책들은 모두 토스카나어로 저술됐다. David Wootton은 재치 있게 도발적인 자신의 저서 〈갈릴레오: 창공의 관찰자〉에서, 갈릴레오는(혹은 갈릴레오의 주장에 의하면) 자신의 피렌체 동료들이 자신을 어떻게 생각하는지에 주로 관심이 있었다고 한다. 그러다 자신의 저서들이 금지되자 갈릴레오는 자신의 저서들이 유럽에서는 라틴어로 읽힐지 몰라도 이탈리아에서는 사람들에게 잊힐 것이 두려웠다. 토스카나어는 이탈리아 북방 전역에 거주하는 학식 있는 평신도들이 읽을 수 있는 언어였으며, 라틴어는 아리스토텔레스의 사고가 지배하는 대학에서 사용되는 언어였다.

16 다음 중 본문에서 밑줄 친 단어를 가장 잘 대체할 수 있는 단어는?
① 다른 곳으로 돌림, 전환
② 강등, 격하
③ 증대, 증가
④ 기본, 기초

| 정답 | ②

| 해설 | 밑줄 친 demotion의 반대말은 promotion으로 승진이나 촉진 등의 뜻을 지닌다. demotion은 승진이 아닌 '직위의 강등'을 뜻하며, 갈릴레오 이전 사람들은 지구가 우주의 중심이라는 자만(cosmic egotism)에 빠져 있었는데, 사실 지구도 한낱 행성에 지나지 않았다는 사실이 밝혀졌기 때문에 이를 '강등'이란 단어를 사용해 표현하고 있다. 따라서 정답은 ②가 된다.

17 다음 중 본문으로부터 추론될 수 없는 것은?
① 〈별에서 온 메신저(Sidereus Nuncius)〉는 우주에서 인간이 가진 최상의 지위에 대한 생각을 뒤엎었다.
② 갈릴레오는 자신의 피렌체 동료들에게 간과되는 것을 두려워했다.
③ 〈별에서 온 메신저(Sidereus Nuncius)〉의 출판은 우주에 대한 아리스토텔레스적 사고를 다시 부활시켰다.
④ 갈릴레오 시대의 라틴어는 주로 학문 연구와 저술에 이용되는 언어였다.

| 정답 | ③

| 해설 | 본문에서 보기 ①에 대한 내용은 "gravely downgraded humanity's place in the universe"에 나와 있다. ②의 내용도 본문 중간에 등장하는데, "Galileo feared they would be forgotten in Italy"라는 구절을 통해 알 수 있다. ④의 경우, 대학에서 사용되는 언어가 라틴어라는 마지막 문장을 통해 유추할 수 있다. ③의 경우 갈릴레오의 책이 아리스토텔레스가 갖고 있던 '지구는 우주 중심'이라는 생각을 되살린(rejuvenate) 것이 아니라 반대로 그런 생각을 뒤엎은(debunk) 것이므로 정답은 ③이 된다.

| 어휘 |
publish ⓥ 출판하다
gravely ⓐⓓ 중대하게, 진지하게
previously ⓐⓓ 이전에
doctrine ⓝ (종교의) 교리, 주의
firmament ⓝ 창공
invisible ⓐ 보이지 않는
rugged ⓐ 울퉁불퉁한, 주름진
candidate ⓝ 후보
cosmic ⓐ 우주의
Tuscan ⓐ 토스카나의 ⓝ 토스카나 사람, 토스카나어
be concerned with – ~에 관련 있다, 관심 있다
Florentine ⓐ Florence의 ⓝ 피렌체 사람
Aristotelian ⓐ 아리스토텔레스의
relegation ⓝ 강등, 격하
rudiment ⓝ 기본, 기초
supremacy ⓝ 최고, 우월, 패권
contemporary ⓐ 같은 시대의
medium ⓝ 수단, 매개물

astronomical ⓐ 천문학의
downgrade ⓥ 강등시키다
blindfold ⓝ 눈가리개
volume ⓝ 책, 권; 부피
be crowded with – ~로 복잡하다, 붐비다
naked eye – 육안
ludicrously ⓐⓓ 웃기게도, 어처구니없게도
demotion ⓝ 강등
egotism ⓝ 자만, 이기주의
laity ⓝ 평신도, 문외한
diversion ⓝ 다른 곳으로 돌림, (기분) 전환
accretion ⓝ 증대, 증가
debunk ⓥ 정체를 폭로하다
overlook ⓥ 빠뜨리고 못 보다; 너그럽게 봐주다
rejuvenate ⓥ 다시 젊어지게 하다, 원기를 회복시키다

[18-20] 성균관대 2006

모든 언어에는 '언급할 수 없는 특정한 말', 즉 점잖은 대화에서 사용할 수 없을 정도의 아주 강한 정서를 내포하는 단어가 있는 듯하다. 영어에서 바로 생각나는 첫 번째 단어는 물론 배변과 성의 내용을 다루는 단어이다. 돈은 또 다른 주제로 이것에 대한 언급이 특정한 방식으로 억제된다. 채권자가 청구서를 보낼 때, 이들은 바로 그런 이유에서 이것을 작성하는 것이지만, 실질적으로 돈을 절대 언급하지 않는다. 죽음에 대한 공포는 넓게 퍼진 상징되는 사물과 상징의 혼동의 관점에서 충분히 죽음과 관련된 단어의 공포로 전이된다. 그러므로 많은 이들은 '죽었다'라는 말 대신 '돌아가셨다'라는 표현으로 대체한다. 우리가 억제하는 말 중에서 특정 단어, 특히 종교적인 것은 성경의 권위를 지닌다. 하나님을 지칭하는 이름은 너무나 거룩하고, 악령을 드러내는 말은 가볍게 말하기에는 너무 두렵다는 감정이 존재하는 것처럼 보인다. 금언(금지된 말)은 이것이 노골적으로 성적인 문제를 논하는 것을 막는 의미에서 심각한 문제를 야기할 수 있다는 것 또한 사실이다. 그러나 더 강한 금언일수록 진정한 사회적 가치를 지닌다. 우리가 아주 화가 나 폭력을 통해 이를 표현할 필요성을 느낄 때, 이러한 금지된 말을 하는 것은 우리가 광포해지는 것의 상대적으로 덜 해로운 대체안을 제공한다.

18 본문에 따르면 채무자는 청구서를 보낼 때, 돈에 대해서 거의 언급하지 않는데, 이는 돈을 언급하는 것이 _____.

① 부도덕하기 때문이다
② 금언이기 때문이다
③ 법에 의해 금지되어 있기 때문이다
④ 프로답지 않기 때문이다
⑤ 관습이기 때문이다

| 정답 | ②

| 해설 | 'Money is another subject about which communication is in some ways inhibited.'에서 알 수 있듯이, 채권자가 돈에 대해서 언급하는 것은 '금기'시되기 때문이다.

19 빈칸에 적절하지 않은 것은?

① 돌아가셨다
② 떠나셨다
③ 불필요한 비용을 절감하다
④ 천국으로 가셨다
⑤ 쇠약하여 가셨다

| 정답 | ③

| 해설 | 죽음(death)을 나타내는 단어를 직접 언급하지 않고, 완곡어법으로 'pass away'와 같은 표현을 사용한다는 내용이다. 보기 ③은 '불필요한 비용을 절감하다'의 의미이고, 나머지는 모두 '죽다'를 의미하는 표현이다.

20 본문에 따르면 금기의 말은 _____.

① 남자만 사용한다
② 위기의 순간에 안전밸브로 작용한다
③ 친근한 의사소통을 조장할 수 있다
④ 세상을 이해하는 상상의 방법이다
⑤ 성에 대한 건설적인 논쟁을 장려한다

| 정답 | ②

| 해설 | 금언이 때론 사회적 가치를 지닌다고 본문 마지막에 드러난다. 폭력으로 이어질 수 있는 상황에서 상대적으로 덜 해로운 금언이 대안으로 작용한다고 말하고 있다. '위기의 순간에 안전밸브의 역할'을 한다는 보기 ②가 이와 같은 맥락의 진술이다.

| 어휘 | unmentionable ⓐ 말로 형용하기 힘든 ⓝ 언급할 수 없는 말
connotation ⓝ 함축
bill ⓝ 청구서
substitute ⓥ 대체하다
holy ⓐ 신성한
genuine ⓐ 진짜의
forbidden ⓐ 금지된
excretion ⓝ 배설물
confusion ⓝ 혼동, 당황, 혼란
reticence ⓝ 과묵
taboo ⓝ 금기
utter ⓥ 말하다
berserk ⓐ 미쳐 날뛰는, 길길이 뛰는

[21-22] 중앙대 2010

영어를 모국어로 쓰는 모든 국가 중에서 남아프리카 공화국의 상황은 상당히 독특하다. 영어는 이곳에서 사용 인구로 따져 봤을 때는 5위에 머무르는 언어이기 때문이다. 남아프리카 공화국 대다수의(3/4의) 사람들이 흑인인 상황에서, 영어는 소수 인종인 백인들 사이에서 사용되는 소수 언어이다. 또한 영어는 이곳에서 10% 미만의 사람들에게만 모국어임에도 불구하고, 정부 고위직이나 기업, 과학기술, 고등교육, 방송 등에서 영어의 위치는 지배적이다. 대부분의 남아프리카 공화국 사람들은 반투(Bantu)족 언어를 사용한다. 그러나 둘 중 한 명의 남아프리카 공화국 사람들은 영어를 어느 정도 안다고 추정된다. 아프리칸스어(Afrikaans)는 남아프리카 공화국의 수백만 시민의 모국어 또는 제2외국어이다. 남아프리카 공화국에서 영어가 성공한 데에는 몇 가지 다른 이유들이 있다. 한 가지 이유는 영어에 대한 태도에 긍정적인 변화가 있어 왔다는 점이다. 영어가 사실상 제도적으로 고착화되어 있고, 공용어로써 널리 사용되고 있다고 하더라도, 다른 언어가 특정 지위를 차지하도록 선택되어 있지 않다는 점이다. 영어를 지지해 주는 또 다른 이유는 영어를 사용하면 특정 아프리카어를 사용함으로써 야기되는 잠재적인 불화를 피할 수 있다는 사실이다. 민족성과 언어적 동질성은 강력하게 연관되어 있어서, 예를 들어 코사(Xhosa)족 언어를 사용하는 정치들은 줄루(Zulu)족 언어를 사용하는 이들의 지지를 잃게 될 수도 있다. 따라서 영어를 중립적 선택의 일환으로 선택하게 된다. 나아가 다양한 언어를 사용하는 다수의 흑인들에게, 아프리칸스어는 억압의 언어로 간주되어 왔다. 아직까지 아프리카 흑인들에게 영어가 인기 있는 이유는 언어에 대한 열광적인 감정이라든가 영어가 대변하는 문화에 바탕을 두고 있다고 보기는 어렵다. 오히려 이는 더 나은 미래에 대한 그들의 꿈이 실현되기를 바라는 소망에 기반을 둔다. 수많은 다른 나라에서 그러하듯이, 이곳 남아프리카 공화국에서도 식민지 시절의 언어인 영어가 어떤 면에서 자유와 세상의 창을 상징하곤 하는데, 이는 참으로 역설적이라고 할 수 있다.

21 윗글에서 논지의 흐름상 가장 불필요한 것을 고르시오.
① ㉮ ② ㉯
③ ㉰ ④ ㉱

| 정답 | ③

| 해설 | 위 문제는 논리적으로 잘못된 문장을 골라내라는 말이 아니다. 상대적으로 글의 흐름에 불필요한 문장을 찾으라는 것이 문제의 핵심이며, 이는 문제를 해결하는 과정에서 깨닫게 된다. 먼저 ①의 경우 남아프리카 공화국 사람들이 가장 많이 사용하는 언어에 대해 말하고 있다. 바로 다음 문장이 두 번째로 많이 사용되는 언어이므로 흐름상 ①은 반드시 필요하다. ②는 영어가 이곳에서 성공한 이유들이 있다고 말하면서, 이후 첫 번째 이유와 두 번째 이유가 잇달아 등장한다. ② 부분이 없다면 글의 흐름이 이상해질 수 있다. ③은 영어에 대한 이곳 사람들의 태도에 있어서의 변화를 예를 들어 설명하고 있는 부분이다. 그런데 영어 중심으로 태동의 변화를 설명하는 예로 적절하지 못하므로 삭제해도 상관없는 부분이다. 마지막으로 ④의 경우 이곳에서 영어가 인기 있는 이유는 ④의 바로 앞 내용이 아니라 바로 ④의 내용이라는 것이 글의 전개이다. 따라서 이 부분도 생략될 수 없다. 따라서 답은 ③이 된다.

22 윗글을 통해 추론할 수 있는 것으로 가장 적합한 것을 고르시오.
① 남아프리카 공화국에서 코사족 언어는 줄루족 사람들의 모국어가 아니다.
② 언어를 본래 사용하는 인구수로 따진다면 영어는 남아프리카 공화국에서 지배적인 언어이다.
③ 남아프리카 공화국에서는 영어와 코사족 언어가 가장 자주 사용되는 언어이다.
④ 남아프리카를 제외한 많은 국가에서 영어는 자유의 상징으로 여겨진다.

| 정답 | ①

| 해설 | 영어는 남아프리카 공화국에서 다섯 번째로 많은 인구가 사용하는 언어라고 했다. 따라서 ②에서와 같이 'dominant language'라고 할 수 없으며, ③의 내용도 맞지 않게 된다. 그리고 다른 나라와 마찬가지로 남아프리카 공화국에서도 영어가 자유의 상징으로 사용된다고 했으므로, except 대신 including과 같은 표현을 사용해야 한다. 답은 ①로, 본문에서 "인종과 언어적 정체성이 매우 강하게 묶여 있다(ethnicity and linguistic identity are strongly linked)"라는 표현을 사용했는데, 이는 인종마다 각각 다른 고유의 언어를 사용함을 말한다. 따라서 코사족 언어와 줄루족 언어를 사용하는 이들은 각기 다르며, 정치인이 한쪽의 언어를 사용하면 다른 쪽의 지지를 잃게 될 수도 있다고 본문에서 밝히고 있다.

| 어휘 | in terms of – ~에 의하여, 관하여
Bantu ⓝ (아프리카 남부, 중부의) 반투족
Afrikaans ⓝ 아프리칸스어 (네덜란드어에서 발달한 언어로 남아프리카공화국에서 사용됨)
mother tongue – 모국어
single out for – ~을 위해 선발[지목]하다
in practice – 실제로는
entrenched ⓐ ~에 자리 잡은
lingua franca – 국제 공용어, 동 지중해에서 쓰는 이탈리아어·프랑스어·그리스어·스페인어의 혼합어
potential ⓐ 잠정적인
ethnicity ⓝ 민족성
Xhosa ⓝ 코사족 언어
resort to – ~에 의지하다, ~에 호소하다
colonial ⓐ 식민지의

dominant ⓐ 지배적인
shift ⓝ 변화 ⓥ 방향을 바꾸다
status ⓝ 지위
institutionally ⓐⓓ 제도상으로
divisiveness ⓝ 불화
linguistic ⓐ 말의, 언어의, 언어학(상)의
Zulu ⓝ 줄루족 언어
oppression ⓝ 차별, 억압, 학대

[23-27] 서강대 2009

문화 제국주의는 비난을 받기에 너무나 뻔하고 쉬울 정도로 지나친 정치와 군사 제국주의보다 그 자체로 덜 명백한 경제 제국주의보다도 훨씬 더 미묘하다. 영어가 세계를 지배한다는 것은 정치적 주도자와 공모한 앵글로 색슨의 강대국에 계획적으로 조직되고 지지된다거나 자신의 초국적 회사에 의한 세계 경제 침투라고 말하는 것은 옳지 않다. "언어 전쟁"은 전쟁으로 좀처럼 간주되지 않을 뿐 아니라 어디서도 선포된 적이 없다. 주된 강대국의 군사, 외교, 정치, 경제적 전략은 연구된 후 비판될 수 있지만, 언어 전략은 두드러지지 않고 암묵적이며, 심지어 해롭지 않거나 존재하지 않는 것 같이 보이기도 한다. 나라들이 단일 언어에 의한 지배에 저항할 것인가?

23 본문의 주제를 가장 잘 설명한 것은?
① 세계 경제와 초국적 회사
② 영어의 세계 주도
③ 국제 관계에서 영어의 역할
④ 앵글로 색슨의 힘

| 정답 | ②

| 해설 | 문화 제국주의 중 특히 영어의 세계 지배를 다루는 내용을 주제의 폭을 좁히고 있다. 글의 도입부에서 정치·군사 제국주의와 다른 문화 제국주의를 언급한 후 그중에서도 영어의 세계 지배로 그 주제의 폭을 좁히고 있다. 따라서 정답은 ②이다.

24
본문의 요지는 _____ 에 의해서 주로 뒷받침되고 있다.
① 비교
② 예시
③ 인과
④ 일화

| 정답 | ①

| 해설 | 기존의 제국주의와 비교하면서 문화 제국주의 중 문화 제국주의의 특징을 언급하고 있다.

25
본문에 따르면 다음 중 옳은 것은?
① 주된 강대국의 군사적·외교적 제국주의는 공공연하게 비판하기 힘들다.
② 인간의 문명은 언어 전쟁을 겪은 적이 없다.
③ 경제 정책은 언어 정책보다 더 뚜렷하다.
④ 점차적으로 증가하는 영어의 중요성은 세계 경제 지배를 위한 영어권 국가가 세운 계획의 일부분이다.

| 정답 | ③

| 해설 | 본문에서 군사 및 외교 제국주의의 경우 'obvious and easy to denounce'라고 했으므로 보기 ①은 잘못된 진술이다. 보기 ②와 ④ 또한 본문과 일치하지 않는다. 보기 ③의 경우 "The military, diplomatic, political and economic strategies of the major powers can be studied and criticized, but linguistic strategies seem to be inconspicuous and tacit, even innocent or nonexistent."로 보아 옳은 진술이다.

26
밑줄 친 ⓐ inconspicuous와 가장 근접한 뜻을 가진 것은?
① 범상하지 않은
② 쉽사리 믿지 않는
③ 버릇없는
④ 남의 눈을 끌지 않는

| 정답 | ④

| 해설 | 'inconspicuous'라는 표현을 몰랐어도 A and B가 A=B임을 활용하여 바로 뒤에 이어지는 tacit과 동의어를 고르는 문제로 이해할 수 있다. 보기 ④가 가장 근접한 의미를 전달한다.

27
㉮에 들어갈 가장 적절한 단어는?
① (stand) for: ~을 나타내다, 의미하다
② (stand) by: 방관하다, 대기하다
③ (stand) up to: ~에 용감히 맞서다
④ (stand) up for: ~을 옹호하다

| 정답 | ③

| 해설 | 문화 제국주의 언어 전략은 'inconspicuous'하다고 했다. 그러므로 다른 나라들이 단일어에 의한 지배에 맞설 저항할 수 있을지 묻는 내용이다. 따라서 보기 ③ 'stand up to'가 가장 적절하다.

| 어휘 | imperialism ⓝ 제국주의
subtle ⓐ 미묘한
tangible ⓐ 만질 수 있는, 실제의
denounce ⓥ 비판하다
deliberately ⓐⓓ 의도적으로
initiative ⓝ 창의력
penetration ⓝ 통찰력
transnational ⓐ 범국가적인
firm ⓝ 회사
tacit ⓐ 암묵의

[28-29] 한국외대 2007

1969년 달에서 닐 암스트롱이 말한 유명한 첫 마디는 "(한) 사람을 위한 작은 한 걸음이지만 인류를 위한 거대한 진보이다"이다. 그러나 정말 이렇게 말한 것이었나? 문법학자들은 오랫동안 세계적으로 이렇게 중요한 순간에 문법적 실수에 의해서 오점이 생겼다고 오랫동안 불편함을 드러냈는데, 주장하길 '인간' 앞에 '한'이 있어야 했다고 말한다. 암스트롱은 오랫동안 그가 '한'을 실질적으로 말했다고 주장했지만, 녹취는 이를 뒷받침하지 못한다. 이 기록을 바로 잡기 위해서 시드니에 기반을 둔 컴퓨터 프로그래머인 Peter Shann Ford는 자신의 최첨단 탐지 작업을 실행했다. 일반적으로 마비된 사람들용의 신경 기반으로 목소리를 분석하는 고도 소프트웨어로 NASA의 기록을 분석한 후 Ford는 들리지 않던 단어를 발견했다. 암스트롱은 실제로 "한 인간을 위한 작은 한 걸음"을 말했지만, Ford에 따르면 '한'이란 단어는 단지 35밀리세컨드만 지속되었다고 한다. Roger Launius는 워싱턴에서 항공 우주 박물관의 우주 역사 부서의 의장으로 "전 세계 역사에서 이것은 아마도 그리 중요하지 않을 것이다. 그러나 그가 말했다고 생각한 것이 실질적으로 그가 말했다는 것과 그 당시의 전자 및 통신 시스템의 특성으로 인해, 이것이 들리지 않았다는 것을 알게 되어 기쁘다."라고 말했다.

28 밑줄 친 표현 [A] the acoustic record begged to differ와 가장 가까운 의미를 전달하는 것은?
① 그는 다른 방법으로 음성 레코드를 사용하기 위해 허락을 구했다.
② 그가 주장한 것은 문법학자가 주장했던 것과 달랐다.
③ 그의 주장은 음향 레코드가 나타냈던 것과는 달랐다.
④ 음향 레코드는 그의 말을 인식하기에 충분히 분명하지 않았다.
⑤ 문법학자들은 음향 레코드가 틀렸다고 생각했다.

| 정답 | ③

| 해설 | 'beg to differ'는 '반대하다, 일치하지 않다'라는 의미이다. 이 표현을 모른다 하더라도 문맥을 통해 답을 유추할 수 있다. 논리적 반전을 이끄는 양보의 although를 기점으로 암스트롱은 자신이 'a'를 말했다고 주장하고 있으므로 뒤에선 이러한 점과 반대되는 내용이 전개되어야 한다. 따라서 정답은 ③이다.

29 문맥을 볼 때 [B]에 들어갈 가장 적절한 것은?
① 레코드가 감지하지 못했을 뿐이다   ② 아무것도 아닌 것으로 드러났다
③ 기다리기에 충분히 가치가 있었다   ④ 우리에겐 전혀 문제가 되지 않았다
⑤ 그의 주장을 받아들이기로 결정되었다

| 정답 | ①

| 해설 | 최신의 장비를 통해서 암스트롱이 'a'를 발음했음이 밝혀졌다. 암스트롱에 대한 문법 전문가들의 비판은 사실 그 당시의 장비가 아주 작은 소리의 그의 말을 잡아내기에 충분하지 못했음에 비롯된 것이다. '통과하다, 이해하다'라는 'get through'가 쓰인 보기 ①이 빈칸에 들어가기에 가장 적절하다.

| 어휘 | leap ⓝ 도약   annoy ⓥ 짜증나게 하다
mar ⓥ 손상시키다, 훼손하다   assert ⓥ 주장하다
acoustic ⓐ 청각의, 음향의   beg to differ – 반대하다, 견해의 차이를 보이다
set something straight – 무언가를 바로 잡다   high-tech ⓐ 첨단의
detective ⓐ 탐정의, 검출의, 탐지의   nerve-based ⓐ 신경에 기반을 둔
paralyse ⓥ 마비시키다   significant ⓐ 중요한

[30-31] 서강대 2017

언어의 음성 체계는 크게 두 가지의 범주로 분류된다. 즉, 자음과 모음(분절적 특성으로 알려진)이 그 하나이고, 강세와 리듬, 억양과 같은 좀 더 포괄적 측면(초분절적 특징 또는 운율체계라고 알려진)이 다른 하나에 속한다. 전통적으로 음성 체계는 음성 > 음절 > 단어 > 구절 > 문장 > 연장 담화라고 하는 구성요소적 방식으로 기술되고 교육되어 왔다. 분석적 관점에서 보면 이것이 타당해 보이지만, 언어 학습자들은 이런 방식으로 언어를 체득하지 않는다. 말을 하는 화자로, 우리가 말하는 것을 음성 단위로 혹은 음절 단위로 생각하려고 하는 순간, 우리의 의사소통은 무너지게 된다. 그래서 한 번에 한 가지의 음성을 마스터하여 최종적으로 음성들을 하나로 결합하는 상향식 접근방식이 하향식 접근방식으로 대체되어 왔다. 하향식 접근방식에서는 일련의 언어적 흐름 속에서 음성 체계가 다루어진다.

30
다음 중 빈칸 Ⓐ에 올 수 있는 가장 적합한 것을 고르시오.
① ~하지 않도록 ② 만약 ~ 아니라면
③ 만약 ~라면   ④ ~처럼, ~로서

| 정답 | ②

| 해설 | 우리가 하는 말을 음성 단위로 쪼개거나 음절 단위로 쪼개어서 생각하려고 하면 우리가 주고받는 대화는 제대로 되지 않고 중단된다는 내용이다. 여기서는 ② unless를 포함한 'not A unless B' 구문을 사용해, 'A 하려고 하면 반드시 B 하게 된다'는 의미를 형성한다.

31
다음 중 본문의 내용과 가장 일치하지 않는 것을 고르시오.
① 자연 담화에서 운율체계는 분절적 특성보다 더 중요한 것으로 간주된다.
② 자음과 모음은 음성의 분석적 관점에서 구성요소에 해당한다.
③ 언어의 기술과 언어의 학습은 서로 상당한 차이가 있다.
④ 의사소통의 중단은 언어의 분석적 성질을 보여준다.

| 정답 | ④

| 해설 | ① 일상의 대화에서는 우리가 하는 말을 음성이나 음절 단위로 쪼개서 생각하지 않으므로, 분절적 특성보다는 초분절적 특성에 해당하는 운율체계가 더 중요하다는 것을 알 수 있다. ② 분석적 관점에서 자음과 모음은 음성의 기본 구성요소에 해당한다. ③ 언어의 기술은 분석적 관점을 통해 상향식 접근방식을 취할 수 있지만, 언어의 학습은 일련의 언어적 흐름 속에서 음성 체계를 다루는 하향식 접근방식을 취한다고 마지막 부분에서 설명하고 있다. 정답은 ④로, 분석적 방식을 취할 때 의사소통이 중단되는 것이므로, 의사소통의 중단은 언어의 연속적 특성을 보여주는 것에 해당한다.

| 어휘 | consonant ⓝ 자음
vowel ⓝ 모음
segmental ⓐ (음의) 분절의
global ⓐ 전반적인, 포괄적인
intonation ⓝ 억양
suprasegmental ⓐ 초분절적인(강세, 억양 등과 관련된)
prosody ⓝ 운율체계; 시형론, 운율학, 작시법
in a ~ fashion ~한 방식으로, ~한 태도로
building block ⓝ 구성요소, 기초 단위; (장난감) 집짓기 블록
syllable ⓝ 음절
discourse ⓝ 담론, 담화
analytical ⓐ 분석적인

break down	– 고장 나다, 좌절되다; 분해하다; 나누다, 분류하다		
bottom-up approach	– 상향식 접근 방식	one at a time	– 한 번에 하나씩
string together	– 연결하다, 결합시키다	top-down approach	– 하향식 접근 방식
address ⓥ	(문제 등) 다루다, 처리하다; 연설하다; 호칭을 쓰다		
a stream of	– 끊임없이 계속되는	not A unless B	– A하려고 하면 반드시 B하게 된다
provided ⓒⓞⓝⓙ	만약 ~라면	disparate ⓐ	다른, 이종의

[32-34] 한국외대 2013

지금, "흰머리", "주름", "빙고 게임", "플로리다 주" 같은 것들을 떠올려 보라. 만일 당신이 지금 의자에서 일어나 주방으로 걸어갈 생각이라면, 당신은 이러한 단어를 읽지 않았을 때보다 읽었을 때 더 천천히 걷게 될 것이다. "흰머리", "주름", "빙고 게임", "플로리다 주"는 모두 노인에 대한 고정관념을 표현하는 것들의 일부이다. 뉴욕대학의 사회심리학자인 존 바그가 참가자들에게 이 단어 및 다른 단어를 마구 뒤섞은 문장 속에 삽입한 형태로 제시했을 때, 꽤나 주목할 만한 일이 발생했다. 노인에 대한 고정관념이 담긴 단어를 담고 있는 문장을 이리저리 뒤섞은 다음에 참가자들은 연구가 끝났으니 가도 좋다는 말을 들었다. 사실, 연구는 아직 끝난 상황이 아니었다. 실험자들은 참가자들이 실험실에서 부근의 승강기로 걸어갈 때 몰래 시간을 측정했다. 바그는 사회심리학 분야 연구에서 지난 수십 년 동안 수행된 연구 가운데 가장 흥미로운 연구 결과 중 하나인 이번 연구를 통해 노인에 대한 고정관념이 담긴 단어에 노출된 참가자들은 마구 뒤섞이지 않은 문장에 중립적 의미의 단어가 포함된 통제 환경하에서의 참가자들보다 승강기에 도달하는 시간이 훨씬 오래 걸렸음을 발견했다.

이전에 제시된 것과 마찬가지로 이러한 효과는 점화효과의 또 다른 사례이다. 사람들이 "플로리다 주" 및 "주름" 같은 단어에 노출이 되면, 이들 단어로부터 다른 연관 개념으로 활성화 현상이 확산되며, 그 이유는 이러한 단어는 노인에 대한 고정관념의 일부이기 때문이다. 바그의 연구에 따르면 노인에 대한 고정관념에 노출이 되면 "느림"이라는 개념이 점화되는 현상이 발생하며, 이렇게 이루어지는 활성화 현상은 행동으로 유출되어 들어가서 실험 참가자들의 행동이 느려지게 만든다. 따라서 심지어 의도적으로 생각하지 않더라도 느림에 관해 생각하는 것이 우리가 행동하는 방식에 영향을 미친다.

32 다음 중 본문의 제목으로 가장 알맞은 것은 무엇인가?
① 연구 참가자들을 실험에서 통제하는 방법
② 문장을 마구 뒤섞는 실험에서 언어 처리 과정이 작동하는 방식
③ 뇌 속에서 특정 단어가 조합이 되는 이유
④ 고정관념을 야기하는 단어를 보게 되는 것이 어떻게 행동에 영향을 미치는가

| 정답 | ④

| 해설 | 본문을 통해 노인에 대한 고정관념을 연상시키는 단어에 노출된 실험 참가자들은 그렇지 않은 대조군에 비해 행동이 노인처럼 느려졌음을 알 수 있다. 즉, 어떤 단어를 보고 형성된 개념이 다른 연관 개념을 활성화시키고, 그 결과 행동에도 영향을 주는 것이다. 따라서 답은 ④이다.

33 문맥상 위 본문보다 먼저 등장하는 지문에 담겨 있을 가능성이 높은 내용은 무엇인가?
① "점화" 효과를 실증하는 사례 ② 노인에 대한 여러 고정관념
③ 존 바그 교수의 프로필 ④ 존 바그의 실험 디자인

| 정답 | ①

| 해설 | "이전에 제시된 것과 마찬가지로 이러한 효과는 점화효과의 또 다른 사례이다(This effect, just like the one presented earlier, is another example of priming)." 여기서 말하는 '이러한 효과'가 본문 첫 번째 단락에 해당되는 사례이므로, '이전에 제시된 것'은 본문보다 먼저 등장한 점화효과의 사례일 것이다. 따라서 답은 ①이다.

34

문맥상 다음 중 빈칸에 가장 알맞은 것은 무엇인가?
① 실험 참가자들을 편견에 노출시키기
② 실험 참가자들의 행동이 느려지게 만들기
③ 고정관념을 더욱 강화시키기
④ 실험 참가자들이 노년에 관해 곰곰이 생각하게 만들기

| 정답 | ②

| 해설 | "노인에 대한 고정관념에 노출이 되면 '느림'이라는 개념이 점화되는 현상이 발생하며, 이렇게 이루어지는 활성화 현상은 행동으로 유출되어 들어간다(exposure to the elderly stereotype primed the concept 'slow,' and this activation leaked out into behavior)." 즉, 느림을 나타내는 단어에 노출이 되면 실제 행동에도 영향을 미치기 때문에, 실험 참가자들도 마찬가지로 '느려지는' 것임을 알 수 있다. 따라서 답은 ②이다.

| 어휘 | stereotype ⓝ 고정관념　　　　　　　　　embed ⓥ 끼워 넣다, 묻다
scramble ⓥ 뒤죽박죽으로 만들다, 마구 뒤섞다　surreptitiously ⓐⓓ 몰래, 남모르게
time ⓥ 시간을 측정하다　　　　　　　　　fascinating ⓐ 대단히 흥미로운
priming effect – 점화효과　　　　　　　　activation ⓝ 활성화
ponder ⓥ 숙고하다, 곰곰이 생각하다

[35-36] 한국외대 2014

비록 영어는 필리핀의 공용어이지만 영어에 비해 스페인어가 지닌 필리핀의 역사 및 문화적 중요성 덕분에 스페인어는 여전히 중요 언어로 취급된다. 사실 메스티조 가정이나 어린 학생들은 아직도 스페인어를 사용하며, 특히 세부・삼보앙가・바콜로드 주에서 많이 사용한다. 이는 스페인어가 처음 도입된 1565년부터 시작되어 미국의 패권하에 놓이게 된 20세기 초까지 지속된 필리핀의 식민지 시절 전체에 걸쳐 스페인어의 근원이 필리핀어에 남겨진 결과이다. 1990년에 필리핀에는 대략 2,700명의 스페인어 사용자가 있었다. 이는 필리핀에서 사용되는 170개의 언어 중 하나이면서 스페인어와 가장 흡사한 언어인 차바카노어를 사용하는 1,200,000명의 현지인들은 포함되지 않은 수치이다. 현재 필리핀에는 스페인어에서 온 차용어가 많이 존재한다. 문화적 근원과 역사적 이유때문에 필리핀은 법률 문서와 법정에서 스페인어를 사용하는 것을 지지한다. 하지만 스페인어는 1973년부터 공용어로서의 지위를 상실했고 1980년부터는 더 이상 학교의 필수과목이 아니다.

35

다음 중 본문의 제목으로 가장 알맞은 것은 무엇인가?
① 필리핀에서의 스페인어의 우세
② 필리핀 사람들의 국가 정체성을 위협하는 스페인어
③ 필리핀에서의 스페인어의 지위
④ 필리핀 사람들 사이에서의 스페인어 부흥

| 정답 | ③

| 해설 | 본문은 필리핀에서 스페인어가 어떤 위상을 점하고 있는지에 관해 설명하고 있다. 따라서 답은 ③이다.

36

다음 중 본문과 일치하는 것은 무엇인가?
① 스페인어는 필리핀의 특정 메스티조 가정에서 사용된다.
② 스페인어에서 온 차용어는 필리핀에서 드물다.
③ 스페인어는 미국의 패권 하에 놓이던 동안에는 금지되었다.
④ 스페인어는 필리핀 법정에서 배제되는 언어이다.

| 정답 | ①

| 해설 | "사실 메스티조 가정이나 어린 학생들은 아직도 스페인어를 사용하며(In fact, Mestizo families and young students continue to use Spanish)"에서 답은 ①임을 알 수 있다.

| 어휘 | **hegemony** ⓝ 패권　　　　　　**borrowing** ⓝ 차용어
compulsory ⓐ 의무적인, 필수적인　　**revitalization** ⓝ 부흥, 활성화
loanword ⓝ 차용어, 외래어

[37-38] 한양대 2015

피진어와 크리올어는 의사소통을 위한 언어를 공유하지 않는 사람들의 필요에 의해 생겨난 결과이다. 피진어가 이러한 목적을 충족시키기 위해 이미 존재하던 언어나 방언의 형태로 시작된 것이 아니라는 점에서 이들 피진어와 크리올어는 어느 한 국가의 언어나 국제적으로 통용되는 언어와는 차이가 있다. 피진어는 그보다는 두 언어가 특별하게 결합된 것이다. 로레토 토드는 피진어와 크리올어에 관해 다음의 사항을 언급했다.

피진어는 공통된 언어를 갖추지 못한 사람들 간의 제한적이면서 특정한 의사소통의 필요성을 충족시키기 위해 생겨난 주변적인 언어이다. 초기 접촉 단계에서 의사소통은 거래 정도로 제한되는 경우가 많고, 이 경우 구체적인 생각의 교환을 필요로 하지는 않으며 한 언어에서만 독점적으로 추출한 소규모의 어휘만으로도 충분하다. 피진어는 처음 접했을 당시의 언어의 구조와 비교하면 구문적으로 구조가 덜 복잡하면서도 덜 유연하다. 그리고 피진어의 특성 가운데 많은 부분은 접촉이 이루어진 언어들의 용례를 분명히 반영하고 있지만, 피진어 고유의 특성도 존재한다.

크리올어는 피진어가 어느 한 언어 공동체의 모국어가 될 때 생성된다. 피진어의 특징인 단순한 구조는 크리올어에도 이어지지만 크리올어도 모국어로서 인간 체험의 모든 영역을 표현할 수 있어야만 하기 때문에 어휘가 확장되며, 더 정교한 구문론적 체계가 형성되는 경우도 빈번하다.

크리올어는 종종 "진짜" 언어로 취급되지 않고 그 결과 열등한 언어로 여겨지기 때문에, 예를 들어 프랑스어와 영어도 피진어의 결과일 수 있다는 점에 주목할 필요가 있다. 즉, 프랑스어의 경우는 토착민인 갈리아족과 정복자인 로마인 사이의 접촉을 통해 형성된 언어이며 영어의 경우는 토착민인 앵글로색슨족과 잉글랜드 동부 해안에 정착한 데인족 간의 접촉을 통해 형성된 언어이다.

37

윗글의 내용으로 추론할 수 있는 것은?
① 프랑스어는 크리올어일 수 있다.
② 영어는 피진어일 수 있다.
③ 피진어는 철학적 생각의 교환을 촉진하기 위해 성장하였다.
④ 언어 공동체가 크리올어를 모국어로 받아들이게 되면 크리올어는 피진어가 된다.

| 정답 | ①

| 해설 | 두 문화가 만나 피진어가 형성되고, 피진어가 모국어가 되면서 크리올어로 변한다. 때문에 네 번째 문단의 "피진어의 결과(outcome of pidgins)"라 함은 바로 크리올어를 뜻한다. 피진어는 모국어가 아닌 언어이지만 크리올어는 모국어이기도 하다. 프랑스어는 갈리아 문화권의 사람들이 로마 문화와 접촉하고 나서 피진어가 형성된 이후에 모국어가 된 언어이다. 즉, 프랑스어는 피진어라기보다는 "피진어의 결과", 즉 크리올어이다. 따라서 답은 ①이다.

38 윗글의 내용과 일치하지 않는 것은?

① 피진어는 보통 두 개의 서로 다른 언어로부터 발전했다.
② 피진어의 어휘는 보통 서로 접촉하는 두 개의 언어로부터 획득된 것이다.
③ 크리올어는 보통 피진어에 비해 인간의 체험을 더 폭넓게 표현한다.
④ 서로 접촉 중인 언어의 구조는 대체로 피진어의 구조에 비해 더욱 유연하다.

| 정답 | ②

| 해설 | "한 언어에서만 독점적으로 추출한 소규모의 어휘만으로도 충분하다(a small vocabulary, drawn almost exclusively from one language, suffices)." 즉, 피진어의 어휘는 양쪽 언어로부터 획득된 것이 아니라 주로 한쪽으로부터 획득된 것이다. 따라서 답은 ②이다.

| 어휘 | **pidgin** ⓝ 피진어(주로 공통점이 없는 두 언어가 섞이면서 발생하는 일종의 사투리)
creole ⓝ 크리올어(피진어로 의사소통하는 사람들의 다음 세대가 쓰는, 피진어를 기반으로 한 언어)
marginal ⓐ 주변적인, 별로 중요하지 않은   **transaction** ⓝ 거래
exclusively ⓐⓓ 배타적으로, 독점적으로   **suffice** ⓥ 충분하다
syntactic ⓐ 구문론의, 통사론의   **speech community** – 언어 공동체
carry over – (다른 상황에서 계속) 이어지다, ~을 가져가다
lexicon ⓝ 어휘   **elaborate** ⓐ 정교한

[39-40] 성균관대 2016

사람들이 이해하기 매우 어려운 것으로 생각되는 개념 중 하나는, 언어는 좋거나 나쁜 특성을 가질 수 없다는 것이다. 즉, 다른 언어 체계보다 더 명확하고 논리적인 (혹은 더 아름답거나 더 추한) 언어 체계는 없다는 사실이다. 명확성과 논리의 차이점이 발생하는 것은 언어 그 자체가 아니라 언어를 효과적으로 다룰 수 있는 능력을 가진 서로 다른 개인에 있다. 일부 프랑스어 사용자는 명료성이 뛰어난 언어를 구사하지만, 다른 사용자는 매번 이해할 수 없는 횡설수설한 말을 내뱉는다. 그러나 우리의 칭찬이나 비난을 받아야 하는 대상은 화자이지 언어가 아니다.

너무나도 명백하게 근거 없는 생각인 프랑스어가 논리적이라는 생각은 어떻게 해서 프랑스에 그리고 어느 정도는 이웃 국가들 사이에서 그렇게 강력한 뿌리를 내리게 되었을까? 프랑스어에 대한 외부의 인식은 그다지 어렵지 않게 설명이 가능하다. 100년 전 유럽에서 발전했고 안타깝게도 오늘날까지 사라지지 않고 있는 국가의 고정관념과 연관이 있을 것으로 생각된다. 이탈리아어는 '음악적 언어'가 되었는데, 이는 의심할 여지없이 이탈리아 오페라와의 연관성 때문이다. 독일어는 프로이센의 군국주의로 인해 '거칠고 쉰 목소리의 언어'가 되었다. 투우사와 플라멩코 춤 때문에 스페인어는 '낭만적인 언어'가 되었다. 프랑스어는 데카르트와 같은 뛰어난 철학자 덕분에 거의 필연적으로 '논리적인 언어'가 되었다. 데카르트의 사고방식은 '실용적인 영국인들'의 사고방식과 크게 대조되는 것처럼 느껴졌다.

39

빈칸에 들어갈 가장 적절한 표현은 _____ 이다.
① 지도자의 통찰력
② 국가의 고정관념
③ 국민의 상상력
④ 국가의 경제
⑤ 국민의 희망사항

| 정답 | ②

| 해설 | 프랑스어가 왜 논리적인 언어로 인식되는가에 대해 설명하고 있는 부분이다. 빈칸 뒤에는 여러 국가들의 언어에 대한 인식이 '예시'로 등장하고 있으므로, 이를 포괄적으로 설명할 수 있는 표현이 와야 한다. 예를 들어 이탈리아는 오페라로 인해 음악적인 언어로 생각되고, 독일은 국군주의로 인해 거친 언어로 인식된다는 등 특정 국가에 대한 고정관념이 언어에 대한 인식으로 이어진 것을 알 수 있으므로, 정답은 ②가 된다.

40

저자에 따르면 영국인은 _____.
① 로맨틱한 사람이 될 수 없다
② 그렇게 현실적이지 않을 수 있다
③ 오페라를 못 부른다
④ 프랑스어를 할 수 없다
⑤ 논리적이지 않다

| 정답 | ②

| 해설 | 마지막 문장의 'pragmatic English'를 통해 영국인들에 대한 고정관념을 설명하고 있다. 실용적인 영국인이라는 것도 하나의 고정관념에 불과하므로 영국인들이 그렇게 현실적(실용적)이지 않을 수 있다고 저자는 생각하고 있다.

| 어휘 | clarity ⓝ 명료성, 명확성
lucidity ⓝ 명료, 명석; 평정
impenetrable ⓐ 들어갈 수 없는; 눈앞이 안 보이는, 불가해한
gibberish ⓝ 횡설수설
logicality ⓝ 논리성, 논리적 타당성
guttural ⓐ 목 뒷부분에서 나오는 (듯한), 후두음의, 쉰 목소리의
militarism ⓝ 군국주의
inevitably ⓐⓓ 필연적이다시피, 아니나 다를까
mode of thinking – 사고방식
stereotype ⓝ 고정관념, 정형화된 생각

marvellous ⓐ 기막히게 좋은, 경탄할 만한
mythical ⓐ 신화 속에 나오는, 가공의, 사실이 아닌
takc root – 뿌리를 내리다[널리 받아들여지다]
flamenco dancing – 플라멩코 춤
prestigious ⓐ 명망 있는, 일류의
pragmatic ⓐ 실용적인

CHAPTER 05 심리

01	①	02	④	03	③	04	⑤	05	④	06	①	07	③	08	②	09	③	10	①
11	②	12	④	13	①	14	②	15	④	16	④	17	④	18	②	19	③	20	④
21	④	22	④	23	②	24	②	25	②	26	①	27	②	28	②	29	③	30	②
31	③	32	②	33	①	34	②	35	②	36	②	37	③	38	②	39	④	40	③
41	②	42	④	43	①	44	④	45	⑤	46	③	47	②	48	①	49	③	50	①
51	④	52	③	53	④	54	④	55	③	56	④	57	②	58	②	59	②	60	②

[01-04] 성균관대 2008

행복의 심리에 대한 연구가 심술궂은 사람들 편을 들어주었다. (남의 불행을 보고 행복감을 느끼는 것이 사람들이 심술궂어서만은 아니라는 사실이 연구 결과에 의해 나왔다는 뜻 - 옮긴이) Kahneman과 Tversky는 흔히 일상에서 볼 수 있는 예를 다음과 같이 보여주고 있다. 당신이 급여를 확인한 후 5% 인상된 급여를 보면 기뻐하겠지만, 동료들에게는 급여가 10% 인상되었다는 사실을 알고 나면 그 기쁨은 곧 사라진다. 한 일화에 따르면, 여가수 Maria Callas는 자신이 노래하는 어떤 오페라 극장이건 그곳에서 가장 많은 돈을 받는 가수보다 자신에게 1달러 더 많은 돈을 지불해야 한다는 조건을 요구했다고 한다.

오늘날의 사람들은 역사상 그 어떤 시기보다 더 안전하고, 더 건강하며, 더 잘 먹고, 더 오래 산다. 하지만 우리는 뛸 듯이 기뻐하며 하루하루를 살고 있지 않다. 그렇다고 우리 선조들이 만성적으로 우울하게 살지만도 않았을 것으로 추정된다. 오늘날 서구 국가의 많은 가난한 사람들이 과거 귀족들은 상상도 못한 환경에서 살고 있다고 지적한다 해서 반발을 가져올 일은 아니다. 다양한 계층과 국가의 사람들이 자신들을 더 부유한 이들과 비교하기 전까지는 자신들의 운명에 대체로 만족해한다. 한 사회에서 발생하는 폭력의 규모는 그 사회의 가난과 관련 있다고 하기보다는 그 사회의 불평등과 보다 더 밀접한 관련이 있다. 20세기 후반에 나타난 제3세계의 불만과 그 이후 제2세계의 불만은 모두 제1세계의 대중매체를 통해 알게 되었기 때문이다.

01 다음 중 본문에 의하면 사람들이 행복하다고 느낄 수 있는 것은 오직 어느 경우겠는가?

① 사람들이 서로 비교할 대상이 없을 경우에
② 사람들이 자신이 노력한 것을 성취할 때
③ 사람들이 모든 것을 원할 때
④ 사람들이 더 이상 잃을 것이 없을 때
⑤ 사람들이 누군가와 사랑에 빠졌을 때

| 정답 | ①

| 해설 | 본문에 따르면 행복의 심리에는 어떤 것이 자리 잡고 있는지 연구해 봤더니, 거기에는 상대에 대한 비교를 통해 행복감을 느낀다는 사실이 밝혀졌다고 서술하면서, 여러 예를 들고 있다. 따라서 진정으로 행복하려면 비교 대상이 없을 경우에만 가능하다는 ①이 정답이 된다.

02

다음 중 행복에 대해 다른 말을 하고 있는 것은?

① 다른 사람의 눈을 통해 행복을 들여다보는 것은 얼마나 씁쓸한 일인가!
② 행복이란 다른 사람들의 불행을 생각하면서 생겨나는 기분 좋은 감정이다.
③ 성공만으로는 부족하다. 다른 사람들은 실패해야 한다.
④ 당신이 잘하는 그 어떤 것이라도 있다면 그것은 행복으로 이어진다.
⑤ 꼽추는 언제 기쁨을 느낄까? 바로 등에 더 큰 혹을 달고 다니는 꼽추를 볼 때이다.

| 정답 | ④

| 해설 | 나머지 보기들은 모두 자신과 상대방을 서로 비교를 하고 있으나, ④의 경우는 잘하는 것이 어떤 것이건 간에 자신이 잘하는 것이 행복으로 이어진다는 말이므로 비교 대상이 없어서 나머지 보기와 차이가 있다. 따라서 정답은 ④가 된다.

03

다음 중 빈칸의 (가)와 (나)에 들어갈 단어가 가장 잘 짝지어진 것은?

① 가난 – 독재
② 독재 – 잔혹 행위
③ 불평등 – 가난
④ 잔혹 행위 – 정치
⑤ 정치 – 불평등

| 정답 | ③

| 해설 | 바로 앞 문장을 보면 사람들이 자신들의 운명에 만족하다가도 더 잘 사는 사람들과 비교하는 순간 그런 만족감이 사라진다고 말하고 있다. 따라서 사회에서 폭행이나 폭동이 발생하는 것은 (나)보다는 (가)와 더 밀접한 관계가 있다고 했으므로, 사람들이 서로 비교하게 되는 것, 즉 '불평등(inequality)'이 (가)에 와야 하며, (나)에는 우리가 흔히 생각하는 이유인 '가난(poverty)'이 적합하므로 정답은 ③이 된다.

04

본문에 따르면, 다음 중 대중매체의 발달이 가져올 수 있는 것은?

① 일반 사람들의 사생활을 침해할 수 있다.
② 평등한 사회를 가져올 수 있다.
③ 엔터테인먼트 사업이 활성화되게 만들 수 있다.
④ 제3세계의 불만을 가라앉힐 수 있다.
⑤ 불행한 사람을 보다 더 많이 양산할 수 있다.

| 정답 | ⑤

| 해설 | 본문의 마지막 문장을 보면 제3세계와 제2세계 사람들이 제1세계의 대중매체를 들여다보면서 상대적 박탈감을 느끼면서 불만족이 생긴 것이라고 했으므로, 정답은 ⑤가 적합하다.

| 어휘 | bear out – ~이 옳음[사실임]을 증명하다
　　　paycheck ⓝ 급여, 봉급
　　　raise ⓝ 급여 인상
　　　stipulate ⓥ (계약서·조항 등이) 규정하다; 조건으로서 요구하다; 명기하다
　　　long-lived ⓐ 오래 사는
　　　presumably ⓐⓓ 아마, 추측건대
　　　glum ⓐ 우울한, 낙담한
　　　curmudgeon ⓝ 괴팍한 사람(보통 노인)
　　　co-worker ⓝ 동료
　　　walk on air – 기뻐 날뛰다, 들뜨다, 대단히 기쁘다
　　　chronically ⓐⓓ 만성적으로

reactionary ⓐ (정치 사회적 변화를 반대하는) 반동의, 보수적인	
aristocrat ⓝ 귀족	be content with – ~에 만족하다
affluent ⓐ 부유한	be related to – ~와 관련되어 있다
be attributed to – ~ 탓이다, ~ 때문이다	glimpse ⓝ 힐끗 봄, 짧은 경험[접촉]
hunchback ⓝ 꼽추	atrocity ⓝ (특히 전시의) 잔혹 행위

[05-07] 한국외대 2008

> 대중 연설에서 사람들의 관심을 끌기 위해 가장 빈번히 사용되는 방법은 아마도 '공통 기반(common ground)'이라고 알려진 기법일 것이다. 연설자는 자신과 청중 사이의 정치적, 종교적 배경이나 출생지, 민족성, 또는 특정 스포츠에 대한 관심 중에서 유사점들을 발견해 연설을 시작한다. 영국의 Margaret 공주가 켄터키 더비를 방문해 경마 우승자에게 우승컵을 수여해 달라는 요청을 받았을 때, 공주는 켄터키 더비와 영국 더비가 서로 유사하다는 점을 되살리면서 연설을 시작했다. 이렇게 함으로써 공주는 자신이 외국에서 건너온 공주라는 특이성은 줄이고 자신이 청중들과 공유하고 있는 경마에 대한 관심을 강조할 수 있었다. 이러한 형태의 연설자와 청중 사이의 '동일성 인식(recognition of sameness)'은 청중의 관심을 끌기 위해 흔히 사용되는 방법이다. 만약 연설자가 자신과 청중들 간에 공통으로 언급할 만한 사항이 거의 없는 경우에는, 차라리 다른 방법을 모색하는 것이 현명하다. 연설자가 공감대를 형성하기 위해 실제로 자신이 겪지 않은 특정 경험을 가진 것처럼 암시하는 것은 위험한 방법일 뿐 아니라 비윤리적이기도 하다.

05 다음 중 저자가 답변을 준 것이 아닌 질문은?
① 연설자와 청중 사이의 유사점을 드러낼 수 있는 방법은 어떤 것이 있는가?
② 영국 Margaret 공주가 켄터키 더비에서 연설을 위해 사용한 기법은 무엇인가?
③ '동일성 인식'이라는 방법을 사용하는 목적은 무엇인가?
④ 정직하지 못한 대중 연설의 한 종류에 대한 명칭은 무엇인가?
⑤ '공통 기반' 기법의 목적은 무엇인가?

| 정답 | ④

| 해설 | ①의 경우 'common ground' 기법을 예로 들었으며, ②의 경우 켄터키 더비와 영국 더비의 유사성에 대한 말로 연설을 시작해서 'common ground' 기법을 공주가 사용했다고 밝히고 있다. ③과 ⑤의 경우 모두 청중의 관심을 끌기 위해서라고 했다. 정답은 ④로, 정직하지 못한 연설에는 어떤 것이 있는지는 지칭하지 않았다.

06 다음 중 본문의 제목으로 적절한 것은?
① 대중의 관심을 얻는 방법
② 대중이 보이는 반응의 유형
③ 연설 주제를 배열하는 방법
④ 윤리적인 주제의 실용적 사용
⑤ 대중 연설을 마무리 짓는 방법

| 정답 | ①

| 해설 | 본문은 대중의 관심을 끌기 위해 대중 연설에서 주로 사용되는 공통 기반(common ground) 기법에 대해 설명하고 있으므로 정답은 ①이 된다.

07 다음 중 ⓐ에 들어갈 것으로 가장 적절한 것은?

① 마침내
② 예를 들어
③ 이렇게 함으로써
④ 반면
⑤ 불행하게도

| 정답 | ③

| 해설 | 빈칸 앞에는 공주가 켄터키 더비와 영국 더비의 공통점을 서두로 연설을 시작했다는 내용이고, 빈칸 뒤에는 이를 통해 결과적으로 청중과의 공감대를 이끌어 냈다는 내용이기 때문에 원인과 결과를 이어 줄 수 있는 연결어구가 적당하다. 따라서 정답은 ③이 된다.

| 어휘 | attention device – 주의를 끄는 장치
common ground – 공통되는 기반, 공통점
identify ⓥ 찾다, 발견하다; (신원을) 확인하다
similarity ⓝ 유사점
ethnic ⓐ 민족의
heritage ⓝ 전통, 유산
Kentucky Derby – 켄터키 더비(Kentucky주 Louisville에서 매년 5월에 열림)
thoroughbred ⓝ 순종
deemphasize ⓥ ~을 강조[중시]하지 않다
highlight ⓥ 강조하다
recognition of sameness – 동일성 인식
in order to – ~하기 위하여
practice ⓝ 실행, 실천; 관행, 관례
unethical ⓐ 비윤리적인

[08-10]

외향적인 사람은 전형적으로 사교적이고, 파티를 좋아하고, 친구들이 많으며, 같이 대화할 상대를 필요로 하며, 혼자서 독서나 공부하는 것을 좋아하지 않는다. 외향적인 사람은 흥분되는 일을 갈망하고, 모험을 즐기며, 가끔은 위험도 무릅쓰며, 순간적 충동에 따라 행동하기도 하며, 대개는 충동적인 사람이다. 외향적인 사람은 짓궂은 장난을 좋아하고 항상 준비된 답변이 있으며, 대개는 변화를 즐긴다. 외향적인 사람은 걱정 근심이 없고, 태평스러우며, 낙천적이고, "웃고 즐거워하는 것"을 좋아한다. 외향적인 사람은 계속 움직이면서 무언가 하는 것을 선호하며, 쉽게 공격적인 성향을 보이거나 화를 내는 경향이 있다. 전체적인 측면에서 외향적인 사람은 감정 통제가 잘 되지 않으며, 항상 신뢰할 만한 사람은 아니다. 내성적인 사람은 전형적으로 매우 수줍음이 많고 남들과 잘 어울리지 않는 그런 부류의 사람으로, 사색적이며, 사람보다는 책을 좋아한다. 내성적인 사람은 말수가 적고, 아주 가까운 친구가 아니면 사람들과는 거리를 둔다. 내성적인 사람은 미리 계획하고 행동하는 경향이 있으며, "돌다리도 두들겨 보고 건너는" 편이며, 순간의 충동을 신뢰하지 않는다. 내성적인 사람은 흥분되는 일을 좋아하지 않고, 일상적인 문제들도 적당히 진지하게 대하며, 잘 정돈된 삶의 방식을 좋아한다. 내성적인 사람은 자신의 감정을 잘 통제하고, 공격적인 태도로 행동하지 않으며, 쉽게 화를 내지도 않는다. 내성적인 사람은 신뢰할 수 있는 편이며, 다소 비관적이고, 도덕적 규범에 많은 가치를 부여한다.

08 다음 중 본문에서 유추할 수 없는 것은?

① 내성적인 사람들은 외향적인 사람들처럼 역동적이지 않다.
② 외향적인 사람들은 내성적인 사람들보다 더 신중한 경향이 있다.
③ 내성적인 사람들과 비교할 때 외향적인 사람들은 즉흥적이다.
④ 외향적인 사람들은 친구가 많다고 봤을 때 내성적인 사람들은 친구가 별로 없다.

| 정답 | ②

| 해설 | 본문은 외향적인 사람들과 내성적인 사람들의 성향을 서로 비교 분석한 것이다. 정답은 ②로, 신중한(cautious) 경향을 보이는 사람들은 외향적인 사람들이 아닌 내성적인 사람들이다.

09 다음 중 저자가 본문을 쓴 목적은?
① 외향적인 사람들과 내성적인 사람들의 정의가 다소 추상적이라고 말하기 위해
② 외향적인 사람들이 내성적인 사람들보다 더 좋은 성격을 가지고 있다는 것을 시사하기 위해
③ 내성적인 사람들과 외향적인 사람들은 거의 극단의 성격을 보인다는 사실을 암시하기 위해
④ 사람들은 외향성과 내향성을 모두 가지고 있다는 사실을 주장하기 위해

| 정답 | ③

| 해설 | 본문을 보면 외향적인 사람들과 내성적인 사람들은 성격이 정반대라는 것을 보여주고 있기 때문에 정답은 극과 극의 성격(polar characteristics)을 보인다는 ③이 정답이 된다.

10 다음 중 내성적인 사람의 성격이 아닌 것은?
① 남들과 어울리기 좋아한다.
② 책임감이 강하다.
③ 감정 표출을 거의 하지 않는다.
④ 도덕적이다.

| 정답 | ①

| 해설 | ①의 'gregarious'는 sociable(사교적)이란 단어와 동의어이기 때문에 외향적인 사람의 성격에 속하므로 정답은 ①이 된다.

| 어휘 | typical ⓐ 전형적인   extrovert ⓐ 외향적인
sociable ⓐ 사교적인   crave ⓥ 열망하다, 갈망하다
take chances - 위험을 무릅쓰다, 운에 맡기고 해 보다
stick one's neck out - 무모한 짓을 하다, 위험을 자초하다
spur ⓝ 자극   on the spur of the moment - 준비 없이 무작정
impulsive ⓐ 충동적인   practical joke - 짓궂은 장난, 몹쓸 장난
carefree ⓐ 근심 없는, 태평한   easygoing ⓐ 태평한, 게으른
optimistic ⓐ 낙천적인   aggressive ⓐ 공격적인
lose one's temper - 화내다   reliable ⓐ 신뢰할 수 있는
introvert ⓐ 내성적인   retiring ⓐ 남과 잘 어울리지 않는, 내성적인
introspective ⓐ 자기성찰적인   reserved ⓐ 말을 잘 하지 않는, 내성적인
well-ordered ⓐ 질서가 잘 잡힌   pessimistic ⓐ 비관적인, 염세적인
ethical ⓐ 윤리적인   spontaneous ⓐ 즉흥적인, 자발적인
gregarious ⓐ 남과 어울리기 좋아하는, 사교적인

[11-13]

뇌 가운데서 지각과 사고를 처리하고, "두려워해라, 아주 두려워해라!"라는 꼬리표를 그곳에 붙이는 역할을 하는 곳이 편도체 (amygdala)이다. 뇌의 중앙 부근에 위치하며, 아몬드처럼 생긴 신경다발인 편도체는 의식적 자각의 소재지인 대뇌 신피질 (neocortex)보다 더 오래전에 진화했다. 두려움에 대한 회로가 최초로 자리 잡게 된 데에는 그만한 이유가 있다.

잘 다듬어진 공포 반응을 갖지 못한 원인(原人)들은 모두 고도의 사고를 할 수 있도록 진화할 만큼 오래 살아남지 못했다. 바스락거리는 덤불이나 접근해 오는 그림자에 신속하고 직감적으로 반응하지 못한다면, 원인들은 육식동물의 저녁거리가 되어야 했기 때문이다. 구체적으로 말하면, 공포가 진화한 이유는 공포가 위협에 즉각적으로 반응하도록, 즉 호랑이가 달려들기 전에 맹수의 공격에 대해 깊이 생각하지 않고도 즉각적으로 반응하도록 해서 생존의 가능성을 높여 주기 때문이다. 공포를 감지하고 그에 대응하는 인간의 뇌는 궁극적으로 우리 자신에게 이익이 되는 방향으로 작동하며, 이를 통해 자신과 가족을 안전하게 지킬 수 있도록 해 준다. 진화적 관점에서 뇌의 공포 회로를 구축하는 것이 가장 중요했기 때문에 뇌의 인지적 능력보다는 뇌의 공포 반응 능력이 훨씬 더 강력해졌다. 공포는 이성을 ⓐ지배한다. 편도체가 우리의 논리적·이성적인 회로를 가로막기 때문이다. 그래서 이성보다 공포가 훨씬 더 강력한 것이다. 공포는 생명을 위협하는 상황들로부터 우리를 보호해 주는 기제로 진화했으며, 진화적 관점에서 이보다 더 중요한 것은 없다고 할 수 있다.

11 윗글의 제목으로 가장 적절한 것은?
① 뇌의 힘
② 공포의 힘
③ 공포의 열기
④ 우리에게 적대적인 공포

| 정답 | ②

| 해설 | 본문을 보면 공포를 관장하는 편도체(amygdala)가 이성을 관장하는 신피질(neocortex)보다 진화적 관점에서 훨씬 먼저 진화했기 때문에 더 강력한 힘(more powerful)을 가진다고 설명하고 있으므로 정답은 ②가 된다.

12 윗글의 내용과 일치하지 않는 것은?
① 편도체는 의식적 자각이 자리 잡고 있는 신피질보다 훨씬 전에 뇌 안에 자리를 잡았다.
② 공포 반응은 뇌의 한 기제로 생명을 위협하는 위험으로부터 우리를 지켜준다.
③ 공포는 이성보다 더 파괴적이고 육식성이기 때문에 이성보다 훨씬 더 강력하다.
④ 공포는 개인들이 위협에 즉각 반응하게 해서 생존의 가능성을 높여 준다.

| 정답 | ③

| 해설 | ①의 경우 본문 초반의 "this almond-shaped bundle of neurons evolved long before the neocortex" 부분에 나오는 내용이며, ②의 경우 본문 후반의 "It evolved as a mechanism to protect us from life-threatening situations" 부분을 통해 알 수 있다. ④의 경우 본문 중간의 "it promotes survival by triggering an individual to respond instantly to a threat" 부분을 통해 알 수 있다. 정답은 ③으로, 앞부분의 내용은 본문과 부합하지만 because 이하의 내용, 즉 공포가 파괴적이고 육식성이라는 부분은 본문과 전혀 무관하다.

13 빈칸 ⓐ에 들어갈 가장 적절한 단어는?
① 강화하다
② 전달하다
③ 인도하다
④ 지배하다

| 정답 | ④

| 해설 | 빈칸의 앞뒤 문장이 모두 '공포가 이성보다 더 강력'하다는 내용이다. 그리고 빈칸 바로 뒤의 접속사 as로 이어지는 부분은 주절에 대한 이유를 설명하고 있다. 공포를 관장하는 편도체가 이성적 회로를 방해한다는 것이다. 따라서 빈칸에는 공포가 이성보다 더 우위에 있다는 것을 나타내는 단어가 와야 하며, '지배하다, 무효화하다'라는 뜻을 지닌 ④의 overrule이 정답이 된다.

| 어휘 |
perception ⓝ 지각, 자각
amygdala ⓝ 편도체
evolve ⓥ 진화하다
circuitry ⓝ 전기 회로망
hone ⓥ (기술 등을) 연마하다, 갈고 닦다
rustling bushes – 바스락거리는 덤불
carnivore ⓝ 육식동물
trigger ⓥ 촉발시키다, 작동시키다
pounce ⓥ 갑자기 달려들다; 맹렬히 비난하다
faculty ⓝ 능력
standpoint ⓝ 관점

tag ⓥ 꼬리표를 붙이다
neuron ⓝ 신경
neocortex ⓝ 신피질
proto-human ⓝ 원인, 원시인
intuitively ⓐⓓ 직관에 의해
advancing shadows – 점점 다가오는 그림자
specifically ⓐⓓ 명확하게, 구체적으로 말하면
cogitate ⓥ 숙고하다, 명상하다
primacy ⓝ 최고, 으뜸
hobble ⓥ 방해하다; 다리를 절다, 절뚝거리다
overrule ⓥ 지배하다; 번복하다, 기각하다(=override)

[14-16] 숭실대 2013

우리의 과거 모습을 떠올려 보면 지금과는 꽤 차이가 있다. 우리는 오랜 세월 동안 우리의 성격과 취향이 얼마나 변했는지를 알고 있다. 하지만 목요일 일군의 심리학자들은 사람의 자아 인식에 관해 자신들이 수행한 연구에 관해 기술하면서, 우리들은 미래를 내다보면서 왠지 앞으로도 지금과 같은 모습을 유지할 것이라 기대한다고 밝혔다.

학자들은 이러한 현상을 "역사의 종언이라는 착각"으로 묘사했으며, 여기에 따르면 사람들은 "자신들이 미래에 얼마나 바뀌게 될 것인지 과소평가"하는 성향이 있다. 이들이 18세에서 68세 사이의 19,000명 이상의 사람들을 대상으로 수행한 이번 연구에 따르면 사람들의 착각은 10대 시절부터 은퇴 연령이 될 때까지 지속된다.

하버드 대학 소속 심리학자이자 이번 연구의 저자 중 하나인 다니엘 T. 길버트는 다음과 같이 말했다. "저처럼 중년인 사람들은 10대 당시 자신의 모습을 어느 정도 즐거움과 실망감이 뒤섞인 형태로 바라봅니다. 하지만 우리가 미래에 과거를 되돌아보면 우리 자신에 관해 정확히 같은 생각을 할 것이라는 사실을 우리는 결코 깨닫지 못할 것으로 보입니다. 나이가 몇 살이 되었건 우리는 지금 하는 말이 가장 중요한 말이라고 생각하지만, 나이가 몇 살이 되었건 우리는 그것이 잘못임을 깨닫게 됩니다."

다른 심리학자들은 목요일 학술지 "사이언스"에 발표되는 연구 결과에 흥미를 느꼈으며 이를 뒷받침하는 증거의 규모에 깊은 감명을 받았다고 밝혔다.

참가자들은 과거와 현재에 자신의 성격적 특성과 좋아하는 음식·휴양지·취미·밴드 등과 같이 선호하는 것들에 관해 질문을 받았고, 앞으로 어떨 것인지에 관해 예측을 해 달라는 요청을 받았다. 당연하게도, 연구에 참가한 젊은 사람들은 나이가 든 응답자들에 비해 지난 10년 동안 더 큰 변화를 보여줬다.

하지만 앞으로 10년 후에 자신의 성격이나 취향이 어떻게 변할 것인지에 관해 예측해 달라는 요청을 받았을 때, 일관적으로 모든 연령대의 사람들이 앞으로 닥칠 수 있는 변화에 관해 폄하했다.

따라서 일반적인 20세 여성이 향후 10년에 관해 예측한 사항은 일반적인 30세 여성이 자신이 20대 시절에 얼마나 변해 왔는지 회상한 것과 비교해 그다지 근본적으로 차이 난다고 할 수는 없다. 이러한 유형의 불일치는 60대의 참가자들도 포함해 전 연령대에 걸쳐 포괄적으로 지속되었다.

14 다음 중 (1)을 가장 잘 패러프레이즈한 것은 무엇인가?

① 우리의 미래는 결코 지금과 같이 않을 것이다.
② 우리의 미래는 지금과 많이 변하지 않을 것이다.
③ 우리의 미래에 있어 아직 최고의 순간은 오지 않았다.
④ 우리는 우리 삶의 최종적인 승자가 될 것이다.

| 정답 | ②

| 해설 | have the last word는 "토론 등에서 마지막 말을 하다"라는 의미로, 가장 마지막에 말을 한다는 것은 모든 상황을 포괄하는 '결정적 발언'을 한 다음에 토론을 마무리한다는, 즉 가장 중요한 취지의 발언을 한다는 의미이다. 이를 본문의 문맥에 맞게 해석하면, 우리가 미래에도 지금의 모습과 별반 다르지 않을 것으로 생각한다는 것은 지금의 모습이 최종적이고 궁극적인 형태이며, 앞으로도 내 모습은 바뀔 것이 없다고 생각하는 것이다. 그러므로 정답은 ②이다.

15 다음 중 (2)에 가장 알맞은 것은 무엇인가?

① 환상을 품다
② 과대평가하다
③ 걱정하다
④ 폄하하다

| 정답 | ④

| 해설 | 사람들이 자신의 미래 모습이 지금과 큰 차이가 없을 것이라고 생각한다는 것은 앞으로 자신에게 닥칠 수 있는 변화는 자신에게 큰 영향을 미치지 못할 만큼 별것 아닌 것으로 치부한다는 의미이다. 즉, 변화를 "경시하거나 폄하한다"는 의미이다. 따라서 답은 ④이다.

16 본문에 따르면 다음 중 사실이 아닌 것은 무엇인가?

① 과거를 회상하는 것은 쉬운 일이다.
② 미래를 예측하는 것은 힘든 일이다.
③ 우리는 삶에 있어 긍정적이면서 부정적인 부분을 모두 기억한다.
④ 삶은 50세 이후에는 거의 같을 것이다.

| 정답 | ④

| 해설 | 지금 우리가 미래의 자신의 모습을 상상한 것과 세월이 흐른 후 실제 자신의 모습을 비교해 보면 차이가 크며, 이는, 즉 우리는 지속적으로 변화를 겪는다는 것이 본문의 중심 주제이다. 이러한 변화 폭은 연령에 따라 차이는 있으나 ["연구에 참가한 젊은 사람들은 나이가 든 응답자들에 비해 지난 10년 동안 더 큰 변화를 보여줬다(the younger people in the study reported more change in the previous decade than did the older respondents)"]. 본문 어디에도 나이든 사람들은 거의 변화를 겪지 않는다는 내용은 없다. 즉, 변화는 정도 차이는 있을지언정 연령에 무관하게 일어나는 일이다. 따라서 답은 ④이다.

| 어휘 | somehow ⓐ 왠지
self-perception ⓝ 자아 인식
persist ⓥ 계속되다, 지속되다
have the last word – 마지막 말을 하다, 결정적 발언을 하다
intrigued ⓐ 흥미로워하는
trait ⓝ 특성
consistently ⓐ 일관되게, 지속적으로
play down – 폄하하다, 깎아내리다

prediction ⓝ 예측 discrepancy ⓝ 불일치, 차이
fantasize ⓥ 환상을 품다

[17-18] 중앙대 2013

사회적 순응을 연구하기 위해 필립 짐바르도와 크레이그 헨리는 (1977) 신문에 가상 교도소 실험에 참여하고자 하는 지원자들을 신문 광고로 모집했다. 지원자들에게는 무작위로 "죄수"와 "간수"의 역할이 할당되었다. 죄수와 간수 양 집단은 스탠퍼드 대학 심리학과 건물 지하에 배치되어 최소한의 지침을 받았다. 즉, 이들은 할당받은 역할을 맡으라는 지침을 받았고 여기에 간수는 "법과 질서를 유지"하라는 지침을 받았다. 몇 시간 만에 한쪽 집단의 행동이 다른 집단의 행동과 급격한 차이를 보였다. 간수는 경비가 매우 삼엄한 교도소의 간수가 취하는 전형적인 행동 양식과 태도를 취했다. 대부분의 죄수는 수동적이며 의존적이고 우울하게 변했지만 일부는 간수에 격분했다. 죄수들은 너무 극심한 고통을 겪은 나머지, 어떤 죄수는 36시간이 되기 전에 석방되어야 했고, 그 외 다른 죄수들도 원래 의도했던 2주의 기간이 끝나기 전인 6일 만에 석방되어야 했다.

전형적인 사회적 규범이 양 집단의 행위를 통제했다. 간수들은 자신들의 역할을 모방하면서 질서를 유지하기 위해 필요하다고 생각한 방식을 채택했다. 간수의 학대 대상이 된 죄수들은 교도소에서의 삶 하면 떠오르는 스스로의 이미지와 일치하는 태도를 취했다. 양 집단이 서로에게 적대적으로 변할수록 각자 다른 집단의 행위를 강화시켰다. 죄수들은 간수들이 비열하고 잔인할 것으로 예상했고 그런 추정에 따라 간수들을 대했다. 간수들은 죄수들이 반항적이라 예상했고 제멋대로의 행동을 예방하기 위한 행동을 취했다. 실험 참가자들의 인식 때문에 실제로는 위장에 불과했던 상황이 관련된 모든 이의 감정과 행동에 실제로 영향을 미치게 되었다. 이 실험이 나타난 바와 같이 사회적 규범에 대한 순응은 단순히 자신이 속한 집단으로부터의 사회적 압력만의 결과는 아니다. 사회내의 다른 집단의 영향이 규범에 순응하라는 압력을 확대하는 것이다.

17 윗글의 제목으로 가장 적합한 것을 고르시오.
① 수감자의 심리적 불안
② 전형적인 사회적 규범의 효능
③ 새로운 환경에서의 행동 변화
④ 사회적 행동에 있어 순응이 미치는 영향

| 정답 | ④

| 해설 | 본문은 스텐퍼드 대학의 심리 실험을 통해 사회적 규범에 순응하라는 압박이 어떻게 형성되고 있는지를 다루고 있다. "이 실험이 나타난 바와 같이 사회적 규범에 대한 순응은 단순히 자신이 속한 집단으로부터의 사회적 압력만의 결과는 아니다. 사회 내의 다른 집단의 영향이 규범에 순응하라는 압력을 확대하는 것이다(As this experiment shows, conformity to social norms is not simply the result of social pressures from one's own group; the influence of other groups in society magnifies the pressure to conform)." 즉, 규범에 순응하라는 압박은 자신이 속한 집단뿐만이 아니라 다른 집단으로부터도 내려지는 것이다. 그리고 구성원들의 사회적 행동도 이렇게 내려지는 압박의 영향을 받아 압박에 순응하는 행위를 하게 된다. 따라서 답은 ④이다.

18 윗글의 내용과 일치하는 것을 고르시오.
① 순응이 상황의 악화를 막았다.
② 참가자들은 전형적인 사회적 규범에 따라 행동했다.
③ 죄수 집단은 지침 대문에 수동적인 것처럼 가장했다.
④ 규범에 순응하라는 집단 내의 사회적 압력은 다른 집단과의 접촉을 통해 완화되었다.

| 정답 | ②

| 해설 | "전형적인 사회적 규범이 양 집단의 행위를 통제했다(Stereotypical social norms controlled the behavior of both groups)." 따라서 답은 ②이다.

| 어휘 | conformity ⓝ 순응, 동조성
assume ⓥ (권력·책임을) 맡다
stereotypical ⓐ 전형적인, 진부한
antagonistic ⓐ 적대적인
vicious ⓐ 잔인한, 포악한
by virtue of - ~에 의해서
magnify ⓥ 확대하다, 강화하다
inmate ⓝ 수감자, 재소자
mitigated ⓥ 완화[경감]시키다
mock ⓐ 가짜의
enrage at - ~에 격분하다
accord with - ~와 일치하다
mean ⓐ 비열한
unruly ⓐ 제멋대로의, 다루기 힘든
pretense ⓝ 위장, 허위
insecurity ⓝ 불안
efficacy ⓝ 효능, 효력

[19-20] 한국외대 2007

기억에 더 오래 남는 이미지일수록, 그런 이미지를 잊어버리기란 쉽지 않다. 하지만 의미 있는 정보라 하더라도 정보의 양이 방대한 경우에는 이를 모두 기억하기란 쉬운 일이 아니다. 그렇기 때문에 암기 대회 참가자들은 자신들이 암기할 이미지들을 가상의 경로를 따라 배치시킨다. 위치법(loci method)이라고 불리는 이 기법은 전해지는 바에 의하면 기원전 447년 고대 그리스 시인인 케오스(Ceos) 지방의 시모니데스(Simonides)에 의해 유래했다고 한다. 왕실 연회에서 지붕이 무너져 내리는 바람에 모든 참석자들이 목숨을 잃었는데 그때 유일하게 시모니데스만 살아남게 됐다. 시신들은 사고로 뭉개져 거의 알아볼 수 없을 정도로 훼손된 상태였지만, 시모니데스는 눈을 감고 저녁 식사 테이블 주위의 참석자들을 다시 기억해 내서 참석했던 이들의 목록을 복원할 수 있었다. 우리의 뇌는 이미지와 공간 정보를 처리하는 데 매우 우수하다는 사실을 그때 그가 발견한 것이다. 진화심리학자들의 이에 대해, 아마도 우리 조상들은 마지막으로 먹을거리를 보았던 곳이나 동굴로 다시 돌아가는 길을 기억하는 것이 매우 중요하다고 생각했기 때문에 이미지와 공간 정보를 인간이 잘 처리하게 된 것이라고 설명한다. 시모니데스의 발견 이후로, 위치법은 고대 그리스 전역에 걸쳐 연설과 글을 암기하는 수단으로 큰 인기를 얻게 되었다. 이에 대해 아리스토텔레스가 글을 쓰기도 했고, 이후 로마에서는 이 기억술에 대한 수많은 논문들이 쏟아져 나오기도 했다. 책이 인쇄되어 나오기 전 기억술은 문법, 논리, 수사학과 견줄만한 ⓐ 고대 교육의 주요 항목으로 간주되었다.

19 다음 중 ⓐ에 들어갈 것으로 알맞은 것은?
① 자극들에 수동적으로 반응하는 방법
② 원재료를 안전한 곳에 보관하는 방법
③ 마지막으로 먹을거리를 보았던 곳이나 동굴로 다시 돌아가는 길
④ 저녁 식사 테이블을 둘 장소와 식사를 하고 싶은 시간
⑤ 자신들의 어머니들이 안아 줄 때 웃음으로 대하는 방법

| 정답 | ③

| 해설 | ⓐ가 들어간 문장의 바로 앞 문장을 보면 인간의 뇌가 이미지와 공간 정보(image and spatial information)에 매우 뛰어나다는 설명을 하고 있다. 이에 대한 진화심리학자들의 답변에 ⓐ가 포함되는 것이기 때문에 그 내용은 이미지와 공간 정보가 포함되어 있어야 한다. 따라서 정답은 ③이 된다.

20 다음 중 본문에 언급되거나 함축되어 있는 것이 아닌 것은?

① 시모니데스는 머릿속으로 순간 이미지를 저장해서 상당한 정확도로 기억해 낼 수 있었다.
② 뇌의 우반구는 시각 이미지와 공간 정보에 관여한다고 알려져 있다.
③ 어떤 이들은 시각 이미지와 공간 정보를 이용해 기억을 되살릴 수 있다.
④ 아리스토텔레스는 기억법을 사용해 연설문의 일부를 기억했다.
⑤ 인쇄물이 출판되기 전에는 로마 학교의 사람들은 기억법을 이용했다.

| 정답 | ②

| 해설 | ①의 시모니데스 설명은 본문과 부합하며, 시모니데스가 이 기억법을 발견한 이후 사람들이 이를 이용했다고 나오므로 ③도 적절하다. ④의 아리스토텔레스에 관한 내용도 본문 후반부에 등장하며, 로마에서는 기억술에 관한 많은 논문(treatise)이 나왔다고 했으므로 학교에서 이를 사용했다는 내용인 ⑤도 적절하다. 정답은 ②로, 본문에서는 뇌의 우반구나 좌반구에 대해서 설명하고 있지는 않다.

| 어휘 | **resonant** ⓐ 공명하는, 울려 퍼지는, 반향을 일으키는
competitive ⓐ 경쟁하는, 경쟁적인   **imaginary** ⓐ 가상의
route ⓝ 경로
loci method – 장소법(기억을 돕는 전략의 하나로 기억을 위해 장소를 사용함)
originate ⓥ 기원하다
Simonides – 시모니데스(고대 그리스의 시인으로 경이로운 기억력으로 유명했음)
survivor ⓝ 생존자   **collapse** ⓝ 붕괴
royal ⓐ 왕의   **banquet** ⓝ 연회
mangle ⓥ 난도질하다, 엉망으로 만들다   **beyond recognition** – 알아보기 어려운
reconstruct ⓥ 재구성하다   **exceptionally** ⓐⓓ 매우, 특별히
spatial ⓐ 공간의   **presumably** ⓐⓓ 아마, 짐작건대
trick ⓝ 요령   **treatise** ⓝ 논문
consider ⓥ 간주하다   **staple** ⓝ 주성분; 주요 산물
on a par with – ~와 같은, 견줄 만한   **rhetoric** ⓝ 수사학
stimulus ⓝ 자극 (pl. stimuli)   **fidelity** ⓝ 정확도, 충실도; 충실함; (배우자에 대한) 정절
activate ⓥ 활성화시키다, 작동시키다   **retain** ⓥ 보유하다, 간직하다

[21-24] 이화여대 2009

청소년기의 자존감 상실은 심리학 분야를 주도하고 있는 Richard Robins 교수에게는 전혀 놀라운 현상이 아니었지만 "노년기의 자존감 상실은 매우 이례적인 현상"이라고 교수는 밝혔다. Robins 교수는 청소년기와 노년기에 접어드는 사람들 사이에서 나타난 자존감 수준이 서로 유사하다는 점에 특히 주목했다. "노년기와 청소년기 양 시기에는 갑작스레 자존감 상실이 축적되어 나타난다." Robins 교수가 말을 이었다. "이 시기에 임계 수치에 이르는 변화가 진행되고 있는 것이다." 우리 모두는 각각 하나의 개체이며, 그렇기 때문에 각 사람들의 자존감은 생물학적, 사회적, 상황적인 수많은 요인들에 의해 영향을 받지만, 우리 모두가 직면하는 특정 변화의 단계가 있는데, 그 단계들은 우리의 자아의식에 중대한 영향을 미칠 수 있다고 교수는 강조했다. "청소년기 아이들에게 있어, 이들이 느끼는 자존감은 종종 피상적 정보에 기반을 둔다." 교수는 이어 설명했다. "하지만 나이가 들어감에 따라 실제 성취한 것들과 다른 사람으로부터 받는 피드백에 기반을 두고 스스로의 자존감을 우리는 평가하게 된다."

21

다음 중 ⓐ를 대체할 수 있는 단어는?

① 분석했다
② 심사숙고했다
③ 비판했다
④ 조직했다, 체계화했다

| 정답 | ④

| 해설 | 'spearhead'는 원래 뾰족한 창의 끝부분을 지칭하는 단어로 동사로 사용되어 '주도하다, 선도하다' 등의 뜻을 지니며, 특정 분야에서 선봉에 위치하고 있다는 뜻을 나타낸다. 따라서 비슷한 단어로는 '체계화하다, 조직하다' 등의 뜻을 지닌 ④ organized가 정답이 된다.

22

다음 중 ⓑ에 들어갈 단어로 가장 적절한 것은?

① 기분이 언짢은
② 구역질 나게 하는
③ 새로운
④ 착취하는

| 정답 | ③

| 해설 | 바로 앞에 나온 내용과 역접의 접속사인 but으로 연결되어 있기 때문에 내용이 서로 반대라는 것을 알 수 있다. 따라서 앞에 나온 '청소년기의 자존감 상실은 놀랍지 않다(no surprise)'고 한 부분과 역접을 이루려면, '노년기의 자존감 상실은 놀랍다'라는 의미가 되어야 하므로 정답은 ③이 된다.

23

다음 중 ⓒ에 들어갈 것으로 가장 적절한 것은?

① 통계적 증거
② 피상적 정보
③ 또래의 반응
④ 특정 결과

| 정답 | ②

| 해설 | 역접의 접속사나 연결어(transition)가 직접 사용된 것은 아니지만 문맥의 흐름으로 볼 때 대조라는 사실을 알 수 있다. 즉, 청소년기와 노년기에 자존감을 가늠할 때 어디에 기반을 두고 있는지를 대조를 통해 나열하고 있다. 노년기에는 실제로 성취한 것들(actual achievements)과 남들의 평가(feedback from other people)와 같은 실질적이거나 현실적인 것에 기초하는 반면, 청소년기에는 비실질적이거나 비현실적인 것에 기초하는 경향이 있다고 서술하는 것이 자연스럽다. 따라서 정답은 ②가 된다. 참고로 보기 중 ③과 ④는 노년기에 해당하는 것이라고 할 수 있다.

24

다음 중 저자가 채택해서 사용하고 있는 글쓰기 방법이 아닌 것은?

① 인용문
② 비교와 대조
③ 일화
④ 원인과 결과

| 정답 | ③

| 해설 | ①의 경우 계속해서 Robins 교수의 말을 인용한 것으로 알 수 있고, ②의 경우 청소년기와 노년기의 자존감 상실에 대해 '비교'하면서도, 다른 측면이 있다는 사실을 서술해 '대조' 기법을 사용하고 있다. 원인과 결과에 대해서는 본문

중반에 "Everybody is an individual, so self-esteem can be affected"에 해당하는 부분에서 사용되었다. 따라서 정답은 ③ anecdote로, 일화에 대한 내용은 본문에 등장하지 않았다.

| 어휘 | self-esteem ⓝ 자존감, 자존심   adolescence ⓝ 청소년기
  spearhead ⓥ 선두에 서다, 선봉에 서다   specifically ⓐⓓ 구체적으로
  intrigue ⓥ 호기심을 자극하다   similarity ⓝ 유사점
  accumulation ⓝ 축적   critical ⓐ 중대한
  critical mass – 임계 질량(물리학에서 핵분열 물질이 연쇄 반응을 할 수 있는 최소의 질량을 의미하며, A에서 B로의 상태 변화에 필요한 최소한의 양을 의미함)
  transition ⓝ 변화, 전환   affect ⓥ 영향을 미치다
  situational ⓐ 상황에 따른
  passage ⓝ 단계, 경과(본문에서는 청소년기, 노년기 등을 겪는 것을 의미함)
  face ⓥ 직면하다   effect ⓝ 영향
  feedback ⓝ 반응   analyze ⓥ 분석하다
  contemplate ⓥ 숙고하다   criticize ⓥ 비판하다
  organize ⓥ 조직하다, 체계화하다   dour ⓐ 기분이 언짢은
  sickening ⓐ 구역질 나게 하는   novel ⓐ 새로운
  exploitative ⓐ 착취하는, 남을 이용해 먹는   superficial ⓐ 표면상의, 피상적인
  quotation ⓝ 인용   comparison and contrast – 비교와 대조
  anecdote ⓝ 일화   cause and effect – 원인과 결과

[25-27] 숭실대 2009

청소년기의 특징으로는 자아의식, 자기지각, 자기본위 등이 있다. 이와 함께 내적 갈등을 들 수 있는데, 이는 성인으로 성장하는 데 선행 조건으로 추측된다. 자기 주관을 내세우려는 고집스런 결의는 정서적으로나 경제적 측면에서 어른들의 지원에 계속 의존해야 하는 필요와 충돌을 일으킨다. 이 시기의 청소년들은 전형적으로 부모의 행동과 가치관에 의문을 제기하고 비판할 수 있는 권리를 요구하며, 자신들의 행동을 형성하려 하거나 통제하려는 부모의 시도에 분개한다.

청소년들이 부모의 가치관을 전면적으로 거부하는 것은 아니지만 전면적으로 수용하려 들지도 않는다. 때로는 조용하고 순응적인 10대라 하더라도 반항심을 외적으로 표출하는 형제자매와 마찬가지로 그들도 내적 갈등을 겪으며, 불안이나 발달 장애를 속으로 겪고 있을 수 있다. 부모와 정상적인 10대 자녀가 종종 충돌하는 것은 불가피하다.

10대들은 때로 변덕스럽고 무뚝뚝하다. 또한 10대들은 자신들이 마치 모든 것을 알고 있는 것처럼 행동하고, 어른들의 충고는 무시하거나 자신들만의 관점에서 상황을 바라보려고 하는 경향이 있다. 하지만 이들도 겉으로 보기보다는 내적 확신이 부족하다. 예를 들어, 10대들은 외모를 지나치게 중시하기도 한다. 괴상한 옷을 입거나 최신 유행의 헤어스타일로 꾸미는 것이 어른들에게는 관례를 비웃는 불쾌한 일로 생각될 수 있다. 하지만 이런 행동은 사실 주위 친구들의 관례를 수용하는 것이라고 보는 것이 합당하다. 자신들의 있는 그대로의 모습에 대해서는 자기 확신이 부족하기 때문에, 대부분의 10대들은 다른 아이들과 같이 옷을 입고 행동함으로써 느끼는 안도감이 필요한 것이다.

25

빈칸 ⓐ에 들어갈 적절한 표현은?

① as they seem   ② than they seem
③ as they are   ④ than they are

| 정답 | ②

| 해설 | 빈칸 앞에 less가 있기 때문에 비교급이라는 것을 알 수 있으며, 문맥상 10대들이 확신에 차 있는 것 같지만 실제로는 그렇지 않다는 의미가 되어야 하기 때문에, 사실을 말하는 are가 아닌 추측을 의미하는 seem이 되어야 한다. 따라서 정답은 ②가 된다.

26 다음 중 본문에 따르면 사실이 아닌 것은?
① 청소년기는 자기 확신의 시기이다.
② 청소년들은 자기 주관을 기어코 내세우려 한다.
③ 청소년들은 부모의 충고를 쉽게 받아들이지 않는다.
④ 청소년들은 정서적으로나 경제적으로 어른들에게 의존해야 한다.

| 정답 | ①

| 해설 | 본문에서는 청소년들이 겉보기와는 달리 속으로는 자기 확신이 부족하다고 서술하고 있다. 그렇기에 또래들과 같이 행동하고 옷을 입는다고 설명하고 있다. 따라서 정답은 ①이 된다. 나머지는 모두 본문에 등장하는 내용이다.

27 다음 중 본문의 ⓑ 'in'과 같은 의미로 사용된 문장은?
① 그 시간에는 나의 룸메이트가 안에 있었다.
② Simpson은 놀라서 그들을 바라봤다.
③ 몇 년 전에는 조깅이 유행이었다.
④ 어린 Raphael은 레오나르도 다빈치의 스타일로 작품을 그렸다.

| 정답 | ③

| 해설 | 본문에서 'in'은 '유행하고 있는'의 의미를 가진 형용사로 사용되었으므로 정답은 ③이 된다.

| 어휘 |
hallmark ⓝ 특징
self-consciousness ⓝ 자아의식
self-centeredness ⓝ 자기본위
inner conflict - 내적 갈등
stubborn ⓐ 완고한
conflict with - ~와 충돌하다
question ⓥ 의문을 제기하다
parental ⓐ 부모의
reject ⓥ 거부하다
rebellious ⓐ 반항적인
disorder ⓝ 무질서
inevitable ⓐ 피할 수 없는
sullen ⓐ 무뚝뚝한, 시무룩한
viewpoint ⓝ 관점
adoption ⓝ 채택
flout ⓥ 비웃다
adolescence ⓝ 청소년기, 사춘기
self-awareness ⓝ 자기인식, 자기지각
coupled with - ~와 함께
prerequisite ⓝ 선행 조건
determination ⓝ 결심
typical ⓐ 전형적인
resent ⓥ 분개하다
shape ⓥ 형성하다
outwardly ⓐⓓ 외견상, 겉보기에는
underlying ⓐ 근원적인, 기초가 되는
clash ⓝ 충돌
moody ⓐ 변덕스러운, 언짢은, 뚱한
elder ⓝ 연장자
outward appearance - 외모
outrageous ⓐ 아주 별난, 터무니없는
convention ⓝ 관례, 관습

[28-29] 한양대 2007

아리스토텔레스는 니코마코스 윤리학에서 우정을 3종류로 구분했다. 이득을 얻기 위해 친분을 맺는 사업가들과 같은 "실리에 기반을 둔 우정", 파티 참석에 관심이 있는 젊은이들과 같은 "쾌락에 기반을 둔 우정", 그리고 "완벽한 우정"이 바로 그것이다. 아리스토텔레스는 첫 번째와 두 번째 우정을 제한적이며 피상적 우정이라고 지칭하는데, 그 이유는 그 두 우정이 쉽게 변할 수 있는 환경적 요소에 기반하고 있기 때문이다. 다른 사람의 선한 인격에 대한 존경심에 바탕을 둔 마지막 종류의 우정은 더 오래 지속되지만 매우 드물게 찾아볼 수 있는데, 이는 좋은 인격을 갖춘 사람이 "드물기 때문"이다. 우정에 관해 최고의 글을 남긴 키케로(Cicero) 또한 진실한 친구들이 되도록 엮어 주는 것은 "상대의 선의에 대한 서로의 믿음"이라고 주장했다. 미덕이야말로 진정한 우정의 전제 조건이라는 이 주장은 요즘 우리들에게는 거의 불가능할 것 같은 과도한 요구라고 생각될 수 있다. 생각해 보면 요즘 시대에 스스로를 좋은 사람으로 여기는 이가 얼마나 되겠는가? 하지만 솔직히 말해 내가 가장 오래도록 우정을 나누고 있는 이들은 청렴하고 인간적이며 자신들의 역경을 감당할 수 있는 힘이 있는 사람들이었다고 나는 그들의 그런 점을 지금도 여전히 존경한다. 반대로 내가 누군가에 대한 존경심을 잃었을 때는, 그 사람이 다른 면에서 얼마나 매력이 있든지 간에 그 사람과의 우정은 거의 순식간에 사라졌다. 키케로(Cicero)는 "우정에서 존경심을 없앤다는 것은 우정이 지닌 가장 아름다운 장식을 없애는 것과 같다"고 말했다.

28 이 글의 흐름상 빈칸에 들어갈 가장 알맞은 것은?
① 마침내
② 반대로
③ 인정하건대
④ 그런 이유로, 그래서

| 정답 | ②

| 해설 | 빈칸의 앞 내용을 보면 존경할 만한 미덕을 가진 사람들과의 우정은 오래 지속되었다고 말하고 있다. 뒤의 내용은 반대로 그 존경심이 사라졌을 때를 말하고 있으므로 정답은 ②가 적합하다.

29 이 글의 내용과 일치하는 것은?
① 아리스토텔레스는 "쾌락에 기반을 둔 우정"은 예외로 여겼다.
② 아리스토텔레스는 완벽한 우정은 좋은 관계에 기반을 두어야 한다는 사실을 부정했다.
③ 키케로는 우정이야말로 상호 신뢰에 기반을 두어야 한다고 믿었다.
④ 저자는 키케로가 드물지만 진귀한 우정을 드러내는 방식을 가치 있게 생각했다고 판단하고 있다.

| 정답 | ③

| 해설 | ①의 경우 아리스토텔레스가 구분한 우정의 세 범주의 하나이므로 예외라고 할 수 없으며, ②의 경우 아리스토텔레스가 옳다고 생각한 것이지 부정(deny)한 것은 아니므로 정답이 될 수 없다. ④는 본문과 관련이 없다. 정답은 ③으로, 본문의 중반부에 나온 "a mutual belief in each other's goodness." 부분을 재서술한 내용이다. 이때 mutual과 reciprocal은 동일한 의미를 지닌다.

| 어휘 | distinguish ⓥ 구별하다　　　　　　　　ethics ⓝ 윤리학
The Nicomachean Ethics - 니코마스 윤리학(아리스토텔레스가 직접 세운 학원 리케이온에서 강의한 내용을 그의 아들 니코마스가 정리한 윤리학 입문서)
based on - ~에 토대를 둔　　　　　　　utility ⓝ 유용성, 실리
cultivate ⓥ (누구와의 관계를) 구축하다; 경작하다　qualified ⓐ 단서[조건]를 다는, 제한적인; 자격이 있는
superficial ⓐ 표면상의, 외면의　　　　　be founded on - ~에 기초해 세워지다

circumstance ⓝ 상황, 환경
permanent ⓐ 불변의, 영구적인
mutual ⓐ 서로의, 상호의
virtue ⓝ 미덕, 덕행, 선행
strike ⓥ ~하다는 인상[느낌]을 주다
after all – 따지고 보면, 결국
integrity ⓝ 청렴, 고결, 성실, 정직
bear ⓥ 견디다, 참다
peter ⓥ 없어지다, 점차 소멸하다
ornament ⓝ 장식
admittedly ⓐⓓ 틀림없이, 확실히, 명백하게
reciprocal ⓐ 상호 간의

Cicero – 키케로(고대 로마의 정치가, 철학자, 웅변가)
treatise ⓝ 논문
goodness ⓝ 선의, 선량함
precondition ⓝ 전제 조건
demanding ⓐ 부담이 큰, 힘든; (사람이) 요구가 지나친
last ⓥ 계속하다, 지속[존속]하다
humanity ⓝ 인성, 인간애
winning ⓐ 마음을 끄는, 매력 있는
splendid ⓐ 화려한, 훌륭한
conversely ⓐⓓ 반대로
exceptional ⓐ 예외적인

[30-32]

인간 본성의 특정한 충동을 탐구하도록 고안된 컴퓨터 게임에 참여한 사람들은 돈을 가장 많이 할당받은 플레이어로부터는 지속적으로 돈을 가장 많이 빼앗았지만 돈을 가장 적게 할당받은 플레이어에게는 지속적으로 돈을 제공했다고 과학자들이 밝혔다. 이 실험은 컴퓨터실에서 120명의 지원자들을 활용해 수행되었다. 일단 4인 그룹으로 무작위로 배치된 다음, 각각의 사람들은 상당량의 돈을 할당받았고 다른 세 사람이 돈을 얼마나 갖고 있는지를 들었다. 그리고서 플레이어들은 다른 사람들이 보유한 돈의 양을 늘리거나 줄일 수 있도록 자신의 돈을 쓸 기회를 얻게 되었는데, 이러한 행동은 자기 자신에겐 어떤 금전적 이익을 주는 것은 아니었다. 플레이어들은 게임을 5번 했는데, 이전에 속한 그룹의 사람들과는 전혀 게임을 하지 않았다. 이는 플레이어가 스스로의 평판을 높이는 노력을 할 가능성이나 자신에게 돈을 가져간 다른 플레이어에게 복수할 가능성을 없애기 위한 것이었다. 연구에 따르면 대략 70퍼센트의 참가자가 다른 사람의 돈을 줄이거나 더했는데, 여기서 가장 흔한 경우는 돈이 제일 많은 플레이어로부터 돈을 뺏은 경우나 가장 가난한 플레이어에게 돈을 기증하는 경우였다.

30 본문에 따르면 실험은 무엇을 밝혔는가?
① 인간은 끝없이 적응이 가능하다.
② 인간 본성에는 평등주의적 충동이 존재한다.
③ 컴퓨터 게임은 궁극적으로는 인간의 본성을 손상시킨다.
④ 인간은 종종 돈에 대해 꽤나 이기적인 태도를 취한다.

| 정답 | ②

| 해설 | 본문 가장 처음의 "돈을 가장 많이 할당받은 플레이어로부터는 지속적으로 돈을 가장 많이 빼앗았지만 돈을 가장 적게 할당 받은 플레이어에게는 지속적으로 돈을 제공했다(People ... consistently robbed from players assigned the most money while giving money to those with the least)" 부분과, 가장 마지막의 "가장 흔한 경우는 돈이 제일 많은 플레이어로부터 돈을 뺏는 경우나 가장 가난한 플레이어에게 돈을 기증하는 경우(by taking from the richest players or by donating to the poorest players)" 부분을 보면 실험 참가자들을 통해 인간은 보편적으로 가진 사람에게 좀 뺏고 못 가진 사람에게 좀 주는 평등주의적 충동이 있음을 알 수 있다. 따라서 답은 ②가 된다.

31 본문의 문맥에 따라서 밑줄 친 ㉮ design의 올바른 형태를 고르시오.
① design
② designing
③ designed
④ have designed

| 정답 | ③

| 해설 | 문제의 design이 들어 있는 첫 번째 문장을 보면, 동사가 robbed이고 한 문장에서 동사가 두 개 이상 올 수는 없기 때문에 design은 동사가 아님을 알 수 있다. design 앞에 명사가 위치하고 있으므로 명사 computer game을 수식하는 분사임을 유추할 수 있다. 여기서 design의 의미가 능동이냐 수동이냐에 따라 현재분사(designing)인지, 과거분사(designed)인지 형태를 정할 수 있다. 문맥상 'a computer game design to explore'는 '~을 탐구하도록 고안된 컴퓨터 게임'을 의미하므로, design은 수동의 의미를 가진 'designed(고안된)'가 되어야 한다. 따라서 답은 ③이다.

32 다음 중 빈칸 ㉯와 ㉰에 들어갈 가장 알맞은 것은 무엇인가?
① ㉯ 증가시키다 – ㉰ 감소시키다
② ㉯ 최소화하다 – ㉰ 증가시키다
③ ㉯ 증가시키다 – ㉰ 확대시키다
④ ㉯ 최소화시키다 – ㉰ 감소시키다

| 정답 | ①

| 해설 | 본문 첫 부분에서 실험 참가자들이 서로 돈을 주거나 뺏었음을 알 수 있으므로, ㉯에는 바로 뒤 decrease에 대응하는 increase가 와야 한다. 따라서 답은 ① 아니면 ③이다. ㉰의 경우 본문 가장 마지막 문장을 보면 "가장 가난한 플레이어에게 돈을 기증하는(donating to the poorest players)" 행위는 "다른 사람의 돈을 더하는 것(added to another person's money)"에 해당하므로, "돈이 제일 많은 플레이어로부터 돈을 뺏는(taking from the richest players)" 행위는 다른 사람의 돈을 '줄이는' 것임을 유추할 수 있다. 따라서 답은 ① 아니면 ④이다. 이 두 사항을 종합하면 답은 ①이 된다.

| 어휘 | designed ⓐ ~하도록 고안된
consistently ⓐⓓ 지속적으로
randomly ⓐⓓ 무작위로
reputation ⓝ 평판, 명성
adaptable ⓐ (새 환경에) 적응할 수 있는
impair ⓥ 손상시키다
impulse ⓝ 충동, 자극
assign ⓥ 할당하다
an amount of – 상당량의
infinitely ⓐⓓ 무한히, 한없이
egalitarian ⓐ 평등주의의

[33-34] 덕성여대 2011

공약하거나 약속한 것을 지키는 것은 대규모 예금(deposit)과 같고, 그것을 지키지 않는 것은 대규모 인출(withdrawal)과 같다. 사실 누군가에게 중요한 약속을 했다가 그것을 지키지 않는 것만큼 더 큰 규모의 인출은 아마도 없을 것이다. 다음에 그들과 다시 약속을 한다 하더라도, 그들은 믿지 않을 것이다. 사람들은 약속을 기반으로 자신들의 소망을 쌓는 경향이 있는데, 기본적인 생계에 관한 약속이라면 더욱 그렇다.

부모 된 사람으로서 나는 내가 지키지 못할 약속은 절대로 하지 않는다는 철학을 견지하려고 노력해 왔다. 그렇기 때문에 나는 매우 신중하고도 매우 절제해서 약속하려 노력하며, 최대한 많은 변수들과 돌발 상황들을 염두에 두려고 노력한다. 그래서 갑자기 어떤 일이 생겨서 약속을 지키지 못하는 경우가 발생하지 않도록 한다.

그러나 가끔, 이런 모든 노력에도 불구하고, 예상치 못한 일이 일어나 내가 한 약속을 지키는 것이 현명하지 못하거나 불가능한 상황이 발생하기도 한다. 그러나 나는 그런 약속도 중요하게 여긴다. 그런 경우에 어찌됐든 약속을 지키거나, 아니면 약속한 사람에게 그 상황을 충분히 설명하고 약속에서 해방될 수 있는지 요청한다.

당신이 만약 스스로 한 약속을 언제나 지키는 습관을 기른다면, 나는 당신이 당신과 자녀 사이의 이해의 격차를 이어 주는 신뢰의 다리를 건설하고 있는 것이라고 믿는다. 만약 당신이 원하지 않는 것을 당신의 자녀가 하고자 할 때, 그리고 당신은 이미 성인이기 때문에 당신의 자녀는 보지 못하는 예상되는 결과를 당신은 볼 수 있을 때, 아마 이렇게 말할 것이다. "아들아, 만약 네가 이것을 한다면 이런 결과가 나타날 것이란다." 만약 아이가 당신의 말과 약속에 신뢰를 쌓았다면, 그 아이는 당신의 조언을 따를 것이다.

33 다음 중 이 글에서 저자가 말하고자 하는 주제는 무엇인가?
① 약속을 지키는 것은 신뢰의 다리를 짓게 해 준다.
② 아이들은 약속이 깨지는 것으로 인해 부모만큼이나 부정적인 영향을 받는다.
③ 자녀와의 약속을 지키는 것은 부모에게 특히 중요하다.
④ 사람이 할 수 있는 가장 나쁜 일은 약속을 깨는 것인데, 다른 사람이 다음번에 당신을 믿지 않을 것이기 때문이다.

| 정답 | ①

| 해설 | 이 글은 약속을 잘 지키는 것의 중요성에 대해 말하고 있다. 물론 보기의 ③과 같이 본문 후반부에 자녀와의 관계에 약속이 미치는 영향에 대해서도 서술하고 있지만, 자녀와의 약속에 대해서만 서술한 글은 아니기 때문에 이를 주제라고 할 수는 없다. 따라서 약속을 잘 지키는 것은 서로의 신뢰를 형성해 주기 때문에 중요하다는 ①이 정답이 된다.

34 다음 중 당신이 일상생활에서 약속을 지키는 것과 관련이 없는 것은?
① 약속을 지키는 것은 당신의 철학의 일부가 되어야 한다.
② 당신은 자녀들에게 그들이 성인이 되어 결과를 충분히 이해하게 되기 전까지는 약속을 하지 못하게 해야 한다.
③ 당신은 약속을 지키지 못하게 할 수 있는 가능한 모든 예상치 못한 변수에 대해 고려해야 한다.
④ 당신은 약속을 신중하게 해야 하며, 만약 약속을 지키지 못할 때는 충분한 설명을 해야 한다.

| 정답 | ②

| 해설 | ②에서는 아이들이 성인이 되어 결과를 이해할 수 있기 전까지는 약속을 하지 못하게 하라고 했지만, 본문에서 이런 식으로 언급한 부분은 없다. 본문 후반부에서 자녀가 어리기 때문에 결과를 예상할 수 없는 것을 부모는 예상할 수 있다는 부분이 나오지만, ②와는 전혀 관계가 없으므로 정답은 ②가 된다.

| 어휘 | commitment ⓝ 공약, 약속   deposit ⓝ [은행] 예금

withdrawal ⓝ [은행] 인출, 회수, 철수
livelihood ⓝ 생계
sparingly ⓐ 삼가서, 절제해서
variable ⓝ 변수
keep A from B – A가 B하지 못하도록 (방해)하다
fulfill ⓥ 이행하다
value ⓥ 소중하게 생각하다
span the gap – 격차를 이어 주다, 간극을 연결하다
maturity ⓝ 성숙
act on – ~대로 실행하다

come through – 약속을 이행하다
philosophy ⓝ 철학
be aware of – ~을 알아차리다, 인식하다
contingency ⓝ 만일의 사태, 돌발 상황
come up – 갑자기 발생하다
cultivate ⓥ 경작하다, 일구다
consequence ⓝ (좋지 않은) 결과

[35-37] 광운대 2007

David Weeks 박사가 진행한 심도 깊은 연구에서, 사회에서 "괴짜"라는 낙인을 받은 사람들에 대해 몇 가지 매우 긍정적인 정보가 발견됐다. 책으로도 출판된 연구 보고서는 괴짜들이 보통 사람들보다 5~10년 정도 더 오래 살며, 이들이 보통 사람들보다 일반적으로 더 행복감을 느끼고, 보다 건강하며, 지능도 더 높다는 결론을 내리고 있다. 보고서에 따르면, 괴짜들의 몇몇 전형적 특징을 보면, 이들은 창의적이고, 비순응적이며, 호기심에 단단히 사로잡혀 있으며, 하나 이상의 취미에 몰두하고, 지적이고, 자기 주관이 뚜렷하며, "자신이 옳고 세상의 다른 사람들이 이상하다는 강한 확신"을 지니고 있다는 것이다. 괴짜들은 종종 약간 미친 사람들로 오해를 받는다. 하지만 괴짜들이 특이한 방식으로 행동하는 것은 사실 그런 행동이 자신들에게 긍정적 즐거움을 주기 때문이다. "괴짜들은 다른 이들보다 더 행복감을 느끼기 때문에 더 건강하다. 솔직히 말해, 괴짜들은 무엇인가에 순응할 필요를 느끼지 않기 때문에 스트레스를 훨씬 적게 받으며, 낮은 스트레스로 인해 이들의 면역체계가 보다 효과적으로 작동한다"고 Weeks 박사는 설명한다. 따라서 일 년 중 가장 무더운 날에 우비를 입고 돌아다니고 싶다거나, 수염을 절반만 깎고서 쉬운 과목을 대학에서 공부하고 싶다면, 그렇게 하라! 당신은 미친 것이 아니라 그저 별난 것이기 때문이다. 그리고 이는 다시 실제 건강으로 이어진다!

35 윗글의 제목으로 가장 적절한 것을 고르시오.
① 약간 미친 괴짜들
② 괴짜 기질 받아들이기
③ 자기주장이 강한 괴짜들
④ 모든 개인은 괴짜들

| 정답 | ②

| 해설 | 본문은 괴짜라고 해서 일반인들이 생각하는 것처럼 약간 미친 사람들이 아닌, 나름의 그들만의 방식으로 세상을 살기 때문에 유익한 점이 있다는 것을 말하고 있다. 본문 후반부에는 괴짜처럼 하는 것도 나쁘지 않다고 말하고 있으므로 정답은 ②가 된다. ①은 본문과 다르며, ③은 본문에 나온 내용이지만 제목이기에는 너무 단편적인 내용이며, ④는 본문과 무관해서 정답이 될 수 없다.

36 윗글의 ⓐ에 가장 적절한 표현을 고르시오.
① 친구와 상의하라
② 다시 한 번 생각해 봐라
③ 한 번 시도해 봐라
④ 인내심을 가져라

| 정답 | ③

| 해설 | 본문에서 저자는 괴짜의 행동들의 긍정적 측면을 부각했다. 그리고 빈칸 뒤에 이어지는 문장에서도 건강에 좋은 점을 설명하고 있다. 따라서 빈칸에는 긍정적 어감의 말이 와야 한다. 따라서 정답은 ③이 되며, 나머지 보기들은 모두 그렇게 하지 말라는 내용이므로 정답이 될 수 없다.

37

다음 중 괴짜 기질에 대한 저자의 태도는?
① 회의적인   ② 무관심한
③ 긍정적인   ④ 부정적인

| 정답 | ③

| 해설 | 본문에서 저자는 괴짜의 행동을 긍정적으로 바라보고 있으므로 정답은 '긍정적인'의 의미인 ③이 된다.

| 어휘 | positive ⓐ 긍정적인
eccentric ⓐ 괴상한, 괴짜의
nonconforming ⓐ 관행을 따르지 않는
opinionated ⓐ 자기 의견을 고집하는, 독선적인
insane ⓐ 미친
conform ⓥ 순응하다, 따르다
underwater basket-weaving – 대단히 쉽거나 쓸모없는 (대학) 과목
in turn – 차례로, 번갈아
skeptical ⓐ 회의적인
affirmative ⓐ 긍정적인, 찬성의
label ⓥ (특히 부당하게) 딱지[꼬리표]를 붙이다
trait ⓝ 특성, 특색
obsessed ⓐ 사로잡힌, 몰두하는
out of step – 보조를 맞추지 않고, 조화되지 않고
outlandish ⓐ 이상한, 기이한
immune ⓐ 면역의
embrace ⓥ 받아들이다, 수용하다; 껴안다, 포옹하다
indifferent ⓐ 무관심한

[38-40] 한국외대 2012

인간 본성에 관한 우리의 이해는 우리가 자녀를 키우는 방식에서부터 우리가 수용하는 정치 운동에 이르기까지 우리 삶의 모든 요소에 영향을 미친다. 하지만 과학을 통해 우리가 인간의 본성을 이해할 수 있는 황금기에 도달했음에도 많은 사람들은 인간 본성을 이해한다는 생각 그 자체를 강력히 거부하고 있다. 이들은 선천적인 사고 패턴과 감정 패턴에 관한 발견이 불평등의 정당화, 사회적 변화의 전복, 개인적 책임의 해소, 삶이 의미와 목적의 상실 등에 이용될 수 있다고 우려한다.
스티븐 핑커는 자신의 책 "백지상태"에서 인간 본성에 대한 견해와 함께 도덕적·정서적·정치적으로 인간 본성을 어떻게 바라보는지에 관해 탐구했다. 저자는 얼마나 많은 지식인들이 세 가지의 서로 연계된 신조를 받아들이면서 어떻게 인간 본성의 존재를 부인했는지를 보여줬는데, 구체적으로 첫 번째 신조는 인간 정신은 선천적 특성이 존재하지 않는다는 내용의 "백지상태"이고, 두 번째 신조는 인간은 태어날 때는 선하지만 사회에 의해 타락한다는 내용의 "고결한 야만인"이며, 세 번째 신조는 인간 각각은 생명 작용과는 무관하게 자유로이 선택할 수 있는 영혼을 보유하고 있다는 내용의 "기계 속의 유령"이다. 각각의 신조마다 도덕적으로 부담이 따르므로, 이를 수호하는 사람들은 이에 이의를 제기하는 과학자들의 신용을 떨어뜨리고자 필사적인 전략을 구사해 왔다.
핑커는 다채로운 인간 본성을 발견함으로서 평등·진보·책임·목적 등의 측면에서 두려워할 일은 전혀 없음을 보여주었고, 이를 통해 상기 언급된 논의와 관련해 침착함과 이성을 찾을 수 있게 하였다. 핑커는 명료한 사고와 상식 그리고 과학과 역사로부터 근거를 둔 적절한 진실 등을 통해 가장 험악한 위협조차도 무력화한다. 핑커의 주장에 따르면 "백지상태" 신조는 20세기 전반에 걸쳐 지식인들 사이에서 인기를 얻었지만 유익하기는커녕 유해했을 가능성이 있다.

38 왜 많은 사람들은 인간의 본성을 이해하고자 과학적 노력에 반감을 갖는가?
① 이들은 자신의 이론이 새로운 과학적 발견에 기여하기를 원한다.
② 이들은 과학이 인간의 정신을 탐구하기에 적절하지 않다고 생각한다.
③ 이들은 인간의 정신이 더 철저하게 연구되어야 할 것이라고 믿는다.
④ 이들은 이러한 노력의 결과가 남용될 수 있다고 우려한다.

| 정답 | ④

| 해설 | "이들은 선천적인 사고 패턴과 감정 패턴에 관한 발견이 불평등의 정당화, 사회적 변화의 전복, 개인적 책임의 해소, 삶이 의미와 목적의 상실 등에 이용될 수 있다고 우려한다(They fear that discoveries about innate patterns of thinking and feeling may be used to justify inequality, to subvert social change, to dissolve personal responsibility, and to strip life of meaning and purpose)." 여기서 말하는 '선천적인 사고 패턴과 감정 패턴에 관한 발견'은 인간 본성의 이해를 위한 시도이며, 따라서 이 문장은 인간 본성의 이해를 위한 시도가 오히려 남용되거나 악영향을 미칠 수 있다는 의미이다. 그러므로 답은 ④이다.

39 핑커는 과학이 인간 본성에 대한 우리의 이해를 높인다고 믿는다.
① 정신에는 선천적인 특성이 존재하지 않는다
② 사람은 태어날 때는 선하지만 사회에 의해 타락한다
③ "기계 속의 유령" 신조는 올바른 신조이다
④ 과학이 인간 본성에 대한 우리의 이해를 높인다

| 정답 | ④

| 해설 | "핑커는 명료한 사고와 상식 그리고 과학과 역사로부터 근거를 둔 적절한 진실 등을 통해 가장 험악한 위협조차도 무력화한다(He disarms even the most menacing threats with clear thinking, common sense, and pertinent facts from science and history)." 즉, 핑커는 과학을 활용하여 인간 본성의 파악에 방해가 되는 요인들을 제거하고 그 결과 인간 본성에 대한 이해를 높일 수 있었다. 따라서 답은 ④이다.

40 다음 중 본문에서 언급되거나 암시되지 않은 것은 무엇인가?
① 우리가 아이들을 키우는 방식은 인간 본성에 대한 우리의 생각에 달려 있다.
② 우리는 이제 선천적인 사고 패턴에 관해 더 잘 이해하고 있다.
③ 일부 사상가들은 인간은 태어날 때 악하지만 교육을 통해서 개선된다고 믿는다.
④ "백지상태"는 인간 정신에 관한 이론으로 20세기에 큰 영향력을 보였다.

| 정답 | ③

| 해설 | 본문에는 인간은 선하게 태어나지만 사회에 의해 타락한다는 내용의 '고결한 야만인' 이론은 제시되었지만 이와는 반대되게 인간은 태어날 때 악하지만 교육을 통해서 개선된다는 내용은 등장하지 않는다. 따라서 답은 ③이다.

| 어휘 | embrace ⓥ 받아들이다, 수용하다　　innate ⓐ 타고난, 선천적인
　　　　subvert ⓥ 뒤집어엎다, 전복하다　　dissolve ⓥ 해소시키다, 해제하다
　　　　blank slate – 백지상태, 빈 서판　　coloring ⓝ 채색, 견해

dogma ⓝ 신조
discredit ⓥ 신임[신용]을 떨어뜨리다
disarm ⓥ 무력하게 하다, 무장 해제시키다
pertinent ⓐ 적절한
biology ⓝ 생명 작용[활동]
inject A into B – A를 B에 더하다[투입하다]
menacing ⓐ 위협적인, 험악한
disapprove ⓥ 반감을 갖다, 못마땅해 하다

[41-43] 홍익대 2012

> 마돈나처럼 바비도 일단은 열성적인 팬과 적대적인 비판가들을 동시에 보유하게 되었다. 미국뿐만 아니라 전 세계에서 어른, 아이 할 거 없이 수백만의 사람들에게 바비는 제일 유명하면서 모든 장난감 중에서도 가장 생명력이 강한 인형으로, 아이뿐만 아니라 수집가들이 가장 얻고 싶어하는 인형이다. 그 외 다른 사람들에게는, 특히 걱정 많은 부모님이나 페미니스트 학자들에게 있어 바비는 여성을 겨냥한 위험한 무기이자 이상화된 여성성의 아이콘으로, 이들이 매우 싫어하거나 최소한 추궁하고 파괴하지는 못할지언정 해체하고 싶어하는 대상이다. 바비 인형이 지닌 과장된 몸매 비율과 병적으로 마른 체형에 맞춰 정해진 기준 등이 논란의 핵심이다. (바비 인형을 실물 크기에 맞출 경우, 측정하는 사람이 누구냐에 따라 다르겠지만, 치수가 36-18-33 정도가 될 것이며, 몸에는 정기적으로 생리를 할 수 있을 만큼의 지방도 쌓이지 못할 것이다.) 실제로 바비는 많은 사람들에게 종종 머리가 비었고, 자신에게만 관심을 가지며, 거식증을 앓고, 물욕에 사로잡힌 소녀로서 병리학적으로 묘사되는 젊은 여성을 칭하는 은유로 통하며, 이런 상황에서 오랫동안 페미니스트들의 분노를 샀다. 페미니스트들은 바비를 여성의 아름다움과 여성의 몸매에 대해 가부장제가 소녀와 여성에게 강요하는 유해하고 잘못된 믿음을 실제로 드러내게끔 만드는 또 다른 예시로 보고 매도하고 있다.

41

다음 중 사실이 아닌 것은 무엇인가?
① 바비는 아이들뿐만 아니라 어른들 사이에서도 유명하다.
② 부모는 이상적 여성성의 아이콘에 대한 페미니즘 학자들의 분노를 우려하고 있다.
③ 페미니스트들은 바비가 소녀와 여성에게 해를 끼칠 수 있다고 경고한다.
④ 바비의 과장된 몸매 비율은 거식증을 앓고 물욕에 사로잡힌 소녀의 이미지와 관련이 있다.

| 정답 | ②

| 해설 | 걱정 많은 부모와 페미니스트 학자들 모두 바비가 드러내는 이상적 여성상에 관해 우려하고 있다. 즉, 이 둘은 서로 뜻을 같이하므로 ②는 본문의 내용과는 다르다.

42

위 본문에서 유추할 수 있는 것은 무엇인가?
① 페미니즘 학자들은 완구 산업에 종종 적대적인 시선을 던진다.
② 사람들이 바비에 보이는 반응은 둘 이상으로 나뉜다.
③ 마돈나는 바비의 치수에 매료된 팬 가운데 하나이다.
④ 가부장제는 여성의 아름다움에 대한 잘못된 믿음을 재생산하는 책임으로부터 자유롭지 못하다.

| 정답 | ④

| 해설 | 본문의 "가부장제가 소녀와 여성에게 강요하는 유해하고 잘못된 믿음(damaging myths of female beauty and the feminine body that patriarchy thrusts upon girls and women)"이란 문장을 통해 답은 ④임을 알 수 있다.

43 다음 중 바비를 둘러싼 논란에 있어 저자가 보이는 태도는 무엇인가?

① 분석적인 ② 단호한
③ 애증이 엇갈리는 ④ 냉담한

| 정답 | ①

| 해설 | 저자는 바비 인형을 둘러싼 논쟁에 있어 수치를 제공하고 반대 진영의 의견과 그 근거를 제시하는 등 분석적 태도로 글을 작성하고 있다. 따라서 답은 ①이다.

| 어휘 | posse ⓝ 무리, 패거리
enduring ⓐ 오래가는, 지속되는
womankind ⓝ 여성, 부녀자
interrogate ⓥ 심문하다, 추궁하다
morbidly ⓐⓓ 병적으로
menstruate ⓥ 생리하다
pathologically ⓐⓓ 병리학적으로, 비정상적으로
anorexic ⓐ 거식증의
revile ⓥ 매도하다
patriarchy ⓝ 가부장제
determined ⓐ 단단히 결심한, 단호한
aloof ⓐ 냉담한
devoted ⓐ 헌신적인, 열정적인
wary ⓐ 경계하는, 걱정하는
femininity ⓝ 여성성, 여성다움
deconstruct ⓥ 해체하다, 분해하다
measurement ⓝ 치수
metaphor ⓝ 은유, 비유
pathological ⓐ 자신에게만 관심을 갖는
ire ⓝ 분노, 노여움
manifestation ⓝ 징후, 현현
antagonistic ⓐ 적대적인
ambivalent ⓐ 애증이 엇갈리는

[44-45] 성균관대 2015

연구진은 만족감을 얻는 일을 나중으로 회피하거나 미룰 수 있는 능력이 인생을 살면서 거두게 되는 성과와 연관이 있는지 여부에 큰 흥미를 느끼고 있다. 이와 관련하여 가장 잘 알려진 것이 바로 "마시멜로" 실험이다. 이 실험에서는 마시멜로를 15분 동안 먹지 않고 자제할 수 있었던 아이는 마시멜로를 하나 더 받을 수 있었다. 기다리지 못한 아이들은(참을 수 있었던 아이들에 비해) 성인이 되었을 때 소득이 더 낮았고 건강도 나쁜 경향을 보였다. 스톡홀름 대학의 데이비드 린달(David Lindahl) 박사는 스웨덴에서 수행된 한 조사의 데이터를 활용했는데, 이 조사에서는 13,000명이 넘는 13세의 아동들에게 지금 140달러를 받는 것이 좋은지 아니면 5년 동안 총 1,400달러를 받는 것이 좋은지를 물었다. 아이들 가운데 5분의 4가 자신들은 기다릴 준비가 되어 있다고 밝혔다. 이전의 연구진과 달리 린달 박사는 모든 아이들을 추적할 수 있었고 아이들의 부모의 배경과 인지 능력을 설명할 수 있었다. 린달 박사는 적은 양의 돈을 즉시 받길 원했던 아이들은 더 큰 보상을 받기 위해 기다리는 편이 낫겠다고 답한 아이들에 비해 이후 18년 동안 범죄로 기소될 확률이 32% 더 높다는 사실을 발견했다. 박사의 생각으로는 참을성이 없는 사람은 즉각적인 보상을 선호하며 따라서 앞으로 처벌을 받을지도 모른다는 두려움으로 인해 주저하게 될 가능성이 낮다. 하지만 어떤 사람이 범죄자의 길을 걷게 될지 여부는 10대 때 이미 정해진다고 걱정하며 안절부절못하는 사람들에게는 절망하지 말 것을 전하고자 한다. 린달 박사는 해결책을 제시하였다. 응답자의 교육에 관한 사항을 분석에 포함시킨 결과, 린달 박사는 높은 수준의 학업성취는 만족감을 뒤로 미루는 것을 선호하는 것과 서로 관계가 있음을 발견했다. 린달 박사는 다음과 같이 설명했다. "저는 따라서 학교 교육은 사람들이 미래를 더욱 가치 있게 여기도록 하여 범죄를 저지르지 않도록 한다고 추정합니다."

44 위 본문의 제목으로 가장 알맞은 것은 무엇인가?
① 유혹과 처벌
② 인간의 행동과 법의 허점
③ 참을성 없는 아이들을 교육시키는 법
④ 시간선호와 범죄행동
⑤ 고등교육의 한계

| 정답 | ④

| 해설 | 본문에 따르면 즉각적인 만족감을 추구하는 아이보다 참을성 있게 기다릴 줄 아는 아이가 어른이 되어 성공할 가능성이 높으며, 그렇지 않은 아이들은 범죄의 유혹에 빠질 가능성이 높다. 현재의 이익과 미래의 이익을 비교하면서 현재의 이익을 중시하는 것은 "시간선호" 개념과 관련이 있으며, 현재를 중시한 아이들이 범죄를 저지를 확률이 높다는 것은 범죄행동과 연관이 있다. 따라서 답은 ④이다.

45 본문에 따르면 린달 박사의 주장은 다음과 같다.
① 교육적 배경과 인내는 관련이 없다.
② "마시멜로" 실험은 더 이상 아이의 자제력을 효과적으로 측정하는 역할을 다하지 못한다.
③ 보상을 늦추는 아이는 나중에 범죄자가 될 확률이 높다.
④ 인내가 항상 미덕인 것은 아니다.
⑤ 학교 교육은 사람들이 보상을 미루게 될 가능성을 높일 수 있다.

| 정답 | ⑤

| 해설 | "린달 박사는 높은 수준의 학업성취는 만족감을 뒤로 미루는 것을 선호하는 것과 서로 관계가 있음을 발견했다(he found that higher educational attainment was linked to a preference for delayed gratification)." 즉, 교육을 통해 보상을 뒤로 미루는 법을 배우게 되면서 향후 어른이 되어 성공할 확률도 올라가는 것이다. 따라서 답은 ⑤이다.

| 어휘 | intrigued ⓐ 아주 흥미로워하는
defer ⓥ 미루다, 연기하다
outcome ⓝ 결과, 성과
confection ⓝ 과자, 단 것
track ⓥ 추적하다, 뒤쫓다
parental ⓐ 부모의
be convicted of – ~로 유죄판결을 받다, ~로 기소되다
deter ⓥ (공포·염려하게 하여) 주저시키다, 그만두게 하다
fret ⓥ 조바심치다, 안절부절못하며 지내다
remedy ⓝ 처리 방안, 해결[개선]책
schooling ⓝ 학교 교육
time preference – 시간선호(각 개인이 현재의 소비를 미래의 소비보다 상대적으로 얼마나 더 선호하는가를 나타내는 개념)
postpone ⓥ 미루다, 연기하다
as to – ~에 관해서
gratification ⓝ 만족(감)
refrain from – ~을 삼가다[자제하다]
survey ⓝ (설문)조사
account for – ~의 소재를 확인하다, ~을 설명하다
cognitive ⓐ 인지의, 인식의
despair ⓥ 절망하다, 체념하다
educational attainment – 학업성취
loophole ⓝ (빠져나갈) 구멍, 허점

[46-47] 한국외대 2013

용서하는 것은 신이라는 말이 있지만, 아무도 용서가 쉽다는 말은 한 적이 없다. 누군가가 여러분에게 깊은 상처를 주었을 경우, 여러분이 마음속에 간직한 원한을 놓아 버리는 것은 극도로 힘들다. 하지만 용서하는 것은 가능한 일이며 용서는 여러분의 신체적 건강뿐만 아니라 정신적 건강에도 놀랄 만큼 이롭다. "용서: 나를 위한 선택"이란 책의 저자인 프레드 러스킨 박사는 다음과 같은 말을 했다. "용서하는 사람은 우울증, 분노, 스트레스를 덜 보이는 대신 희망에 찬 모습을 보여줍니다. 따라서 용서는 우리의 장기가 마모되지 않도록 아끼는 데 기여하며, 면역체계가 손상되는 경우를 줄여 주며, 사람들이 더 활력을 느끼도록 합니다." 만일 여러분이 치유 과정을 시작하고 싶다면 먼저 시작해야 할 것이 있다. 바로 마음을 가라앉히는 일이다. 화를 진정시키기 위해서는 간단한 스트레스 관리 기법을 시도해 본다. 몇 번 심호흡을 한 다음 여러분에게 기쁨을 주는 것을 떠올려 본다. 예를 들면 자연의 아름다운 풍경이나 여러분이 사랑하는 사람 등이 있다.

46. 다음 중 (A)와 의미상 가장 가까운 것은 무엇인가?
① 학대
② 흠
③ 손상
④ 외관의 손상

| 정답 | ③

| 해설 | 밑줄 친 (A)는 "마모"를 의미하며, 보기 중에서 의미상 가장 가까운 것은 마모하여 못 쓰게 되었다는 의미에서 ③의 "손상(damage)"이다.

47. 다음 중 본문에 따르면 사실이 아닌 것은 무엇인가?
① 용서는 장애로부터 건강을 회복하는 데 도움이 된다.
② 용서를 통한 치료는 우선 마음의 평화를 필요로 한다.
③ 용서는 때로는 놀랄 만큼 간단하고 쉽다.
④ 분한 감정을 없애기란 힘들다.

| 정답 | ③

| 해설 | "아무도 용서가 쉽다는 말은 한 적이 없다(no one ever said it was easy)"와 "여러분이 마음속에 간직한 원한을 놓아 버리는 것은 극도로 힘들다(it can be extremely difficult to let go of your grudge)"는 보기 ③과 정면으로 충돌한다. 따라서 답은 ③이다.

| 어휘 | divine ⓐ 신성한, 신의
grudge ⓝ 원한, 유감
beneficial ⓐ 유익한, 이로운
wear and tear – 마모, 소모
wearing-out ⓝ 손상, 파손
calm oneself – 마음을 가라앉히다
defuse ⓥ 진정시키다, 완화시키다
abuse ⓝ 남용, 학대
blemish ⓝ 티, 흠
disfigurement ⓝ (외관의) 손상, 결점
impairment ⓝ 장애
resentment ⓝ 분함, 억울함

[48-49] 성균관대 2013

TV 소리는 요란하게 울리고, 화장실에서 물 내리는 소리가 들리고, 이따금 머리 위에서 비행기가 날아가는 상황에서는 밤에 한 번도 방해받는 일 없이 계속 잠을 자는 것이 희귀한 일이다. 수면 중인 뇌는 소리로 인해 정신이 산란해지는 것을 무시할 수 있도록 만들어져 있다. 하지만 일부 사람들의 뇌는 다른 이들에 비해 이 일을 더 잘 수행할 수 있다. 이제 연구진은 그 이유를 이해할 수 있는 첫 번째 단서를 찾게 되었다.

매사추세츠 종합병원 소속 과학자들은 스스로 잠을 잘 잔다고 말하는 12명의 사람들의 뇌파를 수면 연구실에서 3일 밤 동안 분석했다. 자원자들에게는 아늑한 침대가 제공되었지만, 밤마다 자동차 소리, 비행기 소음, 문두드리는 소리 같은 다양한 음량으로 스피커를 통해 보내지는 14개 종류의 소리에 시달렸다.

실험 결과 가장 시끄러운 소리에도 졸던 사람은 뇌전도 기록에서 "수면 방추"가 가장 빈번하게 나타난 사람이었다. 과학자들에 따르면 (뇌 속 깊이 위치해 들어오는 자극을 처리하는 부위인) 시상에서 벌어지는 활동을 통해 생성되는 수면 방추는 수면 중에 뇌가 소리를 얼마나 잘 차단하는지를 측정할 수 있는 수단으로 사용된다. 그리고 과학자들은 언젠가는 잠을 깊이 못 드는 사람들이 더 푹 잘 수 있도록 수면 방추 활동을 조종할 수 있을 것이라고 한다.

48 본문에 따르면 몇몇 사람들은 소음을 덜 듣기 때문에 잠을 더 잘 잔다.
① 소음을 덜 듣는다
② 조용한 이웃을 뒀다
③ 낮 시간에 일을 열심히 한다
④ 편안한 침대에서 잠을 잔다
⑤ 다른 사람들보다 꿈을 더 많이 꾼다

| 정답 | ①

| 해설 | "수면 중인 뇌는 소리로 인해 정신이 산란해지는 것을 무시할 수 있도록 만들어져 있다. 하지만 일부 사람들의 뇌는 다른 이들에 비해 이 일을 더 잘 수행할 수 있다(The sleeping brain is designed to tune out these auditory distractions, but some people's brains do so a lot better than others')." 즉, 어떤 사람들은 소리를 다른 사람에 비해 더 잘 차단할 수 있으므로 소음을 덜 듣게 되는 것이다. 따라서 답은 ①이다.

49 본문에 따르면 수면 방추가 더 빈번하게 등장한다는 것은 더 잠을 잘 잔다는 의미이다.
① 더 많은 소음
② 더 많은 꿈
③ 더 잠을 잘 잠
④ 더 많은 자극
⑤ 더 긴 잠

| 정답 | ③

| 해설 | "실험 결과 가장 시끄러운 소리에도 졸던 사람은 뇌전도 기록에서 '수면 방추'가 가장 빈번하게 나타난 사람이었다. 과학자들에 따르면 (뇌 속 깊이 위치해 들어오는 자극을 처리하는 부위인) 시상에서 벌어지는 활동을 통해 생성되는 수면 방추는 수면 중에 뇌가 소리를 얼마나 잘 차단하는지를 측정할 수 있는 수단으로 사용된다(It turned out that those who dozed through the loudest noises were those whose brains recorded the most 'sleep spindles' on an EEG. Scientists say the spindles, produced by activity in the thalamus (a region deep in the brain that processes incoming stimuli), can be used as a measure of how well the brain blocks

out sound during sleep).” 즉, 수면 방추가 빈번하게 등장하면 뇌가 소리를 더 잘 차단하게 되므로 잠 또한 더 잘 자게 되는 것이다. 따라서 답은 ③이다.

| 어휘 | uninterrupted ⓐ 연속된, 중단되지 않는   commodity ⓝ (유용한) 것
blare ⓥ 요란하게 울리다   tune out – 듣지 않다, 무시하다
auditory ⓐ 청각의   distraction ⓝ 집중을 방해하는 것
assault ⓥ (청각·후각 등을) 괴롭히다   pipe ⓥ (유선으로 소리 등을) 송신하다[보내다]
sleep spindle – 수면 방추   EEG – 뇌전도
thalamus ⓝ 시상   manipulate ⓥ 조종하다, 다루다

[50-51] 단국대 2016

> 비록 심리학은 19세기 말까지는 자체적인 학문 분야로 인정받지 않았지만 심리학의 초기 기원은 고대 그리스 시대로 거슬러 올라갈 수 있다. 예를 들어, 플라톤(Plato)과 아리스토텔레스(Aristotle)는 인간 정신의 본성에 관해 관심을 보인 철학자였다. 17세기에 르네 데카르트(René Descartes)는 정신과 육체를 구분하였는데, 데카르트는 이 둘을 서로 영향을 미친 끝에 인간의 경험을 창출하는 측면으로 바라봤고, 이리하여 현대 심리학이 생겨날 수 있도록 길을 터놓았다. 철학자들은 결론을 도출하기 위해 관찰과 논리에 의존한 반면, 심리학자들은 인간의 생각과 행동을 연구하기 위해 과학적 방법을 사용하기 시작했다. 독일의 심리학자 빌헬름 분트(Wilhelm Wundt)는 1879년 라이프치히 대학(University of Leipzig)에서 세계 최초의 심리학 연구소를 열었다. 분트는 반응 시간 같은 정신 과정을 연구하기 위해 실험을 통한 방법을 활용했다. 이러한 형태의 연구는 별도의 학문 분야로서 심리학이 탄생되었음을 나타낸 것으로 여겨진다. '정신의학'이란 용어는 1808년 독일 의사인 요한 라일(Johann Reil)에 의해 처음으로 사용되었다. 하지만 하나의 학문 분야로서의 정신의학은 지그문트 프로이트(Sigmund Freud)가 무의식에 초점을 맞춘 새로운 성격이론을 제안한 후에야 대중적으로 알려지게 되었다. 그 이전에는 심리학자들은 사람이 인식하고 있는 분야인 지각, 생각, 기억, 환상 등 정신의 의식적 측면에 주로 관심을 보였다.

50 본문에 따르면 다음 중 사실인 것은 무엇인가?
① 플라톤은 마음을 이해하는 일에 관심이 있었다.
② 지그문트 프로이트는 현대 심리학이 생겨날 수 있도록 길을 터놓았다.
③ 현대의 철학자들은 인간의 정신을 연구하기 위해 과학적 방식을 사용하기 시작했다.
④ 요한 라일은 무의식의 역할에 집중하는 새로운 성격이론을 제안했다.

| 정답 | ①

| 해설 | "라톤(Plato)과 아리스토텔레스(Aristotle)는 인간 정신의 본성에 관해 관심을 보인 철학자였다(Plato and Aristotle, for instance, were philosophers concerned with the nature of the human mind)." 이는 보기 ①에 해당되는 내용이며, 따라서 답은 ①이다.
현대 심리학의 탄생을 위한 길을 열어놓은 사람은 프로이트가 아니라 데카르트이며 따라서 ②는 답이 아니다. "철학자들은 결론을 도출하기 위해 관찰과 논리에 의존한 반면, 심리학자들은 인간의 생각과 행동을 연구하기 위해 과학적 방법을 사용하기 시작했다(While philosophers relied on observation and logic to draw their conclusions, psychologists began to use scientific methods to study human thought and behavior)." 이는 ③의 내용과 반대되며, 따라서 ③은 답이 아니다. 새로운 성격이론을 제안한 사람은 라일이 아니라 프로이트다. 따라서 ④는 답이 아니다.

> **51** 빈칸 Ⓐ와 Ⓑ에 가장 알맞은 것은 무엇인가?
> ① 예를 들어 – 그 동안에
> ② 그렇지 않으면 – 동시에
> ③ 그 결과 – 그 이후에
> ④ 하지만 – 그 이전에

| 정답 | ④

| 해설 | Ⓐ: 빈칸 앞에서는 '정신의학'이란 용어가 1808년에 처음 등장했음을 말하고 있으며, 빈칸 뒤에서는 프로이트의 등장과 함께 정신의학이 새로운 학문 분야로 대중에게 인식되었음을 말하고 있다. 프로이트가 활동한 시기는 19세기 말이며 여기서 정신의학이 처음 등장했을 때와 이후 대중에게 널리 알려진 때의 간격이 크다는 사실을 알 수 있다. 즉, 빈칸을 기준으로 빈칸 앞의 분위기가 뒤에서 반전되기 때문에 빈칸에 적합한 접속하는 역접의 접속사임을 유추할 수 있다. 따라서 빈칸에는 However가 적합하다.

Ⓑ: 빈칸 앞에서는 프로이트가 정신의 무의식적 측면에 초점을 맞췄음을 말하고 있으며 빈칸 뒤에서는 심리학자들이 정신의 의식적 측면에 초점을 맞췄음을 말하고 있다. 여기서 빈칸 앞뒤 내용은 프로이트 등장 '이전'에는 의식적 측면에 집중했지만 그의 등장 이후 무의식적 측면에 집중하는 새로운 이론이 제시되었다는 내용인 것으로 판단 가능하다. 따라서 빈칸에는 Before that time이 적합하다.

이러한 점들을 감안했을 때 답으로 가장 적합한 것은 ④이다.

| 어휘 | psychology ⓝ 심리학
be traced to – ~로 거슬러 올라가다
observation ⓝ 관찰
mark ⓥ ~일 것임을 보여주다[나타내다]
personality ⓝ 성격
perception ⓝ 지각
otherwise ⓐⓓ 그렇지 않으면[않았다면]
field ⓝ 분야
aspect ⓝ 측면, 양상
experimental ⓐ 실험적인, 실험의
psychiatry ⓝ 정신의학
unconscious ⓝ 무의식
in the meantime – 그 동안에, 한편

[52-53] 성균관대 2016

하버드 경영대학원의 우마 카마카(Uma Karmarkar) 교수와 듀크대 푸쿠아 경영대학원의 브라이언 볼링어(Bryan Bollinger) 교수의 최근 논문은 식료품을 사러 올 때 쇼핑 봉투를 직접 가져온 구매자는 자신을 보상하기 좋아한다는 사실을 발견했다. 저자들은 2년 동안 미국의 슈퍼마켓에서 발생한 거래를 추적했다. 자신의 쇼핑 봉투를 직접 가져온 고객들이 상점의 봉투를 사용한 사람들보다 더 많은 친환경 제품을 구입했는데, 이는 그다지 놀랍지 않은 일이다. 그러나 이것 외에도 친환경 구매자들은 과자, 아이스크림, 감자칩 등을 구입할 가능성이 더 많았다.

심리학자들은 이러한 종류의 행위를 "도덕적 허가"라고 지칭한다. 앞에서 든 예는 무해한 것처럼 보일 수 있지만, 그 결과는 왜곡될 수도 있다. 매사추세츠 주의 수자원 보존에 관한 2011년 연구는 어떻게 해서 왜곡되는지를 잘 보여 준다. 실험에서 약 150가구의 아파트 거주민들이 두 그룹으로 나뉘었다. 절반의 사람들은 물 절약에 대한 팁과 주간 사용량에 대해 통보받았다. 다른 절반은 대조군 역할을 했다. 물을 절약하기로 요구받은 가구는 실제 물을 절약했다. 그들의 물 소비량은 대조군과 비교해 평균 6% 정도 떨어졌다. 문제는 그들의 전력 소비가 5.6% 증가했다는 사실이다. 다른 말로 하자면 도덕적 허가가 너무 강해서, 그것이 본래의 도덕적 행동보다 다소 더 중요해졌다는 것이다.

도덕적 허가는 도덕적 행동이 의무가 아닌 경우에 나타나는 것으로 보인다. 한 연구에서 참가자들은 자신들이 지역봉사활동에 참여하고 있다고 상상하도록 했다. 그런 다음 그들에게 두 가지 보상 중 하나를 선택하도록 했다. 관대한 보상(유명 디자이너가 만든 고가의 청바지)과 실용적인 보상(진공청소기)이 제시됐다. 교통 위반으로 사회 봉사를 선고받았다고 상상해 보라는 지시를 받은 경우, 그들이 고가의 청바지를 선택할 가능성은 자원봉사자로 자신을 상상할 경우에 비해 적었다.

52 밑줄 친 표현 "moral licensing"은 다음 중 _____ 경향을 의미한다.
① 다른 사람들 앞에서 도덕적으로 행동하려고 하는
② 다른 사람들보다 도덕적으로 우월함을 느끼는
③ 좋은 어떤 일을 한 것에 대한 보상으로 무엇인가를 탐닉하는
④ 고결한 어떤 일을 하도록 스스로에게 허용을 하는
⑤ 나쁜 어떤 일을 한 것에 대해 스스로 자책하는

| 정답 | ③

| 해설 | 본문에서는 두 번째 문단과 세 번째 문단에서 각각 도덕적 허가의 예를 들고 있다. 물 절약이나 사회봉사와 같은 도덕적 행위를 한 경우 행위자들은 다른 행위로 그에 대한 보상을 받으려고 한다는 것이다. 물을 절약한 경우 오히려 전기를 좀 더 사용하거나, 사회봉사 활동을 한 경우 생필품보다는 사치품을 선택해서 스스로의 행위를 보상받고 싶어 한다는 것이다. 따라서 좋은 일을 한 이후 보상으로 무엇인가에 탐닉한다고 설명한 ③이 정답으로 적합하다.

53 다음 중 빈칸에 가장 적절한 것은 무엇인가?
① 사람들이 타인에 대해 나쁘게 느끼다
② 사람들이 법을 위반하다
③ 사람들이 희생을 하려고 하지 않다
④ 도덕적 행동이 의무가 아니다
⑤ 소비 패턴이 변하다

| 정답 | ④

| 해설 | 빈칸 뒤의 내용이 예시로 등장한다. 사회봉사 활동을 예로 들면서, 교통법규를 위반해 사회봉사 활동을 해야 할 경우와 자원봉사자로 사회봉사 할 경우를 비교하고 있다. 두 경우 사회봉사 활동(도덕적 행동)이 의무인지 아닌지의 여부를 따지고 있으므로 정답은 ④가 된다. 그리고 법을 위반한 경우가 아닌 떳떳한 경우 도덕적 허가가 더 잘 발생하는 것을 알 수 있다.

| 어휘 | transaction ⓝ 거래　　　　　　　　　　　　crisp ⓝ 감자칩
license ⓝ 면허, 인가; (행동의) 자유; 지나친 자유, 방종
perverse ⓐ (사고방식·태도가) 비뚤어진[삐딱한]　　control group – 제어 집단, 통제군
hitch ⓝ (뜻밖의) 장애, 문제　　　　　　　　　　outweigh ⓥ ~보다 더 크다[대단하다]
virtue ⓝ 미덕
community service – 지역[사회] 봉사 활동(자원 활동의 형태로나 법원에 의한 처벌의 한 형태로 이뤄짐)
indulgent ⓐ 멋대로 하게 하는, 관대한　　　　　practical ⓐ 현실[실질/실제]적인
be sentenced to – ~형을 받다　　　　　　　　virtuous ⓐ 도덕적인, 고결한
indulge oneself – ~에 빠지다, (특히 좋지 않다고 여겨지는 것을) 마음껏 하다

[54-55] 한양대 2017

기분이 적응적(adaptive) 기능을 수행하는 것으로 나타났다. 긍정적인 기분은 주변 상황이 안전하고 친숙하며, 기존의 지식에 의지할 수 있음을 나타낸다. 이와 대조적으로 부정적인 기분은 가벼운 경보 신호와 같은 기능을 하며, 주변 상황이 새롭고 익숙하지 않다는 것을 나타내며, 새로운 외부 정보를 주의 깊게 감시할 필요가 있다는 것을 나타낸다. 이를 뒷받침하는 증거가 있으며, 이 증거는 긍정적 감정은 증가하고 부정적 감정은 줄어든다는 것을 보여준다. 인지적 작업에서 외적 정보보다는 내적 지식에 의존하는 경향이 있으며, 이런 경향은 스스로 만든 정보에 대해 선택적 기억 편향(selective memory bias)을 유발한다. 따라서 이 이론은 긍정적인 기분과 부정적인 기분이 모두 상황을 처리하는 데 있어서 이점이 있다는 것을 예측해 주고 있다. 물론 서로 다른 처리 스타일을 요구하는 다양한 상황에 대응할 때 각각의 이점이 있다. 우리가 사는 문화권에서는 긍정적인 감정이 주는 이점에 대해서만 거의 독점적으로 강조하고 있는데, 이런 사실을 감안해 볼 때, 이것은 흥미로운 실제적 함의가 있는 중요한 메시지일 수 있다. 수많은 연구 결과에 따르면, 부정적인 기분은 새로운 외적 정보의 면밀한 감시가 필요한 상황에서 명백한 처리상의 이점을 만들어 낸다는 것을 보여주고 있다.

54 문맥상 밑줄 친 "adaptive"가 의미하는 것으로 가장 적절한 것은?
① 우리를 정보의 홍수에서 보호해 주는
② 우리가 다목적 인지 기술을 개발할 수 있게 도와주는
③ 매우 오랜 시간에 걸쳐 서서히 우리가 변하는 것을 가능하게 해 주는
④ 서로 다른 환경적 문제에 대응하도록 준비해 주는

| 정답 | ④

| 해설 | 기분의 적응적(adaptive) 기능에 대해 설명하고 있다. '적응적'이란 말 그대로 각 상황에 대해 각각 다른 방식으로 적응하도록 해 준다는 것으로, 바로 다음 문장에서 각각 긍정적인 기분과 부정적인 기분을 나누어 어떻게 서로 다른 방식으로 환경에 반응하는지를 보여주고 있다. 따라서 정답은 ④가 된다.

55 빈칸에 들어갈 가장 적절한 것은?
① 노력을 최소화하는 기술
② 스스로 만든 정보
③ 새로운 외적 정보의 면밀한 감시
④ 인지적, 심리적 결과에 대한 분석

| 정답 | ③

| 해설 | 본문은 부정적인 감정(기분)이 갖는 장점에 대해 서술하고 있다. 부정적인 감정이 주변 상황에 대해 대응하는 방식을 본문의 "negative mood functions like a mild alarm signal, indicating that the situation is novel and unfamiliar, and that the careful monitoring of new, external information is required." 부분을 통해 설명하고 있다. 여기서 부정적인 감정은 새로운 외부 정보의 면밀한 감시가 요구되는 상황에서 일종의 위험 신호를 보내면서 처리한다는 내용이므로 빈칸에 ③이 적합하다는 것을 알 수 있다.

| 어휘 | **adaptive** ⓐ 조정의; 적응할 수 있는
affect ⓝ [심리학] 감정, 정서
selective memory bias – 선택적 기억 편향
exclusive ⓐ 독점적인, 전용의
implication ⓝ 영향, 결과; 함축
novel ⓐ 새로운
cognitive ⓐ 인지의
albeit ⓒⓞⓝ 비록 ~일지라도
intriguing ⓐ 아주 흥미로운

[56-58] 한국외대 2018

1996년 심리학자인 로이 바우마이스터(Roy Baumeister)는 하나의 실험을 수행했는데, 실험 결과 우리 인간의 의지력은 고갈될 수 있는 자원과 같다는 사실이 나타났다. 해당 연구의 첫 번째 단계에서 참가자들은 갓 구운 초콜릿 칩 쿠키 한 묶음이 군침이 돌게 놓인 방 안에서 테스트를 받았다. 하지만, 참가자 전체가 쿠키를 먹도록 허용된 것은 아니었다. 참가자들 가운데 반은 단 것을 마음껏 먹을 수 있다는 허가를 받았지만, 나머지 반에게는 대신 무 한 묶음이 먹으라고 주어졌다. 연구의 두 번째 단계에서는 모든 참가자들에게 인내력을 테스트하는 퍼즐이 주어졌고, 이 퍼즐은 수많은 시도 끝에 최대한 집중을 해야만 풀 수 있는 것이었다. (위와 같이) 참가자들은 두 집단으로 구성되었는데, 퍼즐의 성과를 (두 집단 간에) 서로 비교해 보면 현저하게 대조적인 결과가 나왔다. 무를 먹으라고 받은 참가자들은 쿠키를 받은 참가자들에 비해 시도 횟수가 훨씬 적었고, 포기도 더 빨리했고, 평균적으로 퍼즐 해결 성공률이 떨어졌다. 바우마이스터는 자제력과 의지력은 매우 많은 종류의 업무에서 활용 가능한 자원이지만 과도하게 활용할 경우 고갈될 수 있다는 결론을 내렸다. 실험의 첫 단계에서 단 것들을 먹지 않고 참아야 했던 참가자들은 의지라는 이름의 이용 가능 자원을 고갈시키고 말았고 더 이상 퍼즐에 집중할 만큼의 의지를 갖고 있지 못했다. 이러한 연구 결과는, 자제력을 일종의 숙달이 가능한 기술로 보고 결과에 거의 영향을 미치지 않는 것으로 여기던, 기존의 자제력과 의지력에 대한 견해를 반박한다. 바우마이스터의 연구는 자기 통제가 근육을 사용하는 것에 더 가깝다는 사실을 보여준다. 열심히 운동하고 나면 피로해질 가능성이 크다. 좋은 소식은 어쩌면 의지력은 근육처럼 규칙적인 운동과 훈련을 통해 강화될 수도 있다는 점이다.

56 본문에 따르면 왜 무를 먹은 참가자들은 퍼즐 해결의 성공률이 떨어졌는가?
① 맛없는 무를 먹느라 너무 많은 시간을 보냈다.
② 다른 집단에 비해 지능 수준이 높았다.
③ 쿠키를 먹지 못하게 되었기 때문에 화가 났다.
④ 쿠키를 먹지 않으려 하다가 의지력을 다 써 버렸다.

| 정답 | ④

| 해설 | 본문에 따르면 의지력은 일종의 자원으로 고갈될 가능성이 있다. 때문에 맛있는 쿠키가 아니라 맛없는 무를 억지로 먹기 위해 의지력을 발휘했던 사람들은 그 결과 의지력이 소모되어 나중에 까다로운 퍼즐을 풀 수 있을 만큼의 의지력이 고갈될 수 있다. 따라서 답은 ④이다.

57 본문에 따르면 다음 중 사실인 것은 무엇인가?
① 쿠키를 먹은 참가자들은 퍼즐을 풀기 위한 시도를 더 많이 했다.
② 자제력은 개인 성격의 타고난 부분이다.
③ 과거에는, 자기 통제는 강화가 가능한 근육과 같은 것으로 여겨졌다.
④ 강한 의지력을 갖춘 사람은 운동 없이도 계속 끈질기게 버틴다.

| 정답 | ①

| 해설 | "무를 먹으라고 받은 참가자들은 쿠키를 받은 참가자들에 비해 시도 횟수가 훨씬 적었고, 포기도 더 빨리했고, 평균적으로 퍼즐 해결 성공률이 떨어졌다(The participants who were given radishes to eat made far fewer attempts, gave up faster, and, on average, were less successful at solving the puzzle than the participants who had been given cookies)." 이는 역으로 보면 쿠키를 먹은 참가자들이 퍼즐을 풀기 위해 시도를 훨씬 더 많이 했다는 소리와 같다. 따라서 답은 ①이다.

58

(A)에 가장 알맞은 것은 무엇인가?
① 영구적인 부상에 시달리기 쉽다
② 피로해질 가능성이 크다
③ 신속하게 채워지다
④ 다음번에 사용하기가 더 쉽다

| 정답 | ②

| 해설 | 자제력은 소모될 수 있는 일종의 자원이다. 근육을 자제력에 비유한다면 근육 운동을 열심히 하고 나면 당연히 "피로해질 가능성이 크고" 마찬가지로 자제력을 소모하게 되면 결국에는 고갈될 수 있다. 여기서 답은 ②임을 알 수 있다.

| 어휘 |
- deplete ⓥ 비우다, 고갈시키다
- invitingly ⓐⓓ 시선을 끌게, 군침이 돌게, 솔깃하게
- sweet tooth – 단 것[과자]을 좋아함
- strikingly ⓐⓓ 현저하게, 두드러지게
- self-control ⓝ 자제력
- a pool of resources – 이용 가능 자원
- self-regulation ⓝ 자기 통제
- unsavory ⓐ 맛없는
- persistent ⓐ 끈질긴, 집요한; 영속하는, 영존하는
- replenish ⓥ (원래처럼) 다시 채우다, 보충하다
- a batch of – 한 묶음의, 한 무리의
- indulge ⓥ 마음껏 하다, 갖고 싶은 대로 갖게 하다
- persistence ⓝ 고집, 인내력
- contrastive ⓐ 대조적인, 대비되는
- resist ⓥ (몹시 하고 싶은 것을 하지 않고) 참다[견디다]
- contradict ⓥ ~와 상반하다; ~을 부인하다, 반박하다
- strenuously ⓐⓓ 활기차게, 열심히
- innate ⓐ 타고난, 선천적인
- liable ⓐ ~의 영향을 받기[~당하기] 쉬운

[59-60] 한국외대 2017

최근 한 연구에서 아버지와 딸의 관계에 관해, 딸의 자존감과 삶의 만족이라는 관점에서, 3가지 영역(참여, 접근 가능성, 책임감)을 조사했다. 연구자들은 참여(engagement)를 아버지가 딸과 갖는 직접적인 교류로 정의했으며, 접근 가능성(accessibility)은 신체적 혹은 심리적 이용 가능성으로, 책임감(responsibility)은 자녀에게 양육을 제공하는 것으로 정의했다. 이러한 유형의 개입이 아이의 행복과 직접적으로 관련되어 있다고 연구자들은 추정했다. "아이의 현재와 미래의 행동에 가장 큰 영향을 미치는 것은 아이의 내면에 장기적으로 남아 있는 부모의 '잔영'으로, 이는 부모에 대한 아이의 회상적 인식 안에 간직되어 있다."고 연구 저자들은 밝히고 있다. <u>이 연구의 독특한 점은 그것이 아버지의 개입에 대한 딸의 '인식'에 관한 것이지, 아버지가 개입한 객관적 '사실들'에 관한 것은 아니라는 점이다.</u> 이 연구 조사를 위해서 우선 18~21세 사이의 여성 참가자들을 모집한 후, 이들에 대해 심층적인 심리 설문조사를 마쳤다. 연구결과는 전반적으로 아버지의 개입에 대한 회상적 인식이 성인이 되는 딸의 자존감과 다소 강한 양의 상관관계가 있다는 예측을 뒷받침해 주었다. 사춘기 시절 아버지의 개입에 대한 성인이 되는 딸의 회고적 인식이 더 높을수록 딸의 자존감도 더 높게 나타났다. 이와 마찬가지로, 아버지의 개입에 관한 인식 수준과 딸의 삶의 만족 사이에도 양의 상관관계가 있었다.

59

다음 문장이 들어갈 곳으로 알맞은 위치는?

> 이 연구의 독특한 점은 그것이 아버지의 개입에 대한 딸의 '인식'에 관한 것이지, 아버지가 개입한 객관적 '사실들'에 관한 것은 아니라는 점이다.

① Ⓐ
② Ⓑ
③ Ⓒ
④ Ⓓ

| 정답 | ②

| 해설 | 주어진 문장은 아버지의 개입에 대해 딸이 느끼는 '인식'이 중요한 것이지, 아버지가 얼마나 많이 실제 개입했는지에 관한 객관적 '사실'이 중요한 것은 아니었다고 말하고 있다. 즉, 아버지에 대한 딸의 회상적 인식에 관한 특이점을 서술한 것이므로, 이 내용 앞에는 '아버지에 대한 딸의 회상적 인식'이 등장해야 하므로, 정답은 ②가 적합하다.

60

다음 중 본문의 내용과 일치하는 것은?
① 접근 가능성이란 아버지가 자녀와 갖는 교류로 정의 내려진다.
② 연구자들은 성인이 되는 참가자들이 완성한 철저한 설문조사를 이용했다.
③ 이 주제에 대한 연구자들의 가정이 연구 결과와 모순되게 나타난다.
④ 아버지의 참여가 딸의 행복에 근본적인 요소는 아니다.

| 정답 | ②

| 해설 | ① 아버지가 자녀와 갖는 교류로 정의 내려진 것은 접근 가능성(accessibility)이 아니라 참여(engagement)이다. ③ "Overall, results supported the prediction that ..."을 통해, 실험 결과가 연구자들의 가정을 뒷받침해 주고 (supported) 있다는 것을 알 수 있다. ④ 본문 후반에서 아버지의 개입이 딸의 자존감 및 삶의 만족과 양의 상관 관계를 보이고 있다고 했으므로, 아버지의 참여는 딸의 행복과 밀접한 관련이 있는 토대가 됨을 알 수 있다. 정답은 ②로, 본문 중반의 "For the study, female participants between the ages of 18 and 21 were recruited and completed an in-depth psychological questionnaire."를 재진술한 내용에 해당한다.

| 어휘 | examine ⓥ 시험하다, 검사하다, 조사하다   engagement ⓝ 교전; 참여; 약속; 업무; 약혼
accessibility ⓝ 접근 (가능성), 접근하기 쉬움; 이해하기 쉬움
self-esteem ⓝ 자존감   define ⓥ 정의하다
psychological ⓐ 심리학적인   provision ⓝ 공급, 제공; 대비, 준비
residue ⓝ 나머지, 잔여
encapsulate ⓥ 캡슐에 싸다[넣다], (캡슐에 싸듯이) 조심스럽게 보호하다; 요약하다, 압축하다
retrospective ⓐ 회고의, 회상하는   perception ⓝ 인지, 인식, 지각, 이해
questionnaire ⓝ 설문조사, 설문지
moderately ⓐⓓ 중간 정도로, 적당히; 적정하게, 알맞게
adolescence ⓝ 청소년기, 사춘기   belie ⓥ 모순되다, 딴판이다

에듀윌 편입영어 **기출심화 완성 독해**

PART 04

문화 · 예술

CHAPTER 01   문화
CHAPTER 02   정보 · 기술
CHAPTER 03   지역 · 지리
CHAPTER 04   음악 · 미술
CHAPTER 05   영화 · 스포츠

CHAPTER 01 문화

01	③	02	②	03	①	04	①	05	③	06	②	07	⑤	08	③	09	①	10	④
11	③	12	④	13	②	14	④	15	④	16	②	17	④	18	②	19	④	20	②
21	④	22	①	23	③	24	②	25	③	26	④	27	②	28	⑤	29	③	30	③
31	④	32	①	33	③	34	②	35	③	36	①	37	③	38	④	39	④	40	④
41	②	42	⑤	43	④	44	②	45	①	46	①	47	②	48	③	49	②	50	①

[01-03] 이화여대 2009

문화이론들은 개인이 따라야 하는 기존의 가치관들에 완전히 둘러싸여 있다고 결론짓곤 한다. 일부 보수적인 비평가들에 따르면, 이런 관점은 개인의 도덕적 책임을 축소한다는 문제점이 있다. 다른 한편에선, 인간에게 반대할 자유, 협상, 전복의 여지가 전혀 없는 무거운 짐이라는 숙명론적이고 비관적인 문화관을 초래한다는 비판이 있다. 미국의 인류학자이자 문화비평가인 James Clifford는 "19세기 중반 이후, 문화 이론들은 집단적 경험에 연속성과 깊이를 부여하는 특징들을 결합하면서, 문화를 논쟁적이고 파편화되고 상호텍스트적이고 혼합적인 것이 아니라 완전한 것으로 간주했다."고 썼다. 그에 따르면, 모든 인간에게 일반적이지도 않고 개인에게만 특수하지도 않은 행동 패턴을 설명하기 위해서는 '문화' 같은 용어가 반드시 필요하다. 그러나 우리는 문화가 본질적으로 불안정하고 분열적이라는 것을 인식해야 한다. 문화의 경계선은 규정할 수 없고 논란의 여지가 많기 때문이다.

01

다음 중 빈칸 (A)에 가장 적절한 것은?

① 극복하다 ② 초과하다
③ 종속되다 ④ 풀려나다

| 정답 | ③

| 해설 | 다음 문장에 문화의 특징이 상술되어 있다. "culture as an immoveable burden that leaves us no freedom for dissent, negotiation and subversion." 반대와 협상과 전복의 자유를 박탈하는 문화이므로 인간이 종속된 (become subordinate) 문화임을 알 수 있다. 답은 ③이다.

02

다음 중 빈칸 (B)와 대체할 수 있는 것은?

① 소생 ② 감소
③ 과장 ④ 지체

| 정답 | ②

| 해설 | 단순한 어휘 문제이다. reduction(감소)과 동의어는 ② diminishment(감소)이다.

03

다음 중 빈칸 (C)와 (D)에 가장 적절한 것은?

① 숙명론적인 – 비관적인
② 실존적인 – 불가피한
③ 끝에서 두 번째의 – 무시하는
④ 평등주의적인 – 인도주의적인

| 정답 | ①

| 해설 | "culture as an immoveable burden that leaves us no freedom for dissent, negotiation and subversion." 에 문화의 특징이 부연되어 있다. 반대와 협상과 전복의 자유를 박탈하는 문화이므로 숙명적(fatalistic)이고 비관적인(pessimistic) 문화이다. 따라서 정답은 ①이다.

| 어휘 |
enclose ⓥ 에워싸다
subordinate to – ~에 종속적인
reduction ⓝ 감소
fatalistic ⓐ 숙명론적인, 체념하는
immoveable ⓐ 부동의
negotiation ⓝ 협상
anthropologist ⓝ 인류학자
collective ⓐ 집단적인
torn ⓐ 찢어진, 분열된
syncretic ⓐ 혼합적인
specific ⓐ 특수한, 구체적인
internally ⓐⓓ 내적으로
riven ⓐ 분열적인
unmappable ⓐ 지도에 표시할 수 없는

pre-existing ⓐ 기존의
conservative ⓐ 보수적인
responsibility ⓝ 책임
pessimistic ⓐ 비관적인
dissent ⓝ 반대
subversion ⓝ 전복
continuity ⓝ 연속
disputed ⓐ 논쟁적인, 논란이 되는
intertextual ⓐ 상호텍스트적인[상호 관련된]
generically ⓐⓓ 일반적으로
recognize ⓥ 인식하다
unstable ⓐ 불안정한
perimeter ⓝ 주변, 외곽
contested ⓐ 논쟁적인, 경쟁적인

[04-06] 숭실대 2006

서로 다른 문화권의 사람들은 서로의 제스처를 종종 오해한다. Athabaskan 인디언들의 대화에서, 1.5초 정도의 침묵은 반드시 할 말이 끝났다는 것을 의미하지는 않는다. 이들은 말하는 도중에도 그 정도의 시간 동안 잠시 멈추곤 한다. 반면에 유럽계 미국인들은, 물론 사회마다 정도 차이는 있겠지만, 1초 이상의 침묵이면 할 말이 끝났다는 충분한 신호라고 생각한다. Athabaskan 인디언들과 유럽계 미국인들이 대화할 때, 후자는 인디언들이 말하는 도중에 멈추는 것을 할 말이 끝났다는 신호로 오해해서 마음 놓고 말을 하려 한다. 그러나 Athabaskan 인디언들이 볼 때는, 그 순간에 유럽계 미국인들이 말을 하려 하는 것은 자신이 말하는 중간에 끼어드는 것이다. 이런 상황이 계속 반복되면서, 서로 간에 부정적인 고정관념이 생긴다. 전자는 후자를 무례하고, 고압적이고, 심하게 수다스럽다고 생각하는 반면, 후자는 전자가 대화에 소극적이고, 퉁명스럽고, 논리적인 대화를 못한다고 생각한다. 자신도 모르게 이런 고정관념을 교실에서까지 보이는 유럽계 미국인 교사들은 학생들이 크게 말하고, 서로 대화하고, 즉시 대답해야 한다는 암묵적인 문화적 기대를 갖고 있기 때문에, Athabaskan 인디언 학생들이 무반응에 우둔하다고 생각한다. 이런 것들은 주로 유럽계 미국인 문화에서 자란 학생들의 행동인 반면, 자신들의 문화적 규범을 중시하는 Athabaskan 학생들은 그런 식으로 행동하지 않는다. 대부분의 사람들은 그런 미묘한 문화 간 차이를 인식하지 못하지만, 그 차이는 심각한 사회적 결과를 초래할 수 있다.

04

다음 중 빈칸 ⓐ에 가장 적절한 것은?

① 문화적 기대 ② 개인의 직관
③ 인종적 태도 ④ 사회적 능력

| 정답 | ①

| 해설 | 앞부분의 내용에 대한 예시가 되도록 빈칸을 완성한다. 앞부분에서 학생들의 태도가 문화에 따라 다르다고 했으므로, 교사도 학생들의 태도를 문화적 관점에서 예상하고 해석할 것이다. '학생들의 적극적 태도에 대한 문화적 기대(cultural expectation) → 실제 태도에 대한 실망', 따라서 보기 ①이 적절하다. ②는 앞부분의 내용과 무관하므로 선택하지 않도록 주의한다.

05

지문에 따르면, 다음 중 비교 문화적 언어 습관을 잘못 설명한 것은 무엇인가?

① 유럽계 미국인 교사들은 Athabaskan 학생들이 과묵하다고 생각한다.
② Athabaskan 인디언들은 유럽계 미국인들이 무례하다고 생각한다.
③ 유럽계 미국인들은 Athabaskan 인디언들보다 말할 기회를 더 자주 양보한다.
④ 유럽계 미국인 교사들은 Athabaskan 학생들이 말을 조리 있게 하지 못한다고 생각한다.

| 정답 | ③

| 해설 | 문화권이 다르면 언어 습관이 다르고, 다른 문화의 언어적 관습을 오해하기도 한다는 비교문화적 관점과 그 예시가 지문의 내용이다. 내용이 일치하지 않는 보기를 찾을 때 "When Athabaskan Indians and European Americans interact with each other, the latter often misinterpret the Athabaskans' midturn pauses as end-of-turn signals and feel free to claim the floor."를 참조하면, 유럽계 미국인들은 Athabaskan 인디언들이 말하는 중간에 끼어드는 경우가 많으므로 ③의 내용이 일치하지 않는다.

06

다음 중 빈칸 ⓑ에 적절한 결론은 무엇인가?

① 그 차이를 통해 소통 능력이 향상될 수 있다
② 그 차이는 심각한 사회적 결과를 초래할 수 있다
③ 그 차이는 사람들의 평판에 도움이 될 수 있다
④ 그 차이는 단일어 사회로 발전될 수 있다

| 정답 | ②

| 해설 | though를 중심으로 대조의 논리를 완성하는 것이 출제 의도이다. "Though most people are unaware of such subtle cross-cultural differences(문화적 차이를 인식하지 못하지만), ↔ they can have profound social consequences(문화적 차이가 심각한 결과를 가져올 수 있다)." '문화적 차이에 대한 무지'와 '문화적 차이로 인한 심각한 결과'가 대조를 이룬다. 따라서 답은 ②이다.

| 어휘 | **misinterpret** ⓥ 오해하다 **pause** ⓝ 정지
indicate ⓥ 나타내다 **turn** ⓝ 말할 차례[순서]
sufficient ⓐ 충분한 **variation** ⓝ 차이, 변화
interact ⓥ 대화하다, 상호작용하다 **claim the floor** – 발언권을 요구하다

perspective ⓝ 관점
interruption ⓝ 방해
stereotype ⓝ 고정관념
rude ⓐ 무례한
talkative ⓐ 수다스러운
coherent ⓐ 일관성 있는
judge ⓥ 판단하다
unspoken ⓐ 언외의
quick ⓐ 재빠른
honor ⓥ 존중하다
be unaware of - ~을 모르다
cross-cultural ⓐ 비교문화적인, 문화 간의

constitute ⓥ ~이 되다, ~을 구성하다
time and again - 반복해서
arise ⓥ 발생하다
pushy ⓐ 고압적인
sullen ⓐ 퉁명스러운
unwittingly ⓐⓓ 부지불식간에
unresponsive ⓐ 묵묵부답의, 반응 없는
speak up - 크게 말하다
mainstream ⓐ 주류(의)
norm ⓝ 규범
subtle ⓐ 미묘한

[07-09] 한국외대 2010

한 세기 이상 동안, 서양의 철학자들과 심리학자들은, 동일한 기본적 과정이 인간의 모든 사고의 기본이 된다는, 이 하나의 주요한 가정에 정신적 삶에 대한 논의의 기반을 두었다. 문화적 차이점은 사람들이 무엇에 관해 생각하는지를 가리킬 것이다. 하지만 서양의 철학자들은, 사람들이 정보를 가공하고 자신 주변의 세상에서 벌어지는 일을 이해하기 위해 채택한 전략인, 사고 습관이 모든 사람들에게 동일하다고 가정했다. 여기엔 논리적 추론, 범주화, 원인과 결과라는 선형적 관점에서 사건을 이해하기 등이 있다.

하지만 Michigan 대학의 한 사회심리학자가 행한 연구는 이처럼 오랫동안 품어져 온 정신적 기능에 관한 관점을 뒤집어엎었다. 유럽계 미국인들과 동아시아인들을 비교한 일련의 연구에서, Richard Nisbett 박사와 그의 동료들은 다른 문화에서 자란 사람들은 다른 것들을 생각할 뿐 아니라 다르게 생각한다는 것을 발견했다. "우리는 모두가 동일한 방식으로 범주를 활용하고, 매일의 삶을 이해하는 데 있어 논리가 모두에게 동일한 종류의 역할을 하고, 기억이나 지각 그리고 기타 것들이 모두 동일하다고 생각했었습니다. 하지만 지금 우리는 인지과정 그 자체도 심리학계 주류가 가정했던 것과 많이 다르다고 주장하고 있습니다."라고 Nisbett 박사는 말했다.

07 다음 중 본문의 주제로 가장 알맞은 것은 무엇인가?
① 주류 서양철학에 가해진 문화적 영향
② 상식에 대한 서양철학자들의 관념 변화
③ 심리학에서의 논리적 추론에 관한 다양한 관점
④ 서양철학 및 심리학에서의 오랫동안 지속된 관점
⑤ 사고 과정에 있어서의 새로 발견된 문화적 영향

| 정답 | ⑤

| 해설 | 서양철학과 심리학에서는 인간의 사고 습관이나 과정은 문화적 차이와는 상관없이 모두 동일할 것이라고 생각해 왔는데, 실제 실험을 해 보니 다른 것들을 생각하는 정도에서 벗어나 아예 생각하는 방식이 다르다는 결과가 나와서 기존에 가졌던 관념을 모두 뒤집어야 하는 상황이 되었다는 것이 본문의 주 내용이다. 또한 연구진이 새로이 발견한 것은 "people who grow up in different cultures do not just think about different things, they think differently(다른 문화에서 자란 사람들은 다른 것들을 생각할 뿐 아니라 다르게 생각한다)"는 점이고, 이는 달리 말하면 문화적 요소가 사람의 사고에 상당히 큰 영향을 끼친다는 것을 의미한다. 따라서 보기 중에서 본문의 주제에 가

장 적합한 것을 고르면 ⑤가 된다. ①과 ③은 본문과 별 관련이 없다. ②는 본문이 "Common Sense(상식)"에 관한 내용은 아니기 때문에 답으로 볼 수 없다. ④의 경우는, 본문이 "Long-held Views(오랫동안 지속된 관점)"에 관해 논하는 정도로 끝나는 것이 아니라 그 관점이 뒤집어졌다는 것까지 언급하기 때문에 결국 본문의 주제로 보기에는 미흡하다.

08

㉮에 가장 알맞은 것은 무엇인가?
① 특이한
② 뿌리 깊이 배어든
③ 동일한
④ 물려받은
⑤ 조종할 수 있는

| 정답 | ③

| 해설 | 서양철학과 심리학에서 가장 기본적인 전제로 삼은 것은 "the same basic processes underlie all human thought(동일한 기본적 과정이 인간의 모든 사고의 기본이 된다)"이다. 비록 문화적 차이에 따라 생각하는 내용이 다를 수는 있지만, 결국 "habits of thought(사고 습관)"은 모두에게 '동일'하다는 것이 서양철학과 심리학의 기본 개념이었던 것이다. 따라서 빈칸에 들어갈 말은 ③의 "identical(동일한)"이다. 다른 보기는 대입해 봤을 때 본문의 내용과 맞지 않기 때문에 답으로 볼 수 없다.

09

㉯가 나타내는 것은 무엇인가?
① 사고 과정은 기본적으로 모든 문화에서 동일하다.
② 논리적 추론의 방식은 다른 세대에 따라 좌우된다.
③ 우리의 일상적 삶은 논리적 사고에 의해 지배된다.
④ 사람들은 원인과 결과를 인식하기 위해 사건을 순환적 방식으로 이해한다.
⑤ 예측하기 위해 사람들이 사용한 방법은 그 사람들이 어떻게 생각하는가에 영향을 받는다.

| 정답 | ①

| 해설 | 기존에 문화별로 생각하는 내용이 다를 수는 있어도 사고의 과정 차제는 모두 동일하다는 것이 서양철학 및 심리학의 기본 전제였으나, 이것이 최근 연구의 결과 뒤집히게 되었다는 것이 본문의 핵심 내용이다. 따라서 ㉯의 "what mainstream psychology assumed(심리학계 주류가 가정했던 것)"은 ①의 "thinking processes are basically the same in all cultures(사고 과정은 기본적으로 모든 문화에서 동일하다)"임을 쉽게 추론할 수 있다. 다른 보기는 그럴듯해 보이지만 모두 본문과는 관련이 없는 내용이므로 답이 될 수 없다.

| 어휘 | cardinal ⓐ 기본적인, 주요한
linear ⓐ 선의
long-held ⓐ 오랫동안 지속된
cognitive ⓐ 인식의, 지적 작용의
common sense – 상식
ingrained ⓐ (편견·미신·습관 등이) 깊이 배어든
inherited ⓐ 상속받은, 물려받은
comprehend ⓥ 이해하다; 함축하다
dictate ⓥ (조건·방침 등을) 명령하다
turn ~ upside down – ~을 뒤집다
perception ⓝ 지각, 인식
mainstream ⓐ 주류의
peculiar ⓐ 특이한
, 타고난
manipulable ⓐ 다룰 수 있는, 조종할 수 있는
calculation ⓝ 계산, 추정; 숙고

[10-12] 숭실대 2008

금기는 사회 구성원들을 불안하거나 당황스럽게, 혹은 수치스럽게 만드는 해로운 행동에 대한 금지나 기피이다. 따라서 언어에 있어서도, 절대 말해서는 안 되거나, 특정한 사람이 특정 상황에서만 언급할 수 있거나, 의도적으로 돌려서 완곡하게 표현해야 하는 것들이 있다. 물론 자신이 사회적 제약으로부터 자유롭다는 것을 과시하거나, '표현의 자유'를 추구하는 사회운동에서처럼 금기가 불합리하고 부당하다는 것을 알리기 위해 금기를 깨트리는 사람들도 언제나 있다.

금기시되는 주제는 성, 죽음, 배설, 신체적 기능, 종교적 문제, 정치 등 매우 다양하다. 반드시 피해야 하거나 신중을 기해야 할 금기 대상은 장모, 특정 사냥감, 왼손['sinister(사악한)'의 어원]의 사용 등이다. 영어에도 금기어가 있다. 영어를 사용하는 대부분의 사람들은 금기어가 무엇인지 잘 알고 있고 이 '규칙들'을 잘 지킨다. 누군가가 규칙을 어길 경우, Shaw가 희곡 Pygmalion에서 'bloody(빌어먹을)'란 표현을 사용하거나 영화 "Gone with the Wind"에 'damn(제기랄)'이란 표현이 등장했을 때만큼 대대적인 비난은 받지는 않겠지만, 그 일탈 행위에 대한 많은 비판이 뒤따를 것이다. 금기에 대한 기준과 규범은 변한다.

10 (A), (B), (C), (D) 중, '금기'로 채우기에 적절하지 않은 것은?
① (A) ② (B)
③ (C) ④ (D)

| 정답 | ④

| 해설 | 빈칸 (A), (B), (C) 이후 금기들이 구체적으로 예시되므로 빈칸에는 taboos가 적절하다. 빈칸 (D)는 금기어 'bloody'와 'damn'를 사용한 결과로 완성해야 하므로, 'comments(비난, 지적)'이 적절하다. 따라서 적절하지 않은 보기는 ④이다.

11 지문에 따르면, 다음 중 금기시되는 주제로 간주되지 않은 것은?
① 당신은 왜 신을 믿습니까?
② 당신은 이번에 노동당에 투표했습니까?
③ 당신은 새 집을 얼마에 구입했습니까?
④ 당신은 하루에 얼마나 자주 소변을 봅니까?

| 정답 | ③

| 해설 | 두 번째 단락의 "Tabooed subjects can vary widely: sex, death, excretion, bodily functions, religious matters, and politics."에서 상술된 금기에 해당하지 않는 주제는 money이다.

12 지문에 따르면, 사실인 것은?
① 금기는 엄격하게 지켜진다.
② 금기는 오늘날 더 중요하다.
③ 사람들은 아무 이유 없이 금기를 깬다.
④ 금기에 대한 판단은 시대에 따라 변한다.

| 정답 | ④

| 해설 | 마지막 문장 "Standards and norms change."에서 "금기에 대한 판단은 시대마다 변한다(Judgment about

taboos changes over time.)"는 것을 알 수 있다. 첫 번째 단락에 금기를 깨는 사람들은 언제나 있다는 점과 금기를 깨는 이유가 상술되어 있으므로 ①, ②를 선택하지 않도록 주의한다.

| 어휘 | taboo ⓝ 금기
prohibition ⓝ 금지
avoidance ⓝ 회피
anxiety ⓝ 불안
shame ⓝ 수치, 부끄러움
so far as ~ is concerned – ~에 관한 한, ~에 있어서
refer to – ~을 지칭하다
deliberate ⓐ 의도적인, 신중한
circumlocution ⓝ 완곡한 표현
euphemistically ⓐⓓ 완곡하게
constraint ⓝ 제약
irrational ⓐ 불합리한
unjustified ⓐ 부당한
free speech – 표현의 자유
excretion ⓝ 배설
game animal – 사냥감
sinister ⓐ 사악한
rupture ⓝ 파열(일탈), 결렬
arouse ⓥ 불러일으키다, 야기하다
comment ⓝ 비판, 지적
formerly ⓐⓓ 예전에
norm ⓝ 규범

[13-15] 명지대 2008

Istanbul Blue Mosque의 가장 유명한 특징 중 하나는 멀리서도 눈에 띄는 그 6개의 첨탑이다. 이것은 매우 독특한 특징인데 대부분의 모스크(이슬람 성전)에는 첨탑이 4개, 2개 혹은 1개만 있기 때문이다. 한 가지 설에 의하면, 금(터키어로 altin) 첨탑을 만들라는 Sultan의 명령을 건축가가 여섯(터키어로 alti) 개의 금탑을 만들라는 것으로 오해했다고 한다. 이 독특한 특징의 유래가 무엇이든 간에, 6개의 첨탑은 상당한 물의를 일으켰다. Mecca의 모스크도 첨탑이 6개였기 때문이다. 이 문제는 Mecca의 모스크에 7번째 첨탑이 추가되면서 해결되었다. 서측 주 출입구는 화려하게 장식되어 있으므로 놓쳐서는 안 된다. 그러나 성전의 경건함을 지키기 위해서, 비신도들은 Hippodrome(대예배당)에서 떨어진 북측 입구를 이용해야 한다. 이 문에는 들어설 때 모든 사람들이, 심지어 말에 탄 Sultan조차도 고개를 조아리게 하는 상징적 사슬들이 달려 있다. 내부의 높은 천장은 20,000여 개의 푸른 타일로 장식되어 있는데 Blue Mosque라는 별칭은 이 푸른 타일에서 유래한 것이다.

13 윗글의 내용과 다른 것은?
① 이슬람교도만이 서측 출입구를 이용할 수 있다.
② 두 입구에는 들어오는 사람이 고개를 숙이도록 낮게 걸어 놓은 상징적 사슬이 걸려 있다.
③ 주 출입구는 화려하게 장식되었다.
④ Blue Mosque의 첨탑들은 멀리서도 보인다.

| 정답 | ②

| 해설 | "However, to preserve the mosque's sanctity, non-worshippers are required to use the north entrance, off the Hippodrome. Hanging from this gate are symbolic chains"를 참조하면, 상징적 사슬이 걸려 있는 곳은 북측 입구이다.

14 현재 메카에 있는 이슬람 사원의 첨탑 수는 몇 개인가?
① 4개
② 5개
③ 6개
④ 7개

| 정답 | ④

| 해설 | "The problem was solved by adding a seventh minaret to Mecca's mosque."를 참조하면, 메카의 모스크에는 원래 6개의 첨탑이 있었지만 이후 1개가 추가되어 현재 7개이다. 따라서 ④가 답이다.

15 이스탄불에 있는 이슬람 사원이 지금의 명칭을 갖게 된 이유는?
① 주 출입구의 색
② 첨탑들의 색
③ 북측 입구에 걸려 있는 상징적 사슬의 색
④ 사원 내부의 높은 천장을 장식한 타일의 색

| 정답 | ④

| 해설 | 마지막 문장 "The interior's high ceiling is lined with about 20,000 blue tiles that give the mosque its popular name."를 참조하면, Blue Mosque라는 명칭이 천장을 장식한 푸른 타일에서 유래했음을 알 수 있다. 따라서 답은 ④이다.

| 어휘 | notable ⓐ 유명한
visible ⓐ 보이는, 눈에 띄는
account ⓝ 설명
scandal ⓝ 물의, 추문
decorate ⓥ 장식하다
sanctity ⓝ 경건함, 신성함
bow ⓥ 머리를 숙여 절하다
popular name - 속칭
feature ⓝ 특징
minaret ⓝ 첨탑
direct ⓥ 명령하다
entrance ⓝ 입구
preserve ⓥ 보존하다
non-worshipper ⓝ 비신도
be lined with - ~으로 안을 대다[채우다]

[16-17] 한국외대 2007

영국인들이 생각하는 이민은 외국인들이 일자리와 임대 아파트를 찾아서 국내로 이민하는 것이다. 그러나 그 반대 방향의 이민이 늘고 있다는 사실은 잘 모른다. 이것은 얼마나 많은 영국인들이 해외에 살고 있는지 제대로 알고 있는 사람이 없기 때문이다. 이 주제에 대한 정확한 데이터는 19세기 이래로 수집된 적이 없을 정도이다. 최근 조사에 따르면, 2006년 약 20만 명의 영국인들이 귀국 계획 없이 영국을 떠났고 550만 명은 현재 해외 거주 중이다.
왜 사람들은 영국을 떠나는 걸까? 해외로 떠난 사람들은 더 좋은 일자리와 더 나은 삶 때문이라고 말한다. 해외 이민을 아직 고려 중인 사람들 중 4분의 1은 영국의 높은 물가 때문이라고 말한다. 비싼 주택도 원인이다. 영국의 집을 팔면 해외에서 더 넓은 집을 살 수 있기 때문에 청년층과 무주택자들은 해외 이민을 고려하게 된다. 대부분의 이주자들은 해외가 더 좋아 보이기 때문에, 즉 기후가 더 온화하고 삶의 질이 더 높기 때문에 이주한다. 누가 그들을 비난할 수 있겠는가? 영국의 실질 가처분 소득은 2003년과 2005년 사이에 거의 늘지 않았고 삶의 질은 평범한 수준에 불과하다.

16

지문에 따르면, 영국인들이 영국의 이민에 있어서 (자국민의) 해외 이민보다 (외국인의) 국내 이민에 더 관심을 갖는 이유는 무엇인가?

① 데이터 조작
② 통계의 결여
③ 정부의 정책들
④ 유럽의 통합
⑤ 재정적 문제들

| 정답 | ②

| 해설 | "That is because no one really knows how many Britons live abroad. No proper data on the subject have been gathered since the 19th century."를 참조하면, 영국인들이 이민 현황에 무지한 것은 이민 추세에 대한 정확한 통계가 없기 때문이다. 따라서 답은 ②이다. ①은 비약이므로 타당하지 않다.

17

지문에 따르면, 다음 중 사실은?

① 최근 영국에서 해외 이민자들이 국내 이민자보다 많아졌다.
② 영국의 낮은 연금이 해외 이민의 주 원인이다.
③ 영국인의 민족성은 해외 이주를 꺼린다.
④ 더 높은 삶의 질이 해외 이민을 고려하는 주요인 중 하나이다.
⑤ 청년층은 장년층에 비해 영국을 떠나려는 경향이 덜하다.

| 정답 | ④

| 해설 | 두 번째 단락에 해외로 이민하는 여러 이유가 제시되었고 "Most leave because other countries sound better: a nicer climate, a higher quality of life."를 참조하면, 그중 하나가 더 높은 삶의 질이므로 ④가 정답이다. 해외 이민자가 증가 추세이기는 하지만 국내 이민자보다 많은지는 언급되지 않았으므로 ①을 선택하지 않도록 주의한다.

| 어휘 | migration ⓝ 이주, 이민
take notice of – ~에 주목하다, ~을 알아채다
the other way – 반대 방향으로
quarter ⓝ 4분의 1
cite ⓥ 언급하다
blame ⓥ 비난하다, 탓하다
mediocre ⓐ 평범한, 중간밖에 안 되는
immigration ⓝ 국내로의 이민[이주]

council flat – 임대 아파트
proper ⓐ 적절한
flirt with – ~을 장난삼아 생각해 보다
move ⓝ 이동
disposable income – 가처분 소득
emigration ⓝ 해외로의 이민[이주]

[18-19] 가톨릭 2013

문화충격은 사회적 교류와 관련한 모든 친숙한 신호와 상징을 잃게 되면서 발생하는 불안에 의해 촉발된다. 여기서 말하는 신호란 우리가 스스로를 일상의 상황에 적응시키기 위한 다양한 방식을 가리킨다. 예를 들어 언제 악수를 할 것인가, 사람들을 만나면 무슨 말을 해야 하는가 등이 있다. 이들 신호는 말, 몸짓, 얼굴 표정, 관습, 규범 등의 형태를 지닐 수 있으며, 성장 과정에서 우리 모두가 습득하고, 우리가 말하는 언어나 우리가 수용한 믿음과 마찬가지로 우리 문화의 일부가 된다.

어느 한 개인이 낯선 문화권에 속하게 되면, 이러한 친숙한 신호는 사라지게 된다. 그 개인은 마치 물 밖의 물고기와 같은 존재가 된다. 이 사람은 아무리 마음이 넓거나 선의에 가득한 존재일지라도 자신을 지탱하는 것들이 아래부터 무너져 버린 것이다. 이후 좌절감과 불안감이 뒤따르게 된다. 사람들은 아주 유사한 방식으로 좌절감에 대응한다. 우선 불쾌함을 야기하는 환경을 거부하게 된다. "우리를 손님으로 맞이한 국가의 방식에 문제가 있고 그 이유는 이들 방식이 우리의 기분을 나쁘게 하기 때문이다." 문화충격의 또 다른 단계는 퇴행이다. 고향의 환경이 갑자기 엄청난 중요성을 지니게 된다. 고향의 모든 것들이 비이성적으로 미화된다. 모든 어려움과 문제가 잊혀지고 고향에서의 좋은 것들만이 기억된다. 보통 고향으로 돌아가야만 현실로 복귀하게 된다.

18 빈칸에 들어갈 가장 적절한 표현을 고르시오.
① 건초 더미에서 바늘 찾기
② 물 밖의 물고기
③ 공중누각
④ 주객전도

| 정답 | ②

| 해설 | ②의 "물 밖에 벗어난 물고기"는 자신의 익숙한 환경을 벗어나서 낯선 상황에 처했을 때 쓰는 표현이다.

19 다음 문장이 들어갈 가장 적절한 곳을 고르시오.

고향의 모든 것들이 비이성적으로 미화된다.

① (A)
② (B)
③ (C)
④ (D)

| 정답 | ④

| 해설 | 제시된 문장 뒤에는 그러한 상황에서 빠져나와서는 정상적일 때와 다르게 좋은 측면만을 보려고 한다는 문장으로 이어져야 하므로 보기 ④가 적절하다.

| 어휘 | precipitate ⓥ 촉발시키다　　　orient ⓥ ~에 맞추다, ~에 적응시키다
norm ⓝ 규범　　　cue ⓝ 신호, 단서
prop ⓝ 지주, 버팀목　　　regression ⓝ 퇴행, 회귀
irrationally ⓐ 비이성적으로　　　glorify ⓥ 미화하다

[20-21] 단국대 2013

과거 우리를 서로 공유된 놀라움 속에서 하나로 묶어 주었던 그 수많은 은유가 우리에 대한 영향력을 잃어 가고 있다. 영화는 더 이상 우리 가운데 다수의 사람들을 사로잡지 못하고 있다. 논파가 불가능한 것으로 보였던 단체 스포츠마저도 점차 번영을 누릴수록 그리고 이들 단체 스포츠가 참가자들을 착취하는 방식에 관해 우리가 점차 많이 알아 가게 되면서 더 큰 논란에 휩싸이고 있다. 그리고 어떤 경우에서든 언론에 과도하게 노출되면서 친숙함이 오히려 오래된 비유를 향한 경멸까지는 아니더라도 초조함을 낳고 있다. 우리는 뭔가 신선하고 흠 없는 것을 찾는 과정에서 과거 애호가나 마니아들의 분야였던 영역으로 희망을 품고 진출하고 있다. 물론 우리는 참신함을 찾고 있지만 그러면서도 어느 정도 순수함을 빌고 있으며, 이런 순수함은 유명인 중심으로 돌아가는 체제로 인해 뒤틀린 압박으로부터 벗어날 경우에만 생겨나는 유형의 것이다. 과거 대중오락의 한 형태였던 서커스는 이제 우리 자신의 과거에 대한 의무감으로 그리고 어쩌면 실제와 다른 추억을 자녀들이 공유하게끔 하려는 희망을 품고 자녀들을 데리고 가는 변방에 불과하며, 순수하며 세속적이지 않지만 시대착오적인 곳으로서 실존하는 곳이기도 하다.

20
다음 중 본문에서 유추할 수 있는 것은 무엇인가?
① 기술은 과거를 향한 향수를 키우고 있다.
② 사람들은 세월이 흐르면서 오락에 대한 스스로의 취향을 바꿔 오고 있다.
③ 전통적 비유에 관해 여러 세대가 동일한 관점을 갖고 있다.
④ 영화와 스포츠는 애호가와 마니아만이 즐길 수 있는 분야이다.

| 정답 | ②

| 해설 | 세월이 흐르고 지식이 많아질수록 사람들은 영화, 단체 스포츠, 서커스 등에 관해 과거와는 다른 시선을 품고 있다. 그리고 "어떤 경우에서든 언론에 과도하게 노출이 되면서 친숙함이 오히려 오래된 비유를 향한 경멸까지는 아니더라도 초조함을 낳고 있다(in any event, familiarity, due in part to media overexposure, breeds restlessness, if not contempt, with the old metaphors)"는 말은 친숙한 것들에 대한 취향이 변화했음을 말하고 있다. 이 모두가 세월이 흐르면서 사람들의 취향이 변화했음을 보여주고 있다. 따라서 답은 ②이다.

21
저자에 따르면 서커스는 현재의 가치를 공유할 수 없으므로 시대착오적이다.
① 무리를 이룬 동물들이 등장하는 쇼이다
② 아이들에게 즐거움과 흥분을 불러일으킨다
③ 유명인 중심 체제를 반영한다
④ 현재의 가치를 공유할 수 없다

| 정답 | ④

| 해설 | 본문 마지막 부분에서 저자는 서커스를 "시대착오적인 것(anachronism)"으로 지칭한다. 시대착오적이라는 말은 현재와 더 이상 맞지 않는 것을 의미하며, 과거가 아닌 '현재의 가치를 더 이상 공유할 수 없는 것'을 의미한다. 따라서 답은 ④이다.

| 어휘 | metaphor ⓝ 은유, 비유   hold ⓝ 영향력, 지배력
　　　 unassailable ⓐ 난공불락의, 논파할 수 없는   prosperous ⓐ 번영한, 번창한
　　　 sophistication ⓝ 지식, 교양, 세련   restlessness ⓝ 동요, 초조함
　　　 untainted ⓐ 때 묻지 않은, 흠 없는   province ⓝ 분야

buffs ⓝ 애호가, ~광	aficionado ⓝ ~광, 마니아
novelty ⓝ 새로움, 참신함	backwater ⓝ 후미진 곳, 변두리
unworldly ⓐ 세속적이지 않은, 순진한	anachronism ⓝ 시대착오적인 것

[22-24] 명지대 2013

50명의 서양 출신 미국 어머니와 48명의 중국 이민자 출신 어머니를 대상으로 이루어진 한 연구에 따르면 70% 가량의 서양 어머니는 "학업의 성공을 강조하는 것은 아이에게 좋지 못하다"라고 답하거나 "부모는 배움이 재미있는 것이라는 생각을 키워 줘야 한다"고 답했다. 대조적으로 이런 식으로 생각하는 중국 어머니는 거의 0%였다. 대신에 중국 어머니의 절대 다수는 자신의 자녀가 "최고의" 학생이 될 수 있다고 생각한다고 밝혔고, "학업의 성취는 성공적 자녀 양육을 반영한다"고 말했으며, 만일 자녀가 학교에서 두각을 나타내지 않는다면 이는 "문제"가 되며 부모는 "할 일을 하지 않은 것"이라고 생각한다고 말했다.

그 외 다른 연구를 보면, 서양 부모와 비교해 중국 부모는 매일 반복 학습을 위해 자녀와 함께 하는 시간이 최대 열 배에 달한다. 대조적으로 서양 아이들은 다양한 스포츠 활동에 참여할 확률이 높았다. 여기서 나는 다음의 사항을 최종적으로 강조하고자 한다. 일부는 미국의 스포츠 부모는 중국 어머니와 유사하다고 생각할 수 있다. 하지만 결코 그렇지 않다. 일반적으로 여러분이 알고 있으며 자녀에게 과도한 스케줄을 강제하는 서양의 사커맘과 달리, 중국 어머니는 학교 공부가 언제나 가장 우선시된다고 생각한다. 중국 어머니의 시선에 따르면, A-는 형편없는 성적이며, 수학에서 최소 2년은 선행 학습이 이루어져야 하며, 공개적으로 자녀를 칭찬해서는 결코 안 되며, 자녀가 교사나 감독의 뜻에 따르지 않을 경우 언제나 교사나 감독의 편에 서야 하며, 자녀가 할 수 있도록 허용되는 유일한 활동은 자녀가 결국에는 메달을 획득할 수 있는 것이어야 하고, 획득한 메달은 반드시 금메달이어야 한다.

아시아 어머니는 종종 주도면밀하고, 냉담하며, 열정이 과도하며, 자녀의 진정한 관심사에는 무관심한 사람으로 묘사된다. 중국 어머니들의 경우, 꽤나 많은 이들이 스스로가 서양 어머니에 비해 자녀를 더 많이 신경 쓰며 자녀를 위해 더 많은 것을 기꺼이 희생할 것이라고 믿고 있지만, 이를 드러내지는 않고 있다. 나는 이런 생각은 양측 모두에게 있어 오해라고 본다. 제대로 된 부모는 자녀를 위해 최선의 행위를 하고 싶어 한다. 중국 어머니는 단지 최선의 행위를 하기 위한 방법에 관한 생각이 서양 어머니와 완전히 다를 뿐이다.

22 빈칸 (A)에 가장 적합한 것을 고르시오.
① 유사체
② 보충물
③ 대리인
④ 반대

| 정답 | ①

| 해설 | 빈칸 뒤를 보면 "하지만 결코 그렇지 않다(This is so wrong)" 다음에 중국 엄마와 서양 엄마의 차이점을 말하고 있음을 알 수 있다. 때문에 빈칸이 들어간 문장은 이와 내용이 반대이어야 하며, 즉 중국 엄마와 서양 엄마가 서로 유사하다는 내용을 말해야 한다. 따라서 답은 ①이다.

23 본문에 따르면 사실이 아닌 것은 무엇인가?
① 서양 어머니 및 중국 어머니의 자녀 양육에 대한 태도를 주제로 연구가 수행되었다.
② 중국 어머니는 거의 완벽에 가까운 점수도 만족스러워하지 않는다.
③ 저자는 서양 어머니의 시각보다 중국 어머니의 시각을 지지한다.
④ 서양 어머니는 자녀의 학업 성취를 과도하게 강조하지 않는 경향이 있다.

| 정답 | ③

| 해설 | "나는 이런 생각은 양측 모두에게 있어 오해라고 본다. 제대로 된 부모는 자녀를 위해 최선의 행위를 하고 싶어 한다. 중국 어머니는 단지 최선의 행위를 하기 위한 방법에 관한 생각이 서양 어머니와 완전히 다를 뿐이다(I think it's a misunderstanding on both sides. All decent parents want to do what's best for their children. The Chinese just have a totally different idea of how to do that)." 여기서 저자는 어느 한쪽을 옹호하기보다는, 서양 엄마든 중국 엄마든 각자 자신만의 방식으로 아이를 아끼고 있으며 단지 방법의 차이임을 말하고 있다. 따라서 저자가 어느 한쪽의 시각을 지지한다는 내용의 ③은 본문의 내용과 다르다.

24

다음 중 나머지와 다른 것을 하나 고르시오.

① they ② they
③ they ④ them

| 정답 | ②

| 해설 | ②는 중국인 엄마를 가리키고, 그 외 나머지는 자녀를 가리킨다. 따라서 답은 ②이다.

| 어휘 | drill ⓥ 반복 연습[훈련]시키다   analogue ⓝ 유사체
compliment ⓥ 칭찬하다   scheming ⓐ 주도면밀한
callous ⓐ 냉담한   overdriven ⓐ 과열된, 열성을 다하는
supplement ⓝ 보충물   surrogate ⓝ 대리(인)
antithesis ⓝ 반대, 대립   endorse ⓥ 지지하다, 홍보하다

[25-27]

여러분이 만약 지난 몇 년간 인터넷상의 아마추어 성향에 관한 논란과 논평 등을 숙독해 왔다면, 논쟁이 결국 다음의 두 가지로 귀결된다는 사실을 깨달을 것이다. 기존의 저널리즘에 블로깅이 미치는 영향과 기존의 학문에 위키피디아가 미치는 영향 말이다. 이 두 경우를 보면 훈련받고, 제도적으로 공인받은 엘리트들이 블로거인 글렌 레이놀드의 표현을 빌면 "다윗의 군단"의 도전을 받고 있으며, 여기에 양측 모두 이기면 다는 생각과, 조롱과, 수동적인 태도가 혼재되어 있다. 이러한 논쟁은 전적으로 타당한 것으로 볼 수 있는데, 그 이유는 블로거들과 위키피디아 편집자들은 전문가들로 불리는 자신들의 상대(언론인, 학자)보다 더 잘하는 것도 있고, 훨씬 못하는 것도 있기 때문이며, 우리 입장에서는 어떤 것이 잘했고 못했는지 파악하는 편이 제일 낫기 때문이다. 이 문제를 계속 논의하느라 시간을 많이 보내게 되면, 인터넷이 열어 놓은 광대한 아이디어의 시장에서 아마추어 저널리즘과 백과사전 작업의 중요성을 과대 포장하는 것이 되는 점이 문제가 된다. 사실 인터넷상에서 사용자가 창조한 콘텐츠 중 대다수는 전통적인 전문가의 권위의 상대가 되지 못한다. 이런 사례가 먹히는 영역은 전문가가 없는 영역이나 사용자들 자신이 전문가인 영역일 뿐이다.

25

밑줄 친 "다윗의 군대"의 의미와 가장 가까운 것을 고르시오.

① 권위를 가진 사람 ② 무력 성향을 지닌 사람
③ 보통 사람 ④ 모험심이 강한 사람

| 정답 | ③

| 해설 | 성경에서 소년 다윗이 골리앗이라는 거인을 물리친 것을 떠올려 보면, 위키피디아 편집자들이나 블로거들은 '아마추어주의'를 상징하는 '보통' 사람들로 비유할 수 있고 기존의 전문가 및 권위자 또는 엘리트들은 골리앗과 같은 존재로 비유할 수 있다. 그리고 이 여러 '다윗'이 모여 기존의 권위에 도전하고 있는 것이다. 따라서 답은 ③이다.

26 빈칸에 가장 알맞은 것을 고르시오.
① 인터넷 중독
② 인터넷 서핑
③ 인터넷 접속
④ 인터넷상의 아마추어 성향

| 정답 | ④

| 해설 | 빈칸 뒤에서부터는 본문의 핵심인 '아마추어주의'와 '엘리트주의' 또는 '비전문가' 대 '전문가'의 대결을 다루고 있다. 그리고 이러한 대결은 결국 인터넷상에서 위키피디아와 블로거로 상징되는 '아마추어주의'가 대두된 탓이다. 따라서 답은 ④이다.

27 본문의 목적은 무엇인가?
① 인터넷상에서 다양한 유형의 글쓰기 장소를 대조한다
② 인터넷은 아무 제약 없는 활동의 공간임을 제시한다
③ 인터넷상의 전문 지식은 좀 더 조성되어야 한다고 주장한다
④ 사람들에게 잘못된 정보를 개시하지 말 것을 설득한다

| 정답 | ②

| 해설 | 본문에 따르면 인터넷이 가능케 한 것은 "광대한 아이디어의 시장(the vast marketplace of ideas)"이다. 인터넷상의 아마추어주의라든지 기존의 전문성에 대한 도전은 어디까지나 인터넷을 통해 온갖 아이디어의 표출이 가능해졌기 때문이고, 이는 즉 인터넷이야말로 제약 없는 아이디어의 표출이 가능하게 한 존재라는 것이다. 따라서 답은 ②이다.

| 어휘 | op-ed ⓝ 논평 기사면, 칼럼 기사면
scholarship ⓝ 학문
accredited ⓐ 승인받은, 인가받은
derision ⓝ 조롱, 조소
legitimate ⓐ 타당한
hash out – 계속 논의하여 끝을 보다
inclination ⓝ 경향, 성향
uninhibited ⓐ 아무 제약을 받지 않는
foster ⓥ 조성하다, 발전시키다
refrain ⓝ 자주 반복되는 말
institutionally ⓐⓓ 제도적으로
triumphalism ⓝ 승리주의
defensiveness ⓝ 방어적임, 수동적임
equivalent ⓝ 상대, ~에 대응되는 것
overstate ⓥ 과장하다
venue ⓝ 장소
expertise ⓝ 전문 지식
refrain ⓥ 삼가다

[28-29] 이화여대 2013

인구가 서로 섞이면서 지역적 차이점이 융합되는 현상은 미국인들의 특징이라 할 수 있는 특정한 이동성을 통해 촉진되었다. 성년이 된 미국인들이 태어난 곳에서 계속 사는 경우는 발견하기 힘들다는 말이 있었고, 비록 이는 분명히 말해 과장되었지만, 그럼에도 불구하고 거주지 변경이 분명히 말해 흔히 일어나는 것임은 사실이다. 게다가 미국의 영토가 광대하다는 바로 그 사실이 공간에 대한 감각을 축소하려는 마음가짐을 갖게 하는 경향이 있다. 미국인들은 거리에 익숙해져 있기 때문에 거리를 무시한다. 미 서부에 거주하는 사람이 사소한 용건에도 500마일에서 1,000마일을 기꺼이 이동하려는 모습이나 휴가 목적으로 미 대륙을 기꺼이 횡단하려는 모습을 보라. 과거 미국인들은 웹스터의 철자 교본과 린들리 머레이의 문법책의 영향력을 감안해야 했고, 언제나 미국의 공교육은 표준화를 추구하는 방향으로 영향을 미쳤다. 우리는 언어에 있어 뭔가를 알고 있을 것으로 여겨지는 이들의 권위를 존중한다. 이것이 바로 우리가 외과의사나 "홍보 전문가" 같은 전문가들에 관해 품고 있는 신뢰의 일부이다. 그리고 우리는 순응에 대한 미국인들의 본능을 잊지 말아야 하며 미국인들은 집과 자동차 및 여러 다른 것들뿐만 아니라 언어 관련 문제에 있어서도 표준화를 기꺼이 수용할 것임을 잊어서도 안 된다.

28 [A]를 대체할 수 없는 것은 무엇인가?
① 거주지
② 거주지
③ 거주지
④ 거주지
⑤ 감소

| 정답 | ⑤

| 해설 | 보기 가운데 '감소, 축소'를 의미하는 ⑤를 제외하면 모두 '거주지'란 의미를 지니며, [A]에 대입해 보면 미국인들 사이에서 거주지 주소를 바꾸는 일은 흔하다는 사실을 알 수 있는데, 이는 미국인들의 특징이라고 일컬어진 '이동성(mobility)'과 뜻이 통한다. 따라서 답은 ⑤이다.

29 [B]에 가장 알맞은 것은 무엇인가?
① 흔한 발음이 런던 및 그 부근의 고등 교육을 받은 계층의 발음과 비슷하다.
② 미국 영어의 균일성은 19세기 초에 일반적으로 인식되었던 것으로 보인다.
③ 우리는 순응에 대한 미국인들의 본능을 잊지 말아야 하며 미국인들은 집과 자동차 및 여러 다른 것들뿐만 아니라 언어 관련 문제에 있어서도 표준화를 기꺼이 수용할 것임을 잊어서도 안 된다.
④ 우리는 국민으로서 자체적인 유지 관리 과정보다 미국화 과정에 더 많은 관심을 보여 왔다.
⑤ 이렇게 서로 차이나는 문화적 배경이 지역 내에서 그 이후 이어진 영어의 역사에 반영되었다.

| 정답 | ③

| 해설 | 빈칸 앞에서 미국인들의 공교육이 "표준화를 추구하는 방향으로 영향을 미쳤다(standardizing influence)"고 나와 있으며, 웹스터의 철자 교본과 린들리 머레이의 문법책은 이러한 표준화가 얼마나 큰 영향을 미쳤는지에 대한 예로 볼 수 있다. 그리고 이러한 표준화는 "지역적 차이점의 융합(merging of regional differences)"과 같은 맥락으로 볼 수 있다. 따라서 빈칸에도 이런 표준화와 융합과 뜻이 통하는 내용이 들어가야 하며, 보기 중에서 이에 해당되는 것은 "순응(conformity)"과 표준화에 관해 말하는 ③이다.

| 어휘 | **merge** ⓥ 합치다, 융합되다　　**promote** ⓥ 촉진하다
characterize ⓥ ~의 특징이 되다, 특징짓다　　**distinctly** ⓐ 명백하게, 참으로

extensiveness ⓝ 광대, 대규모	**diminish** ⓥ 줄이다
witness ⓥ ~을 보다(앞서 한 말의 예를 들기 위해 사용함)	
reckon with - ~을 감안하다, ~을 무시할 수 없는 존재로 여기다	
publicity ⓝ 홍보(업)	**conformity** ⓝ 순응, 동조
abode ⓝ 거주지, 집	**habitation** ⓝ 거주지, 주거
dwelling ⓝ 거주지, 주택	**residence** ⓝ 주택, 거주지
abatement ⓝ 감소, 감퇴	**approximate** ⓥ 비슷하다, 가깝다
vicinity ⓝ 부근, 인근	**uniformity** ⓝ 균일함, 획일성
nation ⓝ 국민	**subsequent** ⓐ 이후의, 그 다음의

[30-32] 광운대 2006

오늘날 많은 사람들은 영웅이 없다고 말한다. 오늘날 정상급 정치인들 중 실제보다 위대해 보이는 인물이 설사 있다고 할지라도 거의 없다. 사생활을 파헤치는 기자들과 TV 시대의 대중들이 있는 오늘날의 세계에서는, 누구든 영웅의 지위를 얻기는 힘들다. 게다가, 우리는 과거 영웅들의 추문까지 들춰내서 그들의 영웅성을 없애고 만다. John Kennedy에게 여성 편력이 있었다는 것, Martin Luther King도 마찬가지였다는 것은 이제 다 알려진 사실이다. 그리고 오늘날 점점 더 많은 영웅들이 그들의 사생활이 공개되면서 영웅으로서의 지위를 포기할 수밖에 없다.

이렇게 영웅이 사라지면, 존경할 만한 사람이 누가 있을까? 요즘 유행어인 "롤 모델"은 그 행동이 "모범이 되긴 하지만" 반드시 "용감하거나", "영웅적"이라고는 할 수 없는 인물을 뜻한다. 운동선수들을 롤 모델로 여기는 사람들은 팬들과, 선수들의 영웅적 자질을 "팔아서 돈을 벌려는" 구단주들이다. 그러나 오늘날에는 롤 모델이 되기도 쉽지 않다. 대부분의 대중들은 운동선수들의 불량한 행동과 약물 복용을 비판하면서, 이들을 롤 모델로 인정하지 않는다. 선수들이 공정한 대우와 급여를 받을 권리를 대변하는 선수 협회의 입장에 따르면, 야구선수들은 일반인들과 마찬가지로 평범한 사람일 뿐, 어떤 특별 대우도 원치 않는다.

이처럼 과거의 영웅들은 이미 죽었고 현재의 롤 모델들은 검증을 받아야 한다면, 우리 사회는 어떻게 되는 걸까? 문제의 핵심은 미국인들이 언제나 영웅과 롤 모델이 전통적인 미국적 가치관을 구현해 주기를 바랐다는 데 있다. 그러나 오늘날 대중은 공인들에 대해 고마워하지도 너그럽지도 않다. 대중들은 공인들이 완벽한 인간이 아닌데도 부와 명예를 얻는 것을 용납하지 못한다.

30 지문에서 유추할 수 있는 것은?

① 영웅은 신과 같은 존재일 수 있다.
② 야구선수들은 선수 연합에 의해서 롤 모델로 지나치게 이용되고 있다.
③ 사람들은 공인에 대해서 더 관대해져야 한다.
④ 야구선수들은, 결함이 있긴 해도 영웅으로 인정받아야 한다.

| 정답 | ③

| 해설 | 영웅에게 지나치게 인색하고 비판적인 현대인의 태도를 우려하는 글이므로, "Yet today's public has become ungrateful and ungenerous toward its public figures."를 참조하면, 영웅이나 롤 모델이 될 수 있는 공인들에 대해 더 관대해지기를 바라는 필자의 입장을 유추할 수 있다. 따라서 정답은 ③이다.

31 오늘날 세계에서 영웅이 되기 힘든 이유는 무엇인가?

① 사람들이 영웅주의를 중요하게 생각하지 않기 때문에
② 사람들이 영웅보다 롤 모델을 더 선호하기 때문에
③ 사람들이 영웅을 특별 대우하지 않기 때문에
④ 사람들이 타인의 사생활을 들춰내기 때문에

| 정답 | ④

| 해설 | 첫 단락에 오늘날 영웅이 되기 힘든 이유로, "we now dredge up information about our past heroes, only to take away their heroism"를 참조하면, 사생활을 들춰내는 언론과 사람들의 비판적 태도가 언급되었다. 따라서 정답은 ④이다. ①은 비약이므로 선택하지 않도록 주의한다.

32 밑줄 친 부분에 가장 적절한 표현은?

① 영웅적 지위　　　　　　② 표현의 자유
③ 부와 명성　　　　　　　④ 롤 모델로서의 지위

| 정답 | ①

| 해설 | 주제와 관련 있도록 인과관계를 완성하는 것이 출제 의도이다. 공인의 사생활이 파헤쳐지면, 영웅적 지위가 퇴색되거나 사라질 것이다. 답은 ①이다. 사생활 노출의 결과로서 ③은 주제와 무관하고, ④는 영웅적 지위만을 다루는 단락의 통일성을 해치므로 정답이 될 수 없다.

| 어휘 | figure ⓝ 인물
pry ⓥ (추문 등을) 파헤치다
dredge up – (사생활 등을) 들춰내다
run around with – ~와 어울려 다니다
status ⓝ 지위
imitate ⓥ 모방하다
quality ⓝ 자질
drug use – 약물 복용
union ⓝ 노조, 협회
fairly ⓐⓓ 공정하게
special treatment – 특혜, 특별 대우
crux ⓝ 핵심
ungrateful ⓐ 고마움을 모르는, 배은망덕한
public figure – 공인

larger than life – 실물보다 큰
attain ⓥ 얻다
take away – ~을 제거하다
abdicate ⓥ 포기하다, 양도하다
buzzword ⓝ 유행어
courageous ⓐ 용감한
critical of – ~에 대해 비판적인
reject ⓥ 거부하다
represent ⓥ 대표하다; 표현하다
equitable ⓐ 공정한, 동등한
scrutinize ⓥ 면밀히 조사하다
exemplify ⓥ 구현하다; 예시하다
ungenerous ⓐ 인색한
get away with – ~을 훔쳐 달아나다

[33-34] 서울여대 2009

40년 전, 한 젊은 급진적 저널리스트의 선구적인 저서 The Other America는 "빈곤과의 전쟁"의 시발점이 되었다. 그 책에서 Michael Harrington은 당시 주장되던 풍요의 시대는 환상일 뿐이고, 미국의 번영 이면에는 수천만 명의 사람들이 오직 대대적인 정부 개입만이 해결할 수 있는 극심한 빈곤에 시달리고 있다고 경고했다. 오늘날의 신진 저널리스트들도 Harrington의 위업을 재연하기 위해, 현대 미국의 경제 시스템이 수백만 미국인들에게는 효과가 없으며 오직 정부만이 그들을 빈곤으로부터 해방시킬 수 있다는 것을 알리기 위해 애쓰고 있다. 그러나 이 신진 저널리스트들은 Harrington보다 더 어려운 난관에 봉착해 있다. Harrington의 책이 출간된 이후로 범정부적으로 약 10조 달러가 빈곤 정책에 쓰였지만, 결과는 실망스러웠고 심지어 역효과도 있었기 때문이다. 지난 40년 동안, 수백만의 빈곤층은 이민자와 본토 미국인 모두 Harrington이 제시한 정부 정책에 의존하지 않고 빈곤에서 벗어났다.

33 지문에 따르면, 다음 중 사실이 아닌 것은?
① Michael Harrington은 빈곤에 대한 정부 개입을 요구했던 저널리스트이다.
② The Other America에 따르면, 많은 미국인들이 빈곤에 시달리고 있다.
③ 오늘날 저널리스트들은 Harrington의 주장에 영향을 받았다.
④ 정부의 빈곤 정책 덕분에 수백만 명이 빈곤에서 벗어났다.

| 정답 | ④

| 해설 | 마지막 문장 "millions of poor people, immigrants and native-born alike, have risen from poverty"를 참조하면, 수백만 명이 정부의 빈곤 정책의 도움 없이 빈곤에서 벗어났음을 알 수 있다. 따라서 정답은 ④이다.

34 다음 중 이 단락 다음에 이어질 내용으로 적절한 것은?
① Harrington의 확고한 신념이 이뤄 낸 성취
② Harrington의 주장에 대한 재평가
③ 미 정부 빈곤 정책의 성공 사례
④ 미 정부의 노력이 경제에 미치는 긍정적 영향

| 정답 | ②

| 해설 | 이 글의 주제는 Harrington의 주장이 현실에서는 설득력이 없다는 것이다. "These new journalists face a tougher task than Harrington's"가 그 근거이다. 따라서 다음 단락에서는 보기 ②의 내용인 Harrington 주장의 문제점을 상술하는 "재평가, 재검토(reevaluation)"가 이어질 것이다.

| 어휘 | radical ⓐ 급진적인
pioneering ⓐ 선구적인
affluence ⓝ 풍요, 부유
surface ⓝ 표면
stuck ⓐ 갇힌
massive ⓐ 대규모의
strain to – ~하기 위해 애쓰다
feat ⓝ 업적, 위업
ignite ⓥ 불붙이다, 촉발하다
proclaim ⓥ 선언[공표]하다
mirage ⓝ 신기루, 환상
prosperity ⓝ 번영
poverty ⓝ 빈곤
intervention ⓝ 개입
duplicate ⓥ 재연하다, 복제하다
convince ⓥ 설득하다

disappointing ⓐ 실망스러운
immigrant ⓝ 이민자
counterproductive ⓐ 역효과의
recourse ⓝ (도움을 얻기 위한) 의지, 부탁

[35-37] 한국외대 2010

미국인의 가장 큰 결점 세 가지는 효율성, 시간 엄수, 업적과 성공에 대한 욕구이다. 이 세 가지야말로 미국인들을 매우 불행하고 불안하게 만드는 것들이다. 이러한 것들은 미국인들로부터 빼앗을 수 없는 권리인 빈둥거리며 보낼 수 있는 권리를 앗아갔고, 미국인들로부터 좋고, 한가하며, 아름다운 저녁 시간의 대부분을 빼앗아 갔다. 사람들은 세상의 파국은 없을 것이라는 믿음을 가지고, 일을 완료하는 고귀한 기술뿐 아니라, 일을 마치지 않고 놔두는 고귀한 기술도 있다는 신념을 갖고 일을 시작해야 한다. 만약 여러분이 편지에 바로 답장을 보내면, 대체로 결과는 편지에 전혀 답장을 하지 않을 때만큼 좋을 수도 있고 나쁠 수도 있다. 만약 편지를 서랍에 세 달간 보관하고 나서 나중에 읽으면, 여러분은 편지에 일일이 다 답장을 보내는 것이 애초에 시간 낭비였었다는 것을 깨닫게 될 수도 있다. 편지만 쓰다 보면 우리의 저술가들은 세련된 판매 촉진 세일즈맨과 마찬가지로 바뀌고, 우리의 대학교수들은 뛰어나고 효율적인 회사의 경영진과 마찬가지로 바뀐다. 이런 차원에서, 나는 항상 우체국으로 가는 미국인을 향해 가졌던 Thoreau의 경멸을 이해할 수 있다.

35
다음 중 저자가 가장 존중하는 것은 무엇인가?
① 우수함을 추구함
② 동기부여를 유지함
③ 페이스를 늦춤
④ 행동 전에 많이 생각함
⑤ 인생의 헛됨을 인정함

| 정답 | ③

| 해설 | 저자는 "three great American vices(미국인의 가장 큰 결점 세 가지)"를 "efficiency, punctuality and the desire for achievement and success(효율성, 시간 엄수, 업적과 성공에 대한 욕구)"라고 꼽고 있으며, "loafing(빈둥거리기)"를 "inalienable right(빼앗을 수 없는 권리)"로 묘사한다. 이를 통해 저자는 과도하게 꽉 맞춰 숨 가쁘게 돌아가는 삶보다는 느슨하게 지낼 줄 아는 것도 필요하다고 말한다. 이러한 사항을 고려해 보면 답은 ③이 된다.

36
㉮에 가장 알맞은 것은 무엇인가?
① 일을 마치지 않고 놔두기
② 일을 조직하기
③ 일을 완벽하게 끝내기
④ 제대로 된 일을 높이 평가하기
⑤ 일에 작용될 것들을 준비하기

| 정답 | ①

| 해설 | 저자는 "noble art of getting things done(일을 완료하는 고귀한 기술)"에 덧붙여 "there is a nobler art(다른 고귀한 기술이 있음)"을 말하고 있는데, 바로 앞 문제에서 저자가 가장 존중하는 것이 "slowing down the pace (페이스를 늦추는 것)"임을 미루어 보면 결국 또 다른 "고귀한 기술"은 ①인 "leaving things undone(일을 마치지 않고 놔두기)"임을 알 수 있다. 그 외의 다른 보기는 저자가 결점으로 보는 "efficiency, punctuality and the desire for achievement and success(효율성, 시간 엄수, 업적과 성공에 대한 욕구)"와 관련 있는 사항이기 때문에 빈칸에 들어간다면 전체 내용과 모순을 일으킨다. 따라서 답으로 볼 수 없다.

37

㉯에 알맞은 것은 다음 중 무엇인가?
① 찬사　　　　　　　　　② 무시
③ 인가　　　　　　　　　④ 경멸
⑤ 동정

| 정답 | ④

| 해설 | 저자는 미국인들이 편지를 받자마자 일일이 다 답장을 보내기 때문에, 저술가도, 대학교수도 마치 세일즈맨과 다를 바 없이 변한다고 한탄하고 있다. 보기를 살펴보면 빈칸에 들어갈 내용은 감정에 관한 것임을 유추할 수 있으며, 따라서 Thoreau가 "Americans who always go to the post office(항상 우체국으로 가는 미국인)"을 향해 가졌던 감정이 어떤 것인지 유추해야 할 것이다. 본문의 흐름상 Thoreau가 가졌던 감정은 긍정적일 리가 없기 때문에 ①, ③, ⑤는 답이 될 수 없다. 또한 ②의 "neglect(태만)"과 결합되는 전치사는 "for"가 아니라 "of"이고, ④의 "contempt(경멸)"과 결합되는 전치사는 "for"이기 때문에 본문의 빈칸 뒤에 "for"가 있는 것으로 미루어 보면 답은 ④가 됨을 알 수 있다.

| 어휘 |
vice ⓝ 악덕; 결점
inalienable ⓐ 양도할 수 없는, 박탈할 수 없는
cheat A of B – A에게서 B를 사취하다, 속여서 빼앗다
start out with – ~와 함께 시작하다
noble ⓐ 고귀한
turn A into B – A를 B로 바꾸다
prize ⓥ ~을 존중하다
futility ⓝ 무용함, 헛됨
sanction ⓝ 제가, 인가

punctuality ⓝ 시간 엄수
loaf ⓥ 빈둥거리다, 놀며 지내다
catastrophe ⓝ 대참사, 파국
art ⓝ 기술
promotion ⓝ 승진; 판매 촉진
excellence ⓝ 우수함, 뛰어남
appreciate ⓥ 가치를 인정하다; 고맙게 생각하다

[38-40] 덕성여대 2011

세계 각지의 기독교 국가에서 건너온 이민자들로 이루어져 있는 미국이라는 나라에 걸맞게, 미국에는 미국인들만의 고유한 크리스마스 상징물이 없다. 하지만 우리 미국인들은 세계 각국의 크리스마스 상징물을 모아서 우리만의 것으로 만들었다. 크리스마스트리와 선물 교환, 산타클로스 이야기, 그리고 선국에서 불려 퍼지는 크리스마스 캐럴 등이 20세기 중반 미국 크리스마스를 구성하는 요소들이다. 비록 우리에게 고유한 크리스마스 상징물이 없기는 하지만, 두 가지 특징적 요소 때문에 미국의 크리스마스에는 적어도 다른 것들과는 확연히 구별되는 독특한 매력이 있다.

그중 하나는, 미국과 같이 기업 경영에 열성적인 국가에서 기대될 수 있는 것으로, 크리스마스 축제의 주요 기능 중에 하나는 소매 유통업(사람들의 쇼핑을 의미함)의 자극제 역할을 수행하는 것이다. 크리스마스 광고 테마들이 이르면 9월 초부터 등장하기 시작하고, 크리스마스 쇼핑은 11월부터 시작된다. 50년 전에는 추수감사절(11월 4째주 목요일)이 크리스마스 쇼핑의 시작을 알리는 날로 여겨졌지만, 요즘은 할로윈(10월 마지막 날)이 끝나면 바로 크리스마스 시즌이 시작된다. 그래서 사실상 크리스마스 시즌에 한 달이 쇼핑 목적으로 더 늘어났다.

두 번째는, 크리스마스 축제 시즌이 부지불식간에 새해 축제와 결합되어 마치 농신제(Saturnalia)와 같은 하나의 긴 축제 기간이 되었다. 이 축제는 크리스마스가 시작되기 며칠 전 "오피스 파티"로 시작해서 크리스마스이브까지 지속되는데, 크리스마스이브는 시즌을 대표하는 두 개의 가장 큰 떠들썩하게 노는 축제 중 하나이다. 예외적으로 크리스마스이브의 흥청거림은 크리스마스 자정에 큰 성당의 자정 미사를 드리기 위해 방문하는 것으로 흐름이 끊기는데, 이런 예배도 점차 시즌을 즐기는 오락의 한 요소로 변화되고 있다. 그리고 이런 흥청거림은 희열에 들떠 두 번째로 큰 축제인 새해 전날까지 이어진다. 새해 첫날은 휴식을 취하고, 아마도 자신의 과했던 모습을 반성하고, 미식축구를 보고, 스스로 정한 마음을 가라앉히는 것에 탐닉해 시간을 보낸다.

38 다음 중 본문의 내용에서 유추할 수 있는 것은?

① 19세기 후반부터 20세기 초반에 많은 나라에서 건너온 이민자들의 거대한 물결이 미국의 크리스마스 축제에 중대한 영향을 미쳤다.
② 미국의 크리스마스 축제의 기반이 되는 전통들은 주로 초창기 이민자들에 의해 도입된 것이다.
③ 크리스마스가 들어 있는 주의 흥청거림은 크리스마스 쇼핑 시즌의 고된 노동으로부터의 해방을 의미한다.
④ 현 시점에서 새해 첫날은 크리스마스이브와 분리해서 생각할 수 없다.

| 정답 | ④

| 해설 | ①의 경우, 이민자들이 각국에서 가져온 크리스마스의 전통이 합쳐진 것은 맞지만 시기적으로 19세기 후반이나 20세기 초반에 대한 설명은 본문에 등장하지 않는다. ②의 경우도 이민자들은 맞지만 초창기(earliest) 이민자에 대한 내용은 본문과 무관하다. ③은 전체 내용이 모두 본문과 전혀 관련이 없다. 정답은 ④로. 크리스마스이브 며칠 전부터 시작된 축제 시즌이 새해까지 이어지기 때문에 서로 분리해서 생각할 수 없다고 유추할 수 있다.

39 다음 중 저자가 미국의 크리스마스 시즌만의 특징으로 언급한 것은 무엇인가?

① 크리스마스 선물의 교환
② 축제 중 식사와 음주
③ 크리스마스 이른 아침에 참석하는 미사
④ 상업에 대한 기여

| 정답 | ④

| 해설 | 본문에서 저자는 미국만의 독특한 요소로 2가지를 들고 있는데, 하나는 상업적으로 발달해서 방대한 쇼핑을 한다는 점과 두 번째로는 크리스마스 축제와 새해 축제가 합쳐져서 긴 축제의 기간이 되었다는 것을 들고 있다. 따라서 정답은 ④가 된다.

40 본문에 따르면, 미국인들의 크리스마스 시즌 축하는 어떠하다고 볼 수 있는가?

① 대단한 상징적인 독창성을 보여주었다.
② 존재에 대한 정당성이 거의 없다.
③ 초기 이민자들의 선례에서 완전히 벗어났다.
④ 다른 나라들의 전통에서 광범위하게 빌려 온 것이다.

| 정답 | ④

| 해설 | 미국의 크리스마스에는 미국만의 전통이나 상징은 없지만, 두 가지 요소로 인해 미국만의 독특한 매력을 지닌다고 했으므로 ①과 ② 모두 올바른 설명이 될 수 없다. 또한 ③의 경우 이전에 하던 것과 완전히 다르다는 내용은 본문에 등장하지 않는다. 캐럴이나 산타클로스, 선물 교환 등은 지금도 행해지기 때문이다. 정답은 ④로, 이민자들의 나라답게 다양한 요소를 차용했다고 본문 서두의 "we have taken the symbols of all the nations" 부분에서 밝히고 있다.

| 어휘 | befit ⓥ 걸맞다, 적합하다   distinctive ⓐ 특유의
      aura ⓝ 기운, 매력, 독특한 분위기   virtue ⓝ 미덕; 장점

by virtue of sth — ~ 덕분에, ~ 때문에, ~의 힘으로
characteristic ⓐ 특유의, 특징적인
carry on the business — 회사를 경영하다
stimulus ⓝ 자극제
add A to B — A를 B에 더하다(= A is added to B)
insensibly ⓐⓓ 눈에 띄지 않을 정도로
Saturnalia ⓝ 농신제(지금의 크리스마스 무렵 행해지던 고대 로마의 축제), 진탕 마시고 노는 잔치
revel ⓝ 흥청망청 즐김, 술 마시고 흥청거림
spirited ⓐ 기운이 넘치는, 활발한
indulge in sth — (특히 좋지 않다고 여겨지는 것을) 마음껏 하다
lenitive ⓝ 진정제, 완화제
depart ⓥ 떠나다, 출발하다, 벗어나다

be dedicated to — ~에 헌신하다
dominant role — 지배적인 역할
virtually ⓐⓓ 사실상, 거의

be punctuated — (경기 등이) 여러 번 중단되다
euphoria ⓝ 행복함, 희열

demonstrate ⓥ 입증하다

[41-43] 숙명여대 2017

사우디아라비아에서 볼 수 있는 베일의 유래는 알려져 있지 않다. 사우디아라비아의 동부 연안 지역을 터키가 지배하고 있을 당시, 사회적 지위가 높은 여성들은 아마도 가혹한 사막의 태양으로부터 얼굴을 보호하기 위해 베일을 착용했을 것이라는 설명이 사우디아라비아의 특정한 베일 관행에 대해 가장 널리 인정받는 이론이다. 다른 이론은 베두인 종족들이 서로 전쟁을 벌이고 경쟁 부족의 가축을 약탈했을 때 여성들이 베일을 착용해 아름다운 여성들이 염소와 함께 잡혀가는 것을 막았을 것이라고 설명한다. 또 다른 이론들은 베두인 여성이 이런 습격에서 맹렬한 전사의 모습을 보여 사막의 기사도 정신에 따라 여성들에게 성 정체성을 타나내는 형태로 베일을 쓰게 해서 전투에 참여하지 못하게 했고, 그 결과 두려움을 모르는 남성들이 이들과 싸울 위험을 모면하게 해 주었다고 설명한다. 베일의 기원과 관계없이 오늘날 사우디 여성들은 베일을 착용하지 않고 집 밖에 나가는 것이 남성들에 의해 허용되지 않는다. 이 규칙은 모든 사회 계층의 여성에게 적용된다. 공공장소에서 여성들은 모든 개성과 특성을 상실하고 거리를 지나가는 너무도 많은 검은 물체로 변한다. 각각의 여성들은 검은색으로 덮여 있고, 그들의 얼굴은 뚫을 수 없는 검은색 거즈 뒤에 가려져 있다. 서양인들의 눈에 그 베일은 사우디아라비아의 모든 생활 영역에서 여성들이 남성에 종속된 분명한 상징으로 보인다. 베일은 여성들이 감금당한 분위기를 형성하며, 사회 일원으로 기능할 수 있는 여성의 능력을 통제하는 가족의 남성 구성원들에게 여성이 완전히 의존하고 있음을 말해 준다.

41 다음 중 본문의 제목으로 가장 적합한 것은?
① 사우디아라비아 여성들의 이론적 역사
② 사우디아라비아의 베일: 허구와 실상
③ 사우디아라비아 여성들이 착용하는 베일의 유래
④ 베일의 신비
⑤ 사우디아라비아 베일에 대한 여러 이론

| 정답 | ②

| 해설 | 1단락에서 베일의 기원에 대해 여러 가지 가설을 제시하고, 2단락에서 베일의 실제 현실에 대해 서술하고 있다. 가설은 현실을 고려하지 않은 허상이고, 현실은 뒤에 나온다. 그러므로 가장 근접한 보기는 ②가 된다.

42

다음 중 밑줄 친 부분 'intrepid'와 가장 가까운 의미에 해당하는 것은?

① 존경하는
② 지배적인
③ 본의 아닌
④ 기사도적인
⑤ 두려움을 모르는

| 정답 | ⑤

| 해설 | 밑줄 친 'intrepid'는 '용감무쌍한, 두려움을 모르는' 등을 의미하므로, 동일한 의미를 지닌 ⑤ fearless가 동의어가 된다.

43

본문의 마지막 밑줄 친 부분은 다음 중 누구의 관점이 드러난 것인가?

① 사우디 여성들
② 사우디 남성들
③ 아시아 남성들
④ 서양인들
⑤ 위 모두 해당

| 정답 | ④

| 해설 | 본문 후반의 "In the eyes of a Westerner …" 이후의 내용에 연결되는 것으로 베일을 쓴 여성의 모습을 부정적인 측면에서 바라보게 되는 서양인들의 시선을 드러내고 있으므로 정답은 ④가 된다.

| 어휘 |
origin ⓝ 기원, 출처
theory ⓝ 이론
coastal ⓐ 해변의
complexion ⓝ 용모, 안색
raid ⓥ 급습하다, 침입하다 ⓝ 습격, 급습, 불시 단속
livestock ⓝ 가축
chivalry ⓝ (특히 여자에 대한 남자의) 정중함[예의 바름], 기사도
intrepid ⓐ 두려움을 모르는, 용맹스러운
spare ⓥ (불쾌한 일을) 모면하게[겪지 않아도 되게] 하다
regardless of – ~와 상관없이
individuality ⓝ 개성, 특성
glide down – 무심코 지나가다
gauze ⓝ 가볍고 투명한 천, (상처에 붙이는) 거즈[가제]
starkly ⓐⓓ 순전하게, 완전히
subservience ⓝ 복종, 종속; 아첨
set the tone – 분위기를 조성하다, 풍조를 만들다[확립하다]
confinement ⓝ 갇힘, 얽매임, 가둠
function as – ~로서의 기능을 하다
myth ⓝ 허구, 신화, 낭설
involuntary ⓐ 본의 아닌, 마음 내키지 않는, 무심결에, 무의식적
chivalrous ⓐ 기사도적인

veil ⓝ 베일, 면사포
practice ⓝ 관행, 관습
standing ⓝ 지위[평판]
brutality ⓝ 잔인한 행위, 만행
code ⓝ (사회적) 관례[규칙], 법규; 암호
personality ⓝ 성격, 인격, 개성
blob ⓝ 작은 방울, 작은 덩이; 윤곽이 뚜렷하지 않은 것
impenetrable ⓐ 불가해한, 관통할 수 없는
symbolic ⓐ 상징적인, 상징하는
regulate ⓥ 조정하다, 통제하다, 규제하다, 단속하다
theoretical ⓐ 이론상의
dominating ⓐ 지배하는, 우세한, 우위를 차지하는

[44-45] 성균관대 2016

영국은 오랫동안 어느 국가에서 이혼할지 선택할 수 있는 여유가 되는 아내들이 이혼의 선택지로 가장 선호해 오던 국가였다. 영국 법률은 평생의 필요와 공정함에 균형을 두려고 노력하기 때문이다. 경제적으로 여유가 없는 배우자(일반적으로 아이들을 양육하는 아내들)는, 특히 결혼으로 직장 생활을 유지하다가 그만둔 경우, 이혼 후 집과 몇 년간의 수입을 기대할 수 있다. 그럼에도 불구하고 2월 23일의 법정 판결은 남편들에게 약간 유리한 방향으로 기울어져 온 최근의 추세를 이어 갔다. 트레이시 라이트(Tracey Wright)는 2008년 11년간의 결혼 생활이 실패로 돌아간 후 그녀에게 지급해 왔던 연간 7만 5천 파운드의 양육비를 줄이고자 하는 전남편의 시도에 반대해 소송을 제기했다. 그녀는 두 아이를 돌보는 일이 너무 바빠서 직장을 알아볼 수조차 없다고 주장했다. 하지만 그녀는 항소심에서 패소했다. 재판관인 피치포드(Pitchford)는 전남편 라이트의 정년이 다가오기 때문에 전처에게 지불하고 있는 비용 또한 점점 줄어들어야 하며, 전처도 직업을 구해야 한다고 주장했다. 이 판결은 기념비적인 판결이었는데, 주요인은 이 판결에서 이혼 후 직업을 구하려고 노력해야 한다는 이혼한 여성의 의무를 명시하고 있기 때문이다. 이혼 전문 변호사인 데이비드 허드슨(David Hodson)의 언급에 따르면, 그 원칙은 복지 혜택 청구와 관련해서 가난한 여성들에게 오랫동안 적용돼 왔다. 하지만 이혼한 여성은 자신에게 마땅한 일자리가 없으며, 자신과 아이들이 이혼 이전의 생활수준을 계속 유지하기 위해서는 전남편의 도움이 필요하다고 계속 주장할 수 있을 것이다. 그런 주장은 대부분의 다른 나라에서는 거의 효과가 없다. 이번 판결이 이혼의 세계적 중심지로서의 런던의 매력에 흠집을 내지는 않을 것이다. 영국 이혼법은 비용이 많이 드는 법적 논쟁을 거친 후에야 이혼법이 마련한 해결책에 다다를 수 있어서, 대단히 부유한 소수의 사람들을 제외한 대부분의 사람들에게는 이용이 제한되어 있는 사치스러운 서비스로 계속해서 남을 가능성이 여전히 높다.

44 다음 중 빈칸에 가장 적절한 것은 무엇인가?
① 그 판결은 복지 혜택을 지급해야 할 이혼한 남성의 의무를 명시하고 있다
② 그 판결은 이혼 후 직업을 구하려고 노력해야 한다는 이혼한 여성의 의무를 명시하고 있다
③ 그 판결은 처음으로 남편들을 더 가난한 배우자로 인정하고 있다
④ 그 판결은 아이들이 있는 전처를 더 가난한 배우자로 인정하고 있다
⑤ 그 판결은 부모를 선택할 수 있는 아이들의 권리를 인정하고 있다

| 정답 | ②

| 해설 | 바로 앞 문장에서 "his ex-wife should get a job"이라고 말하고 있고, 빈칸 뒤의 내용 중 "no suitable work is available for her and that she needs her ex-husband's help"라고 주장할 수 있다는 내용을 통해, 이혼한 여성이 자신과 아이들을 부양하기 위해 직장을 가져야 한다고 명시했다는 것을 추론할 수 있다.

45 이 글에 따르면, _____.
① 영국은 게으른 전처에게 약간 불리한 곳이 되었다
② 영국은 전업주부에게 더 좋은 곳이 되었다
③ 대부분의 다른 국가들은 직업이 없는 이혼 여성들에게 영국보다 더 좋은 국가들이다
④ 대부분의 국가들은 은퇴한 이혼 남성들에게 나쁜 곳이다
⑤ 대부분의 다른 나라에서 남편들은 복지 혜택을 받을 자격이 주어지지 않는다

| 정답 | ①

| 해설 | 영국의 이혼법은 여성들에게 유리해서 여유가 되는 여성들은 영국에서 이혼하려고 한다고 설명하고 있다. 그런데 최근의 판결이 이혼한 여성에게 불리한 판결이 나왔으며(전남편이 지급하는 비용이 퇴직 시점이 다가오면서 줄어들고,

전처 또한 직업을 가져야 한다는 판결), 최근 이혼한 남성들에게 유리하게 진행되는 경향과 일치한다고 했으므로 이혼 여성들이 불리해졌다는 내용이 본문과 일치하게 된다. 따라서 정답은 영국이 게으른 전처에게 약간 불리한 곳이 되었다는 ①이 된다.

| 어휘 | jurisdiction ⓝ 관할권, 관할 구역; 사법권
have the luxury of ~ing – ~할 여유가 있다
bring up – ~을 양육하다
tilt ⓥ 기울어지게 하다
appeal ⓝ 항소
landmark ⓝ 획기적 사건, 주요 지형지물, 랜드마크
welfare benefit – 복지 혜택
keep up the living standards – 생활수준을 유지하다
cut little ice – 효과가 거의 없다
bespoke ⓐ (개인 주문에 따라) 맞춘
out of reach – 힘이 미치지 않는 곳에

of choice – (~에 의해/~용으로) 선택되는[고르는]
fairness ⓝ 공정함
ruling ⓝ 판결
bid ⓝ 시도, 노력
taper off – (수·양·정도가) 점점 줄어들다

dent ⓥ 손상시키다, 약화시키다
wrangling ⓝ 논쟁

[46-47] 한국외대 2018

프랜시스 스콧 피츠제럴드(F. Scott Fitzgerald)는 그가 재즈 시대(the Jazz Age)라는 별명을 붙인 1920년대 미국의 모습을 기록한 작가 가운데 가장 유명한 인물이다. 1925년작 "위대한 개츠비(The Great Gatsby)"는 당시의 가장 위대한 문학작품 중 하나이다. 당시 미국 경제는 호황을 맞이했고 덕분에 미국 전역이 전례 없는 수준의 번영을 누렸다. 술의 판매와 소비를 금하는 법인 금주법은 밀주업자들을 백만장자로 만들어 줬고, 흥청대며 먹고 마시며 파티를 하는 음지의 문화가 우후죽순처럼 싹텄다. 비공개 파티는 경찰의 눈을 피해 무질서하게 사방에서 개최되었고, 술을 파는 비밀 클럽이 번성했다. 1차 세계 대전의 혼란과 폭력은 미국을 충격 상태로 몰아넣었고, 전쟁에 참여해 싸웠던 세대는 보상심리에서 무모하고 사치스러운 생활에 의지하게 되었다. 돈과 부유함 그리고 윤택함이 그 시대를 풍미했다. "위대한 개츠비"의 닉(Nick)과 마찬가지로 피츠제럴드도 자신의 새로운 생활 방식이 유혹적이면서 흥미진진하다는 것을 깨달았고, 개츠비와 마찬가지로 갑부들을 숭배했다. 이제 피츠제럴드는 억제되지 않은 물질만능주의가 사회의 풍조를 확립한 시대에 스스로가 속해 있음을 깨달았다. 그럼에도 피츠제럴드는 재즈 시대의 화려함 속에 감춰진 도덕적 공허함과 위선을 꿰뚫어 봤고, 그의 일부는 이처럼 사라진 도덕적 중심을 갈망했다. 많은 면에서 보면 "위대한 개츠비"는 피츠제럴드가 재즈 시대에 대한 자신의 모순된 감정과 마주하려 시도했음을 상징한다.

46 다음 중 (A)와 (B)에 가장 알맞은 것은 무엇인가?

① 사라진 – 모순된
② 얼빠진 – 관대한
③ 확고한 – 모호한
④ 집요한 – 냉소적인

| 정답 | ①

| 해설 | (A): 재즈 시대는 화려함과 물질만능주의가 팽배한 시기였지만 도덕적 공허함과 위선의 시대이기도 했다. 이런 시대는 도덕적 중심이 "사라진" 시대라 할 수 있다.
(B): 피츠제럴드는 갑부들을 숭배하고 화려함과 윤택함에 매력을 느낀 사람이었다. 그러면서도 그는 도덕적인 중심을 갈망한 사람이기도 했다. 그가 재즈 시대에 대해 품은 감정은 "모순된" 감정이라 할 수 있다.
이러한 점들을 감안했을 때, 답으로 가장 적합한 것은 ①이다.

47

본문에 따르면 다음 중 사실이 아닌 것은 무엇인가?

① 피츠제럴드의 책은 재즈 시대에 대한 뛰어난 연대기이다.
② 술은 1920년대에 비공개 파티를 제외한 장소에서 불법이었다.
③ 1차 세계 대전 이후 향락주의가 새로운 삶의 방식이 되었다.
④ 닉과 개츠비는 피츠제럴드가 1920년대에 대해 갖고 있던 태도를 상징한다.

| 정답 | ②

| 해설 | 술을 취급하는 비공개 파티가 경찰의 눈을 피해 열린 이유는 비공개 파티를 포함해 모든 장소에서 술이 불법이었기 때문이다. 따라서 답은 ②이다. "프랜시스 스콧 피츠제럴드(F. Scott Fitzgerald)는 그가 재즈 시대(the Jazz Age)라는 별명을 붙인 1920년대 미국의 모습을 기록한 작가 가운데 가장 유명한 인물이다(F. Scott Fitzgerald was the most famous chronicler of 1920s America, an era he dubbed 'the Jazz Age')"는 ①의 근거가 된다. "1차 세계 대전의 혼란과 폭력은 미국을 충격 상태로 몰아넣었고, 전쟁에 참여해 싸웠던 세대는 보상심리에서 무모하고 사치스러운 생활에 의지하게 되었다. 돈과 부유함 그리고 윤택함이 그 시대를 풍미했다(The chaos and violence of World War I left America in a state of shock, and the generation that fought the war turned to wild and extravagant living to compensate. Money, opulence, and exuberance became the order of the day)"는 ③의 근거가 된다. "'위대한 개츠비'의 닉(Nick)과 마찬가지로 피츠제럴드도 자신의 새로운 생활 방식이 유혹적이면서 흥미진진하다는 것을 깨달았고, 개츠비와 마찬가지로 갑부들을 숭배했다. 이제 피츠제럴드는 억제되지 않은 물질만능주의가 사회의 풍조를 확립한 시대에 스스로가 속해 있음을 깨달았다(Like Nick in *The Great Gatsby*, Fitzgerald found this new lifestyle seductive and exciting and, like Gatsby, he had always idolized the very rich. Now he found himself in an era in which unrestrained materialism set the tone of society)"는 ④의 근거가 된다.

| 어휘 | chronicler ⓝ 연대기 작자[편자]; (사건의) 기록자　dub ⓥ 별명을 붙이다
unprecedented ⓐ 전례 없는, 미증유의　　Prohibition ⓝ 미국 금주법 시행 시대
bootlegger ⓝ (특히 미국의 금주법 시대의) 주류 밀매[밀수, 밀조]자
revelry ⓝ 흥청대며 먹고 마시는 파티, 흥청대며 놀기
sprawling ⓝ 제멋대로 뻗어[퍼져] 나가는, 무질서하게 확산된
turn to – ~에 의지하다　　　　　　　　　extravagant ⓐ 낭비하는, 사치스러운
compensate ⓥ 보상하다, 메우다　　　　　opulence ⓝ 풍부, 부유
exuberance ⓝ 풍부, 윤택　　　　　　　　order of the day – 시대의 풍조, 유행
seductive ⓐ 마음을 끄는, 유혹적인　　　　unrestrained ⓐ 억제되지 않은, 거리낌 없는
materialism ⓝ 물질만능주의　　　　　　　set the tone – 풍조를 만들다[확립하다]
glitter ⓝ 화려함, 반짝임　　　　　　　　hypocrisy ⓝ 위선
conflicting ⓐ 모순되는, 상충하는　　　　confront ⓥ (정면으로) 마주하다
vacuous ⓐ 멍청한, 얼빠진　　　　　　　fixed ⓐ 고정된, 확고한
persistent ⓐ 끈질긴, 집요한　　　　　　cynical ⓐ 냉소적인
chronicle ⓝ 연대기, 연대순 기록　　　　hedonism ⓝ 쾌락주의, 향락주의
embody ⓥ (사상·특질을) 상징[구현]하다

[48-50] 서강대 2010

> 모든 문화권에서는 내면의 자기비판의 목소리, 즉 양심의 가책을 느낀다. 그러나 서구 기독교 문화권에서는 소위 '스테로이드를 복용한 양심(conscience on steroids)'을 지니고 있다. 우리의 죄의식은 상당히 극단적이며, 원죄 및 이로 인한 인간의 지위의 추락(역자 주: 성경의 아담과 하와가 금지된 선악과를 먹고 원죄를 지은 후 에덴동산에서 쫓겨난 것을 의미한다.)에 기반을 둔 우리 문화권에서는 우리의 존재 그 자체에도 죄의식을 느낀다. 서구 문화의 중심에 우리는 무가치한 존재라는 생각이 자리 잡고 있다. 왜 이런 생각들이 존재하는 것일까?
>
> 이런 모든 내재화된 자기혐오는 문명화를 위해 우리가 지불한 비용인 것이다. 다수의 이익을 보호하는 매우 잘 조직화된 사회에서는, 우리는 매일 우리의 자연스런 본능을 억제해야 한다. 우리는 스스로의 이기적이고 공격적인 충동을 항상 억제해야 하며, 성인으로서 우리는 이런 것들에 매우 익숙해져 있기 때문에 이런 사실을 항상 의식하는 것은 아니다. 하지만 만약 내가 습관처럼 충동적으로 행동했다면, 카페에서 휘핑크림을 얹어서 이런저런 방식으로 모카 음료를 만들어 달라고 주문하는 사람들을 볼 때마다 그들을 늘 살해했을지 모른다. 사실 나는 긴 줄에 서서 기다리는 것을 개의치 않지만, 헐레벌떡 매장으로 들어와 사람들을 밀치고 주문하고 싶은 충동이 있는 것도 사실이다. 하지만 내 마음 속에서 작은 갈등의 순간이 오고, 이로써 나는 내 자신의 본능적인 공격성을 억제할 수 있다. 이는 마치 한잔의 모닝커피와 같은 역할을 한다. 대중교통을 이용하면서 얼마나 자주 누군가의 목을 조르고 싶었는지를 생각해 보라.

48
다음 중 본문에 나온 양심의 개념을 가장 잘 표현한 것은?
① 자연스런 본능 ② 이기적이고 공격적인 충동
③ 내재화된 자기혐오 ④ 충동

| 정답 | ③

| 해설 | 본문에서는 서구 문화권의 양심에 대해 말하고 있다. 서구 문화권에서의 양심이란 매우 극단적이라고 말하면서, 성경과 관련된 문화로 인해 인간의 존재 자체에도 죄의식을 느낀다고 말하고 있다. 하지만 이런 내재화된 자기혐오(internalized self-loathing)가 문명사회의 기반을 이루고 있다고 필자는 설명하고 있다. 따라서 본문에서 말하는 양심의 개념은 ③이 된다.

49
밑줄 친 ㉮의 문장이 암시하는 것은?
① 우리는 항상 우리의 양심을 억제한다.
② 서구 문화권에서는 죄책감을 지나치게 강조한다.
③ 사람들의 일상적 생각에 종종 양심이 자리 잡고 있지 않다.
④ 사람들은 근본적으로 범죄자의 본성을 갖고 있다.

| 정답 | ②

| 해설 | 스테로이드(steroid)는 성장 호르몬으로 이를 복용한 경우 단기간에 '과도'한 근육을 만들 수 있다. ㉮의 문장("But Western Christian culture has conscience on steroids, so to speak.")을 보면, 모든 문화권이 양심의 가책을 느끼지만, 유독 서구 기독교 문화권에서는 소위 "스테로이드를 복용한 양심(conscience on steroids)"을 지니고 있다고 말하면서, 양심이 과도하게 부풀려져 있다고 주장하고 있다. 그러면서 바로 뒤의 문장에서 필자는 양심의 가책이 다른 문화권에 비해 상대적으로 과한 측면이 있다(comparatively extreme)고 주장한다. 따라서 답은 ②가 된다.

50 밑줄 친 ㉯의 의미는?

① 혼합물
② 작은 빈터, 습지
③ 회선, 얽힘
④ 무리

| 정답 | ①

| 해설 | concoction은 혼합물(something, especially a drink or food, made by mixing different things, especially things that are not usually combined)을 말하는 것으로, 본문에서는 '혼합 음료'를 말한다. 매장에서 음료를 주문하려는데, 바로 앞에 있는 사람이 휘핑크림이나 저지방 우유 등 독특한 방식으로 이것저것 섞어 달라고 할 때 미운 생각이 든다는 뜻으로 concoction이란 단어를 사용하고 있다. 따라서 답은 ① blends가 된다.

| 어휘 |
conscience ⓝ 양심
on steroid – 스테로이드를 복용하는
internalized ⓐ 내재화된, 내면화된
interest ⓝ 이익
instinct ⓝ 본능
be accustomed to – ~하는 데 익숙하다
elaborate ⓐ 공들인, 정교한, 복잡한
queue ⓝ 줄
muscle people out of my way – 내가 가려는 길에 있는 사람들을 힘으로 밀쳐내다
psyche ⓝ 정신, 마음
overemphasize ⓥ 지나치게 강조하다, 지나치게 중시하다
glade ⓝ (숲 속의) 작은 빈터, 습지, 늪지
drove ⓝ 떼 지어 가는 무리
so to speak – 말하자면
comparatively ⓐⓓ 상당히, 비교적
loathing ⓝ 혐오
refrain ⓥ 삼가다
urge ⓝ 욕구, 충동
impulse ⓝ 충동
concoction ⓝ (특히 음료나 약물의 특이한) 혼합물
storm ⓥ 쿵쾅대며 가다
strangle ⓥ 목 졸라 죽이다
convolution ⓝ 회선; 얽힘

CHAPTER 02 정보·기술

01	③	02	①	03	①	04	②	05	③	06	①	07	③	08	①	09	⑤	10	⑤
11	②	12	①	13	②	14	②	15	④	16	④	17	③	18	①	19	⑤	20	①
21	①	22	④	23	①	24	④	25	①	26	①	27	④	28	①	29	①	30	④

[01-03]

1993년 뉴욕타임스에 "인터넷에서는 네가 개라는 사실을 누구도 모른다"는 내용을 담은 기억에 남을 만한 만화가 실렸던 적이 있다. 2010년 익명성은 사라지게 될지 모르는 길을 향해 가고 있다. 2010년 8월 4일에 열렸던 〈Techonomy 컨퍼런스〉에서 구글 CEO인 Eric Schmidt는 "당신 사진 14장을 보여주면 우리는 당신이 누구인지 맞출 수 있다. 인터넷에 14장의 사진이 없을 것이라고 생각하는가? 페이스북에 사진을 가지고 있잖은가!"라는 말을 남겼다. 이 같은 현상은 돌이킬 수 없을 뿐만 아니라, 그의 눈에는 필요한 것이었다. 왜냐하면 그가 "비대칭 위협이 존재하는 세상에서, 진정한 의미의 익명성은 매우 위험하다 … 여러분들은 사람들에 대한 이름 서비스를 필요로 한다 … 정부들도 이런 서비스를 요구하게 될 것이다"라고 말했기 때문이다.

사람들을 속이는 것이 여전히 가능하지만, 앞으로는 점점 더 어려워질 전망이다. 세계에서 가장 막강한 온라인 설계자들과 정치 지도자들이 자유로운 인터넷 세상(이들은 여전히 이와 같은 세상을 무법 지대로 보고 있다)을 "교화"하려는 계획을 세우고 있기 때문이다. 그들이 인터넷을 길들이는 데 성공한다면, 당신의 실제 신분을 밝히는 것이 인터넷의 모든 접근을 즐기기 위해 치러야 할 대가가 될 것이다. 거미줄(web)이라는 단어는 원래 실타래처럼 얽힌 정보 네트워크의 분산형 시스템을 묘사하기 위해 사용한 이미지였다. 하지만 거미줄의 거미가 실제로 중앙에 터를 잡고 모든 인터넷 사용자들의 활동들을 감시하기 시작할 것이라고는 누구도 상상하지 못했던 일이다.

01 윗글의 첫 문단에서 1993년으로부터 2010년까지라는 세월의 경과가 갖는 의미는?
① 수년에 걸쳐서, 인터넷의 영향력 증가로 우리의 일상적 업무를 처리하는 방식이 혁명적으로 바뀌었다.
② 과거에는 뉴욕타임스와 같은 신문들이 누리던 사회적 권위가 이제는 구글과 같은 IT 회사들의 CEO들에게 넘어갔다.
③ 한때는 긍정적 장점으로 인식되던 인터넷의 속성이 이제는 몇몇 영향력 있는 사람들에 의해 사회의 심각한 위협으로 인식되고 있다.
④ 정치인들은 Eric Schmidt와 같은 사람들의 사회적 영향력이 커져 가는 것을 시기하고 있다.

| 정답 | ③

| 해설 | 1993년에는 인터넷상의 익명성(anonymity)이 문제가 되지 않았지만, 이제는 폐지(being abolished)를 향해 나아가고 있고, 비대칭 위협으로 인해 이제는 익명성이 매우 위험한(too dangerous) 것이라는 말이 있으므로, 인터넷의 장점이 아닌 단점에 초점을 맞추고 있다는 것을 알 수 있다. 따라서 정답은 ③이 된다.

02 빈칸 ㉮에 알맞은 단어는?
① 길들이는 데
② 범람시키는데, 물에 잠기게 하는 데
③ 분개하게 만드는 데
④ 누그러뜨리는 데

| 정답 | ①

| 해설 | 빈칸 앞의 they는 "the world's most powerful online architects and its political leaders"가 되며, 이들이 빈칸을 성공한다면 인터넷을 사용하는 데 있어서 익명성을 보장받을 수 없다는 내용이 뒤에 나오므로, 이들의 목적은 인터넷의 익명성을 허용하지 않는 데 있다. 빈칸 바로 앞 문장에서 'civilise'라는 단어와 비슷한 어감이 들어가야 하므로, 정답은 '길들이다'라는 의미의 ①이 된다.

03 두 번째 문단에서 가장 핵심적으로 대비되는 한 쌍의 이미지는?

① 분산형 시스템 vs. 법치 지대
② 설계자 vs. 거미
③ 정치인 vs. IT 기업의 CEO들
④ 오프라인상의 신분 vs. 온라인상의 신분

| 정답 | ①

| 해설 | 익명성을 지향하는 분산형 시스템이 과거 인터넷의 모습이라면[이를 달가워하지 않는 측에서는 이를 무법 지대(lawless zone)이라고 부름], 이제는 이런 인터넷을 길들여 익명성을 허용하지 않는 방식으로 변해 가고 있으므로 이를 법치 지대(law-governed zone)로 명명할 수 있다. 따라서 정답은 ①이 된다.

| 어휘 | **anonymity** ⓝ 익명성
abolish ⓥ 폐지하다
irrevocable ⓐ 돌이킬 수 없는, 취소할 수 없는
asymmetric threat – 비대칭 위협[서로 다른 두 국가 사이에 어느 한쪽에만 있는 요소로 인해 힘의 균형이 깨지고 이것을 무기 삼아 우세에 있는 쪽이 열세에 있는 쪽을 위협하는 행위를 말한다. 전면전이 아닌 테러나 대량 살상 무기 등을 이용한 공격을 지칭한다. 비슷한 용어로는 '비군사적 위협(non-military threat)', '초국가적 위협(transnational threat)' 등이 있다.]
civilise ⓥ 개화하다, 교화하다, 세련되게 하다
pay the price – 대가를 지불하다
take up residence – 주거를 정하다, 자리를 차지하고 살다
social authority – 사회적 권위(사회적 권위는 한 개인이나 조직이 어떤 특정한 분야에서 전문가로 인정받아 그 분야에 영향력을 미칠 수 있는 개인이나 조직이 되는 것을 의미한다.)
asset ⓝ 자산, 장점(↔ liability ⓝ 부채, 단점)
domesticate ⓥ 길들이다, 사육하다
inundate ⓥ 범람시키다, 침수시키다, 감당 못할 정도로 주다
scandalize ⓥ (충격적인 행동으로) 분개하게 만들다
be on the way to sth – ~을 향해 나아가다
the state of affairs – 상황, 정세, 현상
asymmetric ⓐ 비대칭의
lawless zone – 무법 지대
decentralised ⓐ 분산형의, 분권의
mollify ⓥ 누그러뜨리다, 완화시키다

[04-06] 숙명여대 2011

인터넷은 인류에게 셀 수 없이 많은 혜택을 가져다주었다. 하지만 이와 동시에, 우리가 잘 알고 있듯, 헤아릴 수 없을 만큼 심각한 악용의 가능성 또한 열어 주었다. 인터넷은 교정에서 약자를 괴롭히는 불량 학생들의 위협을 증폭시키고 있으며, 테러리스트와 비주류 무리들에 더 큰 권한을 부여하고 있으며, 첨단 기술에 능수능란한 범죄자들에게 새로운 거대한 장을 열어 주고 있다. 정보들이 서로 공유될 수 있고, 링크를 통해 연결되어 있으며, 거의 순식간이라고 할 수 있을 만큼 쉽고 빠르게 악용될 수 있기 때문에, 정보의 공개에 수반된 위험들은 몰라볼 정도로 매우 빠르게 커져 가고 있다. 그리고 그 어떤 편집자도, 설사 그가 아무리 좋은 의도를 가지고 있다고 하더라도, 이 같은 종류의 막대한 양의 기밀 유출에 수반된 향후 반향에 대해 제대로 된 판단을 내릴 방법이 결코 존재하지 않는다. 하지만 이런 시대에 우리가 살고 있는 것이 현실이며, 하지 말라고 설교한다고 해서 어느 정도 효과가 있을지는 의문이다. 기술이 윤리를 앞질렀기 때문이다.

모든 정보에 대한 공개를 옹호하는 사람들은 언론인들과 정부 사이의 줄다리기가 한쪽으로 치우쳐져 있다는 사실을 내가 간과하고 있다고 항의할지 모른다. 그들은 정부 관료들이 막대한 자원과 폐쇄적인 문화를 가지고, 비밀 정보를 유출하는 그 어떤 개인보다 훨씬 더 막강한 정보 통제력을 지녔다고 주장할지도 모른다. 웹상에서 게릴라처럼 정보를 누출하는 이들은 운동장의 땅을 고르게 하듯 단지 공정한 경쟁 환경을 조성하려고 노력하는 것일 뿐이다.

04 빈칸에 가장 적합한 표현은?
① 양심
② 윤리
③ 세대
④ 정의
⑤ 법

| 정답 | ②

| 해설 | 본문에서는 인터넷의 발달로 기술이 해악을 가져올 수 있다고 전제하고 있다. 학교에서 폭력을 행사하는 아이들이 이제는 인터넷을 이용해 더 큰 폭력을 휘두를 수 있고, 알카에다 같은 비주류 집단의 힘이 더 막강해졌으며, 해커와 같은 이들에게 인터넷 공간은 새로운 악용의 장이 되고 있다. 이런 상황에서 좋은 의도로[위키리크스(WikiLeaks)가] 비밀 자료를 공개했다고 하더라도 이런 자료가 어떤 식으로 악용될지는 아무도 모른다는 것이다. 이것이 현실이고, 자제하라고 해서 될 일도 아니라고 말하고 있다. 왜냐하면 기술이 '빈칸'을 이미 앞질렀기 때문이라고 말하고 있다. 따라서 문맥으로 봤을 때 이 빈칸에는 ① 또는 ②가 가능하다. ①의 양심(conscience)은 무엇이 옳고 그른지에 대한 문제로 '개인'에 국한된 문제이고, ②의 윤리(ethics)는 '집단'에 해당하는 문제라고 할 수 있다. 기술의 발달로 우리가 흔히 생각하는 옳고 그름을 무색하게 하고 있다는 뜻이 되어야 하므로, 정답은 ②가 된다.

05 다음 중 밑줄 친 even을 대체할 수 있는 가장 적절한 것은?
① 방해하다
② 무효로 만들다
③ 평평하게 하다, 고르다
④ 조직하다
⑤ 보여주다

| 정답 | ③

| 해설 | even은 형용사로 '평평한'의 의미를 지니며, 동사로는 '평평하게 하다'라는 뜻을 지닌다. 본문에 나온 'even the playing field'는 '경기장의 표면을 고르게 하다'는 뜻으로, 두 팀이 경기장에서 경기를 하는데, 한쪽 팀이 상대적으로 높은 곳에 위치할 경우 그 팀이 유리하게 경기를 진행하는데, 이런 부정의 요소가 될 수 있는 부분을 근본적으로 차단한다는 것을 의미하는 숙어이다. 따라서 답은 ③이다. even 대신 level을 동사로 사용하기도 하며, 뜻은 동일하다.

06 본문의 저자는 인터넷상의 모든 정보들의 공개에 대해 _____.

① 회의적이다
② 침통해 있다
③ 확신하고 있다
④ 장난으로 대하고 있다
⑤ 낙관적이다

| 정답 | ①

| 해설 | 본문에서 저자는 계속해서 인터넷과 정보 공개에 대해 우려의 목소리를 내고 있다. "incalculable potential for mischief"나 "the risks ... develop very quickly out of all recognition" 등을 통해 이를 알 수 있으며, 후반부에서는 정보 공개에 대해 찬성하는 이들과 자신의 입장을 비교해 서술하고 있다. 따라서 정답은 ①이 된다.

| 어휘 |
countless ⓐ 셀 수 없이 많은, 무수한
mischief ⓝ 해악, 나쁜 짓, 장난
empower ⓥ 권한을 주다
technologically savvy – 첨단 기술에 정통해 있는, 첨단 기술을 잘 아는
exploit ⓥ 이용하다, 악용하다
ease ⓝ 용이함, 편함
out of (all) recognition (=beyond recognition) – 몰라보게, 몰라볼 정도로
informed judgement – 정통한 판단, 모든 정보를 알고 내리는 제대로 된 판단
repercussion ⓝ 영향, 반향
preach ⓥ 설교하다, 설파하다
outpace ⓥ 앞서다, 앞지르다
object that ~ – ~라고 항의하다
tug-of-war ⓝ 줄다리기
contend ⓥ 주장하다, 싸우다
leak ⓥ 유출시키다, 새게 하다
even/level the playing field – (경기장의 표면을 고르게 만들어) 공평한 경쟁이 될 수 있도록 하다
conscience ⓝ 양심
skeptical ⓐ 회의적인
convinced ⓐ 확신하는

incalculable ⓐ 헤아릴 수 없는, 무수한
threat ⓝ 협박, 위협
fringe group – 비주류파
instantaneous ⓐ 즉각적인
entail ⓥ 수반하다
confidential data – 기밀문서, 기밀 자료
restraint ⓝ 규제, 통제, 제한
advocate ⓝ 옹호자, 지지자
overlook ⓥ 간과하다, 눈감아 주다
lopsided ⓐ 한쪽으로 치우친
bureaucracy ⓝ 관료
even ⓥ 평평하게 하다
disrupt ⓥ 방해하다
solemn ⓐ 침통한, 근엄한

[07-08] 한양대 2013

스마트 차량도 문제가 있다. 한 가지 문제로는 어떻게 이 모든 자동차 기술을 제어할 수 있을지이다. 버튼이 많을수록 운전자의 주의를 많이 빼앗기 된다. 음성 제어도 운전자의 집중력을 저하시킨다. 최근 연구에 따르면 손에다 휴대전화를 들고 대화를 하는 운전자는 그렇지 않은 운전자에 비해 네 배나 더 사고에 휘말릴 가능성이 높다고 한다. 사실 휴대전화를 사용하는 운전자는 법적으로 음주 운전을 범한 것으로 분류되는 운전자들만큼이나 사고에 휘말릴 가능성이 높다. 핸즈프리 장치라도 음성 제어 기능을 사용하는 것이 전화로 대화를 나누는 것만큼이나 집중력을 떨어뜨리는 것으로 나타날 수 있다. 그럼에도 불구하고 이런 제어 관련 문제에 있어 자동차 업계의 답변은 지금까지는 음성 제어뿐이다. 라디오 채널을 바꾸거나 트렁크를 여는 것 같이 간단한 작업의 경우 음성 제어는 충분히 잘 작동한다. 하지만 인터넷 활용이나 자동차 자체를 제어하는 것 같이 한층 까다로운 작업을 총괄하는 데에는 음성 제어가 최고의 방법이라 할 수는 없을 것이다. 엔진 소음, 고속도로에서의 소음, 차량 스테레오에서의 소음 등이 지시 사항을 왜곡시키고, 음성 인식 시스템은 종종 센 억양을 판독하지 못한다.

07 윗글의 바로 앞에 나올 내용으로 가장 알맞은 것을 고르시오.
① 스마트 차량의 전자적 결함
② 스마트 차량의 미덕과 악덕
③ 현대 차량의 영리한 기능
④ 스마트 차량의 기계적 고장

| 정답 | ③

| 해설 | 첫 번째 문장을 해석하면 "스마트 차량도 문제가 있다(Smart cars create problems as well)"인데, 여기서 "~도(as well)" 덕분에 첫 번째 문장 앞에는 스마트 차량의 장점 내지는 기능 등이 설명되었을 것으로 유추 가능하다. 따라서 답은 ③이다.

08 윗글의 내용과 일치하는 것을 고르시오.
① 휴대전화를 이용하면서 운전하는 것은 음주 운전만큼이나 위험하다.
② 음성 제어는 다양한 소음을 이겨낼 수 있을 만큼 효율적이다.
③ 새로운 기술은 자동차 제어를 위해 필요한 버튼의 수를 줄여 준다.
④ 음성제어는 자동차 사고의 횟수를 급격하게 줄이기 위해 도입될 수 있다.

| 정답 | ①

| 해설 | "사실 휴대전화를 사용하는 운전자는 법적으로 음주 운전을 범한 것으로 분류되는 운전자들만큼이나 사고에 휘말릴 가능성이 높다(In fact, drivers using cell phones were almost as likely to be involved in accidents as those who were legally intoxicated)." 따라서 답은 ①이다.

| 어휘 | distract ⓥ 집중이 안 되게 하다, 주의를 딴 곳으로 돌리다
intoxicated ⓐ (술·마약에) 취한　　garble ⓥ 왜곡시키다, 잘못 전하다
decipher ⓥ 판독하다, 해독하다　　malfunction ⓝ 기능 부전, 고장

[09-10] 성균관대 2014

현재 미국의 공공 도로에서 안테나와 카메라가 빽빽하게 장착된 차량을 시험 운행하고 있는 구글에 따르면 운전자가 필요 없는 자동차가 곧 출현할 것이다. 하지만 (아직까지는) 구글은 차량을 만들지 않는다. 따라서 무인 자동차 기술을 시장에 선보이는 역할은 자동차 생산 기업에 달려 있다. 그리고 자동차 업체들은 보수적인 무리이다. 그렇지만, 자동운전 보조장치의 수가 점차 증가하면서 느리지만 꾸준하게 자동운전 차량이 등장할 것이다. 최근에 볼보가 이러한 기능을 하나 보였는데, 바로 스스로 주차가 가능한 차량이다. 이미 일부 차량은 주차를 돕는 시스템을 갖추고 있으나 완전 자동 주차는 아니다. 이들 주차보조 시스템은 평행 주차가 가능한 공간을 식별한 다음에 운전자가 브레이크를 밟고 있는 동안 차량을 주차 공간으로 인도하여 들어가게 한다. 하지만 볼보의 자동 주차 시스템은 운전자가 차량 밖으로 나와서 스마트폰 앱을 활용해 차량이 주차할 수 있도록 지시하는 것이 가능하다. 그렇게 하면 차량은 서서히 움직여서, 주차 공간으로 이동한 다음 운전자에게 자신이 어디에 위치해 있는지를 알려주는 메시지를 보낸다. 나중에 운전자는 직접 차를 가지러 가거나 차를 놔둔 장소에 전화로 다시 부를 수 있다. 따라서 자동주차 기능은 툭 트인 큰 도로에 비해 자동으로 움직이는 차량을 더 쉽게 관리할 수 있는 통제된 장소인 쇼핑몰이나 공항 같은 곳에서 제공이 가능하다.

09 다음 중 빈칸에 가장 알맞은 것은 무엇인가?
① 충분히 안전하지 않다
② 자동운전이 아닌 차량과 별반 차이가 없다
③ 아직 판매 중이 아니다
④ 너무 비싸다
⑤ 완전 자동 주차는 아니다

| 정답 | ⑤

| 해설 | 빈칸 뒤 내용을 보면 "이들 주차보조 시스템은 평행 주차가 가능한 공간을 식별한 다음에 운전자가 브레이크를 밟고 있는 동안 차량을 주차 공간으로 인도하여 들어가게 한다(They can identify an empty parallel-parking space and steer into it while the driver uses the brake)." 여기서 "운전자가 브레이크를 밟고 있는 동안"이란 표현을 통해 운전자가 필요 없는 완전 자동주차 시스템은 아님을 알 수 있다. 따라서 답은 ⑤이다.

10 본문에 따르면 다음 중 맞는 것은 무엇인가?
① 자동차 제조업체는 신기술을 빠르게 상업화하고 있다.
② 운전자 없는 차량끼리의 통신에는 문제가 존재한다.
③ 구글의 소프트웨어 앱의 지원을 받는 볼보는 자동 대리 주차 시스템을 개발했다.
④ 자율운전 차량은 안전 문제 때문에 근 미래에는 공공 도로에서는 허용이 되지 않을 것이다.
⑤ 자동주차는 통제된 장소에서는 비교적 쉽다.

| 정답 | ⑤

| 해설 | "따라서 자동주차 기능은 툭 트인 큰 도로에 비해 자동으로 움직이는 차량을 더 쉽게 관리할 수 있는 통제된 장소인 쇼핑몰이나 공항 같은 곳에서 제공이 가능하다(Autonomous parking could thus be provided at places like shopping centers and airports, which are controlled areas in which automated vehicles can be managed more easily than on open highways)." 즉, 볼보의 자동주차 기능은 통제된 장소에서 더 적합함을 알 수 있다. 따라서 답은 ⑤이다.

| 어휘 | **just around the corner** – 아주 가까이에 있는, 곧 다가오는
bristle with – ~이 빽빽하게 있다, ~으로 가득하다
aerial ⓝ 안테나
bunch ⓝ 무리, 묶음
parallel parking – 평행 주차
steer into – ~쪽으로 돌리다, 조종하다
trundle ⓥ (천천히 소리를 내며) 굴러가다
manoeuvre ⓥ 움직이다, 이동하다
collect ⓥ 데리러[가지러] 가다
drop off – ~을 내려놓다
valet parking – 대리 주차

[11-12] 명지대 2014

테이프는 현재에도 사용 중인 저장매체 중에서 가장 오래된 것이다. 테이프는 1951년 UNIVAC 컴퓨터에 처음으로 사용되었다. 유럽 입자 물리 연구소(CERN)의 데이터 및 저장 분야 책임자인 알베르토 페이스(Alberto Pace)에 따르면 테이프는 데이터의 장기 보존에 있어 하드디스크에 비해 네 가지 이점을 갖고 있다. 첫 번째는 속도이다. 자료 보관소 관리 로봇이 올바른 테이프를 찾은 다음에 판독 장치에 넣기까지 40초나 걸리지만, 일단 로딩이 완료되면 이 테이프에서 자료를 추출하는 데 걸리는 시간은 하드디스크에서 판독하는 시간보다 대략 네 배 빠르다. 두 번째 장점은 신뢰성이다. 테이프는 뚝 끊어져도 다시 이어 붙일 수 있다. 이로 인한 손실은 몇 백 메가바이트 분량의 수준을 넘는 경우가 거의 없다. 이와는 대조적으로 테라바이트 용량의 하드디스크가 망가질 경우 하드디스크에 담긴 모든 데이터가 날아갈 수 있다. 테이프의 세 번째 이점은 테이프에 담긴 데이터를 보존하기 위해서 전원이 필요하지 않다는 점이다. 네 번째 이점은 보안이다. 악의를 품은 해커가 CERN의 데이터 센터에 침입할 경우, 이 해커는 수십 분 내에 디스크에 담긴 50페타바이트 분량의 모든 데이터를 삭제할 수 있다. CERN이 보유한 테이프에 담긴 동일한 분량의 데이터를 삭제하려면 수년이 걸릴 수 있다. 테이프는 또한 추가적으로 두 개의 이점이 존재한다. 테이프는 디스크에 비해 싸며 수명이 더 길다. 테이프에 담긴 정보는 30년이 지난 후에도 확실하게 판독할 수 있지만, 이와는 대조적으로 디스크에 담긴 정보는 5년이 기한이다.

11 본문에 따르면 사실이 아닌 것은 무엇인가?
① 테이프는 1951년에 처음을 컴퓨터용 저장장치로 사용되었다.
② 하드디스크에서 보다는 테이프에서 데이터를 삭제하는 데 시간이 덜 걸린다.
③ 테이프에 데이터를 보존하는 일은 전원을 필요로 하지 않는다.
④ 테이프는 하드디스크에 비해 값이 더 싸고 수명이 더 길다.

| 정답 | ②

| 해설 | 네 번째 장점으로 제시된 것은 보기 ②의 것과 정반대되는 사실이다. 따라서 답은 ②이다.

12 빈칸 (A)와 (B)에 가장 적합한 것을 고르시오.
① 내구성 – 안정성
② 처리 용이성 – 보호
③ 속도 – 보안
④ 판독 가능성 – 내구성

| 정답 | ③

| 해설 | (A): 하드디스크에서 자료를 판독하는 시간보다 테이프에서 자료를 추출하는 시간이 더 빠르다는 것은 테이프가 '속도' 면에서 장점을 갖고 있다는 의미이다.
(B): 해커가 테이프에 담긴 자료를 삭제하는 데 걸리는 시간이 하드에 담긴 동일한 용량의 자료를 삭제하는 데 걸리는 시간에 비해 오래 걸린다는 것은 테이프가 '보안' 차원에서 장점을 갖고 있다는 의미이다.
이러한 점들을 감안했을 때 답으로 가장 적합한 것은 ③이다.

| 어휘 | in use – 쓰이고 있는, 사용 중인
long-term ⓐ 장기적인
archive ⓝ (데이터 등의) 보관, 보존 기록 보관소
load ⓥ 보조[외부]기억장치에서 주기억장치로 넣다, 로드하다
extract ⓥ 뽑아내다, 추출하다
snap ⓥ 딱[똑] 부러지다, 툭 끊어지다
grudge ⓝ 악의, 적의, 원한
advantage ⓝ 이점, 장점
preservation ⓝ 보존, 저장
reliability ⓝ 신뢰성, 확실성
splice ⓥ (필름, 테이프 등의 두 끝을) 붙이다[잇다]
last ⓥ 계속[지속, 존속]하다

reliably ⓐ 확실하게, 신뢰할 수 있게
stability ⓝ 안정성
readability ⓝ 가독성, 판독 가능성
durability ⓝ 내구성
manageability ⓝ 처리 용이성

[13-15] 한국외대 2014

1938년 수천 명의 미국인이 H.G. 웰스의 소설 "우주전쟁"의 라디오판 각색을 진짜 뉴스 방송으로 착각한 유명한 사건이 있었다. 경찰서에는 미국이 화성인의 침공을 받았다고 생각한 시민들의 전화가 쇄도했다. 인터넷 시대인 지금에 와서는 라디오 연극이 이 정도의 오해를 불러일으킬 것이라는 생각은 하기 힘들다. 하지만 1938년에 라디오가 그랬던 것처럼 지금의 인터넷은 비교적 젊은 매체이다. 소셜 미디어에 오해의 소지가 있는 글을 띄울 경우 이와 비교할 수 있을 만큼의 공황을 불러일으킬 수도 있다. "디지털상에 들불처럼 번지는 소문"이 생길 가능성을 생각할 수 있는 것이다. 지금처럼 과다 싶게 연결된 세상에서 정보는 전례 없는 속도와 범위로 뻗어나갈 수 있다. 소셜 미디어는 오해의 소지가 있거나 도발적인 정보를 의도적이든 그렇지 않든 급속하게 확산시킬 수 있다. 이러한 상황에 대한 우려가 인터넷 규제에 대한 광범위한 논쟁에 불을 붙였다. 그렇지만 온라인상의 표현의 자유에 관해 모두가 용인할 수 있는 법적 규제에 도달할 가능성은 없어 보인다. 디지털상에 소문이 들불처럼 번지지 못하게 막거나 억제하려면, 그 가능성은 소셜 미디어의 사용자와 소비자에 주로 달려 있는 것으로 보인다. 역설적으로 들릴지 모르지만 이러한 소문에 대처하는 가장 효과적인 방법 중 하나는 오해를 바로잡기 위해 소셜 미디어라는 동일한 수단을 사용하는 것임이 드러났다. 산불로 비유한 것을 좀 더 확대하여 이와 같은 자율 수정 행위를 (디지털상에 들불처럼 번지는 소문을 바로잡아 주는) "디지털 비"로 기술할 수 있을지 여부는 두고 봐야 할 것이다.

13 저자가 "우주전쟁"을 언급한 이유는 무엇인가?
① 디지털 정보 교환을 규제하는 방법을 설명하기 위해
② 잘못된 정보가 빠르게 확산되는 사례를 보여주기 위해
③ 대중매체가 대중에 져야 할 책임을 강조하기 위해
④ 상업적인 소셜 미디어의 근원적 역할이 무엇인지 예를 들기 위해

| 정답 | ②

| 해설 | "우주전쟁" 드라마판이 사람들 사이에서 엄청난 난리를 불러일으킨 것은 "소셜 미디어에 오해의 소지가 있는 글을 띄울 경우 이와 비교할 수 있을 만큼의 공황을 불러일으킬 수도 있다(It is conceivable that a misleading post on social media could spark a comparable panic)"는 사실을 제시하기 위해 사례를 든 것이다. 즉, 라디오가 그랬던 것처럼 요즘은 인터넷을 통해 잘못된 정보가 빠르게 확산될 수 있다는 것이다. 따라서 답은 ②이다.

14 저자에 따르면 다음 중 "디지털상에 들불처럼 번지는 소문"의 책임을 져야 할 쪽은 누구인가?
① 정책 입안자
② 인터넷 이용자
③ 서비스 제공 업체
④ 사이버상의 권리 운동을 벌이는 사람

| 정답 | ②

| 해설 | "디지털상에 소문이 들불처럼 번지지 못하게 막거나 억제하려면, 그 가능성은 소셜 미디어의 사용자와 소비자에 주로 달려 있는 것으로 보인다(If a digital wildfire is to be avoided or contained, it seems that the responsibility lies mainly with users and consumers of social media)." 따라서 답은 ②이다.

15 다음 중 "디지털상에 들불처럼 번지는 소문"과 "디지털 비" 간의 관계를 가장 잘 특징지어 설명한 것은 무엇인가?

① 원인 – 결과　　　　　　② 질문 – 대답
③ 근원 – 결과　　　　　　④ 문제 – 해결

| 정답 | ④

| 해설 | "디지털상에 들불처럼 번지는 소문"은 사이버 공간에 퍼지는 잘못된 소문을 의미하고 "디지털 비"는 산불을 진화하는 데 도움을 주는 비처럼 잘못된 소문을 진압할 수 있는 해결 방안을 의미한다. 즉, 이 둘은 '문제'와 문제에 대한 '해결책'을 의미한다. 따라서 답은 ④이다.

| 어휘 |
adaptation ⓝ 각색　　　　　　　　　　conceivable ⓐ 가능한, 상상할 수 있는
misleading ⓐ 오해의 소지가 있는, 오해를 불러일으키는
comparable ⓐ 비교할 만한　　　　　　wildfire ⓝ 들불
unprecedented ⓐ 전례 없는　　　　　　provocative ⓐ 도발적인
contain ⓥ 억누르다, 억제하다　　　　　avenue ⓝ 방안, 수단
set the record straight – 기록을 바로잡다, 오해를 바로잡다
exemplify ⓥ 예를 들다

[16-17] 단국대 2017

'인공신경망', '기계학습', '딥러닝'이 실제로 의미하는 것은 무엇일까? 최근 들어 이 세 용어를 들어 봤을 가능성이 크다. 인공신경망은 컴퓨터 아키텍처의 한 종류로 그 위에 인공지능이 생성된다. 인공신경망은 마치 뇌의 그림처럼 컴퓨터를 조직하는 것으로, 그물망에서 서로 연결된 뉴런처럼 생긴 노드들로 구성되어 있다. 개별적으로 이런 노드들은 매우 기초적인 질문에 대답하는 바보 같지만, 집단적으로는 어려운 문제를 해결할 수 있다. 더 중요한 점은 알고리즘만 제대로 갖추면 신경망이 학습할 수 있다는 것이다. 기계학습은 인공신경망에서 실행할 수 있는 프로그램으로, 컴퓨터가 수많은 데이터에서 특정 답변을 찾도록 학습시킨다. 딥러닝은 저렴한 학습 처리 능력과 풍부한 데이터(달리 말하면 인터넷으로 알려진)라는 두 가지 새로운 자원 덕분에 지난 10년에 걸쳐 인기를 얻게된 특별한 유형의 기계학습이다. 만약 딥러닝 시스템이 그림을 보고 있다면, 각 계층은 사실상 서로 다른 배율을 다루고 있다. 가장 밑바닥에 있는 층에서는 5x5 격자픽셀을 보면서, 격자 안에 무언가가 나타나는지에 관해서만 "예" 또는 "아니오"로 답한다. 만일 예라는 답변을 한다면, 그 위의 층은 이 격자가 좀 더 큰 패턴에 어떻게 들어맞는지를 살핀다. 예를 들어, 이게 선이 시작하는 부분일까 아니면 모서리가 시작하는 부분일까? 이런 과정이 점차 쌓이면서 소프트웨어는 가장 복잡한 데이터라도 그것을 구성 부분들로 쪼개는 방식을 통해서 이해할 수 있게 된다.

16 다음 중 본문의 내용과 일치하는 것은?

① 딥러닝 시스템에서는 가장 복잡한 데이터도 가장 밑바닥 층으로부터 이해될 수 있다.
② 딥러닝은 기계학습을 가능하게 만드는 일종의 컴퓨터 아키텍처이다.
③ 저렴한 처리 능력과 풍부한 데이터가 인공신경망의 개발을 가능하게 했다.
④ 인공신경망 시스템에서는 각각의 노드가 집단을 이루어 어려운 문제를 해결한다.

| 정답 | ④

| 해설 | ① 딥러닝은 가장 밑바닥 층에서 시작해 계속 위의 층으로 올라가면서 문제를 해결하므로, 가장 밑바닥 층에서 바로 문제를 이해할 수 있다는 말은 본문과 일치하지 않는다. ② 기계학습을 가능하게 만드는 컴퓨터 아키텍처는 딥러닝

이 아니라 인공신경망이다. ③ 저렴한 처리 능력과 풍부한 데이터로 인해 인공신경망이 아닌 딥러닝이 가능하게 되었다. 정답은 ④로, "These networks are a way of structuring a computer so that it looks like a cartoon of the brain ... collectively they can tackle difficult problems." 부분에 해당한다.

17 다음 중 밑줄 친 부분과 가장 가까운 의미를 가지는 것은?
① 가장 마지막에 있는 층에서 복잡한 데이터를 처리하는 것
② 집단으로 어려운 문제를 해결하는 것
③ 더 낮은 층에서 간단한 문제에 답하는 것
④ 복잡한 데이터를 구성 부분으로 쪼개는 것

| 정답 | ③

| 해설 | 밑줄 친 'This process'는 앞부분의 "The bottom layer might look at just a 5 x 5 grids of pixels ... Is this the beginning of a line, for example, or a corner?"를 지칭한다. 낮은 층에서 간단한 문제를 해결하고, 한층 한층 올라가면서 더 복잡한 문제에 답하는 것을 의미하므로, 이에 대한 내용은 ③에 해당한다.

| 어휘 | **neural** ⓐ 신경(계통)의
computer architecture - 컴퓨터 구조
be comprised of - ~로 구성되다
dumb ⓐ 벙어리의, 얼간이의, 우둔한
pots of - 많은, 거액의, 큰돈의
magnification ⓝ 확대
complicated ⓐ 복잡한, 정교한
lately ⓐⓓ 최근에, 얼마 전에
artificial intelligence - 인공지능
node ⓝ (연결망의) 교점[접속점], 노드
tackle ⓥ (일에) 달려들다, (문제와) 씨름하다
layer ⓝ 층
build up - 점점 커지다[강력해지다/많아지다]
break down - ~을 나누다, 분류하다

[18-20] 이화여대 2017

스티븐 호킹, 빌 게이츠, 엘론 머스크, 닉 보스트롬 및 다른 수많은 과학계 거장들의 인공지능(AI) 관련 공포가 실현된다면, 인간의 삶은 훨씬 더 단축될 것이다. 통제 불능의 인공 일반 지능(AGI) 무기에서부터 기계가 계속적인 자기 향상이 가능해지고 이런 과정에서 인간 두뇌의 지적 능력과 그것을 통제할 수 있는 인간의 능력을 뛰어넘는 것을 의미하는 '지능 폭발'에 이르기까지 (인공지능과 관련한) 폭넓은 우려가 존재한다. 만일 초인공지능 재난이 곧 닥칠 것처럼 보인다면, 너무 늦기 전에 인공지능 군비 경쟁에서 물러날 수 있는 선견지명을 그때쯤 우리가 이미 갖추었을 것이라는 신뢰할 만한 지표를 역사에서는 결코 찾을 수 없다. 로버트 오펜하이머는 "기술적으로 감미로운 것을 보면 우리는 서둘러 그것을 해 보고, 기술적 성공을 거둔 후에야 비로소 그 기술을 가지고 무엇을 할 것인지를 논의한다"고 말한 적이 있다. 몇십 년이 지난 후 보스트롬은 "우수한 인공지성이 결코 인간을 해치지 않을 것이라는 보장이 있다면, 그러면 그런 인공지성이 만들어질 것이다. 그런 것을 보장해 주는 방법이 없다면, 그래도 인공지성은 만들어질 것이다."라고 말했다. 호킹은 가장 최근에 "인공지능을 만드는 것에 성공하는 것은 인류 역사상 최대의 성과일 것이다. 불행하게도 그것이 마지막 성과일 수 있다."라는 말로 깔끔하게 요약한 바 있다.

딥마인드의 CEO 데미스 하사비스는 무표정한 얼굴로 "글쎄요, 나는 그렇지 않기를 바란다"고 말한다. 그는 초인공지능과 관련한 질문에 "우리는 목표가 명확히 명시됐는지, 그리고 거기에 모호한 것이 없고 목표가 시간이 지남에 따라 안정적인지 확실히 할 필요가 있다. 우리의 모든 시스템에서 최상위 목표는 여전히 설계자에 의해 명시될 것이다. 인공 일반 지능은 그 목표에 도달하기 위한 자신만의 방법을 생각해 낼 것이다. 그러나 인공 일반 지능이 스스로 목표를 만들어 내는 것은 아니다."라고 말한다. 그의 목소리는 여전히 확신에 차 있다. "이것들은 모두 흥미롭고 어려운 문제이다. 모든 새롭고 강력한 기술과 마찬가지로 이것 또한 윤리적이고 책임감 있게 사용되어야 하며, 그렇기 때문에 우리가 적극적으로 토론을 요구하고 있고, 현재 이 문제점들을 연구하고 있는 것이다. 결과적으로 그 시기가 오면 우리는 충분히 준비되어 있을 것이다."

18	다음 중 빈칸 [A]와 [B]에 올 수 있는 가장 적합한 것은?

① 자아 성찰 – 주장을 뒷받침하다　　② 자기 비판 – 용해하다
③ 자기 개선 – 뛰어넘다　　　　　　　④ 자기 착각 – 딴 데로 돌리다
⑤ 자체 회복 – 객관화하다

| 정답 | ③

| 해설 | 인공지능에 대해 많은 우려가 있다는 내용으로, 빈칸은 그 우려 중 하나인 지능 폭발을 설명하는 대목이다. 'in doing so'를 이용해 앞뒤 내용이 인과관계로 묶여 있다. 기계가 계속 [A]해서 그 결과 인간의 지능과 통제를 [B]하는 지능 폭발의 위험이 있다는 내용이다. 정답은 ③으로 기계가 계속 자가 학습과 같은 '자기 개선'을 통해 인간의 능력과 통제를 '뛰어넘는다'는 내용이 가장 적합하다.

19	다음 중 본문을 통해 가장 잘 추론할 수 있는 것은?

① 호킹의 발언은 인공지능의 개발을 인류 역사상 최고의 성과로 축하하는 것이다.
② 오펜하이머에 따르면 고도로 발전된 인공지능이 개발되면 인간이 개입할 여지는 더 이상 없어진다.
③ 보스트롬은 초인공지성이 무슨 일이 있어도 개발될 수 없다는 것을 보증한다.
④ 하사비스는 인공지능이 윤리적인 결정을 내릴 것이라고 알려준다.
⑤ 하사비스에 따르면, 인공지문에 할당된 애매한 목표는 긍정적 효과를 보장하지 못할 수도 있다.

| 정답 | ⑤

| 해설 | ① 호킹은 인공지능의 개발이 '인류 최대의 성과이자 마지막 성과'라고 했으므로 인공지능의 개발은 그에게 축하가 아닌 경고의 대상이 된다. ② 오펜하이머는 인간은 좋아 보이는 기술이 있으면 일단 만들고 나서 그 이후의 일을 생각하는 경향이 있다고 했으므로, 보기의 내용과는 다르다. ③ 보스트롬은 인공지능에 두려움을 느끼는 이들 중 하나이며, 초인공지성이 인간을 해친다는 보장이 있든 없든 초인공지성은 개발될 것이라고 했으므로, 무슨 일이 있어도 개발될 수 없다는 것과 반대가 된다. ④ 인공지능이 윤리적인 결정을 내리는 것이 아니라 인간이 인공 지능과 같은 기술을 윤리적으로 사용해야 한다고 하사비스는 주장한다. ⑤ 본문의 "We need to make sure the goals are correctly specified" 부분을 통해 목표가 정확히 명시되는 것이 중요하다는 것을 알 수 있다. 따라서 명확하지 않고 애매하게 부여된 목표는 좋은 결과를 보장할 수 없다는 ⑤가 본문에서 추론할 수 있는 내용에 해당한다.

20	다음 중 빈칸 [C]에 올 수 있는 가장 적합한 것은?

① 우리는 충분히 준비되어 있을 것이다
② 인공지능은 자율적으로 작동해야 한다
③ 과학적 성공이 이루어질 수 있다
④ 인간은 인공지능을 고용해야 한다
⑤ 인간의 두뇌는 인공지능처럼 강력하게 기능해야 한다

| 정답 | ①

| 해설 | 일단 [C] 앞의 'the time'이 무엇을 지칭하는지 파악할 필요가 있다. 본문의 내용은 크게 양측의 입장이 대조를 이루는 것으로, 앞부분은 인공지능의 위험성에 대해 우려하는 측이고, 뒷부분은 대비만 잘하면 인공지능이 위험한 것이 아니라고 주장한다. 여기서 the time은 진정한 의미의 인공지능이 개발된 상황을 의미한다. 앞부분의 사람들은 그런

상황이 오면 인간은 손을 쓸 수 없게 된다고 우려하고 있다. 따라서 목표를 잘 명시하고, 예상 문제를 논의하고 연구하면, 인공지능이 개발된 상황이 오더라도 '충분한 준비가 되어 있을 것'이므로 문제가 되지 않는다는 ①이 적합하다. ③의 경우 이미 과학적 성공(인공지능의 개발)이 끝난 상황을 the time이 내포하고 있으므로, 논리적으로 어색하다.

| 어휘 | AI – 인공지능(artificial intelligence)
mind ⓝ (지성이 뛰어난) 사람, 지성(인)
unchecked ⓐ 억제되지 않은
AGI – 인공 일반 지능[artificial general intelligence, 인간이 할 수 있는 어떠한 지적인 업무도 성공적으로 해낼 수 있는 (가상적인) 기계의 지능을 말함]
intelligence explosion – 지능 폭발(인공지능이 더 뛰어난 인공지능을 만드는 것을 의미함)
recursive ⓐ 반복[되풀이]되는
reliable ⓐ 믿을 수 있는
foresight ⓝ 선견지명, 통찰(력)
arms race – 군비 경쟁
observe ⓥ 주장하다, 논평하다; 목격하다, 관찰하다; 준수하다
guarantee ⓥ 보증하다, 보장하다
deadpan ⓥ 무표정한 얼굴로 말하다 ⓐ 무표정한
ambiguous ⓐ 애매한, 분명치 않은
over time – 시간이 흐르면서
relentlessly ⓐⓓ 가차 없이
ethically ⓐⓓ 윤리(학)적으로
underpin ⓥ 버팀목을 대다, 주장을 뒷받침하다
dissolve ⓥ 녹다, 용해되다
surpass ⓥ 능가하다
divert ⓥ (딴 데로) 돌리다
objectify ⓥ ~을 객관화[대상화]하다, ~을 물건 취급하다
autonomously ⓐⓓ 자체적으로; 독자적으로

a host of – 많은
range from A to B – 범위가 A에서 B까지 이어지다

loom ⓥ 어렴풋이 나타나다 ⓝ 베틀
indicator ⓝ 지표
withdraw ⓥ 철수하다, 철회하다, 인출하다

summarize ⓥ 요약하다
specify ⓥ 명시하다
stable ⓐ 안정적인
come up with – (아이디어를) 생각해 내다
reassuring ⓐ 안심시키는, 걱정[불안감]을 없애 주는
self-reflection ⓝ 자아 성찰
self-critique ⓝ 자기 비판
self-improvement ⓝ 자기 개선
self-illusion ⓝ 자기 착각

potently ⓐⓓ 강력하게

[21-22] 성균관대 2016

우리의 온라인 생활을 추적하는 기술은 단순한 쿠키로 시작됐다. 쿠키는 당신의 웹브라우저로 웹사이트가 보내는 작은 양의 데이터로, 당신이 어디를 방문했었는지를 기억한다. 인터넷 초기 시절 전자상거래 회사는 쿠키를 이용해 당신이 누구인지 식별하는 태그를 붙이는 데 일조했다. 당신이 어떤 사이트에 로그인하거나, 온라인 장바구니에 물품을 담거나, 암호화된 신용카드 번호를 보낼 경우, 당신이 계속 거래하고 있다는 사실을 웹사이트에 알려주는 역할을 하는 것이 바로 이 쿠키이다.

"쿠키를 이해하는 가장 쉬운 방법은 손목 밴드와 쿠키를 서로 비교해 보는 것입니다. 여러분이 콘서트장에 가면 손목 밴드는 당신이 누구인지 안전 요원에게 알려주고, 제지당하지 않고도 바로 재입장할 수 있도록 도와줍니다"라고 온라인 사업가인 샘 오(Sam Oh)는 말한다.

하지만 온라인 마케팅 담당자들은 즉시 쿠키가 당신이 해 온 다른 것들도 그들에게 알려줄 수 있다는 것을 알게 됐다. 나는 온라인에서 무엇을 공유할 것인가에 대해 내 스스로 결정내리는 것을 더 좋아하기 때문에 쿠키와 브라우저의 기록을 정기적으로 지우는 버릇이 생겼다. 그러나 이것은 양날의 검과 같다. 이런 기록을 추려내 없애면 나의 기록을 숨길 수는 있지만, 이로 인해 내가 종종 이용한 서비스에 반복해서 접속해야 하는 것을 의미하며, 더구나 이런 사이트들은 내가 과거에 구매한 것과 관련한 기록이 없기 때문에 나는 나중에 다시 들어왔을 때 위시리스트와 장비구니에 있던 물품들을 저장할 수 없게 된다.

21

다음 중 빈칸에 들어갈 가장 적합한 것은?
① 양날의 검
② 첨단 기기
③ 뜨거운 감자
④ 골칫거리
⑤ 독재자

| 정답 | ①

| 해설 | 빈칸 바로 앞부분에는 쿠키를 지워서 나의 활동을 삭제해 보안을 높일 수 있다고 설명한다. 하지만 빈칸 뒷부분에서는 이런 기록을 지우게 되면 과거의 활동 기록도 사라지게 되기 때문에 불편한 점도 발생한다고 설명하고 있기 때문에 쿠키 삭제와 관련한 긍정과 부정에 대해 설명하고 있는 ①이 정답이 된다.

22

쿠키를 사용하는 장점은 ＿＿＿＿＿＿ 하는 것에 있다.
① 당신이 새로운 컴퓨터를 살 필요가 없다
② 당신의 컴퓨터가 정기적으로 업데이트 된다
③ 당신은 당신의 생각을 온라인상에 누구에게든 보낼 수 있다
④ 당신이 좋아하는 웹사이트에 다시 접속할 필요가 없다
⑤ 인터넷 검색 기록이 자동으로 삭제된다

| 정답 | ④

| 해설 | 인터넷에서 쿠키의 역할이 손목 밴드와 비슷하다고 설명하면서 재입장을 용이하게 해 준다는 내용이 등장한다. 후반부에도 쿠키를 지울 경우 자주 사용하는 서비스에 계속 로그인해야 한다고 설명하고 있다. 이를 통해 쿠키는 당신이 좋아하는 웹사이트에 다시 접속할 필요가 없게 만들어 준다는 ④가 정답임을 알 수 있다.

| 어휘 | track ⓥ 추적하다 humble ⓐ 시시한, 변변찮은
cookie ⓝ 쿠키(사용자가 네트워크나 인터넷을 사용할 때마다 중앙 서버에 보내지는 정보 파일)
chunk ⓝ 상당한 양, 대량 tag ⓥ 꼬리표를 붙이다
encrypted ⓐ 암호화된 transact ⓥ 거래하다
wrist band – 손목 밴드 disruption ⓝ 파괴
cull ⓥ 고르다, 추려내다; 추려서 죽이다, 도태하다
a double-edged sword – (긍정과 부정의) 양면성을 지닌 상황[결정]
gadget ⓝ (작고 유용한) 도구[장치] hot potato – 뜨거운 감자, 난감한 문제[상황 등]
a pain in the neck – 아주 귀찮은 사람[것], 골칫거리
big brother – 독재자

[23-25] 한국외대 2017

자동차 기술과 관련해, 자율주행 자동차가 요즘 대유행이다. 자율주행 자동차는 인간이 운전하는 자동차보다 더 안전하고, 더 깨끗하며, 연비 또한 더 뛰어나다. 하지만 이런 자동차가 100% 안전한 것은 아니며, 알고리즘의 도덕성과 관련한 해결할 수 없는 윤리적 딜레마를 제기한다. 피할 수 없는 사고가 발생한 경우 자동차가 어떻게 행동하도록 프로그래밍해야 할 것인가? 설사 탑승자를 희생하는 경우라도 인명의 손실을 최소화해야 하는가, 아니면 무슨 일이 있어도 탑승자를 보호해야 할까? 차량의 소유주를 희생하도록 설계된 차를 누가 사려고 하겠는가? 일부 과학자들은 새로운 실험 윤리의 과학을 활용해서 대중의 견해를 알아보는 일에 착수했다. 이 실험은 많은 사람에게 이들이 어떻게 반응하는지를 알아보기 위해 윤리적 딜레마를 제기하는 것을 포함하고 있다. 실험 결과는 예측할 수 있는 것이긴 해도 흥미롭다. 일반적으로 사람들은 자율주행 자동차가 사망자 수를 최소화하도록 프로그래밍되어 있다는 사실에 안도감을 느낀다. 이런 공리주의적 접근법은 분명 칭찬할 만한 것이지만, 실험 참가자들이 기꺼이 수긍하는 것은 거기까지였다. 참가자들은 자율주행 자동차가 실제로 그런 방식으로 프로그래밍되리라는 것에 대해서는 앞서와 같은 확신은 갖지 못했으며, 거기에는 그럴듯한 이유가 존재했다. 참가자들은 자신이 직접 공리주의적인 자율주행 자동차를 구매하길 원하는 것보다는, 자신이 아닌 다른 사람들이 그런 자동차를 운전하길 희망했다. 바로 이 지점에서 역설이 존재한다. 참가자들은 자신이 직접 운전할 필요가 없는 한에서만, 다른 사람들의 생명을 구하기 위해 탑승자를 희생시키는 차를 더 선호하는 것이다.

23
다음 중 글의 주제로 적합한 것은?
① 자율주행 자동차에 대한 찬반
② 자율주행 자동차의 불완전한 알고리즘
③ 자율주행 자동차의 윤리적 딜레마
④ 비윤리적 사용자를 위한 윤리적으로 프로그래밍된 차량

| 정답 | ③

| 해설 | 자율주행 차량 주행 중 회피할 수 없는 사고가 발생할 경우 일어날 수 있는 주행 알고리즘의 윤리적 딜레마를 다루고 있는 글이므로, 정답은 ③이 된다.

24
다음 중 밑줄 친 Ⓐ가 의미하는 것은?
① 사람들은 실험자에게 약삭빠르게 반응한다.
② 사람들은 컴퓨터화된 세상에 적응했다.
③ 최근 들어 사람들은 점점 공리주의적인 사고를 갖게 되었다.
④ 사람들은 다른 사람을 구하기 위해 자신을 희생하는 데에는 주저한다.

| 정답 | ④

| 해설 | 밑줄 이후의 내용을 통해, 자율주행 차량이 사고가 날 경우 인명 피해를 최소화하도록 프로그래밍되어 있는 것에는 사람들이 찬성하지만, 사고가 발생할 경우 인명 피해를 최소화하는 과정에서 탑승자가 다칠 수 있는 선택을 하는 것은 주저한다는 것을 지적하고 있으므로, 정답은 ④가 적합하다.

25
다음 중 공리주의적 자율주행 자동차의 역설을 설명한 것은?
① 다른 사람이 그런 차를 운전해야 하지만, 나는 아니다.
② 그런 차는 사람의 생명을 구하지만 비용이 든다.
③ 나는 그런 차를 운전하고 싶지만, 그런 차를 사고 싶지는 않다.
④ 나를 제외한 그 어떤 사람도 그런 차를 운전할 수 없다.

| 정답 | ①

| 해설 | 본문 후반의 "참가자들은 자신이 직접 공리주의적인 자율주행 자동차를 구매하길 원하는 것보다는, 자신이 아닌 다른 사람들이 그런 자동차를 운전하길 희망했다."라고 한 이후 이 지점에 역설이 존재한다고 했으므로, 이 부분이 역설에 해당한다. 즉, 다른 사람이 그런 차를 운전했으면 좋겠지만, 그런 차에 탑승자가 되고 싶지는 않다는 것이 역설에 해당하므로, 정답은 ①이 된다.

| 어휘 |
automotive ⓐ 자동차의
fuel-efficient ⓐ 저연비의, 연료 효율이 좋은
and yet – 그렇다 하더라도
dilemma ⓝ 딜레마, 진퇴양난
morality ⓝ 도덕성
sacrifice ⓥ 희생하다
occupant ⓝ (특정 시간에 차량·의자 등에) 타고[앉아] 있는 사람
at all costs – 어떤 희생을 치르더라도, 기어코
pose ⓥ (문제 등을) 제기하다, 주장하다 ⓝ 자세
utilitarian ⓐ 공리주의의, 실용의, 실익의 ⓝ 공리주의자
laudable ⓐ 칭찬할 만한, 훌륭한
autonomous ⓐ 자율의, 자치의
paradox ⓝ 역설
all the rage – 대단한 인기로, 대유행으로
counterpart ⓝ 상대, 대응 관계에 있는 사람[것]
ethical ⓐ 윤리적인, 도덕적인
algorithmic ⓐ 알고리듬의
minimize ⓥ 최소화하다
set out – 출발하다, (일·과제 등에) 착수하다[나서다]
death toll – 사망자 수
so far – (제한된) 어느 정도까지만
therein lies – ~ 바로 그 안에 ~이 있다
in favor of – ~에 찬성[지지]하여

[26-27] 가톨릭대 2018

뚜렷한 이유 없이 고속도로에서 갑자기 차들이 급정거하는 유령 정체가 오랫동안 운전자들의 속을 썩여 왔다. 흥미롭게도 MIT 연구원들은 최근 이러한 가다 서기를 반복하게 만드는 운전을 완화하는 데 도움이 되는 해결책을 제시했다. 해결책의 논리는 다소 단순하다. 문제는 우리가 운전하는 방식에 내재되어 있다. 만약 어떤 차가 갑자기 브레이크를 밟는다면, 뒤에 있는 차는 브레이크를 밟아야 하고 다시 뒤에 있는 차는 또 브레이크를 밟아야 한다. 제동은 거리가 늘어나면서 점점 길어져 차가 실제로 멈추게 된다. MIT의 컴퓨터 과학 및 인공지능 연구소 교수인 혼스타인 박사는 차량의 크루즈 컨트롤 기능을 차량의 앞뒤 공간을 고려해 다시 설계할 것을 제안한다. 물론 오늘날 시장에 선두 차량의 속도에 적응하여 추종 거리를 일정하게 유지할 수 있는 진보된 크루즈 컨트롤 시스템이 존재한다. 그러나 선행 차량과 후행 차량의 간격은 고려되지 않는다. 선행 차량과 후행 차량 간의 간격을 동일하게 유지하면 교통 체증을 방지할 수 있다. 교통 체증을 막을 수 있는 기술의 정식 명칭은 '양방향 제어(bilateral control)'이다.

26 다음 중 본문을 통해 추론할 수 있는 것은?
① 교통 체증은 크루즈 컨트롤을 재설계하여 해결할 수 있다.
② 바람직하지 않은 운전 습관이 고속도로 교통 체증을 일으키는 경우가 있다.
③ 연구 결과에 따르면 고속도로상의 교통 체증은 우리의 통제를 벗어난 것이다.
④ 기존의 크루즈 컨트롤은 교통 사고를 증가시킬 수 있다.

| 정답 | ①

| 해설 | 정답은 ①로, 본문의 "Dr. Hornstein ... proposes redesigning the cruise control feature on our car to consider the space in front and behind the vehicle" 부분을 통해 확인할 수 있다. 뚜렷한 교통 체증의 원인이 없어도 발생하는 교통 체증을 유령 정체라고 말하면서, 이 현상을 해결하려면 기존의 차량에 사용되는 크루즈 기능을 재설계해야 한다고 말한다.

27 다음 중 제시문이 들어갈 가장 적합한 곳은?

> 그러나 선행 차량과 후행 차량의 간격은 고려되지 않는다.

① Ⓐ
② Ⓑ
③ Ⓒ
④ Ⓓ

| 정답 | ④

| 해설 | 제시문의 연결사 'But'과 선행 차량과 후행 차량의 이야기가 앞서 등장한 것을 통해 위치를 찾아갈 수 있다. 정답은 ④로, 바로 앞에서는 일반 차량의 크루즈 기능에 대해 말한 후, 좀 더 진화한 형태의 크루즈 기능을 갖춘 차량도 있다고 말한다. 정속으로 이동하지 않고 앞차의 속도에 반응하는 반응형 크루즈 기능을 말한다. 그리고 그 이후 제시문이 들어간다. 그런 기능 조차도 앞뒤 차량의 간격은 고려되지 않았다는 것이다. 그리고 이후 내용에서 앞뒤 간격을 일정하게 하도록 하는 크루즈 기능을 개선하면 유령 정체는 사라질 수 있다는 것으로 글을 마치고 있다.

| 어휘 | phantom traffic jam – 유령 정체(뚜렷한 원인을 알 수 없는 교통 체증)
screech to a stop – 끽하는 소리를 내며 멈추다   for no apparent reason – 명백한 이유 없이
alleviate ⓥ 완화하다, 경감하다   inherent ⓐ 고유한, 선천적인
cruise control – (차량의) 자동 주행 속도 유지 장치
adapt to – ~에 적응하다   trail ⓥ (자취를 따라) 뒤쫓다, 추적하다
bust ⓥ 부수다, 고장내다, 파멸시키다   bilateral ⓐ 쌍방의, 쌍무적인

[28-30] 숭실대 2017

제이슨 주크(Jason Zook)는 매일 트위터, 인스타그램, 바인, 자신의 블로그, 페이스북 등을 살펴보며 아침을 시작한다. 이런 습관이 33세 기업가인 그의 정신 건강에 영향을 미치기 시작했다. 샌디에이고에서 거주하고 있는 그는 스트레스를 받고, 주의가 산만해지고, 자신의 팔로워 수가 3만 3천 명이 넘는 디지털 세상에서 자신이 보여 주었던 기대감을 충족하지 못할 수 있을 것 같다는 생각을 하게 됐다. "당신은 매일 남들과 비교되는 자신을 보며 하루를 시작한다. 그러면 당신은 뒤처지는 느낌을 받고 당신만의 의견을 갖기도 전에 남들의 의견에 자신이 짓눌리는 상황이 온다."고 그는 말한다.

그래서 그는 과감히 모두 중단하기로 하고, 30일간 소셜미디어의 중독치료를 받기(소셜미디어를 일절 하지 않는 것을 의미함)로 했다. 현명한 조치였다. 최근 피츠버그 대학의 미디어, 기술, 건강 연구센터는 다수의 소셜미디어 플랫폼을 사용하는 것이 우울증과 불안 위험을 증가시킬 수 있다는 사실을 발견했다. 연구에 따르면 7~10개의 소셜미디어 플랫폼을 사용하는 사람은 2개의 플랫폼을 넘지 않은 사용자에 비해 우울증이나 불안 증상을 가질 확률이 3배 더 높았다. 이런 증상을 보고한 사람들은 자신의 프로필을 관리하는 데 필요한 다중작업에 압도된다. 관리할 프로필이 많으면 많을수록 부담은 더 늘어나게 된다.

7개의 소셜미디어 프로필을 유지하는 것은 한계점에 다다른 것이기는 하지만 가능은 하다. 오늘날 사용자들은 이용 가능한 여러 옵션이 있기 때문이다. "사람들은 소셜미디어에 올라온 글들을 보면서 자신과 비교한다. 그리고 자신을 무능하다고 느낀다."고 온라인 치료 업체인 톡스페이스(Talkspace)의 임상개발 수석인 니콜 에임즈베리(Nicole Amesbury)는 말한다. "다른 이유는 생물학적인 요인에 기반을 둔다. 사람들이 소셜미디어 앱을 열고 긍정적인 답변을 볼 때마다, 그들은 뇌에서 소량의 도파민이 분비된다. 그런데 도파민 분비를 일으키는 '좋아요(Like)'를 충분히 받지 못하면, 그들은 상실감을 느낀다."고 덧붙였다.

소셜미디어 컨설턴트이자 퀸즈(Queens) 거주민인 35세의 조쉬 스프링거(Josh Springer)는 플랫폼 사용을 3개로 제한할 것을 충고한다. 그런데도 주크에게 휴식은 정말 필요한 것이었다. "30일간 소셜미디어를 하지 않은 후 머리가 마치 안개가 걷힌 듯 맑아진 것 같다. 나는 이 모든 정신적 공간을 되찾았다."고 그는 말한다.

28 다음 중 밑줄 친 (A)를 가장 잘 재진술한 것은?
① 그는 시골 농장에 가서 칠면조들과 친구가 됐다.
② 그는 진정하기 위해 차가운 음료를 마셔야 했다.
③ 그는 즉시 소셜미디어 게시물을 확인하는 습관을 멈추었다.
④ 그는 치유할 수 없을 만큼 소셜미디어에 중독되었다.

| 정답 | ③

| 해설 | (A)의 'go cold turkey'는 이디엄으로 '(마약이나 흡연을) 갑자기 끊다'라는 의미를 지닌다. 따라서 소셜미디어를 자주 이용하는 습관을 멈추었다는 ③이 가장 적합하다.

29 다음 중 본문의 주크(Zook)에 관한 내용과 일치하지 않는 것은?
① 그는 소셜미디어 플랫폼에 기반한 사업을 운영한다.
② 그는 소셜미디어에 3만 명이 넘는 팔로워가 있다.
③ 그는 소셜미디어로 인해 우울증과 불안증세를 느낀다.
④ 그는 30일간 소셜미디어를 중단했다.

| 정답 | ①

| 해설 | ①이 정답으로 주크의 직업은 기업가(entrepreneur)로 나와 있으며, 소셜미디어 플랫폼을 기반한다는 내용은 등장하지 않는다. 그는 팔로워가 3만이 넘는 소셜미디어를 많이 사용하는 사용자로 우울증과 불안감을 느껴 소셜미디어를 30일간 끊어보기로 했던 사람이다.

30 다음 중 본문의 내용과 일치하지 않는 것은?
① 주크의 사례는 우리에게 소셜미디어 중독에 대한 위험 가능성에 대해 경고한다.
② 필요한 경우 소셜미디어 플랫폼의 수를 제한해야 한다.
③ 소셜미디어에 너무 많은 시간을 보내면 우울증과 불안감을 느낄 수 있다.
④ 주크의 사례는 팔로워가 너무 많기 때문에 예외적인 경우이다.

| 정답 | ④

| 해설 | ① 주크의 사례는 소셜미디어 중독에 대한 위험에 대해 경고하고 있는 내용이며, ② 본문 마지막에서 소셜미디어 플랫폼을 3개로 줄이도록 권고하고 있다. ③ 소셜미디어 플랫폼이 7~10개인 사람은 2개 이하인 사람에 비해 불안과 우울증상을 겪을 확률이 3배가 높다고 나온다. 정답은 ④로, 본문에서는 팔로워의 수가 많고 적음은 고려하지 않았다.

| 어휘 | scroll through - (컴퓨터 화면 등을) 스크롤해서 움직이다
entrepreneur ⓝ 기업가
fulfill the expectation - 기대를 충족시키다
go cold turkey - (마약이나 흡연을) 갑자기 끊다
depression ⓝ 우울증; (경제) 침체, 공황
symptom ⓝ 징후, 증상
be overwhelmed by - ~에 눌리다, 압도당하다, 어찌할 줄 모르다
high end - 상한선; 고급[고가]품
keep from something - ~하지 않다[~을 참다]
distract ⓥ 주의를 산만하게 하다; 즐겁게 하다
amass ⓥ 모으다, 축적하다, 쌓다
detox ⓝ (인체 유해 물질의) 해독
no more than - 단지 ~에 지나지 않다, ~일 뿐(only)
bevy ⓝ (여자, 새) 무리, 떼

CHAPTER 03 지역·지리

| 01 | ① | 02 | ② | 03 | ② | 04 | ① | 05 | ④ | 06 | ② | 07 | ① | 08 | ① | 09 | ④ | 10 | ③ |
| 11 | ① | 12 | ① | 13 | ② | 14 | ③ | 15 | ① | 16 | ① | 17 | ③ | 18 | ① | 19 | ② | 20 | ④ |

[01-03] 한국외대 2016 C형

정신적 외상을 초래할 정도로 고달프지만 풍성한 역사를 자랑하고, 굉장히 아름다운 풍경과 남아메리카 대륙 국민 가운데 외부인들을 가장 반갑게 맞이해 주는 사람들이 사는 국가인 콜롬비아는 남아메리카 대륙 여행객들의 마음을 자연스럽게 끄는 곳이다. 40년 동안 내전이 진행 중에 있지만 보안 상태가 개선된 덕분에 관광객이 급격히 증가했다. 외국인들 및 콜롬비아인들 모두가 구름에 뒤덮인 숲속의 산들과 주위가 야자수로 둘러싸인 해변 그리고 아주 멋진 식민지 시대 도시들로 이루어진 콜롬비아의 황홀한 낙원을 이제는 답사할 수 있게 되었다. 콜롬비아는 남아메리카 대륙에서 태평양과 카리브해를 접하고 있는 유일한 국가로 아마존 열대 우림에서 정상이 눈으로 덮인 산들과 열대의 섬에 이르기까지 매우 다양한 생태계를 자랑한다. 황금빛의 카리브해 해변과 자갈이 깔린 식민지 시대 도시가 전하는 매력에서부터 여러 곳의 커피 농장에 이르기까지 콜롬비아라는 하나의 국가 속에 라틴아메리카의 모습이 압축적으로 드러나고 있다. 콜롬비아의 활기를 되찾은 주요 도시로 소설가 가브리엘 가르시아 마르케스(Gabriel Garcia Marquez)가 작품의 무대로 삼은 마법과도 같은 도시인 카르타헤나(Cartagena)을 놓쳐서는 안 된다. 카르타헤나보다 더 신비에 둘러싸인 곳은 바로 산 아구스틴(San Agustí)으로, 500개 이상의 등신대 조각상이 인근 시골 지역에 산재하여 있다. 콜롬비아의 다양한 지형은 다이빙, 등산, 래프팅, 트래킹 등 야외에서 모험을 즐기기에 아주 좋은 근간이 된다. 남아메리카 대륙을 상징하는 트래킹 코스 중 일부는 이곳 콜롬비아에 존재한다. 시우다드 페르디다(Ciudad Perdida)는 타이로나(Tayrona) 문명의 고대 유적지로 향하기 위해 며칠 동안 정글 속을 걷는 도보 여행이며 한편 국립공원 내의 수많은 오르막길은 겁 없는 도보 여행자들을 안데스(Andes) 산맥의 최정상 지역으로 인도해 준다. 프로비덴시아(Providencia)가 자랑하는 세계 최고의 암초는 스쿠버 다이버들에겐 물속의 천국을 의미하고, 태평양 해변의 고래 연구가들은 야생 상태의 위풍당당한 혹등 고래를 관찰할 수 있다.

01 다음 중 Ⓐ의 예로 알맞지 않은 것은 무엇인가?
① 40년 동안 진행된 내전
② 여러 곳의 커피 농장
③ 아마존 열대우림
④ 고대 유적지로 향하는 정글 속 도보 여행

| 정답 | ①

| 해설 | ①은 콜롬비아로 사람들의 마음을 끄는 요인이 될 수 없다. 따라서 답은 ①이다.

02 다음 중 본문의 주제는 무엇인가?
① 콜롬비아의 자연사
② 콜롬비아에서 방문할 만한 장소
③ 콜롬비아의 국가안보
④ 콜롬비아에서의 스포츠 활동 기회

정답과 해설 • 409

| 정답 | ②

| 해설 | 본문은 장기간의 내전의 상처를 극복하고 있는 콜롬비아의 유명 관광 명소에 관해 설명하고 있다. 따라서 답은 ②이다.

---

03 다음 중 본문에서 언급되거나 암시되지 않은 것은 무엇인가?
① 콜롬비아는 과거엔 여행하기에 안전하지 않은 장소였다.
② 콜롬비아는 주변국들과 공통된 점이 거의 없다.
③ 안데스 산맥의 정상까지 도보로 올라갈 수 있다.
④ 콜롬비아는 카리브해에 인접한 국가이자 태평양에 인접한 국가이다.

| 정답 | ②

| 해설 | "황금빛의 카리브해 해변과 자갈이 깔린 식민지 시대 도시가 전하는 매력에서부터 여러 곳의 커피 농장에 이르기까지 콜롬비아라는 하나의 국가 속에 라틴아메리카의 모습이 압축적으로 드러나고 있다(From gilded Caribbean coasts and cobblestoned colonial charm to clusters of coffee plantations, Colombia encapsulates Latin America in a single country)." 여기서 즉 콜롬비아란 국가에서는 다른 라틴아메리카 국가들이 지니고 있는 특성을 엿볼 수 있음을 알 수 있다. 따라서 답은 ②이다.
"40년 동안 내전이 진행 중에 있지만 보안 상태가 개선된 덕분에 관광객이 급격히 증가했다(Despite its four-decade-long civil war, improved security conditions have led to a sharp increase in tourism)"는 ①의 근거로 볼 수 있다. "국립공원 내의 수많은 오르막길은 겁 없는 도보 여행자들을 안데스(Andes) 산맥의 최정상 지역으로 인도해 준다(numerous ascents inside national parks place fearless hikers on the highest reaches of the Andes)"는 ③의 근거로 볼 수 있다. "남아메리카 대륙에서 태평양과 카리브해를 접하고 있는 유일한 국가(The only country in South America to border both the Pacific and the Caribbean)"는 ④의 근거로 볼 수 있다.

| 어휘 |
traumatic ⓐ 정신적 외상의, 정신적 충격이 큰
welcoming ⓐ 따뜻이[반갑게] 맞이하는
tourism ⓝ 관광객
fringe ⓥ 둘레[가장자리]를 형성하다
border ⓥ (국경·경계를) 접하다
gilded ⓥ 도금의, 황금빛의
charm ⓝ 매력
plantation ⓝ (특히 열대 지방에서 커피·설·고무 등을 재배하는 대규모) 농장
encapsulate ⓥ 요약[압축]하다
shrouded ⓐ 뒤덮인, 싸인
sculpt ⓥ 조각하다
surrounding ⓐ 인근의, 주위의
iconic ⓐ 상징이 되는, 상징적인
ascent ⓝ 오르막길
aquatic ⓐ 물의, 물과 관련된
majestic ⓐ 장엄한, 위풍당당한
stunning ⓐ 굉장히 아름다운[멋진]
draw ⓝ 인기를[마음을] 끄는 사람[것]
thrilling ⓐ 황홀한, 아주 신나는
gorgeous ⓐ 아주 멋진[아름다운]
a range of – 다양한
cobblestoned ⓐ 조약돌[자갈]을 깐
cluster ⓝ 무리, 떼, 집단
rejuvenated ⓐ 회춘한, 활기를 되찾은
life-sized ⓐ 실물 크기의, 등신대의
dot ⓥ 여기저기 흩어져 있다, 산재하다
fertile ⓐ 결실을 낳는 활동하기에 좋은
ruins ⓝ 폐허, 유적
spell ⓥ ~을 가져오다[의미하다]
watcher ⓝ 관찰자, 연구가

[04-05] 한국외대 2010

사회학자 Edwin Burgess의 동심원 지대 가설은 미국의 도시가 중심에서 주변부로 일련의 동심원 지대를 따라가면서 성장한다고 설명한다. 각 동심원 지대마다 사회적인 그리고 거주 관련 특징이 구분되어 나타난다. 하나의 가족만이 거주하는 집, 아파트, 가게, 공장, 창고 등 다른 토지 이용자들은 느리면서도 지속적으로 생태학적 과정인 경쟁, 분리, 침입, 계승 등을 거치면서 비슷한 용도의 지대가 부상하는 방식을 따라 스스로를 분류해 나간다. 이 지대는 정부의 계획, 지대 설정, 노력보다는 특히 경제적 비용 같은 생태학적 경쟁을 반영한다. 그러므로 중심가의 토지 이용은 돈, 혼잡, 오염 등으로 환산된 비용을 지불할 의도가 가장 높은 백화점이나 업체 사무실에게 돌아가게 된다. Burgess는 또한 각 지대는 구별되는 사회적 특성을 보이며, 각기 다른 종류의 사회적 문제를 갖게 된다고 언급했다. 범죄, 정신병, 가족 붕괴 및 그 외의 다른 사회적 문제는 대도시권 전역에 걸쳐 무작위로 분포되지 않았다. Burgess의 설명은 왜 대부분의 미국 도시가 비슷해 보이는지 설명이 된다.

04 빈칸 ㉮에 가장 잘 알맞은 것은 다음 중 무엇인가?
① 왜 대부분의 미국 도시가 비슷해 보이는지
② 왜 도시에 사는 사람들은 자신의 지대에 빠르게 적응하는지
③ 왜 중심가 다른 모든 지대의 특성을 공유하는지
④ 왜 몇몇 대도시는 다른 도시보다 더 오염이 심한지
⑤ 왜 중심가는 천천히 발전이 이루어지는지

| 정답 | ①

| 해설 | Burgess의 이론에 따르면 미국의 도시가 동심원을 그려 가며 성장하고, 각 동심원마다 각기 다른 속성을 보이게 된다고 한다. 미국의 도시가 단지 한두 군데만 동심원 형태의 성장을 하는 것이 아니기 때문에 전체적인 공통점을 찾는 과정에서 Burgess는 가설을 세운 것일 테고, 따라서 그의 가설에 따라 미국 도시의 성장 패턴이 동일하다면 결국 미국의 도시는 대부분이 비슷해 보일 것이라고 추론할 수 있다. 따라서 답은 ①이 된다.
다른 보기는 본문에 언급이 되어 있지 않은 내용이거나, 본문에는 중심가가 "distinct(구별되는)" 특징을 가지고 있다고 나옴에도 "shares characteristics(특징을 공유)"한다고 나온 ③처럼 본문과는 동떨어진 것들이기 때문에 답이 될 수 없다.

05 다음 중 Burgess의 가설에서 제시되지 않은 것은 무엇인가?
① 대도시권은 중심에서 주변부로 확장된다.
② 각 지대마다 각기 구별되는 사회적 문제가 있다.
③ 다른 토지 이용자는 다른 지대에 거주한다.
④ 도시는 정부가 계획한 대로 동심원 지대를 따라 성장한다.
⑤ 아파트와 창고는 다른 지대에 위치한다.

| 정답 | ④

| 해설 | Burgess의 이론은 도시의 성장을 "planning, zoning, or the efforts of government(정부의 계획, 지대 설정, 노력)"과 같은 인위적인 것을 통한 것이 아니라 마치 "ecological(생태학적)" 관점에서 자라나는 생물과 같이 비유하고 있다. 따라서 '정부의 계획'에 따라 동심원이 형성된다는 ④가 답이 된다. 다른 보기는 모두 본문에서 언급되는 사항이므로 답이 될 수 없다.

| 어휘 | sociologist ⓝ 사회학자
zonal ⓐ 지대의, zone의
periphery ⓝ (원·곡선 등의) 주위, 주변, 바깥 둘레
housing ⓝ 주거, 거주
sort out – ~을 분류하다, 가려내다, 추려 내다
ecological ⓐ 생태학의
invasion ⓝ 침입
be willing to – 기꺼이 ~하다
congestion ⓝ 혼잡
breakdown ⓝ 붕괴
distribute ⓥ ~을 보급하다
adapt to – ~에 적응하다
be located in – ~에 위치하다

concentric ⓐ 동심원의
hypothesis ⓝ 가설
distinct ⓐ 별개의, 뚜렷한
feature ⓝ 특징
constant ⓐ 불변의, 지속되는
segregation ⓝ 분리
zoning ⓝ 지대 설정
in terms of – ~으로 환산하여
distinctive ⓐ 뚜렷이 구별되는
randomly ⓐⓓ 무작위로
metropolitan area – 수도권, 대도시권
reside in – ~에 (장기간) 거주하다

[06-07] 한양대 2010

사해에는 왜 염분이 많을까? Great Rift Valley를 따라 위치한 수역인 사해는 오랫동안 고요한 물 위에서 힘들이지 않고도 둥둥 떠다니기 위해 찾아오는 관광객들을 매혹시켜 왔다. 하지만 그렇게 엄청난 크기의 소금 호수에서 어떻게 이처럼 쉽게 떠 있을 수 있는지 이유를 아는 사람은 거의 없다. 비록 요르단 강과 그보다 소규모의 지맥들이 사해에 흘러들어 가고 있지만, 사해에는 물이 빠져나갈 곳이 없다. 따라서 사해로 흘러드는 모든 물은 최소한 증발 과정이 실시되기 전까지는 그대로 사해에 머무른다. 사해가 위치한 지역의 열기로 인해 사해의 물은 빠른 비율로 증발한다. 모든 광물 침전물이 그대로 남게 되며, 그 결과 사해의 물은 소금기를 띠게 된다. 이렇게 조합된 소금기 풍부한 물에는 해양 생물이나 식물이 살 수 없다. 사실 사해에서 발견 되는 유일한 생명체는 물의 비중을 증가시키는 광물성 염분인데, 덕분에 둥둥 떠서 수영하는 사람들뿐이다.

06 밑줄 친 "tranquil"이 의미하는 것은 무엇인가?
① 깊은
② 고요한
③ 신선한
④ 투명한

| 정답 | ②

| 해설 | 'tranquil'은 '고요한'이란 의미를 가지며, 보기 중에서 이에 가장 흡사한 의미를 가진 단어는 역시 '고요한'이란 의미를 가진 ②의 'calm'이다.

07 본문의 목적은 무엇인가?
① 독특한 현상을 살피기 위해
② 거슬리는 개념을 설명하기 위해
③ 오랫동안 가져온 가정에 도전하기 위해
④ 오해받아 온 사실에 의문을 표하기 위해

| 정답 | ①

| 해설 | 본문은 왜 사해에 사람이 물 위에 떠다닐 수 있을 정도로 염분이 많은지에 관해 설명하고 있는 글이다. 즉, 사실을 있는 그대로 설명하는 글이기 때문에 ②의 '개념을 설명'하거나 ③의 '가정에 도전'하거나 ④의 '의문을 표하는' 글로는 볼 수 없다. 보기 중에서 본문의 목적을 잘 설명한 것은 사람이 물에 뜨는 '독특한 현상'을 살피는 ①이다.

| 어휘 |
body of water – 수역(水域) ≪바다 · 호수 등≫
drift ⓥ 표류하다, 떠돌다
tranquil ⓐ 조용한, 고요한
tributary ⓝ 지류(支流)
evaporation ⓝ 증발
take effect – 효력을 발휘하다, 실시되다
concoction ⓝ 조제물, 수프, 혼합 음료
density ⓝ 비중, 농도, 밀도
irksome ⓐ 진저리나는, 거슬리는

fascinate ⓥ 매혹시키다
effortlessly ⓐⓓ 노력하지 않는, 힘들이지 않고
saline ⓐ 염분을 함유한 ⓝ 염류
outlet ⓝ 출구, 배출구
evaporate ⓥ 증발하다
brackish ⓐ 소금기가 있는
buoy ⓥ 띄우다, 띄워 두다
transparent ⓐ 투명한, 명쾌한
long-held ⓐ 오랫동안의; 기존의

[08-10] 광운대 2011

수리남(Suriname)은 남미에서 가장 작은 독립 국가이다. 수리남의 면적은 165,000가 조금 안되고, 대략 47만 명이 살고 있는 것으로 추정되며, 이들 중 대부분은 수도 Paramaribo가 위치한 북부 해안가에 살고 있다. 가이아나 순상지(Guiana Shield)에 위치한 수리남은 크게 두 지역으로 구분될 수 있다. 북부 해안가 저지대 지역에서 경작이 이루어지며, 이 지역 주민들 대부분이 이곳에서 살고 있다. 남부 지역은 열대우림과 거주민이 적은 대초원으로 이루어져 있으며, 남부 지역 면적은 수리남 전 국토의 약 80%를 차지한다. 남부 국경은 브라질과 접하고 있으며 북부 국경은 대서양 해안과 접해 있다. 수리남은 매우 무더운 열대성 기후를 지니며, 연간 기온은 크게 변동하지 않는다. 일 년에 두 차례의 우기가 있으며, 한 번은 4월부터 8월에 다른 한 번은 11월부터 2월에 해당한다. 또한 일 년에 두 차례의 건기가 있으며, 8월부터 11월까지 그리고 2월부터 4월까지 건기가 지속된다.

수리남의 경제는 GDP의 15% 이상을 차지하며 수출 수입의 70%를 차지하는 알루미늄 산업에 의해 주도된다. 이 밖의 주요 수출 품목으로는 쌀, 바나나, 새우 등이 있다. 수리남은 최근 상당한 크기의 원유 및 금 매장지 일부를 개발하기 시작했다. 대략 주민 중 1/4이 농업 분야에 종사한다. 수리남 경제는 주로 상업에 의존하고 있으며, 주요 교역국으로는 네덜란드, 미국, 캐나다, 카리브 연안국들이 있다.

08

윗글의 내용과 일치하지 않는 것을 고르시오.

① 수리남의 인구는 백만 명을 넘으며, 수도 Paramaribo 근처에 살고 있다.
② 인구 대부분은 북부 해안가에 살고 있는 반면, 남부 지역은 인구 밀도가 낮다.
③ 대부분의 육지는 열대우림과 거의 사람이 서식하지 않는 대초원 지역으로 이루어져 있다.
④ 수리남의 기후는 매우 습하며, 온도는 연중 내내 비슷하게 유지된다.
⑤ 수리남은 원유나 금 같은 풍부한 천연자원을 개발하기 시작했다.

| 정답 | ①

| 해설 | ①의 경우 백만이 아닌 47만 명을 넘지 않는다고 했으므로 일치하지 않아서 정답이 된다. ②의 경우 북부와 남부 지역을 설명하는 대목에 나오며, ③의 경우 열대우림과 대초원 지역은 남부 지방에 있다고 했으며, 전 국토의 80%를

차지한다고 했으므로 대부분(most)이라고 할 수 있다. ④의 경우 기후가 열대성 기후라고 했으므로 무덥고 습하다는 것을 알 수 있으며, 기온도 연중 내내 비슷하다고 나온다. ⑤도 본문 후반에 나오며 본문의 'exploit'를 'make use of'로 대체해서 사용했다.

09

윗글에서 Suriname의 경제에 대하여 옳게 설명한 것을 고르시오.
① 알루미늄 수출은 수리남 수출 수익의 15%를 차지하며, GDP의 70%를 차지한다.
② 쌀이나 바나나, 새우 등의 수출품은 수출 수익에서 주요한 역할을 담당하지 못한다.
③ 또한 원유와 금의 수출은 수리남에 상당한 수익을 가져다주고 있다.
④ 대략 25%의 인구가 농업 부분에 종사하고 있다.
⑤ 네덜란드, 미국, 캐나다, 카리브 연안국들은 수리남에 경제 원조를 제공하고 있다.

| 정답 | ④

| 해설 | ①의 경우 숫자가 서로 바뀌어 있으므로 정답이 아니며, ②의 경우 쌀이나 바나나, 새우를 본문에서 'other main export products'라고 했으므로 주요 수출품이라는 것을 알 수 있다. ③의 경우 본문 후반부에서 이제 개척하기 시작했다고 나오고 있지 수익에 대한 내용은 등장하지 않는다. ④의 경우 농업에 종사하는 인구는 전체의 1/4(a quarter)이라고 했으므로, 25%가 되어 정답이 된다. ⑤의 경우 이 나라들은 경제 원조를 제공하는 나라가 아니라 주요 교역국(trading partners)이라고 나오므로 정답이 될 수 없다.

10

윗글의 제목으로 가장 적합한 것을 고르시오.
① 수리남의 지리 ② 수리남의 기후
③ 수리남의 소개 ④ 수리남의 인구
⑤ 수리남의 경제

| 정답 | ③

| 해설 | 본문에서는 수리남의 지리나 기후, 인구, 경제 등에 대해 포괄적으로 설명하고 있으므로 정답은 ③이 된다.

| 어휘 | estimated ⓐ 추정의, 대략의   approximately ⓐⓓ 대략
Guiana Shield - 가이아나 순상지(남미 북부의 거대한 순상지)
lowland ⓝ 저지대   cultivate ⓥ 경작하다, 재배하다
consist of - ~로 구성되다   tropical ⓐ 열대성의
sparsely inhabited - 인구가 희박한, 거주민이 드문
dominate ⓥ 지배하다, 압도적으로 우세하다   account for - (비율이) ~ 정도 차지하다
exploit ⓥ 개척하다, 개발하다, 이용하다, 착취하다 reserve ⓝ 매장지
exceed ⓥ 넘다, 초과하다   uninhabited ⓐ 사람이 살지 않는, 무인의
humid ⓐ 날씨가 습한   make use of - ~을 이용하다, 활용하다

[11-13] 경희대 2012

한때 세계에서 네 번째로 가장 큰 호수였던 웅장한 아랄해는 지금은 단말마의 고통을 겪고 있다. 생명선이었던 아무다리야 강과 시르다리야 강의 물이 말라 버리면서, 아랄해는 지난 40년 동안 크기가 줄어들고 있다. 1930년대부터 구소련은 면화 수출을 크게 늘리기 위한 장대한 계획의 일환으로 대규모의 목화밭에 관개용수를 대기 위해 물의 방향을 바꾸는 엄청난 크기의 운하를 건설하기 시작했다. 이러한 목표는 달성되어서 현재 우즈베키스탄은 여전히 대규모 면화 수출국이다. 하지만 이로 인해 생태계와 인간의 건강에 끼친 영향은 천문학적이었다.

1960년부터 25에서 50입방 킬로미터의 강물이 매년 관개용수로 쓰이기 위해 전환되었고 자연히 호수의 물가가 후퇴하기 시작했다. 평균 수위가 10년 동안 1년에 20cm(8인치)씩 줄기 시작했고, 그 이후 감소율이 70년대에서는 1년에 60cm로 가속화되었다. 그 이후 80년대에는 1년당 거의 1미터씩 줄었다. 1990년대가 되면 계속되는 물의 전환과 증발로 인해 크기가 줄어들던 아랄해는 두 동강이 났고 호수의 염도가 1리터에 10그램에서 45그램으로 증가했다. 남아랄해의 일부는 염도가 2001년에 리터당 98그램에 달한다. 바닷물의 평균 염도는 1리터당 33그램이다. 한때 번성하던 어업은 물고기 및 대부분의 동식물과 함께 파괴되었다. 염전과 오염된 유출수로 된 호수가 등장했고, 겨울은 더욱 가혹하고 길어졌으며 여름은 더욱 덥고 짧아졌다.

11 윗글의 제목으로 가장 적당한 것은?
① 죽어가는 아랄해
② 아랄해의 염도
③ 아랄해의 물을 전환시키는 계획
④ 아랄해의 부활

| 정답 | ①

| 해설 | 본문은 거대한 아랄해가 1960년대 이후 어떻게 죽어 가고 있는지를 설명하는 글이다. 따라서 답은 ①이다.

12 윗글의 빈칸 ⓐ에 들어갈 단어로 가장 적당한 것은?
① 동물
② 식물
③ 나뭇잎
④ 곤충

| 정답 | ①

| 해설 | flora and fauna는 한 묶음으로 '동식물'이란 의미를 갖는 표현이다. 따라서 답은 ①이다.

13 윗글에서 과거의 대형 사업이 Aral Sea에 미친 영향으로 언급되지 않은 것은?
① 아랄해의 염도 증가
② 면화 생산의 증가
③ 생물 다양성의 변화
④ 기후의 변화

| 정답 | ②

| 해설 | 아랄해가 죽어 간 이유는 구소련이 아랄해로 가는 물길을 면화 생산을 늘리기 위해 다른 곳으로 돌렸기 때문이다. 그런데 면화가 생산되는 지역이 아랄해라는 언급은 본문에 전혀 등장하지 않는다. 따라서 답은 ②이다. 그 외 보기에 해당하는 내용은 본문 두 번째 단락에 전부 등장한다.

| 어휘 | death throes – 단말마의 고통, 최후의 발악 lifeblood ⓝ 생명선
shrink ⓥ 줄어들다 diversion ⓝ 방향 전환
irrigate ⓥ 관개하다, 물을 대다 ecological ⓐ 생태계의
astronomical ⓐ 천문학적인

divert ⓥ 방향을 바꾸게 하다[전환시키다], 다른 곳으로 돌리다
shoreline ⓝ 물가, 해안선
mean ⓐ 평균의
salinity ⓝ 염도
contaminated ⓐ 오염된
rebirth ⓝ 부활
biodiversity ⓝ 생물 다양성
recede ⓥ 물러나다, 후퇴하다
evaporation ⓝ 증발
flora and fauna – (한 지역의) 동식물
runoff ⓝ 유출수
foliage ⓝ 나뭇잎

[14-15] 한양대 2013

시에라리온은 분쟁 이후 재건의 모델이라 할 수 있다. 2002년까지 11년 동안 지속된 내전으로 대략 5만 명이 사망했으나, 푸른색 모자를 쓴 UN 평화유지군의 도움을 받아 내전의 상처를 극복할 수 있었다. 2007년에 시에라리온 역사상 두 번째에 불과한 공정한 선거를 거쳐 권력 교체가 이루어졌으며 올해 11월에 국민들은 다시 투표를 했다. 하지만 모든 일이 잘 진행되는 것은 아니다. 시에라리온의 대통령 어니스트 바이 코로마는 자신의 재선 기회를 늘리기 위해 UN 현지 코디네이터를 강제로 물러나게 만들었다. 현지 코디네이터인 마이클 본 더 슈런버그는 시에라리온 대통령의 탄원으로 인해 뉴욕에 있는 UN 고위직의 명령에 따라 갑작스럽게 다른 곳으로 옮겨졌다. 타국의 외교관들은 9월에 시에라리온 대통령이 UN에게 마이클 본 더 슈런버그를 해임할 것을 요구했음을 확인했으며, 아마도 슈런버그가 공정성에 문제가 있는 인사라고 주장했을 것이라고 말했다. 2개월 후 대통령은 문서를 통해 다시 요청을 했지만, 현재는 요청했다는 사실 자체를 부인하고 있다.

마이클 본 더 슈런버그는 훌륭히 임무를 수행한 것으로 보인다. 그는 UN 주둔군의 규모를 상당히 감축했는데, 이는 자신이 할 일이 없어지는 상황을 종종 꺼려 하는 조직의 입장에서 희귀한 업적이라 할 수 있다. 그는 또한 아직도 논쟁이 쉽게 폭력적으로 변하는 환경에서 정당들 사이의 존중받는 중재자 역할을 했다. 그는 야당 지도자들을 만났지만 이들을 편애하지도 않았다. 하지만 그의 공명정대함만으로도 대통령의 분노를 유발하기엔 충분했던 것으로 보인다. UN이 마이클 본 더 슈런버그를 다른 곳으로 옮기기로 동의한 것은 나쁜 선례가 되었다. UN이 시에라리온에서 얼마나 많은 생명(인명)과 재산을 소모했는지 생각해 보면 이번 일은 UN의 신뢰성을 손상시켰고, 또한 앞으로 있을 선거에 나쁜 징조라 할 수 있다.

14 밑줄 친 (A)에 들어갈 가장 알맞은 것을 고르시오.
① 변덕스러움
② 완고함
③ 공명정대함
④ 가혹함

| 정답 | ③

| 해설 | 두 번째 단락에서 빈칸 (A) 앞부분의 내용은 시에라리온의 대통령에 의해 쫓겨난 마이클 본 더 슈런버그가 임무를 훌륭히 수행했으며, 그중에서도 특히 "정당들 사이의 존중받는 중재자(valued mediator between political parties)"이자 "편애하지 않는(did not favor)" 등 '공명정대한' 역할을 했음을 설명하고 있다. 하지만 그랬기 때문에 현직 대통령의 눈 밖에 나서 쫓겨나게 된 것이다. 따라서 답은 ③이다.

15 문맥상 밑줄 친 (B)에 들어갈 가장 알맞은 것을 고르시오.
① 앞으로 있을 선거에 나쁜 징조라 할 수 있다.
② UN의 국제적인 지도력을 강화한다.
③ 대통령의 재선 가능성을 위태롭게 한다.
④ 이 나라의 민주주의가 급성장할 수 있도록 길을 닦아 준다.

| 정답 | ①

| 해설 | 공명정대하게 일을 하던 UN 현지 코디네이터가 재선에 유리한 고지를 점하려는 현직 대통령에 의해 물러나게 되면, 자연히 앞으로 있을 선거에는 부정적 영향이 가해질 것이다. 따라서 답은 ①이다.

| 어휘 |
reconstruction ⓝ 재건
impartiality ⓝ 공명정대, 공평무사
even-handedness ⓝ 공평함, 공명정대함
credibility ⓝ 신뢰성
lightheadedness ⓝ 변덕스러움, 경솔함
heavy-handedness ⓝ 가혹함, 엄함
burgeoning ⓐ 급성장하는
mission chief – 대사, 현지 코디네이터
presence ⓝ 주둔군
precedent ⓝ 선례, 전례
bode ill for – ~에 나쁜 징조이다
strongheadedness ⓝ 완고함, 고집 셈
compromise ⓥ ~을 위태롭게 하다

[16-17] 한국외대 2016

아이슬란드는 명칭이라든지 위치가 북극권에 인접해 있다는 점에서 시사되는 것보다는 훨씬 온화한 기후를 누리고 있다. 멕시코 만류의 지류 중 하나가 남부 및 서부 해안을 따라 흘러서 기후를 크게 완화시킨다. 하지만 이 덕분에 온화한 대서양 공기가 차가운 북극 공기와 접촉하게 되면서 빈번한 날씨 변화와 거센 풍랑을 특징으로 삼는 기후가 야기된다. 더군다나, 이로 인해 아이슬란드 섬의 북부보다 남부 및 서부의 강우량이 높다. 여름 여행철은 5월 말부터 9월 초까지이다. 이 기간 동안 태양은 24시간 내내 지평선 위에 떠 있고 산과 용암층 및 빙하에서 전개되는 빛과 그림자의 상호 작용이 변화무쌍한 광경을 낳는다. 겨울철은 긴 밤과 혹독한 겨울 폭풍이 체류하는 기간이다. 하지만 넓게 트인 얼어붙은 지면의 고요함과 청명한 밤하늘에 소위 북극광(northern light)이란 명칭으로 불리는 북극 오로라(aurora borealis)의 춤은 점차 많은 수의 관광객들을 끌어당기고 있다.

16 다음 중 아이슬란드의 기후가 예상보다 따뜻한 원인은 무엇인가?
① 멕시코 만류
② 북극의 공기
③ 용암층
④ 북극광

| 정답 | ①

| 해설 | "멕시코 만류의 지류 중 하나가 남부 및 서부 해안을 따라 흘러서 기후를 크게 완화시킨다(A branch of the Gulf Stream flows along the southern and the western coasts greatly moderating the climate)." 따라서 답은 ①이다.

17 다음 중 아이슬란드에 대해 사실인 것은 무엇인가?
① 아이슬란드 겨울 여행은 인기가 떨어지고 있다.
② 강우량은 전국에 고르게 분포되어 있다.
③ 아이슬란드의 날씨는 매우 변화무쌍하다.
④ 여름철 관광객들은 태양이 지평선 아래로 내려가는 모습을 볼 수 있다.

| 정답 | ③

| 해설 | 아이슬란드 날씨는 생각보다는 훨씬 온화하지만, "온화한 대서양 공기가 차가운 북극 공기와 접촉하게 되면서 빈번

한 날씨 변화와 거센 풍랑을 특징으로 삼는 기후가 야기된다(this brings mild Atlantic air in contact with colder Arctic air resulting in a climate that is marked by frequent changes in weather and storminess)." 여기서 답은 ③임을 알 수 있다.

| 어휘 | adjacent ⓐ 인접한
imply ⓥ 암시하다, 시사하다
Gulf Stream – 멕시코 만류
in contact with – ~와 접촉하다
interplay ⓝ 상호 작용
glacier ⓝ 빙하
abode ⓝ 거주, 체류
expanse ⓝ 넓게 트인 지역, 광활한 공간
the northern lights – 북극광
the Arctic circle – 북극권
branch ⓝ 지류, 분기
moderate ⓥ 완화하다, 누그러뜨리다
mark ⓥ 특징짓다, 눈에 뜨이게 하다
lava field – 용암층, 용암원
ever-changing ⓐ 변화무쌍한, 늘 변화하는
serenity ⓝ 고요함, 맑음
aurora borealis – 북극광

[18-20] 국민대 2016

이탈리아의 토스카나(Tuscany)는 세계에서 가장 유명한 장소 중 하나이다. 이 아름다운 풍경은 르네상스 시대의 회화와 이탈리아 소설 및 영화를 통해 우리에게 익숙해졌다. 토스카나는 지구상의 낙원으로 많은 관광객에게 진정으로 그 매력을 호소한다. 매년 3,200만 명이 넘는 관광객이 토스카나를 방문하고 고국으로 돌아가 그 아름다움에 대해 열심히 이야기한다. 물론 광고주와 사진작가도 이 지역에 관심이 있다. "아름다움 때문에 우리는 이 지역을 선택했다. 다른 어떤 곳도 이곳과 비교할 수 없다."고 대형 광고 대행사에서 일하고 있는 린다 패브리스(Linda Fabris)는 말한다.

그러나 주민들은 중세 이래로 거의 그대로 남아 있는 자신들의 유산을 잃을까 봐 걱정이 많다. 토스카나 주민들은 그 지역이 광고에 사용되는 방식을 제한하기 위해 토스카나 풍경에 대해 저작권으로 보호하겠다는 안을 생각해 냈다. 토스카나 출신의 사업가인 로베르트 디토마소(Robert DiTommaso)는 "우리는 토스카나와 무관한 브랜드가 이곳에서 광고되는 것을 금지하려고 한다. 우리는 수 세기 동안 우리가 누렸던 풍경을 보호해야 한다. 이곳은 우리의 유산이다." 이와 동시에 토스카나에서 온 올리브 오일, 치즈 및 포도주의 품질을 보장하기 위해 자발적인 상표인 "Made in Tuscany"가 생겨났다. 목표는 토스카나라는 이름을 사용하는 많은 제품, 특히 식품이 실제로 그 지역에서 오지 않는다는 것을 사람들에게 보여주는 것이다.

18 본문에 의하면 보기 중 다음 문장의 빈칸에 들어가기에 가장 알맞은 것은?

토스카나가 우리에게 알려지게 된 것은 _____ 덕분이다.

① 토스카나의 풍경을 보여주는 예술 작품들
② 자신들만의 상표를 고집하는 토스카나 주민들
③ 토스카나와 같은 낙원에 관심 있는 광고 대행사
④ 고국의 사람들에게 토스카나의 사진을 보내는 관광객들

| 정답 | ①

| 해설 | 본문 서두의 "Its beautiful landscape has become familiar to us through Renaissance paintings and Italian novels and movies." 부분에서 토스카나의 아름다움은 르네상스 시대의 작품과 이탈리아 소설이나 영화를 통해 알려지게 되었다고 말하고 있으므로, 정답은 ① 예술작품이 된다.

19

다음 중 빈칸 Ⓐ에 적합한 것은?

① 고안하다　　　　　　　　② 제한하다
③ 팽창하다　　　　　　　　④ 설립하다

| 정답 | ②

| 해설 | 빈칸 바로 앞의 'to copyright their landscape'에서 토스카나의 풍경을 저작권으로 설정한다는 것은 토스카나가 광고에 사용되는 방식을 '제한'하겠다는 것이다. 빈칸 뒤에 이어지는 'stop non-Tuscan brand names from advertising here' 부분을 통해서도 재확인할 수 있다.

20

다음 중 본문의 내용과 일치하는 것은?

① 토스카나 사람들은 다른 나라에서 자신의 제품을 광고하는 것이 금지되어 있다.
② "Made in Tuscany"라는 상표는 이 지역의 광고를 늘리는 데 사용된다.
③ 토스카나 주민들은 중세 이후 관광객이 너무 많아서 어려움을 겪었다.
④ 토스카나 주민들은 그들의 유산을 지키기 위해 지역 풍경을 저작권으로 보호하기를 원한다.

| 정답 | ④

| 해설 | 두 번째 문단의 서두에서 "주민들은 중세 이래로 거의 그대로 남아 있는 자신들의 유산을 잃을까 봐 걱정이 많다"고 서술하며, 그곳의 경치를 저작권으로 보호하려는 계획을 세운다. 따라서 ④가 본문의 내용과 일치한다.

| 어휘 |
landscape ⓝ 풍경, 경치, 풍경화(법)　　　　appeal to – ~에 호소하다
rave about – ~에 대해 열심히 이야기하다, 격찬하다
resident ⓝ 거주자　　　　heritage ⓝ (국가·사회의) 유산
virtually ⓐⓓ 사실상, 거의　　　　untouched ⓐ 훼손되지 않은, 본래 그대로의
come up with – (해답·돈 등을) 생각해 내다[내놓다]
copyright ⓥ (무엇에 대한) 저작권[판권]을 얻다　　　stop A from ~ing – A가 ~하는 것을 막다
voluntary ⓐ 자발적인, 자진한; 임의적인　　　trademark ⓝ (등록) 상표
devise ⓥ 창안[고안]하다　　　restrict ⓥ (크기·양·범위 등을) 제한[한정]하다

CHAPTER 04 음악·미술

01	②	02	①	03	④	04	③	05	④	06	②	07	①	08	①	09	④	10	④
11	③	12	②	13	④	14	②	15	④	16	③	17	③	18	③	19	②	20	④
21	④	22	②	23	④	24	④	25	②	26	②	27	①	28	③	29	②	30	②
31	②	32	②	33	④	34	②	35	①	36	③	37	②	38	②	39	④	40	②
41	②	42	②	43	④	44	④	45	①	46	②	47	③	48	④	49	④	50	①

[01-03] 단국대 2006

우리가 음악을 감상하는 것은 학습에 의한 결과라고, 다시 말해 인간의 본성이 아니라 육성이 감상 능력을 결정한다고 믿는 것은 아마도 논리적으로 보일 것이다. 하지만 이제 본성 또한 중요한 역할을 한다는 것이 분명히 드러났다. 최근 연구에 따르면 인간의 뇌는 음악과 '연결되어' 있다는 사실이 드러난다. 캐나다 토론토 대학에서는 심리학자들이 생후 6개월에서 9개월 된 유아들을 대상으로 연구를 진행하고 있다. 이 아이들은 연구원들이 화음이 잘 맞는 음악을 연주하면 미소를 지었지만, 불협화음이 나는 음악은 싫어하는 것으로 보였다. 대부분의 사람들은 성인이 되면 시나 산문 구절은 단 몇 편 정도만 기억할 수 있지만, 음악의 선율은 최소 수십 가지를 기억할 수 있고 수백 가지 정도를 알아볼 수 있는 능력을 보유하게 된다. 아마도 더 흥미로운 점은 음악에는 실제로 몇 가지 유형의 지능을 향상시킬 수 있는 가능성이 있다는 점이다. 1999년의 한 연구에서는 아이들이 수학을 더 잘하는 데 음악이 도움을 준다는 사실을 입증했다. 이상하게도 다른 과목도 아닌 바로 수학에서만 말이다. 음악과 관련된 많은 두뇌 활동이 대뇌의 측두엽에서 일어난다는 사실은 그다지 놀랄 만한 일은 아닐 것이다. 보스턴에 위치한 베스 이스라엘 디커너스 메디컬 센터의 연구원들은 또한 음악인의 경우 비음악인에 비해 뇌량의 앞부분이 실제로도 더 크다는 점을 발견했다.

01 다음 중 본문에서 유추할 수 있는 것은 무엇인가?
① 음악은 오로지 교육의 결과이기 때문에 아이들이 수학을 잘하는 데 도움이 될 수도 있다.
② 뇌량은 음악과 관련된 두뇌 활동과 연계되었을 가능성이 있다.
③ 음악에 거의 노출된 바 없는 아이들은 단지 몇 편의 시나 산문 구절만 기억할 수 있을 것이다.
④ 음악과 관련된 두뇌 활동은 뇌량의 성숙과는 관계가 없을 것이다.

| 정답 | ②

| 해설 | "보스턴에 위치한 베스 이스라엘 디커너스 메디컬센터의 연구원들은 또한 음악인의 경우 비음악인에 비해 뇌량의 앞부분이 실제로도 더 크다는 점을 발견했다(Researchers at Beth Israel Deaconess Medical Center in Boston have also discovered that the front part of the corpus callosum is actually larger in musicians than in non-musicians)." 여기서 뇌량은 음악과 관련된 두뇌 활동과 연계되었을 가능성이 있음을 유추할 수 있다. 따라서 답은 ②이다.

02

빈칸 ⓐ에 가장 알맞은 것은 무엇인가?

① 학습한
② 천부적인
③ 통제받은
④ 보존된

| 정답 | ①

| 해설 | 빈칸 ⓐ 뒤 대시(dash)는 이미 언급된 사항을 다른 말로 부연하거나 보충할 때 쓰이는 문장 부호이다. 따라서 대시 뒤 문장은 빈칸 ⓐ를 보충 설명하고 있음을 유추할 수 있다. 대시 뒤 문장을 읽어 보면 "인간의 본성이 아니라 육성이 감상 능력을 결정한다(nurture, not nature, determines this)"를 통해 음악 감상은 '육성', 즉 '학습'을 통해 키워진다는 의미가 된다. 따라서 답은 ①이다.

03

빈칸 ⓑ와 ⓒ에 들어갈 것으로 가장 알맞은 것은 무엇인가?

① 협화음의 - 즐거운
② 즐거운 - 협화음의
③ 불협화음의 - 협화음의
④ 협화음의 - 불협화음의

| 정답 | ④

| 해설 | ⓑ한 음악을 들려주면 아이들은 "미소를 지었고(smile)" ⓒ한 음악을 들려주면 아이들은 "싫어했다(hate)". smile과 hate가 서로 대조적인 관계이므로 ⓑ와 ⓒ 역시 대조적인 관계임을 유추할 수 있다. 그리고 아이들이 불협화음을 들으면서 '미소를 지었을' 리는 없기 때문에 답으로 가장 적합한 것은 ④이다.

| 어휘 |
appreciation ⓝ 감상
consonant ⓐ 협화음의, 조화로운
tune ⓝ 곡조, 선율
temporal lobe – 측두엽
maturation ⓝ 성숙, 성장
nurture ⓝ 육성, 양성
dissonant ⓐ 불협화음의, 귀에 거슬리는
oddly ⓐⓓ 이상하게, 특이하게
corpus callosum – 뇌량
endow ⓥ 부여하다

[04-07] 서강대 2009

매일 1억 명이 넘는 사람들이 배경음악을 듣는다. 사람들은 사무실에서 일하는 동안, 가게에서 물건을 사는 동안, 식당에서 식사를 하는 동안 배경음악을 듣는다. 사람들은 심지어 치과 의자에 앉아 있는 동안에도 배경음악을 듣는다. 왜 배경음악이 이렇게나 많은 곳에서 연주되는 것일까? 답은 간단하다. 음악이 사람들의 행동에 영향을 줄 정도로 강력한 힘을 갖고 있기 때문이다.

연구에 따르면 배경음악은 업체의 판매량에 영향을 미친다. 마케팅 교수인 로널드 밀리만은 빠른 음악이 흐를 때, 느린 음악이 흐를 때, 아무 음악도 흐르지 않을 때 이 세 가지 경우가 슈퍼마켓을 찾은 손님에게 미치는 영향을 측정했다. 그는 빠른 음악은 아무 음악도 없었을 경우와 비교하면 판매에 크게 영향을 주지 않는다는 사실을 발견했다.

하지만 느린 음악에서는 큰 차이가 발생했다. 천천히 연주되는 음악을 들으면 쇼핑객들이 더 천천히 움직였다. 느린 음악이 연주되는 동안 쇼핑객들은 더 많이 구매했고 판매량은 38%가 증가했다.

또한 밀리만은 식당 주인들이 음악을 자신들의 이익이 될 수 있게 사용할 수 있음을 발견했다. 저녁에 느린 음악을 연주하면 고객이 식당에서 보내는 시간을 늘린다. 점심때 식당에서는 손님이 식사를 빨리해서 더 많은 손님을 받을 수 있기를 원한다. 점심시간에 활기 넘치는 음악을 들려주면 고객이 빨리 먹고 떠나도록 부추긴다.

04
빈칸 (A)에 가장 알맞은 것은 무엇인가?
① 짧게 줄이다
② 짧게 하다
③ 길게 늘이다
④ 길어지다

| 정답 | ③

| 해설 | "천천히 연주되는 음악을 들으면 쇼핑객들이 더 천천히 움직였다(Listening to music played slowly made shoppers move more slowly)." 쇼핑뿐만 아니라 식당에서 식사하는 사람들 역시 천천히 연주되는 음악을 들으면 식당 안에 더 오래 머물렀을 것이다. 따라서 답은 ③이 가장 적합하다. ④는 문제에서처럼 '시간'을 연장할 때 쓰기보다 물건이나 사물의 길이를 늘이는 것을 표현하기 위해 더 많이 사용되므로 답으로 보기 힘들다.

05
로널드 밀리만은 누구인가?
① 슈퍼마켓 체인의 마케팅 담당 중역
② 음악이 다이어트에 미치는 영향에 관심을 보인 심리학자
③ 식사하면서 음악을 즐기는 단골 고객
④ 음악이 미치는 영향을 연구하는 마케팅 전문가

| 정답 | ④

| 해설 | "마케팅 교수인 로널드 밀리만은 빠른 음악이 흐를 때, 느린 음악이 흐를 때, 아무 음악도 흐르지 않을 때 이 세 가지 경우가 슈퍼마켓을 찾은 손님에게 미치는 영향을 측정했다(Ronald Milliman, a marketing professor, measured the effects that fast music, slow music, and no music had on customers in a supermarket)." 여기서 답은 ④가 됨을 유추할 수 있다.

06
만약 여러분이 패스트푸드 음식점의 주인이라면 주어진 정보에 의거해 어떤 종류의 음악을 들려주겠는가?
① 소울 음악
② 신나는 음악
③ 위로해 주는 음악
④ 자극적인 음악

| 정답 | ②

| 해설 | "점심때 식당에서는 손님이 식사를 빨리해서 더 많은 손님을 받을 수 있기를 원한다. 점심시간에 활기 넘치는 음악을 들려주면 고객이 빨리 먹고 떠나도록 부추긴다(At lunch time, restaurants want people to eat more quickly so that they can serve more customers. Playing lively music at lunchtime encourages customers to eat quickly and leave)." 즉, 회전율을 높이기 위해서는 의도적으로 빠른 음악을 틀 것이다. 따라서 답은 ②이다.

07
본문의 주제를 가장 잘 표현한 것은 무엇인가?
① 로널드 밀리만은 음악이 인간 행동에 미치는 영향을 발견했다.
② 느린 음악이 연주되면 슈퍼마켓에서의 판매량이 증가한다.
③ 배경음악은 가게의 판매에 보탬이 되거나 방해가 된다.
④ 음악은 고객이 돈을 더 쓰고 더 많이 먹도록 부추긴다.

| 정답 | ①

| 해설 | 본문에 따르면 로널드 밀리만은 빠른 음악이 흐름, 느린 음악이 흐름, 음악 없음 이 세 가지 경우 인간의 행동이 어떤 영향을 받는지를 연구를 통해 밝혔다. 따라서 답은 ①이다. 참고로 ③의 경우를 보면 "빠른 음악은 아무 음악도 없었을 경우와 비교하면 판매에 크게 영향을 주지 않는다(fast music did not affect sales very much when compared with no music)"를 통해 빠른 음악이 최소한 악영향은 미치지 않는다는 점에서 답이 될 수 없음을 알 수 있다.

| 어휘 | background music – 배경음악　　　　　　to one's advantage – ~의 이익이 되도록
　　　　truncate ⓥ 길이를 줄이다　　　　　　　　elongate ⓥ 길어지다
　　　　irritating ⓐ 자극적인, 짜증 나게 하는

[08-10] 서울여대 2012

1919년 10월 10일 "그림자 없는 여인"이란 의미를 가진 오페라 "Die Frau ohne Schatten"가 빈의 빈 주립 오페라에서 초연되었다. 곡은 리하르트 슈트라우스가 작곡하였으며 대본, 즉 원고는 휴고 폰 호프만스탈이 작성하였다. 이 오페라에 관한 아이디어는 초연으로부터 8년 전에 등장했다. 호프만스탈과 슈트라우스는 한동안 자신들의 다음 오페라의 소재를 찾고 있었다. 이들은 자신들의 오페라를 모차르트의 "마적"에 필적하는 20세기판 마적으로 만들고 싶어 했다. 1911년 3월 3일 호프만스탈은 슈트라우스에게 편지로 새로운 오페라에 대한 아이디어를 제시했다. "이번 작품은 마법 동화로 하세 … 그리고 신중하게 고려해 본 결과 등장 여성 가운데 한 명은 자네 부인을 모델로 삼는 편이 좋겠네." 호프만스탈은 슈트라우스의 부인인 파울린을 기초로 한 등장인물을 제안했다. 호프만스탈은 그 등장인물에 관해 다음과 같이 말했다. "그녀는 괴짜이면서 영혼이 매우 아름다운 인물로, 특이한 성격에다 기분파이고 자기주장이 강한 사람이지만 그러면서도 동시에 호감 가는 성격을 갖고 있다네."
슈트라우스가 자신의 부인이 괴짜라는 의견에 기분이 상하는 것도 당연한 일이었다. 슈트라우스와 호프만스탈의 업무관계는 말썽 많은 것으로 유명했고, 때로 이 둘의 모습은 고양이가 개와 사이좋게 지내려고 노력하는 모습에 비유되곤 했다. 하지만 슈트라우스는 기분이 상하지 않았다. 어쩌면 이는 슈트라우스도 호프만스탈의 성격 묘사에서 어느 정도 진실이 있음을 알고 있기 때문일 수도 있다. 파울린 슈트라우스는 저명한 오페라 가수였으며 종종 성격이 특이했던 것으로 묘사되었다. 파울린은 사람들 앞에서도 말을 공격적으로 하던 것으로 유명했으며 대부분이 보기에 큰 존재감을 자랑하던 사람이었다.

08 다음 중 빈칸에 가장 알맞은 것은 무엇인가?
① 슈트라우스의 부인이 괴짜이다
② 호프만스탈은 슈트라우스의 부인에 매료되었다
③ 슈트라우스의 부인은 모델로 받아들여야 했다
④ 호프만스탈은 아마도 작곡을 주도할지도 모른다

| 정답 | ①

| 해설 | 빈칸 뒤 "하지만 슈트라우스는 기분이 상하지 않았다. 어쩌면 이는 슈트라우스도 호프만스탈의 성격 묘사에서 어느 정도 진실이 있음을 알고 있었기 때문일 수도 있다(Strauss, however, did not take offense, probably because he knew there was some truth to the characterization)."의 다음 내용을 보면 슈트라우스의 부인이 특이한 사람임을 알 수 있다. 이는, 즉 슈트라우스는 자신의 부인이 특이한 사람이라 기분이 상하지 않았다는 내용이다. 이를 감안하고 보기의 문장을 빈칸에 대입해 보면, "슈트라우스는 호프만스탈이 자신의 부인이 특이한 사람이라

고 말한 것 때문에 기분이 상했을 수 있지만, 사실 슈트라우스도 그렇게 생각했기 때문에 기분이 상하지 않았다"는 내용이 글의 흐름상 맞다. 따라서 답은 ①이다.

09

슈트라우스는 호프만스탈의 의견에 기분이 상하지 않았고, 그 이유는 _____ 때문이다.
① 슈트라우스는 호프만스탈이 자신보다 현명하다고 생각했다
② 슈트라우스는 더 이상 자신의 부인에 관해 말하고 싶어 하지 않았다
③ 슈트라우스는 자신의 부인이 다소 호감 가는 성격을 가진 오페라 가수임을 알고 있었다
④ 슈트라우스 자신도 부인이 다소 특이한 데다 기분파이고 자기주장이 강한 사람임을 알고 있었다

| 정답 | ④

| 해설 | 슈트라우스 부인의 성격에 기초한 오페라 속 등장인물을 호프만스탈은 "특이한 성격에다 기분파이고 자기주장이 강한 사람(strange, moody, domineering)"으로 묘사했다. 그리고 앞 문제 해설에서도 언급된 바와 같이, 슈트라우스는 "호프만스탈의 성격 묘사에서 어느 정도 진실이 있음을 알고 있었고(knew there was some truth to the characterization)", 자신의 부인이 "종종 성격이 특이했던 것으로 묘사되었음(was often described as odd)"을 알고 있었다. 즉, 슈트라우스가 보기에 자신의 부인은 호프만스탈이 제시한 등장인물과 별 다를 바 없던 것이었다. 따라서 답은 ④이다.

10

다음 중 본문에 따르면 사실인 것은 무엇인가?
① 호프만스탈은 1911년 3월 3일이 돼서야 파울린 슈트라우스를 알게 되었다.
② 슈트라우스와 호프만스탈은 서로를 업무의 경쟁자로 여겼다.
③ "마적"은 성격 묘사에 있어 "그림자 없는 여인"을 모델로 삼았다.
④ "그림자 없는 여인"은 최초 구상된 이후 8년이 지나 초연되었다.

| 정답 | ④

| 해설 | "이 오페라에 관한 아이디어는 초연으로부터 8년 전에 등장했다(The idea for the opera had come eight years earlier)." 따라서 답은 ④이다.

| 어휘 | premiere ⓥ 개봉하다, 초연하다   libretto ⓝ 오페라의 대본
         discretion ⓝ 자유재량, 신중   bizarre ⓐ 특이한, 괴짜의
         moody ⓐ 기분파의, 기분 변화가 심한   domineering ⓐ 지배하려 드는, 자기주장이 강한
         likeable ⓐ 호감이 가는   take offense at – ~에 기분이 상하다
         contentious ⓐ 논쟁이 많이 벌어지는, 말썽 많은   characterization ⓝ 성격 묘사
         verbally ⓐⓓ 말로, 구두로   combative ⓐ 전투적인
         a force to be reckoned with – 무시할 수 없는 존재, 존재감이 큰 사람

[11-12] 서강대 2011

거의 모든 사람들은 "Greensleeves(영국의 전통 민요이자 곡조)"가 슬픈 노래라고 생각한다. 하지만 왜 그럴까? 우수에 찬 가사도 한몫 하겠지만, 이 곡의 멜로디가 단3도(minor third)라 불리는 음악적 구성을 두드러지게 담고 있기 때문이다. 음악가들은 적어도 17세기부터 슬픔을 표현하기 위해 단3도를 이용해 왔다. 사람들은 적어도 서양 음악에서는 장조로 구성된 노래들(예를 들어 생일 축하곡)이 일반적으로 쾌활한 반면, 단조로 구성된 노래(예를 들어 비틀즈의 Eleanor Rigby)는 음울한 경향이 있다고 생각하는데, 단3도가 감정에 미치는 영향은 바로 이런 대중들의 생각과 밀접한 연관성을 지닌다.

단조 음계와 슬픔 사이에 어느 정도 연관성(이 연관성은 우리의 특정한 음악적 전통에 의해 강화된 것이다)이 있을 수 있겠지만, 음악이 불러일으키는 감정이 음색(tonality) 그 자체만으로 생겨난다고 확신에 차 있다면 이는 잘못된 것이다. Jonathan Richman의 "Egyptian Reggae"라는 곡을 생각해 보자. 이 곡의 단조 멜로디는 묘하게도 이 곡을 듣는 서양인들에게 이 곡이 무언가 이집트와 관련성이 있다는 생각을 갖게 하는데, 이 곡이 재미있는 이유가 바로 이런 이국적이면서도 묘하게 이집트를 연상시키는 것에서 나온 것이다. 곡의 정서가(emotional valence)를 단순히 단조 음색으로만 들릴 수는 없는 것이다. 사실 음색과 감정 간의 대중적 생각을 거부하는 이런 고집스런 단조 음색을 가진 곡들이야말로 대중의 생각에 순응하는 곡들보다 음악에 대해 더 심오한 것을 우리에게 말해 준다고 할 수 있다.

11 다음 중 본문의 주요 요지에 해당하는 것은?
① 음악가들은 단3도를 슬픔과 불행한 감정을 표현하기 위해 사용해 왔다.
② 동양적 전통과는 달리, 서양 음악은 단조 음을 사용하는 것을 기피한다.
③ 음악이 감정에 미치는 영향을 단순히 단조 음의 음색으로만 국한시킬 수는 없을 것 같다.
④ 단조 음의 곡들은 특히나 슬픈 감정에 특히 효능이 있다.

| 정답 | ③

| 해설 | 첫 번째 문단에서는 어떤 노래가 슬프게 느껴지는 것은 단3도와 같은 음색과 관계가 있다고 말하고 있다. 하지만 다음 문단에서 필자는 약간의 연관성은 있겠지만 오로지 음색만이 감정과 관계있다고 생각하는 것은 잘못(mistake)이라고 주장하고 있다. 따라서 두 번째 문단이 이 글의 주요 요지에 해당한다. 이를 토대로 보기를 보면, ①의 경우 본문에 나온 내용이지만 필자가 말하고자 하는 바는 아니다. ②는 본문과 무관한 내용이므로 답이 될 수 없으며, ③이 두 번째 문단의 핵심 내용이 되므로 정답이 된다. ④도 본문과 무관하다.

12 다음 노래 중에서 본문에서 논의되고 있는 내용으로 봤을 때 다른 노래와 다른 것은?
① Greensleeves ② Happy Birthday
③ Eleanor Rigby ④ Egyptian Reggae

| 정답 | ②

| 해설 | 단조로 이루어진 노래(Greensleeves, Eleanor Rigby)는 장조로 이루어진 노래(Happy Birthday)에 비해 슬픈 감정을 느끼게 한다. 하지만 Egyptian Reggae는 단조로 이루어진 노래이지만 묘하게 이집트를 연상시키면서 슬픔이 아닌 즐거움을 주는 노래이다. 따라서 감정으로 보면 나머지 셋과 다른 보기를 고를 수 없다. 감정이 아닌 장조/단조의 개념으로 접근하면 정답은 나머지 단조 곡과 다른 장조 곡인 ②가 정답이 된다.

| 어휘 | apart from - ~은 그렇다고 치고, ~ 외에도
　　　 lyric ⓝ 가사
　　　 feature ⓥ ~을 특징으로 하다
　　　 melancholy ⓝ 우울, 애수
　　　 prominently ⓐd 두드러지게
　　　 minor third - 단3도

sway ⓝ 지배, 영향, 흔들림
popular idea – 대중들의 생각
major key – 장조 음
minor key – 단조 음
doleful ⓐ 서글픈
loose correlation – 느슨한 상관관계(상관관계가 별로 없다는 뜻)
reinforce ⓥ 강화하다
evoke ⓥ 불러일으키다
A is reduced to B (= A is reducible to B) – A를 줄이고 줄였더니 B만 남다, A는 결국 B라고 할 수 있다
tonality ⓝ 음색
in and of itself – 그 자체로
spring from – ~로부터 나오다
exotic ⓐ 이국적인
association ⓝ 연관성
emotional valence – 정서가
recalcitrant ⓐ 완강하게 반항하는, 고집 센
conform ⓥ 따르다, 순응하다
Oriental ⓐ 동양의
be reluctant to – ~하기에 마음이 내키지 않다, 마지못해 ~하다
employ ⓥ 사용하다, 이용하다, 고용하다
efficacious ⓐ 효과 있는, 효능 있는

[13-14] 숙명여대 2012

토스카니니가 속도, 리듬, 음색의 쾌적함 등의 문제를 올바로 다루었는지 아니면 잘못 다루었는지에 관해 음악가들끼리 거의 논의하지 않고 있다는 점은 특이한 일이다. 다른 음악가들과 마찬가지로 토스카니니는 이러한 속도, 리듬, 음색의 쾌적함 등을 능숙하게 잘 다루는 경우가 빈번했으면서도 실수하는 경우 또한 빈번했다. 이보다 더 중요한 것은 각 곡을 지휘하면서 청중에게 자신의 인상을 심어 줄 수 있는 토스카니니의 변치 않는 능력이었다. 그는 뻔뻔스러울 만큼 박자를 자극해 속도를 높여 명확함을 희생시키고 기본적인 리듬을 무시하면서, 만일 청중의 주의가 점차 분산된다 싶으면 마치 자신의 지휘봉처럼 음악을 빙빙 돌아가게 만든다. 어떤 곡도 구체적인 무언가를 의미해서는 안 되며, 모든 곡은 청자에게 즉흥적으로 받아들여지는 상황을 유발해야 한다. 이는 내가 "감탄을 불러일으키는 기법"이라 부르는 것이다.

13 빈칸에 가장 알맞은 것은 무엇인가?
① ~인 척하다
② 따르다
③ ~인 상황에 처하다
④ 무시하다
⑤ 올리다

| 정답 | ④

| 해설 | 토스카니니는 속도, 리듬 등을 철저히 지키는 지휘자가 아니었으며 박자를 자극시키는 지휘자였으므로 기본적인 리듬 또한 준수하기보다 "무시(ignore)"했을 것으로 유추 가능하다. 따라서 답은 ④이다.

14 저자에 따르면 토스카니니의 "와우 테크닉"의 가장 중요한 요소는 무엇인가?
① 진실성
② 즉흥
③ 서정적 꾸밈음
④ 음악적 철저함
⑤ 연습

| 정답 | ②

| 해설 | 토스카니니에 있어 곡은 "구체적인(specific)"인 것을 의미하기보다, 청자에게 "spontaneous acceptance(즉흥적

으로 받아들여지는)"것이다. 이를 저자는 토스카니니의 "감탄을 불러일으키는 기법"이라 불렀다. 따라서 답은 ②이다.

| 어휘 | tonal ⓐ 음조의, 음색의
amenity ⓝ 쾌적함, 즐거움
apt ⓐ 능숙한, 이해가 빠른
unvarying ⓐ 불변의, 한결같은
put over – 성공시키다, [청중]에게 자기의 인상을 심다
shamelessly ⓐⓓ 뻔뻔하게
whip up – ~을 자극시키다[선동하다]
tempo ⓝ 박자
baton ⓝ 지휘봉
waver ⓥ 약해지다; 흔들리다
provoke ⓥ 유발하다
spontaneous ⓐ 자발적인; 즉흥적인
feign ⓥ 가장하다, ~인 척하다
authenticity ⓝ 진짜임, 진실성
improvisation ⓝ 즉흥
lyrical ⓐ 서정적인
coloration ⓝ 꾸밈음, 착색법
rigour ⓝ 철저함, 엄격함

[15-17] 숭실대 2012

실제로 프란츠 슈베르트의 "대(Great)" 교향곡 다장조에 관한 이야기는 말 그대로 너무 광대하기(great) 때문에 이야기를 할 수밖에 없다. 우리는 슈베르트의 교향곡에 관해 논할 때 음악학 연구자들이 슈베르트의 교향곡의 번호를 매기기 위해 취한 눈물겨운 노력에 관해 말하지 않을 수 없다. 이를 이해하려는 사람은 누구든지 계산법에 관해 호된 훈련을 받을 준비가 되어 있어야 할 것이며, 그 이유는 슈베르트의 교향곡에 일반적으로 매겨진 번호가 응당 혼란을 일으키게 되기 때문이다. 예를 들어, 슈베르트 교향곡의 역사에 관해 잘 알지 못하는 사람들이 보기에 "대" 교향곡은 정렬된 슈베르트의 교향곡 순서에 따르면 그의 아홉 번째 교향곡일 것으로 생각된다. 하지만 이 "대" 교향곡은 때로는 여덟 번째 교향곡으로도 지칭된다. 이처럼 이례적인 일이 벌어지게 된 배경으로 꽤나 혼란스러운 이야기가 존재한다.

1818년에 작곡된 "소(Little)" 교향곡 6번 다장조까지는 순서가 모두 확실하다. 슈베르트가 완성한 처음 여섯 개의 교향곡은 모두 시간 순으로 번호를 부여받았다. 이 다음부터 혼란이 생겨난다. 슈베르트는 6번 교향곡을 완성한 이후 두 개의 악장을 추가로 작곡했는데, 이 두 악장은 훨씬 나중에 하나로 합쳐져서 그 유명한 "미완성" 교향곡이 된다. 이 두 악장은 세월이 꽤 흐른 다음에도 발견되지 않았기 때문에, 6번 교향곡 다음의 교향곡은 7번 교향곡으로 불리게 되었다. 이 7번 교향곡은 "대" 교향곡이란 이름이 붙었는데, 그 이유는 7번과 같은 다장조 교향곡인 6번 "소" 교향곡과 구별하기 위해서였다. 슈베르트의 "미완성" 교향곡이 발견된 이후, 슈베르트 교향곡의 새로운 판본이 준비되었고, 그 당시 이 "미완성" 교향곡을 8번 교향곡으로 부르기로 결정되었기 때문에, "대" 교향곡은 9번으로 숫자가 올라갔다. 이 글을 주의 깊게 읽었다면 7번이 비어 있음을 눈치챘을 것이다. 이 부분은 아직 명쾌한 해결책이 나오지 않았기 때문에 숫자가 누락되었다. 따라서 슈베르트의 (존재하지 않는) 7번 교향곡은 음악사에서 가장 잘 알려진 유령 작품이 될 가능성이 있다.

15 다음 중 제목으로 가장 알맞은 것은 무엇인가?
① 교향곡에 번호를 매기는 일의 복잡함
② 슈베르트의 교향곡에 이름을 붙이는 데 있어 겪게 되는 모순
③ 슈베르트의 사라진 교향곡의 중요성
④ 슈베르트의 교향곡에 번호 매기기

| 정답 | ④

| 해설 | 본문은 슈베르트가 작곡한 교향곡에 어떻게 번호를 매기게 되었는지, 그리고 번호를 매기면서 어떻게 혼란이 벌어지게 되었는지를 말하고 있다. 따라서 답은 ④이다.

16 본문에 따르면 다음 중 사실인 것은 무엇인가?
① 음악학 연구자들은 슈베르트의 작품을 다룰 때 다소 안심한다.
② 슈베르트는 "유령"이라 이름 붙여진 교향곡을 작곡했다.
③ 슈베르트의 "미완성" 교향곡은 "대" 교향곡보다 훨씬 나중에 발견되었다.
④ 슈베르트는 자신의 교향곡에 번호를 매기는 일에 관해 거의 신경 쓰지 않았다고 한다.

| 정답 | ③

| 해설 | "미완성" 교향곡은 "대" 교향곡보다 먼저 작곡되었지만, 발견은 시간이 훨씬 흐른 다음에야 이루어졌다. 따라서 답은 ③이다.

17 본문에 다르면 다음 중 ⓐ this one이 나타내는 것은 무엇인가?
① "소" 교향곡 다장조
② "대" 교향곡 다장조
③ "미완성" 교향곡
④ "유령" 교향곡

| 정답 | ③

| 해설 | 문맥상 this one은 바로 앞의 '미완성 교향곡'을 나타낸다. 따라서 답은 ③이다.

| 어휘 | touching ⓐ 감동적인 desperation ⓝ 필사적임, 자포자기
musicologist ⓝ 음악학 연구자 mathematics ⓝ 계산
line-up ⓝ 정렬(된 것) anomaly ⓝ 이례, 변칙
chronological ⓐ 시간 순서대로 된 subsequently ⓐⓓ 뒤에, 나중에
movement ⓝ 악장 subsequent ⓐ ~ 다음의, 차후의
numeric ⓐ 수의 hiatus ⓝ 누락, 빠진 틈
elegant ⓐ (계획, 생각이) 명쾌한 composition ⓝ 작품, 곡
inconsistency ⓝ 불일치, 모순

[18-20] 가천대 2007

[1] 대부분의 그래피티 예술가들은 자신의 개성이나 예술적 능력을 표현하기 위해 언론의 자유 같은 어떤 권리를 가지고 있다고 생각할지 모른다. 하지만 그래피티는 아름다운 것들을 창조하거나 학습이나 연습에 의해 획득되는 기술을 요하는 그런 예술 형식은 아니다. 그래피티 예술가들은 그냥 스프레이 통 하나 들고서 건물, 길거리, 심지어는 도시의 기차들 위에다가 자신들의 이름이나 이상한 그림들을 그린다. 그래피티는 건물의 가치를 떨어뜨리고 단번에 한 지역을 추하고 황폐한 지역으로 변모시킨다. 때문에 나는 그래피티를 도시 문화의 일부로 받아들일 수 없다고 생각한다.

[2] 그래피티는 아름답고 창조적일 수 있으며 사람들이 자신을 표현하는 비폭력적인 방법이 될 수 있다. 그래피티의 관례은 일반적으로 사회적 권위에 반항하는 하위문화와 관련이 있다. 그래피티는 힙합 문화의 한 요소로 여겨진다. 우리는 그래피티가 없었더라면 알 수 없었던 사회의 다른 요소에 관해 배울 수 있다. 게다가 그래피티 예술가들은 자신들의 실력을 향상시키기 위해 노력하고 있으며, 이들의 실력은 꾸준히 발달하고 있다. 일부 도시에서는 합법적으로 그래피티를 그릴 수 있도록 특정 공동체의 벽이나 구역을 따로 떼어 놓았다. 이를 통해 그래피티 예술가들은 위대한 예술 작품을 창조할 수 있다.

18 윗글 [1], [2]의 핵심 쟁점으로 가장 적절한 것은?
① 그래피티 기술을 향상시키는 방법
② 그래피티 예술가들의 역할
③ 예술의 형태인 그래피티 그림
④ 합법적인 그래피티를 그릴 장소

| 정답 | ③

| 해설 | [1]과 [2]는 과연 그래피티 회화를 예술의 일부로 받아들일 것인가에 관한 상반된 입장을 제시한 글이다. 따라서 핵심 쟁점 사항은 ③이 된다.

19 윗글 [1]의 빈칸에 들어갈 말로 가장 적절한 것은?
① 자아 표현의 행위로 활용된다
② 도시 문화의 일부로 받아들일 수 없다
③ 가난한 구역에서는 덜 유명한 경향이 있다
④ 수천 년 동안 전혀 발전하지 않았다

| 정답 | ②

| 해설 | "그래피티는 건물의 가치를 떨어뜨리고 단번에 한 지역을 추하고 황폐한 지역으로 변모시킨다(Graffiti reduces property values and instantly makes an area look ugly and rundown)." 즉, [1]의 주장을 하는 사람의 입장에서 그래피티를 받아들일 수는 없다. 따라서 답은 ②이다.

20 윗글의 내용과 맞지 않는 것은?
① graffitists는 그래피티 예술가를 의미한다.
② 사회적 권위에 반항하는 것은 힙합 문화의 한 요소이다.
③ 일부 도시에서는 그래피티를 부분적으로 허용한다.
④ 그래피티 예술가는 어디서든 자신들의 예술을 표현할 권리가 있다.

| 정답 | ④

| 해설 | "대부분의 그래피티 예술가들은 자신의 개성이나 예술적 능력을 표현하기 위해 언론의 자유 같은 어떤 권리를 가지고 있다고 생각할지 모른다(Most grafftists may think they have some right like free speech to express their individualism or artistic ability)." 그러나 이는 '생각'일 뿐이지 실제 이들에게 권리가 있는 것은 아니라는 것이 [1]의 내용이다. 따라서 답은 ④이다.

| 어휘 | graffitist ⓝ 낙서 예술가
individualism ⓝ 개성
run-down ⓐ 황폐한, 쇠퇴한
set aside – 따로 떼어 놓다
free speech – 언론의 자유
graffiti ⓝ (공공장소에서 하는) 낙서, 그래피티
rebel ⓥ 반항하다

[21-23] 한양대 2007

모든 예술의 주된 목표가 즐거움에 있다면, 우리들 대부분이 거리낌 없이 즐거움을 무심하게 받아들이고 우리가 감동받은 수단에 대해 별 생각이 없다고 해서 우리에게 비난이 쏟아질 일은 거의 없다. 아주 당연히도 우리 대부분이 누리는 즐거움은 별 생각 없이 누리는 것들이다. 그리고 일부 걸작 예술품을 감상하는 과정에서, 이러한 경이로운 작품을 창조한 사람들의 기교, 손재주, 예술적 기교의 정통함, 기술에 대한 완벽한 지식 등에 관해 호기심을 갖고 고려해 보려는 습관을 지닌 사람은 거의 없다. 우리의 관심사는 명작에 관한 좀 더 큰 요소, 즉 명작의 의미와 진실성, 지적인 고상함, 도덕적인 매력 등에 다소 집중되어 있다. 이것이 최선임에는 의심의 여지가 없다. 그 이유는 예술 작품은 이렇게 고귀한 특성을 소유함으로서 오래 지속될 수 있기 때문이다. 반면에 보다 고귀한 이런 특징들이 숙련된 장인의 여러 기교적 수단에 의해 지탱되지 않을 경우, 이러한 고귀한 특징 그 자체만으로는 작품에 불멸성을 부여하기엔 충분치 않을 것이다.

21

밑줄 친 wont와 뜻이 가장 가까운 것은?

① 가능한　　　　　　　　　② 강요받은
③ 기뻐하는　　　　　　　　④ ~하려 하는

| 정답 | ④

| 해설 | 밑줄 친 be wont to는 '~하는 습관을 가지다, ~하려 하다'의 의미를 갖는다. 보기 중에서 이와 가장 유사한 의미를 나타내는 것은 ④이다.

22

이 글에 나타난 우리들의 일반적 예술 작품 감상의 태도는?

① 예술가의 장인 정신을 깊이 있게 헤아려 본다.
② 깊은 생각 없이 다만 작품에서 즐거움을 찾는다.
③ 작품의 진실성이나 의미에 대하여 많이 고려하지 않는다.
④ 우리를 감동시키는 것이 무엇인가에 대하여 깊이 생각한다.

| 정답 | ②

| 해설 | "아주 당연히도 우리 대부분이 누리는 즐거움은 별 생각 없이 누리는 것들이다(Properly enough, the enjoyment of most of us is unthinking)"와 "일부 걸작 예술품을 감상하는 과정에서, 이러한 경이로운 작품을 창조한 사람들의 기교, 손재주, 예술적 기교의 정통함, 기술에 대한 완벽한 지식 등에 관해 호기심을 갖고 고려해 보려는 습관을 지닌 사람은 거의 없다(in the appreciation of the masterpieces of the several arts few of us are wont to consider curiously the craftsmanship of the men who wrought these marvels, their skill of hand, their familiarity with the mechanics of their art, their perfect knowledge of technique)"를 고려해 봤을 때 우리는 작품을 감상할 때 즐거움에 중점을 둘 뿐 작품이 만들어지기 위한 기교는 거의 고려하지 않음을 알 수 있다. 따라서 답은 ②이다.

23

이 글의 요지를 가장 잘 나타낸 것은?

① 예술 작품은 내용뿐만 아니라 기교도 중요하다.
② 예술 작품의 성공 여부는 예술가의 성품에 달려 있다.
③ 예술가의 완벽한 기교만이 최고의 예술품을 창조한다.
④ 예술 작품에서 즐거움을 찾는다고 해서 비난받을 수는 없다.

| 정답 | ①

| 해설 | "반면에 보다 고귀한 이런 특징들이 숙련된 장인의 여러 기교적 수단에 의해 지탱되지 않을 경우, 이러한 고귀한 특징 그 자체만으로는 작품에 불멸성을 부여하기엔 충분치 않을 것이다(On the other hand, these nobler qualities by themselves will not suffice to confer immortality, if they are not sustained by the devices of the skillful craftsman)." 이 부분은 예술 작품에 있어 기교 또한 내용만큼 중요하다는 의미이다. 따라서 답은 ①이다.

| 어휘 |
end ⓝ 목표
be attached to - ~에 소속되다, ~와 결부되다
whereby ⓐⓓ (그것에 의하여) ~하는
unthinking ⓐ 생각[분별]없는, 경솔한
masterpieces ⓝ 걸작, 명작
craftsmanship ⓝ 기교, 솜씨
marvel ⓝ 경이(로운 업적)
mechanics ⓝ 기교, 솜씨
center on - ~에 초점을 맞추다
appeal ⓝ 호소, 매력
confer ⓥ 수여하다, 주다
inclined ⓐ ~하려 하는, ~할 것 같은
delight ⓝ 기쁨
carelessly ⓐⓓ 무심하게
properly ⓐⓓ 타당하게도, 적절히
appreciation ⓝ 감상
wont ⓐ ~하는 습관을 가진, ~하려 하는
wrought ⓥ 초래하다, 일으키다
familiarity ⓝ 친숙함, 친밀
regard ⓝ 관심, 고려
elevation ⓝ 기품, 고상함
suffice ⓥ 충분하다
immorality ⓝ 불멸성, 불후의 명성

[24-28] 서강대 2009

앙리 마티스와 마르크 샤갈은 둘 다 유명한 예술가이다. 이 두 사람은 20세기 초 프랑스에서 회화를 그렸다. 이들의 회화는 당시 많은 예술가들에게 영향을 주었다.
앙리 마티스는 1869년 프랑스의 한 소도시에서 태어났다. 그는 부유한 가정에서 자랐고 처음에는 예술에 그리 흥미를 보이지 않았다. 그러다가 1890년 수술에서 회복되는 과정에서 회화를 그리면서 시간을 보냈다. 그때 이후 화가가 되는 것을 고려하게 된다.
마티스는 자신의 회화에 이전 어떤 예술가도 사용해 본 적 없는 방식으로 색을 사용했다. 그는 색을 과감하면서 특이한 방식으로 사용했고 이를 통해 그의 회화를 본 사람들은 세상을 새로운 방식으로 볼 수 있었다. 마티스는 병에 걸려서 더 이상 그림을 그릴 수 없게 되었어도 예술가로서의 길을 포기하지 않았다. 그는 다채로운 색의 커다란 모양 종이를 잘라다가 캔버스에 배열했다. 이런 방식으로 그는 죽을 때까지 아름다운 예술 작품을 만들어 낼 수 있었다.
마르크 샤갈은 1887년 러시아의 소도시에서 태어났다. 그의 가족은 가난했지만 어린 샤갈은 예술을 배울 수 있도록 부모님께 간청했다. 샤갈은 예술가로 한동안 활동한 다음에 파리로 가기로 결심했다. 그는 러시아로 돌아가기 전까지 4년 동안 파리에서 공부하고 작업했고, 러시아로 돌아가서 부인을 만나 결혼했다. 그는 결국에 가족과 함께 파리로 이주했고, 죽을 때까지 대부분의 시간을 파리에서 지냈다. 그의 후기 작품에는 벽화와 스테인드글라스 창이 포함된다.
샤갈의 회화는 사람들에게 꿈속에서 본 장면을 떠올리게 했다. 동물과 사람이 공중에 떠다녔다. 놀랍도록 특이한 색이 꿈과 같은 느낌을 더했다. 샤갈은 수많은 작품 속에서 러시아 동화와 유대의 설화를 소재로 활용했다.
마티스와 샤갈은 구상한 것을 보여주기 위해 새롭고 특이한 방식으로 예술과 색을 활용했다. 오늘날 이들의 회화는 유명 박물관에 전시되어 있다. 모네와 피카소 같은 예술가와 함께 마티스와 샤갈은 현대 미술의 선구자로 여겨진다.

24 마티스와 샤갈의 공통점은 무엇인가?
① 둘 다 러시아에서 살다가 파리로 이주했다.
② 둘 다 부유한 가정 출신이다.
③ 둘 다 평생 꿈과 같은 장면을 그렸다.
④ 둘 다 20세기 초에 프랑스에서 회화를 그렸다.

| 정답 | ④

| 해설 | "이 두 사람은 20세기 초 프랑스에서 회화를 그렸다(The two men painted in France in the early twentieth century)." 따라서 답은 ④이다. ①과 ③은 샤갈에게만 해당되는 사항이며, ②는 마티스에게만 해당되는 사항이다.

25
> 샤갈의 회화와 마티스의 회화 간의 유사성은 무엇인가?
> ① 모두 동화 속 장면이 담겨 있다.
> ② 모두 특이한 방식으로 색을 표현했다.
> ③ 모두 대체로 초상화이다.
> ④ 모두 잘라낸 모형으로 만들어져 있다.

| 정답 | ②

| 해설 | "마티스는 자신의 회화에 이전 어떤 예술가도 사용해 본 적 없는 방식으로 색을 사용했다. 그는 색을 과감하면서 특이한 방식으로 사용했고 이를 통해 그의 회화를 본 사람들은 세상을 새로운 방식으로 볼 수 있었다(In his paintings, Matisse used color in a way that no artist had before. His bold and unusual use of color let the viewer see the world in a new way)." 그리고 샤갈의 경우 "놀랍도록 특이한 색이 꿈과 같은 느낌을 더했다(Wonderfully unusual colors add to the dream-like quality)." 따라서 두 화가 모두 색을 "특이하게(unusual)" 사용했음을 알 수 있으므로 답은 ②이다.

26
> 젊은 시절의 마티스와 샤갈이 지닌 공통점은 무엇인가?
> ① 둘 다 대가족을 거느렸다.
> ② 둘 다 소도시에서 성장했다.
> ③ 둘 다 어렸을 때부터 예술에 관심을 보였다.
> ④ 둘 다 프랑스에서 성장했다.

| 정답 | ②

| 해설 | "앙리 마티스는 1869년 프랑스의 한 소도시에서 태어났다(Henri Matisse was born in a small town in France in 1869)." "마르크 샤갈은 1887년 러시아의 소도시에서 태어났다(Marc Chagall was born in a small Russian town in 1887)." 두 사람 모두 소도시에서 태어났으므로 답은 ②이다.

27
> 샤갈과 마티스는 말년에 어떤 차이를 보였는가?
> ① 마티스는 오려낸 것으로 작품을 만들었고 샤갈은 벽화를 그렸다.
> ② 마티스는 동화 속 장면을 그렸고 샤갈은 초상화를 그렸다.
> ③ 마티스는 프랑스에서 작업을 했고 샤갈은 러시아에서 작업을 했다.
> ④ 마티스는 흑백이 주는 효과를 발견했고 샤갈은 더 과감한 색을 사용했다.

| 정답 | ①

| 해설 | "마티스는 더 이상 회화를 그릴 수 없게 되자 다채로운 색의 커다란 모양 종이를 잘라다가 캔버스에 배열했다(cut out large and colorful paper shapes and arranged them on a canvas)." 샤갈의 경우 "그의 후기 작품에는 벽화와 스테인드글라스 창이 포함된다(His later work included murals and stained-glass windows)." 따라서 답은 ①이다.

28 저자에 따르면 마티스 및 샤갈이 모네 및 피카소와 공통적으로 지닌 것은 무엇인가?
① 모두 죽을 때까지 회화를 그렸다.
② 모두 예술의 다른 분야에서 작업을 하기 위해 회화를 그만뒀다.
③ 모두 현대 미술의 선구자이다.
④ 모두 어렸을 때 예술에 대한 사랑을 깨달았다.

| 정답 | ③

| 해설 | "모네와 피카소 같은 예술가와 함께 마티스와 샤갈은 현대 미술의 선구자로 여겨진다(Along with artists like Monet and Picasso, they are considered pioneers of modern art)." 따라서 답은 ③이다.

| 어휘 | arrange ⓥ 배열하다　　　　　　　　mural ⓝ 벽화
pioneer ⓝ 개척자, 선구자　　　　portrait ⓝ 초상화

[29-30] 한국외대 2006

[1] 르네상스 시대의 화가인 Giotto는 자연을 너무나 정확하게 묘사한 나머지 Giotto의 스승이 그의 작품 속 파리 그림을 찰싹 때린 적도 있었다. 이것이야말로 대단히 훌륭한 예술적 업적이 아니겠는가? 예술가의 목적은 모사에 있는 것이다. 모사는 르네상스 시대부터 예술적 업적의 정점으로 여겨졌다. 하지만 현대 미술은 세상의 겉모습을 묘사하는 데 집중할 뿐 아니라 추상적 사고와 느낌이라는 내면세계의 묘사에도 집중한다. 현대 미술은 작품 속 요소가 상호작용을 일으키는 방식에 집중하며 이들 요소가 어떤 느낌을 불러일으키는지에 집중한다. 지난 세기에 제작된 예술 작품을 빠르게 살짝 훑어보면 모사는 대다수의 예술가들에게서 버림받았음이 드러난다.

[2] 1880년부터 1차 세계 대전의 발발까지 기술과 문화 분야에 일어난 일련의 광범위한 변화로 인해 시간과 공간에 관해 생각하고 경험하는 독특하고 새로운 방식이 등장했다. 전화, 자동차, 비행기, 엑스레이 기계, 영화, 그리니치 표준시 등의 근본적인 발명품이 사람들로 하여금 수 세기 동안 자리가 잡혀 있던 세상에 대한 개념을 다시 수립하게끔 만들었다. 거리는 좁혀진 느낌이 들었다. 시간은 더 세부적으로 나뉘게 되었고 자연의 영향을 덜 받게 되었다. 예술가들도 동일한 방식으로 반응했다. 흐르는 모래와 같은 현실을 나타내고자 화가와 소설가는 사실처럼 보이는 모습은 포기하고 인간이 자연과 새로운 관계를 생성하는 새로운 예술의 형태를 구축했다.

29 위의 두 지문에서 알게 된 내용으로 가장 적합한 것을 고르시오.
① 르네상스 이전의 예술은 모사를 통해 표현하려는 욕구에 의해 추진되었다.
② 현대 예술은 모사를 통한 세상의 표현으로부터 벗어나 다른 곳에 관심을 보였다.
③ 현대의 기술적 발명품은 현대 예술의 변화는 거의 관계가 없다.
④ 1880년에서 1914년까지의 사회적 변화는 속도로 상징된다.

| 정답 | ②

| 해설 | 우선 있는 그대로 사실을 모사하는 행위는 과거에는 미술의 대세였지만 현재엔 "대다수의 예술가들에게서 버림받았다(has been abandoned by the vast majority of artists)." 그리고 시대의 변화와 함께 등장한 "근본적인 발명품이 사람들로 하여금 수 세기 동안 자리가 잡혀 있던 세상에 대한 개념을 다시 수립하게끔 만들었으며(Such radical inventions ... forced people to reconsider perceptions of the world that had been in place for

centuries)" "화가와 소설가는 사실처럼 보이는 모습은 포기하고 인간이 자연과 새로운 관계를 생성하는 새로운 예술의 형태를 구축했다(painters and novelists abandoned verisimilitude and forged new art forms that explored man's new relationship with his environment)." 즉, 단순한 모사에 그치지 않고 세상을 보는 다른 시각을 지닌 새로운 예술의 형태가 현대에 구축된 것이다. 따라서 답은 ②이다.

모사는 르네상스 시대부터 중심으로 부각된 것이지 그 이전이 아니므로 ①은 답이 아니다. 현대의 발명품이 예술의 변화를 야기했다는 것이 본문의 내용이므로 ③은 답이 될 수 없다. ④에 관한 사항은 본문에 등장하지 않으므로 역시 답이 될 수 없다.

30 [1]의 저자와 달리 [2]의 저자는 예술 스타일의 변화를 가져온 문화적 요소를 지적한다.
① 전통적인 사고방식의 상실에 한탄한다
② 예술 스타일의 변화를 가져온 문화적 요소를 지적한다
③ 관점의 중대한 변화가 일어난 정확한 순간을 정한다
④ 예술이 취한 형태의 혁신을 언급한다

| 정답 | ②

| 해설 | [2]에서는 "기술과 문화 분야에 일어난 일련의 광범위한 변화(a series of sweeping changes in technology and culture)"로 인해 예술에도 크나큰 변화가 이루어졌음을 말하고 있다. 따라서 답은 ②이다.

| 어휘 | accurately ⓐd 정확하게, 정밀하게
superb ⓐ 최상의, 대단히 훌륭한
pinnacle ⓝ 정점, 절정
glance ⓥ 힐끗 보다, 살짝 훑어보다
sweeping ⓐ 전면적인, 광범위한
radical ⓐ 급진적인; 근본적인
shrink ⓥ 줄어들다
in kind – 동일한 것으로
verisimilitude ⓝ 그럴듯함, 사실처럼 보임
propel ⓥ 추진하다, 몰다
perspective ⓝ 관점
swat ⓥ 찰싹 때리다
mimesis ⓝ 모사, 모방
evoke ⓥ 불러내다, 일깨우다
reveal ⓥ 드러내다
distinctive ⓐ 독특한
perception ⓝ 개념
particularize ⓥ 상세히 설명하다, 하나씩 열거하다
intent on – ~을 꾀하는[작정한]
forge ⓥ 구축하다
lament ⓥ 한탄하다, 애통하다

[31-33] 가톨릭대 2011

한 친구가 내게 말하길, 한 번은 레오나르도 다빈치 작품의 사본을 박물관에 가져가서 그곳 큐레이터에게 그 사본을 보여줬다고 한다. 큐레이터가 사본을 한 번 보더니 그 사본이 만들어진 연도와 그 사본을 만든 사람의 국적까지 정확하게 말해 주었다고 한다. 세계에서 가장 뛰어난 모조품 식별 기술을 마주하게 되었다고 생각한 그 친구는 "어떻게 그런 사실을 알 수 있느냐"고 물었다. 알고 보니 거기에는 다른 무엇인가가 더 있었다. "우리는 모두 우리 시대의 죄수들"이라고 그 큐레이터는 말하면서, "창조적인 능력이 정의상 제한적일 수밖에 없는 사본가는 특히 그렇다"고 덧붙였다. 또한 그는 "모방할 대상의 선정과 붓의 놀림, 강조가 모두 시대적으로 유행하는 취향과 스타일을 반영"하며, "이런 증거들이 그를 마치 진흙이 묻은 부츠와 같이 그를 뒤따라가며, 캔버스에서 이런 증거들이 비명을 지르고 있다"고 말했다. "자신의 피부를 벗어날 수 있는 사람이 누가 있겠느냐"며 반문했다.

31

윗글의 내용과 일치하는 것은?

① 그 큐레이터는 다빈치 작품이 사기라는 사실을 깨닫지 못했다.
② 거의 대부분의 사본가들은 자신들이 살던 시대와 장소에 갇혀 있었다.
③ 사본가의 창의력은 종종 원작 화가의 창의력을 뛰어넘곤 한다.
④ 그 큐레이터는 캔버스에서 진흙 묻은 부츠의 흔적을 발견했다.

| 정답 | ②

| 해설 | 친구가 가져간 작품을 사본이라고 큐레이터는 바로 알아차리고, 그 작품을 필사한 작가의 국적과 연도까지 알려 주었으므로 ①은 사실이 아니다. ③의 경우 사본가(copyist)의 창의력은 copyist라는 말의 사전적 의미를 통해 알 수 있듯이 제한적(limited)이라고 말하고 있으므로 본문의 내용과 다르며, ④에 나온 진흙 묻은 부츠(muddy boots)는 캔버스에서 발견했다는 것이 아니라 사본가임을 알려주는 자취와 같다는 뜻의 비유로 사용한 것으로 이 또한 정답이 될 수 없다. 답은 ②로, 사본가들은 자신이 살던 시대의 유행을 쫓는 등 다분히 시대와 분리될 수 없다는 것을 강조하고 있다.

32

㉮가 구체적으로 의미하는 것은?

① 다빈치 모조 기술   ② 모조품 식별 기술
③ 미술관 관리 기법   ④ 미술품 복원 기법

| 정답 | ②

| 해설 | 친구가 깜짝 놀라며 자신이 세상에서 가장 뛰어난 것을 우연히 보게 되었다(run across)고 말하는 부분이므로 이 부분은 매우 긍정적이며 놀라운 것이란 것을 알 수 있다. 그리고 뒤이어 copyist에 대한 얘기가 나오고 있는 것을 통해 모조품을 식별한 기술이란 것을 알 수 있으므로 정답은 ②가 된다. parlor trick은 원래 마술에서 나온 것으로 stage trick보다는 작은 규모의 마술로 탁자에 둘러앉아 보여 주는 마술 등으로 '숨은 재주'라는 뜻을 지닌다.

33

빈칸 ㉯에 가장 적절한 것은?

① 제한적인   ② 강력한
③ 유연한, 융통성이 있는   ④ 견딜 수 있는

| 정답 | ①

| 해설 | 주어가 사본가(copyist)의 창조적 능력이며, 사본가에 대해서 시대를 벗어나기 어려운 사람으로 규정하고 있기 때문에 부정적인 어감의 단어가 와야 한다. 이에 어울리는 답은 ①밖에 없다.

| 어휘 | nationality ⓝ 국적
run across – ~을 우연히 마주치다
turn out to be – ~로 밝혀지다
in vogue – 유행하는
shriek ⓥ 비명을 지르다
copyist ⓝ 사본가, 복제 담당자
parlor trick – [마술] 숨은 재주
by definition – 정의상, 사전적인 의미로
track behind – ~의 뒤를 쫓다
potent ⓐ 강력한

[34-37]

모든 이집트 예술은 기하학적 규칙성과 자연에 대한 예리한 관찰의 조화를 특징으로 둔다. 무덤 벽을 장식한 부조와 회화를 통해 이를 가장 잘 배울 수 있다. 여기서 사용된 "장식했다"는 말은, 장식이 된 것은 사실이지만, 오직 죽은 이의 혼령만이 볼 수 있도록 의도된 것이기 때문에 예술이라 하기엔 잘 맞지 않을 수도 있다. 사실 이들 예술품은 감상을 위한 것이 아니었다. 이들 예술품 또한 "부활"을 위한 의도로 제작된 것들이다. 예전 암울했던 먼 과거에는 권력자가 죽으면 무덤에 권력자의 하인들도 동반시키는 것이 풍습이었다. 이후 이런 참혹한 행위는 너무 잔인하거나 너무 대가가 큰 것으로 여겨졌고, 따라서 예술이 사람들을 구원하게 되었다. 현세의 위대한 인물들에겐 실제 살아 있는 하인들 대신에 그림이나 조각이 대용품으로 주어졌다. 이집트의 무덤에서 발견되는 그림과 모형은 죽은 자의 영혼에게 사후 세계에서 지낼 동료를 제공하겠다는 생각과 연관이 있다.

우리들의 입장에서 보면 이런 부조와 벽화는 수천 년 전 이집트에 살았던 사람들의 삶의 모습을 매우 생생히 전해 준다. 그럼에도 처음 이들 예술 작품을 보면 다소 당황스럽다는 인상을 받을 것이다. 그 이유는 이집트의 화가들은 실제 생물을 묘사할 때 우리와는 꽤나 다른 방식을 사용했기 때문이다. 아마도 이는 이집트의 그림이 기여하는 목적이 지금과는 다르다는 것과 연관이 있을 것이다. 당시 가장 중요했던 것은 아름다움이 아니라 완전성이었다. 가능한 한 모든 것을 명확하게 그리고 영구불변하도록 보존하는 것이 당시 이집트 예술가들의 임무였다. 따라서 그들은 우연히 어떤 각도에서 바라보던지 간에 자신들이 보는 대로 자연을 묘사하려고 들지 않았다. 그들은 그림에 들어가야 할 모든 것이 완벽하고 명확하게 두드러질 수 있도록 하는 엄격한 규칙에 따라 기억에 의존해 그림을 그렸다. 이 같은 방식은 실제로는 화가의 작업방식이라기보다 지도 제작자의 작업 방식과 흡사했다.

34 빈칸에 가장 잘 알맞은 것을 고르시오.
① 손재주 　　　　　　　　② 장식
③ 완전성 　　　　　　　　④ 불투명함

| 정답 | ③

| 해설 | 빈칸 바로 다음 문장을 보면 이집트 시대 예술가는 "가능한 한 모든 것을 명확하게 그리고 영구불변하도록 보존(preserve everything as clearly and permanently as possible)"해야 했음을 알 수 있고, 좀 더 뒤를 보면 "그림에 들어가야 할 모든 것이 완벽하고 명확하게 두드러질 수 있도록(everything that had to go into the picture would stand out in perfect clarity)"해야 했음을 알 수 있다. 즉, 엄격한 규칙에 따라 꼭 들어가야 할 요소가 꽉 들어 차 있는 것이 당시의 그림이었다. 따라서 답은 '완전함, 완전성'을 의미하는 ③이다.

35 다음 중 "이집트식 무덤"에 관해 유추할 수 있는 것은 무엇인가?
① 벽을 장식하던 예술은 미적으로 보기 좋아야 할 필요가 없었다.
② 사자는 죽기 전에 자신에 대한 예술 작품을 의뢰했다.
③ 사자를 위해 가장 큰 공간이 배정되었다.
④ 사막에는 출토해야 할 것이 많이 있다.

| 정답 | ①

| 해설 | 당시 이집트식 예술에 있어 "가장 중요했던 것은 아름다움이 아니었음(what mattered most was not prettiness)"을 알 수 있다. 따라서 이집트식 무덤을 장식했던 벽화나 부조 또한 "미적으로 보기 좋은(aesthetically pleasing)" 것은 아니었을 것이다. 따라서 답은 ①이 된다.

36 본문에 따르면 다음 중 무덤에 있는 예술 작품의 용도는 무엇인가?
① 미래 세대를 위해 사자의 추억을 유지하기 위해
② 사자의 영혼을 정화하는 방법을 제공하기 위해
③ 사자는 사망 이후에 다른 사람들과 동반한다는 믿음을 뒷받침하기 위해
④ 사자와 사자의 가족에 대한 일대기를 기록하기 위해

| 정답 | ③

| 해설 | "이집트의 무덤에서 발견되는 그림과 모형은 죽은 자의 영혼에게 사후 세계에서 지낼 동료를 제공하겠다는 생각과 연관이 있다(The pictures and models found in Egyptian tombs were connected with the idea of providing the soul with helpmates in the other world)." 즉, 그림과 모형에 묘사된 사람이 죽은 자와 함께 사후 세계에서 지낸다는 의미이다. 따라서 "사자는 사망 이후에 다른 사람들과 동반한다는 믿음을 뒷받침하기 위해" 무덤에 예술 작품을 새기거나 그렸다는 의미의 ③을 답으로 볼 수 있다.

37 본문에 따르면 왜 이집트 예술가들은 지도 제작자들과 비교가 되었는가?
① 이들은 자연을 고려해야 했다.
② 이들은 정확한 방식으로 세부 사항을 기록하기 위해 노력했다.
③ 이들은 지도 제작자들로부터 그림을 그리는 기법을 배웠다.
④ 이들은 몇 년 단위로 그림을 수정해야 했다.

| 정답 | ②

| 해설 | 이집트 예술가들은 "그림에 들어가야 할 모든 것이 완벽하고 명확하게 두드러질 수 있도록 하는 엄격한 규칙에 따라(according to strict rules which ensured that everything that had to go into the picture would stand out in perfect clarity)" 그림을 그렸고, 때문에 저자는 이들을 지도 제작자와 비슷하다고 묘사한 것이다. 이는 보기 중에서 "정확한 방식으로 세부 사항을 기록했다"는 의미에서 ②와 가장 흡사하고 따라서 답은 ②가 된다.

| 어휘 | combination ⓝ 조합
regularity ⓝ 규칙성
observation ⓝ 관찰
adorn ⓥ 장식하다
keep alive – 살려 주다, 부활시키다
custom ⓝ 관습, 풍습
come to the rescue of – ~을 구원하다
helpmate ⓝ 동료, 배우자
vivid ⓐ 생생한
bewildering ⓐ 당황하는, 어리둥절하게 만드는
permanent ⓐ 영구적인
fortuitous ⓐ 우연한; 행운의
craftsmanship ⓝ 손재주
completeness ⓝ 완전함; 완전성
aesthetically ⓐⓓ 미적으로
the deceased – 죽은 사람, 사자

geometric ⓐ 기하학의
keen ⓐ 예리한
relief ⓝ 부조
fit ⓥ (꼭) 맞다, 적합하다
grim ⓐ 암울한
accompany ⓥ 동반하다
substitute ⓝ 대용품
extraordinarily ⓐⓓ 유별나게, 엄청나게
and yet – 그럼에도
preserve ⓥ 보존하다
sketch ⓥ 묘사하다
stand out – 두드러지다, 눈에 띄다
decoration ⓝ 장식
opaqueness ⓝ 불투명함
pleasing ⓐ 보기 좋은, 즐거운
commission ⓥ 의뢰하다, 주문하다

excavate ⓥ 출토하다, 발굴하다
uphold ⓥ 유지시키다; 옹호하다
take ~ into consideration – ~을 고려하다
precise ⓐ 정확한

purify ⓥ 정화하다
life history – 일대기
details ⓝ 세부 사항
no one but = only

[38-40] 단국대 2012

카미유 클로델(1864~1943)은 프랑스의 조각가였으며, 유명한 조각인 "입맞춤"을 창작한 예술가인 오귀스트 로댕의 도제로 일했다. 클로델은 로댕의 모델이자 조수로 활동했고 또한 로댕의 정부로서 로댕의 아이 둘을 낳았다. 하지만 클로델은 동시에 수많은 대리석 및 청동 조각을 창작하기도 했다. 이들 작품을 통해 클로델은 사후에 현재의 여러 예술 비평가들과 역사가들의 찬사를 얻게 되었다. 하지만 당시에 클로델의 동시대 사람들 중에서 그녀의 작품의 진가를 알아본 사람은 거의 없었다. 일부 예술사가들은 클로델의 재능이 그녀의 멘토이자 연인인 로댕에 의해 가려졌다고 주장한다. 이들은 로댕은 사람들로부터 존경을 받던 유명 인사였으며 프랑스 문화계에서 상당한 지위를 점하고 있었고, 비록 클로델이 자신만의 평판을 구축하려 노력했지만 결국 로댕의 그림자에서 벗어날 수는 없었다는 언급을 했다. 클로델은 로댕이 자신의 아이디어 중 일부를 도용했다고 주장했지만, 그 당시에 클로델은 사람들로부터 공공연하게 제정신이 아닌 것으로 치부되며 묵살당했다. 다른 역사가들과 비평가들은 클로델이 성공을 못한 이유는 그녀가 여성이었기 때문이라고 주장한다. 19세기 여성 예술가들은 제대로 된 대우를 거의 받지 못했고 동등한 기회가 주어지지도 못했다. 클로델은 로댕과 누드모델을 연구하면서 인간의 형상에 대해 깊이 감탄 하게 되었고, 클로델과 로댕 모두 이러한 감탄을 반영한 조각품을 창작했다. 예를 들어 클로델의 "성숙"은 떠나는 남자에게 무릎을 꿇고 애원하는 벌거벗은 여성의 모습을 묘사했다. 하지만 당시 일반 대중과 언론은 클로델의 조각을 외설적이라 부적절하며 전시에 적합하지 않다는 이유로 거부했다.

38
본문의 주된 목적은 무엇인가?
① 어려움에 처한 여성 조각가를 지원하도록 독자를 설득하기
② 여성 예술가들이 과거 어떤 대우를 받았는지 알려주기
③ 클로델이 어떻게 예술적 상상력을 개발해 왔는지 설명하기
④ 여성 예술가들이 직면한 어려움 가운데 일부를 보여주기

| 정답 | ②

| 해설 | 본문은 카미유 클로델을 예로 들어 당시에는 재능 있는 여성 예술가가 사회로부터 제대로 된 대우를 받지 못하고 잊혀졌으며, 그 진가가 사후에서나 알려졌음을 말하고 있다. 따라서 답은 ②이다. 참고로 ④의 경우는, 시제가 현재이기 때문에 과거의 사례를 말하는 본문의 시제와는 맞지 않아서 답이 될 수 없다.

39
다음 중 빈칸에 가장 적합한 것은 무엇인가?
① 한 가지 사례를 보여줬다.
② 하지만 이것이 유일한 이유는 아니었다.
③ 남성 예술가의 경우도 마찬가지였다.
④ 동등한 기회가 주어지지도 못했다.

| 정답 | ④

| 해설 | 빈칸 다음 내용을 보면, 로댕과 클로델이 같은 주제를 가지고 조각품을 만들었지만 클로델의 작품은 외설적이란 이

유로 거부당했음을 알 수 있다. 그 원인은 클로델이 여자였기 때문에 제대로 된 대우도 받지 못했을 뿐만 아니라 '동등한 기회가 주어지지도 못한' 것이다. 따라서 답은 ④이다.

40

다음 중 밑줄 친 단어인 posthumous의 의미를 가장 잘 설명한 것은 무엇인가?
① 성공적인　　　　　　　　　　② 사후의
③ 거의 불가능한　　　　　　　　④ 단독으로

| 정답 | ②

| 해설 | posthumous는 '사후의, 죽은 이후의' 등의 의미를 가진 단어이며 보기 중에서 이와 의미상 가장 가까운 것은 ②이다. 이 단어의 의미를 모를 경우엔, 다음 문장인 "하지만 당시에 클로델의 동시대 사람들 중에서 그녀의 작품의 진가를 알아본 사람은 거의 없었다(However, few of her own contemporaries appreciated her work)"는 말은 역으로 생각하면, 당시에는 아니지만 '사후' 현재엔 진가를 알아보게 되었다는 의미임을 유추할 수 있다. 따라서 답은 ②이다.

| 어휘 | apprentice ⓝ 견습생, 도제　　　　　mistress ⓝ 정부
　　　　bear ⓥ 아이를 낳다　　　　　　　　creation ⓝ 창작품, 창조물
　　　　posthumous ⓐ 사후의　　　　　　　acclaim ⓝ 찬사, 칭찬
　　　　contemporary ⓐ 동시대인　　　　　appreciate ⓥ 진가를 알아보다
　　　　eclipse ⓥ 빛을 잃게 하다, 가리다　　note ⓥ 언급하다; 주목하다
　　　　prominent ⓐ 두드러진, 유명한　　　deranged ⓐ 제정신이 아닌
　　　　be attributed to – ~에 기인하다, ~ 때문이다　　admiration ⓝ 감탄, 칭찬
　　　　plead ⓥ 애원하다, 간청하다　　　　lewd ⓐ 외설적인, 선정적인
　　　　single-handed ⓐ 혼자서, 단독으로

[41-43] 동덕여대 2012

다다이즘 예술가들은 기존 문화와 예술적 전통에 대해 반감과 경멸을 드러냈고 지속적으로 이들을 깎아내리려고 노력했다. 마르셀 뒤샹이 레오나르도 다빈치의 "모나리자"의 복제품에 콧수염을 그린 악명 높은 행위는 이를 극명하게 드러낸 사례로 볼 수 있으며, 이런 행위를 기성 예술계에서는 불경스럽고 분별없는 행위로 취급했다. 다다이즘은 예술이 상징하는 모든 것으로부터 반대되는 것을 표현하려 했다. 만일 기존의 예술이 적어도 한 가지 정도 암시적인 메시지를 품고 있다면, 다다이즘은 아무 의미도 나타내지 않으려 했다. 따라서 다다이즘 작품을 해석하는 일은 전적으로 작품을 보는 사람에 달려 있다.

다다이즘은 창조성에 대한 완전히 새로운 접근법을 만들어 냈고 이를 탐구했다. 예술적 전통에 더 이상 제약받지 않던 다다이즘 예술가들은 창조적 과정을 자유로이 실험해 볼 수 있음을 깨닫게 되었다. 예를 들어, 화가인 한스 아르프는 종이를 대충 정사각형 모양으로 자른 다음에 바닥의 종이 위에 떨어뜨리고 떨어진 자리에 풀을 발라 고정했다. 아르프는 이 기법이 제공하는 무작위성과 즉흥성에 만족한 나머지 자신의 가장 잘 알려진 작품 가운데 하나인 "우연성의 법칙에 따라 정리된 콜라쥬(Collage Arranged According to the Laws of Chance)"를 창작하기 위해 해당 기법을 활용했다.

아마도 다다이즘 예술가 중에서 가장 광범위한 영향력을 지녔을 마르셀 뒤샹은 레디메이드로 유명했으며, 그는 예술계 내에서 매체를 엄격하게 관례적인 범위 내에서 사용하는 것을 공공연하게 비난하려는 의도에서 레디메이드를 활용했다. 레디메이드는 수프 캔이나 보틀랙처럼 대량 생산되는 흔한 오브제로 예술가가 어떤 방식으로든 변형하였거나 다른 오브제와 결합한 것을 의미한다. 예술가는 레디메이드를 화랑에 전시하는 것만으로 레디메이드에 예술 작품의 지위를 부여하게 된다. 뒤샹의 레디메이드 조각품 가운데 가장 터무니없는 것인 "샘"은 그저 자기로 된 소변기에 불과했다. 소변기에 다른 예술 작품처럼 서명과 날짜가 기록된 것이었다.

41

첫 번째 단락에 따르면 다음 중 다다이즘 예술가에 관해 사실인 것은 무엇인가?
① 이들은 작품에 고전적 예술 기법을 활용했다.
② 이들은 기성 예술계와 반목했다.
③ 이들은 유명 예술 작품을 파괴하려 했다.
④ 예술가들의 메시지가 작품 속에 암시되어 있다.

| 정답 | ②

| 해설 | "다다이즘 예술가들은 기존 문화와 예술적 전통에 대해 반감과 경멸을 드러냈고 지속적으로 이들을 깎아내리려고 노력했다(Dada artists showed their disapproval of and contempt for traditional culture and artistic conventions and continually tried to undermine them)." 따라서 답은 ②이다. 참고로, 이들은 "예술적 전통에 더 이상 제약받지 않던(No longer constrained by artistic traditions)" 사람들이라서 ①처럼 고전적 예술 기법을 활용했을 리는 없고, 작품이 "아무 의미도 나타내지 않으려 했기(was to have no meaning)" 때문에 ④를 답으로 볼 수는 없다. 그리고 전통에 대한 반감을 드러냈어도 유명 작품을 파괴하려 한 적은 없었기 때문에 ③도 답이 될 수는 없다.

42

다음 중 한스 아르프에 관해 본문에서 유추할 수 있는 것은 무엇인가?
① 그는 콜라주 기법을 최초로 창안한 사람이다.
② 그는 스스로의 예술에 대해 통제력을 행사할 필요는 없다고 생각했다.
③ 그는 최소한의 노력으로 예술 작품을 창조하는 것을 선호했다.
④ 그는 과학적 지식을 예술에 적용하는 것이 중요하다고 생각했다.

| 정답 | ②

| 해설 | 우선 "예술적 전통에 더 이상 제약받지 않던 다다이즘 예술가들은 창조적 과정을 자유로이 실험해 볼 수 있음을 깨닫게 되었다(No longer constrained by artistic traditions, Dada artists found themselves free to experiment with the creative process)." 따라서 이들은 작품을 창작하는 데 있어 기존의 방식에 얽매이지 않고 하고 싶은 대로 맘껏 시험을 해 봤고, 그 결과 한스 아르프는 "무작위성과 즉흥성(randomness and improvisation)"에 따른 작품 창작 방법을 고안했다. 즉, 그는 작품을 통제하려 하기보다 그냥 흘러가는 대로 놔둔 것이었다. 따라서 답은 ②이다. 참고로 무작위성과 즉흥성을 최소한의 노력이라 볼 수 있는 근거는 본문에 없으므로 ③은 답이 될 수 없다.

43

아래 주어진 문장이 들어가기에 가장 적합한 곳을 고르시오.

소변기에 다른 예술 작품처럼 서명과 날짜가 기록된 것이었다.

① Ⓐ   ② Ⓑ
③ Ⓒ   ④ Ⓓ

| 정답 | ④

| 해설 | It은 단수 비인칭대명사이며 문맥상 뒤샹의 '샘', 즉 소변기를 지칭한 것으로 볼 수 있다. 소변기에 서명과 날짜가 기

록되면서 ⓑ 다음 문장이 말하는 '레디메이드가 예술 작품의 지위를 부여받게 된' 한 가지 사례가 되었다. 따라서 답은 ④이다.

| 어휘 | disapproval ⓝ 반감
irreverent ⓐ 불손한, 불경한
stand for – ~을 상징하다
ready-made ⓝ 레디메이드
confer ⓥ 주다, 부여하다
porcelain ⓝ 자기
be at odds with – ~와 반목하다, ~와 사이가 나쁘다

striking ⓐ 두드러진, 극명한
ill-conceived ⓐ 계획이 잘못된, 분별없는
improvisation ⓝ 즉흥
overt ⓐ 명시적인, 공공연한
outrageous ⓐ 너무나 충격적인, 터무니없는
urinal ⓝ 소변기

[44-45] 인하대 2014

페이션스 웹(Patience Webb)은 오래 전에 미술 분야에서 아이를 격려하는 방법은 무엇이 아이를 움직이게 하는지를 파악하는 것임을 깨달았다. 27년 동안 매사추세츠 주의 여러 학교에서 예술을 가르친 웹은 처키(Chuckie)란 이름의 7세 소년의 이야기를 들려주었다. 처키는 미술 수업에서 자신이 제대로 할 수 있는 것은 아무것도 없다고 생각했고 따라서 아예 시도조차 하지 않았다. 하지만 그 이후 웹은 처키가 치타를 좋아한다는 사실을 발견했다. 그래서 웹은 처키에게 치타를 습작 삼아 그려보라고 요청했다. 처키는 몇 주 동안 치타의 그림을 그렸고, 자신이 그린 그림을 자랑스러워했으며, 대형 고양이과 동물을 주제로 한 학교 과제물의 표지로 그 치타 그림을 사용했다. 웹은 아이가 무엇에 관심을 갖는지를 파악하라고 말하며, 심지어는 무의식적 단계에서도 그래야 한다고 말한다. 아이는 어떤 색을 좋아할까? 아이는 무엇을 수집할까? 아이의 삶에 있어 변함없이 등장하는 주제는 무엇일까? 아이가 좋아하는 것을 미술 프로젝트의 근거로 삼으라. 이를 위해서는 어느 정도 생각해 둘 것들이 있다. 아이가 자동차를 매우 좋아하고 자동차를 그리는 것을 좋아하는가? 아이의 장난감 차가 다닐 길이 있는 마을 지도를 아이와 함께 만들라. 미술가가 되기를 주저하는 아이이거나 이미 미술을 좋아하는 아이일 경우, 이 아이는 이따금 이루어지는 미술 프로젝트에서 당신이 제공하는 사려 깊은 지침을 통해 혜택을 볼 수 있다.

44 본문의 제목으로 가장 알맞은 것은 무엇인가?
① 아이를 창조적인 아이로 만드는 방법
② 아이가 학습 과정에서 겪는 불안감을 줄이기
③ 미술 교육의 시작점으로서의 집
④ 미술 프로젝트를 아이가 신나하는 것에 맞추기

| 정답 | ④

| 해설 | 본문은 미술 분야에서 아이의 참여를 유도하기 위해서는 아이가 흥미진진해 하는 것에 맞춰 미술 프로젝트를 진행해야 한다는 사실을 말하고 있고, 하나의 예로 처키란 이름의 소년의 경우를 들고 있다. 따라서 답은 ④이다.

45 다음 중 빈칸에 가장 적합한 것은 무엇인가?
① 관심을 갖다
② 걱정시키다
③ 기력을 떨어뜨리다
④ 축하하다

| 정답 | ①

| 해설 | 미술과 관련하여 제대로 할 수 있는 게 아무 것도 없다고 생각한 나머지 미술 수업을 포기한 처키를 위해, 페이션스 웹은 처키에게 처키가 좋아하는 대상인 치타를 소재로 그림을 그리라고 했다. 그 결과 처키의 미술 실력은 크게 상승했다. 이는, 즉 아이가 '관심을 갖는' 대상을 가지고 미술 활동을 하게 하면 나중에 아이의 미술 실력은 상승하고 미술 프로젝트를 통한 혜택을 누릴 수 있다는 의미이다. 따라서 답은 ①이다.

| 어휘 | tick ⓥ (사람·기구 따위가) 움직이다, 작동하다
big cat – 대형 고양이과 동물
constant ⓐ 변함없는
direction ⓝ 지도, 지침
tailor ⓥ (특정한 목적·사람 등에) 맞추다[조정하다]
enervate ⓥ 기력을 떨어뜨리다
study ⓝ 습작품 (그림)
unconscious ⓐ 무의식적인
hesitant ⓐ 주저하는, 망설이는
occasional ⓐ 이따금의, 가끔의

[46-47] 한국외대 2017

밥 딜런(Bob Dylan)으로 잘 알려진 음악계 최고의 시인인 로버트 앨런 지머맨(Robert Allen Zimmerman)이 노벨 문학상을 수상했다. 그의 영향력은 여전히 록(rock)과 팝에서부터 포크와 솔(soul)에 이르기까지 여러 음악 장르에 걸쳐 퍼져 있지만, 그의 놀라운 서정적 능력은 자신만의 영향력을 발휘하길 원하는 수많은 가수 겸 작곡가들에게 영감을 불러일으키고 있다. 딜런의 음악 경력은 50년 이상 이어진다. 그의 가슴이 저미는, 강력하고 격렬한, 가슴이 찢어질 듯한, 그러면서도 가끔은 재치 있게 단어를 다루는 그의 솜씨가 그의 특유의 거칠고 느릿한 말투보다 의심의 여지없이 더 많은 감탄을 불러일으키며, 능수능란한 언어 구사가 실제로 세상을 바꿀 수 있음을 입증하고 있다. 딜런은 스스로 많은 노래의 의미를 신비로 간직했다. 한 번은 인터뷰 진행자에게 자신의 노래 가사가 무엇에 관한 것인지 자신은 모른다고 답변했다. 그는 "어떤 노래는 약 4분, 어떤 것은 약 5분 분량이다…."라고 말하면서 가사의 의미를 캐묻는 것을 회피하고, 매혹적이며 난해한 수수께끼로 남는 것을 선택했다.

46 다음 중 딜런이 단어를 구사하는 방식이 보여주는 것으로 적합한 것은?
① 50년에 걸친 음악 경력
② 능수능란한 언어 구사의 힘
③ 그의 노래의 비밀스런 의미
④ 그의 음악적 기교에 대한 더 많은 존경

| 정답 | ②

| 해설 | 본문 중반의 "His poignant ... and often witty way with words arguably sparks more admiration ..." 부분을 통해 그의 단어 구사 방식이 사람들에게 존경심을 불러일으켰다는 것을 알 수 있으므로 정답은 ②가 적합하다.

47 다음 중 빈칸 (A)에 올 것으로 가장 적합한 것은?
① 패러디
② 금욕주의자
③ 수수께끼
④ 믿음

| 정답 | ③

| 해설 | 앞부분의 "The man himself has kept the meaning of many of his songs a mystery"에서 이어지는 내용을 다루고 있다. 딜런은 자신의 노래 가사 의미를 비밀에 부쳤다. 의미의 대한 질문을 회피(eluding probing)한다고 했고, 순접의 and를 이용해 같은 내용을 다시 부연설명하고 있다. 이런 질문을 피해 신비한 'mystery'로 남는 전략을 취했다는 의미가 적합하므로, 이와 가장 유사한 ③ enigma가 정답이 된다.

| 어휘 | poet laureate – (특히 영국에서) 계관 시인, 국민[최고] 시인
pervade ⓥ 퍼지다
lyrical ⓐ 서정적인, (표현이) 아름답고 열정적인
inspire ⓥ 영감을 불러일으키다
span ⓥ 걸치다
fiery ⓐ 불 같은, 열렬한, 격렬한
drawl ⓝ 느린 말투
elude ⓥ 회피하다
ascetic ⓝ 금욕주의자, 수도자
stunning ⓐ 놀랄 만큼 아름다운[멋진]
pinnacle ⓝ 절정, 정점
a host of – 많은
poignant ⓐ 감동적인; 통렬한, 신랄한
gravelly ⓐ 목소리가 걸걸한, 귀에 거슬리는; 자갈의
a command of language – 언어 구사력
probe ⓥ 캐묻다, 캐다, 조사하다
enigma ⓝ 수수께끼

[48-50] 중앙대 2017

아마도 당신은 그 그림을 본 적이 있을 것이다. 사진적 사실주의로 묘사된 파이프가 "이것은 파이프가 아니다(Ceci n'est pas une pipe)."라고 적힌 세심하게 작성된 문구 위에 놓여져 있다. 르네 마그리트(René Magritte)는 1920년대에 〈이미지의 배반〉이라는 작품을 그렸는데, 그 이후 사람들은 그 작품의 의미가 무엇인지를 두고 계속 이야기해 왔다.

재현한 것은 그 재현이 묘사한 실제 대상이 아니라는 것, 즉 그의 작품은 '오직' 그림에 불과하며 실제 파이프는 아니라는 것을 마그리트는 우리에게 상기시키려고 의도한 것일까? 그와 같은 해석이 대학생들에게 널리 가르쳐지는 것이지만, 만일 그것이 사실이라면 마그리트는 우리가 이미 알고 있는 것을 말하기 위해, 특별히 우아한 디자인의 마감 처리된 파이프를 신중하게 선택하고, 파이프를 수십장 스케치하고, 내부 구조에 친숙해지기 위해 파이프를 분해해 보고, 세심한 주의와 솜씨로 파이프의 정물화를 그리는 등의 엄청난 수고를 감수한 것이 된다. 〈두 개의 수수께끼〉라는 다른 작품에서 마그리트는 훨씬 더 고집스러운 모습을 보인다. 문구가 들어가 있는 원래 파이프 그림이 판자 바닥 위에 서 있는 이젤에 놓여 있는 모습이 보인다. 하지만 그 그림 바로 위에, 그리고 전체 작품에서는 왼편에, 두 번째 파이프가 앞서 캔버스와 프레임보다 더 크게 (혹은 더 가깝게) 그려져 있다. 우리가 여기서 보는 것은 역설의 그림이다. 분명 작은 파이프는 그림이고, 파이프가 아니다. 하지만 재현된 그림 바깥에 놓여있는 두 번째 파이프는 무엇이란 말인가? 만일 그것 또한 그림에 불과하다면, 그렇다면 그 그림은 어디서 끝이 나는 것일까?

나에게는 역설의 핵심이 프레임의 개념에 있다고 생각된다. 우리가 역사적 인물의 초상화와 같은 사실적 그림을 바라볼 때 우리는 관례적으로 그 초상화가 실제 사람과 실제 대상을 재현하고 있다고 받아들인다. 마그리트의 파이프 그림에서와 같이 그런 관례가 거부될 때, 그림이 실재가 아니라는 것을 떠올리는 것이 핵심이 아니다. 그것도 맞는 말이지만 사소한 것에 해당한다. 핵심은 프레임 밖의 모든 것은 실재하는 것이라는 생각에 도전하는 것이다.

마그리트와 같은 예술가들의 적은 소박한 실재론(naïve realism)이다. 소박한 실재론이란 인간의 감각 기관이 하나밖에 없는 실제 세계를 정확히 기록하며, 인간의 뇌가 그 세계로부터 하나의 정확한 모델을 만들어 낼 수 있다고 끈덕지게 믿는 것을 말한다. 물론 실제로는 그 누구도 실재를 전체적으로 파악할 수 없으며, 각자의 우주가 어느 정도 특별하며, 이런 환경이 단 하나의 참된 실재가 있다는 것을 우리가 증명하지 못하도록 만든다.

48

윗글에서 어법상 가장 적합하지 않은 것을 고르시오.
① (A) ② (B)
③ (C) ④ (D)

| 정답 | ④

| 해설 | 정답은 ④로, (D)의 'which'를 'of which'로 수정해야 한다. 관계대명사 which 이하의 내용이 불완전한 문장이 아닌 완전한 문장을 이루고 있으므로, 관계대명사가 전치사를 포함하거나 관계부사가 와야 한다. 이 문장의 기본 구조는 〈make A (out) of B〉로 'B를 A로 만들다; B를 A로 이해(생각)하다'의 뜻을 지닌다. 즉, 'make A(model) of B(reality)'에서 'of B'가 'of which'로 관계대명사가 되어 앞으로 이동하게 되면서 'make A'만 남게 되는 형태를 취하고 있다.

49

윗글을 통해 추론할 수 있는 것으로 가장 적합한 것을 고르시오.
① 마그리트의 그림은 많은 대학생들에게 친숙하지 않다.
② 마그리트는 〈이미지의 배반〉을 그리는 데 불필요한 노력을 기울였다.
③ 마그리트의 두 작품은 서로 다른 메시지를 전달한다.
④ 마그리트가 파이프 그림을 그린 의도가 종종 오해를 받는다.

| 정답 | ④

| 해설 | ① 본문의 "Such an interpretation is widely taught to college students"을 통해 대학생들에게 친숙한 그림이라는 것을 알 수 있다. ② "if it is true, Magritte went to an awful lot of trouble ..." 이하의 내용을 지칭하고 있는데, 앞에 '그것이 사실이라면'의 전제를 붙이고 있으므로, 마그리트가 실제로 불필요한 수고를 했다는 것을 의미하는 것은 아니다. ③ 두 작품은 모두 같은 메시지를 전달하고 있다. 정답은 ④로 "Did Magritte intend to remind us that a representation is not the object it depicts — that his painting is 'only' a painting and not a pipe?"를 통해 일반인들이 마그리트의 작품을 보고 생각하는 것에 대해 기술한다. 하지만 후반부의 "That much is true but trivial. The point is to challenge the belief that everything outside the frame is real."을 통해 실제로는 그런 생각은 매우 사소한 것에 해당하며, 마그리트가 전달하고자 하는 핵심은 프레임 밖의 모든 것은 사실이라는 기존의 관념에 도전장을 내미는 것이라고 밝히고 있다.

50

윗글의 요지로 가장 적합한 것을 고르시오.
① 현실에 대한 우리의 이해는 제한적이고 다양하다.
② 현대 예술작품은 다양한 해석이 가능하다.
③ 현대 예술가들의 궁극적인 목표는 현실 내에 존재하는 역설을 묘사하는 것이다.
④ 우리는 공동의 노력을 통해서만 진정한 실재에 도달할 수 있다.

| 정답 | ①

| 해설 | 글의 마지막 부분인 "nobody can grasp reality whole, that each person's universe is to some extent unique, and that this circumstance makes it impossible for us to prove that there is but one true

reality"를 통해 마그리트가 두 작품을 통해 의도한 바를 짐작할 수 있다. 현실을 전체적으로 이해할 수 있는 사람은 존재하지 않으며, 각자의 세계는 저마다 독특한 부분이 있으며, 이런 현실적인 한계로 인해 우리는 단 하나의 참된 현실이 있다는 것을 증명할 수 없다는 것이 이 글의 요지에 해당한다. 따라서 정답은 "현실에 대한 우리의 이해는 제한적이고 다양하다"는 ①이 된다.

| 어휘 | **depict** ⓥ 설명하다, 묘사하다
float ⓥ 표류하다, 떠오르다
treachery ⓝ 배반, 반역
representation ⓝ 표시, 표현, 주장, 대표, 대리, 대의 제도
interpretation ⓝ 해석, 이해, 설명; 통역
familiarize ⓥ 익숙하게 하다, 정통하게 하다
insistent ⓐ 고집[주장]하는, 우기는
caption ⓝ 제목, 자막
loom ⓥ 어렴풋이 나타나다 ⓝ 베틀
by convention – 관례상
naïve ⓐ 순진한
sensory apparatus – 감각 기관
variegated ⓐ 다양한 종류로 이뤄진; 얼룩덜룩한

photographic realism – 극사실주의, 사진적 사실주의
script ⓝ 문자

go to trouble – 애쓰다
anatomy ⓝ 해부, 해부학
complete with – ~이 완비된, ~로 완벽한
hover ⓥ 공중을 떠돌다, 배회하다
paradox ⓝ 역설
trivial ⓐ 하찮은, 대단치 않은
dogged ⓐ 완강한, 끈덕진
to some extent – 어느 정도는

CHAPTER 05 영화·스포츠

01	②	02	①	03	②	04	④	05	④	06	③	07	⑤	08	③	09	④	10	③
11	②	12	③	13	③	14	④	15	②	16	③	17	①	18	②	19	①	20	④
21	①	22	④	23	①	24	④	25	②	26	④	27	③	28	①	29	①	30	②
31	①	32	①	33	②	34	④	35	②	36	①	37	③	38	①	39	②	40	①

[01-04] 삼육대 2007

"웨스트 사이드 스토리"는 윌리엄 셰익스피어의 시공을 초월한 러브스토리인 "로미오와 줄리엣"을 원작으로 한 뮤지컬 비극이다. 이 작품은 대도시 갱단들 간의 항쟁으로 인해 부상을 입거나 심지어 사망하는 경우도 발생했던 1950년대 초반을 배경으로 한다. "웨스트 사이드 스토리"에서는 셰익스피어의 희곡 "로미오와 줄리엣"에 등장하는 몬터규 가문과 캐플렛 가문을 경쟁 관계의 거리 갱단인 제트파와 샤크파로 변화시켰다. 샤크파는 푸에르토리코에서 막 건너온 이민자들이었고 제트파는 뉴욕 토박이들이었다. 줄거리는 오빠인 베르나르도가 샤크파의 리더인 푸에르토리코 소녀인 마리아와 제트파의 일원인 토니의 이야기이다. 두 대립하는 갱단이 뉴욕의 길거리에서 싸우는 와중에 이 두 사람은 사랑에 빠진다. 토니는 거리 싸움을 막으려는 와중에 의도치 않게 마리아의 오빠 베르나르도를 죽이게 되고 결국 자살하게 된다.

"웨스트 사이드 스토리"는 공연계의 전설적인 3인조의 재능이 꽃피운 결과였다. 멋진 배경음악을 작곡한 레너드 번스타인은 클래식 작곡가이자 뉴욕 필하모닉의 지휘자였다. 이 작품이 자신의 브로드웨이 데뷔작이었던 스티븐 손드하임은 작사 능력에 뛰어난 재능이 있음을 드러냈다. 이 작품에 수록된 히트곡들에는 "Tonight", "Maria", "America", "Gee Officer Krupke", "I Feel Pretty" 등이 있다. 안무가인 제롬 로빈스의 열광적인 안무는 1950년대 뮤지컬계에 신기원을 열었다. "웨스트 사이드 스토리" 이전에는 춤이 음악이나 가사만큼 극의 서술 과정에 필수적인 역할을 할 수 있을 것이라고 생각한 사람은 아무도 없었다. 하지만 "웨스트 사이드 스토리" 내에서 춤은 가장 흥미진진한 요소 중 하나이다.

이 작품은 1957년 9월 26일에 초연되었다. 734회의 공연을 하였고, 10개월간 순회공연을 하였으며, 그 다음에 뉴욕으로 복귀해 246회의 추가 공연을 하였다. 1961년에는 나탈리 우드를 주연으로 한 이제는 고전으로 불리는 영화판이 개봉되었다. 그 영화는 작품상과 감독상을 포함하여 10개의 아카데미상을 수상하였다. 이 작품은 1980년에 그리고 초연되고 거의 40년 만인 1995년에 뉴욕에서 성공적으로 재공연되었다.

01 본문에 따르면 "웨스트 사이드 스토리"에서 벌어진 사건은 언제의 일인가?
① 셰익스피어의 연극 속 시대
② 1950년대 초반
③ 1957년
④ 1980년

| 정답 | ②

| 해설 | "이 작품은 … 1950년대 초반을 배경으로 한다(It is set in the early 1950s)." 따라서 답은 ②이다.

02 본문에 따르면 몬터규 가문과 캐플렛 가문은 <u>셰익스피어의 연극에 등장하는 가문</u>이다.
① 셰익스피어의 연극에 등장하는 가문
② 1950년대의 거리 갱단
③ 제트파와 샤크파에 맞서 싸웠다
④ 연기자, 무용가, 가수 등의 집단

| 정답 | ①

| 해설 | "셰익스피어의 희곡 '로미오와 줄리엣'에 등장하는 몬터규 가문과 캐플렛 가문(the Montagues and Capulets of Shakespeare's play)"을 통해 답은 ①임을 알 수 있다.

03 "웨스트 사이드 스토리" 이전에 만들어진 뮤지컬에 관해 유추할 수 있는 것은 무엇인가?
① 노래 수가 적었다.
② 춤이 그다지 중요한 특징으로 여겨지지 않았다.
③ 줄거리 보다 춤과 노래에 좌우되었다.
④ 전설적인 재주꾼들이 극의 창작에 도움을 주지 않았다.

| 정답 | ②

| 해설 | "'웨스트 사이드 스토리' 이전에는 춤이 음악이나 가사만큼 극의 서술 과정에 필수적인 역할을 할 수 있을 것이라고 생각한 사람은 아무도 없었다. 하지만 '웨스트 사이드 스토리' 내에서 춤은 가장 흥미진진한 요소 중 하나이다(Before West Side Story, no one thought that dance could be as integral to a narrative as the music and the lyrics. But the dances in West Side Story are among the most thrilling elements of the play)." 이를 통해 '웨스트 사이드 스토리' 이전에는 춤이 그다지 중요한 요소로 취급되지 않았음을 알 수 있다. 따라서 답은 ②이다.

04 "웨스트 사이드 스토리"는 최초 뉴욕에서 상영되는 기간 동안 얼마나 많이 상영되었는가?
① 10
② 26
③ 246
④ 734

| 정답 | ④

| 해설 | "이 작품은 1957년 9월 26일에 초연되었다. 734회의 공연을 하였다(The play opened on September 26, 1957. It ran for 734 performances)." 여기서 답은 ④임을 알 수 있다. 참고로 246은 순회공연 이후 뉴욕 브로드웨이에 복귀한 다음에 한 공연 횟수이다.

| 어휘 | timeless ⓐ 영원한, 시공을 초월한 transform A into B - A를 B로 변형시키다[바꿔 놓다]
opposing ⓐ 대립하는 inadvertently ⓐ 무심코, 우연히
feature ⓥ 특징으로 삼다, 특별히 포함하다 score ⓝ (영화·연극의) 음악
lyric ⓝ (노래의) 가사 electrifying ⓐ 열광시키는, 흥분시키는
choreography ⓝ 안무 break new ground - 신기원을 이룩하다
theater ⓝ 극장 연극계 integral ⓐ 필수적인
narrative ⓝ 서술 thrilling ⓐ 흥미진진한, 아주 신나는
starring ~ - ~이 주연인 release ⓥ 발표하다, 공개하다
premier performance - 초연 garner ⓥ 모으다, 획득하다

[05-07] 성균관대 2012

카메라는 우리가 본 모든 것에, 그리고 이미 전문가들이 아주 잘 기록해 놓았고 서점이나 가판대 어디에서나 판매 중인 '세계의 불가사의'를 기록한 표지에다 우리를 박아 넣기 위한 수단이다. 하지만 완벽한 사진이 많이 들어간 화보집이 우리에게 무슨 소용일까? 우리가 사진엽서 속에 들어 있지 않은데 타지마할, 콜로세움, 피사의 사탑 등의 엽서를 집에 돌아간 다음 친구에게 보여준들 무슨 소용일까? 우리가 사원 옆에 미소 지은 표정을 보이지 않는다면 어떤 사원도 관심의 대상이 아니다. 대부분의 아마추어 사진작가들은 있는 그대로의 세상에는 아무 관심을 보이지 않고 오직 이상적으로 비춰져야만 하는 세상에만 관심이 있다. 예를 들어 여러분은 아주 오래된 옛날 그대로의 진정한 모로코의 장면을 사진으로 찍고 싶어 한다. 여러분에겐 안됐지만 유리로 된 현대식 건물이 모스크 높이까지 접근해 올라가고 있고, 사원의 뾰족탑 뒤에는 TV 안테나가 하늘을 찌르고 있으며, 낙타 옆에는 두 명의 모로코 사람들이 어울리지 않는 서양식 복장을 하고 서서 사업을 논의하고 있다. 따라서 여러분은 일어서서 카메라를 비틀고서 옆으로 카메라를 떠받치고 자세를 바꿔야 한다. 이렇게 하면 작은 노란색 선이 나머지 요소는 그대로 유지시키면서 건물을 가려 버리고, 안테나랑 전선을 잘라내 버리고, (사업을 논의하던) 사업가들은 제외시켜 버린다. 그리고 이렇게 만들어진 소중한 순간 동안 (모로코답지 않은) 이질적 요소들이 없어져 버릴 때 찰칵하고 사진을 찍는다. 이제 진정한 모로코의 모습이 찍혔다. 이것이 바로 아마추어 사진작가 예술의 최고봉인 완전한 비현실성이다. 있는 그대로의 세상이 아닌 것이다.

05 본문의 어조는 어떠한가?
① 유익한
② 감상적인
③ 미안해하는
④ 풍자적인
⑤ 우울한

| 정답 | ④

| 해설 | 저자는 아마추어 사진작가들이 "있는 그대로의 세상에는 아무 관심을 보이지 않고 오직 이상적으로 비춰져야만 하는 세상에만 관심이 있다(show no interest in the world as it is, only in the world as it ideally should be)"고 보고 있으며, 이들이 찍은 사진은 "있는 그대로의 세상이 아닌(The World As It Isn't)" "완전한 비현실성(total unreality)"으로 보고 있다. 그리고 모로코의 진짜 모습을 찍겠다고 피사체를 왜곡하는 경우를 예로 들면서 아마추어 사진작가들의 행태를 풍자하고 있다. 따라서 답은 ④이다.

06 다음 중 빈칸에 가장 알맞은 것은 무엇인가?
① 우리의 사진은 초점이 빗나갔다
② 우리는 제대로 된 곳을 방문하지 못했다
③ 우리는 사진에 들어 있지 않다
④ 우리는 카메라를 가져 오는 것을 잊었다
⑤ 우리는 전문 사진작가가 아니다

| 정답 | ③

| 해설 | 빈칸 다음 문장은 "우리가 사원 옆에 미소 지은 표정을 보이지 않는다면 어떤 사원도 관심의 대상이 아니다(No temple is of interest without our faces beside it, grinning)"인데, 이는 즉 어떤 관광 명소이든 우리가 그 옆에 서 웃으며 찍은 사진이 없다면 의미가 없다는 뜻이다. 즉, "타지마할, 콜로세움, 피사의 사탑 등의 엽서(postcards of the Taj Mahal, the Coliseum, the Leaning Tower of Pisa)"는 우리가 찍은 사진보다는 잘 나왔을지 모르지만 우리의 모습이 사진에 없다면 아무리 잘 빠진 사진이든 소용이 없다는 의미이다. 따라서 답은 ③이다.

07 본문에 따르면 다음 중 사실은 무엇인가?
① 모로코에서는 진짜 모로코 사람을 찾기가 매우 어렵다.
② 아마추어 사진작가의 뒤떨어진 사진 기술이 종종 현실을 왜곡한다.
③ 여행객들은 구식 모로코보다 현대식 모로코를 더 선호하는 경향이 있다.
④ 카메라를 가지고 여행하는 것은 여행객들이 예상치 못한 것들을 경험하도록 권장한다.
⑤ 카메라를 가지고 여행하는 것은 종종 여행객의 시야를 좁힌다.

| 정답 | ⑤

| 해설 | 본문에 언급된 아마추어 사진작가가 '진정한(Real)' 모로코를 찍겠다고 피사체를 왜곡한 행위는 결국은 사물을 있는 그대로 보지 않는 자신의 좁은 시야를 드러낸 행위이다. 따라서 답은 ⑤이다. 참고로 ②가 답이 될 수 없는 것은, 본문의 사진작가는 기술이 모자라서 왜곡된 사진을 찍은 것이 아니라 의도적으로 왜곡된 사진을 찍은 것이기 때문이다.

| 어휘 | means ⓝ 수단
newsagent ⓝ 가판대
grin ⓥ (소리 없이) 웃다
minaret ⓝ (이슬람교 사원의) 뾰족탑
spike ⓥ 찌르다
sideways ⓐd 옆으로
obliterate ⓥ 없애다, 지우다
sentimental ⓐ 감상적인
satirical ⓐ 풍자적인

stamp ⓥ 찍다, 새기다
illustrated ⓐ 사진이 들어간
edge up – 점차 증가하다
aerial ⓝ 안테나
unsuitable ⓐ 알맞지 않은
retain ⓥ 유지하다
informative ⓐ 유익한
apologetic ⓐ 미안해하는
gloomy ⓐ 우울한

[08-10] 단국대 2006

나는 짜임새가 좋고, 정말로 무섭고, 서스펜스가 넘치는 영화만큼 재밌는 것을 상상할 수조차 없다. 나 자신도 공포 소설을 쓰고 있으며 공포 영화를 체험하는 과정에서 수반되는 일시적인 현실 이탈을 매우 좋아한다. 90여 분 동안 나에겐 걱정거리도 사라지고, 해야 할 설거지나 빨랫감도 없고, 지불해야 할 계산서도 없다. 나는 항상 이런 장르에 매료되었지만, 그 이유가 무엇인지는 확신이 들지 않는다. 어쩌면 적대감이 공포 장르를 통해 이런 식으로 무해하게 배출되는 것과 관계있을지도 모른다. 어쨌든 괜찮은 공포 영화나 살인 사건을 다룬 미스터리 소설은 항상 내게 꼭 맞는 것이다.

공포 영화에겐 다른 어떤 것을 변충할 만한 가치가 없다고 주장하는 사람들에게 나는 그들에겐 과연 공포 영화 말고 다른 변충할 만한 것이 있는지 묻고 싶다. 영화는 예술의 한 형태이며 제대로 만들어져야 한다. 영화가 자신의 장르에 충실하다면, 나머지 사항은 단지 개인적인 선택의 문제일 뿐이다. 푸른색이 붉은색보다 꼭 낫다고 할 수는 없다. 두 색은 그냥 색이 다를 뿐이다. 영국 영화인들은 미국 영화인들에 비해 호러 장르를 더 진지하게 받아들였다. 크리스토퍼 리와 피커 쿠싱은 사이코패스와 음울한 괴물을 의지 있고 품위 있게 연기했다. 이렇게 보면 호러 쪽에서는 영국이 더 나은 것 같다. 오로지 미국 공포 영화계에만 힘을 쏟던 빈센트 프라이스 정도를 제외하고 말이다.

공상과학, 서스펜스, 공포 영화들은 모두 현대 영화계에서 나름대로의 위치를 점하고 있다. 죽은 자들이 도심의 거리를 활보한다고? 그럴 수도 있다. 어쩌면 단지 좋은 영화를 찾아다니는 정도일 것이다. 이런 장르에 로드니 데인저필드가 말했던 "약간의 존중"을 표해 본다.

08
본문의 목적은 무엇인가?
① 유명한 공포 영화의 홍보
② 공포 영화 관람은 무해하다는 점을 주장
③ 무서운 영화에도 나름 가치가 있음을 강조
④ 영국의 공포 영화사를 연대기순으로 기록

| 정답 | ③

| 해설 | 나름의 가치가 있고 영화계에서도 적절한 위치를 점유하고 있음을 설명하는 글이다. 따라서 답은 ③이다.

09
영화에 대한 저자의 태도는 어떠한가?
① 공포 영화는 성인 관객들에게만 제한되어야 한다.
② 영화는 영화일 뿐이고 사람들은 영화를 가볍게 받아들여야 한다.
③ 영화에는 귀중한 교훈이 들어가야 한다.
④ 일부 영화에 대한 선호도는 개인 선택의 문제이다.

| 정답 | ④

| 해설 | "영화가 자신의 장르에 충실하다면, 나머지 사항은 단지 개인적인 선택의 문제일 뿐이다. 푸른색이 붉은색보다 꼭 낫다고 할 수는 없다. 두 색은 그냥 색이 다를 뿐이다(Movies are an art form and should be done well. If they are true to their genre, then it all becomes a matter of personal choice. Blue isn't necessarily better than red; it's just different.)." 즉, 저자의 입장에서 영화의 장르는 서로 다를 뿐 어떤 우열이 있는 것은 아님을 알 수 있다. 따라서 답은 ④이다.

10
저자는 푸른색이 붉은색보다 낫다고 할 수는 없다고 말하며 그 이유는 저자는 영화의 종류가 많다는 것을 시사하기 때문이다.
① 이 두 색은 같은 색에 속하지 않는다
② 저자는 붉은색을 개인적으로 선호한다
③ 저자는 영화의 종류가 많다는 것을 시사한다
④ 흑백 영화는 컬러 영화만큼 좋다

| 정답 | ③

| 해설 | 본문에서 색깔을 비유로 삼은 이유는 영화에는 색깔만큼 많은 종류가 있으나 그 종류 간에 어떤 우월함은 존재하지 않으며 단지 선택의 문제임을 말하기 위함이다. 따라서 답은 ③이다.

| 어휘 |
| well-crated ⓐ 잘 만들어진, 짜임새가 좋은 | suspenseful ⓐ 서스펜스가 넘치는
| suspension ⓝ 중지, 정지 | accompany ⓥ 동반하다, 동반되다
| attracted to – ~에 매료되다 | vent ⓝ (감정의) 분출구, 배출구
| one's cup of tea – 기호에 맞는 것, 맘에 드는 것 | redeeming ⓐ 보완하는, 벌충하는
| true to – ~에 충실한 | portray ⓥ 연기하다
| moody ⓐ 변덕스러운; 음울한 | exclusively ⓐⓓ 오직, 독점적으로
| assert ⓥ 주장하다 | merit ⓝ 가치, 장점
| chronicle ⓥ 연대순으로 나열하다 | preference ⓝ 선호도

[11-12] 중앙대 2006

1915년까지는 영화는 거의 값싼 오락거리에 불과했다. 기술적으로 조잡하고 부실하게 제작되고 전반적으로 줄거리도 없었기 때문에 영화는 분명히 예술로 간주되지는 않았다. 그러다가 D.W. 그리피스의 작품 "국가의 탄생"이 등장한다. 사실상 하룻밤 사이에 영화가 존경의 대상이 된 것이다. 그리피스는 클로즈업 같이 기술적으로 참신한 기법을 도입했다. 그리피스의 영화에는 또한 스토리가 있었다. 또한 진정한 감정을 전하던 배우도 있었다. 즉, 배우가 연기를 할 수 있었다. "국가의 탄생"은 거의 순식간에 극장가에서 성공을 거두었지만 그럼에도 불구하고 완전한 승리를 거두었다고는 결코 말할 수 없었다. "국가의 탄생"은 철저하게 인종차별적인 영화였다. "국가의 탄생"은 미국 흑인들에 대한 고정관념을 소재로 삼아 이들을 조잡하면서 무자비하게 묘사하는 것에 몰두했다. 실제로 쿠 클럭스 클랜 조직원들이 영화의 주인공으로 등장했다. 새로 결성된 NAACP(National Association for the Advancement of Colored People; 전미 흑인 지위 향상 협회)는 이에 격분하여 "국가의 탄생" 영화가 상영되고 있는 극장에서 팻말을 들고 시위했다. 사회사업가인 제인 애덤스 같은 일부 우려하는 시민들은 항의의 편지를 썼다. 불행히도 그러한 항의는 단지 그 영화에 대한 흥미를 자극할 뿐이었다. 이 모든 야단법석이 어찌된 영문인지 알아보기 위해 영화팬들이 무더기로 표를 구매했던 것이다.

11 윗글의 빈칸에 들어가기에 가장 적당한 것을 고르시오.
① 정부 관리들은 극장을 폐쇄할 수밖에 없었다
② 영화팬들이 무더기로 표를 구매했다
③ 의원들이 영화 상영을 금지하기로 결정했다
④ 많은 사람들이 항의의 편지를 썼다

| 정답 | ②

| 해설 | '국가의 탄생'을 둘러싸고 큰 논란이 일었지만, "불행히도 그러한 항의는 단지 그 영화에 대한 흥미를 자극할 뿐이었다(Unfortunately, the protests only stimulated interest in the film)." 영화팬들이라면 "이 모든 야단법석이 어찌된 영문인지 알아보기 위해(To see what all the fuss was about)" 당연히 직접 표를 사서 확인했을 것이다. 따라서 답은 ②이다.

12 윗글의 내용과 일치하지 않는 것을 고르시오.
① 1915년 이전 초창기 영화는 줄거리도 없고 기술적으로도 조잡했기 때문에 예술로 취급되지 않았다.
② "국가의 탄생"은 흑인에 대한 고정관념을 소재로 이들을 무자비하게 묘사했기 때문에 인종차별적 영화이다.
③ 제인 애덤스는 "국가의 탄생"에 등장하는 인종차별에 항의하기 위해 NAACP를 창립했다.
④ 역설적으로 "국가의 탄생"을 둘러싼 소란이 영화에 대한 관심을 불러일으켰다.

| 정답 | ③

| 해설 | 본문에는 제인 애덤스가 "사회 운동가(social worker)"라는 언급은 있지만, NAACP를 창립했다는 말은 없다. 따라서 답은 ③이다.

| 어휘 | crude ⓐ 조잡한, 날것의
practically ⓐⓓ 사실상, 실질적으로
respectable ⓐ 존경받을 만한, 부끄럽지 않은
showcase ⓥ 공개하다, 전시하다
to the core – 속속들이, 철저히
plotless ⓐ (소설 등) 줄거리 없는
overnight ⓐⓓ 갑자기, 하룻밤 사이에
novelty ⓝ 새로운 것, 참신한 것
convey ⓥ 전달하다, 전하다
revel in – ~에 골몰하다[빠지다]

Ku Klux Klan – 쿠 클럭스 클랜(미국의 남북전쟁 이후 생겨난 인종차별집단의 총칭)
outrage ⓥ 위반하다; 격분케 하다
picket ⓥ 팻말을 들고 시위하다
stimulate ⓥ 자극하다
in droves – 떼를 지어, 무더기로
outraged ⓐ 격분한
concerned ⓐ 걱정하는, 우려하는
fuss ⓝ 야단법석, 소란

[13-14] 명지대 2009

연극에서 성격 묘사는 거의 전적으로 행동과 대사에 기반을 둔다. 행동에는 몸짓이나 표정 변화같이 감지하지 힘든 기법이 포함되며, 대사에는 생각과 느낌을 표현하는 것과 유사한 독백이 포함된다. 연극에서 의상의 역할 또한 중요하다. 하지만 무대에선 등장인물에 대한 주된 인상은 그 등장인물이 취하는 행동과 다른 사람에게 하는 말에 따라 형성된다. 이는 소설에 등장하는 기법과 비교 가능하다. 더 유연한 장르인 소설에서는 저자인 당신은 등장인물의 생각, 다른 등장인물의 생각, 회상 기법을 통해 과거를 잠깐 엿보기, 직접적인 해설 등을 사용할 수 있다. 극작가가 활용할 수 있는 기법은 이보다는 제한적이기 때문에, 기법을 좀 더 과감하게 사용하는 경향이 있다. 청중은 이런 경향에 익숙해져 있다. 연극에서 분장이 짙어지고 목소리가 커질수록 성격 묘사는 더욱 직설적으로 이루어진다. 성격이 발랄하고 인상적인 사람을 묘사하는 언어로 '연극조의(theatrical)'란 말을 사용하는 게 자연스러워 보인다.

13 윗글의 제목으로 가장 적절한 것은?
① 극장 발전사
② 소설 작성의 이점
③ 연극에서 성격 묘사의 본질
④ 저자와 청중 간의 관계

| 정답 | ③

| 해설 | 본문은 연극에서 '성격 묘사'가 무엇이고 어떻게 이루어지는지에 관해 말하고 있다. 따라서 답은 ③이다.

14 윗글의 내용과 일치하지 않는 것은?
① 소설은 연극보다 저자에게 더 많은 유연성을 제공한다.
② 독백은 극작가가 성격 묘사를 위해 사용하는 방법 중 하나이다.
③ 소설가는 회상과 직접 설명을 종종 사용하는데, 이들 기법은 극작가가 쉽게 사용할 수 있는 것이 아니다.
④ 배우들이 무대에서 해야 하는 짙은 화장에 관해 청중이 가장 많은 불평을 한다.

| 정답 | ④

| 해설 | "더 유연한 장르인 소설에서는 저자인 당신은 등장인물의 생각, 다른 등장인물의 생각, 회상 기법을 통해 과거를 잠깐 엿보기, 직접적인 해설 등을 사용할 수 있다. 극작가가 활용할 수 있는 수단은 이보다는 제한적이기 때문에, 수단을 좀 더 과감하게 사용하는 경향이 있다(In that more flexible genre you as author can use the character's own thoughts, the thoughts of others, quick glimpses into the past through flashbacks, and direct exposition Since the devices available to the dramatist are more limited, the tendency is to use them more boldly)." 여기서 소설이 극작품보다 성격 묘사를 위해 더 많은 유연성을 제공하고(①), 극작가 입장에서 소설의 기법을 그대로 사용하기란 어려움을 알 수 있다(③). "생각과 느낌을 표현하는 것과 유사한 독백(a monologue

that resembles the expression of thoughts and feelings)"이 의미하는 것은 극작가는 생각과 느낌을 표현하기 위해 독백을 활용한다는 의미이다(②). 하지만 ④에 관한 사항은 본문 어디에도 등장하지 않기 때문에 답은 ④이다.

| 어휘 | characterization ⓝ 성격 묘사
subtle ⓐ 미묘한, 감지하기 힘든
costuming ⓝ 의상
dramatist ⓝ 극작가
theatrical ⓐ 연극조의, 과장된
striking ⓐ 인상적인, 두드러지는
entirely ⓐⓓ 전적으로, 완전히
monologue ⓝ 독백
exposition ⓝ 설명, 해설
bluntly ⓐⓓ 직설적으로
vivid ⓐ 강렬한, 발랄한
readily ⓐⓓ 쉽게

[15-18]

우리는 공포 영화를 보러 가서 근본적으로 정상적인 감정을 재정립한다. 이것(공포 영화)은 분석하려는 좀 더 문명화된 성인들의 성향을 없애고, 다시 아이와 같이 되어 사물을 흑백으로 보도록 촉구한다. 그리고 우리는 가서 즐긴다. 이 점이 공포 영화의 기반이 무너지기 시작하는 점인데, 이는 이것이 아주 독특한 종류의 즐거움이기 때문이다. 이 즐거움은 다른 이가 괴롭힘을 당하거나 때로 죽임을 당하는 것을 보는 것에서 발생한다. 비평가들은 공포 영화는 현대판 공개처형이 되었다고 말한다.

이런 잠재적인 공개 처형을 하는 사람은 거의 모든 우리에게 존재하고 한 번씩 그를 놓아 주어야 한다. 우리의 감정과 두려움을 통해 이들은 자신의 몸을 형성하고 우리는 이것이 적절한 근육 상태를 유지하기 위해 운동을 요구한다. 특정 종류의 이런 감정적 근육은 우리 사회에서 받아들여지고, 심지어 찬양되기도 한다. 사랑, 우정, 충성, 친절함과 같은 감정은 우리가 찬양하는 것이다. 우리가 이러한 감정을 드러낼 때, 사회는 우리에게 긍정적 강화를 부여 준다. 그러나 반시민적 감정은 사라지지 않고 주기적인 실천을 요구한다.

공포 영화는 손을 더럽히는 일을 해야 한다. 이것은 의도적으로 우리 속에 거하는 가장 악한 것에 호소한다. 이것은 고삐 풀린 병적인 것으로 우리의 가장 영악한 본능이 자유롭게 되고, 우리의 가장 지저분한 공상이 실천되는 것이다. 아주 공격적인 공포 영화의 성향은 문명화된 전뇌의 뚜껑문을 열고 지하 깊숙한 강 아래서 주위를 돌아다니는 배고픈 악어에게 한 바구니의 생고기를 던져 준다. 이것으로 인해 이들은 밖에 나가지 않는다. 이것으로 이들은 아래에 있고 나는 위에 있게 되는 것이다.

15 빈칸에 들어갈 것을 고르시오.
① 공포 영화는 도덕적 기준을 바꾼다
② 공포 영화는 내재적으로 인습적이다
③ 공포 영화는 반사회적 욕망을 거부한다
④ 공포 영화는 아이에겐 충격을 줄 수 있다

| 정답 | ②

| 해설 | 바로 뒤에 이어지는 내용을 바탕으로 빈칸의 내용을 유추할 수 있다. "It urges us to put away our more civilized and adult penchant for analysis and to become children again"의 내용을 보면, 공포 영화는 우리가 나중에 습득하게 되는 교양(civilized)과 어른이 되면서 가지게 되는 분석적 성향(penchant for analysis)을 없애고 다시 어린아이로 돌아간다고 말하고 있다. 즉, 공포 영화는 'civilized'와 'penchant for analysis'의 속성인 학습된 것과 대조되는 상태로 이끌어 줌을 유추할 수 있다. 인간이 태어나면서 내재적으로 드러내는 속성을 나타내는 'innate'가 표현된 보기 ②가 가장 적절한 답안이다.

16

본문에서 유추할 수 없는 것은?

① 우리는 사회적으로 받아들일 수 없는 감정의 배출구로 공포 영화를 사용하는 경향이 있다.
② 공포 영화의 단순성은 어느 정도 정신적 안정을 제공해 줄 수 있다.
③ 주기적으로 비합리성에 빠지는 것은 우리가 우리의 공포를 없애도록 도와준다.
④ 우리를 움츠리게 하는 것은 동시에 우리의 무의식의 욕망을 만족시킬 수 있다.

| 정답 | ③

| 해설 | 사회적으로 받아들여지지 않는 폭력적 행위의 일시적 대안으로 공포 영화를 본다고 했다. 이런 진술은 우리가 공포 영화를 통해서 정신적 안정과 함께 근본적으로 우리를 움츠리게 만드는 영상이 무의식 속에 억눌린 감정을 간접적으로 표출하는 역할로 볼 수 있다. 보기 ①, ②, ④는 모두 이런 맥락에서 본문과 일치한다. 보기 ③의 경우 비이성적인 것, 즉 사람을 죽이는 행위가 같은 것이 우리의 공포를 없애 준다고 했는데, 본문에서 언급된 공포 영화는 우리 내면에 존재하는 폭력적 성향을 잠재워 주는 기능을 한다. 그러므로 정답은 ③이다. 참고로, 본문 마지막의 악어의 비유에서 악어가 바로 우리 내면에 잠재된 '폭력적 성향'을 나타낸다.

17

본문의 목적은 무엇인가?

① 왜 사람들이 공포 영화를 보려고 하는지를 설명하기 위해서
② 다양한 정신 이상의 종류를 분석하기 위해서
③ 모든 사람은 폭력의 경향이 있음을 증명하기 위해서
④ 사람들에게 공포 영화를 보도록 설득하기 위해서

| 정답 | ①

| 해설 | 본문은 공포 영화를 보는 이유를 밝히면서, 어떤 역할을 하는지를 기술하고 있다. 따라서 답은 ①이다.

18

본문의 어조는?

① 고발적인   ② 분석적인
③ 영감을 주는   ④ 비판적인

| 정답 | ②

| 해설 | 우리가 공포 영화를 보는 근본적인 원인을 분석적으로 기술하고 있다. 따라서 답은 ②이다.

| 어휘 | **re-establish** ⓥ 재정립하다
normality ⓝ 정규, 정상 상태
put away – ~을 밀어내다, 쫓아내다
ground ⓝ 기반, 근거, 이유
public lynching – 공개 제제(특히 교수형)
applaud ⓥ 박수갈채하다, 성원하다
positive reinforcement – 긍정 강화
deliberately ⓐⓓ 의도적으로
abject ⓐ 영락한, 비참한, 절망적인

essential ⓐ 중요한, 필수적인
urge ⓥ 재촉하다, 노력하게 하다, 추진하다
penchant ⓝ 성향, 경향, 취미
slope away – 내려가다, 도망가다
let loose – ~을 놓아 주다, 해방하다, 마음대로 하게 하다
exhibit ⓥ 전람하다, 나타내다, 보이다, 드러내다
periodic ⓐ 주기적인, 정기의
morbidity ⓝ 병적임, 불건전; 사망률
aggressive ⓐ 공격적인, 호전적인

forebrain ⓝ 전뇌　　　　　　　　　　alligator ⓝ 악어
subterranean ⓐ 지하의, 지중의, 숨은

[19-21] 국민대 2013

> 슈퍼히어로는 엄청난 힘을 갖고 있지만 강점과 약점을 동시에 지니고 있는 사람들이다. 이들은 보통 하늘을 날거나 높은 빌딩 사이를 뛰어다니는 것 같은 슈퍼파워를 갖고 있다. 하지만 이런 "슈퍼"한 면은 분명히 인상적이지만 우리는 결코 "히어로"의 요소 또한 잊어서는 안 된다. 슈퍼히어로는 훌륭한 위업을 달성하도록 스스로를 인도해 주는 숭고한 품성을 보유해야 한다. 이들은 다른 보통의 인간과 마찬가지로 어두운 생각을 품고 있을 수도 있지만, 이러한 어두운 면은 옳은 일을 하겠다는 스스로의 욕구를 통해 억제되어야 한다. 따라서 복장을 착용하고 범죄에 싸우는 모든 사람이 반드시 히어로인 것은 아니며, 슈퍼파워를 보유한 인물들이 반드시 슈퍼히어로인 것도 아니다. 슈퍼히어로는 영감과 열망을 불러일으키는 이미지를 품고 있다. 슈퍼히어로는 이야기 및 영화 속에서 우리들 모두가 열망하는 어떤 것을 우리에게 제시해 준다. 플라톤은 선은 본질적으로 매력적이라고 생각했다. 때문에 슈퍼히어로는 도덕적인 힘으로 묘사되며, 선과 옳음을 위한 힘으로 묘사된다. 이들은 우리에게 선과 숭고함을 위해 스스로를 절제하고 희생하며 삶을 바치는 일의 중요성을 상기시켜 준다. 간단히 말해 우리 모두가 좋아하는 슈퍼히어로는 우리에게 즐거움을 줌과 동시에 교훈을 제공한다.

19 다음 중 아래 문장이 들어가기에 가장 적합한 곳은 어디인가?

> 하지만 이런 "슈퍼"한 면은 분명히 인상적이지만 우리는 결코 "히어로"의 요소 또한 잊어서는 안 된다.

① (A)　　　　　　　　　　② (B)
③ (C)　　　　　　　　　　④ (D)

| 정답 | ①

| 해설 | 제시된 문장을 분석해 보면, "하지만 이런 '슈퍼'한 면은 분명히 인상적이지만"을 통해 제시된 문장 앞에서는 '슈퍼'한 부분에 관한 내용이 등장하고, "우리는 결코 '히어로'의 요소 또한 잊어서는 안 된다"를 통해 제시된 문장 뒤에서는 '히어로'에 관한 내용이 등장함을 알 수 있다. 그리고 (A)의 뒤는, 슈퍼히어로의 '히어로', 즉 영웅적 품성인 '숭고함'에 관해 언급되고 있다. 따라서 답은 ①이다.

20 빈칸 ⓐ에 가장 알맞은 것은 무엇인가?

① 완화시키다　　　　　　　② 미연에 방지하다
③ 못마땅해하다　　　　　　④ 즐거움을 주다

| 정답 | ④

| 해설 | 본문은 슈퍼히어로의 영웅적 모습과 숭고함, 즉 '교훈적'인 모습을 강조하고 있다. 그렇지만, 슈퍼히어로물이 어떤 장르일지를 생각해 보면, 보통 인간이 할 수 없는 힘, 즉 슈퍼파워를 발휘하여 악당을 무찌르는 슈퍼히어로의 모습을 쉽게 연상할 수 있다. 여기서 '교훈적'인 모습에 대비하여 우리가 느낄 수 있는 것은 '즐거움'과 만족감일 것으로 유추 가능하다. 따라서 답은 ④이다.

21 다음 중 본문에 따르면 사실이 아닌 것은 무엇인가?
① 플라톤은 슈퍼히어로의 도덕적 완벽함을 강조했다.
② 슈퍼히어로는 도덕적 행동을 위해 스스로의 약점을 제어한다.
③ 우리는 슈퍼히어로로부터 고무되어 스스로를 개선한다.
④ 슈퍼파워는 슈퍼히어로가 되기 위해 요구되는 유일한 것이 아니다.

| 정답 | ①

| 해설 | "플라톤은 선은 본질적으로 매력적이라고 생각했다(Plato believed that good is inherently attractive)." 그렇지만 이외에 플라톤이 슈퍼히어로의 도덕적 완벽함을 강조했다는 내용은 본문에 등장하지 않는다. 따라서 답은 ①이다.

| 어휘 | extraordinarily @ 비상하게, 엄청나게
character ⓝ 품성, 인격
inspirational ⓐ 영감을 주는
aspire ⓥ 열망하다, 염원하다
self-discipline ⓝ 자기 절제, 수양
mitigate ⓥ 완화시키다
disapprove ⓥ 못마땅해하다
impressive ⓐ 인상적인
constrain ⓥ 억제하다, 제약하다
aspirational ⓐ 열망을 일으키는
inherently @ 선천적으로, 본질적으로
entertain ⓥ 즐거움을 주다
preempt ⓥ 선취하다, 미연에 방지하다
better ⓥ 개선하다, 더 낫다

[22-24] 명지대 2013

1968년 파라마운트 픽처스는 뉴욕 출신의 소설가 마리오 푸조가 저술한 소설 "대부"의 초안에 대한 영화화 옵션을 취득했지만, 따로 작업을 하지는 않고 소설이 베스트셀러가 되기 전까지 그냥 방치했었다. 1970년이 되자 파라마운트 픽처스의 경영진은 마리오 푸조의 소설에 기초한 영화를 만들 감독을 찾고 있었다. 다수의 영화 제작자들이 영화화 프로젝트를 거부하자, 이 영화사는 프란시스 포드 코폴라에게 도움을 요청했다. 코폴라는 영화업계 경력은 있었지만 자신의 이름을 내걸고 성공한 경력은 없던 감독이었다.

[A] 전하는 바에 따르면 영화 제작 과정에서 코폴라는 업무 진행 과정 전체에 걸쳐 잘해 낸 일이 없다고 생각했다고 한다. 그렇지만 이 과정에서 몇 가지 작은 일은 성공하기도 했는데, 그중에서도 알 파치노와 말론 브란도를 캐스팅하도록 파라마운트 픽처스를 설득한 것과 영화사로 하여금 뉴욕 시와 시칠리아에서 야외 촬영을 위한 자금을 제공하도록 한 것을 들 수 있다. 1971년 9월에 제작이 마무리되자 코폴라는 골치 아픈 일은 모두 뒷일로 남기를 바라면서 유럽을 향해 다시 배를 타고 떠났다.

[B] "대부"는 1972년 3월 15일 맨해튼에서 개봉되었고, 사람들은 한 블록에 걸쳐 나란히 여섯 줄을 서서 기다렸다. 영화는 상업적으로도 비평적으로도 완전히 성공적이었다. 4월 중순이 되자 영화는 하루에 백만 달러를 벌어들였다. 첫 번째 상영 기간이 종료된 다음에 영화는 8,620만 달러를 거두었고, 그 결과 역사상 최대의 수익을 올린 영화가 되었다. 두 번째 상영 기간이 종료된 시점에 "대부"는 1억 5천만 달러를 넘게 벌었고, 이를 통해 코폴라는 할리우드에서 가장 높은 수익을 거두고 가장 영향력이 큰 감독으로서 자리매김했다.

[C] 영화사는 코폴라가 이탈리아계 미국인이기 때문에 영화의 주제에 관해 선천적인 감각을 갖고 있을 것이며 따라서 영화의 줄거리 및 제작에 있어 진실성을 부여할 것이라고 파악했다. 코폴라는 감독 업무를 맡는 것을 주저했지만, 당시 "조이트로프(Zoetrope)"란 명칭의 자신이 소유한 영화사를 금전적으로 지탱하기 힘들었고, 할리우드의 채권자들에게 진 빚을 갚을 돈이 필요했다. 코폴라는 대서양을 순항중인 배 안에서 업무를 받아들였고, 책을 말 그대로 장별로 쪼갠 다음에 배의 방 창문에 붙이는 것으로 일을 착수했다.

22
첫 단락 이후 단락의 순서로 가장 적합한 것을 고르시오.
① [A] – [B] – [C] 　　　　② [B] – [A] – [C]
③ [B] – [C] – [A] 　　　　④ [C] – [A] – [B]

| 정답 | ④

| 해설 | 우선 첫 번째 단락에서 코폴라에게 감독 제의가 갔음이 언급되며, [C]에서 코폴라가 처음에는 제의에 주저했으나 돈 때문에 수락하였고 이후 배 안에서 제작에 착수했음이 언급된다. 그 다음 [A]에서 코폴라의 뜻대로 제작이 잘 되지는 않았지만 어쨌든 완성은 했고 코폴라는 다시 배를 타고 떠났다는 내용이 나오며, 마지막으로 [B]에서 영화가 엄청난 성공을 거두었다는 내용이 나온다. 따라서 순서는 [C] – [A] – [B]가 되고 답은 ④가 된다.

23
위 본문의 제목으로 가장 적합한 것을 고르시오.
① 코폴라와 "대부"에 관한 알려지지 않은 이야기
② "대부"가 성공한 유일한 비결
③ "대부" 소설보다 영화
④ "대부"는 여전히 헐리우드의 뇌리에서 떠나지 않고 있다

| 정답 | ①

| 해설 | 본문은 영화 '대부'가 제작되기까지 일반 대중에게 알려지지 않은 뒷이야기를 다루고 있다. 따라서 답은 ①이다.

24
다음 중 다른 나머지와 가리키는 대상이 다른 것을 고르시오.
① Ⓐ 영화사 　　　　② Ⓑ 영화사
③ Ⓒ 영화사 　　　　④ Ⓓ 조이트로프

| 정답 | ④

| 해설 | Ⓓ의 조이트로프는 코폴라 감독이 소유했던 영화사를 의미하며, 그 외 나머지는 모두 파라마운트 픽처스를 의미한다. 따라서 답은 ④이다.

| 어휘 | option ⓥ (출판, 영화화를 위한) 옵션[선택 매매권]을 취득하다
dormant ⓐ 휴면 중의, 활동을 중단한　　studio ⓝ 영화사
reportedly ⓐd 전하는 바에 따르면, 소문에 의하면　　wrap up – 마무리 짓다
abreast ⓐd 나란히; 따라서　　unmitigated ⓐ 완전한
gross ⓥ 수익을 올리다　　lucrative ⓐ 수익성이 좋은
innate ⓐ 타고난, 선천적인　　authenticity ⓝ 진실성
untold ⓐ 알려지지 않은　　haunt ⓥ (오랫동안) 괴롭히다, 뇌리에서 떠나지 않다

[25-26] 명지대 2009

야구의 기원은 애브너 더블데이가 쿠퍼스타운에서 다이아몬드 모양의 경기장을 설치하고 경기 운영을 위한 규칙을 표준화하려 했던 1839년으로 거슬러 올라간다. 남북전쟁 말기엔 200개가 넘는 야구팀이나 야구클럽이 존재했으며 서로 경기를 하기 위해 지속적으로 이동을 했다. 이들 팀과 클럽은 전미 "야구선수" 협회에 속해 있었고, 처음에는 아마추어였다가 야구가 점차 인기를 얻으면서 이익을 거둘 수 있는 기회도 생겨나게 되면서 1869년엔 최초의 프로팀인 신시내티 레드 스타킹스가 등장했다. 다른 도시에서도 프로팀을 설립하기 시작했고, 1876년엔 현재의 내셔널 리그가 알버트 스폴딩의 주도로 설립되었다. 얼마 있지 않아 경쟁 리그인 아메리칸 어소시에이션이 등장했다. 이 두 리그 간의 경쟁은 치열했고 1883년에 포스트 시즌 시합을 벌였는데, 이것이 바로 최초의 "월드 시리즈"이다. 아메리칸 어소시에이션은 결국 무너졌지만 1900년에 아메리칸 리그가 설립되었다.

25 1869년 이전의 야구선수들의 특성과 일치하지 않는 것은?
① 이들은 광범위한 거리를 여행했다.
② 이들이 속한 클럽의 수는 그리 많지 않았다.
③ 이들은 합의된 규칙에 따라 운동했다.
④ 이들은 프로선수가 아니었다.

| 정답 | ②

| 해설 | 1869년 이전 남북전쟁 직후엔 "200개가 넘는 야구팀이나 야구클럽이 존재했다(over 200 teams or clubs existed)." 즉, 클럽이나 팀의 수가 상당했음을 알 수 있으며 따라서 답은 ②이다. ①의 근거는 "지속적으로 이동을 했다(constantly on the road)", ③의 근거는 "경기 운영을 위한 규칙을 표준화하다(standardize the rules governing the game)", ④의 근거는 "처음에는 아마추어였다(These teams were amateurs)"이다.

26 다음 중 National League에 대한 설명으로 옳지 않은 것은?
① 최초의 프로팀은 레드 스타킹스였다.
② 내셔널 리그는 1876년 이전에는 존재하지 않았다.
③ 알버트 스폴딩은 내셔널 리그의 설립에 중요한 역할을 했다.
④ 결국에는 아메리칸 리그로 대체되었다.

| 정답 | ④

| 해설 | "아메리칸 어소시에이션은 결국 무너졌지만 1900년에 아메리칸 리그가 설립되었다(The American Association eventually collapsed, but in 1900 the American League was organized)." 여기서 아메리칸 리그가 대체한 것은 아메리칸 어소시에이션이지 내셔널 리그가 아님을 알 수 있다. 따라서 답은 ④이다. ①의 근거는 "최초의 프로팀인 신시내티 레드 스타킹스(the first professional team, the Cincinnati Red Stockings)," ②와 ③의 근거는 "1876년엔 현재의 내셔널 리그가 알버트 스폴딩의 주도로 설립되었다(in 1876 the present National League was organized chiefly by Albert Spalding)"이다.

| 어휘 | date back to – ~까지 거슬러 올라가다　　lay out – 배치하다, 설치하다
　　　　on the road – 이동 중인　　　　　　　　wax ⓥ 차츰 커지다(≠ wane)
　　　　intense ⓐ 치열한　　　　　　　　　　　　eventually ⓐⓓ 결국, 마침내
　　　　extensively ⓐⓓ 널리, 광범위하게　　　　instrumental ⓐ 중요한
　　　　supercede ⓥ 대신하다, 대체하다

[27-28] 중앙대 2009

미식축구 스타플레이어의 경력상의 궤적을 연구하는 일이 어떻게, 그리고 왜 기업의 조직과 경력을 더 잘 관리할 수 있는 기회를 제공하게 되었는가? 전미 미식축구 연맹(National Football League; NFL)을 대상으로 한 조사 결과가 드러낸 바와 같이, 때로는 어떤 직업이 지닌 구체적인 특성이 한 회사에서 높은 성과를 보인 사람이 다른 회사에서도 높은 성과를 재현할 수 있을지 여부를 결정한다. 스포츠 팀은 다른 수많은 조직과 마찬가지로 다른 곳에서도 흔히 발생하는 실수를 범하기 쉽다. 하지만 스포츠 팀의 성공과 실패는 매우 눈에 잘 띄고 증폭되기도 쉬운데 그 이유는 스포츠 팀들은 제로섬 구조 속에서 경기를 치르기 때문이다. 즉, 어느 한 팀이 승리하려면 다른 팀은 져야 한다. 그 결과 스포츠 팀의 초점은 특히나 성적 지향으로 맞춰지게 된다. 스포츠 팀은 재능을 토대로 스타플레이어를 영입하는데, 이는 다른 많은 조직도 마찬가지이다. 따라서 만약 한 스타플레이어의 성적이 매우 정확한 통계 데이터로 자료화가 이루어진다면, 조사자들은 자료를 가지고 NFL의 많은 팀들이 믿는 것처럼 새로운 환경에서도 스타플레이어의 성적이 재현 가능한지 여부를 점검할 수 있게 된다. 기업 경영자에게 있어 스타플레이어의 성적을 재현할 수 있는 포지션과 재현할 수 없는 포지션이 있다는 사실은 알아 둘 필요가 있다.

27 밑줄 친 (A)의 문맥상의 의미로 가장 적합한 것을 고르시오.
① 구별할 수 있는　　② 측정할 수 있는
③ 재현 가능한　　④ 분명히 실재하는

| 정답 | ③

| 해설 | 'portable'은 '이식 가능한, 휴대 가능한'의 의미를 갖는데, 문맥상 '이전 환경에서 새로운 환경으로 이전에 이룬 성취를 이식하다. 즉, '이전의 성취를 다시금 재현하다' 정도의 의미를 갖는다. 따라서 답은 ③이다.

28 위의 지문의 내용과 가장 일치하는 것을 고르시오.
① 스타플레이어의 성적을 재현하기 위해서는 적절한 포지션을 배정하는 것이 중요하다.
② 뛰어난 성적을 거두는 사람은 어느 조직에서도 최선을 다한다.
③ 뛰어난 성적을 거두는 사람은 새로운 조직에서 살아남기가 매우 힘들다.
④ NFL의 최종 연구 결과에 따르면 스타플레이어는 재능을 토대로 선정되어야 한다.

| 정답 | ①

| 해설 | 본문 마지막 문장인 "스타플레이어의 성적을 재현할 수 있는 포지션과 재현할 수 없는 포지션이 있다는 사실은 알아 둘 필요가 있다(the fact that the star's performance is portable for some positions and not portable for others is necessary to know)"는 단순히 스타플레이어를 영입하는 것으로 모든 것이 끝나는 것이 아니며 적절한 포지션에 배치해야만 성공을 보장할 수 있다는 의미이다. 이는 보기 ①의 내용과 일치하기 때문에 답 역시 ①이다. 보기 나머지 사항은 본문 내용과는 직접적 관계가 없다.

| 어휘 | trajectory ⓝ 궤적, 경로
replicate ⓥ 복제하다; 반복하다
amplify ⓥ 증폭시키다, 확대하다
performance ⓝ 성적, 성과
measure ⓥ 측정하다, 재다
reveal ⓥ 드러내다, 밝히다
subject to – ~하기 쉬운
zero-sum ⓝ 제로섬(한쪽이 잃으면 다른 한쪽이 따는 구조)
-oriented ⓐ ~ 위주의, ~ 지향의
portable ⓐ 이식 가능한, 휴대 가능한

distinguishable ⓐ 구별할 수 있는, 분간할 수 있는
measurable ⓐ 측정할 수 있는
replicable ⓐ 재현 가능한, 복제 가능한
tangible ⓐ 분명히 실재하는, 유형의

[29-30] 숙명여대 2012

노 젓는 사람 하나만의 힘으로는 옥스퍼드 대학과 캠브리지 대학 간의 조정 경주에서 우승할 수 없다. 한 명의 노 젓는 사람에게는 여덟 명의 동료가 필요하다. 각각의 선수들은 전문가로서 기술, 정조수, 키잡이 등의 역할을 하면서 보트의 특정한 위치에 각자 자리를 잡는다. 보트의 노를 젓는 것은 협력을 요하는 일이지만, 그럼에도 어떤 이는 다른 이들에 비해 노를 더 잘 젓곤 한다. 감독이 지원자들 가운데 자신의 이상에 맞는 팀원들을 선정해야 하는 상황에서, 어떤 이는 기수 일을 전문적으로 잘하는 사람이 있고, 다른 이는 키잡이 일을 전문적으로 잘하는 사람이 있는 등, 각기 차이가 난다고 가정해 보자. 그리고 감독이 다음 과정을 통해 선발을 했다고 가정해 보자. 감독은 매일 각 위치마다 후보자들을 무작위로 섞은 다음, 시범적으로 세 명의 시범 팀원들을 새로 모은 다음에 이들이 서로 경쟁하게 하는 것이다. 이렇게 몇 주가 지나고 나면, 이기는 조정팀의 구성원이 동일해지는 경향을 보이는 경우가 종종 있다. 이들은 잘하는 사람으로 표시된다. 그 외 잘 못하는 사람들은 계속해서 느린 팀에 속한 것으로 보이며, 이들은 결국에는 탈락된다. 하지만 두드러지게 잘하는 사람도 어떨 때는 느린 팀에 속하기도 하며, 이는 다른 팀원들의 수준이 떨어지기 때문이거나 역풍이 강하게 부는 것 같이 운이 없어서이기 때문이다.

29

빈칸에 가장 적합한 것은 무엇인가?
① ~ 후에
② ~ 전에
③ ~에도 불구하고
④ ~ 안으로
⑤ ~ 밖으로

| 정답 | ①

| 해설 | 이기는 팀의 구성원이 같아 보이고, 못하는 사람과 잘하는 사람으로 구분되는 결과가 나온 것은 팀을 섞어서 시험 한 지 몇 주 "후에" 나온 결과로 볼 수 있다. 따라서 정답은 ①이다.

30

이기는 보트에 가장 잘 타는 사람들이 있는 것은 단지 평균적인 일일 뿐이다.
① 잘 알고 있는
② 평균적으로
③ 장난삼아
④ 작동이 안 되는
⑤ 필요상

| 정답 | ②

| 해설 | "하지만 두드러지게 잘 하는 사람도 어쩔 때는 느린 팀에 속하기도 하며, 이는 다른 팀원들의 수준이 떨어지기 때문이거나 역풍이 강하게 부는 것 같이 운이 없어서이기 때문이다(But even an outstandingly good oarsman might sometimes be a member of a slow crew, either because of the inferiority of the other members, or because of bad luck — say a strong adverse wind)." 즉, 이기는 보트에 항상 가장 잘 타는 사람만 있는 것은 아니고, 잘 타는 사람이 운이 없어서일 수도 있기 때문에, 이기는 보트에는 잘 타는 사람이 '항상' 있는 것은 아니고 '평균적으로' 있는 것으로 볼 수 있다. 따라서 답은 ②이다.

| 어휘 | **oarsman** ⓝ 노 젓는 사람
stroke ⓝ 정조수 조정에서 속도나 방향을 조정하는 사람
cox ⓝ 키잡이, 타수
consistently ⓐ 일관하여, 항상
adverse wind – 역풍
on a lark – 장난삼아
out of necessity – 필요상
bow ⓝ 뱃머리, 기수
crew ⓝ 조정 경기 팀
outstandingly ⓐ 두드러지게, 현저히
in the know – 잘 알고 있는
out of action – 작동이 안 되는

[31-33] 한국외대 2014

미국 관객은 서부영화를 엄청난 열정을 가지고 본다. 백인들이 서부영화를 좋아하는 이유는 알기 쉬운데, 그 이유는 영화 속에서 사나운 황야를 지배하며, 파괴에 열중하는 잔인하고 야만스러운 미국 원주민들로부터 스스로를 보호하는 영웅으로 묘사되는 사람들이 바로 자기 자신들이기 때문이다. 그런데 왜 미국 원주민들은 서부영화를 좋아하는 것일까? 이에 매우 흥미를 느낀 사회학자 조엘렌 쉬블리는 성인이 된 미국 원주민들과 백인들에게 서부영화를 보여주는 방식으로 이 문제를 조사해 보리라 결심했다. 그리고 놀라운 점을 발견했다. 미국 원주민들도 백인들도 모두 카우보이와 자신을 동일시했으며, 아무도 영화 속 미국 원주민들과 자신을 동일시하지 않았다. 하지만 백인들이 카우보이와 자신을 동일시하는 방식은 미국 원주민들이 동일시하는 방식과 꽤 큰 차이가 있었다. 백인들은 영화가 옛 서부를 정확히 묘사했으며 영화가 자신의 사회적 위치를 정당화하는 것으로 여겼지만 미국 원주민들은 영화를 자유롭고 자연스러운 삶의 방식을 구현한 것으로 여겼다. 카우보이처럼 자유롭고 독립적인 삶에 대한 환상이 서부영화가 미국 원주민들에게 의미 있는 대상이 되게 한 것으로 보인다. 미국 원주민들은 카우보이의 이야기 속에서 삶에 대한 카우보이 방식의 주요 부분이 승리를 거두고 도덕적으로도 옳은 것으로 나오는 것을 보며 환상을 발견하고, 극적으로 만족스러운 이야기의 맥락에서 자신이 속한 문화 집단을 인정하게 된다. 쉬블리는 "핵심은 민족성이 아니라 가치에 있습니다"라고 밝혔다. 만일 미국 원주민 영화 업계에서 백인 영화 업계가 카우보이를 대상으로 투사하는 가치와 동일한 가치를 가지고 미국 원주민을 묘사할 경우, 미국 원주민은 아마도 스스로를 자신이 속한 집단과 동일시할 것이다.

31 다음 중 본문을 가장 잘 뒷받침하는 것은 무엇인가?
① 다른 민족성을 지닌 사람들이 유사한 가치를 공유할 수 있다.
② 사람들의 영화에 관한 취향은 민족성과 관련이 있다.
③ 서양인들은 미국 원주민에 대한 편견이 있다.
④ 미국 원주민들은 서부영화 속에서 다양하게 묘사된다.

| 정답 | ①

| 해설 | 본문의 핵심은 "핵심은 민족성이 아니라 가치에 있습니다(Values, not ethnicity, are the central issue)"이다. 백인이 미국 원주민을 지배하는 서부영화에 백인도 미국 원주민도 같이 좋아하는 모습을 보이는 것은, 백인과 미국 원주민이라는 서로 다른 민족성을 지닌 사람들 간에도 뭔가 같은 가치를 공유하고 공감할 수 있다는 의미이다. 따라서 답은 ①이다.

32 본문에 따르면 미국 원주민들은 카우보이가 자신들이 마음속에 그린 삶의 방식을 대표하기 때문에 카우보이와 자신을 동일시한다.
① 카우보이가 자신들이 마음속에 그린 삶의 방식을 대표한다
② 카우보이가 인디언들의 지위를 정당화한다
③ 카우보이가 황량한 서부를 나타낸다
④ 카우보이는 항상 승리한다

| 정답 | ①

| 해설 | "미국 원주민들은 영화를 자유롭고 자연스러운 삶의 방식을 구현한 것으로 여겼다. 카우보이처럼 자유롭고 독립적인 삶에 대한 환상이 서부영화가 미국 원주민들에게 의미있는 대상이 되게 한 것으로 보인다(Native Americans saw it as embodying a free, natural way of life. What appears to make Westerns meaningful to Indians is the fantasy of being free and independent like the cowboys)." 즉, 미국 원주민들은 서부영화 속 카우보이가 자신들이 원하는 삶의 방식을 구현한 존재로 보는 것이다. 따라서 답은 ①이다.

33 다음 중 빈칸에 가장 알맞은 것은 무엇인가?
① 꽤 실용적이다
② 꽤 큰 차이가 있다
③ 매우 효과적이다
④ 다소 근거가 빈약하다

| 정답 | ②

| 해설 | 백인과 미국 원주민은 카우보이와 자신을 동일시했지만, 동일시하는 방식에는 다음과 같은 큰 차이가 있었다. 즉, "백인들은 영화가 옛 서부를 정확히 묘사했으며 영화가 자신의 사회적 위치를 정당화하는 것으로 여겼지만 미국 원주민들은 영화를 자유롭고 자연스러운 삶의 방식을 구현한 것으로 여겼다(While Anglos saw the movie as an actual portrayal of the Old West and a justification of their own status in society, Native Americans saw it as embodying a free, natural way of life)." 따라서 답은 ②이다.

| 어휘 | devour ⓥ 걸신 들린 듯 먹다, (엄청난 열의를 갖고) 집어삼킬 듯이 보다[읽다]
Anglo ⓝ 백인
tame ⓥ 길들이다, 다스리다
intrigued ⓐ 아주 흥미로워[궁금해]하는
justification ⓝ 정당화
validate ⓥ 입증하다, 인정하다
have to do with – ~와 관련이 있다
envision ⓥ 상상하다, 마음속에 그리다
western ⓝ 서부 영화
intent on – ~에 열중하는
identify with – ~와 동일시하다
embody ⓥ 구현하다, 표현하다
ethnicity ⓝ 민족성
be prejudiced against – ~에 대한 편견이 있다
victorious ⓐ 승리하는

[34-35] 에리카 2018

야구는 세상에서 가장 널리 관람되고 플레이되는 스포츠 중 하나로, 플레이되는 국가의 수 측면에서 그리고 게임에 참여하는 사람들의 수 측면에서 축구 및 농구와 어깨를 나란히 한다. 원래 "타운볼(townball)"이란 명칭으로 알려졌던 야구는 19세기 초 미국 북동부에서 개발되었다. 야구는 영국의 크리켓과 라운더스 같은 게임 및 어린이들의 놀이인 "원 올드 캣(one old cat)"에서 차용하여 만들어졌다. 1840년대에 알렉산더 카트라이트(Alexander Cartwright)가 오늘날 사용되는 야구장의 치수를 표준화했다. 1858년 스포츠 기자인 헨리 채드윅(Henry Chadwick)이 최초의 야구 규칙서를 작성했다. 미국 남북전쟁(1861~1865) 기간 동안에는 북군 병사들이 야구의 인기를 확산시키는 데 기여했다. 그 이후 1869년에 야구 사상 최초의 프로 야구팀인 신시내티 레드 스타킹스(Cincinnati Red Stockings)가 조직되었다. 내셔널 리그는 1876년에 설립되었고 라이벌인 아메리칸 리그는 1901년에 설립되었다. 최초의 월드 시리즈는 1903년 내셔널 리그 우승팀인 피츠버그 파이어리츠(Pittsburgh Pirates)와 아메리칸 리그 우승팀인 보스턴 필그림스(Boston Pilgrims) 사이에서 진행되었다. 야구는 미국의 "국민오락"으로 자리잡았다.

34 빈칸에 들어갈 가장 알맞은 것을 고르시오.
① 증가시키다
② 다각화하다
③ 미루다
④ 표준화하다

| 정답 | ④

| 해설 | 본문은 야구의 역사에 관해 다루고 있으므로, 알렉산더 카트라이트란 인물은 야구의 역사와 관련이 있기 때문에 언급된 것으로 볼 수 있다. 1840년대가 야구 역사의 초창기였다는 점을 감안하면 이 사람이 '야구장의 치수'를 가지고 할 일은 치수를 '표준화'하는 일일 것이고, 이렇게 표준화된 치수가 지금도 쓰이고 있는 것임을 유추할 수 있다. 따라서 답은 ④이다.

35 윗글의 내용과 맞지 않는 것을 고르시오.
① 야구는 크리켓과 라운더스 같은 영국의 게임의 영향을 받았다.
② 아메리칸 리그는 내셔널 리그보다 훨씬 이전에 설립되었다.
③ 야구는 본래 미국에서 19세기 초에 타운볼이라는 명칭으로 알려졌다.
④ 최초의 월드 시리즈는 피츠버그 파이어리츠와 보스턴 필그림스 사이에서 진행되었다.

| 정답 | ②

| 해설 | 아메리칸 리그는 1901년 내셔널 리그는 1876년에 설립되었다. 이는 ②의 내용과 반대이며, 따라서 답은 ②이다. "원래 '타운볼(townball)'이란 명칭으로 알려졌던 야구는 19세기 초 미국 북동부에서 개발되었다. 야구는 영국의 크리켓과 라운더스 같은 게임 및 어린이들의 놀이인 '원 올드 캣(one old cat)'에서 차용하여 만들어졌다(The game — originally known as 'townball' — developed in the early nineteenth century in the northeastern United States. It borrowed from the English games of cricket and rounders, and from children's games such as 'one old cat.')" 이는 ① 및 ③의 내용과 일치한다. "최초의 월드 시리즈는 1903년 내셔널 리그 우승팀인 피츠버그 파이어리츠(Pittsburgh Pirates)와 아메리칸 리그 우승팀인 보스턴 필그림스(Boston Pilgrims) 사이에서 진행되었다(The first World Series was played between the Pittsburgh Pirates, the champions of the National league, and the Boston Pilgrims, American league champions, in 1903)"는 ④의 내용과 일치한다.

| 어휘 | rank with ~와 어깨를 나란히 하다   borrow ⓥ 차용하다
rounders ⓝ 라운더스(야구와 비슷한 구기 종목)   standardize ⓥ 표준화하다

field ⓝ [특정 스포츠를 하는] ~장, 경기장
sportswriter ⓝ 스포츠 기자
national pastime – 국민오락
temporize ⓥ (결정·확답을 하지 않고) 미루다[시간을 끌다]
dimension ⓝ (높이·너비·길이의) 치수
rule book – 규칙서
diversify ⓥ 다각화하다

[36-38] 명지대 2017

많은 사람들은 스포츠 팀이나 대회 주최자에게 비용을 지급하지 않고서도 스포츠가 제공하는 편익(benefits)을 즐긴다. 메이저리그 팀이 있는 도시에 살고 있다는 이유로 그들은 시민으로서의 자부심을 느끼거나, 국가대표 선수들이 올림픽 메달을 획득한 경우에는 국민으로서의 자부심을 느낀다. 뉴욕 양키스가 월드 시리즈에서 우승할 경우 그들은 색종이가 휘날리는 카퍼레이드에 참여하기 위해 맨해튼 거리에 줄지어서며, 자신들이 사는 도시가 올림픽 개최지로 선정된 것을 축하하기 위해 그들은 런던의 트라팔가 광장과 리우데자네이루의 해변을 가득 메운다.

이것은 스포츠를 지원하는 정부 정책의 편익-비용 분석(benefit-cost analysis)을 복잡하게 만든다. 원칙적으로는 티켓 구매와 케이블 채널 가입으로부터 얻는 편익을 측정하는 것은 쉬운 일이다. 예를 들어, 티켓 가격 및 매출에 관한 시장 데이터는 수요함수, 소비자 잉여, 생산자 잉여 등을 산정할 수 있게 해 준다. 이런 방법들은 현시 선호(revealed preference) 데이터를 사용하는데, 이런 이름이 붙여진 이유는 사람들의 구매가 대체 상품 및 서비스보다 스포츠에 대한 이들의 선호를 더 드러내기 때문이다.

하지만 색종이가 휘날리는 퍼레이드와 어젯밤 경기에 대한 사무실 대화 등을 취급하는 시장은 존재하지 않는다. 그 어떤 리그나 팀에서도 국민적 자부심을 측정하거나, ESPN.com에 나온 명장면들이나 지역신문에 실린 리그 순위 확인에 팬들이 거는 가치를 측정하는 통계자료를 수집하지 않는다. 크롬프튼(Crompton)은 그러한 편익을 '심리적 소득(psychic income)'이라 부르며, 그러한 편익이 아마도 스포츠에 의해 생산되는 가장 큰 무형의 편익일지 모른다고 말한다.

이런 관점에서, 스포츠는 환경과 유사하다. 스포츠와 환경은 모두 비경합적(non-rival)이고 비배제적인(non-excludable) 공공재 성격의 중요 편익을 생산해 낸다. 많은 사람들이 아름다운 풍경이나 멸종 위기 동식물의 생존, 깨끗한 공기와 같은 공공재를 가치 있게 여긴다는 사실에 대해 반박할 사람은 아무도 없다. 하지만 그런 공공재를 구매하기 위해 동네 구멍가게나 온라인 판매업체를 방문해야 하는 것도 아니다. 다시 말하면, 스포츠에서 그런 것처럼, 많은 편익들은 가치를 평가하기 어려운데, 그 이유는 수요 및 소비자 잉여를 측정할 현시 선호 데이터가 존재하지 않기 때문이다. 스포츠 경제학자들에게는 다행스럽게도, 환경 경제학자들은 거래되지 않는 공공재의 편익을 평가하는 방법을 개발해냈다.

36 다음 중 빈칸에 올 수 있는 가장 적합한 것은?
① 무형의
② 만연하는
③ 화려한
④ 즙이 많은

| 정답 | ①

| 해설 | 스포츠를 통해 사람들이 얻는 편익을 "심리적 소득(psychic income)"이라고 부르고 있는데, 이는 현시 선호 데이터가 없기 때문에 '측정이 불가능하다'고 말한다. 사람들이 정신적으로 얻는 편익이기 때문이다. 따라서 이런 편익을 가장 잘 설명할 수 있는 것은 '형태가 없다'는 뜻의 ① intangible이 된다.

37

다음 중 본문에 언급된 것이 아닌 것은?

① 축하하기 위해 런던 시민들이 모이는 장소
② '현시 선호 데이터'의 정의
③ 자신들이 응원하는 팀의 리그 순위를 팬들이 확인하는 이유
④ 스포츠와 환경의 유사성

| 정답 | ③

| 해설 | ① 'pack Trafalgar Square in London'에 런던 시민들이 축하하기 위해 모이는 장소가 나온다. ② "Such methods use revealed preference data, so called because people's purchases reveal their preferences for sports over alternative goods and services."에서 so called 후반에 'revealed preference'로 불리는 이유가 나오고 있으므로 이를 정의로 볼 수 있다. ④ 마지막 문단의 "In this respect, sport resembles the environment."를 통해 스포츠와 환경은 닮은 점(analogy)이 있다는 것을 알 수 있다. 정답은 ③으로, 팀의 리그 순위를 확인하는 데 팬들이 거는 가치에 대한 통계자료는 없다는 대목이 나오지만, 왜 팬들이 순위를 확인하는지에 대한 '이유'는 본문에 등장하지 않는다.

38

다음 중 본문의 목적으로 가장 적합한 것은?

① '심리적 소득'을 평가하기 위한 방법을 소개하기 위해서
② 스포츠 팀에 정부가 지급하는 보조금을 비판하기 위해서
③ 정부의 스포츠 정책의 중요성을 강조하기 위해서
④ 스포츠 경기의 숨겨진 편익을 설명하기 위해서

| 정답 | ①

| 해설 | 이 글은 스포츠를 통해 얻을 수 있는 무형의 편익에 대해 설명하고 있으며, 이를 본문에서는 '심리적 소득'이라고 부르고 있다. 하지만 이런 편익은 현시 선호 데이터가 없기 때문에 가치를 평가하기 어렵다. 여기까지만 보면 정답을 ④로 생각할 수 있다. 하지만 마지막 문단에서 스포츠는 환경과 유사한 성격의 공공재에 해당한다고 언급하면서, 다행히 환경과 관련한 공공재의 편익을 측정하는 방법을 이미 환경 경제학자들이 개발해 놓았다고 설명한다. 이를 이용해 스포츠의 편익을 알아낼 수 있다는 말이므로, 본문의 목적은 '심리적 소득'을 평가하기 위한 방법을 소개'한다고 한 ①이 적합하다는 것을 알 수 있다.

| 어휘 | bask in – (관심·칭찬 등을) 누리다   civic pride – 시민으로서의 자부심
national pride – 국민으로서의 자부심, 국민적 자부심
athlete ⓝ 운동선수   line ⓥ ~을 따라 늘어서다[줄을 세우다]
tickertape ⓝ (환영을 위해 던지는) 색종이 테이프   pack ⓥ 가득 메우다 ⓝ 무리
complicate ⓥ 복잡하게 만들다   benefit-cost analysis – 편익–비용 분석
estimation ⓝ 판단, 평가   demand function – 수요함수
consumer surplus – 소비자 잉여(시장에서 소비자가 기꺼이 지불하려는 금액보다 적은 비용으로 재화를 구매할 때 생기는 이득을 의미함)
producer surplus 생산자 잉여(생산자가 기꺼이 팔려고 하는 금액보다 많은 값을 받고 재화를 팔 때 얻는 이득을 의미함)
revealed preference [경제] 현시 선호(기존의 소비자 이론에서 실제로 관찰 불가능한 선호, 효용 등의 개념을 버

리고, 단순히 시장에서 관찰 가능한 소비자의 행위만을 가지고 무차별곡선과 수요곡선을 도출해 내자는 사뮤엘슨의 이론을 의미함)

alternative ⓐ 대안적인, 대체의 ⓝ 대안, 양자택일
statistics ⓝ [복수] 통계자료, [단수] 통계학
league standings - 리그 순위
in this respect - 이런 점에서
dispute ⓝ 분쟁, 분규; 논란, 논쟁 ⓥ 반박하다, 이의를 제기하다
scenic ⓐ 경치가 좋은
endangered species - 멸종위기 종
intangible ⓐ 만질 수 없는, 무형의
flamboyant ⓐ (색상이나 문체가) 화려한, 현란한
definition ⓝ 정의
subsidization ⓝ 보조금 지급

place value on - ~에 가치를 두다, ~을 평가하다
psychic income - 심리적 수익, 정신적 이득
public goods - 공공재, 공공시설
vista ⓝ (아름다운) 경치, 풍경
corner shop - (동네) 구멍가게
pervasive ⓐ 만연하는, 스며드는
succulent ⓐ 즙이 많은; 흥미진진한
analogy ⓝ 비유, 유사점, 유추
illustrate ⓥ 보여주다

[39-40] 성균관대 2017

디즈니 영화 속 폴리네시아인 캐릭터에 대한 묘사를 두고 태평양제도 전역에서 분노가 일고 있다. 뉴질랜드의 한 하원의원은 폴리네시아 마우이(Maui) 신을 너무 뚱뚱하게 묘사한 것은 '받아들일 수 없는' 일이라고 말했다. 통가제도 출신의 제니 살레사(Jenny Salesa) 하원의원은 영화 〈모아나(Moana)〉에 나오는 마우이의 모습은 '반은 돼지, 반은 하마'인 생명체의 모습과 흡사하다고 말했다.

폴리네시아 신화 속 마우이는 영웅적인 인물로, 태평양 지역 섬들을 바다에서 건져 올려 태평양 제도를 만들었다. 윌 일로라히아(Will Illohahia)는 와아테아 뉴스(Waatea News)와의 인터뷰에서 디즈니 영화가 그려낸 마우이의 모습은 태평양 창조 신화에 등장하는 그의 영웅적 모습과 어울리지 않는다고 밝혔다. "신화 속 이야기에서, 그리고 특히 내가 살았던 문화권에서, 그는 힘세고 영향력 있는 인물이자, 신성을 지닌 인물로 묘사된다. 마우이를 이런 식으로 뚱뚱하게 묘사한 것은 미국인들의 전형적인 고정관념일 뿐이다. 비만은 이전에는 없었던 새로운 현상으로, 우리 입속에 채워지는 선진국에서 넘어온 음식 때문에 일어난 일이다."라고 일로라히아는 말했다.

하지만 많은 사람들은 소셜미디어에 글을 남기며, 디즈니의 마우이는 힘세고 강해 보이며, 그의 체격은 폴리네시아 남성들에게 흔히 찾아볼 수 있는 모습이라고 말했다. 자신을 '상당히 몸집이 큰 남자'라고 밝힌 통가 출신의 뉴질랜드인 이소아 카바키모투(Isoa Kavakimotu)는 이번 논란과 관련해 유튜브 영상을 만들어 올리며, 디즈니가 묘사한 마우이는 자신이 볼 때 문제 될 게 없다고 밝혔다. "나는 괜찮다고 본다. 내게는 마우이가 뚱뚱해 보이지 않고, 엄청난 일을 해낼 수 있는 대단히 건장한 사람으로 보인다. 그런 이유로 그의 몸집이 큰 것이다. 영화 속에서 그들은 마오리 전통 카누인 와카를 타고 항해를 하는데, 식민지 시대 이전을 배경으로 하고 있어서, 테이크아웃 가게가 갑자기 영화 속에 등장할 것이라는 생각은 전혀 들지 않는다. 내게는 그가 언제든 충돌할 준비가 되어 있는 것처럼 보인다."라고 그는 말했다.

39 다음 중 밑줄 친 "테이크아웃 가게가 갑자기 영화 속에 등장할 것이다"라는 내용이 의미하는 것은?
① 이 영화는 추측에 근거한, 공상과학 기반의 묘사를 사용하고 있다.
② 이 영화의 시대 배경은 식민지 시대 이후의 근대 시기이다.
③ 이 영화에서 사실적인 묘사가 매우 분명하게 나타나고 있다.
④ 이 영화는 일상의 평범한 삶에 초점을 두고 있다.
⑤ 이 영화는 식민지의 인종 문제를 탐색하고 있다.

| 정답 | ②

| 해설 | 마우이 신이 왜 체격이 크고 뚱뚱한 것처럼 묘사되었는지를 옹호하는 관점에서 설명하고 있는 부분이다. 마우이 신이 위대한 일을 할 수 있는 것을 나타내기 위해 몸집이 큰 것이지, 테이크아웃 가게와 같은 곳에서 많이 먹어서 뚱뚱한 것은 아니라고 설명한다. 바로 앞 내용처럼 이 영화는 식민지 시대 이전을 배경으로 하고 있으므로, 영화에 갑자기 테이크아웃 가게가 나타나는 일은, 즉 식민지 이후에 생겨난 테이크아웃 가게가 갑자기 나올 것 같지는 않다(highly doubt)고 말한다. 이런 관점에서 밑줄 친 부분은 영화의 배경이 되는 시점을 말한 ②가 정답이 된다.

40 다음 중 본문의 내용과 일치하지 않는 것은?
① 현재 대부분의 폴리네시아 사람들은 뚱뚱하지 않다.
② 어떤 사람들은 디즈니가 묘사한 마우이의 모습에 동의를 표했다.
③ 마우이에 대한 묘사가 영화에 그려지는 폴리네시아인들에 대한 고정관념과 관련한 논쟁을 촉발시켰다.
④ 디즈니가 묘사한 뚱뚱한 폴리네시아 신의 모습이 폴리네시안 사람들에게 분노를 불러일으켰다.
⑤ 마우이의 신체적 특징은 디즈니 영화 속 (등장인물의) 성격을 나타냈다.

| 정답 | ①

| 해설 | ① 본문의 "This depiction of Maui being obese is typical American stereotyping. Obesity is a new phenomenon …"을 통해 폴리네시아인들이 뚱뚱하다는 것은 미국인들의 편견으로, 비만은 최근에 생겨난 일이라고 말하고 있다. 따라서 현재 뚱뚱한 폴리네시아인들이 많은 것은 어느 정도 사실로 생각할 수 있으므로, ①이 정답이 된다. ② 본문에는 디즈니의 묘사를 찬성하는 측과 반대하는 측이 모두 등장한다. ③과 ④는 본문의 첫 번째 문장인 "The depiction of a Polynesian character in a Disney film has prompted anger across the Pacific islands …"을 통해 확인할 수 있다. ⑤ 신화에서 마우이 신이 태평양 지역 섬들을 바다에서 건져 올려 태평양 제도를 만든 것과 같이 힘세고 강한 모습을 하고 있다고 했으므로, 마우이의 큰 체격(물론 뚱뚱한 모습이라고 생각하는 이들도 있는 것은 사실이지만)은 신화 속 그의 성격(특성)을 반영하고 있다고 할 수 있다.

| 어휘 | **depiction** ⓝ 묘사, 서술
Polynesian ⓐ 폴리네시아(태평양 중·남부에 흩어져 있는 여러 섬)의
prompt ⓥ 자극하다, 촉구하다 ⓐ 신속한, 시간을 엄수하는
MP ⓝ 하원 의원(Member of Parliament) **portrayal** ⓝ 묘사
obese ⓐ 비만의 **Tongan** ⓝⓐ 통가 제도[사람, 말](의)
heritage ⓝ 세습 재산, 혈통, 전승 **rendering** ⓝ 표현, 묘사; 연출, 연주; 번역
mythology ⓝ 신화 **heroic** ⓐ 영웅적인
fit with – ~와 맞다 **endeavor** ⓝ 노력 ⓥ 노력하다
magnitude ⓝ 규모, 크기; 중대(성) **stuff** ⓥ 채워 넣다, 잔뜩 먹다
physique ⓝ (사람의) 체격 **controversy** ⓝ 논쟁
powerhouse ⓝ 강국, 유력[실세] 집단[기관] **extraordinary** ⓐ 비범한, 기이한, 놀라운
waka ⓝ 와카(마오리족이 타는 카누) **set** ⓥ (연극·소설·영화의) 배경[무대]을 설정하다
colonization ⓝ 식민지화[건설]
take-away store – 테이크아웃 전문점(다른 데서 먹을 수 있게 사 가지고 갈 수 있는 음식을 파는 식당)
pop up – 불쑥 나타나다 **speculative** ⓐ 추측에 근거한; 투기적인
overweight ⓐ 과체중의 **attribute** ⓝ 속성, 특질 ⓥ 돌리다, 탓으로 하다
be indicative of – ~을 가리키다

**여러분의 작은 소리
에듀윌은 크게 듣겠습니다.**

본 교재에 대한 여러분의 목소리를 들려주세요.
공부하시면서 어려웠던 점, 궁금한 점,
칭찬하고 싶은 점, 개선할 점, 어떤 것이라도 좋습니다.

에듀윌은 여러분께서 나누어 주신 의견을
통해 끊임없이 발전하고 있습니다.

에듀윌 도서몰 book.eduwill.net
- 부가학습자료 및 정오표: 에듀윌 도서몰 → 도서자료실
- 교재 문의: 에듀윌 도서몰 → 문의하기 → 교재(내용, 출간) / 주문 및 배송

에듀윌 편입영어 기출심화 완성 독해

발 행 일	2022년 9월 8일 초판 ｜ 2022년 11월 30일 2쇄
편 저 자	에듀윌 편입 컨텐츠연구소, 홍준기 공저
펴 낸 이	권대호, 김재환
펴 낸 곳	(주)에듀윌
등록번호	제25100–2002–000052호
주　　소	08378 서울특별시 구로구 디지털로34길 55
	코오롱싸이언스밸리 2차 3층

* 이 책의 무단 인용 · 전재 · 복제를 금합니다.

www.eduwill.net
대표전화 1600-6700